# Communications in Computer and Information Science　　1588

More information about this series at https://link.springer.com/bookseries/7899

Xingming Sun · Xiaorui Zhang · Zhihua Xia ·
Elisa Bertino (Eds.)

# Advances in Artificial Intelligence and Security

8th International Conference
on Artificial Intelligence and Security, ICAIS 2022
Qinghai, China, July 15–20, 2022
Proceedings, Part III

Springer

*Editors*
Xingming Sun ⓘ
Nanjing University of Information Science
and Technology
Nanjing, China

Xiaorui Zhang ⓘ
Nanjing University of Information Science
and Technology
Nanjing, China

Zhihua Xia ⓘ
Jinan University
Guangzhou, China

Elisa Bertino ⓘ
Purdue University
West Lafayette, IN, USA

ISSN 1865-0929          ISSN 1865-0937 (electronic)
Communications in Computer and Information Science
ISBN 978-3-031-06763-1          ISBN 978-3-031-06764-8 (eBook)
https://doi.org/10.1007/978-3-031-06764-8

This Springer imprint is published by the registered company Springer Nature Switzerland AG
The registered company address is: Gewerbestrasse 11, 6330 Cham, Switzerland

# Preface

The 8th International Conference on Artificial Intelligence and Security (ICAIS 2022), formerly called the International Conference on Cloud Computing and Security (ICCCS), was held during July 15–20, 2022, in Qinghai, China. Over the past seven years, ICAIS has become a leading conference for researchers and engineers to share their latest results of research, development, and applications in the fields of artificial intelligence and information security.

We used the Microsoft Conference Management Toolkit (CMT) system to manage the submission and review processes of ICAIS 2022. We received 1124 submissions from authors in 20 countries and regions, including the USA, Canada, the UK, Italy, Ireland, Japan, Russia, France, Australia, South Korea, South Africa, Iraq, Kazakhstan, Indonesia, Vietnam, Ghana, China, Taiwan, Macao, etc. The submissions cover the areas of artificial intelligence, big data, cloud computing and security, information hiding, IoT security, multimedia forensics, encryption and cybersecurity, and so on. We thank our Technical Program Committee (TPC) members and external reviewers for their efforts in reviewing papers and providing valuable comments to the authors. From the total of 1124 submissions, and based on at least three reviews per submission, the Program Chairs decided to accept 166 papers to be published in three LNCS volumes and 168 papers to be published in three CCIS volumes, yielding an acceptance rate of 30%. This volume of the conference proceedings contains all the regular, poster, and workshop papers.

The conference program was enriched by a series of keynote presentations, and the keynote speakers included Q.M. Jonathan Wu and Brij B. Gupta, amongst others. We thank them for their wonderful speeches.

There were 68 workshops organized in ICAIS 2022 which covered all the hot topics in artificial intelligence and security. We would like to take this moment to express our sincere appreciation for the contribution of all the workshop chairs and participants. We would like to extend our sincere thanks to all authors who submitted papers to ICAIS 2022 and to all TPC members. It was a truly great experience to work with such talented and hard-working researchers. We also appreciate the external reviewers for assisting the TPC members in their particular areas of expertise. Moreover, we want to thank our sponsors: ACM, ACM SIGWEB China, the University of Electronic Science and Technology of China, Qinghai Minzu University, Yuchi Blockchain Research Institute, Nanjing Normal University, Northeastern State University, New York University, Michigan State University, the University of Central Arkansas, Dublin City University,

Université Bretagne Sud, the National Nature Science Foundation of China, and Tech Science Press.

April 2022

Xingming Sun
Xiaorui Zhang
Zhihua Xia
Elisa Bertino

# Organization

## General Chairs

Yun Q. Shi                  New Jersey Institute of Technology, USA
Weisheng Ma                 Qinghai Minzu University, China
Mauro Barni                 University of Siena, Italy
Ping Jiang                  Southeast University, China
Elisa Bertino               Purdue University, USA
Xingming Sun                Nanjing University of Information Science and
                              Technology, China

## Technical Program Chairs

Aniello Castiglione         University of Salerno, Italy
Yunbiao Guo                 China Information Technology Security
                              Evaluation Center, China
Xiaorui Zhang               Engineering Research Center of Digital
                              Forensics, Ministry of Education, China
Q. M. Jonathan Wu           University of Windsor, Canada
Shijie Zhou                 University of Electronic Science and Technology
                              of China, China

## Publication Chair

Zhihua Xia                  Jinan University, China

## Publication Vice Chair

Ruohan Meng                 Nanjing University of Information Science and
                              Technology, China

## Publicity Chair

Zhaoxia Yin                 Anhui University, China

## Workshop Chairs

Baowei Wang                          Nanjing University of Information Science and
                                                 Technology, China
Lingyun Xiang                       Changsha University of Science and Technology,
                                                 China

## Organization Chairs

Genlin Ji                              Nanjing Normal University, China
Jianguo Wei                          Qinghai Minzu University and Tianjin University,
                                                 China
Xiaoyu Li                            University of Electronic Science and Technology
                                                 of China, China
Zhangjie Fu                          Nanjing University of Information Science and
                                                 Technology, China
Qilong Sun                           Qinghai Minzu University, China

## Technical Program Committee

Saeed Arif                           University of Algeria, Algeria
Anthony Ayodele                   University of Maryland Global Campus, USA
Zhifeng Bao                          Royal Melbourne Institute of Technology,
                                                 Australia
Zhiping Cai                          National University of Defense Technology,
                                                 China
Ning Cao                             Qingdao Binhai University, China
Paolina Centonze                   Iona College, USA
Chin-chen Chang                   Feng Chia University, Taiwan
Han-Chieh Chao                    National Dong Hwa University, Taiwan
Bing Chen                            Nanjing University of Aeronautics and
                                                 Astronautics, China
Hanhua Chen                         Huazhong University of Science and Technology,
                                                 China
Xiaofeng Chen                       Xidian University, China
Jieren Cheng                         Hainan University, China
Lianhua Chi                          IBM Research Center, Australia
Kim-Kwang Raymond Choo     University of Texas at San Antonio, USA
Ilyong Chung                        Chosun University, South Korea
Martin Collier                       Dublin City University, Ireland
Qi Cui                                Nanjing University of Information Science and
                                                 Technology, China
Robert H. Deng                      Singapore Management University, Singapore
Jintai Ding                           University of Cincinnati, USA

| | |
|---|---|
| Xinwen Fu | University of Central Florida, USA |
| Zhangjie Fu | Nanjing University of Information Science and Technology, China |
| Moncef Gabbouj | Tampere University of Technology, Finland |
| Ruili Geng | Spectral MD, USA |
| Song Guo | Hong Kong Polytechnic University, Hong Kong |
| Mohammad Mehedi Hassan | King Saud University, Saudi Arabia |
| Russell Higgs | University College Dublin, Ireland |
| Dinh Thai Hoang | University of Technology Sydney, Australia |
| Wien Hong | Nanfang College of Sun Yat-Sen University, China |
| Chih-Hsien Hsia | National Ilan University, Taiwan |
| Robert Hsu | Chung Hua University, Taiwan |
| Xinyi Huang | Fujian Normal University, China |
| Yongfeng Huang | Tsinghua University, China |
| Zhiqiu Huang | Nanjing University of Aeronautics and Astronautics, China |
| Patrick C. K. Hung | University of Ontario Institute of Technology, Canada |
| Farookh Hussain | University of Technology Sydney, Australia |
| Genlin Ji | Nanjing Normal University, China |
| Hai Jin | Huazhong University of Science and Technology, China |
| Sam Tak Wu Kwong | City University of Hong Kong, China |
| Chin-Feng Lai | Taiwan Cheng Kung University, Taiwan |
| Loukas Lazos | University of Arizona, USA |
| Sungyoung Lee | Kyung Hee University, South Korea |
| Hang Lei | University of Electronic Science and Technology of China, China |
| Chengcheng Li | University of Cincinnati, USA |
| Xiaoyu Li | University of Electronic Science and Technology of China, China |
| Feifei Li | Utah State University, USA |
| Jin Li | Guangzhou University, China |
| Jing Li | Rutgers University, USA |
| Kuan-Ching Li | Providence University, Taiwan |
| Peng Li | University of Aizu, Japan |
| Yangming Li | University of Washington, USA |
| Luming Liang | Uber Technology, USA |
| Haixiang Lin | Leiden University, The Netherlands |
| Xiaodong Lin | University of Ontario Institute of Technology, Canada |
| Zhenyi Lin | Verizon Wireless, USA |

| | |
|---|---|
| Alex Liu | Michigan State University, USA |
| Guangchi Liu | Stratifyd Inc., USA |
| Guohua Liu | Donghua University, China |
| Joseph Liu | Monash University, Australia |
| Quansheng Liu | University of South Brittany, France |
| Xiaodong Liu | Edinburgh Napier University, UK |
| Yuling Liu | Hunan University, China |
| Zhe Liu | Nanjing University of Aeronautics and Astronautics, China |
| Daniel Xiapu Luo | Hong Kong Polytechnic University, Hong Kong |
| Xiangyang Luo | Zhengzhou Science and Technology Institute, China |
| Tom Masino | TradeWeb LLC, USA |
| Nasir Memon | New York University, USA |
| Noel Murphy | Dublin City University, Ireland |
| Sangman Moh | Chosun University, South Korea |
| Yi Mu | University of Wollongong, Australia |
| Elie Naufal | Applied Deep Learning LLC, USA |
| Jiangqun Ni | Sun Yat-sen University, China |
| Rafal Niemiec | University of Information Technology and Management, Poland |
| Zemin Ning | Wellcome Trust Sanger Institute, UK |
| Shaozhang Niu | Beijing University of Posts and Telecommunications, China |
| Srikant Ojha | Sharda University, India |
| Jeff Z. Pan | University of Aberdeen, UK |
| Wei Pang | University of Aberdeen, UK |
| Chen Qian | University of California, Santa Cruz, USA |
| Zhenxing Qian | Fudan University, China |
| Chuan Qin | University of Shanghai for Science and Technology, China |
| Jiaohua Qin | Central South University of Forestry and Technology, China |
| Yanzhen Qu | Colorado Technical University, USA |
| Zhiguo Qu | Nanjing University of Information Science and Technology, China |
| Yongjun Ren | Nanjing University of Information Science and Technology, China |
| Arun Kumar Sangaiah | VIT University, India |
| Di Shang | Long Island University, USA |
| Victor S. Sheng | Texas Tech University, USA |
| Zheng-guo Sheng | University of Sussex, UK |
| Robert Simon Sherratt | University of Reading, UK |

| | |
|---|---|
| Yun Q. Shi | New Jersey Institute of Technology, USA |
| Frank Y. Shih | New Jersey Institute of Technology, USA |
| Guang Sun | Hunan University of Finance and Economics, China |
| Jianguo Sun | Harbin University of Engineering, China |
| Krzysztof Szczypiorski | Warsaw University of Technology, Poland |
| Tsuyoshi Takagi | Kyushu University, Japan |
| Shanyu Tang | University of West London, UK |
| Jing Tian | National University of Singapore, Singapore |
| Yoshito Tobe | Aoyang University, Japan |
| Cezhong Tong | Washington University in St. Louis, USA |
| Pengjun Wan | Illinois Institute of Technology, USA |
| Cai-Zhuang Wang | Ames Laboratory, USA |
| Ding Wang | Peking University, China |
| Guiling Wang | New Jersey Institute of Technology, USA |
| Honggang Wang | University of Massachusetts-Dartmouth, USA |
| Jian Wang | Nanjing University of Aeronautics and Astronautics, China |
| Jie Wang | University of Massachusetts Lowell, USA |
| Jin Wang | Changsha University of Science and Technology, China |
| Liangmin Wang | Jiangsu University, China |
| Ruili Wang | Massey University, New Zealand |
| Xiaojun Wang | Dublin City University, Ireland |
| Xiaokang Wang | St. Francis Xavier University, Canada |
| Zhaoxia Wang | Singapore Management University, Singapore |
| Jianguo Wei | Qinghai Minzu University and Tianjin University, China |
| Sheng Wen | Swinburne University of Technology, Australia |
| Jian Weng | Jinan University, China |
| Edward Wong | New York University, USA |
| Eric Wong | University of Texas at Dallas, USA |
| Shaoen Wu | Ball State University, USA |
| Shuangkui Xia | Beijing Institute of Electronics Technology and Application, China |
| Lingyun Xiang | Changsha University of Science and Technology, China |
| Yang Xiang | Deakin University, Australia |
| Yang Xiao | University of Alabama, USA |
| Haoran Xie | Education University of Hong Kong, China |
| Naixue Xiong | Northeastern State University, USA |
| Wei Qi Yan | Auckland University of Technology, New Zealand |

| | |
|---|---|
| Aimin Yang | Guangdong University of Technology, China |
| Ching-Nung Yang | National Dong Hwa University, Taiwan |
| Chunfang Yang | Zhengzhou Science and Technology Institute, China |
| Fan Yang | University of Maryland, USA |
| Guomin Yang | University of Wollongong, Australia |
| Qing Yang | University of North Texas, USA |
| Yimin Yang | Lakehead University, Canada |
| Ming Yin | Purdue University, USA |
| Shaodi You | Australian National University, Australia |
| Kun-Ming Yu | Chung Hua University, Taiwan |
| Shibin Zhang | Chengdu University of Information Technology, China |
| Weiming Zhang | University of Science and Technology of China, China |
| Xinpeng Zhang | Fudan University, China |
| Yan Zhang | Simula Research Laboratory, Norway |
| Yanchun Zhang | Victoria University, Australia |
| Yao Zhao | Beijing Jiaotong University, China |
| Desheng Zheng | Southwest Petroleum University, China |

## Organization Committee

| | |
|---|---|
| Xianyi Chen | Nanjing University of Information Science and Technology, China |
| Qi Cui | Nanjing University of Information Science and Technology, China |
| Zilong Jin | Nanjing University of Information Science and Technology, China |
| Yiwei Li | Columbia University, USA |
| Yuling Liu | Hunan University, China |
| Zhiguo Qu | Nanjing University of Information Science and Technology, China |
| Huiyu Sun | New York University, USA |
| Le Sun | Nanjing University of Information Science and Technology, China |
| Jian Su | Nanjing University of Information Science and Technology, China |
| Qing Tian | Nanjing University of Information Science and Technology, China |
| Qi Wang | Nanjing University of Information Science and Technology, China |
| Lingyun Xiang | Changsha University of Science and Technology, China |

Zhihua Xia             Nanjing University of Information Science and
                       Technology, China
Lizhi Xiong            Nanjing University of Information Science and
                       Technology, China
Leiming Yan            Nanjing University of Information Science and
                       Technology, China
Tao Ye                 Qinghai Minzu University, China
Li Yu                  Nanjing University of Information Science and
                       Technology, China
Zhili Zhou             Nanjing University of Information Science and
                       Technology, China

# Contents – Part III

## Information Hiding

## IoT Security

# Encryption and Cybersecurity

# Deep Edge Defense for Industrial Internet Based on Customized Hardware and UOS Architecture

Ming Wan[1] ⓘD, Xinlu Xu[1], Jianming Zhao[2], Jiangyuan Yao[3](✉), Xiu Lin[1],
Tingting Liu[1], and Xingcan Cao[4]

[1] School of Information, Liaoning University, Shenyang 110036, China
wanming@lnu.edu.cn
[2] Shenyang Institute of Automation Chinese Academy of Sciences, Shenyang 110016, China
[3] School of Computer Science and Technology, Hainan University, Haikou 570228, China
yaojy@hainanu.edu.cn
[4] Faculty of Arts, The University of British Columbia, Vancouver, BC V6T 1Z4, Canada

**Abstract.** With the rocketing development of Industrial Internet, the edge control and acquisition networks have become one integral role in determining high-efficiency intelligent manufacturing and flexible production, and the edge security requirements have increasingly drawn widespread attention around the world. In order to strengthen industrial security capabilities, this paper designs a multifunctional deep edge defense system, which is developed on the customized hardware and popular UOS architecture. Furthermore, this system not only supports the basic data routing and forwarding between distinct network boundaries, but also provides some deep content checking and filtering services, which can block malicious attack traffics by setting effective security strategies. Additionally, the multi-scale log audit and authority management can enable the immediate analysis and accurate positioning on abnormal communication behaviors, and further improve the high availability and convenience. The long-term testing shows that this system has fine stability and robust defense capabilities under the comprehensive testing which integrates with different types of data traffics.

**Keywords:** Edge defense · Deep content checking and filtering · Log audit and authority management · UOS

## 1 Introduction

In order to meet the large-scale requirements of industrial automation and maximize the resource utilization and production efficiency, ICSs (Industrial Control Systems) are realizing the integration of networking and intelligence with the driving of various new-generation information technologies, and intelligent manufacturing has reached one important development stage to complete the fourth industrial revolution [1, 2]. In this stage, ICTs (Information Communication Technologies) play a more and more pivotal role in the following changes: firstly, the application of single service has been changed to the integration pattern of multiple services; secondly, the production optimization of local technological process has been changed to the full life-cycle integrated manufacturing;

© The Author(s), under exclusive license to Springer Nature Switzerland AG 2022
X. Sun et al. (Eds.): ICAIS 2022, CCIS 1588, pp. 3–13, 2022.
https://doi.org/10.1007/978-3-031-06764-8_1

thirdly, the traditional production mode has been changed to the function of flexible setting and intelligent control. As a result, Industrial Internet, which has been regarded as a representative industry modality, achieves the interconnection and interoperation of all physical devices in the entire production process [3, 4]. Moreover, Industrial Internet not only implements the interaction and integration of IT (Information Technology) and OT (Operational Technology), but also starts to break the "information isolated island" state in traditional industrial control systems. With all these changes, industrial security flaws and threats reveal a trend of dramatic growth in recent years, and more and more risks of cyber attacks may force the construction of Industrial Internet into stagnation [5–8].

Originally, various edge control and acquisition networks, which can consist of industrial field devices (such as controllers, robots and sensors), always fall into the stable and closed running environment, because they are designed as some self-isolated internal networks. More specifically, they adopt some specialized communication protocols and customized software/hardware platforms, and are forbidden to interact with other external networks [9]. In consequence, both industry and academia put much emphasis on their functional safety and physical security [7, 10]. However, Industrial Internet establishes an entrance to edge control and acquisition networks, and the edge security requirements have increasingly drawn widespread attention around the world. In practice, the security problems in edge control and acquisition networks can be summarized as follows: 1) device security problems: the customized software/hardware platforms inevitably cover various potential system vulnerabilities and hardware failures, which can be exploited as the direct attack targets by the malicious adversaries [11]; 2) network security problems: the inherent design bugs of specialized communication protocols may be utilized to hide the attack tracks by the skilled attackers [12]; 3) the application of some burgeoning industrial information technologies may pose new security challenges due to their novel features, and the number of additional attack entrances and attack paths may be easily increased [6, 13]. Additionally, APTs (Advanced Persistent Threats) have been the most popular and most dangerous attack means in today's ICSs [14], and they may be far easier to launch due to the full interconnection characteristic in Industrial Internet [15].

In order to strengthen industrial security capabilities, some traditional security technologies and popular security viewpoints have been studied based on IT defense mechanisms: for the traditional security technologies, access control and intrusion detection are two representative ones [16–18], which are successfully applied in real-world ICSs, but the boundary conditions between the availability and the confidentiality still require careful consideration; for the popular security viewpoints, on the one hand, trusted computing and software-defined security defense may become two of the most promising researches in industrial cyber security field [19, 20], but it will take time to catch on even if their theoretical exploration survives contact with reality; on the other hand, various artificial intelligence and optimization algorithms have been gradually introduced to enhance security measures [21–23], but it will take a long time to develop and improve. Actually, one common characteristic of all edge control and acquisition networks is that they belong to one kind of regional networks which independently complete one or a series of industrial production processes, and use one or several entrances to communicate with other external networks. From this point, this paper designs a multifunctional deep edge defense system, which is developed on the customized hardware and popular UOS (Unity Operating System) architecture. More narrowly, this system can follow the basic strategy of "Defense in Depth" [24], and establish a data communication pipeline at the entrance of edge control and acquisition networks to analyze and manage the communication data between different network regions. As one special edge gateway, this system not only supports the basic data routing and forwarding between distinct network boundaries, but also provides some deep content checking and filtering services, which can block malicious attack traffics by setting effective security strategies. Also, this system can provide the mechanism to implement and enforce security policies, and support the customized configuration of network topology. Additionally, the multi-scale log audit and authority management can enable the immediate analysis and accurate positioning on abnormal communication behaviors, and further improve the high availability and convenience. Finally, we use different types of data traffics to carry out one long-term and comprehensive test, and the test results show that this defense system has fine stability and robust defense capabilities.

The rest of this paper is organized as follows. In Sect. 2, we present the main description of customized hardware and UOS architecture. In Sect. 3, we provide the details of deep edge defense system, including basic architecture and main functional modules. In Sect. 4, we give a long-term and comprehensive test based on different types of data traffics. Finally, we conclude our contribution and propose the future work in Sect. 5.

## 2 Description of Customized Hardware and UOS Architecture

As noted earlier, this edge defense system is developed on the customized hard-ware and popular UOS architecture. In the customized hardware, the main CPU model is PHYTIUM FT-2000/4 which embedded by the 64-bit ARM instruction set, and its main working frequency ranges from 2.6 GHz to 3.0 GHz. Additionally, this system has 8 GB DDR4 RAM, and integrates 6 Gigabit Ethernet ports. In order to enhance its usability, the customized hardware also supports the Lan Bypass function, which can maintain the network connectivity when the system is suddenly powered off.

In the system architecture, this edge defense system introduces UOS as its underlying operating system which is built on the Linux kernel. Furthermore, UOS can have relatively high stability and satisfactory security, and these characteristics can provide the basal guarantee for the reliable running of this defense system. Remarkably, UOS can support multiple platforms (such as ARM, AMD64 and MIPS), and perfectly match with the above hardware design. Because of their simplicity and compatibility, UOS can provides a wide variety of service interfaces to further maintain and extend the edge defense system.

## 3 Deep Edge Defense System and Functional Modules

### 3.1 Basic Architecture

This edge defense system, which can be distributedly deployed at the entrance of various edge control and acquisition networks, can provide all-round security protections for their key industrial field devices. That is, this system can reinforce the security of internal networks by effectively performing a series of security functions. In this system, all configuration information and logs are stored in a highly customized database, and the security strategies are synchronized and called by one build-in executable program. Based on the access control mechanism, this system can define the allowed accesses from the internal services, and ensure the normal external requests to the internal services. More specifically, this system deeply checks the communication data, and match with the security strategies to execute the following two actions: to block the communication data and to pass the communication data. According to the above mechanism, this system can further accomplish the following services: to protect some vulnerable applications; to control the access between internal and external networks; to centralize the management of edge industrial devices; to enhance the data privacy in internal networks; to log the active conditions of network resources and provide the basis for security planning and network maintenance. Additionally, this system can offer the WEB service interface to achieve the capability of remote management and configuration. Figure 1 shows the basic architecture and functional modules of this edge defense system.

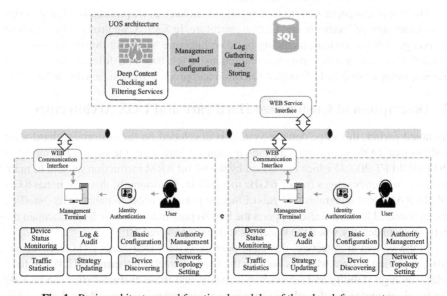

**Fig. 1.** Basic architecture and functional modules of the edge defense system.

## 3.2 Main Functional Modules

**Deep Content Checking and Filtering.** Based on the Linux Netfilter mechanism, this system develops one deep content checking and filtering service by using the DPI (Deep Packet Inspection) technology [25]. More specifically, this module intercepts all communication data from or to edge control and acquisition networks, and checks the data contents according to the configurable security strategies. If the checked contents can exactly match with any security strategy, the corresponding action will be executed. Additionally, this module not only support the basic content checking of network and transport layers (such as source and destination IP addresses, source and destination ports and protocol type), but also perform the in-depth analysis for industrial application protocols, including Modbus/TCP, Modbus/UDP and OPC Classic. For Modbus/TCP and Modbus/UDP, this module can analyze and restore the key data contents (such as function code, register or coil addresses and register or coil values) according to the Modbus protocol specification, and realize the auditing of abnormal Modbus communication behaviors. For OPC Classic, this module can accomplish the dynamic port opening according to the OPC security specification, and track the whole connection and communication process to prevent the illegal access. Also, this module can effectively associate with the real-time alarming and logging operations, and update all security strategies according to the change of security requirements. Figure 2 shows the main function and principle of deep content checking and filtering service.

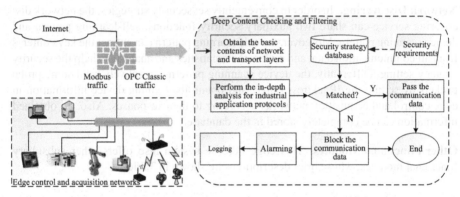

**Fig. 2.** Main function and principle of deep content checking and filtering service.

**Multi-scale Log Audit.** The logging and auditing operation plays a key role in all security defense devices, because it is helpful to trace and identify where the unexpected behaviors occurred. Moreover, this operation can effectively record the communication activities of networks or devices, and offer a posteriori investigation to find their vulnerabilities and improve their security. In general, the logging and auditing operation has the following practical implications: 1) by analyzing the logging records, it can help to discover and resolve the system security problems; 2) by using the auditing information, it can help to determine the attack events and attack sources; 3) by selectively collecting and tracking some security events, it can help to provide strong evidences of their destructive behaviors; 4) by combining with security policies and specifications, it can help to implement disaster recovery and maintain normal system activities. In our edge defense system, the multi-scale log audit service can appropriately meet the above objectives: firstly, the local operating logs can record all user operations in this system, and prevent that the legal users operate over authority and the illegal users viciously attack;

secondly, the general logs can support the comprehensive records of general communication activities, which can be used to exploit network or device vulnerabilities; thirdly, the alarming logs can record malicious attack behaviors, which are prevented because of the unauthorized access to edge control and acquisition networks; fourth, this service can also carry out the traffic monitoring statistics from or to edge control and acquisition networks.

**Authority Management.** In order to obtain more flexible user authorization, this system utilizes three-dimensional authority management service, including user management, role management and authority allocation. Furthermore, the role management can create different roles according to the actual industrial management system, and the authority allocation can allocate the specific security functions for each role. Based on the above settings, the user management can create multiple users under different levels of roles. Through the collaboration among the above three ways, this service can offer the wholescale authority management to achieve various degrees of access and control.

**Network Discovering.** In order to conveniently set security strategies, the network discovering service can share two auxiliary security functions: self-learning pattern and device scanning pattern. Moreover, the self-learning pattern can extract the key contents from all communication data, and realize their statistics and analysis to help the security strategy setting. Differently, the device scanning pattern can actively send some probe packets by setting the IP address range, and obtain the running device information in edge control and acquisition networks according to their responses. Also, all obtained information can be completely stored in the database.

**Other Functional Modules.** This edge defense system also offers other subsidiary functional modules, whose brief descriptions are shown in Table 1.

1) System status: this system can show the real-time running statuses, mainly including the real-time CPU utilization, current memory usage, actual disk space usage and different numbers of various logs.
2) Time configuration: this system can configure the system time by using the following two ways: manual time configuration and automatic time configuration based on NTP.
3) Forwarding mode: this system can set different forwarding modes according to the actual network structure. Moreover, the basic routing forwarding mode can perform and verify the default or basic routing configuration tasks between different edge network segments, which also involve SNAT and DNAT strategies. Differently, the transparent bridging forwarding mode can accomplish the two-layer interconnectivity in the same edge network segment, which never change any IP address.
4) Working pattern: this system has three working patterns, including the bypass pattern, the defense pattern and the self-learning pattern, and these three patterns can be seamlessly switched according to the actual usage requirements.
5) Network topology setting: this system can dynamically configure the network topology and physical layout of industrial devices according to the actual industrial

field network structure, and customize the setting of industrial device information, including: its name, device type, IP address, MAC address et al.

6) Basic configuration: this system can configure the basic system information (such as the system ID and network card information), and provide the fault recovery function when the system appears a major failure or a catastrophic event.

**Table 1.** Main features and items of other functional modules.

| Functional module | Features and items |
| --- | --- |
| System status | 1) Real-time CPU utilization;<br>2) Current memory usage;<br>3) Actual disk space usage;<br>4) Different numbers of various logs |
| Time configuration | 1) Manual time configuration;<br>2) Automatic NTP time configuration |
| Forwarding mode | 1) Basic routing forwarding mode;<br>2) Transparent bridging forwarding mode |
| Working pattern | 1) Bypass pattern;<br>2) Defense pattern;<br>3) Self-learning pattern |
| Network topology setting | 1) Dynamical configuration of network topology;<br>2) Customized device information setting |
| Basic configuration | 1) Basic system information configuration;<br>2) Fault recovery configuration |

## 4 Long-Term and Comprehensive Test Based on Different Types of Data Traffics

In order to evaluate the system's availability and stability, we use different types of data traffics to carry out one long-term and comprehensive test, and the testing environment is shown in Fig. 3. In this test, we fully integrate the white-listing testing approach with the black-listing testing approach, and four different types of data traffics are constructed to pass through this defense system. Moreover, these four types of data traffics can be briefly descripted as follows:

1) Basic TCP/UDP data traffic: we use the TCP/UDP testing tool to create the corresponding test cases, and these test cases includes normal TCP connections and connectionless UDP packets, which can conform to the security strategies based on the white-listing testing approach. Additionally, we adopt the automatic sending operation whose period is set to 1000ms, and judge whether the TCP connections are successfully established and the data transmission has no mistake.

2) Modbus/TCP data traffic: we use Modbus Slave and Modbus Poll simulation software to create Modbus/TCP test cases, and respectively perform the white-listing test and the black-listing test for five different testing objects, including function code, register address, register value, coil address and coil value. Furthermore, we configure 5 pairs of Modbus client and Modbus server: the first 4 pairs establish normal Modbus/TCP communications to complete the white-listing test, and the last pair sends malicious communication data by using a forbidden function code to complete the black-listing test. By comparing the consistency between client and server, we judge whether normal Modbus/TCP communications are successfully established and the malicious Modbus/TCP communication data can be effectively blocked.

**Fig. 3.** Testing environment based on different types of data traffics.

3) OPC Classic data traffic: we use KEPServerEx V4.0 software to create OPC Classic test cases, and perform the white-listing test to track the dynamic port. Moreover, this software can use the known port 135 to negotiate a new port, which can be further utilized to transmit the OPC data. In this test, we set that the OPC Quick Client executes one data access operation per 1000ms, and judge whether the data values can be successfully obtained from the OPC server.

4) Malicious attack data traffic: we design a script to simulate one malicious attack, which can be regarded one stress test due to its massive data flow. More specifically, this script continuously sends 10000 packets per 60s, and the data size of each packet includes 5000 bytes. Additionally, the destination port and source IP address change

randomly on a big scope. In this test, we perform the black-listing test, and judge whether all malicious attack packets can be effectively blocked.

It is worth mentioning that the forwarding modes in this test are set to the basic routing mode and the transparent bridging forwarding mode for OPC Classic data traffic and other data traffics, respectively. Based on the above four types of data traffics, we run this testing environment for more than three months, and the defense system can achieve the anticipated protection effect. That is, for the normal communication data, this defense system can successfully forward these traffics by using the white-listing testing approach. For the malicious communication data, this defense system can effectively prevent the corresponding attacks by using the black-listing testing approach. Through the long-term and comprehensive test, it can directly prove that this defense system has fine stability and robust defense capabilities.

## 5  Conclusion and Future Work

Based on the customized hardware and popular UOS architecture, this paper design a multifunctional deep edge defense system for Industrial Internet, and this system can meet the requirements of distributed deployment at the entrance of various edge control and acquisition networks. Based on the access control mechanism and the basic principle of "Depth in Defense", this system can define the allowed accesses from the internal services, and ensure the normal external requests to the internal services. Moreover, this system provides some deep content checking and filtering services which can block malicious attack traffics by setting effective security strategies, and enable the immediate analysis and accurate positioning on abnormal communication behaviors by using the multi-scale log audit and authority management. Also, this system offers some additional functions to enhance its availability and convenience. long-term and comprehensive test fully demonstrates that this defense system has fine stability and robust defense capabilities. In the future work, we will apply this defense system in real-world ICSs, and further verify the feasibility of its practical application.

**Acknowledgement.** The authors are grateful to the anonymous referees for their insightful comments and suggestions.

**Funding Statement.** This work is supported by the National Key R&D Program of China: "Key technology and application of safety and credibility for industrial control system" (Grant no. 2020YFB2009500), the Scientific Research Project of Educational Department of Liaoning Province (Grant No. LJKZ0082), the Natural Science Foundation of Liaoning Province Department of Science and Technology (Grant No. 2020-BS-082), the Hainan Provincial Natural Science Foundation of China (Grant No. 620RC562) and the National Natural Science Foundation of China (Grant No. 61802092).

## References

1. Park, I., Yoon, B., Kim, S., Seol, H.: Technological opportunities discovery for safety through topic modeling and opinion mining in the fourth industrial revolution: the case of artificial intelligence. IEEE Trans. Eng. Manage. **68**(5), 1504–1519 (2021)

2. Fakhri, A.B., et al.: Industry 4.0: architecture and equipment revolution. Comput. Mat. Continua **66**(2), 1175–1194 (2021)
3. Li, J., Yu, F.R., Deng, G., Luo, C., Ming, Z., Yan, Q.: Industrial Internet: a survey on the enabling technologies, applications, and challenges. IEEE Commun. Surv. Tutor. **19**(3), 1504–1526 (2017)
4. Sahu, P., Singh, S.K., Singh, A.K.: Blockchain based secure solution for cloud storage: a model for synchronizing Industry 4.0 and IIoT. J. Cyber Secur. **3**(2), 107–115 (2021)
5. Ahmadian, M.M., Shajari, M., Shafiee, M.A.: Industrial control system security taxonomic framework with application to a comprehensive incidents survey. Int. J. Crit. Infrastruct. Prot. **29**, 1–22 (2020)
6. Wan, M., Li, J., Liu, Y., Zhao, J., Wang, J.: Characteristic insights on industrial cyber security and popular defense mechanisms. Chin. Commun. **18**(1), 130–150 (2021)
7. Jhanjhi, N., Humayun, M., Almuayqil, S.N.: Cyber security and privacy issues in industrial internet of things. Comput. Syst. Sci. Eng. **37**(3), 361–380 (2021)
8. Ma, L., Wang, X., Wang, X., Wang, L., Shi, Y., et al.: TCDA: truthful combinatorial double auctions for mobile edge computing in industrial internet of things. IEEE Trans. Mob. Comput. 1–14 (2021). https://doi.org/10.1109/TMC.2021.3064314
9. Galloway, B., Hancke, G.P.: Introduction to industrial control networks. IEEE Commun. Surv. Tutor. **15**(2), 860–880 (2013)
10. Chen, Y., Cui, L., Wang, C.: T application of MES system in the safety management of offshore oil and gas fields. J. Quant. Comput. **1**(1), 41–48 (2019)
11. Yang, J., Zhou, C., Tian, Y., An, C.: A zoning-based secure control approach against actuator attacks in industrial cyber-physical systems. IEEE Trans. Industr. Electron. **68**(3), 2637–2647 (2021)
12. Volkova, V., Niedermeier, M., Basmadjian, R., Meer, H.: Security challenges in control network protocols: a survey. IEEE Commun. Surv. Tutor. **21**(1), 619–639 (2019)
13. Benias, N., Markopoulos, A.P.: A review on the readiness level and cyber-security challenges in industry 4.0. In: 2017 South Eastern European Design Automation, Computer Engineering, Computer Networks and Social Media Conference, pp. 1–5, Kastoria, Greece (2017)
14. Ahmed, Y., Asyhari, A., Rahman, M.A.: A cyber kill chain approach for detecting advanced persistent threats. Comput. Mater. Continua **67**(2), 2497–2513 (2021)
15. Alshamrani, A., Myneni, S., Chowdhary, A., Huang, D.: A survey on advanced persistent threats: techniques, solutions, challenges, and research opportunities. IEEE Commun. Surv. Tutor. **21**(2), 1851–1877 (2019)
16. Cheminod, M., Durante, L., Seno, L., Valenzano, A.: Performance evaluation and modeling of an industrial application-layer firewall. IEEE Trans. Industr. Inf. **14**(5), 2159–2170 (2018)
17. Zhao, J., Zeng, P., Chen, C., Dong, Z., Han, J.: Deep learning anomaly detection based on hierarchical status-connection features in networked control systems. Intell. Autom. Soft Comput. **30**(1), 337–350 (2021)
18. Han, S., Wu, Q., Zhang, H., Qin, B., Hu, J., et al.: Log-based anomaly detection with robust feature extraction and online learning. IEEE Trans. Inf. Forensics Secur. **16**(23), 2300–2311 (2021)
19. Maene, P., Gotzfried, J., Clercq, R., Muller, T., Freiling, F., et al.: Hardware-based trusted computing architectures for isolation and attestation. IEEE Trans. Comput. **67**(3), 361–374 (2018)
20. Du, M., Wang, K.: An SDN-enabled pseudo-honeypot strategy for distributed denial of service attacks in industrial internet of things. IEEE Trans. Industr. Inf. **16**(1), 648–657 (2020)
21. Ma, L., Huang, M., Yang, S., Wang, R., Wang, X.: An adaptive localized decision variable analysis approach to large-Scale multiobjective and many-objective optimization. IEEE Transactions on Cybernetics (2021). https://doi.org/10.1109/TCYB.2020.3041212

22. Ma, L., Cheng, S., Shi, Y.: Enhancing learning efficiency of brain storm optimization via orthogonal learning design. IEEE Trans. Syst. Man Cybern. Syst. **51**(11), 6723–6742 (2021)
23. Cho, J.: Efficient autonomous defense system using machine learning on edge device. Comput. Mat. Continua **70**(2), 3565–3588 (2022)
24. Nugraha, Y., Brown, I., Sastrosubroto, A.S.: An adaptive wideband Delphi method to study state cyber-defence requirements. IEEE Trans. Emerg. Top. Comput. **4**(1), 47–59 (2016)
25. Xu, C., Chen, S., Su, J., Yiu, S.M., Hui, L.C.K.: A survey on regular expression matching for deep packet inspection: applications, algorithms, and hardware platforms. IEEE Commun. Surv. Tutor. **18**(4), 2991–3029 (2016)

# A Blockchain-Based Risk Assessment Model for Heterogeneous Identity Alliance

Yanbo Yang[1], Wunan Wan[1,2(✉)], Shibin Zhang[1,2], Jinquan Zhang[1,2], Zhi Qin[1,2],
and Jinyue Xia[3]

[1] School of Cybersecurity, Chengdu University of Information Technology, Chengdu 610225,
China
nan_wwn@cuit.edu.cn
[2] Advanced Cryptography and System Security Key Laboratory of Sichuan Province,
Chengdu 610255, China
[3] International Business Machines Corporation (IBM), New York 10041 NY 212, USA

**Abstract.** Heterogeneous identity alliance technology solves the identity management problem under heterogeneous networks by building a unified and trusted identity management system, while the risk assessment system of heterogeneous identity alliance can analyze potential security problems in heterogeneous identity alliance in advance, so as to realize timely supervision and maintenance of identity when crossing domains and reduce the proliferation of security problems. A blockchain-based risk assessment model for heterogeneous identity alliance is proposed for existing risk assessment systems that are generally centralized architectures with single point of failure, internal mischief, and loss of control of user data. The model uses attribute encryption to guarantee the secure storage of privacy data, while ensuring that the control of risk assessment-related data is always in the hands of the data owner, and simplifies the three-stage PBFT (Practical Byzantine Fault Tolerance) consensus to two stages to improve the efficiency of risk assessment result processing. Finally, a comparison experiment shows that compared to the three-stage PBFT, the two-stage PBFT reduces the number of communications to reach consensus and improves the throughput by about 7%.

**Keywords:** Blockchain · Risk assessment · Attribute-based encryption · PBFT · Heterogeneous identity alliance

## 1 Introduction

During the widespread use of Internet technology, the problem of information non-interoperability and identity information misuse among various network identity platforms has emerged, which seriously hinders the monitoring and management of identity information in cyberspace [1, 2], and the concept of heterogeneous identity alliance has been proposed to solve the above problems [3].

The heterogeneous identity alliance solves the problem of non-uniform network identity information in different domains by building a cross-domain unified network identity

© The Author(s), under exclusive license to Springer Nature Switzerland AG 2022
X. Sun et al. (Eds.): ICAIS 2022, CCIS 1588, pp. 14–27, 2022.
https://doi.org/10.1007/978-3-031-06764-8_2

system and associating multiple independent heterogeneous identity management systems, but it still suffers from identity impersonation and misuse, and data tampering and theft [4, 5]. Therefore, in order to improve the trustworthiness problem of heterogeneous identity alliance as a whole, scholars have proposed a heterogeneous identity alliance risk assessment system.

The heterogeneous identity alliance risk assessment system [6], is a system that analyzes the weak points and potential threats of members in a heterogeneous identity alliance by establishing a common index system and having a risk assessment organization evaluate their assets and user behavior, etc. This system can not only prevent attacks that occur in heterogeneous identity alliance, but also provide important information basis for future supervision and maintenance [7, 8].

In traditional risk assessment systems for heterogeneous identity alliance, alliance members lose control over the data they possess after submitting their own asset information and relevant data required for risk assessment, such as user behavior, to risk assessment organizations and regulators, and such private data often involve vulnerabilities and vulnerabilities of alliance members, which can endanger individual heterogeneous identity alliance member organizations and even the entire heterogeneous identity the security of the alliance as a whole. In addition, due to the centralized architecture, there are also issues of downtime and internal mischief, including but not limited to modifying the risk values of alliance members and tampering with the data required for risk assessment, which is difficult to trace.

Blockchain technology, as a decentralized database that cannot be tampered with and possesses traceability [9, 10], has the following advantages when combined with a heterogeneous identity alliance risk assessment system: blockchain technology, as a decentralized distributed database, can reduce the possibility of attacks on confidential data due to centralized storage; the nature of data on the blockchain that cannot be tampered with ensures the secure storage of confidential data, and the traceable The nature of traceability can realize the audit of risk assessment results by regulators more quickly and precisely, trace the source of risk and risky behaviors for processing at any time, and realize the assessment of recourse when the assessment results are disputed; moreover, the research related to the combination of blockchain and cryptography technology to protect privacy has also made a lot of achievements, which can ensure the safe storage of risk assessment data and realize efficient sharing and calculation at the same time.

The popular combination areas of blockchain are still in logistics, finance, and medical industries, while there are fewer studies combining blockchain technology with risk assessment. In 2018, Yonggui Fu and others constructed a cyber-physical system information security risk assessment system based on blockchain and big data, and blockchain technology was used to ensure the authenticity and reliability of cyber-physical system data and data from related systems outside the cyber-physical system [11]. In 2019, Zhao Yang and others utilized blockchain technology to store data generated by a heterogeneous identity alliance risk assessment system and used an improved DPoS algorithm to mobilize each risk assessment node [12].

At present, the popular combination areas of blockchain are still in logistics, finance, medical and other industries, while the research combining blockchain technology with risk assessment is less. The current research direction is mainly in designing blockchain models that are more compatible with risk assessment, but the models that have been studied simply use the decentralization ability of blockchain to change the traditional centralized architecture, as well as use blockchain technology to store important data related to risk assessment, guaranteeing that it cannot be tampered with, and does not consider the protection of user data control rights and the high requirements of risk assessment on data processing efficiency.

So this paper proposes a new risk assessment model for heterogeneous identity alliance based on blockchain for heterogeneous identity alliance risk assessment system, in summary, we make the following contributions:

1) Using attribute encryption to guarantee the secure storage of private data, while ensuring the data owner's control rights over risk assessment data.
2) Based on the PBFT consensus mechanism and combined with the heterogeneous identity alliance risk assessment system, a two-stage PBFT-based improved consensus mechanism is proposed, which reduces the number of communications required for node consensus and improves the block-out efficiency.

In Sect. 2, we introduce the technology related to the blockchain-based heterogeneous identity alliance risk assessment system. In Sect. 3, we propose a blockchain-based risk assessment model for heterogeneous identity alliance, including the logical framework and consensus process of the model. The model is evaluated in Sect. 4 and Sect. 5 is the conclusion.

## 2 Related Work

### 2.1 Heteronormative Identity Alliance

Heterogeneous identity alliance is a network identity management technology that is responsible for maintaining the entity identity credentials of all users within multiple identity management platforms with different application domains, architectures, and independence from each other, and providing trust transfer services for users across identity management platforms, while meeting the regulatory requirements of regulators for multiple identities and multiple behaviors of a single entity user. Cyber identity management and authentication technologies have attracted worldwide attention as the construction focus and strategic cornerstone for national maintenance of cyberspace security, and the United States released the National Strategy for Trusted Identities in Cyberspace [13] and the National Action Plan for Cybersecurity [14] in 2011 to carry out identity authentication services in healthcare, e-commerce, and other industries in various states, and European Union countries, in order to unify the European e identity management technical standards and management framework, the FutureID project was carried out and implemented in 2017 [15], and the eID framework was proposed in 2018 [16], which promoted the development of cross-border network identity service technology, and the Chinese government also promulgated the National Strategy for Cyberspace Security [17] and the Cyber Security Law in 2016, which raised the importance of cyberspace security elevated to a national strategic level. Therefore, the research on the design of the underlying model of heterogeneous identity alliance, including trust transfer, cross-domain access, trustworthy evaluation, privacy protection and regulatory analysis, is in urgent need of strengthening.

The traditional heterogeneous identity alliance is a centralized architecture, as shown in Fig. 1, where a trust domain is first constructed from heterogeneous identity management systems within a domain or organization, and then a unified heterogeneous identity alliance management system is used as the center, responsible for maintaining the alliance unified identity credentials of users in different heterogeneous identity management systems within the alliance, so as to support cross-domain authentication, access, trust evaluation, and other services of users.

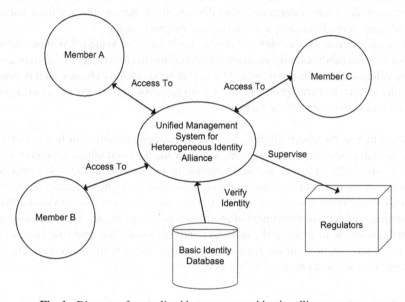

**Fig. 1.** Diagram of centralized heterogeneous identity alliance system.

## 2.2  Risk Assessment System of Heterogeneous Identity Alliance

Risk assessment of heterogeneous identity alliance is to count the resources of heterogeneous identity alliance members and predict the number of possible losses to the overall network after an attack on different resources according to their vulnerability, which can be used as an active defense means to learn the potential security risks of heterogeneous identity alliance in advance and solve them, and at the same time provide clear information security construction goals of heterogeneous identity alliance for regulators and alliance members, and the main processes of risk value calculation is as follows [18]:

1) Establishing risk assessment index system: the risk assessment agency makes reference to the traditional risk assessment index system and combines the recommendations of information security risk assessment experts to establish the risk

assessment index system of the heterogeneous identity alliance based on the characteristics of heterogeneous identity alliance members with targeted optimization and improvement.

2) Asset identification: according to the determined risk assessment index system, the risk assessment organization makes the entry of assets and assigns values to the confidentiality, integrity and availability of assets and the weights of the above three security attributes, so as to calculate the asset value.

3) Vulnerability identification: risk assessment personnel make entries and assign values to the vulnerability of assets using penetration tests and expert scoring.

4) Threat identification: based on user behavior data recorded in the logs of firewalls, intrusion detection systems and other devices, the behaviors that are more harmful and occur more frequently are entered and assigned values.

5) Risk calculation: In accordance with the prescribed risk value calculation method, assets, vulnerabilities and threats are correlated and the risk values of different assets are calculated. The final risk value of heterogeneous identity alliance members generally adopts the barrel principle, i.e., the highest risk value of system assets is used as the final risk value of the member.

According to the above process, the risk assessment organization first establishes a unified risk assessment index system, and then the assessed alliance member sends its own assets and data such as user behavior in log records to the risk assessment organization and grants the risk assessment organization the right to conduct penetration tests on its own system, so as to complete the risk assessment of its own system. When the data required for risk assessment of an alliance member changes, the risk assessment organization needs to evaluate the new data and recalculate the final risk value of the alliance member in time for the regulator to analyze and control the security situation of the entire heterogeneous identity alliance.

## 2.3 Blockchain

Once Bitcoin was proposed by Satoshi Nakamoto in 2008 [19], the underlying blockchain technology has gradually become familiar to people. Blockchain has the features of "decentralization", "traceability of ledger data", and "immutability of ledger data", and so on [20], and it has gradually become familiar with its ability to build a foundation of trust between multiple unfamiliar interests at a low cost. It is gradually becoming familiar with the characteristics of building a foundation of trust between multiple unfamiliar interests at low cost [21]. Blockchain technology is not only limited to cryptocurrencies, but also has great potential for fund traceability in the financial industry, copyright protection in the cultural industry, and privacy data protection in the medical industry, etc. [22–24]. Blockchain is changing the transaction mode in the current untrustworthy network step by step, and steadily moving toward the goal of reconstructing a trustworthy society.

In blockchain, although different blockchain platforms have differences in data structure, the overall structure is similar. In Bitcoin, as shown in Fig. 2, a block is divided into two parts: the block header, which includes the merkle root, the current protocol version, a hash pointer to the previous block, the difficulty target threshold for mining, a random number (Nonce) and a timestamp, and the block body, which contains a list of transactions. The blocks are generated in order to form a complete block chain using the hash pointer to the previous block [25], and the characteristics of the Merkle tree ensure the integrity and tamper-proof data on the block chain.

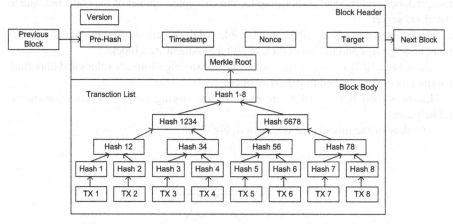

**Fig. 2.** Structure of data block.

## 3    A Blockchain-Based Risk Assessment Model for Heterogeneous Identity Alliance

### 3.1    Logical Framework

In this paper, we propose a blockchain-based risk assessment model for heterogeneous identity alliance, which is designed mainly for risk assessment agencies and regulators to control the risk situation of heterogeneous identity alliance members. Since the number of members of the heterogeneous identity alliance may increase and the continuous existence of members in the network will lead to the growing amount of risk assessment related data, if all data is stored directly on the chain, it will cause the waste of storage resources and the efficiency of node data synchronization will become less and less, which will be a burden to the network, so this model adopts a hybrid data storage method of blockchain+cloud server; in order to meet the principle of confidentiality, while keeping the access control of the data in the hands of the data owner all the time, using attribute encryption technology to guarantee the security of the data in the model; and using the improved consensus mechanism to ensure the block-out efficiency to meet the requirements of risk assessment related data need to be processed as soon as possible.

The model in this paper consists of five components:

Identity Authority (IA): It has government qualification endorsement, so it can act as a trusted center with the highest management authority, and take the role of certificate authority in the model at the same time. Its main responsibility is to carry out global settings, including the system master public key and master private key. It is also responsible for vetting the identities of evaluated enterprises and risk assessment organizations and assigning identities to them after verification.

Evaluated Node (EN): member of the heterogeneous identity alliance, provider of data required for the risk assessment process (enterprise assets, presence of vulnerabilities, risk behaviours) and responsible for the encrypted upload of the collected data to the cloud server.

Risk Assessment Node (RA): responsible for the election of representative assessment node groups and the generation of risk assessment data blocks.

Consortium Blockchain (CB): responsible for storing summary values and important parameters of data related to risk assessment.

Elastic Cloud Server (ECS): responsible for storing encrypted risk assessment-related data.

The flow of the model runs is shown in Fig. 3:

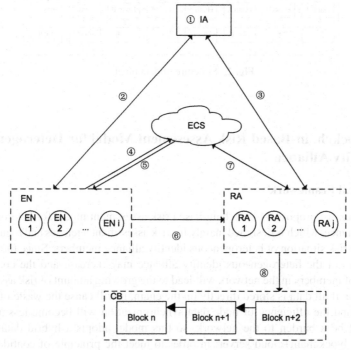

**Fig. 3.** Logical framework of model.

1) When the system is initialized, *IA* generates the master key pair *(MPK, MSK)* ←
   *Setup*(λ), where λ is the security parameter. The system's master public key *(MPK)*
   is public and the master private key *(MSK)* is kept by the *IA* which is kept secret.

2) *EN* Submit an application to join *CB*, *IA* review *EN*'s identity and assign him ID book (*Identity* $= (ID, < pubkey, privkey >)$) where *ID* is the global unique identity of the node, and (*pubkey, privkey*) is the key pair of the node.

3) *RA* Submit an application to join *CB*, *IA* review qualifications and pass for *RA* assign the ID book (*Identity* $= (ID, A_p, < pubkey, privkey >)$) and generate the node attribute private key($ASK = KeyGen(MPK, MSK, A_p)$) for *RA*, where *ID* is the node's globally unique identity, and (*pubkey, privkey*) is the node's key pair, and $A_p = (a_1, a_2, a_3, ..., a_n)$ is the set of attributes possessed by the *RA*.

4) After a data update occurs on $EN_i$, first create an *index*, which is used to identify the specific serial number of the data in the cloud server storage path, for each updated risk assessment related data *m*, *index* is usually generated in chronological order. Then encrypt *m* with a randomly selected symmetric file key ($key_m$) in the key space to obtain a ciphertext *CT*, and according to the node's customized access policy $A_s$, use encrypted symmetric file key ($key_m$) to get $key'_m \leftarrow Encrypt(MPK, A_s, key_m)$, ensuring that only risk assessment node can decrypt the correct file key. $EN_i$ combines each piece of *CT* with its *index* to form a *M* set. Along with the access policy in plaintext form ($A_s$), the symmetric key ($key'_m$) after the attribute encryption, the digest value of the *M* (*MD*), and the signature of $EN_i$ on $MD(sig_{EN_i})$, compose the *file$_j$* and send it to *ECS*.

5) *ECS* receives the above message, verifies $EN_i$'s signature and calculates *M*'s hash value to verify *MD*. After ensuring the correctness and integrity of the data, the storage path ($sl_j$) of *file$_j$* is returned to $EN_i$.

6) $EN_i$ gets $sl_j$ and sends a message ($update = (ID_{EC_i}, MD, sig_{EC_i}, sl_j)$) to *RA* that it has updated its data.

7) After receiving *update*, master node $RA_k$ first uses $EN_i$'s public key ($pubkey_{EN_i}$) to verify the signature of $sig_{EN_i}$, Then request to the cloud server to download the *file$_j$* stored in the $sl_j$, *ECS* will determine whether $RA_k$ satisfies the condition based on the access policy corresponding to the requested file. If it does, $RA_k$ is allowed to download *file$_j$* to get *M* and compare *update* with $sig_{EC_i}$ and *MD* in *file$_j$* to ensure that the source is genuine and that the data stored on the cloud server has not been tampered with. Since the role attributes of $RA_k$ satisfy the access policy set by $EN_i$, so you can decrypt $key'_m$ to get the file key ($key_m \leftarrow Decrypt(MPK, ASK_{RA_k}, key'_m)$), And use $key_m$ to obtain plaintext data *m*, select a risk evaluation algorithm for the calculation of risk values.

8) After packaging the risk assessment results into blocks, consensus is reached within all risk assessment nodes and uploaded to the chain.

### 3.2 Consensus Process

Since the model in this paper uses a consortium blockchains, the number of nodes on the chain is small and basically fixed. In order to meet the requirement of efficient block generation, this model uses the improved PBFT consensus mechanism to reach consensus among multiple risk assessment nodes.

For the sake of simplicity and efficiency, the generation and consensus of the blocks on the chain are initiated directly by the master node after collecting the data, and all nodes work together to complete the process, so the C/S mode of the client sending requests in the classical PBFT can be changed to the P2P mode, and the purpose of consensus in this model is to synchronize all nodes local area block chain contains risk assessment related data and results, in the Pre-prepare and Prepare stage, the consensus message has been broadcasted within all nodes, so the three stage process in the classical PBFT consistency protocol can be simplified to two stages, and the improved PBFT flow chart is shown in Fig. 4:

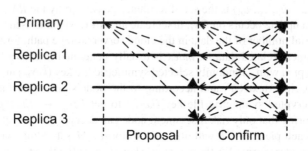

**Fig. 4.** Flow chart of improved PBFT.

1) Set the number for all *RA* nodes, and use the view number $v$ and the total number of *RA* nodes ($N$) to get the number of the master node in the current view ($p = v$ mod $|N|$).
2) $EN_i$ sends its own update message to the master node $RA_k$, together with a signature for the message.
3) After $RA_k$ receives *update*, it checks the signature of *update* and discards the request if it is illegal, and downloads the data related to risk assessment if it is legal.
4) $RA_k$ verifies the authenticity and integrity of the data related to the risk assessment, and then records it in the update request table of the master node (*Utable0*). $RA_k$ selects a risk assessment algorithm for each recently updated $m$ to evaluate the respective risk value $VaR_m$, and updates the final risk value $VaR$ of $EN_i$. At the same time, it generates a risk value change message $tx$, which is packed into the block. A $tx$ in this model includes $ID_{EN_i}$, $sl_j$, $index, VaR_m$, $< VaR_p$, $VaR_a >$, $ID_{a\lg}$ and *Height*, where $VaR_p$ is the final risk value before the change, initialized to 0, $VaR_a$ is the updated final risk value, $ID_{a\lg}$ is the ID of the risk algorithm on which the current evaluation result is based, and *Height* is the height of the block to which the current $tx$ belongs.
5) After a certain time $t$ of collection by $RA_k$, the collected $tx$ is composed into Block, The *Blockheader* $=<$ Pr *ehash*, *Timestamp*, *Height*, $ID_{RA_k}$, $sig_{RA_k}$, *TX Root* $>$, where Pr *ehash* is the hash pointer to the previous block, *Timestamp* is the outgoing block timestamp, *Height* is the current block height, $sig_{RA_k}$ is the signature of the $RA_k$ on the block, and *TX Root* is the root of the Merkle tree consisting of all $tx$ of the current block.
6) $RA_k$ sends consensus proposal $<Proposal, Blockheader, Utable0>$ to each $RA$ replica node.
7) After the $RA$ replica node receives the consensus proposal from $RA_k$, it needs to perform the block checksum, which is as follows:

1) Signature verification of the node responsible for generating the block.
2) Verify the legitimacy of the parent block by hashing the block header of the current block.
3) Check if there is an abnormal assignment of $tx$ in the block and verify that its root hash is the same as the TX Root in the block header.

After verification, send consensus confirmation message ($<Confirm, Blockheader, ID_{RA_d}, sig_{RA_d}>$) to other $RA$ nodes, where $ID_{RA_d}$ is the ID of current replica $RA$ node, $sig_{RA_d}$ is the signature of consensus confirmation message to current replica $RA$ node.

8) All $RA$ nodes collect consensus confirmation messages in the network, and when they collect more than or equal to $2f + 1$ legitimate consensus confirmation messages ($f$ is the number of Byzantine nodes in the network), the block is added to the chain of this node and the next round of consensus is opened.

# 4 Safety and Performance Analysis

## 4.1 Security Analysis

In the traditional heterogeneous identity alliance risk assessment system, the heterogeneous identity alliance user, as the data provider, loses control over the data after providing its own risk assessment-related data to the risk assessment organization. In this model, uploads the data to the cloud server after attribute encryption, and can operate on its own data at any time, and realize the change of data accessibility by modifying the access policy.

Since $ECS$ is "honest but curious", there is a risk of privacy leakage when storing data directly to $ECS$. In this model, $ECS$ stores the data after encrypting the attributes, and $ECS$ cannot decrypt the file content, so it can guarantee the invisibility of the data to the cloud server.

The invisibility of the data to unrelated third parties is guaranteed because access policies are established and only identity attributes that match the policies can correctly decrypt the encrypted data stored in the $ECS$.

When $ECS$ receives the above data, it verifies the signature and compares the summary values to ensure that it has received the risk assessment data from a legitimate source and that the content has not been tampered with.

After receiving $update$, the node avoids malicious nodes from impersonating $EN$ nodes by checking whether the message is real and valid, and reduces the time wasted by $RA$ nodes in processing invalid update messages, saving system resources.

Based on $update$, the node is able to verify that the encrypted data stored in the $ECS$ has not been tampered with before the evaluation is performed, ensuring the integrity and reliability of the data on which the evaluation is based.

## 4.2 Analysis of Improved Consensus Mechanisms

The improved PBFT consensus mechanism chosen for this model has the following advantages:

The *RA* nodes on the chain are strictly audited and endorsed by IA, so the possibility of malicious behavior will be greatly reduced compared to the nodes in the public chain. Moreover, as an important part of the cyber security industry, the network and database of the Risk Assessment Agency are more complete and secure compared to other blockchain application areas, thus providing a more secure and stable environment for the operation of PBFT.

The number of *RA* nodes required in this model is much smaller than the number of consensus nodes in medical and financial blockchains, and the PBFT consensus mechanism has the best performance compared to other consensus algorithms with fewer nodes, and its data throughput and block-out efficiency can meet the requirements of new risk assessment-related data to be processed as soon as possible.

The same probability of all nodes in PBFT becoming the master node, avoiding the block-out right to be gradually centralized as the blockchain runs.

The *RA* nodes on the chain do not need to perform constantly repeated hash calculations to compete for bookkeeping rights, reducing the power consumption of each node.

Communication volume analysis: when the system nodes for n, the classical PBFT algorithm consistency protocol in the three stages of Pre-prepare, Prepare, Commit communication number of $n - 1$, $(n - 1)(n - 1)$ and $n(n - 1)$, respectively, the total number of communication is $2n^2 - 2n$.

The consensus request in this model is directly initiated by the master *RA* node, and the consensus result does not need to be fed back to the *EN* node, so the communication in the Propose and Reply stages can be eliminated. In addition, since the message has been broadcasted within all RA nodes in the Pre-prepare and Prepare stages, this model simplifies the three-stage process in the PBFT consistency protocol into two stages of consensus proposal and consensus confirmation. The number of communications in the two phases is $n - 1$ and $n(n - 1)$, respectively, and the total number is $n^2 - 1$. According to Fig. 5, it can be seen that with the increase in the number of nodes, the number of communications required for nodes to reach consensus is significantly reduced with the improved PBFT algorithm.

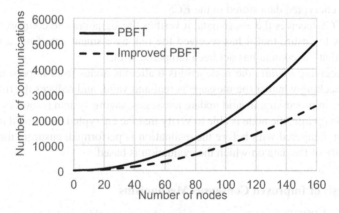

**Fig. 5.** Comparison of communication volume.

Throughput analysis: An important indicator to judge the performance of the consensus mechanism is the throughput, i.e., the number of completed transactions processed per second, according to $TPS = \frac{SUM(tx)}{T}$, where $T$ is the time consumed from issuing a transaction to consensus reaching and generating a block, and $SUM(tx)$ is the total number of transactions within this time, by using the same number of nodes in the same experimental environment and multiple threads for simulation experiments to compare the three-stage PBFT with the two-stage PBFT, the experimental results are shown in Fig. 6:

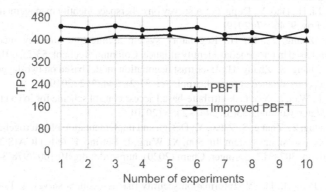

**Fig. 6.** Comparison of throughput

## 5  Conclusion

Research on blockchain technology has been devoted to exploring the organic combination of its decentralized architecture, anti-tampering, traceability and other capabilities with industries with high privacy needs. Risk assessment itself is an important part of information security, and the privacy of its related data is of paramount importance. Combining heterogeneous identity alliance risk assessment system with blockchain can not only improve the security of data in the system, but also increase the resistance of the system to external attacks and internal mischief. The blockchain-based heterogeneous identity alliance risk assessment model proposed in this paper decentralizes the traditional architecture while ensuring the control of data owners over data and the invisibility of private data to unrelated third parties. However, the application combination of blockchain and risk assessment system as a new attempt still has issues to be solved, such as the future research on risk assessment model with more efficient traceability and how to make the model consensus algorithm support dynamic changes of members while ensuring the block-out efficiency.

**Acknowledgement.** This work is supported by the Key Research and Development Project of Sichuan Province (No. 2021YFSY0012, No. 2020YFG0307, No. 2021YFG0332), the National Natural Science Foundation of China (No. 62076042), the Science and Technology Innovation Project of Sichuan (No. 2020017), the Key Research and Development Project of Chengdu (No.

2019-YF05–02028-GX), the Innovation Team of Quantum Security Communication of Sichuan Province (No. 17TD0009), the Academic and Technical Leaders Training Funding Support Projects of Sichuan Province (No. 2016120080102643).

# References

1. Jing, J.: The development status and tendency of internet trusted identity management. J. Inf. Secur. Res. **2**(7), 666–668 (2016)
2. Jiang, W., Li, H., Hao, Y., Dong, G.: A survey on cyberspace identity management. Inf. Secur. Commun. Priv. **9**, 46–57 (2019)
3. Dong, G., Zhang, Z., Li, H.: Regulatory system architecture and key mechanisms of blockchain-based heterogeneous identity alliance. Commun. Technol. **53**(2), 401–413 (2020)
4. Yang, M., Zhang, S., Zhang, H.: User trust negotiation model based on two-layer blockchain in heterogeneous alliance system. J. Appl. Sci. **37**(2), 244–252 (2019)
5. Chen, W.H., Wan, J.: Xia: task-attribute-based access control scheme for IoT via blockchain. Comput. Mater. Continua **53**(3), 2441–2453 (2020)
6. Gan, J., Sheng, Z., Zhang, S., Zhao, Y.: Design and implementation of heterogeneous identity alliance risk assessment system. In: Sun, X., Wang, J., Bertino, E. (eds.) ICAIS 2020. LNCS, vol. 12240, pp. 307–317. Springer, Cham (2020). https://doi.org/10.1007/978-3-030-57881-7_28
7. Zhang, L., Peng, J., Du, Y.: Information security risk assessment survey. J. Tsinghua Univ. (Sci. Technol.) **52**(10), 1364–1369 (2012)
8. Feng, D., Zhang, Y., Zhang, Y.: Survey of information security risk assessment. J. Commun. **7**, 10–18 (2004)
9. Yuan, Y., Wang, F.: Blockchain: the state of the art and future trends. Acta Automatica Sinica **42**(4), 481–494 (2016)
10. Zeng, S., Huo, R., Huang, T.: Survey of blockchain: principle, progress and application. J. Commun. **41**(1), 134–151 (2020)
11. Fu, Y., Zhu, J., Gao, S.: CPS information security risk evaluation based on blockchain and big data. Tehnicki Vjesnik **25**(6), 1843–1850 (2018)
12. Zhao, Y., Zhang, S., Yang, M.: Research on architecture of risk assessment system based on block chain. Comput. Mater. Continua **61**(2), 677–686 (2019)
13. Kask, R.J.: Cyberspace policy review: assuring a trusted and resilient information and communications infrastructure pp. 49–127 (2011)
14. Li, C.: Review of the U.S. national action plan on cybersecurity. E-Government **12**, 98–109 (2016)
15. Ronagel, H., et al.: Futureid-shaping the future of electronic identity (2012)
16. Stevens, T., et al: The state of the electronic identity market: technologies, infrastructure, services and policies. JRC Working Papers (2010)
17. National Cyberspace Security Strategy. China Information Security **1**, 26–31 (2017)
18. Chen, S., Wang, G., Liu, X.: Study on security risk assessment for information system. Communications Technology **45**(1), 128–130 (2012)
19. Nakamoto, S.: Bitcoin: a peer-to-peer electronic cash system. https://bitcoin.org/bitcoin.pdf (2008)
20. Wang, P., Susilo, W.: Data security storage model of the internet of things based on blockchain. Comput. Syst. Sci. Eng. **36**(1), 213–224 (2021)
21. Hsiao, S., Sung, W.: Utilizing blockchain technology to improve wsn security for sensor data transmission. Comput. Mater. Continua **68**(2), 1899–1918 (2021)

22. Alsalamah, S.A., Alsalamah, H.A., Nouh, T., Alsalamah, S.A.: Healthyblockchain for global patients. Comput. Mater. Continua **68**(2), 2431–2449 (2021)
23. Kara, M., Aydın, M.A., Balık, H.H.: Bcvop2p: decentralized blockchain-based authentication scheme for secure voice communication. Intell. Autom. Soft Comput. **31**(3), 1901–1918 (2022)
24. Ali, A., Pasha, M.F., Fang, O.H., Ali, J., Alzain, M.A.: An efficient blockchain-based healthcare system using artificial intelligence. Comput. Mater. Continua **71**(2), 2721–2738 (2022)
25. Wang, Q., Li, F., Wang, Z.: Principle and core technology of blockchain. J. Front. Comput. Sci. Technol. **14**(10), 1621–1643 (2020)

# The Principle and Implementation of Sentiment Analysis System

Jiani Xue and Yuqi Chen[✉]

Department of Computer Information and Network Security, Jiangsu Police Institute, Nanjing 210000, China
734541846@qq.com

**Abstract.** The sentiment analysis system is one of the most classic applications in natural language processing and enduring. The development of the mobile Internet has greatly increased people's participation, and everyone can make their own comments on social media platforms such as Weibo. Through public opinion mining and emotional analysis of text information, a rich potential value of information can be obtained. However, in the face of a large number of comment data, how is it more convenient for public opinion workers to see the whole picture and take timely measures? This is the practical problem to be addressed in this article. The main work of this article is to build a public opinion emotional analysis system about Jiangsu Police Institute, to realize the emotional analysis of the comments related to Jiangsu Police Institute in Weibo and post bar. Then related workers are able to screen out the comments of negative emotions. The experimental dataset in this article is a training dataset composed of positive and negative reviews selected from JD commodity reviews, and the test data are random reviews selected from the microblog of Jiangsu Police Institute. This article details the processing of the Chinese comment text dataset. Because Chinese text is involved, the data is first partitioned using the jieba participle. After the data pre-processing, we input the processed data into the Word2Vec model, and set the relevant parameters according to the formatting rules of the word2vec, so that the dataset of text can be quantized to facilitate code learning.

**Keywords:** Natural language processing · Text emotion analysis · Bi-directional short-term and long-term memory recurrent neural networks

## 1 Introduction

Weibo is a commonly used social media platform for people, gathering text, pictures and videos full of people's subjective emotions, storing a large amount of text information. By mining, processing and analyzing the microblog short text books, we can obtain a rich potential value of information [1–3]. Therefore, it is a top priority to conduct public opinion mining and emotional analysis of the complex microblog information. This article selects Sina Weibo as a data collection platform to analyze the public opinion of the hot events in Weibo.

X. Sun et al. (Eds.): ICAIS 2022, CCIS 1588, pp. 28–39, 2022.
https://doi.org/10.1007/978-3-031-06764-8_3

The main work of this article is to build a sentiment analysis system on the public opinion comments of Jiangsu Police Institute, to realize the sentiment analysis of the comments text of Jiangsu Police Institute in Weibo and post bar. Then related workers are able to screen out the comments of negative emotions. The experimental dataset in this article is a training dataset composed of positive and negative reviews selected from JD commodity reviews, and the test data are random reviews selected from the microblog of Jiangsu Police Institute.

This article details the processing of the Chinese comment text dataset. It uses a model of emotion classification based on word2vec and bidirectional long, short-term memory recurrent neural networks. The text was first used to vectorize [4] with Tokenizer function, and then the vectorized text was removed to prevent small errors during training. Then the vocabulary was constructed, string token was converted to index and the data was processed. Since a word index with a frequency of less than 10 would default to 0, we added 1 after such words. And for some words with an index of 0, we set the word vector to 0. We started with the word of index 1 and each word corresponded to its word vector. Finally, our model was trained on the training set, and the accuracy was tested on the validation set.

In conclusion, we successfully built a system of sentiment analysis on public opinion comments in this article, completing the emotional analysis of short texts such as social platform comments.

## 2   Related Work

### 2.1   Research Background

The text classification is the most basic core task of natural language processing (NLP). The sentiment analysis is to automatically identify the opinion tendency, attitude, mood, evaluation, etc. according to the input text, voice or video. It is widely used in consumer decisions, public opinion analysis, personalized recommendation and other fields [5]. This article involves sentiment analysis, also known as textual emotion analysis, a piece of content involved in the natural language processing and text mining processes.

In short, we can use the algorithm to judge the emotional bias of a paragraph of text and comment, so as to quickly understand the subjective emotions of the original author expressing this text. In reality, when we make our own remarks online, there may be emotions such as joy, excitement, loss, depression, tension, doubt. But in the world of natural language processing, we can not reach such a small classification due to manually annotated complex emotion training sets. So here we only deal with two emotional states: positive and negative. Currently, there are two approaches for textual emotion analysis, one dictionary-based and the other based on machine learning.

### 2.2   Dictionary-Based Affective Analysis

The Dictionary-based sentiment analysis is a very simple and easy to understand approach. To summarize, we first have a manually annotated dictionary, and each of the

**Table 1.** Dictionary.

| Word | Lable |
|------|-------|
| Good | Positive |
| Bad | Negative |
| Sad | Negative |
| Happy | Positive |
| ... | ... |

dictionary corresponds to this negative or positive label [6]. The dictionary reference is shown in Table 1.

This dictionary can reach hundreds of thousands of articles, which is commonly used in the collection of words for sentiment analysis (beta version). After collecting the user's comments, we divide the sentence, and then take the sorted words to match the dictionary and assign the sentence score to judge the mood of the sentence according to the score. The method of sentiment analysis through a dictionary is simple, but the disadvantages are also obvious. We often need a large dictionary and keep it updated. This is a great test of both human and material resources. In addition, the method has emotional judgment problems that cannot be solved by expanding the dictionary. For example, when we judge the mood of a sentence, we tend to grasp the overall language environment, especially pay attention to the influence of some tone aids on the mood. But methods based on dictionary sentiment analysis cannot do this, and splitting sentences into words is likely to affect the overall emotional expression of the sentence. Because the simple dictionary comparison method is not highly accurate, this experiment will not achieve user comment sentiment analysis through this method.

### 2.3 Machine Learning-Based Text Emotion Analysis

**TF-IDF**

TF-IDF is one of the most widely used text representation techniques, which is based on text representation methods based on statistical ideas [7, 8]. First, statistics the number of text each word appears in the text and standardized processing, that is, "word frequency" (TF), and then assign a "reverse document frequency" (IDF) weight to each word, its size is inversely proportional to the prevalence of a word. The formulas for word and inverse document frequencies are shown in Eqs. 1 and 2:

$$\text{tf}_{i,j} = \frac{n_{i,j}}{\sum_k n_{k,j}} \tag{1}$$

$$\text{idf}_i = \lg \frac{|D|}{|\{j : t_i \in d_j\}|} \tag{2}$$

Multimultiplying the word frequency by the inverse document frequency yields a TF-IDF value of a word. The larger the TF-IDF value of a word, the more important the word is to the article. The TF-IDF calculation formula is shown in Eqs. 3.

$$\text{tfidf}_{i,j} = \text{tf}_{i,j} \times \text{idf}_i \qquad (3)$$

The advantages of TF-IDF algorithm are small computation, fast operation speed, and the calculation results are close to reality. The disadvantage is that the TF-IDF algorithm is not considered comprehensively enough, and the importance of a certain word cannot be measured only by the word frequency. Not only does it fail to identify certain important but less appearing keywords, nor does it distinguish between synonyms where different representations are used. For example, NLP and emotional analysis are actually a meaning word, but TF-IDF counts two different words. The TF-IDF algorithm is also unable to represent the location information of a word, and the effect of the location where a word appearing in the text on its importance is self-evident.

**Emotion Analysis Based on a Long and Short-Term Memory Neural Network (LSTM) + Word2vec**

This article chose to base on the sentiment analysis of long and short-term memory neural network (LSTM) + word2vec. Many deep learning models in NLP need the results of word embedding as input features. Word embedding is a technique for language modeling and feature learning that transforms words in a vocabulary into a vector [9] of continuous real numbers. This technique usually involves a mathematical embedding from a high-dimensional sparse vector space to a low-dimensional dense vector space. Each dimension of the embedded vector represents a latent feature of the word, and the vector can encode the laws and patterns of the language. A commonly used word embedding system is the Word2Vec, which is essentially a computationally efficient neural network prediction model [10–12].

Some methods of Word Embedding existed before Word2vec, but previous methods were not mature and were not applied on a large scale. Word2vec, a word vector training model proposed by Mikolov in two articles published in 2013, simplified the network structure of neural language models above the n-gram language model proposed by Bengio et al., and proposed CBOW and Skip-gram models, which could obtain more efficient word vectors through large amounts of data.

Word2vec is characterized that each word in the corpus corresponds to a vector in the vector space, words with contextual relations and mapping to a closer distance in the vector space. The core models of Word2vec are all three-layer neural network structures with the input, hidden, and output layers. Where the CBOW model is used to predict the word vector of a given word, so the input of its trained model is the word vector corresponding to the relevant words before and after the desired predicted word. The Skip-Gram model, on the contrary, is trained with a word vector of a word and output as a word vector of the context word of the word.

Word2vec has less dimensions, faster speed than previous neural language model methods and it has better word vector construction and strong versatility. It has been widely used in the NLP field after 7 years of development. It can take into account the order of words and meaning of the text. However, the disadvantage of the Word2vec model is that the words and vectors have a one-to-one relationship, so the problem of polysemy words cannot be solved, and the Word2vec cannot be dynamically optimized for a specific task. By comparing the advantages and disadvantages of TF-IDF and Word2vec, this article decided to conduct textual emotion analysis using Word2vec.

## 2.4 Bidirectional Long and Short-Term Memory Network

Bidirectional long, short-term memory network (BiLSTM) is a combination of forward LSTM and reverse LSTM. Its core idea is to split the LSTM definition into two directions, one of which is in chronological order from beginning to end, the other is in chronological order from the last to start, just like the writing technique of flashback and flashback, in this way, any certain moment of the model output will refer to the forward and reverse timing information at the same time, and the circular neural network RNN can only obtain one-way information. The structural model diagram of the BiLSTM is shown in Fig. 1.

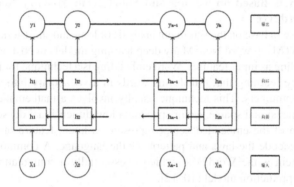

**Fig. 1.** BiLSTM structural model Fig.

Its forward and backward vectors are indicated as follows.

$$\overrightarrow{h}t = f(\overrightarrow{w}xt + \overrightarrow{v}\,\overrightarrow{h}t - 1 + \overrightarrow{b}) \tag{4}$$

$$\overleftarrow{h}t = f(\overleftarrow{w}xt + \overleftarrow{v}\,\overleftarrow{h}t + 1 + \overleftarrow{b}) \tag{5}$$

The output is obtained by stitching the results of the pair sum, as shown in Eq. 6.

$$yt = g(U[\overrightarrow{h}t \cdot \overleftarrow{h}t] + c) \tag{6}$$

This feature of BiLSTM coincides with the task requirements of many natural language processing. Because text is sequential, a word understanding requires reference context, and BiLSTM can just get two-way information through forward LSTM and reverse LSTM, which is why BiLSTM will achieve better results in many text processing tasks than both LSTM and RNN. This system used this structure in the process of the annotation algorithm of subject words and emotional words.

## 2.5 Research Status

Pang, one of the first engaged in sentiment analysis research, used N metasyntax and word sex of selected text as emotional features. He used supervised machine learning methods to classify movie comments into positive and negative categories with naive Bayes, maximum entropy model and support vector machine as classifier [13] for supervised learning algorithms. The results showed that the SVM works best among several classification methods, with a classification accuracy of 80%. In a machine learning-based emotion classification algorithm, each article is transformed into a corresponding eigenvector to represent it. The quality of feature selection will directly affect the performance of the emotion analysis task.Follow-up studies focused emotion classification as a feature optimization task on the basis of Pang et al. With the addition of semantic feature information and the development of the training corpus, machine learning-based classification will have broad prospects.

Since 2014, it is the centralized development stage of network public opinion research based on text mining technology. For example, in the emotional analysis study of 2000–2015 in social media by Kumarawi et al., the main tasks, methods and applications of emotion analysis were summarized, and the application of text mining in social media has gradually been paid attention to [14]. Asarmanick used a 2017 SVM-based Kini index feature selection method to classify emotion [15] on the movie review dataset in social media. In recent years, deep learning-based social media text mining has been valued by researchers. For example, in 2019, CNN, LSTM, Bi-LSTM, and found that CNN models using functions such as word embedding and POS tags had the best effect.

However, the accuracy of text emotion classification is difficult to reach the level of ordinary text classification, which is mainly caused by the complex emotional expression and a large number of emotional ambiguity in emotional text. Since the expression mode of Chinese text is more diverse and flexible, Chinese sentiment analysis still has a long way to go in the direction of good development.

Domestic scholars have continued to advance and improve the emotional dictionary research. They have been working hard in bettering emotion dictionary and determining the seed vocabulary of praise and criticism with the use of the TF-IDF weighted way. They have successfully taken a big step in the research of Chinese emotion analysis. Chen Guolan further studied the existing emotional dictionary, and obtained an effective way of emotional analysis on Weibo. We can also learn from the foreign researchers' methods, including Japanese scholar Nasukaw and American scholar Kim.

## 3 Code Module Introduction

The code used in this article will be presented. First, we will introduce the training dataset used in this experiment. They came from the review dataset of JD Commodity, with a total of 21,105 reviews. Among them, there were 10677 positive samples and 10428 bad reviews, so the sample categories were relatively balanced. The cumulative distribution map of the expected sentence lengths was obtained using the Matplotlib library, the numpy library, and the library's own plot () function(as shown in Fig. 2).

**Fig. 2.** Code.

The sentence length accepted in the LSTM algorithm was the sequence length, which was like a container with a fixed volume, and the amount of the liquid it could withstand was also fixed. Therefore, the sentence needed to be trimmed to the same length in the data processing, and we sought the sentence length of 90% probability in the sample as the unified length of the trimmed sentence according to the cumulative distribution of the corpus.

Next, we we officially started our project. As mentioned above, the dataset of this article used the training dataset of JD Commodity Review, which was essentially a Chinese text sequence, so we preprocessed the data in order. Because Chinese text was involved, the data was first typed using the jieba participle. Since the positive and negative evaluations currently in two different files, we combined the samples from the two files during training to facilitate better training of the code. Considering we included both positive and bad reviews, we marked both evaluations as 1 and 0 respectively. In the next step, we abandoned the word frequency and set a minimum word frequency of 10. If the word frequency was less than 10, let its index to 0. Then we made the corresponding word vector to zero vector. In the end, we unified the sentence uniform length is 188.

Then we defined the partition function to divide the sentence. The line change would cause some errors in the data reading, so we did the line change operation. We created a word dictionary, set the eigenvector dimension dictionary truncation and the parallel number of cpu control training, returning the index of each word, the word vector, and the word index corresponding to each sentence(as shown in Fig. 3). After data processing, because the word index with the frequency less than 10 would default to 0, we added 1 after such words. For some words' index is 0, the word vector was set to 0. Then we started with the word of index 1, each word corresponded to its word vector.

After obtaining the processed data above, we began to build our model with the main network of Embedding layer, LSTM layer, LR layer. First, we added the Squential sequential model. Then we added the Embedding layer, converting the annotated words into word vectors. After that we embed the LSTM model, setting the output dimension and the activation function. Because the sigmod function is widely used and has a limited output range and stable optimization, the activation function selected the sigmod function, adding the Dropout layer to prevent overfitting. Finally we added the full

```
def word2vec_train(combined):

    model = Word2Vec(size=vocab_dim,
                     min_count=n_exposures,
                     window=window_size,
                     workers=cpu_count,
                     iter=n_iterations)
    model.build_vocab(combined)
    model.train(combined, total_examples=model.corpus_count, epochs=10)
    model.save('D:/AiStudio/sik/DeepLearn/Word2vec_model.pkl')
    index_dict, word_vectors,combined = create_dictionaries(model=model, combined=combined)
    return index_dict, word_vectors,combined
```

**Fig. 3.** Create the dictionary.

connection layer and defined the network structure. After the completion, we trained the model and saved it in the specified path to visually show the training process.

## 4   Experimental Results and Analysis

The length distribution histogram of the text occurring during the code run are shown below (as shown in Fig. 4). The resulting loci in the code and the required uniform sequence lengths are shown below (as shown in Fig. 5).

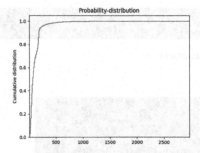

**Fig. 4.** Cumulative distribution histogram.

**Fig. 5.** Operation results.

Here we used the octopus crawler software to crawl the comments on the official micro blog and the institute post bar. We pasted the comment data under the test code and displayed it with the lstm_predict() function. The we placed the comments that needed to be tested in string and the remaining text waiting to test in the annotation information.

We tested sample, selected negative semantics and judged the results by code (as shown in Fig. 6).

The test procedure of the training results is shown below (as shown in Fig. 7).

The test results, such as " the police, the police are great? Don't cancel them? Do you think you are great?" were shown below. This sentence was marked as negative (as shown in Fig. 8).

Then we selected the positive code to try, and the results of the code test are shown below (as shown in Fig. 9).

The training procedure is shown below (as shown in Fig. 10).

**Fig. 6.** Comments presentation.

**Fig. 7.** The test procedure.

**Fig. 8.** A negative statement test.

**Fig. 9.** The test samples.

**Fig. 10.** The training process.

As for the comments about our school canteens, such as "I feel the incense pot and chicken leg rice is the best when I have gone to work", the test results shown below was positive (as shown in Fig. 11).

**Fig. 11.** A positive statement test.

## 5  Discussion

Although the system has been completed and tested to be used normally, which can analyze the comment data and show the results, due to constraints in time and technical reasons, some details of the system function are not perfect, and there are some places needing to be improved:

(i)   Improve the data source problem.The test data set of this system came from the network. In the actual production process, the merchants rely on the network crawler to obtain the comment data, while the learning cost of the network crawler is high. This article will later design the climbing function of the network data, automatically climb the data needed by the merchants from the network and clean the data.

(ii)  Improves the system visualization implementation. Due to the short time and the ability is not widely involved enough, the visualization and aesthetic function of the system cannot be realized.

(iii) Realize the early warning function of the system. Due to the limited time problems and limited research ability, the early warning function of the system cannot be fully implemented, which will be better improved and implemented in the next stage.

In the next step, the authors will improve the above aspects and constantly improve the emotional analysis system of Weibo user comments.

## 6  Conclusion

Nowadays, with the rapid development of the Internet, the amount of data in various related fields is increasing, and so is the comment data on online platforms. The traditional mode of comment data analysis is outdated, and how to obtain and analyze the comment data for specific objects on the network has increasingly become a hot research problem.

Entity recognition technology is a basic level and a very important work in natural language processing research. It is the cornerstone of other processing tasks, and has a very broad application prospects and scope. In this article, the LSTM algorithm transforms the evaluated sentiment analysis problem into the problem of the recognition and matching of subject words and emotional words, namely the sequence annotation problem of entity recognition techniques. Compared with the existing algorithms, some degree of optimization and improvement is made. Multiple tests were conducted on the experimental dataset, the accuracy of the algorithm was successfully verified, and the sentiment analysis system based on microblog comments was successfully designed based on the system demand analysis and overall design, and the system algorithm.

The specific results are summarized as follows:

(i)According to the system demand analysis and overall design, the Python and other technical frameworks, we have successfully designed and realized the data preprocessing function, data analysis function and data visualization function. (ii)A set of emotional analysis algorithm process has been designed. Through data preprocessing, the identification and matching of theme words and emotional words, theme word classification and emotional tendency score, the user comment data has been transformed into < theme words, theme classification, emotional words, emotional tendency > quadruples, so that the user comments can realize visual display.

(iii)This article transformed the extraction of subject words and emotional words into the problem of entity recognition sequence annotation. It improved algorithm based on LSTM entity recognition model algorithm. With the use of the experimental dataset, the improved algorithm demonstrated superior accuracy.

**Funding Statement.** The authors received no specific funding for this study.

**Conflicts of Interest.** The authors declare that they have no conflicts of interest to report regarding the present study.

# References

1. Wei, S., Yue, F.: Considers the context of microblog short text mining: the method of emotion analysis. Comput. Sci. **S1** (2021)
2. Balahur, A., Jesús, M., Hermida, A.: Montoyo: Detecting implicit expressions of emotion in text: a aomparative analysis. Dec. Supp. Syst. **53**(4), 742–753 (2012)
3. Li, b., Zhou, X., Sun, Y., Zhang, H.: Research and realization of emotional analysis. Software J. **12** (2017)
4. Cortes, C., Vapnik, V.: Support-vector networks. Mach. Learn. **20**, 273–293 (1995). https://doi.org/10.1007/BF00994018
5. Greco, F., Polli, A.: Emotional text mining: consumer analysis in brand management. Int. J. Inf. Manage. **51**, 1–8 (2020)
6. Chao, Y., Shi, F., Xiaoling, W., Nan, Y., Ge, Y.: Analysis based on emotion dictionary extension technology. Small Microcomput. Syst. **04** (2010)
7. Shi, C., Xu, C., Yang, X.: TFIDF algorithm research review. Comput. Appl. **S1** (2009)
8. Kim, D., Seo, D., Cho, S., Kang, P.: Multi-co-training for document classification using various document representations: TF-IDF, LDA, and Doc2Vec. Inf. Sci. **477**, 15–29 (2018)
9. Pasua, S.T.S.N.: Deep learning-based thai emotion analysis: comparative study based on word embeddings, pos-tag and affective characteristics. Cities and Society, p. 50 (2019)

10. Tang, M., Zhu, L., Zou, X.: Based on a word2vec document vector representation. Comput. Sci. **06** (2016)
11. Li, H., Zhang, L.: Deep learning based text sentiment analysis during epidemic. Int. Core J. Eng. **7**, 467–472 (2021)
12. Su, X., Meng, H.: Based on neural network. Comput. Technol. Dev. **12** (2015)
13. Pang, B., Lee, L., Vaithyanathan, S.: Thumbs up: senti-ment classification using machine learning techniques. In: Proceedings of the ACL-02 Conference on Empirical Methods in Natural Language Processing-Volume 10, Stroudsburg, Association for Computational Linguistics, pp. 79–86 (2002)
14. Kumarawi, A.B., Wallamilawi, A.: Opinion mining and emotional analysis: task, methods and application. Knowl. Base Syst. **89**, 14–46 (2015)
15. Asarmanik, D., Mohan, C.: Large movie review emotion analysis term word extraction based on the Gini exponential feature selection method and the SVM classifier. World Wide Web Internet, World Wide Web Inf. Syst. **20**, 135–154 (2017)

# Linkable Ring Signature Scheme from NTRU Lattice

Qing Ye[1][(✉)] , Nannan Zhao[1] , Xiaojun Wang[2] , and Deng Pan[1]

[1] School of Computer Science and Technology, Henan Polytechnic University,
Jiaozuo 454000, China
z546246@163.com
[2] School of Electronic Engineering, Dublin City University, Dublin 9, Ireland

**Abstract.** There are two serious security problems existing in blockchain: privacy protection problem and quantum attack problem. In order to address them, this paper studied the privacy protection technology of blockchain based on linkable ring signature (LRS) from NTRU lattice, and proposed a new LRS scheme from NTRU lattice whose signature length is $O(\log M)$, where $M$ is the number of members in the ring. Firstly, the GGH standard method is used to construct the homomorphic commitment scheme on NTRU lattice based on the CVP problem of NTRU lattice. Then, based on the homomorphic commitment scheme, the Sigma-protocol on NTRU lattice is constructed. Finally, the protocol is transformed into a LRS scheme through Fiat-Shamir heuristic. The analysis shows that the LRS scheme proposed in this paper not only satisfies the anonymity and unforgeability, but also resists quantum computing attack. In terms of efficiency, since the proposed scheme is constructed based on Sigma-protocol on NTRU lattice, the signature length is $O(\log M)$.

**Keywords:** NTRU lattice · Ring signature · Commitment scheme · Blockchain

## 1 Introduction

In recent years, with the rapid development of cryptocurrency represented by Bitcoin, blockchain [9,19], as the underlying technology of Bitcoin, has also received widespread attention. The earliest definition of blockchain comes from the paper published by Nakamoto in 2009 [13]. The two most important features of blockchain, "decentralization" and "anonymity", make Bitcoin the most popular digital currency. However, blockchain still faces two major problems at present. One is privacy protection. Data in blockchains are visible on the whole network. Although this is conducive to the "decentralization" of blockchain, it will make the transaction records and related information of both sides public, bringing privacy protection problem. The method adopted by current Bitcoin system is to generate one (address, signature key) pair for each transaction and for each user. The transaction information that all users can see is that a sum of concurrency is transferred from one address to another, while the actual user's identity corresponding to the address is unseen for every user. However, since using ECDSA (elliptic curve digital signature algorithm), Bitcoin only partially solves the privacy protection problem. The white paper [15] also mentioned that "At present, the industry generally believes that zero-knowledge proof, ring signature and homomorphic encryption are more promising to solve the privacy problem of blockchain."

Another problem of Bitcoin is quantum attack problem [16,17,20]. The emergence of quantum computers will make the traditional cryptosystem based on number-theoretic assumption (such as large integer factorization problem and finite field discrete logarithm problem) be broken in polynomial time. Therefore, if the cryptosystem based on number-theoretic assumption is still used in blockchain, the security of blockchain will be difficult to be guaranteed in the quantum age. In recent years, the new cryptosystem based on lattice theory has become a research hotspot in the post-quantum cryptography field because of its advantages of good asymptotic efficiency, simple operation, parallelism, anti-quantum attack and stochastic instances in the worst case, and has achieved a series of research results [1,10,22].

Ring signature was first proposed by Rivest et al. [18]. Ring signature allows a user to sign messages on behalf of a group of users. The verifier can be sure that the real signer is a member of a group of users, but cannot specify which one the signer is. Considering the anonymity in blockchain, ring signatures are obviously more suitable for blockchain than standard digital signatures. It is worth noting that if the standard digital signature in blockchain is simply replaced by the general ring signature, since the anonymous protection of ring signature, the user who signs the same currency twice will not be detected, which will lead to the problem of "double-spending". In order to solve this problem, it is necessary to enable the public to determine whether two or more ring signatures are generated by the same signer. Traceable ring signature [3] provides the ability to track key pairs that sign different messages, and has been modified to be a one-time signature used in Monero. Linkable ring signature (LRS) proposed by Liu et al. [11] protects the anonymity of the signer. Meanwhile, in LRS, anyone can determine whether two signatures are issued by the same ring member. Generally, LRSs are enough to solve the "double-spending" problem in cryptocurrency.

NTRU is a public key cryptosystem based on polynomial rings, which was proposed by Hoffstein et al. [8] in 1996. Compared with ideal lattice and general lattice, NTRU lattice public-key cryptosystem has shorter public-private key length and faster operation speed because it only involves multiplication over polynomial rings and modular operation of small integers. For example, the earliest lattice-based signature scheme GGH [5] with key length of $O\left(n^3 \log n\right)$ ($n$ denotes the security parameter) can be reduced to the one with key length of $O\left(n \log n\right)$ by using NTRU lattice-based signature scheme. NTRU lattice-based cryptosystem is considered by cryptographers to be the most likely alternative to the existing public key cryptosystem in the post-quantum era. NTRU system requires less bandwidth, processor and memory, and is more suitable for blockchain which involves large amounts of data transmission, computation and storage. At present, there is only a little literature about ring signature on

NTRU lattice. To the best of our knowledge, the work of [21,24] is the only one. Reference [21] based on NTRUSign signature algorithm [7], using ingenious randomization technology, designed a ring signature scheme on NTRU lattice. The signature length of this scheme can reach $O(1)$, but it lacks rigorous security proof. Reference [24] proposed a ring signature scheme from NTRU lattice and proved its security in random oracle model and standard model respectively, and the signature length of the scheme is $O(n)$. All the ring signature schemes of [21,24] are not linkable or traceable, which is not suitable for the privacy protection of blockchain.

In this paper, aiming at the problems of "privacy protection" and "quantum attack" existing in blockchain, combined with NTRU lattice, homomorphic commitment scheme [14] and Sigma-protocol ($\Sigma$-protocol) [6], we proposed a LRS scheme from NTRU lattice. The scheme is based on the idea and method of [6,23], that is, the $\Sigma$-protocol on NTRU lattice is used to construct a ring signature scheme. Firstly, the homomorphic commitment scheme on NTRU lattice is established. Secondly, based on the homomorphic commitment scheme, an efficient NTRU lattice-based LRS scheme is constructed. Our scheme satisfies anonymity, unforgeability, linkability, and can resist quantum attacks. Moreover, since our scheme is based on NTRU lattice, the length of the public key and the private key is shorter and the signature length is shorter than other related schemes, and our scheme has faster computation speed and higher efficiency.

## 2   Preliminaries

For the convenience of description, the symbols used in the text are explained in Table 1.

**Table 1.** Symbol description

| Symbol | Meaning |
| --- | --- |
| $b$ | Column vector |
| $b_i$ | The $ith$ component of vector $b$ |
| $A^{m \times n}$ | Matrix of $m$ rows and $n$ columns |
| $A^T$ | Conversion of matrix $A$ |
| $negl(n)$ | Negligible function: $f(n) < (n^{-c})$, $c$: Constant |
| $N$ | Dimension of lattice, prime number |
| $q$ | Modulus, $n$-th power of 2 |
| $R$ | Polynomial ring, equal to $Z[x]/(x^N - 1)$ |
| $R_q$ | Polynomial ring, equal to $Z_q[x]/(x^N - 1)$ |
| $a * b$ | Convolution of polynomials, $a, b \in R_q$ |
| $a + b$ | Polynomial addition, $a, b \in R_q$ |
| $\lceil t \rceil$ | Rational number $t$ integrates upwards |

## 2.1  Relevant Definitions of Lattices

**Definition 1** *(Lattice). Let $B = \{b_1, b_2, \ldots, b_m\} \subset \mathbb{R}^n$ consist of $m$ linearly independent vectors. The $m$-dimensional lattice $\Lambda$ generated by the basis $B$ is*

$$L = \{a \in \mathbb{Z}^m : a_1 b_1 + a_2 b_2 + \ldots + a_m b_m\}$$

**Definition 2** *(q-Lattice). Let $q, n, m \in \mathbb{Z}, A \in \mathbb{Z}_q^{m \times n}, u \in \mathbb{Z}_q^n$, defined as follows*

$$\Lambda_q^\perp(A) = \{e \in \mathbb{Z}_q^m : Ae = 0(\bmod q)\},$$

$$\Lambda_q^u(A) = \{e \in \mathbb{Z}_q^m : Ae = u(\bmod q)\},$$

$$\Lambda_q(A^T) = \{y \in \mathbb{Z}_q^m : y = A^T w(\bmod q), \forall w \in \mathbb{Z}_q^n\}.$$

$\Lambda_q^\perp(A)$ *is the orthogonal lattice of $\Lambda_q(A^T)$, if $t \in \Lambda_q^u(A)$, then $\Lambda_q^u(A) = \Lambda_q^\perp(A) + t$; that is $\Lambda_q^u(A)$, which is the coset of $\Lambda_q^\perp(A)$.*

**Definition 3** *(NTRU Lattice). Let $n, q \in \mathbb{Z}^+$, polynomials $f$, $g$, $F$, $G \in R$ satisfies $f * G - g * G = q$, the NTRU lattice generated by $f, g, F, G$ is the lattice generated by the rows of the block matrix*

$$\begin{pmatrix} A(f) & A(g) \\ A(F) & A(G) \end{pmatrix},$$

*where $A(x)$ represents the convolution polynomial corresponding to the polynomial $x$.*

**Definition 4** *(Discrete Gaussian distribution). The discrete Gaussian distribution density function of $m$-dimensional $L$ can be defined:*

$$\forall x \in L, \rho_{s,c}(x) = \frac{1}{s^m} \exp\left(-\pi \left(\frac{\|x - c\|}{s}\right)^2\right),$$

*where $s$ is the standard deviation and $c \in \mathbb{R}^+$ is the center of the lattice. Then the discrete Gaussian distribution of any point $x$ on lattice $L$ is:*

$$D_{L,s,c}(x) = \frac{\rho_{s,c}(x)}{\sum_{y \in L} \rho_{s,c}(y)}.$$

## 2.2  Hard Assumption

**Definition 5** *(Shortest vector problem, SVP). Find a non-zero vector $v$ on the lattice so that $\|v\| \leq \|u\|$ is true for any vector $u$ on the lattice.*

**Definition 6** *(Closest vector problem, CVP). For a given vector $w$, find a vector $v$ on the lattice so that for any vector $u$ on the lattice, $\|v - w\| \leq \|u - w\|$ holds.*

**Definition 7** *(Gap shortest vector problem, GapSVP). Input any basis for n dimensional lattice L, a rational number d and a gap function $\gamma$, if there is a non-zero vector $v$, such that $\|v\| \leq d$, then output "Yes", otherwise, if for any vector $v$ there is $\|v\| \geq \gamma d$, output "NO".*

**Definition 8** *(Approximate closest vector problem, aCVP). Input any set of basis B on n-dimensional lattice L, an approximate parameter $\gamma$, for a given vector $w$, find a vector $v$ on the lattice, such that $\|v-w\| \leq \gamma \|u-w\|$ for any vector $u$ on the lattice.*

## 3   LRS Scheme and Its Security Model

This section will introduce the system framework of LRS and two important securities: anonymity and unforgeability, and give the formal definition of security model.

### 3.1   LRS

Generally speaking, the LRS scheme consists of five basic polynomial time algorithms.

1. Parameter setting algorithm $(pp \leftarrow Setup(1^\lambda))$: A probabilistic polynomial time algorithm, which inputs the security parameter $\lambda$ and outputs a common parameter set $pp$.
2. Key generation algorithm $((pk, sk) \leftarrow KenGen(pp))$ : A probabilistic polynomial time algorithm, which inputs the common parameter $pp$, outputs the user's signature public key $pk$ and signature private key $sk$.
3. Ring signature algorithm $(\sigma \leftarrow RingSign(sk, R, m))$ : A probabilistic polynomial time algorithm that inputs the user's signature private key $sk$, the public key set $R$ of all users in the ring, a message $m$, and outputs the ring signature $\sigma$.
4. Verification algorithm $(0/1 \leftarrow RingVerify(R, m, \sigma))$ : The algorithm is a deterministic algorithm, which inputs all public key set $R$, message $m$ and corresponding signature $\sigma$. When ring signature is legal, output 1 indicating that the signature is accepted, and when output 0, the signature is illegal and rejected.
5. Linkable algorithm $(0/1 \leftarrow RingLink(R, R', m, m', \sigma_1, \sigma_2))$ : The algorithm is a deterministic algorithm, which inputs all public key sets $R, R$, two messages $m, m'$, two legal signatures $\sigma_1, \sigma_2$, and outputs 1, indicating that the two signatures are linkable, that is, the signature signed by the same user; output 0, indicating that the two signatures are not linked, that is, the signature signed by the different user.

A ring signature scheme needs to ensure that the message m and the signature $\sigma$ produced by each user in the ring can be successfully verified by the verifier. That is, it needs to satisfy the correctness, which is defined as follows:

Given the ring size $l$, for $\forall i \in [l]$ and $\forall m \in \{0,1\}^*$, the following formula holds for all key pairs $\left\{(pk_i, sk_i)_1^l\right\} \leftarrow KenGen\,(pp)$

$$RingVerify\,(R, m, RingSign\,(sk_i, R, m)) = 1$$

where $R = (pk_1, pk_2, \ldots pk_l)$.

## 3.2  Security Model of Ring Signature

The ring signature scheme has two important features: one is anonymity, which requires that users outside the ring cannot obtain any information about the identity of the signer. Another is unforgeability, which requires that no one who has obtained multiple message-signature pairs can forge a valid signature for a new message. The formal definitions of anonymity and unforgeability are as follows:

Anonymity: Anonymity of a ring signature scheme can be defined by Game, which describes the game between a challenger $B_1$ and an attacker $A_1$: Given the security parameter $\lambda$, the ring size $l$, the challenger $B_1$ and the probabilistic polynomial time attacker $A_1$ perform the following game. If the advantage of the attacker $A_1$ winning the game is negligible, then the ring signature scheme is anonymous and secure.

The specific steps of the game are as follows:

1. Parameter setting: Given the security parameter $\lambda$, the challenger $B_1$ runs the algorithm $Setup\,(1^\lambda)$ to generate the parameter set $pp$; then, the Challenger $B_1$ runs the algorithm $KenGen\,(pp)$ to generate the key pair $(pk_l, sk_l)$ for all members in the ring, and sends all the public keys $pk_i\,(i \in [l])$ to the attacker $A_1$, while the challenger $B_1$ keeps the private keys secret.
2. Query stage: Attacker $A_1$ can issue a key query and a signature query. The signature query means that the attacker $A_1$ initiates a query request to the challenger $B_1$ in the form of $(i, R, M)$, where $M$ is the message to be signed, $R$ is the set of public keys of all members in the ring, and $i$ is the index $(pk_i \in R)$ of the user in the ring, and when the challenger $B_1$ receives the query request from $A_1$, it sends $\sigma \leftarrow RingSign\,(sk_i, R, m)$ to $A_1$ as the response. The key query means that the attacker $A_1$ sends $i$ to the challenger $B_1$, which means to initiate the private key of the user whose query number is $i$, and the challenger $B_1$ sends $sk_i$ to $A_1$ as the response.
3. Challenge: After the attacker $A_1$ finishes the query phase, it outputs the user $i_0, i_1$ to be challenged and the message $M^*$ that needs to be signed by the user, that is, the data tuple $(i_0, i_1, R^*, M^*)$, and sends the tuple to Challenger $B_1$. The challenger randomly selects a bit $b \leftarrow \{0,1\}$, and calculates the challenge signature $\sigma \leftarrow RingSign\,(pk_{i_b}, sk_{i_b}, R^*, m^*)$ and sends the challenge signature to attacker $A_1$.
4. Guess: The attacker outputs the guessed bit $b'$ at this stage, and if $b' = b$, the attacker wins the game.

In the above game, if the probability of $A_1$ winning the game is set to $\Pr[Succ]$, then when the following conditions are satisfied, the ring signature scheme satisfies the anonymity:

$$Adv^{anon}(A_1) = |\Pr[Succ] - 1/2| \leq negl(\lambda)$$

The formal definition of unforgeability is also defined by game, and unforgeability game is basically the same in parameter setting stage and query stage as in anonymity game. The difference between them is that attackers only do signature query in query stage. In the challenge stage, the game steps are completely different. Given the challenger $B_1$, the attacker $A_1$, the challenge stage is as follows:

Challenge Stage: Attacker $A_1$ ends the query phase and outputs forged signatures $(R^*, M^*, \sigma^*)$. If $RingVerify(R^*, M^*, \sigma^*) = 1$ and $M^*$ never be asked from the signature oracle, we call the attacker wins the game.

In the above game, if the probability of $A_1$ winning the game is $\Pr[Succ]$, then the ring signature scheme satisfies the unforgeability when the following condition is satisfied:

$$Adv^{unfor}(A_1) = |\Pr[Succ]| \leq negl(\lambda)$$

## 4   Our Scheme

The scheme in this paper is similar to that in reference [23]. Firstly, the homomorphic commitment scheme is constructed, and then the $\Sigma$-protocol is designed based on the commitment scheme and transformed into a LRS scheme. The difference between our scheme and reference [23] is that the algorithms in reference [23] are based on ideal lattice, while the algorithms of our scheme (including homomorphic commitment scheme, $\Sigma$-protocol and LRS) are based on NTRU lattice. Therefore, the scheme of this paper has higher computational efficiency and shorter public and private keys and signature length, and is more suitable for the scenario of blockchain which requires a large amount of transmission, computation and storage resources.

### 4.1   Homomorphic Commitment Scheme on NTRU Lattice

The LRS scheme of this paper requires a homomorphic commitment scheme. The following is a detailed homomorphic commitment scheme based on NTRU lattice:

$G(1^\lambda)$: Input security parameter $\lambda$, randomly and uniformly select polynomial $u, v \in R_q$, set message space $\mathcal{M}$, random number space $\mathcal{R}$ and commitment space $\mathcal{C}$ as $\mathcal{M} = \mathcal{R} = \mathcal{C} = R_q$, output commitment key $ck = \{q, u, v, \mathcal{M}, \mathcal{R}, \mathcal{C}\}$.

$com_{ck}(m, r)$: Input commitment key $ck$, message $m \in M$. The algorithm randomly selects polynomial $r \in R_q$. Firstly, $m$ and $r$ are mapped to an NTRU lattice point $(m', r')$ by GGH standard method of reference [5]. (Reference [5,7] has introduced that $m$ and $r$ can be mapped to an NTRU lattice point when a set of "good basis" are obtained, that is, approximately solving the CVP problem on NTRU lattice, and this set of "good basis" are also easy to get), and then calculate the commitment

$$c = (u * m' + v * r') \bmod q \in C$$

**Hiding.** The hiding property of the commitment algorithm is related to the approximate CVP problem of NTRU lattice. When a set of "good basis" on NTRU lattice are known, the approximate CVP problem can be solved, that is, the nearest NTRU lattice with $m, r \in R_q$ are easy to solve, but if the private basis is not known, only $c, u, v \in R_q$ is given to solve(m', r') or (m, r), even under the quantum computing model, it is still a difficult problem.

**Binding.** Given different pairs of message and random number $(m_0, r_0) \neq (m_1, r_1)$, assuming that the private basis is the same, the probability that two arbitrary polynomial points $(m_0, r_0)$, $(m_1, r_1)$ are mapped to the same NTRU lattice is negligible according to the GGH standard method, so the probability that $c_0 = Com_{ck}(m_0, r_0)$, $c_1 = Com_{ck}(m_1, r_1)$, $c_0 = c_1$ is negligible.

**Additive Homomorphism.** Due to

$$\begin{aligned}
(c_0 + c_1) \bmod q &= [\mathrm{Com}_{ck}(m_0; r_0) + \mathrm{Com}_{ck}(m_1; r_1)] \bmod q \\
&= (u * m_0 + v * r_0 + u * m_1 + v * r_1) \bmod q \\
&= [u * (m_0 + m_1) + v * (r_0 + r_1)] \bmod q \\
&= \mathrm{Com}_{ck}(m_0 + m_1; r_0 + r_1),
\end{aligned}$$

the proposed commitment scheme satisfies additive homomorphism.

### 4.2   LRS Scheme on NTRU Lattice

Based on the commitment scheme in 4.1, this section proposes a LRS scheme on NTRU lattice. Regarding the ring signature scheme on NTRU lattice, this scheme uses the method of constructing ring signature in reference [6,23], and adopts the idea of "homomorphic commitment scheme- $\Sigma$-protocol-ring signature". Based on the homomorphic commitment scheme of 4.1, a $\Sigma$-protocol on NTRU lattice is constructed.

$\Sigma$-protocols are proposed in [6]: $\Sigma_1$-protocol and $\Sigma_2$-protocol $\Sigma_1$-protocol can prove that a commitment is about message "0" or "1" in a zero-knowledge way. If $\Sigma_1$-protocol is successfully implemented, $\Sigma_2$-protocol can prove that one of the M commitments is a commitment to message "0" in a zero-knowledge way. Assuming that the l-th user wants to prove his commitment is about message "0" secretly, the $\Sigma_2$-protocol first undertakes every binary bit $lj(j = 1, 2, ...,$ $n$, $n = \lceil \log_2 M \rceil$) of integer l, and then runs $\Sigma_1$-protocol to prove that the $n$ commitment is about 0 or 1 in a zero-knowledge way. Then the $\Sigma_2$-protocol proves that the $l$-th user can open the $l$-th commitment in zero knowledge (a commitment about 0).

Figure 1 shows the construction of the NTRU lattice-based $\Sigma_2$-protocol based on the commitment scheme in 4.1. In Fig. 1, P algorithm is the proof algorithm, V algorithm is the verification algorithm. The prover make use of $c_{lj}, c_{bj}, f_j, z_{aj}, z_{bj}$ in the P algorithm to prove $c_{lj}$ $(j = 1, 2, ..., n, n = \left\lceil \log_2{}^M \right\rceil])$ is a commitment to polynomial 0 or 1 based on $\Sigma_1$-protocol on NTRU lattice in a zero knowledge way. The Comck( ) function in Fig. 1 is the homomorphic commitment function on NTRU lattice proposed in 4.1, $c_{aj}, c_{dj-1}, z_d$ proves that the l-th user can open cl (a commitment about 0), which is the public key of $U_1$.

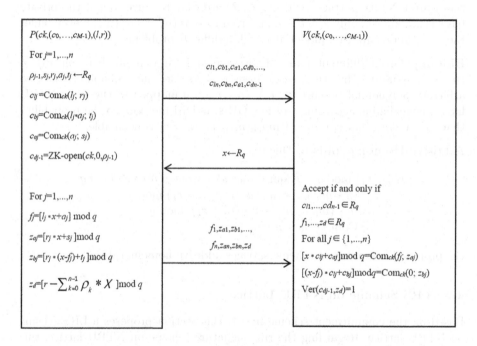

**Fig. 1.** $\Sigma_2$-protocol based on NTRU lattice

The $M$ commitment of message "0 and random number $r_i$ in the $\Sigma_2$-protocol mentioned above are regarded as the public key of $M$ ring members, and the corresponding random number $r_i$ is regarded as the private key of Ui member. The commitment and random numbers in the $\Sigma_2$-protocol are associated with the public and private keys of ring signatures. Then, by Fiat-Shamir transformation method [2], the challenge message $x \leftarrow R_q$ sent by the verifier is replaced by the hash value of all initial messages, and the interactive $\Sigma_2$-protocol on NTRU lattice can be changed to a non-interactive ring signature scheme. Figure 2 is a ring signature scheme on NTRU lattice.

| Setup($1^\lambda$) | Sign$_{pp,sk}(m,R)$ | Vfy$_{pp}(m,R,\sigma)$ |
|---|---|---|
| $ck \leftarrow G(1^\lambda)$ | Input $R=(c0,...,c_{M-1})$ | Input $R=(c0,...,c_{M-1})$ |
| $H \leftarrow H(1^\lambda)$ | Where $c_i$=Com$_{ck}(0;sk)$ | Input $\sigma=(a,z)$ |
| Return $pp=(ck,H)$ | | |
| | $a \leftarrow P(ck,R,(l,sk))$ | $x=H(ck,m,R,a)$ |
| | $x=H(ck,m,R,a)$ | |
| KGen($pp$) | $z \leftarrow P(x)$ | |
| $c$=Com$_{ck}(0;r)$ | Return $\sigma=(a,z)$ | |
| Return $(vk,sk)=(c,r)$ | | Return $V(ck,R,a,x,z)$ |

**Fig. 2.** LRS based on NTRU lattice

## 5   Security Analysis

**Theorem 1.** *Under the random oracle model, if the underlying commitment scheme has perfect hiding property, then the ring signature scheme satisfies anonymity. Moreover, if the underlying commitment scheme has perfect hiding and computable binding properties, then the ring signature scheme satisfies unforgeability.*

**Correctness.** This ring signature scheme is obtained by applying Fiat-Shamir transformation technology to $\Sigma_2$-protocol on NTRU lattice. On the premise that the homomorphic commitment scheme is correct and the $\Sigma_2$-protocol on NTRU lattice is correct, the correctness of this ring signature scheme is obvious.

**Anonymity.** This ring signature scheme is anonymous because the $\Sigma_2$-protocol on NTRU lattice proves identity through zero knowledge, and the Fiat-Shamir transformation process does not lead to the disclosure of confidential information.

*Proof.* Assuming that given a challenger $B_1$ and an adversary $A_1$, the probability that the adversary wins the game is negligible. They play the following games:

1. Parameter setting: the number of ring members is $l$, the security parameter is $\lambda$, and the challenger $B_1$ runs the algorithm *Setup* $(1^\lambda)$ to generate the parameter set $pp = (ck, H)$; then, the challenge $B_1$ runs the $l$-time algorithm, firstly randomly selecting the polynomial $r$, namely $r \leftarrow R_q$, from the polynomial ring; secondly, the commitment algorithm $Com_{ck}(0; r) = c$ is implemented to form the key pair $(pk_1, sk_1), \ldots (pk_l, sk_l) = (c_1, r_1), \ldots, (c_l, r_l)$; finally,

the challenger sends all the public key $(pk_i = c_i)_{i=1}^{l}$ to the attacker $A_1$, and challenger $B_1$ keeps the private key.

2. Query stage: attacker $A_1$ issues key query and signature query. In the query phase, as described in Sect. 3.2, the attacker performs key query, that is, attacker $A_1$ sends $i$ to challenger $B_1$ and Challenger $B_1$ sends $sk_i$ as a response to $A_1$. Then, the attacker launches a signature query request to challenger $B_1$ in the form of $(i, R, M)$. Challenger $B_1$ receives the query request from $A_1$ and sends it to $A_1$ in response to $(a, z) \leftarrow Sign_{pp,sk_i}(R, m)$.

3. Challenge: after attacker $A_1$ finishes the query phase, Challenger $B_1$ randomly selects a bit $b \leftarrow \{0, 1\}$ and calculates Challenge Signature, $(a^*, z^*) \leftarrow Sign_{pp,sk_i}(R^*, m^*)$, and sends Challenge Signature to Attacker $A_1$.

4. Guess: Attacker outputs guessed bit $b'$ at this stage, and if $b' = b$, Attacker $A_1$ wins the game. However, because the opponent's probability of winning the game is negligible, the ring signature scheme is anonymous.

**Unforgeability.** On the basis of the successful construction of $\Sigma_2$-protocol on NTRU lattice, assuming that hash function H is a random oracle, the ring signature scheme can be proved unforgettable by Fiat-Shamir transformation technology.

*Proof.* The hypothesis of unforgeability and anonymity is consistent, and this proof can be described from the second stage.

1. Parameter setting: this phase is consistent with the first phase of anonymity.

2. Query stage: the opponent signs query $(a, z) \leftarrow Sign_{pp,sk_i}(R, m)$ on $j$, the Challenger chooses $x \leftarrow \{0, 1\}^{\lambda}$ randomly, implements the $\Sigma_2$-protocol, gives the zero-knowledge proof of $(a, z)$, make $H(ck, M, R, a) = x$ and send $(a, z) \leftarrow Sign_{pp,sk_i}(R, m)$ as the response.

3. Challenge: After the attacker $A_1$ finishes the query phase, the attacker forges a signature $(R^*, M^*, \sigma^*)$, where $\sigma^* = (a^*, z^*)$ is not questioned by the signature oracle. If $A_1$ fails to forge signatures successfully, the challenge fails. Otherwise, we use a signature $\sigma^* = (a^*, z^*)$ that is forged successfully on $M$, which is obtained on the ring using the random oracle query $H(ck, M, R, a) = x^{(0)}$ for obtaining challenge $x^{(0)}$. Similarly, the same query is used for the challenge value $x^{(1)}, \dots, x^{(l)}$ to generate l forged ring signatures. If the opponent gives different answers to the $n+1$ challenge value, it can attack the binding of commitment scheme and open commitment value $Com_{ck_i}(0; r) = c_i$ through the sound attribute of $n+1$, that is, the opponent wins the game. Because the opponent's probability of winning the game is negligible, it satisfies the unforgeability.

**Linkability.** The direct way to guarantee the linkability of ring signature is to embed an encryption value $t = u * sk$ on the user's private key in the P algorithm. Add $t$ part in the output signature, so that the verifier can determine whether the two ring signatures are generated by the same user by comparing with the $t$ value parts of the two ring signatures are the same, and it guarantees the anonymity of the signer, while ensuring the linkability of the signature. However, this direct approach will lead to an increase in the length of the signature, but also need to adjust the entire ring signature scheme, so there is still a better way to continue to explore and study.

## 6    Efficiency Analysis

The central part of this scheme is about the construction of $\Sigma$-protocol based on NTRU lattice, and its hiding and binding properties enhance the security of privacy protection. Because the protocol is constructed based on NTRU lattice, the length of public key, private key and signature of this scheme are shorter than those of reference [2,5].

In this paper, we selected Aguilar-Melchor et al.'s [12] and Gao et al.'s [4] ring schemes for comparison in terms of signature private key, signature public key and signature length, and the comparison results are shown in Table 2. Aguilar-Melchor et al. proposed to improve Lyubashevsky's signature scheme to ring signature scheme [12] in 2013 and Gao et al. proposed undeniable ring signature scheme [4] based on lattice in 2019. In Table 2, m and n are related to the security parameter $\lambda$, and in reference [4,12], $\rho = mn^{1.5}\log n - \sqrt{n}\log n > 1$, $q$ are large prime numbers, and $M$ represents the number of ring members.

**Table 2.** Comparison of key and signature sizes

| Scheme | Public key size | Private key size | Signature size |
|---|---|---|---|
| Reference [4] | $mn\log q$ | $2mn$ | $2Mnm\log\rho + 2Mn + (m+M)nM\log p$ |
| Reference [12] | $nm\log q$ | $2mn$ | $2Mnm\log + 2n$ |
| Ours | $n\log q$ | $n\log q$ | $7\log_2^M$ |

Table 2 shows that the size of the public key and private key in this paper is obviously shorter than that in reference [4,12], so it takes up less storage space. Table 2 also shows that the signature size in reference [4,12] is linearly related to the number of ring members, and the signature size is related to parameters. The signature length in this paper includes two parts $(a, z)$, the size of part a is $4\log_2^M$, and the length of part $z$ is about $3\log_2^M$, so the total length of the signature is about $7\log_2^M$. Therefore, it can be seen that the signature length is only related to the number of ring members and is logarithmic. Therefore, the signature length in this paper is relatively shorter and it is the minimum signature length of all provably secure ring signature schemes at present.

## 7    Conclusion

Our study proposed a LRS scheme from NTRU lattice, which can determine whether two or more ring signatures are issued by the same user, and it can be applied to many scenarios of blockchains. It also enhances the privacy protection function in blockchains and solves the problem of double-spending. Our scheme also has a great improvement in efficiency. Compared with other relevant schemes, the length of ring signature of our scheme is also shorter.

**Acknowledgements.** Supported by the National Natural Science Foundation of China (61802117), Support Plan of Scientific and Technological Innovation Team in Universities of Henan Province (20IRTSTHN013), the Youth Backbone Teacher Support Program of Henan Polytechnic University under Grant (2018XQG-10).

# References

1. Duan, R., Gu, C., Zhu, Y., Zheng, Y., Chen, L.: Efficient identity-based fully homomorphic encryption over NTRU. J. Commun. **38**(1), 66–75 (2017)
2. Fiat, A., Shamir, A.: How to prove yourself: practical solutions to identification and signature problems. In: Odlyzko, A.M. (ed.) CRYPTO 1986. LNCS, vol. 263, pp. 186–194. Springer, Heidelberg (1987). https://doi.org/10.1007/3-540-47721-7_12
3. Fujisaki, E., Suzuki, K.: Traceable ring signature. In: Okamoto, T., Wang, X. (eds.) PKC 2007. LNCS, vol. 4450, pp. 181–200. Springer, Heidelberg (2007). https://doi.org/10.1007/978-3-540-71677-8_13
4. Gao, W., Chen, L., Hu, Y., Newton, C.J.P., Wang, B., Chen, J.: Lattice-based deniable ring signatures. Int. J. Inf. Secur. **18**(3), 355–370 (2018). https://doi.org/10.1007/s10207-018-0417-1
5. Goldreich, O., Goldwasser, S., Halevi, S.: Public-key cryptosystems from lattice reduction problems. In: Kaliski, B.S. (ed.) CRYPTO 1997. LNCS, vol. 1294, pp. 112–131. Springer, Heidelberg (1997). https://doi.org/10.1007/BFb0052231
6. Groth, J., Kohlweiss, M.: One-out-of-many proofs: or how to leak a secret and spend a coin. In: Oswald, E., Fischlin, M. (eds.) EUROCRYPT 2015. LNCS, vol. 9057, pp. 253–280. Springer, Heidelberg (2015). https://doi.org/10.1007/978-3-662-46803-6_9
7. Hoffstein, J., Howgrave-Graham, N., Pipher, J., Silverman, J.H., Whyte, W.: NTRUSign: digital signatures using the NTRU lattice. In: Joye, M. (ed.) CT-RSA 2003. LNCS, vol. 2612, pp. 122–140. Springer, Heidelberg (2003). https://doi.org/10.1007/3-540-36563-X_9
8. Hoffstein, J., Pipher, J., Silverman, J.H.: NTRU: a ring-based public key cryptosystem. In: Buhler, J.P. (ed.) ANTS 1998. LNCS, vol. 1423, pp. 267–288. Springer, Heidelberg (1998). https://doi.org/10.1007/BFb0054868
9. Kara, M., Aydın, M.A., Balık, H.H.: Bcvop2p: decentralized blockchain-based authentication scheme for secure voice communication. Intell. Autom. Soft Comput. **31**(3), 1901–1918 (2022)
10. Ling, S., Nguyen, K., Wang, H., Xu, Y.: Constant-size group signatures from lattices. In: Abdalla, M., Dahab, R. (eds.) PKC 2018. LNCS, vol. 10770, pp. 58–88. Springer, Cham (2018). https://doi.org/10.1007/978-3-319-76581-5_3
11. Liu, J.K., Wong, D.S.: Linkable ring signatures: security models and new schemes. In: Gervasi, O., Gavrilova, M.L., Kumar, V., Laganà, A., Lee, H.P., Mun, Y., Taniar, D., Tan, C.J.K. (eds.) ICCSA 2005. LNCS, vol. 3481, pp. 614–623. Springer, Heidelberg (2005). https://doi.org/10.1007/11424826_65

12. Aguilar Melchor, C., Bettaieb, S., Boyen, X., Fousse, L., Gaborit, P.: Adapting Lyubashevsky's signature schemes to the ring signature setting. In: Youssef, A., Nitaj, A., Hassanien, A.E. (eds.) AFRICACRYPT 2013. LNCS, vol. 7918, pp. 1–25. Springer, Heidelberg (2013). https://doi.org/10.1007/978-3-642-38553-7_1
13. Nakamoto, S.: Bitcoin: a peer-to-peer electronic cash system. https://bitcoin.org/en/bitcoin-paper
14. Pedersen, T.P.: Non-interactive and information-theoretic secure verifiable secret sharing. In: Feigenbaum, J. (ed.) CRYPTO 1991. LNCS, vol. 576, pp. 129–140. Springer, Heidelberg (1992). https://doi.org/10.1007/3-540-46766-1_9
15. Ping, Z., Yu, D., Bin, L., et al.: White paper on china's blockchain technology and application development. Ministry of Industry and Information Technology of People's Republic of China, Beijing (2016)
16. Qu, Z., Huang, Y., Zheng, M.: A novel coherence-based quantum steganalysis protocol. Quantum Inf. Process. **19**(10), 1–19 (2020). https://doi.org/10.1007/s11128-020-02868-2
17. Qu, Z., Sun, H., Zheng, M.: An efficient quantum image steganography protocol based on improved EMD algorithm. Quantum Inf. Process. **20**(2), 1–29 (2021). https://doi.org/10.1007/s11128-021-02991-8
18. Rivest, R.L., Shamir, A., Tauman, Y.: How to leak a secret. In: Boyd, C. (ed.) ASIACRYPT 2001. LNCS, vol. 2248, pp. 552–565. Springer, Heidelberg (2001). https://doi.org/10.1007/3-540-45682-1_32
19. Shraddha, R., Khonde, V.U.: Blockchain: secured solution for signature transfer in distributed intrusion detection system. Comput. Syst. Sci. Eng. **40**(1), 37–51 (2022)
20. Sun, L., Wang, Y., Qu, Z., Xiong, N.N.: BeatClass: a sustainable ECG classification system in IoT-based eHealth. IEEE Internet Things J. (2021). https://doi.org/10.1109/JIOT.2021.3108792
21. Wang, C., Wang, H.: A new ring signature scheme from NTRU lattice. In: 4th International Conference on Computational and Information Sciences, pp. 353–356. IEEE (2012)
22. Wang, S., Zhang, X., Zhang, Y.: Efficient revocable and grantable attribute-based encryption from lattices with fine-grained access control. IET Inf. Secur. **12**(2), 141–149 (2018)
23. Zhang, H., Zhang, F., Tian, H., Au, M.H.: Anonymous post-quantum cryptocash. In: Meiklejohn, S., Sako, K. (eds.) FC 2018. LNCS, vol. 10957, pp. 461–479. Springer, Heidelberg (2018). https://doi.org/10.1007/978-3-662-58387-6_25
24. Zhang, Y., Hu, Y., Xie, J., Jiang, M.: Efficient ring signature schemes over NTRU Lattices. Secur. Commun. Networks **9**(18), 5252–5261 (2016)

# A Fair Blockchain Transaction Based on Commitment

Yu Jinxia[1], Mu Ruijie[1], Qin Rongxia[1], Zhang Jing[1]($\boxtimes$),
and Wang Xiaojun[2]

[1] School of Computer Science and Technology, Henan Polytechnic University,
Jiaozuo 454003, China
zj_jsj@hpu.edu.cn
[2] School of Electronic Engineering, Dublin City University, Dublin 43016, Ireland

**Abstract.** Aiming at the problems of the correctness of transaction information and the fairness between participants, a FBT (fair blockchain transaction) scheme based on commitment is proposed. Firstly, a FOC-EC (FO commitment scheme based on elliptic discrete logarithm) scheme is designed to hide the transaction amount to ensure its correctness. At the same time, the scheme improves the computational efficiency and security of the FBT scheme. Secondly, use the FOC-EC and the SM9 signature technology, the new scheme realizes the binding between the commitment value and the participants' identity information to prevent participants' denial behaviors. Finally, through the smart contract, the scheme verifies the signatures of both parties and commitment values in order to prevent participants' cheating behaviors, and punished them in cash. Which ensure fairness between participants in the scheme. The analyses of security and performance show that the scheme not only ensures the correctness of transaction information, but also realizes the punishment of dishonest participants. Moreover, the scheme has better the computational efficiency.

**Keywords:** Blockchain · Smart contract · Commitment · SM9 ·
Signature · Punishment mechanism

## 1 Introduction

With the rapid development of mobile internet, internet of things, big data and other technologies, the traditional digital transaction modes are optimized continuously. For its decentralized feature, blockchain can be used to verify the transaction data instead of trusted third parties, which can be widely used in finance [14]based on quantum technology [17,18], medical care [3,5,7], Internet of things [4] and supply chain management [8]. For example, in the smart grid [19], most smart payment systems replace trusted third parties with the decentralization of blockchain to verify and save data, so that the amount of payment can safely reach the recipient's account. However, for their own interests, participants may have dishonest behaviors such as denials, which will undermine the fairness of the participants. So it is important to solve the fairness of participants. On the other hand, the decentralization and distributed storage of blockchain make transaction information open and transparent. Any user can supervise and verify the transaction information. However, because some sensitive information such as users' ID and Amount of electricity is contained in transaction information, the event will be happened that malicious users tamper with the sensitive information. Therefore, it is another important problem to make sure the correctness of transaction information.

Reference [9] uses paillier encryption algorithm, zero knowledge proof and smart contract constructed by FO commitment scheme to hide transaction information, and ensure the correctness of the transaction amount in the blockchain transaction process. Reference [10] analyzes the system abstract framework on the blockchain, which has hidden properties of balance and transaction amount. By non-interactive zero-knowledge proof and signature technology, the correctness of transaction information is guaranteed. Reference [12] puts forward some solutions to the existing user identity authentication problems, and summarizes the transaction privacy protection. The solutions include zero knowledge proof, ring signature, commitment and other technologies. Reference [13] hides the transaction amount by using the paillier cryptographic algorithm. The creation of secret accounts is based on the homomorphism of the algorithm. Make it possible to prove that the input and output transaction amounts are equal through commitment. The above scheme ensures the correctness of the transaction amount, but there may be acts of cheat by the transferor or denial by the receiver. Therefore, it will damage the interests of honest participants. To ensure the interests of honest participants, it is necessary to punish malicious participants need to be punished to achieve fairness among participants. Reference [2] proposed a timed commitment scheme on the blockchain system. It requires participants to reveal their commitment value within the specified time, otherwise they need to pay a fine. If most of the participants are dishonest, the scheme lacks fairness. That is, it has certain limitations. To improve this defect, reference [1] proposes a new method based on blockchain time commitment on the basis of reference [2]. Before the agreement begins, participants must submit a deposit. If participants want to get the money back, they need to execute the protocol honestly until the end. To guarantee fairness between the two parties. If one party terminates the agreement after understanding the output, the other party will receive economic compensation. However, the participants are forced to execute the agreement and enforce the mandatory deposit transfer. Reference [16] designed a fair deposit agreement. This protocol is used to resist the dual expenditure of blockchain participants, so as to punish the malicious party and reward the honest party. Although the above scheme can ensure the fairness between participants, there are still problems of high calculation cost.

Our contribution: In this paper, we proposed a fair blockchain transaction scheme based on commitment. Transactions can be completed only if participants did not engage in dishonest behaviors; Otherwise, the dishonest party will be punished in cash.

1. A FO commitment scheme is designed based on elliptic discrete logarithm, through the idea that the addition operation on the elliptic curve corresponds to the modular multiplication operation in the discrete logarithm and the multiplication operation corresponds to the modular exponentiation operation. The aim is improving the security and computational efficiency of the new scheme in the construction of commitment value.
2. The scheme combines the improved commitment scheme with SM9 signature technology, which not only hides the transaction amount in the commitment value to ensure that the scheme can be carried out safely and effectively, but also ensures that the transaction amount of both parties is consistent. At the same time, the scheme associates the commitment value with the identity of the participant to prevent the participants' denial and dishonest behavior effectively.
3. The scheme use the smart contracts and blockchain punishment mechanisms to verify the dishonest behavior and identity of participants, and ensure the fairness of both parties through holding dishonest participants accountable.

## 2    Preliminaries

### 2.1    Elliptic Curve Discrete Logarithm

For an elliptic curve $M$ given over field $GF(p)$ by the equation

$$y^2 \equiv x^3 + ax + b \,(\mathrm{mod}\,p) \tag{1}$$

We define the discrete logarithm problem: for given $P, Q \in M\,(GF(p))$, find

$$x : 0 \leq x \leq M\,(GF(p))\ suchthat Q = xP \tag{2}$$

Given $x$ and point $P$, it is easy to find point $Q$. On the contrary, it is difficult to find $x$ with known points $P$ and $Q$. This problem is called the discrete logarithm problem of point groups on elliptic curves [11]. Therefore, operations in the group of points of an elliptic curve allow to implement a number of cryptographic primitives.

### 2.2    Fujisaki-Okamoto Commitment Scheme

In 1997, Fujisaki E, Okamoto T first proposed FO commitment scheme [6]. In FO commitment, set three security parameters: $t, l$ and $s$, two large composite numbers $n_1$ and $n_2$ whose factorizations are unknown by users. Let $g$ be an element of large order, $h$ be an element of the group generated by $g$. Alice hold $x \in [0, b]$, the FO commitment scheme as follow:

Set $E = E_1(x, r_1) = g_1^x h_1^{r_1} \bmod n$ and $F = E_2(x, r_2) = g_2^x h_2^{r_2} \bmod n$ are FO commitment, where $r_1$ and $r_2$ are randomly selected over $\{-2^s n + 1, ..., 2^s n - 1\}$.

The purpose of Alice is to prove to Bob that she knows the value of $x, r_1, r_2$ and that the commitment values $E$ and $F$ hide that same secret $x$. The Proof of equality of two committed numbers states as follow:

Protocol: $PK\{x, r_1, r_2 | E = E_1(x, r_1) \bmod n_1 \wedge F = E_2(x_2, r_2) \bmod n_2\}$.

1. Alice randomly selects $\omega \in \{1, ..., 2^{i+t}b - 1\}$ and $\eta_1 \in \{1, ..., 2^{l+t+s}n - 1\}$, $\eta_2 \in \{1, ..., 2^{l+t+s}n - 1\}$, and computes $W_1 = g_1^{\omega} h_1^{\eta_1} \bmod n_1$, $W_2 = g_2^{\omega} h_2^{\eta_2} \bmod n_2$;

2. Alice computes $u = H(W_1 || W_2)$;

3. Alice computes $D = \omega + ux$, $D_1 = \eta_1 + ur_1$, $D_2 = \eta_2 + ur_2$, and send $(u, D, D_1, D_2)$ to Bob;

4. Bob computes $u' = H\left(g_1^D h_1^{D_1} E^{-u} \bmod n_1 || g_2^D h_2^{D_2} F^{-u} \bmod n_2\right)$, and verify $u = u'$.

### 2.3 SM9 Digital Signature Algorithm

SM9 signature algorithm includes three stages: system master key establishment, signature generation and signature verification [15].

$Setup(s, P_{pub})$: KGC generates the random number $s \in [1, N - 1]$ as the master private key, calculates the master public key is $P_{pub} = [s]P_2$, and the system master key pair is $(s, P_{pub})$.

$Sig(M, d_A)$: The SM9 digital signature to a message $M$, calculates user's the master private key $(Q_A, d_A)$, randomly select integer $r \in [1, N - 1]$, calculate $g = e(P_1, P_{pub})$, $w = g^r$, $Z = H_2(M||w, N)$ and $L = (r - Z) \bmod N$, check whether $L = 0$, if it is, select randomly $r$ to again calculates $S = [L]d_A$, then $(Z, S)$ is the SM9 digital signature to massage $M$.

$Verify(Z, S)$: Check $Z'$ is an integer in $[1, N - 1]$, if not, the verification fails, otherwise proceeds; calculate $t = g^{Z'}$, where $g = e(P_1, P_{pub})$; calculate $P = [Z_1]P_2 + P_{pub}$, where $Z_1 = H_1(ID_A||hid, N)$; calculate $u = e(S', P)$, $w' = u \cdot t$ and $Z_2 = H_2(M'||w', N)$, the verification will pass $Z_2 = Z'$, otherwise it fails.

## 3 Our Scheme

### 3.1 Overview

The transaction fairness of blockchain means that the transfer amount $m$ of participant A can correctly reach the recipient's account. In the process of trading, transfer amount $m$ is not revealed, and there is no deception between the participants. If there is deception between the participants, the dishonest participants will be punished, so as to ensure the fairness of the transaction.

In the process of blockchain transaction, to solve the correctness of the transaction amount and fairness between participants in the process of blockchain transaction, a FBT scheme based on the commit technology is designed, as shown in Fig. 1. First of all, the FOC-EC scheme and SM9 signature technology are used to solve the correctness of the transaction amount. From this perspective, we can say that the transfer amount is hidden in the equation $E = mG + rH$, and calculate its commitment value $(E_1, E_2)$. The SM9 signature technology is used to realize the association between the commitment information and the identity of the participants, so as to prevent the denial of dishonest participants. Since the commitment value of transaction information will change with the change of blind factor $r$, no one can modify the committed message. This achieves the purpose of hiding the transfer amount and ensures the correctness of the transaction amount. Second, it uses a punishment mechanism to resolve the fairness between participants. In other words, the smart contract verifies the signature and the commitment value. It punishes dishonest participants according to the verification results to ensure the fairness between participants.

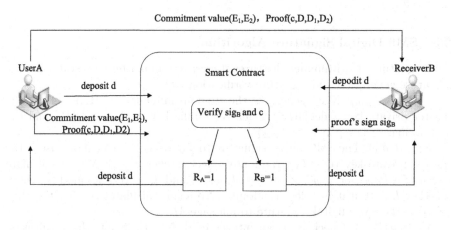

**Fig. 1.** Party interaction in our FBT scheme.

## 3.2   The FO Commitment Scheme Based on Elliptic Curve

This section mends the FO scheme in reference [9] to improve the security of hidden transaction amount. The addition operation in elliptic curve corresponds to the modular multiplication operation in discrete logarithm, and the multiplication operation in elliptic curve corresponds to the modular exponentiation operation in discrete logarithm, which is the main change of the scheme. The transformation of the corresponding algorithm is to map $g$ and $h$ of the discrete logarithm to two points $G$ and $H$ on the elliptic curve through the mapping function $varphi\,(t) : t \to \left( \frac{4t}{(t-1)^2}, \frac{8t^2}{(t-1)^3} \right) (t \neq 1, t \in F_p)$. The specific transformation method can be seen in the reference [11]. According to the addition on the elliptic curve, calculating $H$ is easy if $r$ and $G$ are given. On the contrary, given $G$ and $H$, it is difficult to calculate $r$, which satisfies the discrete logarithm difficulty assumption $H = rG$ on the elliptic curve. Therefore, the FOC-EC scheme is designed as follows:

1. A selects random numbers $r_1, r_2 \in F_p$ to contrast a new commitment equation $E_1(m, r_1) = mG + r_1H$, $E_2(m, r_2) = mG + r_2H$;
2. A random selection blinding factor $\omega, \eta_1, \eta_2 \in F_p$, computing $W_1 = \omega H_1 + \eta_1 G_1$, $W_2 = \omega H_2 + \eta_2 G_2$, $c = H(W_1 \| W_2)$. At the same time, A need to

compute $D = \omega + cm$, $D_1 = \eta_1 + cr_1$, $D_2 = \eta_2 + cr_2$, and send evidence $(c, D, D_1, D_2)$ to B;

3. B compute $c' = H(DH_1 + D_1G_1 - cE_1||DH_2 + D_2G_2 - cE_2)$, and verify that equation $c = c'$ holds.

The correctness and security of FOC-EC scheme can be inferred from the following two theorems.

**Theorem 1.** *The FOC-EC scheme is correct.*

*Proof.* Suppose A uses the FOC-EC scheme to hide the secret message $m$, and verifies that equation $c = c'$ is valid, then the FOC-EC scheme is correct. The process of verifying the validity of equation $c = c'$ is as follows:

1. Hiding secret message $m$ correspond to building commitment $E(x, r) = mG + rH$. In step 1 of the scheme, the random number $r_1, r_2$ is selected to generate the commitment value $(E_1, E_2)$ of the transfer amount $m$. Therefore, step 1 is correct;
2. Generate evidence $(c, D, D_1, D_2)$, where $c = H(W_1||W_2)$, $W_1 = \omega H_1 + \eta_1 G_1$, $W_2 = \omega H_2 + \eta_2 G_2$, $D = \omega + cm$, $D_1 = \eta_1 + cr_1$, $D_2 = \eta_2 + cr_2$, and send evidence $(c, D, D_1, D_2)$, it can be seen that step 2 is correct.
3. In the verification phase, B calculates equation $c'$ and verifies whether equation $c = c'$ is true. If the equation is true, step 3 is correct, where

$$
\begin{aligned}
c &= H(W_1||W_2) \\
&= H(\omega H_1 + \eta_1 G_1 || \omega H_2 + \eta_2 G_2)
\end{aligned}
\tag{3}
$$

$$
\begin{aligned}
c' &= H(DH_1 + D_1G_1 - cE_1 || DH_2 + D_2G_2 - cE_2) \\
&= H\left(\begin{array}{l}(\omega + cm)H_1 + (\eta_1 + cr_1)G_1 - c(mH_1 + r_1G_1) \\ || (\omega + cm)H_2 + (\eta_2 + cr_2)G_2 - c(mH_2 + r_2G_2)\end{array}\right) \\
&= H(H_1\omega + G_1\eta_1 || H_2\omega + \eta_2 G_2) \\
&= c
\end{aligned}
\tag{4}
$$

Therefore, the equation $c = c'$ holds, this step is correct. In summary, the FOC-EC scheme is correct.

**Theorem 2.** *The security condition of FOC-EC scheme is to satisfy the hiding and binding properties.*

*Proof.* It is necessary for commitment scheme to satisfy the binding and hiding. Binding means that after the commitment party makes a commitment, it cannot deny the content of the commitment. If the commitment party A uses the random number $r$ and secret message $m$ is not true, the commitment party A forges data to deceive verifier B. In other words, the commitment party needs to forge $m'$ and $r'$ to calculate $E' = m'G + r'H$. Making equation $mG + rH = m'G + r'H$ is true. It is difficult to solve two points $G$ and $H$ on elliptic curve, because the commitment scheme is concerned with the discrete logarithm problem of elliptic curve. Therefore, $m' \neq m$ cannot be found so that $mG + rH = m'G + r'H$, and the assumption is not tenable. To sum up, the FOC-EC scheme meets the binding. Hiding means that the recipient does not reveal any information about secret after receiving the commitment value. In other words, in the process of commitment value calculation, since $r_1$ and $r_2$ are random number, $E_1(m, r_1) = mG + r_1H$ and $E_2(m, r_2) = mG + r_2H$ are computationally indistinguishable. Above all, the scheme is hidden.

### 3.3   Fair Transaction Scheme

In this section, a FBT scheme based on commitment technology is proposed. The specific design of the scheme is as follows:

Input: Transferor A inputs the transfer amount $m$ and deposit $d$; Receiver B inputs the deposit $d$;

Output: The smart contract obtains the verification result $R$ and reasonably outputs the deposit $d$.

**Commit phase**

1. A and B submit deposit $d$ to the smart contract through the secure channel.
2. The step of A to calculate to commitment value of $m$ is as follows:
1) A select the random number $r_1, r_2$ to generate the commitment value $E_1(m, r_1) = mG + r_1H$, $E_2(m, r_2) = mG + r_2H$ of the transaction amount $m$, and select the random number $\eta_1, \eta_2, \eta_3$ to generate the evidence $(c, D, D_1, D_2)$ of opening the commitment, where $c = H(W_1 \| W_2)$, $W_1 = \omega H_1 + \eta_1 G_1, W_2 = \omega H_2 + \eta_2 G_2$, $D = \omega + cm$, $D_1 = \eta_1 + cr_1$, $D_2 = \eta_2 + cr_2$;
2) A select the random number $r \in F_p$, calculate the signature $sig_A = (Z_A, S_A)$ of commitment evidence $c$;
3. A send evidence $(c, D, D_1, D_2)$ and signature $sig_A = (Z_A, S_A)$ to B, send commitment value $(E_1, E_2)$, evidence $(c, D, D_1, D_2)$ to smart contract;
4. B records the received evidence as $c_B$, and sends its signature $sig_B = (Z_B, S_B)$ to the smart contract;

**Verify phase**

5. According to the received message, the smart contract verifies the equality of commitment values as follows:
1) The smart contract verifies whether equation $Z_B = Z'_B$ is true. If it is true, execute 2). Were it not true, record the calculation result as $R_B = 1$, and receiver B will be punished;
2) The smart contract uses the evidence $(c, D, D_1, D_2)$ to calculate the commitment value $c' = H(DH_1 + D_1G_1 - cE_1 \| DH_2 + D_2G_2 - cE_2)$, judge whether $c'$ and $c_B$ are equal, and record the judgement result as $R_A$ (if $c' = c_B, R_A = 0$, otherwise $R_A = 1$).

**Punish phase**

6. If the smart contract gets $R_B = 1$, receiver B accepts the penalty and sends the deposits $d$ of receiver B to A;
7. If the smart contract get $R_A = 0$, return the deposit submitted by receiver respectively; If $R_A = 1$ is obtained, the smart contract sends the deposit $d$ of transferor A to receiver B, and the transaction ends.

# 4  Scheme Analysis

## 4.1  Correct Analysis

**Theorem 3.** *The FBT scheme based on commitment technology is correct.*

*Proof.* A transfer to B is equivalent to building commitment $E(x, r) = mG + rH$.

In step 1, A and B respectively submit deposit $d$ to the smart contract. The deposit is used to punish dishonest participants, Therefore, step1 is correct.

In step 2, A calculate the commitment value of transfer amount $m$, commitment evidence $(c, D, D_1, D_2)$ and commitment signature $sig_A = (Z_A, S_A)$. The steps are:

1) A choose the random number $r_1, r_2$ to calculate the commitment value $E_1(m, r_1) = mG + r_1 H$, $E_2(m, r_2) = mG + r_2 H$ of the transaction amount $m$;
2) Calculate the evidence $(c, D, D_1, D_2)$, where $c = H(W_1 \| W_2)$, $W_1 = \omega H_1 + \eta_1 G_1$, $W_2 = \omega H_2 + \eta_2 G_2$, $D = \omega + cm$, $D_2 = \eta_2 + cr_2$. It can be seen from equation (3) that this step is correct.

In step 3, A use SM9 signature scheme to sign the commitment value $sig_A$ and send the signature to B. The steps are as follows:

1) The commitment value $c$ is regarded as M in SM9 signature scheme. Firstly, the key $(Q_A, d_A)$ of A is generated by the system key $(s_A, P_{pubA})$. Where $Q_A = [H_{1A}(ID_A \| hid)]P + P_{pubA}$, $d_A = [t_2]P = [s/H_{1A}(ID_A \| hid + s)]P_1$, $P_{pubA} = [s_A]P_2$, $t_2 = s \cdot t^{-1}$;
2) Randomly select $r \in [1, N-1]$, calculate $g = e(P_1, P_{pubA})$, $w = g^r$, $Z_A = H_A(c \| w_A, N)$, $L = (r - Z_A) \bmod N$ and $S_A = [L]d_A$. Send proof $(c, D, D_1, D_2)$ and signature $sig_A = (Z_A, S_A)$ to B, where

$$
\begin{aligned}
Z_A &= H_A(c \| w_A, N) \\
&= H_A(c \| e(P_1, P_{Pub})^r, N) \\
&= H_A(c \| e(P_1, sP_2)^r, N) \\
&= H_A(c \| e(P_1, P_2)^{rs}, N)
\end{aligned}
$$

Therefore, step 3 is correct.

In step 4, B receives the commitment value $c$ and records it as $c_B$. It uses SM9 signature technology to sign the commitment value $c_B$ to obtain $sig_B(Z_B, S_B)$.

It can be seen from step 3 that B's calculation using SM9 signature technology is correct. Thus, step 4 is correct;

In step 5, according to the received commitment value $(E_1, E_2)$, the evidence $(c, D, D_1, D_2)$ for verifying the commitment and the signature $sig_B = (Z_B, S_B)$ of receiver B, the verification process of the smart contract is as follows:

$$
\begin{aligned}
w'_B = u_B t_B &= e(S_B, [Z_{1B}]P_2 + P_{pub}) \cdot e(P_1, P_{pub})^{Z_B} \\
&= e([r - Z_B] d_B, [Z_{1B}]P_2 + [S_B]P_2) \cdot e(P_1 \cdot [S_B]P_2)^{Z_B} \\
&= e\left((r - Z_B) \cdot s \cdot (Z_{1B} + s)^{-1} P_1, [Z_{1B} + S_B]P_2)\right) \cdot e(P_1, P_2)^{sZ_B} \\
&= e(P_1, P_2)^{\frac{(r - Z_B)s}{Z_{1B}+s}(Z_{1B}+s)} \cdot e(P_1, P_2)^{sZ_B} \\
&= e(P_1, P_2)^{(r - Z_B)s + sZ_B} \\
&= e(P_1, P_2)^{rs}
\end{aligned}
$$

The B signature verification result is denoted as $R_B$. If $R_B = 1$, receiver B will be punished. Otherwise, the smart contract will verify the commitment value of transferor A. In fact, the smart contract calculates the commitment value $c'$ according to $(E_1, E_2)$ and $(c, D, D_1, D_2)$, and judge whether equation $c' = c_B$ is valid. The equation verification process is the same as equation (4). The smart contract will record the result as $R_A$, according to the verification. If $c' = c_B$, then $R_A = 0$; If $c' \neq c_B$, then $R_A = 1$. So step 5 is correct.

In step 6, the smart contract punishes the party who violates the protocol according to the verification results. For one, when the verification result is $R_B = 1$, the deposit of receiver B will be rewarded to transferor A. For other, when the verification result is $R_A = 1$, the smart contract rewards the deposit of transferor A to receiver B. However, if the verification result is $R_A = 0$, both parties involved execute the agreement honestly, and the smart contract return the deposit of both parties. So step 6 is correct.

To sum up, the FBT scheme based on commitment technology is correct.

## 4.2  Security Analysis

**Theorem 4.** *The FBT scheme based on commitment technology is secure.*

*Proof.* If the scheme satisfies the hiding, binding of the commitment scheme and the unforgettable of SM9 signature technology, the scheme is secure.

1. The hiding of the commitment scheme means that the commitment value will not disclose any information about secret $m$, also the commitment values $E_1(m, r_1) = mG + r_1 H$ and $E_2(m, r_2) = mG + r_2 H$ are indistinguishable in calculation. Assuming that there is a promiser to deceive the verifier, the secret message $m'$ needs to be forged so that $m'$ satisfies $m \neq m'$ and $E(m, r') = E(m', r')$. In the light of the definition of hiding of commitment scheme, the probability of finding $m \neq m'$ is negligible, which can be proved

by a challenge experiment. Supposing that commitment $E(m, r) = mG + rH$ is the real commitment value, there will be the following challenges:

1) The opponent calculates the commitment value $E(m', r') = m'G + r'H$ of $m'$;
2) If the opponent can forge $m'(m \neq m')$, so that $E(m, r)$ and $E(m', r')$ are indistinguishable, the opponent wins;
3) The probability of an opponent winning:

$$\Pr[Advwin] = \Pr[E(m, r) = E(m', r') \wedge m \neq m']$$
$$= \Pr[mG + rH = m'G + r'H \wedge m \neq m']$$

Referring to the addition operation on the elliptic curve, it can see that $m' \cdot G$ can be transformed into $G^{m'}$, making $m' = \log_G G^{m'}$. That is, the difficulty of solving $m'$ is equivalent to solving the discrete logarithm problem. Therefore, the probability of the opponent winning is negligible, which satisfied the hiding of the commitment scheme.

2. The binding of the commitment scheme mean that after the commitment party makes a commitment, it cannot deny the commitment content. Assuming that commitment party A forges data to deceive verifier B, using available forged $m'$ and $r'$ to calculate commitment value $E' = m'G + r'H$, so that $mG + rH = m'G + r'H$. If there is a negligible function $\varepsilon(k)$, then

$$\Pr\left(\begin{array}{c} Verify(Params, E, m, r) = 1 \\ Verify(Params, E', m', r') = 1 \\ m \neq m' \end{array} \middle| \begin{array}{c} (E, \langle m, r \rangle, \langle m', r' \rangle) \\ \leftarrow \mathcal{A}(Params) \end{array}\right) \leq \varepsilon(k)$$

Therefore, for all non-uniform polynomial time interactive adversaries, there is a negligible function $\varepsilon(k)$, which can meet the binding of the commitment scheme.

3. If the signature technology based on SM9 is unforgeable and the smart contract correctly allocates the deposit reasonably, the deposit submitted by the participants is secure.

   During the transaction, on the one hand, it is necessary to verify the signature $sig_A = (Z_A, S_A)$ of commitment party A on the commitment evidence. On the other hand, it is also necessary to verify the signature $sig_B = (Z_B, S_B)$ of the commitment result calculated by receiver B. Both parties can redeem their deposit only if the signature and commitment results are correct. Otherwise, the dishonest party will be punished.

It is assumed that in the process of transaction, there are opponents forged signatures $sig'_A = (Z'_A, S'_A)$ and $sig'_B = (Z'_B, S'_B)$, secret value $m'$, and the commitment evidence $(c, D, D_1, D_2)'$. In order to obtain the deposit, the opponent sends the forged message to the smart contract. The specific operations are as follows:

1) Obtain the commitment value $(E_1, E_2)$;

2) Sending forged information $sig'_A$, $sig'_B$ and $(c, D, D_1, D_2)$ to smart contract;
3) The smart contract verifies whether the signature and commitment value are correct: $Verify\left(sig'_A = (Z'_A, S'_A)\right) == ture, Verify\left(sig'_B = (Z'_B, S'_B)\right) == ture \ \& \ \& \ c = c'$.

If the opponent finally obtains the deposit, the signature is forgery successful. And the false secret value can pass the commitment algorithm, which is contrary to the assumption. Therefore, it is impossible for the enemy to successfully forge the signature and pass the verification. All in all, the deposit submitted by the participants is safe.

In summary, the proposed scheme not only satisfies the hiding and binding properties of the commitment scheme, but also satisfies the unforgeability of SM9 signature technology. Therefore, the FBT scheme based on commitment technology are safe.

## 5  Property Analysis

### 5.1  Theoretical Analysis

This section mainly evaluates the computing cost, communication efficiency and performance optimization. We set $T_E$, $T_S$, $T_H$, $T_M$ to represents the modular exponentiation, signature calls, hash function calculation, and multiplication on the elliptic curve. The comparative analysis between the scheme in this paper and that in reference [1,9], is shown in Table 1.

**Table 1.** Property analysis

| | Computational cost | | Calculate total cost | Communication cost | Punishment mechanism |
|---|---|---|---|---|---|
| | Commit phase | Verify phase | | | |
| Reference [9] | $15T_E + 2T_H$ | $9T_E + 2T_H$ | $24T_E + 4T_H$ | 4 | No |
| Reference [1] | $16T_E + 2T_S + 2T_H$ | $12T_E$ | $28T_E + 2T_H + 2T_S$ | 6 | Yes |
| Ours | $11T_M + 2T_S + 1T_H$ | $6T_M + 1T_H$ | $17T_M + 2T_H + 2T_S$ | 5 | Yes |

(1) Computational cost analysis

In the commitment phase of this article, the transferor A needs to calculate the commitment value and related evidence of the transfer amount. To calculate the commitment value and evidence once requires 11 multiplications and 2 hash operations. The participants need to call the signature algorithm once respectively, so the calculation cost of the commitment phase is $11T_M + 2T_S + 1T_H$. In the verification phase, the smart contract needs to verify the signature equation and the commitment equation of the receiver B. requiring a total of 6 multiplication operations and 1 hash operation. The calculation cost of the verification phase is $6T_M + 1T_H$. Therefore, the total computational cost of this scheme is $17T_M + 2T_H + 2T_S$.

In the commitment phase of the scheme in reference [9], the transferor A needs to keep the transaction amount confidential and calculate the 2 modular exponentiations. In the process of calculating the commitment value and verifying the commitment, it needs the 13 modular exponentiation calculations and 2 hash operations. Therefore, the calculation cost in the commitment phase is $15T_E + 2T_H$. In the verification phase, the smart contract needs to verify whether the same secret is hidden in the commitment value and the legitimacy of the transaction amount. It needs 9 modular exponentiation calculations and 2 hash operations. The calculation cost in the verification phase is $9T_E + 2T_H$. Therefore, the total cost of the scheme in reference [9] is $24T_E + 4T_H$.

In the commitment phase of the scheme in reference [1], the promisor needs to calculate the amount of commitment value and the evidence of the verification commitment. It take16 modular exponentiation calculations and 2 hash operations. In order to investigate the responsibility of dishonest participants, the scheme calls the 2 signature algorithms, the calculation cost in the commitment phase is $16T_E + 2T_s + 2T_H$; In the verification phase, the verifier needs to verify the commitment value of the promisor and punish the dishonest party. It needs 12 modular exponentiation operations, and the calculation cost in the verification phase is $12T_E$. Therefore, the total cost of the scheme in reference [1] is $28T_E + 2T_H + 2T_S$.

(2) Communication cost analysis

In FOC-EC scheme, A and B need to submit a deposit $d$ to the smart contract respectively. A needs to send the committed value and evidence of commitment to B, and the smart contract. B needs to send the signature of the verification result to the smart contract. Then the smart contract allocates the deposit. Therefore, a total of 5 data transfers are required to complete the implementation process of the scheme. Reference [9] needs 4 data transfers to complete the implementation process of the scheme. Reference [1] needs 6 data transfers to complete the implementation process of the scheme.

As can be seen from Table 1, compared with reference [9], this paper has two more signature call algorithms in terms of total calculation cost. However, it can ensure the security and integrity of the sent data and the authenticity of the identity of the participants. In addition, the introduction of punishment mechanism can achieve fairness among participants. Compared with reference [1], both schemes have punishment mechanism. But the FOC-EC scheme is superior to the reference [1] in terms of communication overhead. It can be seen from the whole that the scheme in this paper is not only better in computational overhead and communication efficiency, but also has a punishment mechanism. Therefore, the comprehensive advantages are more obvious.

## 5.2   Simulation and Analysis

This section evaluates different schemes through the operating system windows10 ultimate 64bit, processor AMD A10-8700P, Radeon R6, 10 Compute Cores

4C+64G, 1.80GHz and eclipse 2017 compilation environment. The time consuming of the scheme is mainly affected by modular exponentiation operations, multiplication operations under the elliptic curve, and the number of signature calls. Therefore, through experiments, we can get: under the modulus of 128, 256, 512, 1024 bit, the average time required to calculate the 1 modulus exponentiation is 0.0392ms, 0.0488ms, 0.051ms, 0.0538ms, respectively. Similarly, the average time required for 1 multiplication operation under the elliptic curve is 0.0261ms, 0.0277ms, 0.0185ms, and 0.0168ms. The time for calling a signature is 0.1722ms under different moduli. Therefore, a comparison chart of FO commitment time-consuming based on different difficult problem assumptions can be obtained, as shown in Fig. 2. The total time consuming calculation of different schemes under different modulus is shown in Table 2, and the corresponding broken line chart is shown in Fig. 3. The time-consuming of commitment algorithm and verification algorithm of different schemes are shown in Fig. 4 and Fig. 5 respectively. Among them, the abscissa represents different modulus (bit), and the ordinate represents the total time (ms) of modulus exponentiation.

First of all, it can be seen from Fig. 2 that under different moduli, the FO commitment time based on the discrete logarithm of the elliptic curve is lower than that of the discrete logarithm. Then in the commitment phase, when the modulus is 128 bit, the time-consuming solution of this paper is higher than that of reference [9], as shown in Fig. 3. However, with the increase of the modulus, the time-consuming of this proposal in the commitment phase gradually decreases. Next, we can see from Fig. 4 that the experimental curve of the verification stage is lower than that of reference [9] and reference [1]. Finally, it can be seen from 5 that the total computational cost of the proposed scheme becomes less and less time-consuming as the modulus increases, while reference [9] and reference [1] consume more time as the modulus increases. In short, although the FOC-EC scheme has higher computational cost in the commitment phase when the modulus is 128 bit than in the reference [9], but the scheme has a penalty mechanism. From an overall point of view, the computational cost of the proposed scheme is better than that of reference [9] and reference [1]. In addition, the scheme in this paper constructs the FO commitment scheme based on the assumption of the elliptic curve discrete logarithm difficulty, and improves the calculation efficiency of the scheme. In summary, the comprehensive advantages of this project are more obvious.

**Table 2.** Property analysis.

|               | 128bit | 256bit | 512bit | 1024bit |
|---------------|--------|--------|--------|---------|
| Reference [9] | 0.9408 | 1.1712 | 1.224  | 1.2912  |
| Reference [1] | 1.442  | 1.7108 | 1.7724 | 1.8508  |
| Ours          | 0.8932 | 1.0276 | 1.0584 | 1.0976  |

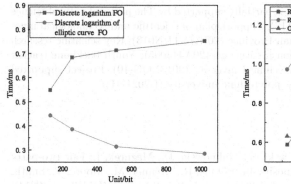

**Fig. 2.** Comparision of commitment schemes.

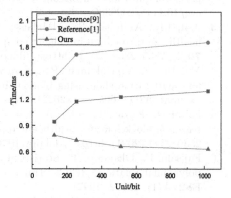

**Fig. 3.** Total running times

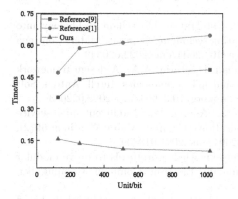

**Fig. 4.** The verification phase takes time.

**Fig. 5.** Commitment phase takes time.

## 6  Conclusion

This paper proposes a FBT scheme based on commitment technology for the correctness of transaction information and the fairness between participants in the process of blockchain transactions. It first designs a FOC-EC scheme. Next, the SM9 signature technology is combined to realize the association between the participants and the promised value, so as to prevent malicious parties from denying and dishonest behavior. Then use smart contracts to verify the signature and promise value, punish dishonest participants, and ensure fairness between participants. Finally, compared with the existing schemes, the FO promise based on the discrete logarithm of the elliptic curve reduces the computational cost and improves the safety of the scheme. The comprehensive advantages of the scheme are more obvious. In the next step, we will study the combination of polynomial commitments and zero-knowledge proofs on the blockchain. Consider how to reduce the computational overhead of polynomial commitments while ensuring the privacy of transaction information.

**Acknowledgement.** This work is partially supported by The national natural science foundation of China (No. 61802117); Support plan of scientific and technological innovation team in university of Henan Province (20IRTSTHN013); Key scientific research project of Henan higher education institutions (20A413005); Youth backbone teacher support program of Henan Polytechnic University (2018XQG-10); Project supported by the PhD foundation of Henan polytechnic university (B2021-41).

# References

1. Andrychowicz, M., Dziembowski, S., Malinowski, D., Mazurek, Ł: Fair two-party computations via bitcoin deposits. In: Böhme, R., Brenner, M., Moore, T., Smith, M. (eds.) FC 2014. LNCS, vol. 8438, pp. 105–121. Springer, Heidelberg (2014). https://doi.org/10.1007/978-3-662-44774-1_8

2. Andrychowicz, M., Dziembowski, S., Malinowski, D., Mazurek, L.: Secure multi-party computations on bitcoin. Commun. ACM **59**(4), 76–84 (2016). https://doi.org/10.1145/2896386

3. Asif, I.K., Abdullah, S., AlMalaise, A.: Integrating blockchain technology into healthcare through an intelligent computing technique. Comput. Mater. Continua **70**(2), 2835–2860 (2022). https://doi.org/10.32604/cmc.2022.020342

4. Malathi, D., Vijayakumar, P.S., Saravanan, D., Tariq, A.A.: A design framework for smart ration shop using blockchain and IoT technologies. Intell. Autom. Soft Comput. **32**(1), 605–619 (2022). https://doi.org/10.32604/iasc.2022.022083

5. Faisal, J., Faiza, Q., Soha, A., Farjeel, J., Ammar, M.: Intelligent microservice based on blockchain for healthcare applications. Comput. Mater. Continua **69**(2), 2530–2543 (2021). https://doi.org/10.32604/cmc.2021.018809

6. Fujisaki, E., Okamoto, T.: Statistical zero-knowledge protocols to prove modular polynomial relations. IEICE Trans. Fundam. Electron. Commun. Comput. Sci. **E82–A**(1), 81–92 (1997)

7. Jiang, S., Cao, J., Wu, H., Yang, Y., Ma, M., He, J.: Blochie: a blockchain based platform for healthcare information exchange. In: 2018 IEEE International Conference on Smart Computing (SMARTCOMP), Taormina, pp. 49–56. IEEE (2018). https://doi.org/10.1109/SMARTCOMP.2018.00073

8. Kang, J., Xiong, Z., Niyato, D., Ye, D., Kim, D.I., Zhao, J.: Toward secure blockchain-enabled internet of vehicles: optimizing consensus management using reputation and contract theory. IEEE Trans. Veh. Technol. **68**(3), 2906–2920 (2019). https://doi.org/10.1109/TVT.2019.2894944

9. Li, G.L., He, D.B., Guo, B.: Blockchain privacy protection algorithms based on zero-knowledge proof. HuaZhong Univ. Sci. Tech. (Nat. Sci. Ed.) **48**(07), 112–116 (2020). https://doi.org/10.13245/j.hust.200719

10. Qi, F., Debiao, H., Sherali, Z.: A survey on privacy protection in blockchain system. J. Netw. Comput. Appl. **126**(15), 45–58 (2019). https://doi.org/10.1016/j.jnca.2018.10.020

11. Trimoska, M., Ionica, S., Dequen, G.: A SAT-based approach for index calculus on binary elliptic curves. In: Nitaj, A., Youssef, A. (eds.) AFRICACRYPT 2020. LNCS, vol. 12174, pp. 214–235. Springer, Cham (2020). https://doi.org/10.1007/978-3-030-51938-4_11

12. Wang, D., Zhao, J., Wang, Y.: A survey on privacy protection of blockchain: the technology and application. IEEE Access **8**, 108766–108781 (2020). https://doi.org/10.1109/ACCESS.2020.2994294

13. Wang, Q., Qin, B., Hu, J., Xiao, F.: Preserving transaction privacy in bitcoin. Futur. Gener. Comput. Syst. **107**, 793–804 (2020). https://doi.org/10.1016/j. future.2017.08.026
14. Xie, J., et al.: A survey of blockchain technology applied to smart cities: research issues and challenges. IEEE Commun. Surv. Tutor. **21**(3), 2794–2830 (2019). https://doi.org/10.1109/COMST.2019.2899617
15. Ye, W., Long, Y.: Two party generation of SM9 digital signature. In: 2020 IEEE 20th International Conference on Communication Technology (ICCT) on Proceedings, Nanning, China, pp. 1556–1560. IEEE (2020). https://doi.org/10.1109/ ICCT50939.2020.9295863
16. Yu, X., Thang, M.S., Li, Y., Deng, R.H.: Collusion attacks and fair time-locked deposits for fast-payment transactions in bitcoin. J. Comput. Secur. **27**(3), 375–403 (2019). https://doi.org/10.3233/JCS-191274
17. Qu, Z.G., Sun, H.R., Zheng, M.: An efficient quantum image steganography protocol based on improved EMD algorithm. Quantum Inf. Process. **20**(53), 1–29 (2021). https://doi.org/10.1007/s11128-021-02991-8
18. Qu, Z.G., Huang, Y.M., Zheng, M.: A novel coherence-based quantum steganalysis protocol. Quantum Inf. Process. **19**(362), 1–19 (2020). https://doi.org/10.1007/ s11128-020-02868-2
19. Zhou, Y., Guan, Y., Zhang, Z., Li, F.: A blockchain-based access control scheme for smart grids. In: 2019 International Conference on Networking and Network Applications (NaNA), Daegu, Korea (South), pp. 368–373. IEEE (2019). https:// doi.org/10.1109/NaNA.2019.00070

# Identification of Experts in the Security Field Based on the Hypernet S-edgeRank Algorithm

Yurui Zhang[1] , Lei Hong[1(✉)] , Fan Xu[2], and Yiji Qian[1] 

[1] Jiangsu Police Institute, Nanjing 210000, China
814338895@qq.com
[2] Nanjing Police Department, Nanjing 210000, China

**Abstract.** In recent years, national security has become increasingly important. However, since most security fields are still in their infancy and expert resources are scarce, governments and enterprises often fall into the predicament of not being able to effectively select experts and the evaluation system for experts is not scientific and objective. This paper draws on the PageRank algorithm, improves the transition matrix M and the damping coefficient d, and improves to the S-edgeRank algorithm, which is more suitable for the hypernet, which is a complex network, to calculate various metrics of the hypernet. Crawl CSSCI security-related papers, and build a hypernet with four layers of subnets of citation subnet, domain subnet, and keyword subnet. The S-edgeRank algorithm is used to rank experts and scholars in the thesis database, so as to effectively select experts in related fields, and provide a reference for more accurate and objective evaluation of the ability of experts and scholars in the follow-up.

**Keywords:** Hypernet · Superedge rank · Expert identification · PageRank · Security field

## 1 Introduction

With the development of modern information technology, the Internet has become the fourth largest media after newspapers, radio, and television. Under the integration of the three major academic journal databases of CNKI, VIP and Wanfang, China has formed a relatively complete and comprehensive journal database [1]. At the same time, how to distinguish the authenticity from the massive amount of information, and to remove the false and preserve the true, has also become an indispensable part of providing knowledge services today.

Hypernet is a complex network composed of multiple subnets, and has unique advantages in the field of research with multiple systems and multiple networks [2, 3]. Due to the particularity of the hypernet, the general network sorting algorithm cannot be directly applied. Previously, research on the identification of public opinion leaders based on SuperedgeRank algorithm improved from PageRank [4] in the field of online public opinion proved its feasibility in the hypernet [5]. Therefore, this paper will use the hypernet and the improved S-edgeRank algorithm in the field of expert recognition, committed to creating an objective and comprehensive expert identification system, to make an effective assessment of scholars' influence, research ability and other academic abilities, and to help discover experts and scholars in the field.

## 2 Research Summary

Hypernet was first proposed by·Sheffi in 1985 [6], and defined it as a multi-layer, multi-level, multi-dimensional, and multi-attribute network, which is a network beyond the existing network. Hypernet can be used to describe and express the relationships and influences between networks, and at the same time provide tools for the research on the relationships and influences between networks. At this stage, the research and application of hypernet mainly exist in the following three aspects: hypernet model based on hypergraph, multi-layer optimized hypernet model based on variational inequality, and multi-network integration model based on multi-subnet integration [7].

Due to its simple structure, the hyper-network model based on the hyper-graph is more suitable for studying the characteristics and applications of the hypernet. At present, the main applications include hypergraph-based scientific research cooperation networks, knowledge expression and information dissemination, and hyperlink prediction [8]. Hypernet based on variational inequalities have focused their research on Internet finance, online advertising resources, supply chain and other fields in recent years, mainly to solve problems such as system equilibrium [9] and resource optimization [10–12]. The multi-network integrated hypernet model based on multiple subnet is composed of multiple different subnets. Compared with the other two, it is more flexible and changeable, and is more suitable for the needs of different situations. It is often used in the field of public opinion [13], media information dissemination [14, 15] etc.

Expert identification is to detect scholars based on certain evaluation criteria, in order to have a more objective, fair and comprehensive evaluation of scholars' academic influence. At present, there are three main methods for identifying experts [16]: based on bibliometric indicators, that is to evaluate scholars based on the two perspectives of scholars' published articles and cited; based on the perspective of knowledge interaction, that is to evaluate scholars based on the cooperative relationship between individual scholars, groups or institutions to conduct joint research. Usually, people evaluate their influence based on the location of the authors in the collaborative network [17]; based on topic identification and scholar clustering, that is, based on the authors' published literature. Based on topic identification and scholar clustering, that is, using topic models to identify the author's research topics based on the literature published by the author [18], so as to carry out the analysis and evaluation of the author's cross-field cross-fusion and other innovative capabilities, which can not only evaluate the author's research content inclination but also represent the breadth of its research content.

# 3 Expert Recognition Method Based on S-edgeRank Algorithm

## 3.1 S-edgeRank Algorithm

The PageRank algorithm [19] proposed by Page and Brin in 1996 is already the most representative algorithm for graph link analysis. The original formula of PageRank is as follows (1):

$$R = \frac{1-d}{N} + dMR \tag{1}$$

R is the PageRank value matrix of the directed graph, each component of which is the PageRank value of each directed graph node. M is the transition matrix, d is the damping coefficient, and N is the number of directed graph nodes.

It can be seen from the above that the PageRank algorithm is an effective algorithm for calculating the link analysis of the directed graph, and it is a simple network algorithm. But the hypernet is a complex network, so its transfer matrix M and damping coefficient d are improved to make it suitable for hypernet. The improved formula is as (2):

$$R = \frac{1-I}{N} + IMR \tag{2}$$

In the formula, R is the S-edgeRank value matrix of the hypernet, and N is the total number of superedges in the hypernet. I is the Impact(P) matrix of superedges in the hypernet, where each component is the $I(P_i)$ value of each super edge, and $I(P_i)$ is the document node of the citation subnet lay-er corresponding to the super edge connection.

$$R = \begin{bmatrix} SER(SE_1) \\ SER(SE_2) \\ SER(SE_3) \\ \vdots \\ SER(SE_N) \end{bmatrix}, I = \begin{bmatrix} I(p_1) \\ I(p_2) \\ I(p_3) \\ \vdots \\ I(p_N) \end{bmatrix}$$

M is the transfer matrix of in the hypernet, the formula of MR is as follows (3)

$$MR = \sum_{SE_j \in M(SE_j)} \frac{SER(SE_j) \times Sim_{D_iD_j} \times Sim_{SE_iSE_j}}{L(SE_j)} \tag{3}$$

Therefore, the formula of S-edgeRank value can also be written as (4):

$$SER(SE_i) = \frac{1 - I(p_i)}{N} + I(p_i) \sum_{SE_j \in M(SE_j)} \frac{SER(SE_j) \times Sim_{D_iD_j} \times Sim_{SE_iSE_j}}{L(SE_j)} \tag{4}$$

## 3.2 Expert Recognition Based on Hypernet

After calculating the S-edgeRank value of each superedge in the hypernet, calculate the sum of all the superedge scores that each author $A_i$ participates in, thereby obtaining the author's average superedge score $S(A_i)$ and sorting it. The calculation formula is as follows (5):

$$S(A_i) = \frac{\sum_{SE_i \in M(SE_i)} SER(SE_i)}{SD_{Ai}} \tag{5}$$

# 4 Construction of Expert Recognition Model Based on S-edgeRank Algorithm

## 4.1 Construction of Author Subnet

Take authors as nodes, and the relationship between authors in co-writing papers is the connecting edge to establish an author network. Define the author's subnet with $SN_A = \{A, E\}$, Where A is Author (abbreviated as A) and is the collection of all nodes in the network, and $A_1, A_2, \cdots, A_n$ in A are author nodes in the network, as shown in formula (6).

$$A = \{A_1, A_2, \cdots, A_n\} \tag{6}$$

E is the set of edges connecting each node in the subnet, as shown in formula (7).

$$E = \{(A_i, A_j)\}A_i, A_j \in A, A_i \neq A_j \tag{7}$$

When nodes $A_i$ and $A_j$ have a cooperative paper writing relationship, $(A_i, A_j) = 1$, otherwhise $(A_i, A_j) = 0$. That is, there is no cooperative relationship between the two nodes.

## 4.2 Construction of Citation Subnet

Use documents as network nodes and citation relationships between documents as connecting edges to construct a directed citation network. Define the citation subnet expressed by $SN_C = \{P, E\}$, where P is the set of all nodes in the network, $P_1, P_2, \cdots, P_n$ are the document nodes in the network, as shown in formula (8).

$$P = \{P_1, P_2, \cdots, P_n\} \tag{8}$$

E is the set of edges connecting each node in the subnet, as shown in formula (9):

$$E = \{(P_i, P_j)\}P_i, P_j \in P, P_i \neq P_j \tag{9}$$

When there is a literature citation relationship between nodes $P_i$ and $P_j$, $(P_i, P_j) = 1$, otherwise $(P_i, P_j) = 0$.

Comparing the citation network and the author network, the author network is an undirected network and exists $(A_i, A_j) = (A_j, A_i)$. However, in the citation network, $(P_i, P_j)$ represents a one-way citation relationship between documents, which can only be a later-published document citing a previously-published document, and there is no $(P_i, P_j) = (P_j, P_i) = 1$.

## 4.3 Construction of Domain Subnet

Take the academic field as the node in the network and the relationship between the academic fields as the edge to construct the field subnet. The defined domain subnetwork is represented by $SN_D = \{D, E\}$, where D is the set of all nodes in the network, $D_1, D_2, \cdots, D_n$ are domain nodes in the network, as shown in formula (10).

$$D = \{D_1, D_2, \cdots, D_n\} \tag{10}$$

E is the set of edges connecting each node in the subnet, as shown in formula (11).

$$E = \{(D_i, D_j)\}D_i, D_j \in D, D_i \neq D_j \tag{11}$$

When the domain nodes $D_i$ and $D_j$ have a mutual relationship between the domains $(D_i, D_j) = 1$, otherwise $(D_i, D_j) = 0$.

## 4.4 Construction of Keyword Subnet

Use keywords as network nodes, and the co-occurrence relationship between keywords is an undirected edge to construct a keyword subnet. Define the keyword subnet with $SN_K = \{D, E\}$, where K is the set of all nodes in the network, $K_1, K_2, \cdots, K_n$ are the keyword nodes in the network, as shown in the following formula (12).

$$K = \{K_1, K_2, \cdots, K_n\} \tag{12}$$

E is the set of edges connecting each node in the subnet, as shown in the following formula (13).

$$E = \{(K_i, K_j)\}K_i, K_j \in K, K_i \neq K_j \tag{13}$$

When the keyword nodes $K_i$ and $K_j$ have a co-occurrence relationship between keywords, $(K_i, K_j) = 1$, otherwise it is $(K_i, K_j) = 0$.

## 4.5 Subnet Collaboration

After analysis, in the 4 subnets, there are the following 3 types of synergy relations among the subnets:

(1) The collaborative relationship between the author subnet and the citation subnet (A-C) indicates the relationship between the author and the document, and has the following formula (14):

$$E(A_i) = \{P_j | P_j \in P, \delta(A_i, P_j) = 1\} \tag{14}$$

When there is a relationship between $A_i$ and $P_j$ that author i wrote document j, $\delta(A_i, P_j) = 1$, otherwise $\delta(A_i, P_j) = 0$.

(2) The collaborative relationship between the citation subnet and the domain subnet (C-D) indicates the relationship between the literature and the subject area, and has the following formula (15):

$$E(P_i) = \{D_j | D_j \in D, \delta(P_i, D_j) = 1\} \tag{15}$$

When there is a relationship between $P_i$ and $D_j$ that the research content of document i belongs to domain j, $\delta(P_i, D_j) = 1$, otherwise $\delta(P_i, D_j) = 0$.

(3) The collaborative relationship between the domain subnet and the keyword subnet (D-K) indicates the relationship between the domain and the keyword, and has the following formula (16):

$$E(D_i) = \{K_j | K_j \in K, \delta(D_i, K_j) = 1\} \tag{16}$$

When there is a relationship between $D_i$ and $K_j$ that the domain i contains the keyword j, $\delta(D_i, K_j) = 1$, otherwise $\delta(D_i, K_j) = 0$.

Take 5 author nodes A in the author subnet, 3 document nodes P in the citation subnet, 2 domain nodes D in the domain subnet, and 6 keyword nodes in the topic subnet as an example, as the Fig. 1 below shows the visual diagram of the hypernet model.

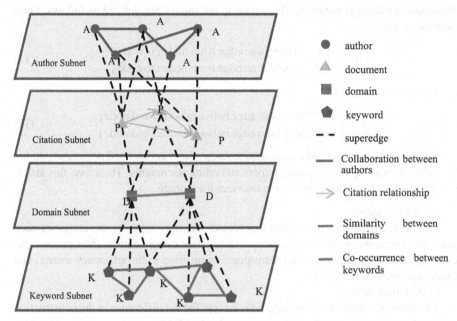

**Fig. 1.** Hypernet model example diagram.

According to the corresponding relationship between the nodes of each layer in the hypernet model, several different superedges are formed.

## 5   Experimental Verification

### 5.1   Experimental Methods and Procedures

**Data Acquisition and Cleaning.** The Chinese Social Sciences Citation Index (CSSCI) is selected as the data source of this experiment, and the titles, authors, keywords, source journals, references, abstracts, etc. of all the searched documents on the platform that use "safe" as the keyword are crawled.

Delete the information irrelevant to this experiment, such as comments and biographical materials in the papers and the paper data whose abstract information cannot be crawled. Experiment with the data after cleaning.

**The Construction of the Hypernet.** The network is a realistic concept. The storage and calculation of the network in the computer need to be converted into data. Graph provides a way to represent various actual networks with abstract points and lines. Using the adjacency matrix to represent the network can clearly determine whether there is an edge connection between any two nodes in the network. Because the security field covers a wide range, most authors and documents do not have the relationship of co-writing papers and citing documents. Therefore, this article converts ordinary matrices into sparse matrices for storage. Define: For a network with N nodes, an N × N two-dimensional matrix is required. The values in the matrix are defined as follows. For a directed graph:

$$a_{ij} = \begin{cases} 1, & \text{There is an edge from node i to node j} \\ 0, & \text{There is no edge from node i to node j} \end{cases} \quad (17)$$

For undirected graphs:

$$a_{ij} = \begin{cases} 1, & \text{There is an edge between node i and node j} \\ 0, & \text{There is no edge between node i and node j} \end{cases} \quad (18)$$

Because the security field covers a wide range, most authors and documents do not have the relationship of co-writing papers and citing documents. Therefore, this article converts ordinary matrices into sparse matrices for storage.

(1) Author subnet

The author subnet is a weighted undirected network. Take out the author of each academic literature, build an adjacency matrix after deduplication, then process the query result, assign a value to the corresponding position in the adjacency matrix, and finally compress and store it.

(2) Citation subnet

The citation subnet is a directed graph. Except for the difference in the construction of the adjacency matrix, it is similar to the author's subnet.

(3) Domain subnet

The Chinese stop word list, the stop word list of Harbin Institute of Technology, Baidu stop word list, and the stop word database of the Machine Intelligence Laboratory of Sichuan University are combined to form a stop word dictionary. In addition, a user-defined dictionary is constructed based on the literature keywords obtained during the previous data collection. The results of Jieba word segmentation are filtered using the stop vocabulary table to generate the top 10 keywords and their weights for a single text TF-IDF value.

(4) Keyword subnet

According to the word segmentation results generated during the segmentation of the domain subnet, the cosine formula is used to calculate the similarity between the subject words, from the established keyword subnet.

**S-edgeRank Algorithm for Superedge Sorting.** In the final hypernet, the author subnet has 15,096 nodes, the citation subnet has 10678 nodes, and the domain subnet has 150 nodes. The S-edgeRank algorithm is used to calculate the obtained super edges to obtain the S-edgeRank value of each super edge, and then calculate the average super edge score $S(A_i)$ of each author, according to the average score $S(A_i)$ to sort, so as to get the most influential experts and scholars in the field.

## 5.2  Analysis of Experimental Results

The results of the superedge sorting of the security field data collected in this experiment show that the security field, as an emerging interdisciplinary subject, contains multiple traditional disciplines in the fields of social science and natural science.

In terms of the scope of the ranking results, the research fields of the top 20 experts and scholars rarely overlap, and the results basically cover most of the disciplines involved in the security field. In terms of disciplines, the research fields of the top 20 experts and scholars are food science, agricultural economic management, soil science, history of science and technology, political science, cartography and geographic information system, accounting, hydrology and water resources, water conservancy and hydropower engineering, international relations, Communication and information systems, ancient literature, criminal law, information science, space physics. Popular fields are mainly concentrated in the more mature disciplines that have been developed for a long time, such as geography, agriculture, and politics. Among them, agriculture and geography are more prominent. 8 of the top 20 experts are related to these two disciplines. However, the amount of literature on topics related to emerging fields such as Internet information is less, and the impact is far less than that of mature fields.

In terms of comparison with existing experts and scholars measure indicators, the H index measures the citations of all scholars' articles, the G index is the largest paper ranking based on the citations of the literature, The S value of S-edgeRank has a certain correlation with these indicators. Part of the top 20 experts and scholars are shown in Table 1 below. The H-index and G-index of these experts and scholars are high, indicating that these experts and scholars have a high academic influence. However, the security field is a subsidiary research field of many disciplines. At present, only a few of the large number of published documents of most experts and scholars are related to the field of security, so it is not that the H index and G index are high to get a high S value.

**Table 1.** Examples of H index and G index。

| Rank | Name | H index | G index |
| --- | --- | --- | --- |
| 6 | LI Qing | 31 | 58 |
| 8 | WANGHuaimin | 33 | 65 |
| 10 | RUAN Benqing | 37 | 71 |
| 11 | XIE Jiancang | 36 | 64 |
| 14 | WANG Ning | 28 | 59 |
| 15 | SHU Hongshui | 25 | 46 |
| 18 | LYU Aifeng | 19 | 46 |
| 19 | LIU Manfeng | 21 | 46 |
| 20 | ZENG Fusheng | 39 | 58 |

In summary, the expert identification system in the security field based on hypernet established in this paper uses the superedge sorting algorithm to identify expert according to the collected data. The results obtained have a certain correlation with the H index and G index, and at the same time they have made breakthroughs. There is a certain degree of rationality and objectivity for the identification of such interdisciplinary experts in the security field.

## 6 Summary

In this article, we improved the PageRank algorithm and used the improved S-edgeRank algorithm to calculate, sort and analyze the superedges of the academic literature hypernet in the security field inter-grated by the author subnet, citation subnet, domain subnet, and keyword subnet. We also analyzed the connection relationship among the four-layer subnets. As a result, an expert recognition system based on the hypernet was designed, and the experimental results were analyzed through the collected author data, which verified the effectiveness and rationality of the algorithm, and achieved the expected purpose.

The expert recognition system based on the hypernet constructed in this paper still has certain shortcomings. In the system constructed in this paper, the three processes of data collection, data cleaning, and construction of a hypernet cannot be fully automated. Paper data is also lacking. For the academic field of security, which has a large research scope, the sample size does not have a very good effect, and there is a certain gap between the actual published articles and citations of the experts in the network, which leads to a certain difference between the results and the actual situation.

In addition, the network structure can be further optimized. The hypernet constructed in this paper is composed of four layers: author, document, domain, and keywords. In reality, publishing often has to consider many factors such as the institution, the impact factor of the publishing journal, and so on. The above four layers alone cannot describe a more realistic network completely and in detail. Follow-up research can consider adding elements such as published journals for deeper evaluation.

## References

1. Jia, W.J.: A comparative study on the searching function of Chinese periodical full-text databases. Inf. Res. **31**(10), 70–72 (2012)
2. Afzal, H.R., Luo, S., Ramadan, S., Lechner-Scott, J., et al.: Automatic and robust segmentation of multiple sclerosis lesions with convolutional neural networks. Comput. Mater. Continua **66**(1), 977–991 (2021)
3. Li, Y., Wang, X.: Person re-identification based on joint loss and multiple attention mechanism. Intell. Autom. Soft Comput. **30**(2), 563–573 (2021)
4. Hong, L., Yin, J., Xia, L., Gong, C., Huang, Q.: Improved short-video user impact assessment method based on PageRank algorithm. Intell. Autom. Soft Comput. **29**(2), 437–449 (2021)
5. Ma, N., Liu, Y.J.: Recognition of network public opinion leaders based on the super-edge sorting algorithm in the super network. Syst. Eng. **31**(9), 1–10 (2013)
6. Sheffi, Y.: Urban Transportation Networks: Equilibrium Analysis with Mathematical Programming Methods. Prentice Hall, Upper Saddle River (1985)
7. Xi, Y.J., Yang, Q., Liao, X.: A brief introduction to the research on hypernetworks and knowledge hypernetworks. Mod. Manag. **9**(4), 557–565 (2019)

8. Ma, T., Suo, Q.: Summary of research on hypernetwork based on hypergraph. Oper. Res. Manag. **30**(2), 232–239 (2021)
9. Nagurney, A., Ke, K.: Financial networks with intermediation: risk management with variable weights. Eur. J. Oper. Res. **172**(1), 40–63 (2006)
10. Zhou, S.B.: Research on super network model of online advertising based on variational inequality. Ph.D. thesis, Dalian Maritime University (2007)
11. Sheffi, Y.: Transportation network equilibrium with discrete choice models. Ph. D Thesis. Civil Engineering Department, Massachusetts Institute of Technology Cambridge, Massachusetts (19780
12. Zhang, L.: Establishment of weibo hypernet model and research on key nodes identification method. Ph.D. thesis, Nanjing University of Aeronautics and Astronautics (2016)
13. Qu, J., Liu, J., Yu, C.: Adaptive multi-scale hypernet with bi-direction residual attention module for scene text detection. J. Inf. Hiding Privacy Prot. **3**(2), 83–89 (2021)
14. Dong, J., Nagurney, A.: A supernetwork model for commuting versus telecommuting decision making. Hong Kong: Transportation Planning and Management in the 21st Century (2001)
15. Nagurney, A.: On the relationship between supply chain and transportation network equilibria supernetwork equivalence with computations. Transp. Res. Part Elogistics Transp. Rev. **42**(4), 293–316 (2006)
16. Lu, W.H., Jing, L.B.: Scholar clustering and academic influence evaluation method based on author topic model. Inf. Documentation Serv. **41**(4), 60–66 (2020)
17. Li, C.L., Ji, X.M., Zhi, L.: Identification of enterprise internal knowledge experts based on social network analysis. Inf. Theory Pract. **34**(11), 64–66 (2011)
18. Xue, Y., Tang, Y.H., Xu, X.: Multi-objective feature selection with missing data in classification. IEEE Trans. Emerg. Top. Comput. Intell. (2021). https://doi.org/10.1109/TETCI.2021.3074147
19. Page, L., Brin, S.: The PageRank citation ranking.: bringing order to the Web. Stanford Digital Library Technologies Project (1998)

# A Search Cryptographically Significant S-Boxes with Improved DPA Resistance Based on Genetic Algorithm

Tingxiu Qiu[1] and Qichun Wang[1,2]

[1] School of Computer and Electronic Information/School of Artificial Intelligence,
Nanjing Normal University, Nanjing 210023, China
[2] Shanghai Key Laboratory of Intelligent Information Processing,
School of Computer Science, Fudan University, Shanghai 200433, China
qcwang@fudan.edu.cn

**Abstract.** Finding an S-box that is resistant against DPA attacks is an important research topic in cryptography. Until now, the notion of the transparency order including transparency order (TO) and modified transparency order (MTO) has received considerable attention and is one of the best metrics to measure the resistance of S-boxes against DPA attacks. Recently, Li et al. revisited the concepts of TO and MTO. They spotted a flaw that is overlooked and provided a revised definition (revised transparency order, RTO). There are few works on evolving cryptographically strong S-boxes with good RTO values. In fact, generating high nonlinear balanced S-boxes with low differential uniformity and improved DPA resistance is an extremely challenging problem. In this paper, we propose to use the genetic algorithm to search cryptographically significant S-boxes. Particularly, we generate an $8 \times 8$ balanced S-box, with algebraic degree of 7, nonlinearity of 112 and differential uniformity of 4, absolute indicator 32, RTO 7.5222, SNR 8.8869 (the RTO of the S-box of AES is 7.5402 and SNR is 9.6000), which improves the resistance to DPA attack.

**Keywords:** S-box · Differential power analysis · Revised transparency order · Nonlinearity · Differential uniformity

## 1 Introduction

Cryptographic algorithms consist of symmetric key algorithms and asymmetric key algorithms. Symmetric key algorithm is further divided into two fields: stream cipher and block cipher. The S-box (Substitution box) is an important cryptographic component in block cipher system, which essentially is a vector

Supported by National Natural Science Foundation of China (No. 62172230), National Natural Science Foundation of Jiangsu Province (No. BK20201369) and Open Research Program of Shanghai Key Lab of Intelligent Information Processing (No. IIPL201901).

Boolean function. When we discuss the security of a symmetric cryptosystem, we often start from the cryptographic security index of its designed S-box. The main reason is that S-box is almost the only nonlinear component in symmetric cryptosystem, which provides important functions of confusion and partial diffusion. Generally speaking, the design of cryptographic function needs to select different cryptographic indicators for different attacks. In the ordinary way, the traditional attacks against cryptographic functions mainly include the linear analysis proposed by Mitsuru Matsui at the 1993 EUROCRYPT [1], and the differential attack proposed by Eli Biham and Adi Shamir [2]. With the development of attack methods, there are algebraic attack [3], best affine attack [4], fast correlation attack [5] and so on. For example, in order to resist linear attack, optimal affine attack and fast correlation attack, the nonlinearity of cryptographic function must be as high as possible. In order to resist differential attacks, the differential uniformity of cryptographic functions should be as low as possible. Some other cryptographic properties which need to be considered in S-box design include high algebraic degree [6], correlation immunity of high order [7] and low absolute indicator value of global avalanche characteristics (GAC) [8]. However, it is a challenge that these indexes all reach a better solution because of some constraints between these cryptographic indicators. In the year of 1996, Kocher [9] introduced single cryptanalysis Side-Channel Attacks (SCAs). In this attack, the physical leakage through the hardware device can be used to extract the whole confidential information. In addition, the efficiency of SCAs is usually much higher than that of traditional attacks. Therefore, SCAs has become a very active research topic. Among the side-channel attacks, differential power analysis (DPA) [10] is one of the most powerful and effective attacks. This attack originated from the simple power attack and differential power attack carried out by Kocher et al. [11] in the Block Cipher Encryption Standard DES algorithm in 1999. Consequently, some scholars [12] have put forward some countermeasures against DPA attacks. Nevertheless, these countermeasures integrated into the hardware implementation are impractical for those areas limited by devices. What's more, as the main target of DPA attacks, some scholars find that S-box does have an inherent resistance to SCAs [13–15]. Thus, scholars have been trying to design anti-DPA algorithms by selecting relevant S-boxes, the reason why is that it's an effective way to reduce the complexity and improve the ability to resist DPA attacks by updating the cryptographic characteristics of S-boxes. In 1999, Thomas and Ezzy studied the phenomenon characteristics of power signals and proposed the method of modeling signal-to-noise ratio (SNR) [16], which is the first guide to improve the anti-power analysis attack ability of S-box. Then, Guilley [15] analyzed and gave the SNR formula in 2004, which is used to evaluate the ability of S-box to resist DPA attack. The following year, Prouff [13] showed some characteristics of the S-box on which DPA attack depends, and proposed the concept of transparent order (TO) to quantify the resistance of S-box to DPA attack. Since then, many works involving the original transparency order (TO) have been explored. In the year of 2017, Chakraborty [17] and others found that the original definition had shortcomings and made a detailed definition of the transparency order. In addition, they actually verified that the modified transparency order (MTO) had a significant impact on the ability of S-box to resist side channel attacks. Specifically, the low signal to noise ratio (SNR) and low transparency order (TO) can be considered excellent. Surprisingly, a defining flaw has been ignored. Very recently, Li et al. [18] revisited the notions of TO and MTO. They found a flaw in the definition that affected the robustness of TO and investigated that MTO takes a variant of multi-bit DPA attacks into consideration, which was mistakenly thought to appropriately serve as an alternative powerful attack. Finally, they also provided a revised definition, which also considers a stronger opponent. Li et al. [18] verified that revised transparency order (RTO) has better representation for DPA resistance through simulation and actual experiments. So far, a large amount of research has done some work on the concepts of original transparent order (TO) and MTO, and contributed many results with good cryptographic properties. However, little work has been done on the revised transparent order (RTO) concept proposed by Li et al. [18]. Moreover, the RTO model provides a more accurate ability to evaluate the DPA resistance of cryptographic function than TO and MTO. In view of this, our paper is mainly committed to looking for S-boxes with superior RTO. Generally, these criteria for evaluating the ability of S-box to resist DPA attacks cannot be nonlinear at the same time. Therefore, finding a highly nonlinear balanced S-box with low differential uniformity and relatively low revised transparency order (RTO) is a very challenging issue.

## 1.1  Related Work

In 2005, the same year when the concept of original transparency order (TO) was put forward, Carlet found many S-boxes obtained by mathematical construction methods, such as gold function, Kasami function, inverse function and Niho function, although they have high nonlinearity, the transparency order (TO) of these S-boxes is pretty poor [19]. Mazumdar and Mukhopadhyay et al. have generated some S-boxes with better DPA-resistivity than AES (but other properties are much worse than AES), such as 20. [14,20,21] by using simulated annealing algorithm. In 2014, Picek et al. [22,23] used genetic programming and genetic algorithm to search for some $8 \times 8$ S-boxes with high nonlinearity and relatively low transparency order (TO). In the same year, Evci and Kavut applied the heuristic search algorithm designed to study $8 \times 8$ and $6 \times 6$ S-boxes, and gave a rotationally symmetric S-box with better transparency order (TO) than AES [24]. Others have also done some work on the heuristic search algorithm based on design, and their work have obtained good results [25–27]. Subsequently, Jain et al. [28] used Cartesian genetic programming algorithm, genetic algorithm and particle swarm optimization algorithm to generate better results than Picek et al. on NSS 2015. As a result, the safety and practicability of these S-boxes are not enough. However, in 2020, Xu [29] et al. searched the S-boxes with high nonlinearity, low difference and MTO value better than AES. Unfortunately, these are only for the work carried out by TO and MTO.

## 1.2 Our Contribution

As far as we know, we are the first to study the $8 \times 8$ S-box based on heuristic search algorithm with the revised transparency order (RTO) given in [18] as the reference index. In this paper, we use genetic algorithm to search the S-box with high nonlinearity, low differential uniformity and good RTO, so as to improve the anti-DPA performance. Under the S-box standard of nonlinearity 112, differential uniformity 4, algebraic degree 7, absolute indicator 32, RTO is 7.5259 and SNR is 8.8879. For comparison, the RTO of the S-box of AES is 7.5402 and SNR is 9.6000. Meanwhile, with the same nonlinearity and differential uniformity as the S-box in Xu [29], their RTO is 7.54325 and SNR is 9.6457. Obviously, our results have better RTO values which indicate our results have better resistance of DPA. We organize the rest of this paper as follows. In Sect. 2, we introduce the symbols and preliminary knowledge of the properties of S-box. Section 3 describes the genetic algorithm. Then, we show some S-boxes with cryptographic significance, and give some comparisons in Sect. 4. Finally, Sect. 5 briefly summarizes the research results of this paper.

## 2 Preliminaries

### 2.1 Boolean Functions

A Boolean function is in mathematics usually defined as a mapping from $\{0,1\}^2$ to $\{0,1\}$. Usually, we also use $\mathbb{F}_2^n \Rightarrow \mathbb{F}_2$ to refer to it. Among we denote by $\mathbb{F}_2^n$ the *n-dimensional* vector space over $\{0,1\}$. Where $\mathbb{F}_2$ is the Galois field with two elements ($n$ is a positive integer). The addition in $\mathbb{F}_2$ will be denoted by $\oplus$. The set of all Boolean functions $f:\mathbb{F}_2^n \Rightarrow \mathbb{F}_2$ will be denoted as usual by $BF_n$. The Hamming weight $\omega_H(v)$ of a binary vector $v \in \mathbb{F}_2^n$ being the number of its nonzero coordinates.

An *n-variable* Boolean function $f$ can be uniquely represented as a multivariate polynomial over $\mathbb{F}_2$ called the Algebraic Normal Form (ANF) as,

$$f(x) = \bigoplus_{I \in P(n)} a_I \left( \prod_{i \in I} x_i \right). \tag{1}$$

where $P(n)$ denotes the power set of the set $\{1, 2, \ldots, n\}$.

For an *n-variable* Boolean function, the Walsh-Hadamard transform is defined as,

$$\mathcal{W}_f(\omega) = \sum_{x \in \mathbb{F}_2^n} (-1)^{f(x) \oplus \omega \cdot x}, \tag{2}$$

where $\omega \in \mathbb{F}_2^n$ and $\omega \cdot x$ is an inner product, for instance, $\omega \cdot x = \omega_1 \cdot x_1 + \omega_2 \cdot x_2 + \ldots + \omega_n \cdot x_n$.

Any $n \times m$ S-box is a function from $\mathbb{F}_2^n$ into $\mathbb{F}_2$. The form of S-box $F$ can be described as $F(x) - (f_1(x), f_2(x), \ldots, f_m(x))$, which is a combination of m

Boolean functions $f_i : \mathbb{F}_2^n \Rightarrow \mathbb{F}_2$ for $i = 1, 2, ..., m$. These Boolean functions are called coordinate functions of $F$.

Similarly, where $a_u \in \mathbb{F}_2^m$, Any $n \times m$ S-box has the Algebraic Normal Form (ANF) as,

$$F(x_1, x_2, ..., x_n) = \sum_{u \in \mathbb{F}_2^n} a_u \left( \prod_{i=1}^n x_i^{u_i} \right), \tag{3}$$

The algebraic degree $deg(F)$ of $F$ equals the maximum Hamming weight of $u$ such that $a_u \neq 0$.

Obviously, the Walsh-Hadamard transform of an $n \times m$ S-box $F$ with respect to two vectors $u, v \in \mathbb{F}_2^n$ is defined as,

$$\mathcal{W}_f(u, v) = \sum_{x \in \mathbb{F}_2^n} (-1)^{u \cdot F(x) \oplus v \cdot x}, \tag{4}$$

## 2.2   Cryptographic Properties

Then we list some basic knowledge about the cryptographic properties of the S-boxes we need next.

The nonlinearity of an $n \times m$ S-box is defined as the minimum Hamming distance between all non-zero component functions of $F$ and all $n$-*variable* affine Boolean functions [30]. The nonlinearity of component functions can be measured using the maximum absolute value of its Walsh spectra, that is,

$$\mathcal{N}_F = 2^{n-1} - \frac{1}{2} \max_{u \in \mathbb{F}_2^m, \omega \in \mathbb{F}_2^n} |W_f(u, \omega)|. \tag{5}$$

Here, the hamming distance between two Boolean function $f, g$ equals $w_H(f \oplus g)$. The larger the minimum distance to any affine function, the greater the nonlinearity (that is, $nl(f) = \min d(f, g)$ and $\mathcal{A}_n$ is the set of all the n-variable affine functions). Ideally, a cryptographically significant S-box should have high nonlinearity to possess good confusion characteristics.

The derivative of S-box $F$ with regard to vector $a \in \mathbb{F}_2^n$ is the function $\mathcal{D}_F(x, a) = F(x \oplus a) \oplus F(x)$. Let $\delta_F(a, b)$ denote the number of the solutions to the equation $\mathcal{D}_F(x, a) = b$, namely,

$$\delta_F(a, b) = |\{x \in \mathbb{F}_2^n \,|\, F(x \oplus a) \oplus F(x) = b\}|. \tag{6}$$

The differential uniformity of an $n \times m$ S-box is expected to have a lower value, if there exist at most $\delta_F$ solutions to the equation for every non-zero $a \in \mathbb{F}_2^n$ and every $b \in \mathbb{F}_2^m$, which is viewed as,

$$\delta_F(a, b) = \max_{a \in \mathbb{F}_2^{n*}, b \in \mathbb{F}_2^m} \delta_F(a, b). \tag{7}$$

Except that $\omega, u = (0, 0, ..., 0)$, the global avalanche characteristics (GAC) [8], which can measure the diffusion capacity of S-box, is expressed as,

$$\rho_F = \max_{u \in \mathbb{F}_2^{n*}, \omega \in \mathbb{F}_2^{m*}} \left| \sum_{x \in \mathbb{F}_2^n} (-1)^{u \cdot (F(x) \oplus F(\omega \cdot x))} \right|. \tag{8}$$

The signal-to-noise ratio [11] of an $n \times m$ S-box $F$ is an original property to measure the ability of anti-DPA, and a low signal-to-noise ratio suggests that S-boxes have good resistance towards DPA, which is formulated in terms of the Walsh spectrum as follow,

$$SNR(F) = n2^{2m} \left( \sum_{u \in \mathbb{F}_2^m} \left( \sum_{\omega \in \mathbb{F}_2^n, w_H(\omega)=1} \mathcal{W}(u, \omega) \right)^4 \right)^{-\frac{1}{2}}. \tag{9}$$

S-boxes with low RTO values indeed have much better DPA resistance than those with high RTO values. According to [15] the revised transparency order (RTO) of S-boxes can be determined by,

$$\tau_F = \max_{\beta \in \mathbb{F}_2^m} \left( m - \frac{1}{2^{2n} - 2^n} \sum_{\alpha \in \mathbb{F}_2^{n*}} \left| \sum_{j=1}^m \sum_{i=1}^m (-1)^{\beta_i \oplus \beta_j} \mathcal{C}_{f_i, f_j}(\alpha) \right| \right) \tag{10}$$

where $\mathcal{C}_{f_i, f_j}(\alpha) = \sum_{x \in \mathbb{F}_2^n} (-1)^{f_i(x) \oplus f_j(x \oplus \alpha)}$ is the cross-correlation function.

We are committed to looking for S-boxes with high security, which means we are devoted to search a S-box with higher nonlinearity, lower differential uniformity, higher global avalanche characteristics, higher algebraic degree and lower RTO. However generally speaking, it's difficult for a S-box to have lower differential uniformity in high nonlinearity level. When the S-boxes have high nonlinearity and low differential uniformity, it's hard have a lower transparency.

## 3    Search Strategy

In this section, we describe briefly a generic overview of evolutionary computation methods GA that are used in this paper for evolving DPA-resistant Boolean functions.

### 3.1    Simulated Annealing Algorithm

Before that we use simulated annealing algorithm to find some sub-optimal S-boxes as input of GA.

Simulated annealing algorithm is a process of gradually generating the optimal solution through the continuous decline of temperature. It is a sequence of lemarkov chains, which continuously repeats the metropolis process at a certain temperature, and the value of the objective function satisfies the Boltzmann probability distribution. When the temperature drops slowly enough, the Boltzmann distribution converges to the uniform distribution of the global minimum state, so as to ensure that the simulated annealing algorithm converges to the global optimum with a probability of 1.

## 3.2  Heuristic Based on GA

Based on the concept of imitating the evolution of a species, The genetic algorithm (GA) is modelled, which is a heuristic search algorithm that directly operates on structural objects. The application of GA to cryptology is tested showing better results.

The core step is the iteration of "individual evaluation → selection operation → crossover operation → mutation operation → acting mutation operator on the group". Firstly, an initial pool of solutions (in our case regular S-boxes) is generated. In our experiment, we adopt simulated annealing algorithm to generate some "better-than-random" S-boxes which are still sub-optimal. Once a pool has been established, a loop consisting of parental selection, breeding strategy, mutation and the selection of survivors for the next generation is iterated until a satisfactory solution is obtained. For detailed information about genetic algorithms and their applications in optimization problems, we refer the interested reader to [31,32].

After the initial pool is established, the term $B_f$ gets a value 'zero', if the corresponding truth table is balanced, otherwise $B_f$ is equal to the 'amount of bits need to be inverted for balancing the truth table multiplied by a fixed value $X$. In the experiment, we fixed the value of $X = 5$ which refers to [33].

As for crossover operation, we use a simple one-point crossover operate to generating a new population, where at each call this operator generates an offspring from two best individuals among three. Here, each time a simple tournament selection procedure is called that returns three individuals of the parent population by the uniform random selection procedure. In the experiment, we fixed $\mathcal{N}_{max} = 112$, $\delta_{min} = 4$ and in order to obtain a lower revised transparency order under the same conditions, the modified transparency order is considered in the cost function.

Then apply a specific mutation operator (Method 1). However, individuals that are unbalanced or have nonlinearity less than $\mathcal{N}_{max}$ and differential uniform more than $\delta_{min}$, we apply another mutation operator (Method 2).

**Method 1:** If balanced and to preserve it, this operator just changes two bits of the corresponding individual.

**Method 2:** Divide the operator into three sub mutation operators. For each individual, one-third times (of the size of the population) a single bit is inverted. Another one-third times, the order of a small subset of bits is inverted. The remaining one-third times a small subset of bits is shuffled.

The small subset is chosen between two random points of an individual. We limited the size of subset to 15% of the size of the individual and the probability of mutation for each individual was fixed to 0.33.

## 3.3    Cost Function

An extremely important component of any evolutionary process is the cost function, which is used to quantitatively evaluate proposed solutions. In order to improve the characteristics (in our case refer to cryptographic properties) of the elements in the loop, A cost function must be as representative as possible.

Based on the cost function provided by [29], we design a cost function composed of nonlinearity, differential uniformity, and revised transparency order (RTO) as below,

---

**Algorithm 1:** Genetic Algorithm for Highly Nonlinear Balanced S-boxes with Low Differential Uniformity and Low Revised Transparency Order

---

**Input:** an initial pool of S-boxes $(S)$ as a population of
m-individuals, in the form of truth tables of n-variable Boolean functions.
**Output:** $n \times n$ balanced S-boxes $(S_best)$ with desired cryptographic characteristic.
1:  **repeat**
2:  **for** each $S$ $im$ **do**
3:      **if** the S-box is balanced $(\omega_H(S_i) = 2^{n-1})$ **then**
4:          $B_f = 0$
5:      **else**
6:          $B_f = -(2^{n-1} - w_H(S_i)) \cdot X$
7:      **end if**
8:      $max_{walsh\_W_f} = Cal\_walsh(S_i)$
9:      $\mathcal{N}_F = 2^{n-1} - \frac{1}{2}max_w alsh\_W_f$
10:     $\delta_F = Cal\_uniformity(S_i)$
11:     $\tau_F = Cal\_tof(S_i)$
12:     $Cost_f inal = B_f + Cost(S_i)$
13:     Store the value of calculated properties in the list.
14:  **end for**
15:  Load the best individual of current population in next generation population (by lower $Cost_f inal$)
16:  **for** each new $S$ $im$ **do**
17:      Select three individuals of old population using tournament selection.
18:      Generate the offspring by applying one point crossover between two best individuals among three that are selected in the previous step.
19:  **end for**
20:  **for** each offspring $S$ $im$ **do**
21:      **if** $w_H(S_i) = 2^{n-1} \& \mathcal{N}_F \geq \mathcal{N}_m ax \& \delta_F \leq \delta_m in$ **then**
22:          $Cost(S_i) = \tau_F$ (change cost function only have $\tau_F$)
23:          Method1: changing two bits of the corresponding individual.
24:      **else**
25:          Method2: $\frac{1}{3}$a single bit is inverted.
26          $\frac{1}{3}$a small subset of bits is inverted.
27          $\frac{1}{3}$a small subset of bits is shuffled.
28:      **end if**
29:  **end for**
30:  Load the next generation population in the evolution process (by lower $Cost_f inal$).
31:  **until** "termination condition of are satisfied"

$$Cost(F) = \sum_{u \in \mathbb{F}_2^{n*}} ( \sum_{v \in \mathbb{F}_2^n} (\mathcal{W}_F^4(u,v) - 2^n)^2) + \frac{1}{2^{2n} - 2^n} \sum_{a \in \mathbb{F}_2^n, b \in \mathbb{F}_2^{n*}} N_{g4}(\delta_F(a,b)) + \frac{\tau_F}{n^2}.$$

(11)

The lower value of cost implies better cryptographic properties in terms of nonlinearity, differential uniformity, and DPA resistivity. Obviously,

The first term $\sum_{u \in \mathbb{F}_2^{n*}} (\sum_{v \in \mathbb{F}_2^n} (\mathcal{W}_F^4(u,v) - 2^n)^2)$ of the cost function can improve the nonlinearity of S-boxes to be closed to that of Bent functions.

The term $\sum_{a \in \mathbb{F}_2^n, b \in \mathbb{F}_2^{n*}} N_{g4}(\delta_F(a,b))$ aims to find S-boxes having more potential to be converted to S-boxes with differential uniformity 4, which is to restrict the spread of differential spectra of the given S-box, among $N_{g4}(\delta_F(a,b))$ represents the number of $\delta_F(a,b) > 4$.

The last term $\frac{\tau_F}{n^2}$ of $Cost(F)$ is designed for searching S-boxes with lower revised transparency order. Clearly, the higher value of the third term is, the higher modified transparency order will be.

In case the S-box nonlinearity equals 112 and differential uniformity equal 4, we suggest that cost function only have $\tau_F$.

### 3.4   Discuss of Search Strategy

Similar to nature, genetic algorithm (GA) knows nothing about the problem itself and has no requirements for the search space (such as function derivability, smoothness, connectivity, etc.). It can be used to solve the optimization problems without numerical concept or difficult to have numerical concept, and has a wide range of applications. What's more, The GA search process does not directly affect variables, but directly encodes parameter sets (the operation objects can be sets, sequences, matrices, trees, graphs, chains and tables). The search process is to iterate from one set of solutions to another, and deal with multiple individuals in the group at the same time, therefore, the GA has the characteristics of parallelism. Most importantly, GA has strong fault tolerance and it can effectively avoid falling into local extreme points and has the characteristics of global optimization.

Among many heuristic search algorithms, these are the reasons why we use genetic algorithm. Meanwhile, many scholars use GA to find Boolean functions with better cryptographic properties, that is, there have been applications to prove the feasibility of this algorithm in searching Boolean functions.

But genetic algorithm (GA) has some defects, such as poor local search ability and easy to fall into premature convergence. In order to solve this problem, we use simulated annealing algorithm, which has the advantages of simple calculation structure, good universality and strong robustness, to generate some sub-optimal solutions at first. Then these sub-optimal solutions are used as the input of GA, which enhance the search ability and efficiency in the global and local sense.

## 4   Experimental Results

Our experiments are performed on a PC(Intel(R) Core(TM) i5-10500 CPU, 3.10 GHz 3.10 GHz, 4 cores, Windows10), realized by C++.

In this section, the results of $8 \times 8$ S-boxes using the genetic algorithm (GA) are provided. We define the profiles of an S-box as its nonlinearity, differential uniformity, algebraic degree, RTO, signal-to-noise ratio (SNR), and absolute indicator. In Table 1, we exhibit the profiles of the major proposed S-boxes found by the algorithm of Sect. 3.

In the case of nonlinearity that equals to 112 and differential uniformity equals to 4, we acquired an $8 \times 8$ balanced S-box with the cryptographic profile (112, 4, 7, 7.5221, 8.8869, 32), which is much better than AES S-box with (RTO 7.5402, SNR 9.6000), and better than the S-box with (RTO 7.5433, SNR 9.1092) given by [29] (in this case, our the value of RTO is lower than AES and the S-box given by [29], which means our result has better anti-DPA ability.). And **Ourresult1** truth table is given in Appendix.

At the level of the S-box standard of nonlinearity 110, differential uniformity 4, algebraic degree 7, absolute indicator 32, our RTO is 7.5126 and SNR is 8.9854, which has a better performance in anti-DPA. And **Ourresult2** truth table is given in Appendix.

**Table 1.** Comparison of cryptographic properties between our proposed S-boxes and those of the AES S-box and the known S-boxes in the literatures.

| S-box | $\mathcal{N}_F$ | $\delta_F$ | $deg(F)$ | $RTO_{TF}$ | SNR | $\rho_F$ |
|---|---|---|---|---|---|---|
| AES | 112 | 4 | 7 | 7.5402 | 9.6000 | 32 |
| **Ourresult1** | 112 | 4 | 7 | 7.5222 | 8.8869 | 32 |
| **Ourresult2** | 112 | 4 | 7 | 7.5126 | 8.9854 | 32 |
| Reference [29] shows | 112 | 4 | 7 | 7.5433 | 9.1092 | 32 |
| | 110 | 4 | 7 | 7.5370 | 9.0664 | 32 |
| | 108 | 4 | 7 | 7.5016 | 8.8068 | 48 |
| | 106 | 4 | 7 | 7.4975 | 9.0669 | 48 |
| Reference [34] shows | 110 | 6 | 7 | 7.5392 | 9.8501 | 40 |
| | 108 | 6 | 6 | 7.5670 | 9.4585 | 40 |
| | 106 | 6 | 6 | 7.5424 | 9.4585 | 40 |
| | 104 | 6 | 7 | 7.5290 | 9.4048 | 48 |
| Reference [20] shows | 102 | 8 | 7 | 7.4017 | 7.4181 | 96 |
| | 102 | 10 | 7 | 7.4618 | 5.5173 | 64 |
| | 102 | 12 | 7 | 7.5252 | 7.1316 | 96 |
| Reference [35] shows | 96 | 10 | 7 | 7.5272 | 9.2600 | 72 |
| Reference [25] shows | 100 | 10 | – | – | – | 104 |
| | 98 | 14 | – | – | – | 96 |
| | 92 | 12 | – | – | – | 96 |

Since some known S-boxes, e.g., [14,21,22,24,26] do not provide the RTO or true table of S-boxes they attained, we cannot make a direct comparison. But the nonlinearity of those work is not high (98–106), the differential uniformity is too high (8,10,12). From Table 1, it is clear to see that our S-boxes have the best trade-off between all the important cryptographic criteria, among all currently known S-boxes of [20, 25, 29, 34, 35].

## 5   Conclusions

To the best of our knowledge, we are the first to take the revised transparency order (RTO) given by [18] into the account in $8 \times 8$ S-boxes and contribute some cryptographically interesting results. In this paper, we propose the genetic algorithm to search for S-boxes with very high nonlinearity, low differential uniformity, relatively good RTO values, and therefore improved resistance against DPA attacks. With this new algorithm, we generate some balanced S-boxes with cryptographic profile (112, 4, 7, 7.5221, 8.8869, 32), which have improved values of RTO and SNR (whereas the AES Rijndael S-box has RTO 7.5402 and SNR 9.6000), even better than the cryptographic properties of S-boxes by [29]. The proposed S-boxes possess much better RTO values and signal-to-noise ratio (SNR), which are the best guidance to quantify the resistance of S-boxes against DPA attacks up to now. So to speak, our proposed S-boxes have the best trade-off among all the important cryptographic properties than those of previous works.

## Ourresult1:

[223,111,11,172,204,121,120,159,144,128,222,33,107,8,103,139,250,4,56,239,
106,171,155,142,36,202,65,102,52,2,138,30,21,169,81,6,211,245,77,185,145,
130,218,14,72,109,16,84,1,221,135,220,115,208,129,119,195,151,70,25,63,
134,148,73,38,132,226,49,177,248,105,3,207,244,136,20,99,153,32,71,79,75,
0,124,69,41,86,233,249,122,51,182,188,255,43,123,203,62,231,234,154,127,
82,199,217,168,66,173,141,55,246,165,13,193,88,35,209,180,54,15,113,149,
47,197,213,235,76,137,57,167,23,252,232,80,89,22,31,192,45,183,28,170,243,
10,29,198,61,108,7,161,147,224,27,190,112,212,46,104,100,175,91,210,116,
228,126,67,68,42,92,9,164,95,19,18,90,238,152,184,83,58,97,74,189,37,186,
206,143,191,156,44,230,166,50,110,196,160,114,64,215,93,253,236,201,176,60,
241,34,162,200,117,87,94,254,194,205,229,157,17,78,240,5,158,242,118,219,
40,53,85,59,237,163,146,247,48,133,125,251,12,227,174,225,131,96,39,179,
24,26,187,216,181,98,101,214,140,178,150].

## Ourresult2:

[235,112,155,127,83,107,74,72,12,185,159,90,124,210,49,242,34,195,103,136,
230,243,39,9,46,6,58,214,32,115,126,69,157,84,53,47,196,59,207,106,15,111,
188,176,141,28,129,142,132,88,161,191,224,33,13,240,145,153,170,30,8,131,
100,246,19,244,202,7,149,24,17,16,38,110,128,105,235,215,156,71,29,160,221,
14,97,86,121,218,166,205,117,253,138,52,226,1,251,194,199,186,45,122,93,42,

228,146,75,125,184,204,57,162,37,44,79,151,68,21,142,64,225,43,89,61,233,
236,51,73,180,173,154,134,78,249,40,130,104,76,20,4,211,95,144,22,41,217,
177,223,181,174,175,201,197,109,70,237,87,222,183,219,63,232,152,0,27,187,
208,198,252,167,77,254,113,182,250,31,62,10,227,169,192,133,165,60,193,50,
116,216,168,25,140,189,66,147,212,118,65,241,35,190,229,172,200,238,123,11,
114,137,18,3,135,239,23,36,54,143,81,92,220,203,101,163,213,245,98,48,234,
2,96,94,119,209,148,179,91,139,178,80,158,231,26,55,99,255,247,150,108,67,
56,82,5,102,248,120,85,164].

# References

1. Matsui, M.: Linear cryptanalysis method for DES cipher. In: Helleseth, T. (ed.) EUROCRYPT 1993. LNCS, vol. 765, pp. 386–397. Springer, Heidelberg (1994). https://doi.org/10.1007/3-540-48285-7_33

2. Biham, E., Shamir, A.: Differential cryptanalysis of DES-like cryptosystems. In: Menezes, A.J., Vanstone, S.A. (eds.) CRYPTO 1990. LNCS, vol. 537, pp. 2–21. Springer, Heidelberg (1991). https://doi.org/10.1007/3-540-38424-3_1

3. Knudsen, L.R.: Truncated and higher order differentials. In: Preneel, B. (ed.) FSE 1994. LNCS, vol. 1008, pp. 196–211. Springer, Heidelberg (1995). https://doi.org/10.1007/3-540-60590-8_16

4. Ding, C., Xiao, G., Shan, W. (eds.): The Stability Theory of Stream Ciphers. LNCS, vol. 561. Springer, Heidelberg (1991). https://doi.org/10.1007/3-540-54973-0

5. Meier, W., Staffelbach, O.: Fast correlation attacks on certain stream ciphers. J. Cryptol. 1(3), 159–176 (1988). https://doi.org/10.1007/BF02252874

6. Kocher, P.C., Jaffe, J., Jun, B.: Differential power analysis. In: Advances in Cryptology - CRYPTO 2000, Santa Barbara, pp. 515–532 (2000)

7. Braeken, A., Borissov, Y.L., Nikova, S., Preneel, B.: Classification of cubic (n-4) - resilient Boolean functions. IEEE Trans. Inf. Theory 52(4), 1670–1676 (2006)

8. Zhang, X., Zheng, Y.: GAC - the criterion for global avalanche characteristics of cryptographic functions. J. Univ. Comput. Sci. 1(5), 316–333 (1995)

9. Kocher, P.C.: Timing attacks on implementations of Diffie-Hellman, RSA, DSS, and other systems. In: Koblitz, N. (ed.) CRYPTO 1996. LNCS, vol. 1109, pp. 104–113. Springer, Heidelberg (1996). https://doi.org/10.1007/3-540-68697-5_9

10. Kocher, P., Jaffe, J., Jun, B.: Differential power analysis. In: Wiener, M. (ed.) CRYPTO 1999. LNCS, vol. 1666, pp. 388–397. Springer, Heidelberg (1999). https://doi.org/10.1007/3-540-48405-1_25

11. Nyberg, K.: Differentially uniform mappings for cryptography. In: Helleseth, T. (ed.) EUROCRYPT 1993. LNCS, vol. 765, pp. 55–64. Springer, Heidelberg (1994). https://doi.org/10.1007/3-540-48285-7_6

12. Mangard, S., Oswald, E., Popp, T.: Power Analysis Attacks - Revealing the Secrets of Smart Cards, 1st edn. Springer, Heidelberg (2017)

13. Prouff, E.: DPA attacks and S-boxes. In: Gilbert, H., Handschuh, H. (eds.) FSE 2005. LNCS, vol. 3557, pp. 424–441. Springer, Heidelberg (2005). https://doi.org/10.1007/11502760_29

14. Carlet, C.: On highly nonlinear S-boxes and their inability to Thwart DPA attacks. In: Maitra, S., Veni Madhavan, C.E., Venkatesan, R. (eds.) INDOCRYPT 2005. LNCS, vol. 3797, pp. 49–62. Springer, Heidelberg (2005). https://doi.org/10.1007/11596219_5

15. Guilley, S., Hoogvorst, P., Pacalet, R.: Differential power analysis model and some results. In: Quisquater, J.-J., Paradinas, P., Deswarte, Y., El Kalam, A.A. (eds.) CARDIS 2004. IIFIP, vol. 153, pp. 127–142. Springer, Boston, MA (2004). https://doi.org/10.1007/1-4020-8147-2_9

16. Messerges, T.S., Dabbish, E.A.: Investigations of power analysis attacks on smartcards. In: Proceedings of the 1st Workshop on Smartcard Technology, Chicago, pp. 1–12 (1999)

17. Chakraborty, K., Sarkar, S., Maitra, S., Mazumdar, B., Mukhopadhyay, D., Prouff, E.: Redefining the transparency order. Des. Codes Cryptogr. (3), 95–115 (2016). https://doi.org/10.1007/s10623-016-0250-3

18. Li, H., Zhou, Y., Ming, J., Yang, G., Jin, C.: The notion of transparency order. Comput. J. **63**(12), 1915–1938 (2020)

19. Mazumdar, B., Mukhopadhyay, D.: Construction of rotation symmetric S-boxes with high nonlinearity and improved DPA resistivity. IEEE Trans. Comput. **66**(1), 59–72 (2017)

20. Mazumdar, B., Mukhopadhyay, D., Sengupta, I.: Design and implementation of rotation symmetric S-boxes with high nonlinearity and high DPA resilience. In: 2013 IEEE International Symposium on Hardware-Oriented Security and Trust, Austin, pp. 87–92 (2013)

21. Mazumdar, B., Mukhopadhyay, D., Sengupta, I.: Constrained search for a class of good bijective S-boxes with improved DPA resistivity. IEEE Trans. Inf. Forensics Secur. **8**(12), 2154–2163 (2013)

22. Picek, S., Ege, B., Batina, L., Jakobovic, D., Chmielewski, U., Golub, M.: On using genetic algorithms for intrinsic side-channel resistance: the case of AES S-box. In: Proceedings of the First Workshop on Cryptography and Security in Computing Systems, Vienna, pp. 13–18 (2014)

23. Picek, S., Ege, B., Papagiannopoulos, K., Batina, L., Jakobovic, D.: The case of 4x4 S-boxes. In: 2014 IEEE International Symposium on Hardware-Oriented Security and Trust, Arlington, pp. 80–83 (2014)

24. Evci, M.A., Kavut, S.: DPA resilience of rotation-symmetric S-boxes. In: Advances in Information and Computer Security, Hirosaki, pp. 146–1574 (2014)

25. Picek, S., Mazumdar, B., Mukhopadhyay, B., Batina, L.: Modified transparency order property: solution or just another attempt. In: International Conference on Security, Privacy, and Applied Cryptography Engineering, Jaipur, pp. 210–227 (2015)

26. Spain, M., Varia, M.: Evolving S-boxes with reduced differential power analysis susceptibility. IACR Cryptology ePrint Archive https://eprint.iacr.org/2016/1145, p. 1145 (2016)

27. Kavut, S., Baloglu, S.: Classification of 6x6 S-boxes obtained by concatenation of RSSBs. In: International Workshop on Lightweight Cryptography for Security and Privacy, Aksaray, pp. 110–127 (2016)

28. Jain, A., Chaudhari, N.S.: Evolving highly nonlinear balanced Boolean functions with improved resistance to DPA attacks. In: NSS 2015. LNCS, vol. 9408, pp. 316–330. Springer, Cham (2015). https://doi.org/10.1007/978-3-319-25645-0_21

29. Xu, Y., Wang, Q.: Searching for balanced S-boxes with high nonlinearity, low differential uniformity, and improved DPA-resistance. In: Susilo, W., Deng, R.H., Guo, F., Li, Y., Intan, R. (eds.) ISC 2020. LNCS, vol. 12472, pp. 95–106. Springer, Cham (2020). https://doi.org/10.1007/978-3-030-62974-8_6

30. Braeken, A.: Cryptographic properties of Boolean functions and S-boxes. Ph.D. thesis, Catholic University of Leuven, Belgium (2006)

31. Goldberg, D.: Genetic Algorithms in Search, Optimization, and Machine Learning, 2nd edn. Addison-Wesley Professional, New Jersey (1988)
32. Srinivas, M., Patnaik, L.M.: Genetic algorithms: a survey. Computer **27**(6), 17–26 (1994)
33. Picek, S., Batina, L., Jakobovic, D.: Evolving DPA-resistant Boolean functions. In: Bartz-Beielstein, T., Branke, J., Filipič, B., Smith, J. (eds.) PPSN 2014. LNCS, vol. 8672, pp. 812–821. Springer, Cham (2014). https://doi.org/10.1007/978-3-319-10762-2_80
34. Ivanov, G., Nikolov, N., Nikova, S.: Reversed genetic algorithms for generation of bijective S-boxes with good cryptographic properties. Cryptogr. Commun. **8**(2), 247–276 (2016)
35. Gérard, B., Grosso, V., Naya-Plasencia, M., Standaert, F.-X.: Block ciphers that are easier to mask: how far can we go? In: Bertoni, G., Coron, J.-S. (eds.) CHES 2013. LNCS, vol. 8086, pp. 383–399. Springer, Heidelberg (2013). https://doi.org/10.1007/978-3-642-40349-1_22
36. Kh, A., Akay, B.: A survey on the metaheuristics for cryptanalysis of substitution and transposition ciphers. Comput. Syst. Sci. Eng. **39**(1), 87–106 (2021)
37. Sanam, N., Ali, A., Shah, T., Farooq, G.: Non-associative algebra redesigning block cipher with color image encryption. Comput. Mater. Continua **67**(1), 1–21 (2021)
38. Ramadan, R.A., Aboshosha, B.W., Yadav, K., Alseadoon, I.M., Kashout, M.J., et al.: LBC-IoT: lightweight block cipher for IoT constraint devices. Comput. Mater. Continua **67**(3), 3563–3579 (2021)
39. Muthumari, A., Banumathi, J., Rajasekaran, S., Vijayakarthik, P., Shankar, K., et al.: High security for de-duplicated big data using optimal Simon cipher. Comput. Mater. Continua **67**(2), 1863–1879 (2021)
40. Zheng, H., Shi, D.: A multi-agent system for environmental monitoring using Boolean networks and reinforcement learning. J. Cyber Secur. **2**(2), 85–96 (2020)

# An Efficient Quantum Private Comparison Protocol Based on Cluster State and Bell State

Chaoyang Li[1] , Hua Qing[1] , Gang Xu[2] , Xiubo Chen[3] , Xiangjun Xin[1(✉)] ,
Mianxiong Dong[4] , and Kaoru Ota[4]

[1] College of Software Engineering, Zhengzhou University
of Light Industry, Zhengzhou 450002, China
`xin_xiang_jun@126.com`
[2] School of Computing Science and Technology, North China University
of Technology, Beijing 100144, China
[3] Information Security Centre, State Key Laboratory of Networking and Switching Technology,
Beijing University of Post and Telecommunications, Beijing 100876, China
[4] Department of Sciences and Informatics, Muroran Institution
of Technology, Muroran 050-8585, Japan

**Abstract.** Quantum private comparison (QPC) is the quantum method that can compare the equality of the distrustful participants' private information without leaking them. The 4-particle cluster state has a strong violation of local reality and shows to be robust against decoherence than any other 4-particle state. In this paper, a new efficient QPC protocol based on the entanglement swapping between the 4-particle cluster state and Bell state has been proposed. With the pre-shared secret key sequence between the two participants, the semi-honest third party (TP) can only execute the protocol's processes without obtaining information about the participants' secrets and the final comparison results. Then, we show that the proposed QPC protocol is secure against outside or participant attacks and more efficient than similar literature.

**Keywords:** Quantum private comparison · 4-particle cluster state · Bell state · Semi-honest third party

## 1 Introduction

In recent years, quantum cryptography has been widely concerned in many studies, especially the first quantum key distribution protocol proposed by Bennett and Brassard in 1984 [1]. From then on, there are existing more and more exciting applications about quantum secure protocols and experimental researches [2–5].

Secure multiparty computation (SMC) is that many users cooperate in obtaining the result of a function without leaking their secret information in a distributed trustless network. As Yao first proposed the concept of SMC, which was widely used to implement the following tasks [6, 7]: electronic voting, joint decryption, geometric calculation and digital signature. Therefore, many SMC protocols have been proposed, which play an essential role in classical information security. However, the SMC protocols' security

© The Author(s), under exclusive license to Springer Nature Switzerland AG 2022
X. Sun et al. (Eds.): ICAIS 2022, CCIS 1588, pp. 94–105, 2022.
https://doi.org/10.1007/978-3-031-06764-8_8

is still based on the classical mathematical difficulty assumption, and Shor [8] pointed out that it can be solved by models based on the quantum setting with higher efficiency. Therefore, designing an SMC protocol by the quantum method should be a significant way to resist quantum attacks along with the development of quantum Shor, Grover, and other deformation algorithms [8–10]. Since then, more and more special SMC problems have been solved in a quantum setting, such as quantum protocol for anonymous voting [11], quantum homomorphic encryption [12, 13], quantum private comparison [14–16], the quantum secret sharing [17], and so on.

Quantum private comparison (QPC) is one important branch of SMC, which mainly can compare the equality of the private information of the distrustful parties by quantum methods. In general, there is also a semi-honest third party (TP) in the QPC protocol, who has the ability to help the participants to compare their secret inputs. However, he cannot obtain anything about the comparison results and the participants' private information. In 2009, Yang [18] proposed the first QPC protocol based on two-particle entangled state, and she also used the classical Hash function to realize private comparison. From then on, a new chapter of the private comparison by the quantum method has been started. Then, the design and analysis of QPC protocols have attracted much interest and attention in recent years. As a consequence, lots of QPC protocols based on different entangled states have been presented, such as Bell state, GHZ state, W state, and cluster state, etc. [19–32].

As we all know, the cluster states have been thought to have a strong violation of local reality and shown to be robust against decoherence [33, 34]. The two-particle and three-particle cluster state are the Bell state and GHZ state respectively, which are popular to us. Then, the formal definition of an $N$-particle cluster state was proposed in Reference [35]:

$$|C_N\rangle = \frac{1}{2^{N/2}} \otimes_{a=1}^{N} (|0\rangle_a \delta_z^{(a+1)} + |1\rangle) \tag{1}$$

Note that $\delta_z^{(N+1)} = 1$. Then, there are many QPC protocol based on 4-particle or five-particle cluster state. In this paper, we proposed an efficient QPC protocol based on the entanglement swapping of the 4-particle cluster state and Bell state. Comparing with some previous similar protocols, the 4-particle cluster state $|C_4\rangle$ is different in that it is hard to destroy the entanglement than that of the 4-particle W-state by local operations [36]. It also shows a strong violation of local reality and is shown to be robust against decoherence. Therefore, taking the entanglement swapping of the 4-particle cluster state and Bell state as the information carrier can preferably perform the QPC protocol. Then, for better implementing the scheme, a semi-honest TP is introduced in the proposed QPC protocol, who only can obey the duty to perform the rules of the protocol without knowing the comparison results and participants' secret information. Furthermore, with the decoy photons and pre-shared random sequence, it can detect the malicious eavesdropper Eve and forbid him knowing the actual comparison results and the length of the secret inputs.

## 2  The Proposed QPC Protocol

In this section, we present a detailed description of the proposed QPC protocol. Meanwhile, the 4-particle cluster state is described as following, where $N = 4$ in Eq. (1):

$$|C_4\rangle_{1234} = \frac{1}{2}(|0000\rangle + |0110\rangle + |1001\rangle - |1111\rangle)$$

Here, we choose the Bell state $|\phi^+\rangle_{56} = (|00\rangle + |11\rangle)\big/\sqrt{2}$ to construct the entangled state. The Bell basis is $\{|\phi^\pm\rangle = (|00\rangle + |11\rangle)\big/\sqrt{2}, |\psi^\pm\rangle = (|01\rangle + |10\rangle)\big/\sqrt{2}\}$, which was used for measuring the 2-qubit system. Then, the entanglement swapping of the 4-particle cluster state $|C_4\rangle_{1234}$ and the Bell state $|\phi^+\rangle_{56}$ is given in Eq. (2):

$$|C_4\rangle_{1234} \otimes |\phi^+\rangle_{56}$$
$$= \frac{1}{2}(|0000\rangle + |0110\rangle + |1001\rangle - |1111\rangle) \otimes \frac{1}{\sqrt{2}}(|00\rangle + |11\rangle)$$
$$= \frac{1}{4}(|\phi^+\rangle_{12}(|\phi^+\rangle_{35}|\phi^-\rangle_{46} + |\phi^-\rangle_{35}|\phi^+\rangle_{46} + |\psi^+\rangle_{35}|\psi^-\rangle_{46} + |\psi^-\rangle_{35}|\psi^+\rangle_{46})$$
$$+ |\phi^-\rangle_{12}(|\phi^+\rangle_{35}|\phi^+\rangle_{46} + |\phi^-\rangle_{35}|\phi^-\rangle_{46} + |\psi^+\rangle_{35}|\psi^+\rangle_{46} + |\psi^-\rangle_{35}|\psi^-\rangle_{46})$$
$$+ |\psi^+\rangle_{12}(|\psi^+\rangle_{35}|\phi^+\rangle_{46} - |\psi^-\rangle_{35}|\phi^-\rangle_{46} + |\phi^+\rangle_{35}|\psi^+\rangle_{46} - |\phi^-\rangle_{35}|\psi^-\rangle_{46})$$
$$+ |\psi^-\rangle_{12}(|\psi^+\rangle_{35}|\phi^-\rangle_{46} - |\psi^-\rangle_{35}|\phi^+\rangle_{46} + |\phi^+\rangle_{35}|\psi^-\rangle_{46} - |\phi^-\rangle_{35}|\psi^+\rangle_{46}) \quad (2)$$

The proposed QPC protocol can be described with the input: Given Alice's private integer $X$ and Bob's private integer $X$. Then, the binary representation of the two participants' private information $X$ and $Y$ in $F_{2^L}$ can be written as: $X = (x_0, x_1, ..., x_{N-1})$, $Y = (y_0, y_1, ..., y_{N-1})$, where $x_i, y_i < 2^L$. They also can be described as $X = \sum_{i=0}^{L-1} x_i 2^i$, $Y = \sum_{i=0}^{L-1} y_i 2^i$, $2^L - 1 < \max\{X, Y\} < 2^L$. Meanwhile, it is with the output $X = Y$ or $X \neq Y$.

Additionally, there also needs a semi-honest third party (TP) Charlie, who only can help the two participants Alice and Bob compare their secrets without obtaining anything about the secrets of Alice and Bob through the protocol. Beforehand, Alice (Bob) and Charlie should share a common secret key $K_{AC}(K_{BC})$ by a secure QKD protocol. The two participants, Alice and Bob, share a secret key sequence $K : (k_0, k_1, ..., k_{L-1})$, where $k_i \in \{0, 1\}, i = 0, 1, ..., (L - 1)$ through a secure QKD protocol.

### 2.1  Preparing Step

In order to accurately compare the two secrets of Alice and Bob, the $N$-bit binary string $X(Y)$ has been divided into $\lceil N/2L \rceil$ groups, and each group has $2L$ bits. If $N \bmod 2 \neq 1$, Alice (Bob) always adds $2L - (N \bmod 2L)$ 0 at the end of last group. Then, the two $N$-bit binary strings $X$ and $Y$ will be denoted as $X = A_{\lceil N/2L \rceil - 1}..A_1 A_0$ and $Y = B_{\lceil N/2L \rceil - 1}..B_1 B_0$, where $A_j$ and $B_j$ $(j = 0, 1, ..., \lceil N/2L \rceil - 1)$ are

$$\begin{cases} A_j = (x_j^{2L-1}, ..., x_j^1, x_j^0) \\ B_j = (y_j^{2L-1}, ..., y_j^1, y_j^0) \end{cases}$$

For each group $A_j(B_j)$, the $2L$ bits will be divided into $L$ pairs with every two adjacent bits composing a pair, such as $Q_A^i = (x_j^{2i}, x_j^{2i+1})$, $Q_B^i = (y_j^{2i}, y_j^{2i+1})$. Then, the group $A_j(B_j)$ can be denoted as

$$\begin{cases} A_j = (Q_A^{L-1}, ..., Q_A^1, Q_A^0) \\ B_j = (Q_B^{L-1}, ..., Q_B^1, Q_B^0) \end{cases}$$

Charlie prepares $N$ ordered states $|C_4\rangle_{1234}$ and $|\phi^+\rangle_{56}$ for the $j$-th round comparison, by which he constructs two ordered sequences $S_1$ and $S_2$ as following:

$$\begin{cases} S_1 : [P_1^0 P_2^0 P_3^0 P_4^0, \ P_1^1 P_2^1 P_3^1 P_4^1, \ ..., \ P_1^{L-1} P_2^{L-1} P_3^{L-1} P_4^{L-1}] \\ S_2 : [P_5^0 P_6^0, \ P_5^1 P_6^1, \ ..., \ P_5^{L-1} P_6^{L-1}] \end{cases}$$

where the subscripts $\{1, 2, 3, 4 \ (5, 6)\}$ denote the different particle in each quantum sequence $S_1(S_2)$, and the superscripts $\{0, 1, ..., L-1\}$ denote the $i$-th entangle quantum state which was prepared by Charlie.

In this step, Charlie will divide sequences $S_1$ and $S_2$ into three parts, and send different parts to different parties. The first two particles of all $|C_4\rangle_{1234}$ states in $S_1$ will be formed into sequence $S_C$ owned by himself, and the third particles of all $|C_4\rangle_{1234}$ states in $S_1$ and the first particle of all $|\phi^+\rangle_{56}$ states in $S_2$ will be formed into sequence $S_A$ and sent to Alice, while the fourth particles of all $|C_4\rangle_{1234}$ states in $S_1$ and the second particle of all $|\phi^+\rangle_{56}$ states in $S_2$ will be formed into sequence $S_B$ and sent to Bob. Then, the sequences $S_C$, $S_A$, $S_B$ are depicted as following:

$$\begin{cases} S_C : [P_1^0 P_2^0, \ P_1^1 P_2^1, \ ..., \ P_1^{L-1} P_2^{L-1}] \\ S_A : [P_3^0 P_5^0, \ P_3^1 P_5^1, \ ..., \ P_3^{L-1} P_5^{L-1}] \\ S_B : [P_4^0 P_6^0, \ P_4^1 P_6^1, \ ..., \ P_4^{L-1} P_6^{L-1}] \end{cases}$$

Before sending $S_A(S_B)$ to Alice (Bob), the sequence should be pre-processed for the anti-eavesdrop. Here two bunches of decoy photons $D_A$ and $D_B$ will be mixed into the sequences $S_A$ and $S_B$, which randomly chosen from states $\{|0\rangle, |1\rangle, |+\rangle, |-\rangle\}$. Then, the new sequences $S_A'$ and $S_B'$ will be sent to Alice and Bob, respectively.

## 2.2  Checking Step

For the eavesdropper checking, Charlie should announce the positions and measuring basis of $D_A(D_B)$ after that Alice (Bob) has received the sequence $S_A'(S_B')$.

Then, the participant Alice (Bob) picks out the decoy particles $D_A(D_B)$ from sequence $S_A'(S_B')$, and measures them with the announced corresponding basis by Charlie.

Next, Alice (Bob) sends the measuring results to Charlie, and Charlie compares them with his initial decoy photons states. If the error rate exceeds a suitable threshold, Charlie will terminate this communication and restart one new communication from the preparing step. Otherwise, the protocol will continue.

## 2.3  Coding Step

After passing the eavesdropping detection, the decoy photons will be discarded, and the veritable sequence $S_A(S_B)$ will be recovered by Alice (Bob).

Alice (Bob) measures the $i$-th pair $P_3^i P_5^i (P_4^i P_6^i)$ in $S_A(S_B)$ with the basis $\{|\phi^\pm\rangle, |\psi^\pm\rangle\}$, and the measurement results can be denoted by $M_A^i(M_B^i)$. According to the measurement results, Alice(Bob) will obtain a two-bit value by the following corresponding relation: $C_A^i(C_B^i) = 00$ with $M_A^i(M_B^i) = |\phi^+\rangle$, $C_A^i(C_B^i) = 01$ with $M_A^i(M_B^i) = |\phi^-\rangle$, $C_A^i(C_B^i) = 10$ with $M_A^i(M_B^i) = |\psi^+\rangle$ and $C_A^i(C_B^i) = 11$ with $M_A^i(M_B^i) = |\psi^-\rangle$.

Alice (Bob) encodes her(his) secrets $Q_A^i(Q_B^i)$ with $C_A^i(C_B^i)$ and the pre-shared secret keys $K_i$ by calculating

$$\begin{cases} R_A^i = Q_A^i \oplus C_A^i \oplus K_i \\ R_B^i = Q_B^i \oplus C_B^i \oplus K_i \end{cases} \tag{3}$$

Then, she(he) can get the sequence $R_A^0, R_A^2, ..., R_A^{l-1} (R_B^0, R_B^2, ..., R_B^{l-1})$.

After the former coding processes, the two sequences $R_A^0, R_A^2, ..., R_A^{l-1}$ and $R_B^0, R_B^2,$ ..., $R_B^{l-1}$ will be encrypted with the pre-shared secret keys $K_{AC}$ and $K_{BC}$, respectively. Then, the two encrypted sequences $E_{K_{AC}}(R_A^0, R_A^2, ..., R_A^{l-1})$ and $E_{K_{BC}}(R_B^0, R_B^2, ..., R_B^{l-1})$ will be sent to Charlie through the quantum-one-time pad.

## 2.4  Decoding Step

When receives the two encrypted sequences from Alice and Bob, Charlie will use the corresponding secret keys $K_{AC}$, $K_{BC}$ to decrypt them. The two sequences $R_A^0, R_A^2, ...,$ $R_A^{l-1}$ and $R_B^0, R_B^2, ..., R_B^{l-1}$ can be recovered from the two encrypted sequences. Then, Charlie calculates

$$R_{AB}^i = R_A^i \oplus R_B^i \tag{4}$$

The $i$-th pair in $S_C$ also should be measured by Charlie with the same basis $\{|\phi^\pm\rangle, |\psi^\pm\rangle\}$, and the measurement results can be denoted as $M_C^i$. Through calculating and summarizing for all cases, the relations between $Q_A^i$, $Q_B^i$'s value according to $R_{AB}^i$ and $M_C^i$ are shown in Table 1.

As shown in Table 1, if $R_{AB}^i = 01$ and $M_C^i = |\phi^+\rangle$, $R_{AB}^i = 00$ and $M_C^i = |\phi^-\rangle$, $R_{AB}^i = 10$ and $M_C^i = |\psi^+\rangle$ or $R_{AB}^i = 11$ and $M_C^i = |\psi^-\rangle$, the relation $Q_A^i = Q_B^i$ holds. Otherwise, $Q_A^i \neq Q_B^i$. If all of the $Q_A^i = Q_B^i$ holds, the relation $Q_A = Q_B$ is valid. Once at least one data element $Q_A^i \neq Q_B^i$, then $Q_A \neq Q_B$. Moreover, Table 2 shows two cases of the detail results.

**Table 1.** Relations between $Q_A^i$, $Q_B^i$'s value according to $R_{AB}^i$ and $M_C^i$.

| $M_C^i/R_{AB}^i$ | 00 | 01 | 10 | 11 |
|---|---|---|---|---|
| $\lvert\phi^+\rangle$ | $\neq$ | $=$ | $\neq$ | $\neq$ |
| $\lvert\phi^-\rangle$ | $=$ | $\neq$ | $\neq$ | $\neq$ |
| $\lvert\psi^+\rangle$ | $\neq$ | $\neq$ | $=$ | $\neq$ |
| $\lvert\psi^-\rangle$ | $\neq$ | $\neq$ | $\neq$ | $=$ |

## 3 Security Analysis

Two primary attacks should be considered for the security analysis, the outside attack and the dishonest participant's attack. They all attempt to steal the participants' private information or the comparison results by all means.

### 3.1 Outside Attack

The outside attack is a vital scenario that should be paid more attention to, as there are many kinds of attacks that once grew in previous QPC protocols, such as the intercept-resend attack, the entanglement-measure attack, and the coordinated and the Trojan horse attack. However, the entanglement-measure attack and the coordinated attack will be detected with nonzero probability during the checking step. The Trojan horse attack also can be automatically prevented due to the one-way transmission.

Unfortunately, in the preparing step and coding step, the secret inputs may be quickly stolen by the intercept-resend attack through the transmission of $S_A'(S_B')$ and $E_{K_A}(E_{K_B})$. However, we will show Eve cannot obtain any information about the participants' secrets $X$ or $Y$ even though he stole some results from these two steps, which are show in the following two cases.

**Case 1: In the Preparing Step.** Eve first intercepts the photon sequence $S_A'$ (from Charlie to Alice in the final step of preparing phase), then he measures $S_A'$ with the basis $\{\lvert\phi^\pm\rangle, \lvert\psi^\pm\rangle\}$. Then, a measurement result $M_A'$ has been obtained by Eve. According to the measurement result sequence $M_A'$, Eve generates the new quantum sequence $S_A''$ and resends it to Alice to preventing Charlie from perceiving the attack. Nevertheless, Eve does not know the position of the decoy photons in $S_A'$, and he cannot abandon the decoy photos when he measures the quantum sequence $S_A'$. Therefore, the decoy photons will destroy the correctness of the measurement results and Eve's new quantum sequence $S_A''$, so the sequence $S_A''$ will be quite different from sequence $S_A'$. Once Alice starts the eavesdropping detection process when she received the photon sequence $S_A''$, the attack will be easily detected for the states of the decoy photons that has been damaged.

**Case 2: In the Decoding Step.** Alice (Bob) sends the sequence $E_{K_A}(R_A^0, R_A^2, ..., R_A^{l-1})(E_{K_B}(R_B^0, R_B^2, ..., R_B^{l-1}))$ to Charlie. It cannot reveal any information about $X$ and $Y$ from $R_A^i$ and $R_B^i$, so the outside eavesdropper cannot get anything. In the decoding

**Table 2.** Two cases of $Q_A^i$, $Q_B^i$'s value.

| $Q_A^i$ | $Q_B^i$ | $M_A^i$ | $M_B^i$ | $C_A^i$ | $C_B^i$ | $R_A^i$ | $R_B^i$ | $R_{AB}^i$ | $M_C^i$ |
|---|---|---|---|---|---|---|---|---|---|
| 00 | 00 | $\lvert\phi^+\rangle$ | $\lvert\phi^-\rangle$ | 00 | 01 | 00 | 01 | 01 | $\lvert\phi^+\rangle$ |
| | | $\lvert\phi^-\rangle$ | $\lvert\phi^+\rangle$ | 01 | 00 | 01 | 00 | 01 | $\lvert\phi^+\rangle$ |
| | | $\lvert\psi^+\rangle$ | $\lvert\psi^-\rangle$ | 10 | 11 | 10 | 11 | 01 | $\lvert\phi^+\rangle$ |
| | | $\lvert\psi^-\rangle$ | $\lvert\psi^+\rangle$ | 11 | 10 | 11 | 10 | 01 | $\lvert\phi^+\rangle$ |
| | | $\lvert\phi^+\rangle$ | $\lvert\phi^+\rangle$ | 00 | 00 | 00 | 00 | 00 | $\lvert\phi^-\rangle$ |
| | | $\lvert\phi^-\rangle$ | $\lvert\phi^-\rangle$ | 01 | 01 | 01 | 01 | 00 | $\lvert\phi^-\rangle$ |
| | | $\lvert\psi^+\rangle$ | $\lvert\psi^+\rangle$ | 10 | 10 | 10 | 10 | 00 | $\lvert\phi^-\rangle$ |
| | | $\lvert\psi^-\rangle$ | $\lvert\psi^-\rangle$ | 11 | 11 | 11 | 11 | 00 | $\lvert\phi^-\rangle$ |
| | | $\lvert\psi^+\rangle$ | $\lvert\phi^+\rangle$ | 10 | 00 | 10 | 00 | 10 | $\lvert\psi^+\rangle$ |
| | | $\lvert\psi^-\rangle$ | $\lvert\phi^-\rangle$ | 11 | 01 | 11 | 01 | 10 | $\lvert\psi^+\rangle$ |
| | | $\lvert\phi^+\rangle$ | $\lvert\psi^+\rangle$ | 00 | 10 | 00 | 10 | 10 | $\lvert\psi^+\rangle$ |
| | | $\lvert\phi^-\rangle$ | $\lvert\psi^-\rangle$ | 01 | 11 | 01 | 11 | 10 | $\lvert\psi^+\rangle$ |
| | | $\lvert\psi^+\rangle$ | $\lvert\phi^-\rangle$ | 10 | 01 | 10 | 01 | 11 | $\lvert\psi^-\rangle$ |
| | | $\lvert\psi^-\rangle$ | $\lvert\phi^+\rangle$ | 01 | 10 | 01 | 10 | 11 | $\lvert\psi^-\rangle$ |
| | | $\lvert\phi^+\rangle$ | $\lvert\psi^-\rangle$ | 00 | 11 | 00 | 11 | 11 | $\lvert\psi^-\rangle$ |
| | | $\lvert\phi^-\rangle$ | $\lvert\psi^+\rangle$ | 11 | 00 | 11 | 00 | 11 | $\lvert\psi^-\rangle$ |
| 01 | 10 | $\lvert\phi^+\rangle$ | $\lvert\phi^-\rangle$ | 00 | 01 | 01 | 11 | 10 | $\lvert\phi^+\rangle$ |
| | | $\lvert\phi^-\rangle$ | $\lvert\phi^+\rangle$ | 01 | 00 | 00 | 10 | 10 | $\lvert\phi^+\rangle$ |
| | | $\lvert\psi^+\rangle$ | $\lvert\psi^-\rangle$ | 10 | 11 | 11 | 01 | 10 | $\lvert\phi^+\rangle$ |
| | | $\lvert\psi^-\rangle$ | $\lvert\psi^+\rangle$ | 11 | 10 | 10 | 00 | 10 | $\lvert\phi^+\rangle$ |
| | | $\lvert\phi^+\rangle$ | $\lvert\phi^+\rangle$ | 00 | 00 | 01 | 10 | 11 | $\lvert\phi^-\rangle$ |
| | | $\lvert\phi^-\rangle$ | $\lvert\phi^-\rangle$ | 01 | 01 | 00 | 11 | 11 | $\lvert\phi^-\rangle$ |
| | | $\lvert\psi^+\rangle$ | $\lvert\psi^+\rangle$ | 10 | 10 | 11 | 00 | 11 | $\lvert\phi^-\rangle$ |
| | | $\lvert\psi^-\rangle$ | $\lvert\psi^-\rangle$ | 11 | 11 | 10 | 01 | 11 | $\lvert\phi^-\rangle$ |
| | | $\lvert\psi^+\rangle$ | $\lvert\phi^+\rangle$ | 10 | 00 | 11 | 10 | 01 | $\lvert\psi^+\rangle$ |
| | | $\lvert\psi^-\rangle$ | $\lvert\phi^-\rangle$ | 11 | 01 | 10 | 11 | 01 | $\lvert\psi^+\rangle$ |
| | | $\lvert\phi^+\rangle$ | $\lvert\psi^+\rangle$ | 00 | 10 | 01 | 00 | 01 | $\lvert\psi^+\rangle$ |
| | | $\lvert\phi^-\rangle$ | $\lvert\psi^-\rangle$ | 01 | 11 | 00 | 01 | 01 | $\lvert\psi^+\rangle$ |
| | | $\lvert\psi^+\rangle$ | $\lvert\phi^-\rangle$ | 10 | 01 | 11 | 11 | 00 | $\lvert\psi^-\rangle$ |
| | | $\lvert\psi^-\rangle$ | $\lvert\phi^+\rangle$ | 11 | 00 | 10 | 10 | 00 | $\lvert\psi^-\rangle$ |
| | | $\lvert\phi^+\rangle$ | $\lvert\psi^-\rangle$ | 00 | 11 | 01 | 01 | 00 | $\lvert\psi^-\rangle$ |

*(continued)*

**Table 2.** (*continued*)

| $Q_A^i$ | $Q_B^i$ | $M_A^i$ | $M_B^i$ | $C_A^i$ | $C_B^i$ | $R_A^i$ | $R_B^i$ | $R_{AB}^i$ | $M_C^i$ |
|---------|---------|---------|---------|---------|---------|---------|---------|------------|---------|
|         |         | $\lvert\phi^-\rangle$ | $\lvert\psi^+\rangle$ | 01 | 10 | 00 | 00 | 00 | $\lvert\psi^-\rangle$ |

step, Charlie announces only one $c$-bit $F$ to compare secret messages. From this one $c$-bit, outside eavesdropper cannot deduce any information about $X$ and $Y$.

In addition, if Eve can get the accurate particle pairs, he will serve as a malicious TP. Then, he attempts to steal the private information of the participants. As the participants' secret information $Q_A^i(Q_B^i)$ was encoded into the entanglement state by Eq. (3), Eve only can get the information of $R_A^i(R_B^i)$ and $C_A^i(C_B^i)$. However, since the sequence ($K_0$, $K_1$, ..., $K_{L-1}$) between Alice and Bob was pre-shared by a secure QKD protocol, Eve cannot obtain anything about $K_i$. Then, he can get nothing about the participants' secret information $Q_A^i(Q_B^i)$.

Hence, this proposed QPC protocol is secure against outside attack.

### 3.2 Participant Attack

The participant attack is another important scenario that should be paid more attention to. In general, the participants always have more opportunities and advantages to steal other participants' private information than an outside eavesdropper. Now, we give three cases to prove that the proposed QPC protocol can resist the participant attack, and the adversary cannot obtain any information about $X$ and $Y$.

**Case 1: Alice (Bob) Attempts to Obtain Bob (Alice)'s Secrets.** In the whole process of the proposed QPC protocol, the two participants do not transmit any information to each other except the pre-shared sequence $K$. The $K$ is the pre-shared secret key, and it is used to secure the encoding message against the malicious TP. As in the coding step, the private information is encoded in an entanglement state by Eq. (3). The $R_A^i(R_B^i)$ was encrypted by a pre-shared secret key, and sent by a secure QKD protocol to Charlie. Thus, it cannot be obtained by the other participant. The $C_A^i(C_B^i)$ was a classical bit corresponding to the measurement results. Since one participant cannot obtain anything about the other participant's private information, no matter the entanglement state generated and distributed by Charlie or the measurement basis which the participants themselves selected. Therefore, the participant cannot derive any information about $Q_A^i(Q_B^i)$ by the Eq. (3). Therefore, the two participants Alice and Bob, cannot infer any information about each other's secrets.

**Case 2: Charlie Attempts to Obtain Alice (Bob)'s Secrets.** The malicious TP is curious about the participants' secret information, and he will try every means to obtain that. At the same time, the intermediate date $R_A^i$ and $R_B^i$, which relate to the participants' secret information, can be easily used by Charlie. Here, TP can obtain the measurement results with the following probability.

$$P(R_A^i(R_B^i) = 00) = P(R_A^i(R_B^i) = 01) = P(R_A^i(R_B^i) = 10) = P(R_A^i(R_B^i) = 11) = \frac{1}{4}$$

$$P(M_C^i = |\phi^+\rangle) = P(M_C^i = |\phi^-\rangle) = P(M_C^i = |\psi^+\rangle) = P(M_C^i = |\psi^-\rangle) = \frac{1}{4} \qquad (5)$$

Here, we know that TP cannot infer any information of the participants' secret with the undistinguishable probability of the measurement results.

In addition, if TP obtains the $C_A^i(C_B^i)$ by a fake single attack, he will derive the value of $Q_A^i \oplus K_i(Q_B^i \oplus K_i)$ from Eq. (3). However, he cannot get any information about $Q_A^i(Q_B^i)$ since that $K_i$ is secretly pre-shared by a secure QKD protocol between Alice and Bob. Moreover, the secret input is divided into $\lceil N/2L \rceil (L = 1, 2, ...)$ groups, while each group has $2L$ bits. Alice (Bob) always adds $2L - (N \bmod 2L)$ 0 at the end of the $N$-bit binary string $X(Y)$. Therefore, although Charlie can infer the participants' secret inputs, he cannot know the real length of their secret information.

**Case 3: Charlie Attempts to Obtain the Comparison Results.** TP is a semi-honest participator, he only can help the two participants to compare their secret inputs, and he cannot obtain anything about their secret information, even the comparison results. As the comparison principle is secretly established between Alice and Bob, when Charlie announces the results $R_{AB}^i$ and $M_C^i$, Alice and Bob will know the comparison results according to Table 1. Charlie has no information about the relationship between the value of $R_{AB}^i$ and $M_C^i$ and the comparison results, and then he can obtain nothing about the comparison results.

Hence, this proposed QPC protocol is secure against participant attack.

## 4   Efficiency Comparison

Compared with similar QPC protocols, this protocol has many advantages for comparing private information by quantum methods. As the 4-particle cluster state $|C_4\rangle_{1234}$, it is hard to destroy the entanglement by local operations, which is different from the 4-particle $W$-state, and has a strong violation of local reality and robust against decoherence. Therefore, this paper takes the entanglement swapping between the 4-particle cluster state and Bell state as the information carrier, which will make the QPC protocol more practical for private comparison. Then, the proposed QPC protocol has no unitary operations and Hash functions and compares two bits of private information simultaneously, which shows better performance on operability, efficiency, and security as details of the comparison results have been shown in the Table 3.

In addition, we compare the computational costs in this scheme with other kinds of literature. Here, we mainly consider the classical bit-wise exclusive-OR $\oplus$ operations, the quantum measurement, and unitary operations involved in the protocol. In one group comparison, there need $3L$ classical operations. In the whole scheme, there needs $3L *$ $\lceil N/2L \rceil$ classical operations with $\lceil N/2L \rceil$ groups. As the classical operations of the pre-shared sequence in the coding step can be calculated in the spare time, it does affect the time complexity. Then, there need $D + 3L * \lceil N/2L \rceil$ quantum measurements operated by the three participants, where $D$ denotes the measurement of decoy photons. The detailed comparison results in Table 4 have shown that our scheme is more efficient than other protocols.

**Table 3.** Efficiency comparison of the similar schemes.

| Protocol | QR | UO | HF | BC | CT | RD |
|---|---|---|---|---|---|---|
| Ref. [20] | 4-qubit cluster state | No | No | No | No | Yes |
| Ref. [21] | 4-qubit cluster states | Yes | No | 1 | $N$ | Yes |
| Ref. [23] | 3-particle $W$-class state and Bell state | No | No | 2 | $\lceil N/2L \rceil$ | No |
| Ref. [24] | 5-particle cluster state | Yes | No | 1 | $N$ | No |
| Ref. [29] | 4-Particle GHZ States | No | No | 3 | $\lceil N/3 \rceil$ | No |
| **Our protocol** | **4-qubit Cluster-state and Bell state** | No | No | **2** | $\lceil N/2L \rceil$ | Yes |

QR: Quantum resource; UO: Unitary operation; HF: Hash function; BC: Bit compared; CT: Comparison times; RD: Resist decoherence.

**Table 4.** Computational costs comparison.

| Protocol | Classical computations | Quantum measurements | Unitary operations |
|---|---|---|---|
| Ref. [20] | $2N$ | $D + 2N$ | $2N$ |
| Ref. [21] | $2N$ | $D + 2N$ | $2N$ |
| Ref. [23] | $3L * \lceil N/2L \rceil$ | $D + 3L * \lceil N/2L \rceil$ | 0 |
| Ref. [24] | $4N$ | $D + 4N$ | $2N$ |
| Ref. [29] | $3 * \lceil N/3 \rceil$ | $D + 3 * \lceil N/3 \rceil$ | 0 |
| **Our protocol** | $3L * \lceil N/2L \rceil$ | $D + 3L * \lceil N/2L \rceil$ | **0** |

# 5  Conclusion

This paper proposed an efficient QPC protocol based on the entanglement swapping of the 4-particle cluster state and Bell state. This cluster is more robust and practical than the other 4-particle clusters and W-state. With the help of semi-honest TP, two participants can compare the equality of their private information without leaking them. This scheme is secure against the outside and participants' attacks with the decoy photons and pre-shared random sequence. Then, from the efficiency standpoint, our scheme is more efficient than other protocols by only using single particles, Bell states, and GHZ states since that it compares double bits at one time and uses less classical and quantum operations. Additionally, the quantum channel is vulnerable to noise, such as collective-dephasing noise and collective-rotation noise. So, it is more important to design a new noise-resisting QPC protocol in future work.

**Acknowledgement.** This work was supported by the National Natural Science Foundation of China under Grant 92046001, 61962009, the Fundamental Research Funds for the Central Universities under Grant 2019XD-A02, JSPS KAKENHI Grant Numbers JP19K20250, JP20F20080, and JP20H04174, Leading Initiative for Excellent Young Researchers (LEADER), MEXT, Japan, and JST, PRESTO Grant Number JPMJPR21P3, Japan. Kaoru Ota is the corresponding author, and the Doctor Scientific Research Fund of Zhengzhou University of Light Industry under Grant 2021BSJJ033, Key Scientific Research Project of Colleges and Universities in Henan Province (CN) under Grant No. 22A413010.

# References

1. Bennett, C.H., Brassard, G.: Quantum cryptography: Public key distribution and coin tossing. arXiv preprint arXiv:2003.06557 (2020)
2. Li, J., Li, N., Zhang, Y., et al.: A survey on quantum cryptography. Chin. J. Electron. **27**(2), 223–228 (2018)
3. Chen, S., Xu, G., Chen, X., Ahmad, H., Chen, Y.: Measurement-based quantum repeater network coding. Intell. Autom. Soft Comput. **30**(1), 273–284 (2021)
4. Li, J., Li, H., Wang, N., et al.: A quantum key distribution protocol based on the EPR Pairs and its simulation. Mob. Netw. Appl. **26**(2), 620–628 (2021)
5. Xin, X., Ding, L., Li, C., Sang, Y., Yang, Q., Li, F.: Quantum public-key designated verifier signature. Quantum Inf. Process. **21**(1), 1–16 (2021). https://doi.org/10.1007/s11128-021-03387-4
6. Yao, A.C.: Protocols for secure computations. In: Proceedings of the 23rd Annual Symposium on Foundations of Computer Science, pp. 160–164 (1982)
7. Du, W., Atallah, M.J.: Secure multi-party computation problems and their applications: a review and open problems. In: Proceedings of the 2001 Workshop on New Security Paradigms, pp. 13–22 (2001)
8. Shor, P.W.: Polynomial-time algorithms for prime factorization and discrete logarithms on a quantum computer. SIAM Rev. **41**(2), 1484–1509 (1999)
9. Grover, L.K.: A fast quantum mechanical algorithm for database search. In: Proceedings of the Twenty-Eighth Annual ACM Symposium on Theory of Computing, pp. 212–219 (1996)
10. Gao, P., Perkowski, M., Li, Y., Song, X.: Novel quantum algorithms to minimize switching functions based on graph partitions. Comput. Mater. Continua **70**(3), 4545–4561 (2022)
11. Bonanome, M., Buzek, V., Hillery, M., et al.: Toward protocols for quantum-ensured privacy and secure voting. Phys. Rev. A **84**(2), 022331 (2011)
12. Xu, G., Yun, F., Xiao, K., et al.: A securing multi-party quantum summation protocol based on quantum homomorphic encryption. CMC-Comput. Mater. Continua (2021)
13. Yang, Y.G., Naseri, M., Wen, Q.Y.: Improved secure quantum sealed-bid auction. Opt. Commun. **282**(20), 4167–4170 (2009)
14. Xu, G., Shan, R.T., Chen, X.B., et al.: Probabilistic and hierarchical quantum information splitting based on the non-maximally entangled cluster state. CMC-Comput. Mater. Continua **69**(1), 339–349 (2021)
15. Tian, Y., Li, J., Chen, X.-B., Ye, C.-Q., Li, C.-Y., Hou, Y.-Y.: An efficient semi-quantum private comparison without pre-shared keys. Quantum Inf. Process. **20**(11), 1–13 (2021). https://doi.org/10.1007/s11128-021-03294-8
16. Hou, Y., Li, J., Chen, X.B., et al.: Quantum algorithm for help-training semi-supervised support vector machine. Quantum Inf. Process. **19**(9), 1–20 (2020)
17. Li, C., Ye, C., Tian, Y., Chen, X.-B., Li, J.: Cluster-state-based quantum secret sharing for users with different abilities. Quantum Inf. Process. **20**(12), 1–14 (2021). https://doi.org/10.1007/s11128-021-03327-2
18. Yang, Y.G., Wen, Q.Y.: An efficient two-party quantum private comparison protocol with decoy photons and two-photon entanglement. J. Phys. A Math. Theor. **42**(5), 055305 (2009)

19. Chen, X.B., Xu, G., Niu, X.X., et al.: An efficient protocol for the private comparison of equal information based on the triplet entangled state and single-particle measurement. Opt. Commun. **283**(7), 1561–1565 (2010)
20. Xu, G.A., Chen, X.B., Wei, Z.H., et al.: An efficient protocol for the quantum private comparison of equality with a four-qubit cluster state. Int. J. Quantum Inf. **10**(04), 1250045 (2012)
21. Sun, Z.W., Long, D.Y.: Quantum private comparison protocol based on cluster states. Int. J. Theor. Phys. **52**(1), 212–218 (2013)
22. Siddhu, V.: Quantum private comparison over noisy channels. Quantum Inf. Process. **14**(8), 3005–3017 (2015)
23. Li, J., Jia, L., Zhou, H.F., et al.: Secure quantum private comparison protocol based on the entanglement swapping between three-particle W-class state and bell state. Int. J. Theor. Phys. **55**(3), 1710–1718 (2016). https://doi.org/10.1007/s10773-015-2810-0
24. Chang, Y., Zhang, W.B., Zhang, S.B., et al.: Quantum private comparison of equality based on five-particle cluster state. Commun. Theor. Phys. **66**(6), 621 (2016)
25. Xu, L., Zhao, Z.: Quantum private comparison protocol based on the entanglement swapping between $\chi$ state and W-Class state. Quantum Inf. Process. **16**(12), 302 (2017)
26. Liu, B., Xiao, D., Huang, W., Jia, H.-Y., Song, T.-T.: Quantum private comparison employing single-photon interference. Quantum Inf. Process. **16**(7), 1–13 (2017). https://doi.org/10.1007/s11128-017-1630-y
27. Chongqiang, Y., Jian, L., Xiubo, C., Yuan, T.: Efficient semi-quantum private comparison without using entanglement resource and pre-shared key. Quantum Inf. Process. **20**(8), 1–19 (2021). https://doi.org/10.1007/s11128-021-03194-x
28. Li, C., Chen, X., Li, H., Yang, Y., Li, J.: Efficient quantum private comparison protocol based on the entanglement swapping between four-qubit cluster state and extended Bell state. Quantum Inf. Process. **18**(5), 1–12 (2019). https://doi.org/10.1007/s11128-019-2266-x
29. Xu, Q.-D., Chen, H.-Y., Gong, L.-H., Zhou, N.-R.: Quantum private comparison protocol based on four-particle GHZ states. Int. J. Theor. Phys. **59**(6), 1798–1806 (2020). https://doi.org/10.1007/s10773-020-04446-9
30. Chongqiang, Y., Jian, L., Zheng-wen, C.: A class of protocols for multi-party quantum private comparison based on traveling mode. Quantum Inf. Process. **20**(2), 1–18 (2021). https://doi.org/10.1007/s11128-020-02986-x
31. Gianni, J., Qu, Z.G.: New quantum private comparison using hyperentangled GHZ state. J. Quantum Comput. **3**(2), 45–54 (2021)
32. Sun, Y., Yan, L., Sun, Z., Zhang, S., Lu, J.: A novel semi-quantum private comparison scheme using bell entangle states. Comput. Mater. Continua **66**(3), 2385–2395 (2021)
33. Hein, M., Dur, W., Briegel, H.J.: Entanglement properties of multipartite entangled states under the influence of decoherence. Phys. Rev. A **71**(3), 032350 (2005)
34. Walther, P., Resch, K.J., Rudolph, T., et al.: Experimental one-way quantum computing. Nature **434**(7030), 169 (2005)
35. Briegel, H.J., Raussendorf, R.: Persistent entanglement in arrays of interacting particles. Phys. Rev. Lett. **86**(5), 910 (2001)
36. Khokhlov, D.L.: Interpretation of the entangled states. Journal of Quantum Computing **2**(3), 147–150 (2020)

# Pairing-Free Certificateless Key-Insulated Encryption with Keyword Search

Qing Miao[1], Yang Lu[1(✉)], Lan Guo[1], Qi Sun[1], and Zhongqi Wang[2]

[1] School of Computer and Electronic Information,
Nanjing Normal University, Nanjing 210046, China
luyangnsd@163.com
[2] Graduate School of Science and Technology,
University of Tsukuba, Tsukuba, Ibaraki 305-8577, Japan

**Abstract.** Public key encryption with keyword search (PEKS) allows a user to make searches on ciphertexts without disclosing the information of encrypted messages and keywords. The certificateless public key encryption with keyword search scheme avoids the problems of public key certificate management and key escrow based on the realization of ciphertext retrieval. But in practice, key leakage is often difficult to avoid, and key leakage will threaten the security of the entire cryptographic system. Considering the key leakage problem in the scheme, we are desirable to incorporate the key insulation mechanism into the certificateless public key encryption with keyword search scheme. In this work, a new scheme named pairing-free certificateless key-insulated encryption with keyword search (KI-CLPEKS) is designed. This scheme realizes two functions of key insulation and ciphertext search at the same time. The security notions for KI-CLPEKS are formally defined and then a concrete KI-CLPEKS scheme is proposed. The security proofs demonstrate that the KI-CLPEKS scheme guarantees the keyword ciphertext indistinguishability against adaptive chosen keyword attacks under the complexity assumption of the computational Diffie-Hellman problem in the random oracle model. The experimental results and comparisons show that the proposed scheme is practicable.

**Keywords:** Certificateless public key encryption · Keyword search · Key insulation · Ciphertext indistinguishability

## 1 Introduction

In recent years, cloud computing technology has developed rapidly, which provides a quick and convenient solution to data management problems. Cloud storage allows users to store a large amount of data in the cloud, solving local data management problems and insufficient storage problems. However, for data owners, the storage servers are not completely trustworthy. Therefore, the data owner usually encrypts the data before uploading it to the cloud storage server to protect the security and privacy of the data. When data is stored in the storage server in the form of cipher-text, how to retrieve the ciphertext has become a new problem. Users can choose to download all ciphertexts

X. Sun et al. (Eds.): ICAIS 2022, CCIS 1588, pp. 106–118, 2022.
https://doi.org/10.1007/978-3-031-06764-8_9

to local storage, and get the data plaintext after decryption. However, this method not only requires high communication and computation overhead, but also occupies a large amount of local storage space. Another method is that the user sends the private key to the storage server, and then the storage server decrypts the ciphertexts and searches the plaintexts, which obviously loses the meaning of encryption.

Searchable Encryption (SE) [1] is a very effective method to solve the problem of ciphertext retrieval. Searchable encryption technology allows users to retrieve data ciphertexts by keywords on the storage server without leaking any information about the data plaintexts and the search keywords. Searchable encryption can be achieved through symmetric encryption or public key encryption. In 2000, Song *et al.* [1] first proposed a symmetric searchable encryption (SSE) scheme. Subsequently, many improved symmetric searchable encryption schemes [2–5] were proposed. Although the symmetric searchable encryption scheme has higher efficiency, there is a problem of key distribution.

In 2004, Boneh *et al.* [6] proposed public key encryption with keyword search (PEKS). In the PEKS scheme, the data sender generates the data ciphertext and the keyword ciphertext, and sends them to the storage server, where the keyword ciphertext is appended to the data ciphertext. When the receiver wants to obtain a ciphertext containing a specific keyword, the receiver can use its own private key to generate a trapdoor for that keyword, and then sends the trapdoor to the storage server. Once the storage server receives the trapdoor, it can use the trapdoor to match the keyword ciphertext. If the match is successful, the corresponding data ciphertext will be returned to the receiver. In this process, the storage server knows nothing about the data content and keyword information, so the security and privacy of the data are effectively protected. After the concept of searchable public key encryption was proposed, it attracted great attention from scholars all around the world. Various improved searchable public key encryption schemes [7–17] have been proposed one after another. However, many of these schemes are constructed under the traditional public key cryptography (PKC) system, which results the certificate management problem. In order to solve this problem, identity-based encryption with keyword search (IBEKS) [18, 19] and attribute-based encryption with keyword search (ABEKS) [20, 21] were proposed, which introduce searchable encryption technology into identity-based cryptography (IBC) and attribute-based cryptography, respectively. However, the users' private keys in IBEKS and ABEKS are generated by a trusted third party. Therefore, IBEKS and ABEKS suffer from the key escrow problem.

In 2014, Peng *et al.* [22] proposed a certificateless public key encryption with keyword search (CLPEKS) scheme to solve the key escrow problems. This method follows the idea of certificateless public key encryption (CLPKC) proposed by Al-Riyami *et al.* [23]. In the certificateless searchable public key encryption system, the user's private key is composed of a partial private key and a secret value. Among them, the partial private key is generated by a trusted third party, and the secret value is generated by the user. Obviously, for a trusted third party, it only knows part of the user's private key, and knows nothing about the secret value selected by the user, thus effectively solving the key escrow problem. At the same time, in the certificateless public key encryption with keyword search system, the user can decrypt only if he knows the complete private key, so there is no need to use a public key certificate for authentication, which is effectively solve the certificate management problem. Later, Zheng *et al.* [24] proposed a certificateless keyword search on encrypted data (CLKS) scheme, and proved its security under the Decisional Linear assumption in the standard model. Recently, Ma *et al.* [25, 26] respectively proposed a CLPEKS scheme and a designated server CLEKS scheme.

The security of a cryptographic system mainly depends on the confidentiality of the key. If the key is leaked, the security of the entire cryptographic system will be threatened. However, cryptographic calculations are often performed on relatively insecure devices, which cannot guarantee the confidentiality of keys. Therefore, the key leakage seems inevitable, and the methods proposed by cryptographers are no longer limited to preventing the key leakage, but to minimize the harm it brings after the key leakage occurs. The concept of key-insulated was first proposed by Dodis *et al.* [27], which can effectively reduce the harm caused by key leakage. In the key-insulated cryptosystem, the lifetime of the system is divided into N time periods, the user's private key is updated by communicating with the physical security device at every time period. The private key consists of two parts: one part is created by the helper key from the physical security device, and the other part is created by the user. At the same time, the public key is fixed during the entire process of key update. In this way, even if the adversary steals the private key in the current time period, it cannot threaten the security of the system in other time periods.

In 2014, Peng *et al.* [22] proposed a CLPEKS scheme, which solved the key escrow problem. Lu *et al.* [28] proposed a pairing-free certificateless public key encryption with keyword search (PF-CLEKS) scheme, which had obvious advantages in terms of computing performance and communication bandwidth. Besides, Lu *et al.* [29] proposed a new CLEKS scheme, which provided resistance to both the outside KG attack and the inside KG attack. He *et al.* [30, 31] introduced the key-insulated mechanism into the certificateless public key encryption system, which solved the problem of key leakage. However, how to simultaneously realize the two functions of key-insulated and ciphertext search in a certificateless public key encryption system is still a problem to be solved.

In this work, a pairing-free certificateless key-insulated encryption with keyword search is designed. Specifically, the contributions are as follows:

1) This scheme not only avoids the problems of public key certificate management and key escrow, but also effectively reduces the harm caused by key leakage.
2) This study gives the definition and security model of the KI-CLPEKS scheme, and the scheme satisfies the ciphertext indistinguishability security under the adaptive chosen keyword attack.
3) The simulation experiment results show that the proposed KI-CLPEKS scheme is practical, it has obvious performance advantage compared with the existing related schemes.

## 2 Preliminaries

In this section, some preliminaries that used in the paper are reviewed.

Assuming that G and G1 denote two cyclic groups both with a prime order p, P denotes a random generator of G, and e: $G \times G \to G1$ is a bilinear map satisfying the following characteristics:

(1)  Bilinearity: $\forall m, n \in G$ and $x, y \in Z_p^*$, $e(m^x, n^y) = e(m, n)^{xy}$.
(2)  Non-degeneracy: $\exists m, n \in G$, $e(m, n) \neq 1$.
(3)  Computability: $\forall m, n \in G$, $e(m, n)$ can be calculated by an efficient algorithm.

**Definition 1.** The CDH problem is: Inputting three elements $(P, xP, yP)$, to calculate $xyP \in G$, where $x, y \in Z_p$.

## 3  Framework Definition and Security Definitions

### 3.1  Framework Definition

A KI-CLPEKS scheme includes five entities: a key generation center (KGC), a storage server, a physical security device, a data sender and a data receiver. The KGC is responsible for producing the master key, the global parameters for the whole system and the partial private key for the data receiver. The physical security device produces the helper's public-private key pair and the update key. The data sender produces the keyword ciphertext and the data ciphertext, then transmits the keyword ciphertext and the data ciphertext to the storage server. The data receiver produces the secret value, the initial private key, the public key, the private keys of different time periods and the search trapdoors, then it transmits the search trapdoors to the storage server. When the storage server gets a search trapdoor from the data receiver, it seeks out and returns all matching data ciphertexts.

**Definition 2.** A KI-CLPEKS scheme is specified by eleven algorithms that are shown below:

(1)  $Setup(\lambda)$: This algorithm takes the security parameter $\lambda$ as input, it returns the KGC's master key $mk$ and a set of global parameters $gp$.
(2)  $HelperKeyGen(gp)$: This algorithm takes $gp$ as input, it returns the helper's public-private key pair $(HK, PK_{helper})$.
(3)  $PartialKeyGen(gp, mk, ID)$: This algorithm takes $gp$ as input, master key $mk$, a user's identity $ID$, it returns a partial private key $D_{ID}$.
(4)  $SecretValGen(gp, ID)$: This algorithm takes $gp$ and a user's identity $ID$ as input, it returns a secret value $s_{ID}$.
(5)  $InitialPrivateKeyGen(gp, D_{ID}, s_{ID})$: This algorithm takes gp as input, a partial private key $D_{ID}$ and a secret value $s_{ID}$, it returns an initial private key $SK_{ID,0}$.
(6)  $PublicKeyGen(gp, s_{ID}, SK_{ID,0}, PK_{helper})$: This algorithm takes $gp$ as input, the secret value $s_{ID}$, initial private key $SK_{ID,0}$, and the helper's public key pair $PK_{helper}$, it returns a public key $PK_{ID}$.
(7)  $KeyUpd(gp, HK, ID, i)$: This algorithm takes $gp$ as input, the helper's private key $HK$, a user's identity $ID$ and a time period $i$, it returns a update key $UK_{ID,i}$ at time period $i$.
(8)  $PrivateKeyGen(gp, i, UK_{ID,i}, SK_{ID,i-1})$: This algorithm takes $gp$, a time period $i$, a update key $UK_{ID,i}$ of time period $i$ and a private key $SK_{ID,i-1}$ of time period $i-1$ as input, it returns the private key $SK_{ID,i}$ at a time period $i$.

(9)  *Encrypt(gp, w, i, ID, PK$_{ID}$)*: This algorithm takes $gp$, a keyword $w$, a time period $i$, a user's identity $ID$ and a public key $PK_{ID}$ as input, it returns a keyword ciphertext $C_w$.

(10) *Trapdoor(gp,w', ID, SK$_{ID,i}$)*: This algorithm takes $gp$, a keyword $w'$, a user's identity $ID$ and the private key $SK_{ID,i}$ of a time period $i$ as input, it returns a keyword trapdoor $T_{w'}$.

(11) *Test(gp, C$_w$,T$_{w'}$)*: This algorithm takes $gp$, a keyword ciphertext $C_w$ and a keyword trapdoor $T_{w'}$ as input, it returns 1 if $w = w'$ or 0 otherwise.

If the following formulas are satisfied for any keyword $w$, then a KI-CLPEKS scheme is correct.

If $gp \leftarrow GlobalSetup(\lambda)$, $(HK, PK_{helper}) \leftarrow HelperKeyGen(gp)$, $D_{ID} \leftarrow PartialKey\text{-}Gen(gp, mk, ID)$, $s_{ID} \leftarrow SecretValGen(gp, ID)$, $SK_{ID,0} \leftarrow InitialPrivateKeyGen(gp, D_{ID}, s_{ID})$, $PK_{ID} \leftarrow PublicKeyGen(gp, s_{ID}, SK_{ID,0}, PK_{helper})$, $UK_{ID,i} \leftarrow KeyUpd(gp, HK, ID, i)$, $SK_{ID,i} \leftarrow PrivateKeyGen(gp, i, UK_{ID,i}, SK_{ID,i-1})$, $C_w \leftarrow Encrypt(gp, w, i, ID, PK_{ID})$, $T_w \leftarrow Trapdoor(gp, w, ID, SK_{ID,i})$, then $1 \leftarrow Test(gp, C_w, T_{w'})$.

## 3.2  Security Definitions

To formalize the security model of KI-CLPEKS, we define these random oracles as follows:

(1) Public key generation oracle $O_{pk}$: With the input of a user's identity $ID$ by the adversary, the challenger runs $PublicKeyGen(gp, s_{ID}, SK_{ID,0}, PK_{helper})$ to produce a public key $PK_{ID}$ of the user and then gives $PK_{ID}$ to the adversary.

(2) Helper's key generation oracle $O_{hk}$: With the input of a user's identity $ID$ by the adversary, the challenger runs $HelperKeyGen(gp)$ to produce the helper's public-private key pair $(HK, PK_{helper})$ and then returns it to the adversary.

(3) Partial private key generation oracle $O_{psk}$: With the input of a user's identity $ID$ by the adversary, the challenger runs $PartialKeyGen(gp, mk, ID)$ to produce a partial private key $D_{ID}$ and then returns it to the adversary.

(4) Initial private key generation oracle $O_{ik}$: With the input of a user's identity $ID$ by the adversary, the challenger runs $InitialPrivateKeyGen(gp, D_{ID}, s_{ID})$ to produce an initial private key $SK_{ID,0}$ and then returns it to the adversary.

(5) Replace public key oracle $O_{rpk}$: With the input of a user's identity $ID$ and a false public key $PK_{ID,R}$ by the adversary, the current public key associated with identity $ID$ is replaced by $PK_{ID,R}$. The challenger outputs a private key $SK_{ID,R}$ corresponding to the false public key to the adversary, and the challenger does not know the corresponding private key if the public key is replaced. This oracle is only queried by Type I adversary.

(6) Update key generation oracle $O_{uk}$: With the input of a user's identity $ID$ and a time period index $i$ by the adversary, the challenger runs $KeyUpd(gp, HK, ID, i)$ to produce a update key $UK_{ID,i}$ at time period $i$ and then returns it to the adversary.

(7) Private key generation oracle $O_{sk}$: With the input of a user's identity $ID$ and a time period index $i$ by the adversary, the challenger runs $PrivateKeyGen(gp, i, UK_{ID,i},$

$SK_{ID,i-1}$) to produce the private key $SK_{ID,i}$ at a time period $i$ and then returns it to the adversary.

(8) Trapdoor generation oracle $O_{td}$: With the input of a user's identity $ID$ and a keyword $w$ by the adversary, the challenger runs $Trapdoor(gp, w, ID, SK_{ID,i})$ to produce a keyword trapdoor $T_w$ and then returns it to the adversary. If the Type I adversary has replaced the public key of the identity $ID$, the challenger should use the private key corresponding to the replacement public key to generate a keyword trapdoor.

A KI-CLPEKS scheme should meet the keyword ciphertext indistinguishability against adaptive chosen keyword attacks (IND-CKA). To formalize the security definitions of KI-CLPEKS, two games between an adversary $A_i$ ($i = 1, 2$) and a challenger $B$ are defined, where the adversary $A_1$ is a Type I adversary and the adversary $A_2$ is a Type II adversary. The Type I adversary represents an inside storage server or an outside attacker who cannot access the master key but can replace the public key for an entity with its choice. The Type II adversary represents the malicious KGC who can access the master key but cannot replace the public key by itself.

**Game 1**: In this game, $B$ plays with the Type I adversary $A_1$ who models an inside storage server or an outside attacker as below:

**Setup**: Given a security parameter $\lambda$, the challenger generates $(mk, gp)$ by running $GlobalSetup(\lambda)$. Then, the challenger gives adversary $gp$.

**Phase 1**: The adversary adaptively queries the oracles $\{O_{pk}, O_{hk}, O_{psk}, O_{ik}, O_{rpk}, O_{uk}, O_{sk}, O_{td}\}$.

**Challenge**: Once the Phase 1 is finished, the adversary inputs two distinct keywords $(w_0, w_1)$ with the equal length on the challenger identity $ID^*$ and a time period index $i^*$ to $B$. The restrictions are (1) $A_1$ did not previously ask queries $O_{td}(i^*, w_0)$ and $O_{td}(i^*, w_1)$; (2) $A_1$ did not previously ask the queries either $O_{sk}$ or $O_{psk}$ on the time period $i^*$. $B$ randomly selects $b \in \{0, 1\}$, calculates a challenge ciphertext $CT_{i^*}^{w_b} = Encrypt(gp, w, i^*, ID^*, PK_{ID})$ and sends it to adversary $A_1$.

**Phase 2**: $A_1$ makes more oracle queries as in Phase 1.

**Guess**: At last, $A_1$ outputs a guess $b'$ and wins if $b = b'$. Its advantage is defined as

$$Adv_{A_1}^{IND-CKA}(\lambda) = |\Pr[b = b'] - 1/2|. \tag{1}$$

**Game 2**: In this game, $B$ plays with the Type II adversary $A_2$ who models the malicious KGC as below:

**Setup**: Given a security parameter $\lambda$, the challenger generates $(mk, gp)$ by running $GlobalSetup(\lambda)$. Then, the challenger gives adversary $gp$ and $mk$.

**Phase 1**: The adversary adaptively queries the oracles $\{O_{pk}, O_{hk}, O_{ik}, O_{uk}, O_{sk}, O_{td}\}$.

**Challenge**: Once the Phase 1 is finished, the adversary inputs two distinct keywords $(w_0, w_1)$ with the equal length on the challenger identity $ID^*$ and a time period index $i^*$ to $B$. The restrictions are (1) $A_2$ did not previously ask queries $O_{td}(i^*, w_0)$ and $O_{td}(i^*, w_1)$; (2) $A_2$ did not previously ask the queries $O_{sk}$ on the time period $i^*$ if it is a Type II adversary. $B$ randomly selects $b \in \{0, 1\}$, calculates a challenge ciphertext $CT_{i^*}^{w_b} = Encrypt(gp, w, i^*, ID^*, PK_{ID})$ and sends it to adversary $A_2$.

**Phase 2**: $A_2$ makes more oracle queries as in Phase 1.

**Guess**: At last, $A_2$ outputs a guess $b'$ and wins if $b = b'$. Its advantage is defined as

$$Adv_{A_2}^{IND-CKA}(\lambda) = |\Pr[b = b'] - 1/2|. \tag{2}$$

**Definition 3.** For a KI-CLPEKS scheme, if the advantage $Adv_{A_1}^{IND-CKA}(\lambda)$ and $Adv_{A_2}^{IND-CKA}(\lambda)$ of any polynomial time adversary $A_1$ and $A_1$ is negligible, then the scheme is IND-CKA secure.

## 4 The Proposed KI-CLPEKS Scheme

The description of the proposed KI-CLPEKS scheme is as below.

(1) *GlobalSetup*($\lambda$): With the input of security parameter $\lambda$, the algorithm generates a cyclic group $G$ of order $p$. It selects a generator $P \in G$ and four cryptographic hash functions $H_1: \{0, 1\}^* \to Z_p^*$ and $H_2: \{0, 1\}^* \times Z^+ \to Z_p^*$, $H_3: \{0, 1\}^* \to Z_p^*$, $H_4: G \to Z_p^*$. It then randomly chooses $s \in Z_q$, and computes $P_{pub} = sP$, and the corresponding $s$ can be regard as the master key $mk$. Finally, it returns a global parameter $gp = \{p, P, G, P_{pub}, H_1, H_2, H_3, H_4\}$.

(2) *HelperKeyGen*($gp$): With the input of $gp$, the algorithm randomly chooses $v \in Z_q$, sets the helper's private key $HK = v$ and computes its public key $PK_{helper} = vP$.

(3) *PartialKeyGen*($gp$, $mk$, $ID$): With the input of $gp$, the master key $mk$, a user's identity $ID$, the algorithm computes the user's partial private key $D_{ID} = sH_1(ID)$.

(4) *SecretValGen*($gp$, $ID$): With the input of $gp$ and a user's identity $ID$, the algorithm randomly chooses $s_{ID} \in Z_p^*$ as the secret value for the user.

(5) *InitialPrivateKeyGen*($gp$, $D_{ID}$, $s_{ID}$): With the input of $gp$, a partial private key $D_{ID}$ and a secret value $s_{ID}$, the algorithm randomly chooses $y \in Z_p^*$, computes $SK_{0,1} = s_{ID} + sH_1(ID)$ and sets the initial private key $SK_{ID,0} = (SK_{0,1}, SK_{0,2}) = (s_{ID} + sH_1(ID), y)$.

(6) *PublicKeyGen*($gp$, $s_{ID}$, $SK_{ID,0}$, $PK_{helper}$): With the input of $gp$, the secret value $s_{ID}$, the initial private key $SK_{ID,0}$ and the helper's public key $PK_{helper}$, the algorithm sets the public key $PK_{ID} = (PK_1, PK_2, PK_3) = (s_{ID}P, yP, vP)$.

(7) *KeyUpd*($gp$, $HK$, $ID$, $i$): With the input of $gp$, the helper's private key $HK$, a user's identity $ID$ and a time period $i$, the algorithm computes the update key $UK_{ID,i} = vH_2(ID, i) - vH_2(ID, i - 1)$, where $UK_{ID,1} = vH_2(ID, 1)$.

(8) *PrivateKeyGen*($gp$, $i$, $UK_{ID,i}$, $SK_{ID,i-1}$): With the input of $gp$, a time period $i$, a update key $UK_{ID,i}$ of time period $i$ and a private key $SK_{ID,i-1}$ of time period $i$-1, the algorithm computes the private key $SK_{ID,i} = (SK_{i,1}, SK_{i,2}) = (SK_{i-1,1} + UK_{ID,i}, SK_{i-1,2}) = (s_{ID} + sH_1(ID) + vH_2(ID, i), y)$ at a time period $i$.

(9) *Encrypt*($gp$, $w$, $i$, $ID$, $PK_{ID}$): With the input of $gp$, a keyword $w$, a time period $i$, a user's identity $ID$ and a public key $PK_{ID}$, the algorithm randomly chooses $r \in Z_p^*$, computes $C_1 = rP$, $C_2 = H_4(rH_3(w)(PK_1 + PK_2 + H_1(ID)P_{pub} + H_2(ID, i)PK_3))$, and outputs the keyword ciphertext $C_w = (C_1, C_2)$.

(10) *Trapdoor*($gp$, $w'$, $ID$, $SK_{ID,i}$): With the input of $gp$, a keyword $w'$, a user's identity $ID$, the private key $SK_{ID,i}$ of a time period $i$, the algorithm computes $T_{w'} = (SK_{i,1} + SK_{i,2})H_3(w')$.

(11) *Test*($gp$, $C_w$,$T_{w'}$): With the input of $gp$, a keyword ciphertext $C_w$ and a keyword trapdoor $T_{w'}$, The algorithm checks whether $C_2 = H_4(T_{w'} C_1)$ holds. If it does, output 1; otherwise, output 0.

Correctness: Assume the ciphertext of keyword $w$ is $C_w = (rP, H_4(rH_3(w)(PK_1 + PK_2 + H_1(ID)P_{pub} + H_2(ID, i)PK_3))$ and the trapdoor associated to keyword $w'$ is $T_{w'} = (SK_{i,1} + SK_{i,2})H_3(w')$. If $w = w'$, then $H_4(T_{w'} C_1) = H_4((SK_{i,1} + SK_{i,2})H_3(w')rP) = H_4((s_{ID} + sH_1(ID) + vH_2(ID, i) + y)H_3(w')rP) = H_4(rH_3(w')(PK_1 + PK_2 + H_1(ID)P_{pub} + H_2(ID, i)PK_3)) = C_2$. Therefore, the KI-CLPEKS scheme is correct.

Next is main result about the security of our KI-CLPEKS scheme.

**Theorem 1.** The KI-CLPEKS scheme satisfies the IND-CKA security under the hardness assumption of the CDH problem in the random oracle model.

Due to the space limitation, the full proof of this theorem is omitted here and will be written in the final version of this paper.

# 5  Performance Evaluation

To evaluate the properties of the proposed KI-CLPEKS scheme, we compare it with the previous schemes [28–31]. We denote these schemes by PF-CLEKS, CLEKS, PF-CL-KIE and CL-KIE, respectively. The details are shown in Table 1. From the table, it is easy to see that the KI-CLPEKS framework enjoys some good properties such as supporting key update and ciphertext search at the same time.

**Table 1.** Properties of the KI-CLPEKS framework and other framework.

| Frameworks | Supporting key update | Supporting ciphertext search | IND-CKA |
|---|---|---|---|
| PF-CLEKS | N | Y | Y |
| CLEKS | N | Y | Y |
| PF-CL-KIE | Y | N | N |
| CL-KIE | Y | N | N |
| KI-CLPEKS | Y | Y | Y |

Table 2 and Table 3 respectively give the computational efficiency comparison and the communicational efficiency comparison of the five schemes, where $T_H, T_{GH}, T_P,$ $T_{MP}, T_{ZM}, T_{GM}, T_{ZE}$ and $T_{GE}$ are the running time of a cryptographic hash operation, a hash function operation that maps an element in $G$ to an integer in $Z_p^*$, a bilinear pairing operation, a map-to-point encoding operation, a modular multiplication operation in $Z_p^*$, a modular multiplication operation in $G$, an exponent operation in $Z_p^*$ and a modular multiplication operation in $G$ respectively, $l$ and $|G|$ respectively denote the bit-size of a hash value and the bit-size of an element in $G$.

**Table 2.** Computational efficiency of the compared schemes.

| Schemes | PartialKeyGen | KeyUpd | Encrypt | Trapdoor | Test |
|---|---|---|---|---|---|
| PF-CLEKS | $T_{ZM}$ | – | $2T_{GM} + T_{ZM} + T_H$ | $T_{ZM} + T_H$ | $T_{GM}$ |
| CLEKS | $T_{GM}$ | – | $T_{GM} + 3T_{ZM} + 2T_H + T_P$ | $T_{GM} + T_H$ | $T_P + T_H$ |
| PF-CL-KIE | $T_{ZM} + T_{HE}$ | $T_{ZM} + T_H$ | $3T_{ZE} + 4T_{ZM} + 2T_H$ | – | – |
| CL-KIE | $T_{GE}$ | $T_{GM} + T_{MP}$ | $4T_{GM} + 3T_P + T_{GE} + T_H + T_{GH}$ | – | – |
| KI-CLPEKS | $T_{ZM}$ | $2T_{ZM} + T_H$ | $3T_{GM} + T_{ZM} + T_H$ | $T_{ZM} + T_H$ | $T_{GM}$ |

**Table 3.** Communicational efficiency of the compared schemes.

| Schemes | Length of a keyword ciphertext | Length of a trapdoor |
|---|---|---|
| PF-CLEKS | $2|G|$ | $|Z_q^*|$ |
| CLEKS | $|G| + 1$ | $|G|$ |
| PF-CL-KIE | $|G| + 1$ | – |
| CL-KIE | $|G| + 1$ | – |
| KI-CLPEKS | $2|G|$ | $|Z_q^*|$ |

**Table 4.** Time cost of each basic operation and bit-length of an element/hash value.

| Running time (ms) | | | | | | | | Bit-length (bit) | | |
|---|---|---|---|---|---|---|---|---|---|---|
| $T_{ZM}$ | $T_{GM}$ | $T_{HE}$ | $T_{GE}$ | $T_H$ | $T_{MP}$ | $T_P$ | $T_{GH}$ | $|G|$ | $|Z_q^*|$ | 1 |
| 0 | 0.223 | 0.228 | 0.223 | 0.005 | 1.13 | 8.512 | 23.387 | 512 | 160 | 256 |

To evaluate the computational efficiency, the schemes are tested by the miracl library. The experiments are carried out on a laptop and Linux OS with an Intel Core i5-4210U CPU of 1.7 GHz and 3.0 GB RAM. The bilinear group $G$ is 512 bits. Besides, the hash functions are implemented by SHA-256. We simulate the CLEKS scheme and the CL-KIE scheme by applying the Type-A bilinear pairing, which is defined on the curve $y^2 = x^3 + x$ over the finite field $F_q$ for prime $q \equiv 3 \mod 4$. Table 4 gives the time cost of each basic operation and bit-length of a group element or a hash value.

The experimental results (see Fig. 1, 2, 3, 4 and Fig. 5) show that the costs of the *PartialKeyGen* algorithm, the *Encrypt* algorithm, the *Trapdoor* generation algorithm and the *Test* algorithm in the KI-CLPEKS scheme are all equivalent to the PF-CLEKS scheme.

Furthermore, the costs of the *PartialKeyGen* algorithm and the *Encrypt* algorithm are lower than that of the PF-CL-KIE scheme. Since the CLEKS scheme and the CL-KIE scheme are based on bilinear pairing, the costs of all algorithm of the KI-CLPEKS scheme are much lower than these two schemes. Specifically, the time for generating a partial private key in the KI-CLPEKS scheme is about 0 ms, while that in the PF-CLEKS, CLEKS, PF-CL-KIE and CL-KIE schemes are 0 ms, 0.223 ms, 0.228 ms and 0.223 ms, respectively. The time for encrypting a keyword in the KI-CLPEKS scheme is about 0.674 ms, while that in the PF-CLEKS, CLEKS, PF-CL-KIE and CL-KIE schemes are 0.451 ms, 8.745 ms, 2.353 ms and 27.674 ms, respectively. The time for updating private key in the KI-CLPEKS scheme is about 0.005 ms, while that in the PF-CL-KIE and CL-KIE schemes are 0.005 ms and 1.353 ms, respectively. The time for generating a search trapdoor in the KI-CLPEKS scheme is about 0.005 ms, while that in the PF-CLEKS and CLEKS schemes are 0.005 ms and 0.228 ms, respectively. The time for matching a keyword ciphertext with a search trapdoor in the KI-CLPEKS scheme is about 0.223 ms, while that in the PF-CLEKS and CLEKS schemes are 2.2 ms and 8.517 ms, respectively.

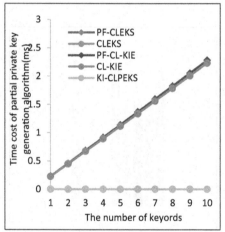
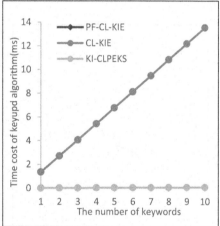

**Fig. 1.** Time cost of partial private key generation algorithm.

**Fig. 2.** Time cost of keyupd algorithm.

Regarding the communication overhead (as illustrated in Fig. 6), the keyword cipher-text length in KI-CLPEKS scheme is 1024 bits, while the keyword ciphertext length in the PF-CLEKS, CLEKS, PF-CL-KIE and CL-KIE schemes are 1024 bits, 768 bits, 768 bits and 768 bits, respectively. Besides, the size of a search trapdoor in KI-CLPEKS scheme is 160 bits, while that in the PF-CLEKS and CLEKS schemes are 160 bits and 512 bits, respectively. Compared with other schemes, the KI-CLPEKS scheme not only realizes the ciphertext search function and the key isolation function at the same time on the basis of the certificateless cryptosystem, but also has certain advantages in terms of computational efficiency and communication efficiency.

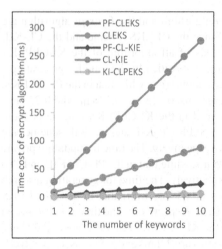

**Fig. 3.** Time cost of encrypt algorithm.

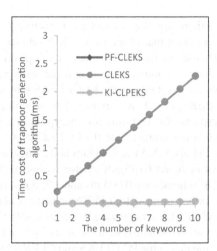

**Fig. 4.** Time cost of trapdoor generation algorithm.

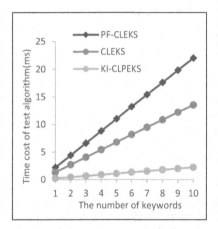

**Fig. 5.** Time cost of test algorithm.

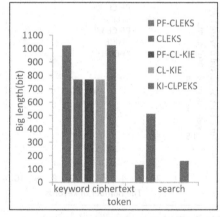

**Fig. 6.** Bit-length of keyword ciphertext and search token.

# 6    Conclusion

This article proposes a pairing-free certificateless key-insulated encryption with keyword search (KI-CLPEKS). After formally defining its security, a specific KI-CLPEKS scheme that has been proven to be secure in the random oracle model is given. The KI-CLPEKS scheme realizes two functions of key isolation and ciphertext search at the same time, and it not only avoids the problems of public key certificate management and key escrow, but also effectively reduces the harm caused by key leakage. The experimental results and comparisons show that the KI-CLPEKS scheme is feasible and applicable.

**Acknowledgments.** This work was supported in part by the National Natural Science Foundation of China under Grant No. 61772009, the Natural Science Foundation of Jiangsu Province under Grant No. BK20181304.

# References

1. Song, D.X.S., Wagner, D., Perrig, A.: Practical techniques for searches on encrypted data. In: IEEE Symposium on Security and Privacy, USA, pp. 44–55. IEEE (2000)
2. Golle, P., Staddon, J., Waters, B.: Secure conjunctive keyword search over encrypted data. In: Jakobsson, M., Yung, M., Zhou, J. (eds.) ACNS 2004. LNCS, vol. 3089, pp. 31–45. Springer, Heidelberg (2004). https://doi.org/10.1007/978-3-540-24852-1_3
3. Curtmola, R., Garay, J., Kamara, S., Ostrovsky, R.: Searchable symmetric encryption: improved definitions and efficient constructions. J. Comput. Secur. **19**(5), 895–934 (2011)
4. Fu, Z.J., Wu, X.L., Guan, C.W., Sun, X.M., Ren, K.: Toward efficient multi-keyword fuzzy search over encrypted outsourced data with accuracy improvement. IEEE Trans. Inf. Forensics Secur. **11**(12), 2706–2716 (2016)
5. Xia, Z.H., Wang, X.H., Sun, X.M., Wang, Q.: A secure and dynamic multi-keyword ranked search scheme over encrypted cloud data. IEEE Trans. Parallel Distrib. Syst. **27**(2), 340–352 (2016)
6. Boneh, D., Di Crescenzo, G., Ostrovsky, R., Persiano, G.: Public key encryption with keyword search. In: Cachin, C., Camenisch, J.L. (eds.) EUROCRYPT 2004. LNCS, vol. 3027, pp. 506–522. Springer, Heidelberg (2004). https://doi.org/10.1007/978-3-540-24676-3_30
7. Baek, J., Safavi-Naini, R., Susilo, W.: Public key encryption with keyword search revisited. In: Gervasi, O., Murgante, B., Laganà, A., Taniar, D., Mun, Y., Gavrilova, M.L. (eds.) ICCSA 2008. LNCS, vol. 5072, pp. 1249–1259. Springer, Heidelberg (2008). https://doi.org/10.1007/978-3-540-69839-5_96
8. Rhee, H.S., Park, J.H., Susilo, W., Lee, D.H.: Trapdoor security in a searchable public-key encryption scheme with a designated tester. J. Syst. Softw. **83**(5), 763–771 (2010)
9. Shao, Z.Y., Yang, B.: On security against the server in designated tester public key encryption with keyword search. Inf. Process. Lett. **115**(12), 957–961 (2015)
10. Park, D.J., Kim, K., Lee, P.J.: Public key encryption with conjunctive field keyword search. In: Lim, C.H., Yung, M. (eds.) WISA 2004. LNCS, vol. 3325, pp. 73–86. Springer, Heidelberg (2005). https://doi.org/10.1007/978-3-540-31815-6_7
11. Lai, J.Z., Zhou, X.H., Deng, R.H., Li, Y.J., Chen, K.: Expressive search on encrypted data. In: ASIA CCS 2013, pp. 243–252. ACM, USA (2013)
12. Zhang, B., Zhang, F.G.: An efficient public key encryption with conjunctive-subset keywords search. J. Netw. Comput. Appl. **34**(1), 262–267 (2011)
13. Lv, Z., Hong, C., Zhang, M., Feng, D.: Expressive and secure searchable encryption in the public key setting. In: Chow, S.S.M., Camenisch, J., Hui, L.C.K., Yiu, S.M. (eds.) ISC 2014. LNCS, vol. 8783, pp. 364–376. Springer, Cham (2014). https://doi.org/10.1007/978-3-319-13257-0_21
14. Chen, Y.C.: SPEKS: secure server-designation public key encryption with keyword search against keyword guessing attacks. Comput. J. **58**(4), 922–933 (2015)
15. Chen, R.M., Mu, Y., Yang, G.M., Wang, X.F.: Dual-server public-key encryption with keyword search for secure cloud storage. IEEE Trans. Inf. Forensics Secur. **11**(4), 789–798 (2015)
16. Li, L., Xu, C., Yu, X., Dou, B., Zuo, C.: Searchable encryption with access control on keywords in multi-user setting. J. Cyber Secur. **2**(1), 9–23 (2020)

17. Xu, L., Xu, C.G., Liu, J.K., Zuo, C., Zhang, P.: Building a dynamic searchable encrypted medical database for multi-client. Inf. Sci. **527**, 394–405 (2020)
18. Abdalla, M., et al.: Searchable encryption revisited: consistency properties, relation to anonymous IBE, and extensions. In: Shoup, V. (ed.) CRYPTO 2005. LNCS, vol. 3621, pp. 205–222. Springer, Heidelberg (2005). https://doi.org/10.1007/11535218_13
19. Mei, L., Xu, C., Xu, L., Yu, X., Zuo, C.: Verifiable identity-based encryption with keyword search for IoT from lattice. Comput. Mater. Continua **68**(2), 2299–2314 (2021)
20. Ali, M., Xu, C., Hussain, A.: Authorized attribute-based encryption multi-keywords search with policy updating. J. New Media **2**(1), 31–43 (2020)
21. Feng, T., Pei, H., Ma, R., Tian, Y., Feng, X.: Blockchain data privacy access control based on searchable attribute encryption. Comput. Mater. Continua **66**(1), 871–890 (2021)
22. Peng, Y.G., Cui, J.T., Peng, C.G., Ying, Z.B.: Certificateless public key encryption with keyword search. China Commun. **11**(11), 100–113 (2014)
23. Al-Riyami, S.S., Paterson, K.G.: Certificateless public key cryptography. In: Laih, C.-S. (ed.) ASIACRYPT 2003. LNCS, vol. 2894, pp. 452–473. Springer, Heidelberg (2003). https://doi.org/10.1007/978-3-540-40061-5_29
24. Zheng, Q., Li, X., Azgin, A.: CLKS: certificateless keyword search on encrypted data. In: Qiu, M., Xu, S., Yung, M., Zhang, H. (eds.) Network and System Security, NSS 2015. LNCS, vol. 9408, pp. 239–253. Springer, Cham (2015). https://doi.org/10.1007/978-3-319-25645-0_16
25. Ma, M., He, D.B., Khan, M.K., Chen, J.H.: Certificateless searchable public key encryption scheme for mobile healthcare system. Comput. Electr. Eng. **65**, 413–424 (2018)
26. Ma, M., He, D.B., Kumar, N., et al.: Certificateless searchable public key encryption scheme for industrial Internet of Things. IEEE Trans. Industr. Inf. **14**(2), 759–767 (2017)
27. Dodis, Y., Katz, J., Xu, S., Yung, M.: Key-insulated public key cryptosystems. In: Knudsen, L.R. (ed.) EUROCRYPT 2002. LNCS, vol. 2332, pp. 65–82. Springer, Heidelberg (2002). https://doi.org/10.1007/3-540-46035-7_5
28. Lu, Y., Li, J.-G.: Constructing pairing-free certificateless public key encryption with keyword search. Front. Inf. Technol. Electron. Eng. **20**(8), 1049–1060 (2019). https://doi.org/10.1631/FITEE.1700534
29. Lu, Y., Li, J.G.: Constructing certificateless encryption with keyword search against outside and inside keyword guessing attacks. China Commun. **16**(7), 156–173 (2019)
30. He, L.B., Yan, D.J., Xiong, H., Qin, Z.G.: Pairing-free certificateless key-insulated encryption with provable security. J. Electron. Sci. Technol. **16**(1), 50–56 (2018)
31. He, L., Yuan, C., Xiong, H., Qin, Z.: Certificateless key-insulated encryption: cryptographic primitive for achieving key-escrow free and key-exposure resilience. In: Wang, Y., Yu, G., Zhang, Y., Han, Z., Wang, G. (eds.) Big Data Computing and Communications. BigCom 2016. LNCS, vol. 9784, pp. 387–395. Springer, Cham (2016)

# A Blockchain-Based IoT Data Secure Vickery Auction System

Haohui Wang[2], Xiubo Chen[1,2], Haseeb Ahmad[3], Gang Xu[1,4(✉)], and Yixian Yang[2]

[1] Guizhou Provincial Key Laboratory of Public Big Data, Guizhou University, Guiyang 550025, Guizhou, China
gangxu_bupt@163.com
[2] Information Security Center, State Key Laboratory of Networking and Switching Technology, Beijing University of Posts and Telecommunications, Beijing 100876, China
[3] Department of Computer Science, National Textile University, Faisalabad 37610, Pakistan
[4] School of Information Science and Technology, North China University of Technology, Beijing 100144, China

**Abstract.** Traditional centralized architectures for IoT data suffer from single points of failure in terms of data storage and access control, and IoT data does not fully realize its value as a digital asset. In response to the above challenges, we propose a decentralized storage and lightweight access control method for IoT data based on blockchain technology, and put forward an auction system to commercialize the IoT data. Firstly, a blockchain-based data storage method proposed using Inter Planetary File System (IPFS), which ensures the data is immutable and traceable. Secondly, in this paper, we propose a distributed lightweight Capability-Based Access Control (CapBAC) based on blockchain, in which a time dimension is added so that no additional token revocation operation is required. Thus, lightweight access control is achieved under IoT devices with limited computing power. Finally, we come up with a blockchain-based Vickery auction system to sell the data to the highest bidder in demand. This auction effectively protects the privacy of bidders and does not require third-party intermediary fees. And it can ensure fairness and non-repudiation of the auction. By analyzing the entire system process, we guarantee secure storage of IoT data. Besides, we can achieve lightweight access control and realize the value of the data based on the blockchain technology.

**Keywords:** Blockchain · Iot · Decentralized storage · Access control · Vickery auction

## 1 Introduction

In recent years, with the development of the IoT industry, the number of IoT devices has grown rapidly. The IoT technology has profoundly affected all aspects of human production and life, from smart homes and smart security to smart transportation and smart cities, generating massive amounts of IoT data. In the era of big data, data storage and security issues cannot be ignored [1, 2]. In general, data generated by IoT devices is usually stored in a centralized database, which leads to single point of failure and data security issues. In addition, the IoT generates huge amounts of private data. Access control, as one of the main techniques for data privacy protection, ensures that data is accessed by users with access rights. However, traditional access control methods use a centralized entity for access authorization, where each access request is directed to the same central trusted entity. It is insecure to have all information kept by the central trusted entity. Blockchain technology, which has developed rapidly in recent years, has brought new ideas to solve the above problems. Blockchain was initially known as the underlying endorsement system of Bitcoin [3], with characteristics such as decentralization and immutability. In this paper, we come up with a decentralized storage method for IoT data based on blockchain technology, and propose a lightweight CapBAC to achieve distributed access control. Besides, a blockchain-based Vickery auction system is put forward to empower the data, where IoT data is used as a commodity to be auctioned and data demanders act as blockchain nodes.

The single point of failure problem of traditional IoT data storage refers to the storage of data through a centralized database. Many IoT devices involve private data, leading to privacy leakage issues. Illegal access problem refers to IoT data being accessed or even modified by users who do not have access rights. For individuals, the popularity of smart home has brought privacy issues while improving the quality of life. Data generated by IoT devices like smart cameras and smart door locks that involve privacy will have serious consequences if the data is accessed illegally. To address these issues, distributed storage methods using blockchain technology have been developed rapidly, which eliminates the need for third-party data centers while ensuring that data is immutable. Reference [4] used a combination of blockchain and IPFS to store and manage industrial IoT data. And [5] proposed a Cipherchain, which can process and maintain transaction data in the form of ciphertext to securely store data. In this paper, we propose a distributed storage method by uploading the data to IPFS. At the same time, the data owner decides whether to put the data into auction or not. Then, design smart contracts to automatically execute operations.

Besides, to solve the problem of illegal access to private data, access control as an effective security management method. The main access control methods are: Role-Based Access Control (RBAC) [6], Attributes-Based Access Control (ABAC) [7], Usage Control (UCON) [8], and Capability-Based Access Control (CapBAC) [9]. The core of RBAC is the association of roles with a set of permissions, and users obtain the corresponding permissions according to the roles. Since RBAC is a static access control method, the correspondence between {user, role} and {role, permission} cannot be set in advance, so it can't solve the problem of dynamic access to IoT nodes [10]. In contrast, ABAC is a dynamic access control method [11], which uses attributes as the deciding element of access control. Attributes are inherent to the subject and object, so there is no need to enter the correspondence manually. Besides, UCON not only solves the problem of dynamic node access, but also considers continuity and variability in the access control process. But RBAC, ABAC and UCON all require a centralized server for authorization decisions, while CapBAC [12–14] has been implemented for lightweight distributed access control in IoT environments. In this case, the capability token is a transferable and unforgeable identifier and supports scalability and dynamism. However,

CapBAC cannot solve the problem of access control in untrustworthy environments. Therefore, a combination of blockchain and CapBAC can enable fine-grained access control. Nakamura et al. [15] proposed a scheme to manage the tokens in units of access rights. They use a delegation graph instead of a delegation tree to simplify the delegation relationship. Bouras et al. [16] introduced the concept of statement, which can be used as a token to grant subject privileges. They focused on CapBAC in a smart city, which required additional overhead. Besides, [17, 18] described quantum-based encryption schemes that are useful for our paper. In order to reduce the communication overhead of IoT devices and improve the blockchain performance, Li et al. [19] proposed a blockchain-based access control model for IoT applicability using cross-chain technology and linear secret sharing scheme. And [20] used searchable attribute encryption to preserve data privacy based on blockchain. This scheme uses Fisco Bcos as the underlying blockchain development platform. In this paper, we propose a blockchain-based CapBAC with a time parameter. By adding a start time and an end time to a token, it is automatically invalidated after the valid time. Therefore, there is no need to design revocation operations, reducing the overhead. This lightweight access control is suitable for use in IoT devices with limited computing power.

In addition, data generated by IoT devices is a valuable digital asset that should be more fully utilized to realize its true value. For example, the data generated by the camera, on the one hand, can be used as powerful evidence to monitor illegal acts such as robberies. On the other hand, camera data can be used as test data for smart security, contributing to the training of more accurate models. Besides, with the development of industrial IoT, the upper layer model needs real and effective sensor data for training and learning to produce the best manufacturing benefits. For example, temperature sensor data is a valuable training set and test set for the manufacturing industry that strictly controls temperature. Hence, IoT data owners can sell the data to the data demander to realize the value of the data asset. To better improve railroad services, Gbadamosi et al. [21] proposed a prediction strategy to use IoT to collect data, use IoT sensors to monitor the status in real time, and then use this data for conceptual modeling and analysis. Therefore, the data owners can commercialize these data and realize the actual value of the data by auctioning them through the blockchain-based Vickery auction system proposed in this paper. In the traditional auction process, there are some problems such as privacy leakage of members participating in the auction, high fees for third-party auction centers, and inflated prices due to collusion between third-party auction centers and bidders. The blockchain-based Vickery auction system can avoid these problems. Vickery auction [22] is known as second-price sealed-bid auction, where bidders bid without knowing the bids of others. And the highest bidder is successful, but only costs the next highest bid. The advantage of this auction method is that the buyer tends to bid slightly lower than the psychological price in order to protect their own interests. Vickery auction can make everyone report their own true valuation, thus realizing the effective allocation of items to the highest bidder. In addition, combined with blockchain technology, the privacy of each participating auction member can be protected. Since no third party is required to act as an intermediary, no additional costs are incurred. Liu et al. [23] proposed a secure and efficient auction system for decentralized cross-blockchain asset transactions that transfer user assets to another blockchain. In this paper, we propose a blockchain-based Vickery auction system, in which the data owner decides whether to put the data up for auction. By designing the bid contract to ensure that each auction participant gets the needed data fairly and non-repudiation.

In summary, in order to ensure the security of IoT data storage and access control, this paper proposes decentralized storage and lightweight CapBAC. Besides, we also propose a blockchain-based Vickery auction system to realize the value of the data. The main contributions of this paper are as follows.

1. We propose a blockchain and IPFS-based data storage approach that combines on-chain-off-chain decentralized storage to ensure that data is immutable and traceable. Moreover, the data owner can decide to auction the data.
2. We propose a distributed CapBAC with a time dimension, which enables lightweight access control in resource-constrained IoT devices. By specifying the validity time of tokens, there is no need for token revocation operations. It is implemented by smart contracts and is publicly verifiable on the blockchain.
3. We propose a blockchain-based Vickery auction system to realize the value of IoT data and protect the privacy of auction participants. Without third-party agencies, this system saves on intermediary costs and avoids collusion between third-party agencies and auction participants, ensuring a fair transaction.

The remainder of this paper is organized as follows. In Sect. 2, some basic knowledge is introduced. Then, the specific design of our system is placed in Sect. 3. Section 4 analyzes the whole system process. Finally, in Sect. 5, we summarize our work and plan for future research.

## 2 Preliminaries

### 2.1 IoT

Internet of Things (IoT) refers to connecting any object to the network through various devices and technologies such as radio frequency identification technology, GPS, infrared sensors, etc. In accordance with agreed protocols to realize intelligent sensing, identification, positioning, and management of objects. IoT is an information carrier based on Internet, traditional telecommunication network, etc. It allows all physical objects that can be independently addressed to form an interconnected network.

For protocols of IoT devices, they can be specifically divided into Zigbee, Bluetooth, WiFi, MQTT, HTTP [24] etc. Among them, Zigbee, Bluetooth, WiFi need hardware support. And MQTT, HTTP are protocols that need to connect to a server. Different protocols have different characteristics. Zigbee is a low cost and low power consumption wireless networking communication technology. WiFi technology is a communication technology with high power consumption and fast transmission rate. HTTP protocol is a typical client/server communication mode, which is used to a high degree in the Internet. Therefore, many vendors choose to develop IoT system based on HTTP protocol. However, there are some disadvantages in IoT application, including poor security and high overhead cost. Ordinary IoT devices have limited computing power and generally require gateways to convert their respective networks to Internet. The process is shown in Fig. 1 below.

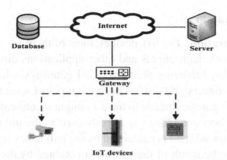

**Fig. 1.** Relationship between IoT devices and Internet.

## 2.2 Blockchain, Ethereum, Smart Contract and IPFS

Blockchain is one of the most revolutionary emerging technologies in recent years, with the prominent feature of building trust in a decentralized manner. Blockchain technology refers to a combination of technologies for data exchange, process and storage between multiple participants, where the technologies mainly include modern cryptography, distributed consistency protocols, peer-to-peer network communication technologies and smart contract programming languages. The core of blockchain technology is the consensus mechanism, that is, in the case of decentralization, a consensus is reached on the legality of transactions between individuals who do not trust each other.

The concept of smart contracts was first introduced by Nick Szabo [25], the purpose of a smart contract is to provide a secure method that is superior to traditional contracts. Smart contracts are digital contracts stored on a blockchain that are automatically executed when conditions are met.

Ethereum [26] achieves the complete fit of blockchain and smart contracts for the first time, and is known as a new blockchain-based smart contract development platform with Turing completeness. It has efficient consensus mechanism, and supports for more application scenarios. Any smart contract can be written on Ethereum to achieve powerful functions through smart contracts for decentralized application development.

IPFS is a peer-to-peer distributed file system protocol [27], called "Inter Planetary File System", whose core technology is to store files in a certain format and then generate a unique hash value. IPFS ensures the security of the data and makes the data permanently stored and immutable.

## 3 System Model

### 3.1 System Architecture

This section describes the overall system architecture. Firstly, for the data generated by IoT devices, distributed storage is achieved using blockchain technology. In addition, the data owner decides whether to put the data up for auction. Then, add time dimension in CapBAC to realize the lightweight access control. Finally, the blockchain-based Vickery auction system proposed in this paper can realize the value of the data. During the valid auction time, the data demanders act as blockchain nodes for the auction. After each round of the auction, the highest bidder pays the next highest price for the data.

## 3.2   System Configuration

**IoT Gateway Configuration.** For IoT devices, most of them are computationally limited and cannot run blockchain clients and other applications directly on the devices. Therefore, we will deploy Ethereum platform in IoT gateways, which act as a link. And it can realize protocol conversion between different types of sensing networks.

Therefore, each IoT gateway needs to have a unique identification. Considering the security, the Ethereum account address is directly used as the unique identifier of each device. Ethereum account address is calculated by the public key through hash function, while the public key is the result of the operation obtained by the private key through elliptic curve cryptography. Then only the last 20 bits are retained as the Ethereum address after using the one-way hash function Keccak-256.

**Data Storage.** Design smart contracts to implement storing data on IPFS. By utilizing the relevant functions of IPFS, we can get the hash value after uploading the data. The process is shown in the Fig. 2 below.

**Fig. 2.**  Process of data saved to IPFS.

In the meantime, the data owner decides whether the data will be used for auctions. If so, the specific auction start time, duration and starting price need to be set. As Vickery auction adopted, the current second highest price needs to be kept during each round of the auction. Therefore, the data structure needs to contain parameters related to the auction. Define the IoTData data structure as follows.

```
struct IoTData
{
        uint id;
        string type;
        string dataHash;
        bool ifAuction;
        uint startPrice;
        uint startTime;
        uint endTime;
        address topBidder;
        uint topBidPrice;
        uint secondBidPrice;
}
mapping (address => uint) Owner;
```

**Data Structure 1**: IoTdata structure

Among them, *id* is the unique identifier and *type* is a description of the data. It is also necessary to use a mapping (a data structure in solidity) to record what data has been uploaded for each account address, forming a mapping between account addresses and data numbers.

The *Algorithm 1* implements the function of uploading data to IPFS. It mainly uses IPFS's client method *ipfs.add* in node.js, and saves the returned hash.

| *Algorithm 1. saveDataToIPFS* |
| --- |
| Input: data |
| Output: dataHash |
| Step 1: ipfs.add(data); |
| Step 2: **if** (error) |
| Step 3: **then** return console(error); |
| Step 4: **else** |
| Step 5: save dataHash; |

**Algorithm 1**: Algorithm to save data to IPFS

After uploading the data to IPFS, it needs to design the algorithm to get the data off the IPFS. In *Algorithm 2*, we can get the original data from IPFS. Either by accessing the official link of the ipfs and adding the hash value or by adding the hash value after the local link.

| *Algorithm 2. getDataFromIPFS* |
| --- |
| Input: dataHash |
| Output: data |
| Step 1: Get "https://ipfs.io/ipfs/" + hash; |
| Step 2: **OR** |
| Step 3: Get "http://localhost:8080/ipfs/" + hash; |

**Algorithm 2**: Algorithm to get data from IPFS

Since the data is stored using on-chain-off-chain method, it is also essential to record the data to the blockchain. According to the *IoTData* data structure, the owner assigns each field. This process is implemented by a smart contract, which means that a transaction is sent. Then start *miner* for mining to package the transaction onto the blockchain.

| Algorithm 3. saveDataToBlockchain |
| --- |
| Input: IoTData |
| Output: Transaction Hash |
| Step 1: **if** (ifAuction == true) |
| Step 2: **then** set startPrice, startTime, endTime **AND require** (startTime < endTime); |
| Step 3: id+1; |
| Step 4: type = _type; |
| Step 5: dataHash = _dataHash; |
| Step 6: Owner(address , id); |
| Step 7: save IoTData to blockchain; |
| Step 8: miner.start(); |

**Algorithm 3**: Algorithm to save data to blockchain

**Capability-Based Access Control and Smart Contract.** CapBAC as a distributed access control method, each subject is associated with a capability list, which records the subject's access rights to other objects. In the actual process, the object creates a capability token for the subject, the subject carries the token and the object verifies it. Due to the limited computing power of IoT devices, in this paper, the IoT gateway is used as the object, and the account in Ethereum is used as its unique id. Besides, the distribution, verification, and management of the token are realized by smart contracts. For the design of capability tokens, Hernández-Ramos et al. [28] used JSON format. However, we add time parameters to the token so that no revocation operation is required, making it more lightweight to apply to IoT devices with limited computing power. The token is designed as follows:

$$\text{token}_{owner} \rightarrow \{Owner, Device, Time, Sig\} \tag{1}$$

- Owner: a registered account address of a device owner;
- Device: a registered account address used to represent device;
- Time: a time period within which a token is valid;
- Sig: owner's signature to verify tokens.

In this paper, CapBAC is designed to prevent unauthorized users from accessing data illegally. We innovatively propose that when data owners upload the data, they decide whether to commercialize the data. And the data requester auctions the data according to the demand. Consequently, the data is either accessed by the final auctioneer or by the account that gets access rights. Moreover, through the blockchain-based Vickery auction system proposed in this paper, the privacy of participants can be effectively protected and the problems caused by inflated bids can be avoided.

In addition to adding a valid parameter in the token to prove whether the token is valid or not, we also add a time dimension to indicate the validity time of the capability token. So that the token can be automatically revoked after the set end time. At the same time, the token's delegation operation is cancelled because too many delegations may reduce the readability of the capability delegation tree and increase the algorithm overhead. As for the token data structure, there is an address (a data structure in solidity) to point out the owner of the token. Use a string array *operations* to represent the specific operation permissions assigned, such as read, write, and execute. Therefore, a double mapping is needed to represent the token of the specific device for which permissions. The *token* data structure is defined as follows.

```
struct token
{
    bool valid;
    uint startTime;
    uint endTime;
}
Address owner;
String[] operations;
mapping(address => mapping(string => token)) tokenMapping;
```

**Data Structure 2**: CapBAC token structure

The Fig. 3 below illustrates that when a requester carries a token to access data, the object needs to verify the validity of the token before it can be accessed properly.

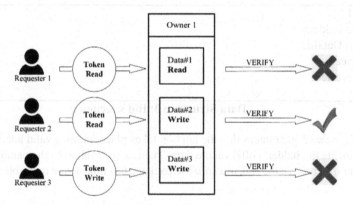

**Fig. 3.** CapBAC token verification

Once the specific structure of the token is available, the *tokenCreate* algorithm needs to be designed to initialize a token. The algorithm first checks the validity of the token and ensures that the token did not exist before. Then assign initial values to specific operation permissions, and return the token object. [29] proposed a data storage method based on cloud storage and blockchain.

---

*Algorithm 4. tokenCreate*

---

Input: Owner Address, Valid Time, String _operations
Output: Token Object
Step 1: **if** (this.valid == true)
Step 2: **then** return;
Step 3: **else**
Step 4:  tokenMapping[owner][_operations].valid = true;
Step 5:  tokenMapping[owner][_operations].startTime = current;
Step 6:  tokenMapping[owner][_operations].endTime = current + PERIOD;
Step 7:  return token;

---

**Algorithm 4**: Algorithm to create tokens

**Vickery Auction.** As for the auction process, this section designs the *Bid* data structure, and proposes the *bid* algorithm and *revealBid* algorithm according to the Vickery auction. Firstly, we define the *Bid* structure. This structure contains the bidder's account address, the *IoTData* number of the bid and the *price* of the bid, and a bool named *revealed* to indicate whether the bid has been revealed before.

```
struct Bid {
    address bidder;
    uint IoTDataId;
    uint price;
    bool revealed;
}
```

**Data Structure 3**: Bid structure

The *algorithm 5* guarantees that the auction takes place within a valid auction time and implements the bidder's offer on the data. Then, assign values to the parameters in the *Bid* data structure. In the end, use *miner* to package this transaction to the blockchain.

---

*Algorithm 5. Bid*

---

Input: IoTDataId, price
Output: Transaction Hash
Step 1: **if** (this.revealed == true)
Step 2: **then** return;
Step 3: **else**
Step 4: **require**( now < endTime **AND** now > startTime );
Step 5: **input** _IoTDataId, _price;
Step 6: IoTDataId = _IoTDataId, price = _price, bidder = this.address;
Step 7: **require**( price > startPrice );
Step 8: miner.start();

---

**Algorithm 5**: Algorithm to bid during auction

After the bidding time is over, the highest bidder and the second highest bid need to be found. Therefore, we need to traverse all the auction rounds and compare all the offers to get them. Finally, using the web3.eth.sendTransaction function of Ethereum, the highest bidder pays successfully and gets the hash of the data.

---

*Algorithm 6. revealBid*

---

Input: Every Bid
Output: Bid Winner
Step 1: **require**( now < endTime **AND** now > startTime );
Step 2: **require**( this.revealed == false );
Step 3: **for**( every bid )
Step 4:    **if**( first bid )
Step 5:    **then** set topBidPrice = bid.price, secondBidPrice = startPrice;
Step 6:    **else if**( new bid.price > topBidPrice )
Step 7:       **then** secondBidPrice = topBidPrice, topBidPrice = new bid.price;
Step 8:    **else if**( new bid.price > secondBidPrice **AND** new bid.price < topBidPrice )
Step 9:       **then** secondBidPrice = new bid.price;
Step 10: **sendTransaction**({from: topBidder, to:IoTDataOwner, value: secondBidPrice});
Step 11: this.revealed = true **then** send hash to topBidder;

---

**Algorithm 6**: Algorithm to reveal bid

The specific process is shown in Fig. 4 below. Within the effective auction time, the highest bidder gets the data and pays only the second highest price. Then the consensus mechanism of the blockchain ensures the data consistency. After successful transaction, the hash of the data is returned to the highest bidder.

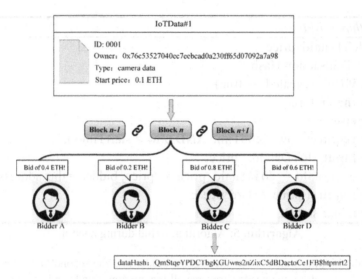

**Fig. 4.** Blockchain based auction process.

# 4  Analysis

This section analyzes our system in several aspects. First, blockchain technology is utilized to decentralize the storage of IoT data. Using IPFS to upload data to the local node, a hash value is returned after successful upload. Thus, the data is available locally through localhost. As shown in the Fig. 5 below. The upload and download functions can be implemented by smart contracts. The data is then recorded on the blockchain, guaranteeing its immutability and traceability. After analysis, using IPFS to store data can guarantee data integrity, and the upload and download speed is generally faster than the centralized data storage method.

**Fig. 5.** Data upload to IPFS.

Besides, we put forward a lightweight CapBAC in which a time parameter is added. Therefore, once the valid time is exceeded, the token expires. So there is no need to implement the token revocation operation in CapBAC, which reduces the overhead of the algorithm and makes it possible to run access control in IoT devices with limited computing power. And use blockchain technology to accomplish decentralized access control.

After analysis, a comparison between our lightweight CapBAC and other approaches is shown in Table 1 below.

Table 1. Comparison with other CapBAC approaches.

| Approach | Innovation | Scenarios | Security |
|---|---|---|---|
| Proposed | No token revocation operations | IoT data access control and auction | Resistant to SPOF |
| [12] | Decentralized identifiers to manage access control | IoT device rental on campus | Resistant to association attack |
| [14] | Context-awareness in access policy | IoT devices and operations on the cloud server | Resistant to MITM attack |
| [15] | One token per action | IoT data access control | Resistant to MITM attack |
| [16] | Introduce the concept of Statement as a token | Waste management in a smart city | Resistant to MITM attack |

In addition, the blockchain-based Vickery auction method proposed in this paper reduces the risk of adversary attack with decentralized storage compared to traditional auctions. Besides, this system does not require the participation of third-party auction institutions. Through the analysis, the specific advantages are as follows:

(1) Fairness. Bidders as the nodes of the blockchain to bid on real data. Without the participation of third-party auction institutions, so fraud is avoided.
(2) Protection of privacy. Using the Vickery auction method, each bid is sealed and the bidders' privacy is protected.
(3) Time validity. The data owner determines the start time and end time of the auction, and the auction will be invalid if the valid time is exceeded, and the time is strictly enforced.
(4) Non-repudiation. Using the non-tampering feature of blockchain, the auction results are guaranteed to be true and immutable. Each round of the bidding process is recorded on the blockchain and is publicly verifiable.

## 5  Conclusion

With the development of IoT technology, a large amount of data has been generated, and a lot of private data is involved. Traditional data storage methods have security problems, like single point of failure problem. Besides, private data are at risk of illegal access, and data are not fully utilized. The development of blockchain technology has brought solutions to the above problems. In this paper, we propose a blockchain-based decentralized storage method of IoT data. Moreover, we put forward a lightweight CapBAC to achieve fine-grained access control on IoT devices with limited computing resources. Apart from these, owners of different types of IoT data can decide to put the data up for auction through a blockchain-based Vickery auction system proposed in this paper. In this auction system, the privacy of the bidders can be protected and there is no need for third party auction organizations. In the future, we need to design more user-friendly interaction interface of our auction system. Furthermore, optimizing the CapBAC algorithm is another focus of our future work.

**Funding Statement.** This work was supported by the Open Fund of Advanced Cryptography and System Security Key Laboratory of Sichuan Province (Grant No. SKLACSS-202101), the Fundamental Research Funds for Beijing Municipal Commission of Education, Beijing Urban Governance Research Base of North China University of Technology, the Natural Science Foundation of Inner Mongolia (2021MS06006), Baotou Kundulun District Science and technology plan project (YF2020013), and Inner Mongolia discipline inspection and supervision big data laboratory open project fund (IMDBD2020020).

**Conflicts of Interest.** The authors declare that they have no conflicts of interest to report regarding the present study.

# References

1. Alaba, F.A., Othman, M., Hashem, I.A.T., Alotaibi, F.: Internet of Things security: a survey. J. Netw. Comput. Appl. **88**, 10–28 (2017)
2. Wazirali, R.: A review on privacy preservation of location-based services in Internet of Things. Intell. Autom. Soft Comput. **31**(2), 767–779 (2022)
3. Nakamoto, S.: Bitcoin: a peer-to-peer electronic cash system. Decentralized Bus. Rev. 21260 (2008)
4. Zheng, X., Lu, J., Sun, S., Kiritsis, D.: Decentralized industrial IoT data management based on blockchain and IPFS. In: Lalic, B., Majstorovic, V., Marjanovic, U., von Cieminski, G., Romero, D. (eds.) APMS 2020. IAICT, vol. 592, pp. 222–229. Springer, Cham (2020). https://doi.org/10.1007/978-3-030-57997-5_26
5. Chen, H., et al.: Cipherchain: a secure and efficient ciphertext blockchain via mpeck. J. Quantum Comput. **2**(1), 57 (2020)
6. Sandhu, R.S.: Role-based access control. In: Advances in Computers, vol. 46, pp. 237–286. Elsevier (1998)
7. Hu, V.C., Kuhn, D.R., Ferraiolo, D.F., Voas, J.: Attribute-based access control. Computer **48**(2), 85–88 (2015)
8. Park, J., Sandhu, R.: Towards usage control models: beyond traditional access control. In: Proceedings of the Seventh ACM Symposium on Access Control Models and Technologies, pp. 57–64 (2002)
9. Sandhu, R.S., Samarati, P.: Access control: principle and practice. IEEE Commun. Mag. **32**(9), 40–48 (1994)
10. Hasebe, K., Mabuchi, M., Matsushita, A.: Capability-based delegation model in RBAC. In: Proceedings of the 15th ACM Symposium on Access Control Models and Technologies, pp. 109–118 (2010)
11. Lu, X., Fu, S., Jiang, C., Lio, P.: A fine-grained IoT data access control scheme combining attribute-based encryption and blockchain. Secur. Commun. Netw. **2021** (2021)
12. Liu, Y., et al.: Capability-based IoT access control using blockchain. Digital Commun. Netw. **7**, 463–469 (2020)

13. Gusmeroli, S., Piccione, S., Rotondi, D.: A capability-based security approach to manage access control in the internet of things. Math. Comput. Model. **58**(5–6), 1189–1205 (2013)
14. Sivaselvan, N., Asif, W., Vivekananda, B.K., Rajarajan, M.: Authentication and capability-based access control: an integrated approach for IoT environment. In: 2020 12th International Conference on Communication Software and Networks (ICCSN), pp. 110–117. IEEE (2020)
15. Nakamura, Y., Zhang, Y., Sasabe, M., Kasahara, S.: Exploiting smart contracts for capability-based access control in the internet of things. Sensors **20**(6), 1793 (2020)
16. Bouras, M.A., Xia, B., Abuassba, A.O., Ning, H., Lu, Q.: IoT-CCAC: a blockchain-based consortium capability access control approach for IoT. PeerJ Comput. Sci. **7**, e455 (2021)
17. Chen, X.B., Sun, Y.R., Xu, G., Yang, Y.X.: Quantum homomorphic encryption scheme with flexible number of evaluator based on (k, n)-threshold quantum state sharing. Inf. Sci. **501**, 172–181 (2019)
18. Xu, G., Cao, Y., Xu, S., Xiao, K., Liu, X.: A novel post-quantum blind signature for log system in blockchain. Comput. Syst. Sci. Eng. **41**(3), 945–958 (2022)
19. Li, Z., Hao, J., Liu, J., Wang, H., Xian, M.: An iot-applicable access control model under double-layer blockchain. IEEE Trans. Circuits Syst. II Express Briefs **68**(6), 2102–2106 (2020)
20. Feng, T., Pei, H., Ma, R., Tian, Y., Feng, X.: Blockchain data privacy access control based on searchable attribute encryption. Comput. Mater. Continua **66**(1), 871–884 (2021)
21. Gbadamosi, A.Q., et al.: IoT for predictive assets monitoring and maintenance: an implementation strategy for the UK rail industry. Autom. Constr. **122**, 103486 (2021)
22. Vickrey, W.: Counterspeculation, auctions, and competitive sealed tenders. J. Financ. **16**(1), 8–37 (1961)
23. Liu, W., Wu, H., Meng, T., Wang, R., Wang, Y., Xu, C.Z.: AucSwap: a Vickrey auction modeled decentralized cross-blockchain asset transfer protocol. J. Syst. Architect. **117**, 102102 (2021)
24. Polianytsia, A., Starkova, O., Herasymenko, K.: Survey of the IoT data transmission protocols. In: 2017 4th International Scientific-Practical Conference Problems of Infocommunications. Science and Technology (PIC S&T), pp. 369–371. IEEE (2017)
25. Szabo, N.: Formalizing and securing relationships on public networks. First Monday **2** (1997)
26. Wood, G.: Ethereum: a secure decentralised generalised transaction ledger. Ethereum Project Yellow Paper **151**, 1–32 (2014)
27. Benet, J.: IPFS-content addressed, versioned, P2P file system. arXiv:1407.3561 (2014)
28. Hernández-Ramos, J.L., Jara, A.J., Marín, L., Skarmeta Gómez, A.F.: DCapBAC: embedding authorization logic into smart things through ECC optimizations. Int. J. Comput. Math. **93**(2), 345–366 (2016)
29. Zhang, J.S., Xu, G., Chen, X.B., Ahmad, H., Liu, X., Liu, W.: Towards Privacy-preserving cloud storage: a blockchain approach. Comput. Mater. Continua **69**(3), 2903–2916 (2021)

# Formal Verification and Testing of Data Plane in Software-Defined Networks: A Survey

Jiangyuan Yao[1], Min Jing[1], Shengjun Lin[1], Deshun Li[1(✉)],
and Xingcan Cao[2]

[1] Hainan University, Haikou 570228, Hainan, China
lideshunlily@qq.com
[2] University of British Columbia, Vancouver, BC V6T1Z1, Canada

**Abstract.** Software-defined network (SDN) separates the control plane and the data plane, which provides the programmability of the network and is widely deployed in data center networks. As the foundation of SDN, the data plane needs to be fully verified and tested to ensure its correctness and reliability. At present, formal verification and testing methods have been applied to SDN networks. The goals of verification and testing are to find the design defects and the implementation errors of the data plane, respectively. In this paper, we conduct a survey of the state-of-art methods and tools of formal verification and formal testing for SDN data plane. According to support for online verification, the related works of formal verification for the data plane fall into static verification and real-time verification. According to the requirement of source code, the existing works of formal testing for the data plane fall into white-box testing and black-box testing. Based on the state-of-art approaches of verification and testing, we also discuss the research trends of verification and testing for SDN data plane, such as artificial intelligence (AI)-based model construct and property definition, and scalable support for the stateful data plane.

**Keywords:** Software-defined network (SDN) · Data plane · Verification · Testing · Formal method

## 1 Introduction

SDN is a new network paradigm, which separates the control plane and the data plane and realizes the centralized control of the network through a central controller. Data plane also known as the forwarding plane, which consists of switches and other forwarding equipment. Compare with traditional networks, these forwarding devices are simple forwarding components without embedded intelligence to make their own decisions. The programmability of control plane is supported by data plane which is the foundation of SDN. SDN also makes it easier to apply machine learning strategies. Based on this, some scholars have

© The Author(s), under exclusive license to Springer Nature Switzerland AG 2022
X. Sun et al. (Eds.): ICAIS 2022, CCIS 1588, pp. 134–144, 2022.
https://doi.org/10.1007/978-3-031-06764-8_11

proposed Intelligent Software Defined Network (ISDN) to deal with new challenges [3].

The programmability brings new possibilities to the future network, which introduces the risk of network errors. Although some methods have been proposed [1] to effectively handle network congestion and load balancing in SDN networks, it is still necessary to verify and test SDN networks. Due to the difference of network properties, the technology of verification and testing in traditional network cannot be directly applied to SDN data plane. SDN has been paid more and more attention by the academia, and this paper focuses on the verification and testing with formal methods of data plane. The formal methods employ rigorous logical reasoning to check whether the model meets the system specifications, which has high accuracy and efficiency of verification and testing in data plane.

The formal verification in data plane of is used to check whether the packet forwarding path is consistent with the expectation of controller. The main methods include reading a snapshot of the flow table of the switch at a certain time, and monitoring the communication between the controller and the switch in real time, which constructing a formal model to verify the model. With a lot of effort, a lot of work has been done to help users find design flaws in data planes, such as HSA [15], VeriFlow [16], and NetPlumber [14], and more.

The formal testing of the SDN data plane is to check the forwarding behavior of each switch by generating probe packets. According to whether the source code is needed, these works are divided into the white-box testing methods and the black-box testing methods. Testing is used to find implementation errors in the data plane devices, thereby helping users or developers to improve the reliability of the data plane. Stand for Monocle [18], RuleScope [8], RuleChecker [24], and more.

Based on the survey, we believe that the future development direction of SDN data plane verification and testing may include the following three aspects. (1) AI-based model construct, (2) AI-based property definition, (3) scalable support for the stateful data plane.

The remainder of this paper is organized as follows. In Sect. 2, we introduce the formal verification of the SDN data plane. In Sect. 3, we introduce the formal testing of the SDN data plane. In Sect. 4, we put forward a vision for future work. Section 5 concludes this paper.

## 2   Verification

When verifying the data plane of traditional networks, we can collect FIB (Forwarding Info Base) through SNMP (Simple Network Management Protocol), a terminal, or a control session, representing Anteater [17], NETSAT [25], and so on. For SDN data plane verification, the main idea is to read the information of the flow tables from the data plane devices and monitor the real-time communication between the controller and the devices, as shown in Fig 1. We roughly divide the verification works into two categories: one is static verification, and the other is real-time verification.

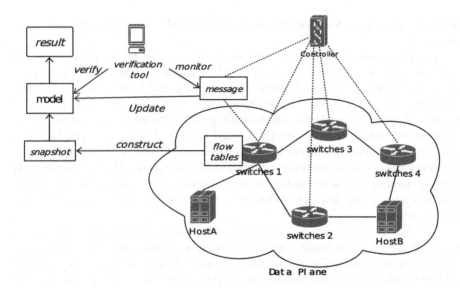

**Fig. 1.** Workflow of SDN data plane verification

### 2.1  Static Verification

The static verification of the SDN data plane is mainly to construct a snapshot at a certain moment by reading the flow table of the switch, and then build a model based on the snapshot, and then use a verification tool to check whether the model meets the defined rules, and then find possible data plane design.

Ehab et al. propose FlowChecker [2], which first applies model checking to SDN networks, and can accurately detect the correctness of the data plane. They code the flow tables as the Binary Decision Diagram (BDD), encode the forwarding rules as Boolean expressions. FlowChecker use the model checking tool NuSVM to verify the invariants of the network. Although FlowChecker can check the correctness of protocol deployment, its poor scalability indicated that it can only be used on small-scale networks.

Natali et al. propose a verification method based on the OpenFlow Specification. They propose a general OpenFlow switch model based on first-order logic. Use Alloy [19] to model and verify the OpenFlow switch, and finally use the SAT solver to solve it. It can well detect the violation of invariants such as black holes and forwarding loops, but it also has the common shortcomings of other model-based checking tools such as state space explosions, etc.

HSA [15], proposed by the Kazemian team, combines the formal methods and the network domain features to verify the data plane by checking the network boxes. First, it abstracts the data packet header as a subset of the geometric space, then uses the network transfer function and the topology transfer function to model different individual network boxes, and finally combines all the individual network boxes into a large network box, which contains all network behaviors. It can use several algorithms to check network invariants, such as reachability failure, loops, and so on. However, when the number of bits in the header space is large, the cost of exploring the header space state of an exponential packet is enormous.

Son et al. proposed FLOVER [20], a model checking system that verifies that the set of instantiated flow policies in an OpenFlow network does not violate the network security policy. They proposed a formal approach to demonstrate the consistency of dynamically generated OpenFlow flow rules with non-by-pass security attributes, including those with set and goto table actions. Using FLOVER, OpenFlow rules and network security policies are converted to an assertion set, which is then processed and validated by the SMT solver. FLOVER can detect violations that override and modify up to 200 rules in more than 100 ms.

Static verification summary: As SDN was just beginning to be known to the public, so the initial verification work was not much, and was limited to static verification. They all verify the accuracy of the network to a limited extent, but these tools find problems after the data plane goes wrong, these errors may have caused damage to the network. More importantly, static verification is not efficient and cannot be applied to dynamically change networks.

## 2.2   Real-Time Verification

The network changes with time due to the addition and deletion of the rules for the controller to issue the flow table. Previous tools were not sufficient to check the correctness of each network update. To implement real-time verification, it is necessary to get the continuous update in real-time and improve the performance of the verification methods. Fortunately, in SDN networks, forwarding rules can be obtained by monitoring the control messages, such as insertion, deletion, or modification, between the controller and switch, to achieve real-time verification.

VeriFlow [16], proposed by Khurshid, is the first real-time verification system that can check network invariants in a few hundred microseconds. It observes state changes between the control plane and the data plane, and dynamically checks the validity of network-wide invariants as each rule is inserted. The network is divided into a set of equivalent classes, and the packets belonging to the equivalent class go through the same forwarding path in the whole network. VeriFlow iterates through the paths of the equivalent classes to determine the state of one or more invariants. Then it can find where the failure occurred. However, when a rule has multiple matching fields to check, the number of equivalent classes may be too large for quick verification.

Different from VeriFlow, Yang et al. give a new method for the division of equivalence classes. They use PreCherker [9] to dynamically identify conflicting rules and classify them into equivalence classes. A multi-terminal BDD (MTBDD) structure is proposed to express the equivalent classes. This significantly improves the efficiency of network verification.

Kazemian et al. have improved on HSA and propose NetPlumber [14] a new real-time policy checking tool. They run HSA checks incrementally and use NetPlumber to check for updates in real-time. It does not have to write new code for each policy check like HSA. Once Netplumber detects the occurrence of an error, it prevents the new policy from taking effect Although it is generally fast enough, it takes a long time to update the dependency diagram when a link is up or down.

Yang et al. also inspired by HSA, proposes a new approach, NetV [10]. They redefine the rule function based on packet header space and present the BDD transformation and inverse transformation algorithm, which speeds up the rule updating, and can verify invariants among domains.

In the SDN real-time verification methods, there are some works based on atomic predicates. Atomic predicates, first proposed by the Yang [21] team, use atomic predicates to quickly calculate the intersection and union of data packets. The Zhang [26] team proposes a new verification method based on atomic predicates. First, the reachability of packets is verified, and then the reachability result of packets is used to verify the cyclic degree of freedom and the absence of black hole. In addition, they modeled the network as a directed graph, adopted the concept of atomic predicates. To improve scalability, they also proposed a parallel computing method Apache Spark to compute atomic predicates.

To solve the problem of a large number of equivalent classes that VeriFlow cannot solve, the Horn group proposes a new real-time data plane checker, Delta-net [13]. It does not construct multiple forwarding graphs to represent the packets in the network. Instead, the packets are incrementally transformed into a single edge-labelled graph that can represent all packet flows across the network. In addition, the first provable quasi-linear algorithm is proposed, which is influenced by Yang's atomic predicate verifier. The algorithm maintains the concept of atomic predicate incrementally. It analyzes all of the Boolean combinations of the IP prefix forwarding rules in the network with a set of disjoint packets.

Vermont [5], proposed by the Altukho team, is a set of tools for real-time verification. Vermont can be installed on the control plane. It intercepts the messages sent by the switch to the controller and the commands sent by the controller to the switch to observe the state changes of the network. It establishes an appropriate formal model of the entire network and checks each event, such as rule installation, deletion, or modification, against a set of formal requirements of the Packet Forwarding Policies (PFP). Before sending the network update command to the switch, Vermont predicts its execution and checks that the new network state meets the PFP. If this condition is met, the command will be passed to the corresponding switch. When a violation of the PFP is detected, VERMONT will prevent the change, warn the network administrator, and provide some additional information to locate the possible source of the error.

Due to the lack of detailed behavior of each hop, the previous work required a complicated fault location process. Zhao et al. proposed SERVE [27], a method that can automatically identify network problems in the data plane and periodically compare each rule and network behavior. SERVE provides all existing rules and generates a set of probes. After each probe is input, the actual network behavior of the output is compared with the expected network behavior of the control plane to verify the validity of each rule. They proposed a new detection generation method that can perform real-time verification in time when rules are added or deleted, which improves the verification efficiency. They considered the characteristics of pipeline processing and modeled the stateful multi-rooted tree (SMRT) in the network equipment of the data plane. The verification efficiency of SERVER is very high.

Summary of real-time verification: Formal real-time verification tools support real-time monitoring of the evolving SDN data plane of the network. They turn the packet reachability verification problem into a graph problem by modeling data packets or flow rules as graphs. This makes verification fast enough, but the existing tools each have different shortcomings, they cannot achieve all of the intended goals, such as good scalability, detection range, easy deployment, easy modeling, and detection speed. In addition, some hardware failures cannot be detected by these tools.

## 3   Testing

Data plane verification in the SDN network can check whether the devices of the data plane forward the packets according to the rules issued by the controller. However, switch failure may still exist, so it is necessary to test the data plane in the SDN network. Testing checks the forwarding behavior of each switch by generating probe data packets, thereby discovering failures in the data plane, as shown in Fig. 2. We divide this testing works into white-box testing and black-box testing according to the need for source code.

### 3.1   White-Box Testing

White-box testing needs to obtain source codes from the vendors to build formal models for checking the invariants of the data plane.

Zeng et al. propose ATPG [23], which is an automated and systematic method for testing data planes. ATPG reads the router configurations and builds a device-independent model which is used to generate a minimum set of test packets. Test packets are sent periodically to detect the failures. And then a mechanism will be triggered to locate the failures. Instead of matching rules, ATPG pays attention to whether the physical paths of the data plane are the same as the expected paths of the control plane policies. When the number of data packets exceeds a certain number, the detection speed will slow down.

Peter et al. propose Monocle [18], a system for monitoring the SDN data plane in real-time. Monocle is used as a proxy between the SDN controller and its corresponding switches, which allows Monocle to intercept all rules changes sent to any switch. Monocle maintain the desired global forwarding status on the network, and the expected content of the flow tables in each switch. After determining the expected state of the switches, Monocle can calculate the packet header space of running rules. Finally, Monocle injects these generated packets into the network as a proxy and sees how they are processed. But it requires a

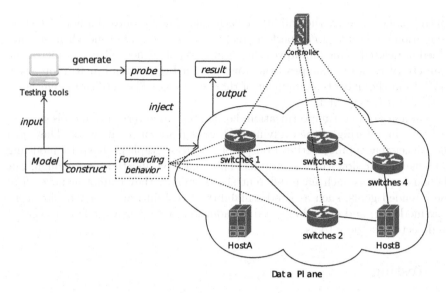

**Fig. 2.** Workflow of SDN data plane testing

Boolean satisfiability problem solution for each probe, resulting in slow probe generation. And when there are multiple missing rules associated with them, they may produce false negatives and do not support incremental probe updates.

Bu et al. propose RuleScope [8], a more comprehensive solution to check the transmission of SDN packets, mainly to detect rule missing fault and priority fault in switches. It checks the forwarding behavior with a probe, based on the established system. RuleScope accomplishes how to generate probe packets and how to handle the results of probes by introducing a monitoring application on the probe core. At the heart of the monitoring, the application is a set of algorithms they propose to detect and troubleshoot rules. However, RuleScope cannot handle rule updates, and its deployment scope is limited.

In response to previous deficiencies, Zhang et al. propose RuleChecker [24]. It is a fast SDN data plane testing tool. Unlike previous tools that solve the SAT problem by generating each probe for each data packet, RuleChecker takes the flow table as a whole and generates all probe data packets iteratively through a simple set operation. By encoding the set with a binary decision graph, RuleChecker is very fast. It is nearly 20 times faster than RuleScope and can update detections in 90.

White-box test summary: In SDN data plane formal testing, there are many methods based on white-box testing. In general, SDN data plane white-box testing can accurately detect and locate the errors, suitable for small and medium-sized networks. But it also has many shortages. On the one hand, not all source codes of data plane devices are available. On the other hand, for large networks, the model built from source codes has too many details and cost too much for testing.

## 3.2 Black-Box Testing

White box testing requires access to source code, but it is difficult for most users to obtain it, which gives white box testing certain limitations. Therefore, it is necessary to use black box testing without obtaining the source code during the testing.

Yao et al. [22] proposed a black-box testing method for the SDN data plane. They defined an extended finite state machine model for the pipeline to describe the OpenFlow switch. The data graph is extracted from the pipeline extended finite state machine model, and the data path that does not contain component details are searched on the data graph. This method can effectively reduce the cost. A leading sequence generation algorithm for I/O matching is proposed, which can process the components on each data path one by one. This method does not need to combine all the state machines in the model, thus effectively alleviating the space explosion.

Fayaz et al. proposed FlowTest [11], a test scheme for testing stateful and dynamic network strategies. They capture different DPFs by establishing abstract models, then model the network topology and forwarding strategies, and then use CBMC to generate counterexamples. Finally, these counterexamples are used as the input of the tracking generator to detect the fault and locate the location of the fault.

Fayaz et al. propose a stateful data plane testing framework BUZZ based on symbolic execution [12]. To establish an expressible and extensible data plane model, BUZZ introduces a novel network traffic abstraction called BUZZ Data Unit (BDU). It models network properties as a collection of finite state machines and triggers forwarding policies by generating test traffic. They also developed an optimized workflow based on symbolic execution to generate test traffic. To deal with the problem of state space explosion, they reduced the number and scope of symbolic variables. However, the process of BUZZ is too complicated, and it is easy to fail in the modeling process.

Summary of black-box testing: In this subsection, we introduce the SDN data plane black-box formal testing. We think that black-box testing is complementary to white-box testing. But due to the limitations of formal methods, and the strategic problems with their testing methods, they are not fast enough. In a word, the black-box testing of SDN data has made great progress, but the current testing method cannot deal with large-scale networks and hybrid networks well.

## 4  Future Research Prospects

At present, many works on formal testing and verification of SDN data planes has been recognized by the industry. But with the widespread deployment of SDN, the data plane will become more complex, so its accuracy and reliability will encounter more challenges. The current work urgently needs to be optimized, and their cost and time also need to be reduced. We divide the future development direction into the following three points. In the future, we will also work to combine AI and formal methods and apply them to the formal verification and testing of the SDN data plane. We learned that AI can effectively balance the load and improve quality of service (QoS) of SDN [7], and we will use it in combination with the related method proposed by some scholars. [4,6], thereby helping us to obtain more traffic.

(1) **AI-based model construct:** Model is the basis of formal verification and testing. Building a model requires specific knowledge. It is so difficult, that only computer experts can implement. This requirement hinders the promotion of formal methods in the industry. Some researchers are currently trying to use AI to assist model construction and have achieved preliminary results. They construct a concrete model based on the abstract model input by the user based on the AI method. We plan to apply AI-based model construct to the real-world SDN data plane verification and testing works. By comparing with existing expert modeling methods, this type of method is expected to gain advantages in ease of use and efficiency.

(2) **AI-based property definition:** In the formal method of verification and testing, researchers define attributes according to the general rules of the network. The attributes are further used as the basis for the correctness of verification and testing. So, defining attributes is very important. But defining attributes requires a lot of professional knowledge. This can only be done by highly professional people. We plan to apply AI-based property definition for formal verification and testing. By giving AI a small number of predefined attributes and network traffic, we let it learn independently and generate a large number of attributes that can be used for verification. Compared with the existing methods that completely define attributes by humans, this type of method is expected to gain advantages in accuracy and efficiency.

(3) **Scalable support for stateful data plane:** As SDN may enable richer network data processing services, the SDN network environment will be more complex and changeable. The correctness and reliability of the stateful data plane need more attention. As the scale of the data plane grows, the state space will become larger and larger, which brings challenges to the scalability of the model. For complex stateful data planes, a new formal model needs to be proposed to accurately describe the data plane while controlling the model scale.

## 5    Conclusion

Since 2010 when Flowchecker applied model checking to SDN data plane verification, more and more work has been done on SDN data plane formal verification and testing. In this paper, the existing works are divided into data plane verification and data plane testing. We have the following conclusions: data plane verification can find the defects of the data plane design in a short time and evaluate whether the design supports ideal invariants; data plane testing can check network behavior by generating probes to find implementation errors in the network. The current short-coming is that the manual construction of models and definitions of attributes re-quire professional knowledge, which hinders the promotion of formal verification and testing. And it needs to be improved in terms of verifying the stateful data plane. In the future, we will apply AI to assist modeling and attribute definition work, and make efforts to explore feasible verification and testing methods for stateful data planes.

**Acknowledgement.** This work was supported by the Hainan Provincial Natural Science Foundation of China (620RC562, 2019RC096, 620RC560), the Scientific Research Setup Fund of Hainan University (KYQD(ZR)1877), the Program of Hainan Association for Science and Technology Plans to Youth R&D Innovation (QCXM201910), and the National Natural Science Foundation of China (61802092, 62162021).

# References

1. Ahmad, S., Jamil, F., Ali, A., Khan, E., Ibrahim, M., Whangbo, T.K.: Effectively handling network congestion and load balancing in software-defined networking. CMC-Comput. Mater. Continua **70**(1), 1363–1379 (2022)
2. Al-Shaer, E., Al-Haj, S.: Flowchecker: Configuration analysis and verification of federated openflow infrastructures. In: Proceedings of the 3rd ACM workshop on Assurable and usable security configuration. pp. 37–44 (2010)
3. Alhaidari, F., et al.: Intelligent software-defined network for cognitive routing optimization using deep extreme learning machine approach (2021)
4. Ali, J., Roh, B.h.: Quality of service improvement with optimal software-defined networking controller and control plane clustering. CMC-Comput. Mater. Continua **67**(1), 849–875 (2021)
5. Altukhov, V., Podymov, V., Zakharov, V., Chemeritskiy, E.: Vermont-a toolset for checking SDN packet forwarding policies on-line. In: 2014 International Science and Technology Conference (Modern Networking Technologies) (MoNeTeC), pp. 1–6. IEEE (2014)
6. Babbar, H., Rani, S., Masud, M., Verma, S., Anand, D., Jhanjhi, N.: Load balancing algorithm for migrating switches in software-defined vehicular networks. Comput. Mater. Continue **67**(1), 1301–1316 (2021)
7. Belgaum, M.R., Ali, F., Alansari, Z., Musa, S., Alam, M.M., Mazliham, M.: Artificial intelligence based reliable load balancing framework in software-defined networks. CMC-Comput. Mater. Continua **70**(1), 251–266 (2022)
8. Bu, K., Wen, X., Yang, B., Chen, Y., Li, L.E., Chen, X.: Is every flow on the right track?: Inspect SDN forwarding with rulescope. In: IEEE INFOCOM 2016-The 35th Annual IEEE International Conference on Computer Communications, pp. 1–9. IEEE (2016)
9. Fang, Y., Lu, Y.: Checking intra-switch conflicts of rules during preprocessing of network verification in SDN. IEEE Commun. Lett. **23**(9), 1547–1550 (2019)
10. Fang, Y., Lu, Y.: Real-time verification of network properties based on header space. IEEE Access **8**, 36789–36806 (2020)
11. Fayaz, S.K., Sekar, V.: Testing stateful and dynamic data planes with flowtest. In: Proceedings of the Third Workshop on Hot Topics in Software Defined Networking, pp. 79–84 (2014)

12. Fayaz, S.K., Yu, T., Tobioka, Y., Chaki, S., Sekar, V.: {BUZZ}: Testing context-dependent policies in stateful networks. In: 13th {USENIX} Symposium on Networked Systems Design and Implementation ({NSDI} 2016), pp. 275–289 (2016)
13. Horn, A., Kheradmand, A., Prasad, M.: Delta-net: real-time network verification using atoms. In: 14th {USENIX} Symposium on Networked Systems Design and Implementation ({NSDI} 17), pp. 735–749 (2017)
14. Kazemian, P., Chang, M., Zeng, H., Varghese, G., McKeown, N., Whyte, S.: Real time network policy checking using header space analysis. In: 10th {USENIX} Symposium on Networked Systems Design and Implementation ({NSDI} 2013), pp. 99–111 (2013)
15. Kazemian, P., Varghese, G., McKeown, N.: Header space analysis: static checking for networks. In: 9th {USENIX} Symposium on Networked Systems Design and Implementation ({NSDI} 12), pp. 113–126 (2012)
16. Khurshid, A., Zou, X., Zhou, W., Caesar, M., Godfrey, P.B.: VeriFlow: verifying network-wide invariants in real time. In: 10th {USENIX} Symposium on Networked Systems Design and Implementation ({NSDI} 2013), pp. 15–27 (2013)
17. Mai, H., Khurshid, A., Agarwal, R., Caesar, M., Godfrey, P.B., King, S.T.: Debugging the data plane with anteater. ACM SIGCOMM Comput. Commun. Rev. 41(4), 290–301 (2011)
18. Perešíni, P., Kuzniar, M., Kostić, D.: Rule-level data plane monitoring with monocle. ACM SIGCOMM Comput. Commun. Rev. 45(4), 595–596 (2015)
19. Ruchansky, N., Proserpio, D.: A (not) nice way to verify the openflow switch specification: formal modelling of the openflow switch using alloy. In: Proceedings of the ACM SIGCOMM 2013 Conference on SIGCOMM, pp. 527–528 (2013)
20. Son, S., Shin, S., Yegneswaran, V., Porras, P., Gu, G.: Model checking invariant security properties in openflow. In: 2013 IEEE International Conference on Communications (ICC), pp. 1974–1979. IEEE (2013)
21. Yang, H., Lam, S.S.: Scalable verification of networks with packet transformers using atomic predicates. IEEE/ACM Trans. Network. 25(5), 2900–2915 (2017)
22. Yao, J., Wang, Z., Yin, X., Shiyz, X., Wu, J.: Formal modeling and systematic black-box testing of SDN data plane. In: 2014 IEEE 22nd International Conference on Network Protocols, pp. 179–190. IEEE (2014)
23. Zeng, H., Kazemian, P., Varghese, G., McKeown, N.: Automatic test packet generation. In: Proceedings of the 8th International Conference on Emerging Networking Experiments and Technologies, pp. 241–252 (2012)
24. Zhang, P., Zhang, C., Hu, C.: Fast data plane testing for software-defined networks with rulechecker. IEEE/ACM Trans. Network. 27(1), 173–186 (2018)
25. Zhang, S., Malik, S.: SAT based verification of network data planes. In: Van Hung, D., Ogawa, M. (eds.) ATVA 2013. LNCS, vol. 8172, pp. 496–505. Springer, Cham (2013). https://doi.org/10.1007/978-3-319-02444-8_43
26. Zhang, Y., Li, J., Kimura, S., Zhao, W., Das, S.K.: Atomic predicates-based data plane properties verification in software defined networking using spark. IEEE J. Sel. Areas Commun. 38(7), 1308–1321 (2020)
27. Zhao, Y., Zhang, P., Wang, Y., Jin, Y.: Troubleshooting data plane with rule verification in software-defined networks. IEEE Trans. Netw. Serv. Manag. 15(1), 232–244 (2017)

# A Blockchain-Assisted Key Generation Electric Health Records Sharing Scheme

Qiao Zhang[2], Xiubo Chen[1,2], Haseeb Ahmad[3], Gang Xu[1,4(✉)], and Yixian Yang[2]

[1] Guizhou Provincial Key Laboratory of Public Big Data, GuiZhou University, Guizhou 550025, Guiyang, China
gangxu_bupt@163.com

[2] State Key Laboratory of Networking and Switching Technology, Information Security Center, Beijing University of Posts and Telecommunications, Beijing 100876, China

[3] Department of Computer Science, National Textile University, Faisalabad 37610, Pakistan

[4] School of Information Science and Technology, North China University of Technology, Beijing 100144, China

**Abstract.** Electronic health records (EHRs) contain a large amount of private data of patients. Once these data are compromised during the process of sharing, it may threaten the patients' privacy. In this paper, a novel blockchain-assisted electronic health record sharing scheme is proposed, which utilizes attribute-based encryption (ABE) based on the consortium blockchain to realize the privacy protection in the sharing process of EHRs. Firstly, the master key is negotiated by all consensus nodes of consortium blockchain, no one knows the specific value of the master key. Consensus nodes are acted by medical institutions, they also responsible for generating and managing users' private keys. Secondly, with the help of powerful cloud services, pre-decryption and ciphertext retrieval assignments are outsourced to cloud services for reducing the burden of blockchain. Thirdly, this scheme is also based on searchable encryption, which allows for quick ciphertext lookup from cloud services. Data owners can generate ciphertext indexes for their private data, and data users with retrieval trapdoors can quickly retrieve ciphertexts. Finally, the security and performance of blockchain-assisted electronic health record sharing scheme are analyzed in detail, the results show that our scheme is safe and feasible.

**Keywords:** Blockchain · Electronic health records · Attribute-based encryption · Data sharing

## 1 Introduction

With the development of technology in healthcare systems, the scale of medical data has grown rapidly. Among them, EHRs [1] are widely used because they contain all health data of patients, including medical records, medications, and experience reports, etc. In the traditional medical system, EHRs are stored on the internal networks of medical institutions [2] and managed by dedicated internal staff only, resulting in the following problems. On the one hand, the EHRs data between different medical institutions do not interoperate, which triggers the data island effect. Patients need to carry multiple

X. Sun et al. (Eds.): ICAIS 2022, CCIS 1588, pp. 145–157, 2022.
https://doi.org/10.1007/978-3-031-06764-8_12

copies of cases for inter-hospital visits, which brings inconvenience to the cross-hospital diagnosis and treatment [3]. On the other hand, EHRs are used without the patients' consent, which may lead to the leakage of patient privacy. Furthermore, EHRs data are also of great value and easy to be attacked by attackers [4]. To address the above issues and enable secure sharing of EHRs data, a challenging problem is how to achieve fine-grained access control for patients to their EHRs.

ABE is one of the most effective methods to ensure confidentiality while achieving fine-grained access control. ABE was first proposed by Sahai et al. [5], which refers to that the ciphertext can only be decrypted if it meets specific attribute requirements. When in the healthcare system, patients can set adequate attributes for their EHRs data to allow access, such as attending hematologist, nurse-in-charge, etc. Doctors can take their access control structure to match the attributes set by patients. Once the patients' attribute requirements are met, doctors can decrypt and access the data. Blockchain was first proposed by Nakamoto [6] in 2008. It is considered to be a distributed database [7] with decentralization, transparency, and non-tamper ability. There is a special program that can interact with the blockchain called smart contract [8]. It can execute automatically according to a pre-determined program. Since the execution process does not require the involvement of a third party, the results of the execution of smart contracts are trusted. To enable secure sharing of EHRs, the existing solutions [2, 9–13] mainly use ABE for fine-grained access control, where encrypted data are stored on a special server and all access actions are recorded on the blockchain with a smart contract. Wang et al. [2] proposed a C-AB/IB-ES scheme combined with ABE and Identity-based encryption (IBE) to achieve access control. In their scheme, patients first sign their data using Identity-Based Signatures (IBS) to ensure data integrity. All data are stored on a healthcare cloud server and the encryption process is handled by the hospital. Wang et al. [9] believed that the patient can also be the subject of access control. The patient generates and distributes the attribute private key to those who are allowed to access it. And the smart contract records the list of users who are allowed to access it. Huang et al. [10] write every query and write operations of EHRs into the blockchain, which ensures traceability. Naresh et al. [11] utilize the consortium chain to store the hash value of EHRs to ensure integrity. Searchable encryption [14] technology can realize fast retrieval of ciphertext without revealing the plaintext. When there are large-scale encrypted EHRs stored on the server, searchable encryption can be used to accelerate the search. Reference [12, 13] also combines searchable encryption into attribute encryption to improve the speed of ciphertext retrieval. In these schemes, the blockchain is used only as a decentralized database to store access records, not involved in trusted computing. And they all rely on a centralized third-party authority to generate and manage the private keys. In reality, there is no guarantee that a third-party authorized authority will always be credible.

With the rise of the cloud servers, some services related to EHRs are transferred to cloud servers. Cloud servers are generally considered to have the unlimited computing power and can perform assigned tasks as required. The low price, as well as infinite storage space have drawn more people's attention. They [15–18] store the encrypted data on it, or use cloud services to assist in computing. Hua et al. [15] pointed out that the EHRs ought to be outsourced to cloud for storage after encryption, which ensures patients' privacy safety while reducing the strain on local systems. To address the issue of high computational overhead in ABE decryption, Zhang et al. [16] proposed a matching stage before decryption scheme, which improves decryption efficiency for outsourced data storage in cloud computing. IPFS is also one of cloud storage services. It allows data to be shared across multiple organizations while also avoiding single points of failure. References [17, 18] store the encrypted data on IPFS. Despite the tremendous benefits, security and privacy remain cloud servers' most important considerations. On the one hand, cloud servers allow access on the public network, which means that an attacker can also access the data. On the other hand, cloud services are often provided by third parties. It is unknown whether third-party institutions are always credible [19, 20]. Hence, the security of cloud services is significant and worth considering.

Through the analysis of the existing schemes, we remark that the security of the existing EHRs sharing systems is mostly based on a centralized third-party authority. However, a single third-party authority will also have a single point of failure, especially, it's difficult to find an always trusted third-party authority in reality. To address this problem, we propose a blockchain-assisted key generation EHRs sharing scheme. Our specific contributions are listed below.

1. We propose a EHRs sharing scheme without the third-party trusted authorized authority. Compared with the existing EHRs scheme, our scheme removes the third-party trusted authorized authority. Medical institutions play the role of consortium chain nodes to realize the safe sharing of EHRs among them. We use the consortium blockchain nodes to generate and manage the master key and attribute private key. All access operations need to be recorded on the chain.
2. In our scheme, we outsource the attribute pre-decryption and ciphertext retrieval assignments that consume a lot of computing power to the cloud servers, which takes pressure off the blockchain system while ensuring security.
3. We propose a EHRs sharing scheme also based on a searchable encryption. Data users with search trapdoors can retrieve data quickly from cloud servers.
4. The proposed scheme is feasible in practice. We implement our scheme based on the open-source cryptographic library and build a consortium blockchain network on Hyperledger Fabric. Performance analysis shows that our scheme can achieve fine-grained access control and fast decryption of EHRs.

The structure of this paper is as follows: Sect. 2 briefly introduced the basic knowledge. Our scheme architecture, system procedure, and security model are presented in Sect. 3. We introduced our scheme in detail in Sect. 4. After security proof and performance analysis in Sect. 5, we summarize the scheme in the last section.

## 2 Preliminaries

### 2.1 Bilinear Map

For two cyclic groups $G_a$ and $G_b$ with prime order $p$. Suppose that $e : G_a \times G_a \rightarrow G_b$ is a general map, we call $e$ as a bilinear map [21] if $e$ satisfies the following three properties.

- Bilinearity: $e(g_1^a, g_2^b) = e(g_1, g_2)^{ab}$ for all $g_1$, $g_2 \in G_a$ and $a$, $b \in Z_p$.

- Non-degeneracy: There exits $g_1$, $g_2 \in G_a$ such that $e(g_1, g_2) \neq 1$, where 1 is the unit of $G_b$.
- Computability: For all $g_1$, $g_2 \in G_a$, $e(g_1, g_2)$ can be calculated quickly in a polynomial-time.

### 2.2 Pedersen $(k, N)$ Secret Share (PSS)

Suppose there are $n$ participants $P_1$, $P_2$, $P_3$..., $P_n$ who are equal to each other. They select a sub-secret $S_i$ respectively, and all sub-secrets add up to the main secret $S$ in the form of an algebraic sum. Denote $G_p$ is a finite field with a large prime order $p$. The Pedersen $(k, n)$ Secret Share [22] protocol is composed of the next four steps.

1. Main-secret production: Each participant picks a random number $N_i \in Z_p$ as the sub-secret, and adds them to generate the main-secret $S$ by Eq. (1).

$$S = \sum_{i=1}^{n} N_i \tag{1}$$

2. Sub-share production: All participants independently execute the Shamir secret sharing algorithm [23]. Each participant $P_j$ randomly selects a $k$-1 degree of polynomial $f_j(x)$ and sets $f_j(0) = N_j$. Then, $P_j$ computes $n$ sub-shares $ss_{ji} = f_j(x_i)$ for $i = 1, 2, 3..., n$ and sends $ss_{ji}$ to $P_i$ through a secret channel.

3. Main-share production: After receiving $n$ sub-share $ss_{ij}$ for $i = 1, 2, 3..., n$, $P_j$ calculates its master-share $ms_j$ with Eq. (2).

$$ms_j = \sum_{i=1}^{n} ss_{ij} \tag{2}$$

4. Main-secret recovery: If there are more than $k$ participants $P_i \in P_R$, the main-secret can be recovered with Eq. (3).

$$S = \sum_{P_i \in P_R} ms_i \prod_{P_j, P_i \in P_R, j \neq i} \frac{j}{j - i} (\mathrm{mod} p) \tag{3}$$

### 2.3 Decision Bilinear Diffie-Hellman (DBDH) Assumption

Let $G$ and $G_T$ be two cyclic groups with prime order $p$, and $e$ is a bilinear map. Randomly select $x$, $y$, $z \in Z_p$ and $T \in G_T$, denote $X = g^x$, $Y = g^y$, $Z = g^z$. It is difficult to determine whether $T$ is equal to $e(g, g)^{xyz}$ in any probabilistic polynomial-time [24].

## 3  System Design

### 3.1  System Architecture

The architecture of our scheme is shown in Fig. 1, which contains five participants, BC, Patients, IPFS, CSP, Data Users and CSP.

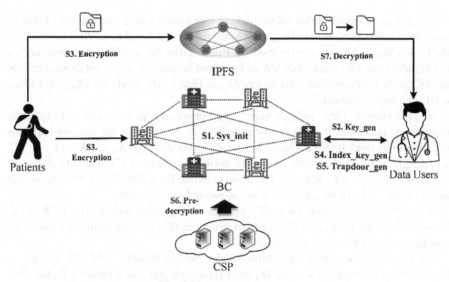

**Fig. 1.** System architecture.

BC: A consortium blockchain composed of multiple medical institutions including regulatory authorities. BC is responsible for generating and managing the master key and users' private keys. And it is also in charge of assigning outsourced decryption or retrieval assignments, and recording all users' operations on the chain.

Patients: The data owner in the system. After the treatment in the hospital, patients get medical data from the doctor, such as their own cases or medication status. Then they select appropriate keywords and attribute sets according to the data content. After encrypting the data and calculating the index, patients upload the encrypted data to IPFS, index to BC for recording.

DU: Data user in the system. DU can be doctors in other hospitals, staff from regulatory authorities, etc. If attribute set embedded in DU's access structure satisfies the patient's attribute requirement, he/she can obtain the Patient's data. At the same time, DU can also generate search trapdoors to search ciphertexts.

CSP: Cloud service provider. It is responsible for the index-retrieval and pre-decryption tasks assigned by BC. We assume that CSP has high computing power and always keeps online. In addition, we suppose that CSP is honest and curious about security.

IPFS: The IPFS is built by multiple medical institutions. We use IPFS to store EHRs from various healthcare facilities, avoiding the single point of failure associated with centralized storage.

### 3.2 System Procedure

S1. *System initialization*: All blockchain nodes perform $SysInit(1^{\lambda}) \rightarrow (MK, PK)$ to generate the public key $PK$ and master key $MK$. Especially, $MK$ is generated through all blockchain nodes by PSS protocol, no one knows the exact master key value.

S2. *Key generation*: In this subsection, all blockchain nodes generate two kinds of keys: outsourced private key $SK_{out}$ and attribute private key $SK_{attr}$. $KeyGen(\mathbb{A}, PK, MK) \rightarrow (SK_{attr}, SK_{out})$ is performed by BC. It takes the user's access structure $\mathbb{A}$, global public key $PK$, master key $MK$ as input and outputs the user's outsourced private key $SK_{out}$, the user's attribute private key $SK_{attr}$. Finally, BC sends the $SK_{attr}$ and $SK_{out}$ to DU in a secret channel.

S3. *Encryption*: First, patients select appropriate access attributes and keywords according to data content. Then he/she runs AES encryption over the data, and uploads the AES ciphertext to IPFS. Next, he/she executes $Encrypt(K_{aes}, PK, w) \rightarrow CT$ for fine-grained access control, and gets attribute ciphertext CT. Patients also execute $IndexGen(PK, CT, KW) \rightarrow Ix(kw)$ to generate the index $Ix(kw)$. Finally, he/she submits tuple $(CT, Ix(kw))$ to BC for recording and latter search.

S4. *Index key generation*: First, BC executes the algorithm $IndexKeyGen(PK, BF_\beta, \mathbb{A}) \rightarrow IK$. Among them, $\mathbb{A}$ is DU's access structure, $BF_\beta$ is a commitment value. This algorithm outputs the query private key $IK$.

S5. *Trapdoor generation*: DU performs the algorithm $TrapDoor(PK, IK, kw, \beta) \rightarrow Td_{kw}$. Among the inputs, $kw$ is the keyword for search and $\beta$ is a blinding factor. This algorithm outputs the trapdoor $Td_{kw}$.

S6. *Pre-decryption*: Pre-decryption is run by CSR. Firstly, DU submits trapdoor $Td_{kw}$ to BC. Then BC commissions CSR to execute the algorithm $Search(Td_{kw}, (CT, Ix(kw))) \rightarrow \bot/CT$. If keywords in $Td_{kw}$ satisfies one of the index-set of $Ix(kw)$, CSR will run $Pre-decrypt(CT, PK, SK_{out}) \rightarrow Q_{pre}$ to gain partial ciphertext $Q_{pre}$ and return it to BC. Finally, BC sends $Q_{pre}$ to DU.

S7. *Local decryption*: After receiving the partial ciphertext $Q_{pre}$, DU executes algorithm $Decrypt(Q_{pre}, CT, PK, SK_{attr}) \rightarrow K_{aes}$ to obtain AES key $K_{aes}$. Then, DU downloads the ciphertext from IPFS, decrypts it with $K_{aes}$, and verifies its integrity.

### 3.3  Security Model

The security requirement for our blockchain-assisted key generation electric health records sharing scheme is based on Li et al.' scheme [25]. The difference is that we use blockchain to generate and manage all keys, and there are no curious KG-CSP and TypeII-Adversary in [25]. Replayable chosen ciphertext attack (RCCA) security was put forward in [26], which allows modifying the ciphertext, and cannot effectively change the implicit information. The adversary $\mathscr{A}$ can be described as a malicious DU, it will conspire with curious CSR to decrypt the data stored on the cloud servers. The $\mathscr{A}$ is permitted to obtain all users' outsourced private key $SK_{out}$ and trapdoor $Td_{kw}$. The definition of the game between challenger and adversary $\mathscr{A}$ is as follows.

*Setup:*  Challenger executes the System initialization method in Sect. 3.1 to get $PK$ and $MK$. Then the challenger sends $PK$ to $\mathscr{A}$ and saves $MK$ as a secret.

*Query Phase:*  Challenger first creates an empty collection $C$ and the adversary $\mathscr{A}$ repeatedly initiate the following queries:

1. KeysGeneration. Upon receiving an access structure $\mathbb{A}$, challenger runs key-generation algorithm to get $SK_{attr}$ and $SK_{out}$. Challenger stores key tuple ($SK_{attr}$, $SK_{out}$) with $\mathbb{A}$ in collection $C$ and sends it to $\mathscr{A}$.
2. TdGeneration. After receiving an access structure $\mathbb{A}$, challenger performs $IndexKeyGen(PK, BF_\beta, \mathbb{A}) \rightarrow IK$ and $TrapDoor(PK, IK, kw, \beta) \rightarrow Td_{kw}$ to generate a trapdoor $Td_{kw}$. Challenger stores $Td_{kw}$ in collection C and sends $Td_{kw}$ to $\mathscr{A}$.
3. Decrypt. After receiving $\mathbb{A}$ and ciphertext tuple ($CT$, $Q_{pre}$), challenger checks whether the access structure exits in the tuple ($\mathbb{A}$, ($SK_{attr}$, $SK_{out}$), $Td_{kw}$) of collection $C$. If so, it executes algorithm $Decrypt(Q_{pre}, CT, PK, SK_{attr})$ and sends $K_{aes}$ to $\mathscr{A}$. Else, it returns null value.

*Challenge:* The adversary $\mathscr{A}$ sends two plaintexts $M_0, M_1$ of equal length and a challenging attribute set $w^*$ to challenger. It should be noted that $w^*$ can't satisfy the access structure $\mathbb{A}$. The challenger chooses $\mu \in \{0, 1\}$, and runs $Encrypt(M_\mu, PK, w) \rightarrow CT$. Then challenger returns the challenge ciphertext $CT$ to the adversary.

*Restrictions:*

Since $w^*$ can't satisfy the access structure $\mathbb{A}$, the adversary $\mathscr{A}$ can't launch the KeysGeneration algorithm.

The adversary $\mathscr{A}$ can't launch TdGeneration query that the result equals to neither $M_0$ nor $M_1$.

*Guess:* The adversary $\mathscr{A}$ gives a guess $\mu' \in \{0, 1\}$ for $\mu$.

Our scheme can meet RCCA-security. If the adversary's advantage in winning the game is negligible at best in any polynomial-time, such as $\left|P(\mu' = \mu) - \frac{1}{2}\right| < \varepsilon$.

## 4 System Scheme

Before introducing the detailed definition of the system, we firstly define the Lagrange coefficient $\Delta_{i,S}(x) = \sum_{i=0}^{n-1} S(i) \prod_{j \in S, i \neq j} \frac{x-j}{i-j}$ for $i, j \in S$, $n$ is the length of $S$.

Our scheme is based on the Outsourced Attribute-based Encryption (OABE) [25] and the tree-based access structure. The user's private key contains a tree-based access structure $\mathbb{A}$, the attribute set $w$ is embedded in ciphertext, and $U$ is the set of all attributes, $d$ is a pre-set threshold value. If $\gamma(w, \mathbb{A}) = 1$, $S$ is an attribute set that satisfies $S \in \{w \cap \mathbb{A}\} \wedge |S| = d$. Based on the above structure, we use blockchain to take the place of authorized authority (AA) to generate and manage the user's private key, and add integrity verification phase in the scheme.

*SysInit*($1^\lambda$): All blockchain nodes of BC run this algorithm, and $\lambda$ is a secure parameter. BC chooses two multiplicative cyclic groups of prime order $p$: $G_a$ with generator $g$, $G_b$, and a bilinear map $e : e(G_a, G_a) = G_b$. Each consensus node of BC cooperates to generate a parameter $x \in Z_p$ by the PSS protocol. BC calculates $g_1 = g^x$, randomly chooses $g_2$, $h \in Z_p$. BC chooses $\{u_i \in U\}_{0 < i \leq n} \in Z_p$ to build the attribute universal $U$ with length $n$. BC also selects secure hash functions: $H_a : \{0, 1\}^* \rightarrow Z_p, H_b : G_b \rightarrow \{0,$

$1\}^{\log p}$. Finally, BC sets $PK = \{G_a, G_b, g, g_1, g_2, h, \{u_i\}_{0<i\leq n}, H_a, H_b\}$, $MK = x$, and publishes $PK$ as the global public key, keeps the $MK$ as a secret.

$KeyGen(\mathbb{A}, PK, MK)$: This algorithm is run by blockchain nodes of BC. When receiving the access structure $\mathbb{A}$, BC selects a random value $x_a \in Z_p$ and calculates $x_b = x - x_a \bmod p$. Then BC randomly selects a $d - 1$ degree of polynomial $f(x)$ and sets $f(0) = x_a$. For $i \in \mathbb{A}$, BC randomly chooses $\forall r_i \in Z_p$, calculates $d_{i_0} = g_2^{f(i)}(g_1 h_i)^{r_i}$, and $d_{i_1} = g^{r_i}$. Denote DU's outsourced private key $SK_{out} = \{d_{i_0}, d_{i_1}\}_{i\in\mathbb{A}}$. Next, BC computes $d_{\theta_0} = g_2^{x_b}(g_1 h)^{r_\varphi}$ and $d_{\theta_1} = g^{r_\varphi}$ where $r_\varphi \in Z_p$. Denote $\varphi$ as the default attribute. Let DU's attributed private key $SK_{attr} = \{d_{\theta_0}, d_{\theta_1}\}$. Finally, BC returns $SK_{attr}$, $SK_{out}$ to DU in a secret channel.

$IndexKeyGen(PK, BF_\beta, \mathbb{A})$: On receiving index-key generation request with DU's access structure $\mathbb{A}$ and a commitment $BF_\beta = g_2^{1/\beta}$ (DU randomly chooses $\beta \in Z_p$ and keeps it as secret). BC searches $(g_1 h)^{r_\varphi}$ associated with $\mathbb{A}$ and calculates $IK = g_2^{x/\beta}(g_1 h)^{r_\varphi}$. Then BC returns the IK to DU.

$Encrypt(K_{aes}, PK, w)$: After treatment, patients get their case plaintext $PT$ from the doctor. Patients use AES encryption PT with random $K_{aes} \in G_2$ to obtain AES ciphertext $M'$, compute $H_a(PT) = h'$, and update $M'$ to IPFS to get IPFS address $p'$. Patients choose an attribute set $w$ associated with PT. Patients also choose $\eta \in Z_p$ randomly and compute $C_0 = K_{aes}e(g_1, g_2)^\eta$, $C_1 = g^\eta$, $C_i = (g_1 h_i)^\eta$ for $i \in w$, and $C_\varphi = (g_1 h)^\eta$. Denote ciphertext $CT = (\omega \cup \{\varphi\}, C_0, C_1, \{C_i\}_{i\in\omega}, C_\varphi)$.

$IndexGen(PK, CT, KW)$: According to the ciphertext $CT$, patients select the appropriate keyword set $KW$. For each keyword $i \in KW$, patients compute $k_i = e(g_1, g_2)^\eta \cdot e(g, H_a(kw_i))^\eta \in G_2$ and let $K_i = H_b(k_i)$. Patients also let $K_1 = C_1 = g^\eta$, $K_2 = C_\theta = (g_1 h)^\eta$ and $Ix(KW) = (K_1, K_2, K_i)$. Patients send $(CT, Ix(KW))$ with $h'$, $p'$ to BC, then BC sends $(CT, Ix(KW))$ to CSR.

$TrapDoor(PK, IK, kw, \beta)$: To generate trapdoor $Td_{kw}$ with keyword $kw$. DU computes $T_q(kw) = H_a(kw)IK^\beta$, $D_1 = d_{\theta_1}^\mu$ and let $I = (I_{i_0} = d_{i_0}, I_{i_1} = d_{i_1})$, $Td_{kw} = (T_q(kw), I, D_1)$.

$Search(Td_{kw}, (CT, Ix(kw)))$: This algorithm is run by CSR, it runs Eq. (5) to get $k_{kw}$.

$$
\begin{aligned}
k_{kw} &= \frac{e(K_1, T_q(kw))}{e(D_1, K_2)} \\
&= \frac{e(g^\eta, H_a(kw)g_2^x(g_1 h)^{r_\varphi \mu})}{e(g^{r_\theta \mu}, (g_1 h)^\eta)} \\
&= \frac{e(g^x, g_2) \cdot e(g, H_a(kw))^\eta \cdot e(g^\eta, (g_1 h)^{r_\varphi \mu})}{e(g^{r_\varphi \mu}, (g_1 h)^\eta)} \\
&= e(g, g_2)^{\eta x} \cdot e(g, H_a(kw))^\eta
\end{aligned}
\tag{4}
$$

Then computes $H_b(k_{kw})$ and compares it with each of $K_i$ in index $Ix$. If equals, CSR then tries to run pre-decrypt algorithm. Else CSR returns null value.

$Pre - decrypt(CT, PK, SK_{out})$: BC sends $CT, PK, SK_{out}$ to CSR. If attributes in ciphertext match with $\mathbb{A}$ that corresponding to $SK_{out}$ ($SK_{out}$ can be found in $Ix(KW)$), CSR performs Eq. (5) to gain the pre-decrypted ciphertext $Q_{pre}$, then CSR returns it to BC. Otherwise, CSR returns none. BC takes $Q_{pre}$ with $h'$, $p'$, and returns them to DU.

*Decrypt*($Q_{pre}$, *CT*, *PK*, $SK_{attr}$): After receiving $Q_{pre}$ from CSR, DU first performs Eq. (6) to get $K_{aes}$. Then he/she downloads AES ciphertext $M'$ with $p'$, runs AES decryption, and gains plaintext $PH'$. DU compares $H_a(PH')$ with $h'$. If equals, indicating that $PH'$ has not been tampered with, otherwise $PH'$ will be discarded.

$$Q_{pre} = \frac{\prod_{i \in S} e(C_1, I_{i_0})^{\Delta_{i,s}(0)}}{\prod_{i \in S} e(I_{i_1}, C_i)^{\Delta_{i,s}(0)}}$$

$$= \frac{\prod_{i \in S} e(g^\eta, g_2^{f(i)}(g_1 h_i)^{r_i})^{\Delta_{i,s}(0)}}{\prod_{i \in S} e(g^{r_i}, (g_1 h_i)^\eta)^{\Delta_{i,s}(0)}}$$

$$= \frac{\prod_{i \in S} e(g^\eta, g_2)^{f(i)\Delta_{i,s}(0)} \cdot \prod_{i \in S} e(g^\eta, (g_1 h_i)^{r_i})^{\Delta_{i,s}(0)}}{\prod_{i \in S} e(g^{r_i}, (g_1 h_i)^\eta)^{\Delta_{i,s}(0)}}$$

$$= e(g, g_2)^{\eta x_a} \tag{5}$$

$$K_{aes} = \frac{C_0 \cdot e(d_{\theta_1}, C_\theta)}{Q_{pre} \cdot e(C_1, d_{\theta_0})}$$

$$= \frac{K_{aes} e(g_1, g_2)^\eta \cdot e(g^{r_\varphi}, (g_1 h)^\eta)}{e(g, g_2)^{s x_a} \cdot e(g^s, g_2^{x_b}(g_1 h)^{r_\varphi})}$$

$$= \frac{K_{aes} e(g^x, g_2)^\eta \cdot e(g^{r_\varphi}, (g_1 h)^\eta)}{e(g, g_2)^{\eta x_a} \cdot e(g^\eta, g_2^{x_b}) \cdot e(g^\eta, (g_1 h)^{r_\varphi})}$$

$$= \frac{K_{aes} e(g^x, g_2)^\eta \cdot e(g^{r_\varphi}, (g_1 h)^\eta)}{e(g, g_2)^{\eta(x_a + x_b)} \cdot e(g^\eta, (g_1 h)^{r_\varphi})} \tag{6}$$

## 5   Security and Performance Analysis

### 5.1   Security Proof

Compare with the scheme [25], our scheme utilizes distributed consortium blockchain rather than a centralized trusted authority to generate, manage master key and secret keys. We assume the consortium blockchain nodes always keep honest. Although there are some nodes that may betray, due to the PSS protocol, as long as no more than $n$ nodes defected at the same time, the security of master key MK can still be guaranteed. The security of PSS protocol has been proved in [22]. We also use the integrity verification algorithm to check whether the data is tampered with.

Suppose that CSR is curious about security, with the help of available resources, CSR can recovery $e(g, g_2)^{\eta x_a}$. But it still can't restore $e(g_1, g_2)^\eta$ without getting $x_b$ from $SK_{attr}$. Under certain circumstances, the curious CSR and malicious user may collude to decrypt others' data. However, due to the random division of $MK$, this collusion attack could be defended. Specifically, $MK$ is randomly divided into different $x_a$ and $x_b$ for each user, and $x_a + x_b = x \mod p$. $x_a$ is used for generating $SK_{out}$, and $x_b$ for $SK_{attr}$. If and only if $SK_{out}$ matches with $SK_{attr}$, the ciphertext can be fully decrypted. Therefore, although CSR can get all users' $SK_{out}$, it cannot decrypt others' ciphertexts without corresponding $SK_{attr}$.

*Theorem* 1: Our scheme is RCCA security if DBDH problem can't be solved in any polynomial-time.

The proof of security is not our main content, for a more detailed proof to outsourced attribute-based encryption, refer to Li et al. in [25]. Next, we give the security analysis to demonstrate the security of our system.

## 5.2 Security Analysis

*Confidentiality:* Our scheme can meet the confidentiality requirements. Firstly, the patients' EHRs are encrypted by AES with a random AES key, and the ciphertext is uploaded to IPFS for sharing. AES is a popular symmetric encryption algorithm whose security depends on the security of the AES key. However, the AES key is encrypted by attribute encryption. DU can obtain the AES key only if the attribute requirements set by the patients are met, then DU download the ciphertext from IPFS and decrypt it. The AES key is random for every ciphertext, even though DU decrypts a ciphertext, they cannot decrypt other ciphertext of this patient.

*Integrity:* Comparing with [25], we have added an integrity verification step. Before encrypting EHRs, patients use the hash function like SHA-1 to calculate the message digest. After that, the message digest will be uploaded to the blockchain for recording. After DU downloads the decrypted data, the digest is calculated in the same way. Only if it is the same as the digest stored on the blockchain, which shows that the patients' data has not been tampered with.

*Non-repudiation:* In our scheme, blockchain is the central authority. All encryption, decryption, and access operations are recorded on blockchain. Because the data on the blockchain can't be tampered, it is always possible to determine who accessed what data and when by querying the blockchain.

## 5.3 Performance Analysis

Our scheme is based on the java pairing-based cryptography library (JPBC) of version 1.2.1. For the consortium blockchain, we use version 1.4.4 of Hyperledger Fabric to build. And version 1.4.4 of fabric-java-sdk is used to execute the contract. More specifically, our system is deployed on a 64-bit Ubuntu 20.04 system with 3.4 GHz i7-6700 CPU and 8G RAM. Consortium blockchain architecture is configured for 2 organizations with total of 4 nodes, which can represent 4 medical institutions in 2 sectors. In terms of security, the elliptic curve in our scheme uses the default parameters provided by JPBC, which are based on the curve $y^2 = x^3 + x$.

To simplify the experimental, we write the intermediate parameters of the PSS protocol on the blockchain. The master key and public key are generated later and can be queried directly from the chain. Figure 2 illustrates the user's private key generation performance of our system. Note that this also includes the fabric-java-sdk initialization time, which is about 300ms.

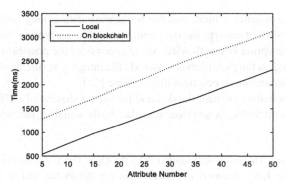

**Fig. 2.** Key generation time consumed.

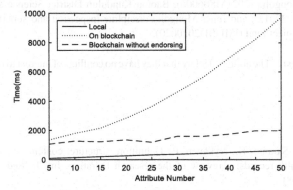

**Fig. 3.** Pre-decryption time consumed

In Fig. 3, the solid line indicates the time consumption only for pre-decryption at the local machine. Due to the constraints, note that we are only performing the pre-decryption computation with smart contract locally, rather than assigning it to CSR. The solid line can also represent the time consumed for pre-decryption on cloud servers. The dotted line here indicates that the smart contract performs the pre-decryption operation and all the nodes are involved in the endorsement. In contrast, the dashed line indicates that only one node executes the contract. We can conclude that endorsement will have some impact on the performance of key generation. However, there are few people who set 50 attributes on EHRs data. With attribute values limited to 15 or less, endorsements have a lesser impact on the system's performance.

After simulation experiments, it is proved that our system is feasible in practice.

## 6 Conclusion

We propose a novel blockchain-assisted key generation electric health records sharing scheme. Compared to scheme [25], we remove the Decryption CSP, and replace Key Generation CSP, Storage CSP with BC and IPFS. While remove the TypeII-Adversary type attackers, our scheme is more suitable for sharing data among multiple organizations. To do this, we first encrypt the data with symmetric encryption, and then encrypt the symmetric encryption key with ABE. We also consider the possibility of tampering with the data stored on the cloud servers, and add the integrity verification phase. Hence, our scheme is safer and more practical than scheme [25].

In short, our scheme can meet the demand for secure sharing of EHRs among multiple healthcare institutions. In addition, it is also easily scalable, just add nodes on the blockchain.

**Funding Statement.** This work was supported by the Open Fund of Advanced Cryptography and System Security Key Laboratory of Sichuan Province (Grant No. SKLACSS-202101), the Fundamental Research Funds for Beijing Municipal Commission of Education, Beijing Urban Governance Research Base of North China University of Technology, the Natural Science Foundation of Inner Mongolia (2021MS06006), Baotou Kundulun District Science and technology plan project (YF2020013), and Inner Mongolia discipline inspection and supervision big data laboratory open project fund (IMDBD2020020).

**Conflicts of Interest.** The authors declare that they have no conflicts of interest to report regarding the present study.

# References

1. Häyrinen, K., Saranto, K., Nykänen, P.: Definition, structure, content, use and impacts of electronic health records: a review of the research literature. Int. J. Med. Inform. **77**(5), 291–304 (2008)
2. Wang, H., Song, Y.: Secure cloud-based EHR system using attribute-based cryptosystem and blockchain. J. Med. Syst. **42**(8), 1–9 (2018)
3. Uddin, M., et al.: Hyperledger fabric blockchain: Secure and efficient solution for electronic health records. Comput. Mater. Continua **68**(2), 2377–2397 (2021)
4. Peng, X., Zhang, J., Zhang, S., Wan, W., Chen, H., Xia, J.: A secure signcryption scheme for electronic health records sharing in blockchain. Comput. Syst. Sci. Eng. **37**(2), 265–281 (2021)
5. Sahai, A., Waters, B.: Fuzzy identity-based encryption. In: Cramer, R. (ed.) EUROCRYPT 2005. LNCS, vol. 3494, pp. 457–473. Springer, Heidelberg (2005). https://doi.org/10.1007/11426639_27
6. Nakamoto, S.: Bitcoin: a peer-to-peer electronic cash system. Decentralized Bus. Rev. 21260 (2008)
7. Chen, H., Xu, G., Chen, Y., Chen, X., Yang, Y., et al.: Cipherchain: a secure and efficient ciphertext blockchain via mpeck. J. Quant. Comput. **2**(1), 57 (2020)
8. Wang, S., Yuan, Y., Wang, X., Li, J., Qin, R., Wang, F.Y.: An overview of smart contract: architecture, applications, and future trends. In: 2018 IEEE Intelligent Vehicles Symposium (IV), pp. 108–113. IEEE (2018)
9. Wang, S., Zhang, D., Zhang, Y.: Blockchain-based personal health records sharing scheme with data integrity verifiable. IEEE Access **7**, 102887–102901 (2019)
10. Huang, H., Sun, X., Xiao, F., Zhu, P., Wang, W.: Blockchain-based eHealth system for auditable EHRs manipulation in cloud environments. J. Parallel Distrib. Comput. **148**, 46–57 (2021)

11. Naresh, V.S., Reddi, S., Allavarpu, V.D.: Blockchain-based patient centric health care communication system. Int. J. Commun. Syst. **34**(7), e4749 (2021)
12. Zhang, J., Xu, G., Chen, X., Ahmad, H.: Towards privacy-preserving cloud storage: a blockchain approach. Comput. Mater. Continua **69**(3), 2903–2916 (2021)
13. Ali, M., Xu, C., Hussain, A.: Authorized attribute-based encryption multi-keywords search with policy updating. J. New Media **2**(1), 31–43 (2020)
14. Bellare, M., Boldyreva, A., O'Neill, A.: Deterministic and efficiently searchable encryption. In: Menezes, A. (ed.) CRYPTO 2007. LNCS, vol. 4622, pp. 535–552. Springer, Heidelberg (2007). https://doi.org/10.1007/978-3-540-74143-5_30
15. Hua, J., Shi, G., Zhu, H., Wang, F., Liu, X., Li, H.: CAMPS: efficient and privacy-preserving medical primary diagnosis over outsourced cloud. Inf. Sci. **527**, 560–575 (2020)
16. Zhang, Y., Chen, X., Li, J., Wong, D.S., Li, H., You, I.: Ensuring attribute privacy protection and fast decryption for outsourced data security in mobile cloud computing. Inf. Sci. **379**, 42–61 (2017)
17. Kumar, R., Tripathi, R.: Towards design and implementation of security and privacy framework for internet of medical things (IoMT) by leveraging blockchain and IPFS technology. J. Supercomput. 1–40 (2021)
18. Gao, H., Ma, Z., Luo, S., Xu, Y., Wu, Z.: BSSPD: a blockchain-based security sharing scheme for personal data with fine-grained access control. Wirel. Commun. Mob. Comput. (2021)
19. Han, K., Li, Q., Deng, Z.: Security and efficiency data sharing scheme for cloud storage. Chaos Solitons Fract. **86**, 107–116 (2016)
20. Hwang, Y.W., Lee, I.Y.: A study on data sharing system using ACP-ABE-SE in a cloud environment. Int. J. Web Grid Serv. **17**(3), 201–220 (2021)
21. Beimel, A.: Secure schemes for secret sharing and key distribution (1996)
22. Pedersen, T.P.: A threshold cryptosystem without a trusted party. In: Davies, D.W. (ed.) EUROCRYPT 1991. LNCS, vol. 547, pp. 522–526. Springer, Heidelberg (1991). https://doi.org/10.1007/3-540-46416-6_47
23. Shamir, A.: How to share a secret. Commun. ACM **22**(11), 612–613 (1979)
24. Zhang, J., Zhang, Z., Chen, Y.: PRE: stronger security notions and efficient construction with non-interactive opening. Theoret. Comput. Sci. **542**, 1–16 (2014)
25. Li, J., Lin, X., Zhang, Y., Han, J.: KSF-OABE: outsourced attribute-based encryption with keyword search function for cloud storage. IEEE Trans. Serv. Comput. **10**(5), 715–725 (2016)
26. Canetti, R., Krawczyk, H., Nielsen, J.B.: Relaxing chosen-ciphertext security. In: Boneh, D. (ed.) CRYPTO 2003. LNCS, vol. 2729, pp. 565–582. Springer, Heidelberg (2003). https://doi.org/10.1007/978-3-540-45146-4_33

# HuntFlow: Search the Arithmetic Vulnerability in Ethereum Smart Contract

Ke Zhou[1,3], Jieren Cheng[2,3(✉)], Le Liu[2,3], and Victor S. Sheng[4]

[1] School of Cyberspace Security (School of Cryptology), Hainan University, Haikou 570228, China

[2] School of Computer Science and Technology, Hainan University, Haikou 570228, China
cjr22@163.com

[3] Hainan Blockchain Technology Engineering Research Center, Haikou 570228, China

[4] Department of Computer Science, Texas Tech University, Lubbock, TX 79409, USA

**Abstract.** With the development of blockchain technology, smart contracts have been applied in more and more industries. Smart contracts are immutable once deployed, so unaudited smart contracts can easily cause economic losses. Arithmetic vulnerabilities usually refer to integer overflow vulnerability in smart contracts, and integer calculations in smart contracts are usually related to the transfer of digital assets. However, most of the existing smart contract auditing methods are inefficient and cannot be applied to the rapidly developing blockchain technology. To address these problems mentioned above, we propose a lightweight Ethereum smart contract arithmetic vulnerability detection model called HuntFlow, which can automatically detect the arithmetic vulnerabilities in the smart contract on a lightweight computer without expert knowledge. We first obfuscate 142 original opcodes into a set of 28 vulnerability features based on the characteristics of arithmetic vulnerabilities. And then we use Long-Short-Term-Memory (LSTM) network with attention mechanism for training and testing. The experimental result shows that the vulnerability features is better than original opcode for detecting arithmetic vulnerabilities. Moreover, the detection time of HuntFlow is greatly shortened than traditional tools, it costs only 0.028 s for each smart contract.

**Keywords:** Blockchain · Ethereum · Smart contract · Arithmetic vulnerability

## 1  Introduction

With the introduction of Bitcoin [1], blockchain technology has also been proposed, which has attracted attention from academia and industry because of its unique decentralized and immutable properties. But the purpose of Bitcoin is to achieve the decentralization of currency, and its ultimate function cannot exceed the scope of currency functions. So Vitalik Buterin proposed Ethereum [2] and smart contracts in 2014. Smart contract was first proposed by Nick Szabo at the end of the twentieth century [3]. It mainly refers to a set of commitments defined in digital form. Each participant in the contract can execute these commitments according to predetermined rules in the smart contract protocol. Because of its contractual nature, blockchain-based smart contracts

© The Author(s), under exclusive license to Springer Nature Switzerland AG 2022
X. Sun et al. (Eds.): ICAIS 2022, CCIS 1588, pp. 158–168, 2022.
https://doi.org/10.1007/978-3-031-06764-8_13

have been applied to more and more industries, such as supply chain [4], Internet of Things [5], finance [6], etc. Smart contracts are immutable once deployed, so unaudited smart contracts can easily cause economic losses. Arithmetic vulnerabilities refer to integer overflow problems in smart contracts, and integer calculations in smart contracts are usually related to the transfer of digital assets. Attackers often use this vulnerability to steal assets. In April 2018, hackers exploited the overflow vulnerability of the ERC-20 standard token contract BatchOverFlow to attack the smart contract of the BEC, and generated a huge number of tokens out of thin air, which were then sold in the trading market, causing their market value to plummet by nearly 94% [7]. There are many similar accidents in recent years and the security issues of smart contracts have drawn public attentions [8].

Smart contract vulnerability detection is mainly divided into manual detecting and automated detecting. In the current stage of rapid development of blockchain, manual detecting methods cannot adapt to the rapid development of smart contracts due to low efficiency and have been gradually eliminated [9]. Automated detection is mainly formal analysis and symbolic analysis. Ethereum developer Yoichi Hirai first proposed the use of formal verification for code auditing of smart contracts in 2016 [10], and subsequent researchers Bhargavan [11], Hirai [12], Grishchenko [10], etc. proposed some new formal verification methods and tools. However, the efficiency of formal verification is low, requiring technicians to formulate smart contracts and formal modeling, and some even require technicians to perform secondary verification [13]. Symbolic execution is a popular program analysis technique primarily used to test whether a piece of software violates certain properties. Researchers Luu [14], Nikolic [15] and Tsankov [16], etc. have proposed symbolic analysis tools to detect vulnerabilities in smart contracts. Using symbolic analysis tools can effectively reduce the false positive rate and false negative rate of smart contract vulnerability detection. However, the analysis method is complex and cumbersome and requires a relatively long analysis time, requires high hardware resources and cannot verify the correctness of smart contract functions.

In order to solve the above problems, we propose a lightweight Ethereum smart contract arithmetic vulnerability detection model called HuntFlow. HuntFlow is mainly composed of Long-Short-Term-Memory (LSTM) network with attention mechanism, and its input is the opcode of the smart contract. In the smart contract, an 8-bit representation space is allocated to the opcode, which is represented by 0x00~0xff. Theoretically, there can be 256 types of opcode, but currently there are only 142 types of opcode. Therefore, we analyzed the relationship between smart contract arithmetic vulnerabilities and opcode in the early stage, and made fuzzy representations of smart contract opcode to get features. The 142 types of opcode were obfuscated into a set of 28 vulnerability features, which reduced the model parameters, made the detection speed is faster and the accuracy rate higher.

In general, our main contributions are:

1) We propose a set of smart contract arithmetic vulnerability feature. We obfuscate 142 original opcodes into 28 vulnerability features based on the characteristics of arithmetic vulnerabilities.

2) We propose a lightweight Ethereum smart contract arithmetic vulnerability detection model, which can automatically detect whether the smart contract contains arithmetic vulnerabilities in a very short time.

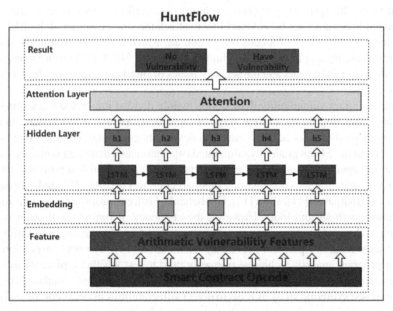

**Fig. 1.** The HuntFlow model.

## 2 Related Work

### 2.1 Smart Contract Vulnerability Detection

Bhargavan et al. [11] proposed a verification framework for Ethereum smart contracts, which uses the F* functional programming language to analyze and formally verify Ethereum smart contracts, and validates smart contracts by converting the smart contract language to F* format various security properties of the contract. Hirai et al. [12] first proposed to use the Isabelle high-order logic interactive theorem prover to formally verify smart contracts. This tool converts the opcodes in the EVM into a formal model using Lem Language, which uses the existing interactive theorems to Check its safety. However, with the development of smart contract technology, the problem of low conversion efficiency of Lem Language has also emerged. Therefore, Grishchenko [10] and Hildenbrandt [17] transformed EVM into a formal model by using F-framework and K-framework, defined the formal semantics of EVM, and conducted security audits by analyzing the formal semantics of smart contracts in EVM, and Formal validation and specification of attributes are supported. Luu et al. [14] designed an OYENTE tool based on symbolic execution technology for issues such as transaction ordering dependencies, reentrancy, timestamp dependencies, and unhandled exceptions. This tool is a static analysis tool for checking smart contract security vulnerabilities. It takes as input the bytecode of the smart contract and the state of the Ethereum blockchain. MAIAN is a dynamic analysis tool that extends the OYENTE method, proposed by Nikolic et al. [15] in 2018. MAIAN can find vulnerabilities directly in the bytecode of smart contracts without accessing the source code and can find vulnerabilities in long sequences of calls to smart contracts.

## 2.2 Smart Contract Vulnerability Detection

With the successful application of neural networks in various fields [18–23], deep learning has received a lot of attention. In the aspect of security, Cao DF et al. [24] proposes a deep convolutional LSTM neural network with Fourier transform for vulnerability detection which is combining convolutional neural network (CNN) with LSTM network to extract local and global features in frequency domain, and utilize attention mechanism to decide the weight of each element in code space. Zhu KL et al. [25] proposes a literal multi-dimensional anomaly detection approach using the distributed LSTM framework for in-vehicle network, especially the Control Area Network (CAN). Tobiyama et al. [26] proposes a malware process detection method based on process behavior, which uses LSTM for feature extraction, and then uses CNN for classification.

# 3  Our Method

## 3.1 Method Overview

HuntFlow is mainly composed of two parts:

1) "Feature": The first part is the vulnerability features. In this part, we obfuscate 142 original opcodes into a set of 28 vulnerability features based on the characteristics of arithmetic vulnerabilities.
2) "Detection Part": The second part is the vulnerability detection part composed of LSTM network with attention mechanism.

The HuntFlow model structure is shown in Fig. 1.

## 3.2 Feature

Smart contract opcode can be divided into the following categories [9]:

1) 0 s: Stop and Arithmetic Operations
2) 1 s: Comparison & Bitwise Logic Operations
3) 20 s: SHA3
4) 30 s: Environmental Information
5) 40 s: Block Information

6)  50 s: Stack, Memory, Storage and Flow Operations
7)  60 s & 70 s: Push Operations
8)  80 s: Duplication Operations
9)  90 s: Exchange Operations
10) a0 s: Logging Operations
11) f0 s: System operations

From the above classification, we can know that the 0s and 1s parts are the operation codes for some arithmetic calculations. The arithmetic vulnerabilities in Ethereum smart contracts are mainly divided into integer overflow and integer underflow vulnerabilities. Although there is a SafeMath library [27] in Ethereum to prevent arithmetic vulnerabilities, in fact, there are still many integer vulnerability many in smart contracts which are have passed security audits [28]. Arithmetic vulnerabilities are mainly caused by addition operations, multiplication operations, and subtraction operations. The 0x01, 0x02, and 0x03 opcode in the smart contract opcode correspond to the operations of addition, multiplication, and subtraction, so they are the important part which we are focus on. First, we directly classify the opcode that we believe are directly related to arithmetic vulnerabilities into feature, so we directly classify 0x01~0x1d and 0x50 opcode into feature without any processing. Then we obfuscate the opcode that we think are indirectly related to arithmetic vulnerabilities to get the corresponding feature, so we obfuscate 0x60~0x7f, 0x80~0x8f, 0x90~0x9f and get the corresponding feature. Finally, we discarded the opcode that we thought were not related to arithmetic vulnerabilities, so we discarded the opcode corresponding to 0x00, 0x20~0x4f, 0x51~0x5f, and 0xa0~0xff. In Table 1, we show the correspondence between smart contract opcode and feature.

**Table 1.** The correspondence between smart contract opcode and feature.

| Opcode | Feature |
| --- | --- |
| ADD(0x01) | ADD |
| MUL(0x02) | MUL |
| SUB(0x03) | SUB |
| ...... | ...... |
| SHL(0x1b) | SHL |
| SHR(0x1c) | SHR |
| SAR(0x1d) | SAR |
| POP(0x50) | POP |
| PUSH1(0x60)~PUSH32(0x7f) | PUSH |
| DUP1(0x80)~DUP16(0x8f) | DUP |
| SWAP1(0x90)~SWAP16(0x9f) | SWAP |

### 3.3   Detection Part

The detection part is mainly composed of LSTM network [29] with attention mechanism. LSTM is composed of multiple cells connected in order address the vanishing gradient belt and long-term dependency issues. The Fig. 2 shows a cell structure in LSTM. There is a storage unit C(t) in each cell, which is mainly Long-term storage and transmission of information. H(t) is the output of the cell and also the input of the next cell.

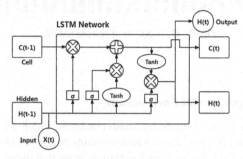

**Fig. 2.**  Schematic of a long short-term memory cell.

The Figs. 3 and 4 show the smart contract opcode length statistics and the features length statistics. As can be seen from the picture, in our dataset, the length of the smart contract opcodes is mainly concentrated on 1200, and the length of the features is mainly concentrated on 900. The LSTM network can pay attention mechanism to the whole part of the sequence, and its cell state contains an information transmission belt, so as to solve the problem of long-term dependence and will not forget the early input. The attention mechanism can evaluate the correlation between different elements in the sequence, and select information that is considered more critical to the target. In our experiments, we expect to use the attention mechanism to make the network more focused on the 01, 02 and 03 opcode which are more related to arithmetic vulnerabilities.

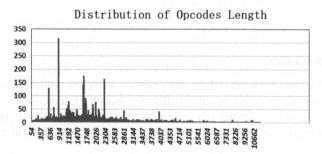

**Fig. 3.**  Distribution of opcodes length.

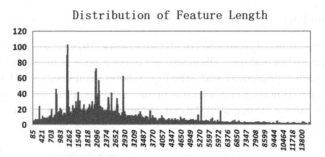

**Fig. 4.** Distribution of feature length.

## 4 Experiments

### 4.1 Dataset and Experimental Environment

In this article, we will focus on Ethereum smart contracts, which are written in Solidity [30]. We test our model on the dataset which contains nearly 45000 smart contracts is provided by the paper [31]. We use label = 0 to indicate that there is no vulnerability, and label = 1 to indicate that there is a vulnerability.

The paper [31] uses Mythril [32], Slither [33] and Smartcheck [34] and other tools to verify the dataset and add vulnerability labels. We randomly selected 80% of the contracts as the training dataset and 20% of the contracts as the testing dataset. The number of arithmetic vulnerabilities in dataset is shown in Table 2.

**Table 2.** The number of vulnerabilities in dataset.

| Vulnerability | Number | | | | | |
|---|---|---|---|---|---|---|
| | Train dataset | | | Test dataset | | |
| | Vulnerable | Invulnerable | Total | Vulnerable | Invulnerable | Total |
| Arithmetic | 14058 | 21605 | 35663 | 3514 | 5401 | 8915 |

### 4.2 Evaluation Index

We use Accuracy and F1-score indicators to judge its detection performance. Accuracy is one of the measurement indexes of classification model. F1-score is an index used in statistics to measure the accuracy of two-classification (or multitask two-classification) model, which takes into account the precision and recall of classification model at the same time.

$$Accuracy = \frac{true\ positive + true\ nagative}{Number\ of\ total\ samples} \quad (1)$$

$$Recall = \frac{true\ positive}{true\ positive + false\ negative} \quad (2)$$

$$Precision = \frac{true\ positive}{true\ positive + false\ positive} \tag{3}$$

$$F1 - score = 2 \times \frac{Recall \times Precision}{Recall + Precision} \tag{4}$$

### 4.3 Experimental Result

We put the opcode into three model for test: HuntFlow, a LSTM with attention mechanism and a classification network constructed by Transformer [35].

In Table 3, we show the test results for the three model. From Table 3, we can see that the result of HuntFlow is better than the result of LSTM and Transformer, and the result of LSTM is better than the Transformer.

**Table 3.** The test results

| Vulnerability | HuntFlow | | LSTM + Attention | | Transformer | |
|---|---|---|---|---|---|---|
| | Acc (%) | F1-score (%) | Acc (%) | F1-score (%) | Acc (%) | F1-score (%) |
| Arithmetic | **82.39** | **85.76** | 81.01 | 84.63 | 72.80 | 78.37 |

In the paper [31], the author uses three servers with 32 vCPUs with 30 GB of RAM to run Mythril [32], Slither [33], Smartcheck [34] and OYENTE [15] on the dataset, the results show that Slither [33] takes 5 s on average to analyze each smart contract, Smartcheck [34] takes 10 s on average to analyze each smart contract, OYENTE [15] takes 30 s on average to analyze each smart contract and Mythril [32] takes 64 s on average to analyze each smart contract. We use a lightweight computer which have i5 Processor with 16 GB of RAM and GeForce GTX 1080 Ti with 12 GB of RAM to run HuntFlow on the dataset, and the experimental result shows that HuntFlow requires fewer resources and can greatly shorten the detection time. It takes about 0.028 s on average to detect each smart contract in dataset. In Table 4, we show the running time of some tools and HuntFlow.

**Table 4.** The running time.

| Tools | Mythril | OYENTE | Smartcheck | Slither | HuntFlow |
|---|---|---|---|---|---|
| Detection time | 64 s | 30 s | 10 s | 5 s | **0.028 s** |

## 5 Discussion

### 5.1 Arithmetic Vulnerability Feature

By analyzing the characteristics of smart contract arithmetic vulnerabilities, we obfuscate 142 original opcodes into a set of 28 vulnerability features. Through the experimental results in Table 3, we can see that the detection accuracy of HuntFlow is higher than LSTM and Transformer. At the same time, due to the reduction of opcode categories, there are fewer network parameters which making the model smaller.

## 5.2 HuntFlow

As shown in the Table 3, HuntFlow has better detection accuracy and F1-score than the other two model, and the Transformer got the worst Accuracy and F1-socre. According to the result of Vision Transformer (ViT) [36] on image classification, we guess it is because Transformer requires a huge dataset, and our dataset is too small, which makes Transformer perform poorly.

## 5.3 Running Time

From Table 4, we can see that compared with traditional tools, HuntFlow greatly shortens the detection time of vulnerabilities. In the experiment, we run HuntFlow on a lightweight computer and it takes about 0.028 s on average to detect each smart contract in dataset. We think the reason is that HuntFlow only detects the arithmetic vulnerabilities trained and cannot detect unknown vulnerabilities without training. Although traditional tools are time-consuming and need much resource, they can analyze unknown vulnerabilities.

## 6  Conclusion

We propose a lightweight smart contract arithmetic vulnerability detection mode called HuntFlow, which can automatically detect smart contract vulnerabilities on a lightweight computer. HuntFlow first obfuscate 142 original opcodes into a set of 28 vulnerability features, then use LSTM network with attention mechanism for detection. The experimental results show that HuntFlow has good arithmetic vulnerability detection ability and it takes very little time.

In the future, we will try to associate different vulnerabilities with the "feature" and explore the most suitable obfuscate method for different vulnerabilities.

**Acknowledgement.** This work was supported by National Natural Science Foundation of China (Grant No. 62162022 and 62162024), Key Projects in Hainan Province (Grant ZDYF2021GXJS003 and Grant ZDYF2020040), the Major science and technology project of Hainan Province (Grant No. ZDKJ2020012).

## References

1. Nakamoto, S., Bitcoin, A.: A peer-to-peer electronic cash system. Bitcoin, vol. 4 (2008). https://bitcoin.org/bitcoin.pdf
2. Buterin, V.: A next-generation smart contract and decentralized application platform. In: White paper, vol. 3, no. 37, pp. 1–36 (2014)
3. Szabo, N.: The Idea of Smart Contracts (2018). http://szabo:best:vwh:net/smart_contracts_idea.html

4. Fda, B., Yg, B., At, C.: Review and analysis of blockchain projects in supply chain management. Procedia Comput. Sci. **180**, 724–733 (2021)
5. Dai, H.N., Zheng, Z., Zhang, Y.: Blockchain for internet of things: a survey. IEEE Internet Things J. **6**(5), 8076–8094 (2019)
6. Chang, S.E., Luo, H.L., Chen, Y.: Blockchain-enabled trade finance innovation: a potential paradigm shift on using letter of credit. Sustainability **12**(1), 188 (2020)
7. Fmichaell, Y.: Building a safer crypto token (2018). https://medium.com/cybermiles/building-a-safer-crypto-token-27c96a7e78fd
8. Atzei, N., Bartoletti, M., Cimoli, T.: A survey of attacks on ethereum smart contracts (SoK). In: Maffei, M., Ryan, M. (eds.) POST 2017. LNCS, vol. 10204, pp. 164–186. Springer, Heidelberg (2017). https://doi.org/10.1007/978-3-662-54455-6_8
9. Gavin, W.: Ethereum: a secure decentralised generalised transaction ledger. In: EthereumProject Yellow Paper, vol. 151, pp. 1–32 (2014)
10. Grishchenko, I., Maffei, M., Schneidewind, C.: A semantic framework for the security analysis of ethereum smart contracts. In: Bauer, L., Küsters, R. (eds.) POST 2018. LNCS, vol. 10804, pp. 243–269. Springer, Cham (2018). https://doi.org/10.1007/978-3-319-89722-6_10
11. Bhargavan, K., Delignat-Lavaud, A., Fournet, C.: Formal verification of smart contracts: short paper. In: Proceedings of the 2016 ACM Workshop on Programming Languages and Analysis for Security, pp. 91–96 (2016)
12. Hirai, Y.: The Palace Hotel. In: International Conference on Financial Cryptography and Data Security, pp. 520–535. Springer, Heidelberg (2017)
13. Wang, S., Ouyang, L., Yuan, Y., Ni, X., Han, X., Wang, F.Y.: Blockchain-enabled smart contracts: architecture. Appl. Future Trends **49**, 2266–2277 (2019)
14. Luu, L., Chu, D.H., Olickel, H., Saxena, P., Hobor, A.: Making smart contracts smarter. In: Proceedings of the 2016 ACM SIGSAC Conference on Computer and Communications Security, pp. 254–269 (2016)
15. Nikolić, I., Kolluri, A., Sergey, I., Saxena, P., Hobor, A.: Finding the greedy, prodigal, and suicidal contracts at scale. In: Proceedings of the 34th Annual Computer Security Applications Conference, pp. 653–663 (2018)
16. Tsankov, P., Dan, A., Drachsler-Cohen, D.: Practical security analysis of smart contracts. In: Proceedings of the 2018 ACM SIGSAC Conference on Computer and Communications Security, pp. 67–82. Association for Computing Machinery (2018)
17. Hildenbrandt, E., Saxena, M., Rodrigues, N.: KEVM: a complete formal semantics of the ethereum virtual machine. In: IEEE 31st Computer Security Foundations Symposium (CSF), pp. 204–217. IEEE (2018)
18. Cheng, J., Yang, Y., Tang, X., Xiong, N., Zhang, Y., Lei, F.: Generative adversarial networks: a literature review. KSII Trans. Internet Inf. Syst. **14**(12), 4625–4647 (2020)
19. Shao, X.: Accurate multi-site daily-ahead multi-step pm2.5 concentrations forecasting using space-shared cnn-lstm. Comput. Mater. Continua **70**(3), 5143–5160 (2022)
20. Dubey, R.: J: An improved genetic algorithm for automated convolutional neural network design. Intell. Autom. Soft Comput. **32**(2), 747–763 (2022)
21. Cheng, J., Liu, J., Xu, X., Xia, D., Liu, L., Sheng, V.: A review of Chinese named entity recognition. KSII Trans. Internet Inf. Syst. **15**(6), 2012–2030 (2021)
22. Lei, F., Cheng, J., Yang, Y., Tang, X., Sheng, V., Huang, C.: Improving heterogeneous network knowledge transfer based on the principle of generative adversarial. Electronics **10**(13), 1525 (2021)
23. Tang, X., Tu, W., Li, K., Cheng, J.: DFFNet: an IoT-perceptive dual feature fusion network for general real-time semantic segmentation. Inf. Sci. **565**, 326–343 (2021)
24. Cao, D., Huang, J., Zhang, X.: FTCLNet: convolutional LSTM with fourier transform for vulnerability detection. In: 2020 IEEE 19th International Conference on Trust, Security and Privacy in Computing and Communications (TrustCom), pp. 539–546 (2020)

25. Cheng, J., Liu, Y., Tang, X.: DDoS attack detection via multi-scale convolutional neural network. Comput. Mater. Continua **62**(3), 1317–1333 (2020)
26. Tobiyama, S., Yamaguchi, Y., Shimada, H.: Malware detection with deep neural network using process behavior. In: 2016 IEEE 40th Annual Computer Software and Applications Conference (COMPSAC), vol. 2, pp. 577–582 (2016)
27. OpenZeppelin (2021). https://github.com/OpenZeppelin
28. Lai, E., Luo, W.: Static analysis of integer overflow of smart contracts in ethereum. In: Proceedings of the 2020 4th International Conference on Cryptography, Security and Privacy, pp. 110–115 (2020)
29. Gers, F.A., Schmidhuber, J., Cummins, F.: Learning to forget: continual prediction with LSTM. Neural Comput. **12**(10), 2451–2471 (2000)
30. Ethereum Foundation: The solidity contract-oriented programming language (2018). https://github.com/ethereum/solidity
31. Durieux, T., Ferreira, J.F., Abreu, R., Cruz, P.: Empirical review of automated analysis tools on 47,587 ethereum smart contracts. In: Proceedings of the ACM/IEEE 42nd International Conference on Software Engineering, pp. 530–541 (2020)
32. Mueller, B.: Smashing ethereum smart contracts for fun and real profit. In: 9th Annual HITB Security Conference (HITBSecConf), vol. 54 (2018)
33. Feist, J., Grieco, G., Groce, A.: Slither: a static analysis framework for smart contracts. In: 2019 IEEE/ACM 2nd International Workshop on Emerging Trends in Software Engineering for Blockchain (WETSEB), pp. 8–15. IEEE (2019)
34. Tikhomirov, S., Voskresenskaya, E., Ivanitskiy, I., Takhaviev, R., Marchenko, E., Alexandrov, Y.: Smartcheck: static analysis of ethereum smart contracts. In: Proceedings of the 1st International Workshop on Emerging Trends in Software Engineering for Blockchain, pp. 9–16 (2018)
35. Vaswani, A., Shazeer, N., Parmar, N.: Attention is all you. In: Advances in Neural Information Processing Systems, pp. 5998–6008 (2017)
36. Dosovitskiy, A., et al.: An image is worth 16x16 words: transformers for image recognition at scale. arXiv preprint arXiv:2010.11929 (2020)

# Review of Security Choreography Research

Jiangping Yu[1], Yanyan Han[2], Wenyu Zhu[2], and Yuan Gao[2(⊠)]

[1] Department of Cryptography and Technology, Beijing Electronics Science and Technology Institute, Beijing 100070, China
[2] Department of Electronics and Communication Engineering, Beijing Electronics Science and Technology Institute, Beijing 100070, China
gy@besti.edu.cn

**Abstract.** Security choreography is a process of automatically detecting, preventing, and recovering network attacks without human interference by using a variety of combination technologies. It is the development trend of future network security and the premise of realizing network security automation. How to effectively arrange security resources and tools is an urgent problem to be solved. Security choreography technology, as an efficient means of security, has outstanding advantages such as script automation, reasonable allocation of resources, small cost, and large benefit, and has attracted more and more attention at home and abroad. This paper first introduces the background and basis of security choreography and analyzes the concept and development of security choreography. Secondly, the main quality attributes of long-term average return and stability of security orchestration are given, and the key technologies of security orchestration are summarized according to the quality attributes. Finally, the challenges of security choreography are summarized and the future research trends are pointed out.

**Keywords:** Security orchestration · Security automation · Rational allocation of resources · Wireless network virtualization

## 1 Introduction

### 1.1 Research Background and Current Situation

As the attack and defense of network security become increasingly fierce, the strategy of network security relying solely on prevention and prevention has become ineffective, and more attention must be paid to detection and response. Enterprises and organizations should build a new security protection system and security solution that integrates prevention, detection, response, and prevention under the assumption that the network has been attacked.

A network security solution can generate thousands of alerts, which are often monitored and acted upon by security personnel, mostly manually or semi-automatically [1–3]. According to a Verizon report, 93 percent of data breach cases take minutes to execute, but it took the company weeks or even months to discover the attacks [4]. According to Baker Hostetler, it takes an average of 61 days for security experts to discover that an incident has occurred, and another 41 days after that to take remedial action,

X. Sun et al. (Eds.): ICAIS 2022, CCIS 1588, pp. 169–182, 2022.
https://doi.org/10.1007/978-3-031-06764-8_14

according to The Report [5]. It can be seen that manual or semi-automatic solutions take too long to discover and deal with problems and are inefficient, thus failing to ensure high system security. To address the potential threat of a security breach, security specialists should offer and facilitate the selection of existing security solutions as soon as possible to provide the required security services and ensure seamless security operations. That said, we need a fully automated response – security choreography.

### 1.2  Significance and Limitations of the Study

Security choreography is often used by practitioners to bring automation, simplify incident response, and integrate security tools. Security choreography solves the problem of human threat analysis, delayed response to security incidents, and timely information on the security status of organizational and communications technology infrastructure. It can automatically identify suspicious activity in an organizational environment and proactively take action to mitigate cyber-attacks. According to a Gartner report, 30% of medium to large enterprises will deploy some form of security automation and choreography capabilities by 2021 [6]. Another study reports a third of organizations plan to deploy or have already deployed a security choreography solution, which can bundle together different security solutions and human expertise for automating security services within an organization said The Report [3].

Security solutions require a thorough look at the choreography platform, as these solutions work in their way and generate alerts in different formats. Existing security choreography solutions do not provide sufficient evidence to support different quality attributes such as flexibility, interoperability, scalability, modifiability, accuracy, and extensibility [7–13]. Given the increasing demand for security choreography, a great deal of research is needed to help better address challenges in security choreography, existing solutions, and practices.

## 2  Fundamentals of Security Choreography

### 2.1  Concept of Security Choreography

Security Choreography is designed to introduce technical and socio-technical solutions that integrate multi-vendor security tools as a unified whole to support security personnel in a security operations center (SOC) [14]. Organizations are increasingly adopting security choreography platforms with proactive, autonomously collaborative solutions that enable security protectors to perform their duties effectively and efficiently. The Security Choreography initiative enables people, practices, and technologies to work together to improve an organization's security intelligence for better security operations and management. Security orchestration is the premise of security automation. It is a process of automatically detecting, preventing, and recovering network attacks without human interference by using information technology, automatic algorithm, and artificial intelligence. Its functions are mainly divided into three areas: integration, orchestration, and automation [15].

## 2.2 Development of Security Choreography

Security orchestration is a relatively new concept first proposed by Gartner in recent years. At that time, Gartner proposed the definition of Security Operations, Analytics, and Reporting. With the rapid development and evolution of security operation technology, Gartner redefined it as security choreography in 2017 and regarded it as security Choreography and automation (SOA, Security Orchestration and Automation, Security Incident Response Platform (SIRP), and Threat Intelligence Platform (TIP, Threat Intelligence Platform) is a fusion of three technologies/tools [16]. Gartner believes that security choreography is still evolving rapidly and its content may change in the future, but its goal of focusing on security response around security operations will not change [17].

And security choreography as a script automation response solution launched in recent years, fully integrated data, human security skills, tools, processes, to achieve the purpose of fast and efficient safe operation [18, 19].

Gartner's latest descriptive definition of security choreography is that security choreography is a collection of technologies that enable enterprises and organizations to collect information monitored by security operations teams, including alarms generated by various security systems, and perform event analysis and alarm triage on this information [20]. Then, guided by a standard workflow, a human-machine approach helps security operations define, prioritize, and drive standardized incident response activities. Security choreography tools enable enterprises and organizations to formalize event analysis and response processes.

## 2.3 Main Quality Attributes of Security Choreography

The quality attributes of security choreography mainly include the success rate of service execution, long-term average revenue, long-term average revenue cost ratio, resource utilization, stability, availability, etc., which are the functional requirements, non-functional requirements, and prerequisites of security choreography system. The following are some of the main quality attributes.

Definition 1 (Security service Execution Success Rate) Insecurity choreography, the ratio of the number of successfully automated user security service requests to the total number of arrival requests, denoted as $\xi$. The larger the $\xi$, the more security choreography can process more security service requests from users within a period T, and the InP (Infrastructure Provider) will also get more benefits.

$$\xi = \lim_{x \to \infty} \frac{\sum_{t=0}^{T} SOAR_{suc}}{\sum_{t=0}^{T} SOAR_{sum}} \tag{1}$$

where $SOAR_{suc}$ represents the number of user security service requests accepted by automation and $SOAR_{sum}$ represents the total number of requests arrived.

Definition 2 (Long Term average Revenue) Long term average revenue is combined with the key technology of security choreography, security service functional chain technology, which will be highlighted in the next chapter. The benefit of security choreography at time t is defined as R(SOAR,t). the resources required by the user's security service request, and the cost of security choreography receiving the user's security service request at time T is defined as the consumption of total physical resources, namely: C(SOAR,t)

$$R(SOAR, t) = \sum_{n_v \in N_v} CP(n_v) + \alpha \sum_{l_v \in L_v} BW(l_v) \tag{2}$$

$$C(SOAR, t) = \sum_{n_v \in N_v} CP(n_v) + \beta \sum_{l_v \in L_v} BW(l_v) \bullet HoP(l_v) \tag{3}$$

where, $CP(n_v)$ and $BW(l_v)$ respectively represent the CPU resources and bandwidth resources required by secure service requests. $\alpha$, $\beta$ Are the relative weights to balance the benefits and costs between CPU and bandwidth respectively, and $HoP(l_v)$ are hops. Therefore, the long-term average revenue R and long-term average cost C are:

$$R = \lim_{x \to \infty} \frac{1}{T} \sum_{t=0}^{T} R(SOAR, t) \tag{4}$$

$$C = \lim_{x \to \infty} \frac{1}{T} \sum_{t=0}^{T} C(SOAR, t) \tag{5}$$

Definition 3 (long-run average revenue cost ratio) is the ratio of long-run average revenue to long-run average cost.

$$\frac{R}{C} = \lim_{x \to \infty} \frac{\sum\limits_{t=0}^{T} R(SOAR, t)}{\sum\limits_{t=0}^{T} C(SOAR, t)} \tag{6}$$

R/C is the resource usage. The higher R/C is, the higher resource utilization is and the more efficient security choreography performance is.

Definition 4 (Stability) Security choreography is mainly embodied in security resource allocation and automation, in which security resource allocation is specifically implemented on the underlying physical nodes and links. The pressure of a physical node $S_N$ can be defined as the number of virtual nodes supported by the physical node, and the pressure of a physical link $S_L$ can be defined as the number of virtual links supported by the physical link. Node pressure ratio $R_N$ and link pressure ratio $R_L$ are defined as:

$$R_N = \frac{\max\limits_{v \in V_s} S_N(v)}{[\sum\limits_{v \in V_s} S_N(v)]/|V_S|} \tag{7}$$

$$R_L = \frac{\max\limits_{e \in E_s} S_L(e)}{[\sum\limits_{e \in E_s} S_L(e)]/|E_S|} \tag{8}$$

The node pressure ratio $R_N$ is the ratio of the maximum node pressure to the average node pressure, and the link pressure ratio $R_L$ is the ratio of the maximum link pressure to the average link pressure. The pressure ratio is an indicator of load balancing performance. A smaller pressure ratio indicates a more balanced load. Therefore, nodes or links cannot be used due to overload, preventing hotspot faults and improving system stability.

## 3 Key Technology of Security Choreography

### 3.1 Wireless Network Virtualization Technology

Under the new network environment such as cloud computing and software-defined network, software-defined security and security resource scheduling emerge at the historic moment. For secure resource choreography, there are only general concepts such as abstraction, automation, business processes, scripts, automatic extensible API applications, and so on. For its specific composition and structure, different organizations have different understandings and schemes. Underlying devices are heterogeneous and have different service capabilities, resulting in poor scalability. Through virtualization, these differences can be masked. Reference [21] shows an accelerated resource scheduling mechanism based on SDN/NFV architecture is proposed to realize unified management and optimal resource scheduling. Reference [22] shows the security protection problem of cloud computing and another virtualization environment, a security service chain automatic arrangement and deployment framework based on SDN/NFV technology was proposed to realize automatic security arrangement and deployment. Virtualization technology mainly includes two aspects: Network Virtualization (NV) and Network function virtualization (NFV). The following is an introduction to these two aspects.

Network virtualization technology has been put forward for a long time and has been widely used in the field of the Internet [23]. Network virtualization technology is believed to be able to effectively solve a series of problems faced by the Internet, can shield the underlying differences of security orchestration, improve orchestration resource utilization and system flexibility [24].

The essence of network virtualization technology is "abstraction" and "isolation". Firstly, the abstraction of physical network and components decouples the underlying network infrastructure from services, so that each virtual network can share the underlying network infrastructure so that security orchestration can focus more on services rather than the bottom layer. Figure 1 describes a diversified Internet based on network virtualization.

Secondly, through isolation of each virtual network, different services are isolated to ensure the security and privacy of security orchestration services. Meanwhile, the resource isolation of different services ensures the demand for security orchestration services on the underlying network resources. The early application of Network virtualization is Virtual Private Network (VPN), which encrypts data packets and translates IP addresses through THE VPN gateway to achieve remote access to the internal network [25]. With the development of data center services, network virtualization technology needs to carry different service applications on the same physical network, and they are isolated from each other. This supports the demand for security orchestration for

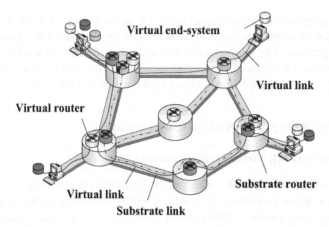

**Fig. 1.** Diversified Internet based on network virtualization.

services and creates conditions for security orchestration service hosting and service stability [26].

With the development of cloud computing technology and its successful application in IT networks, ETSI put forward a network Function Virtualization (NFV) architecture from the perspective of operators in 2012 [27]. In traditional networks, network functions are coupled with dedicated hardware, which increases cost and is not scalable. NFV enables you to decouple network functionality from dedicated hardware and run on VMs (Virtual Machines) or general-purpose hardware servers on cloud platforms [28]. NFV technology enables various security service functions to be flexibly loaded into the security orchestration system by software so that they can be flexibly deployed in different locations such as data centers, network nodes, or the user side. NFV breaks the coupling between the physical device layer and the logical service layer in traditional networks. Each dedicated hardware network device is replaced by virtualized network elements. Carriers can manage and configure virtualized security elements to meet customized requirements [29].

### 3.2 Security Service Function Chain Technology

SFC (Service Function Chain) defines a set of ordered Virtual Security Service functions (VSSF) and instantiates them. Based on a virtual network, the traffic between network middleware can be flexibly scheduled to meet specific network service requirements. The optimal allocation of resources is a key problem in security choreography, which directly determines the effectiveness of the system. Along with the modern network management to the intelligent scheduling and refine the service goal, security services chain technology in optimizing the allocation of resources at the same time, also need to meet the performance requirements, such as load balancing, on-demand scaling, migration network function, energy-saving, and fault recovery, etc., these are arranged to ensure the safety of the system to the efficient and stable operation. For resource management of security service function chain, the existing theoretical research mainly focuses on three aspects: 1) group chain of SFC: how to reasonably describe and construct SFC according to user's personalized needs and attributes of VSSFs. 2) SFC deployment: how to effectively deploy virtual networks on the underlying network while meeting SFC resource requirements and limiting the capacity of the underlying network. 3) SFC scheduling: how to arrange the execution sequence of different SFC security service functions to reduce the total service time. Existing research focuses on the deployment of SFC, also known as the virtual network mapping process.

**Group Chain of the SFC.** The group chain process of SFC is to describe and construct the security service function chain according to the personalized request put forward by users and the attribute characteristics of various VSSFs. Figure 2 provides an example of a chain of security service functions where data flows need to be processed by the corresponding VSSFs in linked order, such as firewall → deep packet detection → encoder → data monitor → decoder to complete a customized network security service. SFC inserts a service chain header containing the required VSSFs when it is sent to the edge router. Its attributes generally include source address, a destination address, type, and number.

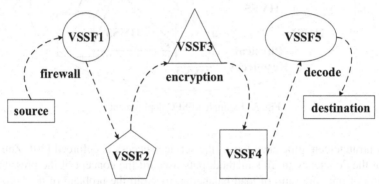

**Fig. 2.** Example of a security service function chain.

**SFC Deployment.** Most of the existing research on security resource choreography of the security service function chain focuses on the deployment phase of SFC. For a group of network service SFC requests, the SFC needs to be instantiated, allocated resources, and routed on the underlying physical network. An assembled chain is a personalized request made by users, which is a virtual network; Each VSSF is a virtual node, and nodes are connected by virtual links. SFC deployment is also called virtual network mapping. The virtual network must be mapped to the underlying physical network, and virtual nodes and link constraints must be met. Figure 3 illustrates an SFC deployment example with resource constraints such as node CPU resources and link bandwidth resources.

Yu et al. in the deployment of nodes, each time you select in the underlying physical network available CPU resources of the largest physical node, its defect is easy to cause the available CPU resources of the larger physical nodes on the physical link is connected to appear bottleneck, making the link load is too high, it will cause the entire

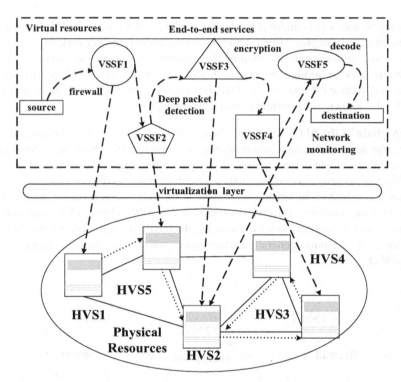

**Fig. 3.** Example of SFC deployment.

security arrangement efficiency lower, the service success is enforced [30]. Zhu et al. aimed at the deficiency in Yu's method, puts forward the concept of the pressure, the evaluation of pressure ratio of load balancing, to avoid the problem of the bottleneck node or link, make security arrangements can perform more services, to enhance the stability of the choreography, but no consider the topological properties of the node, security arrangements resource utilization is not high [31]. Shi Chaowei et al. aiming at the shortcomings of the methods of Zhu, considering the characteristic of node resources and consider node topology characteristics, puts forward the nearby, the center degrees, concentration and CPU and adjacency indices such as bandwidth and, enrich the evaluation method of node, and can be adjusted according to the network environment of adaptive and greatly improving the safety layout resource utilization and service execution success ratio [32]. CHEN et al. show a novel energy consumption optimization model are proposed to reduce the energy consumption of the choreography process, but other performance indicators are not considered [33]. Zhu Guohui et al. combined with the previous research, considering the resource attributes, topological attributes, and energy consumption characteristics of nodes, an efficient and energy-saving virtual network mapping algorithm based on node topological awareness is proposed, which not only reduces energy consumption but also improves resource utilization, achieving very good effect and performance [34].

*SFC Scheduling.* After the SFC is linked and deployed, one physical node can host multiple virtual nodes, namely, virtual security services. Once the virtual security service function is deployed on physical nodes, it takes a certain amount of time for data to pass the virtual security service function. Most physical nodes can process only one virtual security service function at a time, and the process of processing all virtual network functions in a security service chain cannot be interrupted. This means that the security service request occupies a certain physical resource in advance, and the virtual security service function assigned to other chains can only be considered after the virtual security service function on the current security service chain is completed, that is, the request from other chains can only temporarily wait. How to arrange the execution sequence of virtual security service functions on service nodes reasonably for efficient scheduling under the condition of parallel processing of multiple data streams has become a problem worthy of study, which can greatly reduce the total time of security orchestration to provide services [35].

### 3.3 Security Service Function Chain Technology

Because the network can be abstracted as a graph, more and more researches on security resource choreography begin to focus on graph theory. In graph theory, a directed graph is a directed acyclic graph (DAG) if it cannot start from a vertex and return to that point by several edges. Abstract several virtual security service functions contained in the security resource service chain into a directed acyclic graph according to the logical sequence, and arrange security by combining the logical sequence with the service device resources provided on the network, focusing on the optimization and deployment of the logical sequence of virtual security service functions. Zhang et al. show for most of the existing research often only consider the request execution costs while ignoring the era of big data is data transmission by a special focus on cost, this paper proposes a heuristic algorithm based on priority, the priority of the algorithm in the request of fully considering the DAG structure properties, task execution time and data transmission time estimates, was introduced to the safety arrangements in the directed acyclic graph, Significantly improved performance [36].

In addition, the bipartite graph has been used more and more in security resource arrangement. The requester and provider of the resource are the two-point sets of the bipartite graph, and each secure resource scheduling scheme is a match of the bipartite graph. The goal of the scheduling is to find the optimal match of the bipartite graph, focusing on the matching degree between different providers and requesters. The advantage of a bipartite graph is that the modeling is intuitive and it can accurately describe the supply and demand relationship of resources and the dependence relationship between businesses, but the calculation complexity is high when there are a large number of nodes in the graph. Lischka J, et al. based on the two parts graph, this paper proposes a virtual network mapping algorithm based on the technology of subgraph isomorphism, the method based on pattern matching technology through the lookup in the underlying physical network and virtual network structure of the same subgraph, once encountered do not conform to the constraints of directly back to the last successful mapping continue mapping, which greatly improved the efficiency and success of the choreography [37].

## 4   Future Challenges and Development Direction

### 4.1   Future Challenges

The future challenges of secure resource choreography are mainly reflected in four aspects: node and link constraints, access control, online request, and the diverse typology of the virtual network.

1) Node and link constraints: usually including node CPU resources, link bandwidth resources, node location, link reliability, etc., a variety of constraints need to be satisfied by the security choreography system, which makes the embedding problem complicated to solve in computing.
2) Access control: If a large number of requests arrive, the security choreography system cannot accept every request, because resources are limited, so it is necessary to reject or delay the acceptance of extra requests.
3) Online request: Different from offline requests, online requests may arrive at any time, without certain regularity and unpredictability. Therefore, security choreography can not batch process the request, can not execute a large number of requests at the same time, but take corresponding operations when the request comes, this dynamic real-time greatly increases the difficulty of the system to deal with security problems
4) Various virtual network topologies: Different topologies have different optimal processing modes. Each incoming request is an unpredictable structure, and the system needs to come up with an inclusive strategy to handle requests from a variety of topologies. If the policy is too simple or targeted at only a few mainstream topologies, the efficiency and functionality of the choreography system cannot be achieved once the request is complex.

### 4.2   Technical Challenges

The technical challenges of security resource choreography are primarily related to the technical issues that lead to security issues. Different security service providers provide different security services and solutions [7]. These services and solutions are isolated from each other and only focus on security issues of their concern, with a lack of interaction, failing to play an overall role and the efficiency needs to be improved [38, 39]. Studies have found that the existing key tools for security orchestration automation, such as collecting and updating threat intelligence, verifying alerts, investigation tasks, response, and resolution, are missing [6, 40], and the absence of these tools will lead to security experts spending 95% of their time on manually performing repeatable tasks [41]. In addition, it is also found that some existing security tools may not be able to fully protect the security of organizations [42]. For example, the alarm monitoring system will generate a large number of false alarms while protecting early warning, requiring extensive analysis. Security experts deal with a large number of alerts and spend more time investigating and verifying duplicate and false alerts.

### 4.3 Social Challenges

The social challenges of security resource orchestration are related to processes, rules, and policies in cybersecurity. Network security personnel have a wide range of responsibilities, including manual analysis and processing of complex attacks [43], manual consulting and writing custom code to verify alerts through threat intelligence [44], manual extraction of key attributes from threat intelligence data, etc. Handling a large number of alerts manually can spread a lot of effort and can result in the loss of critical attack information or even errors. The Safety Practitioners Report study cited a lack of skilled safety staff as one of the main reasons for failure to address safety violations [45–47]. In addition, one of the major social challenges to organizational security is the lack of a fully developed implementation IRP (Information Resource Planning) framework for coordination and collaboration between incident response, seamless implementation, and deployment policies [48]. The paper reveals that stakeholders from different organizations are unwilling to share threat intelligence. Organizations' fear of losing their reputation is one of the reasons they are reluctant to share their security situation with other organizations [49]. These are the social limitations of the arrangement of security resources.

### 4.4 Future Direction

Although the technology and practice of security resource scheduling are widely used in recent years, the interaction between different security tools needs to be strengthened, and the research scheme of group chain, deployment, and scheduling of security service function chain is single and independent and needs to be integrated. Virtual network mapping, as a key step to realizing security choreography, has been paid more and more attention by experts and scholars. Most of the existing researches focus on the mapping process, and there is little content about group chain and scheduling. In the next step, researches on these aspects should be strengthened. In addition, privacy protection and joint optimization of multiple performance indicators should be considered in the process of security choreography to reduce energy consumption and improve resource utilization, to enhance the comprehensive efficiency of the system.

## 5 Conclusion

As an emerging hot research issue, the research on security choreography has been a very active direction from concept, background to quality attributes and key technologies, from risk and challenge to future development direction, from focusing on theoretical perfection to gradual practice. On the whole, the research on security choreography is not mature at present, and a complete theoretical system has not been established, and there is still a certain gap from the perfection of technical theory to the specific application of the algorithm.

This paper reviews the main achievements in the research field of security choreography in recent years, summarizes all aspects of security choreography, introduces the main quality attributes and key technologies of security choreography in detail, simplifies the security process, and provides power for security automation. As an important trend of network security development in the future, security choreography has broad application prospects, showing great application potential, and has been paid more and more attention.

**Acknowledgement.** We gratefully acknowledge anonymous reviewers who read drafts and made many helpful suggestions. This work is supported by Higher Education Department of the Ministry of Education Industry-university Cooperative Education Project (202002186009) and Chinese College Students' Innovation and Entrepreneurship Training program (X202110018015).

# References

1. Trull, J. https://cloudblogs.microsoft.com/microsoftsecure/2017/08/03/top-5-best-practices-to-automate-security-operations. Accessed 05 Sept 2017
2. Resilient, I. https://www.resilientsystems.com. Accessed 28 Oct 2017
3. TDG.    https://www.turremgroup.com/security-orchestration-fine-tunes-the-incident-response-process. Accessed 25 Oct 2017
4. Verizon 2016 Data Breach Investigations Report. http://www.verizonenterprise.com/verizon-insights-lab/dbir. Accessed 02 Sept 2017/09/02
5. BakerHosteller. https://www.bakerlaw.com/events/webinar-be-compromise-ready-go-back-to-the-basics. Accessed 20 Aug 2017
6. Rochford, O., Proctor, P.E.: Innovation Tech Insight for Security Operations, Analytics and Reporting, Gartner (2015)
7. Digiambattista, E.: Enterprise level security orchestration, US. US. Patent No. Number, Cybric Inc., Boston, MA (US) (2017)
8. Nadkarni, H.: Security orchestration framework, US. US. Patent No. Number, McAfee LLC (2017)
9. Intel Security. https://www.intel.com/content/dam/www/public/us/en/documents/datasheets/open-security-controller-datasheet.pdf. Accessed 23 Oct 2017
10. Koyama, T., Hu, B., Nagafuchi, Y., Shioji, E., Takahashi, K.: Security orchestration with a global threat intelligence platform. NTT Techn. Rev. (2015)
11. Luo, S., Salem, M.B.: Orchestration of software-defined security services. In: 2016 IEEE International Conference on Communications Workshops. ICC 2016, Kuala Lumpur, Malaysia, pp. 436–441 (2016)
12. Poornachandran, R., Shahidzadeh, S., Das, S., Zimmer, V.J., Vashisth, S., Sharma, P.: Premises-aware security and policy orchestration, US. US. Patent No. Number, McAfee LLC (2016)
13. Yu, T., Fayaz, S.K., Collins, M., Sekar, V., Seshan, S.: PSI: precise security instrumentation for enterprise networks. In: Network and Distributed System Security Symposium (NDSS), San Diego, CA, USA (2017)
14. Sun, L.: Research and implementation of security service orchestration system based on blockchain. Beijing Univ. Posts Telecommun. (2021)
15. Liao, W.: Exploration and scenario practice of security orchestration and automated response. In: The Third Institute of the Ministry of Public Security. 2020 "Network Security Technology and Application Innovation" Symposium Proceedings. The Third Research Institute of the Ministry of Public Security: Information Network Security, Beijing Editorial Office (2020)
16. Gartner: How to decide whether endpoint and network security integration is a feature or a fad (2017)
17. Gartner: Endpoint detection and response architecture and operations practices (2018)

18. Gartner: Market guide for security orchestration, automation, and response solutions (2019)
19. Market Guide for Security Orchestration: Automation and Response Solutions (2020)
20. Gartner: Solution comparison for endpoint detection and response technologies and solutions (2020)
21. Duan, T., Lan, J., Hu, Y., Fan, H.: J. Commun. **39**(06), 98–108 (2018)
22. Qi, Z.: Automatic arrangement and deployment framework of security service chain based on SDN/NFV. Journal **27**(03), 198–204 (2018)
23. Wang, A., Iyer, M., Dutta, R., et al.: Network virtualization: technologies, perspectives, and frontiers. Journal **31**(4), 523–537 (2013)
24. Chowdhury, N.M.M.K., Boutaba, R.: A survey of network virtualization. Journal **54**(5), 862–876 (2010)
25. Carapinha, J., Jimenez, J.: Network virtualization: a view from the bottom. In: Proceedings of the 1st ACM Workshop on Virtualized Infrastructure Systems and Architectures, pp. 73–80. ACM (2009)
26. Bradai, A., Rehmani, M.H., Haque, I., Nogueira, M., Bukhari, S.H.R.: Software-defined networking (SDN) and network function virtualization (NFV) for a hyperconnected world: challenges, applications, and major advancements. Journal **28**(3) (2020)
27. ETSI NFV ISG.https://portal.etsi.org/nfv/nfv_white_paper.pdf. Accessed 22 Oct 2012
28. Liu, Y.: Research on security service system and application based on NFV. Beijing Univ. Posts Telecommun. (2017)
29. Han, B., Gopalakrishnan, V., Ji, L.: et aL Network function virtualization: challenges and opportunities for innovations. Journal **53**(2), 90–97 (2015)
30. Yu, M., Yi, Y., Rexford, J., Chiang, M.: Rethinking virtual network embedding: substrate support for path splitting and migration. Journal **38**(2), 17–29 (2008)
31. Zhu, Y., Ammar, M.: Algorithms for assigning substrate network resources to virtual network components. In: Proceedings of the 25th IEEE International Conference on Computer Communications (2006)
32. Chaowei, S., Xiangru, M., Zhiqiang, M., Xiaoyang, H.: Topology comprehensive evaluation and weight adaptive virtual network mapping algorithm. Journal **47**(07), 236–242 (2020)
33. Chen, X., Li, C., Jiang, Y.: Optimization model and algorithm for energy efficient virtual node embedding. Journal **3**, 1327–1330 (2015)
34. Zhu, G., Zhang, Y., Liu, X., Sun, T.: Virtual network mapping algorithm based on node topology awareness. Journal **47**(09), 270–274 (2020)
35. Wang, Z., Zhang, L., Li, D.: Journal **57**(04), 18–27 (2021)
36. Zhang, X., Zhang, D., Zheng, W., et al.: An enhanced priority-based scheduling heuristic for DAG applications with temporal unpredictability in task execution and data transmission. Journal **100** (2019)
37. Lischka, J., Karl, H.: A virtual network mapping algorithm based on subgraph isomorphism detection. In: Proceedings of the 1st ACMSIGCOMM Workshop on Virtualized Infrastructure Systems and Architectures, pp. 81–88 (2009)
38. Sourour, M., Adel, B., Tarek, A.: Collaboration between security devices toward improving network defense. In: Seventh IEEE/ACIS International Conference on Computer and Information Science, Portland, OR, USA, pp. 13–18 (2008)
39. Chen, X., Ma, B., Chen, Z.: NetSecu: a collaborative network security platform for in-network security. In: 2011 Third International Conference on Communications and Mobile Computing, Qingdao, China, pp. 59–64 (2011)
40. Forte, D. https://www.darkreading.com/threat-intelligence/security-orchestration-and-automation-parsing-the-options/a/d-id/1329886?piddl_msgid=329392. Accessed Sept 2017
41. Zahedi, M., Shahin, M., Ali Babar, M.: A systematic review of knowledge sharing challenges and practices in global software development. Int. J. Inf. Manag. **36**(6), Part A, 995–1019 (2016)

42. Bhadra, S. https://techcrunch.com/2016/03/06/process-as-code-security-ops-orchestration-for-a-brave-new-world/. Accessed 13 Oct 2017
43. Koyama, T., Hato, K., Kitazume, H., Nagafuchi, M.: Resilient security technology for rapid recovery from cyber attacks. NTT Tech. Rev. **12**, 6 (2014)
44. Sadamatsu, T., Yoneyama, Y., Yajima, K.: Practice within Fujitsu of security operations center: operation and security dashboard. Journal **52**(3), 52–58 (2016)
45. ForeScout. https://www.forescout.com/wp-content/uploads/2018/07/FS-WP-Automating_System-Wide_Security-Orchestration_073118.pdf. Accessed July 2018
46. FireEye. https://www.fireeye.com/solutions/security-orchestrator/wp-best-practices-in-orchestration.html. Accessed 21 Nov 2017
47. Demisto. https://www.demisto.com/. Accessed 20 Oct 2017
48. Kamal, M., Davis, A.J., Nabukenya, J., Schoonover, T.V., Pietron, L.R., Vreede, G.j.D.: Collaboration engineering for incident response planning: process development and validation. In: 40th Annual Hawaii International Conference on System Sciences, HICSS 2007. Waikoloa, HI, USA, p. 15 (2007)
49. Jeong, K., Park, J., Kim, M., Noh, B.: A security coordination model for an inter-organizational information incidents response supporting the forensic process, pp. 143–148 (2008)

# A High-Efficiency Blockchain Sharded Storage Expansion Model

Jinliang Guo[1], Jinquan Zhang[1,2(✉)], Wunan Wan[1,2], Zhi Qin[1,2], Huailin Pu[1], Shibin Zhang[1,2], and Jinyue Xia[3]

[1] School of Cybersecurity,
Chengdu University of Information Technology, Chengdu 610225, China
zhjq@cuit.edu.cn

[2] Advanced Cryptography and System Security Key Laboratory of Sichuan Province,
Chengdu 610225, China

[3] International Business Machines Corporation (IBM), New York, NY 10041, USA

**Abstract.** Blockchain is a new decentralized storage system that combines cryptography, consensus algorithms, distributed storage and other technologies. The full node redundant storage of data on the blockchain provides extremely high security, but while the redundant storage of the blockchain improves the security of the system, it also puts a lot of storage pressure on the nodes. The storage scalability problem of the blockchain has become a shortcoming restricting the development of blockchain technology. Sharded storage is a solution to the scalability of blockchain storage. While the existing sharded storage solution relieves the storage pressure of nodes, it also increases the computing and communication consumption of nodes, and reduces the efficient of blockchain systems. This article proposes a highly efficient fragmented storage model, which classifies blocks according to the frequency and size of the blocks being accessed, and uses different storage schemes for blocks of different classifications, which reduces the storage pressure of the node while controlling the computing and communication consumption of the node.

**Keywords:** Blockchain · Sharded storage · Distributed storage

## 1 Introduction

In 2008, Satoshi Nakamoto proposed the concept of Bitcoin in "Bitcoin: A Peer-to-Peer Electronic Cash System" [1], which is also the first proposal and application of blockchain technology. In 2015, the emergence of Ethereum made the concept of blockchain become more familiar to more people, and the development of blockchain technology has become more and more rapid.

But there is a triadic paradox in blockchain technology: centralization, security, and scalability. The three cannot be satisfied at the same time, only two of them can be satisfied at the same time. Both Bitcoin and Ethereum prioritize the pursuit of decentralization and security, while sacrificing scalability. Therefore, as the scale of blockchain nodes

© The Author(s), under exclusive license to Springer Nature Switzerland AG 2022
X. Sun et al. (Eds.): ICAIS 2022, CCIS 1588, pp. 183–193, 2022.
https://doi.org/10.1007/978-3-031-06764-8_15

increases, scalability has become the biggest bottleneck for blockchain applications. In different application scenarios, the requirements for blockchain centralization, security, and scalability are different. The traditional blockchain performs fully redundant storage of the data on the chain, which improves the security of the system and reduces the scalability of the system. It has a high storage cost. However, in many application scenarios, excessive security may not be required. And decentralization, but there is a certain demand for scalability.

Based on the existing research, this paper proposes a fragmented storage model based on the frequency and size of the block being accessed. This model adopts different storage schemes according to the different characteristics of different blocks. Compared with the traditional fragmented storage model, Which reduces the computational consumption and communication consumption of block recovery.

The contributions of this article are as follows:

(1) Theoretical analysis of the appropriate value of the number of shard copies, the appropriate number of shard copies can alleviate the storage pressure of nodes, while ensuring the stability and security of the blockchain system.
(2) A fragmented storage model based on block access frequency and size is proposed. This model divides blocks into three categories based on their size and frequency of access. Each category adopts different storage strategies according to its block characteristics. While reducing the storage pressure of the node, it also controls the computational consumption and communication consumption.

## 2 Background

### 2.1 Blockchain Overview

Blockchain is a new application mode of computer technology such as distributed data storage, point-to-point transmission, consensus mechanism, and encryption algorithm. In the blockchain, the writing of data is completed by a distributed consensus algorithm between nodes, such as Proof-of-Work (POW), etc. The data is stored in blocks and form a chain structure in chronological order. In addition, cryptography technology is also used to ensure that the distributed ledger is tamper-proof and traceable.

Block chains can be divided into public chains, alliance chains, and private chains according to the requirements and thresholds for their nodes to join the blockchain network. There are some differences in the degree of decentralization, consensus mechanism, and incentive mechanism of the three, which are suitable for different application scenarios.

Blockchain has attracted widespread attention from financial institutions, investment institutions, regulatory agencies, and government departments due to its decentralized, tamper-resistant, and traceable characteristics. However, the current blockchain still has many technical difficulties, and the storage problem is one of them. In the public chain, because of the large number of nodes, the storage problem is particularly prominent.

## 2.2 Sharded Storage

The sharding technology was initially applied in the database field. The database was divided into multiple parts and stored on multiple servers to relieve the storage pressure of the servers. Sharding in the blockchain refers to dividing a complete blockchain into multiple parts and storing them on different nodes, reducing the redundancy of the overall data storage, so as to alleviate the storage pressure of the nodes. Elastico [2] is a public chain consensus protocol based on sharding. Its idea is to shard transactions, but after the blockchain is sharded, each node still needs to store a complete ledger, which does not effectively alleviate the node's Store pressure. OmniLedger [3] improved the existing problems of Elastico. OmniLedger proposed the RandHound protocol, which automatically allocates nodes to different shards. In order to reduce the storage consumption of nodes, OmniLedger introduced the concept of state blocks. When a consensus cycle ends, the leader of the shard stores UTXO in the Merkle tree and stores the root hash of Merkle in the head of the state block. After the state block is verified, it will be used as the genesis block of the next consensus era However, OmniLedger adopts a regular shard reorganization strategy, so there is a large amount of data migration consumption. Monoxide [4] divides the blockchain network into multiple independent and parallel groups. Each group independently completes the consensus. Each group only uses the transaction data within the group to store and process. For cross-group transactions, the author proposes In order to achieve final atomicity, final atomicity enables transactions across consensus groups to be executed indirectly in multiple consensus groups without blocking. However, with the increase in the number of consensus groups, each full node needs to synchronize and track the block headers in all consensus groups. For each full node, this is still an overhead that cannot be ignored. As the number of consensus groups increases, local bandwidth will be exhausted, which has become a bottleneck that limits the efficiency of the scheme.

Traditional blockchain shard storage has the following problems:

(1) Decreased stability

Sharded storage reduces the redundancy of the blockchain data and improves the storage performance of the blockchain. However, when the number of shard copies is small, the failure of the node or the existence of malicious nodes may cause the blockchain system to fail to integrate. Fragmentation is used to recover block data, which affects the overall performance of the blockchain. Therefore, how to determine the number of shard copies to balance the storage performance and stability of the blockchain system is an unsolved problem.

(2) Reduced efficiency

In the traditional shard storage solution, the shards of the block data are stored in each node. When the block data needs to be accessed, the node stored by the shard will be found according to the index table of the shard, and the corresponding download will be requested to restore the entire block data. However, some blocks may contain certain key transactions, and the access frequency is significantly higher than other blocks. The blockchain system will access the block data multiple times and frequently request the fragments of the block for data recovery. System resources are wasted and the efficiency of the overall blockchain system is reduced.

## 3    Sharded Storage Model Based on Block Access Frequency and Size (BAFS)

Based on the sharding idea and distributed storage method, this paper proposes the BAFS sharding storage model. The core idea is to use different storage strategy for different blocks according to the different access frequency and block size of each block in the blockchain. The storage mode of the block can be dynamically converted according to the access frequency of the block in the last T period. While alleviating the pressure on node storage, it also guarantees the operating efficiency of the blockchain system. Especially in the scenario where the block access rate and block size distribution are uneven, the efficiency advantage of the BAFS shard storage model will be more obvious.

### 3.1   Storage Unit

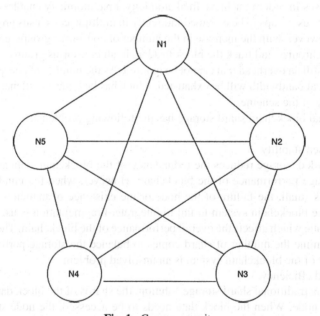

**Fig. 1.** Consensus unit.

There are N nodes in the storage model, which constitute multiple storage units. Each storage unit has n nodes. When the block is fragmented, it will be divided into n fragments and stored in the n nodes of the consensus unit. That is, the node of each storage unit can store the data of the entire blockchain completely without redundancy, and a consensus unit is equivalent to a full node with stronger storage capacity. The entire blockchain has $N/n = m$ storage units, and each slice will have m copies. When $n = 1$, each node stores complete block data. This model degenerates into a traditional blockchain, which is safe the highest performance, but the lowest storage performance. When $n = N$, there is only one storage unit, and the data on the entire blockchain is not redundantly accessed. The storage performance is the highest, but the security is the lowest, and single points of failure are prone to occur (Fig. 1).

Therefore, the number m of storage units has a direct impact on the security and stability of the shard storage model. Next, the value of the number of storage units will be theoretically deduced. The symbol table is as follows (Table 1):

**Table 1.** Symbol table.

| Symbol | Implication |
|--------|-------------|
| $P_r$ | The average node reliability of the blockchain system is the probability that the node will operate normally |
| $P_{sf}$ | The probability that all copies of a slice are unavailable |
| $P_f$ | The probability that the blockchain system fails and is unavailable |
| $P_a$ | The availability of the system, the probability of the blockchain will work properly. |

The reliability of the node in the blockchain system is $P_r$, which is obtained by counting the normal working time of the blockchain node.

$$P_{sf} = \prod_1^m (1 - P_r) \tag{1}$$

$P_{sf}$ is the probability that a slice copy is unavailable.

$$P_f = \sum_{i=1}^n C_N^i \prod_1^m (1 - P_r) \tag{2}$$

$P_f$ is the probability that the blockchain system is unavailable.

$$P_a = 1 - \sum_{i=1}^n C_N^i \prod_1^m (1 - P_r) \tag{3}$$

$P_a$ represents the availability of the blockchain system, which is the probability of the blockchain system operating normally.

Take the logarithm of both sides to get m.

$$m = \frac{\ln(1 - P_a) - \ln(2^n - 1)}{\ln(1 - P_r)} \tag{4}$$

Borel's law [5] defines events with a probability lower than $1/10^{50}$ as impossible events. Therefore, in our fragmentation model, when $Pf \leq 1/10^{50}$, we believe that fragmentation will not affect the area. For the security and stability of the block chain system, $Pf = 1/10^{50}$ is an ideal value. Put $Pf = 1/10^{50}$, and Pr into the equation to find the value of m [6].

## 3.2 Fragmented Storage Model

Block data is stored in shards on each node of the storage unit, which improves storage efficiency while increasing the cost of verifying data in the block, because verifying block data needs to obtain slices from each node of the storage unit to restore complete block data. For some blocks with high access frequency, frequent block restoration puts huge pressure on the bandwidth of the blockchain network [7–9].

This storage model will count the access frequency of blocks. Each node will maintain a table. The table records the number of times each block is accessed during the T period and the size of the storage space occupied by the block. According to the access frequency and block size, this model divides the blocks into four categories, and adopts different storage strategies for different types of blocks (Fig. 2).

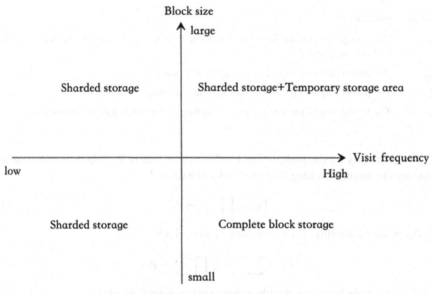

**Fig. 2.** Block type division.

(1) Blocks with low access frequency: fragmented storage

   For blocks with low access frequency, a fragmented storage scheme is adopted to distribute the blocks to each node of the storage unit after fragmentation. When the blockchain system needs to access the block, it will request the storage unit for fragmentation to restore the block [10–12].

(2) High access frequency and small storage space: complete storage

   For blocks with high access frequency and small block size, no sharding operation is performed, but stored in each node like a traditional blockchain. This avoids the overhead of frequent block recovery, and at the same time does not increase a lot of storage pressure [13, 14].

(3) High access frequency and large storage space: fragmented storage + temporary storage

   For blocks with high access frequency and large block size, the blocks are fragmented and distributed to the nodes of the storage unit. At the same time, the storage unit maintains a temporary storage area, which will not be deleted immediately after the block is restored. Instead, it is stored in the temporary storage area. If there is a request to access the block, the block will be downloaded directly from the temporary storage area without restarting the block recovery operation. When the temporary storage area is full, it will be cycled in T according to the block. The number of accesses in the temporary storage area is deleted (Fig. 3) [15, 16].

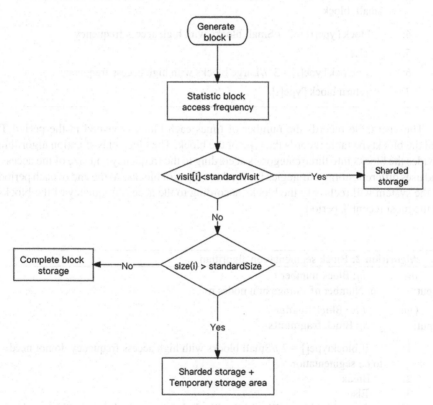

**Fig. 3.** Block storage flow chart.

---

**Algorithm 1:** Block classification algorithm

---

| Input: | $b_i$: Block number i |
|---|---|

| Output: | blocktype[]: Block classification table |
|---|---|

1:     if visit[i] < standardVisit  //Visits Less than standardVisit is a low access frequency block

2:     blocktype[i] = 1  //Blocks with low access frequency

3:     else if b.size() < standardSize  //Block size less than standardSize is a small block

4:     blockType[i] = 2  //Small blocks with high access frequency

5:     else

6:         blockType[i] = 3  //Large blocks with high access frequency

7:     return blockType[i]

---

The visit table records the number of times each block is visited in the period T, and the blocktype table records the type of the block. The block classification algorithm divides the blocks into three categories according to the frequency and size of the access, and uses different storage strategies for the three types of blocks. At the end of each period T, the system will reclassify the blocks according to the access frequency of the blocks in the most recent T period.

---

**Algorithm 2:** Block segmentation algorithm

---

| Input: | $b_i$: Block number i |
|---|---|
|  | n: Number of storage unit nodes n |

| Output: | $bh_i$: Block header |
|---|---|
|  | $S_i$: Block fragments |

1:     if blocktype[] = 2  //Small blocks with high access frequency do not need to be segmentation

2:     Break

3:     Else

4:     $b_i \to bh_i, bb_i$  //Divide the block $b_i$ into a block header $bh_i$, and a block body $bb_i$

5:         $bb_i \to H_i$  //Convert block body $bb_i$ to hexadecimal $H_i$

6:         $H_i \to S_i$  //Divide $H_i$ into n block fragments $S_i$

7:     Return $bb_i, S_i$

The block division algorithm divides the block $b_i$ that needs to be divided into a block header $bh_i$ and a block body $bb_i$, and converts the block body $bb_i$ into a decimal $H_i$ and then divides it into n parts to obtain $S_i$.

This model classifies blocks. For blocks with low access frequency, distributed storage is performed after sharding, which effectively reduces the storage pressure of nodes. For blocks with high access frequency but small block size, complete storage is performed. While increasing the cost of limited storage, it also controls the computing and communication consumption of nodes. According to different application scenarios, there are different requirements for storage and efficiency, and different standardVisit and standardSize can be set to adjust the model.

## 4  Theoretical Analysis

In the traditional block chain sharding scheme, all blocks will be sharded and stored in the storage unit. In the actual block chain system, because some blocks may contain key transactions, while other blocks are not so important, so the frequency of access between blocks is very different. The following is an efficiency analysis of the traditional fragmentation scheme and the BAFS-based fragmentation scheme proposed in this article [17].

Suppose the total number of nodes in the blockchain system is N, the number of storage units is m, and the number of nodes in the storage unit is n. There are x blocks in total. The four types of blocks are evenly distributed in the blockchain:

Low frequency and low size blocks (x/4, accessed k times, block size is y);
Low frequency and high size blocks (x/4, accessed k times, block size is 2y);
High frequency and low size blocks (x/4, accessed 2k times, block size is y);
High frequency and high size blocks (x/4, accessed 2k times, block size is 2y).

The resource consumed for each block reorganization is $w = p * y$, the consumed resource w is proportional to the block size y, and p is a coefficient [18].

Using the traditional sharding scheme, the resources consumed by the block system during block reorganization in period T:

$$C_T = \frac{1}{4} * x * k * y * p + \frac{1}{4} * x * k * 2y * p + \frac{1}{4} * x * 2k * y * p + \frac{1}{4} * x * 2k * 2y * p \tag{5}$$

Figure out $C_T$:

$$C_T = \frac{3}{2} * x * k * p * y \tag{6}$$

Using the BAFS sharding scheme, the resources consumed by the block system during block reorganization in cycle T:

$$C_T = \frac{1}{4} * x * k * y * p + \frac{1}{4} * x * k * 2y * p + \frac{1}{4} * x * 1 * 2y * p \tag{7}$$

Figure out $C_T$:

$$C_T = (\frac{3}{4} * k + \frac{1}{2}) x * p * y \tag{8}$$

It can be seen that in this case, the use of the BAFS fragmentation scheme can effectively reduce the resource consumption during the block recovery process. With the increase of the value of k, the cost of the BAFS fragmentation scheme in block reorganization is close to half of the traditional scheme. And when the variance of the access frequency and block size of different blocks is larger, the effect of the BAFS fragmentation scheme is better. It can be seen that the BAFS fragmentation scheme can effectively reduce the computing and communication consumption of nodes in the process of restoring blocks.

## 5   Conclusion

This paper studies the storage scalability of the blockchain and proposes a BAFS shard storage model. Through statistical analysis of the frequency and size of the block being accessed, the blocks are divided into three categories, which are carried out according to different storage schemes storage. Compared with the traditional sharding scheme, while alleviating the storage pressure of the node, it reduces the calculation and communication consumption of the node in the process of restoring the block, and improves the overall efficiency of the blockchain. It also analyzes the appropriate value of the number of storage units, which can ensure the stability and security of the blockchain system while alleviating the storage pressure of nodes. In the future, it is possible to study the network delay, storage space size, and reliability of nodes as the basis for dividing storage units to further improve the efficiency and stability of the system and better solve the storage problems of the blockchain system.

**Acknowledgement.** This work is supported by the Key Research and Development Project of Sichuan Province (No. 2021YFSY0012, No. 2020YFG0307, No. 2021YFG0332), the Key Research and Development Project of Chengdu (No. 2019-YF05-02028-GX), the Innovation Team of Quantum Security Communication of Sichuan Province (No. 17TD0009), the Academic and Technical Leaders Training Funding Support Projects of Sichuan Province (No. 2016120080102643).

## References

1. Nakamoto, S., Bitcoin, A.: A peer-to-peer electronic cash system. Bitcoin (2008). https://bit coin.org/bitcoin
2. Luu, L., Narayanan, V., Zheng, C., Baweja, K., Gilbert, S., Saxena, P.: A secure sharding protocol for open blockchains. In: Proceedings of the 2016 ACM SIGSAC Conference on Computer and Communications Security, pp. 17–30 (2016)
3. Kokoris-Kogias, E., Jovanovic, P., Gasser, L., Gailly, N., Syta, E., Ford, B.: Omniledger: a secure, scale-out, decentralized ledger via sharding. In: 2018 IEEE Symposium on Security and Privacy (SP), pp. 583–598. IEEE (2018)
4. Wang, J., Wang, H.: Monoxide: scale out blockchains with asynchronous consensus zones. In: 16th USENIX Symposium on Networked Systems Design and Implementation (NSDI 2019), pp. 95–112 (2019)
5. Borel, E.: Probabilities and Life. New, pp.23–87. Dover Publications Inc., York (1962)

6. Zeng, S., Huo, R., Huang, T., Liu, J., Wang, S., Feng, W.: Survey of blockchain: principle, progress and application. J. Commun. **41**(1), 134–151 (2020)
7. Peng, X., Zhang, J., Zhang, S., Wan, W., Chen, H., Xia, J.: A secure signcryption scheme for electronic health records sharing in blockchain. Comput. Syst. Sci. Eng. **37**(2), 265–281 (2021)
8. Wan, W., Chen, J., Xia, J., Zhang, J., Zhang, S., Chen, H.: Clustering collision power attack on RSA-CRT. Comput. Syst. Sci. Eng. **36**(2), 417–434 (2021)
9. Wan, W., Chen, J., Zhang, S., Xia, J.: A cluster correlation power analysis against double blinding exponentiation. J. Inf. Secur. Appl. **48**, 102357 (2019)
10. Zhao, Y., Zhang, S., Yang, M., He, P., Wang, Q.: Research on architecture of risk assessment system based on block chain. Comput. Mater. Continua **61**(2), 677–686 (2019)
11. Yang, M., Zhang, S., Zhao, Y., Wang, Q.: Dynamic negotiation of user behaviour via blockchain technology in federated system. Int. J. Comput. Sci. Eng. **22**(1), 74–83 (2020)
12. Chen, H., et al.: Task-attribute-based access control scheme for iot via blockchain. Comput. Mater. Continua **65**(3), 2441–2453 (2020)
13. Dai, Q., Xv, K., Guo, S., Dai, L., Zhou, Z.: A private data protection scheme based on blockchain under pipeline model. In: 2018 1st IEEE International Conference on Hot Information-Centric Networking (HotICN), pp. 37–45. IEEE (2018)
14. Xu, Z., Han, S., Chen, L.: CUB, a consensus unit-based storage scheme for blockchain system. In: 2018 IEEE 34th International Conference on Data Engineering (ICDE), pp. 173–184. IEEE (2018)
15. Guo, Z., Gao, Z., Mei, H., Zhao, M., Yang, J.: Design and optimization for storage mechanism of the public blockchain based on redundant residual number system. IEEE Access **7**, 98546–98554 (2019)
16. Goh, V.T., Siddiqi, M.U.: Multiple error detection and correction based on redundant residue number systems. IEEE Trans. Commun. **56**(3), 325–330 (2008)
17. Wang, X.J.: Improvement in distributed data storage scheme in wireless sensor networks. Netw. Secur. Technol. Appl. **2012**, 5–7 (2012)
18. Croman, K., et al.: On scaling decentralized blockchains. In: Clark, J., Meiklejohn, S., Ryan, P.Y.A., Wallach, D., Brenner, M., Rohloff, K. (eds.) FC 2016. LNCS, vol. 9604, pp. 106–125. Springer, Heidelberg (2016). https://doi.org/10.1007/978-3-662-53357-4_8

# Reliable Collaboration Mechanism of Side End Resources for Discrete Services of Virtual Power Plants

Jigao Song[1], Bingyang Han[1], Jiahui Guo[2(⊠)], Xiaolu Chen[3], Baozhu Zhao[3], and Shi Wang[2]

[1] Fibrlink Communications Co., Ltd., Beijing 100071, China
[2] State Key Laboratory of Networking and Switching Technology, Beijing University of Posts and Telecommunications, Beijing 100876, China
guojiahui0982@126.com
[3] State Grid Shanghai Electric Power Company Information and Communication Company, Shanghai 200072, China

**Abstract.** With the substantial increase in the number of participants in virtual power plants and the in-depth popularization of power Internet of Things, a large number of IoT terminals will be deployed on the internal and external networks of the system. Service terminals are connected to the network in different ways, and transmitted to the service system and cloud platform via the backbone network. In the process of data transmission and processing, the communication, computing, and storage resources required by the service terminal are highly heterogeneous and different. The bearing relationship between services and resources, and the connection relationship between resources in different network segments are complex, and it is impossible to Realize the integrated management of end-to-end resources. In response to the above problems, this paper proposes a MEC server collaborative computing model, which combines the computing capabilities of the service terminal itself and edge nodes to coordinate the offload rate between different devices to minimize the system's delay and energy consumption, and proposes A load balancing model that transfers tasks between overloaded and lightly loaded edge nodes to maximize system operating efficiency. Through simulation experiments, the method proposed in this paper effectively reduces the service delay and system energy consumption, and improves the reliability of the system.

**Keywords:** Mobile edge computing · Computation offloading · Machine learning · Artificial intelligence · Virtual power plant

## 1 Introduction

At present, renewable energy has become the main direction of global energy development in the future, virtual power plants [1] have become a regional multi-energy aggregation mode that realizes large-scale integration of renewable energy power generation into the grid. With the substantial growth of virtual power plants participating

© The Author(s), under exclusive license to Springer Nature Switzerland AG 2022
X. Sun et al. (Eds.): ICAIS 2022, CCIS 1588, pp. 194–206, 2022.
https://doi.org/10.1007/978-3-031-06764-8_16

subject, the continuous and in-depth popularization of Power Internet of Things, there will be a large number of Internet of Things terminals deployed on the internal and external networks of the system. Business terminals are connected to the network in different ways, and transmitted to the business system and cloud platform via the backbone network. In the process of data transmission and processing, the telecommunications, computing, and storage resources required by services in different network segments are heterogeneous and highly differentiated. The bearing relationship between services and resources, and the connection relationship between resources in different network segments are complicated, so it is hard to realize the integrated management of end-to-end resources. In the traditional centralized management mode, mobile services are sent to the cloud computing platform for processing, which causes greater transmission delay and calculation pressure, and cannot meet the service requirements of a large number of delay-sensitive services. On the other hand, although mobile edge computing [2] can reduce the delay caused by communication, it may cause excessive processing delay due to limited computing power. In the broader perspective of future computing offloading applications, cloud and mobile edge computing servers can coexist and complement each other, resulting in collaborative computing offloading.

The ultimate goal of mobile edge computing (MEC) [3] is to achieve an ultra-low response time. This time interval may include the waiting queue and processing time of the local central processing unit CPU or the CPU in the edge server, as well as the communication delay between the mobile device and the edge service node and the remote cloud. Considering the additional communication overhead brought by offloading, we can get a key technical challenge to find a balance between computing cost and communication cost, so as to satisfy terminal services with lower delay and energy consumption. Therefore, the application of edge computing technology to sink cloud storage [4] and computing capabilities to the access network can effectively alleviate the pressure on the core network channel and improve the service capabilities of the edge network. The integration of edge computing and 5G network architecture and the research on the reliable provision mechanism of edge collaboration services in high-speed mobile scenarios have become a hot spot in the industry [5].

## 2   System Model

This paper proposes a framework for automatic calculation and unloading of business terminals [6], as shown in Fig. 1. The framework consists of terminal equipment and MEC system, which means that some storage resources and computing resources in the cloud center are transferred to the edge of the network or the edge node MEC, and moved closer to the data source.

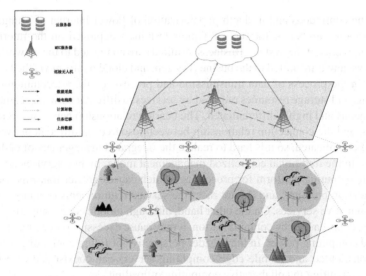

**Fig. 1.** Multi-user computing offload network architecture.

**Table 1.** Parameters of the model.

| Notation | Description |
|----------|-------------|
| $M$ | The set of business terminals |
| $N$ | The set of mobile edge nodes |
| $T_k$ | Computationally intensive tasks |
| $L_t$ | CPU calculation frequency |
| $f_R$ | The computing power of the MEC server |
| $\lambda_t$ | Ratio of result data volume to input data volume |
| $\alpha$ | Offload rate |
| $\delta_i$ | MEC load factor |
| $R(t)$ | Data transfer rate |
| $W(t)$ | Computing performance |
| $E(t)$ | MEC storage resources |
| $C(t)$ | MEC computing resources |

MEC sinks the resources in the cloud to a location closer to the terminal [7], such as a user terminal, and provides cloud services for users at the edge of the network. The users can offload computing tasks to the MEC server for execution, so as to get rid of the limitations of terminal equipment computing capabilities. In the service terminal offloading system, we use to denote the collection of mobile service terminals. The business terminal is at the mobile layer and is responsible for data collection. The mobile terminal can offload data (ID, location, speed, destination, etc.) to the edge layer to ensure that the information collected by the service terminal is credible. The edge nodes are distributed in the edge layer, and we use to denote the set of MEC. MEC needs to further process and analyze the collected information, which will generate computationally intensive tasks, can be calculated independently by the local MEC server or coordinated by neighboring MEC servers. The symbols commonly used in the text are summarized in Table 1.

## 2.1 Calculation Model

In the process of computation offloading for business terminal, there will be different uninstall strategies, and different uninstall strategies will bring different computing models. Therefore, the calculation model mainly depends on the uninstallation decision. The service terminal usually follows the binary uninstallation strategy [8] when uninstalling.

**Local Calculation (Third Level).** Assuming that the processing power allocated by the service terminal to its own calculation, that is, the frequency of the CPU is denoted as $f_i^{local}$, the power consumption of the service terminal to process data locally can be denoted as:

$$p_i^{local} = k_1 \left( f_i^{local} \right)^3 \tag{1}$$

where $k_1$ represents the effective switching capacitance related to the chip structure [9] in the service terminal. It can be seen from the above that the energy consumption calculated locally by the service terminal can be expressed as:

$$E_i^{local} = p_i^{local} \Delta t = k_1 \left( f_i^{local} \right)^3 \Delta t \tag{2}$$

Therefore, the amount of data processed locally by the business terminal is expressed as:

$$D_i^{local} = \frac{f_i^{local} \Delta t}{c} \tag{3}$$

where c is the density of data processing.

**Edge Server Node Computing (Third Level).** When a service terminal generates a computing task, the service terminal can select an edge node within its communication range, and offload the computing data of the task to the edge node for calculation. We assume that the processing capacity of the edge server is $f_k^{edge}$, then the power consumption of the edge node to process data is

$$p_j^{edge} = k_2 \left( f_j^{edge} \right)^3 \tag{4}$$

where $k_2$ represents the effective switching capacitance related to the edge server chip structure. Therefore, the energy consumption of edge node k in one-time calculation and processing of data is

$$E_j^{edge} = p_j^{edge} \Delta t = k_2 \left( f_j^{edge} \right)^3 \Delta t \tag{5}$$

Therefore, the amount of data processed by the edge node is

$$D_j^{edge} = \frac{f_j^{edge} \Delta t}{c}$$  (6)

## 2.2 Communication Model

The communication between the service terminal and the edge node involves offloading data to the edge node. In the network architecture, communication is involved in the process of offloading data to edge nodes. In order to model the offloading process, we denote the path loss as $d$ and $\vartheta$, where $d$ and $\vartheta$ represent the distance from the transmitter to the receiver and the path loss index respectively [10]. The channel fading coefficient is denoted by h, and h is modeled as a circularly symmetric complex Gaussian random variable. When the data is transmitted and offloaded on the channel, the transmission rate is:

$$r_{i,j}^t = B \log_2 \left( 1 + \frac{P_i^{tr}|h|^2}{\omega_0 \left(d_{i,j}^t\right)^\vartheta} \right)$$  (7)

where $p_i^{tr}$ is the transmission power of the service terminal, $\omega_0$ is the Gaussian white noise power, and $d_{i,j}^t$ is the distance from the service terminal to the edge node $k$ in the time slot $t$. But at the same time, when the service terminal is performing data transmission, it will involve offloading to multiple edge nodes for calculation, so the energy consumed in communication will be related to the offloading path.

## 2.3 Communication Model

Compared with cloud centers, the resources of edge nodes are still very limited [11]. With the increase in the number of service terminals, it is difficult for a single MEC server to simultaneously meet the different needs of service terminals for offloading services. Figure 4.1 is a flowchart of edge node load balancing. At the same time, the load status of MEC servers in the cluster is different. For example, in emergencies, a large number of information collection terminals will upload data for processing, causing some MEC servers to process a large number of business requests and a high load rate, while some MEC servers are relatively idle and in a low load state. Therefore, we propose a mode of distributing the tasks of a single service terminal to adjacent MEC servers for collaborative computing to optimize resource utilization and further reduce system delay.

In the local offloading calculation, the task $T_k$ is directly calculated by the local MEC server $n_i$. We use $L_t$ (CPU calculation frequency) to represent the total CPU cycles of task $T_k$, which can be defined as:

$$L_t = D_t X_t$$  (8)

Let $Q_t$ denote the number of CPU cycles required by the MEC server to process one-bit computing tasks. The number of cycles is determined by the type of application and can be obtained by offline measurement. $f_R$ is the computing power of the MEC server, which satisfies $f_R \leq f_{max}$. Therefore, the calculation rate $R_l(t)$ of the local MEC server can be expressed as:

$$R_l(t) = \frac{f_R}{Q_t} \tag{9}$$

Assuming that the tasks generated by the mobile service terminal obey the Poisson distribution [12], the tasks arrive at the scheduler of the MEC server $n_i$ at a rate of $\lambda_i$. We model the MEC server of the access point as an M/M/1 queue. The tasks arriving at the MEC server $n_i$ for calculation follow the Poisson process, and the arrival rate is $\lambda_i$. Therefore, the average delay $\Delta T_l(t)$ for the local MEC server to complete the task can be expressed as:

$$\Delta T_l(t) = \frac{1}{\mu_l - \lambda_i} \tag{10}$$

And, $\mu_l = 1/T_{exe,l}(t)$. $T_{exe,l}(t)$ is the time for the local MEC server to perform the calculation task $T_k$, which can be expressed as:

$$T_{exe,l}(t) = \frac{D_t X_t}{f_R} = \frac{L_t}{f_R} \tag{11}$$

In another model, we optimize the local computing model, and design the model through collaborative offloading between edge nodes. Similar to the assumption in literature [13], we analyze the performance of this model, and the computing task can be Divided into two parts: $(1 - \alpha)D_t$ is used for the calculation of the local MEC server $n_i$, and $\alpha D_t$ is used for the calculation of the adjacent MEC server $n_j$, And $\alpha$ is the offload rate, and the processed result is finally merged into the local MEC server $n_i$. Assuming that the tasks arriving at the MEC server $n_i$ follow the Poisson process, the task scheduler on $n_i$ is determined by the value of the load factor $\delta_i$, and the arrival rate is $(1 - \delta_i)\lambda_i$, and the average task execution time is $T_{exe,i}(t)$. At the $T_{exe,i}(t) \circ$ At the same time, the average delay $\Delta T_i(t)$ for the MEC server $n_i$ to complete the task can be expressed as:

$$\Delta T_i(t) = \frac{1}{\mu_i - (1 - \delta_i)\lambda_i} \tag{12}$$

$\mu_i = 1/T_{exe,i}(t)$, and $T_{exe,i}(t)$ can be defined as:

$$T_{exe,i}(t) = \frac{(1 - \alpha)D_t X_t}{f_R} = \frac{(1 - \alpha)L_t}{f_R} \tag{13}$$

In addition, the offloading task arriving at the neighboring MEC server $n_j$ also follows the Poisson process, and the arrival rate is $\delta_i\lambda_i$. Similarly, the average delay $\Delta T_j(t)$ for MEC serving $n_j$ to complete the task can be expressed as:

$$\Delta T_j(t) = \frac{1}{\mu_j - \delta_i\lambda_i} \tag{14}$$

$\mu_j = 1/T_{exe,j}(t)$, and $T_{exe,j}(t)$ can be defined as:

$$T_{exe,j}(t) = \frac{\alpha D_t X_t}{f_R} = \frac{\alpha L_t}{f_R} \tag{15}$$

When the adjacent MEC server $n_j$ is selected in the time slot $t$, the transmission rate from the MEC server $n_i$ to $n_j$ can be expressed as:

$$R_{i,j}(t) = B_m \cdot \log_2(1 + \frac{P_{i,j}(t)g_{i,j}(t)}{\sigma_{i,j}^2(t)}) \tag{16}$$

And $P_{i,j}(t)$ is the transmission power from $n_i$ to $n_j$ in time slot $t$, $g_{i,j}(t)$ is the channel gain between $n_i$ and $n_j$ in time slot $t$, and $\sigma_{i,j}(t)$ is the noise variance from $n_i$ to $n_j$ in time slot $t$. Therefore, in this mode, the communication delay $T_{i,j}(t)$ of offloading some computing tasks can be defined as:

$$T_{i,j}(t) = \frac{\alpha D_t}{R_{i,j}(t)} \tag{17}$$

Since neighboring MEC server $n_j$ needs to merge results into local MEC server $n_i$ after performing some calculation tasks, the delay $T_{j,i}(t)$ for MEC server $n_j$ to transmit part of calculation results to $n_i$ can be defined as:

$$T_{j,i}(t) = \frac{\alpha \lambda_t D_t}{R_{j,i}(t)} = \frac{\alpha \lambda_t D_t}{R_{i,j}(t)} \tag{18}$$

In this mode, the total time delay $T_{tot,ij}(t)$ can be measured only after uninstalling and completing all calculation tasks $T_k$, which can be expressed as:

$$\begin{aligned} T_{tot,ij}(t) &= \max\{\Delta T_i(t), T_{i,j}(t) + \Delta T_j(t) + T_{j,i}(t)\} \\ &= \max\{\frac{1}{\mu_i - (1 - \delta_i)\lambda_i}, \frac{\alpha D_t}{R_{i,j}(t)} + \frac{1}{\mu_i - \delta_i \lambda_i} + \frac{\alpha \lambda_t D_t}{R_{i,j}(t)}\} \end{aligned} \tag{19}$$

Based on above analysis of two calculation modes, the total time delay for system to execute calculation tasks can be expressed as:

$$T_{tot}(t) = (1 - a_n(t))\Delta T_l(t) + a_n(t)T_{tot,ij}(t) \tag{20}$$

In the above model, the local MEC server performs offloading calculation. In the local offloading calculation, the task is directly calculated by the local MEC server $n_i$.

$$\Delta E_l(t) = \frac{1}{\mu_l - \lambda_i} \bullet P_{power} \tag{21}$$

In another model, we use collaborative offloading between edge nodes to design the model. Similar to the delay model, the calculation tasks $T_k$ are divided into two parts: $(1-\alpha)D_t$ used for local MEC server $n_i$ calculations, $\alpha D_t$ used for adjacent MEC server $n_j$ calculations, among them $\alpha$ is the uninstall rate, and processed results are finally merged into the local MEC server $n_i$. In this mode, we can measure total energy consumption

$E_{tot,ij}(t)$ only after uninstalling and completing all calculation tasks $T_k$, which can be expressed as:

$$E_{tot,ij}(t) = \max\{\Delta E_i(t), E_{i,j}(t) + \Delta E_j(t) + E_{j,i}(t)\}$$

$$= \max\{\{\frac{1}{\mu_i - (1 - \delta_i)\lambda_i}, \frac{\alpha D_t}{R_{i,j}(t)} + \frac{1}{\mu_j - \delta_i\lambda_i} + \frac{\alpha\lambda_t D_t}{R_{i,j}(t)}\} \bullet P_{power}\} \quad (22)$$

## 2.4 Load Balancing Model

In a business terminal offloading environment, MEC server loads generally vary greatly and cluster computing resources are unevenly distributed. Therefore, resource usage of MEC server needs to be considered when computing tasks are offloaded, so that computing resources of MEC server can be used reasonably, and make sure that MEC server is in a load balanced state. We integrate storage resources and computing resources of MEC server to evaluate current operating status. We define the performance of MEC server in the network as $W_{cap,i}(t) = \{E_{cap,i}(t), C_{cap,i}(t)\}$, where $E_{cap,i}(t)$ and $C_{cap,i}(t)$ represent the storage resources and computing resources of MEC server $n_i$ respectively. The load status of MEC server is $F_{cur,i}(t) = \{E_{cur,i}(t), C_{cur,i}(t)\}$, where $E_{cur,i}(t)$ and $C_{cur,i}(t)$ respectively represent the current storage resource usage and computing resource usage of MEC server. Therefore, the storage resource utilization rate $E_i(t)$ and computing resource occupancy rate $C_i(t)$ of MEC server $n_i$ can be expressed as:

$$E_i(t) = \frac{E_{cur,i}(t)}{E_{cap,i}(t)} \quad (23)$$

$$C_i(t) = \frac{C_{cur,i}(t)}{C_{cap,i}(t)} \quad (24)$$

Furthermore, the load rate of MEC server $n_i$ can be defined as

$$F_{load,i}(t) = \beta E_i(t) + \eta C_i(t) \quad (25)$$

Among $\beta + \eta = 1$, $\beta$ and $\eta$ indicate the weight of index, the higher weight value represents the larger proportion of corresponding resources and the stronger dependence.

Suppose $F_s = \{F_{load,1}(t), F_{load,2}(t), \cdots, F_{load,n}(t)\}$ be the set of MEC server load rate in the system. The average load rate reflects load status of entire cluster. The lower average load rate indicates the lower overall load of the cluster and the better load status. The average load rate of the cluster $F_{ave}(t)$ can be expressed as:

$$F_{ave}(t) = \frac{1}{n}\sum_{i=1}^{n} F_{load,i}(t) \quad (26)$$

Suppose $\sigma_F$ is the standard deviation of cluster load rate. The load standard deviation reflects load stability of entire cluster. The lower value it has, the more balanced cluster load and the stronger stability it has. $\sigma_F$ can be defined as:

$$\sigma_F = \sqrt{\frac{1}{n-1}\sum_{i=1}^{n}(F_{load,i}(t) - F_{ave}(t))^2} \quad (27)$$

Therefore, we can use the load factor $\delta_i$ to express the load of MEC server, which can be defined as:

$$\delta_i = \frac{F_{load,i}(t) - F_{ave}(t) + \sigma_F}{2\sigma_F} \tag{28}$$

## 3    Design and Implementation of Algorithm

In the A3C algorithm, the optimizer of neural network uses an asynchronous gradient descent method [14]. The training process is mostly multi-threaded asynchronous mode [15]. The neural network of each thread is independently trained and calculated neural network parameter gradients, and then asynchronously updates to the network parameters of global network. Using multiple CPU threads at the same time can effectively improve learning efficiency. Global neural network and neural network parameters of each thread are continuously synchronized and iterated repeatedly until neural network parameters converge. The A3C algorithm makes full use of computing resources and effectively breaks the correlation between data. Since there are both continuous action space and discrete action space in the system, we use the A3C algorithm to solve the proposed problem.

### 3.1    State Space and State Transition Probability

We express the current state space as a combination of available computing resources $C_s(t) = \{C_1(t), C_2(t), \ldots C_n(t)\}$, available storage resources $E_s(t) = \{E_1(t), E_2(t), \ldots E_n(t)\}$, and channel conditions $G_2(t) = \{g_{i,j}(t)\}$ of MEC server:

$$S_{s2}(t) \triangleq \{C_s(t), E_s(t), G_2(t)\} \tag{29}$$

After performing an action, the probability of leaving the current state $S_{s2}(t)$ to the next state $s_{s2}(t+1)$ can be defined as:

$$\Pr(s_{s2}(t+1)|s_{s2}(t), a_{s2}(t)) = \int_{s_{s2}^t}^{s_{s2}^{t+1}} f(s_{s2}(t), a_{s2}(t), s_{s2}) ds_{s2} \tag{30}$$

### 3.2    Action Space

The action space includes offloading decision $a(t)$ and offloading rate decision $a(t)$. We use $A_{s2}(t)$ to define the action set: $A_{s2}(t) \triangleq \{a(t), a(t)\}$. Among them, $a(t) \in [0, 1]$, and $a(t)$ can be further expressed as:

$$a(t) \triangleq \{a_1(t), a_2(t), \cdots, a_N(t)\} \tag{31}$$

### 3.3 Reward Function

To further optimize the delay of system, we define the reward function as:

$$r_{s2} = \begin{cases} W_{s2}(t) \\ 0, \ otherwise \end{cases}$$

where $W_{s2}(t) = \dfrac{1}{\sum\limits_{n=1}^{N} T_{tot,n}(t)}$.

## 4  Simulations

This paper proposes two models based on artificial intelligence A3C algorithm: the establishment of a collaborative computing model between access points and adjacent edge nodes and a load balancing model. Above two algorithms involve the problem of offloading rate. There are two main forms of offloading rate: the first is offloading mode of service terminals and edge nodes, that is, the offloading and offloading rate formulation between user terminal equipment and edge nodes. The role of the offload rate in the mode is to determine how much data needs to be offloaded to edge nodes for calculation. In this case, offload rate will affect the overall computing load of the system. If the excessive computing demand is burdened on the business terminal device itself, the system will be unreliable; the second is edge node collaborative offloading mode, which involves computing offloading cooperation between edge node and edge node. The offloading rate in this mode needs to balance the load between different nodes to meet the establishment of load balancing model that is, the overloaded nodes unload to the lightly loaded nodes, and the load ratio is used to balance the overall delay and energy consumption of system and minimize the overall consumption of system. In above two kinds of offloading processes, the formulation of offloading rate is involved. In terms of delay, the formulation of an appropriate offloading rate can effectively reduce total transmission delay and improve the reliability of system.

Figure 2 shows the simulation of offloading time delay. In the dual Y-axis graph, the abscissa is offloading rate, the Y1 axis is average reward, and the Y2 axis is average

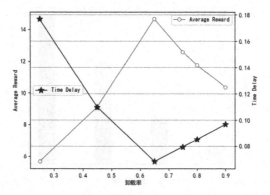

**Fig. 2.** System delay.

offloading time delay. As the offloading rate changes, according to image curve, we can see that system delay first decreases and then increases, and the average reward presents a curve shape that first increases and then decreases. As can be seen from the figure below, when the offloading rate is 0.65, time delay is the smallest, the system is reliable, and the efficiency is the highest.

Figure 3 shows the simulation of offloading energy consumption. The simulation diagram is a dual Y-axis simulation diagram. The Y1 axis is the average system delay, and the Y2 axis is the overall energy consumption of system. As the offloading rate changes, you can see the system tendency according to the image curve. The energy consumption decreases first and then increases, and the average reward presents a curve shape that first increases and then decreases. It can be seen that when the offloading rate is 0.85, the overall energy consumption of system is the smallest.

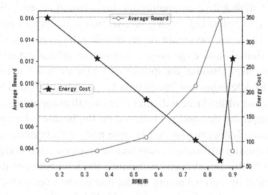

**Fig. 3.** System energy consumption.

Since service terminal IR (Inspection robot) and edge node MEC are randomly distributed in the simulation environment, it is impossible to control the number of service terminals covered by IR-MEC at a certain time. According to Fig. 4, we can see that as the number of service terminals loaded by a single MEC gradually increases, the

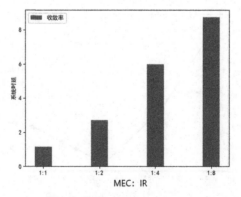

**Fig. 4.** Delay convergence rate.

convergence rate increases accordingly, and the convergence rate is the overall reciprocal of system delay. The higher convergence rate indicates the less overall system delay. As the number of loads increases, the reason for the higher and higher convergence rate is that when too many service terminals are loaded by MEC, it will cause load imbalance, which will lead to an increase in delay. Therefore, when MEC:IR is 1:1, that is, a single MEC only loads one IR, the system delay is optimal.

Figure 5 is a simulation diagram of the system energy consumption convergence rate. The energy consumption convergence rate is reciprocal of the total energy consumption of system. According to the energy consumption convergence rate graph, we can get that when MEC load is only one user terminal, the system energy consumption is the lowest. When the load of different edge nodes is unbalanced, load balance between edge nodes can be performed. It can be concluded that when MEC:IR is 1:1, the total energy consumption of system is the lowest.

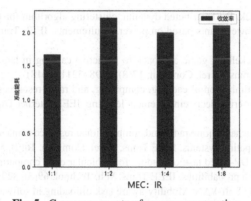

**Fig. 5.** Convergence rate of energy consumption.

Comprehensive analysis of the above offloading rate and edge node load model, we can find that the optimal offloading rate will be different for different time delay and energy consumption models. For the load model, when the MEC:IR is 1:1, the system delay cost and system energy consumption are optimal, but at the same time we can also see that although the overall system performance is the best when the load ratio is 1:1, to achieve a better load effect, the number of loads can be increased as much as possible within the acceptable range of the system energy consumption convergence rate and time delay convergence rate to make system more efficient.

## 5  Conclusion

This paper studies the joint optimization strategy of computing offloading and resource allocation in the multi-access edge computing environment with multi-user terminal equipment and multi-edge server scenarios to achieve the goal of minimizing system energy consumption and overall delay. Through the establishment of a load balancing model and a coordinated computing model of adjacent MEC servers, the final offloading decision is made by combining the computing power between service terminal itself and edge node. In the process of achieving computational load balancing, the offloading rate between different devices is coordinated to minimize delay and energy consumption of system, and a load balancing model is proposed, which will perform the task migration load balancing between overload and light load edge nodes to maximize the efficiency of system operation.

Regarding the research in this direction, this article still has some outstanding problems: when service equipment is moving across domains, there will be problems such as high delay and poor reliability caused by cross-domain communication link switching, interruption, and service retransmission. In the follow-up research, I will conduct further research on the above issues and continue to improve them.

# References

1. Zhang, R., Hredzak, B.: Distributed dynamic clustering algorithm for formation of heterogeneous virtual power plants based on power requirements. IEEE Trans. Smart Grid **99**, 1 (2020)
2. Zheng, Z.: A Stackelberg game approach to proactive caching in large-scale mobile edge networks. IEEE Trans. Wirel. Commun. **17**(8), 5198–5211 (2018)
3. Wei, Y.: Joint Optimization of caching, computing, and radio resources for fog-enabled iot using natural actor-critic deep reinforcement learning. IEEE Internet Things J. **6**, 2061–2073 (2019)
4. Mao, Y., et al.: Stochastic joint radio and computational resource management for multi-user mobile-edge computing systems. IEEE Trans. Wirel. Commun. **16**(9), 5994–6009 (2017)
5. Zhang, X., et al.: DP-based task offloading for vehicular edge computing under certain and uncertain transition probabilities. IEEE Trans. Veh. Technol. **69**(3), 3296–3309 (2020)
6. Misra, S., Bera, S.: Soft-VAN: Mobility-aware task offloading in software-defined vehicular network. IEEE Trans. Veh. Technol. **69**(2), 2071–2078 (2019)
7. Taleb, T., Ksentini, A., Frangoudis, P.A.: Follow-me cloud: when cloud services follow mobile users. IEEE Trans. Cloud Comput. **7**(2), 369–382 (2016)
8. Cao, J., Yang, L., Cao, J.: Revisiting computation partitioning in future 5G-based edge computing environments. IEEE Internet Things J. **6**(2), 2427–2438 (2018)
9. Almutairi, J., Aldossary, M.: Exploring and modelling iot offloading policies in edge cloud environments. Comput. Syst. Sci. Eng. **41**(2), 611–624 (2022)
10. Ning, Z., et al.: Intelligent edge computing in internet of vehicles: a joint computation offloading and caching solution. IEEE Trans. Intell. Transp. Syst. **22**(4), 2212–2225 (2020)
11. Ebrahimzadeh, A., Maier, M.: Cooperative computation offloading in fiwi enhanced 4G hetnets using self-organizing mec. IEEE Trans. Wirel. Commun. **99**, 1 (2020)
12. Bi, S., Huang, L., Zhang, Y.: Joint optimization of service caching placement and computation offloading in mobile edge computing systems. IEEE Trans. Wirel. Commun. **99**, 1 (2020)
13. Liang, G., Wang, Q., Xin, J., Li, M., Xu, W.: Overview of mobile edge computing resource allocation. J. Inf. Secur. **6**(03), 227–256 (2021)
14. Yang, B.: Computation offloading in multi-access edge computing networks: a multi-task learning approach. IEEE Trans. Mob. Comput. **99**, 1 (2020)
15. Li, M., Gao, J., Zhao, L., Shen, X.: Deep reinforcement learning for collaborative edge computing in vehicular networks. IEEE Trans. Cogn. Commun. Netw. **6**(4), 1122–1135 (2020)

# An Improved Certificateless Partial Blind Signature Scheme Based on Homomorphic Encryption

Pengfei Tan[1], Zhi Qin[1,2(✉)], Wunan Wan[1,2], Shibin Zhang[1,2], Jinquan Zhang[1,2], and Jinyue Xia[3]

[1] School of Cybersecurity, Chengdu University of Information Technology, Chengdu 610225, China
cuitqz@qq.com

[2] Advanced Cryptography and System Security Key Laboratory of Sichuan Province, Chengdu 610225, China

[3] International Business Machines Corporation (IBM), New York, NY 10041, USA

**Abstract.** A modified Paillier homomorphic cryptography-based partial blind signature scheme is proposed to address the problems of centralized key generation in traditional blind signature schemes and the fact that the current tamper-proof protection scheme for public messages only protects them after they have been attacked or does not protect public messages. In this scheme, the certificateless idea allows the distribution of keys to be decentralized to the KGC (Public Key Generation) and the user's personal key to be protected, while the partial blind signature idea ensures that the signer's signature is not misused and protects the signed message. The experimental results show that the use of the Paillier homomorphic encryption algorithm not only satisfies the feasible operational efficiency, but also demonstrates that the scheme can be resisted before the public message is tampered with, improving the security of the scheme in terms of security and feasibility.

**Keywords:** Cryptography · Homomorphic encryption · Partially blind signature · Privacy

## 1 Introduction

Blind signatures were first proposed by Chaum [1] in 1983 and after proposing a scheme based on the difficulty of decomposing large integers, various blind signature schemes were proposed over a period of time, and not only that, various improvement schemes were created accordingly after that considering the security factor of blind signatures. In 1996, the problem of complete blindness of blind signatures [2] was discovered and pointed out by Abe, i.e., a malicious requestor can take advantage of the complete blindness property of blind signatures and thus maliciously misuse the signature, but due to the characteristic of blind signatures, the signer himself does not know the signature information associated with the signature and thus is not aware of the misuse caused by

© The Author(s), under exclusive license to Springer Nature Switzerland AG 2022
X. Sun et al. (Eds.): ICAIS 2022, CCIS 1588, pp. 207–221, 2022.
https://doi.org/10.1007/978-3-031-06764-8_17

the signature; therefore, in 1997 Abe proposed another partial blind signature scheme [3] to solve this problem by defining a model in the scheme and introducing public message constraints in it to solve the drawback of complete blindness of blind signatures, allowing partial blind signatures to be further developed.

Xiaoping Zhang [4] proposed an identity-based blind signature scheme, but the efficiency of this scheme is low and unsatisfactory because the use of bilinear operations in many places in the paper leads to an increase in the time consumption and the computational cost. Liu [5] proposed an identity-based partial blind signature scheme, which is based on the CDHP (Computational Diffie- Hellman Problem), but the scheme simply presents the security problem without proof. Later, Yu fang Mao [6] proved the security of the scheme [5] based on the n-CDH problem under the stochastic prediction model in its entirety. Noether [7] proposed the Monero scheme to protect the user's identity and transaction information, which is decentralized, efficient and verifiable, and uses the Pedersen commitment to hide the transaction amount is hidden and the transaction address is hidden by ring signature technique and one-time key technique, which further protects the privacy of both parties of the transaction. However, Kumar [8] performed a validation analysis of the untraceable of the Menero scheme and showed that more than 98% of them can be traced. Er gen Liu [9] improved on the certificateless blind signature scheme, which was considered secure under the random prediction machine model, but a study of it revealed that the scheme is vulnerable to tampering public message attacks and can be misused once the public message is tampered with the signature. Chen [10] built the certificateless digital blind signature scheme into the identity mechanism and introduced the discrete logarithm problem in the scheme, but then the algorithm designed in the concrete implementation is too simple and not highly secure. R.P [11] introduced bilinear technique in blind signature technique to propose a new blind signature scheme, the reference of bilinear technique increases the security of the scheme, but the use of a large number of exponential and modal operations reduces the operational efficiency of the scheme. Suzhen Cao [12] analyzed and improved on the basis of scheme [10], but did not use bilinear in order to reduce the overhead, so the security was reduced, and the secret key of the user of the scheme was decided by the third-party KGC, and the individual user was not involved, so the uncertificated nature was not highlighted and the security was reduced. Cui [13] proposed a restricted scheme for partial blind signatures, which improved the computational efficiency, but it also does not use bilinear, which reduces the overhead but decreases the security. Zheng Tao [14] proposed a quantum blind signature scheme, which guarantees the relative security of the signature process by invoking the blind signature scheme as well as the quantum entanglement property. In 2014, Zhang [15] proposed an identity agent blind signature scheme, which is based on the small integer problem and utilizes the lattice based agent technique and lattice trapdoor technique to prove the unconditional blindness of the scheme as well as its ability to effectively resist selective ciphertext attacks. In 2020, Rawal [16] pointed out that the master key of scheme [15] can be easily stolen by the user and thus the security is significantly reduced, in 2021 Zhou [17] proposed a lattice based identity agent partial blind signature scheme which is based on a standard model and uses cascade matrix technique to address the vulnerability of the master key to theft in scheme [15].

In this paper, we analyze the advantages and disadvantages of the current blind signature and partial blind signature schemes by combining the current privacy protection problems faced by blind signatures and traditional PKG-generated user private keys: the complete blindness of blind signatures leads to great limitations in their applications, while the current partial blind signatures can effectively solve the shortcomings of complete blindness, while the certificate free concept proposed by Rong et al. makes the secret key distribution of traditional blind signatures no longer centralized, allowing the user and the PKG to jointly decide the distribution of the secret key and also resist the public message [18], but only the resistance to the public message is effective after the attack or without any encryption processing of the public message, and the dishonest user can still tamper with the public message [19, 23]. Therefore, an improved privacy-preserving scheme combining a certificateless partially blind signature algorithm with a homomorphic encryption algorithm is proposed, which addresses the problem of tampering with public messages by focusing the problem on the public message before it is tampered with, thus preventing its tampering.

## 2  Preliminary Knowledge

### 2.1  Partial Blind Signature

With the evolution of cryptography, the disadvantages of blind signatures have gradually emerged. The two characteristics of blind signatures make blind signatures too absolute for the signer and the message to be signed, causing the intent of the signer and the signed message to be unknowable, bringing uncontrollability and thus misuse by criminals. The disadvantage of complete blindness of blind signatures in electronic cash or digital currencies can make them more illegal to transact [22].

The application scenario requires controlled operations on the signature and the message to be signed, so partial blind signatures are proposed. Partial blind signature [24], like blind signature, does not require knowledge of the specific content of the signature, but a public message is added to it, which is negotiated between the signer and the request signature, and is a common constraint on the signer and the signature message, which ensures the non-maliciousness of the signature message and the reasonable signature of the signer, and the specific algorithm process is explained in the proposed scheme of this paper.

### 2.2  Paillier Homomorphic Encryption

Homomorphic encryption was introduced by Rivest et al. in 1978, who discovered that some encryption functions are homomorphic in nature so that the data can be encrypted and then operated on to ensure its privacy. Homomorphic encryption is a cryptographic technique based on mathematical conundrums and computational complexity theory, and essentially the results obtained by performing the corresponding operations on the plaintext and ciphertext are equivalent [25]. Therefore, by taking advantage of this special property, one can hand over the data information to an untrustworthy third-party organization that is computationally efficient, while not being afraid of private data leakage. Of course, homomorphic encryption also has limitations such as the efficiency problem in computing, but these problems will be solved with deeper research on it. At present, homomorphic encryption is mainly divided into three categories: additive homomorphic, multiplicative homomorphic and full homomorphic encryption. Tian Jing [20] proposes a protection algorithm that effectively guarantees the location privacy among the entities involved in the swarm intelligence-aware task, and improves the privacy protection of the location by introducing paillier to achieve the secret matching of the task. Yi qing Diao [21] proposes a dual privacy protection method for coalition chains based on group signature and homomorphic encryption, which verifies the legitimacy of transactions and protects the privacy of transaction amounts by introducing the plus homomorphic nature of the paillier algorithm. The Paillier encryption algorithm cited in this paper is additive homomorphic encryption, which itself has the advantages of simple implementation and high efficiency.

The process of Paillier homomorphic encryption algorithm is mainly divided into secret key generation [26], encryption and decryption processes:

1) Secret key generation:first, select two large prime numbers $p$, $q$ at random and they satisfy Eq. (1), then calculating $n = p \bullet q$ and the private key $\lambda = lcm(p-1)(q-1)$ and then randomly selecting an integer $g (g \in z_{n^2}^*)$ and calculating $\mu$(which satisfies Eq. (2)), where the calculation method $L$ can be expressed as Eq. (3). Finally, the public key is obtained as $(n, g)$, and the private key is $\lambda$.

$$gcd(pq, (p-1)(q-1)) = 1 \tag{1}$$

$$gcd(L(g^\lambda \bmod n^2), n) = 1 \tag{2}$$

$$L(v) = (v-1)v^{-1} \tag{3}$$

2) Encryption process: Given a plaintext m and a randomly selected integer w, the encryption process is given by Eq. (4):

$$C = g^m \cdot w^n \bmod n^2 \tag{4}$$

3) Decryption process: be given by Eq. (5)

$$m = gcd(L(c^\lambda \bmod n^2) \cdot \mu, n) \tag{5}$$

Next, the Paillier homomorphic encryption is verified by assuming that there are two plaintexts $m_1$ and $m_2$, which are encrypted to obtain Eqs. (6) and (7), respectively, and Eq. (8) is obtained by the homomorphic encryption property, and the following equation $E$ is the encryption algorithm and $D$ is the decryption algorithm:

$$E(m_1) = g^{m_1} \cdot w_1^n (\bmod n^2) \tag{6}$$

$$E(m_2) = g^{m_2} \cdot w_2^n (\bmod n^2) \tag{7}$$

$$D(E(m_1)E(m_2)) = D(g^{m_1+m_2}(w_1w_2)^n \bmod n^2) = m_1 + m_2 \qquad (8)$$

It can be concluded that the Paillier homomorphic encryption algorithm encrypts two plaintexts and then multiplies the two ciphertexts obtained, and then decrypts them to obtain the same value as the value obtained by adding the two plaintexts, which is consistent with the additive homomorphism property of homomorphic encryption.

# 3 An Improved Certificateless Partial Blind Signature Scheme Based on Homomorphic Encryption

This scheme proposed in this section is to prevent the public message from being tampered with, mainly by introducing homomorphic encryption features to verify the public message for each signature to ensure the authenticity of the public message. The main model of this scheme involves PKG (private key generator), Alice the signer, Bob the requester, and V the verifier, and the specific scheme flow is described as follows:

## 3.1 Building System Parameters

**Definition 1.** The PKG selects a large prime number $q \leq 2^k$, the order of the additive cyclic group $G_1$ is $q$, and the order of the multiplicative cyclic group $G_2$ is $q$. Let a generating element of $G_1$ be $P$, and a bilinear map $e$ of $G_1 \times G_2 \to G_2$, and compute $G = e(P, P)$. The PKG randomly selects a number $s \in {}_RZ_q^*$, computes $P_{pub} = sP$ and uses it as the master public key of the system, and then selects three secure collision-resistant hash functions $H_1 : \{0, 1\}^*, H_2 : \{0, 1\}^* \times G_2 \to {}_RZ_q^*, H_3 : \{0, 1\}^* \to {}_RZ_q^*$. Therefore, the public parameter of the system is $\{G_1, G_2, e, q, P, P_{pub}, H_1, H_2, H_3\}$, and the master key $s$ of the system is kept secret.

## 3.2 Secret Key Generation

**Generate Partial Keys via PKG**
Let the identity of the signer Alice be $Id_A$, first PKG verifies Alice's identity, then calculates $S_A = (s + H_1(Id_A))^{-1}P$ as Alice's partial private key, and sends it to Alice over the secure channel. after Alice receives it, calculates the equation $P_A = P_{pub} + H_1(Id_A)P$, and verifies $G = e(S_A, P_A)$ whether it holds, if it holds then Alice accepts the partial key generated by PKG, if it does not hold, it will reject the partial key, and at the same time tells PKG to generate a new partial key again and repeats the above steps until the equation holds.

**Generate the User's Personal Secret Key**
The signer Alice picks a secret value $x_i \in {}_RZ_q^*$, and computes $S_{Id_A} = sx_iS_A$ as her private key, and then uses the private key to compute the public key: $PK_A = e(S_{Id_A}P, P_A)$, thus obtaining the user's public key as $PK_A$, and the private key pair as $(S_A, S_{Id_A})$.

### 3.3  Signature Process

Let the identity of the requester Bob is $Id_B$, and the signature message is $m \in \{0, 1\}^*$, the requester Bob selects a public message $C_B$ and uses the Paillier homomorphic encryption algorithm to obtain the private key $\lambda_B$ and converts $C_B$ to ciphertext $M_B$, then sends it to the signer Alice, Alice also selects a public message $C_A$ and uses the homomorphic encryption algorithm to obtain the private key $\lambda_A$ and converts $C_A$ to ciphertext $M_A$ and sends it to Bob, finally Alice uses the Finally, Alice uses the homomorphic encryption principle to multiply the $M_A$ and $M_B$ to obtain the final public message $C = D(M_A \bullet M_B)$, and then calculates $PK_A^{H_3(D(M_A \bullet M_B))}$ as the public key parameter and makes it public. The following signature interaction is performed, and it should be noted that before each signature interaction Alice will re-verify the public message using the ciphertext sent by Bob, and Bob will also verify it using the ciphertext sent by Alice (see Fig. 1 for details).

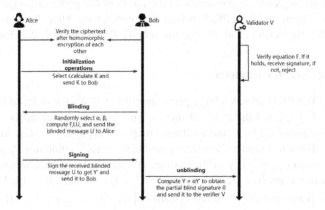

**Fig. 1.** Signature process.

### Initialization
The signer, Alice, selects a random number $r \in {}_R Z_q^*$, and calculates $K = E^r PK_A^{H_3(D(M_A \bullet M_B))}$, then sends $K$ secretly to Bob over a secure channel.

### Blinding
After the requester Bob receives K, he selects two numbers $\alpha, \beta \in_R Z_q^*$ at random again as the blinding factors for the message blinding process, and calculates $F = K^\alpha PK_A^{\alpha\beta}$,

$l = H_2(m, D(M_A \bullet M_B), F)$, $U = (\alpha^{-1}h + PK_3^{-1(D(M_A \bullet M_B))}\beta)$ and finally sends the blinded message $U$ to Alice.

**Signed**

Alice receives the message U from Bob, signs it, computes $Y' = rS_A + H_3(D(M_A \bullet M_B))S_{Id_A}U$, and sends $Y'$ to Bob.

**Unblinding**

Bob starts to unblind the blind signature $Y'$ and computes $Y = \alpha Y'$, obtaining the final partial blind signature as $\theta = (Y, m, l, F, D(M_A \bullet M_B))$.

**Verify**

After receiving a partial blind signature $\theta = (Y, m, l, F, D(M_A \bullet M_B))$, the verifier V verifies that the equation $F = e(Y, P_{pub} + H_1(Id_A)P)PK_A^{-lH_3(D(M_A \bullet M_B))}$ holds, and accepts the signature if it holds, or rejects it if it does not.

## 4 Security Analysis

### 4.1 Correctness Analysis

For the correctness analysis of the scheme, it is sufficient to show that partial blind signatures $\theta$ hold in the verification equation, which is verified as follows:

$$
\begin{aligned}
&e(Y, P_{pub} + H_1(Id_A)P)PK_A^{-lH_3(D(M_A \bullet M_B))} \\
&= e(\alpha Y', P_{pub} + H_1(Id_A)P)PK_A^{-lH_3(D(M_A \bullet M_B))} \\
&= e(\alpha(rS_A + H_3(D(M_A \bullet M_B))S_{Id_A}U, P_A)PK_A^{-lH_3(D(M_A \bullet M_B))} \\
&= e(\alpha rS_A + \alpha H_3(D(M_A \bullet M_B))S_{Id_A}((\alpha^{-1}l + H_3^{-1}(D(M_A \bullet M_B))\beta)P, P_A) \\
&\qquad\qquad PK_A^{-lH_3(D(M_A \bullet M_B))} \\
&= e(P, P)^{\alpha r}PK_A^{\alpha H_3(D(M_A \bullet M_B))}PK_A^{rH_3(D(M_A \bullet M_B))}e(S_{Id_A}P, P)^{\alpha\beta}PK_A^{-lH_3(D(M_A \bullet M_B))} \\
&= (E^r)^{\alpha}(PK_A^{H_3(D(M_A \bullet M_B))})^{\alpha}PK_A^{\alpha\beta}PK_A^{lH_3(D(M_A \bullet M_B)) - lH_3(D(M_A \bullet M_B))} \\
&= K^{\alpha}PK_A^{\alpha\beta} \\
&= F \qquad\qquad\qquad\qquad\qquad\qquad\qquad\qquad\qquad\qquad\qquad\qquad (9)
\end{aligned}
$$

### 4.2 Partial Blindness of the Program

**Theorem 1.** Assume that given a legal partial blind signature $\theta = (Y, m, l, F, D(M_A \bullet M_B))$, and record the intermediate variables generated during the scheme signature process $(r, K, Y', l)$, and the intermediate formulas during the signature process:

$$Y = \alpha Y' \qquad\qquad\qquad\qquad\qquad (10)$$

$$U = (\alpha^{-1}l + H_3^{-1}(D(M_A \bullet M_B))\beta)P \tag{11}$$

$$F = K^\alpha PK_A^{\alpha\beta} \tag{12}$$

From Eq. (10), we can deduce the blind factor $\alpha = \log_{Y'} Y$, and from Eq. (11), we can deduce the blind factor $\beta = \log_P(U - \alpha^{-1}lP)H_3(D(M_A \bullet M_B))$, and then substitute the deduced blind factor $\alpha$, $\beta$ into Eq. (12) to prove that it satisfies Eq. (12). Since the assumed partial blind signature is legitimate, it is satisfying the verification equation $F$ in the signature process, so substituting into the verification equation yields:

$$e(Y, P_{pub} + H_1(Id_A)P)PK_A^{-lH_3(D(M_A\bullet M_B))}$$
$$= e(\alpha Y', P_{pub} + H_1(Id_A)P)PK_A^{-lH_3(D(M_A\bullet M_B))}$$
$$= e(\alpha(rS_A + H_3(D(M_A \bullet M_B))S_{Id_A}U, P_A)PK_A^{-lH_3(D(M_A\bullet M_B))}$$
$$= e(\alpha rS_A + \alpha H_3(D(M_A \bullet M_B))S_{Id_A}((\alpha^{-1}l + H_3^{-1}(D(M_A \bullet M_B))\beta)P, P_A)$$
$$PK_A^{-lH_3(D(M_A\bullet M_B))}$$
$$= e(P, P)^{\alpha r}PK_A^{\alpha H_3(D(M_A\bullet M_B))}PK_A^{rH_3(D(M_A\bullet M_B))}e(S_{Id_A}P, P)^{\alpha\beta}PK_A^{-lH_3(D(M_A\bullet M_B))}$$
$$= (E^r)^\alpha(PK_A^{H_3(D(M_A\bullet M_B))})^\alpha PK_A^{\alpha\beta}PK_A^{lH_3(D(M_A\bullet M_B))-lH_3(D(M_A\bullet M_B))}$$
$$= K^\alpha PK_A^{\alpha\beta} \tag{13}$$

From the derivation process shown above, it is clear that the blindness factor $\alpha$ and $\beta$, introduced by the inverse derivation, is able to satisfy the Eq. (12). This means that there is a uniquely determined blindness factor $\alpha$ and $\beta$, which cannot be changed between any partial blind signature $\theta$ and its corresponding intermediate variables in the signature process as well as the intermediate formula. The existence of the blinded factor $\alpha$ and $\beta$ leads to the inability of the signer to relate his signature to the signature process, thus proving the partial blindness of the scheme.

### 4.3 Non-falsifiability

First of all, since it is a partial blind signature, an ordinary attacker cannot forge the signature of the message $m$ because he does not know the private key $S_{Id_A}$ of the signer, and the private key in the blind signature without a certificate is partly provided by the PKG, which is not fully owned by the user, and at the same time, even if the public key is known to calculate the private key, it is necessary to solve the hash collision, CDHP problem, which is verified as follows:

**Theorem 2.** Under the assumption of the inverse problem based on the bilinear mapping problem under the model of the stochastic prediction machine, the unforgeability of this scheme is considered to exist under identity and adaptive selection attacks. Assume that attacker S successfully forges a valid partial blind signature after a certain number of queries in a bounded polynomial time, which allows challenger T to solve the inverse problem of the bilinear mapping caused when attacker S forges a valid signature with the probability advantage of $\varepsilon \cdot (\sqrt{q_{PG}})^{-1}$.

It is known that $e : G_1 \times G_2 \to G_2$, $P$ is the generating element of $G_1$, $E$ is the generating element of $G_2$, $t \in _R Z_q^*$, then we need to solve $T \in G_1$, such that the bilinear mapping inverse problem $e(T, tP) = E$ is solved. The queries of the attacker S include three hash queries, $H_1$ queries, $H_2$ queries, $H_3$ queries, and public message homomorphic encryption queries, personal public key queries, partial key queries, personal key queries, and signature queries during the signing process, corresponding to the following lists: $L_1(ID_i, h_{1i})$, $L_2(m_i, h_{2i})$, $L_3(D_i(M_S \cdot M_T), h_{3i})$, $L_P(ID_i, M_S, M_{Ti}, D(M_T \cdot M_S))$, $L_{PG}(ID_i, PK_i)$, $L_J(ID_i, S_{Ti})$, $L_{Pj}(ID_i, S_{Id_i})$, $L_\theta(Y_i, m_i, h_i, F_i, D_i(M_S \cdot M_T))$, and the attacker will not ask more than q times for these queries, and the specific interaction process is as follows:

System setup: the identity of the user is represented by $ID'$. The challenger T generates and exposes the system parameters $\{G_1, G_2, e, q, P, P_{pub}, H_1, H_2, H_3\}$, where the master public key is obtained from the formula $P_{pub} = sP$ and $s$ is the master private key.

$H_1$ query: Challenger T sets up table $L_1(ID_i, h_{1i})$, and then attacker S starts to initiate an $H_1$ query to challenger T about identity $ID_i$. After that, challenger T then queries whether there is a record of $(ID_i, h_{1i})$ in table $L_1$. If there is, then challenger T directly returns $h_{1i}$ to attacker S; if not, then judge:

(1) If $ID \neq ID'$, challenger T then picks a random number $y_i \in _R Z_q^*$ and assigns $y_i$ to $h_{1i}$ and then updates $(ID_i, h_{1i})$ the record to table $L_1$.
(2) If $ID = ID'$, challenger T directly updates the value of $h_{1i}$ to $t - s$ and then updates this value to table $L_1$.

$H_2$ query: Challenger T sets up the table $L_2(m_i, h_{2i})$, and then the attacker S starts to initiate a $H_2$ query to Challenger T about the message $m_i$. After that, Challenger T then queries whether there is a record of $(m_i, h_{2i})$ in table $L_2$. If there is, Challenger T returns the value of $h_{2i}$ to the attacker S; if not, Challenger T selects $h_{2i} \in _R Z_q^*$ and returns $h_{2i}$ to the attacker S, and updates this value to table $L_2$. The $H_3$ interrogation process is the same as the $H_2$ interrogation.

Homomorphic encryption interrogation: challenger T sets up table $L_P(ID_i, M_S, M_{Ti}, D(M_T \cdot M_S))$, and then attacker S starts a homomorphic encryption interrogation on decryption parameter $D(M_T \cdot M_S)$ to challenger T:

1) If the record $(ID_i, M_S, M_{Ti}, D(M_T \cdot M_S))$ exists in table $L_P$, and determine if $ID = ID'$, then refuse to answer the query of decryption parameter $D(M_T \cdot M_S)$; if $ID \neq ID'$, then the challenger T will let the attacker S send the other half of the ciphertext $M_T$ of the public message, and then calculate $C = D(M_T \cdot M_S)$ based on its own ciphertext using the homomorphic decryption principle and return it to the attacker S, while updating $D(M_T \cdot M_S)$ to table $L_P$.
2) If the record $(ID_i, M_S, M_{Ti}, D(M_T \cdot M_S))$ does not exist in the table, the challenger T will ask the attacker S to send the other half of the ciphertext $M_T$ of the public message, and then compute $C = D(M_T \cdot M_S)$ based on its own ciphertext using the homomorphic decryption principle and return it to the attacker S, while updating $D(M_T \cdot M_S)$ to the table $L_P$.

Personal public key query: Challenger T sets up table $L_{PG}(ID_i, PK_i)$, and then attacker S initiates a personal public key query to challenger T about the user's identity $ID_i$. Next, challenger S will query table $L_{PG}$. If $(ID_i, PK_i)$ exists in table $L_{PG}$, $PK_i$ will be returned to attacker S. If not, it will determine whether a $H_1$ query was made before that, and if not, a $H_1$ query will be made first, and then:

1) if $ID = ID'$, then the challenger T converts to obtain $P' = sP + h'_1 P = sP + (t-s)P = tP$ according to the formula $P_A = P_{pub} + H_1(Id_A)P$ and assigns the value of $PK_i$ to $E_i = (P', tP)$ of the generating element that initially belongs to $G_2$. Then the challenger T returns $PK_i$ to the attacker S and updates $(ID_i, PK_i)$ to the table $L_{PG}$.
2) If $ID \neq ID'$, then challenger T randomly selects $x_i \in _R Z_q^*$ and obtains $P_i = sP + h_{1i}P = sP + y_i P$, $S_{Id_i} = sx_i S_A$, $PK_A = e(S_{Id_A}P, P_A)$, according to the intermediate variables formula $P_A = P_{pub} + H_1(Id_A)P$, $PK_A = e(S_{Id_A}P, P_A)$ and $S_{Id_i} = sx_i S_A$ in the signature process. Then challenger T returns $PK_i$ to attacker T and updates $(ID_i, PK_i)$ to the table $L_{PG}$.

Partial key interrogation: challenger T sets up table $L_J(ID_i, S_{Ti})$, then attacker S will launch a partial key interrogation about identity $ID_i$ to challenger T. After that, challenger T will query table $L_J(ID_i, S_{Ti})$. If the record $(ID_i, S_{Ti})$ exists in the table, it will directly return the value of $S_{Ti}$ F to attacker S. If the record $(ID_i, S_{Ti})$ does not exist, it will first determine whether $H_1$ interrogation has been conducted before, if not, then $H_1$ interrogation will be conducted first, and then:

1) If $ID \neq ID'$, then the challenger T obtains the formula $S_{Ti} = (s + h_{1i})^{-1}P = (s + y_i)^{-1}P$ based on the formula $S_A = (s + H_1(Id_A))^{-1}P$ and returns $S_{Ti}$ to the attacker S, which then updates $(ID_i, S_{Ti})$ to the table $L_J$.
2) If $ID = ID'$, then the challenger T will get the formula $S_{Ti} = (s + h_{1i})^{-1}P = (s + y_i)^{-1}P$ according to the formula $S_A = (s + H_1(Id_A))^{-1}P$ and returns $S_{Ti}$ to the attacker S, which then update $(ID_i, S_{Ti})$ into the table $L_J$.

Personal key query: challenger T sets up table $L_{Pj}(ID_i, S_{Id_i})$. Then attacker S will initiate a personal key $S_{Id_i}$ query to challenger T about user identity $ID_i$. After that, the challenger will query table $L_{Pj}$. If there is this record of $(ID_i, S_{Id_i})$, the value of $S_{Id_i}$ will be returned to attacker S. If not, the following judgment will be made:

1) If $ID \neq ID'$, challenger T then picks a random $x_i \in _R Z_q^*$ and according to equation $S_{Id_i} = sx_i S_A$ to obtain equation $S_{Id_i} = sx_i S_i$, after which challenger T returns $S_{Id_i}$ to attacker S and updates $(ID_i, S_{Id_i})$ to the table $L_{Pj}$;
2) If $ID = ID'$ Q, then the challenger S will refuse to answer the attacker's query on the personal private key because the ID matches on, which means there is this record in the table $L_{Pj}$ and there is information interaction over, and the query again will be abnormal, the query will be terminated.

Signature query: Challenger T sets up table $L_\theta(Y_i, m_i, h_i, F_i, D_i(M_S \cdot M_T))$, and then attacker S initiates a signature query about message $m_i$ to challenger T. After that, challenger T queries whether there is a signature associated with $m_i$ in table $L_\theta$. If it exists, it directly returns the corresponding signature to attacker S. and if it does not exist, then challenger T determines whether three hash queries have been made before that, and if not, then $H_1, H_2, H_3$ queries are made first, and then the following judgments are made:

1) If $ID \neq ID'$, the challenger T will query the table $L_1, L_2, L_3$ and obtain the values of $h_{1i}, h_{2i}, h_{3i}$ in it, and then randomly select $\alpha, \beta \in _RZ_q^*$ and calculate $F_i = e(Y_i, P_{pub} + h_{1i}P)PK_i^{-h_{3i}h_{3i}}$ by the formula $l = H_2(m, D(M_T \cdot M_S), F)$, $F = K^{\alpha}PK_A^{\alpha\beta}$, $U = (\alpha^{-1}h + PK_3^{-1(D(M_T \bullet M_S))}\beta)P$, $Y' = rS_A + H_3(D(M_T \cdot M_S))S_{Id_A}U$, $Y = \alpha Y'$ and the verification formula, and finally return the calculated signature $\theta$ to the attacker S and update the signature $\theta$ to the table $L_\theta$;

2) if $ID = ID'$, then:

① Challenger T picks any $h_{2i}, h_{3i} \in _RZ_q^*$, and any $\alpha, \beta \in _RZ_q^*$, and computes to obtain $Y_i$;

② The challenger then obtains $F'$ by verifying the equation, and the homomorphic decryption formula to obtain $C = D(M_T \cdot M_S)$;

③ Then through the formula $l_2 = H_2(m, D(M_T \cdot M_S), F), l_3 = H_2(D(M_T \cdot M_S), F)$ to get $h_2, h_2$, If equal to $h_{2i}, h_{3i}$ in ①, then the hash collision occurs, the challenger T then repeat the three steps, if not equal that is, no hash collision occurs, then update the signature $\theta = (Y, m, l, F, D(M_A \cdot M_B))$ to the table $L_\theta$.

Forgery: the attacker S obtains a valid signature $(Y', m', l', F', D'(M_S \cdot M_T))$ associated with the user $ID'$ through the above queries trained continuously (at most q times) and obtains another valid forged signature $(Y'', m'', l'', F'', D''(M_S \cdot M_T))$ through hash replay, and both pass the verification equation because it is valid.

So:

$$F_i = e(Y', P_{pub} + l'P)PK_i^{-l'H_3(D'(M_S \bullet M_T))} \tag{14}$$

$$F_i = e(Y'', P_{pub} + l''P)PK_i^{-l''H_3(D''(M_S \bullet M_T))} \tag{15}$$

Establishing the equation yields:

$$e(Y', P_{pub} + l'P)PK_i^{-l'H_3(D'(M_T \bullet M_S))} = e(Y'', P_{pub} + l''P)PK_i^{-l''H_3(D''(M_T \bullet M_S))}$$

$$e(Y', sP + (t-s)P)E_i^{-l'H_3(D'(M_T \bullet M_S))} = e(Y'', sP + (t-s)P)E_i^{-l''H_3(D''(M_T \bullet M_S))}$$

$$e(Y', tP)e(T, tP)^{-l'H_3(D'(M_T \bullet M_S))} = e(Y'', tP)e(T, tP)^{-l''H_3(D''(M_T \bullet M_S))}$$

$$e(Y', tP)e(-l'H_3(D'(M_T \bullet M_S))T, tP) = e(Y'', tP)e(-l''H_3(D''(M_T \bullet M_S))T, tP)$$

$$e(Y' - l'H_3(D'(M_T \bullet M_S))T, tP) = e(Y'' - l''H_3(D''(M_T \bullet M_S))T, tP)$$

$$Y' - l'H_3(D'(M_T \bullet M_S))T = eY'' - l''H_3(D''(M_T \bullet M_S))T \tag{16}$$

Convert to get:

$$T = (Y' - Y'')[l'H_3(D'(M_T \bullet M_S)) - l''H_3(D''(M_T \bullet M_S))]^{-1}$$

$$= (Y' - Y'')[l'H_3(C') - l''H_3(C'')]^{-1} \tag{18}$$

Thus the solution of the bilinear mapping inverse problem is solved, from which it can be concluded that the challenger T successfully solves the initially mentioned bilinear mapping inverse problem by interrogation, which contradicts the assumption condition at the beginning of this section, so this solution is not breakable by the attacker S. So the attacker S under the adaptive selection message attack as well as the identity attack of this scheme The existential forgery performed is non-existent, so this scheme has unforgeability.

### 4.4  Non-falsifiability of Public Messages

Firstly, this scheme introduces the homomorphic encryption mechanism, unlike the scheme [19] where the attacker directly changes the public message, this scheme divides the public message into $C_A$ and $C_B$ encrypts them as $M_A$ and $M_B$ using the negotiated homomorphic encryption rules, then the user will send the negotiated ciphertext $M_B$ to the signer, and the signer will verify the current public message before signing each one, because the signer has its own public message ciphertext $M_A$ and also the user's, which only needs to be verified by homomorphic encryption. Therefore, in order to tamper with the public message, an attacker needs to obtain both the user's and the verifier's ciphertexts and the homomorphic encryption rules to tamper with the ciphertext, which is not valid from the verifier's perspective. Even if the ciphertext is stolen, it cannot be exploited, and the plaintext cannot be backpropagated without knowing the private key, besides, the backpropagation needs to solve problems such as hash collision. Secondly, each verification is a verification of both the signer and the signer, so it can also resist the attack of dishonest people.

### 4.5  Safety Comparison

The scheme mentioned in this paper is an improvement on the literature [4] by adding a homomorphic encryption scheme. Paillier currently takes about 800 ms to encrypt and decrypt a machine with python version 2.7, intel(R) Xeon(R) E5-2630 24-core 2.6 GHz CPU, and 63 GB RAM when the key length is 8192 bits (key is at least The time used for encryption and decryption is about 800 ms when the key length is 8192 bits (the key is secure at least 2048 bits). The time taken to encrypt and decrypt the C++ code of

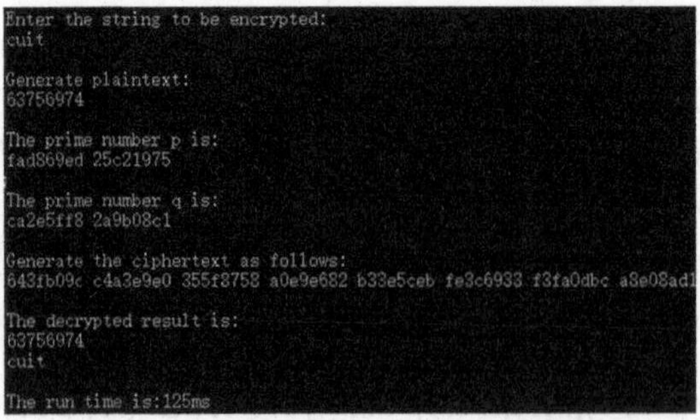

**Fig. 2.** Paillier run result.

paillier is about 125 ms on Visual studio 2015 and a machine with Intel(R) Core(TM) i5-7300HQ CPU@ 2.50 GHz and 16 GB RAM (Fig. 2).

Therefore, there is no significant difference in the efficiency of the scheme operation with other schemes, and thus the safety of the schemes is compared, as detailed in Table 1:

**Table 1.** Safety comparison.

| Program | Improvement | Tamper resistance | Can be breached after tampering | C whether to encrypt | Whether it is breached |
|---|---|---|---|---|---|
| Literature 9 | $K = g_c^{kx}$ | No | Yes | No | Yes |
| Literature 19 | $K = E^K PK_A^{H_3(D(M_T \cdot M_S))}$ | Yes | No | No | No |
| This program | Paillier | Yes | No | Yes | No |

## 5 Conclusion

In this paper, after analyzing the disadvantages of complete blindness of blind signature, we introduce certificate-free partial blind signature, which not only protects user privacy but also prevents signature tampering, making the scheme not only does not destroy the three constraints of blind signature, but also includes a public message negotiated in advance without damaging the blindness, while equally ensuring that the message is unknown to the signer. The scheme also incorporates Paillier homomorphic encryption to achieve verification of each signature request, which is more capable of blocking tampering of the public message. At the same time, the security analysis proves that even if the public message is tampered with, the equation cannot be verified, realizing the unforgeability and greatly improving the security of the scheme. This scheme can be combined with blockchain in the subsequent use scenario to further improve transaction privacy and identity privacy protection by using the traceable and non-tamperable characteristics of blockchain and combining with zero-knowledge proof.

**Acknowledgement.** This work is supported by the Key Research and Development Project of Sichuan Province (No. 2021YFSY0012, No. 2020YFG0307, No. 2021YFG0332), the Key Research and Development Project of Chengdu (No. 2019-YF05-02028-GX), the Innovation Team of Quantum Security Communication of Sichuan Province (No. 17TD0009), the Academic and Technical Leaders Training Funding Support Projects of Sichuan Province (No. 2016120080102643).

# References

1. Chaum, D.: Blind signatures for untraceable payments. In: Chaum, D., Rivest, R.L., Sherman, A.T. (eds.) Advances in Cryptology, pp. 199–203. Springer, Boston (1983). https://doi.org/10.1007/978-1-4757-0602-4_18

2. Abe, M., Fujisaki, E.: How to date blind signatures. In: Kim, K., Matsumoto, T. (eds.) ASIACRYPT 1996. LNCS, vol. 1163, pp. 244–251. Springer, Heidelberg (1996). https://doi.org/10.1007/BFb0034851

3. Abe, M., Camerisch J.: Partially blind signatures. In: 1997 Symposium on Cryptography and Information Security (1997)

4. Zhang, X.P., Yu, J.Y., Liang, B.: Improved identity-based blind signature scheme. Comput. Eng. Des. **27**(21), 4123–4124 (2016)

5. Liu, Z.S., Zhang, F., Chen, X.: ID-based restrictive partially blind signatures and applications. J. Syst. Softw. **80**(2), 164–171 (2007)

6. Mao, Y.F., Deng, L.Z.: An identity-based blind signature scheme and its security proof. Comput. Mod. **04**, 105–108 (2017)

7. Möser, M., Soska, K., Heilman, E.: An empirical analysis of traceability in the Monero blockchain. In: Proceedings on Privacy Enhancing Technologies, no. 3, pp. 143–163 (2018)

8. Kumar, A., Fischer, C., Tople, S., Saxena, P.: A traceability analysis of Monero's blockchain. In: Foley, S.N., Gollmann, D., Snekkenes, E. (eds.) ESORICS 2017. LNCS, vol. 10493, pp. 153–173. Springer, Cham (2017). https://doi.org/10.1007/978-3-319-66399-9_9

9. Liu, E.G., Wang, X., Zhou, H.J.: Analysis and improvement of a certificateless blind signature scheme. Comput. Appl. Softw. **34**(02), 308–312 (2017)

10. Chen, H.B., Zhang, L.: New efficient certificateless blind signature scheme. In: 2016 IEEE Trustcom/BigDataSE/I SPA IEEE, pp. 349–353 (2016)

11. Ribarski, P., Antovski L.: Comparison of lD-based blind signatures from pairings for e-voting protocols. In: International Convention on Information and Communication Technology, Electronics and Microelectronics, pp. 1394–1399. IEEE (2014)

12. Cao, S.Z., Dai, W.J., Wang, C.F., Wang, X.Y., Sun, H., Zuo, W.: Analysis and improvement of an ID-based partially blind signature scheme. Comput. Eng. Sci. **40**(12), 2193–2197 (2018)

13. Cui, W., Jia, Q.: Provably secure pairing-free identity-based restrictive partially blind signature scheme. In: 2019 IEEE 3rd Information Technology, Networking, Electronic and Automation Control Conference (ITNEC), pp. 1038–1042 (2019)

14. Zheng, T., Zhang, S.B., Chang, Y., Li, X.Y.: Quantum blind signature scheme based on bell state entanglement swapping. Comput. Appl. Softw. **37**(03), 310–313 (2020)

15. Zhang, L., Ma, Y.: A lattice-based identity-based proxy blind signature scheme in the standard model. Math. Probl. Eng. **2014**(1) (2014)

16. Rawal, S., Padhye, S.: Cryptanalysis of ID based proxy-blind signature scheme over lattice. In: ICT Express, vol. 6, no. 1, pp. 20–22 (2020)

17. Zhou, Y.H., Dong, S.S., Yang, Y.G.: A lattice-based identity-based proxy partially blind signature scheme in the standard model. Netinfo Secur. **21**(3), 37–43 (2021)

18. Rong, W.J.: Certificateless partially blind signature scheme. J. Zhangzhou Normal Univ. (Nat. Sci. Ed.) **21**(3), 44–47 (2008)

19. Jiang, Y.H., Deng, L.Z.: Analysis and improvement of a partially blind signature scheme. J. Guizhou Normal Univ. (Nat. Sci. Ed.) **38**(02), 85–91 (2020)

20. Tian, J., Du, Y.M., Li, S., Liu Y.: A paillier homomorphic encryption based location privacy protection scheme for crowdsensing task distribution. Comput. Sci. Explor. 1–9 (2021)

21. Diao, Y.Q., Ye, A.Y., Zhang, J.M., Deng, H.N., Zhang, Q., Cheng, B.R.: A dual privacy protection method based on group signature and homomorphic encryption for alliance blockchain. J. Comput. Res. Dev. **59**, 172 (2022)

22. Hwang, Y., Lee, I.: A lightweight certificate-based aggregate signature scheme providing key insulation. Comput. Mater. Continua **69**(2), 1747–1764 (2021)
23. Khonde, S.R., Ulagamuthalvi, V.: Blockchain: secured solution for signature transfer in distributed intrusion detection system. Comput. Syst. Sci. Eng. **40**(1), 37–51 (2022)
24. Xu, G., Cao, Y., Xu, S., Xiao, K., Liu, X., et al.: A novel post-quantum blind signature for log system in blockchain. Comput. Syst. Sci. Eng. **41**(3), 945–958 (2022)
25. Ren, H., Niu, S.: Separable reversible data hiding in homomorphic encrypted domain using POB number system. Multimedia Tools Appl. **81**(2), 2161–2187 (2021). https://doi.org/10.1007/s11042-021-11341-w
26. Dong, D.P., Wu, Y., Xiong, L.Z., Xia, Z.H.: A privacy preserving deep linear regression scheme based on homomorphic encryption. J. Big Data **1**(3), 145–150 (2019)

# Research on Personal Privacy Risks and Countermeasures in the Era of Big Data

Naifu Ye[1], Deyu Yuan[1,2($\boxtimes$)], Yuyan Meng[1], and Meng Ding[3]

[1] School of Information and Cyber Security, People's Public Security University of China,
Beijing 100038, China
yuandeyu@ppsuc.edu.cn

[2] Key Laboratory of Safety Precautions and Risk Assessment, Ministry of Public Security,
Beijing 102623, China

[3] Public Security Behavioral Science Laboratory, People's Public Security University of China,
Beijing 102623, China

**Abstract.** Human society has entered the era of big data, and massive amounts of data and information are exchanged between application platforms at high speed. In contrast to the development of technology, the leakage of citizens' personal privacy information in China has shown a spurt in recent years, and how to protect citizens' privacy has become an urgent issue in today's society. This paper uses model analysis and comparative analysis to explore personal privacy risks, analyses the internal and external factors affecting personal privacy risks in the era of big data and establishes a "trinity" personal privacy risk assessment model consisting of network service providers, Internet users and Internet regulators. This article also analyzes the model of federated learning framework, Secure multiparty computation, decentralization and Hawk block chain platform and DNN, model for privacy preservation. Suggestions and countermeasures are given in the article to strengthen personal privacy protection. It also provides recommendations and countermeasures for strengthening personal privacy protection.

**Keywords:** Big data · Personal privacy · Risk assessment · Protection strategy

## 1 Introduction

In the era of big data, smart terminals are widely popular and data platforms are all-encompassing [1], of which the data contains a large number of personal privacy, different from traditional accounts and passwords, now new types of personal privacy are numerous, specifically: browsing records, user behavior habits, personal preferences, etc. [2], but the vicious cases of personal privacy leakage and illegal use are increasing, and criminals through network technology means Illegal access to citizens' personal privacy information, and the use of social engineering to gradually deceive the trust of victims, followed by the implementation of telecommunications fraud, robbery and other crimes. The risk of personal privacy in the era of big data is caused by various factors, and different responsible subjects should assume corresponding protection responsibilities and clarify the perspectives and methods of personal privacy risk assessment.

X. Sun et al. (Eds.): ICAIS 2022, CCIS 1588, pp. 222–234, 2022.
https://doi.org/10.1007/978-3-031-06764-8_18

This paper analyses the risk of personal privacy in the era of big data, establishes a "trinity" risk assessment model and summarizes and analyses the existing methods for protecting privacy information in the era of big data, and finally proposes the future development trend of privacy protection in the era of big data.

## 2  Overview of Personal Privacy Risks in the Era of Big Data

Personal privacy risk in the era of big data refers to the security risk and hidden danger of citizens' personal information being infringed by unlawful elements during the rapid development stage of big data technology, and personal privacy data being illegally listened to, accessed, controlled, copied by attackers and through other means that may lead to the leakage of personal privacy. The Report on the Protection of Personal Privacy and Security in China [3] covers more than 45 million surveys of people nationwide, of which more than 77% of respondents received unfamiliar calls from people who were familiar with their private information, and about 16% of respondents even received telecommunication fraud calls. The data indicates that there is a security risk to personal privacy information.

The illegal use of personal privacy to commit fraud has a typical division of labor process, as shown in Fig. 1, where hackers exploit loopholes in database systems, break into the system, obtain large amounts of citizen information and sell the personal privacy information to downstream fraudsters, who take advantage of the victim's human weaknesses to commit fraud. The serious consequences of this case have sounded an alarm to the whole society.

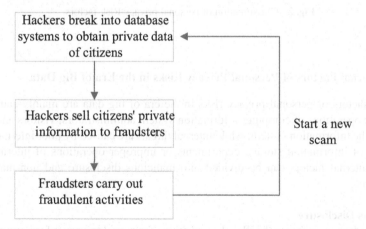

**Fig. 1.**  Using citizens' private information to implement fraud flow chart.

## 3  Personal Privacy Risk Factors in the Era of Big Data

There are many factors affecting personal privacy security. The reason why personal privacy risks are higher in the era of big data is that the scale of data exchange is larger and the security of information platform cannot be guaranteed. Compared with traditional personal privacy security risks, personal privacy risks in the era of big data are potentially harmful. Criminals can extract information with user characteristics from massive data information. They analyze the characteristics of users' social behaviors and get private information.

As it is known to us, Internal inefficient and imprecision management will bring great hidden danger to information security. External criminals' attacks can also make tremendous trouble to private information protection. Personal privacy risk factors in the era of big data can be classified according to sources of risks, as shown in Fig. 2.

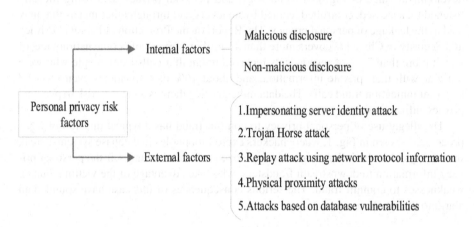

**Fig. 2.** Classification of personal privacy Risk factors.

### 3.1 Internal Factors of Personal Privacy Risks in the Era of Big Data

Internal factors of personal privacy risks in the era of big data are mainly caused by improper operations of computer information system administrators, visitors and other users of the information system, while internal threats are caused by poor internal management of information storage departments or improper operations of internal personnel. Internal factors can be divided into malicious disclosure and non-malicious disclosure.

**Malicious Disclosure**
Malicious leakage refers to the illegal acquisition of personal privacy information stored in computer information systems for illegal purposes, and the copying and leaking of such information. Malicious leaks of citizens' personal privacy information are committed by lawbreakers who, for purposes such as seeking personal gain and influencing public opinion, maliciously obtain citizens' personal privacy, copy it through databases,

duplicate citizens' private and sensitive information and take it out of security-protected information systems.

## Non-malicious Disclosure

Non-malicious leaks, on the other hand, are data information leaks of citizens' privacy and other data information caused by the unsound security awareness or unintentional operational actions of legitimate visitors who do not intentionally intend to leak database information, but due to operational errors, inexperience and inadequate training, illegal actions occur and pose a threat to personal private data information.

### 3.2 External Factors of Personal Privacy Risks in the Era of Big Data

External factors of personal privacy risk in the era of big data mainly originate from the intrusion and infiltration of computer information systems by criminals through editing malicious codes. The main areas are as follows.

## Impersonating Server Identity Attack

The attacker poses as a web server and, based on the principles of social engineering, captures the carelessness of the victim's character and tricks the customer into trusting him by impersonating various application websites. When the user enters his username and password, or enters his personal registration information, the attacker can easily gain access to his private information, thus posing an information security threat.

## Trojan Horse Attack

The attacker implants a Trojan horse virus into a system file that infects the target computer via email, a copy of a removable hard drive and network delivery [4]. Once these files are opened, the Trojan horse virus begins to take hold, silently collecting sensitive information such as personal data on the target computer and transmitting it out of the security domain via the network, resulting in information leakage.

## Replay Attack Using Network Protocol Information

Replay attacks are the most threatening form of network protocol attack against computer networks. They are used to obtain confidential and private information about two parties by collecting the communication records of both parties and impersonating one of them by impersonating an IP address, for example, and sending the information to the other party, making the other party believe that he is communicating with one party.

## Proximity Attacks Based on Physical Factors

Physical access to a network system or device by an unauthorized person for the purpose of modifying, collecting, or denying access. This approach can be secret access or open access, or both.

Attackers take advantage of geographic access to information systems and equipment to actively access and snoop on sensitive private information, and the lack of awareness of privacy protection among information system managers can easily leave the way open for neighboring attacks.

## Attacks Based on Database Vulnerabilities

Attacks based on database vulnerabilities, i.e. SQL injection attacks are very common, where malicious SQL code is inserted into the input parameters of an application and the attacker combines the database structure and type to find system vulnerabilities to retrieve and query sensitive information from the database system and obtain personal private data. The key to this type of attack is to construct SQL statements that are different from those expected by the program design [5].

## 4 Personal Privacy Risk Assessment Model in the Era of Big Data

Whether internal factors from internal data managers or external factors such as malicious attacks from external hackers, these risk factors pose serious challenges to the security of citizens' personal privacy. From the perspective of the main body of personal privacy security protection, the government, enterprises and individual citizens share the responsibility of protection. According to the principle of information security wholeness - the barrel principle, the security level achieved by the protection of personal privacy information depends on the weakest kind of protection measures of various protection capabilities, so in order for the government, enterprises and individuals to achieve the expected Therefore, in order to achieve the expected overall privacy information protection capability, the government, enterprises and individuals should work together to improve the security protection level, and any security loopholes in one of them will affect the overall security.

At the government level, the ability to govern big data is crucial, and the creation of new media elements such as "short videos" requires further improvements in legislation and enforcement capabilities. The lack of science in decision-making is a pressing issue, and the lack of technical knowledge among managers will make top-level design difficult. From the perspective of enterprises, self-security assessment is an important prerequisite for achieving industry self-regulation; confusion in the management of user information repositories and loopholes in security protection technology are factors leading to information leakage; individual citizens, who directly control personal privacy information, and unreasonable use by citizens are important causes of privacy leakage. Therefore, it is

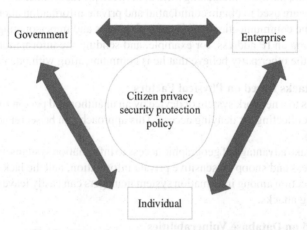

**Fig. 3.** "Trinity" security protection model diagram.

necessary to establish a "trinity" security protection model that includes the government, enterprises and individuals, as shown in Fig. 3, in which the three subjects fulfil their obligations to protect privacy information in their respective areas of responsibility and around privacy information protection strategies. This is the only way to effectively curb the illegal and criminal activities that violate the privacy rights of citizens [6].

## 5 Personal Privacy Security Existing Coping Methods

### 5.1 Federated Learning Framework

Facing the challenge of personal privacy information risk in the era of big data, Google has proposed a machine learning model of federation learning, which uses a central processing device to co-ordinate the application terminals and is a privacy information computing technique established collaboratively by multiple subjects involved to ensure that privacy data is not outside their security control. The training data is stored in a distributed manner to ensure data security. To address the problem of parameters leaking privacy information in federation learning models, the new parameter masking scheme proposed by HongLin Lu [7] uses key exchange and parameter masking protocols to guarantee the security of model parameters after resource aggregation. The following is a brief description of the main federation learning process as is shown in Fig. 4.

(1) Clients downloads the global model $m_0$ from the server. Each client user downloads the global training model from the global server to obtain key information and federated computing methods.
(2) Clients obtains local data training model $m_1$, $m_2$......$m_n$ by training data stored locally.
(3) Client uploads the local training model to the global server.
(4) The global server receives the data and performs weighted aggregation operation to obtain the new global model $m_0'$, completing an iteration.

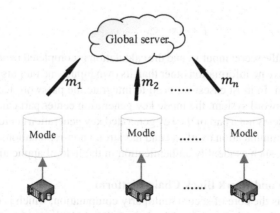

**Fig. 4.** Federated learning model diagram.

Privacy security vulnerabilities still exist in the Federal Learning Framework model, where attackers can obtain private information by constructing clients that generate similar data model updates.

## 5.2 Secure Multiparty Computation

**Definition of Secure Multiparty Computation**

Secure multiparty computation is a collection of interactive high-security protocols based on cryptography, where the two communicating parties jointly compute a security function during the data interaction, thus ensuring that the output result is obtained while ensuring that the original data is not leaked. Multi-party secure computing theory mainly solves the problems of information protection and computing correctness of each data participant.

Yao first proposed the computation of obfuscated circuits [8], which converts the computational logic of a secure protocol into a Boolean circuit, where the possible inputs to the circuit generate a key and encrypt the truth table to complete the obfuscation. complete the obfuscation. The secret sharing strategy, in which the original data is sliced into multiple data segments and the segments are sent to each recipient, each recipient can only get a part of the data segments, and to restore the original data, it is necessary to get a sufficient number of data segments. This method has a low computational overhead and only performs simple operations.

**Secure Multiparty Computation Technical Model**

Secure multiparty computation enables multiple participants to perform distributed computing tasks correctly in a secure manner.

Multiple data communication participants are represented by $\{S_i, i \in [1, n]\}$use their own input information to calculate n-element random function:

$$F(x) = Random(f) \tag{1}$$

$$f = (x_1, x_2, \ldots \ldots, x_n) \tag{2}$$

Each $S_i$ holds the secret input $x_i$, and the calculation is completed to obtain the output $y_i$. Participants have no information other than its own inputs and outputs and what it can deduce from them. In most cases, we need to integrate the password techniques, using no certificate password system, the mode key generation center part can't work out the user's keys, the user is not a part of the key generated key generation center, its advantage lies in the low communication overhead and has strong non-repudiation, suitable for the Internet of things, such as identity authentication in the field of application.

**Decentralization and Hawk Block Chain Platform**

Decentralization is the core of secure multiparty computation, which is of great importance to securing data privacy and value. decentralized block chain technology can be used to monitor the whole process of data, achieve immutable data recording, and ensure log audit and data authenticity. Hawk is a cryptographic-based block chain contract development platform which It does not store private transaction information directly on the block chain. It uses zero-knowledge proofs which means proving statements about a ciphertext without revealing information about the plaintext. Hawk allows programmers to write smart contracts with privacy requirements in an intuitive manner, regardless of the implementation of encryption, which the Hawk compiler automatically generates efficient zero-knowledge proof-based encryption protocols to interact with the block chain. It can be shown in Fig. 5.

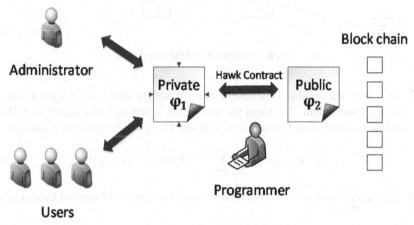

**Fig. 5.** Framework of Hawk.

### 5.3 DNN Model for Privacy Preservation

A person's right to decide who has access to their personal data and how that data is used is called privacy. The data is owned by the data holder, and as such, the data itself represents a danger to individual privacy [9]. DNN model consists four parts includes inputs layer, hidden layer, Iterative hidden layers and output. In this model input can be encrypted through iterative hidden layers. During the training process, the weight of each node is improved by cyclic iteration. Figure 6 illustrated the framework of DNN model.

An activation function is required to enable the model to have non-linear fitness capability. Tan function solves the problem that Sigmoid function is not zero-centered output. Tan function is given as follows [10].

$$\tan(x) = \frac{e^x - e^{-x}}{e^x + e^{-x}} \tag{3}$$

Input data can be defined as x and activated by mapping function $f_m$

$$f_m = \text{sigm}(\alpha_i x + \beta_i) \tag{4}$$

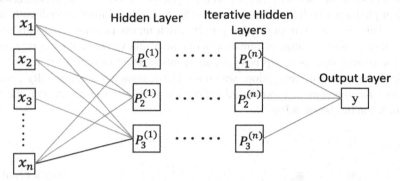

**Fig. 6.** Framework of DNN model.

$\alpha_i$ represents the number i variable's value of weight and $\beta_i$ represents deviation between input and output. To assess the loss value, supervised loss function of DNN also needs to establish, loss function is as follows. Using (x,q) represents parameter

$$L(W_l, b_l, \text{x,q}) = \frac{1}{2k_j} \sum\nolimits_{j=1}^{k} \left| P_j(W_l, b_l, \text{x}) - q_j \right|^2 \tag{5}$$

$W_l$ and $b_l$ represents biases subset and k means the number of input of hidden layer.

## 6  Countermeasures and Suggestions

### 6.1  Internet User Perspective

Internet users should strengthen the security protection of personal privacy, the first person responsible for personal privacy is the user himself, big data era people pursue better quality and more convenient life, but often ignore the protection of personal information security. User subjects need to authorize personal privacy information to APP software in a restrained manner.

**Create Awareness of Personal Privacy Information Protection**
Individual citizens must firmly establish awareness of information security protection and exercise "three cautions". Be cautious about downloading applications and familiarize yourself with genuine software download procedures to protect yourself from pirated software. When registering for an account on an application platform, pay attention to the protection of sensitive information, encrypt it appropriately and be vigilant. Be cautious about providing mobile phone dynamic verification codes. Nowadays, many application platforms verify the identity of users through mobile phone dynamic verification codes, users should screen the websites and pay attention to the domain name of the website to prevent being duped and subjected to man-in-the-middle attacks.

**Strengthen the Password Key Strength**
The key indicator of the security of an encryption algorithm is the key strength, and a

key strength of k indicates that the computational complexity of breaking the key is 2k [11]. Many users usually set their password to a weak type such as birthday date for the convenience of remembering the password, which is extremely weak and easy to crack. Complex passwords using special symbols and case composition are far more secure than weak passwords, and the use of new generation password technologies based on biometric features such as fingerprints can significantly improve password strength and facilitate privacy information protection.

## 6.2   Internet Service Provider Perspective

There are a large number of smartphone applications, and citizens are often asked to provide some of their personal privacy information in order to enjoy the convenient and personalized services of various software. Therefore, Internet service providers, as the collectors of citizens' personal privacy information, need to assume the primary responsibility for maintaining the security of citizens' personal privacy.

The application software platform needs to establish a reliable database management system, a reliable data storage guarantee system, structured management of data [12] and unified implementation of security protection of privacy information. Internet service providers need to conduct statistics on the amount of user data they hold, assess the sensitivity of user information, divide the privacy information security level to carry out, determine the security level of various types of personal privacy information, and graded to take corresponding protection measures. The author summarizes the framework for the protection of privacy information of Internet service providers, as shown in Fig. 7.

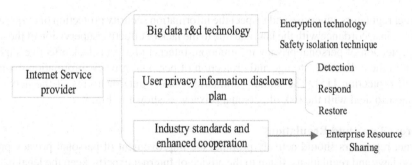

**Fig. 7.** Internet service provider information protection framework diagram.

## Emergency Plan for User Privacy Information Disclosure

The enterprise body needs to do a good job of detection, response and recovery during the operation of the database system, and the information reporting and emergency response of privacy information leakage emergencies follow the strategic principle of "graded and regional management" [13]. For example, in the case of an attack on a server, the enterprise must first find the vulnerability point, close the data connection, check the security level of the data stored on the target machine, determine the response measures and report the situation to the network supervision department in a timely manner.

**Big Data Security Technology Research and Development**
Scientific computer information security analysis platform should be established, through which Netflow traffic information, DNS data, user behavior information and Web application data are analyzed [14]. Adopt deep learning algorithms based on which the adaptability of current security technologies is continuously evaluated, continuously accumulate experience in applying security technologies, and train the adopted personal privacy protection policies by simulating different security events. Deploying a network firewall, the firewall obtains visitor IP addresses through the analysis of request packets and filters them according to the access control policy. The deep learning algorithm is able to mine the behavioral characteristics of attackers and provide a basis for improving the firewall access control list.

**Develop Industry Standards to Enhance Cooperation**
Cooperation brings win-win situation, mutual cooperation between enterprises is conducive to promoting the improvement of the overall privacy information security protection ability of the industry, leading enterprises in the industry should take the initiative to undertake more information security protection standardization work, concentrate the strength of experts and researchers, research and develop user privacy protection rules and regulations, unify equipment equipped with standards, and form a defense synergy.

### 6.3   Internet Regulator Angle

Internet regulators supervise and inspect the information security protection of corporate subjects in accordance with the law, and due to the lack of effective supervision of the use and protection of personal privacy information, Internet platforms lack effective supervision in the collection, storage and protection of personal privacy information mainly by self-protection [15]. The author summarizes the countermeasures of the network regulator to deal with the risk of personal privacy, as shown in Fig. 8.

**Improve Laws and Regulations**
Internet regulators should actively promote the improvement of personal privacy protection laws and regulations, listen to the advice of Internet experts, keep the legal basis up to date, clarify the rights and obligations of privacy protection subjects in the era of big data, scientifically regulate the information security protection work of Internet enterprises, promote the standardization of privacy information protection management, and the state should formulate relevant industry standards to limit the collection and use of personal privacy by enterprises [16].

**Increase Publicity on Personal Privacy Protection**
Media publicity is an important way to improve citizens' awareness of privacy information security protection [17]. New media platforms provide convenient conditions for personal privacy protection publicity [18]. Internet regulators can publicize the importance of personal privacy protection through social public information resource platforms

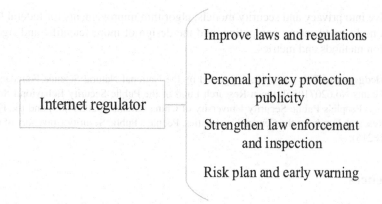

**Fig. 8.**   Internet regulators personal privacy policy map.

such as microblogs, WeChat public numbers and short video APPs. Step up national education on information security.

**Strengthen Law Enforcement and Inspection**
Internet regulators should regularly carry out risk assessment and supervision of enterprise data and information, innovate enforcement models, and conduct special inspections of key enterprises on an ongoing basis through regular inspections and other means. Focusing on the key few key sectors and enterprises, key enterprises classified according to information security protection levels hold core private data affecting people's livelihood and need to take stricter measures to safeguard private data security by stationing security inspectors and other means to investigate and promote improvement.

**Risk Warning and Contingency Plans**
Prepare for a rainy day is an important measure for the scientific management of the Internet supervisory department [19]. The Internet supervisory department can prevent possible security hazards in the network system through effective measures, and at the same time apply scientific and reasonable technology to carry out security evaluation and determination of the network system, which can promptly discover the existence of security hazards, and can monitor the interaction of information in the backbone network of the city region, and make timely risk indication of abnormal data transmission, which can help enterprises repair the loopholes in time.

## 7   Conclusion

The development of big data poses new challenges to personal privacy and security. Privacy and information security need to be effectively protected. Based on an in-depth analysis of personal privacy risk factors in the era of big data, this paper proposes a tripartite protection model based on the government, enterprises and individual citizens, and summarizes existing coping methods as well as countermeasures. Future research will delve into privacy and security models, algorithm improvements for federal learning and multi-party secure computing, and the design of more scientific and rigorous evaluation methods and metrics.

**Acknowledgement.** This work was supported by the National Natural Science Foundation of China [Grants No.62071056], Open Research Fund of the Public Security Behavioral Science Laboratory, People's Public Security University of China [Grants 2020SYS03] and the Fundamental Research Funds for the Central Universities, People's Public Security University of China (2021JKF215).

# References

1. Wang, S.: Discussion on protection strategy of computer network information security in the era of big data. Comput. Programm. Skills Mainten. **9**, 31–32 (2021)
2. Wang, P., Chen, T., Wang, Z.: Research on privacy preserving data mining. J. Inf. Hiding Privacy Protect. **1**(2), 61–68 (2019)
3. Internet Rule of Law Research , Center: China youth university for political sciences. Personal Privacy Secur. Protect. Rep. **1**, 23–24 (2016)
4. Wang, B.J., Tong, H.: Information security technology system. In: 2nd edn. People Public Security of China, Beijing China (2018)
5. Li, T.: Database network security prevention methods under the background of big data. Electron. Technol. Softw. Eng. **6**, 3–4 (2021)
6. Xiong, L.: Overview of mobile internet information security regulation in big data era. Netw. Secur. Technol. Appl. **4**, 5–6 (2021)
7. Lu, H.L., Wang, L.M., Yang, J.: A new parameter masks the federal learning privacy protection scheme. Inf. Netw. Secur. **3**(8), 26–27 (2021)
8. Yao, Q.Z.: Protocols for secure computations. IEEE Comput. Soc. **2**, 160–164 (1982)
9. Nithyanantham, S., Singaravel, G.: Hybrid deep learning framework for privacy preservation in geo-distributed data centre. Intell. Autom. Soft Comput. **32**(3), 1905–1919 (2022)
10. Paulraj, D.: A gradient boosted decision tree-based sentiment classification of twitter data. Int. J. Wavelets Multiresol. Inf. Process. **4**(18), 205027–1–205027–21 (2020)
11. Wen, T.Q.: Research on enterprise information security risk and emergency plan. Wuhan Univ. Technol. **12**, 13–18 (2016)
12. Wu, J.Y.: Computer network information security measures under big data. Electron. Technol. Softw. Eng. **9**, 2–3 (2021)
13. Sun, Q.: Analysis on security intensity and development trend of encryption algorithm. Softw. Ind. Eng. **2**(3), 29–30 (2016)
14. Tian, B.: Data security analysis under the background of big data. Netw. Secur. Technol. Appl. **2**(7), 7–8 (2021)
15. Zhang, Y.T.: Legislation and improvement of personal information protection in the era of big data. Legal Rev. **3**(15), 148–149 (2021)
16. Li, P.R., Zhang, F.Q.: Computer Network information security protection strategy and evaluation algorithm. Netw. Secur. Technol. Appl. **3**(8), 22–23 (2021)
17. Wang, P., Wang, Z., Ma, Q.: Research on the association of mobile social network users privacy information based on big data analysis. J. Inf. Hiding Privacy Protect. **1**(1), 35–42 (2019)
18. Jiang, L., Fu, Z.: Privacy-preserving genetic algorithm outsourcing in cloud computing. J. Cyber Secur. **2**(1), 49–61 (2020)
19. Wazirali, R.: A review on privacy preservation of location-based services in internet of things. Intell. Autom. Soft Comput. **2**(32), 767–779 (2022)

# Byzantine Fault-Tolerant Consensus Algorithm Based on Dynamic Weight Sharding

Wang Zhang[✉], Feng Qi[iD], Ao Xiong, Shaoyong Guo[iD], and Zhenjiang Ma

Beijing University of Posts and Telecommunications, Beijing 100876, China
zhwang1997@bupt.edu.cn

**Abstract.** As a consensus algorithm widely used in the alliance chain, PBFT achieves a good balance between security and fairness, but it can only exert good performance in a network with a small number of network nodes. With the continuous joining of nodes, the efficiency of consensus gradually declines, and it does not have horizontal expansion. In order to solve the horizontal expansion ability of PBFT in order to solve its performance problems in large-scale networks, this paper introduces the Byzantine fault-tolerant consensus algorithm DWS_BFT based on the dynamic weight sharding strategy. Through the sharding technology, the nodes in the alliance chain are divided into different heterogeneous areas, and each area has a parallel consensus to improve the consensus efficiency. And by reasonably adjusting the weight score of the node, and dynamically adjust the sharding members according to the node weight score, the problem of low security of a single shard brought by the sharding technology is solved. At the same time, transactions are divided into different processing between on-chip transactions and inter-chip transactions, to solve the problem of low performance of cross-shard transactions caused by sharding technology.

**Keywords:** Sharding · Dynamic weight · Horizontal expansion · PBFT

## 1 Introduction

Due to the decentralized nature of the blockchain [1], each transaction in the blockchain needs to be confirmed by all nodes participating in the consensus [2], which leads to a sharp decline in the performance of the blockchain as the number of nodes participating in the consensus increases [3]. The sharding technology [4] originated in the application of databases and was used for the horizontal expansion of the database. This technology can also be applied to the blockchain to contribute to the horizontal expansion [5].

The sharding technology cuts all nodes participating in the consensus into different consensus areas [6], and each area independently processes transactions in the area in parallel [7]. Therefore, the number of nodes in each consensus domain is much smaller than the number of nodes participating in the consensus as a whole [8]. Compared with traditional consensus algorithms such as PBFT, the consensus algorithm that introduces sharding technology will improve the consensus efficiency in both transaction processing verification and concurrency [9]. However, the sharding technology also brings two problems:

X. Sun et al. (Eds.): ICAIS 2022, CCIS 1588, pp. 235–244, 2022.
https://doi.org/10.1007/978-3-031-06764-8_19

(1) As the number of nodes in a single area becomes very small, its ability to carry faults or the number of malicious nodes is greatly reduced [10, 11].

(2) Some transaction parties will span two areas [12]. How to deal with cross-area transactions reasonably is also the focus of research on blockchain sharding consensus.

The sharding technology introduced in this article is called dynamic weight sharding. We will score nodes based on each consensus performance and historical performance of the nodes, and reflect them in the form of weights. Increase the weight for good performance, reduce the weight for poor performance, and assign nodes to different shards based on weights to ensure that malicious nodes or faulty nodes are evenly distributed to different shards, and prevent most faulty nodes from being assigned to one shard to destroy the shards. The situation of the film consensus. For cross-shard transactions, we designed a cross-shard transaction verification algorithm to solve this problem.

## 2   Dynamic Shard Allocation Strategy Based on Weight

### 2.1   Overall Structure

In Byzantine fault-tolerant consensus algorithm based on dynamic weight sharding (DWS_BFT), a main chain handles the transaction of each shard and the weight adjustment of the overall node. The overall structure diagram is as follows (see Fig. 1).

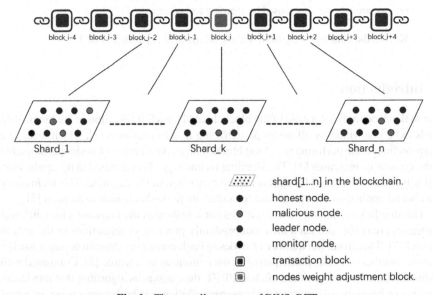

| | |
|---|---|
| ▦ | shard[1...n] in the blockchain. |
| ● | honest node. |
| ◐ | malicious node. |
| ● | leader node. |
| ● | monitor node. |
| ▣ | transaction block. |
| ▣ | nodes weight adjustment block. |

**Fig. 1.** The overall structure of DWS_BFT.

In this system, we divide the nodes into four types:

① Leader node: The leader node is selected according to its own weight, and is responsible for publishing the pre-prepare work in the shard consensus, and at the same time, it is responsible for publishing the consensus results in the shard into the blockchain;

② honest node: responsible for the consensus work in the shard, and will respond correctly to the consensus information;

③ malicious node: including the faulty node in the system and the node that is controlled by the enemy to make an incorrect response to the consensus information;

④ monitor node: Do not participate in the consensus process, and record each consensus process and results.

The transactions in each shard are first voted by the consensus of all nodes in the shard, and then the leader node of each shard conducts another consensus on the transactions in the shards that have reached consensus, and finally the consensus results are put on the chain; The weight of the node is jointly maintained by all nodes, and the weight of the node is composed of two parts: one is the sum of the effective work done by the node on the consensus result, but the frequency of the work. The node weight based on these two aspects can effectively reflect the credibility and robustness of the node. The allocation of shards and leader selection within shards are both selected based on node weights. The update time for node weights is much longer than the transaction consensus update time. For example, a node weight update is performed after dozens of transaction consensus updates, and a reputation fast consensus is generated on the chain. After a consensus update, the nodes are redistributed at the same time. Reducing the update frequency of node weights can reduce the impact of frequent resharding on system performance.

## 2.2 Overall Structure

In order to ensure the safety and reliability of the entire fragmentation scheme, the design of the node weight selection and adjustment scheme is the most important part of the entire system. Generally speaking, for the honest behavior of the node, its weight should be increased as a reward; for the dishonest behavior of the node, its weight should be reduced as a penalty. However, the punishment for dishonest behavior of a node is greater than the reward for honest nodes. For example, if a node submits a misleading consensus result in the consensus, it may cause it to lose all the weight accumulation because of dishonest behavior. Because it may cause devastating results to the entire system. For the rewards of honest nodes, we have adopted the strategies of careful start, quick reward, and smooth end. We choose the sigmoid function as the reward strategy for honest nodes (see Fig. 2).

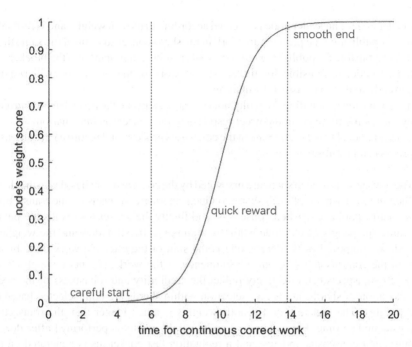

**Fig. 2.** Node's weighted score reward strategy.

The node has done honest work in the first few epochs. This is because we are not completely sure that it must be an honest and reliable node, so the accumulation of weight scores will be very slow at the beginning. But if the continuous honest work time of the node exceeds the threshold we set, we can basically determine its credibility, and can provide it with fast weight rewards, so that it can play an important role in the next work, but if it makes a wrong job in the subsequent work, we will immediately clear its weight score to zero. After the node's weight score accumulates to a sufficient height, we adopt a "smooth end" method for its reward, in order to prevent an honest node from being too high, resulting in uneven rights. Therefore, we adopt Formula (1) as the weight score reward strategy for honest nodes.

$$WS_i = \alpha^* sigmoid(\beta^* T_i) \tag{1}$$

Among them, WSi represents the weight score of node i; $\alpha$ is the maximum weight score, in our scheme $\alpha = 1$; $\beta$ is the parameter to adjust the startup of quick reward, set according to actual needs; Ti is the time of continuous honest work of node i. From the above weight value calculation method, we can use historical work information to calculate its weight score for each node. We can give a threshold $\alpha$ and $\beta$, the threshold $\alpha$ and $\beta$ can be taken into the weight value calculation formula according to the probability of the correct node and the failed node to perform various behaviors. $\alpha$ is the weight value of honest nodes when they work continuously and correctly, and the $\beta$ value can be adjusted to control the threshold of quick reward. In our scheme, nodes can only maintain the accumulated scores if they work correctly all the time. For faulty nodes that have not responded to the consensus information, reduce their weight scores to the threshold of quick reward to ensure their reasonable rights after fault recovery. For a malicious node, once it makes a wrong response to the consensus information, its weight score is cleared to prevent it from destroying the consensus in the subsequent work.

## 2.3 Node Sharding Scheme Based on Weight

After discussing the node weight adjustment strategy, we can further design the node fragmentation strategy according to it. First of all, we have to determine a few basic design goals. The first point is to ensure that each node is assigned to a shard and can only be assigned to one shard; the second point is to ensure that the allocation strategy of the node is unpredictable, if a node can be allocated before the allocation. It is very dangerous for an attacker to guess which shard it will be allocated to. Therefore, we have to introduce a random factor in the allocation process to ensure that the allocation process is random. The third point is to ensure that each shard is similar, that is, the sum of the weight scores of the nodes in the shard is approximately equal. In order to prevent unreasonable allocation of shard nodes, almost all faulty nodes or malicious nodes in a shard are finally divided. The consensus of the film is broken. Based on these three goals, the following fragmentation scheme is designed, see algorithm 1:

---

**Algorithm 1:** Node Distribution Scheme based on Weight

---

**Input:**
A random number generator Rg() and system time t to get random set;
The weight score WS = {$ws_1$, $ws_2$, ..., $ws_n$};
**Output:**
K shards S = {$S_1$, S2, ..., $S_k$};
1  Initialize all parameters;
2  Get random set R = {$r_1$, $r_2$, ..., $r_n$};
3  Sort the weight score WS = sort(WS);
4  **For** each node's weight score $ws_i$ in WS **do**
5      Get reasonable shards S' = {$S_1$', $S_2$', ..., $S_j$'}to be selected which |S'| = min{ $S_1$, $S_2$, ..., $S_k$ } and j is the number of |S'|;
6      Get $r_i$ = Rg($t_i$) ;
7      Select shard Sc' as the shard of node i which c = $r_i$ % j;
8  **End**

---

The weight-based node allocation strategy determines its shard location based on the node's weight score and a random number based on the system time. First, the nodes are sorted in descending order according to their updated weight scores, and the node with the highest score is assigned first each time. For each node, first obtain a list of fragments to be selected S', the number of nodes in each fragment in S' is the minimum number of nodes in all fragments. This ensures that nodes with similar scores are not allocated to the same shard, and keeps the overall score of each shard similar as a whole. Then obtain a random number, and select the shard position of the node based on the random number to prevent it from being predicted. Through this method, the three design goals of the node allocation strategy are met.

# 3   Consensus Algorithm Scheme Based on Sharding

After determining the sharding rules, we need to determine the next consensus process. Because sharding divides the overall node into different areas. In DWS_BFT, the number of shards is equal to one-half of the number of nodes. This ensures that the number of nodes within and between shards will not be large, so the number of nodes in each individual area will become rare. Therefore, we can use the PBFT algorithm for intra-shard consensus. In the PBFT algorithm, the master node presides over the consensus work, so we first introduce the leader node selection process within the shard.

## 3.1   Leader Node Selection

Similar to the sharding process, the selection of the leader node is also an important factor to ensure the safety and feasibility of the entire sharding consensus scheme. Because the leader node is responsible for more responsibilities than other nodes, and once the malicious node is selected as the leader node, the malicious node can tamper with the consensus information and write the wrong consensus information on the blockchain, which causes the entire system the injury is very fatal. Therefore, it is very important to ensure the credibility of the leader node, and the following factors must be met at the same time: ① Randomness, like the sharding rules, the selection of the leader node also requires randomness, for the rights of all trusted nodes it is fair, and it also prevents the enemy from targeting pre-selected nodes; ②Variability, unlike the sharding rules before resharding is performed after multiple transaction consensus, the leader node needs to be re-selected before each transaction consensus to further ensure the distribution security in the on-chip consensus process; ③ Fairness, nodes with high weight scores should be given more opportunities to become leader nodes, and our node weight update scheme ensures that the weight scores of each honest node will not differ much, so it will not lead to the phenomenon of excessive power of a single node. Therefore, we adopted the Proof of Stake (PoS) as the leader node selection algorithm. At the same time, in order to ensure that malicious nodes will not be selected as the leader node, a node preprocessing is performed before PoS. First, arrange the nodes in the shard in descending order of weight, filter out the last 1/3 of the nodes, and use the remaining nodes as candidate nodes for the leader node. Then PoS is performed on the candidate nodes and the leader node is selected.

## 3.2   Consensus Agreement

We use PBFT as the consensus algorithm. Due to the existence of shards, transactions are divided into intra-shard transactions and inter-shard transactions.

**Intra-shard Consensus.** After the master node receives the consensus information from the client, it verifies whether the parties to the transaction are in their own shards. After the verification is successful, the intra-shard consensus is carried out. The following describes the consensus protocol of the intra-shard consensus:

1) PRE-PREPARE phase: The leader node receives the PRE-PREPARE message sent by the client and broadcasts the message to all nodes participating in the consensus.
2) PREPARE phase: The slave node generates a PREPARE message after receiving the PRE-PREPARE message sent by the leader node, and selectively broadcasts the PREPARE message to nodes in its own consensus domain. If more than $2f + 1$ correct preparation messages are received, it will enter the COMMIT phase.
3) COMMIT phase: The node generates a COMMIT message and broadcasts it to the nodes in the consensus domain, and other nodes verify the COMMIT message. After the node receives $2f + 1$ COMMIT messages, it proceeds to the REPLY phase.
4) REPLY phase: After the client receives $f + 1$ identical REPLY information, it can confirm that the message has been agreed, and the message can be written on the blockchain.

**Cross-shard Consensus.** When the master node verifies the received transaction information that one of the parties is in its own shard, it starts to execute the inter-slice transaction consensus. The following describes the consensus agreement between shards:

1) PRE-PREPARE phase: First, the client sends a signed cross-shard transaction request to the leader node li, and after receiving the request, the request is assigned a number si, and the PRE-PREPARE message is broadcast to all the shard nodes involved in the cross-shard transaction $< \ <$ PRE-PREPARE, si, d $> m >$, d represents the hash of transaction m.
2) PREPARE phase: After receiving the PRE-PREPARE request of message m from node r, verify the message signature and transaction hash. Subsequently, the slave node r assigns an intra-slice number sj to the transaction, and broadcasts the PRE-PARE message $<$ PREPARE, si, sj, d, r $>$ d to all related shard nodes, which represents the transaction hash.
3) In-chip COMMIT phase: collect $2f + 1$ consistent PREPARE votes from lj from node r, PREPARE-LOCALlj(m,si,sj,r) status is established, if r receives all related transactions m With $2f + 1$ unanimous votes of all shards, PREPARE (m,l,r) is established. Broadcast $<$ COMMIT, [si,sj,...,sk], d, r $>$ from node r to all nodes related to transaction m.
4) Off-chip COMMIT phase: collect $2f + 1$ consistent COMMIT votes from shard lj from node r, COMMIT-LOCALlj(m,si,sj,r) is established, from node r to all related to transaction m, the node broadcasts $<$ COMMIT, [si,sj,...,sk], d, r $>$.
5) REPLY phase: execute transaction from node r and change state. Return the client execution result $<$ REPLY, tc, c, o, r $>$, tc is the timestamp of transaction m, and r is the execution result. The client waits for $f + 1$ identical REPLY results from each shard to write the consensus into the blockchain.

# 4   Experimental Results and Analysis

This chapter conducts an experimental analysis on the Byzantine fault-tolerant consensus algorithm based on dynamic weights (DWS_BFT), tests the throughput and algorithm security of the algorithm, compares it with some current sharding algorithms, and analyzes the effectiveness of DWS_BFT. Since each committee in the sharding blockchain processes transactions in parallel, the number of committees continues to increase as the number of nodes increases. Therefore, the sharding blockchain has horizontal scalability. The experiment will verify whether DWS_BFT has horizontal scalability and is consistent with the current sharding algorithm to compare. Security is an important feature and basic requirement of the blockchain. In the experiment, the proportion of various nodes in the improved algorithm will be analyzed. At the same time, the security of a single committee will be analyzed to verify the algorithm's anti-attack ability. The experiment simulates a multi-node network environment through a server, and the test system is Ubuntu 18.04.

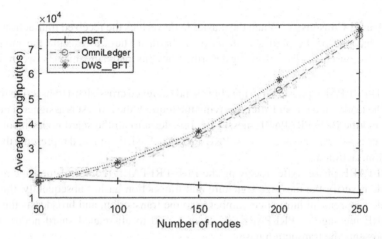

**Fig. 3.** Comparison of throughput of different algorithms under different nodes.

First, test the throughput of the algorithm. In DWS_BFT, the node is divided into multiple shards. In this test, the size of a single shard is first set to 50 nodes. The experiments respectively tested the throughput performance of different consensus algorithms under 50, 100, 150, 200, and 250 nodes. The experiment uses the average throughput within 1 min to measure the performance of the consensus algorithm to prevent accidental situations. It can be seen that the throughput of OmniLedger using sharding technology and the Byzantine fault-tolerant consensus algorithm (DWS_BFT) based on dynamic weights will increase with the number of nodes, while the throughput of the PBFT algorithm will increase with the number of nodes (see Fig. 3). The increase and decrease indicate that the consensus algorithm is scalable after using the sharding technology, and the sharding technology will greatly improve the performance of the consensus algorithm. The average throughput of DWS_BFT in one minute is higher than that of OmniLedger, indicating that DWS_BFT can make full use of the computing resources of each node.

The next experiment observes the proportion of correct nodes in different consensus algorithms when errors occur under continuous operation. In the experiment, the network initially has 50, 100, 150, 200, 250 nodes, and the number of correct nodes when the system fails. The ratio of correct nodes when errors occur in PBFT and DWS_BFT is about 2/3, while OmniLedger is about 1/2 (see Fig. 4). This proves that the dynamic weight can ensure that the proportion of correct nodes in each shard is close to the total proportion of correct nodes in the network, and is due to other sharding schemes. Therefore, DWS_BFT is able to resist attacks from opponents with adaptive capabilities.

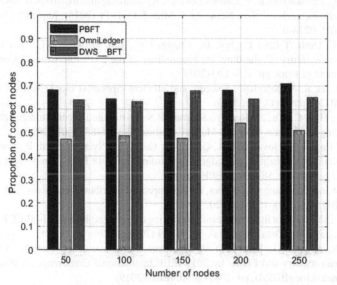

**Fig. 4.** Proportion of correct nodes when the primary selection of different algorithms fails under different nodes

## 5 Conclusion

This paper proposes a Byzantine fault-tolerant consensus based on dynamic weight sharding (DWS_BFT), which achieves both scalability and robustness. DWS_BFT updates the node weight score according to the continuous and correct working conditions of the node, and selects the node to different shards reasonably from the weight score to achieve the balance between the shards and ensure the robustness of the sharding system. Transactions are processed in parallel by each shard to achieve horizontal scalability and improve the performance of the consensus algorithm. And design experiments to verify the above conclusions.

**Acknowledgment.** This work was supported by grants from the National Key Research Program Projects (No. 2018YFB1800704).

# References

1. Watanabe, H., Fujimura, S., Nakadaira, A., Miyazaki, Y., Akutsu, A., Kishigami, J.J.: Blockchain contract: a complete consensus using blockchain. In: 2015 IEEE 4th Global Conference on Consumer Electronics (GCCE), pp. 577–578. IEEE (2015)
2. Alwabel, M., Kwon, Y.: Blockchain consistency check protocol for improved reliability. Comput. Syst. Sci. Eng. **36**(2), 281–292 (2021)
3. Bhat, P.T., Thankachan, R.V., Chandrasekaran, K.: Sharding distributed social databases using social network analysis. Soc. Netw. Anal. Min. **5**(1), 1–11 (2015). https://doi.org/10.1007/s13278-015-0274-0
4. Dang, H., Dinh, T.T.A., Loghin, D., Chang, E.C., Lin, Q., Ooi, B.C.: Towards scaling blockchain systems via sharding. In: Proceedings of the 2019 International Conference on Management of Data, pp. 123–140 (2019)
5. Chen, H., et al.: Cipherchain: a secure and efficient ciphertext blockchain via mPECK. J. Quantum Comput. **2**(1), 57 (2020)
6. Wang, J., Han, C., Yu, X., Ren, Y., Sherratt, R.S.: Distributed secure storage scheme based on sharding blockchain. Comput. Mater. Continua **70**(3), 4485–4502 (2022)
7. Kokoris-Kogias, E., Jovanovic, P., Gasser, L., Gailly, N., Syta, E., Ford, B.: Omniledger: a secure, scale-out, decentralized ledger via sharding. In: 2018 IEEE Symposium on Security and Privacy (SP), pp. 583–598. IEEE (2018)
8. Li, A., Wang, X., Wang, X., Bohan, L.: An improved distributed query for large-scale RDF data. J. Big Data **2**(4), 157–166 (2020)
9. Zhao, H.: Sharding for literature search via cutting citation graphs. In: 2014 IEEE International Conference on Big Data (Big Data), pp. 77–79 (2014)
10. Lee, A.R., Kim, M.G., Kim, I.K.: SHAREChain: healthcare data sharing framework using Blockchain-registry and FHIR. In: 2019 IEEE International Conference on Bioinformatics and Biomedicine (BIBM), pp. 1087–1090. IEEE (2019)
11. Song, L., Wang, X., Wei, P., Lu, Z., Wang, X., Merveille, N.: Blockchain-based flexible double-chain architecture and performance optimization for better sustainability in agriculture. Comput. Mater. Continua **68**(1), 1429–1446 (2021)
12. Zheng, P., Xu, Q., Zheng, Z., Zhou, Z., Yan, Y., Zhang, H.: Meepo: sharded consortium blockchain. In: 2021 IEEE 37th International Conference on Data Engineering (ICDE), pp. 1847–1852. IEEE (2021)

# A Survey of Blockchain-Based Crowd Sensing Incentive Mechanism

Xinbin Xu[1,2], Jieren Cheng[2(✉)], Jingxin Liu[2], Yuming Yuan[3], Hui Li[3], and Victor S. Sheng[4]

[1] School of Cyberspace Security Academy (Cryptography Academy), Hainan University, Haikou 570228, China
[2] Hainan Blockchain Technology Engineering Research Center, Hainan University, Haikou 570228, China
291108957@qq.com
[3] Hainan Huochain Tech Company Limited, Haikou 570100, China
[4] Department of Computer Science, Texas Tech University, Lubbock, TX 79409, USA

**Abstract.** Crowd sensing (CS) is a data acquisition mode using the sensing ability of mobile devices. As a distributed ledger, blockchain (BC) is used for crowd sensing to resist security risks in the incentive process. Therefore, many blockchain-based CS incentive mechanisms have been proposed. In this paper, we summarize the incentive mechanism of the based-blockchain CS system. First, we introduce the background knowledge of crowd sensing and blockchain. Second, we use a two-dimensional incentive mechanism classification framework based on the main incentive goal and the reward form to classify the existing blockchain-based CS incentive mechanisms. In the classification method based on the main incentive goal, the incentive mechanism is divided into service quality, privacy security, and trusted transaction. In the classification method based on reward form, the incentive mechanism is divided into social service, game playing, and monetary reward. Then, we compare and analyze typical incentive mechanisms, discuss the advantages of typical incentive scheme and their existing problems. Finally, we propose the challenges and future directions of the based-blockchain CS incentive mechanism.

**Keywords:** Crowd sensing · Blockchain · Incentive mechanism · Main incentive goal · Reward form

## 1 Introduction

Like generative adversarial networks [1,2], named entity recognition [3], and the internet of thing [4], crowdsensing is an emerging technology. CS is an information sensing method, which enables sensing device holders to get rewards by contributing the data perceived in their mobile devices to provide services for requesters [5]. CS technology is widely used in various fields of daily life and production, including energy [6], transportation [7], and medical treatment [8]. However, CS faces many challenges in service quality, privacy, and participation due to its structural characteristics [9]. And blockchain is a decentralized, traceable, and tamper-proof distributed storage technology, so it is integrated into the CS system [10]. CS incentive mechanism is to actively participate in the project and provide high-quality data under the incentive measures for the holder of the sensing device [11]. To deal with the single point of failure of the centralized CS system, data requesters and task participants in the CS system join the blockchain network as nodes [12]. The addition of blockchain also brings new problems to the CS incentive mechanism, such as difficulty in guaranteeing service quality, leakage of user privacy information, and untrustworthy transactions. Therefore, many scholars have proposed novel CS incentive mechanisms based on blockchain for these problems. However, the traditional incentive mechanism classification framework cannot effectively divide and summarize the CS incentive mechanism in the blockchain environment. So we propose a novel classification framework for the blockchain-based CS incentive mechanism in this paper.

The main contributions of this paper are summarized as follow:

(1) For the first time, we propose a two-dimensional incentive mechanism classification framework based on the main incentive goal and the reward form and use it to classify and sort out the existing blockchain-based incentive mechanisms for crowdsensing.
(2) We discuss the advantages and problems of typical blockchain-based incentive schemes for crowd sensing. And we summarize and compare the important characteristics of different incentive methods in the form of a table.
(3) We analyze the challenges still faced by the blockchain-based crowd sensing incentive mechanism at this stage, and propose possible future development directions.

The rest of this article is as follows. In Sect. 2, we will introduce the background knowledge of blockchain and crowd sensing. In Sect. 3, we use the incentive mechanism classification method based on the main incentive goal and the incentive mechanism classification method based on the reward form to classify and summarize the based-blockchain CS incentive mechanisms. And we compare and discuss the advantages of typical incentive mechanisms and their existing problems. In Sect. 4, we analyze the challenges faced by the blockchain-based crowd sensing incentive mechanism and propose the development direction of future research. In Sect. 5, we summarize the full text.

## 2    Background

### 2.1    Blockchain

Since the publication of the Bitcoin white paper [13] in 2008, blockchain has received extensive attention from industry and academia. Blockchain is a chain structure that combines data blocks in historical order [14]. Its structure is shown in Fig. 1. The blocks are connected by hash pointers in the blockchain system. It is a distributed ledger shared and maintained by all nodes in a decentralized system. The blockchain system can be divided into five layers: data layer, network layer, consensus layer, smart contract layer, and application layer [15]. Blockchain has the following characteristics:

(1) Decentralization: Blockchain participants can publicly access historical transactions or confirm the latest transactions without relying on a trusted third party.
(2) Anti-tampering: Any information generally stored in the blockchain will generate a unique identifier and cannot be tampered with.
(3) Traceability: The blockchain structure stores all historical data based on the genesis block, and any data on the chain can be traced back to its origin.

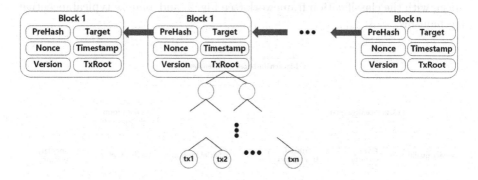

**Fig. 1.** Blockchain structure

Blockchain has the characteristics of decentralization, anti-tampering, and traceability. So it is being widely used in many fields such as medical care, food supply, agriculture, etc. [16–18].

## 2.2 Crowd Sensing

As an emerging data collection mode, the crowdsensing system relies on sensors integrated into mobile devices to collect high-quality data. Compared with traditional sensor networks, the mobility and intelligence of mobile device sensors ensure a higher perceptual coverage and better perceptual context correlation [19]. Nowadays, smart devices are widely used in our daily activities, such as communication, business, and entertainment, which makes the application of crowd sensing technology in many fields possible [20].

At present, the main objects of the crowd sensing system are three: requesters, workers (sensing task participants), and service platforms [21]. The service platform accepts service requests from requesters and assigns tasks.

Workers are selected to join the tasks and return the required data to the service platform. And the service platform returns the data to the requester after verifying. The workers who complete tasks will get the reward from requesters.

Crowd sensing incentive mechanism means that data requesters use rewards through the service platform to encourage workers to actively participate in sensing tasks so that workers can consume sensing equipment resources to collect data according to the requester's wishes [22]. After many transactions, the incentive mechanism maximizes the mutual benefit of the requester and the worker, as shown in Formula (1).

$$Incentive = max(Benefit_r, Benfit_w) \tag{1}$$

## 3   Blockchain-Based Crowd Sensing Incentive Mechanism

In this chapter, we will discuss the existing blockchain-based CS incentive mechanism with the classification framework (see Fig. 2) and analyze typical incentive mechanisms.

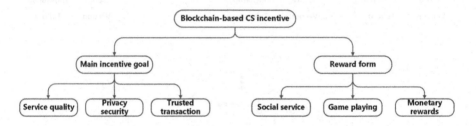

**Fig. 2.** The classification framework for blockchain-based CS incentive mechanism

### 3.1   Incentive Mechanism Based on Main Incentive Goal

**Service Quality.** Promoting participants to provide high-quality service data is the important goal of CS. The data quality is affected by many factors, so incentive mechanisms are needed to encourage users to actively collect data. Wang et al. [23] proposed an incentive mechanism based on two-layer reinforcement learning to encourage high-quality model sharing of drones. Chen et al. [24] proposed an incentive mechanism for car networking crowd sensing based on consortium blockchain and data quality-driven auction model, which uses smart contracts to realize automatic data sharing and encourages users to provide high-quality data. Wei et al. [25] proposed a blockchain-based incentive mechanism for a mixed crowd sensing system, which comprehensively considers data quality evaluation and other factors and encourage participants to actively contribute their sensor data. Zheng et al. [26] proposed a quality of service (QoS) awareness-based incentive mechanism for blockchain-based crowd sensing, using a web service quality model based on non-functional attributes to provide higher rewards to workers who contribute high-quality data. Dimitriou et al. [27] proposed a reward framework that can be used as a block building in crowd sensing applications, allowing workers to submit data and obtain bitcoin rewards through incentive mechanism. Gu et al. [28] proposed a Bitcoin-based CS reward distribution scheme, which maintains the participation enthusiasm of users through sensing capabilities evaluation and transaction verification. Hui et al. [29] developed a blockchain-based collaborative CS scheme that encourages automatic vehicle to perform the sensing tasks cooperatively by alliance games with transferable rewards. Foschini et al. [30] proposed a mobile crowd sensing (MCS) architecture based on multi-access edge computing, which records the task participants' reward status with blockchain to improve the quality of services provided by users. Kadadha et al. [31] proposed a distributed CS task matching mechanism based on the two-way preference, which uses the task quality as the main parameter to select best workers for the task and motivate them. Cheng et al. [32] proposed a blockchain-based CS system, which applies a reputation incentive mechanism to analyze data and effectively reward excellent workers.

**Privacy Security.** With the increase of privacy and security issues, the motivation of users to participate in activities will also decrease. Therefore, some incentive mechanisms have been proposed to protect user privacy and sensitive information from being leaked in the process of CS. Dorsala et al. [33] designed a privacy-preserving aggregation scheme for maintaining crowd sensing data. It deploys aggregator services in intelligent contracts on public blockchain networks, using encryption technology to protect user privacy during the incentive process. Li et al. [34] proposed a blockchain-based incentive mechanism of non-deterministic vehicle crowd sensing, which effectively motivates vehicles to participate in sensing activities under conditions that protect user privacy. Wang et al. [35] proposed a smart privacy protection incentive mechanism, using smart contracts and zero-knowledge evidence to achieve reverse auctions of sensing data based on a limited budget under privacy protection conditions. Peng et al. [36] combined k-anonymity and blockchain to build a MCS system, which allows participants to receive sensing tasks that do not reveal private information and submit corresponding sensing data to obtain corresponding rewards. Chatzopoulos et al. [37] designed an efficient CS optimal auction incentive strategy, which requires workers to perform sensing tasks in specific locations and protect users' privacy with smart contracts. Yang et al. [38] proposed a distributed privacy protection incentive framework, which uses private blockchain to prevent location privacy attacks by connecting payment amounts with user tasks. Moti et al. [39] developed a blockchain-based location crowd sensing incentive mechanism to obtain information services under the condition of privacy protection through six main features for spontaneous location setting. Jia et al. [40] proposed a blockchain-based hybrid incentive mechanism for location privacy protection in a crowd sensing network, which encourages users to participate in sensing tasks without disclosing location information. Lai et al. [41] proposed a secure and privacy-protected map update incentive scheme, which applies the blind signature technology to ensure the safety of the incentive mechanism and protect the privacy of the vehicle users. Wang et al. [42] proposed a based-permission-blockchain location-protected anonymous payment system, which uses the zero-knowledge proof method to realize the security of the anonymous payments system. Lin et al. [43] proposed a distributed location-based services certification incentive mechanism, which encourages witnesses to actively verify the location information provided by CS users and solves the privacy leakage problem of the location proof system.

**Trusted Transaction.** Credible incentives in CS have become an important content of user attention. And incentive methods based on the trust relationship are proposed to avoid malicious behaviors in the CS process. Noshad et al. [44] proposed a blockchain-based distributed reputation incentive mechanism applied to the crowd sensing network, which uses the reputation system to solve trust problems and reward those who complete the perception task. Yuan et al. [45] proposed a reliable distributed CS reward system based on blockchain technology, which allows high-reputation participants are more likely to receive more rewards for completing tasks. Wang et al. [46] proposed a blockchain-based on-board energy information transmission incentive scheme, which uses reputation based on partial trust and credibility calculation to derive and construct an incentive model to stimulate electric vehicles to complete tasks collaboratively. Bellavista et al. [47] proposed an edge-based distributed CS architecture, which supports distributed user incentives in the MCS model and improves the scalability of infrastructure between distrust sensing platforms. Calado et al. [48] proposed a blockchain-based anti-tampering incentive scheme that makes each participant trust others by user participation rewards scores stored in shared records. Weng et al. [49] proposed a federal predictive service incentive framework that provides a real reward prediction and uses blockchain to ensure the fairness of transactions. Xu et al. [50] proposed a CS incentive mechanism based on the reward-punishment model, which is used to build a hybrid crowdsensing platform to avoid malicious activities by minority groups and enable users to trust each other. Gruhler et al. [51] proposed a blockchain-based reputation scheme, which encourages users to cooperate and avoid malicious behavior by providing necessary incentives for task workers. An et al. [52] proposed a blockchain-based CS data transaction system that uses a reliability rating mechanism based on homomorphic cryptography to prevent sellers from reporting false information and manipulating auctions. Yun et al. [53] introduced a private blockchain in the CS system, which establishes a trust relationship between service requesters and workers and makes users act as monitors for each other. An et al. [54] proposed a quality control model of CS based on consensus blockchain, which uses a double consensus method to ensure the fairness of user rewards. Liang et al. [55] proposed a blockchain-based CS application program, which uses a trusted execution environment to solve the problem of malicious requesters deceiving workers by issuing abnormal sensing tasks.

## 3.2  Incentive Mechanism Based on Reward Form

In the blockchain-based CS system, user groups need to use different forms of incentives according to different scenarios. Therefore, we divide the incentive mechanism into social service, game playing, and monetary reward.

**Social Service.** In social-service incentive mechanisms, crowd sensing scenarios are regarded as social networks. All members can act as requesters and workers at the same time, providing services and receiving services, and are encouraged to achieve common community goals. Khalid et al. [56] proposed a data storage system, which uses roadside units as nodes to build a blockchain and provides monetary rewards to vehicles that offer sensing data in the Vehicle Ad Hoc Network. Kim et al. [57] designed a crowd-sensing intelligent parking system based on a multi-blockchain structure, which enables users to transparently trade sensing data in blockchain social networks. Cai et al. [58] proposed a robust and verifiable crowd-testing system framework, which enables blockchain nodes to serve social crowd-testing applications and create a stable network ecosystem through incentive mechanisms.

**Game Playing.** In game-playing incentive mechanisms, the process of crowd sensing is regarded as an entertainment game. The requester and the worker participate in the game as players and maximize each other's benefits through continuous interactive games. Qiu et al. [59] designed a distributed multi-terminal resource allocation incentive mechanism based on the Walras equilibrium theory to ensure that the supply and demand of each terminal in each region are balanced. Jiang et al. [60] proposed a distributed industrial internet of things data-sharing scheme, which models the data transaction between data owners and edge devices as a multistage Stackelberg game. Lv et al. [61] proposed a blockchain-based spectrum sensing system, which models the transaction between requesters and workers as a reward-sensing time game so that both can adopt strategies to maximize their welfare. Xu et al. [62] proposed a smart-contract-based network insurance framework, which can speed up miners' verification and packaging transactions into the blockchain to enable workers to obtain rewards quickly. Zhang et al. [63] proposed an alliance-blockchain-based distributed vehicle-mounted crowd sensing service architecture, which uses the Stackelberg game method to achieve the best task reward distribution. Wei et al. [64] built a smart-contract-based MCS platform, which performs price equilibrium processing through smart contracts and distributed algorithms to achieve the best use of resources and reward fairness in the market. Liu et al. [65] used Q-learning to solve the dynamic game under the sensor model unknown for users, which achieves a balance between the CS platform and participants. Hu et al. [66] proposed a mobile crowd sensing framework based on blockchain and federated learning, which formulates game rules compatible with incentives to maximize the benefits of both requesters and workers. Huang et al. [67] proposed a blockchain-based industrial MCS system, which uses dynamic reward ranking incentive mechanisms to reduce the imbalance of multiple sensing tasks. Hu et al. [68] proposed a three-stage strategy for different participants and task requesters, which ensures the fairness of the sensing data market by the Stackelberg game incentive mechanism.

**Monetary Reward.** In monetary-rewards incentive mechanisms, crowd sensing scenarios are regarded as trading markets. Incentive requesters provide workers with monetary rewards to encourage them to collect data. Xu et al. [69] proposed a role-centered incentive mechanism, which maximizes the utility of participants through a reverse auction incentive mechanism and dynamic programming worker selection method. Wang et al. [70] proposed a prediction-based reverse auction incentive mechanism, which selects the workers with the minimum moving distance and the lowest bidding price according to the prediction results of the semi Markov model. Pang et al. [71] proposed a smart-contract-based crowd sensing framework based, which realizes fair user transactions and efficient task reward allocation by analyzing user information. Liu et al. [72] proposed a cryptocurrency incentive mechanism in a distributed software crowdsourcing system, which rewards workers providing high-quality service.

### 3.3    Comparative Discussion of the Typical Incentive Mechanism

Existing blockchain-based CS incentive mechanisms have their advantages and limitations. For example, the incentive model based on two-layer reinforcement learning [23] can formulate better strategies, but its learning process is time-consuming. Incentives using zero-knowledge proof methods [35] can protect information privacy, but contract execution costs are relatively high. Although the k-anonymous multi-chain architecture [36] can effectively protect the employees' privacy during the reward distribution process, it lacks control over system traffic. Although based-smart-contracts automatic data evaluation [53] can build user trust relationships and achieve credible incentives, the reference factors for data evaluation are not comprehensive. Table 1 summarizes the typical incentive mechanisms in prevtious studies.

**Table 1.** Typical blockchain-based incentive mechanism for crowd sensing.

| Schemes | Challenge | Solution | Scene | BC form | BC type |
|---|---|---|---|---|---|
| Wang et al. [23] | High quality model | Two-tier reinforcement learning | Unmanned aerial vehicle | Single-chain | Consortium blockchain |
| Chen et al. [24] | High quality data | Quality-Driven auction | Internet of vehicle | Single-chain | Consortium blockchain |
| Zheng et al. [26] | High quality model | Incentive based on QoS | Internet of thing | Single-chain | Private blockchain (Ethereum) |
| Wang et al. [35] | Privacy preserving | Zero-knowledge proof | Vehicular network | Single-chain | Public blockchain (Ethereum) |
| Peng et al. [36] | Privacy preserving | k-anonymity and blockchain | General CS | Multi-chain | Public chain and private chain |
| Yang et al. [38] | Location privacy preserving | Blockchain framework | General CS | Multi-chain | Public blockchain |
| An et al. [52] | Truthfulness of Data Trading | Blockchain-based Reverse Auction | General crowd sensing | Single-chain | Consortium blockchain |
| Yun et al. [53] | Trust relationship of users | Smart contract automates data evaluation | General CS | Single-chain | Private blockchain (Ethereum) |
| Khalid et al. [56] | User selfish behavior prevention | Reputation incentive mechanism | Vehicular Networks | Single-chain | Public blockchain (Ethereum) |
| Kim et al. [57] | Real-time data sharing | Multi-Blockchain Structure | Smart parking CS | Multi-chain | Public chain and private chain |
| Lv et al. [61] | Maximize benefits | Reward-Sensing -time game | Spectrum sensing | Single-chain | Public blockchain |

# 4    Challenge and Future Directions

Through the classification introduction and discussion in the previous chapter, we have understood the research work of the crowd sensing incentive mechanism in the current blockchain environment. However, the crowd sensing incentive mechanism in the blockchain environment still faces some challenges.

**Incentive Efficiency.** To improve the accuracy of evaluation and verification, most of the nodes in the blockchain will participate. However, as the number of crowd sensing users increases, the multi-point verification feature of the blockchain may cause the execution efficiency of the incentive mechanism to decrease. The decrease in incentive efficiency will dampen the enthusiasm of the holders of the sensing equipment to participate in the sensing activities. Therefore, in the future, the incentive mechanism needs to be balanced between data reliability and incentive efficiency. For example, design a reasonable verification node selection mechanism to reduce the number of unnecessary verification nodes to improve the efficiency of the incentive mechanism.

**Collaborative Incentives.** As user privacy protection requirements increase and sensing scenarios become increasingly complex and changeable, the single-chain structure can no longer meet user sensing needs. The multi-chain structure will be adopted to cope with the multi-domain complex environment. Therefore, the design of the future incentive mechanism requires a collaborative relationship between perceived users of different chains. For example, the incentive mechanism is combined with a cross-chain consensus mechanism to realize multi-domain crowd sensing and cross-chain collaborative incentives.

**User Trust Evaluation.** The user's trust relationship is a significant factor in the incentive mechanism. The existing trust relationship evaluation parameters are not comprehensive enough, which easily leads to unfair transactions between requesters and workers. The future incentive mechanism needs to refer to the trust relationship established by various factors, such as the incentive mechanism that considers the bidirectional preferences of requesters and workers.

## 5   Conclusion

In this paper, we have reviewed the latest research results of the based-blockchain CS incentive mechanism. Firstly, we have introduced the research background of the CS incentive mechanism based on blockchain. Second, we have used a two-dimensional classification framework based on the main incentive goal and the reward form to summarize the current blockchain-based crowdsensing incentive mechanism. Then, we have discussed and compared typical incentive mechanisms. Finally, we have proposed challenges the blockchain-based CS incentive mechanism faces and future development directions in terms of incentive efficiency, collaborative incentives, user trust evaluation. We hope that this paper can provide a good reference for the research of crowd sensing incentive mechanisms in the blockchain environment.

**Acknowledgements.** This work was supported by National Natural Science Foundation of China (Grant No. 62162022 and 62162024), Key Projects in Hainan Province (Grant ZDYF2021GXJS003 and Grant ZDYF2020040), the Major science and technology project of Hainan Province (Grant No. ZDKJ2020012).

# References

1. Cheng, J., Yang, Y., Tang, X., Xiong, N., Zhang, Y., Lei, F.: Generative adversarial networks: a literature review. KSII Trans. Internet Inf. Syst. **14**(12), 4625–4647 (2020)
2. Lei, F., Cheng, J., Yang, Y., Tang, X., Sheng, V.S., Huang, C.: Improving heterogeneous network knowledge transfer based on the principle of generative adversarial. Electronics **10**(13), 1525 (2021)
3. Cheng, J., Liu, J., Xu, X., Xia, D., Liu, L., Sheng, V.S.: A review of Chinese named entity recognition. KSII Trans. Internet Inf. Syst. **15**(6), 2012–2030 (2021)
4. Tang, X., Tu, W., Li, K., Cheng, J.: DFFnet: an IoT-perceptive dual feature fusion network for general real-time semantic segmentation. Inf. Sci. **565**, 326–343 (2021)
5. Liu, Y., Kong, L., Chen, G.: Data-oriented mobile crowdsensing: a comprehensive survey. IEEE Commun. Surveys Tutorials **21**(3), 2849–2885 (2019)
6. Liu, C.H., Dai, Z., Zhao, Y., Crowcroft, J., Wu, D., Leung, K.K.: Distributed and energy-efficient mobile crowdsensing with charging stations by deep reinforcement learning. IEEE Trans. Mob. Comput. **20**(1), 130–146 (2019)
7. Li, M., Zhu, L., Lin, X.: Privacy-preserving traffic monitoring with false report filtering via fog-assisted vehicular crowdsensing. IEEE Trans. Services Comput. (2019)
8. Simoes, J., et al.: Toward personalized tinnitus treatment: an exploratory study based on internet crowdsensing. Front. Public Health **7**, 157 (2019)
9. Capponi, A., Fiandrino, C., Kantarci, B., Foschini, L., Kliazovich, D., Bouvry, P.: A survey on mobile crowdsensing systems: challenges, solutions, and opportunities. IEEE Commun. Surveys Tutor. **21**(3), 2419–2465 (2019)
10. Chen, Z., Fiandrino, C., Kantarci, B.: On blockchain integration into mobile crowdsensing via smart embedded devices: a comprehensive survey. J. Syst. Architect. **115**, 102011 (2021)
11. She, R.: Survey on incentive strategies for mobile crowdsensing system. In: 2020 IEEE 11th International Conference on Software Engineering and Service Science (ICSESS), pp. 511–514. IEEE (2020)
12. Liang, Y., Li, Y., Shin, B.S.: Distributed trusted computing for blockchain-based crowdsourcing. CMC-Comput. Mater. Continua **68**(3), 2825–2842 (2021)
13. Nakamoto, S.: Bitcoin: a peer-to-peer electronic cash system. Decentralized Bus. Rev. 21260 (2008)
14. Lu, Y.: The blockchain: state-of-the-art and research challenges. J. Ind. Inf. Integr. **15**, 80–90 (2019)
15. Zhang, R., Xue, R., Liu, L.: Security and privacy on blockchain. ACM Comput. Surv. (CSUR) **52**(3), 1–34 (2019)
16. Chang, M.C., Hsiao, M.Y., Boudier-Revéret, M.: Blockchain technology: efficiently managing medical information in the pain management field. Pain Med. **21**(7), 1512–1513 (2020)
17. Köhler, S., Pizzol, M.: Technology assessment of blockchain-based technologies in the food supply chain. J. Cleaner Prod. **269**, 122193 (2020)
18. Chen, Y., Li, Y., Li, C.: Electronic agriculture, blockchain and digital agricultural democratization: origin, theory and application. J. Clean. Prod. **268**, 122071 (2020)
19. Khan, F., Rehman, A.U., Zheng, J., Jan, M.A., Alam, M.: Mobile crowdsensing: a survey on privacy-preservation, task management, assignment models, and incentives mechanisms. Fut. Gener. Comput. Syst. **100**, 456–472 (2019)
20. Xu, Z., et al.: Mobile crowd sensing of human-like intelligence using social sensors: a survey. Neurocomputing **279**, 3–10 (2018)

21. Sarker, S., Razzaque, M.A., Hassan, M.M., Almogren, A., Fortino, G., Zhou, M.: Optimal selection of crowdsourcing workers balancing their utilities and platform profit. IEEE Internet Things J. **6**(5), 8602–8614 (2019)

22. Jiang, W., Liu, X., Shi, D., Chen, J., Sun, Y., Guo, L.: Research on crowdsourcing price game model in crowd sensing. CMC-Comput. Mater. Continua **68**(2), 1769–1784 (2021)

23. Wang, Y., Su, Z., Zhang, N., Benslimane, A.: Learning in the air: secure federated learning for UAV-assisted crowdsensing. IEEE Trans. Netw. Sci. Eng. **8**, 1055–1069 (2020)

24. Chen, W., Chen, Y., Chen, X., Zheng, Z.: Toward secure data sharing for the IoV: a quality-driven incentive mechanism with on-chain and off-chain guarantees. IEEE Internet Things J. **7**(3), 1625–1640 (2019)

25. Wei, L., Wu, J., Long, C.: A blockchain-based hybrid incentive model for crowdsensing. Electronics **9**(2), 215 (2020)

26. Zheng, J., Dong, X., Liu, Q., Zhu, X., Tong, W.: Blockchain-based secure digital asset exchange scheme with QoS-aware incentive mechanism. In: 2019 IEEE 20th International Conference on High Performance Switching and Routing (HPSR), pp. 1–6. IEEE (2019)

27. Dimitriou, T.: Fair and private bitcoin rewards: incentivizing participation in crowd-sensing applications. In: 2020 IEEE International Conference on Decentralized Applications and Infrastructures (DAPPS), pp. 120–125. IEEE (2020)

28. Gu, X., et al.: Using blockchain to enhance the security of fog-assisted crowdsensing systems. In: 2019 IEEE 28th International Symposium on Industrial Electronics (ISIE), pp. 1859–1864. IEEE (2019)

29. Hui, Y., Huang, Y., Su, Z., Luan, T.H., Cheng, N., Xiao, X., Ding, G.: Bcc: blockchain-based collaborative crowdsensing in autonomous vehicular networks. IEEE Internet of Things Journal (2021)

30. Foschini, L., Martuscelli, G., Montanari, R., Solimando, M.: Edge-enabled mobile crowdsensing to support effective rewarding for data collection in pandemic events. J. Grid Comput. **19**(3), 1–17 (2021)

31. Kadadha, M., Otrok, H., Singh, S., Mizouni, R., Ouali, A.: Two-sided preferences task matching mechanisms for blockchain-based crowdsourcing. J. Netw. Comput. Appl. **191**, 103155 (2021)

32. Cheng, J., Long, H., Tang, X., Li, J., Chen, M., Xiong, N.: A reputation incentive mechanism of crowd sensing system based on blockchain. In: Sun, X., Wang, J., Bertino, E. (eds.) ICAIS 2020. CCIS, vol. 1253, pp. 695–706. Springer, Singapore (2020). https://doi.org/10.1007/978-981-15-8086-4_65

33. Dorsala, M.R., Sastry, V., Chapram, S.: Fair payments for privacy-preserving aggregation of mobile crowdsensing data. J. King Saud Univ. Comput. Inf. Sci. (2021)

34. Li, F., Fu, Y., Zhao, P., Li, C.: An incentive mechanism for nondeterministic vehicular crowdsensing with blockchain. In: 2020 IEEE/CIC International Conference on Communications in China (ICCC), pp. 1074–1079. IEEE (2020)

35. Wang, L., Cao, Z., Zhou, P., Zhao, X.: Towards a smart privacy-preserving incentive mechanism for vehicular crowd sensing. Secur. Commun. Netw. (2021)

36. Peng, T., Liu, J., Chen, J., Wang, G.: A privacy-preserving crowdsensing system with muti-blockchain. In: 2020 IEEE 19th International Conference on Trust, Security and Privacy in Computing and Communications (TrustCom), pp. 1944–1949. IEEE (2020)

37. Chatzopoulos, D., Gujar, S., Faltings, B., Hui, P.: Privacy preserving and cost optimal mobile crowdsensing using smart contracts on blockchain. In: 2018 IEEE 15th International Conference on Mobile Ad Hoc and Sensor Systems (MASS), pp. 442–450. IEEE (2018)

38. Yang, M., Zhu, T., Liang, K., Zhou, W., Deng, R.H.: A blockchain-based location privacy-preserving crowdsensing system. Future Gener. Comput. Syst. **94**, 408–418 (2019)

39. Moti, M.H., Chatzopoulos, D., Hui, P., Faltings, B., Gujar, S.: Orthos: a trustworthy AI framework for data acquisition. In: Baroglio, C., Hubner, J.F., Winikoff, M. (eds.) EMAS 2020. LNCS (LNAI), vol. 12589, pp. 100–118. Springer, Cham (2020). https://doi.org/10.1007/978-3-030-66534-0_7

40. Jia, B., Zhou, T., Li, W., Liu, Z., Zhang, J.: A blockchain-based location privacy protection incentive mechanism in crowd sensing networks. Sensors **18**(11), 3894 (2018)

41. Lai, C., Zhang, M., Cao, J., Zheng, D.: SPIR: a secure and privacy-preserving incentive scheme for reliable real-time map updates. IEEE Internet Things J. **7**(1), 416–428 (2019)

42. Wang, H., Yu, Z., Liu, Y., Guo, B., Wang, L., Cui, H.: Crowdchain: a location preserve anonymous payment system based on permissioned blockchain. In: 2019 IEEE International Conference on Smart Internet of Things (SmartIoT), pp. 227–233. IEEE (2019)

43. Lin, Z., Luo, Y., Fu, S., Xie, T.: BIMP: blockchain-based incentive mechanism with privacy preserving in location proof. In: Qiu, M. (ed.) ICA3PP 2020. LNCS, vol. 12454, pp. 520–536. Springer, Cham (2020). https://doi.org/10.1007/978-3-030-60248-2_35

44. Noshad, Z., et al.: An incentive and reputation mechanism based on blockchain for crowd sensing network. J. Sens. 2021 (2021)

45. Yuan, J., Njilla, L.: Lightweight and reliable decentralized reward system using blockchain. In: IEEE INFOCOM 2021-IEEE Conference on Computer Communications Workshops (INFOCOM WKSHPS), pp. 1–6. IEEE (2021)

46. Wang, Y., Su, Z., Zhang, N.: BSIS: blockchain-based secure incentive scheme for energy delivery in vehicular energy network. IEEE Trans. Ind. Inform. **15**(6), 3620–3631 (2019)

47. Bellavista, P., Cilloni, M., Di Modica, G., Montanari, R., Picone, P.C.M., Solimando, M.: An edge-based distributed ledger architecture for supporting decentralized incentives in mobile crowdsensing. In: 2020 20th IEEE/ACM International Symposium on Cluster, Cloud and Internet Computing (CCGRID), pp. 781–787. IEEE (2020)

48. Calado, D., Pardal, M.L.: Tamper-proof incentive scheme for mobile crowdsensing systems. In: 2018 IEEE 17th International Symposium on Network Computing and Applications (NCA), pp. 1–8. IEEE (2018)

49. Weng, J., Weng, J., Huang, H., Cai, C., Wang, C.: FedServing: a federated prediction serving framework based on incentive mechanism. In: IEEE INFOCOM 2021-IEEE Conference on Computer Communications, pp. 1–10. IEEE (2021)

50. Xu, J., Wang, S., Bhargava, B.K., Yang, F.: A blockchain-enabled trustless crowd-intelligence ecosystem on mobile edge computing. IEEE Trans. Ind. Inform. **15**(6), 3538–3547 (2019)

51. Gruhler, A., Rodrigues, B., Stiller, B.: A reputation scheme for a blockchain-based network cooperative defense. In: 2019 IFIP/IEEE Symposium on Integrated Network and Service Management (IM), pp. 71–79. IEEE (2019)

52. An, B., Xiao, M., Liu, A., Xu, Y., Zhang, X., Li, Q.: Secure crowdsensed data trading based on blockchain. IEEE Trans. Mob. Comput. (2021)
53. Yun, J.H., Kim, M.H.: Private blockchain and smart contract based high trustiness crowdsensing incentive mechanism. J. Korea Inst. Inf. Secur. Cryptol. **28**(4), 999–1007 (2018)
54. An, J., Liang, D., Gui, X., Yang, H., Gui, R., He, X.: Crowdsensing quality control and grading evaluation based on a two-consensus blockchain. IEEE Internet Things J. **6**(3), 4711–4718 (2018)
55. Liang, Y., Li, Y., Shin, B.-S.: Blockchain and trusted execution environment based fairness incentive mechanism in crowdsensing. In: Park, J.J., Loia, V., Pan, Y., Sung, Y. (eds.) Advanced Multimedia and Ubiquitous Engineering. LNEE, vol. 716, pp. 33–39. Springer, Singapore (2021). https://doi.org/10.1007/978-981-15-9309-3_5
56. Khalid, A., Iftikhar, M.S., Almogren, A., Khalid, R., Afzal, M.K., Javaid, N.: A blockchain based incentive provisioning scheme for traffic event validation and information storage in VANETs. Inf. Process. Manage. **58**(2), 102464 (2021)
57. Kim, M., Kim, Y.: Multi-blockchain structure for a crowdsensing-based smart parking system. Future Internet **12**(5), 90 (2020)
58. Cai, C., Zheng, Y., Du, Y., Qin, Z., Wang, C.: Towards private, robust, and verifiable crowdsensing systems via public blockchains. IEEE Trans. Depend. Secure Comput. **18**, 1893–1907 (2019)
59. Qiu, G., Zheng, Q., Hu, X.: Multi-terminal collaborative control decision-making mechanism based on blockchain. In: 2019 International Conference on Cyber-Enabled Distributed Computing and Knowledge Discovery (CyberC), pp. 237–244. IEEE (2019)
60. Jiang, Y., Zhong, Y., Ge, X.: IIot data sharing based on blockchain: a multi-leader multi-follower stackelberg game approach. IEEE Internet Things J. (2021)
61. Lv, P., Zhao, H., Zhang, J.: Blockchain based spectrum sensing: A game-driven behavior strategy. In: 2020 IEEE 9th Joint International Information Technology and Artificial Intelligence Conference (ITAIC), vol. 9, pp. 899–904. IEEE (2020)
62. Xu, J., Wu, Y., Luo, X., Yang, D.: Improving the efficiency of blockchain applications with smart contract based cyber-insurance. In: ICC 2020–2020 IEEE International Conference on Communications (ICC), pp. 1–7. IEEE (2020)
63. Zhang, J., Huang, X., Ni, W., Wu, M., Yu, R.: VeSenChain: leveraging consortium blockchain for secure and efficient vehicular crowdsensing. In: 2019 Chinese Control Conference (CCC), pp. 6339–6344. IEEE (2019)
64. Wei, X., Yan, Y., Jiang, W., Shen, J., Qiu, X.: A blockchain based mobile crowdsensing market. China Commun. **16**(6), 31–41 (2019)
65. Liu, Y., Wang, H., Peng, M., Guan, J., Wang, Y.: An incentive mechanism for privacy-preserving crowdsensing via deep reinforcement learning. IEEE Internet Things J. **8**(10), 8616–8631 (2020)
66. Hu, Q., Wang, Z., Xu, M., Cheng, X.: Blockchain and federated edge learning for privacy-preserving mobile crowdsensing. IEEE Internet Things J. (2021)
67. Huang, J., Kong, L., Dai, H.N., Ding, W., Cheng, L., Chen, G., Jin, X., Zeng, P.: Blockchain-based mobile crowd sensing in industrial systems. IEEE Trans. Industr. Inf. **16**(10), 6553–6563 (2020)
68. Hu, J., Yang, K., Wang, K., Zhang, K.: A blockchain-based reward mechanism for mobile crowdsensing. IEEE Trans. Comput. Soc. Syst. **7**(1), 178–191 (2020)

69. Xu, Z., Liu, C., Zhang, P., Lu, T., Gu, N.: URIM: utility-oriented role-centric incentive mechanism design for blockchain-based crowdsensing. In: Jensen, C.S., et al. (eds.) DASFAA 2021. LNCS, vol. 12683, pp. 358–374. Springer, Cham (2021). https://doi.org/10.1007/978-3-030-73200-4_25

70. Wang, Z., Zhu, J., Li, D.: Prediction based reverse auction incentive mechanism for mobile crowdsensing system. In: Li, Y., Cardei, M., Huang, Y. (eds.) COCOA 2019. LNCS, vol. 11949, pp. 541–552. Springer, Cham (2019). https://doi.org/10.1007/978-3-030-36412-0_44

71. Pang, X., Guo, D., Wang, Z., Sun, P., Zhang, L.: Towards fair and efficient task allocation in blockchain-based crowdsourcing. CCF Trans. Netw. **3**(3), 193–204 (2020)

72. Liu, K., Chen, W., Zhang, Z.: Blockchain-empowered decentralized framework for secure and efficient software crowdsourcing. In: 2020 IEEE World Congress on Services (SERVICES), pp. 128–133. IEEE (2020)

# Efficient Quantum Private Comparison Using Locally Indistinguishable Orthogonal Product States

Xi Huang[1], Shibin Zhang[1,2(⊠)], and Jinyue Xia[3]

[1] School of Cybersecurity, Chengdu University of Information Technology, Chengdu 610225, China
cuitzsb@cuit.edu.cn
[2] Advanced Cryptography and System Security Key Laboratory of Sichuan Province, Chengdu 610255, China
[3] International Business Machines Corporation (IBM), Armonk, NY 14201, USA

**Abstract.** In this paper, an efficient quantum private comparison (QPC) for equality comparison using locally indistinguishable orthogonal product states is proposed. In the proposed protocol, two participants can compare the equality of three classical bits in each comparison, which could greatly reduce comparison times and improve efficiency. A semi-honest third party (TP) is involved to help two participants compare the equality of their secrets and she may misbehave on her own, but she is not allowed to conspire with any participants. Additionally, the security analysis shows that the proposed QPC protocol is secure against both outside attacks and participant ones. Compared with the existing QPC protocols, the proposed protocol needs neither swapping entanglement technology nor unitary operations, in which quantum devices are expensive and difficult to implement. Finally, it is generalized to multi-party QPC (MQPC) protocol.

**Keywords:** Quantum cryptography · Quantum private comparison · Local indistinguishability · Orthogonal product states · Semi-honest third-party

## 1 Introduction

Ever since Bennett and Brassard [1] came up with the first quantum cryptography protocol that combined quantum mechanics with classical cryptography in 1984 and proved its unconditional security via the principles of quantum mechanics. Various quantum cryptographic schemes have been developed to solve different tasks. Such as quantum key distribution (QKD) [1–5], quantum key agreement (QKA) [6–9], quantum secret sharing (QSS) [10–13], quantum secure direct communication (QSDC) [14–16], quantum private query (QPQ) [17, 18], quantum information splitting (QIS) [19], quantum image steganography [20] etc.

Secure multi-party computation (SMC) is to calculate a function in a distributed network of mutual distrust without revealing any party's secrets. Private comparison firstly introduced by Yao [21] in the millionaires' problem is an important branch of

SMC, in which two millionaires attempt to judge who is richer without disclosing their actual property. Based on Yao's millionaires' problem, a private comparison protocol aiming to judge whether two millionaires are equally rich was suggested by Boudot et al. [22]. However, as Lo [23] pointed out that it is possible to securely evaluate the equality function in a two-party scenario, a semi-honest third party (TP) should be taken into account when we design a private comparison protocol.

Quantum private comparison (QPC), as the combination of classical private comparison and quantum mechanism, was first proposed by Yang and Wen [24]. It utilized a one-way hash function to encipher the secret data and proved the security of this QPC protocol. In recent years, QPC protocols have aroused much attention, a large number of QPC protocols have been developed on the basis of various quantum states, for example, the QPC protocols with single-particle [25–28], Bell state [24, 29, 30], GHZ state [31–33], W state [34–36], four-particle GHZ state [37], cluster state [38–40], $\chi$-type entangled state [41–43], five-particle state [44–46], six-particle entangled state [47], seven-particle entangled state [48] etc. were proposed.

In recent years, the local distinguishability of orthogonal product states is a research hot in quantum theory. Various properties about the local distinguishability of orthogonal product states were proposed [49–55]. Xu et al. [51] gave different ways to make a set of orthogonal product states that are not be perfectly distinguished by local operations and classical communications (LOCC) in a bipartite or multipartite quantum system. To date, there are few quantum cryptographic schemes based on the local distinguishability of orthogonal product states. Guo et al. [52] designed the first QKD scheme with orthogonal product states. Yang et al. [53] proposed a novel quantum secret sharing protocol with orthogonal product states. It is easier to prepare an orthogonal product state than an entangled state in practice.

To the best of our knowledge, the existing QPC protocols are mainly based on multipartite quantum entangled states, and the QPC protocol using local distinguishability of orthogonal product states has not appeared. The research of the QPC protocol based on local distinguishability of orthogonal product states is blank. Therefore, in this paper, we propose a QPC protocol using local distinguishability of orthogonal product states for the first time. In the proposed QPC protocol, two participants can compare the equality of three classical bits in each comparison, which could greatly reduce comparison times and increase efficiency. A semi-honest third party (TP) is involved to help two participants compare the equality of their secrets and she may misbehave on her own, but she is not allowed to conspire with any participants. Additionally, quantum key distribution (QKD) protocol, decoy particles technology, and orthogonal product states that are not perfectly distinguished are used to ensure the security of the protocol. The efficiency analysis is efficient than the existing QPC protocols. Compared with other similar QPC protocols, there are no swapping entanglement technology and unitary operations needed in our protocol, in which quantum devices are expensive and difficult to implement. All participants must do is to prepare orthogonal product states and measure them with corresponding orthogonal product states.

The rest of our paper is organized as follows. Section 2 describes the proposed QPC protocol using local distinguishability of orthogonal product states in detail. Section 3 gives an analysis of the proposed QPC protocol. Section 4 expands the proposed QPC protocol to MQPC protocol. Finally, the conclusion is given in Sect. 5.

## 2   The Proposed QPC Protocol Using Locally Indistinguishable Orthogonal Product States

As it is described in Ref. [54], Eight states in Eqs. (1–8) cannot be exactly distinguished by LOCC no matter who goes first.

$$|\psi_1\rangle = \frac{1}{\sqrt{2}}(|0\rangle+|1\rangle)_1|1\rangle_2 \tag{1}$$

$$|\psi_2\rangle = \frac{1}{\sqrt{2}}(|0\rangle+|1\rangle)_1|1\rangle_2 \tag{2}$$

$$|\psi_3\rangle = \frac{1}{\sqrt{2}}(|0\rangle+|2\rangle)_1|2\rangle_2 \tag{3}$$

$$|\psi_4\rangle = \frac{1}{\sqrt{2}}(|0\rangle+|2\rangle)_1|2\rangle_2 \tag{4}$$

$$|\psi_5\rangle = \frac{1}{\sqrt{2}}|2\rangle_1(|0\rangle+|1\rangle)_2 \tag{5}$$

$$|\psi_6\rangle = \frac{1}{\sqrt{2}}|2\rangle_1(|0\rangle+|1\rangle)_2 \tag{6}$$

$$|\psi_7\rangle = \frac{1}{\sqrt{2}}|1\rangle_1(|0\rangle+|2\rangle)_2 \tag{7}$$

$$|\psi_8\rangle = \frac{1}{\sqrt{2}}|1\rangle_1(|0\rangle+|2\rangle)_2 \tag{8}$$

The detailed description of the proposed QPC protocol using locally indistinguishable orthogonal product states is as follows.

Input: two participants, Alice and Bob, have their secrets A and B respectively. The binary representations of A and B in $F_2{}^L$ can be written as: $A = (a_{N-1}...a_1a_0)$, $B = (b_{N-1}...b_1b_0)$. where $a_i, b_i \in \{0, 1\}$, $i \in \{0, 1, ..., N-1\}$, $A = \sum_{i=0}^{L-1} a_i 2^i$, $B = \sum_{i=0}^{L-1} b_i 2^i$, $2^L - 1 < \max\{A, B\} < 2^L$.

Output: whether A is equal to B or not.

It must note that a semi-honest third party (TP) is involved to help two participants compare the equality of their secrets and she may misbehave on her own, but she is not allowed to conspire with any participants. In addition, Alice (Bob) and TP share a secret key sequence $K_{AT}$ ($K_{BT}$) via a secure QKD protocol like BB84 protocol respectively. Meanwhile, Alice (Bob) uses a random number generator to generate an L bit raw key $K_A$ ($K_B$) respectively.

## 2.1 Preparing Phase

(1) Alice, Bob, TP agree that $|\psi_1\rangle, |\psi_2\rangle, |\psi_3\rangle, |\psi_4\rangle, |\psi_5\rangle, |\psi_6\rangle, |\psi_7\rangle, |\psi_8\rangle$, represent classical information bit 000, 001, 010, 011, 100, 101, 110, 111, respectively.

(2) Alice (Bob) divides her(his) secrets A (B) into $\lceil N/3L \rceil$ groups. Each group has 3L bits information. If N mod 3 $\neq$ 1, Alice (Bob) adds 3L- (N mod 3L) 0 into the last group. Then, $A = (X_{\lceil N/3L \rceil-1} \ldots X_1 X_0)$, $B = (Y_{\lceil N/3L \rceil-1} \ldots Y_1 Y_0)$. Where $X_j = \left( a_j^{3L-1} \ldots a_j^1 a_j^0 \right)$, $Y_j = \left( b_j^{3L-1} \ldots b_j^1 b_j^0 \right)$, $j = 0, 1, \ldots \lceil N/3L \rceil - 1$.

(3) For each group $X_j$ ($Y_j$), Alice (Bob) makes three adjacent bits to form a pair $Q_A^i = \left( a_j^{3i}, a_j^{3i+1}, a_j^{3i+2} \right)$, $Q_B^i = \left( b_j^{3i}, b_j^{3i+1}, b_j^{3i+2} \right)$ then, $X_j = \left( Q_A^{L-1} \ldots Q_A^1 Q_A^0 \right)$, $Y_j = \left( Q_B^{L-1} \ldots Q_B^1 Q_B^0 \right)$.

(4) In the j-th round of the comparison, Alice (Bob) calculates $R_A^i = Q_A^i \oplus K_A^i \oplus K_{AT}^i$ $\left( R_B^i = Q_B^i \oplus K_B^i \oplus K_{BT}^i \right)$. According to the value of $R_A^i$ ($R_B^i$), Alice (Bob) prepares the corresponding orthogonal product states.

(5) Alice (Bob) takes the first particle of each orthogonal product state to form the sequence $R_{A1}^i$ ($R_{B1}^i$) and the second particles of each orthogonal product state to form the sequence $R_{A2}^i$ ($R_{B2}^i$).

(6) To prevent eavesdropping, Alice (Bob) prepares a set of decoy photons $D_A$ ($D_B$) randomly in one of four states $\{|+y\rangle, |-y\rangle, |+\rangle, |-\rangle\}$ and randomly inserts $D_A$ into $R_{A1}^i$ and $R_{A2}^i$ ($D_B$ into $R_{B1}^i$ and $R_{B2}^i$) to form a new particle sequence $R_{A1}^i{}'$ and $R_{A2}^i{}'$ $(R_{B1}^i{}'$ and $R_{B2}^i{}')$. where $|+y\rangle = 1/\sqrt{2}(|0\rangle + i|1\rangle))$, $|-y\rangle = 1/\sqrt{2}(|0\rangle - i|1\rangle))$, $|+\rangle = 1/\sqrt{2}(|0\rangle + |1\rangle))$, $|-\rangle = 1/\sqrt{2}(|0\rangle + |1\rangle))$.

## 2.2 The First Eavesdropping Detection Phase

Alice (Bob) sends the sequence $R_{A1}^i{}'$ ($R_{B1}^i{}'$) to TP. When TP claims that she has received the sequence $R_{A1}^i{}'$ ($R_{B1}^i{}'$), Alice (Bob) will announce the positions and the corresponding basis of the decoy photons $D_A$ ($D_B$). Then, TP measures the decoy photons according to the correct measurement basis for the first eavesdropping detection and randomly announces half of the measurement results. Alice (Bob) publishes the initial states of the left half of the decoy particles. Then, they check whether the measurement results are consistent with the initial states or not. If the error rate exceeds a predetermined threshold, they abandon the protocol; otherwise, they continue to perform the next step.

## 2.3 The Second Eavesdropping Detection Phase

Alice (Bob) sends the sequence $R_{A2}^i{}'$ ($R_{B2}^i{}'$) to TP. When TP claims that she has received the sequence $R_{A2}^i{}'$ ($R_{B2}^i{}'$), they will make the second eavesdropping detection as they do in the first eavesdropping detection. If the error rate exceeds a predetermined threshold, they abandon the protocol; otherwise, they continue to perform the next step.

### 2.4  Coding and Decoding Phase

(1)  TP first recovers $R_{A1}^i$ and $R_{A2}^i$ ($R_{B1}^i$ and $R_{B2}^i$) by deleting the decoy photons DA (DB). Then, she measures the jth round of each orthogonal product state of $R_A^i$ ($R_B^i$) with the following orthogonal product basis $\{|\psi_1\rangle, |\psi_2\rangle, |\psi_3\rangle, |\psi_4\rangle, |\psi_5\rangle, |\psi_6\rangle, |\psi_7\rangle, |\psi_8\rangle, |\psi_9\rangle = |0\rangle|0\rangle\}$ and obtains the value of $R_A^i$ ($R_B^i$) according to the measurement results.

(2)  Alice and Bob work together to calculate $K_{AB}^i = K_A^i \oplus K_B^i$ and send $K_{AB}^i$ to TP via an authenticated channel.

(3)  When receiving $K_{AB}^i$, TP calculates $R_{AB}^i = R_A^i \oplus R_B^i \oplus K_{AB}^i \oplus K_{AT}^i \oplus K_{BT}^i$. If $R_{AB}$ = 000 for all $i$, then TP announces that the two users' private inputs are identical. Otherwise, it is different.

## 3  Analysis

### 3.1  Correctness Analysis

In this QPC protocol, there has the following equation:

$$
\begin{aligned}
R_{AB}^i &= R_A^i \oplus R_B^i \oplus K_{AB}^i \oplus K_{AT}^i \oplus K_{BT}^i \\
&= \left(Q_A^i \oplus K_A^i \oplus K_{AT}^i\right) \oplus \left(Q_B^i \oplus K_B^i \oplus K_{BT}^i\right) \oplus K_{AB}^i \oplus K_{AT}^i \oplus K_{BT}^i \\
&= Q_A^i \oplus K_A^i \oplus Q_B^i \oplus K_B^i \oplus \left(K_A^i \oplus K_B^i\right) \\
&= Q_A^i \oplus Q_B^i
\end{aligned}
\tag{9}
$$

From Eq. (9), It can be seen that for all $i$, the measurement result $R_{AB}^i$ equals 000, it indicates that $A_i = B_i$. Otherwise, $A_i \neq B_i$.

### 3.2  Security Analysis

**Outside Attacks.** The opportunity for an outside eavesdropper Eve to obtain the secrets is that Alice (Bob) sends $R_{A1}^i{}'$ ($R_{B2}^i{}'$) and $R_{A2}^i{}'$ ($R_{B2}^i{}'$) to TP. Suppose that Eve performs the intercept-resend attack because she doesn't know the positions and the correct measuring basis of the decoy photons $D_A$ ($D_B$) before the sender announces it, she is unable to obtain any useful information of Alice and Bob's private inputs. In addition, Eve can perform the entangling attack. Firstly, she intercepts the transmitted sequence that Alice (Bob) sends to TP. Secondly, she performs the unitary operation U on each intercepted particle and an ancillary qubit $|E\rangle$. In the end, she sends the entanglement results to TP. The effect of the unitary operation U can be written as

$$
\begin{aligned}
U(|0\rangle|E\rangle) = &\, a_0|0\rangle|E_0\rangle + a_1|0\rangle|E_1\rangle + a_2|0\rangle|E_2\rangle \\
&+ a_3|1\rangle|E_0\rangle + a_4|1\rangle|E_1\rangle + a_5|1\rangle|E_2\rangle \\
&+ a_6 2|E_0\rangle + a_7|2\rangle|E_1\rangle + a_8|2\rangle|E_2\rangle
\end{aligned}
\tag{10}
$$

$$
U(|1\rangle|E\rangle) = b_0|0\rangle|E_0'\rangle + b_1|0\rangle|E_1'\rangle + b_2|0\rangle|E_2'\rangle
$$

$$+ b_3 |1\rangle |E_0'\rangle + b_4 |1\rangle |E_1'\rangle + b_5 |1\rangle |E_2'\rangle$$
$$+ b_6 |2\rangle |E_0'\rangle + b_7 |2\rangle |E_0'\rangle + b_8 |2\rangle |E_2'\rangle \tag{11}$$

$$U(|2\rangle |E\rangle) = c_0 |0\rangle |\bar{E}_0\rangle + c_1 |0\rangle |\bar{E}_1\rangle + c_2 |0\rangle |\bar{E}_2\rangle$$
$$+ c_3 |1\rangle |\bar{E}_0\rangle + c_4 |1\rangle |\bar{E}_1\rangle + c_5 |0\rangle |\bar{E}_2\rangle$$
$$+ c_6 |2\rangle |\bar{E}_0\rangle + c_7 |2\rangle |\bar{E}_1\rangle + c_8 |2\rangle |\bar{E}_2\rangle \tag{12}$$

Where

$$|a_0|^2 + |a_1|^2 + \ldots + |a_8|^2 = |b_0|^2 + |b_1|^2 + \ldots + |b_8|^2 = |c_0|^2 + |c_1|^2 + \ldots + |c_8|^2 = 1 \tag{13}$$

$$\langle E_0 | E_1 \rangle = \langle E_0 | E_2 \rangle = \langle E_1 | E_2 \rangle = 0 \tag{14}$$

$$\langle E_0' | E_1' \rangle = \langle E_0' | E_2' \rangle = \langle E_1' | E_2' \rangle = 0 \tag{15}$$

$$\langle \bar{E}_0 | \bar{E}_1 \rangle = \langle \bar{E}_0 | \bar{E}_2 \rangle = \langle \bar{E}_0 | \bar{E}_2 \rangle = 0 \tag{16}$$

From Eqs. (10–12), if Eve wants to obtain the encoded information precisely, she must satisfy the three reduced density matrices

$$\left( |a_0|^2 + |a_3|^2 + |a_6|^2 \right) |E_0\rangle \langle E_0| + \left( |a_1|^2 + |a_4|^2 + |a_7|^2 \right) |E_1\rangle \langle E_1|$$
$$+ \left( |a_2|^2 + |a_5|^2 + |a_8|^2 \right) |E_2\rangle \langle E_2|, \tag{17}$$

$$\left( |b_0|^2 + |b_3|^2 + |b_6|^2 \right) |E_0'\rangle \langle E_0'| + \left( |b_1|^2 + |b_4|^2 + |b_7|^2 \right) |E_1'\rangle \langle E_1'|$$
$$+ \left( |b_2|^2 + |b_5|^2 + |b_8|^2 \right) |E_2'\rangle \langle E_2'|, \tag{18}$$

$$\left( |c_0|^2 + |c_3|^2 + |c_6|^2 \right) |\bar{E}_0\rangle \langle \bar{E}_0| + \left( |c_1|^2 + |c_4|^2 + |c_7|^2 \right) |\bar{E}_1\rangle \langle \bar{E}_1|$$
$$+ \left( |c_2|^2 + |c_5|^2 + |c_8|^2 \right) |\bar{E}_2\rangle \langle \bar{E}_2|, \tag{19}$$

Be discriminated precisely, which means $\langle E_m | E_n' \rangle = \langle E_m | \bar{E}_l \rangle = \langle E_n' | \bar{E}_l \rangle$ for $m, n, l = 0, 1, 2$. Therefore, the universal form of the unitary operation U on the decoy photons and an ancillary qubit $|E\rangle$ can be written as

$$U\left( \frac{1}{\sqrt{2}} (|0\rangle + \gamma |1\rangle) |E\rangle \right) = \frac{1}{\sqrt{2}} (a_0 |0\rangle |E_0\rangle + a_1 |0\rangle |E_1\rangle + a_2 |0\rangle |E_2\rangle + a_3 |1\rangle |E_0\rangle$$
$$+ a_4 |1\rangle |E_1\rangle + a_5 |1\rangle |E_2\rangle + a_6 |2\rangle |E_0\rangle + a_7 |2\rangle |E_1\rangle + a_8 |2\rangle |E_2\rangle)$$
$$+ (b_0 \gamma |1\rangle |E_0'\rangle + b_1 \gamma |0\rangle |E_1'\rangle + b_2 \gamma |0\rangle |E_2'\rangle + b_3 \gamma |1\rangle |E_0'\rangle$$
$$+ b_4 \gamma |1\rangle |E_0'\rangle + b_5 \gamma |1\rangle |E_2'\rangle + b_6 \gamma |2\rangle |E_0'\rangle + b_7 \gamma |2\rangle |E_1'\rangle \tag{20}$$
$$+ b_8 \gamma |2\rangle |E_2'\rangle + c_0 \gamma |0\rangle |\bar{E}_0\rangle + c_1 \gamma |0\rangle |\bar{E}_1\rangle + c_2 \gamma |0\rangle |\bar{E}_2\rangle$$
$$+ c_3 \gamma |1\rangle |\bar{E}_0\rangle + c_4 \gamma |1\rangle |\bar{E}_1\rangle + c_5 \gamma |1\rangle |\bar{E}_2\rangle$$
$$+ c_6 \gamma |1\rangle |\bar{E}_0\rangle + c_7 \gamma |1\rangle |\bar{E}_1\rangle + c_8 \gamma 2\rangle |\bar{E}_2\rangle$$

where $\gamma = 1 - 1, i, -i$. From Eq. (20), the reduced density matrices can be written as

$$\frac{1}{2}[\left(|a_0|^2 + |a_3|^2 + |a_6|^2\right)|0\rangle\langle 0| + \left(|a_1|^2 + |a_4|^2 + |a_7|^2\right)|1\rangle\langle 1|$$
$$+\left(|a_2|^2 + |a_5|^2 + |a_8|^2\right)|2\rangle\langle 2| + \left(|b_0|^2 + |b_3|^2 + |b_6|^2\right)|0\rangle\langle 0|$$
$$+\left(|b_1|^2 + |b_4|^2 + |b_7|^2\right)|1\rangle\langle 1| + \left(|b_2|^2 + |b_5|^2 + |b_8|^2\right)|2\rangle\langle 2| \qquad (21)$$
$$+\left(|c_0|^2 + |c_3|^2 + |c_6|^2\right)|0\rangle\langle 0| + \left(|c_1|^2 + |c_4|^2 + |c_7|^2\right)|1\rangle\langle 1|$$
$$+\left(|c_2|^2 + |c_5|^2 + |c_8|^2\right)|2\rangle\langle 2|]$$

From Eq. (21), we can deduce that the reduced density matrices have nothing to do with $\gamma$, which means that the subsystems of the states on the decoy photons are identical. Therefore, Eve is unable to obtain the secrets without introducing any error. In the end, Eve may perform the typical Trojan horse attacks including the invisible photon eavesdropping (IPE) attack [55, 56] and the delay-photon attack [57]. Because the proposed protocol is a one-way qubit transmission protocol, it is secure against these two kinds of Trojan horse attacks.

**Participant Attacks.** In 2007. Gao et al. [58] first pointed out the concept of participant attack. Compared with outside attacks, participant attacks are more powerful. There are two cases of participant attacks. One case is that dishonest Alice (Bob) tries to obtain Bob's (Alice's) secrets B (A), and the other is that a semi-honest TP attempts to get A and B.

*Case 1 Alice (Bob) Attempts to Obtain Bob's Secrets B (Alice's Secrets A).* In the process of the proposed QPC protocol, Alice (Bob) only works together to compute $K_{AB}$ and there is no information transmission from Alice to Bob. $K_{AB}$ is sent to TP that is utilized to calculate the comparison results. Although Alice (Bob) knows $K_{AB}$, she (he) has no access to know $K_{BT}$ ($K_{AT}$). TP is not allowed to conspire with any participants, without knowing $K_{BT}$ ($K_{AT}$), Alice (Bob) cannot get any information of Bob's (Alice's) secrets. To obtain Bob's (Alice's) secrets, Alice (Bob) may perform her attack on the transmitted sequence that Bob (Alice) sends to TP, she will inevitably be found as an outside eavesdropper which is described in Sect. 3.2.1. Thus, it can be concluded that Alice (Bob) is unable to deduce any information of Bob (Alice)'s secrets.

*Case 2 TP Attempts to Obtain Alice (Bob)'s Secrets.* In this proposed QPC protocol, TP may misbehave on her own, but she is not allowed to conspire with any participants. Although TP can get the value of $R_A^i$ ($R_B^i$) according to the measurement results and $K_{AB}$ that Alice (Bob) sends to her, $K_A$ and $K_B$ are unknown to her, she (he) has no access to know $K_A$ and $K_B$ directly. Thus, TP cannot deduce any information of Bob (Alice)'s secrets. It can be seen that Alice's (Bob's) raw key plays an important role in guaranteeing the security.

### 3.3 Efficiency Analysis

Ref. [47] points out that the qubit efficiency can be defined as

$$\eta_e = \frac{\eta_c}{\eta_t} \tag{22}$$

where $\eta_c$ is the classical bits that compared in each comparison, $\eta_t$ denotes the number of consumed qubits. In our protocol, local distinguishability of orthogonal product states is used as information carriers, it can encode three classical bits so that three-bit private inputs can be compared in each comparison. Therefore, the qubit efficiency is 100%. However, the existing QPC protocols can only compare one or two bits in each comparison. And the comparison between some existing QPC protocols and our protocol is shown in Table 1.

From Table 1, we can conclude that our protocol is more efficient than the existing QPC protocols.

**Table 1.** Comparison between some existing QPC protocols and our protocol.

| Protocol | Ref. [24] | Ref. [28] | Ref. [30] | Ref. [32] | Ref. [34] | Ref. [35] | Ref. [37] | Ref. [40] | Ref. [45] | Our protocol |
|---|---|---|---|---|---|---|---|---|---|---|
| quantum resource | Bell state | Single photon | EPR pair | GHZ state | W state | $\chi^+$ state and W-Class | four-particle GHZ state | 4-qubit Cluster state and $\chi$ state | Five-particle cluster state | orthogonal product state |
| Measurement basis | Bell-basis measurements | single-particle measurements | single-particle measurements | single-particle measurements | single-particle measurements | Bell-basis and extend bell-basis measurements | single-particle and Bell-basis measurements | Bell-basis and extend bell-basis measurements | single-particle measurements | orthogonal product basis measurements |
| Usage of QKD method | No | Yes | No | No | Yes | Yes | Yes | Yes | No | Yes |
| Devices for Trojan horse attacks | Yes | Yes | No | No | Yes | No | Yes | No | No | No |
| Usage of unitary operation | Yes | Yes | No | Yes | Yes | No | Yes | No | Yes | No |
| Usage of entanglement swapping | No | No | No | No | No | Yes | No | Yes | Yes | No |
| Usage of quantum memory | No | No | Yes | Yes | No | No | No | No | No | No |
| Decoy photons | Yes | Yes | Yes | Yes | No | Yes | Yes | Yes | Yes | Yes |
| Bits number compared in each comparison | 1 | 1 | 1 | 1 | 1 | 3 | 3 | 3 | 2 | 3 |
| Comparison times | L | L | L | $\lceil N/L \rceil +1$ | L | $\lceil L/3 \rceil$ | $\lceil N/3L \rceil$ | $\lceil N/3L \rceil$ | $\lceil L/2 \rceil$ | $\lceil N/3L \rceil$ |
| Qubit efficiency | 25% | 25% | 50% | 33% | 16.6% | 60% | 75% | 50% | 40% | 100% |

## 4  Expansibility

We can utilize the proposed two-party QPC protocol to generate the case with M-parties ($M \geq 3$) QPC protocol. In the simplest case, assume that there are three parties Alice, Bob, and Charlie, they have their secrets A, B, and C respectively. The binary representations of A, B, and C in $F_2^L$ can be written as: $A = (a_{N-1}...a_1 a_0)$, $B = (b_{N-1}...b_1 b_0)$, $C = (c_{N-1}...c_1 c_0)$ where $a_i, b_i, c_i \in \{0, 1\}$, $i \in \{0, 1, ..., N-1\}$, $A = \sum_{i=0}^{L-1} a_i 2^i$, $B = \sum_{i=0}^{L-1} b_i 2^i$, $C = \sum_{i=0}^{L-1} c_i 2^i$, $2^L - 1 < \max\{A, B, C\} < 2^L$. They want to judge whether their secrets are equal or not with the help of the semi-honest TP. TP may misbehave on her own, but she is not allowed to conspire with any participants. TP and Alice, TP and Bob, TP and Charlie share a key sequence $K_{AT}$, $K_{BT}$, $K_{CT}$ of length L beforehand, through a secure QKD protocol like BB84 protocol. Meanwhile, Alice,

Bob, and Charlie use a random number generator to generate an L bit raw key $K_A$, $K_B$, $K_C$ respectively.

The following steps are the detailed description of the proposed three-party QPC (MPQC) protocol.

### 4.1 Preparing Phase

(1) Alice, Bob, Charlie and TP all agree that $|\psi_1\rangle, |\psi_2\rangle, |\psi_3\rangle, |\psi_4\rangle,$ $|\psi_5\rangle, |\psi_6\rangle, |\psi_7\rangle, |\psi_9\rangle$, represent classical information bit 000, 001, 010, 011, 100, 101, 110, 111, respectively.

(2) Alice (Bob, Charlie) divides their secrets A (B, C) into $\lceil N/3L \rceil$ groups. Each group has 3L bits information. If N mod 3 $\neq$ 1, Alice (Bob, Charlie) adds 3L- (N mod 3L) 0 into the last group. Then, $A = (X_{\lceil N/3L \rceil -1} \ldots X_1 X_0)$, $B = (Y_{\lceil N/3L \rceil -1} \ldots Y_1 Y_0)$, $C = (Z_{\lceil N/3L \rceil -1} \ldots Z_1 Z_0)$ Where $X_j = \left(a_j^{3L-1} \ldots a_j^1 a_j^0\right)$, $Y_j = \left(b_j^{3L-1} \ldots b_j^1 b_j^0\right)$, $Z_j = \left(z_j^{3L-1} \ldots z_j^1 z_j^0\right), j = 0, 1, \ldots, \lceil N/3L \rceil - 1$.

(3) For each group $X_j$ ($Y_j$, $Z_j$), Alice (Bob, Charlie) makes three adjacent bits to form a pair $Q_A^i = \left(a_j^{3i}, a_j^{3i+1}, a_j^{3i+2}\right)$, $Q_B^i = \left(b_j^{3i}, b_j^{3i+1}, b_j^{3i+2}\right)$, $Q_C^i = \left(c_j^{3i}, c_j^{3i+1}, c_j^{3i+2}\right)$. then $X_j = \left(Q_A^{L-1} \ldots Q_A^1 Q_A^0\right)$, $Y_j = \left(Q_B^{L-1} \ldots Q_B^1 Q_B^0\right)$, $Z_j = \left(Z_C^{L-1} \ldots Z_C^1 Z_C^0\right)$.

(4) In the jth round of the comparison, Alice (Bob, Charlie) calculates $R_A^i = Q_A^i \oplus K_A^i \oplus K_{AT}^i$ ($R_B^i = Q_B^i \oplus K_B^i \oplus K_{BT}^i$, $R_C^i = Q_C^i \oplus K_C^i \oplus K_{CT}^i$). According to the value of $R_A^i$ ($R_B^i$, $R_C^i$), Alice (Bob, Charlie) prepares the corresponding orthogonal product states.

(5) Alice (Bob, Charlie) takes the first particle of each orthogonal product state to form the sequence $R_{A1}^i$ ($R_{B1}^i$, $R_{C1}^i$) and the second particles of each orthogonal product states to form the sequence $R_{A2}^i$ ($R_{B2}^i$, $R_{C2}^i$).

(6) To prevent eavesdropping, Alice (Bob, Charlie) prepares a set of decoy photons $D_A$ ($D_B$, $D_C$) randomly in one of four states $\{|+y\rangle, |-y\rangle, |+\rangle, |-\rangle\}$ and randomly inserts $D_A$ into $R_{A1}^i$ and $R_{A2}^i$ ($D_B$ into $R_{B1}^i$ and $R_{B2}^i$, $D_C$ into $R_{C1}^i$ and $R_{C2}^i$) to form a new particle sequence $R_{A1}^i{}'$ and $R_{A2}^i{}'$ ($R_{B1}^i{}'$ and $R_{B1}^i{}'$, $R_{C1}^i{}'$ and $R_{C1}^i{}'$). where $|+y\rangle = 1/\sqrt{2}(|0\rangle + i|1\rangle))$, $|-y\rangle = 1/\sqrt{2}(|0\rangle - i|1\rangle))$, $|+\rangle = 1/\sqrt{2}(|0\rangle + |1\rangle))$, $|-\rangle = 1/\sqrt{2}(|0\rangle + |1\rangle))$.

### 4.2 The First Eavesdropping Detection Phase

Alice (Bob, Charlie) sends the sequence $R_{A1}^i{}'$ ($R_{B1}^i{}'$, $R_{C1}^i{}'$) to TP. When TP claims that she has received the sequence $R_{A1}^i{}'$ ($R_{B1}^i{}'$, $R_{C1}^i{}'$), Alice (Bob, Charlie) will announce the positions and the corresponding basis of the decoy photons $D_A$ ($D_B$, $D_C$). Then, TP measures the decoy photons according to the correct measurement basis for the first eavesdropping detection and randomly announces half of the measurement results. Alice (Bob, Charlie) publishes the initial states of the left half of the decoy particles Then, they check whether the measurement results are consistent with the initial states or not. If the error rate exceeds a predetermined threshold, they abandon the protocol; otherwise, they continue to perform the next step.

### 4.3  The Second Eavesdropping Detection Phase

Alice (Bob, Charlie) sends the sequence $R_{A1}^{i\prime} R_{A2}^{i\prime}$ $(R_{B2}^{i\prime}, R_{C2}^{i\prime})$ to TP. When TP claims that she has received the sequence $R_{A2}^{i\prime}$ $(R_{B2}^{i\prime}, R_{C2}^{i\prime})$, they will make the second eavesdropping detection as they do in the first eavesdropping detection. If the error rate exceeds a predetermined threshold, they abandon the protocol; otherwise, they continue to perform the next step.

### 4.4  Coding and Decoding Phase

(1) TP first recovers $R_{A1}^{i}$ and $R_{A2}^{i}$ $(R_{B1}^{i}$ and $R_{B2}^{i}$, $R_{C2}^{i\prime}$ and $R_{C2}^{i\prime})$ by deleting the decoy photons DA (DB, DC). Then, she measures the jth round of each orthogonal product state of $R_{A}^{i}$ $(R_{B}^{i}, R_{C}^{i})$ with the following orthogonal product basis $\{|\psi_1\rangle, |\psi_2\rangle, |\psi_3\rangle, |\psi_4\rangle, |\psi_5\rangle, |\psi_6\rangle, |\psi_7\rangle, |\psi_8\rangle, |\psi_9\rangle = |0\rangle|0\rangle\}$ and obtains the value of $R_{A}^{i}$ $(R_{B}^{i}, R_{C}^{i})$ according to the measurement results.

(2) Alice, Bob, and Charlie work together to calculate $K_{ABC}^{i} = K_{A}^{i} \oplus K_{B}^{i} \oplus K_{C}^{i}$ and send $K_{ABC}^{i}$ to TP via an authenticated channel.

(3) When receiving $K_{ABC}^{i}$, TP calculates $R_{ABC}^{i} = R_{A}^{i} \oplus R_{B}^{i} \oplus R_{C}^{i} \oplus K_{ABC}^{i} \oplus K_{AT}^{i} \oplus K_{BT}^{i} \oplus K_{CT}^{i}$. If $R_{ABC} = 000$ for all $i$, then TP announces that the three users' private inputs are identical. Otherwise, it is different.

Now, let us discuss the security of the proposed three-party QPC protocol. As it is analyzed in Sect. 3.2, if Eve performs the intercept-resend attack, she will be caught. Because the positions and the correct measuring basis of the decoy photons are unknown to her. In addition, if Eve performs the entangling attack, she cannot obtain any information about the three user's secrets, as the subsystems of the states on the position of the decoy photons are identical. Meanwhile, the proposed three-party QPC protocol is a one-way qubit transmission protocol, it is secure against the Trojan horse attacks. In terms of participant attacks, because TP is not allowed to conspire with anyone else, without knowing the secret key sequence that TP and other participants pre-share, one party cannot get the other party's secret information. Because the raw key $K_A$, $K_B$, $K_C$ are unknown to TP, TP only knows $K_{ABC}$, she cannot get any useful information about the three users' secrets. Therefore, the proposed three-party QPC protocol is shown to be secure against different kinds of attacks including outside attacks and participant ones.

Next, let us discuss the efficiency of the proposed three-party QPC protocol. Because it utilizes local distinguishability of orthogonal product states as information carriers, which can encode three classical bits so that three-bit private inputs can be compared in each comparison. Therefore, the qubit efficiency is 100%.

## 5  Conclusion

In this paper, with the assistance of the semi-honest third party (TP), an efficient quantum private comparison (QPC) protocol using locally indistinguishable orthogonal product states is proposed. Compared with the existing QPC protocols, the proposed QPC protocol has the following advantages. (1) there are no swapping entanglement technology and unitary operations needed in this protocol. (2) the proposed protocol can compare the equality of three classical bits in each comparison, which could greatly reduce comparison times and increase efficiency, and its efficiency is 100%. (3) the security analysis shows that the proposed protocol is secure against outside attacks and participant ones. The future work will focus on how to compare the sizes in QPC protocol and how to improve the QPC scheme to adapt to the noisy environment.

**Acknowledgement.** This work is supported by the National Natural Science Foundation of China (No. 62076042), the Key Research and Development Project of Sichuan Province (No. 2021YFSY0012, No. 2020YFG0307, No. 2021YFG0332), the Science and Technology Innovation Project of Sichuan (No. 2020017), the Key Research and Development Project of Chengdu (No. 2019-YF05-02028-GX), the Innovation Team of Quantum Security Communication of Sichuan Province (No. 17TD0009), the Academic and Technical Leaders Training Funding Support Projects of Sichuan Province (No. 2016120080102643).

**Conflicts of Interest.**    The authors declare that they have no conflicts of interest to report regarding the present study.

# References

1. Bennett, C.H., Charles, H., Brassard, G.: Quantum cryptography: public key distribution and coin tossing. Theoret. Comput. Sci. **560**(1), 7–11 (2014)
2. Gao, C., Jiang, D., Guo, Y., Chen, L.: Multi-matrix error estimation and reconciliation for quantum key distribution. Opt. Express **27**(10), 14545–14566 (2019)
3. Azuma, H., Ban, M.: Intercept/resend and translucent attacks on the quantum key distribution protocol based on the pre- and post-selection effect. Int. J. Quantum Inf. **19**(01), 661–447 (2021)
4. Wang, M., Lai, H., Pan, L.: Measurement device independent quantum key distribution based on orbital angular momentum under parametric light source. Comput. Mater. Continua **63**(1), 369–387 (2020)
5. Chang, Y., Zhang, S.B., Yan, L.L., Li, X.Y., Cao, T., Wang, Q.R.: Device-independent quantum key distribution protocol based on hyper-entanglement. Comput. Mater. Continua **65**(1), 879–896 (2020)
6. Naresh, V.S., Reddi, S.: Multiparty quantum key agreement with strong fairness property. Comput. Syst. Sci. Eng. **35**(6), 457–465 (2020)
7. Huang, X., Zhang, S.B., Chang, Y., Qiu, C., Liu, D.M., Hou, M.: Quantum key agreement protocol based on quantum search algorithm. Int. J. Theor. Phys. **60**(3), 838–847 (2021)
8. Li, T., Wang, X., Jiang, M.: Quantum key agreement via non-maximally entangled cluster states. Int. J. Theor. Phys. **60**(7), 2429–2444 (2021)
9. Sun, Z., Huang, J., Wang, P.: Efficient multiparty quantum key agreement protocol based on commutative encryption. Quantum Inf. Process. **15**(5), 2101–2111 (2016). https://doi.org/10.1007/s11128-016-1253-8
10. Grice, W.P., Qi, B.: Quantum secret sharing using weak coherent states. Phys. Rev. A **100**(2), 22339 (2019)
11. Liao, Q., Liu, H.J., Zhu, L.J., Guo, Y.: Quantum secret sharing using discretely modulated coherent states. Phys. Rev. A **103**(3), 32410 (2021)

12. Yang, Y.-G., Gao, S., Li, D., Zhou, Y.-H., Shi, W.-M.: Three-party quantum secret sharing against collective noise. Quantum Inf. Process. **18**(7), 1–11 (2019). https://doi.org/10.1007/s11128-019-2319-1

13. Bai, C.-M., Li, Z.-H., Liu, C.-J., Li, Y.-M.: Quantum secret sharing using orthogonal multi-qudit entangled states. Quantum Inf. Process. **16**(12), 1–18 (2017). https://doi.org/10.1007/s11128-017-1739-z

14. Li, T., Long, G.L.: Quantum secure direct communication based on single-photon Bell-state measurement. New J. Phys. **22**(6), 63017 (2020)

15. Bebrov, G., Dimova, R.: Efficient quantum secure direct communication protocol based on Quantum Channel compression. Int. J. Theor. Phys. **59**(2), 426–435 (2020)

16. Huang, X., Zhang, Y.: Chang: Quantum secure direct communication based on quantum homomorphic encryption. Mod. Phys. Lett. A **36**(37), 2150623 (2021)

17. Liu, D.-M., Yan, L.-L., Xu, S.-H., Qiu, C., Huang, X.I.: New flexible quantum private query protocol against rotation noise. Quantum Inf. Process. **20**(2), 1–13 (2021). https://doi.org/10.1007/s11128-020-02983-0

18. Yan, L.L., Liu, D.M., Zhang, S.B., Chang, Y., Wan, G.G.: Practical quantum database private query protocol with classical database owner. Int. J. Theor. Phys. **59**(9), 3002–3008 (2020)

19. Xu, G., Shan, R., Chen, X., Dong, M., Chen, Y.: Probabilistic and hierarchical quantum information splitting based on the non-maximally entangled cluster state. Comput. Mater. Continua **69**(1), 339–349 (2021)

20. Qu, Z., Sun, H., Zheng, M.: An efficient quantum image steganography protocol based on improved EMD algorithm. Quantum Inf. Process. **20**(2), 1–29 (2021). https://doi.org/10.1007/s11128-021-02991-8

21. Yao, A.C.: Protocols for secure computations. In: Proceedings of the 23rd Annual Symposium on Foundations of Computer Science, pp. 160–164 (1982)

22. Boudot, F., Schoenmakers, B., Traore, J.: A fair and efficient solution to the socialist millionaires' problem. Discret. Appl. Math. **111**(1), 23–36 (2001)

23. Lo, H.K.: Insecurity of quantum secure computations. Phys. Rev. A **56**(2), 1154–1162 (1997)

24. Yang, Y.G., Wen, Q.Y.: An efficient two-party quantum private comparison protocol with decoy photons and two-photon entanglement. J. Phys. A: Math. Theor. **43**(20), 209801 (2010)

25. Yang, Y.G., Cao, W.F., Wen, Q.Y.: Secure quantum private comparison. Phys. Scr. **80**(6), 65002 (2009)

26. Liu, B., Gao, F., Jia, H., Huang, W., Zhang, W., Wen, Q.: Efficient quantum private comparison employing single photons and collective detection. Quantum Inf. Process. **12**(2), 887–897 (2013)

27. Lang, Y.F.: Semi-quantum private comparison using single photons. Int. J. Theor. Phys. **57**(10), 3048–3055 (2018)

28. Xu, L., Zhao, Z.: A robust and efficient quantum private comparison of equality based on the entangled swapping of GHZ-like state and $\chi+$ state. Int. J. Theor. Phys. **56**(8), 2671–2685 (2017)

29. Huang, X., Zhang, S.B., Chang, Y., Hou, M., Cheng, W.: Efficient quantum private comparison based on entanglement swapping of bell states. Int. J. Theor. Phys. **60**, 3783–3796 (2021)

30. Tseng, H.Y., Lin, J., Hwang, T.: New quantum private comparison protocol using EPR pairs. Quantum Inf. Process. **11**, 373–384 (2012)

31. Liu, W., Wang, Y.B.: Quantum private comparison based on GHZ entangled states. Int. J. Theor. Phys. **51**(11), 3596–3604 (2012)

32. Chen, X.B., Xu, G., Niu, X.X., Wen, Q.Y., Yang, Y.X.: An efficient protocol for the private comparison of equal information based on the triplet entangled state and single-particle measurement. Optics Commun. **283**(7), 1561–1565 (2010)

33. Gianni, J., Qu, Z.G.: New quantum private comparison using hyperentangled ghz state. J. Quantum Comput. **3**(2), 45–54 (2021)
34. Liu, W., Wang, Y.B., Jiang, Z.T.: An efficient protocol for the quantum private comparison of equality with W state. Optics Commun. **284**(12), 3160–3163 (2011)
35. Xu, L., Zhao, Z.: Quantum private comparison protocol based on the entanglement swapping between $\chi$ state and W-Class state. Quantum Inf. Process. **16**, 1–15 (2017)
36. Li, J., Jia, L., Zhou, H.F., Zhang, T.T.: Secure quantum private comparison protocol based on the entanglement swapping between three-particle W-class state and bell state. Int. J. Theor. Phys. **55**(3), 1710–1718 (2016)
37. Xu, Q.D., Chen, H.Y., Gong, L.H., Zhou, N.R.: Quantum private comparison protocol based on four-particle ghz states. Int. J. Theor. Phys. **59**(6), 1798–1806 (2020)
38. Sun, Z., Long, D.: Quantum private comparison protocol based on cluster states. Int. J. Theor. Phys. **52**(1), 212–218 (2013)
39. Xu, G.A., Chen, X.B., Wei, Z.H., Li, M.J., Yang, Y.X.: An efficient protocol for the quantum private comparison of equality with a four-qubit cluster state. Int. J. Quantum Inf. **10**(4), 1–15 (2012)
40. Li, C., Chen, X., Li, H., Yang, Y., Li, J.: Efficient quantum private comparison protocol based on the entanglement swapping between four-qubit cluster state and extended Bell state. Quantum Inf. Process. **18**(5), 1–12 (2019). https://doi.org/10.1007/s11128-019-2266-x
41. Liu, W., Wang, Y.B., Jiang, Z.T., Cao, Y.Z.: A protocol for the quantum private comparison of equality with $\chi$-type state. Int. J. Theor. Phys. **51**(1), 69–77 (2012)
42. Liu, W., Wang, Y.B., Jiang, Z.T., Cao, Y.Z., Cui, W.: New quantum private comparison protocol using $\chi$-type state. Int. J. Theor. Phys. **51**(6), 1953–1960 (2012)
43. Lin, S., Guo, G.D., Liu, X.F.: Quantum private comparison of equality with $\chi$-type entangled states. Int. J. Theor. Phys. **52**(11), 4185–4194 (2013)
44. Ye, T.Y., Ji, Z.X.: Two-party quantum private comparison with five-qubit entangled states. Int. J. Theor. Phys. **56**(5), 1517–1529 (2017)
45. Chang, Y., Zhang, W.B., Zhang, S.B., Wang, H.C., Yan, L.L., Han, G.H.: Quantum private comparison of equality based on five-particle cluster state. Commun. Theor. Phys. **66**(6), 621–628 (2016)
46. Zha, X.W., Yu, X.Y., Cao, Y., Wang, S.K.: Quantum private comparison protocol with fiveparticle cluster states. Int. J. Theor. Phys. **57**(2), 3874–3881 (2018)
47. Ji, Z.X., Ye, T.Y.: Quantum private comparison of equal information based on highly entangled six-qubit genuine state. Commun. Theor. Phys. **65**(6), 711–715 (2016)
48. Ji, Z.X., Zhang, H.G., Fan, P.R.: Two-party quantum private comparison protocol with maximally entangled seven-qubit state. Mod. Phys. Lett. A **34**(28), 1950229 (2019)
49. Yang, Y.H., Gao, F., Xu, G.B., Zuo, H.J., Zhang, Z.C., Wen, Q.W.: Characterizing unextendible product bases in qutrit-ququad system. Sci. Rep. **5**(1), 1–9 (2015)
50. Zhang, Z.C., Gao, F., Cao, Y., Qin, S.J., Wen, Q.Y.: Local indistinguishability of orthogonal product states. Phys. Rev. A **93**(1), 12314 (2016)
51. Xu, G.B., Wen, Q.Y., Qin, S.J., Yang, Y.H., Gao, F.: Quantum nonlocality of multipartite orthogonal product states. Phys. Rev. A **93**(3), 32341 (2016)
52. Guo, G.P., Li, C.F., Shi, B.S., Li, J., Guo, G.C.: Quantum key distribution scheme with orthogonal product states. Phys. Rev. A **64**(4), 42301 (2021)
53. Yang, Y.G., Wen, Q.Y., Zhu, F.C.: An efficient quantum secret sharing protocol with orthogonal product states. Sci. China, Ser. G **50**(3), 331–338 (2007)
54. Jiang, D.-H., Xu, G.-B.: Multiparty quantum key agreement protocol based on locally indistinguishable orthogonal product states. Quantum Inf. Process. **17**(7), 1–17 (2018). https://doi.org/10.1007/s11128-018-1951-5
55. Deng, F.G., Li, X.H., Zhou, H.Y., Zhang, Z.: Improving the security of multiparty quantum secret sharing against Trojan horse attack. Phys. Rev. A **72**(4), 440–450 (2005)

56. Li, X.H., Deng, F.G., Zhou, H.Y.: Improving the security of secure direct communication based on the secret transmitting order of particles. Phys. Rev. A **74**(5), 54302 (2006)
57. Cai, Q.Y.: Eavesdropping on the two-way quantum communication protocols with invisible photons. Phys. Lett. A **351**(1–2), 23–25 (2006)
58. Gao, F., Qin, S.J., Wen, Q.Y., Zhu, F.C.: A simple participant attack on the brádler-dušek protocol. Quantum Inf. Comput. **7**(4), 329–334 (2007)

# Quantum Gate-Based Quantum Private Comparison Protocol Using Four-Particle GHZ States

Min Hou[1], Shibin Zhang[1,2(✉)], and Jinyue Xia[3]

[1] School of Cybersecurity,
Chengdu University of Information Technology, Chengdu 610225, China
cuitzsb@cuit.edu.cn
[2] Advanced Cryptography and System Security Key Laboratory of Sichuan Province, Chengdu 610255, China
[3] International Business Machines Corporation (IBM), Armonk, NY 14201, USA

**Abstract.** The previous quantum private comparison (QPC) protocols often utilize quantum technology to provide security and the classic computing to perform exclusive-OR operation. In this paper, a secure quantum gate-based quantum private protocol without classical computing is proposed, which uses four-particle GHZ states as quantum resource and quantum circuit to perform computing. Four-particle GHZ states are easy to be prepared with current technology. The proposed protocol doesn't need swapping entanglement technology but single-particle measurement and Bell state measurement. Additionally, a semi-honest third party (TP) is involved to help the two participants accomplish the private comparison. Compared with the previous quantum private comparison protocols with classic computing, the proposed protocol is of simplicity and has a quantity of security. Finally, the analysis shows its correctness and it can withstand various attacks including outside attacks and participant ones.

**Keywords:** Quantum private comparison · Four-particle GHZ states · Quantum circuit · Semi-honest third party

## 1 Introduction

Since Bennett and Brassard [1] came up with the first quantum key distribution protocol (QKD) combined quantum mechanics with cryptography in 1984, various quantum cryptography schemes have been put forward. Such as quantum network coding protocol [2], quantum image steganography protocol [3], quantum information splitting [4]. Quantum secure multiparty computation (QSMC), as an essential ingredient of quantum cryptography, has aroused much attention. It has many actual applications includes quantum protocol for anonymous voting and surveying [5], quantum anonymous ranking [6], quantum auction [7]and so on. In addtion, Yu et al. [8] proposed a phase estimation algorithm for quantum speed-up multi-party computing. Quantum private comparison (QPC) protocol, as an indispensable branch of QSMC, allows two parties to compare the equality of their undisclosed information. In 2009, Yang et al. [9] proposed the pioneering quantum private comparison protocol based on Bell state, which compares the equality of two participants' private inputs without revealing disclosure the other one's information. Its security was guaranteed by the inclusion of decoy photons and it utilizes one-way hash function to encipher the secret data. Since then a large number of quantum private comparison protocols have been proposed, such as the QPC protocol with single particles [10–12], Bell states [13–16], GHZ states [17, 18], W states [19–21], cluster states [22, 23], $\chi$ - type entangled states [24–26], five-particle entangled states [27], five-particle cluster states [28, 29], six-particle entangled states [30], seven-particle entangled states [31].

According to the analysis of many existent QPC protocols, we can conclude that the QPC protocols often utilize quantum technology to provide security and classic computing to perform exclusive-OR operation. Moreover, QPC protocols usually ask the participant do as follows:①perform quantum state measurement and obtain classic results②perform classic exclusive-OR operation③record intermediate computation④announce the computation results via the classic channel, and so on. However, with the leakage probability of the intermediate computations and classic records, they could suffer from classic attacks. So, the classic part has a quantity of insecurity.

In order to solve this problem, a secure quantum gate-based quantum private comparison protocol is proposed, which uses four-particle GHZ states as quantum resources. It utilizes quantum circuit to perform computing instead of using classic computing to perform classic exclusive-OR operation. As Lo [32] pointed out that secure two-party computation is unachievable, a semi-honest third party should be taken into account when we design a quantum private comparison protocol. The third party (TP) can keep the track of all its intermediate computations and try to eavesdrop the users' secret inputs with the limitation that it cannot conspire with any participants. Furthermore, the proposed protocol doesn't need swapping entanglement technology but single-particle measurement and Bell state measurement.

The paper is organized as follows. In Sect. 2, four-particle GHZ states are introduced. In Sect. 3, the proposed protocol is described in detail. Its correctness and security are analyzed in Sect. 4. Finally, conclusion is given in Sect. 5.

## 2   The Introduction of Four-Particle GHZ States

This paper first introduces Z-basis ($|0>,|1>$) and X-basis ($|+>,|->$), where $|+\rangle = \frac{|0\rangle+|1\rangle}{\sqrt{2}}$ and $|-\rangle = \frac{|0\rangle-|1\rangle}{\sqrt{2}}$. So we can conduct that $|0\rangle = \frac{|+\rangle+|-\rangle}{\sqrt{2}}$, $|1\rangle = \frac{|+\rangle-|-\rangle}{\sqrt{2}}$. Bell states are defined as $|\Phi^{\pm}\rangle = \frac{1}{\sqrt{2}}(|00\rangle \pm |11\rangle)$, $|\Psi^{\pm}\rangle = \frac{1}{\sqrt{2}}(|01\rangle \pm |10\rangle)$, so there have the following relationship:

$$|01\rangle = \frac{1}{\sqrt{2}}\left(|\Psi^{+}\rangle + |\Psi^{-}\rangle\right) \tag{1}$$

$$|00\rangle = \frac{1}{\sqrt{2}}\left(|\Phi^{+}\rangle + |\Phi^{-}\rangle\right) \tag{2}$$

$$|10\rangle = \frac{1}{\sqrt{2}}\left(|\Psi^{+}\rangle - |\Psi^{-}\rangle\right) \tag{3}$$

$$|11\rangle = \frac{1}{\sqrt{2}}(|\Phi^+\rangle - |\Phi^-\rangle) \tag{4}$$

In the proposed QPC protocol, we choose four-particle GHZ states as follows:

$$|G_1\rangle_{1234} = \frac{1}{\sqrt{2}}(|0000\rangle + |1111\rangle)_{1234}$$

$$= \frac{1}{\sqrt{2}}\left[\left(\frac{|+\rangle+|-\rangle}{\sqrt{2}}\right)\otimes\left(\frac{|\Phi^+\rangle+|\Phi^-\rangle}{\sqrt{2}}\right)\otimes\left(\frac{|+\rangle-|-\rangle}{\sqrt{2}}\right)+\left(\frac{|+\rangle-|-\rangle}{\sqrt{2}}\right)\otimes\left(\frac{|\Phi^+\rangle-|\Phi^-\rangle}{\sqrt{2}}\right)\otimes\left(\frac{|+\rangle+|-\rangle}{\sqrt{2}}\right)\right] \tag{5}$$

$$= \frac{1}{2}|+\rangle_1 \otimes \left(|\Phi^+\rangle_{23}|+\rangle_4 + |\Phi^-\rangle_{23}|-\rangle_2\right) + \frac{1}{2}|-\rangle_1$$

$$\otimes\left(|\Phi^+\rangle_{23}|-\rangle_4 + |\Phi^-\rangle_{23}|+\rangle_4\right)$$

$$|G_2\rangle_{1234} = \frac{1}{\sqrt{2}}(|0101\rangle + |1010\rangle)_{1234}$$

$$= \frac{1}{\sqrt{2}}\left[\left(\frac{|+\rangle+|-\rangle}{\sqrt{2}}\right)\otimes\left(\frac{|\Psi^+\rangle-|\Psi^-\rangle}{\sqrt{2}}\right)\otimes\left(\frac{|+\rangle-|-\rangle}{\sqrt{2}}\right)+\left(\frac{|+\rangle-|-\rangle}{\sqrt{2}}\right)\otimes\left(\frac{|\Psi^+\rangle+|\Psi^-\rangle}{\sqrt{2}}\right)\otimes\left(\frac{|+\rangle+|-\rangle}{\sqrt{2}}\right)\right] \tag{6}$$

$$= \frac{1}{2}|+\rangle_1 \otimes \left(|\Psi^+\rangle_{23}|+\rangle_4 + |\Psi^-\rangle_{23}|-\rangle_2\right) + \frac{1}{2}|-\rangle_1$$

$$\otimes\left(|\Psi^+\rangle_{23}|-\rangle_4 - |\Psi^-\rangle_{23}|+\rangle_4\right)$$

Four-particle GHZ states are easy to be prepared with current technology, for example, the quantum circuit of generating four-particle GHZ state is presented in Fig. 1.

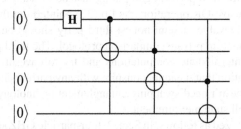

**Fig. 1.** Quantum generating circuit of four-particle GHZ state $|G_1\rangle$.

## 3 The Proposed QPC Protocol

Two participants, Alice and Bob, have their secret data A and B respectively. They desire to know the equality of their private information by performing QPC protocol. The binary representations of A and B in F2L can be written as: $A = (a_{L-1}...a_1a_0)$, $B = (b_{L-1}...b_1b_0)$ where $a_i, b_i \in \{0, 1\}$, $i \in \{0, 1, ..., L-1\}$, $A = \sum_{i=0}^{L-1} a_i 2^i$, $B = \sum_{i=0}^{L-1} b_i 2^i$, $2^L - 1 < \max\{A, B\} < 2^L$. Classic bit 0 (1) can be represented by quantum state $|0>$ ($|1>$), and we can obtain the corresponding quantum sequence of A and B respectively. $QA = (qa_{L-1}, .., qa_{1_1}, qa_0)$, $QB = (qb_{L-1}, ..., qb_1, qb_0)$, where $qa_i, qb_i \in \{|0, |1\}$, $i \in \{0, 1, ..., L-1\}$.

In addition, Alice has a quantum CNOT gate G0, G1 and G2 are possessed by Bob, TP generates Bell state through quantum circuit. The proposed QPC protocol in detail is as follows, and its quantum circuit is shown in Fig. 2.

**Step 1:** TP generates n four-particle GHZ states, which are randomly chosen from the state $\{|G_1\rangle, |G_2\rangle\}$. And he/she divides them into three sequence SA, ST, SB, which are the first, the second and the third, the fourth particle of these four-particle GHZ states. To prevent eavesdropping, TP prepares two sets of decoy photons DA and DB randomly in one of four particle states $\{|0>, |1>, |+>, |->\}$ and randomly inserts DA into SA (DB into SB) to form a new particle sequence SA'(SB'). Then, TP sends SA' to Alice (SB' to Bob) and keeps ST in his/her hand.

**Step 2:** When TP confirms that Alice (Bob) have received the sequence SA'(SB'), he/she will announce the position and measuring basis (X-basis or Z-basis) of the decoy photons DA (DB). Then, Alice (Bob) measures the decoy photons according to the corresponding measurement basis and responds to TP for eavesdropping detection. If the error rate of detection exceeds a predetermined threshold, TP will terminate the protocol. Otherwise, the protocol goes to step 3.

**Step 3:** Alice (Bob) can obtain SA(SB) by discarding the decoy photons DA(DB) respectively. Then, Alice measures the remaining particle SA with X-basis and obtains the measurement result $MA = (ma_{L-1}, ..., ma_1, ma_o)$, where $ma_i \in \{|+, |-\}, i \in \{0, 1, ..., L-1\}$. In order to perform the protocol, if the measurement result $ma_i$ is $|+ > (|- >)$, it can be set as $|0 > (|1 >)$. Alice uses $qa_i$ and $ma_i$ as the control qubits and target qubits of the quantum CNOT gate G0 and the output quantum states sequence is the state $ra_i = qa_i \oplus ma_i$, where $ra_i \in \{|0, |1\}, i \in \{0, 1, ..., L-1\}$. Alice sends RA to Bob.

**Step 4:** When Bob has received Alice's sequence RA, he measures the remaining particle SB with X-basis and obtains the measurement result $MB = (mb_{L-1}, ..., mb_1, mb_o)$, where $mb_i \in \{|+, |-\}, i \in \{0, 1, ..., L-1\}$. As same as Alice, if the measurement result $mb_i$ is $|+ > (|- >)$, it can be set as $|0 > (|1 >)$. Bob uses $mb_i$ and $ra_i$ as the control qubits and target qubits of the quantum CNOT gate G1, the qubits $ra_i$ are transformed into the state $rq_i = mb_i \oplus ra_i = mb_i \oplus qa_i \oplus ma_i$, where $rq_i \in \{|0, |1\}, i \in \{0, 1, ..., L-1\}$. After that, Bob uses $qb_i$ and the generated qubits $rq_i$ as the control qubits and target qubits of the quantum CNOT gate G2. The qubits $rq_i$ are transformed into the state $rb_i = qb_i \oplus rq_i = qb_i \oplus mb_i \oplus qa_i \oplus ma_i$, where $rb_i \in \{|0, |1\}, i \in \{0, 1, ..., L-1\}$. The sequence RB is sent to TP.

**Step 5:** TP uses Bell-basis $\{|\Phi^+\rangle, |\Phi^-\rangle, |\Psi^+\rangle, |\Psi^-\rangle\}$ to measure the sequence ST and obtains the measurement result $MT = (mt_{L-1}, ..., mt_1, mt_0)$. where $mt_i \in \{|\Phi^+\rangle, |\Phi^-\rangle, |\Psi^+\rangle, |\Psi^-\rangle\}, i \in \{0, 1, ..., L-1\}$. After that, TP prepares a sequence $RM = (rm_{L-1}, ..., rm_1, rm_0)$, where $rm_i \in \{|0, |1\}, i \in \{0, 1, ..., L-1\}$. If the measure results $mt_i$ are $|\Phi^+\rangle$ or $|\Psi^+\rangle$ ($|\Phi^-\rangle$ or $|\Psi^-\rangle$), $rm_i$ are set as $|0 > (|1 >)$. Finally, TP utilizes $rm_i$ and $rb_i$ to generate Bell state in the quantum circuit of the proposed protocol. The generates Bell state $R = (r_{L-1}, ..., r_1, r_0)$, where $r_i \in \{|\Phi^+\rangle, |\Phi^-\rangle, |\Psi^+\rangle, |\Psi^-\rangle\}$, $i \in \{0, 1, ..., L-1\}$.

Step 6: TP measures all the generated Bell state with Bell-basis $\{|\Phi^+\rangle, |\Phi^-\rangle, |\Psi^+\rangle, |\Psi^-\rangle\}$. If all the measurement result R is the same as MT. TP announces that the two users' private inputs are identical. Otherwise, the secret data of Alice and Bob will be different.

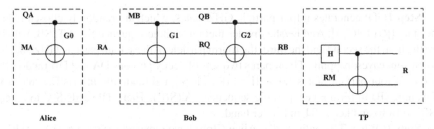

**Fig. 2.** The quantum circuit of the proposed protocol.

## 4   Analysis

In this section, we focus on the correctness of the proposed protocol in Sect. 4.1 and its security in Sect. 4.2.

### 4.1   Correctness

Alice and Bob use quantum circuit to perform private comparison without revealing the other one's secret data. Alice performs quantum CNOT gate G0 on particle sequence QA and MA and obtains the outcome RA. After that, Bob utilizes MB and RA as the control qubits and target qubits of the quantum CNOT gate G1, then performs quantum CNOT gate G2 on particle sequence QB and the generated sequence RQ. So, Bob obtains particle sequence RB. TP uses RB and RM to generate Bell states. According to Table 1, if all the state are equal to the generated Bell state, then we can conduct that the secret data of Alice and Bob will be identical, Otherwise, Alice and Bob's private information will be different.

### 4.2   Security

In this section, we analyze outside attacks and participant one respectively.

**Outside Attack**

The opportunity for an outside eavesdropper Eve to obtain private information of Alice and Bob step by step of our protocol is analyzed.

In step 1, Eve is able to implement different kinds of attacks, such as the measurement-resend attack, the entanglement-measure attack, the intercept-resend attack, man-in-middle attack, etc., to obtain the private information. However, the decoy photon technology [33] is used to prevent eavesdropping. All the attacks will be detected. Those who do not know the positions and measuring bases of the decoy particles will be found by Alice and Bob in step 2. Supposed that Eve implements the intercept-resend attack, she intercepts sequence SA' and SB' that TP sends to Alice and Bob. Unfortunately, Eve doesn't know the position and measuring basis of the decoy particles in SA' and SB'. If Eve uses Z basis to measure a decoy particle in $\{|+\rangle, |-\rangle\}$, the probability of being detected is 50%. In addition, if she uses X basis to measure a decoy particle in $\{|+\rangle, |-\rangle\}$, she will pass the eavesdropping detection.

**Table 1.** The values of various parameter.

| $qa_i$ | $qb_i$ | $ma_i$ | $mb_i$ | $ra_i$ | $rq_i$ | $rb_i$ | $mt_i$ | $r_i$ |
|---|---|---|---|---|---|---|---|---|
| $\lvert 0 >$ | $\lvert 0 >$ | $\lvert + >$ | $\lvert + >$ | $\lvert 0 >$ | $\lvert 0 >$ | $\lvert 0 >$ | $\lvert \Phi^+ > / \lvert \Psi^+ >$ | $\lvert \Phi^+ > / \lvert \Psi^+ >$ |
| | | $\lvert + >$ | $\lvert - >$ | $\lvert 0 >$ | $\lvert 1 >$ | $\lvert 1 >$ | $\lvert \Phi^- > / \lvert \Psi^- >$ | $\lvert \Phi^- > / \lvert \Psi^- >$ |
| | | $\lvert - >$ | $\lvert + >$ | $\lvert 1 >$ | $\lvert 1 >$ | $\lvert 1 >$ | $\lvert \Phi^- > / \lvert \Psi^- >$ | $\lvert \Phi^- > / \lvert \Psi^- >$ |
| | | $\lvert - >$ | $\lvert - >$ | $\lvert 1 >$ | $\lvert 0 >$ | $\lvert 0 >$ | $\lvert \Phi^+ > / \lvert \Psi^+ >$ | $\lvert \Phi^+ > / \lvert \Psi^+ >$ |
| $\lvert 0 >$ | $\lvert 1 >$ | $\lvert + >$ | $\lvert + >$ | $\lvert 0 >$ | $\lvert 0 >$ | $\lvert 1 >$ | $\lvert \Phi^+ > / \lvert \Psi^+ >$ | $\lvert \Phi^- > / \lvert \Psi^- >$ |
| | | $\lvert + >$ | $\lvert - >$ | $\lvert 0 >$ | $\lvert 1 >$ | $\lvert 0 >$ | $\lvert \Phi^- > / \lvert \Psi^- >$ | $\lvert \Phi^+ > / \lvert \Psi^+ >$ |
| | | $\lvert - >$ | $\lvert + >$ | $\lvert 1 >$ | $\lvert 1 >$ | $\lvert 0 >$ | $\lvert \Phi^- > / \lvert \Psi^- >$ | $\lvert \Phi^+ > / \lvert \Psi^+ >$ |
| | | $\lvert - >$ | $\lvert - >$ | $\lvert 1 >$ | $\lvert 0 >$ | $\lvert 1 >$ | $\lvert \Phi^+ > / \lvert \Psi^+ >$ | $\lvert \Phi^- > / \lvert \Psi^- >$ |
| $\lvert 1 >$ | $\lvert 0 >$ | $\lvert + >$ | $\lvert + >$ | $\lvert 1 >$ | $\lvert 1 >$ | $\lvert 1 >$ | $\lvert \Phi^+ > / \lvert \Psi^+ >$ | $\lvert \Phi^- > / \lvert \Psi^- >$ |
| | | $\lvert + >$ | $\lvert - >$ | $\lvert 1 >$ | $\lvert 0 >$ | $\lvert 0 >$ | $\lvert \Phi^- > / \lvert \Psi^- >$ | $\lvert \Phi^+ > / \lvert \Psi^+ >$ |
| | | $\lvert - >$ | $\lvert + >$ | $\lvert 0 >$ | $\lvert 0 >$ | $\lvert 0 >$ | $\lvert \Phi^- > / \lvert \Psi^- >$ | $\lvert \Phi^+ > / \lvert \Psi^+ >$ |
| | | $\lvert - >$ | $\lvert - >$ | $\lvert 0 >$ | $\lvert 1 >$ | $\lvert 1 >$ | $\lvert \Phi^+ > / \lvert \Psi^+ >$ | $\lvert \Phi^- > / \lvert \Psi^- >$ |
| $\lvert 1 >$ | $\lvert 1 >$ | $\lvert + >$ | $\lvert + >$ | $\lvert 1 >$ | $\lvert 1 >$ | $\lvert 0 >$ | $\lvert \Phi^+ > / \lvert \Psi^+ >$ | $\lvert \Phi^+ > / \lvert \Psi^+ >$ |
| | | $\lvert + >$ | $\lvert - >$ | $\lvert 1 >$ | $\lvert 0 >$ | $\lvert 1 >$ | $\lvert \Phi^- > / \lvert \Psi^- >$ | $\lvert \Phi^- > / \lvert \Psi^- >$ |
| | | $\lvert - >$ | $\lvert + >$ | $\lvert 0 >$ | $\lvert 0 >$ | $\lvert 1 >$ | $\lvert \Phi^- > / \lvert \Psi^- >$ | $\lvert \Phi^- > / \lvert \Psi^- >$ |
| | | $\lvert - >$ | $\lvert - >$ | $\lvert 0 >$ | $\lvert 1 >$ | $\lvert 0 >$ | $\lvert \Phi^+ > / \lvert \Psi^+ >$ | $\lvert \Phi^+ > / \lvert \Psi^+ >$ |

Therefore, for n decoy particles, the rate of detection is $1 - \left(\frac{3}{4}\right)^n$. When n is large enough, the rate of detection will approach to 1. Besides, since the proposed protocol is a one-way communication protocol, it is immune to the Trojan horse attack.

In step 2, since there has no qubit transmission, all the eavesdropping attacks will be avoided.

In step 3, Alice utilizes QA and MA as the control qubits and target qubits of the quantum CNOT gate G0, and sends RA to Bob. In step 4, Bob performs quantum CNOT gate G1 on particle sequence MB and RA, sends RQ for quantum CNOT gate G2 to produce RB. RB is sent to TP. In step 5, TP generates Bell state through performing quantum circuit. In these third steps, all operations are performed in quantum circuit, which utilizes quantum mechanics to provide security. Besides, compared with the previous QPC protocols, all participants in the proposed protocol will implement quantum circuit instead of classic computing to perform classic exclusive-OR operation, so the probability of revealing disclosure private information will be reduced.

In a word, the proposed protocol can resist outside attacks.

## Participant Attack

In 2007, Gao [34] first pointed out the concept of participant attack. Compared with outside attacks, participant attack is more powerful. There are two cases of participant attacks. One case is that dishonest Alice (Bob) tries to obtain the secret data of Bob

(Alice), and the other is that a semi-honest TP desires to get the secret data of Alice and Bob.

Case1 Dishonest Alice or Bob's attack.

In this protocol, we analysis the probability of Alice attempts to eavesdrop Bob's secret data. The only way of Alice's attack is that she intercepts the particle sequence SB. Unfortunately, Alice doesn't know the position and measurement basis of decoy particles, she will be found as an outside eavesdropper as described in 4.2.1. Besides, TP cannot conspire with any participants, so that Alice is not able to know the initial four-particle GHZ state. Thus, it is impossible for Alice to steal Bob's secret data. The role of Bob is similar to Alice, if Bob intercepts the particle sequence SA, he will be considered as an outside eavesdropper and be found. Moreover, Bob knows RA, but RA are produced by Alice's secret data GA and MA. Bob doesn't know the measurement result MA, so Alice's secret data will not be revealed to Bob. Thus, one participant is not able to eavesdropper the other one's secret data via launch participant attacks.

Case 2 The semi-honest TP's attack.

Since the initial four-particle GHZ states are generated by TP, she/he can use the initial state to perform attack. Due to the entangled relationship of four-particle GHZ state, TP doesn't know the one-time state SA and SB. Furthermore, RA is produced by GA and MA, she/he doesn't know MA and RA, so she/he is not able to get Alice's secret data. TP receives particle sequence RB and knows the measurement result MT, she/he can only obtain the generated Bell states which are equal to her/his measurement result MT. RB is produced by GB and RQ, but she/he is able to know RQ, so Bob's secret data will not be revealed to TP. Therefore, Alice and Bob's secret data are immune to TP's attack.

## 5   Conclusion

In summary, with the assistance of the semi-honest third party (TP), a secure quantum gate-based quantum private comparison (QPC) protocol using four-particle GHZ states is proposed. Compared with many existent QPC protocols, the proposed protocol adopts quantum circuit instead of the classic computing to perform exclusive-OR operation. The proposed protocol utilizes four-particle GHZ states as quantum resource, which are easy to be prepared with current technology in practice. Besides, the participants of this protocol only utilize single-particles measurement and Bell states measurement. The analysis shows that the proposed protocol is correct and it can resist both outside attack and participant one. Therefore, our protocol is of simplicity and better security. The further work will focus on more quantum gate-based quantum private comparison protocols.

**Acknowledgement.** This work is supported by the National Natural Science Foundation of China (No.62076042), the Key Research and Development Project of Sichuan Province (No.2021YFSY0012, No. 2020YFG0307, No.2021YFG0332), the Science and Technology Innovation Project of Sichuan(No. 2020017), the Key Research and Development Project of Chengdu (No. 2019-YF05–02028-GX), the Innovation Team of Quantum Security Communication of Sichuan Province (No.17TD0009), the Academic and Technical Leaders Training Funding Support Projects of Sichuan Province (No. 2016120080102643).

# References

1. Bennett, C.H., Charles, H., Brassard, G.: Quantum cryptography: public key distribution and coin tossing. Theoret. Comput. Sci. **560**(1), 7–11 (2014)
2. Zhang, Z.X., Qu, Z.G.: Anti-noise quantum network coding protocol based on bell states and butterfly network model. J. Quantum Comput. **1**(2), 89–109 (2019)
3. Qu, Z., Sun, H., Zheng, M.: An efficient quantum image steganography protocol based on improved EMD algorithm. Quantum Inf. Process. **20**(2), 1–29 (2021). https://doi.org/10.1007/s11128-021-02991-8
4. Xu, G., Shan, R., Chen, X., Dong, M., Chen, Y.: Probabilistic and hierarchical quantum information splitting based on the non-maximally entangled cluster state. Comput. Mater. Continua **69**(1), 339–349 (2021)
5. Vaccaro, J.A., Spring, J., Chefles, A.: Quantum protocols for anonymous voting and surveying. Phys. Rev. A **75**(1), 12333 (2007)
6. Huang, W., Wen, Q.Y., Liu, B.: Quantum anonymous ranking. Phys. Rev. A **89**(3), 32325 (2014)
7. Hogg, T., Harsha, P., Chen, K.Y.: Quantum auctions. Int. J. Quantum Inf **5**(05), 751–780 (2007)
8. Yu, W., Feng, H., Xu, Y., Yin, N., Chen, Y.: A phase estimation algorithm for quantum speed-up multi-party computing. Comput. Mater. Continua **67**(1), 241–252 (2021)
9. Yang, Y.G., Wen, Q.Y.: An efficient two-party quantum private comparison protocol with decoy photons and two-photon entanglement. J. Phys. A Math. Theor **42**, 55305 (2009)
10. Yang, Y.G., Gao, W.F., Wen, Q.Y.: Secure quantum private comparison. Phys. Scr **80**(6), 65002 (2009)
11. Liu, B., Gao, F., Jia, H.Y., Huang, W., Zhang, W.W., Wen, Q.Y.: Efficient quantum private comparison employing single photons and collective detection. Quantum Inf. Process **12**(2), 887–897 (2013)
12. Lang, Y.F.: Semi-quantum private comparison using single photons. Int. J. Theor. Phys **57**(10), 3048–3055 (2018)
13. Liu, W., Wang, Y.B., Cui, W.: Quantum private comparison protocol based on bell entangled states. Commun. Theor. Phys **57**(4), 583–588 (2012)
14. Tseng, H.Y., Lin, J., Hwang, T.: New quantum private comparison protocol using EPR pairs. Quantum Inf. Process **11**(2), 373–384 (2012)
15. Lin, J., Yang, C.-W., Hwang, T.: Quantum private comparison of equality protocol without a third party. Quantum Inf. Process. **13**(2), 239–247 (2013). https://doi.org/10.1007/s11128-013-0645-2
16. Sun, Y., Yan, L., Sun, Z., Zhang, S., Lu, J.: A novel semi-quantum private comparison scheme using bell entangle states. Comput. Mater. Continua **66**(3), 2385–2395 (2021)
17. Liu, W., Wang, Y.B.: Quantum private comparison based on GHZ entangled states. Int. J. Theor. Phys **51**, 3596–3604 (2012)
18. Gianni, J., Qu, Z.G.: New quantum private comparison using hyperentangled ghz state. J. Quantum Comput. **3**(2), 45–54 (2021)
19. Li, J., Zhou, H.F., Jia, L., Zhang, T.T.: An efficient protocol for the private comparison of equal information based on four-particle entangled W state and bell entangled states swap-ping. Int. J. Theor. Phys **53**(7), 2167–2176 (2014)
20. Liu, W., Wang, Y.B., Jiang, Z.T.: An efficient protocol for the quantum private comparison of equality with W state. Opt. Commun **284**(12), 3160–3163 (2011)
21. Zhang, W.W., Li, D., Li, Y.B.: Quantum private comparison protocol with W states. Int. J. Theor. Phys **53**(5), 1723–1729 (2014)

22. Xu, G.A., Chen, X.B., Wei, Z.H., Li, M.J., Yang, Y.X.: An efficient protocol for the quantum private comparison of equality with a four-qubit cluster state. Int. J. Quantum. Inf 10, 1250045 (2012)
23. Sun, Z.W., Long, D.Y.: Quantum private comparison protocol based on cluster states. Int. J. Theor. Phys 52(1), 212–218 (2013)
24. Liu, W., Wang, Y.B., Jiang, Z.T., Cao, Y.Z.: A protocol for the quantum private comparison of equality with χ-type state. Int. J. Theor. Phys 51(1), 69–77 (2012)
25. Liu, W., Wang, Y.B., Jiang, Z.T., Cao, Y.Z., Cui, W.: New quantum private comparison protocol using χ-type state. Int. J. Theor. Phys 51(6), 1953–1960 (2012)
26. Lin, S., Guo, G.D., Liu, X.F.: Quantum private comparison of equality with χ-type entangled states. Int. J. Theor. Phys. 52(11), 4185–4194 (2013)
27. Ye, T.Y., Ji, Z.X.: Two-party quantum private comparison with five-qubit entangled states. Int. J. Theor. Phys. 56(5), 1517–1529 (2017)
28. Chang, Y., et al.: Quantum private comparison of equality based on five-particle cluster state. Commun. Theor. Phys. 66, 621–628 (2016)
29. Zha, X.W., Yu, X.Y., Cao, Y., Wang, S.K.: Quantum private comparison protocol with five-particle cluster states. Int. J. Theor. Phys. 57, 3874–3881 (2018)
30. Ji, Z.X., Ye, T.Y.: Quantum private comparison of equal information based on highly entangled six-qubit genuine state. Commun. Theor. Phys. 65(6), 711–715 (2016)
31. Ji, Z.X., Zhang, H.G., Fan, P.R.: Two-party quantum private comparison protocol with maximally entangled seven-qubit state. Mod. Phys. Lett. A 34(28), 1–179 (2019)
32. Lo, H.K.: Insecurity of quantum secure computations. Phys. Rev. A. 56(2), 1154–1162 (1997)
33. Li, C.Y., Zhou, H.Y., Wang, Y., Deng, F.G.: Secure quantum key distribution network with Bell states and local unitary operations. Chin. Phys. Lett. 22(5), 1049 (2005)
34. Gao, F., Qin, S.J., Wen, Q.Y., et al.: A simple participant attack on the Bradler-Dusek protocol. Quantum Inf. Comput. 7(4), 329–334 (2007)

# A Survey on Privacy Protection of Cross-Chain

Jianghao Wang[1,2], Jieren Cheng[1,2(✉)], Yuming Yuan[3], Hui Li[3], and Victor S. Sheng[4]

[1] School of Computer Science and Technology, Hainan University, Haikou 570228, China
2636543988@qq.com
[2] Hainan Blockchain Technology Engineering Research Center, Hainan University, Haikou 570228, China
[3] Hainan Huochain Tech Company Limited, Haikou 570100, China
[4] Department of Computer Science, Texas Tech University, Lubbock, TX 79409, USA

**Abstract.** Blockchain technology has gained widespread attention due to its features of decentralization, tamper resistance, and traceability. Various decentralized applications have formed numerous "value silos" while meeting the unique needs of different industries. Cross-chain technology, as an important technology to realize inter-chain interconnection and value transfer, has also been rapidly developed. However, cross-chain technology faces a number of privacy risks that hinder its practical application. Although numerous surveys have reviewed the privacy protection of blockchain, they fail to reveal its recent progress and fail to provide a comprehensive classification of uniform standards for privacy protection in cross-chain processes. Therefore, in this paper, we review the development of cross-chain technologies and summarize the potential privacy threats. According to different privacy protection objectives, we provide a detailed survey and classification of existing privacy protection technologies. Finally, we propose a few open research questions and future research directions. We hope this work will help future researchers to gain insight into cross-chain privacy protection technologies in terms of concepts, properties and applications.

**Keywords:** Blockchain · Cross-chain · Privacy protection

## 1 Introduction

Due to its decentralized, tamper-proof, and traceable features, blockchain technology is one of the most popular technologies and is widely used in finance, IoT, supply chain, e-government, etc. However, most of the current blockchain projects are designed and implemented by different teams based on the specific use cases of their users, which may not be suitable for other use cases. These different blockchains may have different operation mechanisms and node access mechanisms, so they cannot interoperate with each other, and these projects are isolated from each other like "information silos." Therefore, cross-chain technology has received a lot of attention from researchers. It enables communication and even value exchange between different blockchains, thus alleviating the problem of "information silos" in blockchains.

Compared to a single blockchain, cross-chain technology inevitably brings more computation in pursuit of high performance and scalability, and provides more possibilities for attackers to illegally access users' private information [1]. on November 15, 2020, the Value DeFi protocol was attacked with a net loss of $6 million [2]; on August 10, 2021, the cross-chain interoperability protocol PolyNetwork reported being "attacked" with a total theft of over $610 million [3] and a large number of users' private information being compromised. Thus, achieving privacy protection during cross-chain interactions is a challenge.

There is still a lack of systematic investigation on the recent progress of privacy protection in cross-chain interactions. Considering that all information in cross-chain interactions is transmitted and recorded through transactions, this work will focus on privacy in user cross-chain transactions, which is the main privacy concern of cross-chain systems for practical applications. The main contributions of this paper are manifold: 1) analysis of privacy protection threats in the cross-chain process; 2) classification of cross-chain privacy protection techniques according to their different main privacy goals, and comparison and outlook.

We organize the rest of the paper as follows. Section 2 introduces the development of cross-chain technologies, comparatively analyzes the existing mainstream cross-chain technologies, and gives the privacy protection threats in the cross-chain process. Section 3 discusses different cross-chain data protection techniques and classifies them into three categories with different privacy-preserving purposes. Section 4 provides a detailed comparative analysis and outlook on the classification in the previous section. Finally, we conclude the paper in Sect. 5.

## 2 Overview of Cross-Chain Technology

### 2.1 The Development of Cross-Chain Technology

Cross-chain technology is also developing rapidly to meet the cross-chain demand between different blockchains. In the process of generation, development, and practical application, cross-chain technology has gone through the process from single-chain extension to multi-chain collaboration and has made certain breakthroughs in solving the interoperability, transaction, and scalability problems of blockchains. In 2012, Ripple proposed the InterLedger protocol [4] which solved the problem of collaboration between blockchains across systems; In 2013, Herlihy proposed the concept of atomic swap, pointing out that there are only two situations in the sub-transactions that constitute a complete cross-chain transaction, namely complete success and complete failure. In 2014, BlockSream proposed a side chain mechanism, using two-way anchoring to realize the transfer of cryptocurrency between the main chain and the side chain [5]. In 2015, the Bitcoin Lightning Network used the hash time lock mechanism to realize fast transactions under the Bitcoin chain and improve the transaction efficiency of the

Bitcoin system [6]. In 2016, BTC-Relay used relay cross-chain to realize one-way cross-chain communication between Bitcoin and Ethereum [7]. In 2017, in the Cosmos [8] and Polkadot [9] cross-chain projects, in order to achieve compatibility with all blockchain applications, they proposed a plan to build a cross-chain infrastructure platform. In 2021, Wanchain [10] upgraded the cross-chain mechanism to a "secure deposit sharing multi-chain interchange" mechanism and created the world's first BTC-ETH decentralized direct bridge based on this mechanism. Figure 1 shows the development process of cross-chain technology.

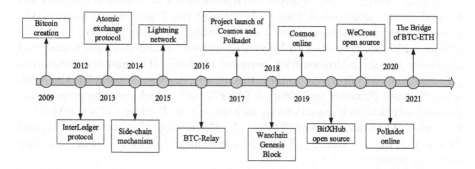

**Fig. 1.** The development process of cross-chain technology.

## 2.2   Main Cross-Chain Technology

Cross-chain technology can be divided into homogeneous and heterogeneous cross-chain based on whether the underlying technology platforms of the crossed blockchains are the same or not. Since the cross-chain interaction of a homogeneous cross-chain is the same across the underlying technology platforms, the consensus algorithm, security mechanism, block generation, and verification logic of the interacting parties are the same, too, so the cross-chain interaction is relatively simple. In contrast, heterogeneous cross-chains are relatively complex and usually require third-party assistance to complete the cross-chain process. Currently, there are four mainstream cross-chain techniques as follows: notary scheme, sidechain/relay, hash locking, and distributed private key control. The performance comparison of the four cross-chain methods is as follows (Table 1):

## 2.3   Privacy Threats for Cross-Chain

In recent years, the large number of transactions on the blockchain network has also generated a large amount of data, but the nature of the blockchain itself makes it possible for illegal users to listen to and analyze the blockchain through de-anonymization techniques, which can reveal the relationship between addresses on the blockchain and user identity information.

**Table 1.** Comparative analysis of cross-chain mechanism performance.

| | Notary Schemes | Sidechains/Relays | Hash-locking | Distributed private key control |
|---|---|---|---|---|
| Trust model | Most notaries are honest | No 51% attack | No 51% attack | No 51% attack |
| Asset exchange | Yes | Yes | Yes | Yes |
| Asset transfer | Yes | Yes | No | Yes |
| Multi-currency smart contracts | Yes | Yes | No | Yes |
| Difficulty of realisation | Easy | Difficulty | Difficulty | Medium |
| Disadvantages | Pseudo-decentralisation | Difficult to achieve | Narrow application scenarios | Smart contracts are difficult to design |
| Typical cases | Corda, InterLedger Protocal | Cosmos, Polkadot | Lighting network | WanChain, Fusion |

Taking Bitcoin as an example, current research on de-anonymization has focused on two approaches. One is Analysis of the Transaction Chain (ATC), which obtains transactions from publicly available blockchain data, classifies bitcoin addresses according to bitcoin anonymity weaknesses into teams, and associates bitcoin addresses with personal identities [11], and the mixed-coin [12] approach can effectively counter this attack. Another approach is the Analysis of Bitcoin Protocol and Network (ABPN [13]), which uses the propagation properties of Bitcoin transactions to infer the source IP address of a new transaction, while The Onion Router (TOR) [14], The Invisible Internet (I2P) [15] and Transaction Remote Release (TRR) [16] can counter this attack by anonymizing routes or addresses.

At the same time, the privacy and security of user data are also threatened due to the participation of third parties in cross-chain interactions and the restrictions of cross-chain protocols. For example, although the interoperability of cross-chain interaction is improved in the notary model, the introduction of a third party reduces the centralization of the blockchain, and the user's identity privacy and transaction privacy are both at risk of leakage; in the hash time lock model, people focus more on ensuring the fairness of atomic exchange and guaranteeing that both parties' assets are transferred or neither is transferred, and the user's data privacy issues are not effectively protected. Thus, it can be seen that different cross-chain approaches also bring new threats to users' data privacy security.

# 3  Methodology for Privacy Preservation in Cross-Chain

This section introduces the cross-chain privacy protection schemes recently proposed by researchers. According to their different privacy goals, they are divided into three categories: obfuscation, cryptographic and data isolation. Figure 2 shows the classification of privacy-preserving methods.

## 3.1  Obfuscation

In this category, solutions for address hiding, data hiding, and routing hiding are included. Privacy protection is achieved mainly through the anonymity of users and the untraceability of transactions.

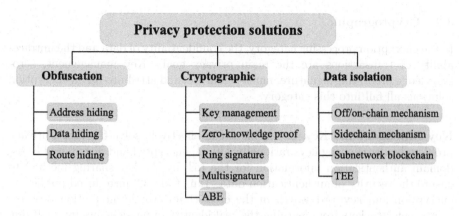

**Fig. 2.** Classification of the privacy-preserving methods.

**Address Hiding.** Address hiding technology is used to provide anonymity on the blockchain. The system generates a new anonymous address randomly for each transaction [17–19] or each user [20], which makes it difficult for an attacker to switch anonymous addresses in the blockchain browser network. Chaisawat et al. [21] introduced a one-time anonymous token to indicate the eligibility of anonymous voters to vote at a specific time. Unterweger et al. [22] proposed a hash time-lock based charging protocol for electric vehicles. An anonymous address is used in the payment phase of the protocol to protect the identity and location privacy of all participants.

**Data Hiding.** Data hiding can prevent the leakage of users' private transaction information by hiding the transaction details. Abidin et al. [23] and Sun et al. [24] protect consumer privacy by hiding details of energy consumption. Zhao et al. [25] use an external chain as a controller to import privacy data into carrier videos, eliminating the need for trusted third parties and achieving autonomous control of privacy data. Hrong et al. [26] combine private information and hashes of original medical images stored on the blockchain to improve the privacy and traceability of images.

**Route Hiding.** In covert routing or anonymous connections, communicating parties can complete transactions without revealing their identities [27]. Kumar et al. [28] used a routing scheme for key management that allows neighboring sensors that communicate with each other to share keys anonymously. Parizi et al. [29] introduced garlic routing (GOR) on a sidechain that can be routed through a network of smart contracts on the sidechain to hide the identity of the user.

## 3.2  Cryptographic

In the encryption processing category, the confidentiality of data and the untraceability of transactions are the main privacy goals. Key management, zero-knowledge proof, ring signature, multi-signature, and attribute-based encryption solutions all fall into this category.

**Key Management.** Key management can effectively solve the user's privacy problem by distributing keys rationally. [30, 31] encrypted and distributed cross-domain authentication information for the IoT by the key sharing method to ensure the security of authentication data. Tan et al. [32] introduced public key encryption and keyword search in the cross-chain atomic interaction protocol to prevent attackers from learning the real identity of participants by analyzing blockchain data. Wang et al. [33] optimized the cross-chain information authentication mechanism of the key management interoperability protocol. Alves et al. [34] protect the data privacy of online ordering customers based on sidechain and key management techniques.

**Zero-Knowledge Proof.** Zero-knowledge proof technology enables the prover to prove to the verifier that a certain assertion is true without revealing any private information. Hawk et al. [35] use zero-knowledge proofs to encrypt transaction information on the blockchain. Hardjono et al. [36] use an enhanced privacy ID (EPID) zero-knowledge proof protocol that allows a device to prove to the source verifier (and device owner) that the device has the correct origin. In [37], enabling drivers to complete secure authentication without revealing the specific location of the vehicle provides privacy protection in terms of location privacy. In [38], zero-knowledge proof technology is integrated into the sidechain to extend the blockchain architecture while guaranteeing user privacy. [39] simplifies the sidechain in a verifiable and scalable manner based on zero-knowledge proofs to protect the privacy of users in cross-chain interactions.

**Ring Signature.** In a ring signature, any member can use a set of public keys and their corresponding private keys to sign a transaction anonymously. The verifier can verify that a signature is indeed a ring signature generated by the owner of one of the private keys in the public key set, but does not know which owner it is. A typical application of ring signatures is CryptoNote [40]. Based on this, Wang et al. [41] designed an optimized ring signature encryption algorithm to resist the malicious phase, and based on this algorithm, they proposed a two-layer energy blockchain network to store private transaction data and public information separately to ensure user privacy.

**Multisignature.** Different from ring signatures, multisignature technology refers to multiple users signing a digital asset at the same time. It can be simply understood as multiple people in an account all having the right to sign and pay.

Users in AgentChain [42] can map assets from other blockchain projects to the agent chain and trade them through a multisignature deposit pool of the selected transaction group, which restricts the behavior of the transaction operator and ensures the privacy and security of the system. Aitzhan et al. [43] can perform secure transactions without relying on trusted third parties by traversing the public history of the distributed transaction chain and voting on the validity of the transactions based on multiple signatures.

**Attribute Based Encryption.** Attribute-based encryption (ABE) is an encryption method that uses attributes as defining and tuning factors and uses the user's key to encrypt or decrypt the cipher text, with the data owner having full control over the data. Attribute encryption not only solves the problem of key leakage caused by symmetric encryption key transmission but also achieves fine-grained access control of encrypted data [44,45]. Gao et al. [46] introduced the ciphertext policy attribute-based encryption (CP-ABE) algorithm in the sidechain to protect user data privacy. Malamas et al. [47] used attribute encryption to ensure that end users from different medical domains (e.g., hospitals or device manufacturers) can access and exchange medical data securely and privately. For the blockchain IoT, Shao et al. [48] proposed an identity-based encryption cross-chain communication mechanism (IBE-BCIOT) to achieve secure and effective cross-domain communication between IoTs.

## 3.3 Data Isolation

In the data isolation category, private data is usually settled separately from the main blockchain ledger, and the protection of transaction anonymity is its main privacy goal. Off/on-chain mechanism, sidechain mechanism, subnetwork blockchain, and trusted execution environment solutions fall into this category.

**Off/On-Chain Mechanism.** Transactions such as user registration in the blockchain not only compromise the privacy of users but also increase transaction costs. The off-chain/on-chain mechanism can perform these transactions off-chain without writing them to the blockchain, which effectively solves the privacy problem of the blockchain. Zhao et al. [49] in their scheme deploy only on-chain processes to the blockchain, which saves resources and hides the private information of off-chain transactions. In the scheme of Darwish et al. [50], the hash of the data is kept in the blockchain to point to the data stored off-chain. Erdin et al. [51] used an off-chain payment system, where non-critical transactions are executed on the blockchain to maximize the privacy leakage problem. Lys et al. [52] reduce protocol complexity and improve privacy by introducing off-chain adapters that eliminate the need for witness chains used in traditional schemes.

**Sidechain Mechanism.** The sidechain mechanism allows ledger assets (such as Bitcoin) to be safely transferred from the main chain to other blockchains and can be safely transferred back. [53–56] designed access control sidechains using smart contracts to protect data privacy when sidechains interact with federated blockchains. [57,58] designed sidechain interactive privacy protection protocols so that each cross-chain connection requires authentication and authorization, enabling secure and private cross-chain interactions. [59–70] ensured the privacy and security of cross-chain transactions by designing different sidechain privacy-preserving models in which different sidechains store different privacy levels of information and encrypt the privacy information with cryptographic knowledge.

**Subnetwork Blockchain.** The subnetwork blockchain is independent from the main chain and is connected through interconnection positions. The main idea is to process p2p transactions of a set of users in a subnetwork blockchain and prevent any private information in the subnetwork from leaking into the main blockchain through interconnection nodes. Firoozjaei et al. [71] proposed the Hy-Bridge framework, which is a hybrid blockchain with local subnetworks to isolate the P2P transactions of IoT users. The subnetwork blockchain is anonymized through the bridge and does not disclose any private information to the main blockchain. Based on Hy-Bridge, the Evchain framework was proposed by [72]. Their framework consists of a main blockchain for billing and payment and one or more subnetwork blockchains for credit sharing. It allows credit sharing within groups of owners and protects the privacy of individual group members under the protection of anonymity.

**Trusted Execution Environment.** The Trusted Execution Environment (TEE) is a secure area in the main processor that operates in a separate environment, parallel to the operating system. It provides a completely isolated environment for the execution of applications and ensures that the confidentiality and integrity of the code and data loaded in the TEE are protected [73]. Ekiden [74] is an SGX-based separation of computation from consensus. It executes smart contract computations in the TEE of off-chain compute nodes and then uses a remote authentication protocol to verify the correctness of the execution of on-chain compute nodes. TrustCross [75] can design a secure key exchange algorithm to generate communication keys for data encryption through the TEE, ensuring that the keys are not compromised.

## 4    Discussion and Analysis

Table 2 summarizes the security goals, main shortcomings, existing applications, and future prospects of the different privacy protection methods in this section.

In the obfuscation category, the anonymity of users and the untraceability of transactions are realized through temporary pseudonyms, data hiding, and routing hiding. However, since this type of method requires obfuscation of privacy, it will cause additional delays while waiting for obfuscation, reduce transaction throughput, and cannot effectively protect the user's data content. Optimizing

**Table 2.** Comparison and analysis of privacy protection methods.

| Classification | Security objectives | Main disadvantages | Existing projects |
|---|---|---|---|
| Obfuscation | Anonymity of users and untraceability of transactions | 1. Higher expansion cost<br>2. Low transaction throughput and high latency<br>3. Not suitable for protecting user data | [17–29] |
| Cryptographic | Confidentiality of data and non-traceability of transactions | 1. Higher storage overhead<br>2. Complex calculations will generate a lot of technical and communication overhead | [30–48] |
| Data isolation | Transaction anonymity | 1. Traceable risk<br>2. The repeater is not completely trusted | [49–66,71–75] |

the confusion algorithm or solving the optimization problem of the configuration combination between the original codes is the direction of future research.

In the cryptographic category, the confidentiality of the data is realized by encrypting the transaction data, and the zero-knowledge proof can realize the untraceability of the transaction. Generally, due to complex cryptographic algorithms, this type of calculation requires a lot of calculations, which will incur additional delay and cost. In the future, lightweight implementations will make these solutions suitable for users' anonymous applications.

In the data isolation category, the user's private data is isolated from the main ledger and recorded separately, thus realizing the anonymity of transactions. However, this type of scheme has traceability risks. For example, by performing correlation analysis on the network traffic on the chain, you can track the private data in the off-chain network. In addition, insider attackers can violate the privacy of users in offline networks. This problem exists in the side chain and sub-network solutions. Both solutions require an intermediate controller or TTP to connect to the main blockchain. At the same time, the interconnection between the side blockchain and the main blockchain leads to traffic correlation, data leakage, and transaction tracking. In the future, the behavior of connectors can be constrained by designing new on-chain and off-chain supervision protocols or using cryptographic techniques such as proxy re-encryption.

## 5   Conclusion

We believe that cross-chain technology is a bridge and hub connecting blockchains, the key to realizing value interconnection, and a favorable means for blockchains to expand outward and break blockchains to form isolated value islands. Therefore, a deep understanding of cross-chain privacy plays a key role in improving the credibility and robustness of cross-chain technology. In this article, we categorize and summarize cross-chain privacy-preserving technologies. First, we review the development history of cross-chain technology, introduce existing cross-chain technologies, and point out existing privacy threats. Then, according to the different privacy goals of privacy protection technologies, we divide the existing cross-chain privacy protection technologies into three categories: obfuscation, encryption and data isolation, and introduce the latest research progress respectively. Based on the analysis and comparison results, we found several issues to be solved, and proposed a series of future research directions, which are helpful for future research on cross-chain privacy protection technology.

**Acknowledgements.** This work was supported by National Natural Science Foundation of China (Grant No. 62162022 and 62162024), Key Projects in Hainan Province (Grant ZDYF2021GXJS003 and Grant ZDYF2020040), the Major science and technology project of Hainan Province (Grant No. ZDKJ2020012).

# References

1. Al-E'mari, S., Anbar, M., Sanjalawe, Y., Manickam, S., Hasbullah, I.: Intrusion detection systems using blockchain technology: a review, issues and challenges. Comput. Syst. Sci. Eng. **40**(1), 87–112 (2022)
2. Wang, B., et al.: Blockeye: hunting for defi attacks on blockchain. In: 2021 IEEE/ACM 43rd International Conference on Software Engineering: Companion Proceedings (ICSE-Companion), pp. 17–20 (2021)
3. Shi, L., Wang, Z., Zeng, Y.: Edge network security risk control based on attack and defense map. J. Circuits Syst. Comput. **30**(03), 2150046 (2021)
4. Hope-Bailie, A., Thomas, S.: Interledger: creating a standard for payments. In: Proceedings of the 25th International Conference Companion on World Wide Web, WWW '16 Companion, International World Wide Web Conferences Steering Committee, Republic and Canton of Geneva, CHE, pp. 281–282 (2016)
5. Kumar, V.A., et al.: A comprehensive survey on privacy-security and scalability solutions for block chain technology (2021)
6. Poon, J., Dryja, T.: The bitcoin lightning network: scalable off-chain instant payments (2016)
7. Robinson, P., Brainard, J.: Anonymous state pinning for private blockchains. In: 2019 18th IEEE International Conference on Trust, Security and Privacy in Computing and Communications/13th IEEE International Conference On Big Data Science and Engineering (TrustCom/BigDataSE), pp. 827–834 (2019)
8. Raychaudhuri, D., et al.: Challenge: COSMOS: A City-Scale Programmable Testbed for Experimentation with Advanced Wireless. Association for Computing Machinery, New York (2020)
9. Wood, G.: Polkadot: vision for a heterogeneous multi-chain framework. White Paper 21 (2016)
10. Robinson, P.: Survey of crosschain communications protocols. Comput. Netw. **200**, 108488 (2021)
11. Wang, Q., Qin, B., Hu, J., Xiao, F.: Preserving transaction privacy in bitcoin. Futur. Gener. Comput. Syst. **107**, 793–804 (2020)
12. Aldamegh, W.F., Alsulaiman, L.A.: T-Mix: a threshold cryptography mixing service for bitcoin. In: Mateev, M., Nightingale, J. (eds.) Sustainable Development and Social Responsibility—Volume 1. ASTI, pp. 291–297. Springer, Cham (2020). https://doi.org/10.1007/978-3-030-32922-8_29

13. Nerurkar, P., Patel, D., Busnel, Y., Ludinard, R., Kumari, S., Khan, M.K.: Dissecting bitcoin blockchain: empirical analysis of bitcoin network (2009–2020). J. Netw. Comput. Appl. **177**, 102940 (2021)
14. Barstad, H.: Deanonymizing communications on the Onion Router (TOR) network with Deep Learning. Master's thesis, The University of Bergen (2021)
15. Cilleruelo, C., de Marcos, L., Junquera-Sánchez, J., Martínez-Herráz, J.J.: Interconnection between darknets. IEEE Internet Comput. **25**(3), 61–70 (2021)
16. Elngar, A.: Bitcoin: a P2P digital currency, pp. 1–17, April 2020
17. Zhang, J., Zhou, G., Wang, J., Huang, L.: Anonymous hidden transaction model for blockchain systems. In: 2021 IEEE Region 10 Symposium (TENSYMP), pp. 1–6 (2021)
18. Lin, C., He, D., Huang, X., Khan, M.K., Choo, K.K.R.: Dcap: a secure and efficient decentralized conditional anonymous payment system based on blockchain. IEEE Trans. Inf. Forensics Secur. **15**, 2440–2452 (2020)
19. Dorri, A., Steger, M., Kanhere, S.S., Jurdak, R.: Blockchain: a distributed solution to automotive security and privacy. IEEE Commun. Mag. **55**(12), 119–125 (2017)
20. Guan, Z., Si, G., Zhang, X., Wu, L., Guizani, N., Du, X., Ma, Y.: Privacy-preserving and efficient aggregation based on blockchain for power grid communications in smart communities. IEEE Commun. Mag. **56**(7), 82–88 (2018)
21. Chaisawat, S., Vorakulpipat, C.: Towards achieving personal privacy protection and data security on integrated e-voting model of blockchain and message queue. Security and Communication Networks 2021 (2021)
22. Unterweger, A., Knirsch, F., Brunner, C., Engel, D.: Low-risk privacy-preserving electric vehicle charging with payments. In: Workshop on Automotive and Autonomous Vehicle Security (AutoSec), vol. 2021, p. 21 (2021)
23. Abidin, A., Aly, A., Cleemput, S., Mustafa, M.A.: Secure and privacy-friendly local electricity trading and billing in smart grid. arXiv preprint arXiv:1801.08354 (2018)
24. Sun, Y., Lampe, L., Wong, V.W.S.: Smart meter privacy: exploiting the potential of household energy storage units. IEEE Internet Things J. **5**(1), 69–78 (2018)
25. Zhao, H., Liu, Y., Wang, Y., Wang, X., Li, J.: A blockchain-based data hiding method for data protection in digital video. In: Qiu, M. (ed.) SmartBlock 2018. LNCS, vol. 11373, pp. 99–110. Springer, Cham (2018). https://doi.org/10.1007/978-3-030-05764-0_11
26. Horng, J.H., Chang, C.C., Li, G.L., Lee, W.K., Hwang, S.O.: Blockchain-based reversible data hiding for securing medical images. J. Healthcare Eng. **2021**, 22 (2021)
27. Wang, N., et al.: When energy trading meets blockchain in electrical power system: the state of the art. Appl. Sci. **9**(8), 1561 (2019)
28. Kumar, P., Bhushan, S., Kumar, M., Alazab, M., et al.: Secure key management and mutual authentication protocol for wireless sensor network using hybrid approach (2021)
29. Parizi, R.M., Homayoun, S., Yazdinejad, A., Dehghantanha, A., Choo, K.K.R.: Integrating privacy enhancing techniques into blockchains using sidechains. In: 2019 IEEE Canadian Conference of Electrical and Computer Engineering (CCECE), pp. 1–4 (2019)
30. Ma, M., Shi, G., Li, F.: Privacy-oriented blockchain-based distributed key management architecture for hierarchical access control in the iot scenario. IEEE Access **7**, 34045–34059 (2019)
31. Chen, H., et al.: Cipherchain: a secure and efficient ciphertext blockchain via mpeck. J. Quantum Comput. **2**(1), 57 (2020)

32. Tan, C., Jing, Z., Bei, S.: Atomic cross-chain swap-based decentralized management system in vehicular networks. In: Xu, G., Liang, K., Su, C. (eds.) Frontiers in Cyber Security, pp. 243–253. Springer, Singapore (2020)
33. Wang, L., et al.: Dynamic adaptive cross-chain trading mode for multi-microgrid joint operation. Sensors **20**(21), 6096 (2020)
34. Alves, D.: Proof-of-concept (POC) of restaurant's food requests in the lisk blockchain/sidechain. J. Phys. Conf. Ser. **1828**(1), 012110 (2021)
35. Kosba, A., Miller, A., Shi, E., Wen, Z., Papamanthou, C.: Hawk: the blockchain model of cryptography and privacy-preserving smart contracts. In: 2016 IEEE Symposium on Security and Privacy (SP), pp. 839–858 (2016)
36. Hardjono, T., Smith, N.: Cloud-based commissioning of constrained devices using permissioned blockchains. In: Proceedings of the 2nd ACM International Workshop on IoT Privacy, Trust, and Security, IoTPTS 2016, pp. 29–36. Association for Computing Machinery, New York (2016)
37. Baza, M., Lasla, N., Mahmoud, M.M.E.A., Srivastava, G., Abdallah, M.: B-ride: ride sharing with privacy-preservation, trust and fair payment atop public blockchain. IEEE Trans. Network Sci. Eng. **8**(2), 1214–1229 (2021)
38. Karaarslan, E., Konacaklı, E.: Data storage in the decentralized world: blockchain and derivatives. arXiv preprint arXiv:2012.10253 (2020)
39. Westerkamp, M., Eberhardt, J.: zkrelay: facilitating sidechains using zksnark-based chain-relays. In: 2020 IEEE European Symposium on Security and Privacy Workshops (EuroS PW), pp. 378–386 (2020)
40. Vijayakumaran, S.: Analysis of cryptonote transaction graphs using the dulmage-mendelsohn decomposition. Cryptology ePrint Archive, Report 2021/760 (2021). https://ia.cr/2021/760
41. Wang, L., Xie, Y., Zhang, D., Liu, J., Jiang, S., Zhang, Y., Li, M.: Credible peer-to-peer trading with double-layer energy blockchain network in distributed electricity markets. Electronics **10**(15), 1815 (2021)
42. Li, D., Liu, J., Tang, Z., Wu, Q., Guan, Z.: Agentchain: a decentralized cross-chain exchange system. In: 2019 18th IEEE International Conference on Trust, Security and Privacy in Computing and Communications/13th IEEE International Conference on Big Data Science And Engineering (TrustCom/BigDataSE), pp. 491–498 (2019)
43. Aitzhan, N.Z., Svetinovic, D.: Security and privacy in decentralized energy trading through multi-signatures, blockchain and anonymous messaging streams. IEEE Trans. Dependable Secure Comput. **15**(5), 840–852 (2018)
44. Zhang, L., Peng, M., Wang, W., Su, Y., Cui, S., Kim, S.: Secure and efficient data storage and sharing scheme based on double blockchain. Cmc -Tech Science Press- 66(1) (2021)
45. Feng, T., Pei, H., Ma, R., Tian, Y., Feng, X., et al.: Blockchain data privacy access control based on searchable attribute encryption (2021)
46. Gao, X., Huang, X., Zhang, W., Yang, R.: A novel cp-abe based sidechain protocol for distributed power system data storage management with the blockchain. In: The 2nd International Conference on Computing and Data Science, pp. 1–8 (2021)
47. Malamas, V., Kotzanikolaou, P., Dasaklis, T.K., Burmester, M.: A hierarchical multi blockchain for fine grained access to medical data. IEEE Access **8**, 134393–134412 (2020)
48. Shao, S., et al.: Ibe-bciot: an ibe based cross-chain communication mechanism of blockchain in iot. World Wide Web **24**(5), 1665–1690 (2021)
49. Zhao, S., Wang, B., Li, Y., Li, Y.: Integrated energy transaction mechanisms based on blockchain technology. Energies **11**(9), 2412 (2018)

50. Darwish, M.A., Yafi, E., Al Ghamdi, M.A., Almasri, A.: Decentralizing privacy implementation at cloud storage using blockchain-based hybrid algorithm. Arabian J. Sci. Eng. **45**, 3369–3378 (2020)
51. Erdin, E., Cebe, M., Akkaya, K., Solak, S., Bulut, E., Uluagac, S.: Building a private bitcoin-based payment network among electric vehicles and charging stations. In: 2018 IEEE International Conference on Internet of Things (iThings) and IEEE Green Computing and Communications (GreenCom) and IEEE Cyber, Physical and Social Computing (CPSCom) and IEEE Smart Data (SmartData), pp. 1609–1615 (2018)
52. Lys, L., Micoulet, A., Potop-Butucaru, M.: Atomic cross chain swaps via relays and adapters. In: Proceedings of the 3rd Workshop on Cryptocurrencies and Blockchains for Distributed Systems, CryBlock 2020, pp. 59–64. Association for Computing Machinery, New York (2020)
53. Jiang, Y., Wang, C., Wang, Y., Gao, L.: A cross-chain solution to integrating multiple blockchains for iot data management. Sensors **19**(9), 2042 (2019)
54. He, Y., Zhang, C., Wu, B., Yang, Y., Xiao, K., Li, H.: A cross-chain trusted reputation scheme for a shared charging platform based on blockchain. IEEE Internet Things J., 1 (2021)
55. Fusco, F., Lunesu, M.I., Pani, F.E., Pinna, A.: Crypto-voting, a blockchain based e-voting system. In: KMIS, pp. 221–225 (2018)
56. Rahman, Z.: Privacy enhancement of the internet of everything (peie) with the integrated blockchain technology (2021)
57. Xiao, X., Yu, Z., Xie, K., Guo, S., Xiong, A., Yan, Y.: A multi-blockchain architecture supporting cross-blockchain communication. In: Sun, X., Wang, J., Bertino, E. (eds.) Artificial Intelligence and Security, pp. 592–603. Springer, Singapore (2020)
58. Robinson, P., Ramesh, R., Johnson, S.: Atomic crosschain transactions for ethereum private sidechains. Blockchain: Research and Applications, p. 100030 (2021)
59. Cao, L., Song, B.: Blockchain cross-chain protocol and platform research and development. In: 2021 International Conference on Electronics, Circuits and Information Engineering (ECIE), pp. 264–269 (2021)
60. Song, L., Wang, X., Wei, P., Lu, Z., Wang, X., Merveille, N.: Blockchain-based flexible double-chain architecture and performance optimization for better sustainability in agriculture. CMC-Comput. Mater. Continua **68**(1), 1429–1446 (2021)
61. Guo, J., Gai, K., Zhu, L., Zhang, Z.: An approach of secure two-way-pegged multi-sidechain. In: Wen, S., Zomaya, A., Yang, L.T. (eds.) ICA3PP 2019. LNCS, vol. 11945, pp. 551–564. Springer, Cham (2020). https://doi.org/10.1007/978-3-030-38961-1_47
62. Sestrem Ochôa, I., Augusto Silva, L., de Mello, G., Garcia, N.M., de Paz Santana, J.F., Quietinho Leithardt, V.R.: A cost analysis of implementing a blockchain architecture in a smart grid scenario using sidechains. Sensors **20**(3), 843 (2020)
63. Jiang, Y., Wang, C., Huang, Y., Long, S., Huo, Y.: A cross-chain solution to integration of iot tangle for data access management. In: 2018 IEEE International Conference on Internet of Things (iThings) and IEEE Green Computing and Communications (GreenCom) and IEEE Cyber, Physical and Social Computing (CPSCom) and IEEE Smart Data (SmartData), pp. 1035–1041 (2018)
64. Hirtan, L., Krawiec, P., Dobre, C., Batalla, J.M.: Blockchain-based approach for e-health data access management with privacy protection. In: 2019 IEEE 24th International Workshop on Computer Aided Modeling and Design of Communication Links and Networks (CAMAD), pp. 1–7 (2019)

65. Hwang, G.-H., Chen, P.-H., Lu, C.-H., Chiu, C., Lin, H.-C., Jheng, A.-J.: InfiniteChain: a multi-chain architecture with distributed auditing of sidechains for public blockchains. In: Chen, S., Wang, H., Zhang, L.-J. (eds.) ICBC 2018. LNCS, vol. 10974, pp. 47–60. Springer, Cham (2018). https://doi.org/10.1007/978-3-319-94478-4_4

66. Li, X., Wu, L., Zhao, R., Lu, W., Xue, F.: Two-layer adaptive blockchain-based supervision model for off-site modular housing production. Comput. Ind. **128**, 103437 (2021)

67. Cheng, J., Yang, Y., Tang, X., Xiong, N., Zhang, Y., Lei, F.: Generative adversarial networks: a literature review. KSII Trans. Internet Inf. Syst. **14**(12), 4625–4647 (2020)

68. Cheng, J., Liu, J., Xu, X., Xia, D., Liu, L., Sheng, V.S.: A review of Chinese named entity recognition. KSII Trans. Internet Inf. Syst. (TIIS) **15**(6), 2012–2030 (2021)

69. Lei, F., Cheng, J., Yang, Y., Tang, X., Sheng, V.S., Huang, C.: Improving heterogeneous network knowledge transfer based on the principle of generative adversarial. Electronics **10**(13), 1525 (2021)

70. Tang, X., Tu, W., Li, K., Cheng, J.: Dffnet: an IoT-perceptive dual feature fusion network for general real-time semantic segmentation. Inf. Sci. **565**, 326–343 (2021)

71. Daghmehchi Firoozjaei, M., Ghorbani, A., Kim, H., Song, J.: Hy-bridge: a hybrid blockchain for privacy-preserving and trustful energy transactions in internet-of-things platforms. Sensors **20**(3), 928 (2020)

72. Firoozjaei, M.D., Ghorbani, A., Kim, H., Song, J.: Evchain: a blockchain-based credit sharing in electric vehicles charging. In: 2019 17th International Conference on Privacy, Security and Trust (PST), pp. 1–5 (2019)

73. Khan, N., Nitzsche, S., López, A.G., Becker, J.: Utilizing and extending trusted execution environment in heterogeneous socs for a pay-per-device ip licensing scheme. IEEE Trans. Inf. Foren. Secur. **16**, 2548–2563 (2021)

74. Cheng, R., et al.: Ekiden: a platform for confidentiality-preserving, trustworthy, and performant smart contracts. In: 2019 IEEE European Symposium on Security and Privacy (EuroS P), pp. 185–200 (2019)

75. Lan, Y., et al.: Trustcross: enabling confidential interoperability across blockchains using trusted hardware. arXiv preprint arXiv:2103.13809 (2021)

# Design and Testing of Source Address Validation Protocols: A Survey

Deshun Li[1]👤, Lu Xiao[1], Ganghua Cao[1], Jiangyuan Yao[1(✉)]👤,
and Xingcan Cao[2]

[1] Hainan University, Haikou 570228, China
yaojy@hainanu.edu.cn
[2] University of British Columbia, Vancouver, BC V6T1Z1, Canada

**Abstract.** In today's Internet, the data packets are forwarded according to the destination addresses without checking source addresses. Therefore, many network attacks based on source address spoofing have occurred, which seriously affects network security. The protocols of source address validation are effective methods to solve the challenge of source address spoofing. At present, many researchers have proposed a variety of source address validation protocols, which can ensure the credibility of source addresses. Based on the source address validation architecture, this paper describes the existing typical protocols in the view of the local subnet, intra-AS, and inter-AS. We summarize the main ideas, advantages, and disadvantages of these protocols. Then we introduce the related works of testing of source address validation protocols. Finally, we discuss the possible future works and research trends of the source address validation protocols, including source address validation protocols in intra-AS with higher deployment incentives, testing of a combination of multiple source address validation protocols, combine validation and testing during the development of protocols.

**Keywords:** Source address spoofing · Source address validation · Protocol testing

## 1 Introduction

During the transmission of data packets, the router only forwards packets according to the destination IP address without verifying the source addresses, which leads to malicious attacks on the network by forging the source address of packets. By source address spoofing, an attacker can disguise itself as a friendly host trusted by the target host and obtain unauthorized services. Then it can import attack traffic, attack network hosts, and achieve the purpose of maliciously stealing network data, spreading malicious software, etc. The attack based on forged source address is difficult to trace and seriously affects the network security.

The validation of the IP source addresses can ensure that each host in the network uses a legal and real address to access the network, which also makes

© The Author(s), under exclusive license to Springer Nature Switzerland AG 2022
X. Sun et al. (Eds.): ICAIS 2022, CCIS 1588, pp. 297–308, 2022.
https://doi.org/10.1007/978-3-031-06764-8_24

it easier to track traffic on the Internet and eliminate attacks on forged source addresses. And can ensure the safety and efficiency of flow scheduling in data centers [24,29,30]. In practical applications, the source address verification technology also has the benefits like the more convenient implementation of fine network management, more simplifier identity authentication and billing based on user address. Researchers have proposed many mechanisms of validation to resist the attack of source address spoofing, where the representative works include SPM [5], HCF [12], IPsec [13], DPF [21], and so on. Due to the lack of deployment incentives for internet service providers (ISPs) and the shortage of support for incremental deployment, these solutions have not been widely deployed over the Internet [25].

To overcome these challenges, Wu et al. proposed a hierarchical source address validation architecture (SAVA) [25] in the trusted Internet. As shown in Fig. 1, the architecture verifies the authenticity of source IP addresses from three levels, i.e., access subnet, intra-AS, and inter-AS. Based on SAVA, this paper summarizes the protocols of source address validation in the view of the three layers. In the local subnet, the source address validation uses packet monitoring to establish rules and locate forged packets. The switch that performs the first hop of forwarding can filter out forged packets and discard them according to the rules, which realize source address authentication of host granularity. In the intra-AS, the source address validation is mainly used to filter forged messages initiated by users in the domain, it has a moderate deployment cost and complicates with the local subnet layer to construct a complete intra-domain defense system. As the unique defense layer that can filter forged packets in foreign domains, source address validation in the inter-AS has the coarsest filtering granularity, lower deployment cost, and better scalability. Source address authentication protocol testing is the validation of source address validation technology, which is crucial in ensuring the accuracy of source IP addresses. We will discuss it in detail in this paper.

The rest of this paper will be organized as follows. We'll introduce source address authentication for the local subnet in detail in Sect. 2. In Sect. 3, we discuss source address authentication protocols within autonomous systems. Section 4 illustrates the source address authentication protocols among inter-AS, and at the end of Sects. 2–4, these protocols are summarized successively. In Sect. 5 of this paper, we summarize the existing source address authentication protocol testing techniques. In Sect. 6, we propose possible future research directions of source address authentication technology, and in Sect. 7 we summarize the whole paper.

## 2   Local Subnet Source Address Validation

The local subnet is located at the bottom of the three-layer SAVA defense architecture. The source address validation protocols of this layer ensure that users of the local subnet cannot initiate source address forgery. The Internet Engineering Task Force (IETF) set up a working group named source address validation

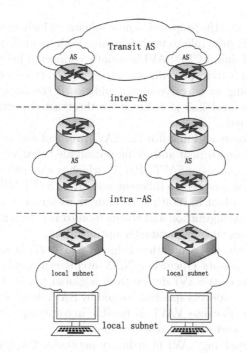

**Fig. 1.** Source address validation architecture [25].

improvement (SAVI) to promote the standardization of source address authentication schemes for access networks. In the recent decade, many scholars proposed a variety of SAVI schemes for different address allocation methods. Some of these schemes have become Request for Comments (RFC) and have been deployed on the networks, such as SAVI-DHCP [4], SAVI-SEND [3], FCFS-SAVI [19], and so on. Other experimental schemes also contribute to the improvement of the local subnet source address authentication scheme. The following briefly introduces several classic local subnet source address validation techniques.

DHCP [7] is the Dynamic Host Configuration Protocol. In DHCP, a host requests an address, and the server responds to the request and allocates available addresses in the address pool. SAVI-DHCP [4] is deployed on SAVI devices to monitor DHCP address assignment and set up the bindings. The forged IP address does not have a valid DHCP allocation process and cannot be bound. Therefore, the SAVI device detects and filters the attack packets with fake source addresses.

Bagnulo M et al. [3] proposed a technology, which uses the secure neighbor discovery (SEND) [2] protocol to provide source address validation. The main principle of this mechanism is that the SEND-SAVI devices form a protection circle. And only when a data packet enters the circle, then the system verifies it, instead of verifying data packets in every SEND-SAVI device that passes through. Therefore, SEND-SAVI prevents the host from generating packets containing IPv6 source addresses that are disconnected from the link.

Nordmark E et al. [19] proposed a new scheme, which uses the First Come First Served (FCFS) principle to provide source address authentication for IPv6 networks. In a local link, FCFS-SAVI is usually connected between a host and a router. And its goal is to inspect the stream generated from a host connected to a local link containing an effective source address. If the data packet generated by the host on the local link is received by the trusted port, it is forwarded, otherwise, it is filtered.

In order to configure and monitor the SAVI protocol and help find configuration errors in SAVI deployment and configuration file behavior of terminal hosts, Changqing An et al. proposed SAVI-MIB [1], which is a management information database that can be adapted to different scenarios. SAVI-MIB is implemented in switches and can adapt to multiple IP address assignment methods, covering all aspects of SAVI configuration and status monitoring. In addition, SAVI-MIB also has multiple uses such as parameter optimization.

Virtual source Address Validation Edge (VAVE) [27] is an improved SAVI mechanism. VAVE adopts OpenFlow/NOX architecture, which can know the verification rules on each SAVI device from a global perspective, which solves the problem of source address spoofing caused by SAVI devices not knowing each other's information. Because VAVE is flexible in verifying source addresses, it reduces processing overhead and resource footprint.

In addition to applying SAVI in ordinary networks, Bingyang Liu et al. [17] also implemented SAVI function in software defined network (SDN). The new scheme SDN-SAVI is a module or application on the controller. Compared with the traditional SAVI scheme, the main feature of this scheme is that there is no need to make the switch support SAVI, only the SDN-SAVI module needs to be integrated on the controller to enforce SAVI.

In order to enable SAVI to be deployed in IPv4/IPv6 transition scenarios and meet all the requirements of various transformation scenarios, Guangwu Hu et al. [10] proposed a source address verification and backtracking framework based on universal SAVI in IPv4/IPv6 transformation scenarios. The principle of the scheme is to extract the basic and universal attributes in the transformation scenes and improve each attribute to form a sub-solution. Then, according to several attributes, researchers can arbitrarily combine them to propose different transformation technologies with corresponding sub-solutions of attributes. The advantage of this technology is that it can be applied to any transition scenario of IPv4/IPv6.

The most important feature of local subnet source address validation is to achieve host-granular source address validation and to defend against the source address forgery attack initiated by the host. Finer-grained source address authentication provides more precise protection and source traceability. Compared with source address validation within and among autonomous systems, local subnet source address validation can achieve finer-grained filtering. However, it is difficult to update all access network devices due to the high overhead of actual deployment and it cannot ensure that the foreign-domain messages it receives will not be forged. At present, the source address validation technology of the local subnet has been standardized, and the related research is also tending to be mature.

# 3 Intra-AS Source Address Validation

The access subnet can achieve more fine-grained source address verification than intra-AS, but its deployment cost is very high. Therefore, validation of source addresses among routers in the autonomous systems is very necessary. The source address validation in the autonomous domain is located in the middle layer of SAVA, it provides source address authenticity authentication at the management domain network prefix level. Following is a brief introduction to the research.

To solve the Denial of Service (DoS) problem, Ferguson P et al. [8] proposed a network ingress filtering method. This method sets ingress filtering on the router so that only specified IP data packets can be forwarded. Forged IP data packets will be discarded. Although the method cannot completely filter packets with forged source addresses, it can lock the attack place within the range of known network prefixes, making tracing easier. This method provides a basis for source address validation and greatly improves the security of the network.

Routing-based distributed packet filtering (DPF) [21] is a new distributed denial of service (DDOS) attack prevention method. This approach relies on routing information to determine whether packets arrive at routers, including those located at the boundaries of autonomous systems. According to the routing information, when forged packets arrive at the router, they are identified and filtered. The method achieves two objectives are that actively preventing spoofed packets from reaching their destination and passively identifying their source.

Pengxu Tan et al. [23] proposed a new defense technology to prevent source address spoofing attacks. It is a hierarchical source address validation (HSAV) technology based on encrypted generated addresses. In HSAV, it uses a hash algorithm to generate IP addresses and then verifies the source address in two layers, namely the local subnet layer and the intra-AS layer. Experimental results show that the technology can verify the accuracy of the source address at a lower cost. But it has not yet been deployed on a large scale. Therefore, researchers can have further progress and breakthroughs in large-scale deployment.

AS the topology of intra-AS is more stable than that of inter-AS, it is not difficult to establish accurate filtering rules by obtaining the address allocation and routing policies of intra-AS. However, it lacks the defense capability against external domain attacks, and the defense cost is higher than inter-AS source address authentication. However, at present, the research of source address authentication in the autonomous system is relatively few.

# 4 Inter-AS Source Address Validation

As the uppermost layer of SAVA, the defense mechanisms of source address authentication among inter-AS are different from the other two layers. In inter-AS, source address authentication shares filtering feature rules between different autonomous systems to identify and filter forged packets from source addresses outside the domain. As source address authentication in inter-AS has the coarsest filtering granularity, it has lower deployment costs, higher deployment incentives, and better scalability in practical applications.

The current inter-AS source address validation schemes can be divided into three categories: schemes based on labeling, schemes based on routing, and incentive deployment. We classify the researches according to these three types as follows.

## 4.1 Based on Labeling

The core idea of the labeling-based verification schemes is to attach verifiable source address information in the form of a label to the data message. The two parties in the communication negotiate beforehand the validation ID that can be verified by each other. This ID is loaded into the data message in the communication process for the receiver to confirm the identity. If a message passes the validation of the receiver, the communication peer is authentic and will receive the message; otherwise, the message is discarded as a forgery. Following are some typical technologies.

Unlike standard ingress filtering technology, which is done close to the source address, Spoofing Prevention Method (SPM) [5] mainly validates the source address authenticity on the router close to the destination. The core idea of SPM is to establish a secure association (SA). In the SA system, each pair of source-destination networks has a unique key mark. ISPs can mark packets with the key in the domain known only to the members of the SA. Each packet arriving at the destination address is checked for the key. If the packet is not from the source network, the packet is discarded. SPM has lower costs and higher deployment incentives compared to ingress filtering.

To achieve a lighter-weight labeling-based packet forwarding and validation, Jie Li et al. [14] proposed an inter-AS source address verification technology VIP based on multi-fence confrontation. VIP improves efficiency by using smart information labels and an extended MPLS-based cloud network. It also can reduce the load of forwarding tables and verification procedures, without negatively affecting the actual network and complicated operations. Experiments show that VIP enhances scalability, and it also promotes incremental deployment from a development perspective.

To enable source address verification to achieve hierarchical, lightweight, and loosely coupled goals, Jie Li et al. [15] proposed a layered, lightweight label replacement source address verification technology SafeZone. This scheme builds a trust alliance at each layer. Within the trust alliance, each member knows and trusts each other's label information, which facilitates the exchange of label information and reduces unnecessary overhead.

Although labeling-based source address authentication can effectively filter spoofing source addresses, it still has some problems such as insecure key negotiation, low efficiency of tag generation, and incompatibility with network functions. To solve the above problems, Yang X et al. [26] Proposed a safe, efficient, and compatible technology SEC. The main advantages of this technique are more convenient label generation and more secure key negotiation.

From the above schemes, it can be concluded that the deployment of labeling-based source address verification has a high incentive and has a good effect of filtering fraudulent traffic. However, this type of solution also has some short-comings, such as the need to add other tags to the data packet, which consumes more bandwidth resources, and therefore has a greater impact on the bandwidth-constrained ASes. In addition, labels are usually placed in extension packet headers, but the router may not recognize some packets with some labels and discard them.

## 4.2 Based on Routing

In a network attack based on source address spoofing, the attacker can only forge the source address information of the data packet, but cannot control the forwarding path of the message. Therefore, an inter-domain source address verification scheme based on the principle of routing technology is proposed. When a data packet with a forged source address enters from an illegal routing port, the router can perform authenticity verification to filter the forged packets.

Source Address Validity Enforcement (SAVE) [16] is a technology that filters forged packets by building an incoming expression on the router. The incoming table contains the interface information of the valid source address on the router, which can identify and filter the packets spoofing the source address. The bandwidth overhead of the SAVE is equivalent to that of the routing protocol, and the memory usage is small. However, there are still some problems, including not being conducive to large-scale deployment and insufficient security.

Routing-based solutions use routing information to construct filtering rules and then perform source address validation. This type of protocol does not need to add additional label information, and there is no risk of being discarded by the router. But they will add extra computational overhead to the router, and at the same time, they will not support some routing features. For example, the asymmetry of routing information between ASes will cause the verification schemes to fail.

## 4.3 Incentive Deployment

Although some source address validation solutions have been standardized by the IETF, few ISPs are willing to adopt them due to insufficient deployment benefits. Some source address validation solutions face the problem of lack of deployability. Therefore, researchers have proposed some frameworks or schemes to reduce deployment difficulty and increase deployment enthusiasm.

Saurabh S et al. [22] proposed a deployment scheme that uses some special path backscatter messages generated by spoofed traffic to study source address validation filtering. Researchers provide a set of spoofing and non-spoofing ASes, and the construction of this list will help ASes to deploy source filtering to combat spoofing. In addition, it will improve the reputation and incentives for AS to deploy source filtering. However, the data set used in this work is not complete and it may be that the result of non-spoofing AS is not accurate enough.

The source address can sometimes be a victim of reflection flooding, causing the correct IP address to be filtered. To prevent this possibility, Yihao Jia et al. [11] proposed a safe and reliable service Inter-AS Source Address Protection (ISAP). The working mechanism of ISAP is to increase the probability that the source address remains within the possible range of the system, to improve the ability to prevent source IP address spoofing, and also improve the ability of incremental deployment. This service has huge commercial prospects, and once it is launched and implemented, it can be launched steadily. However, the ISAP service also has the weakness of being easily replaced by more efficient methods, because it is a completely decoupled structure.

To achieve deployment incentives, Jiamin Cao [6] proposed a decentralized cross-autonomous SAV service framework pSAV. The design principle of the framework is to treat SAV as a paid service and divide participants into service subscribers, providers, and auditors. So that the effect of deployment incentives can be achieved. On the control plane, the pSAV service performance is higher. On the data plane, pSAV can provide various high-throughput SAV services.

From the above source address validation protocols based on incentive deployment, we can draw the following inspiration. To benefit the first-deployed ASes, such as the guarantee of security and the support of finance, researchers need to provide more scalable solutions. These schemes can encourage more ASes to participate in deployment and implementation, which can achieve higher benefits and form a virtuous cycle.

Source address validation in inter-AS can be implemented either by appending information to the packet header or by adding functions on the router. As the only scheme that can resist attacks outside the domain, it is a supplement to source address validation protocol in local access subnet and intra-AS. And it has good performance and high scalability. There are already some incremental deployment schemes that provide some ideas for the promotion of source address validation protocol for inter-AS.

## 5    Testing of Source Address Validation Protocol

The flaws in the source address validation scheme may result in serious security consequences. It may be introduced by incomplete design or conflicts in implementation. The former is more fatal because it makes implementation fragile. The source address verification protocol testing is an important technology to ensure the reliability of the source address. We introduce several classic source address validation protocol testing methods as follows.

Li Zhou et al. [31] proposed a universal technology for protocol testing, incorporating the use of SPIN model checker for validation and the use of formal test language TTCN-3 for protocol testing. This method uses a threat model to model malicious entities and imports information security classification to achieve a complete analysis of the security requirements for protocol validation. The spin tracking to TTCN-3 conversion tool has also been developed to automatically generate test cases based on counterexamples obtained from model checking. This method has been applied in the SAVI, and two versions of the DHCP protocol have been tested for security, and security vulnerabilities have been discovered and tested in the corresponding implementation. However, this method still has the disadvantages that the classification of security requirements is not detailed enough and the test cases generated by st2ttcn only use one test component, and cannot support the distributed test architecture with multiple test components.

Because in the SAVI protocol, there are parallel components that depend on other component variables, it is not feasible to specify such a protocol with a single model. Jiangyuan Yao et al. [28] proposed a method named parallel parameterized extended finite state machine, which includes a new formal model to describe the protocol that depends on parallel work. And they also proposed a new test generation method. Through the actual SAVI protocol test and the test on 10 devices from 4 manufacturers, the effectiveness of the method is verified.

To fill the shortage in the testing of source address validation protocol for SDN, Meena R C et al. [18] proposed a test platform based on the RYU SDN controller. It is mainly used for testing performance and developing source address validation protocols in the SDN environment. The testbed has passed the technical test, the experiments prove that it can successfully test some proposed source address validation protocols, and can support protocol development well. It has the advantages of high efficiency and low cost.

By analyzing the work of source address authentication protocol testing mentioned above, it can be found that the testing process is to build a source address authentication protocol model firstly and then test the protocol on this model to find flaws. Source address authentication protocol testing plays an important role in ensuring the accuracy of source addresses. Researchers have made progress in this area, but there are still many source address authentication schemes that have not been tested, which also provides more opportunities for improvement in our future work.

# 6   Future Research Prospects

Through the above description of the related work, we can see that the protocols of source address validation are improving step by step. But there are few researches on source address validation in intra-AS, and the testing of source address validation protocol needs to be further promoted. This also provides a reference for our possible future research directions.

(1) The protocol of source address validation in the intra-AS is the middle layer of SAVA, which plays an important role in connecting the inter-AS layer and the local subnet layer. It is necessary to ensure the credibility of the source addresses at the prefix level. At the same time, it also has the advantage of lower overhead than the local subnet. However, there are currently few source address verification protocols in the intra-AS. To carry out large-scale deployment, the new intra-AS solutions should have a corresponding

deployment incentive mechanism. Researchers should also consider the coordination of the new protocol of source address validation in the inter-AS with existing protocols in the local subnet and inter-domain.

(2) The testing work of source address validation protocol is mainly concentrated in the local subnet, but it is insufficient within and between autonomous systems. Researchers can devote to the study on testing of these two levels. And they can also consider integrated testing of multiple protocols, such as the combination of local subnets and intra-AS, and the combination of the local subnet and inter-AS, etc.

(3) The validation method helps to find defects in the design and the testing method is helpful for troubleshooting errors in the implementation. For some protocols under development, the design may be imperfect and the implementation may have errors. Therefore, researchers can try to combine protocol verification and protocol testing in the process of protocol development and run logs for exception checking [9,20] at the same time, so that both design defects and implementation errors can be found.

## 7   Conclusion

The protocol of source address validation contributes to the fight against source address spoofing attacks. This paper starts with the SAVA, and then analyzes the related work of source address validation protocols in the view of the local subnet, intra-AS, and inter-AS. Then we summarize the advantages and disadvantages of the existing protocols. On this basis, we review the relevant research on the testing of source address validation protocols, and present the technical challenge in this direction. Finally, we discuss the possible research issues, where we will study these topics in the future.

**Acknowledgement.** This work was supported by the Hainan Provincial Natural Science Foundation of China (2019RC096, 620RC560, 620RC562), the Scientific Research Setup Fund of Hainan University (KYQD(ZR)1877), the Program of Hainan Association for Science and Technology Plans to Youth R&D Innovation (QCXM201910), and the National Natural Science Foundation of China (61802092, 62162021).

## References

1. An, C., Wang, H., Yang, J.: Mib design and application for source address validation improvement protocol. In: 2011 IEEE Symposium on Computers and Communications (ISCC), pp. 677–680. IEEE (2011)
2. Arkko, J., Kempf, J., Zill, B., Nikander, P.: Rfc3971-secure neighbor discovery (send). Internet Engineering Task Force (2005)
3. Bagnulo, M., Garcia-Martinez, A.: Secure neighbor discovery (send) source address validation improvement (savi). A. Garcia-Martinez, Bagnulo (2014)
4. Bi, J., Wu, J., Yao, G., Baker, F.: Source address validation improvement (savi) solution for dhcp. RFC 7513 (2015)

5. Bremler-Barr, A., Levy, H.: Spoofing prevention method. In: Proceedings IEEE 24th Annual Joint Conference of the IEEE Computer and Communications Societies, vol. 1, pp. 536–547. IEEE (2005)
6. Cao, J., Liu, Y., Liu, M., He, L., Jia, Y., Yang, F.: psav: A practical and decentralized inter-as source address validation service framework. In: 2021 IEEE/ACM 29th International Symposium on Quality of Service (IWQOS), pp. 1–7. IEEE (2021)
7. Droms, R.: Stateless dynamic host configuration protocol (dhcp) service for ipv6. Technical report, RFC 3736, April 2004
8. Ferguson, P., Senie, D.: rfc2827: network ingress filtering: defeating denial of service attacks which employ ip source address spoofing (2000)
9. Han, S., Wu, Q., Zhang, H., Qin, B., Hu, J., Shi, X., Liu, L., Yin, X.: Log-based anomaly detection with robust feature extraction and online learning. IEEE Trans. Inf. Forensics Secur. **16**, 2300–2311 (2021)
10. Hu, G., Xu, K., Wu, J., Cui, Y., Shi, F.: A general framework of source address validation and traceback for ipv4/ipv6 transition scenarios. IEEE Network **27**(6), 66–73 (2013)
11. Jia, Y., Liu, Y., Ren, G., He, L.: Revisiting inter-as ip spoofing let the protection drive source address validation. In: 2017 IEEE 36th International Performance Computing and Communications Conference (IPCCC), pp. 1–10. IEEE (2017)
12. Jin, C., Wang, H., Shin, K.G.: Hop-count filtering: an effective defense against spoofed ddos traffic. In: Proceedings of the 10th ACM Conference on Computer and Communications Security, pp. 30–41 (2003)
13. Kent, S., Atkinson, R.: Rfc2401: security architecture for the internet protocol (1998)
14. Li, J., Bi, J., Wu, J., Zhang, W.: A multi-fence countermeasure based inter-domain source address validation method. In: 2012 IEEE 11th International Symposium on Network Computing and Applications, pp. 259–262. IEEE (2012)
15. Li, J., Wu, J., Xu, K.: Safezone: A hierarchical inter-domain authenticated source address validation solution. In: 2011 IEEE Global Telecommunications Conference-GLOBECOM 2011, pp. 1–6. IEEE (2011)
16. Li, J., Mirkovic, J., Wang, M., Reiher, P., Zhang, L.: Save: source address validity enforcement protocol. In: Proceedings. Twenty-First Annual Joint Conference of the IEEE Computer and Communications Societies, vol. 3, pp. 1557–1566. IEEE (2002)
17. Liu, B., Bi, J., Zhou, Y.: Source address validation in software defined networks. In: Proceedings of the 2016 ACM SIGCOMM Conference, pp. 595–596 (2016)
18. Meena, R.C., Bundele, M., Nawal, M.: Ryu sdn controller testbed for performance testing of source address validation techniques. In: 2020 3rd International Conference on Emerging Technologies in Computer Engineering: Machine Learning and Internet of Things (ICETCE), pp. 1–6. IEEE (2020)
19. Nordmark, E., Bagnulo, M., Levy-Abegnoli, E.: Fcfs savi: first-come first-served source address validation improvement for locally assigned ipv6 addresses. Request for Comments 6620 (2012)
20. Park, J., Kim, J., Gupta, B., Park, N.: Network log-based ssh brute-force attack detection model. CMC-Computers Mater. Continua **68**(1), 887–901 (2021)
21. Park, K., Lee, H.: On the effectiveness of route-based packet filtering for distributed dos attack prevention in power-law internets. ACM SIGCOMM Comput. Commun. Rev. **31**(4), 15–26 (2001)

22. Saurabh, S., Sairam, A.S.: Inferring the deployment of source address validation filtering using silence of path-backscatter. In: 2018 Twenty Fourth National Conference on Communications (NCC), pp. 1–6. IEEE (2018)
23. Tan, P., Jia, H., Chen, Y., Mao, J.: A hierarchical source address validation technique based on cryptographically generated address. In: 2011 IEEE International Conference on Computer Science and Automation Engineering, vol. 2, pp. 33–37. IEEE (2011)
24. Wang, Z., et al.: Efficient scheduling of weighted coflows in data centers. IEEE Trans. Parallel Distrib. Syst. **30**(9), 2003–2017 (2019)
25. Wu, J., Ren, G., Li, X.: Building a next generation internet with source address validation architecture. Sci. China Series F: Inf. Sci. **51**(11), 1681–1691 (2008)
26. Yang, X., Cao, J., Xu, M.: Sec: Secure, efficient, and compatible source address validation with packet tags. In: 2020 IEEE 39th International Performance Computing and Communications Conference (IPCCC), pp. 1–8. IEEE (2020)
27. Yao, G., Bi, J., Xiao, P.: Source address validation solution with openflow/nox architecture. In: 2011 19th IEEE International Conference on Network Protocols, pp. 7–12. IEEE (2011)
28. Yao, J., Wang, Z., Yin, X., Wu, J.: Testing of a source address validation protocol with parallel parameterized extended finite state machines. In: Proceedings of the 7th Asian Internet Engineering Conference, pp. 152–155 (2011)
29. Zhang, H., Shi, X., Guo, Y., Wang, Z., Yin, X.: More load, more differentiation-let more flows finish before deadline in data center networks. Comput. Netw. **127**, 352–367 (2017)
30. Zhang, H., Shi, X., Yin, X., Ren, F., Wang, Z.: More load, more differentiation-a design principle for deadline-aware congestion control. In: 2015 IEEE Conference on Computer Communications (INFOCOM), pp. 127–135. IEEE (2015)
31. Zhou, L., Yin, X., Wang, Z.: Protocol security testing with spin and ttcn-3. In: 2011 IEEE Fourth International Conference on Software Testing, Verification and Validation Workshops, pp. 511–519. IEEE (2011)

# Preventing Price Manipulation Attack by Front-Running

Yue Xue[1], Jialu Fu[1], Shen Su[1(✉)], Zakirul Alam Bhuiyan[2], Jing Qiu[1], Hui Lu[1],
Ning Hu[1], and Zhihong Tian[1]

[1] Cyberspace Institute of Advanced Technology,
Guangzhou University, Guangzhou 510006, China
sushen@gzhu.edu.cn

[2] Department of Computer and Information Sciences, Fordham University, Bronx,
NY 10458, USA

**Abstract.** Decentralized finance (DeFi), as one of the fastest growing directions in the field of decentralized applications based on blockchain and smart contract in the past two years, has attracted many participants and institutional investments, and represents a series of decentralized financial projects in the blockchain ecosystem behind it. The most noteworthy one is the Flash-loan based Price Manipulation Attack, which uses a series of new features of DeFi such as flash loan and liquidity pool, and the attack is complex and diverse, leading to the inability of traditional smart contract vulnerability mining means to effectively. In this work, we focus on detecting flash loan-based price manipulation attacks on DeFi applications, which exploit the DeFi project's simple inquiry mechanism to gain large profits by manipulating users' crypto asset prices. To this end, we propose a detector embedded in the blockchain client to detect whether the user's crypto asset price is manipulated by monitoring the transaction execution process in real time, and innovatively propose the use of a front-running attack for remediation based on the amount of profit made by the attacker, solving the problem that the relevant attack can only be detected but not defended against, and reducing the possible financial loss to the DeFi project.

**Keywords:** Blockchain · Smart contract · Decentralized finance · Defi · Security

## 1 Introduction

Decentralized Finance (DeFi) is a broad concept representing a series of application ecologies, technical architectures, and financial models that have emerged in the last two years that combine blockchain and smart contract technologies. DeFi emerged in 2019 and has exploded in the last two years. The total value locked of DeFi reached $160 billion in 2021 and appears hundreds of DeFi projects, with an ecology spanning many public chains such as Ethereum [1], BSC [2], Polygon [3].

However, DeFi is not without its corresponding risks; from February 2020 to 2 to October 2021, the DeFi ecosystem experienced more than 100 security incidents, resulting in financial losses of more than $1.8 billion, costing a large number of participants and causing users to question the DeFi ecosystem seriously.

© The Author(s), under exclusive license to Springer Nature Switzerland AG 2022
X. Sun et al. (Eds.): ICAIS 2022, CCIS 1588, pp. 309–322, 2022.
https://doi.org/10.1007/978-3-031-06764-8_25

Among the security incidents that occurred in DeFi, the flash loan-based price manipulation attack attracted a lot of attention due to its complex logic and severe losses. Where attackers used a large amount of money obtained from flash loans to manipulate the inquiry mechanism of decentralized financial instruments to obtain abnormal rewards, in the past year, such attacks occurred more than 20 times and caused hundreds of millions of dollars in losses, due to the new DeFi features involved and the complex and diverse attack logic, making traditional smart contract vulnerability detection difficult to detect and extremely hard to defend against.

For this reason, many researchers have conducted to detect possible price manipulation attacks, but while related research has proposed more effective and accurate detection methods and found unnoticed price manipulation attacks, it is still impossible to effectively remedy the attacks once they occur because it is only geared towards detection and no corresponding defenses exist.

In summary, our work presents an attack detection method geared towards timely and effective defense against flash loan-based price manipulation attacks in DeFi projects and innovatively proposes the use of preemption to remediate possible attacks and minimize the damage caused by the attacks.

Our work can be divided into three parts: preparation, anomaly detection, and anomaly handling: In preparation, we use the transaction collector embedded in the blockchain client to collect a large amount of detailed transaction information and use it to analyze the liquidity pool address data set, as well as the liquidity pool reserve and the anomaly benchmark of token exchange operation; In anomaly detection, we use the liquidity pool data detector embedded in the blockchain client to perform Anomaly Detection on all operations against the liquidity pool during the execution of a transaction, collect the relevant abnormal information, and build an abnormal money flow tree to obtain the amount of loss caused by the attack; In anomaly handling, we use the robocalls to defend and analyze the feasibility based on the abnormal money flow tree and the loss amount caused by the attack. Section 5 will discuss them. Our main contributions are as follows:

- We propose a real-time anomalous fund flow detection method that generates anomalous money flow trees for detecting possible losses caused by attacks through a transaction detector embedded within the blockchain client.
- We propose a feasible attack defense scheme that minimizes the loss caused by an attack for remediation by pre-empting transactions and using the method of exiting liquidity.

## 2 Background

This section focuses on providing the necessary background information to better understand our work. The relevant background information can be divided into two parts: transaction and smart contracts, DeFi.

### 2.1 Transaction and Smart Contract

A transaction initiated by an external account that triggers a smart contract to modify the blockchain state is called transaction call; such an action triggered by a contract account is called message call. Since contracts can make complex calls to each other, a transaction call contains multiple message calls in the transaction history data, and the data of message calls can also reflect how a transaction is executed in a smart contract project.

In Ethereum and Ethereum-like blockchains, EVM is responsible for handling mutual calls between contracts, and each contract call is preceded by a snapshot backup of the current node database, which is stored in memory.

The global variables in a smart contract are stored in the storage structure, which is reflected in the node database as a key-value pair. Once a smart contract is created, the storage structure is already determined, and its location depends on the order in which the global variables are declared in the contract, while the content can be changed by the call to the contract.

### 2.2 DeFi

Monetary System, Decentralized Exchanges (DEXs) and Flash loan. DeFi utilizes a token system based on ERC-20 [4] standard to implement a monetary system, for represent various financial assets on DeFi. DEXs are token exchange protocols responsible for the free flow of assets on the chain based on smart contract. the current DEXs mainly use the automatic market maker model (AMMs), which are based on smart contracts and are responsible for maintaining a pool of liquid assets using a smart contract token account to provide a liquidity base for token swap.

Flash loan, an extremely innovative mechanism in the DeFi ecosystem, In simple terms, flash loan is an unsecured loan based on smart contracts. The two operations of borrowing and repaying are done in one transaction, without collateralizing any assets and only paying fees. User can use the borrowed assets to perform custom operations, they must return the borrowed money and fees in transaction, otherwise, the transaction will be revert. flash loan mechanism allows the user to obtain a large number of tokens within a transaction for such purposes as arbitrage, collateral exchange, etc.

## 3 Price Manipulation Attacks and Front-Running Attacks

In our work, we protect DeFi projects from Flash loan-based price manipulation attacks by front-running attacks, so it is necessary to introduce these attacks accordingly.

### 3.1 AMM Price Mechanism

In AMM, users can perform liquidity operations, token exchange. users trade through a liquidity pool built with smart contracts, which contains a reserve of two cryptocurrencies, which we call a Token Pair, and users can use the AMM-based pricing mechanism function to determine prices and trade tokens, which is $ReserveX \times ReserveY = K$, called CFMM (Constant Function Market Maker), simply means that when a user makes a token exchange, the user puts in one token of the currency pair to the liquidity pool, the liquidity pool issues another token of the corresponding currency pair to the user, and the code rules of the smart contract ensure that the reserves of the two tokens in the liquidity pool before and after the exchange, The product $K$ of $ReserveX$ and $ReserveY$ remains unchanged:

$$(ReserveX + X_{In}) \times (ReserveY - Y_{Out}) = ReserveX \times ReserveY = K \qquad (1)$$

where $X\_In$ is the number of tokens the user holds before the token exchange, and $Y\_out$ is the number of tokens the user can obtain, based on which any user can freely exchange tokens. At the same time, in the ideal state of infinite liquidity, i.e., when $ReserveX$ and $ReserveY$ are infinite, the exchange ratio of tokens $\frac{X\_In}{Y\_out}$ is approximately equal to the value of $\frac{ReserveX}{ReserveY}$.

### 3.2 Price Manipulation Attack Based on Flash Loan

The steps of this attack have very obvious features: borrowing, attacking, realizing, and returning. A typical case is the flash loan-based Price manipulation attack in Fig. 1. The attacker will obtain a large amount of token for the attack and return after the attack. In addition, the attacker will perform complex operations on the liquidity pool during the attack process, and these operations will significantly affect the liquidity pool's token reserve. The calculation of the value of the user's collateral assets in the inquiry mechanism of most money management applications relies on two kinds of data: (1) the exchange ratio of tokens in liquidity pool; and (2) the number of tokens held in liquidity pool. Due to the lack of effective regulatory mechanism of DeFi and the overly vulnerable design of the inquiry mechanism of DeFi tools, the attacker can conduct token reserve manipulation against the liquidity pool in DEXs to manipulate the inquiry results of DeFi tools and maliciously inflate the value of attacker's collateral assets, To achieve an abnormal number of reward tokens minted or an abnormal number of collateral exchanges.

A representative example is the Pancakebunny attack on May 20, 2021 [5], in which the attacker used the funds obtained from flash loan to indirectly manipulate the amount of BNB in the BUNNY-BNB liquidity pool to make it inflate significantly, thus obtaining a huge BUNNY minting reward (Fig. 1).

The steps of attack is followed: I. The attack gets enough attack funds through flash loan; II. The attacker uses the attack funds to manipulate the BNB-USDT V1 pool, and eventually, the number of BNBs in the BUNNY-BNB liquidity pool expands significantly; III. The victim project Pancakebunny uses The number of BNB in the inflated BUNNY-BNB liquidity pool to calculate the reward and mint an abnormal number of BUNNY tokens, about 6,970,000; IV. The attacker realizes the BUNNY tokens in the BUNNY-BNB pool, withdraws the tokens in the BUNNY-BNB pool before the attack, and returns the flash loan after gaining over 120,000 BNB.

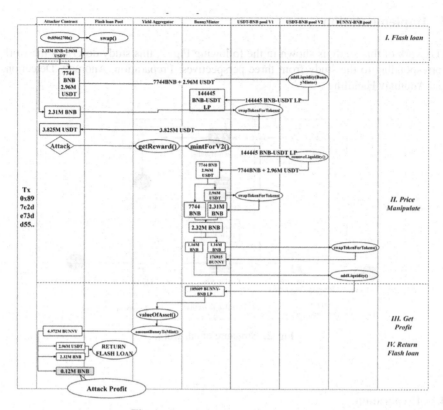

**Fig. 1.** Pancakebunny attack flowchart.

### 3.3 Front-Running Attack

Transactions are open and transparent to anyone in the transaction pool, and the order in which they are sent may be different from the order in which they are packaged, so before a transaction is packaged on the chain, the information of this transaction may be used maliciously and an attack can be reached by changing the order in which transactions are executed by higher gas fee based on packaged standard of miner. which is used to conduct front-running attacks on DEX, also known as sandwich attacks, and the most common front-running attack is the front-running attack based on token exchange.

User usually issues a transaction and makes a token exchange in the AMM-based Dex, using token X to buy token Y at a certain price, while for the Dex, this token exchange process will result in The price of Y to X in the liquidity pool increases. But the attacker sends a transaction to buy Y with X before the victim's transaction is executed by paying a higher gas fee to ensure he buys Y at a lower price. after the victim's transaction is executed, the attacker sends a transaction to sell Y for X and sells the Y in his hand at a higher price than the purchase price to earn the difference.

It is important to note that the front-running attack used in this paper is not based on token exchange behavior, but on liquidity removal behavior for front-running, which will be explained in detail in Sect. 4.3 of this study.

## 4   Implementation

The work of this study is shown in the following Fig. 2, this study describes the work corresponding to the study from three perspectives: Preparation, Anomaly Detection, and Anomaly Handling.

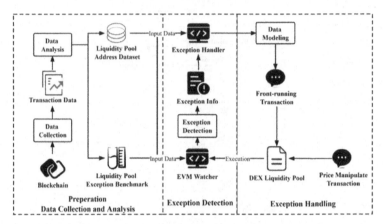

**Fig. 2.** Structure of our work.

### 4.1   Preparation

In preparation, to derive the address of the liquidity pool and the security limit of the liquidity operation, this study needs to collect and analyze the message invocation data of the liquidity pool in the transaction.

**Data Collection.** Some online data query services for Etherscan [6] currently exist, but these services are insufficient to support this study's analysis of message call data in smart contract transactions, our study modified the geth client and collected the metadata of transaction message calls in Etherscan and BSC through full node synchronization, including the caller, the called, the input and output of the message call and the depth of the message call of the transaction, and other information, which helps this study to make a complete judgment of one transaction.

**Data Analysis.** Since most of the attacks on the manipulated pools occurred in Uniswap on the Ethereum chain and Pancakeswap on the BSC chain, this study focuses on the transactions of these two DEXs, and mainly collects the following two kinds of data:

*Liquidity Pool Address of DEX.* In Uniswap or Pancakeswap, when creating Liquidity with Two key data remain unchanged: the called contract address ***Call_Callee*** is a determined Factory Address; the input parameter ***Call_input_data*** is a determined ***byte4*** type variable whose value is the Function selector of function ***createPair(tokenA,tokenB)***. Therefore, this study is based on these two parameters to search.

**Table 1.** Liquidity pool address dataset search method.

| Protocol | Search condition | Factory Address |
| --- | --- | --- |
| Uniswap | (Call_Callee==*Factory Address*)& (Call_input_data==c9c65396(*createPair Function Selector*)) | 0xcA143Ce32Fe78f1f7019d7d551a6402fC5350c73 *(Pancakeswap v2 factory)* |
| Pancakeswap | | 0x5C69bEe701ef814a2B6a3EDD4B1652CB9cc5aA6f *(Uniswap v2 factory)* |

**Liquidity Pool Anomaly Benchmark.** Based on the Liquidity Pool Address dataset collected in the previous step, to ensure that the statistical data are not disturbed by factors such as low liquidity pool transactions and low liquidity, our study selects several tokens commonly used on Ethereum and BSC with frequent liquidity and high transaction volume: ETH, BNB, USDT, and count the coin pair addresses based on ETH-USDT and BNB-USDT ad-dresses. The purpose of this study is to analyze the transaction data for these data to calculate the impact ratio of token exchange and liquidity operation on liquidity pool reserve for these liquidity pools, and to determine the Swap Impact Bench-mark (S) and Liquidity Operation Impact Benchmark (L), where the impact ratio is calculated as follows:

$$S = \left| \frac{\frac{Reserve_{Out}}{Reserve_{In}}}{\frac{Reserve_{Out}+Out}{Reserve_{In}-In}} - 1 \right| \times 100\% \qquad (2)$$

$$L = \left| \frac{Reserve\_0 \times Reserve\_1}{(Reserve\_0 + Token0\_Change) \times (Reserve\_1 + Token1\_Change)} - 1 \right| \times 100\% \qquad (3)$$

In Eq. (2), *Reserve_Out* and *Reserve_In* are the liquidity reserves of the two tokens before the token exchange; *Out* and *In* are the number of tokens decreased and increased during the token exchange process. In Eq. (3), *Reserve_0* and *Reserve_1* are the reserves before liquidity operation, and *Token0_Change* and *Token1_Change* are the numbers of token changes caused by liquidity operation.

Based on the above formula, the results of this study after conducting data statistics are as follows in Fig. 3, taking BNB-USDT and ETH-USDT token exchange data as examples. This study makes certain assumptions to determine the general case of token exchange and liquidity operation limit: taking into account the direction of the curve, Our study considers the ratio below 1% and above 99% as absolutely safe and dangerous, respectively. Based on this and the Dex front-end page limitation(10% in Uniswap, 15% in Pancakeswap), our study mainly counts the data of transactions with an impact ratio of 10%–99% in Uniswap, and the data of transactions with an impact ratio of 15%–99% in Pancakeswap to derive our limitation, below which the behavior is safe. It should be noted that our limitation is not the same for different tokens, take swap action in ETH-USDT and BNB-USDT as example, we conclude the limitation is below 31% and 35%.

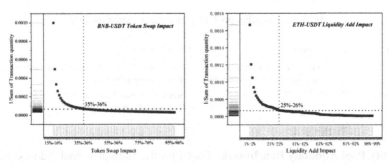

**Fig. 3.** Impact ratio of ETH-USDT and BNB-USDT in token swap and liquidity addition.

## 4.2 Anomaly Detection

Based on the liquidity pool address dataset in 4.1 and the liquidity pool anomaly limitation, our study has inserted a stake in EVM, called EVM Watcher, to monitor the change of token storage in the liquidity pool address before and after the contract call, and if the change exceeds the limitation, the anomaly message will be output and processed.

**Storage in Liquidity Pool Contract.** To obtain the reserve of liquidity pool, The subproblem is how to get the storage of the smart contract in EVM to get the liquidity pool token reserve data. For the contract, once it is written and uploaded, the storage location of the global variables in the contract storage is fixed, depending on the liquidity pool global variable storage address in the table below. *GetState(contract address, storage key)* in the *evm.go* file to obtain the variable data and data judgment of the specified address.

**Table 2.** Mainly storage slot in liquidity pool contract.

| Definition of global variable | Storage key | Description |
|---|---|---|
| uint112 private reserve0/1 | 0x08 | Current reserve of liquidity pool |
| uint public kLast | 0x0b | K value after the last operation |

**Liquidity Pool Anomaly Detection in EVM Watcher.** The process of Anomaly Detection is as follows: EVM Watcher records and evalu-ates the liquidity pool reserves before and after all contract calls based on the liquidi-ty pool address and the anomaly benchmark. If the benchmark value is exceeded, an anomaly message is an output, as follows in Fig. 4.

**Anomaly info Definition and Anomaly Fund Flow Tree.** We define the anomaly information and its storage method, all the anomaly liquidity operation behaviors of one transaction will be depicted as an anomaly fund flow tree. For the output abnormal money flow tree, this study mainly compares the value before the abnormality in the

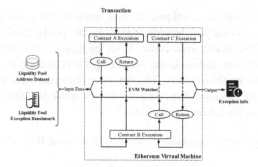

**Fig. 4.** EVM Watcher monitoring process.

first abnormal cash flow in a certain pool and the value after the abnormality in the last abnormal cash flow (as X1 and X7 in Fig. 5), to check whether there is a big change in the data in the liquidity pool after the transaction is executed, to determine whether there is an obvious liquidity behavior, and to extract the attacker's liquidity behavior and determine the attacker's profit token M and profit quantity N.

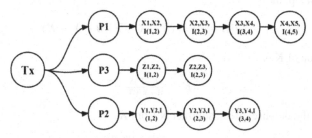

**Fig. 5.** The anomaly cash flow tree from anomaly messages, where *Pi* denotes different liquidity pools, *Xi, Yi, Zi, I(i, i + 1)* denotes the liquidity pool data before and after a message call and the anomaly ratio, including the two token reserves of liquidity pool.

### 4.3 Anomaly Handling

**Analysis.** Through the attacks in Fig. 1, we find that the Flash loan-based price manipulation attack liquidates the gained tokens through the liquidity pool at the end of the attack, and causes a liquidity pool to fluctuate drastically in terms of token reserves and cannot be recovered. Take *Pancakebunny* attack as an example, the attacker finally realizes the obtained BUNNY tokens in the BUNNY-BNB liquidity pool as BNBs, most of which are used to return the flash loan, and a small portion of BNBs are used as attack proceeds, the entire attack can be simplified as the attacker uses flash loan funds as an aid to obtain BUNNY through the price manipulation attack and extracts the BNB that was in the BUNNY-BNB liquidity pool before the attack occurred.

**Defense.** Our study proposes a defense method based on the above analysis: Since the attacker's calculation is based on the project and liquidity pool related data for calculation and flash loan, and the attack profit comes from the liquidity pool token reserve before the attack, so the defender can make the attacker get less attack gain when the attack is realized by withdrawing the liquidity. The defender can make the attacker's calculation go wrong and reduce the loss of the attack, or even make the attacker fail due to the inability to return the flash loan and its fee.

Before liquidity reserves are made to secure the defense, they are related as follows:

$$B = (A + S)(B - N) \tag{4}$$

where the value of N is:

$$N = \frac{BS}{A+S} \tag{5}$$

After liquidity reserve protection, suppose the defender discovers the attack and intends to exit liquidity for defense through front-running transaction, assuming that the platform tokens available to the attacker are still $S$. The state of the liquidity pool after the attack at this point is:

$$(A - X)(B - Y) = (A - X + S)(B - Y - K) \tag{6}$$

where the value of K is:

$$K = \frac{(B-Y)S}{A-X+S} \tag{7}$$

To clarify the defense effect, subtract N from K:

$$N - K = \frac{S(YS+AY-BX)}{(A+S)(A-X+S)} \tag{8}$$

It can be found that if we want to achieve the defense effect, we must satisfy $N - K > 0$, i.e.:

$$YS + AY - BX > 0 \tag{9}$$

Therefore, the liquidity reserve X, Y of the defender must satisfy:

$$\frac{X}{Y} < \frac{A+S}{B} \tag{10}$$

Because before and after adding liquidity reserve, X and Y satisfy the following equation:

$$\frac{X}{Y} = \frac{A}{B} \tag{11}$$

Bringing Eq. (11) into Eq. (10) finds that the equation always holds regardless of the values of X and Y. This means that any amount of controllable liquidity reserve can effectively reduce the attack loss by front-running the exit, so this defense is effective.

# 5  Opening Question and Future Work

Analyzing from the defense, under the precondition that the attacker makes flash loan, the defender can have the following options if he intends to front-running: (1) defense by controlling the liquidity pool price, but there may be a possibility that the defense transaction is monitored and exploited by a third party other than the attacker and the defender; (2) defense by adding liquidity and increasing the number of tokens in the liquidity pool, to reduce the attacker's influence on the liquidity pool price manipulation, however, the tokens paid in this way are far more than the attacker's flash loan funds. Because the amount of flash loan funds is very large, this way is unrealistic. (3) Minimize the loss of tokens when liquidity is realized by exiting liquidity, which is the method of this study, however, this requires the defender to have a certain amount of controllable liquidity within the liquidity pool. Based on the above analysis, this study argues that there are still some key follow-up questions:

- What is the difference between the anomaly benchmarks of different liquidity pools, can the anomaly benchmark be extended to other DeFi projects?
- Is there a better way to prevent liquidity pool manipulation in the defense process based on front-running?
- How to accurately quantify the amount of money lost based on flash loan data input?

# 6  Related Work

## 6.1  Smart Contract Vulnerability Detection and Audit

Since a large number of DeFi security risks such as Smart Contract Vulnerability, Code Reuse, Price Manipulation, and Flash loan contain some of the problems of smart contracts, many people have researched Smart Contract Vulnerability Detection, such as fuzzing-based [7–13]; Tools based on symbolic execution or CFG analysis [14–19]; Studies based on formal validation such as the formal verification framework [20–24]; Research based on machine learning methods [25–28].

However, traditional smart contract vulnerability detection cannot target specific vulnerabilities related to financial logic in DeFi. Therefore, there are studies specifically targeting smart contract security issues that may arise in DeFi. SciviK [29] is a proposed framework for specifying and verifying smart contracts, which uses an expressive annotation system, with EVM low-level execution semantics and SMT solvers to detect vulnerabilities included in DeFi smart contracts.

## 6.2  Transaction Data Analysis

In addition to smart contract vulnerability detection, the analysis of transaction data to determine attacks is an important research direction. The transaction data contain a wealth of token transfer records, so they can be used to analyze the data of DeFi-related operations to identify possible attacks: Chen [30] et al., TXSPECTOR [31], EthScope

[32] and XBlock-ETH [33] found historical attacks caused by Smart contract vulnerability based on transactions in Ethereum; Qin [34] et al. quantifies the pre-emption transactions due to Transaction Order dependency and MEV to identify possible pre-emption transactions based on transaction history data. DeFiRanger [35] proposes a method to prevent Price manipulation by recovering the transaction data as DeFi semantics and detecting attacks with the flow of funds. For the defense of the attack, BlockEye [36] uses the transaction data executed by the DeFi project To perform symbolic inference to detect the presence of Price manipulation vulnerabilities in the contract.

## 7   Conclusion

The objective of this study is to detect and defend against price manipulation attacks on DeFi applications in a timely and efficient manner by telemetry, and to this end, this study proposes a way to detect attacks based on abnormal financial flows of transactions and a defense approach based on front-running transactions to reduce financial, recommended that project owners or liquidity pool developers of DeFi applications should try to reserve controllable liquidity where problems may occur for effective defense.

**Acknowledgement.** This work was supported by National Key Research and Development Plan (Grant No. 2018YFB1800701), Key-Area Research and Development Program of Guangdong Province 2020B0101090003, ccf-nsfocus Kunpeng scientific research fund (CCF-NSFOCUS 2021010), National Natural Science Foundation of China (Grant No. 61902083, 62172115, 61976064), Guangdong Higher Education Innovation Group 2020KCXTD007 and Guangzhou Higher Education Innovation Group (No. 202032854), and Guangzhou fundamental research plan of "municipal-school" jointly funded projects (No. 202102010445), and Guangdong Province Science and Technology Planning Project (No. 2020 A1414010370).

## References

1. Ethereum (2022). https://ethereum.org/en/
2. Binance smart chain (2022). https://www.binance.org/en/smartChain. Accessed
3. Polygon (2022). https://polygon.technology/
4. ERC-20 token standard (2022). https://ethereum.org/en/developers/docs/standards/tokens/erc-20/
5. BSC flash loan attack: pancakebunny (2022). https://coindesk.cc/bsc-flash-loan-attack-Pancakebunny-34593.html
6. Etherscan (2022). https://etherscan.io/
7. Jiangb, L., Contractfuzzer, C.: Fuzzing Smart contracts for vulnerability detection. In: Proceedings of the 33rd ACM/IEEE International Conference on Automated Software Engineering-ASE 2018, pp. 259–269 (2018)
8. Grieco, G.: Echidna: effective, usable, and fast fuzzing for smart contracts. In: Proceedings of the 29th ACM SIGSOFT International Symposium on Software Testing and Analysis, pp. 557–560 (2020)
9. Huang, Y., Jiang, B., Chan, W.K.: EOSFuzzer: fuzzing eosio smart contracts for vulnerability detection. arXiv:2007.14903 (2020)

10. Nguyen, T.D.: sfuzz: an efficient adaptive fuzzer for solidity smart contracts. In: Proceedings of the ACM/IEEE 42nd International Conference on Software Engineering (2020)
11. Torres, F., Christof, Iannillo, A.K., Gervais, A.: Confuzzius: a data dependency-aware hybrid fuzzer for smart contracts (2021)
12. Wüstholz, V., Christakis, M.: Harvey: a greybox fuzzer for smart contracts. In: Proceedings of the 28th ACM Joint Meeting on European Software Engineering Conference and Symposium on the Foundations of Software Engineering (2020)
13. He, J.: Learning to fuzz from symbolic execution with application to smart contracts. In: Proceedings of the 2019 ACM SIGSAC Conference on Computer and Communications Security (2019)
14. Krupp, J., Rossow, C.: Teether: gnawing at ethereum to automatically exploit smart contracts. In: 27th USENIX Security Symposium (USENIX) Security, p. 18 (2018)
15. Luu, L., Chu, D.H., Olickel, H., Saxena, P., Hobor, A.: Making smart contracts smarter. In: Proceedings of the 2016 ACM SIGSAC Conference on Computer and Communications Security, pp. 254–269. (2016)
16. Mueller, B.: Reversing and bug hunting framework for the ethereum blockchain (2017). https://pypi.org/project/mythril/0.8.2/
17. Torres, C., Ferreira, J., Schütte, R., State: osiris: hunting for integer bugs in ethereum smart contracts. In: Proceedings of the 34th Annual Computer Security Applications Conference (2018)
18. Yang, Z.: Seraph: enabling cross-platform security analysis for EVM and WASM smart contracts. In: Proceedings of the ACM/IEEE 42nd International Conference on Software Engineering: Companion Proceedings (2020)
19. Wang, D., Jiang, B., Chan, W.K.: WANA: symbolic execution of wasm bytecode for cross-platform smart contract vulnerability detection. arXiv:2007.15510 (2020)
20. Bhargavan, K.: Formal verification of smart contracts: short paper. In: Proceedings of the 2016 ACM Workshop on Programming Languages and Analysis for Security (2016)
21. Hirai, Y.: Formal verification of deed contract in Ethereum name service (2016). https://yoi chihirai.com/deed.pdf
22. Kalra, S.: ZEUS: analyzing safety of smart contracts. In: NDSS (2018)
23. Tsankov, P.: Securify: practical security analysis of smart contracts. In: Proceedings of the 2018 ACM SIGSAC Conference on Computer and Communications Security (2018)
24. Tian, Z., Li, M., Qiu, M., Sun, Y., Su, S.: Block-DEF: a secure digital evidence framework using blockchain. Inf. Sci. **491**, 151–165 (2019)
25. Momeni, P., Wang, Y., Samavi, R.: Machine learning model for smart contracts security analysis. In: 2019 17th International Conference on Privacy, Security and Trust (PST), pp. 1–6 (2019)
26. Gao, Z., Jayasundara, V., Jiang, L., Xia, X., Lo, D., Grundy, J.: SmartEmbed: a tool for clone and bug detection in smart contracts through structural code embedding. In: 2019 IEEE International Conference on Software Maintenance and Evolution (ICSME), pp. 394–397 (2019)
27. Code coverage for solidity (2022). https://blog.colony.io/code-coverage-for-solidity-eecfa8 8668c2/
28. Lu, H., Jin, C., Helu, X., Zhu, C., Guizani, N., Tian, Z.: AutoD: intelligent blockchain application unpacking based on JNI layer deception call. IEEE Network **35**(2), 215–221 (2020)
29. Lin, S., et al.: SciviK: a versatile framework for specifying and verifying smart contracts. arXiv:2103.02209 (2021)
30. Chen, T., et al.: Dataether: data exploration framework for ethereum. In: 2019 IEEE 39th International Conference on Distributed Computing Systems (ICDCS). IEEE (2019)

31. Zhang, M., et al.: TXSPECTOR: uncovering attacks in ethereum from transactions. In: 29th USENIX Security Symposium (USENIX) Security, p. 20 (2020)

32. Wu, L., et al.: Ethscope: a transaction-centric security analytics framework to detect malicious smart contracts on ethereum. arXiv:2005.08278 (2020)

33. Zheng, P., et al.: Xblock-ETH: extracting and exploring blockchain data from Ethereum. EEE Open J. Comput. Soc. 1, 95–106 (2020)

34. Qin, K., Zhou, L., Gervais, A.: Quantifying blockchain extractable value: how dark is the forest? arXiv:2101.05511 (2021)

35. Wu, S., et al.: DeFiRanger: detecting price manipulation attacks on defi applications. arXiv:2104.15068 (2021)

36. Wang, B.: BLOCKEYE: hunting for defi attacks on blockchain. In: 2021 IEEE/ACM 43rd International Conference on Software Engineering: Companion Proceedings (ICSE-Companion) (2021)

# Information Hiding

# Two-Stage Robust Reversible Image Watermarking Based on Deep Neural Network

Jie Huang[1] , Fengyong Li[2,3,4](✉) , Lei Zhang[1], and Chuan Qin[1]

[1] School of Optical-Electrical and Computer Engineering, University of Shanghai for Science and Technology, Shanghai 200093, China
[2] College of Computer Science and Technology, Shanghai University of Electric Power, Shanghai 200090, China
fyli@shiep.edu.cn
[3] Guangxi Key Lab of Multi-Source Information Mining and Security, Guangxi Normal University, Guilin 541004, China
[4] Computer Science Department, University of Victoria, Victoria, BC, Canada

**Abstract.** This paper proposes a two-stage lossless robust watermarking scheme based on deep neural network. In the first stage, the encoder, noise layer and decoder network are combined to design an end-to-end network framework, which is used to train the input watermark information and cover image. In this framework, the encoder outputs a robust watermarked image whose visual quality is similar to the cover image, and the decoder can extract the embedded watermark information to evaluate robustness. In the second stage, by using reversible information hiding algorithm with extended prediction error, the auxiliary information that can recover the cover image is embedded into the robust watermarked image to ensure reversibility. If the watermarked image does not undergo attack processing, the hidden watermark information can not only be extracted, but also the cover image can be completely recovered. Even if the watermarked image does undergo attack processing, the embedded watermark information can also be extracted correctly because of the strong robustness in the first stage. Experimental results demonstrate the robustness of proposed scheme in terms of JPEG compression, gaussian filtering noise, rotation and shearing operations.

**Keywords:** Reversible information hiding · Robust watermarking · Deep neural network · Two-stage embedding · Noise simulation

## 1 Introduction

With the development of the Internet, digital watermarking technology is more and more widely used in the fields of copyright protection, traceability and integrity authentication of digital media. Traditional digital watermarking technology, including robust watermarking technology and reversible watermarking technology [1]. Robust watermarking technology provides invariable data information for the image without considering the content of the image. On the contrary, reversible watermarking technology is mainly used for the lossless embedding of data information [2], but ignores the anti-attack capability. In satellite images, medical images and micro-images, which require high fidelity and robustness of images, the irreversibility loss of robust watermarking and the vulnerability of reversible watermarking cannot be tolerated [3]. This makes researchers try to develop robust reversible watermarking algorithm. With no attack processing, robust reversible watermarking algorithm can extract the watermark and restore the cover image at the decoding end. Even if the marked image is attacked, although the reversibility is destroyed so that the cover image cannot be restored, the watermark information can be still correctly extracted.

Several robust reversible watermarking algorithms are introduced in the literature. De Vleeschouwer *et al.* early proposed robust reversible watermarking algorithm based on the histogram rotation technology of double mapping transformation [8]. Subsequently, Ni *et al.* improved De Vleeschouwer's scheme to avoid salt-pepper noise caused by histogram rotation. However, such improvement inevitably caused the error bit of overflow/underflow blocks (blocks with pixel value less than 0 or greater than 255) at the decoding end. Furthermore, Ni *et al.* adopted error correction coding to address this problem [9]. Zeng *et al.* divided the cover image into several non-overlapping blocks, calculated the arithmetic difference of each block and generated the corresponding histogram [10]. Gao *et al.* extended Zeng's scheme by using a more efficient statistic: the arithmetic mean, and generated a histogram of the arithmetic mean [11]. An *et al.* proposed a redundant histogram translation method based on wavelet domain, which used the coefficients of images after wavelet transformation to generate histograms [12]. However, this scheme may generate a higher distortion due to the larger offset. In addition, some methods used a location map to mark blocks that produce overflow, and the location map is transmitted to the decoder through an additional channel that is not available in practice [13]. They are also called the general histogram shift methods.

Contrary to the general histogram translation method, Coltuc *et al.* proposed a lossless robust watermarking algorithm based on a two-stage watermarking scheme [15]. As shown in Fig. 1, the algorithm consists of two stages. In the first stage (robust embedding stage), a robust watermarking algorithm is used to embed the watermark into the cover image to obtain the intermediate image. In the second stage (reversible embedding stage), the traditional reversible watermarking method is used to embed the auxiliary information needed to recover the robust embedding stage (difference between the cover and the intermediate image) into the intermediate image, and finally generate the marked image. Wang *et al.* improved Coltuc's two-stage watermarking framework and divided the original image into two independent embedding domains in the integer Haar wavelet transform domain [16]. Xiang *et al.* constructed a two-stage lossless robust watermarking algorithm against common geometric attacks by taking advantage of the geometric invariant features of images [17]. Overall, existing robust reversible watermarking and lossless robust watermarking techniques provide strong robustness for common processing operations, but, these methods cannot adapt to all attacks [19]. The classical robust reversible watermarking algorithm utilizes robust features related to the position of pixels, resulting in decoding failure against geometric attacks.

In this paper, we build an end-to-end trainable data hiding framework and use two convolutional networks to design a lossless robust image watermarking scheme. The

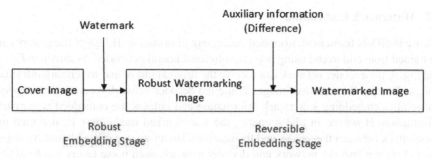

**Fig. 1.** The framework of the two-stage algorithm proposed by Coltuc.

encoder network receives the cover image and watermark information and outputs the encoded image (the robust watermarked image), while the decoder network receives the encoded image to extract the watermark information. In practical application scenario, the image between the sender and the receiver may be attacked by some malicious distortion (such as JPEG compression, rotation, scaling operation), a noise layer is built to simulate the attack processing between the encoder and decoder. We establish the target model of data hiding by minimizing the difference between the cover image and the encoded image and the difference between the input watermark information and the extracted watermark information. Since the difference between the cover image and the encoded image after training is small enough, the difference between the two can be used as auxiliary information to restore the cover image, and the reversible watermarking algorithm is used to embed the difference into the encoded image to obtain the final marked image. Experimental results verify that the robustness of proposed scheme in terms of JPEG compression, gaussian filtering noise, rotation and crop operations.

## 2 Proposed Watermarking Scheme

### 2.1 The Framework of Proposed Scheme

Proposed scheme builds two-stage embedding mode, and combines reversible watermarking algorithm to get the final watermarked image. Specifically, the watermark information is firstly embedded into the original image through HiDDeN network framework [18] to obtain the robust watermarked image. Furthermore, the reversible watermark algorithm is used to embed the difference between the robust watermarked image obtained in the first stage and the original image as auxiliary information into the robust watermarked image. Since there are various kinds of attack noises in real life, we add noise model into the encoding network and decoding network. The noise model is introduced to simulate the attack noise. Since The end-to-end neural network is used to train the encoder, decoder and noise model, the generated watermarked image can greatly improve the performance of noise attacks, such as JPEG compression, Gaussian filtering noise, rotation and other common noise attacks.

## 2.2   Watermark Embedding

We use HiDDeN framework to embed watermark information. HiDDeN framework can be trained from end to end using two convolutional neural networks. As shown in Fig. 2 and Fig. 3, the encoder network can receive the original image and watermark information, and output the encoded image. While the decoder network receives the encoded image after embedding watermark information and outputs the embedded watermark information. However, in real scenario, the watermarked image may be distorted by noise attack between the sender and the receiver. Therefore, we insert alternative noise layers between encoder network and decoder network, such noise layers can be JPEG compression, Gaussian low-pass filtering noise, rotation, etc. Our model is to take advantage of a learnable end-to-end network model that is robust to any noise attack. Therefore, our model includes the encoder $Encoder^\alpha$, the noise layer $Noiser$, the decoder $Decoder^\delta$, and the parameters $\alpha$ and $\delta$. The parameters $\alpha$ and $\delta$ are used for training. The encoder network $Encoder^\alpha$ receives the original image and the watermark information. The size of the original image $I$ is $C \times H \times W$, the watermark information $W$ is a binary string, and the length of the watermark information is $L$. The encoder network $Encoder^\alpha$ outputs the encoded image $I_{en}$ with the size of $C \times H \times W$. The noise layer $Noiser$ inputs the encoded image $I_{en}$, carries on the noise attack to the encoded image, and outputs the noisy image $I_{no}$. The decoder network $Decoder^\delta$ extracts watermark information $W'$ from the noisy image $I_{no}$.

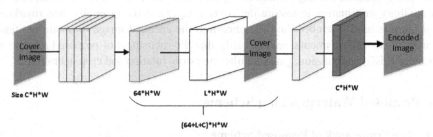

**Fig. 2.** Encoding framework of neural network.

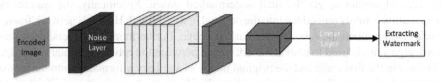

**Fig. 3.** Decoding framework of neural network.

Since the encoded image and the original image should be indistinguishable in the observation of human eyes, the image distortion loss $\mathcal{L}_I(I, I_{en})$ is used to represent the similarity between the original image $I$ and the encoded image $I_{en}$, while the distortion loss $\mathcal{L}_W(W, W')$ of watermark information is used to represent the similarity between the embedded and extracted watermark information.

$$\mathcal{L}_I(I, I_{en}) = \frac{\|I - I_{en}\|_2^2}{CHW} = \frac{\sqrt{\sum (I - I_{en})^2}}{CHW} \tag{1}$$

$$\mathcal{L}_W(W, W') = \frac{\|W - W'\|_2^2}{L} = \frac{\sqrt{\sum (W - W')^2}}{L} \tag{2}$$

where $\|x\|_2^2$ represents the L2 norm, and the Euclidean distance is the sum of squares of the elements of the $x$ vector.

In order to reduce the sum of image distortion loss and watermark distortion loss $S_{I,W}$, we conduct random gradient descent:

$$S_{I,W} = \mu \mathcal{L}_I(I, I_{en}) + \vartheta \mathcal{L}_W(W, W') \tag{3}$$

where $\mu$ represents the relative weight of controlling image distortion loss, and $\vartheta$ is the relative weight of controlling watermark information distortion loss.

Furthermore, we build the end-to-end network architecture. Firstly, for the encoding network, Conv, batch normalization (BN) and activation function (ReLU) are integrated into a Conv-BN-ReLU block. The convolution kernel of each block is $3 \times 3$, step size is 1, filling size is 1, output filter is 64, and the number of channels is 64. The original image with the size of $C \times H \times W$ is transitioned to the image with the size of $64 \times H \times W$ by four Conv-BN-ReLU blocks. Since the size of the watermark information is $L \times 1 \times 1$, in order to embed the watermark information into any position of the original image, the dimension of the watermark information needs to be consistent with the dimension of the transition representation of the original image. Therefore, the watermark information is extended as $L \times H \times W$, which can ensure that the whole watermark information can be accessed by the convolution filter. Then we overlay the previously generated original image transition representation, the extended watermark information and the original image to obtain the joint representation of $(64 + L + C) \times H \times W$. Finally, a Conv-BN-ReLU block and a convolution layer with a convolution kernel of $1 \times 1$, step size of 1 and number of output filters of C are passed. The output size is $C \times H \times W$ encoding image, which is the robust watermark transition image $I_{en}$ mentioned in the second stage.

For the noise layer, when the encoded image $I_{en}$ passes through the noise layer, the number of output channels is C, but the height and width of the noise image $I_{no}$ are not necessarily the same as the original image.

For the decoding network, after passing through 7 Conv-BN-ReLU blocks and a convolution kernel of $3 \times 3$, we can obtain the transition representation of $L \times H \times W$. Then, the watermark $W'$ of $L \times 1 \times 1$ size is extracted through the global spatial average pool homogenized on all spatial dimensions ($H \times W$) and the last $L \times L$ linear layer.

### 2.3 Auxiliary Information Embedding

In order to restore the original image $I$, it is necessary to embed the auxiliary information of the original image with reversible watermarking algorithm. In the first stage, the image distortion loss between the original image and the robust watermarked image $I_{en}$

(encoded image) is set, and a lot of training is carried out to make the loss $\mathcal{L}_1(I, I_{en})$ as small as possible, which also means a high similarity between the original image $I$ and the robust watermarked image $I_{en}$. In this way, the reversible watermarking algorithm can be used in the second stage [4]. If the difference is too large, reversible watermarking algorithm cannot be used to embed the difference in the second stage.

$$A = I - I_{en} \tag{4}$$

$A$ is the difference between the original image and the robust watermark image, which is the auxiliary information to be embedded in the second stage.

We adopted the prediction error expansion algorithm proposed by Thodi et al. [6].

$$p = \begin{cases} max(a, b) & if\ c \le min(a, b) \\ min(a, b) & if\ c \ge max(a, b) \\ a + b - c & otherwise \end{cases} \tag{5}$$

where $x$ in the table represents the original pixel value, $p$ in Eq. (5) represents the predicted pixel value, and a, b and c represent the pixel value around $x$ and $e$ is the prediction error

$$e = x - p \tag{6}$$

Subsequently, the prediction error value is added into auxiliary information $A$, and $n$ is the binary bit length of auxiliary information $A_i, i = 1, 2, \ldots, n$. We move the prediction error to the left by one bit, and insert the auxiliary information bits into the least-significant bits left vacant [5].

$$e' = 2e + A_i \tag{7}$$

where $e'$ represents the prediction error value after embedding information [7]. Therefore, the pixel value $x'$ after embedding information can be obtained as follows:

$$x' = e' + p = 2e + A_i + p = x + e + A_i \tag{8}$$

When extracting auxiliary information, the prediction error value $e'$ after embedding information is firstly calculated by using Eq. (5) and Eq. (6).

According to the inverse process of Eq. (7), the original prediction error value $e$ and embedded auxiliary information bits $A_i$ are obtained.

$$e = \lfloor e'/2 \rfloor \tag{9}$$

$$A_i = mod(e', 2) \tag{10}$$

Finally, the original pixel value $x$ is restored according to the inverse process of Eq. (8).

$$x = x' - e - A_i \tag{11}$$

According to Eq. (8), the size of the prediction error and the pixel value of any position determine whether the position can be expanded and embedded through the prediction error, and overflow may occur. When overflow occurs, these positions are skipped and other positions are embedded with information. At the same time, these overflow positions are recorded by location map and embedded after all auxiliary information is embedded. Finally, after the second stage of auxiliary information and location map embedded, the final watermarked image $I_w$ is obtained.

### 2.4 Watermark Extraction and Image Recovery

The decoding process includes extracting the watermark information and restoring the original image. When the watermarked image $I_w$ is processed without any noise attack, we can extract the watermark information and recover the original cover image by the following steps.

**Step 1:** The position map of the overflow block without embedded auxiliary information $A_i$ and the embedded auxiliary information $A_i$ are extracted by the inverse process of the prediction error extension algorithm.

**Step 2:** Restore the robust watermark transition image $I_{en}$.

**Step 3:** Extract the watermark information $W'$ from the robust watermark transition image $I_{en}$ through the coding network composed of Conv-BN-ReLU block, global spatial mean pool and linear layer.

**Step 4:** Obtain the original image according to the inverse process of Eq. (4):

$$I = A + I_{en} \tag{12}$$

When the watermarked image $I_w$ is attacked by noise, the first and second steps cannot be carried out due to the vulnerability of reversible watermarking algorithm, so we can only extract the watermark information $W'$ from the watermark image $I_w$ according to the decoding network.

## 3 Experimental Results and Discussions

In this part, we mainly test the robustness of the neural network model used in the first stage. COCO data set is used to give the testing results. When watermarked image is attacked by noise in transmission, we test the robustness to evaluate the effective of our scheme. In general, for digital watermarking, the priority of robustness is higher than that of embedding capacity and security. We apply different noise layers in training, and model learning is targeted at different noise layers to improve the robustness so that the final watermark image can still extract watermark information correctly when attacked by noise.

### 3.1 Robustness Test of Watermarking

In the first stage, we randomly choose color images from COCO data set to train our model. The size of color images is $C \times H \times W = 3 \times 128 \times 128$, and the length of watermark information is $L = 50$. We set the weight factors of image distortion loss and watermark distortion loss as $\mu = 0.7, \vartheta = 1$, respectively. During the training, 30-bit watermark information is embedded in original image, and four process models, including JPEG compression, Gaussian filtering noise, rotation and shearing, are used to simulate noise attacking. In this experiment, the rotation angle range is from $10°$ to $30°$ with an interval of $5°$. The crop scale factor is the ratio of the size of the image after cutting to the size of the original image and the range is from 0.3 to 0.9 with an interval of 0.2. For noise attacks, the quality factor for JPEG compression range is from 30 to 90 with an interval of 20, and the core size for Gaussian filtering range is from $2 \times 2$ to $5 \times 5$ with an interval of 1. In addition, robustness is evaluated by Bit Error Rate (BER in short), which is the ratio of the bits of the wrong watermark extracted by the decoding end to the length of the watermark. Generally, when BER is less than 20%, it means that the watermark can be detected.

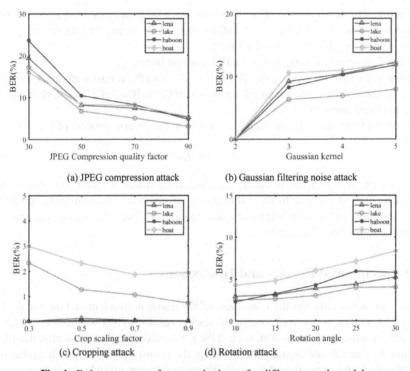

**Fig. 4.** Robustness test of proposed scheme for different attack models.

The corresponding experimental results are shown in Fig. 4. As can be observed from this figure, we can find that Lena, Lake, Baboon and Boat have good performance for JPEG compression attack, Gaussian filtering noise attack, shearing attack and rotation attack. For JPEG compression, when the quality factor is 30, the BER value of Baboon image exceeds 20%, and the BER value of the other three images is also around 20%. With the quality factor increasing, the BER value decreases. For Gaussian filtering noise, with the increase of Gaussian kernel, the BER value of the four images also increases, but it is still lower than 20%. For the crop operation, the BER values of four images in the range of 0.3 to 0.9 are relatively low, it means that proposed scheme has a good performance for crop attack. For the rotation operation, with the increase of rotation angle, the BER value of the four images also increases gradually, but, the BER value is still far less than 20%. Overall, proposed scheme shows a superior performance for different noise attack, this is mainly because when the neural network is trained, a specified noise layer is considered to build the simulation attack model. Even if the image is attacked by some specified noises, the enhanced robustness after a lot of training can effectively resist the noise attack.

## 3.2 Invisibility Test of Watermarking

In the second stage, to recover the original image, we embed the auxiliary information into the watermarked image to achieve the reversibility. Accordingly, the reversible embedding operation inevitably affect the invisibility of the watermark information. In order to verify the invisibility of watermark, we carried out experiments on four classical testing images, Lena, Lake, Baboon and Boat. In the experiment, 30-bits watermark information is used to provide the testing results. We simulate JPEG compression with a quality factor of 50, Gaussian filtering with a Gaussian kernel of $2 \times 2$, rotation of $15°$ and crop scale factor of 0.3, respectively. Table 1 presents PSNR values. From this table, we can see that after different noise attacks, most of the PSNR can maintain a high value, which means that the visual quality of the watermark image is better, and the invisibility of the watermark is higher.

**Table 1.** PSNR values of four images passing through four noise layers.

| Image | JPEG compression ($q = 50$) | Gaussian filter ($2 \times 2$) | Rotate ($15°$) | Crop ($p = 0.3$) |
|---|---|---|---|---|
| Lena | 35.27 | 40.13 | 38.84 | 39.35 |
| Lake | 36.42 | 39.85 | 39.27 | 37.69 |
| Baboon | 32.97 | 41.72 | 36.32 | 38.93 |
| Boat | 34.51 | 41.88 | 37.03 | 37.87 |

In addition, Table 2 presents the PSNR values of both the robust watermarked transition image and the marking image, respectively. As can be seen from this table, the PSNR values for two kinds of image are both greater than 38dB, which indicates that our scheme has a better invisibility for the embedded watermark. In fact, since the neural network model is trained in the first stage, the robust watermarked image (that is, the encoded image) had a better visual effect, while after the auxiliary information was embedded in the second stage, the PSNR values have a slight reduction, which implies that distortion is introduced due to the embedding of auxiliary information in the second stage.

**Table 2.** PSNR values of robust watermarked images $I_{en}$ and marked images $I_w$.

| Image | $I_{en}$ | $I_w$ |
|-------|----------|-------|
| Lena | 40.31 | 39.14 |
| Lake | 39.72 | 39.07 |
| Baboon | 39.58 | 38.59 |
| Boat | 40.71 | 38.67 |

## 4   Conclusions

In this paper, we proposed a two-stage robust reversible information hiding algorithm based on neural network, in order to solve the large difference between the original image and the robust watermark transition image. We used neural network to train a lot of loss values between the two images, so that the difference between the two images can be reduced, which is convenient for us to use reversible watermarking algorithm for embedding. In the proposed scheme, the original image can be recovered without any attack, and the watermark information can be extracted by decoding network. In the case of attack, watermark information can be extracted from the final watermarked image by decoding network. A series of experiments verified the robustness of our scheme in terms of JPEG compression, gaussian filtering noise, rotation and shearing operations. In future work, we will consider how to use the proposed robust reversible watermarking algorithm for audio and video content.

**Acknowledgement.** This work was supported by the Natural Science Foundation of China (62172280, U20B2051), the Shanghai Science and Technology Committee Capability Construction Project for Shanghai Municipal Universities (20060502300), the Natural Science Foundation of Shanghai (21ZR1444600, 20ZR1421600), and the Research Fund of Guangxi Key Lab of Multi-source Information Mining & Security (MIMS21-M-02).

## References

1. Ni, Z., Shi, Y.Q., Ansari, N., Su, W.: Reversible data hiding. IEEE Trans. Circuits Syst. Video Technol. **16**, 354–362 (2006)
2. Li, X., Zhang, W., Gui, X., Yang, B.: A novel reversible data hiding scheme based on two-dimensional difference-histogram modification. IEEE Trans. Inf. Forensics Secur. **8**(7), 1091–1100 (2013)
3. Ou, B., Li, X., Zhao, Y., Ni, R., Shi, Y.Q.: Pairwise prediction-error expansion for efficient reversible data hiding. IEEE Trans. Image Process. **22**(12), 5010–5021 (2013)
4. Ou, B., Li, X., Zhang, W., Zhao, Y.: Improving pairwise pee via hybrid dimensional his- togram generation and adaptive mapping selection. IEEE Trans. Circuits Syst. Video Technol. **29**, 2176–2190 (2018)
5. Tian, J.: Reversible data embedding using a difference expansion. IEEE Trans. Circuits Syst. Video Technol. **13**, 890–896 (2003)

6. Thodi, D.M., Rodriguez, J.J.: Expansion embedding techniques for reversible watermarking. IEEE Trans. Image Process. **16**(3), 721–730 (2007)
7. Coltuc, D.: Improved embedding for prediction-based reversible watermarking. IEEE Trans. Inf. Forensics Secur. **6**(3), 873–882 (2011)
8. Vleeschouwer, C.D., Delaigle, J.F., Macq, B.: Circular interpretation of Bijective doubling in lossless watermarking for media asset management. IEEE Trans. Multimedia **5**(1), 97–105 (2003)
9. Ni, Z., Shi, Y.Q., Ansari, N., Su, W., Sun, Q., Lin, X.: Robust lossless image data hiding designed for semi-fragile image authentication. IEEE Trans. Circuits Syst. Video Technol. **18**, 497–509 (2008)
10. Zeng, X.T., Ping, L.D., Pan, X.Z.: A lossless robust data hiding scheme. Pattern Recogn. **43**(4), 1656–1667 (2010)
11. Gao, X., An, L., Yuan, Y., Tao, D., Li, X.: Lossless data embedding using generalized statistical quantity histogram. IEEE Trans. Circuits Syst. Video Technol. **21**, 1061–1070 (2011)
12. An, L., Gao, X., Li, X., Tao, D., Deng, C., Li, J.: Robust reversible watermarking via clustering and enhanced pixel-wise masking. IEEE Trans. Image Process. **21**(8), 3598–3611 (2012)
13. An, L., Gao, X., Yuan, Y., Tao, D.: Robust lossless data hiding using clustering and statistical quantity histogram. Neurocomputing **77**(1), 1–11 (2012)
14. Yuan, Y., Gao, X., Tao, D., Deng, C., Ji, F.: Content-adaptive robust lossless data embedding. Neurocomputing **79**, 1–11 (2012)
15. Coltuc, D.: Towards distortion - free robust image authentication. J. Phys. Distortion Conf. Ser. **77**, 12005 (2007)
16. Wang, X., Li, X., Pei, Q.: Independent embedding domain based two-stage robust reversible watermarking. IEEE Trans. Circuits Syst. Video Technol. **30**, 2406–2417 (2019)
17. Hu, R., Xiang, S.: Cover-lossless robust image watermarking against geometric deformations. IEEE Trans. Image Process. **30**, 318–331 (2020)
18. Zhu, J., Kaplan, R., Johnson, J., Li, F.F.: HiDDeN hiding data with deep networks. arXiv: 1807.09937v1 (2018)
19. Hu, D., Zhao, D., Zheng, S.: A new robust approach for reversible database watermarking with distortion control. IEEE Trans. Knowl. Data Eng. **31**(6), 1024–1037 (2019)
20. Kocher, I.S.: An experimental simulation of addressing auto-configuration issues for wireless sensor networks. Comput. Mater. Continua **71**(2), 3821–3838 (2022)
21. Lee, S.: A study on classification and detection of small moths using CNN model. Comput. Mater. Continua **71**(1), 1987–1998 (2022)

# Neural Watermarking for 3D Morphable Models

Feng Wang[1] [iD], Hang Zhou[2] [iD], Weiming Zhang[1]([✉]) [iD], and Nenghai Yu[1] [iD]

[1] University of Science and Technology of China, Hefei, China
zhangwm@ustc.edu.cn
[2] Simon Fraser University, Vancouver, Canada

**Abstract.** 3D morphable models (3DMMs) have been widely used in computer graphics applications. Therefore, digital watermarking for 3DMMs can also become a valuable research direction in the near future. However, previous methods on 3D mesh watermarking have their limitations when applied to 3DMMs watermarking. To lift these limitations, in this paper, we propose a novel framework with the data-driven method on 3DMMs watermarking. We make full use of priors of 3DMMs and design an end-to-end network to train the algorithm for watermark embedding and extracting. We design a hierarchical structure to capture and fuse the variations of the watermarks and meshes with multiple scales. To enhance the robustness against various attacks, we design an extra sub-network, randomly generating some adversarial perturbations on watermarked meshes during training. With the adversarial training, the watermarking network can resist many agnostic attacks in the inference stage. Extensive experiments demonstrate the effectiveness of our method, especially more universal robustness compared with traditional methods.

**Keywords:** 3D watermarking · 3D morphable model · Spectral convolution · Adversarial training

## 1 Introduction

3D meshes [1] have been widely used in many emerging social industries, such as computer-aided design(CAD), 3D printing, real-time 3D rendering, etc. 3D morpable models (3DMMs), as a kind of popular 3D format, are constructed with various deformations on a shared 3D mesh template, thus can reflect these variants on special 3D shapes, such as faces [2], bodies [3, 4], hand [5], animals [6], etc. In recent years, these models have been playing an important role in many applications, including shape corresponce [7], shape synthesis [8] and 3D reconstruction from 2D images [9]. Digital watermarking [10–12] can serve as a channel to transmit information and protect the copyright for multimedia products. Considering the population of 3DMMs, exploring digital watermarking technique for them has become a promising task.

Traditionally, 3D mesh watermarking methods are implemented by manually-designed algorithms. These methods can be divided into two categories: spatial domain-based methods [13–18] and transform domain-based methods [19–27]. For the former, the watermark information is directly embedded into the 3D mesh by modifying the

X. Sun et al. (Eds.): ICAIS 2022, CCIS 1588, pp. 336–349, 2022.
https://doi.org/10.1007/978-3-031-06764-8_27

spatial elements, such as the vertex coordinates and topological connection. Cho et al. [15] and Bors et al. [17] proposed to use distance distribution to embed the watermark. First, the distances of all vertices from the mesh gravity are calculated. Then these vertices are grouped into $C$ bins (the watermark capacity is also $C$ bits). For each bin, we normalize the distance values to $(0, 1)$ and adjust the mean value compared with 0.5 based on the input watermark bit '0' or '1'. For watermark extracting, the similar process is implemented, including vertices grouping and judgement for each bin. This type of methods are robust against similarity transformation attacks, yet are vulnerable under other threats such as noise addition attack. For transform domain-based methods, transform domain analysis is first implemented on 3D meshes, such as Laplacian transform and wavelet transform. In general, the watermark bits are embedded by modifying the intermediate frequency coefficients to strike a balance between the imperceptibility and robustness. Cayre et al. [19] first proposed to use Laplacian matrix as the transform tool and applied it on the vertex coordinate matrix. Given the power spectrum of vertices, watermark bit can be embedded by exchanging the spectrum coefficients of x-y-z. And the extracting algorithm is also implemented with the similar procedure. Thus this method is vulnerable to rotation attack. Besides, the visual quality of the watermarked mesh is poor, seriously affecting the usage of the mesh.

With the lack of the specific research on 3DMMs watermarking for previous methods, to lift these limitations and make full use of the priors of 3DMMs, we design a more efficient framework for 3DMMs watermarking. We propose a novel watermarking scheme based on deep neural network (DNN). In our framework, we design an end-to-end network to learn the weights for watermarking algorithm, including embedding sub-network and extracting sub-network. We train our network and move vertices with subtle distance, achieving the watermark embedding in imperceptible ways. Compared with traditional methods, we can leverage the priors of 3DMMs (i.e. fixed topology) and find better solution. Besides, our method has fewer procedures, with the network forward costing less time than complex algorithmic steps, as shown in Fig. 1.

To overcome the irregularity and complexity of 3D mesh, we regard 3D mesh as a graph and introduce the spectral convolution as the convolution operation. We construct a hierarchical network structure, which can extract the features from 3D mesh with multiple scales. Considering that robustness is the most important property for 3D mesh watermarking, to enhance it, we apply adversarial training during the training process. We use a shallow attack sub-network to randomly add some perturbations on the watermarked meshes. Then the attacked meshes are fed into the extracting sub-network. Without the priors about attacks, we can still guarantee sufficient accuracy rate under various attacks.

In summary, our contributions are three-fold:

- We proposed a novel watermarking technique for 3D morphable models via deep neural network.
- We train an end-to-end network for our framework, and we employ the adversarial sub-network to enhance the robustness under various attacks.
- Extensive experiments demonstrate the effectiveness of our method.

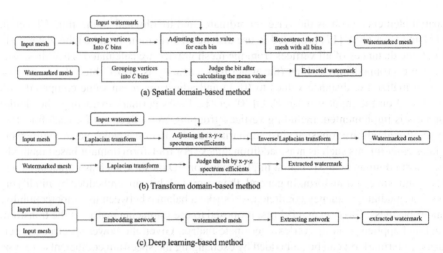

**Fig. 1. Comparisons of three types of methods**: spatial domain-based method [15–17], transform domain-based method [19] and deep learning-based method (proposed). Both traditional methods need complex procedures for watermarking embedding and extracting. Yet deep learning-based method only require the network forward to achieve the watermarking algorithm.

## 2 Method

A 3D mesh can defined as $\mathcal{M} = (\mathcal{V}, \mathcal{F})$, where $\mathcal{V}$ denotes vertices and $\mathcal{F}$ denotes faces. For 3D morphable models, they usually share a fixed topology and the same number of vertices. And we define watermark capacity as $C$ bits.

### 2.1 Priliminary: Chebyshev-Based Spectral Convolution

The convolution operator in the spatial domain can be defined as a Hadamard product in the Fourier domain. To achieve the convolution on 3D mesh, we can use the equivalent operation in the transform domain of 3D mesh by the normalized Laplacian matrix $\mathbf{L}$ [29]. Considering the expensive computation, we use the $K^{th}$ order Chebyshev polynomials $T_k(x)$ to approximate the spectral convolution:

$$g_\theta(\mathbf{L}) = \sum_{k=0}^{K-1} \theta_k T_k(\mathbf{L}) \tag{1}$$

For a 3D mesh with $N$ vertices, we can regard it as a graph with the $N$ nodes. And the connections between nodes indicate the edges of the mesh. For l-layer feature $f_i^l \in \mathbb{R}^N$ of $i^{th}$ channel, we can compute the next layer feature $f_i^{l+1} \in \mathbb{R}^N$:

$$f_i^{l+1} = \sum_{i=0}^{F_{in}-1} g_{\theta_{i,j}}(\mathbf{L}) f_i^l \tag{2}$$

### 2.2 Watermark Embedding and Extracting

We employ two sub-networks to achieve watermarking embedding and extracting respectively. In order to increase the receptive filed and capture the features with multiple scales, we construct a hierarchical architecture. We employ the mesh sampling operation proposed by [2] to change the scale. For vertices with the shape of $N_{in} \times 3$, we use the transformation matrix $\mathbf{Q} \in \mathbb{R}^{N_{in} \times N_{out}}$ to change vertices to $N_{out}$. For the down-sampling process, we calculate the matrix via quadric error metric (QEM) [30]. And for the up-sampling, we seek the nearest triangle for each vertex and calculate the interpolation weights $\tilde{\mathbf{v}} = w_1\mathbf{v}_1 + w_2\mathbf{v}_2 + w_3\mathbf{v}_3 (s.t. w_1 + w_2 + w_3 = 1)$ to acquire the up-sampling matrix.

As shown in Fig. 2, we use Encoder and Decoder to denote the embedding sub-network and extracting sub-network respectively. The input of Encoder module is the mesh $\mathcal{M}_{in}$ and input watermark $\mathbf{wm}_{in} \in [0, 1]^C$. Encoder first encodes the input watermark by the multi-layer perceptron (MLP). Then the input vertices $\mathcal{V}_{in}$ and the encoded watermark are concatenated and fed into the U-Net-based network. The output of the Encoder is the watermarked mesh $\mathcal{M}_{wm}$. Decoder module is responsible for training to extract the watermark message $\mathbf{wm}_{ext}$ from the watermarked mesh. We define the targeted problem as:

$$\min_{\theta_{enc}, \theta_{dec}} ||\mathbf{Dec}(\mathbf{Enc}(\mathcal{M}_{in}; \mathbf{wm}_{in})), \mathbf{wm}_{in}||^2$$
$$\text{s.t.} ||\mathbf{Enc}(\mathcal{M}_{in}; \mathbf{wm}_{in}) - \mathcal{M}_{in}||^2 < \epsilon \tag{3}$$

where $\epsilon$ defines the maximum of modifications on the input mesh, and $\Theta_{enc}, \Theta_{dec}$ denote the network parameters for both modules. Thus we can define the watermark loss $\mathcal{L}_{wm}$ and mesh loss $\mathcal{L}_{\mathcal{M}}$ as:

$$\mathcal{L}_{wm} = ||\mathbf{wm}_{in} - \mathbf{wm}_{ext}||^2 \tag{4}$$

$$\mathcal{L}_{\mathcal{M}} = ||\mathcal{M}_{in} - \mathcal{M}_{in}||^2 \tag{5}$$

where $\mathbf{Dec}(\mathbf{Enc}(\mathcal{M}_{in}; \mathbf{wm}_{in})) = \mathbf{wm}_{ext}$, $\mathbf{Enc}(\mathcal{M}_{in}; \mathbf{wm}_{in}) = \mathcal{M}_{wm}$, and $\mathcal{M}_{wm} - \mathcal{M}_{in}$ implies the difference of vertex coordinates between both meshes.

## 2.3 Adversarial Training

DNNs are vulnerable to adversarial examples [31]: when some imperceptible modifications are added into a targeted carrier, the classifier may produce false result. The similar phenomenon also happens in our network: we find that when the watermarked mesh $\mathcal{M}_{wm}$ is attacked by some tiny perturbations, such as Gaussian noise addition, the extracted message changes a lot. In actual application scenarios, the watermarked meshes may suffer from many agnostic attacks, so we need to improve the robustness of our method as much as possible.

Adversarial training was first proposed by Goodfellow et al. [32] as a method to enhance the generative quality of the targeted network. Luo et al. [33] proposed to use an adversarial network to train against the watermarking network. Inspired by this, in our context, we can employ an adversary which is responsible for training against both watermarking modules and enhance the robustness. Thus, we design the Attacker module which is responsible for adding some subtle perturbations on the watermarked mesh $\mathcal{M}_{wm}$, and generate the attacked mesh $\mathcal{M}_{att}$. We define the targeted problem as:

$$\max_{\Theta_{att}} ||\mathbf{Dec}(\mathbf{Att}(\mathcal{M}_{wm})), \mathbf{wm}_{in}||^2$$
$$\text{s.t.} ||\mathbf{Att}(\mathcal{M}_{wm}) - \mathcal{M}_{in}||^2 < \delta \tag{6}$$

where $\delta$ defines the maximum of the perturbation, and $\Theta_{att}$ denotes the network parameters for Attacker module. The maximization problem guarantees the antagonistic contradiction with the main network. To train the Attacker module, we define the adversarial mesh loss $\mathcal{L}'_{\mathcal{M}}$ and adversarial watermark loss $\mathcal{L}'_{wm}$ for Attacker module as:

$$\mathcal{L}'_{\mathcal{M}} = ||\mathcal{M}_{att} - \mathcal{M}_{enc}||^2 \tag{7}$$

$$\mathcal{L}'_{wm} = ||\mathbf{wm}_{att}, 1 - \mathbf{wm}_{in}||^2 \tag{8}$$

where $\mathbf{Dec}(\mathbf{Att}(\mathcal{M}_{wm})) = \mathbf{wm}_{att}$, and $\mathbf{Att}(\mathcal{M}_{wm}) = \mathcal{M}_{att}$. We minimize the adversarial training loss for Attacker module:

$$\mathcal{L}_{att} = \lambda'_{\mathcal{M}}\mathcal{L}'_{\mathcal{M}} + \lambda'_{wm}\mathcal{L}'_{wm} \tag{9}$$

## 2.4   Network Training

Figure 2 shows the proposed network architecture. Similar to Attack module, we define the adversarial watermark loss $\mathcal{L}''_{wm}$ for the main network as:

$$\mathcal{L}_{wm}'' = ||\mathbf{wm}_{att}, \mathbf{wm}_{in}||^2 \tag{10}$$

Thus we minimized the loss $\mathcal{L}_w$ for Encoder module and Decoder module:

$$\mathcal{L}_w = \lambda_{wm}\mathcal{L}_{wm} + \lambda_{\mathcal{M}}\mathcal{L}_{\mathcal{M}} + \lambda''_{wm}\mathcal{L}''_{wm} \tag{11}$$

---

**Algorithm 1** Network Training

---

**Input**: Mesh dataset $\{\mathcal{M}_i\}_{i=1}^O$, watermark length $C$.

**Output**: Network parameters: $\Theta_{enc}, \Theta_{dec}, \Theta_{att}$.

1: **Initilize** the network parameters

2: **For** step = 1 to max_steps **do**

3:   $\mathcal{M}_{in}$ = **Random Selection** from $\{\mathcal{M}_i\}_{i=1}^O$.

4:   $\mathbf{wm}_{in}$ = **Random Generation** $(\{0,1\}^C)$

5:   $\mathcal{M}_{enc}$ = **Enc**$(\mathcal{M}_{in}, \mathbf{wm}_{in})$

6:   $\mathcal{M}_{att}$ = **Att**$(\mathcal{M}_{enc})$

7:   $\mathbf{wm}_{ext}$ = **Dec**$(\mathcal{M}_{enc})$

8:   $\mathbf{wm}_{att}$ = **Dec**$(\mathcal{M}_{att})$

9:   **Calculate** $\mathcal{L}_W, \mathcal{L}_{att}$

10:   Update $\Theta_{att} = \Theta_{att} + lr \times \text{Adam}(\mathcal{L}_{att})$

11:   Update $\Theta_{enc} = \Theta_{enc} + lr \times \text{Adam}(\mathcal{L}_W)$

12:   Update $\Theta_{dec} = \Theta_{dec} + lr \times \text{Adam}(\mathcal{L}_W)$

13: **Return** $\Theta_{enc}, \Theta_{dec}, \Theta_{att}$.

---

During training, we set $\lambda_{wm} = 1$, $\lambda'_{wm} = 0.001$, $\lambda''_{wm} = 0.5$ and $\lambda_{\mathcal{M}} = \lambda'_{\mathcal{M}} = 8$. We alternately train the main network and adversarial network, with details shown in Algorithm 1. We use Adam 34 algorithm to update the network parameters with the learning rate $lr$. Note that we only need the main network for embedding and extracting process in the inference stage, so adversarial training does not introduce extra computation costs in this stage.

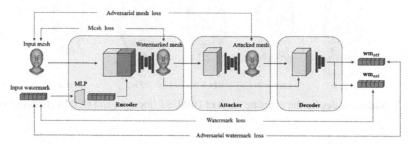

**Fig. 2.** The proposed watermarking network includes three modules: Encoder, Attacker and Decoder.

## 3  Experiments

### 3.1  Setups

We use two datasets to validate out method. COMA [2] is the face expression dataset consisting of 20K + registered 3D face shapes with 5,023 vertices for each shape, and

DFAUST [3] contains 40K + dynamic human body shapes with 6,890 vertices. We train the network on four NVIDIA GeForce RTX 2080Ti GPUs with the batch size of 500 and learning rate $lr = 10^{-4}$. We train each dataset for 300 epochs with initial learning rate $lr = 10^{-4}$ and adjust $lr$ multiplied with 0.95 for every 10 epochs.

We set the sampling factor is 4, with the number of vertices changing correspondingly between adjacent scales. Deep3DMM [35] constructed a five-level hierarchical structure for the template mesh. With the same sampling method, we define the sampling process as shown in Fig. 3.

$$COMA : 5023 \leftrightarrow 1256 \leftrightarrow 314 \leftrightarrow 79 \leftrightarrow 20$$

$$DFAUST : 6890 \leftrightarrow 1723 \leftrightarrow 431 \leftrightarrow 108 \leftrightarrow 27.$$

For the evaluation metrics, we calculate the mean Euclidean error to evaluate the imperceptibility, and we calculate the bit accuracy rate by comparing the extracted watermark and the input watermark to evaluate the robustness.

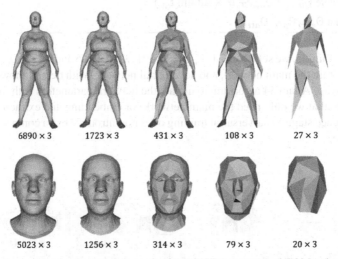

| 6890 × 3 | 1723 × 3 | 431 × 3 | 108 × 3 | 27 × 3 |

| 5023 × 3 | 1256 × 3 | 314 × 3 | 79 × 3 | 20 × 3 |

**Fig. 3.** Various scales for the template mesh of DFAUST (top row) and COMA (bottom row).

### 3.2 Comparisons with Baseline Methods

We compare our methods with two spatial domain-based methods and one transform domain-based method: Bin [15], L-M [17] and Laplacian [19]. For fair comparison, we define the watermark capacity as $C = 64$ bits.

Table 1 shows the results of quantitative comparisons. We can find both our method and Laplacian can achieve 100% of accuracy rate on both datasets. And compared with Laplacian, we can achieve fewer Euclidean errors. There are some watermark errors for Bin and L-M. That is because that the grouping would be changed after watermark embedding (causality problem). And there are some decreases of accuracy rate on COMA dataset for Bin and L-M. That is because the distance distribution of vertices from COMA dataset is relatively consistent (vertices on the head are almost the same distances from the center of the mesh). Qualitative results can be seen in Fig. 4 and Fig. 5. We can find that there are many visual distortions on watermarked meshes with Laplacian method, which have seriously affect the usage of meshes. And we can still guarantee sufficient imperceptibility although there are a little more Euclidean errors compared with Bin and L-M.

**Table 1.** Comparisons on mean Euclidean error (Err) and bit accuracy rate (Acc).

| Method | DFAUST | | COMA | |
|---|---|---|---|---|
| | Err/mm | Acc (%) | Err/mm | Acc (%) |
| Bin [15] | **0.52** | 99.49 | **0.11** | 94.75 |
| L-M [17] | 0.68 | 99.02 | 0.13 | 92.69 |
| Laplacian [19] | 7.56 | **100.00** | 1.17 | **100.00** |
| Proposed | 1.64 | **100.00** | 0.17 | **100.00** |

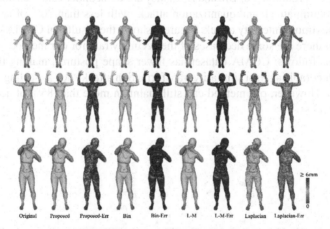

Original    Proposed    Proposed-Err    Bin    Bin-Err    L-M    L-M-Err    Laplacian    Laplacian-Err

**Fig. 4.** Qualitative results on DFAUST dataset. The first line is the original meshes, and others are the watermarked meshes and corresponding Euclidean errors.

The robustness performance under various attacks: To evaluate the robustness under various attacks, we test the performance under several types of attacks with different intensities. With the fixed topology for 3D morphable models, we don't need to consider connection attacks which would change the topological structure and destroy their intrinsic attractiveness [23]. Thus we list several types of attacks: Gaussian noise addition, smoothing, quantization, translation, rotation and scaling. Details about the attacks can be found in the Appendix. Considering the difference of both datasets, we select different attack intensities.

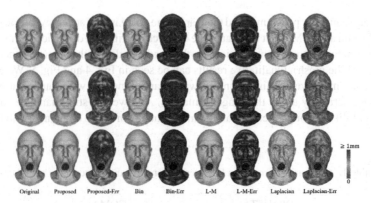

**Fig. 5.** Qualitative results on COMA dataset. The first line is the original meshes, and others are the watermarked meshes and corresponding Euclidean errors.

For DFAUST dataset, as shown in Fig. 6, we can see that our method can achieve more than 95% of accuracy rate under all attacks, which shows the sufficient robustness against these attacks. Laplacian is weak against rotation attack and translation attack, with about 60% of accuracy rate under 0.4m of translation and about 70% of accuracy rate under 45° of rotation. For Bin and L-M, they are weak under Gaussian noise addition attack, smoothing attack and quantization attack, with less than 70% of accuracy rate under the maximum intensity attack. Figure 7 shows the results on COMA dataset. We can find that there are some decreases of the accuracy rate for our method. We analyze the reason as follows: COMA dataset has fewer shape postures, making the network relatively vulnerable against similarity transformation attack such as scaling, translation and rotation. However, our method can still maintain more than 85% of accuracy rate under all attacks.

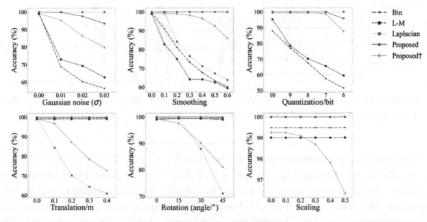

**Fig. 6.** Bit accuracy rate (%) under several attacks with different intensities on DFAUST dataset. Proposed† denotes our method without adversarial training.

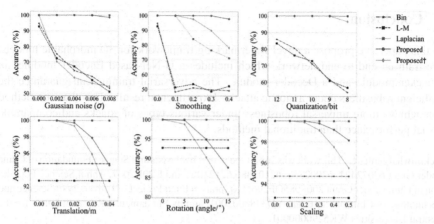

**Fig. 7.** Bit accuracy rate (%) under several attacks with different intensities on COMA dataset. Proposed† denotes our method without adversarial training.

### 3.3 More Analyses

**The Influence of Adversarial Training**: To validate the importance of adversarial training, we remove the Attacker module and re-train the network. And only mesh loss and watermark loss are calculated to update the parameters for Encoder module and Decoder module. Results can also be seen in Fig. 6 and Fig. 7 († denotes our method without adversarial training). We can find that the accuracy rate decreases a lot without adversarial training. On DFAUST dataset, translation for 0.4 m makes the accuracy rate decrease to about 70%. And on COMA dataset, the accuracy rate is close to 55% under the Gaussian noise attack with σ = 0.008 m. That means adversarial training effectively improves the robustness of our method.

**Table 2.** Comparisons with different watermark lengths on DFAUST dataset.

| Capacity/bit | 16 | 32 | 64 | 128 | 256 |
|---|---|---|---|---|---|
| Acc (%) | 100.00 | 100.00 | 100.00 | 97.21 | 84.37 |
| Err/mm | 0.47 | 1.27 | 1.64 | 1.82 | 2.17 |

**The Discussion on the Watermark Length:** Our method can adaptively adjust the watermark capacity. We train our network with different watermark length $C = 16, 32, 64, 128, 256$ and test the performance, as shown in Table 2. It is clear that when the watermark length increases, the disturbance to the input mesh also increases. And we find that we can get no less than 97% of accuracy rate with 128 bits of watermark capacity. Considering the actual usage, we can introduce the error correcting code and extend the watermark capacity to over 64 bits.

## 4   Conclusion

In this paper, we propose a novel watermarking framework for 3D morphable models. We train an end-to-end network which includes a U-Net-based Encoder module, an Attacker module and a Decoder module. The adversarial training can guarantee the sufficient robustness under agnostic attacks. Experimental results show that our method can achieve more universal robustness under various types of attacks and comparable visual performance than traditional methods.

**Acknowledgement.** This work was supported in part by the Natural Science Foundation of China under Grant 62072421, 62002334, 62102386,62121002 and U20B2047, Anhui Science Foundation of China under Grant 2008085QF296, Exploration Fund Project of University of Science and Technology of China under Grant YD3480002001, and by Fundamental Research Funds for the Central Universities WK5290000001.

## Appendix

### A. Detailed Network Architecture

Figure 8 shows the detailed architecture of our network on DFAUST dataset. The number of vertices is adaptively adjusted on COMA dataset. (431, 1723, 6890) denotes three-layer perceptron with output channel 431, 1723,6890 respectively. And (512,C) denotes the corresponding two-layer perceptron.

### B. Details for the Attacks

Various attacks are added during our experiment. In this section, we provide the detailed descriptions for these attacks.

**Gaussian Noise Addition.** We employ a zero-mean Gaussian noise model to generate the noise and attach it to vertices. We use $\sigma$ to control the noise intensity: Gaussian noise $\sim \mathcal{N}(0, \sigma^2)$. Considering the actual size for both datasets, we define $\sigma \in (0, 0.008\,\text{m})$ for COMA dataset and $\sigma \in (0, 0.03\,\text{m})$ for DFAUST dataset.

**Smoothing.** Laplacian smoothing [36] model is employed to simulate smoothing attack. For the watermarked vertices $\mathcal{V}_{wm}$ and the Laplacian matrix $\mathbf{L} \in \mathbb{R}^{N_{in} \times N_{in}}$, we generate the watermarked vertices $\mathcal{V}_{att}$:

$$\mathcal{V}_{att} = \mathcal{V}_{wm} - \alpha_L L \mathcal{V}_{wm} \tag{12}$$

where $\alpha_L$ denotes the smoothing intensity for this attack.

**Quantization.** For the 3D coordinates of vertices, we round the coordinates after the decimal point and represent them in fixed bits, such as 7,8,9 etc.

**Rotation.** We rotate the 3D coordinates in each dimension with random angles sampled in the scope. The sampling scope represents the attack intensity.

**Translation.** We translate the 3D coordinate in each dimension with random distances sampled in the translation scope. For both datasets, we also define different translation intensities.

**Scaling.** We implement the uniform scaling for 3D coordinates of vertices. During the experiment, we define the same scaling scope for both datasets.

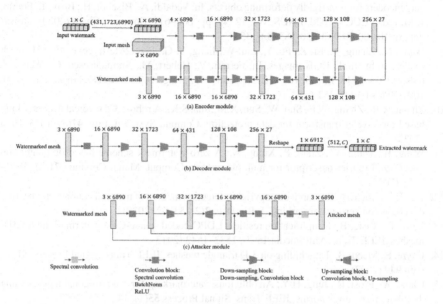

**Fig. 8.** Proposed network architecture.

# References

1. Nguyen-Ngoc, H., Nguyen-Xuan, H., Abdel-Wahab, M.: Three-dimensional meshfree analysis of interlocking concrete blocks for step seawall structure. Comput. Mater. Continua **66**(1), 165–178 (2021)
2. Ranjan, A., Bolkart, T., Sanyal, S., Black, M.J.: Generating 3D faces using convolutional mesh autoencoders. In: Ferrari, V., Hebert, M., Sminchisescu, C., Weiss, Y. (eds.) ECCV 2018. LNCS, vol. 11207, pp. 725–741. Springer, Cham (2018). https://doi.org/10.1007/978-3-030-01219-9_43
3. Bogo, F., Romero, J., Pons-Moll, G., Black, M.J.: Dynamic faust: registering human bodies in motion. In: Proceedings of the IEEE/CVF Conference on Computer Vision and Pattern Recognition (CVPR) (2017)
4. Loper, M., Mahmood, N., Romero, J., Pons-Moll, G., Black, M.J.: SMPL: A skinned multi-person linear model. ACM Trans. Graph. **34**(6), 1–248 (2015)
5. Romero, J., Tzionas, D., Black, M.J.: Embodied hands: modeling and capturing hands and bodies together. ACM Trans. Graph. **36**(6), 1–17 (2017)

6. Zuffi, S., Kanazawa, A., Jacobs, D.W., Black, M.J.: 3D menagerie: modeling the 3d shape and pose of animals. In: Proceedings of the IEEE/CVF Conference on Computer Vision and Pattern Recognition (CVPR), pp. 5524–5532 (2017)

7. Verma, N., Boyer, E., Verbeek, J.: Feastnet: feature-steered graph convolutions for 3d shape analysis. In: Proceedings of the IEEE/CVF Conference on Computer Vision and Pattern Recognition (CVPR) pp. 2598–2606 (2018)

8. Tretschk, E., Tewari, A., Zollhöfer, M., Golyanik, V., Theobalt, C.: DEMEA: deep mesh autoencoders for non-rigidly deforming objects. In: Vedaldi, A., Bischof, H., Brox, T., Frahm, J.-M. (eds.) ECCV 2020. LNCS, vol. 12349, pp. 601–617. Springer, Cham (2020). https://doi.org/10.1007/978-3-030-58548-8_35

9. Wang, N., Zhang, Y., Li, Z., Fu, Y., Liu, W., Jiang, Y.-G.: Pixel2Mesh: generating 3D mesh models from single RGB images. In: Ferrari, V., Hebert, M., Sminchisescu, C., Weiss, Y. (eds.) ECCV 2018. LNCS, vol. 11215, pp. 55–71. Springer, Cham (2018). https://doi.org/10.1007/978-3-030-01252-6_4

10. Zhang, X.R., Zhang, W.F., Sun, W., Sun, X.M., Jha, S.K.: A robust 3-d medical watermarking based on wavelet transform for data protection. Comput. Syst. Sci. Eng. **41**(3), 1043–1056 (2022)

11. Wang, B., Wang, W., Zhao, P., Xiong, N.: A zero-watermark scheme based on quaternion generalized fourier descriptor for multiple images. Comput. Mater. Continua **71**(2), 2633–2652 (2022)

12. Cui, L.L., Xu, Y.B.: Research on copyright protection method of material genome engineering data based on zero-watermarking. J. Big Data **2**(2), 53–62 (2020)

13. Vasic, B., Vasic, B.: Simplification resilient LDPC-coded sparse-QIM watermarking for 3D-meshes. IEEE Trans. Multimedia **15**(7), 1532–1542 (2013)

14. Cayre, F., Macq, B.: Data hiding on 3-D triangle meshes. IEEE Trans. Signal Process. **51**(4), 939–949 (2003)

15. Cho, J.W., Prost, R., Jung, H.Y.: An oblivious watermarking for 3-d polygonal meshes using distribution of vertex norms. IEEE Trans. Signal Process **55**(1), 142–155 (2007)

16. Wang, K., Lavoue, G., Denis, F., Baskurt, A.: Robust and blind mesh watermarking based on volume moments. Comput. Graph. **35**(1), 1–19 (2011)

17. Bors, A.G., Luo, M.: Optimized 3D watermarking for minimal surface distortion. IEEE Trans. Image Process. **22**(5), 1822–1835 (2012)

18. Rolland-Neviere, X., Doerr, G., Alliez, P.: Triangle surface mesh watermarking based on a constrained optimization framework. IEEE Trans. Inf. Forens. Secur. **9**(9), 1491–1501 (2014)

19. Cayre, F., Rondao-Alface, P., Schmitt, F., Macq, B., Maıtre, H.: Application of spectral de- composition to compression and watermarking of 3D triangle mesh geometry". Signal Process. Image Commun. **18**(4), 309–319 (2003)

20. Kanai, S., Date, H., Kishinami, T.: Digital watermarking for 3D polygons using multi-resolution wavelet decomposition. In: Proceedings of Sixth IFIP WG, vol. 5, no. 2, pp. 296–307 (1998)

21. Alface, P.R., Macq, B.: Blind watermarking of 3D meshes using robust feature points detection. In: IEEE International Conference on Image Processing, vol. 1, pp. I-693 (2005)

22. Jing, L., Wang, Y., Ye, L., Liu, R., Chen, J.: A robust and blind 3D watermarking algorithm using multiresolution adaptive parameterization of surface. Neurocomputing **237**, 304–315 (2017)

23. Wang, K., Lavoue, G., Denis, F., Baskurt, A.: Hierarchical watermarking of semiregular meshes based on wavelet transform. IEEE Trans. Inf. Forensics Secur. **3**(4), 620–634 (2008)

24. Uccheddu, F., Corsini, M., Barni, M.: Wavelet-based blind watermarking of 3D models. In: Proceedings of the 6th Workshop on Multimedia & Security, pp. 143–154 (2004)

25. Praun, E., Hoppe, H., Finkelstein, A.: Robust mesh watermarking. In: Proceedings of the 26th Annual Conference on Computer Graphics and Interactive Techniques (SIGGRAPH), pp. 49–56 (1999)

26. Liu, Y., Prabhakaran, B., Guo, X.: Spectral watermarking for parameterized surfaces. IEEE Trans. Inf. Forensics Secur. **7**(5), 1459–1471 (2012)

27. Ohbuchi, R., Takahashi, S., Miyazawa, T.: Watermarking 3d polygonal meshes in the mesh spectral domain. Graph, Interface **2001**, 9–17 (2001)

28. Ronneberger, O., Fischer, P., Brox, T.: U-Net: convolutional networks for biomedical image segmentation. In: Navab, N., Hornegger, J., Wells, W.M., Frangi, A.F. (eds.) MICCAI 2015. LNCS, vol. 9351, pp. 234–241. Springer, Cham (2015). https://doi.org/10.1007/978-3-319-24574-4_28

29. Kipf, T.N., Welling, M.: Semi-supervised classification with graph convolutional networks. International Conference on Learning Representations (ICLR) (2017)

30. Garland, M., Heckbert, P.S.: Surface simplification using quadric error metrics. In: Proceedings of the 24th Annual Conference on Computer Craphics and Interactive Techniques (SIGGRAPH), pp. 209–216 (1997)

31. Szegedy, C., Zaremba, W., Sutskever, I., Bruna, J., Erhan, D., Goodfellow, I., Fergus, R.: Intriguing properties of neural networks. In: 2nd International Conference on Learning Representations (ICLR) (2014)

32. Goodfellow, I.J., Shlens, J., Szegedy, C.: Explaining and harnessing adversarial examples. In: International Conference on Learning Representations (ICLR) (2014)

33. Luo, X., Zhan, R., Chang, H., Yang, F., Milanfar, P.: Distortion agnostic deep watermarking. In: Proceedings of the IEEE/CVF Conference on Computer Vision and Pattern Recognition (CVPR), pp. 13548–13557 (2020)

34. Kingma, D.P., Ba, J.: Adam: A method for stochastic optimization. In: International Conference on Learning Representations (ICLR) (2014)

35. Chen, Z., Kim, T.K.: Learning feature aggregation for deep 3d morphable models. In: Proceedings of the IEEE/CVF Conference on Computer Vision and Pattern Recognition (CVPR) pp. 13164–13173 (2021)

36. Taubin, G.: Geometric signal processing on polygonal meshes. In: 21st Annual Conference of the European Association for Computer Graphics, Eurographics (2000)

# Robust Zero Watermarking Algorithm for Medical Images Using Local Binary Pattern and Discrete Cosine Transform

Wenyi Liu[1] , Jingbing Li[1(✉)], Chunyan Shao[1], Jixin Ma[2], Mengxing Huang[1,3],
and Uzair Aslam Bhatti[1]

[1] School of Information and Communication Engineering, Hainan University,
Haikou 570228, China
Jingbingli2008@hotmail.com
[2] School of Computing and Mathematical Sciences, University of Greenwich,
London SE10 9LS, UK
[3] State Key Laboratory of Marine Resource Utilization in the South China Sea Hainan
University, Haikou 570228, China

**Abstract.** Thanks to the rapid development of the telemedicine, medical treatment has turned in great convenience. However, as the internet network can be addressed by any user, the medical images cannot avoid the defects of suffering from information leakage and require information encryption techniques. To protect the privacy of patients in medical images, a robust watermarking method, which combines medical images with watermark information, is proposed in this paper. First, the low-frequency feature vector of the medical image is extracted by combining local binary pattern (LBP) and transformation with discrete cosine transform (DCT). Second, hash sequence is implemented on to convert feature vector into binary sequences. At last, the medical image is embedded with hash sequence and watermark preprocessed by chaotic encryption technology using the zero-watermark technology. The experimental results show that the method can encrypt the medical images' watermark effectively and has good robustness against geometric attacks.

**Keywords:** Medical image · Local binary pattern · Zero watermark

## 1 Introduction

In today's world, the rapid development of Internet technology has also brought new development opportunities to the medical system [1]. However, the emergence and use of various digital image processing software also provides a way for criminals to maliciously attack and tamper with images, threatening the privacy of patients and the authenticity of medical images. The medical image is related to whether the disease diagnosis is correct or not, once there is a mistake, it is likely to endanger the lives of patients [2]. Consequently, how to improve the security of medical information has become an urgent problem [3, 4]. Digital watermarking technology adds the patient's information

X. Sun et al. (Eds.): ICAIS 2022, CCIS 1588, pp. 350–362, 2022.
https://doi.org/10.1007/978-3-031-06764-8_28

as an invisible watermark to the corresponding medical image, which can also extract the watermark after processing when necessary [5].

Among the most released watermark algorithms on medical images, the zero watermark algorithm is very popular due to well information reserving medical image [6]. Generally, the common zero watermarking algorithm is realized by either changing the pixel value of the image space domain or changing the coefficient value of the image transform domain [7]. The main transformation for watermarking and image security can be classified into four types, i.e. discrete cosine transform (DCT), digital wavelet transform (DWT), contourlet transform and Nonsubsampled Contourlet Transform (NSCT) [8]. Kent mapping algorithm provides more security for images under watermark chaos, using DCT principle to embed the watermark [9]. Another study, used a hybrid algorithm that combined the classic DCT, DWT and SVD to embed the image block watermark [10]. Neetika Soni et al. proposed an image steganography method based on block DCT, which uses chaotic sequences in DCT coefficients to replace secret data [11]. Jing Liang et al. first performed DCT on the image, binarized the high-frequency part, and then performed block Discrete Fourier Transform (DFT) on the host image [12]. Convolutional Neural Networks (CNN), based approach which is popular in recent years, is used to train the small icon recognition and classification data set in the algorithm to achieve the purpose of no modification steganography [13, 14]. These methods can effectively extract image feature vector, but the ability of resisting geometric attack is not very good.

This paper proposes a robust watermarking method for medical images based on the combination of the local binary pattern (LBP) and discrete cosine transform (DCT). First, a local binary pattern (LBP) is applied to the medical image. Then DCT is applied to the LBP response matrix of the image to obtain the low-frequency feature vector of the medical image. At last, the watermark is embedded combing with the logistic map technology, extracting the watermark by inverse transform. This method applies LBP algorithm to medical images and makes use of the advantages of gray invariance and rotation invariance of LBP algorithm. The contribution of this paper is that the zero watermark algorithm is applied to ensure that the visual effect of medical images is not affected and improve the robustness of medical image zero watermarking algorithm. In order to verify the performance of the proposed algorithm, experiments on comparison with Radon-DCT algorithm are conducted. The experimental results show that the performance of the algorithm used in this paper is more robust to geometric attacks compared with Radon-DCT algorithm.

## 2   Materials and Methods

### 2.1   Local Binary Patterns (LBP)

LBP has the advantages of gray invariance and fast feature extraction [15, 16]. The initial LBP defines the image pixel at $3 \times 3$, comparing the gray value of the middle pixel with the gray value of the adjacent 8 pixels, if the value of the middle pixel is larger than that of the adjacent pixel, it is marked as 0 in the region of the adjacent pixel, otherwise it is marked as 1. Finally, the 8-bit binary number starting from the upper left corner is converted to a decimal number with a value range of 0 to 255 [17], as shown in Fig. 1.

LBP is expressed as follows:

$$LBP(x_c, y_c) = \sum_{p=0}^{P-1} 2^P s(i_p - i_c) \tag{1}$$

In the formula, $(x_c, y_c)$ represents the middle pixel, $i_c$ represents the gray value, $i_p$ represents the gray value of the pixels in the adjacent area, and s is the sign function.

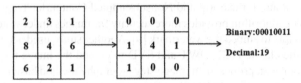

**Fig. 1.** Original LBP operator.

The original LBP Operator covers a small area with a constant radius. Ojala et al. [18, 19]. changed the neighborhood into a circle. When the radius of the circle is R and contains P sampling points, the LBP operator will produce $2^P$ patterns. If there are too many kinds of patterns, the histogram will be too sparse, which is unfavorable to texture extraction. Ojala also proposed a "uniform pattern" to solve this problem, that is, when the number of binary loops corresponding to an LBP has at most two jumps (from 0 to 1 or from 1 to 0), the binary loops corresponding to the LBP are called an equivalent pattern class, otherwise, it is called a mixed-mode class.

## 2.2 Discrete Cosine Transform (DCT)

After LBP based feature extraction on the medical images, DCT is applied to obtain the low-frequency feature vector. Features extracted with LBP are detailed and computationally intensive, while the high frequency part with less information is removed and unnecessary details are reduced by DCT transformation. DCT [20] can transform the signal from the spatial domain to the frequency domain with a small amount of calculation, high accuracy, and good decorrelation. After the DCT transform, the energy of the image will be concentrated in the low-frequency coefficient of the upper left corner, which is conducive to image transmission. The formula of 2D DCT is as follows:

$$F(u, v) = c(u)c(v) \sum_{x=0}^{M-1} \sum_{y=0}^{N-1} f(x, y)$$
$$\cos \frac{(2x + 1)u\pi}{2N} \cos \frac{(2y + 1)v\pi}{2N} \tag{2}$$
$$u = 0, 1, \ldots M - 1 \quad v = 0, 1, \ldots N - 1$$

In the formula:

$$c(u) = \begin{cases} \sqrt{1/M} & u = 0 \\ \sqrt{2/M} & u = 1, 2, \ldots M - 1 \end{cases}$$

$$c(v) = \begin{cases} \sqrt{1/N} & v = 0 \\ \sqrt{2/N} & v = 1, 2, ... N - 1 \end{cases}$$

Generally, in digital image processing, M = N. M and N are the length and width of the image.

## 2.3 Robust Watermarking Method

The robust medical image watermarking algorithm is mainly divided into three steps. The watermark is encrypted firstly, then embedding the watermark into the medical image. Finally, extracting the watermark and calculating the correlation coefficient between the extracted watermarking and the original watermark to verify the effect of the algorithm.

1) Watermark Encryption: Firstly, the watermark is encrypted by a logistic map [21, 22], the formula of the logistic map is as follows:

$$x(i + 1) = u * x(i) * (1 - x(i)) \tag{3}$$

u is the growth parameter, it is set as 4 in this experiment, $x(i)$ and $x(i + 1)$ are chaotic sequences, generated by the initial value of x0, i is the number of iterations, setting as 32 in this experiment.

Then the generated chaotic sequence is changed into 0,1 binary sequence k (n). If the value of $x(i)$ is greater than 0.5, $k(n)$ is recorded as "1", otherwise it is recorded as "0". Then, the binary watermark image w (i, j) is XOR with the binary chaotic sequence $k(n)$, and the chaotic scrambled watermark BW(i, j) is obtained.

2) Watermark Embedding:

Extracting feature vector of the original medical image by LBP-DCT: Firstly, using LBP algorithm to extract the features of the original medical image Ii(i,j), and then global DCT transform is performed on the image to obtain the coefficient matrix F0 (i, j) of the original medical image. Selecting the first L are from the matrix. If F0 (i, j) is greater than 0, it is recorded as "1", otherwise it is recorded as "0", so as to obtain the feature vector K(i) = {k(i)|k(i) = 0,1;1 ≤ i ≤ L}, L is the length of the coefficient, 32 in this experiment.

Embedding watermark: By using XOR operation between the feature vector K (i) and the chaotic scrambled watermark BW (i, j), the watermark can be embedded into the original medical image, and the logical secret key Key (i, j) can be obtained. The formula is as follows:

$$Key(i, j) = BW(i, j) \oplus K(i) \tag{4}$$

Only when the secret key is obtained can the watermark be extracted from the medical image. And this method belongs to zero watermark embedding, after embedding the watermark in the image, the pixel value will not change. The embedding flow chart of the watermark is shown in Fig. 2.

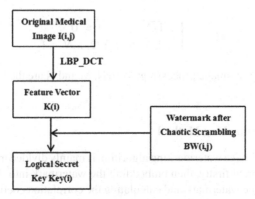

**Fig. 2.** Watermark embedding flow chart.

3) Extraction and Restoration:

Extraction: Using LBP-DCT transform to extract the feature vector K' (i) of the image to be tested, and hash sensing is performed with the obtained secret Key (i, j), then the watermark BW' (i, j) in the medical image to be tested can be obtained.

$$BW'(i, j) = Key(i, j) \oplus K'(i) \tag{5}$$

Restore: During the encryption process, the chaotic sequence x (i) is generated from the initial value x0, and then it is transformed into a binary sequence K(m) by symbol operation. The extracted watermark BW' (i, j) is restored by hash function to obtain W' (i, j). The flow chart of extraction and restoration is shown in Fig. 3.

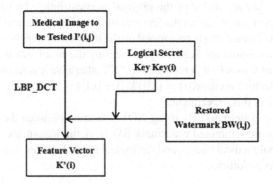

**Fig. 3.** Flow chart of watermark extraction and restoration.

# 3  Results and Discussion

To verify that the algorithm can correctly extract image features, selecting a meaningful binary text image as the watermark of the medical image, noting as W = {w(i, j) | w(i,

j) = 0, 1; 1 ≤ i ≤ M1, 1 ≤ j ≤ M2}. At the same time, we selected six 128 × 128 medical images as the original medical images, denoted as Ii (i, j) (1 ≤ i ≤ 2), w(i, j) represents the pixel gray value of the watermark image. Using LBP-DCT for image feature extraction, and compared the correlation coefficient between different images. The comparison results are shown in Table 1.

**Table 1.** Correlation coefficient of features between different images.

|  | Image 1 | Image 2 | Image 3 | Image 4 | Image 5 | Image 6 |
|---|---|---|---|---|---|---|
| Image 1 | 1.00 | 0.13 | 0.13 | −0.02 | −0.20 | 0.13 |
| Image 2 | 0.13 | 1.00 | 0.00 | −0.13 | −0.06 | 0.00 |
| Image 3 | 0.13 | 0.00 | 1.00 | 0.00 | 0.06 | −0.13 |
| Image 4 | −0.02 | −0.13 | 0.00 | 1.00 | 0.31 | 0.25 |
| Image 5 | −0.20 | −0.06 | 0.06 | 0.31 | 1.00 | 0.31 |
| Image 6 | 0.13 | 0.00 | −0.13 | 0.25 | 0.31 | 1.00 |

From Table 1, the correlation coefficients between the features extracted from different images are lower than 0.5, and the correlation is weak.

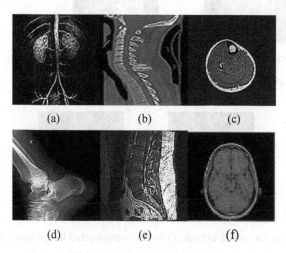

**Fig. 4.** Original medical image.

The results of this paper selected two different medical images for display, the image size is 128 × 128. MATLAB 2018b is used for the development and analysis of the proposed algorithm. After extracting and restoring the watermarks W ′(i, j) from the image to be tested, calculating the normalized correlation coefficient with the original binary watermark image W (i, j). The formula of normalized correlation coefficient [23]

NC is as follows:

$$NC = \frac{\sum_i \sum_j W(i,j)W'(i,j)}{\sum_i \sum_j W^2(i,j)} \tag{6}$$

When the embedded image is not attacked, there is no difference between the two tested images and the original image, as shown in Fig. 5, and the correlation coefficient (NC) between the extracted watermark and the original watermark is 1, as shown in Fig. 6. Next, geometric attacks are carried out on the embedded watermark image to test the robustness of the proposed method.

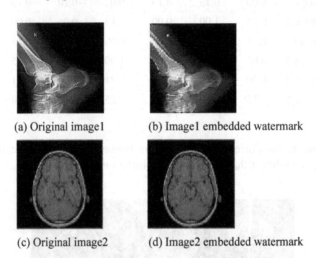

(a) Original image1        (b) Image1 embedded watermark

(c) Original image2        (d) Image2 embedded watermark

**Fig. 5.** The original image without attack and the image embedded with a watermark.

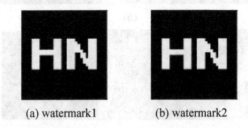

(a) watermark1              (b) watermark2

**Fig. 6.** The watermark extracted from the watermarked image without attack.

1) Rotation attacks: Rotating the two watermarked images clockwise for 5°, and the extracted watermark is shown in Fig. 7. The correlation coefficients are NC1 = 0.93 and NC2 = 0.82 respectively.

The results of the two medical images are shown in Table 2. When the rotation degree is 11°, the normalization coefficient NC of the two images is still greater than

0.5, which indicates that the watermark can be extracted accurately. And the most of the NC values of LBP-DCT algorithm in this paper are greater than Radon-DCT. Therefore, the watermarking method in this paper has better performance than Radon-DCT.

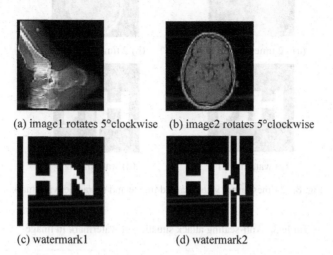

(a) image1 rotates 5°clockwise    (b) image2 rotates 5°clockwise

(c) watermark1                    (d) watermark2

**Fig. 7.** Images with watermark and extracted watermark rotates 5° clockwise.

**Table 2.** Anti-rotation attack situation of the watermark in image.

|         | Degree of rotation° | LBP-DCT NC | Radon-DCT NC |
|---------|---------------------|------------|--------------|
| Image 1 | 1                   | 0.93       | 0.86         |
|         | 3                   | 0.93       | 0.61         |
|         | 5                   | 0.93       | 0.56         |
|         | 7                   | 0.93       | 0.45         |
|         | 9                   | 0.89       | 0.22         |
|         | 11                  | 0.85       | 0.11         |
| Image 2 | 1                   | 0.82       | 0.78         |
|         | 3                   | 0.82       | 0.78         |
|         | 5                   | 0.82       | 0.81         |
|         | 7                   | 0.82       | 0.92         |
|         | 9                   | 0.76       | 0.87         |
|         | 11                  | 0.71       | 0.87         |

2) Scaling attack: The two images embedded with the watermark are enlarged to twice of original, and the extracted watermark is still relatively clear, as shown in Fig. 8 NC1 = 1, NC2 = 0.96.

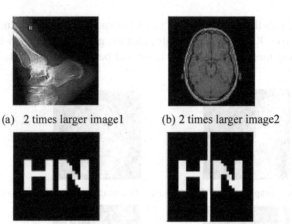

(a)   2 times larger image1          (b) 2 times larger image2

(c) watermark1                       (d) watermark2

**Fig. 8.** 2 times larger watermarked image and extracted watermark.

**Table 3.** Anti-scaling attack situation of watermark in image.

|        | Scaling factor | LBP-DCT NC | Radon-DCT NC |
|--------|----------------|------------|--------------|
| Image1 | 0.5            | 0.83       | 0.72         |
|        | 0.6            | 0.96       | 0.39         |
|        | 0.7            | 0.96       | 0.70         |
|        | 0.8            | 1.00       | 0.34         |
|        | 1              | 1.00       | 1.00         |
|        | 1.5            | 1.00       | 0.23         |
|        | 1.8            | 1.00       | 0.36         |
|        | 2              | 1.00       | 0.39         |
| Image2 | 0.5            | 0.78       | 0.82         |
|        | 0.6            | 0.78       | 0.82         |
|        | 0.7            | 0.91       | 0.72         |
|        | 0.8            | 1.00       | 0.85         |
|        | 1              | 1.00       | 1.00         |
|        | 1.5            | 1.00       | 0.72         |
|        | 1.8            | 0.96       | 0.67         |
|        | 2              | 0.96       | 0.67         |

Performing scaling attacks of different degrees on two medical images and the results obtained are shown in Table 3. When reducing the images to 0.5 of the original, the values of normalized coefficients NC of the two images are NC1 = 0.83, NC2 = 0.78, respectively, and the watermarks can be extracted accurately. While using Radon-DCT algorithm, most of the value of NC are lower.

(a) image1 with a 2% vertical downshift

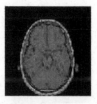

(b)image2 with a 2% vertical downshift

(c) watermark1

(d) watermark2

**Fig. 9.** The watermarked image and the extracted watermarked with a 2% vertical downshift.

**Table 4.** Anti-translational attack situation of the watermark in image.

|  | Downshift distance (%) | LBP-DCT NC | Radon-DCT NC |
|---|---|---|---|
| Image1 | 2 | 1.00 | 0.87 |
|  | 4 | 0.96 | 0.80 |
|  | 6 | 0.93 | 0.80 |
|  | 8 | 0.74 | 0.80 |
|  | 10 | 0.68 | 0.76 |
|  | 20 | 0.35 | 0.80 |
| Image2 | 2 | 1.00 | 0.76 |
|  | 4 | 1.00 | 0.83 |
|  | 6 | 1.00 | 0.64 |
|  | 8 | 1.00 | 0.78 |
|  | 10 | 0.81 | 0.78 |
|  | 20 | 0.61 | 0.64 |

3) Translational attack: Moving the two images with watermarks down vertically by 2%, and the extracted watermark correlation coefficients are all 1, as shown in Fig. 9.

**Table 5.** Anti-shear attack situation of the watermark in image.

|         | Y-direction shear (%) | LBP-DCT NC | Radon-DCT NC |
|---------|-----------------------|------------|--------------|
| Image1  | 3                     | 1.00       | 0.72         |
|         | 6                     | 1.00       | 0.69         |
|         | 9                     | 1.00       | 0.73         |
|         | 11                    | 1.00       | 0.63         |
|         | 15                    | 1.00       | 0.73         |
|         | 20                    | 0.91       | 0.73         |
| Image2  | 3                     | 0.96       | 0.87         |
|         | 6                     | 0.93       | 0.87         |
|         | 9                     | 0.87       | 0.76         |
|         | 11                    | 0.87       | 0.80         |
|         | 15                    | 0.73       | 0.78         |
|         | 20                    | 0.63       | 0.64         |

Two medical images were subjected to different degrees of translational attack, and the results obtained are shown in Table 4. When the image is shifted vertically by 20%, the normalization coefficient of the first image is NC1 = 0.35, which is not very good, but that of the second image is NC2 = 0.61, which is still larger than 0.5.

4) Shear attack: Cut the two images with watermarks from the Y-axis direction by 3%, and the correlation coefficients of the watermarks extracted from image1and 2 are 1 and 0.96, as shown in Fig. 10.

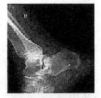

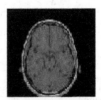

(a) cut 3% of the image1 from the y-axis    (b) cut 3% of the image2 from the y-axis

(c) watermark1                              (d) watermark2

**Fig. 10.** Cut 3% of the watermarked images and extracted watermarked images in the y-axis direction.

Different degrees of y-axis shear attack were performed on two medical images and the results obtained are shown in Table 5. When the image was cut by 20% from the y-axis direction, the first image had a normalized coefficient of NC1 = 0.91, and the second image had a normalized coefficient of NC2 = 0.63, both of which performed well. In addition, we can also see that most of the NC values obtained by LBP-DCT algorithm are greater than Radon-DCT.

# 4 Conclusions

This paper introduces a robust watermarking method for medical images based on LBP-DCT, combing with logistic map technology and zero watermark. The proposed method is robust when facing geometric attacks, and the extracted watermarks have no difference from the original watermarks. Compared with Radon-DCT, the proposed method have better performance, resulting high normalized coefficient. As the images used in this paper are all open pictures on the Internet, the method proposed in this paper is consequently practical in real-world medical systems.

However, the performance of this proposed algorithm needs to be improved, since the performance is not very stable against translational attack. In future work, we will conduce more work on improving in these issues.

**Acknowledgements.** This article was completed under the guidance of my teacher, Professor Li. Thank Mr. Li for your careful guidance and help.

**Funding.** This work was supported in part by Key Research Project of Hainan Province under Grant ZDYF2021SHFZ093, the Natural Science Foundation of China under Grants 62063004 and 61762033, the Hainan Provincial Natural Science Foundation of China under Grants 2019RC018 and 619QN246, and the Major Scientific Project of Zhejiang Lab 2020ND8AD01.

# References

1. Jeslin, T., Linsely, J.A.: Agwo-cnn classification for computer-assisted diagnosis of brain tumors. Comput. Mater. Continua **71**(1), 171–182 (2022)
2. Hu, K., Wang, X., Hu, J., Wang, H., Qin, H.: A novel robust zero-watermarking algorithm for medical images. Vis. Comput. **37**(9–11), 2841–2853 (2021). https://doi.org/10.1007/s00371-021-02168-5
3. Liu, Y.L., Li, J.B.: DCT and Logistic Map based multiple robust watermarks for medical image. Appl. Res. Comput. **30**(11), 333–337 (2013)
4. Shankar, K., Venkatraman, S.: A secure encrypted classified electronic healthcare data for public cloud environment. Intell. Autom. Soft Comput. **32**(2), 765–779 (2022)
5. Singh, K.P., Agarwal, N.: Robust and secure watermarking for propagation of digital multimedia by paillier homomorphic cryptosystem with arnold transformation. Int. J. E-Health Med. Commun. **12**(4), 17–31 (2021)
6. Qi, F.Z., Chang, Q.Z., Na, R., et al.: Zero watermarking algorithm for vector geographic data based on the number of neighboring features. Symmetry **13**(2), 208 (2021)
7. Zhao, J., Liu, Y., Wu, X.Y.: Zero watermarking algorithm based on Radon transform and legendre fourier moment. Inf. Technol. **11**, 50–54 (2020)

8. Wu, J., Ma, X.H.: Blind watermarking algorithm based on tetrolet-Radon transform and Schur decomposition. Modern Electron. Technol. **44**(5), 41–46 (2021)
9. Ou, J.: A digital watermarking technology based on two-dimensional code Kent Mapping and DCT. Comput. Age **11**, 7–10 (2020)
10. Fazli, S.: A robust image watermarking method based on DWT DCT, and SVD using a new technique for correction of main geometric attacks. Optik Int. J. Light Electron Optics **127**(2), 964–972 (2016)
11. Soni, N., Saini, I., Singh, B.: Hybrid chaotic substitution and block-DCT-based ECG steganography with boosted embedding capacity. Res. Biomed. Eng. **37**(2), 201–219 (2021). https://doi.org/10.1007/s42600-021-00146-3
12. Jing, L., Sun, Z.T., Chen, K.X.: Remote sensing image zero watermarking algorithm based on dft. J. Phys: Conf. Ser. **1865**(4), 042034 (2021)
13. Wu, B.J., Zhang, Y., Luo, W.C.: A modification-free steganography algorithm based on image classification and CNN. Int. J. Digital Crime Forens. **13**(3), 47–58 (2021)
14. Nithyanantham, S., Singaravel, G.: Hybrid deep learning framework for privacy preservation in geo-distributed data centre. Intell. Autom. Soft Comput. **32**(3), 1905–1919 (2022)
15. Pal, P., Jana, B., Bhaumik, J.: A secure reversible color image watermarking scheme based on LBP, lagrange interpolation polynomial and weighted matrix. Multimed. Tools Appl. **80**(14), 21651–21678 (2021). https://doi.org/10.1007/s11042-021-10651-3
16. Acharya, S., Nanda, P.K.: Adjacent LBP and LTP based background modeling with mixed-mode learning for foreground detection. Pattern Anal. Appl. **24**(3), 1047–1074 (2021). https://doi.org/10.1007/s10044-021-00967-z
17. Praveen, K., Rajesh, T.M.: Video based sub-categorized facial emotion detection using lbp and edge computing. Revued Intell. Artificielle **35**, 55–61 (2021)
18. Ojala, T., Pietikäinen, M., Harwood, D.: A comparative study of texture measures with classification based on featured distributions. Pattern Recogn. **29**(1), 51–59 (1996)
19. Ojala, T., Pietikainen, M., Maenpaa, T.: Multiresolution gray-scale and rotation invariant texture classification with local binary patterns. IEEE Trans Pattern Anal Mach. Intell. **24**(7), 971–987 (2002)
20. Mosleh, M., Setayeshi, S., Barekatain, B., Mosleh, M.: A novel audio watermarking scheme based on fuzzy inference system in DCT domain. Multimed. Tools Appl. **80**(13), 20423–20447 (2021). https://doi.org/10.1007/s11042-021-10686-6
21. Deng, Z.J., Xiao, D., Tu, F.H.: Design and implementation of chaotic encryption algorithm based on logistic map. JCU **27**(4), 61–63 (2004)
22. Sun, X., Yi, K.Y., Sun, Y.X.: Image encryption algorithm based on chaotic system. J. Comput. Aided Des. Comput. Graph **14**(2), 1–4 (2002)
23. Bhatti, U.A., et al.: New watermarking algorithm utilizing quaternion Fourier transform with advanced scrambling and secure encryption. Multimed. Tools Appl. **80**(9), 13367–13387 (2021). https://doi.org/10.1007/s11042-020-10257-1

# Steganalysis of Content-Adaptive JPEG Steganography Based on Ensemble of Convolutional Neural Networks with Image Preprocessing Using Gabor Filters

Xiaofeng Song[✉], Xinshe Qi, Wanli Kou, and Guopeng Li

School of Information and Communication, National University of Defense Technology, Xi'an 710106, China
xiaofengsong@sina.com

**Abstract.** As we know, compared with the feature-based steganalysis method, deep convolutional neural networks (DCNNs) have firmly established themselves as the superior steganography detectors. In this paper, considering the advantages of Gabor image representation and classifier ensemble, a steganalysis method is proposed based on ensemble of convolutional neural networks with image preprocessing using Gabor filters. First, multiple DCNNs are trained which used different 2D Gabor filter banks in the image preprocessing layers. Then, for a testing image, the steganography detection is performed by combing the total number of votes and the total confidence values which are from the outputs of classification modules of all the trained DNNs. The experiment results show that the proposed steganalysis method can improve the detection performance for content-adaptive JPEG steganography.

**Keywords:** JPEG steganography · Robustness · DCT domain · Singular value · Correlation

## 1 Introduction

JPEG steganography is widely studied and used for covert communication for the ubiquitous presence of JPEG images in the Internet traffic. The existing JPEG steganography algorithms can be roughly divided into two types: non-content-adaptive steganography and content-adaptive steganography [1]. The former performs the steganography embedding by selecting cover elements according to the key while the latter can adaptively select the cover elements according to the embedding cost. The content-adaptive JPEG steganography can constrain the embedding changes to the complex image regions difficult to model and then improve the steganography security greatly. In recent years, the content-adaptive JPEG steganography based minimal distortion framework becomes more and more popular, which defines a suitable distortion function and uses Syndrome-Trellis Codes (STCs) [2] to minimize the distortion. For example, Wang et al. [3] proposed EBS (Entropy Block Steganography) steganography which defines the embedding distortion using the block entropy of DCT coefficient, Holub et al. [4] proposed J-UNIWARD (JPEG UNIversal WAvelet Relative Distortion) steganography which defines the embedding distortion according to the directional residuals obtained using a Daubechies wavelet filter bank, Guo et al. [5] proposed UED (Uniform Embedding Distortion) steganography which defines the embedding distortion based on the magnitude of the DCT coefficients and both their intra- and inter-block neighborhood coefficients, Wang et al. [6] proposed a JPEG steganography algorithm based on a hybrid embedded distortion function.

With the popular of JPEG content-adaptive steganography, the corresponding steganalysis techniques also have attracted increased attention and many steganalysis methods have been proposed. These steganalysis methods can be divided into two categories, one based on steganalysis features and ensemble classifier, and the other based on deep learning. The former extracts the high-dimensional statistical features such JRM (JPEG Rich Model), DCTR (Discrete Cosine Transform Residual), GFR (Gabor Filter Residual) [7], and then the ensemble classifier [8] is trained to perform the detect task. For the latter, the trained DCNN (Deep Convolutional Neural Network) is often used as the final detector. Moreover, the steganalysis methods based on DCNN can achieve the better detection performance. So far, many steganalysis methods based on DCNN have been proposed. For example, Xu et al. [9] designed a 20-layer DCNN that can achieve higher detection accuracy than SCA-GFR(Selection-Channel-Aware GFR), Chen et al. [10] proposed PNet and VNet by porting JPEG-phase awareness into the architecture of a DCNN, Zeng et al. [11] proposed a generic hybrid deep learning framework for JPEG steganalysis which combine hand-crafted stage and DCNN training stage, Boroumand et al. [12] proposed a deep residual network which expand the front part of the network architecture to compute the noise residuals and prevent the suppression of the stego signal, Li et al. [13] proposed a steganalysis method based ensemble of deep residual network and two different strategies are used to combined the outputs of multiple base learners. In general, steganalysis methods based on deep learning have proven their superiority in contrast to the methods based on high-dimensional statistical features. However, it should be noted that the steganalysis methods based on deep learning also utilize the prior experiences from the previous steganalysis features. For example, the high-pass filters for extracting the noise residuals are widely used in the pre-processing layer of different DCNNs for steganalysis, which help to suppress image content and get the stego signal.

In this paper, we proposed a steganalysis method for content-adaptive JPEG steganography through the ensemble of multiple DCNNs which applied 2D Gabor filters with different scale parameters in the image pre-processing layers. The proposed steganalysis method primarily consists of ensemble construction and combination of classifiers. The former is to build an ensemble of DCNNs which have different image pre-processing layers. The latter is to adaptively combine the multiple outputs of the individual DCNN members. For each DCNN, the image pre-processing layer are used to generate the stego noise residuals by applying 2D Gabor filters with different orientation parameters to the input JPEG image and then the network is trained by the cover and stego images. All the outputs of the DCNNs are combined to determine the detection result based on majority voting.

The remainder of this paper is organized as follows. In Sect. 2, image decomposition using 2D Gabor filters is introduced. In Sect. 3, the framework and implementation details of the proposed steganalysis method are described. In Sect. 4, the experimental results and analyses are shown. In Sect. 5, the conclusions and future work are discussed.

## 2  Image Decomposition Using 2D Gabor Filters

The 2D Gabor filters are widely used for the extraction of steganalysis features for content-adaptive JPEG steganography and the competitive detection performance can be got [7]. For steganalysis method based on DCNN, the 2D Gabor filters are also used in the image-preprocessing layer to extract the stego noise residuals. The image can be decomposed into different scales and orientations using 2D Gabor filters. The filter coefficients can reflect the stego noise residual from different scales and orientations. Typically, an input image $I$ is convolved with a 2D Gabor function $g(x, y)$ to obtain a Gabor feature image $u(x, y)$ as follows:

$$u(x, y) = \iint_{\Omega} I(\xi, \eta) g(x - \xi, y - \eta) d\xi d\eta \tag{1}$$

Furthermore, the 2D Gabor wavelet $g(x, y)$ in Eq. (1) use the following family of Gabor functions [14], which are basically a set of differently oriented cosine patterns modulated by a Gaussian kernel,

$$g_{\lambda, \theta, \varphi}(x, y) = e^{-\left(\frac{\left(x'^2 + \gamma^2 y'^2\right)}{2\sigma^2}\right)} \cos\left(2\pi \frac{x'}{\lambda} + \varphi\right) \tag{2}$$

where $x' = x \cos\theta + y \sin\theta$, $y' = -x \sin\theta + y \cos\theta$, $\sigma = 0.56\lambda$, $\gamma = 0.5$.

In Eq. (2), $\sigma$ indicates the scale parameter and the small $\sigma$ value means the high spatial resolution, then the filter coefficients represent the local noise residuals at the fine scale. On the contrary, the large $\sigma$ value means the low spatial resolution and the filter coefficients represent the local noise residuals at coarse scale. The other parameters in Eq. (2) can be described as follows: the parameter $\theta$ represents the orientation of the 2D Gabor wavelet, $\lambda$ represents the wavelength, $\gamma$ represents the aspect ratio of the Gaussian function, and $\varphi$ represent the phase offset value. In order to obtain high-frequency image feature, all the 2D Gabor filters are normalized to zero mean by subtracting the kernel mean from all its elements to remove the DC component of the filter.

The 2D Gabor function in Eq. (2) must be discretized to get the corresponding 2D Gabor filters. First, the filter size $M \times N$ is determined and the sampling points are generated in a certain step such as 1. Then, the parameter value of the 2D Gabor function in Eq. (2) are determined and the corresponding function value of each sample point is calculated. Lastly, the 2D Gabor filter is generated according to the function values and are made zero mean by subtracting the kernel mean from all its elements to form high-pass filter.

Figure 1 shows the decomposition of a test image of "peppers" using 2D Gabor filters with three scales and four orientations. The scale parameter $\sigma$ is set to 0.75, 1.25,

1.75 respectively and the orientation parameter $\theta$ is set to 0, $2\pi/8$, $4\pi/8$ and $6\,\pi/8$ respectively. After steganography embedding, the filter coefficients in different scales and orientations all will change. Then, we can employ the different 2D Gabor filter banks for image pre-processing layers of different DCNNs to get the noise residuals for further steganalysis feature learning and classification.

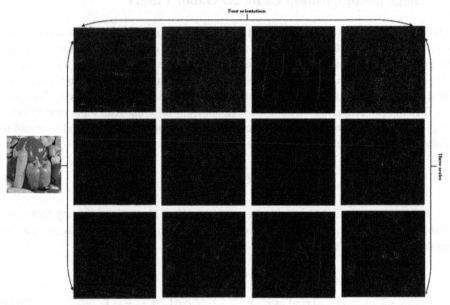

**Fig. 1.** Decomposition of image "peppers" by 2D Gabor filters with three scales and four orientations.

## 3   Proposed Steganalysis Framework

### 3.1   Overall Architecture of Gabor DCNN Ensemble

The overall architecture of the proposed steganalysis method based on Gabor DCNN ensemble is shown in Fig. 2.

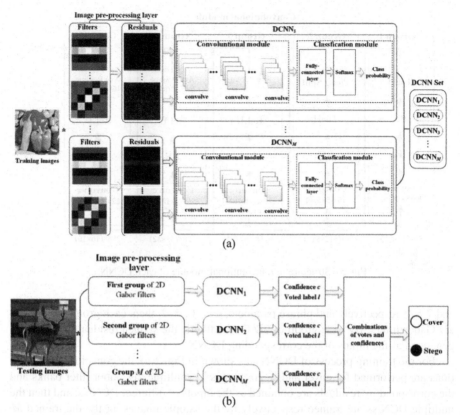

**Fig. 2.** Overall architecture of proposed steganalysis method. (a) Training processing and (b) Testing processing.

The training process of the DCNNs is shown in Fig. 2(a) and the testing process is shown in Fig. 2(b). It can be seen that each DCNN includes a convolutional module and a classification module. In Fig. 2(a), the convolutional module is same to VNet proposed in [10] and the structure is shown in Fig. 3. For each processing unit, the data size follows (number of feature maps) × (height × width), the size of the convolution filters in the boxes follows (number of kernels) × (height × width × number of input feature maps) and the Phase Split indicates that each filtered image is sampled according to the 64 phases in 8 × 8 DCT blocks to obtain 64 sample images. The classification module is a linear classifier formed using a fully-connected layer and a Softmax node. The input of the classification module is the steganalysis feature learned by DCNN, and then the class probability is outputted through Softmax node. Lastly, the sample image is identified as a cover image or a stego image according to the class probability and a threshold value such as 0.5.

In addition, in Fig. 2, it can be seen that one group of 2D Gabor filters is related with one DCNN. Here, the scale parameter $\sigma$ of each group of 2D Gabor filters is different and it is 0.75, 1, 1.25, 1.5, 1.75 respectively. Moreover, for each group of 2D Gabor filters, the orientation parameter $\theta$ is set to 0, $\pi/8$, $2\pi/8$, $3\pi/8$, $4\pi/8$, $5\pi/8$, 6 $\pi/8$

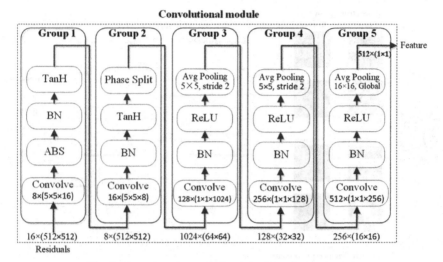

**Fig. 3.** Structure of convolutional module of each DCNN.

and $7 \pi/8$ respectively and phrase parameter $\varphi = 0, \pi/2$, then, each group has sixteen 2D Gabor filters. By each group of 2D Gabor filters, the sixteen residual maps can be generated as the inputs of the corresponding DCNN.

For the training process of DCNNs, as shown in Fig. 2(a), the convolutional operations are performed for cover and stego images by multiple 2D Gabor filter banks and the corresponding residuals are obtained as the inputs of different DCNNs, and then the multiple DCNNs are trained respectively by the sample images, lastly, the trained $M$ DCNNs can be got.

For the testing process, the image preprocessing operation is firstly performed for the test image by the multiple 2D Gabor filter banks and the residuals are inputted into different DCNNs, and then the voted label and classification confidence are outputted, lastly, the test image is classified as cover or stego image by combing the votes and confidence. In other words, the test image is not identified using majority voting which only simply counts the classification results of all the DCNNs. The detailed decision process is given as follows.

## 3.2 Ensemble Combination of Outputs of DCNNs

According to the Fig. 2, the multiple trained DCNNs can be got after the training processing completed. Then, the classification result can be decided using the outputs of all the DCNNs. As we know, the most popular ensemble combination method is the majority voting, in other words, the final class label is the one that receives the maximum number of the votes. This approach is simple and each DCNNs play an equally important role in identifying the stego image. That is to say, it does not consider the class probability or confidence to the vote. For example, the two DCNNs both classified the testing image as a stego image, however, the class probability may be quite different such as 0.55 and 0.95 respectively. Then, the decision of the latter should be paid more attention [15].

Therefore, the votes of class labels and the corresponding probability generated by all DCNNs can be combined to improve the detection performance.

First, the class probability is computed for each DCNN according to Eq. (3),

$$p(x_i = l) = \frac{e^{f_k^l(x_i)}}{\sum_{c=0}^{1} e^{f_k^c(x_i)}} \tag{3}$$

where $f_k^l(x_i)$ denotes the output of the last layer of the $k$-th DCNN corresponding to label $l$, and $l = 0, 1$ for steganalysis task. In other words, the image $x_i$ is classified as a cover image when $l = 0$ and it is stego image when $l = 1$.

Obviously, the probability $p(x_i = l)$ is the output of Softmax layer of DCNN, which measures the degree of belief to which the vote for an image label of $x_i$ is equal to the correct vote. And $p(x_i = l)$ is also referred as the confidence value $c_k^l$.

Second, according to the confidence values $c_k^l, k = 1, 2, \cdots, M$, $M$ denotes the number of DCNNs, the number of votes of DCNNs for cover or stego image can be calculated. Here, the total number of votes given to the image label is denoted as $N_{vote}^l$, which is counted from all the DCNNs and computed using Eq. (4) and (5) as follows,

$$N_{vote}^l = \sum_{k=1}^{M} \delta_k^l(x_i, l) \quad for \ l = 0, 1, \tag{4}$$

$$\delta_k^l(x_i, l) = \begin{cases} 1 \ if \ l = arg \ \max_j c_k^j \\ 0 \quad otherwize \end{cases}. \tag{5}$$

Then, the total confidence value associated with $N_{vote}^l$ can be calculated according to Eq. (6) as follows,

$$C_{conf}^l = \sum_{k=1}^{M} \delta_k^l(x_i, l) c_k^l \tag{6}$$

where $C_{conf}^l$ denotes the sum of confidence values $c_k^l (k = 1, 2, \cdots, M)$ for the vote of the image label of $l$. In other words, $C_{conf}^l$ is the total degree of belief that the label of $x_i$ is assigned to that of $l$.

Lastly, the total number of votes $N_{vote}^l$ and the total confidence value $C_{conf}^l$ can be combined to determine the label of a test image. The specific method is given as follows,

$$l^* = arg \ \max_l \left( C_{conf}^l \times N_{vote}^l \right) \tag{7}$$

According to Eq. (7), it can be seen that the votes $N_{vote}^l$ from DCNNs with high confidence values $c_k^l$ play a more important role in classifying a test image as a cover image or stego image.

## 4   Experimental Results and Analyses

In this section, the image database and experiment settings are introduced firstly, and then the detection performances of different steganalysis methods are compared for J-UNIWARD [5] steganography which is the one of the most security content-adaptive JPEG steganography.

## 4.1 Image Database and Experiment Settings

In the experiments, the image database is BOSSbase 1.01 [16], which includes 10000 grayscale images with PGM format. For J-UNIWARD steganography, the grayscale images are firstly converted into JPEG images with QF (quality factor) of 75, 85 and 95 respectively, and then the stego images are generated with payload 0.05, 0.1, 0.2, 0.3, 0.4, and 0.5 bpnzAC (per non-zero AC DCT coefficient).

For the training of DCNNs, the cross-entropy loss function and the mini-batch stochastic gradient descent are used, the momentum is set to 0.9, the learning rate for all parameters is initially set to 0.001 and is scheduled to decrease 25% every 20 epochs, up to 240 epochs. For each batch, the training samples contain 20 cover images and 20 stego images. All convolution filters are initialized with a zero-mean Gaussian distribution with a standard deviation of 0.01, the bias values of the convolutional layers are fixed to zero, and the bias learning rate of the last fully-connected layer is set to twice the learning rate. The further details for DCNN training can be found in [10].

For the feature-based steganalysis method, the ensemble classifier [8] is trained by the steganalysis feature and used as the final detector. The ratio of training and test images is 0.5:0.5. The detection accuracy is quantified using the minimal total error probability under equal priors $P_E = min_{P_{FA}}(P_{FA} + P_{MD})/2$, where $P_{FA}$ denotes the false-alarm probabilities and $P_{MD}$ denotes the missed-detection probabilities. The value of $\overline{P}_E$ is averaged over ten random image database splits.

## 4.2 Result and Analyses

In Table 1, the detection errors $P_E$ are presented for UED and J-UNIWARD steganography with QF 75 when two different ensemble strategies are used. The experimental results show the weighted ensemble can achieve the better detection performances.

**Table 1.** Detection errors $P_E$ for UED and J-UNIWARD steganography with QF 75 based on DCNNs ensemble using different strategies.

| Payload | UED | | J-UNIWARD | |
|---------|-----------------|-----------------|-----------------|-----------------|
|         | Majority voting | Weighted voting | Majority voting | Weighted voting |
| 0.05    | 0.2781          | 0.2632          | 0.4163          | 0.4022          |
| 0.1     | 0.1478          | 0.1355          | 0.3293          | 0.3113          |
| 0.2     | 0.0590          | 0.0533          | 0.1732          | 0.1593          |
| 0.3     | 0.0261          | 0.0229          | 0.0730          | 0.0632          |
| 0.4     | 0.0150          | 0.0127          | 0.0374          | 0.0321          |
| 0.5     | 0.0090          | 0.0083          | 0.0263          | 0.0244          |

In contrast to majority voting, the weighted voting given in Eq. (7) considers the confidences of votes from all the DCNNs, therefore, the votes with high confidences

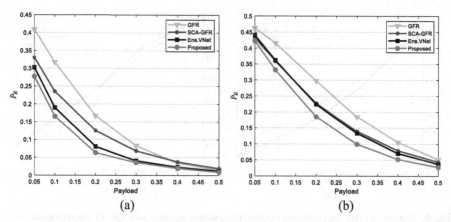

**Fig. 4.** Detection error for content-adaptive JPEG steganography with QF 75 when steganalyzed with different methods. (a) UED steganography and (b) J-UNIWARD steganography.

pay more important role in the classification decision. Obviously, the weighted voting is more reasonable and lower detection error can be achieved.

In Fig. 4, the detection performances of different steganalysis methods are shown. It can be seen that the steganalysis methods based on DCNN have significant advantages over the feature-based steganalysis methods such as GFR and SCA-GFR, and even SCA-GFR has used the selection channel information. Moreover, compared with Ens. VNets, the proposed steganalysis method can achieve the competitive detection performances. It is more because of the use of 2D Gabor filter banks in image pre-processing layer of DCNNs and the ensemble strategy which consider the voting and confidence simultaneously.

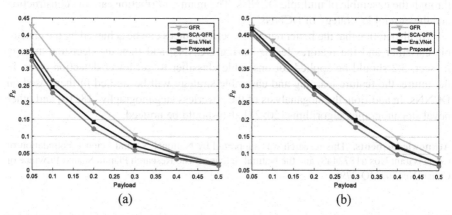

**Fig. 5.** Detection error for content-adaptive JPEG steganography with QF 85 when steganalyzed with different methods. (a) UED steganography and (b) J-UNIWARD steganography.

In Fig. 5 and Fig. 6, the detection performances of different steganalysis methods are shown when the QF of JPEG image is 85 and 95 respectively. It also can be seen that

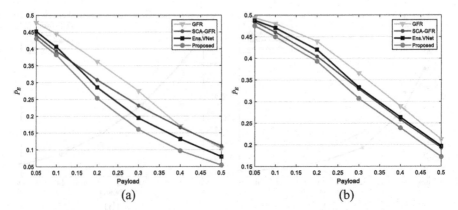

**Fig. 6.** Detection error for content-adaptive JPEG steganography with QF 95 when steganalyzed with different methods. (a) UED steganography and (b) J-UNIWARD steganography.

the steganalysis methods based on DCNN have significant advantages over the feature-based steganalysis methods. Furthermore, compared with other methos, the proposed steganalysis method can achieve the competitive detection performances.

## 5 Conclusions

DCNN is important for image steganalysis. Specially, the design of network structure is key. The existing works have proposed many DCNNs by combing the prior of traditional feature-based steganalysis method and the advances of DCNN in other research field such as computer vision [17]. The improvements in detection accuracy are significant. In this paper, a new steganalysis method is proposed for content-adaptive JPEG steganography through the ensemble of multiple DCNNs. The main contributions are the construction and the ensemble strategy of DCNNs.

We also notice that the better detection performances can be achieved by the ensemble classifier and the features learned using DCNNs, and then the decision strategy in Sect. 3.2 should be applied for ensemble classifier to get lower detection error. In the future, the feature learning and ensemble strategy will be studied further based on DCNNs. In addition, the steganalysis of the coverless steganography [18, 19] and other novel steganography algorithms [20, 21] also should be noticed.

**Acknowledgements.** This research was supported by National Natural Science Foundation of China (Grant Nos 61872448) and the Natural Science Basic Research Plan in Shanxi Province of China (No. 2021JQ-379).

## References

1. Pevný, T., Filler, T., Bas, P.: Using high-dimensional image models to perform highly undetectable steganography. In: Böhme, R., Fong, P.W.L., Safavi-Naini, R. (eds.) Information Hiding. IH 2010. LNCS, vol. 6387, pp. 161–177. Springer, Berlin, Heidelberg (2010). https://doi.org/10.1007/978-3-642-16435-4_13

2. Filler, T., Judas, J., Fridrich, J.: Minimizing additive distortion in steganography using syndrome-trellis codes. IEEE Trans. Inf. Forensics Secur. **6**(3), 920–935 (2011)
3. Wang, C., Ni, J.Q.: An efficient JPEG steganographic scheme based on the block–entropy of DCT coefficients. In: Proceedings of the IEEE International Conference on Acoustics, Speech and Signal Processing, Kyoto, Japan, pp.1785–1788. IEEE (2012)
4. Guo, L., Ni, J., Shi, Y.: Uniform embedding for efficient JPEG steganography. IEEE Trans. Inf. Forensics Secur. **9**(5), 814–825 (2014)
5. Holub, V., Fridrich, J.: Digital image steganography using universal distortion. In: 1st Workshop on ACM Information Hiding and Multimedia Security, Montpellier, France, pp. 59–68. ACM (2013)
6. Wang, Z.C., Zhang, X.P., Yin, Z.X.: Hybrid distortion function for JPEG steganography. J. Electron. Imaging **25**(5), 050501 (2016)
7. Song, X.F., Liu, F.L., Yang, C.F., Luo, X.Y., Zhang, Y.: Steganalysis of adaptive jpeg steganography using 2d gabor filters. In: Proceedings of the 3rd ACM Workshop on Information Hiding and Multimedia Security, Portland, Oregon, USA, pp. 15–23. ACM (2015)
8. Kodovský, J., Fridrich, J., Holub, V.: Ensemble classifiers for steganalysis of digital media. IEEE Trans. Inf. Forensics Secur. **7**(2), 432–444 (2012)
9. Xu, G., Wu, H.Z., Shi, Y.Q.: Structural design of convolutional neural networks for steganalysis. IEEE Signal Process. Lett. **23**(5), 708–712 (2016)
10. Chen, M., Sedighi, V., Boroumand, M., Fridrich, J.: JPEG-phase-aware convolutional neural network for steganalysis of JPEG images. In: Proceedings of the 5th ACM Workshop on Information Hiding and Multimedia Security, Paris France, pp. 75–84. ACM (2017)
11. Zeng, J.S., Tan, S.Q., Li, B., Huang, J.W.: Large-scale JPEG image steganalysis using hybrid deep-learning framework. IEEE Trans. Inf. Forensics Secur. **13**(5), 1200–1214 (2018)
12. Boroumand, M., Chen, M., Fridrich, J.: Deep residual network for steganalysis of digital images. IEEE Trans. Inf. Forensics Secur. **14**(5), 1181–1193 (2019)
13. Li, Q., Feng, G., Wu, H., Zhang, X.: Ensemble steganalysis based on deep residual network. In: Wang, H., Zhao, X., Shi, Y., Kim, H., Piva, A. (eds.) Digital Forensics and Watermarking. IWDW 2019. LNCS, vol. 12022, pp. 84–95. Springer, Cham (2020). https://doi.org/10.1007/978-3-030-43575-2_7
14. Grigorescu, S.E., Petkov, N., Kruizinga, P.: Comparison of texture features based on gabor filters. IEEE Trans. Image Process. **11**(10), 1160–1167 (2002)
15. Choi, J.Y., Lee, B.: Ensemble of deep convolutional neural networks with gabor face representations for face recognition. IEEE Trans. Image Process. **29**, 3270–3281 (2020)
16. Bas, P., Filler, T., Pevný, T.: Break our steganographic system: the ins and outs of organizing BOSS. In: Proceedings of the 13th International Workshop on Information Hiding, Prague, Czech Republic, pp. 59–70 (2011)
17. Zhang, R., Zhu, F., Liu, J.Y., Liu, G.S.: Depth-Wise Separable Convolutions and Multi-Level Pooling for an Efficient Spatial CNN-Based Steganalysis. IEEE Trans. Inf. Forensics Secur. **15**(1), 1138–1150 (2020)
18. Chen, X.Y., Zhang, Z.T., Qiu, A.Q., Xia, Z.H., Xiong, N.N.: A novel coverless steganography method based on image selection and StarGAN. IEEE Trans. Netw. Sci. Eng. **9**(1), 219–230 (2020)
19. Luo, Y.J., Qin, J.H., Xiang, X.Y., Tan, Y.: Coverless image steganography based on multi-object recognition. IEEE Trans. Circuits Syst. Video Technol. **31**(7), 2779–2791 (2021)
20. Wang, Y., Fu, Z.J., Sun, X.M.: High visual quality image steganography based on encoder-decoder model. J. Cyber Secur. **2**(3), 115–121 (2020)
21. Alhomoud, A.M.: Image steganography in spatial domain: current status, techniques, and trends. Intell. Autom. Soft Comput. **27**(1), 69–88 (2021)

# Reversible Data Hiding Based on Stationary Sequence of Pixel Value Ordering

Ningxiong Mao[1], Fan Chen[2], Yuan Yuan[2], and Hongjie He[1(✉)]

[1] School of Information Science and Technology, Southwest Jiaotong University, Chengdu 611756, China
hjhe@home.swjtu.edu.cn
[2] School of Computing and Artificial Intelligence, Southwest Jiaotong University, Chengdu 611756, China

**Abstract.** Pixel value ordering (PVO) is an excellent strategy for improving embedding capacity and visual quality of reversible data hiding (RDH) algorithm. PVO utilize strong correlation between pixel values to improve the prediction accuracy. However, for rough texture blocks the pixel value fluctuates greatly, that resulting correlation between the pixel values is weak. This paper proposed an PVO based on stationary pixel-values sequence (SPS-PVO), which eliminates the fluctuating pixel values according to the context of the block, and obtains a stationary pixel-values sequence to enhance the correlation between pixel values. Furthermore, the adaptive two-dimensional mapping (2D-mapping) of existing pairwise PEE has been further extended, increasing the number of adaptive prediction errors. We will original adaptive prediction errors $\{-2, 1, 0, 1\}$ expanded to $\{-3, -2, 1, 0, 1, 2\}$. Improved 2D-mapping increases the solution space, it is more likely to find the optimal 2D mapping. Experimental results show that the marked images by the proposed scheme have higher visual quality, e.g., the average PSNR for the Kodak image database is 64.45 dB after embedding 10,000bits, and the gain is 0.25 dB against the best result in the literature.

**Keywords:** Reversible data hiding · PVO · Stationary pixel-value sequence · Pairwise PEE

## 1 Introduction

Reversible data hiding (RDH) technology is an important branch in the field of information security. Most data hiding methods will cause irreversible distortion of host image. RDH embeds secret data into the host image in a visually imperceptible way. The key of reversible data hiding is to extract the secret data without distortion and restore the original host image without distortion at the decoding end [1]. Such reversible data hiding can satisfy some areas where unacceptable host images are slightly distorted, such as military, medical, remote sensing image secret communication, content integrity authentication, etc. [2, 3].

Currently, there are many methods of reversible data hiding, including difference expansion (DE) [4, 5], histogram shift [6, 7], and prediction error expansion (PEE) [8].

© The Author(s), under exclusive license to Springer Nature Switzerland AG 2022
X. Sun et al. (Eds.): ICAIS 2022, CCIS 1588, pp. 374–389, 2022.
https://doi.org/10.1007/978-3-031-06764-8_30

The DE method proposed by Tian [6] by expanding the difference between adjacent pixels to replace the least significant bits (LSB) to carry data. The HS technique is proposed by Ni et al. [6], in which the image intensity histogram is first generated and then modified for data embedding. In [8], Thodi and Rodriguez used prediction errors instead of pixel differences for data embedding. RDH based on PEE mainly includes two steps: generation of the prediction error histogram (PEH) and modification of the histogram. Existing research mainly improves these two steps. The first step is to use a high-precision predictor to calculate the prediction error, and then generate a sharp PEH [9–14]. Then, in the second step, according to the generated PEH design excellent expansion rules to obtain higher embedding capacity. So far, there have been many effective strategies, such as adaptive PEE, optimal expansion box selection, pairwise PEE and multiple histogram modification to modify the error embedding data while reducing distortion as much as possible [15–20].

Recently, a strategy called pixel-value ordering (PVO) by combining PEE has been used in RDH. PVO technology was first proposed by Li et al. [21]. By PVO, the host image is divided into non-overlapped blocks, and then the maximum and minimum in each block are modified to embed data. In this method, the maximum (minimum) in each block is either increased (decreased) by 1 in value or unmodified so that the pixel value order is unchanged after data embedding, which guarantees the reversibility. Many improvement scheme have been proposed on the basis of the original PVO [22–28]. He et al. proposed a Multi-Pass IPVO Based PEE in [28], which no longer predicts the maximum/minimum pixels and embeds the data by modifying the maximum/minimum pixels. In [28], the maximum/minimum pixels are used to predict other non-maximum/minimum pixels, and the non-maximum/minimum pixels are modified to embed data.

The key of PVO prediction technology is to use the correlation between pixel values. The higher the correlation between the pixel values, the higher the prediction accuracy of PVO. The higher the stationary pixel-value sequence (SPS) in the block, the more relevant the pixel values. In [28], using the maximum value as the predicted value, the prediction accuracy depends more on SPS. For example, when all pixel values are equal in the pixel-value sequence, Multi-Pass IPVO prediction method has the highest precision. It is rare that all pixel values are equal in a block, and the pixel-values sequence in most image blocks fluctuates. In order to improve the stationary of the pixel-value sequence, this paper proposes a stationary pixel-value sequence based PVO (SPS-PVO) scheme. We adaptively determine the length of SPS according to the complexity of the block to effectively improve the stationary of SPS used in PVO. Then it is combined with pairwise PEE to expand the two-dimensional mapping (2D-mapping) in the paper [20] to increase numbers of 2D bin that can be used to embed data to further improve performance.

The rest of this paper is organized as follows. Section 2 presents the proposed scheme in detail. The experimental results and the comparisons are provided in Sect. 3. Finally, Sect. 4 concludes this paper.

## 2 Proposed Scheme

In this section, the strategy of stationary pixel-value sequence PVO is first introduced. Then, how to determine the length of the sequence based on the block complexity value is described. Finally, the implementation details of the proposed scheme are presented.

### 2.1 Sps-Pvo

In [28], all pixels in the block will involve in IPVO. Use the maximum value as the predicted value to predict other non-maximum pixels, which is effective for smooth blocks but will produce very large prediction errors for texture blocks. In order to overcome this shortcoming, this paper proposes an PVO based on stationary pixel-values sequence. Assuming that the block size of $a \times b$ has $n(n = a \times b)$ pixels sorted as $\{x_{\sigma(1)} \leq x_{\sigma(2)} \leq x_{\sigma(3)} \leq \cdots \leq x_{\sigma(n)}\}$, we will select the predicted value according to the smoothness of the block to improve the stationary of executing PVO pixel-value sequence. We are not only selecting the maximum value as the predicted value, $\{x_{\sigma(n-1)}, x_{\sigma(n-2)}, \cdots, x_{\sigma(2)}\}$ may be selected as the predicted value according to the smoothness of the block. If $x_{\sigma(n-2)}$ is selected as the predicted value, then the $\{x_{\sigma(1)} \leq x_{\sigma(2)} \leq \cdots \leq x_{\sigma(n-2)}\}$ pixel-values sequence will be performed PVO. For coarse blocks, we appropriately compress length of SPS, which can improve the stationary of the sequence. We use the standard deviation (*Std*) to measure the stationary of pixel-value sequence, as shown in Eq. (1), the smaller the *Std*, the more stationary the sequence. As shown in Fig. 1, taking the $2 \times 2$ block size as an example.

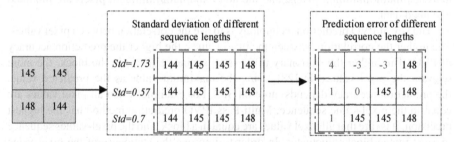

**Fig. 1.** Standard deviation and prediction error of different lengths pixel-value sequences.

Different lengths of the pixel-value sequence are taken to calculate the stationarity. In Fig. 1 we can see that appropriately compressing the sequence length can effectively improve the stationarity of the sequence and the obtained prediction error is also smaller.

$$td = \sqrt{\frac{\sum_{i=1}^{n} (x_i - \overline{x})^2}{n}} \tag{1}$$

where $\overline{x}$ represents the average value of the sequence.

**Calculation of Prediction Error**

We denote the smoothness of the pixel block as $s$, $s \in \{1, 2, \cdots, n-2, n-1\}$ has a total of $n - 1$ smoothness levels. The higher the smoothness level, the smoother the block. Perform IPVO with different sequence lengths for different smoothness levels, and the smoothness level of the block can be according to the complexity of the block. The host image is first divided into a series of non-overlapping blocks, the pixels in the block are $\{x_1, x_2, x_3, \cdots, x_n\}$, where $n$ is the total number of pixels in the block. Sort the pixels in the block in ascending order to get $\{x_{\sigma(1)}, x_{\sigma(2)}, x_{\sigma(3)}, \cdots, x_{\sigma(n)}\}$, and $\{1, 2, 3 \cdots, n\} \rightarrow \{\sigma(1), \sigma(2), \sigma(3), \cdots, \sigma(n)\}$ have a one-to-one correspondence. The prediction error $e_{max}(i)$ for a block with a smoothness of $s$ is calculated as follows.

$$e_{max}(i) = x_u - x_v \tag{2}$$

$$\begin{cases} u = min(\sigma(s+1), \sigma(i)) \\ v = max(\sigma(s+1), \sigma(i)) \end{cases} \quad i \in \{1, 2, \cdots, s\} \tag{3}$$

where $s$ represents the smoothness level of the block.

In Multi-Pass IPVO, it is not to modify the maximum pixel to embed data, but to reduce other non-maximum pixels to embedding data. Ensure that the pixel value ordering remains unchanged. The data embedding and the marker pixel $x_i'$ is as follows

$$x_i' = \begin{cases} x_i - b \ if \ e_{max}(i) = 0 \ or \ e_{max} = 1 \\ x_i - 1 \ if \ e_{max}(i) < 0 \ or \ e_{max} > 1 \end{cases} \tag{4}$$

where $b$ represents secret data.

This paper will inherit the two rounds embedded in [28]. After obtaining the prediction error $e_{max}$, the pixels in the block can be modified to embed data. Reorder the pixels in the block, and the block prediction error $e_{min}(i)$ with smoothness $s$ is calculated as follows

$$e_{min}(i) = x_s - x_t \tag{5}$$

$$\begin{cases} s = min(\sigma(n-s), \sigma(i)) \\ t = max(\sigma(n-s), \sigma(i)) \end{cases} \quad i \in \{n-s+1, n-s+2, \cdots, n\} \tag{6}$$

According to the prediction error $e_{min}(i)$, the non-minimum pixels can be enlarged to modify the embedded data, and the marker pixels $x_i'$ can be obtained as shown below.

$$x_i' = \begin{cases} x_i + b \ if \ e_{min}(i) = 0 \ or \ e_{min} = 1 \\ x_i + 1 \ if \ e_{min}(i) < 0 \ or \ e_{min} > 1 \end{cases} \tag{7}$$

Extracting secret data at the decoding end is the inverse process of embedding data. First, the smallest pixel is used as the predicted value to obtain the marked prediction error $e_{min}'(i)$. The data is extracted as follows

$$b = \begin{cases} e_{min}'(i) - 1 \ if \ e_{min}'(i) \in \{1, 2\} \\ -e_{min}'(i) \ if \ e_{min}'(i) \in \{-1, 0\} \end{cases} \tag{8}$$

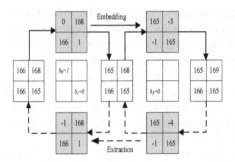 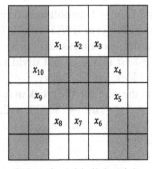

(a) The embedding and extraction process of SPS-IPVO with smoothness level $s=2$.     (b) Context for calculating block complexity.

**Fig. 2.** Illustration of SPS-PVO embedding and extraction process and context of block.

After extracting the secret data b embedded in the second round, the pixel value can be restored to the value after the first round embedding. The specific calculation is shown in Eq. (9).

$$x_i = \begin{cases} x_i' - b \ if \ e_{min}'(i) \in \{-1, 0, 1, 2\} \\ x_i' - 1 \ if \ e_{min}'(i) < -1 \ or \ e_{min}'(i) > 2 \end{cases} \tag{9}$$

After the pixel values are restored in the second round of data embedded, the pixels in the block are reordered. Marks prediction error $e_{max}'(i)$ of the first round can be calculated, according to Eq. (8) secret data $b$ can be extracted in the first round embedded. Restore the pixel value to the original value according to the marker prediction error $e_{max}'(i)$, as shown below

$$x_i = \begin{cases} x_i' + b \ if \ e_{max}'(i) \in \{-1, 0, 1, 2\} \\ x_i' + 1 \ if \ e_{max}'(i) < -1 \ or \ e_{max}'(i)(i) > 2 \end{cases} \tag{10}$$

In Fig. 2(a), we take $2 \times 2$ block size and smoothness level $S = 2$ as an example to show the embedding and extraction process of SPS-PVO in this paper. We can see that the SPS-PVO used in this paper can be embedded with 3bit capacity, and the embedded capacity using Multi-Pass IPVO is 2bit. SPS-PVO has obvious advantages.

**Determination of Block Smoothness Level**
In order to obtain SPS, the determination of the block smoothness level is a key issue. We adaptively determine the smoothness level of the block according to the texture complexity value (denoted as $NL$) of the block. In this paper, a fully enclosed context method is used to calculate the $NL$ of the block. We adopt the checkerboard pattern to embed data in shadow blocks first and then embed data in blank blocks to ensure reversibility. The checkerboard pattern and the context of calculating the block complexity value $NL$ are

shown in Fig. 2(b). The calculation of $NL$ is shown in Eq. (11), and the texture structure of the block can be described more accurately through the closed context.

$$NL = \sum_{j=1}^{11} \left(x_j - x_{j+1}\right)^2 + (x_{10} - x_1)^2 + (x_1 - x_8)^2 + (x_2 - x_7)^2 + (x_3 - x_6)^2$$
$$+ (x_4 - x_{10})^2 + (x_5 - x_9)^2 \tag{11}$$

The texture complexity value of the block can be calculated by Eq. (11), and the texture complexity values of all shadow blocks are collected and sorted in ascending order to obtain the set of complexity values of the shadow blocks, denoted as $SNL$. $SNL = \{NL_1, NL_2, NL_3, \cdots, NL_i, \cdots, NL_k\}$ and $NL_i < NL_{i+1}$, $NL_i$ may correspond to multiple blocks, and blocks with the same complexity value have the same smoothness level ($s$ has the same value). For blocks with every block $n$ pixels, set $(n-2)$ complexity thresholds as $\{T_1, T_2, \cdots, T_{(n-2)}\}$ and $\{NL_1 \leq T_1 \leq T_2 \leq \cdots \leq T_{(n-2)} \leq NL_k\}$, where $NL_1$ and $NL_k$ are the minimum and maximum of the complexity values of all shadow blocks. According to the complexity threshold, we can divide the block complexity value into $(n-1)$ intervals $\{[NL_1, T_1), [T_1, T_2), \cdots, [T_{(n-2)}, NL_k]\}$, and the corresponding smoothness $s$ of each interval is $\{s = n-1, s = n-2, \cdots, s = 1\}$. How to find the optimal complexity threshold $\{T_1, T_2, \cdots, T_{(n-2)}\}$ to make the prediction error sequence optimal is a problem of needs to be solved.

We use the local threshold judgment method to solve the optimal complexity threshold. We define an effective prediction error rate as $P$, the ratio of the prediction error $\{-2, -1, 0, 1\}$ that can be embedded data to the total number of prediction errors. We assume that skipped effective prediction error rate threshold is denoted as $P_S$. The effective prediction error rate corresponding to a every complexity value is denoted as $P_{NL}$. We start from $NL_1$ with the smallest block complexity value. At this time, the highest block smoothness $s = n - 1$. If the $P_{NL}$ obtained from the complexity value $NL_1$ is greater than or equal to $P_S$ i.e. $P_{NL} \geq P_S$, the smoothness level of the block in $NL_2$ continues to maintain the highest level ($s = n - 1$). Otherwise, the smoothness level of the block in $NL_2$ is reduced by one unit ($s = n - 2$), and the first complexity threshold is $T_1 = NL_1$, and similarly $T_2, \cdots, T_{n-2}$ can be obtained. The value of $P_S$ is $P_S \in \{0.05, 0.1, 0.15, \cdots, 0.95\}$, and the value of $P_S$ will be traversed once in the process of solving. The specific details are shown in the following steps. The optimal complexity threshold set $\{T_1^*, T_2^*, \cdots, T_{n-2}^*\}$ can be obtained through the following steps, so that the optimal prediction error sequence can be determined.

Step1. According to the block complexity value Eq. (11), the complexity values of all shadow blocks can be obtained. After the complexity values are sorted in ascending order, the corresponding block sorts can be obtained, and the sorted complexity value set $SNL$ is obtained.

Step2. Starting from $NL_1$ with the smallest complexity value, the block smoothness level corresponding to the complexity value $NL_1$ is $n - 1$. According to Eq. (2) and Eq. (3), the prediction errors of all blocks whose complexity value is $NL_1$ are calculated and $P_{NL}$ is obtained.

Step3. Compare the given skip threshold $P_S(i)$, if $P_{NL}$ is greater than or equal to $P_S(i)$, keep the smoothness level unchanged and return to Step2 to calculate the $P_{NL}$ of the

next complexity value $NL_2$. Otherwise, the smoothing level $s$ is reduced by one unit
($s = n - 2$) and then return to Step2 to calculate the $P_{NL}$ of the next complexity value
$NL_2$, and record the complexity value $NL_1$ at this time and save it in the $i - th$ solution
$\delta_i$.

Step4. When the block corresponding to the maximum complexity value is calculated, a
solution $\delta_i = \{T_1, T_2, \cdots, T_{(n-2)}\}$ of the smoothness level division of the corresponding
block of $P_S(i)$ can be obtained. $\delta_i$ contains multiple complexity values, but it is less than
or equal to $n - 2$. The skip threshold $P_S(i)$ will be updated to $P_S(i + 1)$ and return to
Step2 to recalculate the solution of the next block smoothing level division, and finally
a solution set $\{\delta_1, \cdots, \delta_i, \cdots, \delta_k\}$ can be obtained.

Step5. In the solution set $\{\delta_1, \cdots, \delta_i, \cdots, \delta_{18}\}$, select a solution that satisfies the embedding capacity and has the highest effective prediction error rate $P$ as the optimal solution
$\delta^* = \{T_1^*, T_2^*, \cdots, T_{n-2}^*\}$ for the block smoothness level division.

## 2.2 Experimental Evaluation of SPS-PVO Strategy

In this part, we will verify the effectiveness of the SPS-PVO strategy proposed in this
paper. We used 32 standard images including 8 classic $512 \times 512$ image (Lena, Baboon,
Airplane, Barbara, Boat, Lake, Pepper) and 24 Kodak color images with $512 \times 768$ or
$768 \times 512$ size. Kodak color images will be transformed into gray-scale format in the
following experiments.

In Eq. (1), we mainly use the standard deviation to evaluate the stationary of pixel-
value sequence. In Fig. 3, the Std of Lena images are compared with the block size of
$2 \times 2$ and $3 \times 3$. We calculated the Std of the pixel sequence in each shadow block
that performs PVO. In Fig. 3 we can see that regardless of the $2 \times 2$ or $3 \times 3$ block
size, the Std value of the pixel-value sequence in this paper is smaller, so the sequence
is more stationary, indicating that SPS-PVO has higher prediction accuracy. Figure 4
shows the Std average value of the pixel value sequence performed PVO in the image,
and 32 images are tested. In Fig. 4 we can see that the average Std of the SPS-PVO
strategy is much smaller than the average Std of He et al. [28]. It means that the pixel-
value sequence used by SPS-PVO in this paper is more stationary and can get higher
prediction accuracy. In Fig. 5, the SPS-PVO strategy of this paper is replaced by the

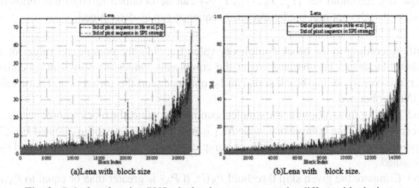

(a)Lena with block size                    (b)Lena with   block size.

**Fig. 3.** Std of performing PVO pixel-value sequence under different block sizes.

prediction method in [28] and the original [28] for PSNR comparison. Comparing the two images Lena, Boat in Fig. 5, we can be seen that the PSNR of [28] after using the SPS-PVO strategy is better than the original [28] scheme at each capacity point. It also proves the superiority of SPS-PVO strategy.

## 2.3   Implementation of the Proposed Scheme

In Sect. 2.1, we can get the optimal prediction error sequence $e_{max}$, and we need embedded data by to modify the pixel according to the prediction error. We will combine the latest pairwise PEE for data embedding. Pairwise PEE is mainly divided into two main steps. The first step is how to effectively pair the prediction errors to obtain a sharp 2D-PEH, the second step is how to design a high-performance 2D-mapping.

**Prediction Error Pairing**
The method of prediction error pairing in pairwise PEE is mainly based on the pairing of adjacent positions and the adaptive pairing of local positions. In this paper, a globally adaptive pairing method is no longer limited to position, but the prediction error sequence sorted according to the complexity value is directly paired according to adjacent positions. In order to improve the embedding capacity of pairwise PEE, this paper first divides the prediction error into an extended set and a shift set similar to the literature [20]. The division of the set is shown in Eq. (12). In Eq. (12), $E_d$ is the expanded set, which can be used for data embedding, and $S_d$ is the shift set, which cannot be used for data embedding, where $d = 3$. The specific process of the global adaptive pairing method is shown in Fig. 6(a).

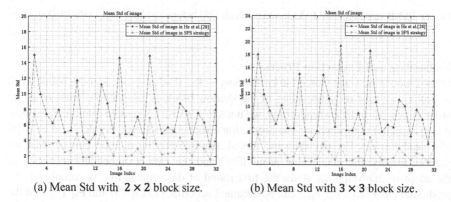

(a) Mean Std with **2 × 2** block size.      (b) Mean Std with **3 × 3** block size.

**Fig. 4.**   Average Std of images.

$$\begin{cases} E_d = \{e_{max} : -d \leq e_{max} \leq d - 1\} \\ S_d = \{e_{max} : e_{max} > d - 1 \text{ or } e_{max} < -d\} \end{cases} \tag{12}$$

**Adaptive 2D-Mapping**
2D-mapping is based on experience in many existing pairwise PEE. Literature [20] proposed an adaptive 2D-mapping method, which can adaptively determine the 2D-mapping
according to the 2D-PEH of the image. In [20], only $\{-2, -1, 0, 1\}$ four prediction errors
are used as the expanded set, but in fact the frequency of $\{-3, 2\}$ prediction errors is
also very high. We expand the range of adaptive prediction error in [20], and expand the
prediction error that can be embedded data to $\{-3, -2, -1, 0, 1, 2\}$. After we expand
the prediction error that can be embedded data, we can use more prediction errors for
data embedding to effectively increase the capacity, and increase the solution space of
the adaptive 2D-mapping, mapping design. The nine red 2D bins need to adaptively
determine the mapping relationship, and the mapping relationship and it is more likely
to obtain the optimal 2D-mapping. Figure 6(b) shows the specific details of other 2D
bins is determined.

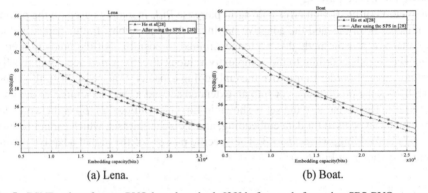

(a) Lena.                                  (b) Boat.

**Fig. 5.** PSNR values for two PVO-based methods [28] before and after using SPS-PVO strategy.

**Embedding and Extraction Process**
In the embedding stage, since the embedding of the shadow block and the blank block
is similar, we take the embedding of the shadow block as an example. First of all, in
order to prevent overflow/underflow, we need to construct a marked bitmap and denote
it as $(LM)$ after compression. The prediction error sequence $e_{max}$ is calculated by SPS-
PVO and Eq. (2), Eq. (3), then the global adaptive pairing method can be used for
pairing. Finally, the pixel value is modified and the data is embedded according to
the adaptive 2D-Mapping. After the first round of data embedding is completed, the
prediction error sequence $e_{min}$ can be obtained according to Eq. (5) and Eq. (6), and the
global adaptive pairing can be performed similarly. Complete pixel modification and
embed data according to adaptive 2D-mapping. In order to ensure reversibility, we need
to embed some auxiliary information including: marks bitmap $(LM)$, block size $(a, b)$,
optimal complexity threshold $\delta^*$, and the end position of the first and second rounds of
embedding. The auxiliary information is embedded in the first line of the image by LSB
replacement. The embedding process of blank blocks is similar.

Data extraction and pixel value restoration at the decoding end are the inverse process
of data embedding. Firstly, the auxiliary information of the blank block is extracted

including: the optimal complexity threshold T, the end position of the embedding, the length of the auxiliary information of the shadow block, and the mark bitmap $(LM)$. Then calculate the mark prediction error $e'_{min}$ according to Eq. (5) and Eq. (6), extract the secret data in the blank block through optimal 2D-mapping, and restore the pixel value of the blank block. After completing the data extraction and pixel value restoration of the blank block, extracting the secret data and restoring the pixel value of the shadow block are similar operations.

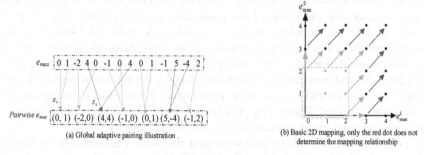

(a) Global adaptive pairing illustration .

(b) Basic 2D mapping, only the red dot does not determine the mapping relationship .

**Fig. 6.** Illustration global adaptive pairing and adaptive 2D-mapping.

## 3 Experimental Results

In this part, the impact of block size on performance will be analyzed, extensive experiments have been conducted to evaluate performance of the proposed scheme by computing the peak signal-to-noise ratio (PSNR) between the cover image and the watermarked images at different embedding rates. A higher PSNR value means that the watermarked image has a higher quality. To better evaluate performance of the proposed scheme, six recently reported state-of-the-art methods [11, 12, 17, 20, 27] and [28] have been implemented for comparison. In the proposed method, the block size a and b take values from {2, 3, 4, 5}, and the optimal onethat produce the highest PSNR is finally utilized for data embedding.

Figure 7 shows the performance comparison of Lena and Boat images under different block sizes. In Fig. 7 we can see that the PSNR is generally higher under large blocks but the embedding capacity of large blocks is small. The main reason is that the texture complexity value of the block under the large block is more accurate, and the very smooth area can be preferentially used. SPS-PVO under large blocks is only effective for smooth blocks. SPS-PVO will produce large prediction errors for general texture blocks and cannot embed data, but there are very few very smooth blocks in natural images, so the capacity of large blocks is low. The texture complexity value of the block under the small block will have error, so the PSNR is lower than the large block under the small capacity. The position correlation between pixels in small blocks is very strong, and the pixel values are also more correlated, so the prediction accuracy is high. The overall prediction accuracy of small blocks is much higher than that of large blocks, so the capacity of small blocks will be higher.

Table 1 and Table 2 show the PSNR comparison of the proposed scheme and other advanced schemes at 10,000bit and 20,000bit capacities, respectively. Table 1 compares 6 test images under 10,000bit. In Table 2, because the capacity of Baboon image is less than 20,000bit, only 5 test images are compared in Table 2. Regardless of Table 1 or Table 2, we can see that the PSNR of this paper scheme is higher than that of other advanced scheme. In Fig. 8 we show the PSNR comparison between the proposed scheme and other advanced schemes under different embedding capacities. In Fig. 8 we can see that the PSNR of the proposed scheme in Lena and Baboon images is lower than other schemes under larger capacity. When the Lena image exceeds the embedding capacity of 22,000bit, the PNSR of this paper scheme will be lower than scheme of the literature [20, 28]. In order to improve the stationary of the pixel-value sequence, SPS-PVO method of this paper will compress the length of the pixel-value sequence, so the number of prediction errors obtained by SPS-PVO is much smaller than the method in [20, 28]. Lena and Baboon images are texture images, the number of prediction errors obtained through SPS-PVO is less, so the performance is low under large capacity. For the four images of Boat, Elaine, Lake and Pepper, the PSNR of the proposed scheme is higher than other advanced schemes at each embedding capacity.

In [28], the maximum value is used as the predicted value, and combined the pairwise PEE method in [20] is used for data embedding. Referring to Fig. 8 we can see that the PSNR of the proposed scheme is lower than [28] in terms of embedding capacity greater than 24,000bit with Lena image. The SPS-PVO in this paper will severely compress the number of prediction errors, so in large capacity, in order to meet the embedding capacity, more invalid shift will be generated. Refer to Table 1 and Table 2 Compared with [28], the average PSNR gains of this paper scheme are 0.47 dB and 0.29 dB, respectively. The gain of the average PSNR is less under the embedding capacity of 20,000bit. The overall performance of the proposed scheme is better compared [28].

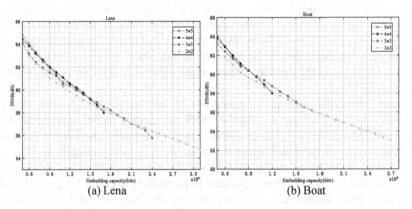

(a) Lena                                    (b) Boat

**Fig. 7.** The impact of different block sizes on performance.

**Table 1.** PSNR comparison between this paper scheme and other advanced schemes with 10000 bits.

| Image | [11] | [12] | [17] | [20] | [27] | [28] | Proposed |
|---|---|---|---|---|---|---|---|
| Lena | 59.08 | 60.08 | 60.99 | 60.42 | 61.15 | 61.16 | **61.46** |
| Baboon | 54.74 | 55.97 | 55.81 | 56.03 | 54.86 | 55.11 | **55.99** |
| Boat | 56.61 | 57.63 | 58.97 | 58.13 | 58.67 | 59.27 | **59.87** |
| Elaine | 57.83 | 58.39 | 58.52 | 58.50 | 58.09 | 59.50 | **59.74** |
| Lake | 57.89 | 58.22 | 59.20 | 59.18 | 59.74 | 60.95 | **61.31** |
| Pepper | 55.63 | 56.94 | 58.67 | 57.02 | 59.60 | 59.87 | **60.30** |
| Average | 56.96 | 57.87 | 58.69 | 58.21 | 58.68 | 59.31 | **59.78** |

**Table 2.** PSNR comparison between this paper scheme and other advanced schemes with 20000 bits.

| Image | [11] | [12] | [17] | [20] | [27] | [28] | Proposed |
|---|---|---|---|---|---|---|---|
| Lena | 55.62 | 56.70 | 57.47 | 57.00 | 57.16 | 57.60 | **57.69** |
| Boat | 52.63 | 53.73 | 54.83 | 54.09 | 54.19 | 55.02 | **55.40** |
| Elaine | 52.52 | 53.13 | 54.12 | 53.47 | 53.25 | 54.39 | **54.78** |
| Lake | 53.17 | 53.65 | 54.64 | 54.31 | 54.59 | 56.08 | **56.40** |
| Pepper | 52.35 | 53.60 | 54.80 | 53.64 | 55.39 | 55.97 | **56.24** |
| Average | 53.26 | 54.16 | 55.17 | 54.50 | 54.92 | 55.81 | **56.10** |

In [27], the traditional prediction method of PVO is used, i.e. the second largest value predicts the maximum value, and then it is also combined with the pairwise PEE in [20]. Use the second largest value to predict the maximum value, because the pixel value correlation between the second largest value and the maximum value is very strong, the prediction accuracy is very high. However, the number of prediction errors obtained by only predicting the maximum/minimum pixels in a block is very small. In [27], 2D-mapping adaptive the numbers of prediction errors is less than this paper scheme. With reference to Fig. 8, the PSNR of the proposed scheme is better under each embedding capacity in the 6 test images. With reference to Table 1 and Table 2, the average PSNR gains of the proposed scheme are 1.1 dB and 1.18 dB under the embedded capacity of 10,000bit and 20,000bit, respectively.

In [20], rhombus prediction is combined with pairwise PEE, and adaptive 2D-mapping method is used to embed data. Rhombus prediction mainly utilize the correlation of pixels positional. In this paper, SPSP-IPVO takes into account the correlation of pixel position and pixel value. The adaptive 2D-mapping in [20] is to adapt to the four prediction errors $\{-2, -1, 0, 1\}$. In this paper, the range of adaptive prediction errors is expanded to $\{-3, -2, -1, 0, 1, 2\}$ total of six prediction errors. In Fig. 8 we can see that

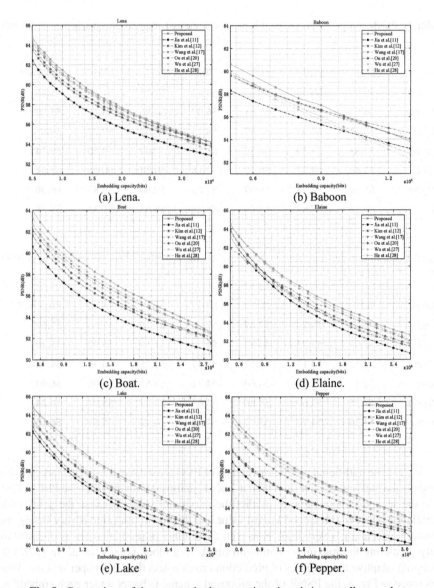

**Fig. 8.** Comparison of the proposed scheme against six existing excellent works.

the PSNR of the proposed scheme is lower than [20] under the large capacity of Lena and Baboon images. In Table 1 and Table 2, we can see that the average PSNR gains of the proposed scheme are 1.57 dB and 1.60 dB under 10,000bit and 20,000bit embedding capacities.

In [17], a fuzzy C-means clustering algorithm is utilized to generate multiple histograms, and the prediction method uses a rhombus predictor. Different types of histograms can adaptively select different shift bins, which can effectively utilize different texture regions of the image. In [17], one-dimensional histogram shift is used, and the accuracy of the prediction method is also lower than SPS-PVO. In Fig. 9 we can see that the PSNR of the proposed scheme is better than [17] at each capacity point, only the PSNR of the Baboon image after 12,000bit capacity is lower than [17] and the reason is similar to before. In Table 1 and Table 2, the average PSNR gain of this paper scheme is 1.09 dB and 0.93 dB, respectively, compared to [17].

Finally, to further illustrate the proposed method superiority, the experiments are conducted on the Kodak image dataset which contains 24 color images sized 512 × 768 or 768 × 512. These images are taken from digital cameras and transformed into gray-scale format in the experiment. Figure 9 shows the PSNR comparison between the proposed scheme and the existing research results [28] and [27] under the 10,000bit and 20,000bit embedding capacity. At 10,000bit embedded capacity, the average PSNR of the proposed scheme is 64.45 dB, and the average PSNR of [28] and [27] are 63.32 dB and 64.20 dB, respectively. Compared with [28] and [27], the average PSNR gains of this paper scheme are 1.13 dB and 0.25 dB, respectively. For the 13-th test image, it is a very complicated texture images, so the PSNR of this paper scheme is slightly lower than [27]. Under the capacity of 20000bit, the average PSNR of this paper scheme, [28] and [27] are 60.53 dB, 60.25 dB and 60.36 dB, respectively. The average PSNR gain is 0.19 dB and 0.28 dB respectively. It demonstrates the proposed scheme has better performance with various kinds of images.

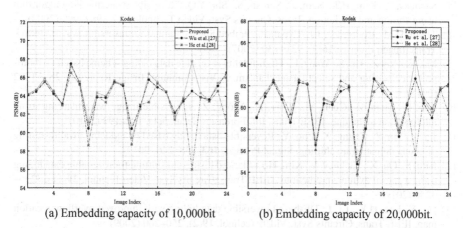

(a) Embedding capacity of 10,000bit       (b) Embedding capacity of 20,000bit.

**Fig. 9.** PSNR comparison between the proposed scheme and methods in [27, 28] on Kodak database with 10,000 bit and 20,000bit.

# 4  Conclusion

In order to improve the stationary of executing PVO pixel-value sequence, this paper proposes an PVO based on stationary pixel-value sequence (SPS-PVO). SPS-PVO can adaptively compress the length of the pixel-value sequence according to the complexity of the block, thereby effectively improving the stationarity of execution PVO pixel-value sequence. In addition, the existing 2D-mapping is improved, the adaptive prediction error $\{-2, -1, 0, 1\}$ is expanded to $\{-3, -2, -1, 0, 1, 2\}$ to increase the number of 2D bins that can be embedded data. The marked images by the proposed scheme have higher visual quality, e.g., the average PSNR values for the six standard images and the Kodak image database after embedding 10,000 bits are 59.78 dB and 64.45 dB, and the gains are 0.47 dB and 0.25 dB against the best result in the literature, respectively.

# References

1. Shi, Y.Q., Ni, Z., Zou, D., Liang, C., Xuan, G.: Lossless data hiding: fundamentals, algorithms and applications. In: Proceedings of the IEEE International Symposium on Circuits and Systems, pp. 33–36 (2004)
2. Honsinger, C.W., Jones, P.W., Rabbani, M., Stoffel, J.C.: Lossless recovery of an original image containing embedded data. U.S. Patent (2001)
3. Shi, Y.Q., Li, X., Zhang, X., Wu, H.T., Ma, B.: Reversible data hiding: advances in the past two decades. IEEE Access 4, 3210–3237 (2016)
4. Tian, J.: Reversible data embedding using a difference expansion. Trans. Circuits Syst. Video Technol. 13(8), 890–896 (2003)
5. Alattar, A.M.: Reversible watermark using the difference expansion of a generalized integer transform. Trans. Image Process. 13(8), 1147–1156 (2004)
6. Ni, Z., Shi, Y.Q., Ansari, N., Su, W.: Reversible data hiding. Trans. Circuits Syst. Video Technol. 16(3), 354–362 (2006)
7. Sachnev, V., Kim, H.J., Nam, J., Suresh, S., Shi, Y.Q.: Reversible watermarking algorithm using sorting and prediction. Trans. Circuits Syst. Video Technol. 19(7), 989–999 (2009)
8. Thodi, D.M., Rodriguez, J.J.: Expansion embedding techniques for reversible watermarking. Trans. Image Process. 16(3), 721–730 (2007)
9. Ma, X., Pan, Z., Hu, S., Wang, L.: High-fidelity reversible data hiding scheme based on multipredictor sorting and selecting mechanism. J. Vis. Commun. Image Represent 28, 71–82 (2015)
10. Luo, L., Chen, Z., Chen, M., Zeng, X., Xiong, Z.: Reversible image watermarking using interpolation technique. IEEE Trans. Inf. Forensics Secur. 5(1), 187–193 (2010)
11. Jia, Y., Yin, Z., Zhang, X., Luo, Y.: Reversible data hiding based on reducing invalid shifting of pixels in histogram shifting. Signal Process. 163, 238–246 (2019)
12. Kim, S., Qu, X., Sachnev, V., Kim, H.J.: Skewed histogram shifting for reversible data hiding using a pair of extreme predictions. IEEE Trans. Circuits Syst. Video Technol. 29(11), 3236–3246 (2019)
13. Hu, Y., Lee, H.K., Li, J.: DE-based reversible data hiding with improved overflow location map. IEEE Trans. Circuits Syst. Video Technol. 19(2), 250–260 (2009)
14. Wu, H., Li, X., Zhao, Y., Ni, R.: Improved PPVO-based high-fidelity reversible data hiding. Signal Process. 56, 167–181 (2020)
15. Wang, J., Ni, J., Zhang, X., Shi, Y.Q.: Rate and distortion optimization for reversible data hiding using multiple histogram shifting. IEEE Trans. Cybern. 47(2), 315–326 (2017)

16. Coatrieux, G., Pan, W., Cuppens-Boulahia, N., Cuppens, F., Roux, C.: Reversible watermarking based on invariant image classification and dynamic histogram shifting. IEEE Trans. Inf. Forensics Secur. **8**(1), 111–120 (2013)
17. Wang, J., Mao, N., Chen, X.: Multiple histograms based reversible data hiding by using FCM clustering. Signal Process. **159**(3), 193–203 (2019)
18. Li, X., Zhang, W., Gui, X., Yang, B.: Efficient reversible data hiding based on multiple histograms modification. IEEE Trans. Inf. Forensics Secur. **10**(9), 2016–2027 (2015)
19. Ou, B., Li, X., Zhao, Y., Ni, R., Shi, Y.Q.: Pairwise prediction error expansion for efficient reversible data hiding. IEEE Trans. Image Process. **22**(12), 5010–5021 (2013)
20. Ou, B., Li, X., Zhang, W., Zhao, Y.: Improving pairwise PEE via hybrid-dimensional histogram generation and adaptive mapping selection. IEEE Trans. Circuits Syst. Video Technol. **29**(7), 2176–2190 (2019)
21. Li, X., Li, J., Li, B., Yang, B.: High-fidelity reversible data hiding scheme based on pixel-value-ordering and prediction-error expansion. Signal Process. **93**(1), 198–205 (2013)
22. Peng, F., Li, X., Yang, B.: Improved PVO-based reversible data hiding. Digit. Signal Process. **25**(6), 255–265 (2014)
23. Ou, B., Li, X., Zhao, Y., Ni, R.: Reversible data hiding using invariant pixel-value-ordering and prediction-error expansion. Signal Process. Image Commun. **29**(7), 760–772 (2014)
24. Weng, S., Shi, Y., Hong, W., Yao, Y.: Dynamic improved pixel value ordering reversible data hiding. Inf. Sci. **489**(8), 136–154 (2019)
25. Wang, X., Ding, J., Pei, Q.: A novel reversible image data hiding scheme based on pixel value ordering and dynamic pixel block partition. Inf. Sci. **310**(68), 16–35 (2015)
26. Ou, B., Li, X., Wang, J.: High-fidelity reversible data hiding based on pixel-value-ordering and pairwise prediction-error expansion. Vis. Commun. Image Represent **39**, 12–23 (2016)
27. Wu, H., Li, X.: Improved reversible data hiding based on PVO and adaptive pairwise embedding. J. Real-Time Image Process. **16**(3), 685–695 (2019)
28. He, W., Cai, Z.: An insight into pixel value ordering prediction-based prediction-error expansion. IEEE Trans. Inf. Forensics Secur. **15**(67), 3859–3871 (2020)

# SVD Mark: A Novel Black-Box Watermarking for Protecting Intellectual Property of Deep Neural Network Model

Haojie Lv, Shuyuan Shen[✉], Huanjie Lin, Yibo Yuan, and Delin Duan

School of Software, South China Normal University, Foshan 528225, China
ssyuan16@m.scnu.edu.cn

**Abstract.** With the rapid development of deep learning technology, more and more researchers have paid attention to protecting the intellectual property rights of the deep neural network (DNN) model. So far, various methods have been proposed to construct black-box watermarking copyright protection based on trigger sets. Since extant black-box watermarking methods are backdoor-based, the watermark embedding process inevitably distorts the decision boundary of the DNN model, which leads to a decline in the performance of the DNN model. We propose a novel scheme for constructing black-box watermarking based on Singular Value Decomposition (SVD) to compensate for shortcomings. We select an appropriate number of image samples as watermark key samples in the training dataset by employing the Mersenne-Twister algorithm, which strengthens the relevance of the process watermarking embedding to the original classification task and extends the perceptual domain of the DNN model. Subsequently, the SVD algorithm extracts the primary feature information of the watermark key samples, thereby constructing more stable and covert watermark samples. Next, the classification labels corresponding to the watermark samples are specified as the classification labels of their corresponding watermark key samples, which is unlike most existing DNN watermarking schemes. It can effectively reduce the distortion of the DNN model decision boundary caused by watermarking during the embedding process. As such, the proposed scheme has a low impact on the performance of the DNN model and is highly robust. We have validated the proposed watermarking scheme on two benchmark datasets. The experimental results show that our scheme, besides meeting the functional requirements of watermarking, also does not affect the test accuracy of the DNN model. Moreover, the proposed watermarking is robust to the common watermarking attacks.

**Keywords:** Watermarking · SVD · DNN models · Ownership verification

## 1 Introduction

Deep learning (DL) techniques have made outstanding achievements in the field of vision processing [9,12], speech recognition [27], natural language processing

(NLP) [24], and robotics. Giant companies such as Microsoft, Apple, and Google have already used the DNN model in their major commercial products. DNN model can provide higher quality and intelligence to their products. That has opened up a new market for Machine Learning as a Service (MLaaS) [18] due to the use of open-source frameworks such as TensorFlow, Pytorch, and the open-source community of pre-trained DNN model. Companies can distribute trained DNN models to users, who can tune them to their needs to improve performance or achieve specified tasks within the scope of the license. Although MLaaS provides more efficient and flexible applications of the neural network models to a broader range of users, these distributed models are inevitably subject to malicious attacks. Attackers build pirated AI services [26] by repackaging the DNN models distributed. They illegally distribute it to other users without the authorization of the DNN model owner to earn profits. As a result, the DNN model owner is at risk of copyright infringement and substantial financial loss arising from the malicious actions of the attackers.

The DNN model is subject to the same hazards of illegal piracy as traditional multimedia products (e.g., images, audio, video, etc.). If effective copyright protection and piracy tracking techniques cannot be established for the DNN model, the casual distribution of the DNN model may threaten human society. It is a crucial issue how to protect the intellectual property rights of the DNN model effectively.

Digital watermarking [3] has been proposed as an effective method of protecting the copyright of digital products in the traditional field of multimedia information [10,20]. It has been widely used in commerce in many countries and is supported by many legal provisions [4]. Although digital watermarking has mature applications in the multimedia field, the traditional watermarking method cannot be directly used to protect DNN model products [25]. The principal reason is that the DNN model relies on internal structure and weight parameters. Since 2017, digital watermarking schemes have been proposed to protect the DNN model based on digital watermarking technology. There are two main types of DNN model watermarking: *white-box* watermarking [2,5,23] and black-box watermarking [1,13,15,26].

The white-box watermarking is mapped to the weight parameters of the hidden layer of the DNN model. The DNN model owner extracts watermarking in the validation phase by mapping the specified model weight parameters to the watermarking information. The differences between extracted watermarking and target's watermarking are compared to complete the ownership validation of the DNN model.

In contrast, the working pattern of black-box watermarking only requires comparing the relationship between the input and output of the DNN model without additional access to the model weight parameters. Consequently, the research of black-box watermarking has been gradually developed in recent years.

The construction of black-box watermarking relies heavily on a dataset called a trigger set, in which a set of samples can trigger a specific output. The embedding process of black-box watermarking is analogous to a backdoor attack. The trigger set and the marked DNN model correspond to the trigger part and the model with a backdoor part of the backdoor attack, respectively. Specifically, the embedding of watermarking is achieved by the DNN model classifying the samples of the trigger set to the (generally incorrect) labels specified. The DNN model owner sends a remote query containing the trigger set to access the target model's Application Programming Interface (API) when a copyright dispute happens. If the label output from the target DNN model is always a predefined label for the trigger set sample, the black-box watermarking verification is successful.

In recent years, several black-box watermarking schemes have been proposed. In 2018, Zhang et al. [26] processed the training dataset's images using Gaussian noise, explicit logos (possibly company names), and other methods to generate watermark samples. Subsequently, Adi et al. [1] picked several abstract images not relevant to the classification task and labeled them with a specified classification label as watermarking. Merrer et al. [13] constructed adversarial samples using the feature information of the decision boundary and pointed the adversarial examples to a specified classification label to obtain watermarking.

Various schemes [8,22,28] have been proposed to construct watermarking. In general, we can divide the types of watermark samples into two main categories: Constructed on an example of the training dataset or not. However, the labels of these watermark samples are specified by the owner or are wrong. These intentionally modified labels deviate from the actual labels of the watermark samples. Worse still, black-box watermarking constructed in their way can largely distort the decision boundary of the DNN model, causing the model to converge less than optimally during training. If this happens, it will result in, for example, the degraded performance of the DNN model and vague generality or robustness of the watermarking, etc.

We propose a novel SVD-based scheme for constructing black-box watermarking that can be effectively applied to copyright protection. Specifically, a certain number of samples in the original training dataset are picked for SVD processing, called watermark key samples. Meanwhile, the labels corresponding to these watermark key samples are not modified so that the samples still point to the correct classification labels to construct watermarking. The advantage is that the watermark samples complete the dimensionality reduction of the image data. Although these samples become more abstract, blurred, and cannot be correctly identified by a clean DNN model, the primary feature information of the training dataset samples is retained. Such primary feature information is always present in the parameters of the first few hidden layers of the DNN model. As a result, the update of the DNN model weight parameters is slowed down during the watermark embedding process, which reduces the impact of the watermarking embedding on the accuracy of the original classification task of the DNN model. Because assigning specific classification labels to watermark samples would lead to distortions in the decision boundary of the DNN model, we do not assign specific or incorrect classification labels to watermark samples. Keeping the original classification labels of the watermark samples ensures the reliability of the source of sample construction. It expands the DNN model's perceptual field, thus improving the DNN model's accuracy by a small margin.

Our proposed watermarking scheme has faster convergence during the embedding process, better robustness of watermarking, and is less prone to erasure by attackers. **In summary, the contributions of our work are as follows:**

1. We generate the pseudo-random sequence to select the watermark key samples using the Mersenne-Twister algorithm. The sequence is more representative and stochastic, stemming from having a more extended period and less correlation between its elements. Further, the seed of the pseudo-random sequence, owner signature, and timestamp are bound together and submitted to a certificate authority (CA) for storage, which strictly guarantees the traceability and uniqueness of the watermark key samples.
2. The processed image samples by SVD are equivalent to a data dimensionality reduction, which effectively eliminates the sensitive regions of the human visual system to the image samples while extracting most of the content feature information of the image samples. We apply SVD to the watermark key samples to produce more hidden and robust watermark samples.
3. We propose a novel watermarking construction scheme based on the DNN model operation pattern. The "watermarking" pattern is tightly linked to the classification task pattern in this scheme, making the watermarking embedding process faster to convergence and more robust to watermarking attacks such as pruning, fine-tuning, etc.

The rest of the paper is structured as follows. In Sect. 2, we introduce the main contents of SVD, black-box watermarking, and deep learning. Next, Sect. 3 shows the implementation of our proposed watermarking framework and the details of the watermarking algorithm. Section 4 provides the experimental results and analysis. Section 5 further discusses the proposed watermarking with the existing watermarking schemes. The conclusion is given in Sect. VI.

## 2   Related Works

### 2.1   Deep Learning

Deep learning is a novel approach in the field of machine learning [12], and its structure is called the DNN model, characterized by complex structure and deep neural hidden layers. Currently, popular DNN model included Res-Net [7], VGG [21], Capsule Network [19] etc. DNN model transforms the input data into feature information as it passes through each hidden layer and finally integrates the feature information to output results.

In this paper, we consider a categorical DNN model whose task is to classify the input samples with labels. $x$ and $y$ represent the set of input samples and the corresponding set of classification labels for the samples, respectively. Specifically, we denote the input $x_i \in \mathcal{R}$, representing an image matrix or text string information. $x_i$ corresponds to a label $y_i \in \mathcal{M}$, where $\mathcal{M}$ is a set of non-negative integers $\{0, 1, 2....l\}$ being in general the number of categories of labels. The input $x_i$ and the label $y_i$ in the DNN model are independently identically distributed.

We use $D_{train} = \{(x_i^{tr}, y_i^{tr}) | i < N_1\}$ to denote the training dataset of the DNN model, with $N_1$ being defined as the number of elements in the dataset. The DNN model is functionally equivalent to a classifier $\mathcal{O}$ for input $x_i$. $\mathcal{O}$ takes input $x$ for feature extraction and finally goes through the output layer to obtain a classification result $y_i \in \mathcal{M}$. We measure the performance of a DNN model in terms of the classification accuracy of a test dataset. For example, the accuracy of a test dataset $D_{test} = \{x_i^{te}, y_i^{te} | i < N_2\}$ is defined as:

$$acc_{test} = \frac{1}{N_2} \sum_{(x_i^{te}, y_i^{te}) \in D_{test}} \Delta\{\mathcal{O}(x_i^{te}) = y_i^{te}\} \tag{1}$$

In Eq. (1), $N_2$ indicates the number of $D_{test}$ samples. $\Delta$ means the indicator function that outputs 1 if $\{\mathcal{O}(x_i) = y_i\}$ is true, 0 otherwise.

## 2.2 Singular Value Decomposition (SVD)

SVD is a solid tool to handle matrix diagonalization. Its arithmetic result represents the most basic variations of the matrix. SVD is widely used in the field of image processing. Suppose $A$ is a binary image matrix of size $m \times n$. Performing SVD on $A$, Eq. (2) is satisfied to hold.

$$\forall A \in R^{n \times n}, \exists U \in R^{m \times m}, \exists V \in R^{n \times n}, s.t$$

$$A = USV^T \tag{2}$$

In Eq. (2), $U$ and $V^T$ are left singular value matrix and right singular value matrix respectively, and both are orthogonal matrices $U \times U^T = 1$ and $V = V^{-1}$. $S = diag(\sqrt{\lambda_i})$ is a matrix whose elements have values $\lambda_i (i = 1, 2, 3 \cdots, r)$ on the diagonal, $\lambda_1 > \cdots > \lambda_r > 0$, the values of the elements in all other positions of $S$ are 0.

Implementing SVD is equivalent to performing a principal component analysis process (PCA). The example in Fig. 1 shows a 3-D feature matrix $A$, where each feature is represented as $v \in (v_1, v_2, v_3)$. The process of SVD implies finding the vector bases $pca1$ and $pca2$ in the low-dimensional space closest to the original matrix $A$. In turn, the 2-D feature matrix $M$ is derived after dimensionality reduction of $A$.

SVD can extract the energy of the matrix to be decomposed and reuse the coefficients of the part of the energy aggregation part to obtain the feature information that describes the specific content of the image. The main features of SVD are as follows.

1. The image processed by SVD does not indicate visual characteristics but the brightness characteristics of the image, which are not easily recognized by the human visual system and machine learning model for image content.
2. SVD can describe the whole image with a small number of singular values.
3. SVD has excellent stability. When the image is attacked, the singular value of the image will not change significantly.

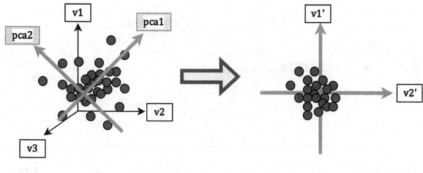

**Three-dimensional matrix A**          **Two-dimensional matrix M**

**Fig. 1.** Example of data dimensionality reduction

4. Among the singular values obtained by SVD, the first one is larger than the other singular values.

With fewer singular value coefficients to describe the feature information of an image, SVD has an outstanding representation in the field of image processing.

## 2.3   DNN Black-Box Watermarking

The work on black-box watermarking does not involve the internal structure and weighting parameters of the DNN model but relies on the input-output relationship of the DNN model. Black-box watermarking is a specific "watermarking" (trigger) pattern resulting from training a particular dataset developed by the owner on a DNN model. In normal circumstances, the relationships in a black-box watermarking are usually contradictory. For example, a sample of image content "cat" in a dataset has the corresponding label "dog".

Figure 2 is shown to provide a more transparent overview of how black-box watermarking works. The marked DNN model will learn the "watermarking" pattern to achieve black-box watermarking and learn the original task's "classification" pattern. A black-box marked DNN model is when a target model works perfectly for a particular "watermarking" pattern and "classification" pattern.

## 2.4   DNN Watermarking

In this section, we describe the proposed watermarking framework in detail. We use SVD to generate watermark samples. The watermarking is embedded during the retraining of the DNN model, and the ownership of the DNN model is verified by sending a remote query carrying watermarking. The marked DNN model has learned and remembered the "watermarking" pattern. As a result, the marked DNN model is perfectly able to predict the output when a remote query is received. In contrast, any unrelated DNN model would not accurately predict the output.

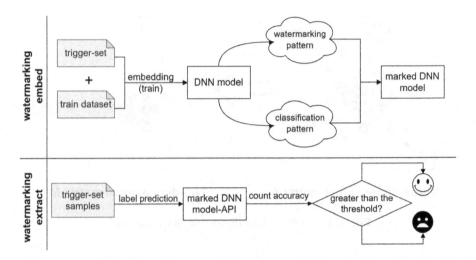

**Fig. 2.** Implementation framework for the black-box watermarking

Figure 3 illustrates the workflow of our DNN watermarking framework. Note that the DNN model generally refers to the classification model. For ensuring the uniqueness of watermarking, we bind the digital signature of the DNN owner, the pseudo-random sequence that generated the watermark key sample, and the timestamp as a key. The key will be sent to the CA for registration.

## 2.5   DNN Watermarking Generation

In this subsection, we display how to generate a watermarking. We take several samples from the training dataset $D_{train}$, called watermark key samples $D_{key}$. Concretely, we employ the Mersenne-Twister algorithm [16] to extract $T$ image samples as watermark key samples by generating pseudo-random numbers among the 50,000 training image samples.

Specifically, we employ the Mersenne-Twister algorithm as a generator of pseudo-random sequences, as this algorithm implements a pseudo-random sequence closer to an irregularly distributed state. The selection of the watermark key samples is depicted in the right part of Fig. 4. There is a sequence seed whose parameters are predefined by the DNN model owner, and it is necessary to describe it before feeding it into the pseudo-random sequence generator, which will cultivate the seed and output a pseudo-random sequence. This pseudo-random sequence will select a certain number of samples in the training dataset as the watermark key samples.

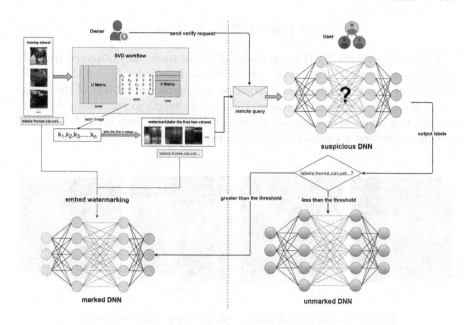

**Fig. 3.** Workflow of the proposed DNNs watermarking

**Fig. 4.** The watermark key sample generator and encryption

In addition, the left part of Fig. 4 depicts the encryption process for the sequence seed. The owner's signature, the sequence seed and the timestamp are combined to obtain a key string uploaded to a CA for storage. In the event of a watermarking forgery attack, the DNN model owner can use the key string to acquire the unique sequence seed at the CA to prove the uniqueness of the watermark samples.

$$D_{key} = \{(x_1^{key}, y_1^{key}), ..., (x_T^{key}, y_T^{key})\} \qquad D_{key} \in D_{train}$$

$T$ is the total number of elements of the pseudo-random sequence. The corresponding classification labels in the $D_{key}$ remain unchanged. Next, the $D_{key}$ is processed by SVD to obtain the watermark samples $D_{wm}$. It is noted that we still refer the labels of the classification labels in the $D_{wm}$ to the classification labels in the $D_{key}$. The specific expression of $D_{wm}$ is :

$$D_{wm} = \{(x_1^{svd}, y_1^{key}), ..., (x_T^{svd}, y_T^{key})\}$$

Figure 5 shows the SVD images with different intensities obtained from the original training dataset's images with different intensities $K = 1, 2, 3..., k$. As the value of $K$ gets smaller, the abstraction and un-recognizability of the images get greater. $k$ is expressed as the maximum side length of the image. The true classification labels of the samples are barely discernible, both in the DNN model without embedded watermarking and the human visual system.

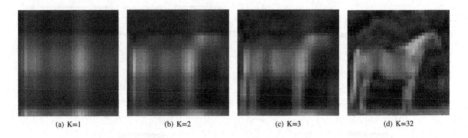

(a) K=1          (b) K=2          (c) K=3          (d) K=32

**Fig. 5.** The watermark key sample generator and encryption

**Example:** To facilitate understanding, we use a simple example to describe the process of the proposed watermarking generation. Suppose there exists a binary image $A$ belonging to $D_{key}$, whose size is $2 \times 3$. It corresponds to a classification label of "2" ($A \rightarrow 2$).

$$A = \begin{bmatrix} 1 & 1 & 0 \\ 0 & 1 & 1 \end{bmatrix} \rightarrow 2$$

Next, the SVD splits the pair $A$ into three matrices $U$, $S$ and $V$.
$AA^T = \begin{bmatrix} 2 & 1 \\ 1 & 2 \end{bmatrix}$ take $AA^T$ eigenvalues $\lambda_1^{AA^T} = 1, \lambda_2^{AA^T} = 3$, eigenvectors of $AA^T$ are

$$vector_1^{AA^T} = \begin{pmatrix} 1/\sqrt{2} \\ -1/\sqrt{2} \end{pmatrix}, vector_2^{AA^T} = \begin{pmatrix} 1/\sqrt{2} \\ 1/\sqrt{2} \end{pmatrix}$$

According to the eigenvectors $(vector_1^{AA^T}, vector_2^{AA^T})$ of $AA^T$, the U matrix is

$$U = \begin{bmatrix} 1/\sqrt{2} & 1/\sqrt{2} \\ -1/\sqrt{2} & 1/\sqrt{2} \end{bmatrix}$$

Similarly, the eigenvalues of $A^T A$ are $\lambda_1^{A^T A} = 3, \lambda_2^{A^T A} = 1$. Further, the corresponding eigenvectors of $A^T A$ are

$$vector_1^{A^T A} = \begin{pmatrix} 1/\sqrt{6} \\ 2/\sqrt{6} \\ 1/\sqrt{6} \end{pmatrix}, vector_2^{A^T A} = \begin{pmatrix} 1/\sqrt{2} \\ 0 \\ -1/\sqrt{2} \end{pmatrix}$$

According to the eigenvectors $(vector_1^{A^T A}, vector_2^{A^T A})$ of $A^T A$, the V matrix is

$$V = \begin{bmatrix} 1/\sqrt{6} & 1/\sqrt{2} \\ 2/\sqrt{6} & 0 \\ 1/\sqrt{6} & -1/\sqrt{2} \end{bmatrix}$$

$S = diag(\sqrt{\lambda_i})$ is a matrix whose values are 0 for all elements except the diagonal elements.

$$S = \begin{bmatrix} \sqrt{3} & 0 \\ 0 & 1 \end{bmatrix}$$

Here, the matrix $A$ can be expressed as $A = USV^T$.

$$A = U \times \begin{bmatrix} \sqrt{3} & 0 \\ 0 & 1 \end{bmatrix} \times V^T$$

Each element $s \in \{\sqrt{3}, 1\}$ on the diagonal of $S$ represents the singular value of $A$. Therefore, the matrix $A$ can also be expressed as:

$$A = US_1V^T + US_2V^T$$

$S_i(i \in \{1,2\})$ represents a matrix where all elements are zero except for one specified singular value element. We let the value of K denote taking the first few singular values. When $K = 1$, it means $A' = US_1V^T = U \times \begin{bmatrix} \sqrt{3} & 0 \\ 0 & 0 \end{bmatrix} \times V^T$. The definition of SVD is

$$SVD(A, K) = A'$$

In the end, we obtain the proposed watermark sample, which is the image $A'$ combined with the corresponding label "2" $(A' \rightarrow 2)$.

While the watermark samples of previous work were usually identified with wrong label, our work still retains the correct label to identify the watermark samples. What is more, our work retains the original correct labels corresponding to the watermark key samples.

---

**Algorithm 1.** Watermarking embedding algorithm

---
**Input:**
    traning dataset: $D_{train} = \{x_i, y_i\}_{i=1,2,3...N}$
    watermarking: $D_{wm} = \{x_i^{wm}, y_i^{wm}\}_{i=1,2,3...n}$    $n \ll N$
    target DNNs model: $\mathcal{F}$
**Output:**
    marked DNN model: $\mathcal{F}_{\mathcal{K}}$

1: **function** WATERMARKING_EMBEDDING()
2:     **for** each minibacth **do**
3:       $\mathcal{F}(x) = \hat{y}$      $\mathcal{F}(x^{wm}) = \hat{y}^{wm}$
4:       $Loss_{train} = CrossEntropyLoss(\hat{y}, y)$
5:       $Loss_{wm} = CrossEntropyLoss(\hat{y}^{wm}, y)$
6:       $Optimizer(Loss_{train}, Loss_{wm})$

7: **end function**
8: **when** $\mathcal{F}(x) = y$ and $\mathcal{F}(x^{wm}) = y^{wm}$ **do**
9: **return** $\mathcal{F}_{\mathcal{K}}$

---

## 2.6 DNN Watermarking Embedding

After generating the watermarking $D_{wm}$, in the next stage, we embed the watermarking into the target DNN model $\mathcal{F}$. Specifically, the embedding process of watermarking is the process of learning the $D_{wm}$ samples by the model $\mathcal{F}_{\mathcal{K}}$. The model $\mathcal{F}_{\mathcal{K}}$ will be output after the watermarking embedding is completed. Here, $\forall(x_i, y_i) \in D_{wm}$ as model $\mathcal{F}$ and $\mathcal{F}_{\mathcal{K}}$ inputs, such that

$$\mathcal{F}(x_i) \neq y_i \qquad \mathcal{F}_{\mathcal{K}}(x_i) = y_i$$

In watermarking embedding process, we add loss function to calculate the loss propagation of watermarking $D_{wm}$. We define the loss value of watermarking as

$$Loss_{wm} = \frac{1}{G} \sum_{i=1}^{N_3} [y_i * log(p_i) + (1 - y_i) * log(1 - p_i)] \tag{3}$$

$x_i$ indicates each image sample in $D_{wm}$, $y_i$ denotes the predicted label of sample $x_i$. Positive class is 1, otherwise 0. $p_i$ denotes the probability that the sample label $y_i$ is predicted to be positive. $N_3$ reflects the total number of samples in $D_{wm}$. $G$ stands for the total number of elements within the dataset $D_{wm}$ in each mini-batch. Adding $Loss_{wm}$ as an additional penalty term to the total loss function $Loss_{all}$ in backpropagation.

$$Loss_{all} = Loss_{train} + Loss_{wm} \tag{4}$$

$Loss_{train}$ denotes the loss value of the $D_{train}$, and $Loss_{all}$ denotes the total back propagation loss function of the DNN model when the embedding is performed for watermarking.

Algorithm 1 reveals the specific algorithm of watermarking embedding. The training dataset $D_{train}$ samples and the watermarking $D_{wm}$ samples are used as the inputs to the DNN model $\mathcal{F}$. During the training of $\mathcal{F}$, each input called "mini-batch" contains $D_{train}$ and $D_{wm}$ samples. Specifically, the number of $D_{wm}$ samples in each "mini-batch" is 1/32 of $D_{train}$. The loss values $Loss_{train}$ and $Loss_{wm}$ are calculated using the cross-entropy loss function. These loss values are summed as the total loss value put into the optimizer to adjust the parameters of $\mathcal{F}$.

When the labels of $D_{train}$ and $D_{wm}$ samples can be correctly classified by model $\mathcal{F}$, it indicates that watermarking embedding is completed, and the marked DNN model $\mathcal{F}_\mathcal{K}$ is obtained.

## 2.7   Ownership Verification

When the DNN model owner believes that the marked DNN model has suspicious attack behavior, the model owner can send a remote query which is a dataset consisting of watermarking, to the suspicious DNN model $\hat{\mathcal{F}}$. Then, the model owner observes the suspected DNN model $\hat{\mathcal{F}}$ in response to the remote query to verify whether $\hat{\mathcal{F}}$ infringes. Here, the samples of $D_{wm}$ are embedded as the main content in the remote query message, which also includes the owner's key string. The suspicious DNN model will use the $D_{wm}$ as input to predict the labels. The predicted labels $\hat{y}$ will be compared with the labels y corresponding to the $D_{wm}$ to obtain the accuracy of a watermarking, called $acc_{wm}$ (watermark accuracy).

$$acc_{wm} = \frac{1}{N_4} \sum_{(x_i, y_i) \in D_{wm}} \Delta\{\hat{\mathcal{F}}(x_i) = y_i\} \tag{5}$$

We employ $acc_{wm}$ to determine whether watermarking is successfully embedded in the DNN model. The suspicious DNN model $\hat{\mathcal{F}}$ is verified using the 0 and 1 determination. $N_4$ tallies the number of $D_{wm}$ samples in the remote query command. We realize ownership verification by setting a threshold $\tau$ (a value almost close to 1) to compare the relationship between the threshold $\tau$ and $acc_{wm}$ as follows:

$$Verify(Acc_{wm}, \tau) = \begin{cases} 1 & acc_{wm} \geq \tau \\ 0 & \text{otherwise} \end{cases} \tag{6}$$

According to Eq. 6, the output is **1** indicating successful DNN model $\hat{\mathcal{F}}$ ownership verification and **0** indicating verification failure.

## 3   Experiments

We monitored the performance of the proposed watermarking scheme using the state-of-the-art evaluation criteria for neural network watermarking [5], [6]. The experiments were implemented using Pytorch 1.7 and Python 3.7. Firstly, we introduce the preparation of the dataset and model structure and watermarking evaluation criteria. Secondly, the effectiveness of watermarking is analyzed in terms of both the watermark embedding process and ownership verification. Finally, we demonstrate the robustness of the proposed watermarking scheme against various watermarking attacks (e.g., model parameter pruning attack, model fine-tuning attack, and watermarking overlay attack).

### 3.1 Experimental Setup

**Dataset:** We used two benchmark image datasets to implement the proposed watermarking approach (MNIST [14] and CIFAR10 [11]). MNIST was a handwritten digit recognition dataset with 60,000 training images and 10,000 test images. The dataset has ten categories of image samples representing the numbers 0 to 9. CIFAR10 is a color image classification dataset with 50,000 training images and 10,000 test images, and the dataset has a total of 10 categories of image samples. We selected $T$ image samples from the MNIST dataset as watermark key samples $D_{key}$ to construct the watermarking $D_{wm}$. The value of $T$ is related to the number of samples in the training dataset, $0 < T < \frac{N_1}{2}$. Similarly, we selected $T$ image samples from the CIFAR10 dataset to construct another watermarking.

**Model:** To satisfy the prediction accuracy criteria for different datasets, we evaluated the proposed watermarking scheme using the Le-Net model for the MNIST dataset and the Res-Net18 model for the CIFAR10 dataset. Moreover, the work aims not to achieve high accuracy classification prediction of the model but to demonstrate the model's performance in the original classification task and the watermarking task. For that reason, we do not overly require the DNN model to achieve almost perfect accuracy for the original classification task.

Evaluation metric: To analyze the proposed watermarking method more clearly, we recorded statistics on the test accuracy of the model's original classification task and the accuracy of watermarking classification. **test acc.** generally displays the fidelity and classification accuracy of the DNN model on the original test dataset, while **wm acc.** indicates the effectiveness and the verification performance of the watermarking.

### 3.2 Effectiveness

The effectiveness of watermarking is the main criterion to measure whether a watermarking can be applied to a DNN model for copyright protection. While ensuring the validity of watermarking, we must also minimize the impact on the DNN model when watermarking is embedded.

In our experiments, we generated a watermarking containing $T$ samples on the original training dataset of MNIST and CIFAR10, respectively. The effectiveness of watermarking is verified by observing the classification prediction accuracy of these two sets of watermarking in the specified DNN model. The

**Table 1.** Test accuracy and watermarking accuracy of DNN model.

| Model | Test acc. | wm acc. | Model | Test acc. | wm acc. |
|---|---|---|---|---|---|
| Clean Le-Net | 98.23% | N/A | Clean Res-Net18 | 89.34% | N/A |
| Marked Le-Net | 99.04% | 98.2% | Marked Res-Net18 | 89.80% | 100% |

simulation results are presented in Table 1. The results evidenced that water-marking cannot be monitored on the clean Le-Net and ResNet18 model, while the watermark accuracy of the marked Le-Net and ResNet18 model is 98% and 100%, respectively. Therefore, our proposed watermarking method can be well embedded in the DNN model and act as a form of copyright protection. Furthermore, the proposed watermarking method is based on the original training dataset, not changing the watermark samples corresponding to the original classification labels. As a result, the accuracy of the original test dataset was not lost or even increased due to watermarking to increase the main feature information perception field of the DNN model instead.

**Table 2.** Watermarking performance of two embedding modes with different K values

| Model | Dataset | K-value | wm acc. | Test acc. | Dataset | K-value | wm acc. | Test acc. |
|---|---|---|---|---|---|---|---|---|
| Fine-tuning (30 epochs) | MNIST | 1 | 93.6% | 98.34% | CIFAR-10 | 1 | 96.4% | 87.06% |
| | | 2 | **97.2%** | **99.24%** | | 2 | **100.0%** | **92.71%** |
| | | 3 | 96.8% | 98.94% | | 3 | 99.6% | 91.45% |
| | | 28 | 97.6% | 99.08% | | 32 | 99.6% | 87.12% |
| Scratch (80 epochs) | | 1 | 95.5% | 98.23% | | 1 | 98.4% | 82.49% |
| | | 2 | **99.2%** | **98.54%** | | 2 | 99.6% | **85.82%** |
| | | 3 | 96.9% | 98.67% | | 3 | 100.0% | 85.88% |
| | | 28 | 98.1% | 98.47% | | 32 | 99.2% | 85.23% |

According to the characteristics of SVD, obtaining the first $K$ singular values will produce different image samples. The maximum $K$ value depends on the size of the training dataset sample; for example, the sample of the CIFAR10 dataset is a $32 \times 32$ image, so the maximum $K$ value of the sample is 32. Here, we embed the watermarking generated at different $K$ values into the same DNN model to observe the generalization of watermarking. Our experiments used both fine-tuning and training from scratch to validate the effectiveness of watermarking obtained under different $K$ values. For scratch training, we blend the water-marking with the training dataset into a mini-batch for 80 epochs, where each mini-batch has a size of 64 and contains 62 training dataset samples and two watermark samples. For the fine-tuning, we used a pre-trained DNN model with a baseline prediction accuracy of the original classification task for 30 training epochs, again using the same mini-batch specification as the scratch training approach. However, after every five epochs, the step size in backpropagation would be adjusted to one-tenth of the original to prevent overfitting of the DNN model. For both training methods, we use the cross-entropy optimizer.

The effect of the two embedding modes is seen in Table 2. Analysis of the results suggests that the watermarking generated with different values of $K$ all achieve almost 100% prediction accuracy in both training approaches, and any loss does not cause the accuracy of the original test dataset of the DNN model. The experimental results proved that the watermarking generated at $K = 2$ has the best protective effect. The result here was 100% watermark accuracy and further prediction accuracy. The reason was that the watermark samples generated with $K = 2$ both maximize the retention of the primary feature information of the training dataset's samples and are not classified as training dataset's samples by the clean DNN model. The effectiveness of watermarking embedded by both training modes was guaranteed. Specifically, the watermarking embedded by the fine-tuning mode achieved almost 100% accurate classification and improved the accuracy of the DNN model prediction test dataset. The pre-trained DNN model already has most of the feature information from the training dataset; it learns the "watermarking" pattern faster than the scratch training method when employing fine-tuning.

### 3.3   Robustness

Robustness refers to the resistance of watermarking to attacks. We examined the resistance to attack of the proposed watermarking method using the main current watermarking attacks, including fine-tuning attack, model parameter pruning attack and watermarking overlay attack.

**Fine-Tuning Attack:** The attack is a watermarking attack in which a user intentionally or unintentionally retrains a distributed DNN model using an additional training dataset to achieve erasure of watermarking. The model fine-tuning attack is a very effective watermarking attack for attackers. The attacker usually looks for a dataset close to the training dataset used by the marked DNN model, called the "attack" dataset. Half of the dataset was taken as the training dataset to corrupt watermarking in the DNN model, and the remaining half was taken as the test dataset to evaluate the model's accuracy for the original classification task.

We used 5000 samples in the training dataset and 5000 samples in the test set as the "attack" dataset. The marked Le-Net and ResNet18 models were trained for 30 epochs of fine-tuning. After the fine-tuning attack, the test accuracy and watermark accuracy of the marked DNN model are shown in Table 3.

**Table 3.** Robustness of the proposed watermarking against fine-tuning attack

| Model | Epoch | Test acc. | wm acc. | Model | Test acc. | wm acc. |
|---|---|---|---|---|---|---|
| Le-Net (using MNIST dataset) | 5 | 99.04% | 96.8% | Res-Net18 (using CIFAR-10 dataset) | 93.24% | 100% |
| | 10 | 99.01% | 96.4% | | 93.62% | 99.7% |
| | 20 | 99.07% | 96.1% | | 93.85% | 99.7% |
| | 30 | 99.05% | 95.3% | | 93.38% | 99.2% |

The results display that the watermarking accuracy is still robust, even when suffering a fine-tuning attack of 30 epochs. Since the feature information of watermarking is similar to that of the subject of the "attack" dataset samples, it indicates that the proposed watermarking is robust to the fine-tuning attack.

Parameter pruning attack: There are often many redundant parameters in a DNN model. These parameters do not play a critical role in the original prediction task of the model and also increase the computational cost of classification task. We used the pruning algorithm proposed in [23]. Their method achieves model compression by dropping the parameters of the neurons in the convolutional and fully connected layers within the DNN model. For the marked DNN model, we removed the parameters by setting the parameters of the weights to zero. Additionally, we used p% to denote the model parameter pruning rate, ranging from 10% to 90%. We still used test accuracy and watermark accuracy as the main evaluation criteria of the proposed watermarking framework.

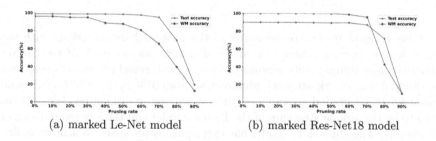

(a) marked Le-Net model                 (b) marked Res-Net18 model

**Fig. 6.** Robustness of the proposed watermarking in parameter pruning attack

We conducted pruning experiments on the DNN model with the results displayed in Fig. 6. The Le-Net model is a DNN model composed of 4 convolutional layers and two fully connected layers, so the model structure is relatively straightforward. The watermark accuracy of the Le-Net model can still maintain more than 80%. The watermark accuracy drops dramatically when the pruning rate is greater than 60%. The primary explanation for the speculation may be due to the simple structure of the Le-Net model, which cannot store watermarking information in a decentralized manner. Besides, the watermark accuracy of the ResNet-18 model can still reach 100% when the pruning rate is even 70%; although the watermark accuracy drops sharply after the pruning rate exceeds

70%, the test accuracy also drops. If an attacker wants to use model parameter pruning to achieve the purpose of watermarking erasure, at least a pruning rate of 60% or higher is needed to process the marked DNN model. An excessive pruning rate is used, which can reduce test accuracy and, hence, the poor performance of the DNN model. Thus, the proposed watermarking is robust to model parameter pruning attacks.

**Watermarking Overlay Attack:** It means that the attacker maliciously generates a small magnitude of forged watermarking and embeds it into the marked DNN model to overwrite watermarking. If the forged watermarking is embedded, the owner cannot prove the uniqueness of watermarking, resulting in DNN model verification failure. In our experiments, we selected other $K$ values from the training dataset to generate forged watermarking samples that do not resemble the original watermarking. The forged watermarking is embedded into the marked DNN model. In order to assess the robustness of the proposed watermarking method, we observed the accuracy of the test dataset as well as the accuracy of the genuine and fake watermarking by conducting experiments using fine-tuning styles (30 epochs).

**Table 4.** Comparison of the accuracy after watermarking overlay attack

| Model | Test acc. | wm acc. | wm2 acc. | Model | Test acc. | wm acc. | wm2 acc. |
|-------|-----------|---------|----------|-------|-----------|---------|----------|
| Le-Net | 99.04% | 98.0% | N/A | Res-Net18 | 93.24% | 100.0% | N/A |
| | 99.01% | 24.4% | 93.2% | | 94.17% | 97.4% | 91.1% |

Table 4 illustrates the performance of the proposed watermarking with the watermarking overlay attack. The original watermark accuracy of the Le-Net model changes dramatically around the forged watermarking embedding, with the original watermark accuracy plummeting from 97% back to 24%. The main reason for the degraded accuracy of the original watermarking has been speculated to be the simple structure of the Le-Net model and the low redundancy of parameters. The ResNet-18 model has extra parameter space to achieve multiple watermarking coexistences, which does not lead to a significant degradation of the original watermark accuracy. The original watermark accuracy of the ResNet-18 model does not change much after watermarking overlay, from 100% to 97%, which can still achieve ownership verification of the DNN model. Due to the complex structure and deep hidden layers of the ResNet-18 model, the original watermarking is not easily covered. Therefore, the proposed watermarking scheme is more widely applicable in large-scale DNN models.

## 4    Comparison with Existing

We compared the performance of our proposed watermarking method with the extant black-box watermarking methods, which include a sample-based noise-generated watermarking method [26], an abstract image-based watermarking method [1], a new label-based watermarking method [28], and a key-based watermarking method [17]. The same experimental setup as in Sect. 4.1 was used to ensure consistency in the experimental environment. The proposed watermarking scheme be compared with the other watermarking schemes above in the following two aspects.

## 4.1 Watermarking Effectiveness

In order to compare the effectiveness of other extant black-box watermarking methods in a uniform manner, we maintained watermark accuracy and training prediction accuracy as validation criteria. We produced watermark samples corresponding to [1, 26, 28], and [17] using the CIFAR10 dataset as a common dataset. Next, these watermark samples were trained with a fine-tuning epoch of 50 to fulfill the embedding.

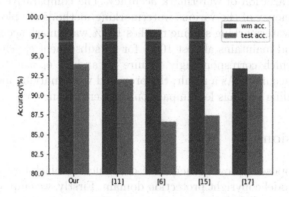

**Fig. 7.** Comparison of the proposed watermarking method with others

The comparative effect of the experiment is revealed in Fig. 7. Since our proposed watermarking scheme can supply additional feature information to the DNN model, the test accuracy (test acc.) is greater than that of other existing watermarking schemes by 1.71–6.09%.

## 4.2 Efficiency of Watermarking Embedding

The watermarking embedding process is similar to a backdoor attack, which inevitably affects the classification prediction accuracy of the DNN model. Thus, the embedding process of any watermarking scheme must be as fast as possible to avoid wasting computer resources. If many epochs are repeated for the watermark, it will degrade the performance of the DNN model.

Our proposed watermarking method was compared with the watermarking scheme proposed by [26] and [1] for watermarking embedding efficiency. Specifically, we compared the embedding rate of each watermarking scheme by

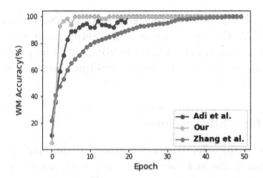

**Fig. 8.** Comparison of the embedding efficiency of the proposed watermarking method with others

observing the variation of watermark accuracy. The comparative results of the embedding efficiency of the various watermarking methods are plotted in Fig. 8. Our proposed watermarking scheme reaches 100% watermark accuracy near ten epoch cycles and maintains almost 100% for all subsequent epochs, followed by [26] and [1], which correspondingly require 43 and 21 epochs to reach 100% watermarking accuracy. As a result, the proposed watermarking method is more agile in embedding and has less impact on the performance of the DNN model.

## 5   Conclusion

This paper proposes a novel scheme for constructing black-box watermarking for the DNN model copyright protection domain. Firstly, we employ the pseudo-random sequence generated by the Mersenne-Twister algorithm, which is tantamount to setting a key for the watermark samples and enhancing the forgery resistance of watermark samples. Secondly, the SVD algorithm processes the watermark key samples to construct more stable and stealthy watermark samples. Finally, the classification labels corresponding to watermark samples are still retained as the classification labels of their corresponding watermark key samples, which effectively reduces the bias in the decision boundary of the DNN model during the watermarking embedding process. Compared with previous work, the proposed black-box watermarking enhances the correlation with the original dataset, which means that watermarking has less impact on the performance of the DNN model. Specifically, we evaluated the proposed watermarking approach on two benchmark datasets. It is clear from sufficient experimental figures that our watermarking scheme does not affect the test accuracy of the DNN model, in addition to meeting the functional requirements of watermarking. Furthermore, the proposed watermarking is robust to major watermarking attacks.

# References

1. Adi, Y., Baum, C., Cisse, M., Pinkas, B., Keshet, J.: Turning your weakness into a strength: watermarking deep neural networks by backdooring. In: 27th {USENIX} Security Symposium ({USENIX} Security 18), pp. 1615–1631 (2018)
2. Chen, H., Rohani, B.D., Koushanfar, F.: Deepmarks: a digital fingerprinting framework for deep neural networks. arXiv preprint arXiv:1804.03648 (2018)
3. Cox, I., Miller, M., Bloom, J., Fridrich, J., Kalker, T.: Digital Watermarking and Steganography. Morgan Kaufmann, Burlington (2007)
4. Cui, L., Xu, Y.: Research on copyright protection method of material genome engineering data based on zero-watermarking. J. Big Data 2(2), 53 (2020)
5. Darvish Rouhani, B., Chen, H., Koushanfar, F.: Deepsigns: an end-to-end watermarking framework for ownership protection of deep neural networks. In: Proceedings of the Twenty-Fourth International Conference on Architectural Support for Programming Languages and Operating Systems, pp. 485–497 (2019)
6. Guo, J., Potkonjak, M.: Evolutionary trigger set generation for dnn black-box watermarking. arXiv preprint arXiv:1906.04411 (2019)
7. He, K., Zhang, X., Ren, S., Sun, J.: Deep residual learning for image recognition. In: Proceedings of the IEEE Conference on Computer Vision and Pattern Recognition, pp. 770–778 (2016)
8. Jebreel, N.M., Domingo-Ferrer, J., Sánchez, D., Blanco-Justicia, A.: Keynet: an asymmetric key-style framework for watermarking deep learning models. Appl. Sci. 11(3), 999 (2021)
9. Zhou, J., et al.: Mixed attention densely residual network for single image super-resolution. Comput. Syst. Sci. Eng. 39(1), 133–146 (2021)
10. Singh, K.U., Abu-Hamatta, H.S., Kumar, A., Singhal, A., Rashid, M., Bashir, A.K.: Secure watermarking scheme for color DICOM images in telemedicine applications. Comput. Mater. Contin. 70(2), 2525–2542 (2022). http://www.techscience.com/cmc/v70n2/44633
11. Krizhevsky, A., et al.: Learning multiple layers of features from tiny images (2009)
12. Krizhevsky, A., Sutskever, I., Hinton, G.E.: Imagenet classification with deep convolutional neural networks. Adv. Neural. Inf. Process. Syst. 25, 1097–1105 (2012)
13. Le Merrer, E., Pérez, P., Trédan, G.: Adversarial frontier stitching for remote neural network watermarking. Neural Comput. Appl. 32(13), 9233–9244 (2019). https://doi.org/10.1007/s00521-019-04434-z
14. LeCun, Y.: The MNIST database of handwritten digits (1998). http://yann.lecun.com/exdb/mnist/
15. Li, Z., Hu, C., Zhang, Y., Guo, S.: How to prove your model belongs to you: a blind-watermark based framework to protect intellectual property of DNN. In: Proceedings of the 35th Annual Computer Security Applications Conference, pp. 126–137 (2019)
16. Matsumoto, M., Nishimura, T.: Mersenne twister: a 623-dimensionally equidistributed uniform pseudo-random number generator. ACM Trans. Model. Comput. Simul. (TOMACS) 8(1), 3–30 (1998)
17. Maung Maung, A.P., Kiya, H.: Piracy-resistant DNN watermarking by block-wise image transformation with secret key. In: Proceedings of the 2021 ACM Workshop on Information Hiding and Multimedia Security, pp. 159–164 (2021)
18. Ribeiro, M., Grolinger, K., Capretz, M.A.: Mlaas: machine learning as a service. In: 2015 IEEE 14th International Conference on Machine Learning and Applications (ICMLA), pp. 896–902. IEEE (2015)

19. Sabour, S., Frosst, N., Hinton, G.E.: Dynamic routing between capsules. In: NIPS (2017)
20. Shady, Y., Yassen, A.M., Alsammak, A.K., Elhalawany, B.M.: Local features-based watermarking for image security in social media. Comput. Mater. Contin. **69**(3), 3857–3870 (2021). http://www.techscience.com/cmc/v69n3/44157
21. Simonyan, K., Zisserman, A.: Very deep convolutional networks for large-scale image recognition (2015)
22. Sun, S., Xue, M., Wang, J., Liu, W.: Protecting the intellectual properties of deep neural networks with an additional class and steganographic images. arXiv preprint arXiv:2104.09203 (2021)
23. Uchida, Y., Nagai, Y., Sakazawa, S., Satoh, S.: Embedding watermarks into deep neural networks. In: Proceedings of the 2017 ACM on International Conference on Multimedia Retrieval, pp. 269–277 (2017)
24. Vaswani, A., et al.: Attention is all you need. In: Advances in Neural Information Processing Systems, pp. 5998–6008 (2017)
25. Xiong, L., Han, X., Yang, C.N., Shi, Y.Q.: Robust reversible watermarking in encrypted image with secure multi-party based on lightweight cryptography. IEEE Trans. Circuits Syst. Video Technol. **32**(1), 75–91 (2021)
26. Zhang, J., et al.: Protecting intellectual property of deep neural networks with watermarking. In: Proceedings of the 2018 on Asia Conference on Computer and Communications Security, pp. 159–172 (2018)
27. Zhang, Y., Pezeshki, M., Brakel, P., Zhang, S., Bengio, C.L.Y., Courville, A.: Towards end-to-end speech recognition with deep convolutional neural networks. arXiv preprint arXiv:1701.02720 (2017)
28. Zhong, Q., Zhang, L.Y., Zhang, J., Gao, L., Xiang, Y.: Protecting IP of deep neural networks with watermarking: a new label helps. Adv. Knowl. Discov. Data Min. **12085**, 462 (2020)

# A High-Capacity and High-Security Generative Cover Steganography Algorithm

Bin Ma[1], Zuowei Han[1], Jian Li[1], Chunpeng Wang[1], Yuli Wang[1(✉)], and Xinan Cui[2]

[1] Shandong Provincial Key Laboratory of Computer Networks, Qilu University of Technology
(Shandong Academy of Sciences), Jinan 250353, China
HanZuoweiqly@163.com
[2] Zhongfu Information Inc., Jinan 250101, China

**Abstract.** Steganography is an important technology in the field of data hiding. The application of deep learning in the field of steganalysis has led to the rapid development of steganalysis techniques, which seriously threatens the security of steganography. In addition, capacity is another important factor that limits the safety of steganography. The larger capacity of the Steganographic image (stego image), the poorer its visual quality and security. To improve the security of steganography, this paper proposes a cover generative steganography, which constructs Generator, Encoder-Decoder, Steganalysis Optimization Network, and Steganalysis Adversarial Network. The Generator input original images output generate covers which more suitable for embedding secret images; Encoder-Decoder uses existing steganographic models to embed and extract secret images from covers and stego images; Steganalysis Optimization Network optimizes the current optimal steganalysis parameters; Steganalysis Adversarial Network evaluates the security of steganography and provides steganalysis adversarial loss (SDO_loss) to the Generator. In addition, we use the stego image and cover loss (SMSE_loss), extract images and secret image loss (XMSE_loss), and steganalysis adversarial loss (SDO_loss) jointly to form the total loss function of the generator. When embedding secret images of the generated cover, it has lower color distortion and higher resistance to steganography through the joint loss function. It is experimentally demonstrated that our model can reduce the color distortion and the steganalysis detection accuracy by about 30–40% with higher security than the previous steganography model for hiding color images based on deep learning.

**Keywords:** Steganography · Steganalysis · Deep learning · Cover generative steganography

## 1 Introduction

Steganography is an important technology in the field of data hiding. It uses the redundancy of cover medium to hide secret information without the detection of a third party [1]. Traditional image steganography algorithms can be divided into three categories: spatial domain model [2], transform domain model, and coverless model. Typical spatial domain steganographic algorithms include LSB [3], S-UNIWARD) [4], WOW [5], and HUGO [6]. transform steganography achieve the hiding of secret information by modifying the frequency domain coefficients of cover, such as DFT [7], DCT [8]; coverless steganography [9–11] does not directly change the cover data but realize the secret information transfer by establishing the mapping between the feature attributes of the image and the secret information.

As a detection and discrimination tool for steganography, steganalysis determines whether an image contains secret information based on the observed changes in its feature information. In recent years, steganalysis technology based on deep learning (such as GNCNN [12], Xu'Net [13], Ye'Net [14], SRNet [15]) have surpassed the traditional steganalysis technology SRM [16] in detection accuracy, which seriously threatens the security of steganography algorithms. In addition, the embedding capacity and steganographic security are negatively correlated, the larger the capacity, the less secure the steganographic model. The existing steganography algorithms limit the embedding capacity of secret information to 0.4 bpp or even below, which sacrifices the embedding capacity for steganography security, resulting in a significant reduction in the practicality of steganography.

Deep learning (CNN) is an important division of machine learning that aims to automatically learn useful and highly abstract features in data by simulating the human brain. Thus, it can learn the basic features of data better than traditional machine learning methods [17]. Deep learning-based steganographic models can be classified into three types: cover generative steganography, real image embedded steganography, and coverless steganography. Cover generative steganography [18–22], using the adversarial training of steganalysis network and generative network to generate the adversarial images and use the generated images as covers to embed the secret messages. The security of the steganography model is improved to some extent, but the capacity of only embedded secret information does not exceed 0.4bpp, which limits the usefulness of the model. Real image embedded steganography also uses a steganalysis network to train against the generative network to reduce the total steganographic distortion of the stego image [23–25]. Some researchers have also tried to embed binary bitstreams or other types of data into the cover through Encoder-Decoder networks [26–28–35], which can achieve an embedding capacity of 4.4 bpp or hide a color image into another color image of the same size. Encoder-Decoder networks don't require additional keys to extract secret information, it's parameters and weights of the network are the key to extracting secret information. Therefore, even if the model structure is publicly shared, others are still unable to extract the secret image due to different network parameters. However, due to the pooling and normalization in the network, the secret information cannot be fully extracted. The deep graph steganography does not affect the receiver's understanding of the semantic information of the extracted secret image even if the embedded secret image cannot be fully recovered. However, it has disadvantages such as poor visual quality of stego images, easy leakage of secret images, and very low steganographic security. The coverless steganography model based on deep learning [36–37] does not need to modify the image and thus has a natural ability to resist steganalysis. However, there are still problems of the weak recovery of steganographic information and low embedding capacity.

Inspired by Volkhonskiy [18], a cover generative steganography model is proposed in this paper. A generator based on U-Net architecture is constructed, and Squeeze and Excitation attention (SE attention) is added to the U-Net architecture. The generator superimposes and fuses the deep and shallow features of the original image in the image feature reconstruction process, which improves the original image feature reconstruction more effectively and the generated image is more suitable for embedding secret information. The generated image has lower color distortion and higher concealment of the secret image after the embedded secret image compared with the original image. On the other hand, considering the problem of poor security of existing steganographic networks for hiding color images, our model achieves good results in parallel steganography detection by adversarial training between the generator and the steganalysis, which can greatly improve the resistance to steganalysis detection. The contributions of this work are as follows.

1. This paper proposes a cover generative steganographic model, which enables the detection of fixed steganalysis resistance at an embedding capacity of 24 bpp. A certain degree of steganographic security at high embedding capacity.
2. Generator inputs the original image and outputs a color image that is similar to the original image, which is more suitable for hiding a secret color image of the same size. The U-Net-based generator is constructed by introducing the SE attention mechanism to output the generated cover closer to the original image and reduce the gradient disappearance during the training process.
3. The experimental results show the practicality and effectiveness of the model. Compared with previous steganography models used to hide color secret images, the generator improves the generated images against steganalysis detection by adversarial training with the steganalysis network and shows good results in parallel steganalysis detection. Please note that the first paragraph of a section or subsection is not indented. The first paragraphs that follows a table, figure, equation etc. does not have an indent, either.

## 2 Related Work

In 2016, Volkhonskiy et al. [18] first proposed the cover generative steganography model (SGAN), which enables the generated cover to resist the detection of steganalysis models to a certain extent after embedding secret information by adding steganalysis networks to DCGAN. However, the quality and steganalysis resistance of generated images are not sufficient, and the embedding capacity is low because only the traditional adaptive steganography scheme can be used to embed the secret information. Based on SGAN, Shi et al. [19] proposed a SSGAN generative steganography scheme, which used WGAN instead of DCGAN network in SGAN, and redesigned the discriminative network and steganalysis network using convolutional neural network-based steganalysis network (GNCNN). The stego image resistance to steganalysis can be improved to a certain extent. However, such schemes are based on the cover generated by normal noise, thus they cannot generate established images with low visual quality, which are semantically not realistic and natural enough. What's more, the resistance to steganalysis of such schemes is difficult to achieve the desired effect, and the capacity of embedding secret information using adaptive steganography is low. In 2018, Zhang et al. [20] proposed a steganography algorithm based on adversarial samples, using Fast Gradient Sign Model to generate an adversarial cover, so that it can gain the ability to actively deceive the steganalyzer and thus achieve data hiding. However, this model only guarantees good security at 0.4 bpp embedding rate, and the embedding capacity is still not high. Moreover, Zhang's steganography model requires repeated training for each cover when the information is embedded, which is time-consuming when facing a large number of images that need to be embeded secret information. In 2019, Zhou et al. [21] constructed a model that can quickly generate counter covers by using a fully convolutional neural network (FCN) as a counter noise generator. The steganography model improved the speed and quality of cover generation and enhanced the security of stego images to a certain extent, but the embedding capacity still was not be improved.

On the other hand, compared with using GAN to generate covers more suitable for information embedding, researchers also proposed an adaptive embedding steganography framework to reduce total steganographic distortion of stego images and image statistical anomalies caused by optimizing distortion function, so that the steganography network can still ensure security under the maximum allowable embedding capacity of 0.4 bpp. In 2018, Tang et al. [22] first proposed an embedded steganographic model with automatic learning distortion function (ASDL-GAN). This model improves the security of stego images in adversarial training of generator and steganalysis, but does not improve the embedding capacity. Yang et al. [23] proposed UT-SCA-GAN based on ASDL-GAN. It uses a more compact U-Net generator and replaced the TES network in ASDL-GAN with Tanh-simulator function. Its model security exceeds that of ASDL-GAN. Compared with the steganography approach that minimizes distortion function at the expense of embedding capacity for security, coding-decoding networks are also widely used in steganography. In 2017, Hayes et al. [24] proposed a SteGAN-based steganography model to apply coding-decoding networks to the field of steganography, but the visual quality of stego images produced by this steganography method is not high. Wang et al. [25] proposed the SteganoGAN model based on this, which uses the adversarial training of steganographer and discriminator to reduce the differences between stego image and cover and improve the quality of stego image. In 2019, Zhang et al. [26] proposed the SteganoGAN steganographic model, which can hide binary bit data up to 4.4 bpp in the cover. The encoding-decoding network can not only hide binary bit data or text information into the cover but even hide color or grayscale images with higher resolution. In 2019, Duan et al. [27] constructed a coding network with a U-Net-like structure using a fully convolutional network. 2020, Fu et al. [28] proposed a steganographic model called HIGAN, in which the encoder is built based on the ResNet network and the steganalysis model is added to the model architecture for adversarial training. However, the PSNR and Structural similarity (SSIM) of their stego images and the extracted secret images are relatively low. In conclusion, the steganographic capacity can be improved by sacrificing part of the security of the steganographic model. However, there are still problems such as color distortion of the stego image, large loss of detail information, and the decoding network cannot fully realize the extraction of the secret image in the specific applications.

## 2.1 Steganalysis Based on Deep Learning

Fundamental features of images can distinguish covers from stego images by using different network structures. In 2015, Qian et al. [12] first combined deep learning with steganalysis and proposed a convolutional neural network-based steganalysis network (GNCNN). In 2016, Xu et al. [13] proposed the Xu'Net steganalysis model. Compared with GNCNN, ReLU activation function, batch normalization layer (BN), and ABS function are added to the model to improve the steganalysis detection accuracy. The model can be applied to the space domain and JPEG domain. In 2017, Ye et al. [14] proposed the Ye'Net steganalysis model, which uses 30 high-pass filters in SRM to initialize the number input information, and introduces selective channel-aware (SCA) to optimize the model and achieve better performance than the SRM [16] steganalysis algorithm. In 2019, Boroumand et al. [15] proposed a SRNet steganalysis model. The model was constructed by residual layers with shortcut connections, which can reuse feature vectors during training and achieve better steganalysis results. From the above analysis, it can be seen that the rapid development of steganalysis has raised new issues for the research of steganography, especially for the safety of steganography under high embedding capacity.

## 3 Model

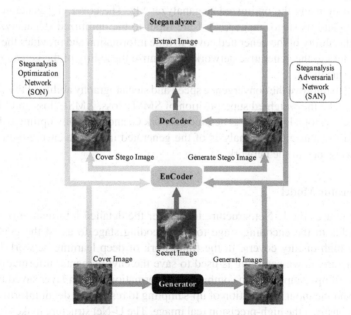

**Fig. 1.** Architecture of the model.

The model in this paper consists of four sub-networks: Generator, steganographer network including secret image embedding network (Encoder), secret image extraction network (Decoder), Steganalysis Optimization Network (SON), and Steganalysis

Adversarial Network (SAN). Steganalyzer optimization network optimizes the current optimal parameters of the steganalyzer. Steganalyzer adversarial network uses the optimized steganalyzer to evaluate the steganographic performance of the generated cover, and provides steganalysis loss to the generative adversarial network, so that the generative adversarial network iteratively generates a cover more suitable for the embedding of the secret image.

As shown in Fig. 1, first, the high-quality cover G_I is generated by Generator (G), G_I is concatenated with the secret image S_I and input to the secret image embedding network (Encoder). Then output the stego image G_S_I, calculate the mean square error between G_S_I and G_I, and use the minimum mean square error loss in pixel space to obtain SMSE_loss. Input G_S_I to the secret image extraction network (Decoder), extract the secret image embedded in the stego image, and output the extracted image X_I. Next calculate the minimum mean square error loss in pixel space between X_I and S_I to obtain XMSE_loss. SMSE_loss and XMSE_loss jointly promote the generator to generate covers with more semantic information and high visual quality.

Second, as shown in the Steganalysis Optimization Network (SON) in Fig. 1, the real image C_I and the secret image S_I are used to generate the stego image C_S_I through the Encoder. Then C_I and C_S_I are jointly input to the SON. SON optimizes its parameters to improve the steganalyzer (SD)'s ability to discriminate specific types of image data.

Third, according to the Steganalysis Adversarial Network (SAN) in Fig. 1, SAN is constructed by using the optimized steganalyzer SD. The cover G_I generated by the generator G and its stego image G_S_I are input to the optimized steganalyzer. SAN evaluates the ability of the generated cover to hide information and provides the gradient loss SDO_loss to the generative network to optimize the ability of the generated image to resist steganalysis.

Finally, to improve the convergence speed and steganography ability of the generated images, we take the weighted superposition of SMSE_loss, XMSE_loss and SDO_loss generated as the total loss of the generated network G, and cyclically optimize the visual quality and resistance to steganalysis of the generated images to ensure the rapid and stable convergence of the network.

### 3.1 Generator Model

This scheme uses the U-Net structure to transfer the detailed information of different sensory fields in the encoding stage to the decoding stage to assist the generator in generating high-quality covers. In the framework of deep learning network based on U-Net structure, down-sampling is used to save the environmental information, while the process of up-sampling is to combine the information of each layer saved by down-sampling and the input information of up-sampling to restore the detail information and gradually construct the high-precision real image. The U-Net structure makes full use of the local and global feature information of the real image by stitching deep and shallow information to ensure the excellent visual performance of the generated image.

As shown in Fig. 2, the U-Net-based generator with the addition of channel attention mechanism contains a total of 16 data processing groups in this scheme. Group 1 to 8 are down-sampling encoding, each includes a convolutional layer for down-sampling with a step size of 2 (convolutional kernel of 3 × 3), batch normalization layer (BN) and Relu activation function with Squeeze and Excitation attention unit (including 1 average pooling layer and 2 fully connected layers with Relu, sigmoid activation functions). Groups 9 to 15 are extended paths, each includes a deconvolution layer with a step size of 2 (DeConv, convolution kernel of 5 × 5), batch normalization layer (BN) and Relu activation function. Group 16 includes a deconvolution layer with a step size of 2 (convolution kernel of 5), Relu activation function and sigmoid activation function. To achieve pixel-level learning and facilitate back propagation, this scheme splices the feature maps of Layer i and Layer 16-i as the input of Layer 16-i + 1 in the decoding stage by skip connections.

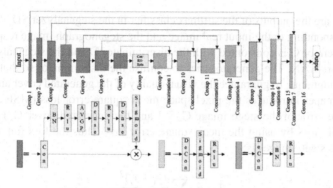

**Fig. 2.** Architecture of the generator network.

## 3.2 Steganalysis Network

The steganalysis network is used to discriminate whether the input image contains secret information or not. With the development of deep learning, the combination of steganalysis and deep learning poses a great threat to the steganography algorithms. In this paper, we use the optimized steganalyzer to build a steganalysis adversarial network (SAN) to improve the steganographic capability of generated images. As shown in the steganalysis optimization network (SON) in Fig. 1, the real image C_I and its stego image C_S_I are firstly used as the input of steganalyzer to optimize the performance parameters of SD and improve its discriminative ability. Then, SD is used to construct SAN, which is used to evaluate the generated cover G_I and its stego image G_S_I, and record its steganalysis adversarial loss SDO_loss. As part of the total loss function for generator optimization, it generates a more suitable cover for steganography and improves the ability of G_S_I to resist steganalysis detection. This scheme optimizes two current excellent deep learning-based steganographic analyzer networks (Xu'Net and SRNet), and constructs the steganalysis network to provide iterative loss SDO_loss for generating the adversarial network and counteract the information hiding ability of the generated covers.

## 3.3 Loss Function

In this model, the generator G learns data distribution characteristics of the real image, SAN detects whether the input image contains secret information and outputs the distribution generated by 2 class labels. The training goal of SAN is to output a [0, 1] distribution (closer to 0) when the input image is an unstego image and a [1, 0] distribution (closer to 1) when the input image is a stego image. Therefore, the loss function of SAN is:

$$L_{SD} = -\sum_{i=1}^{2} z_i' \log(z_i) \tag{1}$$

where $z_1, z_2$ are the outputs of the softmax classifier in the steganalyzer SD, they are the labels corresponding to the input real image and the steganograph image respectively.

The generator G is confronted with the discriminator D and the steganalysis adversarial network SAN. The generator tries to confuse the discriminator so that it outputs the wrong judgment. To guarantee the visual quality of the generated cover and its stego image, this paper introduces the pixel space mean square error loss (MSE_loss). The mean square error of the stego image G_S_I and the generated cover G_I is used to obtain SMSE_loss by using the mean square error loss. Thus the loss function of the cover and its stego images is:

$$L_{SI} = \sum_{i=1}^{n} \frac{(y_i - y_i')^2}{n} \tag{2}$$

where $y_i$ is the value of G_I pixel point, $y_i'$ is the value of G_S_I pixel point, and $n$ is the number of image pixel points. In order to improve the PSNR of extracted image X_I and secret image S_I, it is necessary to calculate their mean square error loss to obtain *XMSE_loss*. Thus the secret image loss function is:

$$L_{XI} = \sum_{i=1}^{n} \frac{(x_i - x_i')^2}{n} \tag{3}$$

where $x_i$ is the value of X_I pixel point, $x_i'$ is the value of S_I pixel point, and n is the number of image pixel points. Thus the total loss of the generator G is:

$$L_G = -L_{SD} + \alpha \cdot \sum_{i=1}^{n} \frac{(y_i - y_i')^2}{n} + \beta \cdot \sum_{i=1}^{n} \frac{(x_i - x_i')^2}{n} \tag{4}$$

where $L_{SD}$ is the steganalysis adversarial loss, $y_i$ is the value of G_I pixel point, $y_i'$ is the value of G_S_I pixel point, $x_i$ is the value of X_I pixel point, $x_i'$ is the value of S_I pixel point and $n$ is the number of image pixel points. In summary, this experiment constructs a weighted combination of steganalysis adversarial loss *SDO_loss*, stego image loss *SMSE_loss* and secret image loss *XMSE_loss* as the total loss $L_G$ of the generation network G.

# 4  Experiment

In this section, we will introduce the details of experiments which include the details of datasets, the parameter settings and the evaluation metrics, and then discuss the results.

## 4.1  Dataset

We use the training sets of ImageNet2012 [27] as the training, validation and test sets of our experiments, in which we randomly choose 50,000 images to form 25,000 pairs of cover-secret images as the training set. We also randomly select 2,000 pictures as the test set. This experiment uses Dell T630, 128 GB memory, RTX3090 GPU with 24 GB memory, python 3.7 and Tensorflow 2.4.0.

## 4.2  Experiments Details

In the training process of our model, the Adam optimizer ($\alpha = 0.5$, $\beta = 0.99$) with the learning rate (lr) of 0.0001 is used to update the parameters of the generator automatically. And we set the initial learning rate of steganalysis to 0.0001, use the Adam ($\alpha = 0.5$, $\beta = 0.99$) optimization method to update the parameters of steganalysis. Moreover, we reduce the generator learning rate by $0.9 * \text{lr}$ each 3 epochs.

## 4.3  Discuss the Results

We perform a comparison with the papers [27, 28] in four aspects in our experiments, including the visual quality of stego images and extracted secret images, the invisibility of the secret image, the resistance to steganalysis detection and the accuracy of reconstruction. To keep the experiments unbiased, we control the variables and use the dataset (Sect. 4.1) to retrain all the relevant steganograpghic methods based on deep learning used to hide color.

**The Quality of Stego and Extracted Images.** The covers are generated by the generator, the stego images and extracted secret images are output by the Encoder and Decoder respectively. Our model used Duan's model as Encoder-Decoder, which is shown in the first and fourth columns of Fig. 3. The results of papers [27, 28] are shown in the second and fifth columns and the third, sixth columns in Fig. 3 respectively. From the images shown in Fig. 3, our model's stego images still do not have the problem of color bias and peak noise points even though the color images are embedded the same size. In the first column, the PSNR of our stego image and cover is 35.2, Fu's [28] is 30.9, and Duan's [27] is 36.1; the PSNR of our secret image and extracted image is 34.6, Fu's is 33.7, and Duan's is 34.3. In the second column, the PSNR of our stego image and cover is 35.0, Fu's is 31.1, and Duan's is 35.7; the PSNR of our secret image and extracted image is 33.5, Fu's is 32.6, and Duan's is 35.1. Our scheme has some improvement in PSNR compared with Fu's model, and we have not exceeded compared with Duan's model. However, we added a steganalysis network to the model to train against the generator to make the generated images in this paper more resistant to steganalysis, which can be seen in The invisibility of the secret images.

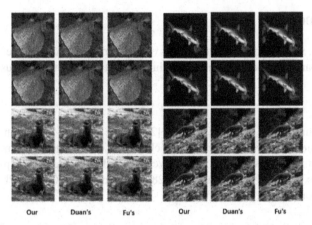

**Fig. 3.** The performance of our model, Duan's model, and Fu's model. The first row in the figure is the cover images, the second row is the corresponding stego images, the third row is the secret images, and the last row is the extracted secret images.

Table 1 shows the PSNR and SIIM values of stego images and extracted images generated by our model, Duan's models and Fu's model. Higher PSNR and SSIM mean a more realistic cover containing secret information and less difference from the original cover. From the results shown in Table 1, we can see that the PSNR values of both stego images and extracted secret images are reduced compared to Duan's model, and the reduction is even lower compared to Fu's model. This is because our generated covers have the effect of anti-steganalysis detection, which will inevitably reduce the visual quality of the images. However, PSNR is reduced by only 1–2 dm and SSIM by 0.1 in our model in the case of ensuring security.

**Table 1.** PSNR and SSIM of stego and extracted images.

|  | Stego (SSIM) | Stego (PSNR) | Extracted (SSIM) | Extracted (PSNR) |
|---|---|---|---|---|
| Duan's model | 0.95 | 36.52 | 0.96 | 36.91 |
| Fu's model | 0.94 | 30.95 | 0.94 | 29.67 |
| Our (Duan's) | 0.94 | 34.36 | 0.95 | 33.94 |
| Our (Fu's) | 0.92 | 30.05 | 0.92 | 28.80 |

**The Invisibility of the Secret Images.** In this subsection, we discuss the invisibility of secret images. We show that the residual image is obtained by subtracting the corresponding pixel values of the stego image and the cover with $5\times, 10\times, 15\times$ and $20\times$ enhancement in Fig. 4. The first row is the cover, the second row is the stego image, the third row is the secret image, and the fourth to seventh rows are $5\times, 10\times, 15\times$ and $20\times$ enhancement respectively. The first and fourth columns are our model, the second and fifth columns are Duan's model, and the third and sixth columns are Fu's model.

First, we can see that in the residual image with 5× enhancement, almost no information about the secret image is visible in all the models in the fourth row of Fig. 4. Second, in the images with 10× and 15× enhancement, the residual image of Fu's model becomes more and more obvious, Duan's model becomes a little obvious, and our model is the least obvious compared to them. Third, in the 20× enhanced residual images, the secret information in our model is still the least obvious compared to Duan's model and Fu's model. This means that the cover generated by our model has higher concealment after embedding the secret image compared to the original cover, and our model has excellent concealment and security.

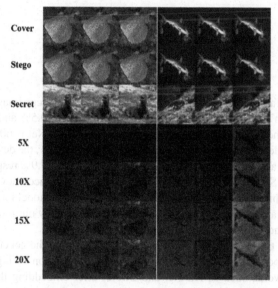

**Fig. 4.** Residual stego images of our, Duan's and Fu's models.

**Resistance to Steganalysis Detection.** In our experiments, we changed the first layer of high-pass filters and the first-layer network structure of the steganalysis, so that the steganalysis models are more suitable for detecting the steganography of color images. Then, we used a dataset (25,000 pairs of cover and secret images) to retrain Duan's model and Fu's model. 150 epochs trained by SRNet and Xu'Net were used as our steganalysis models. There are 10,000 images in total for the test, and we randomly divided them into 5,000 covers and 5,000 secret images in the experiment. The original images and the images generated by our model were used as the covers, and Duan's model and Fu's model were used as the steganographers to embed the secret images respectively. Therefore, in Table 2, we have two columns, the original image column and the proposed column. The original image column uses 5,000 original covers and their corresponding 5,000 stego images as the steganalysis test set; and the proposed column uses 5,000 covers generated by our model and their corresponding 5,000 stego images as the steganalysis test set. The accuracy rate is increased by 0.01% when a cover is judged to be the cover or a secret image is judged to be the secret image by the steganalysis. The accuracy rate remains unchanged when an error occurs.

**Table 2.** Steganalysis detection accuracy.

|  | Original | Proposed |
|---|---|---|
| *Duan's model* |  |  |
| Xu'Net | 99.5% | **60.4%** |
| SRNet | 99.9% | **73.6%** |
| *Fu's model* |  |  |
| Xu'Net | 89.7% | **55.8%** |
| SRNet | 95.9% | **57.2%** |

As shown in Table 2, when using the original image and its stego image, the detection accuracy of Duan's model and Fu's model under Xu'Net is 99.5% and 89.7% respectively; while of the covers generated by our model under Xu'Net is 60.4% and 55.8% respectively, the detection accuracy is greatly reduced. Similarly, the detection accuracy of Duan's model and Fu's model under SRNet is 99.9% and 95.9% respectively, but of our model under SRNet is 73.6% and 57.2% respectively, the accuracy is also reduced by about 30%. This proves that the images generated by our model have strong detection capability against steganalysis, and the covers generated by our model have higher undetectability and security after embedding the secret images.

According to the experimental results, it can be seen that the generated cover proposed in this paper can still effectively cheat the identification of high-performance steganalysis networks such as Xu'Net and SRNet after embedding the same size of secret color images. The reason is that the algorithm adds the jointly trained Steganalysis Optimization Network (SON) into the adversarial model, and builds the Steganalysis Adversarial Network (SAN) based on the optimized steganalyzer, which enhances the steganalysis resistance in the process of generating covers and optimizes some sensitive areas that the steganalysis network "pays attention to". The steganalysis-resistant covers are generated by optimizing certain sensitive areas that are "concerned" by the steganalysis network. On the other hand, the proposed U-Net structure-based generative network uses attention to transfer the detailed information of the real image through the hopping layer to retain as many features of the real image as possible and generate covers with more detailed information, so as to enhance the ability of information hiding.

## 5   Conclusion

In this paper, we propose a cover generative steganography, which uses the U-Net as the generator for constructing covers for steganography. The same steganographic method can achieve higher security by using the generated images than the original images.

To better balance the visual quality of the generated covers with the ability to resist steganalysis detection, we also design a new loss function to obtain different covers by training against different steganalysis networks. We use multiple images sets to verify the effectiveness of our method. By this way, we can not only test the security of the generated images under the same model, but also under different models. In the future, we will do more research in the field of generative steganography.

**Acknowledgement.** This research was funded by the National Natural Science Foundation of China: (No: 61872203, No: 61802212), the Shandong Provincial Natural Science Foundation: (No: ZR2019BF017, No: ZR2020MF054), Jinan City '20 universities' Funding Projects (No: 2019GXRC031, No: 2020GXRC056), Provincial Education Reform Projects: (No: Z2020042), School-level teaching reform project (NO: 201804), and School-level key project (NO: 2020zd24).

# References

1. Wang, J., Cheng, M., Wu, P., Chen, B.: A survey on digital image steganography. J. Inf. Hiding Priv. Prot. **1**(2), 87–93 (2019)
2. Alhomoud, A.M.: Image steganography in spatial domain: current status, techniques, and trends. Intell. Autom. Soft Comput. **27**(1), 69–88 (2021)
3. Mielikainen, J.: LSB matching revisited. IEEE Signal Process. Lett. **13**(5), 285–287 (2006)
4. Pevný, T., Filler, T., Bas, P.: Using high-dimensional image models to perform highly unde-tectable steganography. In: 12th Information Hiding Conference, pp. 161–177. Dept Comp Sci (2010)
5. Holub, V., Fridrich, J.: Designing steganographic distortion using directional filters. In: IEEE International Workshop on Information Forensics and Security, pp. 234–239 (2013)
6. Holub, V., Fridrich, J., Denemark, T.: Universal distortion function for steganography in an arbitrary domain. EURASIP J. Inf. Secur. **2014**(1), 1–13 (2014). https://doi.org/10.1186/1687-417X-2014-1
7. Ruanaidh, J.K., Dowling, W., Boland, F.M.: Phase watermarking of digital images. In: Proceedings of 3rd IEEE International Conference on Image Processing, vol. 3, pp. 239–242 (1996)
8. Cox, I.J., Leighton, K.J., Shamoon, T.: Secure spread spectrum watermarking for multimedia. IEEE Trans. Image Process. **6**(12), 1673–1687 (1997)
9. Luo, Y., Qin, J., Xiang, X., Tan, Y.: Coverless image steganography based on multi-object recognition. IEEE Trans. Circuits Syst. Video Technol. **31**, 2779–2791 (2021)
10. Hussien, A., Mohamed, M.S., Hafez, E.H.: Coverless image steganography based on jigsaw puzzle image generation. Comput. Mater. Continua **67**(2), 2077–2091 (2021)
11. Qiu, A., Chen, X., Sun, X., Wang, S., Wei, G.: Coverless image steganography method based on feature selection. J. Inf. Hiding Prot. **1**(2), 49–60 (2019)
12. Qian, Y., Dong, J., Wang, W., Tan, T.: Deep learning for steganalysis via convolutional neural networks. In: Conference on Media Watermarking, Security, and Forensics (2015)
13. Xu, G., Wu, H.Z., Shi, Y.Q.: Structural design of convolutional neural networks for steganalysis. IEEE Signal Process. Lett. **23**(5), 708–712 (2016)
14. Ye, J., Ni, J.Q., Yi, Y.: Deep learning hierarchical representations for image steganalysis. IEEE Trans. Inf. Forensics Secur. **12**(11), 2545–2557 (2017)
15. Boroumand, M., Chen, M., Fridrich, J.: Deep residual network for steganalysis of digital images. IEEE Trans. Inf. Forensics Secur. **14**(5), 1181–1193 (2018)

16. Fridrich, J., Kodovsky, J.: Rich models for steganalysis of digital images. IEEE Trans. Inf. Forensics Secur. **7**(3), 868–882 (2012)
17. Schmidhuber, J.: Deep learning in neural networks: an overview. Neural Netw. **61**, 85–117 (2015)
18. Vplkonskiy, D., Borisenko, B., Burnaev, E.: Generative adversarial networks for image steganography. In: Proceedings of the Open Review Conference on Learning Representations (2016)
19. Shi, H.C., Dong, J., Wang, W., Qian, Y., Zhang, X.: SSGAN: secure steganography based on generative adversarial networks. In: Proceedings of the Pacific Rim Conference on Multimedia, pp. 534–544 (2017)
20. Zhang, Y.W., Zhang, W.M., Chen, K.J., Liu, J.Y., Liu, Y.J., Yu, N.H.: Adversarial examples against deep neural network based steganalysis. In: Proceedings of the 6th ACM Workshop Information Hiding Multimedia Security, pp. 67–72 (2018)
21. Zhou, L.C., Feng, G.R., Shen, L.Q., Zhang, X.P.: On security enhancement of steganography via generative adversarial image. IEEE Signal Process. Lett. **27**, 166–170 (2019)
22. Tang, W.X., Tan, S.Q., Li, B., Huang, J.W.: Automatic steganographic distortion learning using a generative adversarial network. IEEE Signal Process. Lett. **24**(10), 1547–1551 (2017)
23. Yang, J.H., Liu, K., Kang, X.Q., Shi, E.K.: Spatial image steganography based on generative adversarial network arXiv:1804.07939 (2018)
24. Hayes, J., Danezis, G.: Generating steganographic images via adversarial training. In: 31st NIPS (2017)
25. Wang, Z., Gao, N., Wang, X., Qu, X., Li, L.: SSteGAN: self-learning steganography based on generative adversarial networks. In: Cheng, L., Leung, A.C.S., Ozawa, S. (eds.) ICONIP 2018. LNCS, vol. 11302, pp. 253–264. Springer, Cham (2018). https://doi.org/10.1007/978-3-030-04179-3_22
26. Zhang, K.A., Cuesta-Infante, A., Xu, L., Veeramachaneni, K.: SteganoGAN: high capacity image steganography with gans. arXiv:1901.03892v2 (2019)
27. Duan, X., Jia, K., Li, B., Guo, D.D., Zhang, E., Qin, C.: Reversible image steganography scheme based on a U-Net structure. IEEE Access **7**, 9314–9323 (2019)
28. Fu, Z., Wang, F., Cheng, X.: The secure steganography for hiding images via GAN. EURASIP J. Image Video Process. **2020**(1), 1–18 (2020). https://doi.org/10.1186/s13640-020-00534-2

# Perceptual Image Hashing with Bidirectional Generative Adversarial Networks for Copy Detection

Bin Ma[1], Yili Wang[1], Chunpeng Wang[1], Jian Li[1], Bing Han[1(✉)], and Xinan Cui[2]

[1] Shandong Provincial Key Laboratory of Computer Networks, Qilu University of Technology (Shandong Academy of Sciences), Jinan 250353, China
a1476529663@163.com
[2] Zhongfu Information Inc., Jinan 250101, China

**Abstract.** The traditional perceptual hashing algorithm is generally achieved by artificially extracting features from an image and quantizing them into a hash code. However, it is often hard to capture the inherent features of an image in practice. In order to improve the performance of image perceptual hashing, an unsupervised data-driven generative adversarial framework to generate the image perceptual hash code is proposed in this paper. Firstly, the original image is normalized and the encoder network is employed to generate the perceptual hash code; then, the generator network is used to formulate a data distribution as similar as possible to the original image from random noise in the same dimension as the perceptual hash code. Thirdly, the discriminator network is adopted to distinguish the hash code from the noise modified by the generated network and the source of the generated image and the original image. Finally, the encoder can generate image hash codes with good perceptual robustness and recognition accuracy by jointly training of the three networks. Various experiments have been executed on an extensive test database in this paper. The results show that the proposed perceptual image hashing algorithm has stronger robustness than other state-of-the-art schemes.

**Keywords:** Generative adversarial networks · Perceptual hashing · Copy detection

## 1 Introduction

With the rapid development of intelligent mobile terminals and digital image processing technology, the cost of obtaining high-precision images is declining, and the images in the Internet are increasing exponentially. Image authenticity verification has become a research hotspot in the field of digital image. Cryptography hash is very sensitive to image content, so traditional cryptography hash is only suitable for image copyright authentication of the bit stream level. For images, after specific operations (such as clipping, rotation, etc.) modified images, although the content perception does not change much, the hash function value will change greatly, it is difficult to achieve copyright tracking and source protection of images. Perceptual image hashing based on image visual content to calculate the generated hash sequence should have strong robustness, even after slight changes in the original image can still produce similar hash sequence, resist the attack against the original image tampering operation; on the other hand, the perceptual hashing algorithm also has strong vulnerability. For different sources of images, even without any modification, it can generate hash functions that are quite different from the original image, so as to realize the source authentication of the original image and the monitoring of fake image attacks.

Image perceptual hash was first proposed by Schneider and Chang [1] at the International Conference on Image Processing (ICIP) in 1996. In order to obtain the spatial information in the image, the image is divided into several sub-blocks. The mean value of each sub-block strength histogram is extracted, and the corresponding mean value of all sub-blocks is quantified as the hash value of the image. Since then, there have been a large number of researches on image perceptual hashing. Huang et al. [2] combined gray level co-occurrence matrix and DCT coefficients to generate hash sequences, and achieved good balance between robustness and uniqueness. Hosny et al. [3] generated efficient hash codes by extracting Gauss-Hermite moments and their invariants of grayscale images, which performed well in terms of security and noise attacks. Tang et al. [4] used discrete cosine transform to extract stable features, and then quantified features by local linear embedding. This algorithm is robust to Gaussian filtering and JPEG compression. Tang et al. [5] used logarithmic polar coordinates and DFT to extract feature matrix from normalized images, and then used MDS transform to extract short hash code. This scheme can resist large angle rotation attack, but the uniqueness performance is not good. Li et al. [6] used compressed sampling and random projection to aggregate the spatial layout of low-order approximation and salient components of the input image into hash codes, respectively, and obtained good balance. Tang et al. [7] combined with the image color vector angle matrix and edge statistical characteristics to form a hash code. The algorithm performs well in the face of rotation, brightness, contrast and other attacks.

The above image perceptual hashing methods need to manually design and extract image features, which are difficult to fully describe the perceptual image content features. In recent years, with the development of saliency computing power and deep learning theory, many studies have begun to use deep learning network model to realize image sensing hash algorithm [8–10]. Song et al. [11] proposed a BGAN-based scheme. In the process of adversarial training, adversarial constraints enable the encoder to realize the function from real data distribution to potential inverse representation. Li et al. [12] proposed a perceptual image hashing algorithm based on deep learning network model. Firstly, stacked denoising auto-encoder (DAE) was used to expect that the distorted image could be restored to the original state, and then the whole network was fine-tuned to maximize the robustness and sensitivity of the perceptual hashing algorithm. [11, 12] Both of them adopted pixel-level reconstruction loss. Natural images usually contain many variable details in the reconstruction process, such as size, spot and shape. Pixel-level reconstruction makes the model more sensitive to these details and reduces the robustness of hash code. Overall, the current research on perceptual image hashing algorithm based on deep learning network model is relatively less, and the performance of the algorithm has a large room for improvement.

In this paper, an image perceptual hashing algorithm based on Bidirectional Adversarial Generative Network (BiGAN) is proposed to extract the key information of perceptual image content by BiGAN, so as to improve the robustness of perceptual hash codes against the same images and the vulnerability of different images. The BiGAN-based image perceptual hashing network includes a self-learning encoder, a hash generator and a joint discrimination. The self-learning encoder is responsible for generating hash codes for the input images. The hash generator is responsible for recovering the hash code into the input image; the joint discrimination is responsible for monitoring the quality of the output of the above two components and improving the perceptual hashing performance of the algorithm. Experimental results on datasets such as CeleA show that the BiGAN-based image perceptual hashing algorithm has better balancing performance under high-intensity attacks compared with the current state-of-the-art perceptual hashing algorithms.

## 2 Relate Work

Jeff Donahue *et al.* [13] proposed a Bidirectional Adversarial Generative Network (BiGAN) with the architecture shown in Fig. 1. The main features of BiGAN:

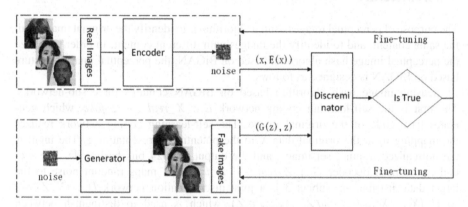

**Fig. 1.** BiGAN structure

Generation network consists of two components. The self-learning encoder $E(x)$ maps the real data space $x$ to the potential data space $z$, forming the distribution $P_E(z|x) = \delta(z - E(x))$; the hash generator $G(z)$ maps the noise variable $P_z(z)$ to the real data space, forming the distribution $P_G(x|z) = \delta(x - G(x))$.

The joint discrimination network performs joint judgments on $G(z)$, $E(x)$ not only in the data space $x$, but also in the data potential representation space $z$ tuple $(x, E(x))$, $(G(z), z)$, forming the distribution $P_D(R|x,z)$. When $x$ comes from the real data, $R = 1$; when $x$ comes from the generated data $G(z)$, $R = 0$.

The value function of BiGAN is:

$$\min_{E,G} \max_{D} V(D, E, G) = E_{X \sim p_{data}(x)}[\log D(x, E(x)] + E_{z \sim pz(z)}[1 - \log D(G(z), z)] \quad (1)$$

BiGAN uses the method of alternately updating the discrimination network and the generation network. Discrimination network is first updated with the requirement to maximize the value function V(D, E, G) to make it more confident in determining the origin of data pairs. Thus, the decoder is guided to learn the real data distribution automatically on the one hand, and the encoder is guided to learn the key feature information of the real data perceptually on the other hand. Secondly, discrimination network is fixed and the generation networks E and G are updated, requiring the minimization of the value function V(D, E, G). According to the guidance of the gradient of the updated discrimination network, the generative network is made to perform better in the double mapping task. When the above process is iterated cyclically until the model converges, the encoder of BiGAN has the reverse decoding capability, and the decoder generation networks is able to generate the same image distribution as the original image, thus deceiving the discriminator. That is, the encoder has the ability to capture the potential features of the input data as it learns to flip. Inspired by the BiGAN network, this paper proposes a bidirectional adversarial generative network to obtain robust image hashing algorithms without pixel-level reconstruction while preserving latent semantic information.

## 3 Architecture

The purpose of perceptual image hashing algorithm is to identify the original image with the same content, and to identify the images with different content. In order to realize the perceptual image hash algorithm based on BiGAN, the perceptual image structure based on BiGAN is designed as follows:

Sensing image hash algorithm based on BiGAN contains three sub-networks. The first is the self-learning coding network $E : X\_real \rightarrow z\_fake$, which generates hash code of the original image. The self-learning coding network realizes the mapping from the original data $X$ to the potential representation $z$. The input is the normalized training set image, and the output is 1024 bits hash code. The second is the hash decoder $G : Z\_real \rightarrow X\_fake$ that maps random noise to the target data distribution; subnet 3 is a joint discrimination network $D : (X, Z) \rightarrow \{0, 1\}$, $(X_{fake}, X_{real} \in X \text{ and } Z_{fake}, Z_{real} \in Z)$, which is used to distinguish between images and potentially represented data pairs from encoders or generators. The overall process is shown in Fig. 2. Firstly, the preprocessed original image is learned through the encoder network to obtain the corresponding potential representation. Then the random noise is used to reconstruct the original image input by the encoder through the generator. The tuple composed of encoder input and output and the tuple composed of generator output and input are put into the discrimination network to guide the next training of the model until the image and the original image are generated, and the image coding and random noise distribution are consistent.

### 3.1 Self-learning Encoder and Hash Decoder

The purpose of self-learning encoder network is to extract compact semantic information from the original image. The self-learning encoder and hash decoder in this paper are

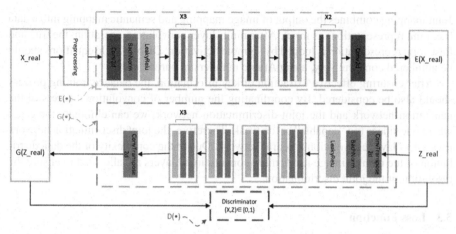

**Fig. 2.** The sensing image hash algorithm architecture based on BiGAN. Conv2d represents convolution layer. BachNorm represents batch normalization layer. LeakyRelu represents activation function.

similar to DCGAN [14] as a whole, and are fully convolutional architectures. However, in the training process, the high-dimensional feature map of the self-learning encoder is retained and transmitted to the hash decoder. After receiving these high-dimensional features, the generator will superimpose these high-dimensional feature maps with the input data of the corresponding deconvolution layer as the new input of the deconvolution layer. The reason for this is mainly to enhance the detail information of the generated image, so that the gradient signal transmitted by the discrimination to the self-learning Encoder and Hash decoder is more sensitive, and finally the frame generates hash codes with higher performance.

## 3.2 Joint Discrimination

The joint discriminator network is used in the model to determine whether the data pair composed of the image and the noise comes from the real data distribution or the generated data distribution. In this pair of data, one element must come from the real data distribution, and the other element must come from the generated data distribution. Since the input of the network consists of two elements, we first perform convolution operations on them, and then distinguish 'true' and 'false'. Equations should be flushed to the left of the column.

In the experiment, the joint discrimination network is divided into three mapping processes, namely, image mapping, semantic mapping and joint mapping. Image mapping will perform multi-layer convolution operation by inputting the original image or reconstructed image. Based on the characteristics of multi-layer volume and network, with the deepening of the network, the number of channels of the image becomes more and more, and the size of the image becomes smaller. Finally, the original input image is compressed into 1024 bit feature representations. Semantic mapping extracts the original image features by multi-layer convolution operation of the input noise or hash code.

Joint mapping combines the output of image mapping and semantic mapping into a data (i.e. joint representation) as input. After multi-layer convolution operation, the true and false joint representation is judged by sigmoid activation. Display style equations should be numbered consecutively, using Arabic numbers in parentheses.

After ensuring effective extraction of key information, the balance training process should also be considered. By coordinating the number of convolutional layers of the generation network and the joint discrimination network, we can eliminate the cases where one side is too "capable" or too weak. Therefore, the joint discrimination network uses a 13 - layer convolutional neural network. Due to the complexity of the data distribution of the natural image itself, more convolutional layers are allocated to ensure the resolution of the joint discrimination.

### 3.3  Loss Function

The core of BiGAN-based perceptual hash algorithm is to generate perceptual hash codes with good robustness and sensitivity by training self-learning encoder network, Hash decoder network and joint discrimination network. Different from the original image reconstruction algorithm based on GAN network, this algorithm aims to generate perceptual hash codes that can represent the original image. In order to ensure that the system generates perceptual hash codes with balanced robustness and sensitivity, and make the distribution of the output image data of the self-learning decoder as consistent as possible with the distribution characteristics of the original image data, the joint discrimination network, self-learning coding network and hash decoding network are required to be optimized according to the loss functions A and B, respectively.

$$Loss_D = -M \text{ean}[\log(D(x, E(x))) + \log(1 - D(G(z), z))] \tag{2}$$

$$Loss_{E,G} = -M \text{ean}[\log(D(G(z), z)) + \log(1 - D(x, E(x)))] \tag{3}$$

where $x \in X\_real, z \in Z\_real$; $E(\cdot)$ represents the output of the self-learning encoder; $G(\cdot)$ represents the output of the hash decoder; $D(\cdot)$ represents the output of the joint discrimination; $M$ean represents the mean operation of batch input. The lower the value of formula (2) is, the larger the value of $D(x, E(x))$, the smaller the value of $D(G(z), z)$, that is, the stronger the discrimination ability; The smaller the value of formula (3) is, the greater the value of $D(G(z), z)$ is, and the smaller the value of $D(x, E(x))$ is, that is, the stronger the generation ability is. After the joint training of the three networks by countering the loss, the encoder and decoder are reciprocal under ideal conditions, namely $G(E(x)) = E(G(z))$. That is to say, the encoder data pair $(x, E(x))$ and the generator data pair $(G(z), z)$ are matched. In other words, the discrimination cannot distinguish the difference between the data pair $(X, E(X))$ and $(G(z), z)$ at this time. At this time, the random noise distribution has been trained to be consistent with the original image coding. Therefore, the trained network model can be used to learn the hash code, and the generated semantic distribution is trained as the perceptual hash of the original image to realize the consistent judgment of the original image and the identification of different source images.

# 4 Experiments

## 4.1 Experimental Setup Details

All images in this experiment are from the CelebAMask-HQ dataset. The CelebAMask-HQ dataset is a large-scale face dataset which contains about 30,000 color face images with 1024 * 1024 pixels. In this paper, 12,000 images are randomly selected as the training set, and the other 18,000 images are used as the test set.

In the preprocessing stage, the images are first resized to $128 \times 128$ uniform size by bilinear interpolation, and then grayed out. The algorithm proposed in this paper is implemented in the experiments through the pytroch framework, and the full convolution (FCN) [14] architecture is used to build the self-learning encoder network, and the parameters are updated using the Adam optimizer for all three network models. Where $\beta_1$ is 0.5, $\beta_2$ is 0.999, the weight decay is 2e−5, the minimum batch is 20, and the learning rate is 1e−4. All parameters of BiGAN generating perceptual hash start learning through random initialization. In addition, the correlation coefficient is used to calculate the correlation between the two hash codes in the experiment. The larger the correlation coefficient of hash codes is, the more similar the image pairs are in visual perception. See Formula for Correlation Calculation (4).

$$\rho(H_1, H_2) = \frac{\sum\limits_{k}^{len} [h_1(k) - u_1][h_2(k) - u_2]}{\sqrt{\sum\limits_{k}^{len} [h_1(k) - u_1]^2 \sum\limits_{k}^{len} [h_2(k) - u_2]^2 + \Delta s}} \tag{4}$$

$h_1(k)$, $h_2(k)$ are the Kth elements of the hash codes $H_1$, $H_2$ respectively. $u_1$, $u_2$ are the mean values of the hash codes $H_1$, $H_2$ respectively. $\Delta s$ is a very small number that prevent the denominator from being 0. From Eq. (4), it is known that the larger the interrelation number $\rho(H_1, H_2)$, the higher the similarity between the perceptual hash codes, the stronger the image discrimination ability of the generated hash codes, and the more accurate the judgment of the same image and the discrimination of different images.

## 4.2 Perceptual Robustness

In order to verify the robustness of the system, 500 images are randomly selected from the test set, and 33500 copies of images are generated after copy attacks such as salt and pepper noise and gamma filtering (see Table 1 for detailed parameters). After this system, 26800 pairs of hash codes are extracted and the correlation coefficients are calculated. The statistical characteristics of all the correlation coefficients are shown in Table 2. From the results of statistical characteristics, the correlation between the generated hash code and the original hash code is close to 1. When the decision threshold T = 0.95, only 536 images have correlation coefficients lower than the threshold. Among the 703 undetected similar images, 349 were generated by rotation, clipping and scaling combined attacks; 274 images are generated by Gaussian noise attacks, and 78 images are generated by gamma correction attacks. The correct source identification rate of images after the above various types of attacks is as high as 95.3%. The experimental results show that the perceptual hash generation network based on BiGAN can effectively determine the copyright ownership of similar copies. That is, the hash code extracted by this system has good robustness to various attacks.

**Table 1.** Correlation coefficients under different content retention operations.

| Operation | Parameter | Parameter value |
| --- | --- | --- |
| Brightness adjustment | Photoshop scale | −20, −10, 10, 20 |
| Contrast adjustment | Photoshop scale | −20, −10, 10, 20 |
| Gaussian filtering | Standard deviation | 0.3, 0.4, 0.5, 0.6, 0.7, 0.8, 0.9, 1.0 |
| Gamma filtering | gamma | 0.7, 0.9, 1.1, 1.3 |
| Image scaling | Scaling ratio | 0.5, 0.7, 0.9, 1.1, 1.3, 1.5 |
| Salt and Pepper noise | Density | 0.001, 0.002, ... , 0.009, 0.01 |
| Gaussian noise | Variance | 0.001, 0.002, ... , 0.009, 0.01 |
| Rotation, cropping, rescaling | Rotation angle | 1, 2, 3, 4, 5 |
| JPEG compression | Quality factor | 30, 40, 50, 60, 70, 80, 90, 100 |
| Watermarking | Quantification step | 0.3, 0.4, 0.5, 0.6, 0.7, 0.8, 0.9, 1.0 |

### 4.3  Discriminative Capability

In order to quantify the ability of the hash code extracted by the system to discriminate images from different sources, four indicators of false positive rate $P_{FPR}$, maximum, mean and minimum are introduced in the experiment to evaluate the performance of the algorithm. Where, represents the probability that it is actually not a similar image but is determined as a similar image.

$$P_{TPR}(T) = \frac{n_1}{N_1}, \rho \geq T \tag{5}$$

$$P_{FPR}(T) = \frac{n_2}{N_2}, \rho < T \tag{6}$$

where $\rho$ represents the correlation coefficient between image pairs, $T$ represents the threshold, $n_1$ represents the number of pairs judged to be similar, and $N_1$ represents the total number of similar images. $n_2$ represents the number of different images that incorrectly judge to be similar. $N_2$ represents the number of different images.

Firstly, 500 images are randomly selected from the test set, and the system is used to extract efficient hash code. A total of $500 \times (500 - 1)/2 = 124750$ hash pairs of different images were obtained. The mean, maximum and minimum values of hash pairs of different images are calculated, which are 0.1732, 0.9916 and −0.2945. The mean value of 0.1745 is much lower than that of 0.9573 for similar images. Calculate the false positive rate of hash pairs in different images (see formula 6). The results are shown in Table 3. It can be seen from Table 3 that when the correlation coefficient threshold decreases, the probability of being misjudged as a similar image increases slightly. In fact, when the threshold $T = 0.9$, only 0.7% of the probability is misjudged as similar images, that is, 99.3% of the probability can correctly identify different images. The experimental results show that the perceptual hash generation model based on BiGAN has good ability to identify different sources of images.

**Table 2.** Statistical characteristics of different content retention operations.

| Operation | Maximum | Minimum | Mean |
|---|---|---|---|
| Brightness adjustment | 0.9998 | 0.9934 | 0.9386 |
| Contrast adjustment | 0.9999 | 0.9981 | 0.9866 |
| Gaussian filtering | 1 | 0.9998 | 0.9974 |
| Gamma filtering | 0.9999 | 0.9836 | 0.7233 |
| Image scaling | 0.9999 | 0.9999 | 0.9998 |
| Salt and Pepper noise | 0.9999 | 0.9969 | 0.9639 |
| Gaussian noise | 0.9999 | 0.9795 | 0.6788 |
| Rotation, cropping, rescaling | 0.9995 | 0.9573 | 0.7015 |
| JPEG compression | 0.9997 | 0.9929 | 0.9646 |
| Watermarking | 1 | 0.9999 | 0.9999 |

### 4.4   Performance Comparison Among Different Methods

In order to evaluate the comprehensive performance of the hash scheme in this paper, this method is compared with other hot hash code algorithms in the experiment. Other hot algorithms choose DCT_GLCM [2] based on frequency domain transform, which combines local features and global features to make hash code have excellent recognition performance and robustness. Based on matrix compression AEU [7], this algorithm is completely immune to rotation attack by combining ring segmentation and edge detection technology. Based on manifold learning DCT_LLE [4], the algorithm combines frequency domain transform and local linear embedding dimension reduction. The application of LLE reduces the data complexity, and DCT ensures the robustness of hash code. And SDAE [12] based on deep learning, the scheme combines deep learning with copy detection for the first time and performs well under various complex attacks. These perceptual hash algorithms show good balance between robustness and sensitivity. All experiments are carried out on the same computer with a P4000. DCT_GLCM, DCT_LLE are implemented by python3.7. SDAE is implemented by MATLAB2018b.

Firstly, 500 images were randomly selected from the CelebAMask-HQ test set, and 8000 similar images were generated after the original image was attacked and modified by brightness adjustment, contrast modification, rotary shear scaling, JPEG compression

**Table 3.** TPR and FPR at different thresholds.

| Threshold | $P_{FPR}$ |
|-----------|-----------|
| 0.96 | $1.02 \times 10^{-3}$ |
| 0.95 | $1.69 \times 10^{-3}$ |
| 0.94 | $2.63 \times 10^{-3}$ |
| 0.93 | $3.61 \times 10^{-3}$ |
| 0.92 | $4.76 \times 10^{-3}$ |

**Table 4.** Correlation coefficients under different content retention operations.

| Operation | Parameter | Parameter value |
|-----------|-----------|-----------------|
| Brightness adjustment | Photoshop scale | −20, 20 |
| Contrast adjustment | Photoshop scale | −20, 20 |
| Gaussian filtering | Standard deviation | 0.6, 1.0 |
| Gamma filtering | Gamma | 0.7, 1.3 |
| Image scaling | Scaling ratio | 0.5, 1.5 |
| Salt and Pepper noise | Density | 0.002, 0.006 |
| Rotation, cropping, rescaling | Rotation angle | 3, 5 |
| JPEG compression | Quality factor | 40, 80 |

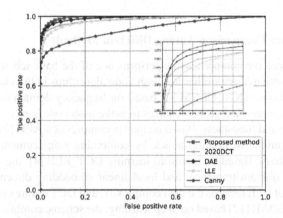

**Fig. 3.** ROC curve comparison of different algorithms.

and other methods (detailed parameters are shown in Table 4). Firstly, the algorithm is used to generate hash codes, and the correlation between each pair of original images and the hash codes of the attached image is calculated by cross-correlation criteria. Then, 20 thresholds are evenly divided from 0% to 100% to calculate 20 $P_{TPR}$, $P_{FPR}$ point pairs (see formula 5, 6), and then the ROC curve is generated. Finally, the ROC curves of all the comparison algorithms are shown in Fig. 3. It can be seen from the graph that our algorithm has a ROC value closer to the upper left corner, which shows that the BiGAN-based generation perceptual hash code algorithm proposed in this paper has more perceptual robustness and strong judgment ability for images of the same source.

## 5 Conclusion

A perceptual hash code generation algorithm based on Bidirectional Adversarial Generative Network is proposed to detect the source of images under multiple attacks. On the one hand, this algorithm uses an unsupervised network model that neither needs to label nor manually extract features, which obviously improves the efficiency of hash code generation. On the other hand, using short hash code instead of large feature database reduces the physical storage space. Experiments on large databases show that the proposed algorithm can not only ensure high recognition rate of different source images, but also has strong perceptual robustness to the same source images, that is, it can achieve good balance between the two performance. However, since this model mainly focuses on 128 * 128 images, we will try to further optimize the performance of hash code algorithm by changing the size of the input image and adjusting the model architecture.

**Acknowledgement.** This research was funded by the National Natural Science Foundation of China: (No: 61872203, No: 61802212), the Shandong Provincial Natural Science Foundation: (No: ZR2019BF017, No: ZR2020MF054), Jinan City '20 universities' Funding Projects (No: 2019GXRC031, No: 2020GXRC056), Provincial Education Reform Projects: (No: Z2020042), School-level teaching reform project (NO: 201804), and School-level key project (NO: 2020zd24).

## References

1. Schneider, M., Chang, S.F.: A robust content based digital signature for image authentication. In: Proceedings of 3rd IEEE International Conference on Image Processing, pp. 227–230 (1996)
2. Huang, Z., Liu, S.: Perceptual image hashing with texture and invariant vector distance for copy detection. IEEE Trans. Multimedia (2020). https://doi.org/10.1109/TMM.2020.2999188
3. Hosny, M., Khalid, K.M., Yasmeen, I.: Walid: Robust image hashing using exact Gaussian-Hermite moments. IET Image Proc. **12**, 2178–2185 (2018)
4. Tang, Z., Lao, H., Zhang, X., Liu, K.: Robust image hashing via DCT and LLE. Comput. Secur. **62**, 133–148 (2016)
5. Tang, Z., Huang, Z., Zhang, X., Lao, H.: Robust image hashing with multidimensional scaling. Signal Process. **137**, 240–250 (2017)
6. Yang, H., Yin, J., Yang, Y.: Robust image hashing scheme based on low-rank decomposition and path integral LBP. IEEE Access **7**(1), 51656–51664 (2019)
7. Tang, Z., Huang, L., Zhang, X., Lao, H.: Robust image hashing based on color vector angle and Canny operator. AEU-Int. J. Electron. C. **70**, 833–841 (2016)
8. Qin, C., Liu, E., Feng, G., Zhang, X.: Perceptual image hashing for content authentication based on convolutional neural network with multiple constraints. IEEE Trans. Circuits Syst. Video Technol. (2020). https://doi.org/10.1109/TCSVT.2020.3047142

9.  Liu, X., Liang, J., Wang, Z.Y., Tsai, Y.T., Lin, C.C., Chen, C.C.: Content-based image copy detection using convolutional neural network. Electronics (2020). https://doi.org/10.3390/electronics9122029

10. Li, Z., Xu, X., Zhang, D., Zhang, P.: Cross-modal hashing retrieval based on deep residual network. Comput. Syst. Sci. Eng. **36**(2), 383–405 (2021)

11. Song, J., He, T., Gao, L., Xu, X., Hanjalic, A.: Binary generative adversarial networks for image retrieval. Int. J. Comput. Vision **2020**, 1–22 (2020)

12. Li, Y., Wang, T.: Robust and secure image fingerprinting learned by neural network. IEEE Trans. Circuits Syst. Video Technol. **30**, 362–375 (2020)

13. Donahue, J., Krhenbühl, P., Darrell, T.: Adversarial feature learning. arXiv:1605.09782 (2016)

14. Radford, A., Metz, L., Chintala, S.: Unsupervised representation learning with deep convolutional generative adversarial networks. arXiv:1511.06434 (2016)

15. Long, J., Shelhamer, E., Darrell, T.: Fully convolutional networks for semantic segmentation. arXiv:1411.4038 (2015)

# Image Tamper Detection and Reconstruction Based on Compressive Sensing and Reversible Data Hiding

Bin Ma[1], Kezhuang Wang[1], Jian Li[1], Chunpeng Wang[1], Xiaoming Wu[1(✉)], and Xinan Cui[2]

[1] Shandong Provincial Key Laboratory of Computer Networks, Qilu University of Technology (Shandong Academy of Sciences), Jinan 250353, China
scwxmsc@163.com
[2] Zhongfu Information Inc., Jinan 250101, China

**Abstract.** Image data is vulnerable to malicious attacks in the process of transmission, especially the region of interest (ROI) of the image. The existing reversible data hiding authentication algorithm is difficult to recover the tamper area after the original image is tampered. To solve this problem, this paper proposes an image tampering detection and reconstruction algorithm based on compressive sensing and reversible data hiding for tampering detection and reconstruction of regions of interest. Firstly, the image is divided into regions of interest and non-interest, and the regions of interest are divided into blocks. The DCT coefficients of the image blocks in the region of interest are sampled by the compressive sensing algorithm, and the watermark is generated according to the sampled data. At the same time, the non-interested region is adaptively partitioned, and the reversible data hiding algorithm is used to embed the watermark information on different positions of the non-interested region. After the watermark is extracted and decoded by the receiver, the measured value of the carrier image is obtained by block compressive sensing measurement, which can be compared with the extracted watermark to locate tampered area, and the decoded watermark is used for compressive sensing to reconstruct the damaged area. By using this method to experiment with images with different texture features, the results show that the algorithm can not only achieve accurate tampering location, but also can recover tamper images of high quality.

**Keywords:** Reversible data hiding · Compressive sensing · Image tampering · Image inpainting

## 1 Introduction

With the development of recent years, digital information is transmitted efficiently in a variety of forms. Although digital multimedia brings people rich life and convenient experience, the problem of information security is becoming more and more serious. For example, images transmitted are vulnerable to illegal tampering and destruction.

X. Sun et al. (Eds.): ICAIS 2022, CCIS 1588, pp. 437–449, 2022.
https://doi.org/10.1007/978-3-031-06764-8_34

In response to this problem, digital watermark has been widely used. People verify the integrity of image content by embedding fragile watermarks into images. On this basis, reversible data hiding can not only deal with copyright protection, tamper detection and other digital security issues, but also can extract watermark lossless, reconstruction the carrier image.

Recently, the combination of compressive sensing and digital watermark has been widely used, and compressive sensing was first proposed by Tao et al. [1, 2]. If the signal satisfies the sparse characteristic in a certain space, the signal can be accurately restored with very few measured values. Traditional compressive sensing reconstruction methods include convex optimization method, greedy algorithm and iterative threshold method [3–6] which are still studied by scholars in recent years [17, 18]. With the continuous development of compressive sensing theory, the concept of sparsity has formed various forms, such as nonlocal sparsity and structural sparsity. Dong et al. [7] used the nonlocal sparsity of images and the low-rank feature of image similarity grouping to regularize the reconstruction of compressive sensing, and proposed the NLR_CS compressive sensing reconstruction method, which can better protect the image details. Yuan et al. [8] further discussed the compression quantification based on NLR_CS to improve the compression effect of compressive sensing. Many researchers have combined compressive sensing with watermark. Huang et al. [9] embedded the watermark into the compressive sensing domain to protect the copyright of image content. Xiao et al. [10] embeds the watermark information into the compressive sensing domain, and extracts the watermark information at the extraction ends to realize the protection of data copyright. Chen et al. [11] proposed a tamper detection algorithm for video frame images by combining semi-fragile watermark with compressive sensing. Most of the above algorithms can achieve more accurate image tampering detection, but cannot achieve the use of watermark information to reconstruction the tampered image. In view of this, the compressibility of compressive sensing and the accuracy of reconstruction can be better applied in image tampering and reconstruction. In the previous image tampering detection and reconstruction methods, the combination of different compression representation methods and reversible data hiding is the most widely used. Yang et al. [12] earlier used vectors quantization to compress information containing images to generate watermarks to achieve image authentication and reconstruction. Qin et al. [13] used the halftone mechanism to compress the image and generate the recovery watermark. The authentication watermark was generated by the hash function and embedded into the image respectively. This method can tolerate high tampering rate. In recent years, tamper detection and reconstruction algorithms with higher performance have been proposed. Li et al. [14] uses chaotic system to realize pseudo-random loop to map image blocks, and adds temporary block recovery, which can withstand a large range of tampering, but cannot guarantee high PSNR. Vishal Rajput et al. [15] proposed the use of pseudo-random code to hide the four compressive versions of the original image in the image to detect tampering. At the same time, the filter and the median image are used to restore the tampered image in the recovery process, which can respond well to different attacks and restore the damaged image. However, this method uses the filter to neutralize the influence of the information hidden in the LSB, which still has a high impact on the quality of the restored image.

To further to enhance the effect of tamper detection and reconstruction, this paper proposes an image tamper detection and reconstruction algorithm based on compressive sensing and reversible data hiding, which can achieve higher performance of image tampered reconstruction. In this paper, the original image is sampled by compressive sensing, and the watermark information is generated after quantitative cod and embedded into the original image. After receiving the image, the receiver extracts the watermark and restores the carrier image. Then the compressive sensing algorithm is used to sense and measure the restored carrier image to generate the contrast watermark. The extracted watermark is decoded and compared with the contrast watermark to achieve image integrity identification and tamper localization, and the extracted watermark can be used to reconstruct and reconstruction tampered images.

## 2   Related Work

In this section, we will introduce the idea sources of some details of our proposed method and their principles. Inspired by the theory of compressive sensing, we generate and compress the watermark information by special methods. In the embedding process, our scheme is mainly based on the change of difference prediction extended reversible information hiding.

### 2.1   Compressive Sensing

Compressive sensing is a new theoretical method proposed by Candes and Tao et al., which can complete the compression at the same time of sampling, and recover the original signal accurately with very few sampling values, which has great advantages over the previous signal processing compress. The theoretical framework of compressive sensing is shown in Fig. 1. After the original signal is represented as a compressible sparse signal on a transformation basis, an observation matrix is used to map the high-dimensional sparse signal to a low-dimensional space. If the observation matrix satisfies the condition that it is not related to the transformation domain, that is, to ensure that the projection contains sufficient information of the original signal, then the original signal can be obtained by a small amount of projection reconstruction in these low-dimensional of projection reconstruction in these low-dimensional spaces.

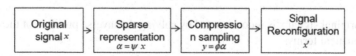

**Fig. 1.**  Compressive sensing process.

Sparse representation is a prerequisite for compressive sensing, and the accurate reconstruction of compressive sensing requires the sparsity of the signal, for an N-dimensional signal x. If only a small number of elements in the signal are not zero, then this signal is a sparse signal. Most signals in nature are not sparse, but a sparse basis $\psi$ can be found. Makes the signal represented on the sparse base as

$$\alpha = \psi x \tag{1}$$

If the above conditions are met, such signals are also called sparse signals. There are many choices of sparse bases, such as Discrete Cosine Transform (DCT), Discrete Wavelet Transform (DWT), and Fast Fourier Transform (FFT), which are commonly used in digital image processing. They can be used for sparse transform of images. The measurement process of compressive sensing is the process of compressive sampling. For the N-dimensional signal x, the M-dimensional measurement value y is obtained by the M-dimensional measurement matrix $\varphi$ dimension reduction projection, namely $y = \varphi x$. Of which $x = \psi \alpha$, $M \ll N$. As shown in Fig. 2.

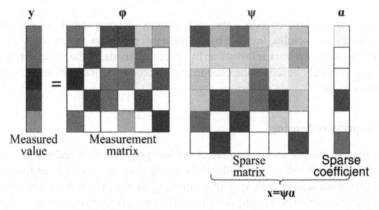

**Fig. 2.** Compressive sensing measurement.

where the perception matrix $\Theta = \varphi \psi$, The N-dimensional original sparse signal $\alpha$ is projected to the M dimensional, so the effect of dimension reduction compression is achieved. Compressive sensing theory proves that when the sensing matrix Q satisfies the Restricted Isometry Property (RIP), the following equation can be solved

$$\Theta = \varphi \psi \tag{2}$$

The original signal x is reconstructed by solving the inverse problem of the formula. In mathematical terms:

$$\alpha = \min \|\alpha\|_0 \ s.t. y = \Theta \alpha \tag{3}$$

where $\|\ \|_0$ represents the $L_0$ norm. However, solving $L_0$ norm is usually a NP-hard problem, but under certain conditions, the problem of solving $L_0$ norm can be transformed into solving $L_1$ norm, namely:

$$\min \|\alpha\|_1 \ s.t. y = \Theta \alpha \tag{4}$$

Since the $L_1$ -norm minimization is a convex optimization problem, the solving process can be transformed into a linear programming problem, so the $L_1$ -norm is used to approximate the $L_0$-norm. In the third section, we will explain the detailed recovery method of compressive sensing and some changes we made to the sampling process to generate watermarks through compressive sensing.

## 2.2  PEE Reversible Data Hiding Algorithm

Reversible data hiding can hide secret information on the carrier image, and recover the carrier image completely after extracting secret information. Early reversible data hiding algorithm is mainly realized by lossless compression, which generates redundant space by lossless compression of original image and hides information by redundant space. Tian [16] first proposed a reversible data hiding algorithm based on Difference Expansion embedding (DE), which extended the difference of a pair of pixels to embed information. Based on the improvement of the Difference Expansion (DE) algorithm, Prediction Error Extension (PEE) appears. The pixels around the target point are used to predict the target point pixels, and then the predicted difference is extended to embed information.

Thodi combines the prediction error expansion with histogram translation, which improves the embedding ability of reversible data hiding. The algorithm calculates the prediction error from the neighborhood of a pixel, and embeds the information into the expanded prediction error. The difference between the value of pixel x and the value of predicted pixel x' is called the prediction error. The carrier image is decomposed into prediction value and prediction error. The image is scanned according to the set sequence. The prediction value of the image is calculated according to the formula (5) from the first pixel of the image. The pixel distribution is shown in Fig. 3.

| k | j |
|---|---|
| h | x |

**Fig. 3.**  Example of pixel distribution.

$$\hat{x} = \begin{cases} \min(h,j) \; if \; c \geq \max(h,j) \\ \max(h,j) \; if \; c \leq \min(h,j) \\ h+j-k \; otherwise \end{cases} \tag{5}$$

the information embedding is expressed as $P'_e = 2P_e + m_i$, where $m_i$ is the information to be embedded, and $m_i \in \{0, 1\}$, the embedded pixel is expressed as

$$x' = x + P_e + m_i \tag{6}$$

Then the positioning matrix of the same size as the image is generated, and the threshold $T$ is set. If the prediction error $P_e \leq T$, the positioning matrix records the value of 1, otherwise 0. The positioning matrix is then encoded to generate a binary bit stream. According to the formula (6), the information is embedded in the lowest effective bit of the image pixel to generate an image with secret information. The information extraction process needs to scan the image according to the order of embedding, extract the lowest effective bit of the image pixel, decode and get the positioning matrix. Starting from the last pixel of the positioning matrix, if the pixel value is 1, then the prediction error value $P'_e = x' - \hat{x}$, the watermark information is extracted by the following formula:

$$m = p'_e - 1 \left\lfloor P'_e / 2 \right\rfloor \tag{7}$$

At the same time, $p_e = \left\lfloor P'_e / 2 \right\rfloor$ is calculated to produce the pixel value $x = x' - p_e - m$ of the original image, and the original image can be restored. In our method, in order to ensure better capacity effect, we divide the image embedding position into different blocks, and then use the above embedding method to embed the watermark information.

## 3 Proposed Algorithm

The flow framework of the algorithm in this paper is shown in Fig. 4. The sender first divides the image of Regions of Interest (ROI) and other non-interest regions, and divides the region of interest in blocks. Then the block DCT transforms is carried out and the compressive sensing measurement is applied to each image. The watermark information to be embedded is generated by the measurement value generated by the compressive sensing after quantitative cod. For non-interested regions, we use them to

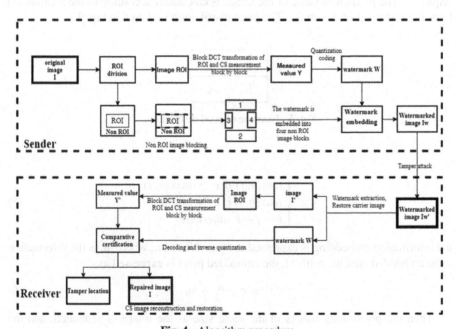

**Fig. 4.** Algorithm procedure.

hide watermark information, and then generate watermarked images. After receiving the watermark image, the receiver can extract the watermark and restore the carrier image. Next, image integrity verification and tamper detection can be carried out. The Region of Interest (ROI) of the carrier image is compressive sensing measured by the same method above to obtain the measured value, which is used as the comparative watermark. By decoding the extracted watermark and performing authentication detection with the comparative watermark, the integrity authentication and tamper localization of the image can be realized. In the image tampered reconstruction, we decode the extracted watermark information to obtain the initial compressive sensing measurement value, and then perform high-performance reconstruction of the tampered image region through the compressive sensing reconstruction algorithm.

## 3.1  Watermark Generation and Embedding

Firstly, the image is preprocessed and divided into regions of interest (ROI) and non-interest regions. Then, the regions of interest are divided into blocks, and the compressive sensing measurement is carried out at the same time of block DCT transformation. In this process, the measurement of compressive sensing does not use the traditional random deterministic measurement matrix, but in the form of JPEG compression, the DCT coefficient is encoded in the 'Z' shape and the first M element value is selected, so it does not require additional storage of the measurement matrix, only the measurement value M can be saved. The next step is to generate the watermark $W = \{w1, w2, w3...wn\}, W \in \{0, 1\}$ to be embedded after the measured values are uniformly quantized and encoded, where $w1, w2, w3...wn$ is the watermark generated by the compressive sensing measurement of each image. The value of M is determined by the compressive sensing sampling rate r. The larger the r, the larger the M value, and the larger the length of the generated watermark information. At the same time, the effect of compressive sensing will be better, but the required embedding capacity will be higher, and the invisibility of the watermark will be worse. In order to meet the larger watermark information compression effect, but also to ensure better image restoration quality, so in our experimental part r value is 0.3.

The non-interest region is used to hide the watermark information. In order to ensure a high embedding capacity, the two long edges of the image ROI are divided into two larger regions, and then the remaining non-ROI is divided into two smaller regions. A total of four regions are used to hide watermark information. The embedding method is shown in Fig. 5. The embedding is carried out step by step according to the regional order, and the reversible data hiding method combining prediction error expansion and histogram translation is used to hide the information of the four parts of the region. The neighborhood of the pixel is used to calculate the prediction error, and the watermark information is embedded into the expanded prediction error. The prediction error is

$$e = x - x'$$ (8)

is the original pixel value, $x'$ is the predicted pixel value. The original image $I$ is decomposed into predicted value $I'$ and predicted error $E$, expressed as

$$I = I' + E$$ (9)

Embed watermark information $W$ into prediction error $E$ to generate watermark image $I_w$.

$$I_W = I' + E_W \tag{10}$$

When extracting, the receiver starts from the first pixel, recovers the context-related pixels of the pixel according to the order of raster scanning, and then recovers the pixel itself, so as to extract the watermark information hidden by the pixel.

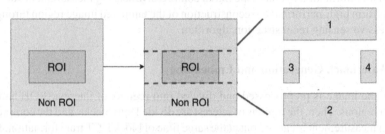

**Fig. 5.** Other regional blocks.

## 3.2  Image Tampering Detection and Reconstruction

Receiver can realize image tamper detection and reconstruction. Firstly, the watermark information is extracted from the received watermarked image and he carrier image $\hat{I}$ is restored. The extracted watermark is decoded to get $\hat{I}$. At the same time, the restored carrier image $\hat{I}$ was subjected to block DCT transform, and the measured value Y was obtained by using the compressive sensing measurement method controlled by the number of measured values M to conduct block compressive sensing measurement on the image.

$$q\hat{w} = \hat{Y} = \{\hat{y}_1, \hat{y}_2...\hat{y}_n\} \tag{11}$$

Comparing $q\hat{w}$ with the decoded watermark $d\hat{w}$ by block matching, the mean square error (MSE) is used as the reference standard. If the MSE of $q\hat{w}$ and $d\hat{w}$ is zero, the image is considered to be complete. If not zero, the second step detection is performed. Because the prediction error expansion method is used for information hiding, after extracting the watermark information hidden in the carrier image, each pixel recovery is affected by the context pixels when the carrier image is restored. If the carrier image pixel to be restored around the tamper pixel recovery effect will have a certain impact, so in the second step of watermark information matching detection, considering the maximum and minimum mean square error is not zero as an auxiliary to set the threshold b:

$$b = \frac{\max Cl - \min Cl}{2c} \tag{12}$$

$$Cl = [cl1, cl2...c\,ln] \tag{13}$$

$c$ ln is the mean square error calculation between the measured values of each block and the measured values obtained by the compressive sensing of the image at the receiving end after the watermark extraction and decoding, and the calculated results are not zero. c is the number of mean square error is not zero, if $cli < b$, the I image block is found to be tamper with.

When the image is tamper, use the obtained image tamper location information. The compressive sensing measurement value of the tamper block is obtained by decoding the watermark extracted from the carrier image, and the nonlocal low rank regularization models (NLR_CS) is used for compressive sensing reconstruction in the image reconstruction. Firstly, the standard compressive sensing DWT reconstruction algorithm is used to obtain the initial estimation of the reconstructed image, and the initial estimation image $Ix$ is matched by blocks. Using nonlocal self-similarity, for each sample block $X_i$, a similar block $Xij$ is found in the search box of its K neighborhood to meet $Gi = \{ij | \|\hat{x}i - \hat{x}ij\| < T\}$. $Gi$ represents the set of blocks similar to the sample block. After grouping, the set of similar blocks corresponding to each sample block is denoted as $Xi = [xi1, xi2...xin]$, which may contain noise, and is expressed as

$$Xi = Li + Wi \tag{14}$$

Where is a low rank matrix, is a noise matrix, can be solved by optimization:

$$Li = \arg\min_{Li} rank(Li), s.t. \|Xi - Li\|_2 <= \sigma_{2}^{\omega} \tag{15}$$

$$\left(\hat{x}, \hat{Li}\right) = \arg\min_{x,Li} \|y - \varphi x\|_2^2 + \eta \sum_i \left\{ \left\|\hat{R}_i x - L_i\right\|_2^2 + \lambda L(L_i, \varepsilon) \right\} \tag{16}$$

$R_i x = [R_{i0}x, R_{i1}x, .....R_n x]$, $R_i x$ matrix consists of a set of similar blocks.

## 4 Experimental Results and Analysis

In this part, we do a lot of experiments on different images to verify the proposed method, and compare the experimental results with the latest high performance image tampering reconstruction algorithm to verify the advancement of this algorithm.

### 4.1 Setting of Experimental Conditions

In order to more comprehensively verify the performance of the algorithm in this paper, we selected several images with different texture features for experiments. As shown in Fig. 6, including Lena, Barbara, Airplane, Baboon, Boat and Goldhill, the image specifications are 256 256 standard gray images. The textures of Lena, Barba-ra and Airplane images are relatively simple, and the textures of Baboon, Boat and Goldhill images are relatively complex. The ROI of the image is selected as the region that includes the theme target in the image and is not less than 48% of the whole image. If there is no image with obvious main objects, select an area not less than 48% of the whole image diffused at the central position. Multiple random location tampering was performed on the ROI region under different tampering rates and different block sizes. The sampling rate of compressive sensing is set to 0.3 to ensure the balance of compression and reconstruction effect. Reconstruction observation results by testing. Peak Signal to Noise Ratio (PSNR) and Structural Similarity (SSIM) are used as the standard to measure the image restoration. Based on the image tamper localization detection and restoration experiments, the algorithm is evaluated.

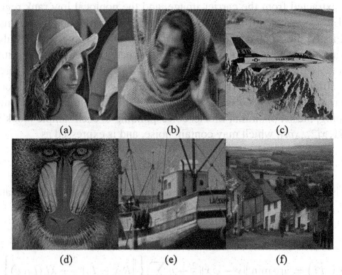

**Fig. 6.** Experimental pictures (a) Lena, (b) Barbara, (c) Airplane, (d) Baboon, (e) Boat, (f) Goldhill.

## 4.2 Algorithm Validation and Performance Evaluation

Firstly, we perform tampering localization and tampering reconstruction experiments on the six images in Fig. 7. We set the tampering rates of 5%, 10%, 15%, 20%, 25%,

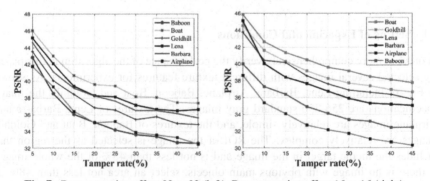

**Fig. 7.** Reconstruction effect 32 × 32 (left), Reconstruction effect 16 × 16 (right).

30%, 35%, 40% and 45%, respectively. Since the textures of different regions of the same image are different, we conduct 10 random-position tampering experiments on each image at the same tampering rate to better verify the effectiveness of our algorithm. At the same time, we also discussed the experimental results of different blocks of the image, and the above conditions were tested respectively in the case of block size of 16 × 16 and 32 × 32. Figure 7 show the average reconstruction effect of each tampering rate (%) under the conditions of 32 × 32 and 16 × 16 blocks, respectively.

In order to more objectively and clearly express the difference of the results of different texture images under different block sizes, we carried out different experimental verification. The results show that for images with complex texture, the effect of 32 × 32 blocks is better than that of 16 × 16 blocks, but for images with simple texture, the effect is opposite. For the Baboon image, although the image texture is extremely complex, but because our ROI selection for the image area is just the baboon's face area, with more similar image blocks, texture relative to other regions is not complex. Therefore, this algorithm can choose 16 × 16 blocks processing for ROI images with complex texture, and 32 × 32 block processing for ROI images with simple texture, so as to achieve the best processing effect.

It can be seen from the above that even under the 45% tampering rate, the average PSNR comparison of the recovery effect of all images in the 32 × 32 blocks are above 32 db, and the lowest PSNR comparison in the 16 × 16 blocks are above 30 db.The highest average PSNR reaches more than 46 db, and most of the image restoration effects can be maintained above 35 db. Therefore, this algorithm has accurate tamper localization and excellent tamper reconstruction effect.

### 4.3 Compared with Other Methods

In order to further prove the superiority of this algorithm, we compare this algorithm with two others latest high-performance tampering reconstruction algorithms. In the case of 32 × 32 blocks in our method, we compared the Lena and Baboon images with the Li et al. [14] method under the tamper rate of 45%, and the following figure is the comparison result.

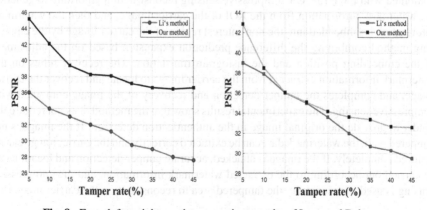

**Fig. 8.** From left to right are the comparison results of Lena and Baboon.

It can be seen from Fig. 8 that under the tamper rate of less than 45%, our method can well concentrate the recovery of damaged images and achieve higher PSNR.

For the comparison with the method in [15], we selected the same experimental objects in this method, including Airplane, Goldhill, Baboon and Sailboat images for quantitative comparison in the multi-region tampering attack of the image. we select the mean PSNR and SSIM of 10 random position attacks under the condition of 16 × 16 blocks to make a quantitative comparison with the method. Keep the tampering rate of each graph unchanged, perform random position selection for cropping tampering, restore the results of 10 tampering experiments and compare the results with the method as shown in Table 1. It can be seen that for complex texture images, we choose the block scheme of 16 × 16. While this is not the best option, it is still better than the method in [15].

Table 1. Mean results.

| Image | Airplane | Goldhill | Baboon | Sailboat |
|---|---|---|---|---|
| Tamper | 5% | 10% | 15% | 20% |
| | PSNR SSIM | PSNR SSIM | PSNR SSIM | PSNR SSIM |
| Proposed method | 42.20 0.9950 | 41.70 0.9926 | 35.51 0.9781 | 40.19 0.9858 |
| [15] method | 41.03 0.9858 | 40.11 0.9761 | 28.65 0.9072 | 32.01 0.9212 |

The above experimental results show that the proposed algorithm is significantly better than other methods in reconstruction the image within 45% tampering rate.

## 5 Conclusion

This paper proposes an image tamper detection and reconstruction algorithm based on compressive sensing and reversible data hiding. The reversible data hiding algorithm is combined with the NLR_CS compressive sensing reconstruction algorithm to generate the watermark information from the ROI of the carrier image, and then the watermark information is embedded into the non-interest region of the carrier image by the embedding method combining the difference prediction expansion based on the adjustment of the embedding position and the histogram translation. The receiver relies on the watermark information extracted from the carrier image to locate and recover the carrier image, and completes the tamper detection and recovery of the image combined with compressive sensing. The experimental results show that the method does not require the sender to provide the original image in the authentication detection. If the image is not tampered with, the watermark data can be extracted correctly and the carrier image can be restored completely. If the image is attacked, accurate tamper detection and location can be carried out according to the extracted watermark information, and the compressive sensing is used to reconstruct the tampered area to reconstruction the carrier image.

**Acknowledgement.** This research was funded by the National Natural Science Foundation of China: (No: 61872203, No: 61802212), the Shandong Provincial Natural Science Foundation: (No: ZR2019BF017, No: ZR2020MF054), Jinan City '20 universities' Funding Projects (No: 2019GXRC031, No: 2020GXRC056), Provincial Education Reform Projects: (No: Z2020042), School-level teaching reform project (NO: 201804), and School-level key project (NO: 2020zd24).

# References

1. Candes, E.J., Romberg, J., Tao, T.: Robust uncertainty principles: exact signal reconstruction from highly incomplete frequency information. IEEE Trans. Inf. Theory **52**(2), 489–509 (2006)
2. Donoho, D.L.: Compressive sensing. IEEE Trans. Inf. Theory **52**(4), 1289–1306 (2006)
3. Chen, S.S., Donoho, D.L., Saunders, M.A.: Atomic decomposition by basis pursuit. reprinted from SIAM. J. Sci. Compute. 20. Siam Revi. **2001**(1), 129–159 (2001)
4. Tropp, J.A., Gilbert, A.C.: Signal recovery from random measurements via orthogonal matching pursuit. IEEE Trans. Inf. Theory **53**(12), 4655–4666 (2007)
5. Dai, W., Milenkovic, O.: Subspace pursuit for compressive sensing: Closing the gap between performance and complexity. Illinois Univ At Urbana-Chamapaign (2008)
6. Cheng, C., Lin, D.: Based on compressed sensing of orthogonal matching pursuit algorithm image recovery. J. Internet Things **2**(1), 37–45 (2020)
7. Dong, W.S.: Ganging: compressive sensing via nonlocal low-rank regularization. IEEE Sig. Process. Soc. **23**(8), 3618–3650 (2014)
8. Yuan, X., Haimi-Cohen, R.: Image compression based on compressive sensing: end-to-end comparison with JPEG. IEEE Trans. Multimedia **22**, 2889–2904 (2020)
9. Huang, H.C., Chang, F.C., Wu, C.H.: Watermarking for compressive sampling applications. In: Eighth International Conference on Intelligent Information Hiding & Multimedia Signal Processing, pp. 223–226 (2012)
10. Xiao, D., Zhou, J., Chang, Y.: Double-domain watermarking algorithm for image sensing data based on compressive sensing. J. Comput. Appl. (2016)
11. Chen, X., Zhao, H.: A novel video content authentication algorithm combined semi- fragile watermarking with compressive sensing. In: 2012 Second International Conference on Intelligent System Design and Engineering Application (2012)
12. Yang, C.W., Shen, J.J.: Recover the tampered image based on VQ indexing. Sign. Process. **90**(1), 331–343 (2010)
13. Yang, S., Qin, C., Qian, Z.: Tampering detection and content recovery for digital images using halftone mechanism. In: 2014 Tenth International Conference on Intelligent Information Hiding and Multimedia Signal Processing. IEEE (2014)
14. Li, Y., Song, W., Zhao, X.: A novel image tamper detection and self-recovery algorithm based on watermarking and chaotic system. Mathematics **7**(10), 955 (2019)
15. Rajput, V., Ansari, I.A.: Image tamper detection and self-recovery using multiple median watermarking. Multimedia Tools and Applications **79**, 2020–2020
16. Tian, J.: Reversible data embedding using a difference expansion. IEEE Trans. Circ. Syst. Video Technol. **13**, 890–896 (2003)
17. Kim, S., Jun, D.: Artifacts reduction using multi-scale feature attention network in compressed medical images. Comput. Mater. Continua **70**(2), 3267–3279 (2022)
18. Kwon, H., Hong, S., Kang, M., Seo, J.: Data traffic reduction with compressed sensing in an AIoT system. Comput. Mater. Continua **70**(1), 1769–1780 (2022)

# An Anti-printing Scanning Watermarking Algorithm Based on Fusion Fonts

He Wang[1(✉)], Qiang Zuo[1], Xiaodong Cao[1], Shuangshuang Zhao[1], and Hengji Li[2,3]

[1] Marketing Service Center of State Grid, Jiangsu Electric Power Co., Ltd., Nanjing 210019, China
fiphoenix@bupt.cn
[2] Beijing University of Posts and Telecommunications, Beijing, China
[3] Quantum Technology Lab and Applied Mechanics, University of Milan, Milan, Italy

**Abstract.** With the development of informatization and digitization in various industries, paper documents are still one of the most direct and effective means of information recording. Therefore, the protection and traceability of paper documents are particularly important. Due to the shortcomings of traditional anti-printing scanning watermarking algorithms in terms of capacity and stability, we combined the characteristics of character fonts to design an anti-printing scanning watermarking algorithm based on fusion fonts. The watermarking algorithm is divided into two stages. The first stage is to use style transfer and generative confrontation network technology to fuse multiple font features to generate new fusion fonts. The second stage is to use the generated fusion font to replace the original font in the file by encoding to realize the embedding of watermark information. In addition to resisting printing and scanning attacks, this watermarking algorithm also has a greater capacity than traditional anti-printing and scanning watermarks.

**Keywords:** Document watermarking · Anti-print scanning · Fusion font generation · Deep learning

## 1 Introduction

The technology of digital watermarking was first proposed by AZTirkel et al. in 1993, and the term "watermark" was first used in public magazines [1]. After that, the digital watermarking technology has attracted the attention of academia and industry and has been widely used. Research has achieved rapid development. At the beginning, the Least Significant Bit (LSB) algorithm proposed by Tirkel [2], the algorithm realizes the embedding of digital watermark information by adjusting the lowest bit of each pixel in the image. This method is simple and has good results. Many people still use this algorithm to hide data. However, the LSB algorithm is relatively primitive and has problems such as poor robustness. In order to solve these problems, people have conducted in-depth research and developed more watermarking algorithms. These watermarks are classified according to their characteristics, mainly including fragile and robust watermarks, and

X. Sun et al. (Eds.): ICAIS 2022, CCIS 1588, pp. 450–463, 2022.
https://doi.org/10.1007/978-3-031-06764-8_35

fragile watermarks. The paper [3] is mainly used to judge whether the file is the original file, because its characteristics make it easy to be destroyed in the process of copying or tampering, etc., while the robust watermark [4] is just the opposite, the embedded robust after copying and other attacks, the original watermark information can still be extracted from the original watermark information, which can be used to determine the identity of the original file. Due to this feature, the watermarking algorithm we use for document traceability is robust.

According to the watermark detection process, it is classified into two types. One type is that the original information is needed in the extraction process, which is called a plaintext watermark; the other is that does not require the original information for auxiliary extraction, which is called a blind watermark [5]. Since it is generally difficult to obtain original documents when tracing paper documents, we generally use blind watermarking technology. According to the hidden position of the watermark, it is generally divided into frequency domain watermark [6] and time domain watermark [7]. As the name implies, frequency domain watermark is to transform the original carrier into frequency carrier through various transformations, and then embed watermark information by fine-tuning the frequency domain removal; And the time domain watermark is to embed the watermark information by changing the spatial segment or spatial structure information. Generally, frequency domain watermarking is mostly used in audio, image, or video that contains or is easily converted into frequency carriers. Because paper files are often converted into multiple times such as printing and scanning, the frequency information in them often changes greatly. The watermark used for the traceability of paper documents is often not a frequency domain watermark, but a combination of frequency domain watermark and time domain watermark. Traditional watermarking technology can realize the traceability of electronic files, but once the files are printed and scanned, the blind watermark information added for traceability cannot be extracted. In order to realize the traceability of paper documents, it is necessary to find watermarking algorithms that can resist printing and scanning, such as watermarking algorithms based on document structure [8, 9] and watermarking based on character pixels [10, 11]. Information such as printer, printing time, etc. is embedded in paper documents, so as to realize the traceability and tracking of paper documents.

Some previous studies have proposed that different fonts can be made by modifying the font library to achieve a paper document traceability and tracking scheme that can resist printing and scanning attacks [12], if you use existing font replacement to achieve The embedding of the watermark will destroy the transparency of the watermark due to the large differences between different fonts. As shown in the figure Fig. 1, we can clearly see the difference between song typeface (a) and boldface type (b). We can also use the small strokes of Chinese characters to modify or adjust the connectivity of the strokes of Chinese characters in a small range, so that the new font is sufficiently different from the original font to facilitate the subsequent embedding of the watermark through the font, and the text will not be more obvious and visible to the naked eye. But the font transformation work is very professional, the workload is large, and the implementation is difficult.

With the development of deep learning, many previously difficult methods have been realized. We can use generative confrontation network and style transfer technology to

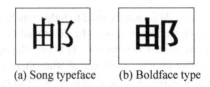

(a) Song typeface    (b) Boldface type

**Fig. 1.** The schematic diagram of the two fonts.

generate new fonts. For example, the original font is song typeface. We can integrate the characteristics of many other fonts into song typeface, and finally generate many fonts similar to song typeface. This process uses a deep learning network for training and generation, and does not require professional designers. The traditional style transfer technology [13] is non-parametric, and is completed by the analysis and synthesis of texture features and the rendering of physical models. These methods have achieved good results in specific fields and applications, but these methods can only extract lower-level features in the image, and the final fusion features are relatively rough, which cannot be applied to font feature fusion. With the rise of deep learning, Efros et al. [14] proposed a style transfer method based on convolutional neural networks, which uses convolutional networks to better extract high-level features of images, such as image style features and content features. Then the style feature of one image is merged with the content of another image, and good results are achieved. This paper combines deep learning algorithms, uses generative confrontation network and style transfer technology to generate new fonts, and chooses font style as an invariant to be used in the document watermarking algorithm.

In summary, the main contributions of the paper are:

(1) Analyze the advantages and disadvantages of traditional digital watermarking technology in anti-printing scanning. Due to the effects of deformation and distortion that are prone to occur during the propagation process, these will cause some features in the document that do not change with printing, scanning, and other operations to disappear.
(2) A watermarking algorithm based on deep learning is proposed to realize the traceability of paper documents, that is, a watermarking algorithm based on fusion fonts. The algorithm uses deep learning technology to realize the style transfer of font images, generate fused fonts that cannot be distinguished by the human eye, and then establish a mapping relationship with the embedded watermark information.
(3) The watermarking algorithm based on fusion font not only has high robustness, but also can improve the capacity of embedding watermark information.

## 2   Related Works

### 2.1   The Impact of the Dissemination Process on Documents

During the dissemination of paper documents, there are two main processes: printing and scanning. From the point of view of digital signals, the process of printing a document can be seen as the conversion of digital signals into analog signals. The process of scanning paper documents can be regarded as the process of converting analog signals to digital signals. In the process of mutual conversion between analog and digital signals, part of the information in the signal will be lost, and because the equipment for digital-to-analog conversion is complex and there are many types, there is no way to express the degree of signal loss with a specific mathematical model. It also increases the difficulty of research.

Generally, document images are affected by gamma correction, halftone process, printer resolution, and other hardware facilities during the printing process. In the scanning process, it will also be affected by gamma compensation, mode conversion, scanner resolution, etc. During these processes, it is difficult to save high-frequency signals in file pictures, and only low-frequency signals can be better preserved. In most cases, low-frequency signals such as the shape of an object in a picture can be better preserved during printing and scanning, while high-frequency signals such as texture details will be destroyed. However, most of the traditional digital watermark information is stored in the high-frequency area of the picture, so most of the watermark information is difficult to save after the document picture is printed and scanned. If you need to use a watermark to record the propagation process of a document, we need to find a watermarking algorithm that can resist printing and scanning attacks.

At present, the most commonly used watermarking algorithms are based on the document structure and character pixels. We can first analyze the performance of these two algorithms, such as the capacity of the watermark information that can be embedded. First of all, the watermarking algorithm based on the document structure embeds traceability information through line spacing. Each line spacing can be embedded with 1 bit of information. Usually a paper document does not exceed 30 lines of text, except for the reference line. In theory, a paper document uses line spacing. The watermark information that can be embedded does not exceed 30 bits. In the actual use process, in order to correctly and completely extract the embedded information and ensure the robustness of the watermarking algorithm, a certain amount of redundant information is also required. Therefore, in actual use, a general file has about 10 lines that can be embedded with valid data, so the traceability information that can be embedded is generally around 10 bits.

The watermarking algorithm based on character pixels uses the invariants in the character pixels in the document to embed traceability information. We can set N prime numbers, adjust the number of pixels of a character to a multiple of the average number of pixels, so that a character can embed $\lfloor logN \rfloor$ bit information. However, considering the robustness and transparency of the algorithm, it is generally still to embed 1-bit information according to one character described in the above algorithm, and the characters that can be used to embed information in a document are generally 100 to 300, so based on The capacity of the watermarking algorithm for character pixel adjustment is 100 to 300 bits. In practice, considering the robustness of the watermarking algorithm, a certain amount of redundant information is required. This part of the information needs to account for about half of the total capacity. Therefore, the effective capacity of the character pixel-based watermarking algorithm is generally 50 to 150 bits.

## 2.2 Generative Adversarial Networks

In recent years, with the continuous development of the information society, human society has accumulated more and more data. In addition, thanks to the improvement of computing power, people have a hardware foundation for processing massive amounts of data. The accumulation of massive amounts of data and the development of hardware devices have made the rapid development of artificial intelligence technology, especially the development of deep learning. According to whether the training samples have labels, deep learning tasks can be divided into three types: supervised learning, semi-supervised learning and unsupervised learning. At present, deep learning has achieved very good results in image recognition, machine translation, speech synthesis and other supervised learning fields, but the cost of obtaining these results is also very expensive [15–19]. This is mainly due to the fact that only a small amount of data has labels when it is generated, and a large amount of raw data has no labels. It takes a lot of manpower and material resources to label the data. Labeling the raw data has become a bottleneck restricting the development of many deep learning.

In order to be able to effectively use the massive unlabeled raw data, many researchers have turned their research direction to unsupervised learning. They believe that unsupervised learning is more in line with the idea of artificial intelligence in form, and it will also be an important development direction for artificial intelligence in the future. Among the many unsupervised learning algorithms, generative models are one of the most important technologies. In 2014, Goodfellow et al. [20] proposed a new generative model-generative adversarial networks (GAN). The main idea of GAN is based on the theory of two-person zero-sum game in game theory [21, 22], its unique adversarial thinking makes it have unique advantages. It has been applied to many fields such as machine learning (ML), computer vision (CV), speech processing (AS), and has become the most popular in the field of artificial intelligence in recent years. The most basic structure of generative adversarial networks are composed of two parts, namely generator and discriminator. The model structure is shown as Fig. 2:

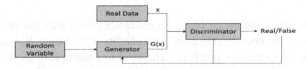

**Fig. 2.** The structure of generative adversarial networks (GAN).

The generator and discriminator in the generative adversarial networks can be regarded as a series of adversarial players in the game. During the model training process, the generator and the discriminator alternately train and update the parameters. Through such continuous iterative updates, finally reach the so-called Nash equilibrium, at this time we believe that the model has reached the optimal state. According to the structure and training method of the generative adversarial networks, the objective function is defined as follows:

$$\min_{G} \max_{D} V(D, G) = E_{x \sim P(x)}[lbD(x)] + E_{z \sim P(z)}[lb(1 - D((G(z))))] \qquad (1)$$

The generation network in the generative adversarial networks is essentially a differentiable function. We input the random variable Z into the generator to obtain the generated sample G(Z). Under normal circumstances, Z is a random code vector of several hundred dimensions, which can be represented by random noise. The generator basically has no requirements for the random variable Z. After training, the generator can theoretically learn any probability distribution, for example, it can learn the approximate distribution of the sample picture, so that it can generate an image similar to the sample image but completely different. The discriminator in the generative adversarial networks is essentially a differentiable function, and its function is to judge whether the input data is a real sample, so it can also be regarded as a binary classifier. During training, the discriminator feeds back the judgment results to guide the training of the generator, and then the generator and the discriminator undergo alternate training until the data generated by the generator is similar to the input sample, and the discriminator can no longer judge that the input sample is real, the generative adversarial networks can be considered as the end of training.

## 3   The Main Work

In this paper, we use existing fonts to generate new fonts, which is inspired by the technical ideas of style migration. The style transfer is applied to the image of the font to realize the generation of the fusion font and to further quantify the difference with the original font. Then we use these new fonts to establish a mapping relationship with the embedded watermark information, and by replacing the fonts in the original document with different fonts, the watermark information can be embedded. In order to quickly and accurately extract the watermark information from the document, that is, to achieve the decoding and extraction of the watermark information, we use a convolutional neural network as a classifier, which can distinguish different font images.

### 3.1   Generation of Fusion Fonts

We mainly use style transfer and generative confrontation network technology to integrate the style characteristics of other fonts into another font, so that the new font has a small number of other font characteristics while maintaining less difference from the original font. The model for generating new fonts uses a generative confrontation network, and the overall network model uses the zi2zi model [23], as shown in Fig. 3.

The model input is the original font image, and the left side of the model is the U-Net [24], which is composed of an encoder and a decoder. U-Net was originally designed for image segmentation tasks. In this article, it is used as a generator of a generative confrontation network to generate new font images. The features of other fonts are spliced in the middle of U-Net [24] as interference, so that the new fonts generated have some of the features of other fonts. The lower right corner of the model is the adversary, which guides the training of the generator by judging whether the input is to generate font images or original font images. In the upper right corner of the model is an encoder, which encodes the generated new font image to constrain the training of the new font. The model is mainly trained through three loss functions, the first is True/Fake Loss, the

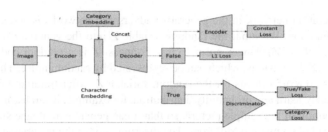

**Fig. 3.** The network model of zi2zi.

function of this loss function is to judge whether the input in the counter is the original font or the generated font; the second loss function Category Loss, the function of The function is to calculate the loss of font style. Once there is confusion or style mixing during training, the discriminator will be penalized; the third loss function is Constant Loss, which is to calculate the distance between the original font and the generated font glyph, the source font and the generated font It should be very close, so the position in the Embedded Space should also be close. This loss can force the decoder to retain the identity of the generated font, narrow the searchable range, and speed up the convergence speed. The fusion font generation algorithm mainly has the following steps:

Step 1: To generate fusion fonts, we need to create a batch of different fonts for training. For example, select 3000 Chinese characters in common use, and then generate images of song typeface and boldface type corresponding to these 3000 Chinese characters, and save them according to the fonts.

Step 2: The choice of original font and characteristic font. In this paper, song typeface is the original font, and boldface is used as the characteristic font. Then send them in pairs to the network for training, so that the new font generated is similar to song typeface but the difference cannot be recognized by the naked eye.

Step 3: Use the trained model and its parameters to generate a new fusion font. In the preparation stage, in addition to using style transfer technology and generative confrontation network to complete the generation of fusion fonts, it is also necessary to classify the generated fusion fonts.

### 3.2  Font Classification Based on Residual Network

The extraction of the watermark depends on the recognition of the font, that is, it is necessary to identify whether each font in the file is the original font or the generated font, so a font classifier is needed. The design of traditional image classifiers is usually based on the prior knowledge of professionals and specific algorithms to extract feature points in the image (such as special corner points, specific textures, etc.), and vectorize the feature points, and then Represent each picture with vectorized features, build data samples, and then send the samples into a classification model for training. With the development of deep learning in recent years, image classification tasks increasingly use convolutional neural networks. As an image classifier, the biggest advantage of convolutional neural network is that it does not need to manually extract features and vectorize the image. Both training and testing can achieve end-to-end, that is, the input original image is directly output after the model calculation. Based on the current mainstream convolutional networks in academia and industry, we choose Residual Network (ResNet) [25]. The most significant feature of this network is that it uses many residual blocks. The residual structure is shown in the figure below:

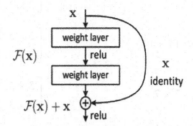

**Fig. 4.** The basic unit diagram of Residual network learning.

The above structure adds a path before and after, so that the gradient can be transmitted without disappearing, which solves the problem of the disappearance of the gradient during the back propagation process of the convolutional neural network due to the excessive number of layers, and also accelerates the network convergence speed. Therefore, the use of residual structure can greatly increase the depth of the network, which can extract more abstract features in the image. Because the font picture is relatively simple, there are not too many complex features, no too deep network, and too many network layers will also affect the recognition speed, so the ResNet-18 network is selected. Table 1 shows its network structure. The process of the font classification algorithm mainly has the following steps: In the first step, first put the generated new fusion font pictures in different folders according to the font category, and separate the training data and test data according to a certain proportion. The second step is to set up the ResNet-18 convolutional network, such as the data loading method, learning rate, maximum number of iterations, batch size, etc. The specific settings need to be set according to the experimental equipment and the size of the data set. The third step is to start training the network until the training Loss function is stable.

**Table 1.** The structure of ResNet-18.

| Layer name | Output size | 18-layer |
|---|---|---|
| Conv1 | $112 \times 112$ | |
| Conv 2_x | $56 \times 56$ | |
| | | $\begin{bmatrix} 3 \times 3, \ 64 \\ 3 \times 3, \ 64 \end{bmatrix} \times 2$ |

*(continued)*

**Table 1.** (*continued*)

| Layer name | Output size | 18-layer |
|---|---|---|
| Conv 3_x | 28 × 28 | $\begin{bmatrix} 3 \times 3, \ 128 \\ 3 \times 3, \ 128 \end{bmatrix} \times 2$ |
| Conv 4_x | 14 × 14 | $\begin{bmatrix} 3 \times 3, \ 256 \\ 3 \times 3, \ 256 \end{bmatrix} \times 2$ |
| Conv 5_x | 7 × 7 | $\begin{bmatrix} 3 \times 3, \ 512 \\ 3 \times 3, \ 512 \end{bmatrix} \times 2$ |
|  | 1 × 1 |  |
| FLOPs |  | $1.8 \times 10^9$ |

### 3.3  Embedding and Extraction of Watermark

After the preparation phase is completed, it is the embedding and extraction part of the watermarking algorithm. The two processes are described below.

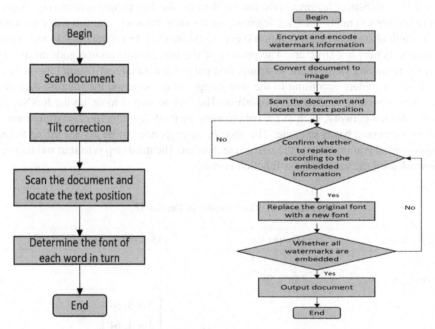

**Fig. 5.** Embedding and extraction of watermark.

The left side of Fig. 5 is the flow chart of watermark embedding. First, encrypt and encode the watermark information, then image the document, scan the entire document, and find the specific position of each word. According to the information to be embedded, determine in turn whether each character should be replaced (if 0 is to be embedded, then no replacement; if it is 1, the new font in the original file is replaced with the corresponding new font), until the watermark of all the information is embedded, the document can be output. The right side of Fig. 5 is the flow chart of watermark extraction. Firstly, scan the document into the computer and saves it as an image, then locate the position of each word after correction and other processing, use the above-mentioned classifier based on residual network training to determine the font of each word in turn.

## 4 Experiments

### 4.1 Training

In this paper, the training process of the fusion font watermarking algorithm based on deep learning is shown in the figure below. The left side of each column is the original font, and the right side is the generated font. It can be seen that as the number of training increases, the generated font becomes clearer and the difference between the original font becomes smaller and smaller.

**Fig. 6.** The training process of fusion fonts.

After 40 batches of training, we can see the stage of the model training. Use the trained model to generate the corresponding 3000 new font images and save them for later embedding of the watermark. After generating the new fusion font, use it together with the original font image as a training sample for the training and testing of the font classifier (ResNet-18 convolutional network). First, randomly select 2000 original song typeface images and 2000 new song typeface images as the training set, randomly select 700 original song typeface images and 700 new song typeface images from the remaining samples as the verification set, and the remaining 300 original song typeface images and 300 new song typeface images were used as a test set. Run the training program, send the data to the network in batches for training randomly. The accuracy of the Classifier is shown as Table 2.

**Table 2.** The accuracy of classifiers.

|  | Training set | Validation set | Test set |
|---|---|---|---|
| Accuracy | 99.99% | 99.7% | 98% |

**Table 3.** Comparison of three watermarking algorithms.

| Watermarking algorithm | Document structure [8] | Character pixels [11] | Our method |
|---|---|---|---|
| Capacity | Around 10 bits | 50–150 bits | Depends on the number of new fonts |
| Robustness | Good | Average | Good |
| Imperceptibility | Average | Average | Good |

## 4.2  Performance Analysis

The preparatory work of the watermarking algorithm based on deep learning is relatively large and complicated. For example, a certain amount of new fonts need to be generated and deleted, and font classifiers need to be trained. But once the preparatory work is completed, the watermarking algorithm only needs to replace the font image without adjusting each character pixel, so the running speed is much faster than the traditional watermarking algorithm mentioned above. This watermarking algorithm can ensure that each word in the file can be embedded with 1 bit of information (replacement and non-replacement), and there is no limitation that the traditional watermarking algorithm can only embed information in some fonts. Therefore, even if each word only embeds 1 bit of information, its watermark capacity is relatively larger. If you need to increase the watermark capacity, you can train the GAN to generate more new fonts, such as generating N types of fusion fonts, so that there are N types of replacement schemes for each word, and the amount of information that can be embedded in each word will greatly increase, and it will not have a greater impact on the transparency of the document. If you want to further increase the watermark capacity, you can also use encoding methods, such as mapping the new font A and new font B to 0 and 1, respectively, encoding the traceability information to be embedded into a binary string, and then encoding the Chinese characters in the file according to the the string is replaced with font A and font B in turn to complete the embedding of traceability information. Theoretically, the capacity of the watermarking algorithm depends on the number of new fonts. In summary, the capacity of the watermarking algorithm depends on the type of new fonts. If there are N new fonts, the amount of information that can be embedded in each character is $\lfloor \log N \rfloor$ bits, and it will not have a major impact on the transparency of the watermark. The following is a comparison between our watermarking algorithm and two traditional watermarking algorithms based on different document characteristics.

According to the comparison in the above table, we can see that the watermarking algorithm based on the new fonts generated by deep learning has greatly improved in terms of capacity, robustness, and imperceptibility, so it can be applied in a wider range. For this paper, embed different information in a document to test whether the traceability can be successfully completed.

**Table 4.** Test results of watermarking algorithm based on fusion font.

| Embedded Information | Traceability time | Result |
|---|---|---|
| 计算机学院 | 20s | success |
| 北京市 | 15s | success |
| 海淀区 | 14s | success |
| 江苏省 | 13s | success |
| 张三 | / | Fail |
| 李雷 | 10s | success |
| 韩梅梅 | 12s | success |

It can be seen from the above Table 4 that the algorithm can better complete the traceability task. The reason for the failure was that the classifier was unable to achieve 100% accuracy, which caused very few fonts to be classified incorrectly, which led to the failure of traceability. The anti-print scanning watermarking algorithm used in this paper is better than the traditional watermarking algorithm based on character pixels. Generally, a paper document has about 300 words. Our algorithm can embed about 300 bits of information for traceability, while a watermark based on character pixels can embed up to 100 bits of information. The more information capacity, the more traceability information can be embedded, and the more detailed record of the dissemination process of paper documents. In addition, the increase in capacity also improves the robustness of the algorithm. We can add more The redundant information can greatly increase the probability of extracting watermark information if the document is severely damaged.

## 5   Conclusions

By analyzing existing watermarking algorithms and learning about style transfer and generative confrontation networks in deep learning, a file watermarking algorithm using GAN network to generate fused fonts is designed, which further improves the capacity and robustness of file watermarking. More information is embedded in paper documents for traceability, which improves the efficiency and accuracy of traceability. Due to the difficulty of training new fonts generated by the generative confrontation network and style transfer technology, this article currently only generates a fusion font, which only meets the capacity requirements of the existing paper document traceability for the file watermarking algorithm. Traceability requires more information to be recorded in the file, and the capacity of the watermark needs to be increased, that is, more new fusion fonts are needed. Subsequent work can improve the efficiency of model training and generate more new fonts that integrate different styles.

**Acknowledgement.** This work was supported by the State Grid science and technology project Research on Power Data Security Collaboration Technology Based on Federated Learning (No.5700–2021-90184A-0-0-00).

# References

1. Hsu, C.S., Tu, S.F.: Enhancing the robustness of image watermarking against cropping attacks with dual watermarks. Multimedia Tools Appl. **2020**, 79 (2020)
2. Van, B., Schyndel, A.Z., Tirkel, C.F.: A Digital Watermark. ICIP (1994)
3. Thanki, R., Borra, S., Kothari, A.: Fragile watermarking framework for tamper detection of color biometric images. Int. J. Digital Crime Forensics **2021**(2), 35–56 (2021)
4. Lin, C.H., Liu, J.C., Shih, C.H.: A robust watermark scheme for copyright protection. In: International Conference on Multimedia & Ubiquitous Engineering, pp. 132–137 (2008)
5. Wang, X., Cai, X., Zhe, K.: A survey of digital image watermarking. Mod. Electron. Tech. **1**, 15–24 (2005)
6. Shih, F.Y., Wu, S.: Combinational image watermarking in the spatial and frequency domains. Pattern Recogn. **36**, 969–975 (2006)
7. Yuan, Z., Su, Q., Liu, D.: Fast and robust image watermarking method in the spatial domain. IET Image Process. **14**, 45–63 (2020)
8. Low, S.H., Maxemchuk, N.F., Brassil, J.T.: Document marking and identification using both line and word shifting. In: Proceedings of INFOCOM 1995, vol. 2, pp. 853–860. IEEE (2002)
9. Brassil, J., Low, S., Maxemchuk, N.: Electronic marking and identification techniques to discourage document copying. In: Infocom Networking for Global Communications (2002)
10. Min, W., Liu, B.: Data hiding in binary image for authentication and annotation. IEEE Trans. Multimedia **6**(4), 526–538 (2004)
11. Qi, G., Li, X., Yang, B., Cheng, D.: File watermarking algorithm for information tracking. J. Commun. **010**, 183–190 (2008)
12. Alkhafaji, A.A., Sjarif, N.N.A., Shahidan, M.: Payload capacity scheme for qurantext watermarking based on vowels with kashida. Comput. Mater. Continua **67**, 3866–3885 (2021)
13. Hertzmann, A., Jacobs, C.E., Oliver, N.: Image analogies. In: Proceedings of the 28th Annual Conference on Computer Graphics and Interactive Techniques, pp. 327–340 (2001)
14. Efros, A.: Image quilting for texture synthesis and transfer. In: Conference on Computer Graphics & Interactive Techniques, pp. 342–346 (2001)
15. Zhang, J.W., Bhuiyang, M.Z.A., Yang, X., Singh, A.K., Hsu, D.F., Luo, E.T.: Trustworthy target tracking with collaborative deep reinforcement learning in edgeai-aided iot. IEEE Trans. Industr. Inf. **18**(2), 1301–1309 (2022)
16. Hang, T.Y., Niu, S.Z., Wang, P.F.: Multimodal-adaptive hierarchical network for multimedia sequential recommendation. Pattern Recogn. Lett. **152**, 10–17 (2021)

17. Ren, H., Niu, S.: Separable reversible data hiding in homomorphic encrypted domain using POB number system. Multimedia Tools Appl. **81**(2), 2161–2187 (2021). https://doi.org/10.1007/s11042-021-11341-w

18. Ushasukhanya, S., Karthikeyan, M.: Automatic human detection using reinforced faster-rcnn for electricity conservation system. Intell. Autom. Soft Comput. **32**(2), 1261–1275 (2022)

19. Dai, Y., Luo, Z.: Review of unsupervised person re-identification. J. New Media **3**(4), 129–136 (2021)

20. Goodfellow, I.J., Pouget-Abadie, J., Mirza, M.: Generative adversarial nets. In: Proceedings of the 27th International Conference on Neural Information Processing Systems, pp. 2672–2680. MIT Press (2014)

21. Mertens, J.F., Zamir, S.: The value of two-person zero-sum repeated games with lack of information on both sides. Int. J. Game Theory **1**(1), 39–64 (1971)

22. Cheng, X., Xie, L., Zhu, J.: Overview of generative adversarial network GAN. Comput. Sc. **46**(03), 80–87 (2019)

23. zi2zi: Master Chinese calligraphy with conditional adversarial networks (2017). https://github.com/kaonashi-tyc/zi2zi

24. Ronneberger, O., Fischer, P., Brox, T.: U-Net: convolutional networks for biomedical image segmentation. In: Navab, N., Hornegger, J., Wells, W., Frangi, A. (eds) Medical Image Computing and Computer-Assisted Intervention – MICCAI 2015. MICCAI 2015. LNCS, vol. 9351. (2015). https://doi.org/10.1007/978-3-319-24574-4_28

25. He, K., Zhang, X., Ren, S.: Deep residual learning for image recognition. In: Proceedings of the IEEE Conference On Computer Vision and Pattern Recognition, pp. 770–778 (2016)

# Steganography Algorithm Based on Transparent Display Principle of Executable Program Icon

Zuwei Tian[1](✉) and Zhichen Gao[2]

[1] College of Computer Science, Hunan First Normal University, Changsha 410205, China
35568625@qq.com
[2] Department of Applied Mathematics and Statistics, College of Engineering and Applied Sciences, Stony Brook University, Stony Brook, NY 11794-2300, USA

**Abstract.** Icon resource is a very important resource in PE file. In order to get the best visual effect when displaying icons under different screen backgrounds and different operating system environments, PE files often store multiple icons of different sizes and different color depths. Because the size of the icon is irregular, the number of bytes filled is often large. These filled byte spaces are redundant and can be used to hide information without affecting the execution result and performance of the program. This paper presents a steganography algorithm based on transparent display principle of executable program icon, which hides secret information in transparent areas of icons. The algorithm has good concealment. The display effect of the embedded icon is the same as that of the original icon. It does not cause any visual distortion neither change the functionality of the executable. The size of the executable and the performance of the executable will not change. It can be widely used in covert data communication.

**Keywords:** Icon resource · XOR bitmap · AND bitmap · Transparent display

## 1 Introduction

With the rapid development of computer software and hardware technology, people's pursuit of software interface is higher and higher. In order to make the user interface of the software more beautiful and visual effect better, PE file usually contains a large number of multimedia resources, including bitmap, icon, cursor, menu, animation, sound, dialog box, toolbar, etc. these multimedia resources are stored in the resource section of PE file in binary form after compiling and linking. Icon is a small graphic used to identify program functions and decorate programs. It is a very important resource in PE files. In order to get the best visual effect when displaying icons under different screen backgrounds and different operating system environments, PE files often store multiple icons of different sizes and different color depths. When users view files, the operating system will select and display the most appropriate icon according to different viewing methods.

Due to the complex structure of PE file resource section, there are few studies on information hiding using resource section. Xiaojing Xu et al. proposed an information hiding algorithm based on the redundancy of PE file resource data [1]. Through the analysis of the data structure of the resource section, there are four kinds of redundancy in the resource section. This scheme hides the information in the redundant space of the resource section. In this way, the length of PE file will not be increased and the problem of over centralized hiding of information is solved, It improves the concealment of the system and makes full use of the redundant space of the resource section. The scheme has high robustness and can resist a variety of attacks. However, changing the structure of the resource section and restoring the value of the redundant field of the resource section will lead to the loss of hidden information and limited hiding capacity. Duanmu qing-feng et al. proposed a new information hiding method based on the storage format and features of icon and bitmap resource [2]. The method embeds secret information into PE resources datum by utilizing the imperceptibility of PE file and by applying effective information hiding algorithms. The experiment shows that it can enhance the information imperceptibility and capacity. In addition, a new palette redundant color allocating algorithm is proposed, which can improve the embedding capacity of information hiding algorithms based on palette color redundancy. Disadvantage: change resource section structure, restore the redundant field values of the resource section, rearrange and modify the color palette entries, etc., these will result in failure to extract the hidden information. Jie Xu et al. proposed an information hiding algorithm based on bitmap resource of portable executable file [3]. This algorithm has higher security than some traditional ones because of integrating secret data and bitmap resources together. Through analyzing the principle of bitmap resources parsing in an operating system and the layer of resource data in PE files, a safe and useful solution is presented to solve two problems that bitmap resources are incorrectly analyzed and other resources data are confused in the process of data embedding. The feasibility and effectiveness of the proposed algorithm are confirmed through computer experiments. Yun Shi proposed an information hiding algorithm for PE file based on image watermarking [4]. A detailed analysis of the structure of the ICO file, and the ICO file display principle, based on an example from which were extracted from the XOR and AND bitmap, further explained the structure of the ICO file and display principle. The paper researches on ICO file characteristics, enumerates four kinds of watermarking algorithm, and then the four algorithm in the ICO file to be realized then a detailed comparison of the advantages and disadvantages of each algorithm and applications.

## 2   PE File Resource Section Structure and PE File Icon Resource

### 2.1   PE File Resource Section Structure

Resource data such as icons, bitmaps, cursors and menus in PE files are stored in resource sections in binary form. The section name of a resource section is generally.rsrc, which adopts tree directory structure for organization and management. From the perspective of data structure, resource section is a four-layer binary sort tree structure. Among them, the data structures of level 1, level 2 and level 3 directories are the same, as shown in Fig. 1.

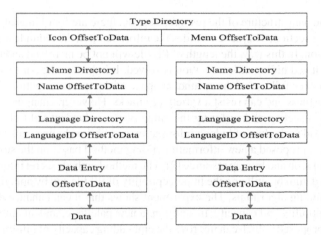

**Fig. 1.** Data organization form of PE file resource section.

## 2.2   PE File Icon Resource

Icon resource is a very important resource in PE file. Windows Explorer provides a variety of viewing methods to browse files, such as tiles, icons, lists, thumbnails, details and so on. When the windows operating system needs to display the icon of a program, the windows operating system according to the display color quality of the current display (256 colors, 16 bit true color, 32-bit true color, etc.), the language of the current operating system (English, simplified Chinese, traditional Chinese, etc.) Different viewing methods (thumbnails, tiles, icons, lists, details, etc.) select the most suitable icon from the program to display. In order to get the best visual effect when displaying icons under different screen backgrounds and different operating system environments, PE files often store multiple icons of different sizes and different color depths. When the program is running, the operating system will select and display the most appropriate icon [5–8]. In the resource section, Icon resources are commonly described by icon group resources (RT_GROUP_ICON) and icon resources (RT_ICON). The RT_GROUP_ICON resource is analogous to the ICONDIR data in the ICO file. Icon resource is composed of the bitmap header, palette, XOR bitmap and AND bitmap (more than 8-bit icon without palette). The XOR bitmap is the color portion of the image and is applied to the destination by using the XOR operation after the application of the AND mask, which describes the basic shape of the image. The AND bitmap is applied to the destination by using the AND operation, to preserve or remove destination pixels before applying the XOR mask, which determines the icon transparent area. The GRPICONDIR structure and GRPICONDIRENTRY structure are defined as:

```
typedef struct
{
  WORD  idReserved;
  WORD  idType;
  WORD  idCount;
} ICONDIR;
typedef struct
{
  BYTE  bWidth;
  BYTE  bHeight;
  BYTE  bColorCount;
  BYTE  bReserved;
  WORD  wPlanes;
  WORD  wBitCount;
  DWORD  dwBytesInRes;
  WORD  nID;
} GRPICONDIRENTRY, *LPGRPICONDIRENTRY;
```

An actual icon data consists of bitmap header, palette, XOR bitmap and AND bitmap. XOR bitmap data describes the basic shape of the image, AND bitmap determines the transparent area of the icon. The length of bitmap header is 40 bytes. The definition type of bitmap header of BMP file with DIB structure is BITMAPINFOHEADER, which is defined as follows:

```
typedef struct tagBITMAPINFOHEADER
{
  DWORD biSize;
  LONG biWidth;
  LONG biHeight;
  WORD biPlanes;
  WORD biBitCount;
  DWORD biCompression;
  DWORD biSizeImage;
  LONG biXPelsPerMeter;
  LONG biYPelsPerMeter;
  DWORD biClrUsed;
  DWORD biClrImportant;
} BITMAPINFOHEADER;
```

The palette data area is located behind the bitmap information header. The number of elements in the palette data area is the same as the number of icon colors. The RGBQUAD structure is used to define the color of pixels (Fig. 2).

```
typedef struct tagRGBQUAD
{
    BYTE rgbBlue;
    BYTE rgbGreen;
    BYTE rgbRed;
    BYTE rgbReserved;
} RGBQUAD;
```

| Icon Group | Icon header | ICONDIR.idReserved<br>ICONDIR.idType<br>ICONDIR.idCount |
|---|---|---|
| | Icon item | ICONDIRENTRY1.bWidth<br>......<br>ICONDIRENTRY1.nID |
| | | ICONDIRENTRY1.bWidth<br>......<br>ICONDIRENTRY1.nID |
| | | ICONDIRENTRY1.bWidth<br>......<br>ICONDIRENTRY1.nID |
| Icon | Icon data | ICONIMAGE1.icheader<br>ICONIMAGE1.iccolors<br>ICONIMAGE1.icxor<br>ICONIMAGE1.icand |
| | | ICONIMAGE2.icheader<br>ICONIMAGE2.iccolors<br>ICONIMAGE2.icxor<br>ICONIMAGE2.icand |
| | | ......<br>ICONIMAGEn.icheader<br>ICONIMAGEn.iccolors<br>ICONIMAGEn.icxor<br>ICONIMAGEn.icand |

**Fig. 2.** Diagram of icon data structure.

The traversal algorithm of icon resources is described as follows:

Step 1: analyze the PE file to get the offset address of the resource section in the file.

Step 2: start from the root directory of the resource section, cycle through each level-1 directory item, get the resource type ID number through the name field, and judge whether there is an icon group (the resource type ID number is 14, i.e. 0eh).

Step 3: if there is an icon group, continue to traverse the secondary directory and tertiary directory of this node to find the offset address size of the icon group in the file, otherwise exit.

Step 4: according to the offset address and size of the icon group in the file, traverse all icons under the icon group through the ID number of the icon.

An actual icon data consists of four parts: bitmap information header, palette, XOR bitmap and AND bitmap (icons with more than 8 bits have no palette) [9–12]. XOR bitmap data describes the basic shape of the image, AND bitmap determines the transparent area of the icon.

The palette data area is located behind the bitmap information header. The number of elements in the palette data area is the same as the number of icon colors. The RGBQUAD structure is used to define the color of pixels, accounting for 4 bytes, that is, 64 bytes for 16 colors and 1024 bytes for 256 colors. Icons with more than 256 colors have no palette. Immediately following the palette data area is the data area of the XOR bitmap. The number of bits recorded in biBitCount refers to the number of bits of data corresponding to each pixel in the XOR bitmap. The 16 color XOR bitmap corresponds to 2 pixels per byte, and the 256 color XOR bitmap corresponds to 1 pixel per byte. The true color icon has no palette. The RGB value of the pixel is directly stored behind the bitmap information header. The 24 bit icon defines 1 pixel value every 3 bytes, and the 3 bytes store the R, G and B values of the pixel in turn. The 32-bit icon defines a pixel value every 4 bytes, and the 4 bytes store the R, G, B values and alpha channel values of the corresponding pixels in turn. Its arrangement rule is: backward (the pixels in the last row are in the front, while the pixels in the first row are in the last, that is, they are organized by the horizontal rows starting from the bottom row of the image and growing upward along the image), and the pixels in each row are arranged from left to right, starting from the leftmost pixel of the image to the right of the image. The arrangement rule of icon pixels with more than 256 colors is the same as that of icons with palette mode. The length of XOR bitmap is related to the size of the icon and the number of colors of the icon. The following figure is 8-bit 16 × 16 icon XOR bitmap data in notepad.exe, the size is 256 bytes, and the file offset address is from 0x43e to 0x53d (Fig. 3).

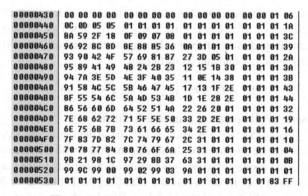

**Fig. 3.** 8-bit 16 × 16 icon XOR bitmap data.

Immediately following the data area of XOR bitmap is the data area of AND bitmap. Each byte of AND bitmap data area corresponds to 8 pixels (each corresponds to 1 pixel), and the arrangement law is the same as that of XOR bitmap. The length of the AND bitmap is only related to the size of the icon, not the number of colors of the icon. The following figure shows 8-bit 16 × 16 icon AND bitmap data in notepad.exe, the size is 64 bytes, and the file offset address is from 0x53e to 0x57d (Fig. 4).

| 00000530 | 01 01 01 01 | 01 01 01 01 | 01 01 01 01 | 01 01 83 FF |
|---|---|---|---|---|
| 00000540 | 17 10 80 3F | DD E8 80 1F | 5A 38 80 07 | 46 46 80 03 |
| 00000550 | 77 76 80 03 | 3A 51 80 03 | 52 61 80 03 | 03 03 80 07 |
| 00000560 | 1A 09 80 07 | DC DB 80 0F | 8B 8C 80 0F | 8C 57 80 0F |
| 00000570 | 46 46 80 0F | 29 2D 80 1F | 3C 5E FF FF | 03 03 □ □ |

**Fig. 4.** 8-bit 16 × 16 icon AND bitmap data.

## 3   Steganography Algorithm Based on Transparent Display Principle of Executable Program Icon

In a 16 × 16 size 256 color icons, where $X = \{x_{ij} | 0 \leq x_{ij} \leq 255, 1 \leq i \leq 16, 1 \leq j \leq 16\}$ represents XOR bitmap,

$Y = \{y_{ij} | y_{ij} \in \{0, 1\}, 1 \leq i \leq 16, 1 \leq j \leq 16\}$ represents XOR bitmap,

$Z = \{z_{ij} | 0 \leq z_{ij} \leq 255, 1 \leq i \leq 16, 1 \leq j \leq 16\}$ represents the screen background. According to the operation rules of AND operation, the AND operation of and 1 will remain unchanged, and the AND operation of 0 will clear 0. Therefore, in the first step, the white part (the pixel represented by 1) in the AND bitmap and the screen background will display the color screen background after AND operation, while black (represented by 0) will mask the color of the icon. In the first step:

$$t_{ij} = x_{ij} \wedge z_{ij}, 1 \leq i \leq 16, 1 \leq j \leq 16 \tag{1}$$

where $\wedge$ represents AND operation. After the first step, a black Icon pattern is generated, that is $T = \{t_{ij} | 0 \leq t_{ij} \leq 255, 1 \leq i \leq 16, 1 \leq j \leq 16\}$. Since the XOR operation with 0 will remain unchanged, the transparent bitmap is obtained after the XOR operation between the screen background and XOR bitmap.

$$b_{ij} = t_{ij} \oplus x_{ij}, 1 \leq i \leq 16, 1 \leq j \leq 16 \tag{2}$$

where $\oplus$ represents XOR operation, transparent bitmap:

$B = \{b_{ij} | 0 \leq b_{ij} \leq 255, 1 \leq i \leq 16, 1 \leq j \leq 16\}$. After the second step, an irregular color icon pattern will be displayed on the screen and fused with the screen background.

In the storage and display of icons, it is carried out according to the scan line. A row of data information in the bitmap is called a scan line. AND bitmap (or XOR bitmap) is a group of 4 bytes, which is called a scan line. Windows operating system stipulates that each scan line must end at a 32-bit boundary, that is, the bit length of a scan line must be divisible by 32, or the byte length must be divisible by 4. For example, if the length of a scan line is 8 bits, 24 bits need to be filled. If there are 48 bits, 16 bits need to be filled. So the size is 16 × 16, the last two bytes of each group in the 16 icon are redundant, that is, the first two bytes correspond to 16 pixels in a row in turn; Size 24 ×

24, the last byte of each group in the icon of 24 is redundant, that is, the first three bytes of the scan line correspond to 24 pixels in a row in turn; 32 × 32, each group of 4 bytes of 32 icons exactly corresponds to 32 pixels in a row, without redundancy; 48 × 48, the last two bytes of each group of 48 icons are redundant, that is, the first six bytes of the scan line correspond to 48 pixels in a row in turn. However, the length of each scan line of the AND bitmap is only related to the width value of the icon image. If the scan line length of AND bitmap is represented by $len_{and}$ and the image width is represented by $w$, then:

$$len_{and} = (\frac{w}{32} + \alpha) \times 4 \tag{3}$$

$$\alpha = \begin{cases} 1, w \bmod 32 = 0 \\ 0, w \bmod 32 \neq 0 \end{cases} \tag{4}$$

The length of each scan line of XOR bitmap depends on two factors: the width value of the image and the number of color bits. If the scanning line length of XOR bitmap is represented by $len_{xor}$, the image width is represented by $w$, and the number of image color bits is represented by $b$, then:

$$len_{xor} = \frac{(w \times b + 31) \wedge 0xFFFFFFE0}{8} \tag{5}$$

where $\wedge$ represents AND operation. Because the size of the icon is irregular, the number of bytes filled is often large. These filled byte spaces are redundant and can be used to hide information without affecting the execution result and performance of the program.

## 4 Conclusion

On the base of icon characteristics of PE file, using transparent display theory icon, we propose a hiding algorithms. This algorithm hides information in the transparent region of icon resource of PE file. In order to get the best visual effect when displaying icons under different screen backgrounds and different operating system environments, PE file resource section includes many different sizes and different color depths icons. Because the size of the icon is irregular, the number of bytes filled is often large. These filled byte spaces are redundant and can be used to hide information without affecting the execution result and performance of the program. This paper presents a steganography algorithm based on transparent display principle of executable program icon. The algorithm has good concealment. The display effect of the embedded icon is the same as that of the original icon, which does not cause any visual distortion, and will not increase the size of the program or affect the performance of the program.

## References

1. Xu, X.J., Xu, X.Y., Liang, H.H.: Research and implementation of information hiding in PE file resource section. Comput. Appl. **27**(3), 621–623 (2007)

2. Duanmu, Q.F., Wang, Y.B., Zhang, K.Z.: Information hiding scheme based on PE file resources datum. Comput. Eng. **35**(13), 128–130 (2009)
3. Xu, J., Li, J.F., Ya, L.Y., Wu, Y.: An information hiding algorithm based on bitmap resource of portable executable file. J. Electron. Sci. Technol. **10**(2), 181–184 (2012)
4. Shi, Y.: Research on PE file information hiding technology based on image watermark. Wuhan University of technology (2012)
5. Wu, Z.Q., Feng, S.D., Ma, J.F.: A scheme and implementation of information hiding based on PE file. Comput. Eng. Appl. **41**(27), 148–150 (2005)
6. Fang, W.S., Shao, L.P., Zhang, K.J.: The research of information hiding technology based on portable executable file format. Microcomput. Inf. **22**(11), 77–80 (2006)
7. Liu, H.M., Zhang, Z.F., Huang, J.W.: A high capacity distortion-free data hiding algorithm for palette image. In: Proceedings of the 2003 International Symposium on Circuits and Systems, pp. 916–919. Bangkok, Thailand (2003)
8. Li, P.C., Liu, Y.F.: Memory forensics method of malicious code based on deleting PE file header. Inf. Network Secur. **21**(12), 38–43 (2021)
9. Luo, Y.B.: 32-bit Windows Assembly Language Programming. Electronic Industry Press, Beijing (2006)
10. Qi, L.: Windows PE: The Definitive Guide. Machinery Industry Press, Beijing (2011)
11. Icons in Win32 (2021). http://msdn.microsoft.com/en-us/library/ms997538.aspx
12. Microsoft portable executable and common object file format specification (2021). http://www.microsoft.com/whdc/system/platform/firmware/pecoff.mspx

# Reversible Data Hiding for JPEG Image Based on Paillier Encryption

Bin Ma[1], Baona Zhang[1], Chunpeng Wang[1], Jian Li[1], Yuli Wang[1(✉)], and Xinan Cui[2]

[1] Shandong Provincial Key Laboratory of Computer Networks, Qilu University of Technology (Shandong Academy of Sciences), Jinan 250353, China
17854112543@163.com

[2] Zhongfu Information Inc., Jinan 250101, China

**Abstract.** With the convenient and rapid development of cloud storage, data privacy violations have become increasingly prominent. Reversible Data Hiding (RDH) can be used to embed additional data in encrypted data stored in the cloud. Most encrypted RDH algorithms are performed in uncompressed images and are not widely employed in popular JPEG images. Therefore, an effective RDH scheme in encrypted JPEG images is proposed in the paper. This algorithm first extracts the distribution characteristics of DCT coefficients, and chaotic encryption is utilized to encrypt the DC coefficients. Then the number of AC coefficients "0" is calculated in each DCT block to generate the embedded sequence in descending order. The paillier encryption and the homomorphic encryption is employed the multiplication feature to embed for the AC coefficient. During the embedding process, the range of the encrypted ciphertexts is determined according to the paillier parameter and the embedding threshold. It ensures that the ciphertexts do not out the range of the DCT coefficient while maintaining a small file increment. The experimental results show that the scheme effectively improves the data embedding capacity and image encryption quality compared to other state-of-the-art encrypted RDH schemed. The scheme also realizes the synchronization of data extraction between the ciphertext image and the original image. The experimental analysis further shows that this scheme has high embedding capacity and good image quality. The scheme can be applied to application scenarios with high embedded capacity and high-security requirements.

**Keywords:** DCT coefficient · Chaotic encryption · Paillier homomorphic encryption · Reversible data hiding

## 1 Introduction

The rapid development and rapid popularization of cloud computing and cloud storage applications have led to a surge in data transmission. Reversible data hiding in the encrypted domain has a high demand in higher application scenarios. Encrypted domain reversible data hiding is to authorize the administrator to embed additional private messages in the encrypted image uploaded by the sender, and it can ensure that the receiver can restore the original image and private messages without loss. At this stage, reversible information hiding in the encryption domain can be divided into the following two categories: inseparable encryption domain reversible information hiding and separable encryption information hiding. In 2011, Zhang et al. [1]. proposed encrypted reversible information hiding, which first uses stream encryption to encrypt the original image, and then divides the secret image into non-overlapping squares, and flips the least significant bits of the pixels in the squares. To embed secret information. The receiver uses the local correlation of the image to extract the secret information and can restore the original image losslessly. The smaller the block size of this method, the larger the embedding capacity, but if the block size is too small, errors are prone to occur in the stages of extracting secret information and image restoration. Based on the Zhang algorithm, Hong et al. [2]. used the spatial correlation between adjacent pixel blocks to embed effective data, which reduced the error rate of data extraction. Liu et al. [3]. proposed a new reversible data hiding method in the encryption domain. The algorithm uses the least significant bit (LSB) to replace the LSB of the region of interest (ROI) as part of the private message and embeds it into the natural image. Ensure that the ROI can be recovered losslessly using the secret key. However, the Liu method is only effective for images with a small area of interest coverage, and other algorithms compress and encrypt images to make the space redundant for embedding. Johnson et al. [4]. designed an efficient encrypted image compression method, whose algorithm is based on low-density parity-check code (LDPC), which has made a huge contribution to the encrypted image compression method.

The above is an inseparable encryption domain reversible information hiding method, and the receiving end can only extract secret information after decryption. To adapt to higher requirements, Ma et al. [6]. proposed a reversible information hiding algorithm based on the strategy of reserving space before embedding. An encryption domain reversible information hiding algorithm based on JEPG image carrier was also proposed in 2014 [7]. To avoid directly processing the plaintext and reduce the computational pressure on the client, Qian et al. [8]. combined distributed source coding to propose a reversible information hiding algorithm that frees up the embedded space after encryption, but the algorithm has high computational complexity and information security. The level is low, and the embedded information is easy to be replaced. Literature [9] proposed an RDH algorithm for medical images under homomorphic encryption, which uses wavelet transform and fast fuzzy algorithms to extract edge pixels from the high and low frequencies of the medical image to reconstruct the medical image, and to block the image. Perform homomorphic encryption on the lower right part of the pixels in the image block, and the information owner can embed the ciphertext information into the ciphertext according to the key. This algorithm has a high embedding capacity and low computational complexity.

The method of storing reversible information in encrypted images has been very common [10, 11]. The algorithms in [5–9] all operate on uncompressed images. Since the JPEG compression method is widely used [12]. Ren et al. [13] also introduces homomorphic encryption into reversible information hiding This paper proposes a new reversible information hiding algorithm based on JPEG image ciphertext domain. Firstly, a multi-coefficient encryption model is constructed by analyzing the quantized DCT coefficients. The DC coefficients are scrambled and encrypted with chaotic encryption, and the AC coefficients are encrypted with homomorphic encryption. Because the quantized DCT coefficients have a certain size range, we are encrypting The threshold T and the parameter r are used to control the encrypted ciphertext range, which can ensure the separable extraction of private data. And this algorithm can use a homomorphic encryption multiplication feature to realize data embedding. This solution has a good embedding capacity and guarantees the visual quality of the image.

The rest of this paper is structured as follows: in the second part, the related work is briefly analyzed and reviewed; Secondly, the specific steps of the encrypted and hidden RDH scheme based on DCT coefficients are explained in detail in the third part; The fourth part is the experimental results and analysis; Finally, the fifth part gives a summary.

## 2 Related Work

This section briefly introduces the key technology of the algorithm, the characteristics of the analysis techniques, and the principle of algorithm use, to facilitate the understanding of the subsequent schemes.

### 2.1 The Principle of Paillier Encryption Algorithm

Paillier encryption system [14] is an additive homomorphic public-key encryption system, and its encryption and decryption mechanisms are as follows:

**Key Generation**

First, select two large prime numbers $p$ and $q$. Ensure that the greatest common divisor of $p \times q$ and $(p-1) \times (q-1)$ conforms to the following formula:

$$\gcd(pg, (p-1)(q-1)) = 1 \tag{1}$$

This ensures that the two prime numbers are equal. Calculate $n = p \times q$ and $\lambda = lcm(p-1, q-1)$, where $lcm(a, b)$ represents the least common multiple of $a$ and $b$. Randomly selected integer $g(g \in Z_{n^2}^*)$, so that $n$ can satisfy the order of dividing $g$. After a series of calculations, the public key is $(n, g)$ and the private key is$\lambda$, which must satisfy $\gcd(L(g^\lambda \mod n^2), n) = 1$, where $L(x) = \frac{(x-1)}{n}$, which means fraction refers to division.

**Encryption Process**

Suppose the original $m$ is a positive integer 0 $n$, and $r$ is randomly selected so that $r$ meets two conditions: 1. $0 < r < n$ 2. $r$ has a multiplicative inverse element in the residual system of $Z_N^*$, namely $r \in Z_N^*$, encrypt $m$ into $c$ according to the following formula.

$$c = E[m, r] = g^m r^N \mod N^2 \tag{2}$$

**Decryption Process**

The decryption process for ciphertext $c$ is as follows:

$$m = D[c] = \frac{L(c^\lambda \mod N^2)}{L(g^\lambda \mod N^2)} \mod N \tag{3}$$

The homomorphic characteristics of Paillier public-key encryption algorithm:

The process of multiplication between ciphertexts. Select two arbitrary original s $m_1$ and $m_2$, randomly select.

parameters $r_1$ and $r_2$ for encryption, and then encrypt them to $E[m_1, r_1], E[m_2, r_2]$, which have the following formula characteristics:

$$E[m_1, r_1] \cdot [m_2, r_2] = g^{m_1} r_1^N \cdot g^{m_2} r_2^N \bmod N^2 = g^{m1+m2}(r_1 r_2)^N \bmod N^2 \qquad (4)$$

$$D[E[m_1, r_1] \cdot [m_2, r_2] \bmod N^2] = m_1 + m_2 \bmod N \qquad (5)$$

We can know from the formula; the multiplication of two ciphertexts is equal to the addition of the original fields.

## 2.2 Chaotic Cipher

Compared with homomorphic encryption [17], an important aspect of the security of chaotic sequence is that even if illegal people master the equation of chaotic sequence, it is difficult to guess the initial value of chaotic sequence and the parameters used in chaotic sequence. In contrast, Logistic chaotic encryption is a simple and important nonlinear iterative equation. Logistic mapping is a dynamic system of statistical population. The equation can be written as follows:

$$x_{n+1} = 1 - \mu x_n^2 \qquad (6)$$

where $x_n$ is the mapping variable, $\mu$ is the system parameter, and their value range is $-1 < x_n < 1, 0 < \mu < 2$.

The basic principle of chaotic encryption is to treat the chaotic system generated by the chaotic system as the key sequence and use the key sequence to encrypt the original. Among them, chaos is determined, which is determined by the equations, initial conditions, and parameters of the nonlinear system. When the system parameters are the same as the initial conditions, they can be completely reconstructed. The receiver can use chaotic synchronization to decrypt the original signal. the logistic chaotic sequence has good characteristics.

## 3 JPEG Homomorphic Encryption Reversible Data Hiding Algorithm

In this section, a new paillier homomorphic encryption separable RDH algorithm will be described in detail. The JPEG homomorphic encryption reversible information hiding algorithm proposed in this paper is shown in Fig. 1.

The original image is compressed by JPEG to obtain the DCT coefficients. For the DC coefficients containing a large amount of information in the image, only chaotic encryption is performed and private data will not be embedded through modification. For the AC coefficients, we are performing paillier encryption At the same time, it uses its multiplication feature to embed private data, and when the receiving end obtains the ciphertext domain image with secret information, it can perform separable processing images.

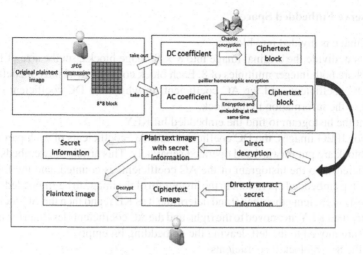

**Fig. 1.** Algorithm flow chart.

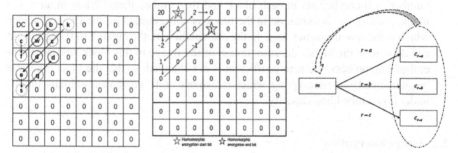

**Fig. 2.** Encryption when the parameter r has different values in each 8 × 8 block.

**Fig. 3.** The start and end bits of homomorphic encryption of AC coefficients.

**Fig. 4.** Encryption of the same key point with different values of r.

Figure 2 shows an 8 × 8 DCT block after quantization of a JPEG image. The first data in the upper left corner of the block is called the DC coefficient, and the other 63 data are called the AC coefficient.

This algorithm performs paillier addition and homomorphic encryption on the AC coefficients. For paillier additive homomorphic encryption, the multiplication operation in the ciphertext domain is equal to the addition operation in the original domain. First, select the bits to be embedded in the AC coefficients. A large number of zero coefficients in the AC coefficients are not considered. We use the number of zero coefficients in each block of DCT as the serial number to identify the 8 × 8 block and embed it. When we embed in the pixels of the original domain image, the corresponding multiplication operation will be performed.

### 3.1 Reserve Embedded Space

1) The image is divided into blocks.

First, divide the original image into $8 \times 8$ image blocks, set the size of I too, M and N are both integer multiples of 8. Each block contains two kinds of coefficients, the DC coefficient, and the AC coefficient, in which the DC coefficient contains most of the information in the block.

2) Count the histogram to find the embedded bit KEY

For JPEG images, the DC coefficients and AC coefficients of each part in the $8 \times 8$ block are put forward and operated separately. This article only embeds the AC coefficients, so the histogram of the AC coefficients is counted, and the following One-step embedded operation. In the histogram of the image to be embedded, find the highest coefficient other than 0 and determine it as KEY, and then the AC coefficients greater than KEY are moved to the right, and the AC coefficients less than the negative KEY are moved to the left, leaving the embedding bit empty.

3) Sort the $8 \times 8$ block 0 coefficients

To avoid the invalid movement of the histogram translation for the unembedded DCT blocks during embedding, we first sort the image blocks according to the number of 0 coefficients in each block and then embed them. When in an $8 \times 8$ block, most of the information in the block is concentrated on the DC coefficient, which is the low-frequency area. In the AC coefficient, the number of 0 coefficients can determine the higher the smoothness of the image in this block, and we In the embedding process, the zero coefficient is not changed, so that the same order can be guaranteed when decrypting, which is also one of the guarantees of image quality under high embedding capacity.

### 3.2 Image Encryption

In the process of Paillier homomorphic encryption, there will be the choice of random parameters $g$ and $r$. The order of parameter $g$ is a non-zero multiple of $n$. The parameter $g$ participates in the process of data encryption and decryption, so we fix the value of $g$. In the quantized DCT coefficients, the range of the coefficients is [−256, 256]. The algorithm in this article selects the parameter $r$ to realize the ciphertext that meets the conditions after encryption. A parameter $r$ is a number that is relatively prime $n$ in the range from 0 to $n$.

To solve this phenomenon and make the encrypted image more meaningful, we will use different ranges of $r$ parameter values for encryption. When $r$ takes different parameters, the effect will be different. Figure 2 is a diagram of homomorphic encryption when $r \in [2, n]$.

Every time you encrypt, a random r is generated for encryption. When $r \in [2, n]$ the encryption is as shown in Fig. 2. At the encryption ends, r circulates from a to d for encryption to achieve control of the encrypted exchange coefficient. Because parameter r is not needed on the decryption side, the loop of the parameter r is to make the data more secure during transmission.

### 3.3  Secret Information Data Embedding

According to the owner, the original image is divided into several non-overlapping $8 \times 8$ blocks, and the quantized DCT blocks are sorted according to the number of 0 coefficients, and the first block is denoted as $B(i)$, in each block There are DC components and AC components. For JPEG images, the low-frequency DC component contains most of the information of the image, and we embed the information into the AC component.

Figure 3 shows the start and end positions of the AC coefficients in an $8 \times 8$ block. The first AC coefficient from the left of the DC coefficient is used as the start bit of homomorphic encryption, scanned in a zigzag pattern, and the end bit is determined by the back The values of the AC coefficients of all scans are "0".

To reduce the file increment that will become larger when the image is encrypted, we do not encrypt the 0 coefficient when encrypting. This will not lead to a rapid increase in file size, and it will ensure the embedding of secret information.

After the first two steps of pre-operation, the DCT AC coefficients have selected the bits to be embedded, that is, the data is hidden in the embedded bits. In this algorithm, the data is embedded by using the homomorphic properties. Assuming the embedded secret information, based on the formula (2), the secret information can be converted into a form that can be embedded using homomorphism.

The encrypted secret information is converted to c, where m is the information to be encrypted, r is the parameter in encryption, and g is the public key.

Suppose A is an initial image sequence of size $N \times N$, we will extract the matrix of DC coefficients to embed using the characteristics of homomorphic encryption, perform zigzag scanning, and embed when encountering the position of AC coefficients.

The exchange coefficient on the embedding bit is homomorphically embedded with the encrypted secret information and brought into the formula of multiplying two numbers.

To enable the image in the ciphertext domain to be directly decrypted, a check and balance factor is determined. When the paillier is encrypted, there is a threshold T and a parameter r that can match the encrypted data to the range of the quantized DCT coefficient $(-1024, 1024)$, when using paillier multiplication homomorphism for embedding, the size of the embedding number cannot be controlled, as shown in the above formula. In this way, after encryption, we operate on the embedded data according to the threshold T, the parameter r, and the check and balance factor.

$$T = ((g^{m_1+m_2} \cdot (r_1 r_2)^N \bmod N^2) - \beta) \bmod 256 \qquad (7)$$

In this way, the embedded encrypted data can be within a certain range, and it can be separated when the recipient extracts the information, that is, the information can be extracted from the ciphertext, or the information can be extracted from the decrypted original.

### 3.4  Overflow Treatment

When the quantized DCT coefficients are encrypted, an image must maintain the same encryption system. After the key is selected, the AC coefficients in the quantized DCT coefficients are encrypted. For natural images, the value range of the pixel AC coefficient is between (–256, 256). When we encrypt beyond this range, we cannot write the encrypted AC coefficients into the JPEG image, so we determine a threshold T. Because the same AC coefficient can be encrypted into different numbers according to the above-mentioned value of r, we take the remainder of the encrypted AC coefficient. If the coefficient after the remainder is between (–256, 256), for this The encrypted AC coefficients can be written into JPEG images. For the encrypted number, the remainder must be T, so that it can be decrypted according to the remainder T when decrypting.

$$c = e \bmod 256 \tag{8}$$

$$T = e/256 \tag{9}$$

where e is the encrypted AC coefficient, c represents the encrypted AC coefficient after the remainder, and T represents the remainder of the encrypted AC coefficient.

### 3.5  Extraction of Secret Information

**Extract Information in Ciphertext.** The same as the embedding process, the receiver first performs $8 \times 8$ blocks on the quantized DCT coefficients of the ciphertext image containing the secret information, sorts them according to the number of 0 coefficients in each block, and uses the threshold T and the secret key Decrypt.

$$m = D[C] = \frac{L((256 \times c \times T)^\lambda \bmod N^2)}{L(g^\lambda \bmod N^2)} \bmod N \tag{10}$$

where c represents the encryption coefficient extracted from the DCT coefficient table, the threshold T represents the multiple g, $\lambda$, N are the keys, decrypted according to the zigzag method, and decrypted to the last non-zero AC coefficient. Get secret information according to KEY.

**Extract Information in Plaintext.** Decrypt the ciphertext image with private information first. First, chaotically decrypt the DC coefficients in the quantized DCT coefficients, and the high-frequency information in the image can be restored to the original position, which contains a large amount of important information of the image. Secondly, directly perform paillier decryption on the AC coefficients

$$m = D[c] = \frac{L(c^\lambda \bmod N^2)}{L(g^\lambda \bmod N^2)} \bmod N \tag{11}$$

Then according to the embedded secret key KEY, the information is extracted, and the image is restored while the information is extracted so that complete reversible data hiding can be realized.

## 4  Experimental Results and Performance Analysis

In our experiment, we downloaded some commonly used $512 \times 512$ images from the USC-SIPI image database (http://sipi.usc.edu/database/), including Baboon, Couple, Boat, and Lena.

## 4.1   The Influence of Parameter R on Encrypted Images

The parameter r only exists in the encryption formula, and the value of the parameter r is no longer needed in the decryption formula. To control the size of the encrypted data, the parameter r is set to a fixed value in the algorithm in this paper. If the parameter r is a fixed value, the waveform of the encrypted image histogram will be similar to the waveform of the original image histogram before encryption.

In Fig. 4, different embedded bit KEY undergoes paillier homomorphic encryption with different parameters r = a, r = b, r = c, and then obtains different encrypted exchange coefficients KEY1, KEY2, KEY3.

Because in the quantized DCT coefficients, the 0 coefficient is the vast majority, when the value of r is only one, the encrypted coefficient is also the highest bit, which is easy to be identified and attacked. Therefore, to keep the encrypted ciphertext within the maximum range of the DCT coefficient and also have a good ciphertext, the r in the encryption process is encrypted within a certain range.

## 4.2   Realizing the RDH Method in the Encryption Process

This experiment first selects the image Lena image to verify the feasibility of the algorithm. An 8-bit grayscale image with an image size of $512 \times 512$ (as shown in Figure a) is used to process the DC coefficients and AC coefficients of the quantized DCT transform, respectively, and the DC coefficients Chaotic encryption is performed after separate extraction, and Paillier encryption is performed after the exchange coefficients are extracted, and information is embedded at the same time. The parameters p = 13 and q = 17 of the Paillier encryption system are used, and the upper limit of the original that can be encrypted is $N = p \times q = 221$. The content owner hides the secret information in the communication coefficient. The specific experimental results are as follows:

## 4.3   Comparison and Analysis

The performance of the algorithm in this article in terms of embedding capacity, file increment, PSNR value, etc. is analyzed below.

According to the description of the proposed method:

1) Embedded capacity:

In our scheme, the size of the encrypted secret key determines the block that cannot be embedded, but in the quantized DCT coefficient, the coefficient must be less than N to ensure the accurate decryption of the original. We performed different Quality Factors on the four images Statistics of the maximum exchange coefficient. As shown in the chart below:

Table 1 describes the maximum exchange coefficient values of Lena, Boat, Baboon, and Couple under different Quality Factors (QF), to ensure the key size during homomorphic encryption.

It can be seen from the table that the maximum value of the exchange coefficient is when the quality factor is QF = 80, and the maximum value in the Lena diagram is 159

(a) original image        (b) ciphertext image with        (c) decrypted image
                              embedded secret
                              information

**Fig. 5.** Lena image encrypted image after algorithm and encrypted image embedded with secret information (a) original image (c) ciphertext image with embedded secret information (d) decrypted image

**Table 1.** The maximum AC coefficient value under different Quality Factors (QF)

| Image | QF = 50 | QF = 60 | QF = 70 | QF = 80 |
|---|---|---|---|---|
| Couple | 48 | 60 | 80 | 122 |
| Baboon | 27 | 32 | 45 | 67 |
| Boat | 42 | 51 | 71 | 111 |
| Lena | 58 | 71 | 91 | 159 |

**Table 2.** The algorithm is different from other algorithms, and the embedded capacity leads to the change of embedded file increment ('–' Indicates that the embedded capacity is not reached)

| Image | Scheme | w = 500 bits | w = 1000 bits | w = 1500 bits | w = 2500 bits |
|---|---|---|---|---|---|
| Baboon | Ref. [18] | 392 | 400 | 416 | – |
| | Ref. [19] (75% APPr) | 12456 | 25856 | 39664 | 67016 |
| | Ref. [20] (N = 16) | 360 | 352 | 384 | 392 |
| | Proposed | 12032 | 25768 | 39944 | 66800 |
| Boat | Ref. [18] | 304 | – | – | – |
| | Ref. [19] (75% APPr) | 920 | 1104 | 1320 | 1504 |
| | Ref. [20] (N = 16) | 512 | 512 | 480 | 576 |
| | Proposed | 10672 | 21416 | 32968 | 57336 |
| Couple | Ref. [18] | 160 | 160 | – | – |
| | Ref. [19] (75% APP,) | 1208 | 1368 | 1536 | 1976 |
| | Ref. [20] (N = 16) | 256 | 248 | 248 | 240 |
| | Proposed | 12032 | 25768 | 39944 | 66800 |
| | Ref. [18] | 168 | – | – | – |
| | Ref. [19] (75% APP,) | 1264 | 1608 | 1920 | 2176 |
| Lena | Ref. [20] (N = 16) | 216 | 232 | 152 | 80 |
| | Proposed | 10888 | 23184 | 35024 | 60184 |

when QF = 80. That is to say, when the value of the secret key N is greater than 159, the ciphertext can be guaranteed to be complete. The decryption of this algorithm will not produce errors, which is also an important reason for the larger embedding capacity of this algorithm than other methods.

Figure 6 shows the comparison between the algorithm proposed in this paper and other algorithm frameworks in terms of embedding capacity. When the Quality Factors are QF = 50, QF = 60, QF = 70, and QF = 80, they are compared to (a) Baboon (b) Boat (c) Couple (d) Lena for comparison. It can be seen from the implementation results that the overall quantity of embedding capacity of the Baboon with a more complex texture is the largest. As the quality factor increases, the embedding capacity also increases. The embedding capacity of the other three images also increases with the increase of the quality factor, and the embedding capacity of the algorithm proposed in this paper is better than other algorithms.

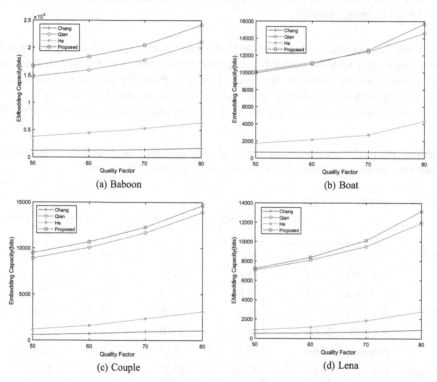

**Fig. 6.** Embedding capacity of the image under different Quality Factors (the truncated line means that a larger capacity cannot be embedded): (a) Baboon(b) Boat (c) Couple (d) Lena.

2) File increment:

The schemes [18] and [20] are the same as the original image except for minor changes. The subtle change after embedding the secret information is due to the byte alignment defined in the JPEG standard. Therefore, these programs are considered to have good file size changes. However, a small increase in file increment corresponds to a decrease in embedding capacity. For literature [19], only 25% of the DCT blocks are inserted into the segment, and cannot be embedded when the secret information is 1500. Literature [20] uses a bitstream-based encryption method. The method of embedding additional data in an encrypted image is to rotate only the selected ZRV pair without any modification so that the size of the encrypted image file after marking remains unchanged. In our algorithm, no matter how large the embedding capacity is, there will be no embedding failure. This can ensure the effect of high embedding capacity, but there is a significant increase in the cost of files to obtain higher embedding capacity.

3)  PSNR

In this paper, the peak signal-to-noise ratio (PSNR) is used to measure the quality of the image containing secret information after decryption. The higher the value of PSNR, the stronger the imperceptibility of embedded secret information and the better the image quality.

Table 3 is a comparison table of the peak signal-to-noise ratio of the algorithm and other algorithms with the embedding capacity can be seen from the table that as the embedding capacity increases, the image quality is gradually decreasing. The multi-factor encryption model adopted in this article is to ensure that the PSNR value of the encrypted image is smaller, and the smaller the PSNR value indicates The similarity with

**Table 3.** The PSNR value of this algorithm and other algorithms increases with the increase of embedding capacity ('–' Indicates that the embedded capacity is not reached)

| Image | Scheme | PSNR | | | | |
|---|---|---|---|---|---|---|
| | | w = 300 bits | w = 600 bits | w = 900 bits | w = 1200 bits | w = 1500 bits |
| Baboon | Ref. [18] | 20.24 | 19.83 | 19.16 | 18.75 | 18.21 |
| | Ref. [16] | 17.00 | 16.83 | 16.66 | 16.33 | – |
| | Proposed | 7.20 | 7.16 | 7.13 | 7.09 | 7.07 |
| Boat | Ref. [18] | 24.10 | 23.56 | 22.75 | 21.75 | 21.81 |
| | Ref [16] | 20.66 | 20.50 | 20.00 | – | – |
| | Proposed | 7.04 | 7.02 | 7.03 | 6.96 | 6.96 |
| Couple | Ref. [18] | 23.97 | 23.16 | 22.35 | 21.67 | 21.13 |
| | Ref [16] | 21.49 | 21.16 | – | – | – |
| | Proposed | 6.82 | 6.80 | 6.80 | 6.78 | 6.77 |
| Lena | Ref. [18] | 26.64 | 25.56 | 24.75 | 24.08 | 23.27 |
| | Ref [16] | 23.00 | – | – | – | – |
| | Proposed | 5.16 | 5.13 | 5.14 | 5.13 | 5.11 |

the original image is even greater. The data in bold in the table is the implementation data of this algorithm, and we have better confidentiality than other algorithms.

## 5 Conclusion

This algorithm proposes a reversible data hiding algorithm in the homomorphic encryption domain of JPEG images based on quantized DCT coefficients. The main contributions of this method are as follows:

1. It is proposed that the quantized DCT coefficients are double-encrypted, the DC coefficients (DC coefficients) are encrypted in a relatively safe manner, the AC coefficients are added and homomorphically encrypted, and the characteristics of paillier homomorphic encryption are adopted (the multiplication characteristics are in the ciphertext domain. The multiplication operation in is equivalent to the addition operation in the original domain) to process the data.
2. The proposed encrypted JPEG original quantized DCT coefficient RDH scheme sorts the number of AC 0 coefficients in each $8 \times 8$ quantized DCT block. First, the smooth block is selected for embedding, and the histogram is shifted in the embedded block. In this way, invalid histograms that are not embedded in blocks can be shifted.
3. When encrypting, think backward and generate a ciphertext that satisfies the range of DCT according to the threshold T and the parameter r, which can not only meet the conditions of Paillier homomorphic encryption but also meet the size range of DCT. According to the multiplication feature of paillier homomorphic encryption, information can be embedded while encrypting. In the future, a more optimized scheme can be selected for Paillier homomorphic encryption in the embedding scheme to achieve a balance between file increment and embedding capacity.

**Acknowledgement.** This research was funded by the National Natural Science Foundation of China: (No: 61872203, No: 61802212), the Shandong Provincial Natural Science Foundation: (No: ZR2019BF017, No: ZR2020MF054), Jinan City '20 universities' Funding Projects (No: 2019GXRC031, No: 2020GXRC056), Provincial Education Reform Projects: (No: Z2020042), School-level teaching reform project (NO: 201804), and School-level key project (NO: 2020zd24).

## References

1. Zhang, X.P.: Reversible data hiding in encrypted image. IEEE Signal Process. Lett. **18**(4), 255–258 (2011)
2. Hong, W., Chen, T.S., Wu, H.Y.: An improved reversible data hiding in encrypted images using side match. IEEE Sign. Process. Lett. **19**(4), 199–202 (2012)
3. Liu, Y., Qu, X., Xin, G.: An ROI-based reversible data hiding scheme in encrypted medical images. J. Vis. Commun. Image Represent. **39**, 51–57 (2016)
4. Johnson, M., Ishwar, P., Prabhakaran, V.M., Schonberg, D., Ramchandran, K.: On compressing encrypted data. IEEE Trans. Signal Process. **52**(10), 2992–3006 (2004)

5. Zhang, X.P.: Separable reversible data hiding in encrypted images. IEEE Trans. Inf. Forensics Secur. **7**(2), 826–832 (2012)
6. Ma, K.D., Zhang, W.M., Zhao, X.F., Yu, N.H., Li, F.H.: Reversible data hiding in encrypted images by reserving room before encryption. IEEE Trans. Inf. Forensics Secur. **8**(3), 553–562 (2013)
7. Qian, Z., Zhang, X., Wang, S.: Reversible data hiding in encrypted JPEG Bitstream. IEEE Trans. on Multimedia **16**(5), 1486–1491 (2014)
8. Qian, Z., Zhang, X.: Reversible data hiding in encrypted image with distributed source encoding. IEEE Trans. Circ. Syst. Video Tech. **26**(4), 636–646 (2015). https://doi.org/10.1109/TCSVT.2015.2418611
9. Xie, D.: Reversible information hiding algorithm of ciphertext CT mechanical scanning image in homomorphic encryption domain. Comput. Inf. Mech. Syst. **3**(2) (2020)
10. Qin, C., Zhang, W., Cao, F., Zhang, X.P., Chang, C.C.: Separable reversible data hiding in encrypted images via adaptive embedding strategy with block selection. Signal Process. **153**, 109–122 (2018)
11. Xiong, L., Han, X., Yang, C., Shi, Y.: Robust reversible watermarking in encrypted image with secure multi-party based on lightweight cryptography. IEEE Trans. Circ. Syst. Video Technol. **32**(1), 75–91 (2021). https://doi.org/10.1109/TCSVT.2021.3055072
12. Chang, C.C., Lin, C.C., Tseng, C.S.: Reversible hiding in DCT-based compressed images. Inf. Sci. **177**(13), 2768–2786 (2007)
13. Ren, H., Niu, S.: Separable reversible data hiding in homomorphic encrypted domain using POB number system. Multimedia Tools Appl. **81**(2), 2161–2187 (2021). https://doi.org/10.1007/s11042-021-11341-w
14. Paillier, P.: Public-key cryptosystems based on composite degree residuosity classes. In: Proceeding of International Conference on the Theory and Application of Cryptographic Techniques, pp. 233–238 (1999)
15. Dong, D.P., Wu, Y., Xiong, L.Z., Xia, Z.H.: A privacy preserving deep linear regression scheme based on homomorphic encryption. J. Big Data **1**(3), 145–150 (2019)
16. Ong, S., Wong, K.: Rotational based rewritable data hiding in JPEG. In: Proc. IEEE VCIP, pp. 1–6 (2013)
17. Yin, Z., Xiang, Y., Zhang, X.: Reversible data hiding in encrypted images based on multi-msb prediction and huffman coding. IEEE Trans. Multimedia **22**(4), 874–884 (2020)
18. Chang, J.C., Lu, Y.Z., Wu, H.L.: A separable reversible data hiding scheme for encrypted JPEG bitstreams. Signal Process **133**, 135–143 (2017)
19. Qian, Z., Xu, H., Luo, X., Zhang, X.: New framework of reversible data hiding in encrypted JPEG bitstreams. IEEE Trans. Circuits Syst. Video Technol. (2018). https://doi.org/10.1109/TCSVT.2018.2797897
20. He, J., et al.: A novel high-capacity reversible data hiding scheme for encrypted jpeg bitstreams. IEEE Trans. Circuits Syst. Video Technol. **29**(12), 3501–3515 (2018)

# IoT Security

# Research on Network Security Situation Assessment Model Based on Double AHP

Wei Wang[1]([✉]), Xuqiu Chen[1], Wei Gan[2], Yi Yang[1], Wenxue Zhang[1], Xiantao Zhang[1], and Fan Wu[3]

[1] State Grid Chengdu Electric Power Supply Company, Chengdu 610000, China
112053432@qq.com
[2] State Grid, Sichuan Electric Power Company, Chengdu 610000, China
[3] Computer Science Department, Tuskegee University, Tuskegee, AL 36088, USA

**Abstract.** Network security situation assessment is an important part of the situational awareness research process and the most important thing. Situation assessment refers to the assessment of the current security status of the system through real-time analysis of network security situation awareness data and the use of appropriate models and methods. The current network boundaries are gradually disintegrating, and the power Internet is moving toward a trend of complex architecture, increased exposure of attack surfaces, and wider business scope. It is necessary to research mobile security monitoring under the zero-trust architecture to improve business security. Business hazard detection and risk prevention capabilities, and network security situation assessment are the focus of mobile security monitoring research. Aiming at the possible risks in network security, this paper proposes an improved AHP (Analytic Hierarchy Process) to comprehensively evaluate situational awareness information. First, build a single-node hierarchical analysis model based on the analytic hierarchy process inside the node, and calculate the evaluation result of the single-node equipment. Subsequently, the single-node equipment is used as a hierarchical analysis factor, and the hierarchical analysis model has been constructed again, and the situation assessment results of the distributed system composed of multiple nodes are comprehensively calculated. This network security situation assessment model based on double AHP provides a concrete and feasible scheme for the distributed system from single-point situation assessment to multi-point integration situation assessment.

**Keywords:** Double analytic hierarchy process · Situation assessment · Network security · Zero trust

## 1 Introduction

With the development of the power Internet, the network structure, scale, data, and applications have become more and more complex and diverse. The network boundary is gradually blurred, and the security problem of the power Internet has become increasingly prominent. Applying zero-trust security protection to the power mobile interconnection business can effectively build "endogenous security" capabilities and provide guarantees for the safe operation of the power mobile business. The implementation of continuous security monitoring for mobile networks is the cornerstone of the concept of a zero-trust security protection framework. Through continuous monitoring of the user terminal equipment environment and the user's access behavior. The monitoring of changes in environmental data can also help realize dynamic authority control. In zero-trust security protection, decision-making and disposal of potential security risks through situation assessment is the key to meeting mobile security monitoring requirements. Therefore, network security situation assessment can provide strong support for mobile network security.

Security situation assessment [1] refers to the collection, filtering, and correlation analysis of security incidents generated by network security equipment, establishing a suitable mathematical model based on constructing security indexes, evaluating the degree of security threats suffered by the network system as a whole. At present, there are many research results on network security situation assessment methods at home and abroad. As shown in Fig. 1, according to the theoretical and technical basis of the assessment basis, it can be divided into three categories, namely based on mathematical models, based on probability and knowledge reasoning, and based on pattern classification.

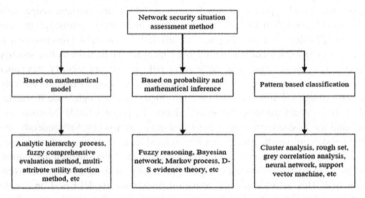

**Fig. 1.** Network security situation assessment method.

The methods based on the mathematical model are represented by the analytic hierarchy process [2], set pair analysis [3], fuzzy comprehensive evaluation method [4], multi-attribute utility function method [5]. It comprehensively considers the factors that affect network security situation awareness, and then establishes the corresponding relationship between the security index set and the security situation, and then assigns the situation assessment problem to issues such as multi-index comprehensive evaluation or multi-attribute set. Its disadvantage is that the evaluation model constructed by this method and the definition of its variables involve many subjective factors and lack objective unity.

The methods based on probability and knowledge reasoning are represented by fuzzy reasoning [6], Bayesian network [7], Markov process [8], DS evidence theory [9]. It builds models based on expert knowledge and experience databases and uses logical reasoning to evaluate the security situation. The use of this method to build a model requires first to obtain prior knowledge. From the practical application point of view, the method for acquiring knowledge is still relatively single, mainly relying on machine learning or an expert knowledge base. Machine learning has the problem of operating difficulties, while an expert knowledge base mainly relies on the accumulation of experience.

The methods based on pattern classification are represented by cluster analysis [10], rough set [11], grey correlation analysis [12], neural network [13], and support vector machine [14]. It is established by training, and then the network security situation is evaluated based on the classification of the model. The advantage of this method is that the learning ability is very good, and the model is established more accurately.

The traditional network situation assessment method is usually based on the information collection module to collect the required situation awareness information and store the results in a unified database after data preprocessing. This operation of centrally and uniformly sending the situational information perceived by the security device to the central database may cause data leakage problems during the transmission process. At the same time, the concurrent upload operation of multiple devices will also have the problem of excessive network load. In addition, for the situation assessment in distributed systems, there is a lack of effective feasible schemes for the fusion calculation of single-point situation value to multi-point situation value.

Based on this, this paper proposes a double AHP analysis method based on distributed architecture to evaluate the security situation of the system. The first level of analysis will directly calculate the situation value inside the node, no longer upload the perception result information to the central database, but rely on the principle of consistency of the distributed system to synchronize the situation weight vector of the node to other nodes. Data leakage caused by direct transmission of situational awareness information is avoided. In the second level of analysis, the single-node equipment is used as the analysis factor, and the level analysis model has been constructed again and combined with the situation weight vector, the situation assessment result of the distributed system composed of multiple nodes is comprehensively calculated. This network security situation assessment model based on double AHP provides a concrete and feasible scheme for the distributed system from single-point situation assessment to multi-point integration situation assessment.

The rest of the paper is arranged as follows. In Sect. 2, the construction of the situation indicator system is introduced. Section 3 introduces the double AHP evaluation model and its improvements. Section 4 gives an example analysis of the model. Section 5 summarizes the full text.

## 2 Construction of the Situation Indicator System

### 2.1 Build a Hierarchical Network Security Situation Indicator System

A group of scholars represented by Wang Juan and Zhang Fengli [15] of the University of Electronic Science and Technology of China has established a relatively complete set of network security situation indicators with a clear level, comprehensive coverage, and strong reference. This set of indexes can cover different levels of the network, different data sources, and different users by comparing various situation influencing factors. This article will use this as a blueprint to construct a network security situation indicator system.

Basic operating status indexes: The basic operating state index is a value calculated by collecting system operating data in a certain time window, performing quantitative evaluation on it, and calculating it. This value reflects the current operating status of the network system. Generally speaking, the larger the value, the worse the operating status of the network system. This part can select the basic operating status as the first-level indexes, and specific indexes such as the CPU usage rate, memory usage rate, and hard disk space usage rate of the security equipment as the basic operating status indexes. As shown in Table 1.

**Table 1.** Description of related fields of basic operating status indexes.

| Index name | Description |
| --- | --- |
| CPU usage | Host CPU usage per unit time of node device |
| Memory usage | Host memory usage rate per unit time of node device |
| Hard disk usage | Host hard disk utilization rate per unit time of node equipment |

Equipment vulnerability status indexes: The equipment vulnerability status index is a comprehensive analysis by quantifying the number of vulnerabilities and other information, and then calculating the vulnerability index, which can measure the degree of loss that may be caused to the system when the network faces an attack [16]. Generally speaking, the larger the value, the more vulnerable the network is and the greater the possibility of loss.

**Table 2.** Description of fields related to device vulnerability status.

| Index name | Description |
| --- | --- |
| Header tracking vulnerability distribution | Header tracking vulnerabilities in node devices as a percentage of total vulnerabilities |
| SQL injection vulnerability distribution | SQL injection vulnerabilities in node devices accounted for the percentage of total vulnerabilities |
| Cross-site scripting vulnerability distribution | The percentage of cross-site scripting vulnerabilities in node devices to the total number of vulnerabilities |
| Distribution of weak password vulnerabilities | The percentage of cross-site weak password vulnerabilities in the node device to the total number of vulnerabilities |

We choose the vulnerability events reported by the vulnerability scanning system as the primary indexes to obtain the hierarchical equipment vulnerability status indicators, as shown in Table 2.

Risk event indexes: Risk event indexes are mainly used to collect various security events caused by cyber-attacks within a certain time and conduct a comprehensive and quantitative assessment of the frequency and degree of harm of these incidents, and then calculate an indication of the harm caused by the network system. A numerical value of the degree. The larger the value, the deeper the degree of this hazard.

Therefore, we combine the types of network security incidents to extract various security incidents such as virus attacks, botnets, Trojan horse attacks, and denial of service as the basic indicators of the risk event indicator system. As shown in Table 3.

**Table 3.** Description of fields related to risk events.

| Index name | Description |
|---|---|
| Virus attack distribution distribution | The percentage of virus attack incidents suffered by node equipment in unit time in total security incidents |
| Botnet distribution | Percentage of botnet attack incidents suffered by node devices per unit time in total security incidents |
| Trojan attack distribution | The percentage of Trojan horse attack incidents per unit time of node equipment in total security incidents |
| Denial of service distribution | The percentage of denial-of-service attack incidents that the node device suffered per unit time to the total security incidents |

Threat event indexes: Threat event indicators are calculated by collecting security events caused by user violations or equipment operation over a while, and quantitatively assessing these events [17].

We can use cyber threat event indicators as the first-level indicators and use various alarm events caused by user operations or abnormal system operation as the second-level indicators to build a threat event indicator system hierarchically, as shown in Table 4.

# 3   Double AHP Evaluation Model

The AHP [18] was first proposed by Professor T.L.Saaty at the International Conference on Mathematical Modeling. In this method, the decision-making problem is decomposed

**Table 4.** Description of fields related to threat event indicators.

| Index name | Description |
|---|---|
| Illegal visits | The percentage of virus attack incidents suffered by node equipment in unit time in total security incidents |
| Offline anomaly | The number of offline abnormalities that the node device suffered per unit time |

into different constituent factors, and the factors are sorted according to the relative importance of the factors, to complete the decision-making on the target problem [19].

### 3.1 The First Level of Analysis

The first analytic hierarchy process obtains the situation assessment result information of the current node through the calculation of the internal perception information of the single node device, and the steps are as follows:

**Establish a Hierarchical Structure Model of Equipment Nodes.** From top to bottom, the target layer A, the criterion layer B, the index layer C, and the plan layer D are constructed progressively. The target layer is expressed as the purpose of decision-making, that is, the security situation of the current node equipment. The target layer is composed of an element and dominant criterion level factors $B_1, B_2, B_3, B_4$. The criterion layer considers various factors that can affect the current decision, including four factors: basic operating status $B_1$, equipment vulnerability status $B_2$, risk events $B_3$, and threat events $B_4$. The index level is a quantitative index that can be calculated by refining the decision-making factors of the criterion level and is limited by the corresponding factors of the criterion level. The various factors at the program level represent the results of the assessment of the node situation, including good $D_1$, warning $D_2$, and critical $D_3$. As Shown in Fig. 2.

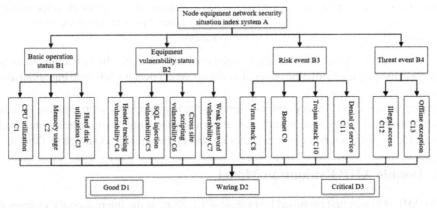

**Fig. 2.** Node equipment network security situation system.

**Construct a Judgment Matrix.** Starting from the criterion level of the hierarchical model structure, for the elements of the same level that belong to each factor of the upper level, the judgment matrix is constructed by the pairwise comparison method until the lowest level. Among them, the pairwise comparison method is the relative importance evaluation formed by comparing the factors representing this level with the factors of the upper level that are dominated by each other. Use Santy 1–9 [20] to evaluate the relative importance of each factor. The details are as follows in Table 5.

**Table 5.** Santy 1–9 scaling method.

| Value | Meaning |
|-------|---------|
| 1 | Compared with A and B, A and B are equally more important |
| 3 | Compared with A and B, A and B are slightly more important |
| 5 | Compared with A and B, A and B are obviously important |
| 7 | Compared with A and B, A and B are strongly important |
| 9 | Compared with A and B, A and B are extremely important |
| 2,4,6,8 | The degree of importance between the above two adjacent levels |

According to the assignment method shown in Table 1, we can determine the value of each element of the matrix, thereby constructing the judgment matrix $A = (a_{ij})_{n \times n}$, which satisfies the following properties:

$$a_{ij} \begin{cases} = 1 & i = j \\ = \frac{1}{a_{ji}} & i, j > 0 \\ > 0 & i, j > 0 \end{cases} \tag{1}$$

**Calculate the Feature Vector.** After constructing the judgment matrix according to the pairwise comparison method, the normalized weights of these indicators should be obtained, that is, the feature vector $W$ is obtained from the judgment matrix to express the relative importance of the elements of the same level to the previous element. First, use the following formula to normalize the elements in matrix A by column to obtain a column-normalized column matrix $Q = (p_{ij})_{m \times n}$:

$$p_{ij} = a_{ij} / \sum_{k=1}^{k=1} a_{ij} \tag{2}$$

The Q matrix elements are added by rows to get $\overline{W} = (\alpha_1, \alpha_2, \ldots, \alpha_m,)^T$. Subsequently use

$$w_i = \alpha_i / \sum_{k=1}^{m} \alpha_k \tag{3}$$

to calculate the feature vector $W = (w_1, w_2, \ldots, w_m)^T$.

**Consistency Inspection.** According to the formula:

$$CI = \frac{\lambda_{max} - m}{m - 1} \tag{4}$$

calculate the consistency index, where $m$ is the order of the judgment matrix. According to the formula:

$$CR = \frac{CI}{RI} \tag{5}$$

calculate the consistency ratio $CR$, which $RI$ [21] is shown in Table 6 below.

When $CR < 0.1$, the judgment that the consistency of the matrix can be accepted, the feature vector is also desired, or required to adjust the judgment matrix until $CR < 0.1$.

**Table 6.** Average random consistency index

| Order ( m) | Average random consistency index ( RI) |
|------------|----------------------------------------|
| 1          | 0                                      |
| 2          | 0                                      |
| 3          | 0.52                                   |
| 4          | 0.89                                   |
| 5          | 1.12                                   |
| 6          | 1.26                                   |
| 7          | 1.36                                   |
| 8          | 1.41                                   |
| 9          | 1.46                                   |
| 10         | 1.49                                   |

## 3.2 The Second Level of Analysis

The situation assessment result information (equipment node situation assessment weight vector) obtained by the first-fold analytic hierarchy process will be sent to other nodes in the network according to the consistency principle of the current distributed system.

Use the received situation assessment result information of other nodes and the security situation assessment result within the node to perform the second-level analysis to calculate the network security situation of the entire distributed system. The steps are as follows:

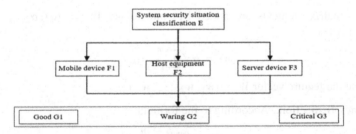

**Fig. 3.** System security situation classification.

**Establish a Hierarchical Model of the Situational Awareness System.** From top to bottom, the target layer E, the criterion layer F, and the scheme layer G are constructed progressively. The target layer is expressed as the purpose of decision-making, that is, the current security situation of the system. The target layer is composed of an element and dominant criterion level factors $F_1$, $F_2$, $F_3$. The factors of the criterion layer are the various sensing entities in the current sensing system, including mobile devices, host devices, server devices, and so on. The program layer represents the evaluation results of the system, including good $G_1$, warning $G_2$, and critical $G_3$. As shown in Fig. 3.

**Sorting of Calculation Levels.** First layer calculation scheme of all the factors $G_1, G_2$, $G_3$ or the rule layer factor $F_i$ level of a single sort $W_{F_iG} = (w_{F_iG_1}, w_{F_iG_2}, w_{F_iG_3})^T$ which

$$W_{F_iG} = W^i = \left(w_1^i, w_2^i, w_3^i\right)^T \tag{6}$$

$W^i$ represents the weight vector of the situation assessment of the i-th device node.

**Constructing the Criterion-Level Judgment Matrix.** According to the different weight status of equipment assets, continue to use the pairwise comparison method to construct the judgment matrix of criterion layer F, and calculate its eigenvector $W_F = (w_{F_1}, w_{F_2}, \ldots, w_{F_i})^T$.

**Total Ranking of Calculation Levels.** Calculate the total ranking of the level G of the scheme $W_G = (w_{G_1}, w_{G_2}, w_{G_3})^T$, where

$$w_{G_j} = \sum_{i=1}^{n} w_{F_i} w_{F_iG_j} \tag{7}$$

$w_{G_j}$ indicates the weight value of the j-th evaluation result, j = 1, 2, 3.

**Consistency Inspection.** According to the formula

$$CR = \frac{\sum_{i=1}^{3} w_{F_i} \times CI_i}{\sum_{i=1}^{3} w_{F_i} \times RI_i} \tag{8}$$

calculate the overall ranking consistency ratio of the hierarchy. Among them, $CI_i$ and $RI_i$ with that of the standard-level device i.

When $CR < 0.1$, the matrix that is determined by the consistency check, or need to adjust the ratio of high consistency judgment matrix until $CR < 0.1$;

The factor corresponding to the highest weight item in the total ranking of levels is the result of the security situation assessment of the requested system.

## 4  Case Analysis

This article takes a small local area network as an analysis example, and the main sensing device nodes include mobile devices, host devices, and server devices. As shown in Fig. 2, this paper mainly uses the basic operating status, equipment vulnerability status, risk events, and threat events perceived in the local area network to evaluate the situation of the internal node equipment of the network. And it establishes the situation indicator system formed by the target layer, the criterion layer, and the indicator layer.

The evaluation model takes the node equipment network security situation indicator system as the target layer $C$. The criterion layer includes basic operating status $B_1$, equipment vulnerability status $B_2$, risk events $B_3$ and threat events $B_4$. The basis of the operating state $B_1$ can be decomposed into CPU usage $C_1$, memory usage $C_2$ and hard drive usage $C_3$. The vulnerability status of the device $B_2$ can be decomposed into four indicators: header tracking vulnerability $C_4$, SQL injection vulnerability $C_5$, cross-site scripting vulnerability $C_6$, and weak password vulnerability $C_7$. Risk events $B_3$ can be decomposed into virus attacks $C_8$, botnets $C_9$, Trojans attacks $C_{10}$ and deny service $C_{11}$. Threat events $B_4$ can be divided into two indicators: illegal access $C_{12}$ and offline abnormality $C_{13}$. The program layer contains three levels of good $D_1$, warning $D_2$ and critical $D_3$.

Because the calculation method is the same, this article only uses mobile devices $F_1$ as an example to calculate the weight vector of the first-level analysis situation assessment, and the other device assessment weight vectors will be directly given.

Determine the judgment matrix and weight of the situation index system according to the pairwise comparison method, establish the judgment matrix and weight vector of the evaluation factors of the first-level analysis criterion layer (as shown in Table 7) and the judgment matrix of the evaluation factors of the index layer And the weight vector (as shown in Table 8). Establish the judgment matrix and weight vector of the evaluation factors of the first level of analysis program level (as shown in Table 9).

Then calculate the combined weight $W_C$ of each factor of the indicator layer according to the above-mentioned obtained criterion layer weight vector $W_B$ and indicator layer weight vector $W_{B_i\_C}$:

**Table 7.** The judgment matrix and weight vector of the evaluation factors at the first level of the criterion layer B.

| Judgment factors set at the criterion layer B | Judgment matrix | Weight vector $W_B(w_{B_i})$ |
|---|---|---|
| $B = [B_1, B_2, B_3, B_4]$ | $A\_B =$ | $W_B = \begin{bmatrix} 0.0535 \\ 0.1123 \\ 0.2913 \\ 0.5429 \end{bmatrix}$ |
| | $\begin{bmatrix} 1.0000 & 0.3333 & 0.1667 & 0.1429 \\ 3.0000 & 1.0000 & 0.2500 & 0.2000 \\ 6.0000 & 4.0000 & 1.0000 & 0.3333 \\ 7.0000 & 5.0000 & 3.0000 & 1.0000 \end{bmatrix}$ | |

**Table 8.** The judgment matrix and weight vector of the evaluation factors at the first level of the index layer C.

| Judgment factors set at the indicator layer C | Judgment matrix $B_i\_C$ | Weight vector $W_{B_i\_C}(w_{B_iC_j})$ |
|---|---|---|
| $B_1 = [C_1, C_2, C_3]$ | $B_1\_C = \begin{bmatrix} 1.0000 & 4.0000 & 0.5000 \\ 0.2500 & 1.0000 & 0.1667 \\ 2.0000 & 6.0000 & 1.0000 \end{bmatrix}$ | $W_{B_1\_C} = \begin{bmatrix} 0.3238 \\ 0.0893 \\ 0.5869 \end{bmatrix}$ |
| $B_2 = [C_4, C_5, C_6, C_7]$ | $B_2\_C = \begin{bmatrix} 1.0000 & 0.3333 & 0.5000 & 4.0000 \\ 3.0000 & 1.0000 & 5.0000 & 6.0000 \\ 2.0000 & 0.2000 & 1.0000 & 3.0000 \\ 0.2500 & 0.1667 & 0.3333 & 1.0000 \end{bmatrix}$ | $W_{B_2\_C} = \begin{bmatrix} 0.1787 \\ 0.5571 \\ 0.1996 \\ 0.0646 \end{bmatrix}$ |
| $B_3 = [C_8, C_9, C_{10}, C_{11}]$ | $B_3\_C = \begin{bmatrix} 1.0000 & 0.1429 & 0.2500 & 0.2000 \\ 7.0000 & 1.0000 & 3.0000 & 4.0000 \\ 4.0000 & 0.3333 & 1.0000 & 0.3333 \\ 5.0000 & 0.2500 & 3.0000 & 1.0000 \end{bmatrix}$ | $W_{B_3\_C} = \begin{bmatrix} 0.0531 \\ 0.5319 \\ 0.1566 \\ 0.2584 \end{bmatrix}$ |
| $B_4 = [C_{12}, C_{13}]$ | $B_4\_C = \begin{bmatrix} 1.0000 & 3.0000 \\ 0.3333 & 1.0000 \end{bmatrix}$ | $W_{B_4\_C} = \begin{bmatrix} 0.7500 \\ 0.2500 \end{bmatrix}$ |

**Table 9.** The judgment matrix and weight vector of the evaluation factors at the first level of the plan layer D.

| Judgment factors set at the plan layer D | Judgment matrix $C_j D$ | Weight vector $W_{C_j D}(w_{C_j D_k})$ |
|---|---|---|
| $D = [D_1, D_2, D_3]$ | $C_1\_D =$ <br><br> $\begin{bmatrix} 1.0000 & 5.0000 & 0.5000 \\ 0.2000 & 1.0000 & 0.1429 \\ 2.0000 & 7.0000 & 1.0000 \end{bmatrix}$ | $W_{C_1 D} = \begin{bmatrix} 0.3338 \\ 0.0755 \\ 0.5907 \end{bmatrix}$ |
| $D = [D_1, D_2, D_3]$ | $C_2\_D =$ <br><br> $\begin{bmatrix} 1.0000 & 5.0000 & 2.0000 \\ 0.2000 & 1.0000 & 0.2000 \\ 0.5000 & 5.0000 & 1.0000 \end{bmatrix}$ | $W_{C_2 D} = \begin{bmatrix} 0.5559 \\ 0.0904 \\ 0.3537 \end{bmatrix}$ |
| $D = [D_1, D_2, D_3]$ | $C_3\_D =$ <br><br> $\begin{bmatrix} 1.0000 & 0.3333 & 6.0000 \\ 3.0000 & 1.0000 & 9.0000 \\ 0.1667 & 0.1111 & 1.0000 \end{bmatrix}$ | $W_{C_3 D} = \begin{bmatrix} 0.2819 \\ 0.6583 \\ 0.0598 \end{bmatrix}$ |
| $D = [D_1, D_2, D_3]$ | $C_4\_D =$ <br><br> $\begin{bmatrix} 1.0000 & 3.0000 & 0.1429 \\ 0.3333 & 1.0000 & 0.1111 \\ 7.0000 & 9.0000 & 1.0000 \end{bmatrix}$ | $W_{C_4 D} = \begin{bmatrix} 0.1549 \\ 0.0685 \\ 0.7766 \end{bmatrix}$ |

(*continued*)

**Table 9.** (*continued*)

| Judgment factors set at the plan layer D | Judgment matrix $C_jD$ | Weight vector $W_{C_jD}(w_{C_jD_k})$ |
|---|---|---|
| $D = [D_1, D_2, D_3]$ | $C_5\_D =$ $\begin{bmatrix} 1.0000 & 0.2500 & 0.2000 \\ 4.0000 & 1.0000 & 0.5000 \\ 5.0000 & 2.0000 & 1.0000 \end{bmatrix}$ | $W_{C_5D} = \begin{bmatrix} 0.0982 \\ 0.3339 \\ 0.5679 \end{bmatrix}$ |
| $D = [D_1, D_2, D_3]$ | $C_6\_D =$ $\begin{bmatrix} 1.0000 & 0.5000 & 2.0000 \\ 2.0000 & 1.0000 & 8.0000 \\ 0.5000 & 0.1250 & 1.0000 \end{bmatrix}$ | $W_{C_6D} = \begin{bmatrix} 0.2584 \\ 0.6380 \\ 0.1036 \end{bmatrix}$ |
| $D = [D_1, D_2, D_3]$ | $C_7\_D =$ $\begin{bmatrix} 1.0000 & 5.0000 & 2.0000 \\ 0.2000 & 1.0000 & 0.1667 \\ 0.5000 & 6.0000 & 1.0000 \end{bmatrix}$ | $W_{C_7D} = \begin{bmatrix} 0.5455 \\ 0.0845 \\ 0.3700 \end{bmatrix}$ |
| $D = [D_1, D_2, D_3]$ | $C_8\_D =$ $\begin{bmatrix} 1.0000 & 2.0000 & 0.2000 \\ 0.5000 & 1.0000 & 0.2500 \\ 5.0000 & 4.0000 & 1.0000 \end{bmatrix}$ | $W_{C_8D} = \begin{bmatrix} 0.1925 \\ 0.1307 \\ 0.6768 \end{bmatrix}$ |

(*continued*)

**Table 9.** (*continued*)

| Judgment factors set at the plan layer D | Judgment matrix $C_jD$ | Weight vector $W_{C_jD}(w_{C_jD_k})$ |
|---|---|---|
| $D = [D_1, D_2, D_3]$ | $C_9\_D =$ $\begin{bmatrix} 1.0000 & 2.0000 & 0.5000 \\ 0.5000 & 1.0000 & 0.1667 \\ 2.0000 & 6.0000 & 1.0000 \end{bmatrix}$ | $W_{C_9D} = \begin{bmatrix} 0.2693 \\ 0.1180 \\ 0.6127 \end{bmatrix}$ |
| $D = [D_1, D_2, D_3]$ | $C_{10}\_D =$ $\begin{bmatrix} 1.0000 & 6.0000 & 2.0000 \\ 0.1667 & 1.0000 & 0.2000 \\ 0.5000 & 5.0000 & 1.0000 \end{bmatrix}$ | $W_{C_{10}D} = \begin{bmatrix} 0.5750 \\ 0.0819 \\ 0.3431 \end{bmatrix}$ |
| $D = [D_1, D_2, D_3]$ | $C_{11}\_D =$ $\begin{bmatrix} 1.0000 & 7.0000 & 4.0000 \\ 0.1429 & 1.0000 & 0.2500 \\ 0.2500 & 4.0000 & 1.0000 \end{bmatrix}$ | $W_{C_{11}D} = \begin{bmatrix} 0.6877 \\ 0.0778 \\ 0.2344 \end{bmatrix}$ |
| $D = [D_1, D_2, D_3]$ | $C_{12}\_D =$ $\begin{bmatrix} 1.0000 & 4.0000 & 7.0000 \\ 0.2500 & 1.0000 & 1.0000 \\ 0.1429 & 1.0000 & 1.0000 \end{bmatrix}$ | $W_{C_{12}D} = \begin{bmatrix} 0.7208 \\ 0.1524 \\ 0.1268 \end{bmatrix}$ |

(*continued*)

**Table 9.** (*continued*)

| Judgment factors set at the plan layer D | Judgment matrix $C_jD$ | Weight vector $W_{C_jD}(w_{C_jD_k})$ |
|---|---|---|
| $D = [D_1, D_2, D_3]$ | $C_{13}\_D =$ | $W_{C_{13}D} = \begin{bmatrix} 0.3700 \\ 0.5455 \\ 0.0845 \end{bmatrix}$ |
| | $\begin{bmatrix} 1.0000\ 0.5000\ 6.0000 \\ 2.0000\ 1.0000\ 5.0000 \\ 0.1667\ 0.2000\ 1.0000 \end{bmatrix}$ | |

$$W_C(w_{C_j}) = \begin{bmatrix} 0.0173 \\ 0.0048 \\ 0.0314 \\ 0.0201 \\ 0.0626 \\ 0.0224 \\ 0.0072 \\ 0.0155 \\ 0.1550 \\ 0.0456 \\ 0.0753 \\ 0.4072 \\ 0.1357 \end{bmatrix}, \text{ where}$$

$$w_{C_j} = w_{B_i} \times w_{B_iC_j}, \{\ i|i \in [1,4], i \in N^+\}, \{\ j|j \in [1,13], j \in N^+\} \qquad (9)$$

According to the calculated solution layer weight vector $W_{C_jD}$ and the index layer combination weight $W_C$, the overall ranking of the solution layer $W_D$ is calculated as follow:

$$W_D(w_{D_k}) = \begin{bmatrix} 0.5027 \\ 0.2717 \\ 0.2256 \end{bmatrix}, \text{ where}$$

$$w_{D_k} = \sum_{j=1}^{13} w_{C_j}w_{C_jD_k}, \{\ j, k|j \in [1, 13], k \in [1, 3], j \in N^+, k \in N^+\} \qquad (10)$$

The hierarchical total sorting $W_D$ is the situation evaluation weight vector of the current device node, which is recorded as the weight vector $W^{F_1}_D$ of the device $F_1$, and the first level of analysis is completed.

Similarly available $W^{F_2}_D = \begin{bmatrix} 0.4517 \\ 0.2105 \\ 0.3378 \end{bmatrix}, W^{F_3}_D = \begin{bmatrix} 0.6521 \\ 0.3110 \\ 0.0369 \end{bmatrix}.$

The second part of the evaluation model, the second level of analysis, takes the system security situation as the target layer E, and the criterion layer F includes mobile devices $B_1$, host devices $B_2$, and server devices $B_3$. Scheme layer $E$ includes three levels: good $G_1$, warning $G_2$, and critical $G_3$, as shown in Fig. 3.

According to the pairwise comparison method, the judgment matrix and weight of the situation index system are determined, and the judgment matrix and weight vector of the evaluation factors of the second-level analysis criterion layer are established (as shown in Table 10).

**Table 10.** The judgment matrix and weight vector of the evaluation factors of the second AHP analysis criterion layer.

| Judgment factors set at the criterion layer B | Judgment matrix | Weight vector $W_F(w_{F_p})$ |
|---|---|---|
| $F = [F_1, F_2, F_3]$ | $E\_F =$ | $W_F = \begin{bmatrix} 0.3537 \\ 0.0904 \\ 0.5559 \end{bmatrix}$ |
| | $\begin{bmatrix} 1.0000 & 5.0000 & 0.5000 \\ 0.2000 & 1.0000 & 0.2000 \\ 2.0000 & 5.0000 & 1.0000 \end{bmatrix}$ | |

Since the scheme level G is the same as the scheme level D in the first-level analysis, the weight vector $W_{F_pG}(w_{F_pG_q})$ of the second level analysis scheme level evaluation factors to the criteria level factors to which they belong is equivalent to the first level analysis of the corresponding equipment node. The total order of levels, namely $W_{F_pG} = W^{F_p}D, \{p|p \in [1, 3], i \in N^+\}$.

According to the weight vector of the solution layer $W_{F_pG}$ and the weight of the criterion layer $W_F$, the total ranking of the solution layer is calculated $W_G$:

$$W_G(w_{G_q}) = \begin{bmatrix} 0.5811 \\ 0.2881 \\ 0.1308 \end{bmatrix}, \text{ where}$$

$$w_{G_q} = \sum_{p=1}^{3} w_{F_p} w_{F_pG_q}, \{ p, q|p \in [1, 3], q \in [1, 3], p \in N^+, q \in N^+\} \quad (11)$$

The hierarchical total sorting $W_G$ is the situation assessment weight vector of the current equipment node, and the second-level analysis is completed.

The analysis results show that the proportion of good evaluation grades is 0.5811, the proportion of warning evaluation grades is 0.2881, and the proportion of critical evaluation grades is 0.1308. According to the criterion of maximum comprehensive evaluation weight, it can be seen that the network security situation assessment is in a good state.

# 5 Conclusion

This paper uses a hierarchical analysis model to evaluate the security situation of the system. The first level of analysis will directly calculate the weight vector of the situational security level of a single node, and will not upload this assessment information to the central database, but rely on the principle of consistency of the distributed system to ensure the synchronization of the assessment information, Effectively avoiding the leakage of assessment information and the tampering of security data. The second-level analysis carried out re-built the level analysis model around the importance of equipment, realized the situation assessment of the system directly within a single node, and provided the situation assessment for the distributed system from single-point situation assessment to multi-point integration. A concrete and feasible solution.

**Acknowledgement.** This work is supported by the State Grid Sichuan Company Science and Technology Project: "Research and Application of Key Technologies of Network Security Protection System Based on Zero Trust Model" (No.SGSCCD00XTJS2101279).

# References

1. Wei, Y., Lian, Y., Feng, D.: Network security situation assessment model based on information fusion. Comput. Res. Dev. **46**(3), 353–362 (2009)
2. Wang, Z., Jia, Y., Li, A., Zhang, J.: Quantitative assessment method of network situation based on fuzzy analytic hierarchy process. Comput. Secur. **1**, 61–65 (2011)
3. Jiang, Y., Xu, C.: Advances in set pair analysis theory and its applications. Comput. Sci. **33**(001), 205–209 (2006)
4. Chen, L., Lv, C.: Research on power risk assessment method based on fuzzy comprehensive evaluation. Electric Power Sci. Eng. **026**(011), 50–54 (2010)
5. Gao, J., Guo, F.: Interval intuitionistic fuzzy multi-attribute decision-making method based on reference point dependent utility function. Statist. Decis. **17**, 45–50 (2019)
6. Qian, B., Cai, Z., Xiao, Y., Yang, J., Liao, N.D., Su, S.: Network security situation awareness of metering automation system based on fuzzy inference. South. Power Grid Tech. **13**(2), 51–58 (2019)
7. Ding, H.D., Xu, H., Duan, R., Chen, F.: Network security situation awareness model based on Bayesian method. Comput. Eng. **46**(514), 136–141 (2020)
8. Mao, Y.: Research on situation prediction method combined with hidden Markov and genetic algorithm. Ph.D. dissertation, Northwest University (2019)
9. Tang, Y.L., Li, W.J., Yu, J.X., Yan, X.X.: Network security situation assessment method based on improved DS evidence theory. J. Nanjing Univ. Sci. Tech. **39**(04), 405–411 (2015)
10. Skopik, F., Wurzenberger, M., Settanni, G., Roman, F.: Establishing national cyber situational awareness through incident information clustering. In: Procedding of International Conference on Cyber Situational Awareness, pp. 1–8 (2015)
11. Dianwen, L., Xiu, J., Xin, T.: Chaos-GA-BP neural network power load forecasting based on rough set theory. J. Phys. Conf. Ser. **1**, 012132. IOP Publishing (2010)
12. Ly, B., Manickam, S.: Novel: adaptive grey verhulst model for network security situation prediction. Proc. Int. J. Adv. Comput. Sci. Appl. **7**(1), 90–95 (2016)
13. He, F., Zhang, Y., Liu, D., Ying, D., Liu, C.Y., Wu, C.S.: Mixed wavelet-based neural network model for cyber security situation prediction using MODWT and Hurst exponent analysis. In: Proceeding of International Conference on Network and System Security, pp. 99–111 (2017)

14. Liu, H., Zhou, L.Q., Rui, J., Zhao, Z.W.: Evaluation model based on support vector machine and the weight of the adaptive network security situation weights. Comput. Syst. **27**(7), 188–192 (2018)
15. Wang, J., Zhang, F.L., Fu, C., Chen, L.S.: Study on index system in network situation awareness. J. Comput. Appl. **27**(8), 1907–1909 (2007)
16. Gong, J., Zang, X.D., Su, Q., Hu, X.Y., Xu, J.: Overview of cyber security situational awareness. J. Softw. **28**(04), 1010–1026 (2017)
17. Zhang, H.B., Yin, Y., Zhao, D.M., Liu, B.: Network security situation awareness model based on threat intelligence. J. Commun. **42**(6), 182–194 (2021)
18. Mustafa, M.A., Al-Bahar, J.F.: Project risk assessment using the analytic hierarchy process. IEEE Trans. Eng. Manage. **38**(1), 46–52 (1991)
19. Saaty, T.L.: The analytic hierarchy and analytic network measurement processes: applications to decisions under Risk. Euro. J. Pure Appl. Math. **1**(1), 122–196 (2008)
20. Shilun, G.: A 1–9 determines coefficient function evaluation scale method. Value Eng. **1**, 33–34 (1989)
21. Hong, Z.G., Li, Y., Fan, Z.H., Wang, Y.: Calculation of high-order average random consistency index (RI) in analytic hierarchy process. Comput. Eng. Appl. **12**, 45–47 (2002)
22. Berguiga, A., Harchay, A.: An IoT-based intrusion detection system approach for TCP SYN attacks. Comput. Mater. Continua **71**(2), 3839–3851 (2022)
23. Ju, X.: An overview of face manipulation detection. J. Cyber Secur. **2**(4), 197–207 (2020)
24. Samad, M.A., Choi, D.: Analysis and modeling of propagation in tunnel at 3.7 and 28 ghz. Comput. Mater. Continua **71**(2), 3127–3143 (2022)
25. Devi, S.K., Subalalitha, C.N.: Deep learning based audio assistive system for visually impaired people. Comput. Mater. Continua **71**(1), 1205–1219 (2022)
26. Al-Adhaileh, M.H., Alsaade, F.W.: Detecting and analysing fake opinions using artificial intelligence algorithms. Intell. Autom. Soft Comput. **32**(1), 643–655 (2022)

# A Privacy-Preserving Scheme by Combining Compressed Sensing and Secret Sharing in Cloud Environment

Junying Liang[1,2], Haipeng Peng[1,2(✉)], and Lixiang Li[1,2]

[1] Information Security Center, State Key Laboratory of Networking and Switching Technology, Beijing University of Posts and Telecommunications, Beijing 100876, China
penghaipeng@bupt.edu.cn

[2] National Engineering Laboratory for Disaster Backup and Recovery, Beijing University of Posts and Telecommunications, Beijing 100876, China

**Abstract.** In the increasingly complex network environment, there are serious security risks in the network environment, the traditional encryption algorithms generally ignore the robustness while considering the security. In order to better deal with the situation that the private information is attacked and stolen, we provide a privacy-preserving scheme by combining compressed sensing and secret sharing in cloud environment in this paper. Message owners compress the private information, which not only realizes once encryption by using a good measurement matrix as the key, but also decreases the resource demand for private information acquisition. Meanwhile, in order to further enhance the reliability and confidentiality of this system and prevent secrets from being too concentrated, secret sharing is an effective method to disperse power, message owners make full use of this method, which not only realizes twice encryption, but also disperses the risk and tolerates the intrusion. In particular, even if several participants work together can recover the secret, they still cannot obtain the private information because they cannot access the cloud server, in other words, they cannot obtain compressed sensing matrix corresponding to the secret. Therefore, they cannot recover the private information by using the reconstruction methods of compressed sensing. Finally, we analyzed our scheme from two aspects.

**Keywords:** Compressed sensing · Secret sharing · Cloud server · Encryption

## 1 Introduction

At the times of information explosion, new technologies such as edge computing, cloud computing, 5G, artificial intelligence and Internet of things have been applied in daily life. With the advent of big data, all kinds of information is growing at a faster and faster speed. Cloud computing platform has the advantages of large scale, high reliability, strong universality, strong scalability and low cost. In order to prevent privacy disclosure, private information need to be uploaded to the cloud service after local encryption. Xia et al. proposed a scheme that supports content-based image retrieval over encrypted

© The Author(s), under exclusive license to Springer Nature Switzerland AG 2022
X. Sun et al. (Eds.): ICAIS 2022, CCIS 1588, pp. 507–517, 2022.
https://doi.org/10.1007/978-3-031-06764-8_39

images without leaking the sensitive information to the cloud server [1]. Tang et al. designed a set of JPEG format-compatible encryption method, making no file expansion to JPEG files [2]. Xia et al. focused on the secure process of image data on cloud servers. Images are stored on cloud servers in encrypted form, and the local binary pattern feature can be directly extracted from the encrypted images for applications [3]. Zheng et al. attempted to provide a joint effort that flexibly addresses the security concerns [4]. Jiang et al. proposed a privacy-preserving outsourced genetic algorithm [5].

Compressed sensing is a new theory of signal acquisition and encoding and decoding. The research on compressed sensing originated from two breakthrough papers published by Donoho [6] and Candes [7]. As soon as this theory was put forward, academia and industry have paid more and more attention to it, especially in the fields of image processing, information theory, microwave imaging, geoscience, pattern recognition, biomedical engineering, wireless communication and so on. Nowadays, the traditional encryption algorithms generally ignore the robustness while considering the security in complex network environment. Compressed sensing has a special property for encryption, that is, compared with traditional methods, it can recover private information with fewer samples. In decryption processing, for different sparse signals, compressed sensing is committed to accurately reconstructing private information by selecting appropriate reconstruction methods, such as greed methods [8, 9], convex optimization methods [10], threshold methods [11] and so on. Therefore, several encryption algorithms based on CS have been proposed [12–18]. The research on compressed sensing is not only to guarantee the security of private information, but also to decrease the resource demand for private information acquisition. Brahim et al. [12] introduced a new image encryption algorithm based on CS. Using Lorenz chaotic system to generate the measurement matrix which works by taking the third equation as a controller to take either the first or the second equation to fill the measurement matrix. Wang et al. [13] designed an image compression encryption algorithm with good reconstruction accuracy and high security by combining with the novel chaotic map and CS. Liu et al. [14] proposed an image encryption method based on CS and arnold transformation. The cipher image has such features, low data volume, strong robustness, key sensitivity, and resistance to brute force attack. Lu et al. [15] proposed an image information encryption scheme combined compressed sensing with optical theory. Not only the security of information was ensured under the premise of decreasing the amount of data transmission and reducing the size of the random phase masks but also the privacy of keys were assured which were gained by rules rather than transmitted from transmitter to receiver. Li et al. [16] presented a CS-based encryption method that associates the quantization with random measurement permutation. An image encryption scheme based on four-wing chaotic system combined with CS and DNA coding was proposed in [17]. In order to enhance the security of optical encryption technology and reduce the data capacity of cipher,an optical image encryption algorithm based on chaotic Gyrator transform and compressive sensing was presented in [18].

Due to the problems of the network environment itself, there are serious security risks in the network environment. In order to avoid that secrets can not be recovered due to the loss, destruction, use or malicious tampering of important information and secret data in the network, researchers suggest using secret sharing mechanism to process secrets. The key of secret sharing is how to better design secret shares and recovery methods. Shamir [19] and Blakley [20] gave the definition of secret sharing respectively, and proposed a $(k, n)$ secret sharing scheme. It divides a secret into several shares and distributes them to the corresponding several participants. The subset composed of at least $k$ participants among these participants can work together to reconstruct the secret. Significantly, this scheme has the following advantages: (1) reasonably creates a backup for the secret messages. (2) prevents abuse caused by excessive concentration of power. (3) guarantees the security and integrity of secret messages. (4) the reliability of the system is improved without increasing the risk. It is one of the most important tools to guarantee secrets security in network application services. Therefore, this study has attracted more and more attention of researchers. Secret sharing has become a hot topic in modern cryptography. At the same time, it has also become an essential research direction in information security. Many researchers have proposed many secret sharing schemes by using polynomials [15–18], vector space [19, 20], Chinese remainder theorem [21–30], codes [31–35] and so on. These schemes greatly enrich the theoretical methods of secret sharing schemes.

The motivation of this paper is that in the increasingly complex network environment, there are serious security risks in the network environment, the traditional encryption algorithms generally ignore the robustness while considering the security. In order to better deal with the situation that the private information is attacked and stolen, the contribution of this paper is to provide a privacy-preserving scheme by combining compressed sensing and secret sharing in cloud environment. Firstly, message owners compresses the private information $S$ by $s$, which not only realizes once encryption by using a good measurement matrix $\Phi$ as the key, but also decreases the resource demand for private information acquisition. Secondly, to prevent secrets from being too concentrated, secret sharing is an effective method to disperses power, message owners make full use of this method, which not only realizes twice encryption, but also disperses the risk and tolerates the intrusion. Finally, we analyze our scheme from two aspects.

This paper is composed of the following sections. Section 2 simple introduces the concepts of compressed sensing, secret sharing, and bilinear mapping. Section 3 presents a privacy-preserving scheme by combining compressed sensing and secret sharing in cloud environment. Section 4 analyzes our scheme from two aspects. Section 5 sums up the conclusions.

## 2  Preliminaries

In this section, we simple introduce some concepts, including compressed sensing, secret sharing and bilinear mapping.

### 2.1  Compressed Sensing

For a sparse signal $x \in R^n$, the standard model of compressed sensing is

$$y = \Phi x \tag{1}$$

where $\Phi$ is an $m \times n$-dimensional $(m < n)$compressed sensing matrix, $y$ is the corresponding compressed signal.

For a compressed signal $y$, we want to reconstruct $x$ by compressed sensing matrix $\Phi$. Generally, this problem is an usually nondeterministic polynomial problem [36].

## 2.2  Secret Sharing

In the following, the two stages of Shamir's $(k, n)$ secret sharing scheme is given.

### 2.2.1  Share Generation Stage

Let $U = \{P_1, P_2, \cdots, P_n\}$, the dealer first randomly selects a polynomial of degree $k - 1$,

$$g(x) = b_0 + b_1 x + \cdots + b_{k-1} x^{k-1} \tag{2}$$

where coefficients $b_i \in Z, i = 0, 1, \cdots, k - 1$, such that the secret $s = g(0)$. Next, the dealer calculates the secret share $g(x_i)i = 1, \cdots, n$, and sends it to the corresponding participant $P_i$.

### 2.2.2  Secret Reconstruction Stage

A subset of $m$ participants $U' = \{P_{i_1}, P_{i_2}, \cdots, P_{i_m}\} \subseteq U, k \le m \le n$, can reconstruct the secret $s$, each participant opens his share to all other participants. Each participant having $m$ shares can calculate the secret $s$ by Lagrange interpolation formula,

$$s = g(0) = \sum_{i \in I} g(x_i) \prod_{j \in I, j \ne i} \frac{-x_j}{x_i - x_j} \tag{3}$$

where $I = \{i_1, i_2, \cdots, i_m\} \subseteq \{1, 2, \cdots, n\}$.

### 2.2.3  Bilinear Mapping

Let $G_1$ and $G_2$ form two cyclic groups of order prime $q$ with respect to addition and multiplication, respectively. If the mapping

$$e : G_1 \times G_1 \to G_2 \tag{4}$$

satisfies three conditions as follows:

1. bilinear: for $\forall a, b \in Z_q^*, P, Q \in G_1, e(aP, bQ) = e(P, Q)^{ab}$.
2. non-degenerative: $\exists P, Q \in G_1, e(P, Q) \ne 1_{G_2}$, where $1_{G_2}$ is the unit element of group $G_2$,
3. computability: for $\exists P, Q \in G_1, e(P, Q)$ is computable.

then $e$ is called a bilinear mapping.

## 3  A Privacy-Preserving Scheme by Combining Compressed Sensing and Secret Sharing in Cloud Environment

This section proposes a privacy-preserving model by combining compressed sensing and secret sharing. The subjects involved in the model include message owners, cloud servers, users and participants, as shown in Fig. 1. When message owners outsource their message to the cloud service, they will still worry about the privacy of outsource message. Therefore, we adopt a method of combining compressed sensing and secret sharing to guarantee that private information are uploaded to the cloud after local encryption. Specifically, we consider that the cloud service is trusted. A specific example of the encryption and recovery process of the privacy information is shown in Fig. 2.

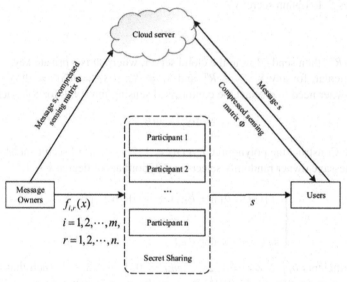

**Fig. 1.** The privacy-preserving model based on compressed sensing and secret sharing.

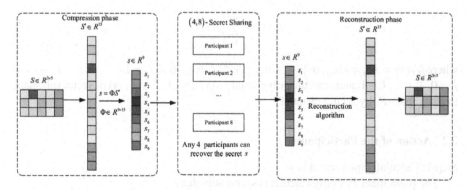

**Fig. 2.** The encryption and recovery process of the private information.

Let $G_1$, $G_2$ and $e$ be described as Sect. 2.2.3, $g \in G_1$ is a generator of additive cyclic group $G_1$. Let $U = \{P_1, P_2, \cdots, P_n\}$ is a set of $n$ participants, and each participant $P_t (t = 1, 2, \cdots, n)$ has a unique open identity $ID_t (ID_t \neq ID_r)$.

### 3.1  Action of the Message Owner

For a private information $S \in R^{p \times q}$, the elements of $S$ are extracted in turn by column and arranged into a column vector, denoted by $S' \in R^n$, where $n = p \times q$. In the processing stage, the message owner obtains the secret $s'$ by compressing $S'$, and further generates the polynomial $f_{i,t}(x)(j = 1, 2, \cdots, m)$ of secret sub share to participant $P_t$.

Step 1: Construct secret $s'$.

The message owner chooses a compressed sensing matrix $\Phi \in R^{m \times n}(m < n)$ and compresses $S'$ to obtain secret $s$,

$$s = \Phi S' \tag{5}$$

where $s \in R^m$, then sends $\Phi$, $s$ to the cloud server, where $\Phi$ is a private key.

In particular, for any $S_1', S_2' \in R^n$, and $S_1' \neq S_2'$, if $s_1 = \Phi S_1' = \Phi S_2' = s_2$, the message owner need to reselect the compressed sensing matrix $\Psi$ for $S_2'$, such that.

$$s_1 = \Phi S_1' \neq \Psi S_2' = s_2$$

Step 2: Construct the polynomial $f_{i,t}(x)(j = 1, 2, \cdots, m)$ of secret sub share.

The message owner randomly selects $m$ polynomials of degree $k - 1$,

$$\begin{cases} g_1(x) = b_{1,0} + b_{1,1}x + \cdots + b_{1,k-1}x^{k-1} \\ \quad\vdots \\ g_m(x) = b_{m,0} + b_{m,1}x + \cdots + b_{m,k-1}x^{k-1} \end{cases} \tag{6}$$

where coefficients $b_{i,j} \in Z, i = 1, 2 \cdots, m, j = 0, 1, \cdots, k - 1$, such that the secret $s$ satisfies, $s = (g_1(0), \ldots, g_m(0))^T$, $s_1 = g_1(0), s_2 = g_2(0), \cdots, s_m = g_m(0)$, the message owner write $g_i(x)(1 \leq i \leq m)$ as

$$g_i(x) = \sum_{t=1}^{n} f_{i,t}(x) \tag{7}$$

where $f_{i,t}(x) = b_{i,t,0} + b_{i,t,1}x + \cdots + b_{i,t,k-1}x^{k-1}, b_{i,t,j} \in Z, i = 1 \cdots, m, t = 1, \cdots, n$, $j = 0, 1, \cdots, k - 1$, and send the polynomial $f_{i,t}(x)(j = 1, 2, \cdots, m)$ of secret sub share to participant $P_t$ by secure channel.

### 3.2  Action of the Participants

Step 1: Calculate open secret keys.

The participant $P_t$ firstly calculates secret sub-share

$$s_{i,t,r} = f_{i,t}(ID_r) = b_{i,t,0} + b_{i,t,1}ID_r + \cdots + b_{i,t,k-1}ID_r^{k-1} \tag{8}$$

then calculates $B_{i,t,j} = b_{i,t,j}g$, $M_{i,t,r} = e(s_{i,t,r}g, g)$ and open them. And $P_t$ sends $s_{i,t,r}$ to other participant $P_r$. If $r = t$, then $P_r$ will retain $s_{i,t,r}$.

Step 2: Verify secret sub share.

Anyone can use the open $B_{i,t,j}$ and $M_{i,t,r}$ to verify whether the secret sub share $s_{i,t,r}$ is valid by the following equation

$$M_{i,t,r} = e(s_{i,t,r}g, g) = \prod_{j=0}^{k-1} e(B_{i,t,j}, g)^{ID_r^j}. \tag{9}$$

Step 3: Reconstruct secret share $s_{i,t}$.

When participant $P_r$ receive the correct secret sub-shares of all other honest participants $P_t(r \neq t)$, they can calculate their own secret share $s_{i,r}$ by the following equation

$$s_{i,r} = \sum_{t=1}^{n} s_{i,t,r} = \sum_{t=1}^{n} f_{i,t}(ID_r) = g_i(ID_r) \tag{10}$$

## 3.3   Action of the User

The access structure $\Gamma = \{P_{i_1}, P_{i_2}, \cdots, P_{i_k}\}$ is a collection of $k$ participants. All participants in $\Gamma$ can reconstruct the secret $s_i$ by their open secret shares,. In the query process, the user generates secret $s$ and sends it to the cloud server; then the user can recover private information $S$ by query result.

Step 1: Verify the secret share $s_{i,i_u}$ of participant $P_{i_u}(u = 1, 2, \cdots, k)$.

After receiving the secret share $s_{i,i_u}$ of participants $P_{i_u}$, other participants first verifies the correctness of the secret share $s_{i,i_u}$ by the following equation

$$e(s_{i,i_u}g, g) = \prod_{t=1}^{n}\prod_{j=0}^{k-1} e(B_{i,t,j}, g)^{ID_{i_u}^j}. \tag{11}$$

Step 2: Reconstruct secret $s$.

Any $k$ participants can reconstruct the secret $s_i$ ans sent $s_i$ to the user,

$$s_i = \sum_{u=1}^{k} s_{i,i_u} \prod_{u=1,l\neq u}^{k} \frac{-ID_{i_l}}{ID_{i_u} - ID_{i_l}} = \sum_{u=1}^{k} g_i(ID_{i_u}) \prod_{u=1,l\neq u}^{k} \frac{-ID_{i_l}}{ID_{i_u} - ID_{i_l}} = g_i(0) \tag{12}$$

Therefore, since $1 \leq i \leq m$, when $i$ takes all values, the user can reconstruction secret.

$$s = (g_1(0), \cdots, g_m(0))^T \tag{13}$$

Step 3: Reconstruct the private information $S$.

The user sends the secret $s$ to the cloud service, and it receives the compressed sensing matrix $\Phi$ from the cloud service. If the private information $S$ is sparse and $\Phi$ satisfies some specific properties, then the user can reconstruct private information $S$ by basis pursuit (BP) algorithm or orthogonal matching pursuit (OMP) algorithm.

### 3.4  Action of the Cloud Server

Step 1: Preserve secret data.

The cloud server receive the secret $s$ and compressed sensing matrix $\Phi$ from the message owner, then preserve $\Phi$, $s$ together.

Step 2: Return query results.

In the user query process, the cloud server received the secret $s$ of the user, then judge whether there is the secret $s$, and return query results to the user. If there is the secret $s$, it sends the corresponding compressed sensing matrix $\Phi$ to the user. Otherwise, it sends "No" to the user, this shows that the secret $s$ of the user is false, in other word, there is less than $k$ participants send the correct secret share to the user. Therefore, the user reveals no information about the secret $s$.

## 4  Analysis of Our Scheme

It is important to evaluate the effectiveness of a privacy-preserving scheme in terms of correctness and security. In the following, we analyze the proposed scheme from this two aspects.

### 4.1  Correctness Analysis

**Theorem 4.1.** In the action of the participants stage, Eq. (9) is correct.

*Proof:* $M_{i,t,r} = e\left(s_{i,t,r}g, g\right) = e\left(\left(b_{i,t,0} + b_{i,t,1}ID_r + \cdots + b_{i,t,k-1}ID_r^{k-1}\right)g, g\right)$

$$= e\left(\sum_{j=0}^{k-1} b_{i,t,j}ID_r^j g, g\right)$$

$$= \prod_{j=0}^{k-1} e\left(B_{i,t,j}, g\right)^{ID_r^j}.$$

**Theorem 4.2.** In the action of the users stage, Eq. (11) is correct.

*Proof:* $s_{i,i_u} = g_i(ID_{i_u}) = \sum_{t=1}^{n} f_{i,t}(ID_{i_u}) = \sum_{t=1}^{n} \left(b_{i,t,0} + b_{i,t,1}ID_{i_u} + \cdots + b_{i,t,k-1}ID_{i_u}^{k-1}\right)$

$$= \sum_{t=1}^{n}\sum_{j=0}^{k-1} b_{i,t,j}ID_{i_u}^j.$$

$$e\left(s_{i,i_u}g, g\right) = e\left(\sum_{t=1}^{n}\left(\sum_{j=0}^{k-1} b_{i,t,j}ID_{i_u}^j\right)g, g\right)$$

$$= \prod_{t=1}^{n} \prod_{j=0}^{k-1} e\left(b_{i,t,j} ID_{i_u}^{j} g, g\right)$$

$$= \prod_{t=1}^{n} \prod_{j=0}^{k-1} e\left(B_{i,t,j}, g\right)^{ID_{i_u}^{j}} .$$

## 4.2 Security Analysis

With the help of cloud serve as a trusted third-party, the security of this scheme depends on compressed sensing and secret sharing.

In the compressed sensing phase, for the private information, we adopts compressed sensing method to encrypt locally and then uploads it to the cloud service. Due to compressed sensing has a special property for encryption, that is, compared with traditional methods, it can recover the private information with fewer samples by selecting a good measurement matrix as key.

In the secret sharing phase, to prevent secrets from being too concentrated, secret sharing is an effective method to disperses power, message owners make full use of this method, which not only realizes twice encryption, but also disperses the risk and tolerates the intrusion. Even if any $k$ participants can recover the secret $s$, they still can not obtain the private information $S$ because they can not access the cloud server.

To sum up, even if the attacker knows the secret $s$, it is still impossible to recover private information. In other words, the method of combining compressed sensing and secret sharing protects the private information security.

## 5 Conclusion

The development of big data is mainly driven by many new technologies. Internet of things is committed to connecting all natural things with each other and building a broad, orderly and intelligent network environment. It relies on various sensing devices to obtain the information of networked objects and complete information interaction in the form of data. In the face of the continuous expansion of the Internet of things, the massive data gushing out all the time is gradually migrating to the cloud. We provides a privacy-preserving scheme by combining compressed sensing and secret sharing in cloud environment in this paper, which not only considers the security, but also considers the robustness.

The analysis results show that with the help of the cloud service, CS is regarded as an encryption method, which can decreases the resource demand for private information acquisition. Meanwhile, in order to further enhance the reliability and confidentiality of this scheme, secret sharing technology is used. We realized double encryption and reconstruction to the privacy information by some of the techniques described.

**Acknowledgement.** We want to thank the editor and all the reviewers.

**Funding Statement.** This work is partly supported by the National Key Research and Development Program of China (Grant No. 2020YFB1805403) and the National Natural Science Foundation of China (Grant Nos. 61771071, 61932005, 61972051).

**Conflicts of Interest.** The authors declare that they have no conflicts of interest to report regarding the present study.

# References

1. Xia, Z., Wang, X., Zhang, L., Qin, Z., Sun, X., Ren, K.: A privacy-preserving and copy- deterrence content-based image retrieval scheme in cloud computing. IEEE Trans. Inf. Forensics Secur. **11**(11), 2594–2608 (2016)
2. Tang, J., Xia, Z.H., Wang, L., Yuan, C.S., Zhao, X.L.: OPPR: an outsourcing privacy- preserving JPEG image retrieval scheme with local histograms in cloud environment. J. Big Data **3**(1), 21–33 (2021)
3. Xia, Z., Jiang, L., Ma, X., Yang, W., Ji, P., Xiong, N.N.: A privacy-preserving outsourcing scheme for image local binary pattern in secure industrial Internet of Things. IEEE Trans. Ind. Inf. **16**(1), 629–638 (2019)
4. Zheng, T., Luo, Y., Zhou, T., Cai, Z.: Towards differential access control and privacy-preserving for secure media data sharing in the cloud. Comput. Secur. **113**, 102553 (2022)
5. Jiang, L., Fu, Z.: Privacy-preserving genetic algorithm outsourcing in cloud computing. J. Cyber Secur. **2**(1), 49–61 (2020)
6. Donoho, D.L.: Compressed sensing. IEEE Trans. Inf. Theory **52**(4), 1289–1306 (2006)
7. Candes, E.J., Romberg, J.K., Tao, T.: Stable signal recovery from incomplete and inaccurate measurements. Commun. Pure Appl. Math. J. Issued Courant Inst. Math. Sci. **59**(8), 1207–1223 (2006)
8. Cai, T.T., Wang, L.: Orthogonal matching pursuit for sparse signal recovery with noise. IEEE Trans. Inf. Theory **57**(7), 4680–4688 (2011)
9. Dai, W., Milenkovic, O.: Subspace pursuit for compressive sensing signal reconstruction. IEEE Trans. Inf. Theory **55**(5), 2230–2249 (2009)
10. Chen, S.S., Donoho, D.L., Saunders, M.A.: Atomic decomposition by basis pursuit. SIAM Rev. **43**, 129–159 (2001)
11. Daubechies, I., Defrise, M., Mol, C.D.: An iterative thresholding algorithm for linear inverse problems with a sparsity constraint. Commun. Pure Appl. Math. J. Issued Courant Inst. Math. Sci. **57**(11), 1413–1457 (2004)
12. Brahim, A., Pacha, A., Said, N.: Image encryption based on compressive sensing and chaos systems. Opt. Laser Technol. **132**, 106489 (2020)
13. Wang, X., Zhang, H., Sun, Y., Wang, X.: A plaintext-related image encryption algorithm based on compressive sensing and a novel hyperchaotic system. Int. J. Bifurcat. Chaos **31**(2), 2150021 (2021)
14. Liu, X., Cao, Y., Lu, P., Lu, X., Li, Y.: Optical image encryption technique based on compressed sensing and Arnold transformation. Optik-Int. J. Light Electron Optics **124**(24), 6590–6593 (2013)
15. Lu, P., Liu, X., Lu, X., Tian, M., Cao, H.: Image information encryption by compressed sensing and optical theory. Acta Photonica Sin. **43**(9), 910002 (2014)
16. Li, Y., Song, B., Cao, R., Zhang, Y., Qin, H.: Image encryption based on compressive sensing and scrambled index for secure multimedia transmission. ACM Trans. Multimed. Comput. Commun. Appl. **12**(4), 1–22 (2016)

17. Wang, X., Su, Y.: Image encryption based on compressed sensing and DNA encoding. Signal Process. Image Commun. **95**, 116246 (2021)
18. Yang, P.: An optical image encryption algorithm based on chaotic gyrator transform and compressed sensing. Comput. Measure. Control (2018)
19. Shamir, A.: How to share a secret. Commun. ACM **22**(11), 612–613 (1979)
20. Blakley, G.: Safeguarding cryptographic keys. In: Proceedings of MARK, p. 313 . IEEE (1979)
21. Çalkavur, S., Sole, P., Bonnecaze, A.: A new secret sharing scheme based on polynomials over finite fields. Mathematics **8**(8), 1200 (2020)
22. Gu, T., Du, W.: Dynamically updatable multi-secret sharing scheme without trusted center. Comput. Eng. **42**(3), 148–155 (2016)
23. Yuan, L., Li, M., Guo, C., C, Choo, K., Ren, Y.: Novel threshold changeable secret sharing schemes based on polynomial interpolation. PloS One **11**(10), 165512 (2016)
24. Yu, L., Du, W.: Secret sharing scheme based on symmetric bivariate polynomial. Comput. Eng. Appl. **56**(13), 120–123 (2020)
25. Wang, Y., Du, W.: Dynamic multi-secret sharing scheme in vector space without trusted center. Comput. Eng. **43**(7), 163–169 (2017)
26. Gao, D., Feng, L., Liu, S., Long, Z.: A secret sharing scheme based on vector space. J. Lanzhou Univ. (Natl. Sci.) **44**(3) (2008)
27. Hou, Z., Chen, Q., Han, J., Liang, D.: Research on verifiable secret sharing based on Chinese remainder theorem. Energy Procedia **13**, 117–123 (2011)
28. Yang, Y., Du, W.: Secret sharing scheme based on Chinese remainder theorem in cloud computing. In: Proceedings of ICMCCE, pp. 618–6183 (2019)
29. Meng, K., Miao, F., Huang, W., Xiong, Y.: Tightly coupled multi-group threshold secret sharing based on Chinese remainder theorem. Discret. Appl. Math. **268**, 152–163 (2019)
30. Meng, K., Miao, F., Ning, Y., Huang, W., Xiong, Y., Chang, C.-C.: A proactive secret sharing scheme based on Chinese remainder theorem. Front. Comp. Sci. **15**(2), 1 (2020). https://doi.org/10.1007/s11704-019-9123-z
31. Nallabothu, S., Rukmarekha, N., Subbarao, Y.: Generalized secret sharing scheme based on MDS codes. In: Proceedings ICCT, pp. 369–378 (2019)
32. Ozadam, H., Ozbudak, F., Saygi, Z.: Secret sharing schemes and linear codes. In: Proceedings of ISC, pp. 101–106 (2007)
33. Wan, S., Lu, Y., Yan, X., Liu, L.: A novel visual secret sharing scheme based on QR codes. Int. J. Digital Crime Forensics **9**(3), 38–48 (2017)
34. Song, Y., Li, Z., Li, Y., Li, J.: A new multi-use multi-secret sharing scheme based on the duals of minimal linear codes. Secur. Commun. Netw. **8**(2), 202–211 (2015)
35. Huang, P., Chang, C., Li, Y., Liu, Y.: Enhanced (n, n)-threshold QR code secret sharing scheme based on error correction mechanism. J. Inf. Secur. Appl. **58**, 102719 (2021)
36. Natarajan, B.: Sparse approximate solutions to linear systems. SIAM J. Comput. **24**(2), 227–234 (1995)

# Dynamic Encryption of Power Internet of Things Data Based on National Secret Algorithm

Jing Zhou[1], Qian Wu[1], Jin Li[2(✉)], and Jiaxin Li[3]

[1] Shenzhen Power Supply Co. Ltd., Shenzhen 518001, China
[2] School of Cyberspace Security, Beijing University of Posts and Telecommunications, Beijing 100876, China
li_jin@bupt.edu.cn
[3] Department of Communication Engineering, University of Science and Technology Beijing, Beijing 100083, China

**Abstract.** The power Internet of Things is the evolution direction of the power industry. While improving the convenience of power grid operations, it also brings emerging network security risks to traditional industries. The national secret algorithm can integrate the characteristics of the power Internet of things for deployment and application, and improve the industry security of the power Internet of things. Based on the characteristics of the power Internet of Things architecture, the security analysis of the interconnection of power grids is carried out, combined with the calculation points of the national secret algorithm, the business application scenarios of the national secret algorithm in the power industry are discussed, and a kind of electricity information encryption is proposed for the communication requirements of the power terminal and the grid platform. In the transmission scheme, SM2 is applied to the encrypted communication between the power terminal and the power grid platform server to solve the security issues such as identity authentication and encrypted transmission, and to improve the security efficiency of the power Internet of Things.

**Keywords:** Power Internet of Things · National secret algorithm · Network security · Encrypted transmission

## 1 Introduction

Electric energy is an important support for social life and production, and the electric power system is a basic industry that guarantees people's livelihood and promotes social and economic development. The power system has a complex structure. From the perspective of equipment composition, the power system mainly includes power generation equipment, power conversion equipment, power transmission equipment, and distribution and consumption equipment; from the perspective of network composition, the power grid is mainly divided into power transmission grids and power distribution networks [1, 2]. In view of the particularity of the power industry, a complete security monitoring system needs to be established, and massive connections need to be built based on new technologies such as 5G industrial network, narrowband Internet of Things, low-power wide area network LPWAN [3], so as to realize the deployment of data collection and monitoring and control systems. And communications, but also provide support for intelligent power services. The power Internet of Things connects the originally isolated power equipment in series and opens up the information channel of the closed network. While improving the convenience of power system operation, it also brings emerging network security risks to the traditional industry of power. As the encryption algorithm of my country's independent intellectual property rights, the national secret algorithm can be deployed and applied by integrating the characteristics of the power Internet of things to improve the industry security of the power Internet of things [4, 5].

This paper combines the development characteristics of the power Internet of Things, carries out the security analysis of the power Internet of Things [6], combines the calculation points of the national secret algorithm, discusses its application in the power Internet of Things industry, designs a typical application scenario, and proposes a kind of electricity based on SM3 and SM9. The information collection and transmission scheme can effectively support the safe development of power information transmission business and provide reference ideas for industry research and industrial production.

## 2 Power Internet of Things Architecture and Security Analysis

### 2.1 Network Architecture

According to the current operating status of power grid transmission, transformation, distribution and power consumption business, the overall framework design of the power Internet of Things is shown in Fig. 1 which according to [7], including 4 layers, of which the perception layer realizes the perception of power terminal equipment information, relying on RFID and other technologies realize the aggregation of terminal status information, realize line monitoring and video monitoring in the transmission link, equipment inspection and video monitoring in the substation link, distribution automation in the power distribution link, equipment monitoring and remote copying in the power utilization link Information collection in various links such as tables and customer relationships; at the network layer, a comprehensive use of wired communications, wireless communications, satellite communications, operator dedicated lines, 5G and other technologies to build a dedicated power communication system has formed a wide-area connection of the power Internet of Things; At the platform layer, the information and data of all links are transmitted to the management platform through the power communication system to realize the integration, analysis and processing of information; at the application layer, through differentiated decision-making on power services in different industries, providing intelligent professional use for different industries Electricity service realizes the high efficiency and intelligence of electric power distribution and power dispatching. Through the power Internet of Things, the existing power system infrastructure resources can be reasonably and effectively integrated, and the efficiency of power utilization can be improved. At the same time, it can promote the rapid access to the grid of new energy industries such as green power, and improve the automation and intelligence of the power system [8].

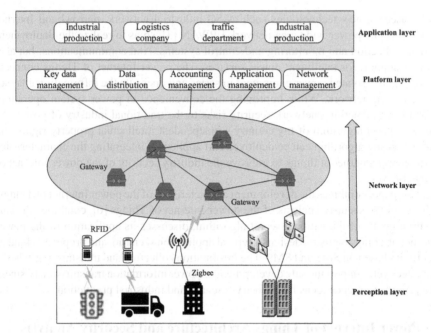

**Fig. 1.**  Power IoT system architecture.

## 2.2  Safety Analysis

An important feature of the power Internet of Things is the ubiquity of the power communication network. A large number of public network protocols are deployed in the power communication network to improve the level of power grid supervision and at the same time provide a suitable platform for most Internet attack methods. Combined with the power Internet of Things architecture, this article believes that its security risks are mainly reflected in the following aspects.

One is identity authentication. With the evolution of the open interconnection of the power Internet of Things, there are massive network connections in the power Internet of Things [9], especially in the mobile, ubiquitous, hybrid, and wide-area interconnection environment. The power Internet of Things has deployed sensor devices, mobile terminals, how to identify a large number of internal and external network data collection, control and management equipment such as video surveillance, smart meters, charging piles, office computers, etc., to realize the accurate positioning of the business system on the massive power equipment, is to prevent the identification of wrong identification and malicious counterfeiting A problem that must be faced when entering.

The second is the network boundary. In the past, the power grid was an isolated network, which used a proprietary protocol to achieve industrial control, and had a clearer boundary with other networks. The Internet of Power Things is an important content of the Industrial Internet, especially the use of cloud platforms, which further dilutes the boundary between the power grid and the public network. At the same time, with the development of the Internet of Power Things, it is bound to use public network resources such as telecom operators 5G slicing or The MPLS VPN network realizes communication networking, which leads to an increase in the scale of the interface between the power grid and the Internet, weakens the network boundary of the industrial network, and increases the source of risk.

The third aspect is encrypted transmission. There is a large amount of communication data in the power Internet of Things. Whether it is the communication between the perception layer RFID terminal perception network, or the communication between the network layer power terminal and the platform layer system, it must face the encryption problem of transmission data to prevent man-in-the-middle hijacking attacks. To realize the tampering of information such as power data, so the demand for data transmission encryption is huge [10].

## 3 National Secret Algorithm Application Analysis

The cryptographic algorithm has the function of data encryption and identity authentication, and the deployment of cryptographic equipment at the network boundary can also play a role in network isolation. The deployment of cryptographic algorithms in the power Internet of Things can achieve network and information security protection.

### 3.1 Overview of National Secret Algorithm

The national secret algorithm is a series of algorithms formulated by the National Cryptography Bureau. The national secret algorithm includes a series of technologies such as cryptographic algorithm programming, algorithm chip, and encryption card implementation. Specific classifications include SM1 symmetric encryption, SM2 cipher hash algorithm, SM3 symmetric encryption algorithm [11], SM4 symmetric encryption algorithm, SM7 block cipher algorithm, SM9 [12] identification cipher algorithm, and ZUC algorithm. The national secret algorithm has a wide range of applications, and is used to encrypt and protect sensitive internal information, administrative information, economic information, etc.: SM1 can be used for enterprise access control management, transmission encryption and storage encryption of various sensitive information within the enterprise to prevent Illegal third parties obtain information content; it can also be used for various security certifications, online banking, digital signatures.

### 3.2 Power Industry Applications

At present, the communication protocol of some business data of the electric power adopts certain security authentication and encryption methods, but the application scenarios are not common. In most business scenarios, there are still security risks such as theft or forgery of protocol data packets, data tampering, and identity forgery by third parties. The use of domestic cryptographic algorithms is conducive to improving security strength and ensuring the safe operation of the power system. Among them, SM1 and SM7 algorithms are widely used in smart meter card communication; SM3 can be used to verify the integrity of sensitive data, for example, SM3 is used to sign during the transmission of meter data to verify that the power data has not been modified; SM2,

SM4, SM9, and ZUC algorithms have good application prospects in the secure transmission of power messages. The following describes the SM2 digital signature generation and verification process, SM2 encryption and decryption process [13, 14].

Generally, users use digital signatures to ensure the non-repudiation of messages. The reliability of messages digitally signed by the signee is determined by the verifier by verifying the signature attached to the message. When the message M needs to be digitally signed, the signer user A first needs to have the public key $P_A$ and the corresponding private key $d_A$, and the signer user B who receives the signed message needs to have the public key $P_A$ of the user A. User A uses $d_A$ to generate a signature, and user B uses $P_A$ for verification. According to the SM2 standard published by the National Cryptographic Administration [15], the hash value $Z_A$ must be calculated for signature verification in the SM2 digital signature algorithm, $Z_A = H_{256}(ENTL_A \parallel ID_A \parallel a \parallel b \parallel x_G \parallel y_G \parallel x_A \parallel y_A)$. Among them, $H_{256}$ () is the password hash function, which calculates a series of parameters of user A, ENTLA is two bytes converted from the length of user IDA, the parameters of a and b elliptic curve equation, the elliptic curve base point $H_{256}$, $x_A$ and $y_A$ are the coordinates of $P_A$. Then user A performs the following operations to realize the digital signature [16]:

(1) Let $M = Z \parallel M$;
(2) Calculate $e = H_v (\overline{M})$ and convert e to an integer;
(3) Generate a random number k in the interval $[1, n-1]$, where n is the order of the base point G;
(4) Calculate $(x_1, y_1) = [k]G$, and convert x1 to an integer;
(5) Calculate $r = (e + x_1) \mod n$, if $r = 0$ or $r + k = n$, then return to step 3;
(6) Calculate $s = ((1 + d_A)^{-1} * (k - r * d)) \mod n$, if $s = 0$, return to step 3;
(7) Convert r and s to byte string, then the signature of message M is (r, s).

In order to verify the received message M' and (r', s'), the sign verifier user B also needs system parameters, $Z_A$ and $P_A$, then implement the following operations:

(1) Does r' belong to $[1, n - 1]$. If yes, proceed to the next step; otherwise, the verification fails;
(2) Does s' belong to $[1, n - 1]$. If yes, proceed to the next step; otherwise, the verification fails;
(3) Set $M' = Z \parallel M'$;
(4) Calculate $e' = H_v (\overline{M'})$, and convert e' to an integer;
(5) Convert r' and s' to integers, calculate $t = (r' + s') \mod n$, if $t = 0$, the verification fails;
(6) Calculate $(x_1', y_1') = [s'] G + [t] P_A$, and convert $x_1'$ to an integer;
(7) Calculate $R = (e + x_1') \mod n$, check whether R and r' are the same, if they are the same, the digital signature verification passes; otherwise, the verification fails.

The public key encryption algorithm means that the key used by the sender to encrypt data is the public key of the receiver, and the receiver needs to use its own private key to decrypt and restore the plaintext. When the message M needs to be encrypted, the encrypting user A first needs to obtain the elliptic curve system parameters and the public key $P_B$ of the recipient user B, and perform the following operations [17]:

(1) Generate a random number k in the interval $[1, N - 1]$, where N is the order of the elliptic curve point group;
(2) Calculate $C_1 = [k]G = (x_1, y_1)$, and convert the elliptic curve point $C_1$ into a bit string;
(3) Calculate $S = [h]PB$, where h is the cofactor of the order, judge whether S is the infinity point, and if so, exit with an error;
(4) Calculate the elliptic curve point $[k]P_B = (x_2, y_2)$, and convert the data types of $x_2$ and $x_2$ into bit strings;
(5) Calculate $t = KDF (x_2 \| y_2, klen)$, judge whether t is a string of all 0 bits, if so, return Step 1;
(6) Calculate $C_2 = M \oplus t$;
(7) Calculate $C_3 = Hash (x2 \| M \| y2)$, and finally get the ciphertext $C = C_1 \| C_2 \| C_3$.

After user B as the decryptor receives the ciphertext C, in order to decrypt the plaintext, the parameters of the elliptic curve system and B's own private key dB are required, and perform the following calculations [18]:

(1) Take out the $C_1$ part of the ciphertext, convert it to a point on the elliptic curve, and verify whether it satisfies Elliptic curve equation, if satisfied, proceed to the next step, otherwise exit with an error;
(2) Calculate the elliptic curve point $S = [h]C_1$, where h is the cofactor of the order, and judge whether S is infinite
    Stay far away, if yes, exit with an error;
(3) Calculate the elliptic curve point $[d_B]C1 = (x_2, y_2)$, and convert the data types of $x_2$ and $y_2$ into bit strings;
(4) Calculate $t = KDF d(x_2 \| y_2, klen)$, if t is a string of all 0 bits, exit with an error;
(5) Take out the bit string $C_2$ from C and calculate $M' = C_2 \oplus t$;
(6) Calculate $u = Hash (x_2 \| M' \| y_2)$, judge whether u is equal to $C_3$, if it is equal to $C_3$, get the plaintext $M'$, otherwise exit with an error.

## 4   Typical Applications

Combining with the main scenarios described in the "5G Network Slicing Enable Smart Grid" [19] issued by China Telecom, Huawei and State Grid, this article discusses the encryption problem of power Internet of Things under the scenario of low-voltage power consumption information collection, and gives a solution based on SM2 Plan and analyze its benefits.

### 4.1   Electricity Acquisition System

As shown in Fig. 2, It's a schematic diagram of the power acquisition system architecture. The access architecture. The power collection system is composed of three parts: power grid platform, data channel, and power terminal. It realizes real-time data collection of power grid and power meter, and completes time-of-use power billing statistics and energy balance. There are many communication methods to realize the transmission of power information, and narrowband communication technology is more commonly used. Through periodic collection, the continuous tracking of the power of important users is realized, and the power service capability is improved.

In the system architecture shown in Fig. 2, there are two practical requirements for security:

One is the problem of encrypted transmission, which requires encrypted transmission protection for the communication between the power grid platform and the power terminal to prevent information from being hijacked and maliciously modified during transmission.

The second is the identity authentication problem of a large number of terminals. Each terminal has a unique code to realize identity identification. However, the power terminal involves a large number of households, and the power grid platform needs to realize the identity authentication of the power terminal.

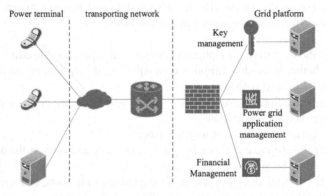

**Fig. 2.** Schematic diagram of power collection and transmission system architecture.

## 4.2 SM2-Based Encrypted Communication

Aiming at the identity authentication problem and encrypted transmission problem raised in the previous section, a SM2-based encrypted transmission scheme is proposed, which can simplify the exchange of digital certificates in the encryption process and make the encryption algorithm easier to deploy and apply.

Electricity data collection is mainly the communication between the electric meter terminal and the grid platform, which has the characteristics of many-to-one communication, that is, a large number of electric meter terminals communicate with the grid platform server. It is divided into two business modes. The first is initiated by the meter terminal and reports power data to the grid platform, which is mainly used for periodic power data reporting; the second is initiated by the power grid platform server and is mainly based on power data query Demand. The collection and transmission of power information is a two-way business, which can be encrypted using symmetric or asymmetric cryptographic algorithm methods. No matter which method is used, key management is a considerable problem. The two methods are analyzed separately as follows.

If the symmetric cipher algorithm uses a pre-shared key, the security of the meter terminal will have an excessive impact on the entire power grid because the keys of the two communicating parties are stored on the side of the meter. At the same time, each time the grid platform server needs to query the corresponding key according to the user's identity, it will bring an additional burden of identity authentication, and it is easy to form a denial of service attack of the grid platform server when a large number of power terminals communicate at the same time.

If an asymmetric cryptographic algorithm is used, the meter terminal needs to store the public key of the power supply station and its own private key, and the power grid platform stores its own private key and the public key of the user's meter. The meter terminal uses the public key of the power grid platform when reporting power data. With key encryption, the power grid platform uses its own private key to decrypt data; when the power grid platform sends data to the meter terminal, it uses the public keys of different meter terminals for encryption, and then the meter terminal uses its own private key to decrypt. Due to the asymmetry of the two-way channel between the electricity meter terminal and the grid platform server in the power communication, the amount of information transmitted by the electricity meter terminal to the server is significantly higher than the amount of data transmitted by the server to the power terminal. Therefore, the server does not decrypt the data. The need for key query can reduce the possibility of service being attacked by denial of service.

The above method solves the problem of information encrypted transmission, but there is still the problem of identity authentication. A large number of electric meter terminal meters use the public key of the power grid platform for transmission, and how to perform information identification is a problem that must be considered. To this end, a digital signature mechanism based on SM2 is further proposed. The main idea is that the meter terminal uses a hash algorithm to generate a message digest from the message during message transmission, and then uses its own private key to encrypt the digest. The summary sends the digital signature of the message and the message to the power grid platform server. The server uses the same hash algorithm to calculate the message summary from the received original message, and then uses the public key of the power terminal to match the message. The attached digital signature is decrypted. If the two digests are the same, the receiver can confirm that the message is from the sender [20].

The SM2-based information transmission mechanism is specifically as follows. Take power information reporting as an example, where the meter terminal is referred to as ET and the grid platform server is referred to as ES:

A1. KGC publishes system parameters, and generates ET public key private key and ES public key private key according to the user's power code;

A2. ET stores the personal private key and the public key of the power platform; ES stores the public key of the meter terminal and its own private key.

A3. ET establishes communication with ES. If it is the first data packet initialized, sign it, see the next step for details; otherwise, use ES public key encryption to obtain encrypted data packet EP, and send EP.

A4. ET uses SM3 to compress the message date. The message data only takes the user information code, and the message digest H = hash(date) is obtained after compression.

A5. ET uses its own private key to use SM2 signature algorithm to sign digest H to obtain signature information SP.

A5. ET attaches the signature information SP to the original information to form a combined data packet, encrypts it to obtain EP, and sends it.

A6. After ES receives the data EP, it uses its own private key to decrypt it, obtains the decrypted data packet DP, and starts the data packet counter to label the received data packet.

A7. If the DP is the first data packet, the combined data packet is obtained, the SP is extracted, the public key corresponding to the ET is calculated, the information to be signed and the signature are input, and SM2 is used to verify whether the signatures are consistent. If they are consistent, the identity is verified the identity of the card.

A8. After the communication ends, the counter of ES is cleared.

## 5 Experiment Analysis

In the hardware environment, as shown in Fig. 3, this article uses two hosts in the LAN to simulate ET and ES. The communication process between ET and ES is implemented using python socket. The transmission layer protocol uses TCP, and Socket is used to simulate the power information transmission between ET and ES. The transmission content is mainly user power code, power information, current time and other information. The encryption code of SM2 uses the GMSSL open-source package [21]. GMSSL is a python implementation of an open-source encryption package that supports SM2/SM3/SM4/SM9 and other national encryption algorithms.

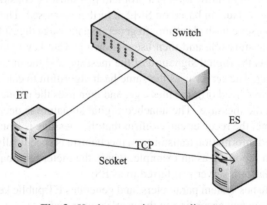

**Fig. 3.** Hardware environment diagram.

Through analysis, unencrypted information can easily cause information leakage and man-in-the-middle attacks in an open network environment. In the local area network environment, the man-in-the-middle attack test frameworks MITMF and Ettercap can be deployed on the third terminal to implement address spoofing technology to achieve session hijacking, which can easily achieve information tampering. However, after encrypting the transmitted information, the ET sends the encrypted data to the ES, which can realize the protection of the data information. In terms of fighting against middleman hijacking, the data is encrypted using the public key of ES, but it can only be decrypted at the ES platform server, and the middleman cannot perform correct decryption. This transmission can effectively ensure the security of information transmission.

In addition, the first data packet of each power user is the signature data, which plays the role of identity authentication. In this process, ET uses its own private key to encrypt the digest information to realize the signature. The ES end receives the signature and needs to use its own private key to decrypt the information. Encoding of ET, and then calculating the public key of ET, there is a problem of ES end response when a large number of users access, but because ES end only verifies the first data packet of each ET, subsequent communication is no longer verified, so ES is also reduced. The response pressure forms the protection of ES.

## 6 Conclusion

The power Internet of Things is the focus of the construction of the power industry. It opens up the originally isolated power equipment network, realizes the communication series of a large number of equipment, builds the information channel of the traditional industry, and improves the operation efficiency of the power system. This article combines the development characteristics of the power Internet of Things, carries out a security analysis of the interconnection and intercommunication of power, combines the calculation points of the national secret algorithm, discusses its application in the power Internet of things industry, and presents the encryption between the SM2-based power terminal and the grid platform server. The communication mode solves security issues such as identity authentication and encrypted transmission, and provides reference ideas for industry research and industrial production. The future work has two aspects. One is to expand the application of encrypted communication in other power business scenarios to further improve the security of the power grid; on the other hand, the current mechanism is only based on the business characteristics of power transmission, and the first data packet is used for identity authentication. In other businesses, the optimization of the number of identity authentication can be studied, and the next step is to seek effective methods to enhance identity authentication under the premise of controlling ES pressure.

## References

1. Fang, X., Misra, S., Xue, G., Yang, D.: Smart grid-the new and improved power grid: a survey. IEEE Commun. Surv. Tutor. **14**(4), 944–980 (2012)
2. Aoufi, S., Derhab, A., Guerroumi, M.: Survey of false data injection in smart power grid: attacks, countermeasures and challenges. J. Inf. Secur. Appl. **54**, 2214–2226 (2020)
3. Yang, W., Mao, W., Zhang, J., Zou, J.: Narrowband wireless access for low-power massive internet of things: a bandwidth perspective. IEEE Wirel. Commun. **24**(3), 138–145 (2017)

4. Kimani, K., Oduol, V., Langat, K.: Cyber security challenges for IoT-based smart grid networks. Int. J. Crit. Infrastruct. Prot. **25**, 36–49 (2019)
5. Shrestha, M., Johansen, C., Noll, J., Roverso, D.: A methodology for security classification applied to smart grid infrastructures. Int. J. Crit. Infrastruct. Protect. **28** (2020)
6. Wang, Y., Wu, L., Yun, Y.: Security authentication method of terminal trusted access in smart grid. Int. J. Secur. Appl. **9**(7), 337–346 (2015)
7. Sun, H., Guo, Q., Zhang, B., Wu, W.: "Integrated energy management system: concept, design, and demonstration in China. IEEE Electrif. Mag. **6**(2), 42–50 (2018)
8. Lu, Q., Cui, W.: Research on security monitoring and analysis technology of ubiquitous power internet of things germinal layer. Inf. Technol. **44**(2), 121–125 (2020)
9. Li, P.Z., Xiao, Z.F., Chen, Z.W.: The research on communication technology matching of power terminal communication access network. Procedia Comput. Sci. **155**, 785–790 (2019)
10. Luo, Z., Xie, J.H., Gu, W.: Development of power grid information security support platform based on SM2 cryptosystem. Autom. Electric Power Syst. **38**(6), 68–74 (2014)
11. Tong, W.: The research of the SM2, SM3 and SM4 algorithms in WLAN of transformer substation. In: 3rd International Conference on Electronic Information Technology and Computer Engineering (EITCE), pp. 276–283 (2019)
12. Tian, C., Wang, L., Li, M.: Design and implementation of SM9 Identity based cryptograph algorithm. In: 2020 International Conference on Computer Network, Electronic and Automation (ICCNEA), pp. 96–100 (2020)
13. Ding, F., Long, Y., Wu, P.: Study on secret sharing for SM2 digital signature and its application. In: 14th International Conference on Computational Intelligence and Security (CIS), pp. 205–209 (2018)
14. Yang, A.: Provably-secure (Chinese government) SM2 and simplified SM2 key exchange protocols. Sci. World J. (2014)
15. National cryptography authority, SM2 elliptic curve public key cryptography algorithm, pp. 65–68 (2010). https://www.oscca.gov.cn/sca/xwdt/2020-12/08/content_1060792.shtml
16. Wang, Z., Zhang, Z.: Overview on public key cryptographic algorithm SM2 based on elliptic curves. J. Inf. Secur. Res. **16**(5), 12–17 (2016)
17. Wang, Z.H., Zhang, Z.F.: Overview of SM2 elliptic curve public key cryptography algorithm. Inf. Secur. Res. **2**(11), 972–982 (2016)
18. Bai, L., Zhang, Y., Yang, G.: SM2 cryptographic algorithm based on discrete logarithm problem and prospect. In: 2012 2nd International Conference on Consumer Electronics, Communications and Networks (CECNet), pp. 1294–1297 (2012)
19. Xia, X.: A survey on 5G network slicing enabling the smart grid. In: 2019 IEEE 25th International Conference on Parallel and Distributed Systems (ICPADS), pp. 911–916 (2019)
20. Hong, X., Zheng: A security framework for internet of things based on SM2 cipher algorithm. In: 2013 International Conference on Computational and Information Sciences, pp. 13–16 (2013)
21. Guo, Q., Ke, Z., Wang, S., Zheng, S.: Persistent fault analysis against SM4 implementations in libraries Crypto++ and GMSSL. IEEE Access **9**, 63636–63645 (2021)

# Mobile Terminal Security Protection Method Based on Community Detection Algorithms and Graph Matching Networks

Mu Chen[1,2(✉)], Zaojian Dai[1,2], Yong Li[1,2], Juling Zhang[3], Sheng Wang[3], Jian Zhou[4], and Fan Wu[5]

[1] Institute of Information and Communication, Global Energy Interconnection Research Institute, Nanjing 210003, China
chenmu@geiri.sgcc.com.cn
[2] State Grid Key Laboratory of Information and Network Security, Nanjing 210003, China
[3] Electric Power Research Institute of State Grid Sichuan, Chengdu 610041, China
[4] State Grid Sichuan Electric Power Company, Chengdu 610041, China
[5] Computer Science Department, Tuskegee University, Tuskegee, AL 36088, USA

**Abstract.** The rapid growth in the number of malware apps poses a great danger to users of power mobile terminals. Among smart devices, devices using the Android system are very popular and thus are easy targets for malware attacks. In this paper, we propose a mobile terminal security protection method based on community detection algorithms and graph matching networks. First, the call relationships between functions are extracted from the decompiled APK files, and runtime information is collected as a supplement to complete the construction of the behavior graph. Second, based on the behavior graph of malware samples, we propose a method to extract the public behavior graph as the features of malware families. Finally, a graph matching network is used to learn and calculate the similarity between the public behavior graph and the software behavior graph, and use it as the basis for detection. Our evaluation of the dataset containing 1274 malware apps and 108 benign apps shows that the selected public behavior graph is effective for Android malware detection, with an overall accuracy of 90.4%. The experimental results show that the method has a high detection rate and a low false rate, and can detect malware and its variants.

**Keywords:** Community detection algorithms · Common behavior graph · Graph matching networks

## 1 Introduction

As an important infrastructure related to the country's livelihood, industrial control systems in key areas such as the power industry have always been the focus of cyber attacks and are easily become the main target of cyber warfare. Therefore, it is necessary to strengthen the security protection of power mobile terminals. Among the mainstream smartphone operating systems, Android has become the world's number one smartphone operating system in just a few years due to its powerful functions. However, driven by economic interests, malicious attacks against Android terminals emerge endlessly. It will seriously infringe the legitimate rights and interests of users and bring huge losses to users.

The graph matching network is the same as the ordinary graph neural network (GNN), which is composed of an encoder, a propagation layer, and an aggregator. The encoder maps the characteristics of nodes and edges to the initial vector of nodes and edges through a separate multi-layer perceptron. The aggregator is used to use the aggregation function to calculate the aggregate information of all nodes and embed it in a new vector space to represent the whole graph, but the graph matching network (GMN) [1] uses an attention-based cross-graph matching mechanism. In the process of node feature propagation, the cross information between the two graphs is used, and the graph pairs are jointly inferred to calculate the similarity coefficient between the graphs. The graph matching network has been proved effective in different fields, including the learning of graph edit distance and the challenging function similarity search based on the control flow graph.

On the Android platform, more than 86% of Android malware samples are applications repackaged by injecting malicious components into legitimate applications [2]. Therefore, the family characteristics of malware can be used to speed up the analysis and identification of malware. It is very important to accurately separate malicious behavior from normal behavior. However, the injected malicious components are hidden in the functions of popular applications and usually only occupy a small part of the application. Existing methods are difficult to distinguish between malicious behavior and normal behavior of malware.

To detect Android malware, many detection methods have been proposed. According to the technology used, these methods can be divided into three categories: static analysis technology, dynamic analysis technology, and analysis technology based on deep learning. The static analysis method can analyze the code and resources of the entire App, so it can achieve a high code coverage, and there is no need to set up an execution environment, and the computational overhead is relatively low. However, since the application program is not executed, the real execution path and related execution context cannot be obtained well, and the code obfuscation and dynamic code loading cannot be handled well. Dynamic analysis is to analyze the malicious behavior of the App according to its runtime behavior. It can analyze the dynamic code loading and code obfuscation that static technology cannot handle, but there are problems such as low code coverage, long analysis time, and low efficiency. The basic principle of the deep learning-based malware detection method is to extract different features to describe the different behaviors of the sample to be analyzed through techniques such as program analysis, and then use existing deep learning algorithms to train samples with known labels and build a classifier. However, most of the existing feature extraction directly analyzes the software itself, resulting in that the features based on the string form are easily tampered with by the existing obfuscation technology, and deep learning itself is a black box method with poor interpretability.

We propose a mobile terminal security protection method based on community detection algorithms and graph matching networks, which can automatically detect known malware and its variants. In the method in this paper, first, decompile the Android application, build a function call graph (FCG), and then collect runtime information to supplement the graph. We also propose a method for extracting public behavior graphs from malware of known families, using the public behavior graphs as the characteristics of the family. Finally, we use graph matching networks to learn and calculate the similarity between software behavior graphs and public behavior graphs.

The rest of this paper is organized as follows: Sect. 2 introduces the research related to malware detection and classification. Section 3 gives an overview of the proposed method. Section 4 elaborates on the method used. Section 5 conducts experimental analysis to test the effect of the method, and Sect. 6 summarizes.

## 2 Related Work

In the past few years, there has been a lot of research work on Android malware analysis. There are many variants or new malware in the real world. Therefore, researchers have proposed many methods, which are divided into the following three categories in this paper. Jaiteg Singh et al. [3] found that static detection is the most widely researched topic in Android malware research, while there is also research focusing on behavioral and structural analysis and more research currently employing machine learning techniques.

### 2.1  Static Detection Method

The static detection method is the earliest proposed method to detect Android malware. Pagnchakneat C. Ouk et al. [4] used a selection algorithm to extract a small set of unique and effective features from applications and native libraries that can detect malware applications quickly and with high detection rates. El et al. [5] realized the machine learning model based on binary feature selection, used the secondary feature selection method of " Principle Component Analysis-Information Gain " to screen the extracted features, selected the lowest number of features more related to the classification results to shorten the classification time, improve the learning accuracy and improve the performance of the classifier. Fan et al. [6] used a community detection algorithm to divide and extract sensitive subgraphs after constructing a sensitive API call graph. The sensitive subgraphs used by most samples in a family were defined as frequent subgraphs of a particular family. Finally, SVM, Algorithms such as decision tree and KNN divide the software. Ge et al. [7] proposed AMDroid, which uses the function call graph representing APK behavior, decomposes each function call graph into root subgraphs by using the graph kernel, generates the graph embedding vector by using the extended model of doc2vec. The classifier uses machine learning algorithms such as SVM, LR, RF, and KNN.

### 2.2  Dynamic Detection Method

To solve the problem that the static detection method will be affected by code confusion, reflection, and other technologies, which will reduce the detection efficiency, the dynamic detection method is proposed. Massarelli et al. [8] obtained the resource consumption index from the proc file system, extracted features from the time series through detrended fluctuation analysis and correlation, used mutual information and principal component analysis to filter out redundant information, and finally adopted an SVM classifies malware into families. This method can collect information on physical equipment without being affected by evasion techniques. Jaiswal et al. [9] established an automatic detection system for Android malicious game software based on system call analysis. According to the frequency that some system calls are called by benign and malicious software programs, the applications are classified as benign or malicious. Taheri et al. [10] analyzed the sequence relationship in the API call collaboration, and appended the network flow characteristics to the extracted API call characteristics, and sent them to the random forest classification model for malware detection, malware classification, and malware Family classification. This method introduces the n-gram concept of natural language processing, and the extraction of the API call mode will not be affected by the sequence of operation tasks requested by the malware.

### 2.3  Detection Methods Based on Deep Learning

With the development of deep learning in recent years, detection methods based on deep learning have been proposed. Zhangjie Fu et al. [11] used static and dynamic analysis techniques to build and train LSTM-based models on samples and constructed a generative adversarial network to generate enhanced examples with 86.5% classification accuracy on real data for new malicious samples. Sohail Khan et al. [12] argue that the translation invariance of popular models of convolutional neural networks (CNNs) in general leaves the true potential of deep learning in this area unrealized, and therefore applies CapsNets to malware analysis. Huizhong Sun et al. [13] extracted multidimensional temporal distribution features, multidimensional word pair correlation features, and multidimensional word frequency distribution features based on statistical analysis to form a feature matrix and built a neural network-based multidimensional temporal distribution model for detecting overall abnormal behaviors within a given time window. Xiao et al. [14] converted Dalvik bytecode into RGB image and input it into the convolutional neural network for classification, and achieved high accuracy and recall. This method will not be affected by the obfuscation technology, but it is inefficient to convert the entire Dalvik bytecode into an RGB image, and it cannot be ruled out that the normal part of the malware sample is affected.

## 3  Proposed Methods

### 3.1  Construction of Behavior Graph

We use the Androguard tool to decompile the APK and generate a function call graph. Subsequently, all Intent call methods are searched. Since there are several attributes used to represent the caller and target in these Intent call methods, we can add an edge to the function call graph by identifying the caller and information transfer target based on these attributes.

Currently, both normal developers and malicious attackers use various encryption or obfuscation techniques to prevent their software from being reverse-analyzed, which can result in incomplete or erroneous information during static analysis. For example, malware can make Intent calls implicitly in the code or obfuscate strings in the Intent calls. Therefore, we also use the collection of runtime information as supplementary information to improve the basic behavior graph generated by static analysis.

We simulate user actions by injecting thousands of pseudo-random events (such as touch events) into the Monkeyrunner tool and execute the Android application in the emulator. The hooking technique is used to get the runtime Intent call information. We use a context-based approach to determine whether the obtained edge already exists in the basic behavior graph: if the captured Intent calls are sent by the same method to the same target, the call in the basic behavior graph is replaced with this call, otherwise, a new edge is created.

Kymie's [15] study of software behavior models showed that a sequence of at least 6 steps of calls is required to discriminate the behavior of software, and many subgraphs with fewer nodes appear when the behavior graph is drawn, so we remove isolated subgraphs (subgraphs with no edges connected to other subgraphs) with less than 6 nodes.

### 3.2 Extraction of Public Behavior Graphs

This section introduces the key technique proposed in this work: the public behavior graph extraction method for malware, which is divided into two steps: community detection and weight-based public behavior extraction.

**Community Detection.** Community is the basic structure existing in various networks and one of the most important characteristics of the network. Finding the community structure in the network is a key step to deeply understanding the network structure. Community detection is to gather the nodes in the graph into groups so that the edge density in groups is higher than that between groups. In the behavior graph, the nodes divided into the same group have strong connections, and they often realize some functions together.

Newman and Girvan first proposed the concept of modularity Q to quantify the quality of the detected community structure. When the Q value is close to 0, it means that the community structure can not be found, and when Q is close to 1, it means that the ideal community structure is obtained. In this paper, Louvain is selected as the community discovery algorithm used in the experiment.

The modularity (Q) [16] can be defined as

$$Q(C) = \frac{1}{2m} \sum \left[ A_{ij} - \frac{k_i k_j}{2m} \right] \delta(c(i), c(j)) \tag{1}$$

where $A_{ij}$ is the weight of the edge between node $i$ and node $j$, $c(i)$ is the community to which node $i$ is assigned, and $\delta(c(i), c(j))$ is the Kronecker $\delta$-function, which is 1 if nodes $i$ and $j$ belong to the same community and 0 otherwise. $k_i$ and $k_j$ are the sum of the weights of the edges connected to nodes $i$ and $j$, respectively, and $m$ is the sum of the weights of all edges in the graph.

**Weight-Based Public Behavior Extraction.** Considering that most of the subgraphs classified by the community detection algorithm are not related to malicious behaviors and are not helpful for malware detection, we propose a method to extract public behaviors from the graph.

In this paper, we take S = {G1, G2,…, Gm} as the set of behavior graphs of malware belonging to the same family that has been processed by the community detection algorithms and denote the ith malware behavior graph in the set S by Gi. These behavior graphs have been processed by the community detection algorithms and are divided into multiple subgraphs.

In this paper, s = {$G_1$, $G_2$,…, $G_m$} is taken as the behavior graph set of malware belonging to the same family processed by the community discovery algorithm, and $G_i$ is used to represent the $i_{th}$ malware behavior graph in the set S. These behavior graphs have been processed by the community discovery algorithm and are divided into multiple subgraphs.

The main idea of extracting common behavior graph is as follows: firstly, we create a weight with an initial value of 1 for each edge of each behavior graph in S. We find the common subgraph of $G_i$ and every other graph in S. Each time we find them, we add 1 to the weights of all edges belonging to the common subgraph in $G_i$. Second, we divide the weights of the edges by | S | to scale them between 0 and 1. Then calculate the weight of subgraphs according to the weight of edges, delete unimportant subgraphs, and merge all remaining subgraphs. Finally, delete unimportant edges.

To filter the unimportant behaviors in $G_i$, we design a method to remove subgraphs and edges. The average weight of the edges in the subgraph is used as the weight of the subgraph, and this is used to evaluate the importance of the subgraph. The formula for calculating the weight of subgraph $g_{ik}$ is shown in (2):

$$W_{g_{ik}} = \sum_{e_l \in E_{ij}} W_{e_l} / |E_{ij}| \tag{2}$$

In Eq. (2), $W_{g_{ik}}$ is the weight of $g_{ik}$, $E_{ij}$ is the set of edges of $g_{ik}$, $e_l$ is the lth edge in $E_{ij}$, $W_{e_l}$ is the weight of $e_l$, and $|E_{ij}|$ is the number of edges in $E_{ij}$.

In this paper, the average weight of subgraphs is used as the threshold for deleting subgraphs. After processing all the behavior graphs, the behavior graphs are merged into one graph. If there are the same edges during merging, the weights of the edges are added. Finally, the average weight of the graph is calculated in the form of similar Eq. (2), and the edges with weight less than the average weight are deleted from the remaining subgraphs to generate a common behavior graph. If a single node has no edges connected, this node is deleted together.

### 3.3  Graph Matching Based Detection Method

We use graph matching networks to calculate the similarity between the behavior graph of the software to be detected and the public behavior graph. The graph matching network is composed of an encoder, propagation layer, and aggregator. The encoder maps the characteristics of nodes and edges to the initial vectors of nodes and edges through a separate multi-layer perceptron. The aggregator is used to calculate the aggregation information of all nodes by using the aggregation function and embed it into a new vector space to represent the whole graph.

The encoder is composed of two separate MLPs, which map the node and edge features to the initial node and edge vector respectively. The structure is shown in Fig. 1.

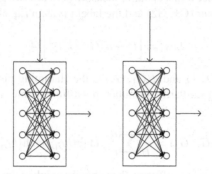

**Fig. 1.** Structure of the encoder.

The propagation layer structure is shown in Fig. 2, which is composed of multiple MLPs and a Gru network to jointly calculate the information between graph pairs and update the representation of nodes.

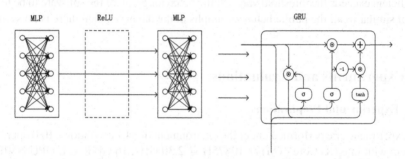

**Fig. 2.** Structure of the propagation layers.

The aggregator is similar to the encoder structure, but it also transforms node representations and then uses a weighted sum with gating vectors to aggregate across nodes.

The graph matching network (GMN) jointly computes the similarity score of a pair of graphs. The representation of a graph pair is calculated jointly over the pair by a cross-graph attention matching-based mechanism. Specifically, the graph matching network model can be expressed as Eq. (3).

$$d(G_1, G_2) = d_H \left( embed_{match(G_1, G_2)} \right) \qquad (3)$$

where $embed\_match(G_1, G_2)$ computes the embedding and matching between $G_1$ and $G_2$ and returns the vector representation of the two graphs. The graph matching network model is based on this to calculate the similarity coefficient between the two graphs.

The graph matching network takes a pair of graphs as input. To train the network, we use a general behavior graph (GBG) and a common behavior graph (CBG) as inputs. If the GBG and CBG belong to the same family, the label "1" is used to indicate similarity, and if they do not belong to the same family, the label "−1" is used to indicate dissimilarity. We use Hamming distance as the distance measure between two graphs, the loss function when given the graph pair (G1, G2) and the label t is as in Eq. (4).

$$Loss = \left[ (t - d(G_1, G_2))^2 \right] / 4 \tag{4}$$

where the label $t \in \{-1, 1\}$ and $d(G_1, G_2)$ is the Hamming distance between G1 and G2. Since the Hamming similarity formula is not differentiable, an approximate formula is used.

$$d(G_1, G_2) = \frac{1}{H} \sum_{i=1}^{H} \tanh\left(h_{G_1 i}\right) \tanh\left(h_{G_2 i}\right) \tag{5}$$

When detecting unknown software, the behavior graph of the software to be detected is fed into the completed training graph matching network together with a public behavior graph in the database, and if the obtained similarity coefficient exceeds the threshold value of the family, the software to be detected is determined to be a security risk; if the obtained similarity coefficient is lower than the threshold value, the comparison with other public behavior graphs in the database continues until the obtained similarity coefficient exceeds the threshold value. If the behavior graph of the software to be tested is not similar to all the public behavior graphs in the database, then there is no security risk.

## 4   Experiments and Evaluations

### 4.1   Experimental Preparations

All experiments are performed under the environment of 64-bit Windows 10.0 operating system with Intel(R) Core (TM) i7-10875H @ 2.30 GHz, 16 GB RAM, GPU NVIDIA GeForce RTX2060.

The experimental dataset is mainly from the Drebin dataset [17]. Since the number of malicious samples under some families is too small to meet the need of extracting public behavior graphs, four families with a high number of malware apps are selected as experimental data. The chosen family names are BaseBridge, DroidKungFu, FakeInstaller, and Plankton, and 108 normal software (downloaded from the official software mall).

### 4.2   Performance Measure

To evaluate the performance of the method proposed in this paper, we apply six performance measures: recall, false-negative rate, precision, false-positive rate, Accuracy, and F-measure. These measures are based on True Positive (TP), False Positive (FP), True Negative (TN), and False Negative (FN) values. The definition of each one is below.

Recall: proportion of malware correctly detected in all malware:

$$recall = TP/(TP + FN) \tag{6}$$

False-negative rate (FNR): proportion of malware detected incorrectly in all malware.:

$$FNR = FN/(TP + FN) \tag{7}$$

precision: proportion of the number of normal software correctly detected in all normal software:

$$precision = TN/(TN + FP) \tag{8}$$

False-positive rate: proportion of normal software detected incorrectly in all benign software:

$$FPR = FP/(TN + FP) \tag{9}$$

Accuracy: proportion of the number of software correctly detected in all software:

$$accuracy = (TP + TN)/(TP + TN + FP + FN) \tag{10}$$

F-measure: weighted harmonic average of accuracy rate and recall rate:

$$F - measure = 2 * precision * recall/(precision + recall) \tag{11}$$

### 4.3 Experiments and Analysis

To verify the effectiveness of the method proposed in this paper, we use a mixture of malicious and normal samples for detection, and the specific distribution of samples is shown in Table 1.

The training set of each family is used for the extraction of the public behavior graph and the training and verification of the graph matching network. The rest is used as test samples to detect the performance of the method.

When building the behavior graph for APKs, we used a mix of static and dynamic approaches. We first extract the function call graph, then install the software in the emulator, simulate user actions by injecting thousands of pseudo-random events (e.g. touch events) into the Monkeyrunner tool, and refine the behavior graph by capturing the intent calls using hook techniques.

**Table 1.** Experimental sample distribution

| Family | Training set | Testing set | |
| --- | --- | --- | --- |
| | | Malware | Normal software |
| BaseBridge | 50 | 211 | 108 |
| DroidKungFu | 50 | 289 | |
| FakeInstaller | 50 | 374 | |
| Plankton | 50 | 546 | |

As can be seen from Table 2, there is little difference between the size of the public behavior graph and the original behavior graph, but it only needs to be calculated once when calculating the similarity, which does not need to be calculated with all samples, which can significantly improve the calculation speed.

**Table 2.** Comparison of public behavior graphs with corresponding behavior graphs.

| Family | Public behavior graph | | Normal behavior graph | |
| --- | --- | --- | --- | --- |
| | Number of nodes | Number of edges | The average number of nodes | The average number of edges |
| BaseBridge | 1554 | 4254 | 1435.4 | 2978.3 |
| DroidKungFu | 4843 | 14875 | 4473.5 | 10988.4 |
| FakeInstaller | 422 | 943 | 294.6 | 521.3 |
| Plankton | 4471 | 12238 | 6954.9 | 17632.9 |

When training the graph matching network, this paper uses the word2vec model to convert the node information into a 100-dimensional vector and uses the One-Hot encoding to convert the feature information of the edges in the graph into a vector representation according to the type of edges. When inputting the graphs into the network, the label of malware in the same family is set to "1", indicating similarity, and malware not in the same family is set to "−1", indicating dissimilarity.

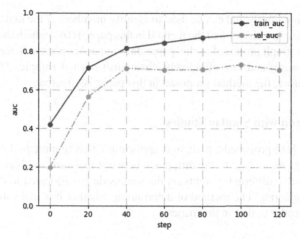

**Fig. 3.** Curve of accuracy change during training.

As shown in Fig. 3, the training is stopped when each performance curve of the graph matching network no longer has significant changes in a longer period. To find the threshold value for judging whether the sample to be detected is malware, we use the model to calculate the similarity between all behavior graphs in the training set and the public behavior graph corresponding to them, and for each family, the smallest similarity is taken as the judgment threshold for that family.

Table 3 shows the detection results under the method of this paper. Taking the Base-Bridge family as an example, a total of 261 samples were used, of which 50 were used for extracting the public behavior graph for extraction and training and validation of the graph matching network, and 211 were used for evaluating the method proposed in this paper. When detected, 33 BaseBridge malware were missed (FN = 33) and no normal software was misidentified (FP = 0). Therefore, the recall rate of BaseBridge family classification is 178/211 = 84.4%, the accuracy rate is 100%, and the F-measure is (2*84.4%*100%)/(84.4% + 100%) = 91.5%.

**Table 3.** Malware detection results

| Family | Recall | FNR | Precision | FPR | Accuracy | F-measure |
|---|---|---|---|---|---|---|
| BaseBridge | 84.4% | 15.6% | 100% | 0% | – | 91.5% |
| DroidKungFu | 87.5% | 12.5% | | | – | 93.4% |
| FakeInstaller | 89.8% | 10.2% | | | – | 94.6% |
| Plankton | 92.9% | 7.1% | | | – | 96.3% |
| #total | 89.7% | 10.3% | 100% | 0% | 90.4% | 94.5% |

In Table 3, the method can effectively detect malware, indicating that the public behavior graph proposed in this paper can effectively contain the behavioral features of the corresponding family and can be used to identify members of the malware family. In addition, the false-positive rate of the method in this paper is 0%, which indicates that the public behavior graph proposed in this paper does not contain more behavioral features of normal software, and can effectively distinguish normal samples from malicious samples. Therefore, the method proposed in this paper is effective.

### 4.4 Comparison with Similar Studies

Jun Guan et al. [18] proposed a malicious application detection method based on sensitive API pairing. According to the difference between malware and benign software in sensitive API calls, different weights on the same side are allocated to detect Android malicious applications. The method of determining whether it is malware according to the weight is similar to that in this paper.

**Table 4.** Comparison of CBG-match and API-match test results

| Name | Measure | | | | | |
|---|---|---|---|---|---|---|
| API-match | TP | FP | TN | FN | Accuracy | F-Score |
| | 1294 | 11 | 97 | 126 | 91.0% | 90.4% |
| | Recall | FNR | Precision | FPR | | |
| | 91.1% | 8.8% | 89.8% | 10.2% | | |
| CBG-match | TP | FP | TN | FN | Accuracy | F-Score |
| | 1274 | 0 | 108 | 146 | 90.4% | 91.5% |
| | Recall | FNR | Precision | FPR | | |
| | 89.7% | 10.3% | 100% | 0 | | |

In Table 4, API-match represents the method proposed by Guan Jun and others, and CBG-match represents the method proposed in this paper. To objectively evaluate the performance of these two methods, when we detect the API match method, the data set selected to participate in API feature extraction is the malware and another 200 normal software (downloaded from the official software mall) used by the CBG match method to extract the public behavior graph in this paper, but. As can be seen from Table 4, the detection rate of the CBG-match method is slightly lower than that of the API-match method, and the false alarm rate is lower than that of the API-match method. The overall performance is the same as that of the API-match method.

From Table 4, we can see that the overall performance of the CBG-match method is the same as that of the API-match method, but the false detection rate is much lower than that of the API-match method. The main reason is that the behavior diagram used by the CBG-match method for matching is more strict, which ensures that some normal software with similar behavior to malware will not be misjudged. For such normal software, the API match method is only a way to match API pairs, which is easy to be false-checked.

When the method in this paper detects malware apps, there is still some malware that can not be found. It may be that some variants only appear in the verification set but not in the training set, resulting in the failure of the public behavior graph to include the behavior characteristics of these malicious samples, which makes some test samples unable to match with the public behavior graph.

## 5 Conclusion

We propose a new Android malware detection method that uses runtime information to complete the construction of behavior graph and propose a method to extract public behavior graph, which takes the public behavior graph as the feature of the malware family. In our experiment, 1274 (89.7%) of 1420 malware were correctly classified, and there was no false detection in 108 evaluated benign applications. This shows that the public behavior graph in this paper can accurately represent the behavior of the malware family.

Although this method uses dynamic information to improve the results of static analysis, it still has some limitations. For example, for malware that can find itself running in a monitored environment to hide malicious behavior, the strategy of dynamically supplementing information may fail. These problems are also the direction of our future research.

**Acknowledgment.** This work is supported by the science and technology project of State Grid Corporation of China Funding Item: "Research on Dynamic Access Authentication and Trust Evaluation Technology of Power Mobile Internet Services Based on Zero Trust" (Grand No. 5700-202158183A-0-0-00).

**Conflicts of Interest.** The authors declare that they have no conflicts of interest to report regarding the present study.

## References

1. Li, Y., Gu, C., Dullien, T., Vinyals, O., Kohli, P.: Graph matching networks for learning the similarity of graph structured objects. arXiv:1904.12787 (2019)
2. Zhou, Y., Jiang, X.: Dissecting android malware: characterization and evolution. In: 2012 IEEE Symposium on Security and Privacy, pp. 95–109. IEEE, San Francisco (2012)
3. Singh, J., Gera, T., Ali, F., Thakur, D., Singh, K., Kwak, K.: Understanding research trends in android malware research using information modelling techniques. Comput. Mater. Continua **66**, 2655–2670 (2021)
4. Ouk, C., Pak, P.: Unified detection of obfuscated and native android malware. Comput. Mater. Continua **70**, 3099–3116 (2022)
5. Fiky, A.H.E., Elshenawy, A., Madkour, M.A.: Detection of android malware using machine learning. In: 2021 international mobile, Intelligent, and Ubiquitous Computing Conference (MIUCC), pp. 9–16. IEEE (2021)
6. Fan, M., et al.: Android malware familial classification and representative sample selection via frequent subgraph analysis. IEEE Trans. Inform. Forensic Secur **13**, 1890–1905 (2018)

7. Ge, X., Pan, Y., Fan, Y., Fang, C.: AMDroid: android malware detection using function call graphs. In: 2019 IEEE 19th International Conference on Software Quality, Reliability and Security Companion (QRS-C), pp. 71–77. IEEE, Sofia (2019)

8. Massarelli, L., Aniello, L., Ciccotelli, C., Querzoni, L., Ucci, D., Baldoni, R.: Android malware family classification based on resource consumption over time. In: 2017 12th International Conference on Malicious and Unwanted Software (MALWARE), pp. 31–38. IEEE, Fajardo (2017)

9. Jaiswal, M., Malik, Y., Jaafar, F.: Android gaming malware detection using system call analysis. In: 2018 6th International Symposium on Digital Forensic and Security (ISDFS), pp. 1–5. IEEE, Antalya (2018)

10. Taheri, L., Kadir, A.F.A., Lashkari, A.H.: Extensible android malware detection and family classification using network-flows and api-calls. In: 2019 International Carnahan Conference on Security Technology (ICCST), pp. 1–8. IEEE, CHENNAI, India (2019)

11. Fu, Z., Ding, Y., Godfrey, M.: An lstm-based malware detection using transfer learning. J. Cyber Secur. **3**, 11–28 (2021)

12. Khan, S., Nauman, M., Ali Alsaif, S., Ali Syed, T., Ahmad Eleraky, H.: Using capsule networks for android malware detection through orientation-based features. Comput. Mater. Continua **70**, 5345–5362 (2022)

13. Sun, H., Xu, G., Yu, H., Ma, M., Guo, Y., Quan, R.: Malware detection based on multidimensional time distribution features. J. Quant. Comput. **3**(2), 55 (2021)

14. Xiao, X., Yang, S.: An image-inspired and cnn-based android malware detection approach. In: 2019 34th IEEE/ACM International Conference on Automated Software Engineering (ASE), pp. 1259–1261. IEEE, San Diego (2019)

15. Tan, K.M.C., Maxion, R.A.: Determining the operational limits of an anomaly-based intrusion detector. IEEE J. Select. Areas Commun. **21**, 96–110 (2003)

16. Blondel, V.D., Guillaume, J.L., Lambiotte, R., Lefebvre, E.: Fast unfolding of communities in large networks. J. Stat. Mech. **2008**, P10008 (2008)

17. Arp, D., Spreitzenbarth, M., Hübner, M., Gascon, H., Rieck, K.: Drebin: effective and explainable detection of android malware in your pocket. In: Proceedings 2014 Network and Distributed System Security Symposium. Internet Society, San Diego (2014)

18. Jun, G., Huiying, M.L., Baolei, J.X.: API-based pairing for Android malicious application detection. J. Northwest. Polytech. Univ. **38**, 965–970 (2020)

# A Method of Firmware Vulnerability Mining and Verification Based on Code Property Graph

Na Xiao[1], Jing Zeng[1], Qigui Yao[2(✉)], and Xiuli Huang[2]

[1] Platform Operation and Security Department, Information and Telecommunication Company, Beijing 100000, China
[2] State Grid Key Laboratory of Information and Network Security, Global Energy Interconnection Research Institute Co. Ltd., Nanjing 210000, China
yaoqigui@geiri.sgcc.com.cn

**Abstract.** With the rapid development of smart power grid, the security of intelligent terminal has been widely concerned. Firmware is the core component of intelligent terminal equipment, and its vulnerability has become one of the main threats to intelligent terminal security. However, the difficulty of obtaining firmware, extracting binary files and analyzing code bring a series of difficulties to firmware vulnerability mining, resulting in low accuracy and high false positive rate of vulnerability mining. Therefore, this paper proposes a firmware vulnerability mining method based on code property graph. First, generate the code property graph of the target program; secondly, abstract syntax tree, control flow graph and data dependency graph are extracted from code property graph. Then the traversal analysis of these three graphs gradually reduces the scope of the vulnerability; Finally, combined with manual analysis and review, the results of vulnerability mining are obtained. In this paper, joern tool is used to verify the DVRF project, mining stack overflow vulnerability, heap overflow vulnerability, command injection vulnerability and heap release vulnerability, and good experimental results are obtained.

**Keywords:** Firmware · Code property graph · Static analysis · Vulnerability mining

## 1 Introduction

As the product of the deep integration of energy system and internet technology, Energy Internet (EI) [1] has been well constructed. Distribution terminals, intelligent fusion terminals and other smart terminals are widely used in power system energy interconnection, it has become an important part of the power system, which supports the full-scale operation state perception, wide-area intelligent cooperative control and natural man-machine interaction [2]. With the increase of the number of intelligent terminals deployed, the location of deployment is extensive [3], and the intelligence of terminals is enhanced. In order to ensure the communication efficiency, the communication protocol of terminals is relatively simple, and the security control of intelligent terminals is more difficult.

© The Author(s), under exclusive license to Springer Nature Switzerland AG 2022
X. Sun et al. (Eds.): ICAIS 2022, CCIS 1588, pp. 543–556, 2022.
https://doi.org/10.1007/978-3-031-06764-8_42

In recent years, the network attacks launched by intelligent terminals are frequent, and the damage caused by the attacks is increasing obviously. In 2017, foreign countries discovered the malicious software aimed at substation intelligent terminals [4], which can control nearly 100 substation intelligent terminals in the world. Gartner predicts that attacks on smart devices will account for 25% of all attacks on businesses by 2020 [5]. Firmware [6] is a core component of an intelligent terminal device, a program stored in a specific component of the device, a program code that is solidified within an integrated circuit, and is responsible for controlling and coordinating the functions of the integrated circuit. According to the open Web application security project, the firmware vulnerability is the 9th most common vulnerability on smart terminal devices. Therefore, the efficiency of firmware vulnerability detection is very important to the security of smart terminals.

Due to the limitation of hardware resources, the complexity of heterogeneous hardware and the non-disclosure of codes and documents, it is a great challenge to exploit the vulnerability of intelligent terminal equipment. Therefore, this paper proposes a method of firmware vulnerability mining based on code property graph, which can reduce the complexity and improve the efficiency of firmware vulnerability mining.

## 2   Related Work

At the firmware level, the object of dynamic analysis is usually the behavior and response of the application. While it is possible to determine if there is a problem, sometimes it is not easy to pinpoint the source of the problem. In addition, the range of applications of dynamic analysis is limited. If we want to use real equipment for analysis, the low performance and low scalability of intelligent terminal equipment make it very difficult to do dynamic analysis on it, and the cost and other reasons are doomed to not cover many equipment. For static analysis, most vendors remove symbolic information at compile time to reduce volume when making firmware for a device, and the source code for the application in the firmware is not easily accessible, these problems make it difficult to get the exact semantic information of the code through static analysis, and the accuracy is greatly affected.

At present, the research of vulnerability mining for binary program has been developed because of its language independence and does not need program source code, however, the unintelligibility of binary program and the diversity of platform architectures restrict the progress of the research on binary program [7]. Source code analysis-based vulnerability mining technology usually does not need to execute the code, data processing operations and feature selection of a wide variety of high program readability. Two of the more popular techniques for source code vulnerability mining are described below.

### 2.1   Source Code Vulnerability Mining Technology Based on Stain Analysis

Stain analysis is to analyze whether the data introduced by the stain source can be transmitted directly to the stain sink without harmless treatment [8]. According to the types of hard-coded vulnerabilities, Thomas et al. [9] put forward a firmware hidden vulnerability mining method based on static data analysis, and identify the static data comparison function in the program, the function is identified by extracting the function features and modeling the static data comparison function. Cheng et al. [10] put forward a method to detect the firmware vulnerability of IOT(Internet Of Things) devices based on the general type of vulnerability, and extract the information of variable description, definition pair, data type and so on through function analysis, and solve the function data-flow analysis, pointer alias analysis, data structure recovery and other problems. The two methods mentioned above have achieved some types of vulnerability mining in a certain scope, but the feature information extracted is not complete enough for the code description. Parasoft C++ Test [11], a tool developed by Parasoft to support C, C++ static analysis, can detect a few semantic defects in addition to coding rules, as well as Test case generation.

## 2.2 Source Code Vulnerability Mining Technology Based on Machine Learning

In recent years, with the increasing demand for data analysis in the era of big data, Machine Learning (ML) has become the main driving force for the development of ML technology. Machine learning-based source code vulnerability mining technology also emerged, providing a more reliable and intelligent research direction for vulnerability mining.

Ban et al. [12] developed a DeepBalance system, which combines deep-code representation learning with a new idea based on fuzzy class rebalancing, using a new fuzzy oversampling method, by generating composite samples of fragile code classes to rebalance the training data, the experimental results show that the system can significantly improve the performance of vulnerability detection. This method is innovative to some extent, but the types and accuracy of vulnerability detection are limited. Russell [13] built an extensive set of C/C++ source code from the Debian and GitHub repositories and flagged up potential vulnerabilities from three different static analyzers, directly explain the lexical analysis source code, using CNN(Convolutional Neural Networks) and RNN(Rerrent Neural Networks) model training. The method combines the static analysis tool with the neural network model to increase the feature description of the vulnerability code, but the training data set is huge and the label is not perfect, which reduces the accuracy of the source code analysis to a certain extent. Fabian et al. [14] proposed pattern-based vulnerability discovery, which is a new approach to design auxiliary methods for vulnerability discovery. Combining static analysis, machine learning and graph mining techniques, this approach provides an imprecise but efficient way for analysts to benefit from the machine's pattern recognition capabilities without sacrificing the advantages of manual analysis. A new vulnerability automatic classification model (TFI-DNN) is proposed by Huang [15] et al. The model uses term frequency-inverse document frequency to calculate the frequency and weight of each word, selects the feature words according to the information gain, obtains the optimal feature words set, and finally builds the DNN(Deep Neural Networks) neural network model to construct the automatic vulnerability classifier, implement effective vulnerability classification. The object described by the source code is the whole program, which increases the difficulty of data set processing and feature extraction.

Based on the research above, this paper presents a method of vulnerability mining based on code property graph. Firstly, the code property graph of all object programs is generated. Secondly, Abstract Syntax Tree(AST), Control Flow Graph(CFG) and Data Dependency Graph(DDG) are extracted from the code property graph, analyze the statements, syntax, structure, function and variables of the code to narrow the scope of the vulnerability. Finally, combine the manual analysis and review to get the result of the vulnerability mining.

## 3   A Vulnerability Mining Method Model Based on Code Property Graph

In order to solve the problem that the data set of the current vulnerability static analysis method is single and the accuracy of mining is reduced when the vulnerability feature extraction is not obvious, a vulnerability static mining method based on code property graph [16] is studied, method model structure as shown in figure Fig. 1, this method is divided into four steps to achieve the code vulnerability mining.

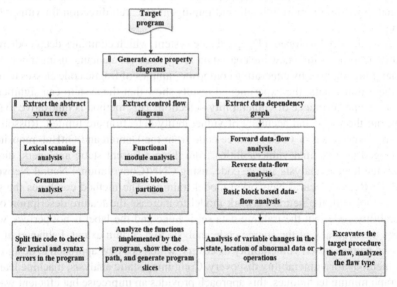

**Fig. 1.** Framework of static vulnerability mining method based on code property graph.

### 3.1   Generation of Code Property Graph

The method of static analysis is very important in the process of vulnerability mining. The code property graph is a kind of comprehensive representation of the target program, it is composed of the abstract syntax tree [17], the control flow graph [18] and the data dependency graph [19], and has the comprehensiveness of information. Each function, in units of the program, generates a code property graph, containing a set of nodes and edges representing the relationships between the nodes, with the following attributes: <Type: node type; code: code for this node; location: node location>. The nodes of code property graph can be divided into function node, abstract syntax tree node, statement node, symbol node, file and directory node and variable declaration node. Take the target program in Fig. 2, which has only one function: main.

```
int main(int argc, char *argv[])
{
    int init_value;
    int loop_counter;
    char buf[10];

    init_value = 0;

    loop_counter = init_value;
    while(++loop_counter)
    {
        /* BAD */
        buf[loop_counter] = 'A';
        if (loop_counter >= 4105) break;
    }


    return 0;
}
```

**Fig. 2.** Target program with vulnerabilities.

## 3.2 Extract the Abstract Syntax Tree

Abstract syntax tree is a tree-like representation of the abstract syntax structure of the target program. Every node in the tree represents a structure in the code. Through the analysis of the abstract syntax tree, we can scan the code and check the basic lexical and syntax errors.

**Lexical Analysis.** Read the code, and then merge it into a single tokens according to predetermined rules [20]. At the same time, remove white space, comments, etc. Finally, the entire code is split into a tokens list (or one-dimensional array). When parsing source code, it reads the code letter by letter, so it's called a scan. When it encounters a space, an operator, or a special symbol, it thinks the word is complete.

The above object program is a function that, first of all, is broken down as a function name: main, the two arguments [ argc, argc[]], the function body: body, and the other method it contains: return. The detachable components are then disassembled until the smallest unit: a single statement or non-detachable method. The tokens of the first statement of the body are: [{value: 'int', type: 'keyword'}, {value: 'init_value', type: 'identifier'},...], to complete the lexical analysis of the entire code.

**Grammar Analysis.** Converts the parsed array to a tree, and validates the syntax. Throw a syntax error if there is a syntax error. When generating a tree, the parser removes unnecessary tokens (such as incomplete parentheses), so the abstract syntax tree does not match the source 100%.

The first level of the abstract parse tree is the method and method ID, the function name: main, and the second level splits the first level main into two parameters, the function body, and the other contained method. For the second level of representation, the argument and the return method can no longer be disassembled, so we continue to disassemble the function body until the last sentence of the code statement forms a complete abstract syntax tree, a preliminary review of the structure and syntax of the target program.

**Extract Control Flow Graph.** Control flow graph is an abstract representation of a process or program, which represents all the paths that a program will traverse during its execution, can also reflect the real-time execution of a process. The program control flow chart is extracted to describe the structure of the program and analyze the function module of the code. The control flow graph extracted from the code property graph of the above target is shown in Fig. 3.

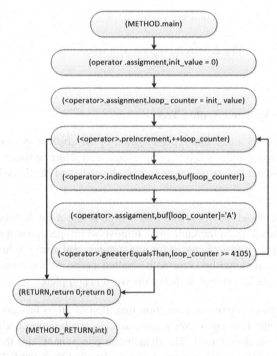

**Fig. 3.** Control flow property of the target program.

A base block is a sequence of statements executed sequentially by a program, with only one entry and one exit. There is only one entry, indicating that no other part of the program can be entered into the base block by a jump class instruction; there is only one exit, indicating that only the last instruction of the program can cause the entry into the other base blocks to be executed. So, a typical feature of a base block is that as long as the first instruction in the base block is executed, all executions within the base block are executed only once in sequence. The basic block partition of the above control flow graph is shown in Fig. 4. Based on the control flow graph, the basic block is divided, the function module of the code is simplified, the program slice is formed, and the detailed analysis of the function and variable data is facilitated.

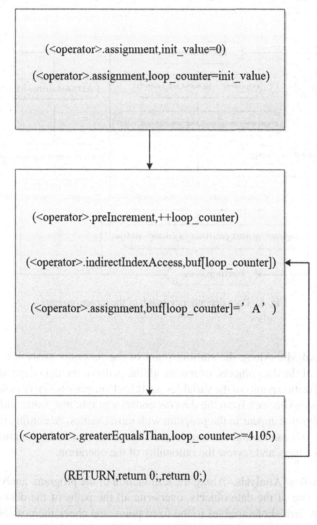

**Fig. 4.** Basic blocks for control flow graph partitioning.

**Extract Data Dependency Graph.** A data dependency graph is a directed graph that represents information about how data flows along the execution path of a program. A node is an array of data operations and variable states filtered from abstract syntax tree nodes, edge points to the data, condition, or result affected, pointing in the direction of the array that causes the variable to change. The method is implemented in three aspects: forward data-flow analysis, reverse data-flow analysis and base block based data-flow analysis. It provides the global information about how the program manipulates its data to locate the vulnerability data and the path of the operation, implementation of code vulnerability mining. The data dependency graph extracted from the code property graph of the above target is shown in Fig. 5.

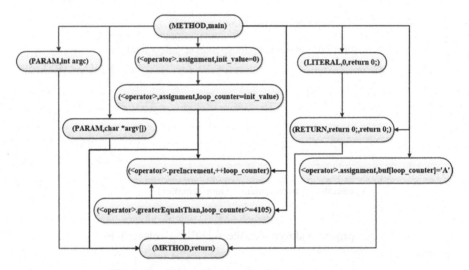

**Fig. 5.** Data dependency graph of the target program.

**Data-flow Analysis.** Along the starting point of the program, analyze the order and possible state of the data objects, overwrite all the paths of the data dependency graph, save the initialization points of the variables, and check the possible error paths of the data operations. As can be seen from the data dependency graph, init_value and loop_count are the variables that appear in the program with initial values. According to the path of the join node, you can look at the statements of the code that make the initial values of the variables change, and review the rationality of the operation.

**Reverse Data-flow Analysis.** Along the termination of the program, analyze the order and possible state of the data objects, overwrite all the paths of the data dependency graph, save the arrival of variables to the fixed point, and check the possible error data operation paths. As you can see from the data dependency graph, the variables pointing to the end of the code include all the variables and parameters in the program, allowing a quick review of the "correct variables" (such as those whose values did not occur) based on a comparison with the initial values, the "incorrect variable" can quickly locate the operation path based on the data flow and narrow the scope of the code vulnerability.

**Base Block Based Data-flow Analysis.** Based on the results of the full path coverage analysis (forward data-flow analysis and reverse data-flow analysis), the basic block where the path with possible vulnerabilities is locked, the state of the variables is checked, and the operations that generate the vulnerabilities are analyzed to determine the types of vulnerabilities.

# 4    Experimental Simulation

In this paper, a method of firmware vulnerability mining based on code property graph is proposed. Joern tool is used to generate code property graph and verify the validity of the model. Since joern usually scans the C++ source code and the firmware is extracted from the binary file, the high level language pseudo code generated by decompiling the files using IDA Pro can not fully reflect the vulnerability information, therefore, this method selects a DVRF project with source code for model validation.

## 4.1    Experimental Environment

In this paper, the lab environment is an Intel(R) Core(TM) i7-10750H CPU @2.60GHz computer, the operating system is Ubuntu 18.04.5, the number of processors is 1, the memory size is 4 GB, the Joern tool version is 1.1.211, and the programming module is Scala.

## 4.2    Introduction to Datasets

The DVRF project is a router firmware based on Linksys E1550, which contains a number of vulnerability binary file written by the developer and their source code forms, directly using the relevant source code to verify the method model, this method avoids the problem of reducing the accuracy of vulnerability detection caused by binary code decompilation. The source code used in the experiment includes heap_overflow_01, stack_bof_01, uaf_01, socket_bof, socket_cmd, and stack_bof_02, which are written in C and can be scanned directly using joern.

## 4.3    Results

In the experiment, we first generate the code property graph of main function of every code using joern tool, then extract the abstract syntax tree, control flow graph and data dependency graph, and then use joern to traverse these three graphs, finally, the result of graph traversal is combined with the result of human review to get the result of hole mining.

**Table 1.** Traversal results of abstract syntax tree.

|  | Number of nodes | Number of edges | Number of method nodes | Number of control structures |
|---|---|---|---|---|
| heap_overflow_01 | 48 | 47 | 16 | 1 |
| stack_bof_01 | 32 | 31 | 9 | 1 |
| uaf_01 | 85 | 84 | 29 | 2 |
| socket_bof | 167 | 166 | 38 | 3 |
| socket_cmd | 155 | 154 | 54 | 4 |
| stack_bof_02 | 32 | 31 | 9 | 1 |

**Table 2.** Traversal results of control flow graphs.

|  | Number of nodes | Number of edges | Number of branches | Number of paths |
|---|---|---|---|---|
| heap_overflow_01 | 42 | 19 | 2 | 2 |
| stack_bof_01 | 12 | 12 | 2 | 2 |
| uaf_01 | 32 | 33 | 4 | 4 |
| socket_bof | 72 | 74 | 6 | 8 |
| socket_cmd | 65 | 69 | 10 | 32 |
| stack_bof_02 | 12 | 12 | 2 | 2 |

**Table 3.** Traversal results of data dependency graphs.

|  | Number of nodes | Number of edges | Number of variables | Number of edges involved in a variable | Effective edge percentage(%) |
|---|---|---|---|---|---|
| heap_overflow_01 | 41 | 47 | 4 | 27 | 57.4 |
| stack_bof_01 | 26 | 29 | 3 | 18 | 62.1 |
| uaf_01 | 68 | 79 | 6 | 49 | 62.0 |
| socket_bof | 131 | 163 | 7 | 113 | 69.3 |
| socket_cmd | 120 | 146 | 6 | 104 | 71.2 |
| stack_bof_02 | 26 | 30 | 3 | 18 | 60.0 |

The results of the abstract syntax trees traversal are shown in Table 1. The traversal includes all the nodes, edges, method nodes and control structures in the graph, and counts the number and information of these features. The number of nodes and the number of edges reflect the size of the source code; the method node traversal records the methods contained in the source code, displays the names and basic operations of these methods, and looks at the code semantics and syntax errors; the number of control structures records the number of loop and conditional structures in the code and the operations that cause them.

The traversal result of the control flow graphs is shown in Table 2. The traversal includes all nodes, edges, branches and paths in the graph, and counts the number and information of these features. The number of nodes and the number of edges reflect the size of each source code control flow graph; the traversal result of branches reflects the number of branches of the control flow graph, and records the operation statements of generating branches and the statements contained in each branch; the path traversal results record all the directions of the source code control flow, and analyze the different path information, the function of the source code and the partition standard of the basic block.

The traversal result of the data dependency graphs is shown in Table 3. The traversal contents include all nodes, edges, variables and the related edges of the graph, and count the number and information of these features. The number of nodes and the number of edges reflect the size of the source code data dependency graph and the number of data manipulation statements; the traversal results record the number, type and name of variables in the source code; the traversal result of the edge involved in the variable records the edge related to the change of the variable in the data dependence graph, and the effective edge ratio reflects the proportion of the number of the edge involved in the variable in all the edges of the graph. In the analysis of abnormal data and operation of abnormal data, only the nodes connected by valid edge and valid edge need to be analyzed.

As can be seen from the table, the data analysis of valid edge can reduce the cost of edge analysis by up to 42.6%, the time consumption of data analysis is reduced, and the efficiency of hole mining is improved.

**Table 4.** Table captions should be placed above the tables.

| References | Analysis object | Detection fine granularity | Code represe-ntation | | | Vulnerability type |
|---|---|---|---|---|---|---|
| | | | AST | CFG | DDG | |
| Reference [19] | Source code | Function level | ✓ | | | SQL injection vulnerabilit-y; Command injection vulnerability |
| Reference [21] | Binary file | Function level | | | ✓ | Buffer overflow; Printf format string; Pomm and injection |

*(continued)*

**Table 4.** (*continued*)

| References | Analysis object | Detection fine granularity | Code represe-ntation | | | Vulnerability type |
|---|---|---|---|---|---|---|
| | | | A S T | C F G | D D G | |
| Reference [22] | Source code | Function level | √ | √ | | Array overstepping vulnerability |
| This paper | Source code | Function leve-l; within and between processes | √ | √ | √ | Stack overflow vulnerabil-ity; Command injection vulnerability; Heap overfl-ow vulnerability; Heap release vulnerability |

### 4.4 Method Comparison

This model is compared with other static analysis methods. As shown in Table 4, the fine granularity detected in references [19, 21, 22] is at function level. The object of this method is firmware source code and the fine granularity detected is at function level and within and between processes. The code property graph is based on function generation and the key information is extracted and filtered in the process to improve the removal rate of useless information and the retention rate of useful information. The code representation of this method is mixed representation, which preserves the comprehensiveness of the code semantic syntax information to the maximum. From the results of model validation, this method can excavate more types of vulnerabilities, and is not limited to these vulnerabilities.

## 5  Summary and Future

At present, the technology of vulnerability mining in power network intelligent terminal equipment has been developed in the fields of static contamination analysis, dynamic fuzzy testing and dynamic-static analysis and verification. Static analysis technology can realize the exploitation of general firmware vulnerability and improve the security of smart grid without running programs. This paper presents a method of firmware vulnerability mining based on code property graph, which is verified by DVRF project. Through four steps of generating code property graph, extracting abstract syntax tree, extracting control flow graph and extracting data dependency graph, the target program is analyzed comprehensively, and the code scope of vulnerability is gradually reduced, by locking the variables, operations and paths that exist in the vulnerability, the problem of reducing the accuracy of the mining is solved when the data set in the static analysis method of vulnerability mining is single and the feature extraction of vulnerability is not obvious, fully using the features of the program described by graph information improves the readability of the target program's syntax, semantics, functions, operations and paths, and improves the efficiency and accuracy of firmware vulnerability mining, it is helpful to the security of intelligent terminal of power network.

The main shortcomings of the method are: (1) the method model mainly aims at the firmware vulnerability source code, but the source code is difficult to find; (2) the process of vulnerability mining still needs some human resources, not fully automated, consume a certain amount of time. The next step will be to improve the above two issues.

**Funding Statement.** This paper is supported by the project of Lightweight security reinforcement and threat perception technologies for energy Internet-oriented smart terminal equipment (52018E20008K).

# References

1. Yong, W., Ning, Z., Yong, G.: Inheritance and expansion of current energy internet and smart grid research topics. Power Syst. Autom. **44**(1), 1–7 (2020)
2. Alotaibi, Y.: A new database intrusion detection approach based on hybrid meta-heuristics. Comput. Mater. Continua **66**(2), 1879–1895 (2021)
3. Bautista-Villalpando, L., Abran, A.: A data security framework for cloud computing services. Comput. Syst. Sci. Eng. **37**(2), 187–203 (2021)
4. Kim, H., Chung, J.: Vanet jamming and adversarial attack defense for autonomous vehicle safety. Comput. Mater. Continua **71**(2), 3589–3605 (2022)
5. Yue, T., Star, T., Benhai, W.: Research and application of endogenous security and defense-in-depth in iot. Power Syst. Equip. **3**, 46–47 (2021)
6. Yingchao, Y., Zoning, C., Shuitao, G.: Research on firmware security analysis technology of embedded device. J. Comput. Sci. **44**(5), 859–881 (2021)
7. Xiajing, W., Changzhen, H., Rui, M.: A survey of key techniques of binary program vulnerability mining. Inf. Netw. Secur. **8**, 1–13 (2017)
8. Yuzhu, R., Youwei, Z., Chengwei, A.: A review of stain analysis techniques. Comput. Appl. **39**(8), 2302–2309 (2019)
9. Thomas, S., Garcia, F., Chothia, T.: A Tool for hidden functionality detection in firmware. Detect. Intrus. Malware Vulnerabil. Assess. **10327**, 279–300 (2017)
10. Cheng, K., Li, Q., Wang, L.: DTaint: detecting the taint-style vulnerability in embedded device firmware. In: 48th Annual IEEE/IFIP International Conference on Depend-able Systems and Networks (DSN), pp. 430–441 (2018)
11. Jack, G.: Using standards and inspections to slash schedules and improve quality. In: Embedded systems conference 2013: ESC Silicon Valley 2013, Design West, San Jose, pp. 22–25. Curran Associates, California (2013)
12. Xinbo, B., Shigang, L., Chao, C.: A performance evaluation of deep-learnt features for software vulnerability detection. Concurr. Comput. Pract. Exp. **31**(19), e5103 (2019)
13. Russell, R., Kim, L., Hamltion, L.: Automated vulnerability detection in source code using deep representation learning. In: The 17th IEEE International Conference on Machine Learning and Applications (ICMLA), pp. 757–762 (2018)
14. Fabian, Y.: Pattern-based methods for vulnerability discovery. Inf. Technol. **59**(2), 101–106 (2017)
15. Huang, G., Li, Y., Wang, Q., Ren, J., Cheng, Y., Zhao, X.: Automatic classification method for software vulnerability based on deep neural network. IEEE Access **7**, 28291–28298 (2019)
16. Tian, X., Jia, C., Ying, X.: Christina Lamb based on code property graph and Bi-GRU. Power Syst. Autom. **44**(1), 1–7 (2020)

17. Jia, J., Jun, C., Ying, X.: A survey of automatic software defect repair technology. J. Softw. Eng. **32**(09), 2665–2690 (2021)
18. Zhang, J., Tian, C., Zhen, D.: Pollution variable graph based taint analysis tool for Android applications. J. Softw. Eng. **32**(09), 1701–1716 (2021)
19. Chen, Q., Cheng, K., Yao, Z.: Functional level data dependency graph and its application in static vulnerability analysis. J. Softw. Eng. **31**(11), 3421–3435 (2020)
20. Jenni, R.S., Shankar, S.: Semantic based greedy levy gradient boosting algorithm for phishing detection. Comput. Syst. Sci. Eng. **41**(2), 525–538 (2021)
21. Liu, X., Yu, M., Guo, Y.: Design and implementation of a static code vulnerability detection system. In: China Conference, Wuxi, Jiangsu, China, pp. 24–27 (2019)
22. Gao, F., Wang, T., Chen, T.: Static detection method of array out-of-bounds defects based on taint analysis. J. Softw. Eng. **31**(10), 2983–3003 (2020)

# Security Access Control of Docker Process Based on Trust

Jing Guo[1]([⊠]), Jianfei Xiao[1], Zesan Liu[2], Zhuo Cheng[1], Xinyi Liu[2], and Yimin Qiang[3]

[1] Aostar Information Technologies Co., Ltd., Chengdu 610041, China
guojing@sgitg.sgcc.com.cn
[2] State Grid Information and Communication Industry Group, Beijing 102211, China
[3] Engineering Research Center of Post Big Data Technology and Application of Jiangsu Province, Research and Development Center of Post Industry Technology of the State Posts Bureau (Internet of Things Technology), Nanjing University of Posts and Telecommunications, Nanjing 210000, China

**Abstract.** Container technology has become a widely recognized server resource sharing method, which can provide system administrators with great flexibility in the process of building operating system instances on demand. Nowadays, container technology, especially Docker technology, is widely used in power systems, but the container manages resources through the kernel C-groups, use namespace to limit the resource visibility of the application in the container, making isolation not as high as traditional virtual machines, this will make the container less secure. And the namespace is currently not perfect, there are still many problems in the deployment configuration of the container. These are also important factors that threaten the security of containers. This paper combines MNT file name/directory randomization technology, access control based on user trust, and CP-ABE algorithm with trusted timestamp verification, dynamically assigning access keys to users to restrict users' access to resources.

**Keywords:** Docker · Container · Namespace · Trust · Access control

## 1 Introduction

As the number of corporate mobile applications increases and the source of users becomes uncontrollable, attackers can register legitimate users frequently through identity theft and other means, cross the border line of defense, in the scope of authority of the account to conduct arbitrary operations, explore business defense vulnerabilities, because mobile users often use the traditional single authentication method of account name/ password to access the company network. Existing protective measures usually assume that the users, equipment, and processes of the intranet are trustworthy, once a terminal device or user that is considered legitimate accesses the network, it is illegally controlled by an attacker, Unable to solve the problem of such devices accessing company data and business resources and performing arbitrary operations with a legal identity will cause significant losses. At the same time, because the system adopts a preestablished trust mechanism for internal personnel if internal personnel conduct illegal operations or initiate malicious attacks, it is difficult to effectively manage and control, and it will also cause huge losses. Therefore, it is necessary to conduct risk prevention for authenticated users based on existing user name/password authentication [1]. The authorization method between the existing mobile terminal-mobile platform-back-end service is mainly based on the role-based static access control mechanism, its authority control granularity is extensive, and its access control strategy is static and solid, therefore, it is necessary to implement dynamic adjustment of access strategy based on continuous risk measurement and trust evaluation results [2]. The container manages resources through the C-groups mechanism and uses the namespace to limit the resource visibility of the application in the container, but this isolation is not as high as traditional virtual machines, this makes the container less secure and the namespace space is currently not perfect. There are still many problems in the deployment configuration of the container. Therefore, strengthening the security protection of containers will be an important aspect of computer security [3].

In the current research and deployment of container security technology, container security technology can be divided into four categories, which are MAC, Sec-comp, capabilities privilege split, and user namespace. MAC (Mandatory Access Control) is not a new security solution, it comes from the access control model developed by the US National Security Agency (NSA) and the military to implement a stricter access control policy than discretionary access control (DAC) [4]. At present, the technologies applied to container security mainly include SE-Linux, App-Armor, SMACK (Simplified Mandatory Access Control Kernel), and RBAC (Role-based Access Control), etc. [5]. The complexity of the policy language brought by fine-grained security access control and the lack of updated policies cause users to lack understanding of it, even some system administrators with high-security permissions are not very familiar with it, this makes MAC not widely used [6]. Sec-comp reduces the number of application-kernel interfaces by limiting the number of valid system calls, putting the running process into "Safe" mode, where it can only use four system calls of read (), write (), exit () and sign return (). When the process tries other system calls, the system will send a SIGKILL signal to terminate the process. Sec-comp application flexibility is greatly restricted; a lot of inter-process communication is required between different micro-processes; the capabilities privilege split is a permission split mechanism proposed for security risks and the excessive concentration of root user permissions in the Linux system. But due to the consideration that its container users may need to use these permissions, the container retains these privileges as default values [7].

In this paper, we propose the security access control of Docker process based on trust, including the following steps: using CP-ABE algorithm for encryption and decryption; using an access control structure based on user trust to distribute private keys; performing trusted timestamp verification before decrypting with the private key; the object of encryption is the filename/directory in MNT-namespace; the object of decryption is the encrypted randomized filename/directory. This method can dynamically control the access and permissions of the process to the created Docker container [8].

## 2   Background Technique

SE-Linux (Security-Enhanced Linux) is a type of MAC, it is based on Linux through independent components or tags to establish a fine-grained security enforcement strategy and type enhancement (TE) [9]. The Android system contains SE-Linux (in mandatory mode) and the corresponding security policy that applies to the entire Android open source code (android open source project, AOSP) by default. In forced mode, illegal operations will be blocked, and all violations attempted will be logged by the kernel to display message and logcat. However, in many cases SE-Linux is disabled or does not implement enhanced strategies, in addition, SE-Linux is often found vulnerabilities or weaknesses in the policy file itself or inappropriately applied tags [10–12]. Like any other MAC system, due to the lack of restrictions on system calls or other kernel boundary conditions, SE-Linux vulnerabilities or weaknesses can also lead to major vulnerabilities, and may even cause the entire system to be attacked.

To achieve access control, the App-Armor security module is inserted into the LSM security framework in a loadable form, App-Armor can identify the two resources of the document and the POSIX.1e capability draft, App-Armor controls all access to these two resources and restricts applications to these two resources [13]. Therefore, App-Armor can effectively prevent restricted programs from accessing these two resources in an unauthorized manner. In the course of use, although the App-Armor module can well limit the configured programs, it recognizes the program file based on the path, once the program file is replaced, it may execute some programs with viruses, which cannot protect the system well, and the intruder can bypass the security module to achieve the purpose of destroying the system [14–16].

In terms of Linux container virtualization technology, Sec-comp can provide a safe operating environment for untrusted pure computing code to protect the normal operation of the system and applications from interference by untrusted code. Sec-comp can filter the system calls in the program and make the process run in a safer mode. In this mode, the process is only allowed to execute a restricted set of system calls. If a system call outside the Sec-comp strategy is executed in the program, the process will be terminated. For a process, there are many systems calls that are not used in its life cycle and some of the systems call it uses are unsafe, many loopholes will be generated in the process of the system call, which will bring opportunities for other untrusted processes and make the system vulnerable to attacks [17]. Conciseness and elegance are the advantages of Sec-comp, but it can only support purely computational code but its application is greatly restricted. For example, the Sec-comp mode process cannot dynamically allocate memory, cannot use shared memory with other processes, cannot use new file descriptors, and so on. If you want to support applications with various functions, you need another method to intercept and process other system calls. For an attacker, the kernel system call interface is an important attack surface. Using Sec-comp to further isolate the container is very useful. But currently, only Docker supports Sec-comp-bpf, and LXCv1.0 only uses Sec-comp as an option. The main reason why Sec-comp-bpf is not widely used is that the whitelist and blacklist of system calls are difficult to set, the required system calls themselves have security vulnerabilities, and the performance loss of Sec-comp is relatively large [18].

# 3    Docker Process Security Access Control Based on Trust

## 3.1    Demand Analysis

The Linux container uses the MNT namespace to implement the installation of the file system in the container. The file name/directory randomization technology based on the MNT namespace is likely to cause security issues such as denial of service attacks, local privilege escalation, and container escape due to the imperfect support of the Linux namespace mechanism for file systems such as proc-fs and sys-fs. It is equivalent to adding a mask to the filename/directory to protect the file name/directory that may be leaked in a targeted manner. [19] However, the file name/directory randomization technology based on the MNT namespace is too static for the key distribution and cannot take the changes in the access rights of the accessing users, and the employee grading system within the company or unit (that is, the employees of the corresponding level have corresponding access permissions, and the high-level permissions include the lower-level permissions) into account. [20] Therefore, we add an access control structure based on the trustworthiness of accessing users on the basis of the file name/directory randomization technology based on the MNT namespace.

The dangers of containers sharing the kernel and the lack of a complete namespace cannot be ignored. Many kernel features of Linux still have not achieved namespace isolation, the namespace mechanism has incomplete support for file systems such as proc-fs, sys-fs, and dev-fs (File systems on a Linux system), making it easy for attackers to bypass inspection protection, forming illegal access and modification, causing information leakage and other loopholes.

For example, proc-fs can display the status information of the system running and the status information of the current process, and proc-fs is located in the memory of the host, therefore, proc-fs lacks namespace support the container needs to inherit this file system from the host to support the operation of the process, but due to its lack of namespace isolation, as a result, the content is easily exposed to user processes without corresponding permissions. [21] Therefore, other methods are needed to protect such files.

In actual operation, the permissions of the user process are not static, in addition to the manual input of the user authorized by the senior authority, it can also rely on the computer to make a comprehensive judgment on the user's initial authority and a series of behaviors of accessing the system to dynamically assign its authority. At the same time, because the system's requirements for user permissions are real-time permissions, therefore, it is necessary to verify the authority of the authority corresponding to the time. Finally, since the access rights to the file are determined by the corresponding attributes of the file, therefore, the permissions granted to the user should be detachable like the attributes of the file.

From the analysis above, it can be seen that the new protection scheme needs to meet the following requirements: 1. Meeting the permission requirements of different users; 2. Strengthening file isolation and file name/directory protection; 3. Meeting the needs of dynamically determining and assigning user permissions; 4. Meeting the requirements for the timeliness of the permissions granted to users; 5. Meeting the requirements of corresponding permits and file attributes and can be spliced.

## 3.2  System Structure

This paper proposes the design idea of Docker process security access control based on trust: 1. The system establishes a dynamic user set according to the needs of users, then set up a character set, file set, and permission set. There is a one-to-one correspondence between permission sets and file sets. The role set and permission set can be matched many-to-many (different roles have different permissions). The system matches users and roles one-to-one according to the user's credibility so that the user can obtain the corresponding authority. 2. Aiming at the trustworthiness of users, and access control structure based on the trustworthiness of users is used to calculate the trustworthiness of users. 3. The CP-ABE algorithm with timestamp is used for encryption and decryption of filenames/directories.

CP-ABE algorithm-specific process:

(1) Initialization Setup: The initialization algorithm is a randomization algorithm, and the initialization only generates the system public key $PK$ and the system master secret key $MSK$.

(2) Revocation mechanism initialization: the input parameter is $PK$, a prime number field $P$ is generated, and $list = 1$ is calculated for each attribute $att$. The algorithm outputs the initialized $P$, $map < user - GID, prime >$ and $map < att, list >$. The list is not our common list, but a large number and a prime number, which is used to record whether it has been revoked.

(3) Secret key generation $KeyGen$: According to the $PK$, $MK$ and the attribute set $S$ submitted by the data requester, the trusted authorization center generates the user secret key $UK$ associated with the attribute set for the data requester. Apply for a prime number prime for the user in the prime number field, delete this prime from $P$, ensure that different users get different primes, then the prime number is stored in the mapping table $map < user - GID, prime >$.

(4) Encrypt: The input parameters of the encryption algorithm (randomization algorithm) are $PK$, the message to be encrypted $M$, and the access control structure associated with the access policy, output encrypted ciphertext based on attributes.

(5) Decrypt: Decryption is a deterministic algorithm, executed by the data requester. Decryption is divided into two steps. Step1: Accessing the leaf node of the policy tree, let $I = att(x)$,$x$ represents the leaf node of the ciphertext policy access tree, (function $att(x)$ returns the attribute corresponding to node $x$), if $I \in S$, the algorithm obtains the revocation list, list corresponding to this attribute and takes the modulus of $list\%prime$. If the value is not 0, it means that the user has not been revoked, if it is 0, it means it has been revoked, and the decryption is over; Step 2: After the first step of verification is passed, the algorithm enters $UK$ and ciphertext $M$. If the attribute set meets the access policy, the algorithm can successfully decrypt the ciphertext $M$.The algorithm principle is shown in Fig. 1:

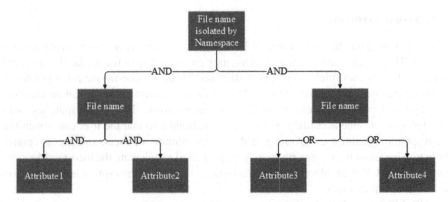

**Fig. 1.** CP-ABE algorithm principle.

The attribute 1–4 in Fig. 1 represents the filename of the previous level. According to the characteristic of attribute decryption in CP-ABE algorithm, a private key is made by combining each indivisible filename。

This paper proposes a randomization technology based on the MNT namespace, which mainly operates on file name/directory, which only changes the file entity name. The overall process is as follows.

(1) Enter the security parameters of the host system where the container is located, and obtain the system public parameters and the system master key and output them. (2) First use Read direct to traverse the filename/directory, then fill it with Fill direct, and then use the system public parameters output in step (1) as the public key to encrypt the filename/directory to get the randomized file name/directory. (3) The access authority corresponding to each file name/directory generates the corresponding private key under the action of the system public parameters and the system master key output in step (1), and stores the private key in the list. (4) Assign the private key stored in the list in step (3) according to the user attribute, and assign it to the user process with the corresponding attribute. (5) Use a trusted timestamp to verify the timeliness and accuracy of the user's private key. (6) When the user process accesses the file name/directory, judging it and decrypts it with the private key.

The specific calculation methods of the user trust are as follows:

**Table 1.** Methods of the user trust.

| Method | Explanation |
| --- | --- |
| $U = (u_1, u_2, u_3, ..., u_a)$ | A collection of users requesting access to filenames/directories in MNT-namespace |
| $R = \{r_1, r_2, r_3, ..., r_b\}$ | A level in the system, representing the qualification to access filenames/directories in MNT-namespace |
| $P = (p_1, p_2, p_3, ..., p_c)$ | Operation permission to access resources in MNT-namespace |
| $F = (f_1, f_2, f_3, ..., f_d)$ | A collection of file names in MNT-namespace |
| $TC = \{1, 2, 3, ..., r\}$ | Trust level |

Initial trust value:

$IT = $ (The initial trust value corresponding to the user's position and level)

Direct trust value calculation:

$$T(u_i, f_j) = \frac{S_{ij}}{N_{ij}} + (S_{ij} - N_{ij}) \times 3^{-N_{ij}} \tag{1}$$

The total number of times the user accesses the file is recorded as $N_{ij}$, The number of successes is recorded as $S_{ij}$, $(S_{ij} - N_{ij}) \times 3^{-N_{ij}}$ is a penalty, The fewer visits a user has, the greater the impact of the penalty item.

Comprehensive trust value calculation:

$$CT = \alpha_1 IT + \alpha_2 T \tag{2}$$

$\alpha_1$ and $\alpha_2$ are weight.

Trust value change: To better motivate users' legitimate behaviors and resist users' illegal behaviors, this mechanism updates the user's trust value after each visiting period. Store the updated trust value in the historical information database as the basis for the start of the next access cycle.

legitimate:

$$UT = CT + \frac{TL}{20} \times \theta \tag{3}$$

Legitimate behavior (successful access) accounted for more than 60% updates to increase trust value.

illegal:

$$UT = CT - \frac{TL}{30} \times \eta \tag{4}$$

Less than 60% of legitimate behaviors update attenuation trust value.

The overall framework is shown in Fig. 2:

The private key given to the user process generated by the CP-ABE algorithm needs to be verified by a trusted timestamp to determine whether it is legal. The process is shown in Fig. 3:

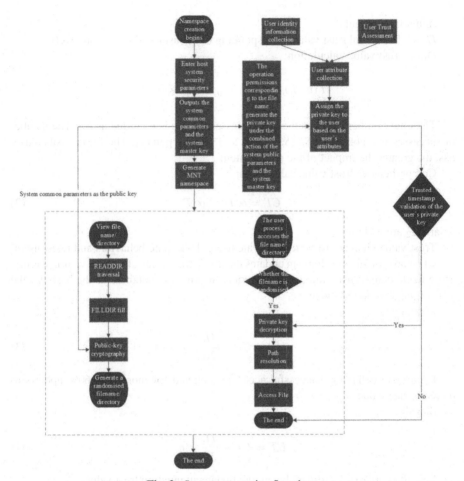

**Fig. 2.** System processing flowchart.

## 4　Experimental Verification

The collection of user identity and position information in this article is based on the user's IP address when accessing the file, the identities of power grid companies collected in this article are divided into 4 levels (IP address: 36.152.116.0–36.152.116.15 are level $A$ employees,36.152.116.16–36.152.116.63 are level $B$ employees, 36.152.116.64–36.152.116.127 are level $C$ employees, and 36.152.116.128–36.152.116.255 are level $D$ employees. The initial trust value of type $A$ employees is 2, type $B$ employees are 1.5, type $C$ employees are 1, and type $D$ employees are 0.5) The calculation of user trust is based on the method of step (4) in Sect. 3. this article divides the user trust level into four levels (1–4), the roles and permissions corresponding to each trust level are shown in Table 2. The higher the trust level, the higher the credibility of the user and the higher the access authority they have.

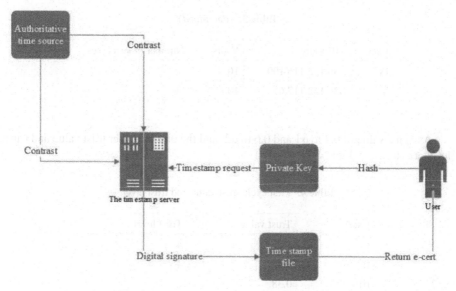

**Fig. 3.** Trusted timestamp verification process.

**Table 2.** Trust level and role authority mapping.

| User trust level | Comprehensive trust value interval | Role | Authority |
|---|---|---|---|
| 4 | [1,1.4] | Highly trusted user | 4 |
| 3 | [0.65,1) | Medium trusted user | 3 |
| 2 | [0.3,0.0.65) | Primary trusted user | 2 |
| 1 | [0,0.3) | Suspect | 1 |

This paper adopts the trust evaluation function in the Docker process security access control based on the user process, Process and evaluate the user's identity information and system access behavior information provided by the grid collected from the Growing IO website, and control the total number of visits to verify the effectiveness of the method. The information collected from the Growing IO website is shown in Table 3.

**Table 3.** User information and behavior.

| User | IP address | Visits | Number of successes |
|---|---|---|---|
| I | 36.152.116.61 | 10 | 7 |
| II | 36.152.116.4 | 10 | 10 |
| III | 36.152.116.244 | 10 | 3 |

(*continued*)

**Table 3.** (*continued*)

| User | IP address | Visits | Number of successes |
|------|------------|--------|---------------------|
| IV | 36.152.116.100 | 10 | 5 |
| V | 36.152.117.61 | 10 | 0 |

Assign a value of 0.4 to $\alpha 1$ and 0.6 to $\alpha 2$, and the obtained user trust value and trust level are shown in Table 4.

**Table 4.** First cycle trust value and trust level.

| User | Trust value | Trust level |
|------|-------------|-------------|
| I | 1.02 | 4 |
| II | 1.4 | 4 |
| III | 0.38 | 2 |
| IV | 0.7 | 3 |
| V | 0 | 1 |

Since the user's access is dynamic, so this function needs to take into account the behavior of the user in the next visit cycle and the change of the user's position/rank, therefore, starting from the second access cycle, after the end of each access cycle, an update of the trust level is required. If the trust level of a single user decreases for two consecutive visit cycles, the identity level is lowered by one level. At the same time, the growth factor of the trust value should be smaller than the decay factor to reflect the "slow rise and fast fall" characteristics of trust. Set the growth factor to 2 and the decay factor to 4. The first update is as shown in Table 5.

**Table 5.** Trust value and trust level update.

| User | Original trust value | Trust value after the update | Original trust level | Trust level after the update |
|------|---------------------|------------------------------|---------------------|------------------------------|
| I | 1.02 | 1.4 | 4 | 4 |
| II | 1.4 | 1.4 | 4 | 4 |
| III | 0.38 | 0.12 | 2 | 1 |
| IV | 0.7 | 0.3 | 3 | 2 |
| V | 0 | 0 | 1 | 1 |

According to the data in the above table, for five users with different initial identities, under the premise of ensuring that each user accesses 10 files in a single access cycle, the trust value and trust level of each user will change with the user's access behavior. Overall, the trust value and trust level of users with high trust levels are generally rising, and the overall trend of users with lower trust values and trust levels is on the decline, which is in line with the actual situation of the distribution of operating rights for internal users in the internal management of enterprises. This proves the feasibility of the method. The details of the changes are shown in Fig. 4.

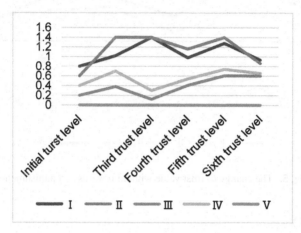

**Fig. 4.** Changes in trust value.

In order to prove the effectiveness and superiority of adding dynamic access control in the experiment, this paper deletes the regular reward and punishment mechanism on the basis of keeping the data of the previous experiment.

As can be seen from the comparison between Figs. 4 and 5, users' trust value fluctuates more when there is a regular reward-punishment mechanism than when there is no regular reward-punishment mechanism, and each visit behavior will affect the subsequent visit results, effectively prevent the illegal behavior impunity, but also to ensure that the user's behavior and user's identity level to bind.

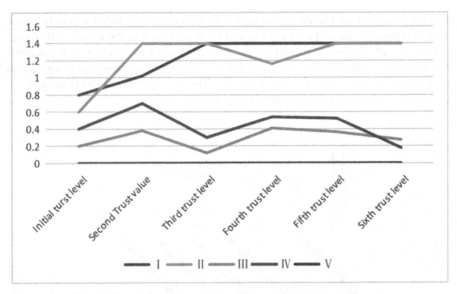

**Fig. 5.** The change of trust value without rewards and punishments.

## 5  Summary

Under the premise that the scale of the power grid is getting larger and larger, the access security of the power grid is becoming more and more important. This article is based on the namespace to improve the method, considering the weak isolation of namespace, this article decided to randomize the file name/directory isolated by MNT namespace, the encryption, and decryption algorithm adopts the CP-ABE algorithm with a trusted timestamp. The distribution of the private key adopts an access control structure based on user trust, which can be dynamically distributed according to the user's trust level. At the same time, the access control structure can ensure that the user's trust level is not static, but changes with the change of their identity and behavior, trusted timestamp verification ensures the authority of the key. This paper verifies the feasibility of the method through experiments on five different entities. The user's position level in the enterprise or system will affect their initial visit, and their visit behavior will dynamically and continuously affect their trust level. The experimental results prove that the trust level of users with high trust levels is relatively stable or even continues to increase, while users with lower trust levels are on the contrary, which conforms to the law in reality. Therefore, the method in this paper can effectively restrict the user's access behavior and prevent the emergence of user unauthorized and escape attacks.

**Acknowledgment.** This work is supported by the science and technology project of State Grid Corporation of China: "Research on Dynamic Access Authentication and Trust Evaluation Technology of Power Mobile Internet Services Based on Zero Trust" (Grand No. 5700-202158183A-0-0-00).

# References

1. Jabbari, A., Mohasefi, J.B.: A secure and LoRaWAN compatible user authentication protocol for critical applications in the IoT environment. IEEE Trans. Ind. In form. **18**(1), 56–65 (2022)
2. Uddin, M., Islam, S., Al-Nemrat, A.: A dynamic access control model using authorizing workflow and task-role-based access control. IEEE Access, **7**, 166676–166689 (2019)
3. Cui, J.B., et al.: A dynamic access control model using authorizing workflow and task-role-based access control. IEEE Trans. Image Process. 8567–8579 (2021)
4. Aymen, F., Mohamed, N., Chayma, S., Reddy, C.H.R., Alharthi, M.M., Ghoneim, S.S.M.: An improved direct torque control topology of a double stator machine using the fuzzy logic controller. IEEE Access **9**, 126400–126413 (2021)
5. Liu, J., Zhu, B.X., Liang, J.H., Ren, N.E., Ji, H.P.: Blockchain access control model strategy based on main-side chain cooperation. In: Computer engineering, pp. 145–152 (2021)
6. Song, X.L., Yang, C.H.: Mobile device management system based on aosp and se-linux. In: 2017 IEEE Second International Conference on Data Science in Cyberspace, pp. 26–29 (2017)
7. Marois, A., Grossetête, L., Chatelais, B., Lafond, D.: Evaluation of evolutionary algorithms under frugal learning constraints for online policy capturing. In: 2021 IEEE Conference on Cognitive and Computational Aspects of Situation Management, pp. 14–22 (2021)
8. Bai, J., Zhai, G.: Study on analysis for SE-Linux security policy. In: 2012 International Conference on Systems and Informatics, pp. 18–20. Yantai, Shandong, China (2012)
9. Kuliamin, V., Khoroshilov, A., Medveded, D.: Formal modeling of multi-level security and integrity control implemented with se-Linux, pp.12–14. Moscow, Russia (2019)
10. Mutti, S., Bacis, E., Paraboschi, S.: An SE-Linux-based intent manager for Android. Florence, Italy (2015)
11. Singh, K.K., Radhika, B.S., Shyamasundar, R.K.: SEFlowViz: a visualization tool for SE-Linux policy analysis. In: 2021 12th International Conference on Information and Communication Systems, pp. 24–26 (2021)
12. Li, Y., Huang, C.L., Yuan, L., Ding, Y., Cheng, H.: ASPGen: an automatic security policy generating framework for apparmor. In: 2020 IEEE Intl Conf on Parallel, pp. 17–19 (2020)
13. Ecarot, T., Dussault, S., Souid, A., Lavoie, L., Ethier, J.: AppArmor for health data access control: assessing risks and benefits. In: 2020 7th International Conference on Internet of Things: Systems, Management and Security, pp. 14–16 (2020)
14. Schweizer, R., Neuhaus, S.: Downright: a framework and toolchain for privilege handling. In: 2019 IEEE Cybersecurity Development, pp. 23–25 (2019)
15. Sultan, S., Ahmad, I., Dimitriou, T.: Container security: issues, challenges, and the road ahead. IEEE Access, **7**, 52976–52996 (2019)
16. Kang, H., Kim, J., Shin, S.: MiniCon: automatic enforcement of a minimal capability set for security-enhanced containers. In: 2021 IEEE International IOT, Electronics and Mechatronics Conference, pp. 21–24 (2021)
17. Wang, X.H., Shen, Q.N., Luo, W., Wu, P.F.: RSDS: getting system call whitelist for container through dynamic and static analysis. In: 2020 IEEE 13th International Conference on Cloud Computing, pp. 122–138 (2020)

18. Zhan, D., Tan, K., Ye, L., Yu, H., Liu, H.: Container introspection: using external management containers to monitor containers in cloud computing. Comput. Mater. Continua **69**(3), 3783–3794 (2021)
19. Lin, X., Shi, J., Wang, Y., Liu, C., Lu, B., et al.: Container application migration algorithm in internet of vehicles. Intelligent Autom. Soft Comput. **29**(3), 915–926 (2021)
20. Javier, J., Higuera, J.B., Ramón, J., Antonio, J., Rubio, M.S.: Mmale-a methodology for malware analysis in linux environments. Comput. Mater. Continua **67**(2), 1447–1469 (2021)
21. Hadi, H.J., Omar, M.A., Rozaini, W.: Investigating the role of trust dimension as a mediator on CC-SAAS adoption. Intelligent Autom. Soft Comput. **29**(2), 373–386 (2021)

# A Review of Crop Recognition Methods Based on Multi-source Remote Sensing Data

Lei Wang[1], Xia Zhao[1,2]([✉]), Bernard Engel[3], Lu Wang[1], Changjun Xu[4], and Yue Zhao[5]

[1] Key Laboratory of Tibetan Plateau Land Surface Processes and Ecological Conservation (Ministry of Education), Qinghai Province Key Laboratory of Physical Geography and Environmental Process, Natural Resources and Environment Modeling Laboratory, College of Geographical Science, Qinghai Normal University, Xining 810008, Qinghai, China
zhaoxia@qhnu.edu.cn

[2] Academy of Plateau Science and Sustainability-Plateau Soil Information Science Research Team, People's Government of Qinghai Province, Beijing Normal University, Xining 810008, Qinghai, China

[3] Purdue University, West Lafayette IN47907, USA

[4] Geomatics Technology and Application Key Laboratory of Qinghai Province, Xining 810000, China

[5] State Key Laboratory of Soil and Sustainable Agriculture, Institute of Soil Science, Chinese Academy of Sciences, Nanjing 210008, China

**Abstract.** How to identify crop types faster and more accurately by integrating multiple sources Remote Sensing (hereafter RS) data has become a key technique in topographic regions, yet few literatures has addressed on this deficiency. By given a detailed review on two major issues of RS data fusion patterns and differentiation algorithms about crop types, this paper extracted three dominant patterns existing in current RS data fusions, which can be named as time-sequential fusion, spatial-resolution fusion, and spatial-temporal fusion; and from which three types of crop recognition methodologies can be concluded, namely time-sequential phenological characteristics method, plant spectral reflection characteristic method, and combined method of spectral and phenological characteristic of crops accordingly. Furthermore, a detailed comparison of those methods on their influencing factors and regional applicability is also illustrated in order to provide a more effective methods selection strategies targeting on RS crop monitoring.

**Keywords:** Crop recognition · Multi-source remote sensing data · Fusion pattern · Technique status and future prospects

## 1 Introduction

Remote sensing recognition of crops is the theoretical foundation of remote sensing of agricultural situations [1, 2], which is usually fulfilled by extracting unique spectral, textural and phenological characteristics of crops, and crop type identification using supervised classification, unsupervised classification and machine learning methods in

© The Author(s), under exclusive license to Springer Nature Switzerland AG 2022
X. Sun et al. (Eds.): ICAIS 2022, CCIS 1588, pp. 571–585, 2022.
https://doi.org/10.1007/978-3-031-06764-8_44

combination with crop growth patterns and conditions [3]. Low spatial resolution remote sensing images such as MODIS data can cover long time series of crop growing period. It can also effectively identify crop phenological crossover phenomenon [4], but cannot identify crop types grown in small plots in complex terrain areas due to the interference of factors such as mixed cropping and plot size. Medium-resolution remote sensing images such as Landsat TM/ETM data can identify relatively more crop types due to the increased resolution. However, it is difficult to obtain long-term sequence images due to adverse weather conditions such as cloud, rain and fog and revisit cycles, which makes it difficult to use growth cycle characteristics (such as growth curve) for crop identification. High spatial resolution remote sensing images, such as GF-1 / 2 data, can extract abundant spectral information and spatial heterogeneity characteristics, which is helpful to improve crop recognition accuracy under complex planting patterns and terrain conditions. However, due to poor data continuity and limited coverage of spatial, the image processing of such images is more difficult [5]. In conclusion, any single remote sensing data source cannot fully reflect the spectral characteristics of different crops throughout the growing season due to the mutual restriction of temporal and spatial resolutions [6]. Therefore, it is of great theoretical research significance and practical application value to study the synergy and fusion of multi-source data in remote sensing recognition of crops.

## 2    Research Overview

Domestic and foreign scholars have used MODIS, Landsat TM / OLI, GF and HJ images to study crop classification. Early data type is single, often using single source image, which is divided into low spatial resolution and high spatial resolution. Low spatial resolution long-term sequence data can be used to detect large-scale crops, and the crop situation is analyzed by calculating the vegetation index. For example, Xiao et al. (2005) and Zheng et al. (2008) used MODIS data and SPOT-5 images to study the planting structure of specific crops. [7, 8]. Ridhika Aggarwal et al. (2014) [9] used remote sensing images of multi-temporal Landsat-8 OLI data to classify wheat of Radaur city, India. Qingyun Xu et al. (2014) [10] reconstructed NDVI time series curve using MOD09Q1 dataset and combined with crop phenology information to identify the types and cropping patterns of major crops in Shanxi Province. Supervised or unsupervised classification and machine learning methods are often used when using multi-temporal data from high spatial resolution images (Kim, 2014) [11]. For example, Huanxue Zhang et al. (2015) [12] used an object-oriented decision tree algorithm to classify crops from multi-temporal environmental satellite NDVI time series data. Wuyundeji et al. (2018) [13] used GF-1 image data to extract the area of spring wheat in the river-loop irrigation area and monitored the crop growth with NDVI, and found that the accuracy of the area extraction results reached 93.51%.

In recent years, in the research of crop classification and agricultural remote sensing, data source has changed from single-source data to multi-source data set [14], and crop identification method based on satellite remote sensing data collaboration has become a research hotspot. For example, Guangxiong Peng et al. (2009) [15] used multiple typical classification methods to identify and extract crops such as sugarcane and maize in Mile

County, Yunnan Province, and the data he used were CBERS02B-CCD and Landsat-5 TM images of CMBR at two times. Songlin Wang (2015) [16] selected low and medium spatial resolution MODIS remote sensing images to extract crop cultivation area in Jiangsu Province, and used medium and high resolution HJ-1A/B images to verify their spatial distribution. Huinan Xin et al. (2016) [17] used a decision tree classification model to monitor crop cropping structure in the Aksu region of Xinjiang. The experimental procedure combined with the spectral information of the higher radiometric resolution multi-temporal Landsat8 OLI images. Aiming at the two key problems of common multi-source image data fusion methods and remote sensing crop recognition methods, this paper makes a systematic review.

**Table 1.** Cases of multi-source remote sensing data fusion applied to crop identification.

| Data source | Identifying characteristics | Research area | Crop type | Accuracy | References |
|---|---|---|---|---|---|
| CBERS02B-CCD and Landsat-5TM | Time series spectral curve | Mile County, Yunnan Province | Corn, rice, sugar cane | 0.655 | [15] |
| HJ-1A/B and MODIS | Comprehensive features | Guangxi Zuojiang River Basin | Sugar cane | 0.8 | [14] |
| | NDVI timing curve | Jiangsu Province | Winter wheat and rape | 0.85 | [16] |
| GF-1 and Landsat | Features such as time series phenology and spectrum | Aksu Region, Xinjiang | Corn, rice, wheat, cotton | 0.83 | [17] |
| | Phenological spectral characteristics | Bei'an City, Heilongjiang | Corn, rice, wheat, soybean | 0.8754 | [41] |
| | NDVI timing and spectral characteristics | Jiutai District, Changchun City | Corn, rice, soybean | 0.88 | [42] |
| MODIS、Landsat and HJ-1 | Vegetation index time series curve | Xinjiang Bole City | Corn, cotton, grapes, melon | 0.9 | [25] |
| HJ CCD and Landsat 8 OLI | NDVI timing and spectral curve | Xining | Wheat, rape, barley, potatoes | 0.882 | [44] |
| Sentinel-1 and Sentinel-2 | Multi-band spectral characteristics | A farm in Dali, Shaanxi Province | Corn, wheat, alfalfa | 0.9 | [64] |
| HJ-1A and GF-1 | Comprehensive features | Sihong County, Jiangsu Province | Corn, rice | 0.9707 | [71] |

## 3   The Fusion Method of Multi-source RS Data

With the rapid development of remote sensing technology, the acquisition of agricultural information gradually tends to the system of Satellite-UAV-Ground Internet of Things

System, which can quickly acquire multi-source and multi-view farmland information data. Multi-source data need to be fused according to certain rules before using [18–20]. Based on the literature review of CNKI in the past decade, this paper introduces the fusion method and recognition method of multi-source remote sensing data. The application and recognition effect of each case are shown in Table 1.

### 3.1 Realization of Multi-source RS Data Fusion for High Temporal Resolution Targets

Multi-source remote sensing image collaboration can expand the frequency of repeated observation on the ground, effectively capture the optimal time window for crop recognition [5, 21], and achieve the goal of "time optimization". Extracting the long time series spectral characteristics of crops by using the image of crop key growth period or whole growth period can solve the phenomenon of crop phenological period crossing and improve the recognition accuracy [22]. Multi-temporal remote sensing data can be divided into multi-phase homologous sensors and heterogeneous sensors according to different data sources [23].

Qinxue Xiong et al. [24] had used multi-period homogenous sensor data for their study. They selected 17 different time-phase MODIS data from May to December 2001 to analyze NDVI time series curves, and then applied hierarchical classification method and BP neural network method to supervise the classification of autumn crop in Jiangling County, Hubei Province. Crop recognition model is a combination of NDVI time series curve data with high temporal resolution extracted from MODIS data and Landsat ETM standard data. This model provides a reliable basis for high precision crop spatial distribution mapping. The study by PengYu Hao et al. [25] is a typical case of crop classification using heterogeneous sensors. They fused 15-view MODIS data and 7-view TM/HJ-1 data into vegetation index time-series data with both 30m spatial resolution, then transformed the TM/HJ-1 vegetation index into MODIS vegetation index by linear regression model. Finally, they used the minimum distance classification method to distinguish cotton, maize and other crops in Bole City, Xinjiang, and the recognition accuracy reached more than 90%. This study uses heterogeneous source data to establish vegetation reference curves. It eliminates the manual collection of training samples compared with the traditional supervised classification, achieves automatic extraction of crop planting area with high spatial resolution for long time series [26].

### 3.2 Realization of Multi-source RS Data Fusion for High Spatial Resolution Targets

The use of high spatial resolution remote sensing data can extract richer spectral information of features, clearer texture features and clearer spatial neighborhood geometric relation-ships, which provides new opportunities for high precision extraction of crop target classification and planting area [27, 28]. Small wave transform methods have been widely used in image fusion because of better spatial scale transformation matching [29], and easier understanding of the synthesized images [30].

For example, Xiaohe Gu et al. [31] used wavelet transform method to fuse MODIS temporal images with 250 m spatial resolution and TM images with 30 m resolution, and obtained time series fusion images with 30 m resolution. The minimum distance classifier combined with crop NDVI growth curve was used to distinguish the main crops in Yuanyang County, Henan Province, and effectively extract maize planting area and spatial distribution. Jie Li [32] and Tao Han et al. [33] found that Sentinel-2A could well extract crop distribution information due to higher spatial resolution in small-scale agricultural areas with complex agricultural structures. In Sentinel-2A, different features show significant differences in spectral characteristics and vegetation indices, which makes Sentinel-2A more suitable for the study of small-scale areas with complex feature structures and fragmented land masses. In addition, Bu and Osler et al. [34] showed that the "pixel-level scale extension" of different resolution data can effectively distinguish mixed pixels and identify feature boundaries, which can be applied in feature classification studies.

### 3.3  Multi-source RS Data Fusion with a Combination of Spatio-Temporal and Spectral Advantages

High spatial and temporal resolution data can improve the accuracy of ground interpretation, and hyperspectral images can obtain the continuous band of feature spectra, which will directly distinguish crop species [35–39]. Therefore, in complex terrain areas with small crop planting area, complex planting pattern and high frag-mentation of farmland landscape [43], it is still urgent to study crop classification by combining temporal and spatial advantages with spectral ad-vantages [40–42]. For example, Feifei Shi et al. (2018) [44] extracted crop NDVI time series data based on HJ CCD and Landsat 8 OLI data, while using HJ-1A HSI data to extract spectral feature variables to form a multi-source dataset. They used classification and regression tree (CART) and support vector machine (SVM) to classify major crops such as oilseed rape, wheat and potatoes in Xining City, a plateau region. Ling Ouyang et al. [45] selected GF-1 data and Landsat8 OLI data as remote sensing data sources, and conducted regression analysis on the spectral reflectance of the same ground object. The decision tree classification method was used to detect crop planting structure in Bei'an City of Heilongjiang Province based on crop phenology and spectral characteristics. Xiaohui Li et al. [46] accurately distinguished the cultivated land area of Datong City, Shanxi Province based on GF-1 image, and extracted the distribution of main crops by using landsat8 OLI image. In summary, it is feasible to use multi-source data fusion for crop identification in complex terrain areas.

## 4  Main Methods of RS Crop Recognition

Extracting important feature parameters of crops based on information such as reflectance spectra, colors, and textures of features and combining them with appropriate classification methods to distinguish crop types [47, 48] is the basis of crop identification from multi-source remote sensing data. In this paper, we introduce three methods for the application of multi-source remote sensing imagery in the field of crop identification, the results of each method and application cases are shown in Table 2.

**Table 2.** Results of remote sensing crop identification methods and application cases

| Identification methods | | | | Classifier | Identify areas | Agrotype | Accuracy | References |
|---|---|---|---|---|---|---|---|---|
| Image analysis | Spectral features | Phenological feature | Comprehensive feature | | | | | |
| Oobject-based classification | Time series spectral curve of 10 band spectral average | NDVI time series curve | | Spectral angle mapping, maximum likelihood, BP neural network, etc | Maile County, Yunnan Province | Sugarcane, maize and rice | Kappa coefficient 0.655 | [15] |
| | Supervised classification of ground object spectrum | | | Spectral Angle Mapping and Decision Tree Classification | Datong City, Shanxi Province | Potato, grain, soybean and spring maize | Classification accuracy 0.8534 | [46] |
| Object-oriented multi-scale segmentation | 9 Spectral Vegetation Index and Reflectivity | Multiple exponential time series curve | | Decision tree classifiers | Bei' an City, Heilongjiang Province | Soybean, maize and wheat | Accuracy greater than 0.85 | [45] |
| Object-oriented Mean Shift segmentation | | HANTS analysis NDVI time series | | SVM | Yongqing County, Langfang City, Hebei Province | Winter wheat, summer maize, spring maize and sweet potato | Overall accuracy 0.9435 | [65] |
| Object oriented classification and four land parcel oriented classification methods | | | 7 Band + 10 Vegetation Index + 3 Texture + 3 Geometric Features | Random forest | The eighth division of xinjiang production and construction corps | Cotton, grape, maize, winter wheat and alfalfa | Kapps coefficients for plots are greater than those for object-oriented plots | [25] |

(continued)

**Table 2.** (*continued*)

| Identification methods | | | | Classifier | Identify areas | Agrotype | Accuracy | References |
|---|---|---|---|---|---|---|---|---|
| Image analysis | Spectral features | Phenological feature | Comprehensive feature | | | | | |
| | | | 5 Spectral + 5 Vegetation Index + 7 Band Difference + 1 Texture Feature | Random forest | Sihong County, Jiangsu Province | Rice, corn | Overall accuracy 0.9707 ( optimized feature subset) | [71] |
| | | | Phenological, temporal and spectral features | Decision tree classifiers | Aksu xinjiang Province | Cotton, maize, wheat and rice | Overall accuracy 0.83 | [17] |
| | Supervisory classification ( mean and variance of multi-band) | | | Minimum distance, maximum likelihood, support vector machine and BP neural network | A farm in Dali, Shaanxi Province | Wheat, corn, alfalfa | Overall classification accuracy greater than 0.9 | [64] |
| | Unsupervised classificationISODATA | | | Spatial geometry semantic constraints | Langfang City, Hebei Province | Fall wheat | Overall classification accuracy 0.9533 | [66] |
| | Maximum, minimum, mean and standard deviation of B1, B2, B3 and B4 | NDVI time series curve | | Simple decision tree | Heilongjiang 852 Farm | Rice, wheat and maize | Kappa coefficient 0.8924 | [8] |

*(continued)*

**Table 2.** (*continued*)

| Identification methods | | | | Classifier | Identify areas | Agrotype | Accuracy | References |
|---|---|---|---|---|---|---|---|---|
| Image analysis | Spectral features | Phenological feature | Comprehensive feature | | | | | |
| Wavelet fusion | Supervised classification | NDVI Standard Growth Curve | | Minimum distance classification | Yuanyang County, Henan Province | Maize | Time series analysis greater than supervised classification | [31] |
| | | Complete phenophase of multitemporal wheat | | Gaussian Kernel(PCM) | Radaur City, India | Wheat | Low entropy value leads to high accuracy of wheat | [9] |
| | | Multiple exponential time series curve | | Multi-index threshold analysis, maximum likelihood, classification regression decision tree, SVM, etc | Agricultural areas | Wheat, corn, rice, etc | Extraction accuracy greater than 0.85 | [10, 13, 15, 17, 25, 57] |

## 4.1 Recognition Methods Based on Temporal Phenological Features

Phenology knowledge show us that different crops are affected by climate, soil, hydrology and other factors in specific areas, and have different periodic growth and development laws [49]. Studies have shown that the time series of Normalized Difference Vegetation Index (NDVI), Enhanced Vegetation Index (EVI) and Normalized Difference Water Index (NDWI) can accurately reflect the dynamic change trend of crops in different periods [50, 51]. It contributes to solving the problem of 'foreign matter congener spectrum' in crop identification and is widely used in monitoring crop annual changes. The key to crop classification based on temporal phenological characteristics is the phenological period and characteristic parameters of crop growth [52]. However, the remote sensing data acquisition and processing are disturbed by many factors such as sensor noise [12] and solar altitude angle, which leads to abnormal fluctuations in the vegetation index curve of time series. Usually, smoothing denoising and eliminating abnormal points are used to reconstruct time series data.

At present, phenological characteristics combined with temporal remote sensing data is the mainstream of remote sensing crop classification research. For example, Ansai, Machao, Rongqun Zhang and Yuepeng Ping et al. [53–56] used MODIS time series data to establish vegetation time series curve, and classify the main crops in plain and hilly areas by extracting phenological indexes such as the beginning and end of crop growth season and the length of crop growth season. Xia Zhao et al. [57, 58] identified crops in Qinghai Province. The results showed that the recognition accuracy of spring wheat, potato and rape was more than 60%. Yanjun Yang [59] used five different classification methods to classify winter wheat, summer maize, rice and peanut through GF-1 WFV satellite images. The results showed that the NDVI time series curve after smoothing treatment could highlight the overall trend of crops.

## 4.2 Recognition Methods Based on Spectral Features

Remote sensing images record the electromagnetic wave information of ground objects. Because the spectral reflection characteristics are different, the images show different brightness, texture features and geometric structures [60]. And hyperspectral can record hundreds of narrow bands from visible light to infrared light, which are close to the actual spectrum of crops in the case of high spatial resolution. Therefore, the difference in spectral reflectance of crops can be used as a basis for judgment [61, 62]. The methods of crop recognition based on spectral features mainly include supervised classification and unsupervised classification. The main difference between them is whether there is prior knowledge.

Supervised classification is the process of using training samples to construct discriminant functions to identify classes of image elements [63], and the main methods are maximum likelihood, SVM and decision tree. Lin Zhu [64] used Sentinel-1 and Sentinel-2 multi-source remote sensing data for crop classification based on minimum distance, maximum likelihood, SVM and BP neural network. Crop classification experiments on a farm in Dali, Shaanxi Province show that the classification results of BP neural network without cloud cover are the best, and SVM with cloud cover are the best, the overall classification accuracy is more than 90%. Unsupervised classification only relies on statistical feature differences to achieve classification purposes, and mainly adopts cluster analysis methods such as iterative self-organizing data analysis algorithm (ISODATA) [65, 66]. Limin Wang et al. [65] used ISODATA to classify multi-temporal GF-1 WFV data in Langfang City, Hebei Province, and established semantic constraints. Winter wheat was identified according to Sigmoid spatial membership. The classification accuracy was 95.33% and the Kappa coefficient was 0.90. In short, supervised classification method has high classification accuracy, but requires prior knowledge, and the workload is large. Methods of crop classification depend on specific circumstances.

### 4.3 Comprehensive Feature Selection for Crop Recognition by Remote Sensing

Auxiliary data are non-image information used to assist image analysis, mainly including parameters such as elevation, slope, slope direction, and various thematic information [67, 68]. Using the spatial characteristics of natural elements and the texture characteristics [69] of measuring the spatial distribution of pixel neighborhood gray can improve the accuracy of crop recognition and effectively avoid the phenomenon of 'same object, different spectrum'. In the hilly areas with high fragmentation, the spatial feature information can help to express the planting area boundary [43]. Crop classification research uses all the feature information to increase the data dimension, which will inevitably lead to Hughe phenomenon, reducing the recognition accuracy. Dimension reduction is the use of specific algorithms to select feature subsets that are important to the classification process, and has become a key step in processing high spatial resolution images. When feature selection is carried out, the classifier is limited by many factors such as the landscape structure of the study area, so the multi-classifier system has been widely used [70].

Na Wang [71] used GF-1 and HJ-1A images to extract the multi-temporal spectral characteristics, vegetation index characteristics (NDVI, perpendicular vegetation index PVI, difference vegetation index DVI, soil-adjusted vegetation index SAVI), texture characteristics (variance, information entropy, second-order distance, etc.) and band difference information of Sihong County, Jiangsu Province. Then, they design six classification schemes based on random forest classifier and SelectKBest method to select the optimized feature subset (A. spectral feature, B. spectral feature + band difference feature, C. spectral feature + vegetation index feature, D. spectral feature + texture feature, E. spectral feature + band difference feature + vegetation index feature + texture feature, and F. optimized feature subset). The classification results show that the recognition accuracy of multi-information comprehensive features of remote sensing crops is higher than that of single original spectral feature classification.

## 5  Accuracy Evaluation of Classification Results and Influencing Factors

The accuracy evaluation of crop classification refers to the comparison of the classification results with the actual data to determine the accuracy of various ground objects [1]. Commonly used methods for evaluation of classification results include confusion matrix, result superposition and ROC curve [72], and indicators for evaluation of accuracy include User's Accuracy, Producer's Accuracy, Overall Accuracy, Kappa coefficient, etc., as well as the calculation of absolute error and root mean square error based on departmental statistics [52]. Usually, the higher the resolution of data is, the stronger the recognition ability is. However, the distinction of crop categories is not entirely dependent on spatial resolution. It is necessary to combine the environmental characteristics of topography, geomorphology and soil in the study area and the relative difference between the brightness and structure of the surrounding objects [61]. We should comprehensively consider the above characteristics to obtain data with optimal resolution. In addition, the rationality of training samples and the heterogeneity within plots will also affect the classification accuracy, and the mixed pixel decomposition method is helpful to improve the classification accuracy of crops [73]. The Table 2 shows that the extraction accuracy of comprehensive features or combination of spectral and phenological features is higher.

## 6  Problems and Prospects

In recent years, with the rapid development of remote sensing technology, the research on crop recognition based on multi-source data has made great progress, but there are still some problems in the classification accuracy and feasibility. In the future, the theoretical system and technical methods of multi-source remote sensing crop identification should be further developed, and its practical application scope should be expanded to promote the development of agricultural remote sensing.

1) Establishing a technical method system for remote sensing crop identification in different ecological zones. The spatial distribution status of crops affects the recognition accuracy of crop types [74]. Because the growing environment of crops has differences, ecological zoning should be carried out according to the agricultural zoning system or farmland landscape, and we should establish a separate system of technical methods for crop identification. Meanwhile, when extracting crop information in areas with abundant crop species and complex terrain, the processing method of image partition can be used to improve the recognition accuracy. However, the size of spatial and temporal scales of different regions or ecological zones and the law of range boundary division need to be further studied, which will determine the selection of remote sensing image types, classification methods, etc.

2) Comprehensive classification features and multi-classifier system application research. There are many characteristic parameters extracted from crop recognition based on multi-source remote sensing data. In addition to the spectral features, temporal phenology differences and texture features, we can also try to classify the area, aspect ratio and shape index as the classification features. However, due to the diversity of information sources, there will be differences in classification, so the comprehensive application of information needs further research. At the same time, it is necessary to consider the contribution rate of different features to the recognition accuracy, and study the influence of feature combination on crop classification, so as to obtain the optimal feature collection in the study area. Studies have confirmed that the multi-classifier system is an effective solution to control the classification uncertainty of remote sensing

images and improve the classification accuracy [75, 76]. Therefore, it's application in crop recognition is a valuable research direction in the future.

3) In-depth exploration of remote sensing technology for crop identification in complex topographic areas. Now the domestic use of optical remote sensing for crop type identification mainly focuses on large area plain agricultural demonstration zone of staple crops such as rice, corn and wheat, cole, potato, soybean and cotton and other crops involved, but there is little research on regional specific crops such as barley and oats in alpine regions such as the Qinghai-Tibet Plateau. Therefore, the potential of remote sensing data to identify crops in complex terrain areas should be further explored, and remote sensing techniques applicable to identify these small crops in complex terrain areas should be studied to provide scientific basis for fine agricultural management of small agricultural areas.

# References

1. Zheng, L.: Crop classification using multi-features of Chinese Gaofen-1/6 sateliite remote sensing images. University of Chinese Academy of Sciences (2017)
2. Liu, Y.: Changes in crop planting Structure of the Heihe river basin in China based on the multi-temporal NDVI from TM/ETM+/OLI images. Chongqing Jiaotong University (2017)
3. Zhang, X., Liu, J., Qin, F.: A review of remote sensing application in crop type discrimination. Chin. Agric. Sci. Bull. 30(33), 278–285 (2014)
4. Liu, M., Wang, Z., Mang, W.: Crop classification based on multitemporal landsat8 oli imagery and MODIS NDVI. Time Series Data. Soil Crops 6(2), 104–112 (2017)
5. Song, Q.: Object-based image analysis with machine learning algorithms for cropping pattern mapping using GF-1/WFV imagery. Dissertation. Chinese Academy of Agricultural Sciences (2016)
6. Dadhwal, V.K., Ray, S.S.: Crop assessment using remote sensing. Part-II. Crop condition and yield assessment (2016)
7. Xiao, X., Boles, S., Liu, J.: Mapping paddy rice agriculture in southern China using multi tempora MODIS images. Remote Sens. 95(4), 480–492 (2005)
8. Zheng, C., Wang, X., Hang, J.: Automatic extraction of rice area information from SPOT-5 satellite image based on characteristic band. Remote Sens. Technol. 2(3), 294–299 (2008)
9. Aggarwal, R., Kumar, A., Raju, P.L.N.: Gaussian kernel based classification approach for wheat identification. ISPRS-Int. Arch. Photogrammetry. Remote Sens. Spat. Inf. 8(1), 671–676 (2014)
10. Xu, Q., Yang, G., Long, H.: Crop planting recognition based on MODIS NDVI multi-year time series data. Trans. Chin. Soc. Agricultural Eng. 30(11), 134–144 (2014)
11. Kim, H.O., Yeom, J.M.: Effect of red-edge and texture features for object-based paddy rice crop classification using RapidEye multi-spectral satellite image data. Int. J. Remote Sens. 35(19), 7046–7068 (2014)
12. Zhang, H., Cao, X., Li, Q.: Research on crop classification based on NDVI time series of multi-temporal environmental stars. Remote Sens. Technol. Appl. 30(2), 304–311 (2015)
13. Wuyun, D., Wulan, T., Yu, L., et al.: Analysis of the growth condition of spring wheat in Hetao irrigation district based on GF-1 WFV-taking Linhe district as an example. J. Northern Agric. 46(2), 123–128 (2018)
14. Han, Z.: Extraction of sugarcane planting areas by fusing environmental satellite and MODIS data. Nanning Normal University (2019)

15. Peng, G., Gong, E., Cui, W.: A comparative study of crop identification and classification methods in typical areas with multi-temporal images. J. Geo-Inf. Sci. **11**(2), 225–230 (2009)
16. Wang, S.: Area extraction of oilseed rape and its coeval major crops in Jiangsu Province based on multi-source remote sensing. Yangtze University (2015)
17. Xin, H.H., Wu, L.: Zhu: crop planting structure extraction based on GF-1 and Landsat8 OLI images-taking Akesu area in Xinjiang as an example. Shandong Agric. Sci. **51**(7), 143–151 (2019)
18. Chen, Z., Ren, J., Tang, H.: Progress and prospects of agricultural remote sensing research applications. J. Remote Sens. **20**(5), 748–767 (2016)
19. Bian, J., Li, A., Wang, Q.: Development of dense time series 30-m image products from the Chinese HJ-1A/B constellation: a case study in Zoige Plateau. China. Remote Sens. **7**(12), 15846 (2015)
20. Roy, D.P., Ju, J., Kline, K.: Web-enabled Landsat data (WELD): Landsat ETM+ composited mosaics of the conterminous United States. Remote Sens. Environ. **114**(1), 35–49 (2010)
21. Wardlow, B.D., Egbert, S.L.: Large-area crop mapping using time-series MODIS 250 m NDVI data: an assessment for the US Central Great Plains. Remote Sens. Environment **112**(3), 1096–1116 (2008)
22. Tu, X.: Global weak Analysis of crop identification methods in multi-temporal remote sensing images. Bulletin of Surveying and Mapping, 4. Surveying and Mapping Press (2012)
23. Song, Q., Zhou, Q., Wu, W.: Recent progresses in research of integrating multi-source remote sensing data for crop mapping. Scientia Agricultura **48**(6), 1122–1135 (2015)
24. Xiong, Q., Hang, J.: Monitoring the acreage of autumn harvest crops using NDVI time-series characteristics. Trans. Chin. Soc. Agric. Eng. **25**(1), 144–148 (2009)
25. Hao, P., Niu, Z., Wang, L.: Automatic crop area extraction method based on historical time-series vegetation index library with multi-source data. Trans. Chin. **28**(23), 123–131 (2012)
26. Zhao, B.: Planting structure extraction and yield estimation based on GF-1 and landsat-8. Hebei University of Engineering (2019)
27. Abdikan, S., Sanli, B., Sunar, F.: F: A comparative data-fusion analysis of multi-sensor satellite images. Int. J. Digital Earth **7**(8), 671–687 (2014)
28. Tang, H., Wu, W., Yang, P.: Recent progresses in monitoring crop spatial patterns by using remote sensing technologies. Scientia Agricultura Sinica **43**(14), 2879–2888 (2010)
29. Zhang, X.: Research on remote sensing inversion technique of land features. Nanjing University of Information Science and Technology (2007)
30. Zhu, M.: Application of wavelet transform in digital image processing technology. J. Shandong Agric. Eng. Univ. **36**(8), 22–23 (2019)
31. Gu, X., Han, L., Wang, J.: Remote sensing estimation of maize planted area by low and medium resolution wavelet fusion. Trans. Chin. Soc. **28**(3), 203–209 (2012)
32. Li, J., Zhang, J., Li, Y.: Differential analysis of Sentinel-2A and GF-1 data in extraction of rape cultivation and comparative study of extraction methods. J. Yunnan **41**(4), 678–688 (2019)
33. Han, T., Pan, J., Zhang, P., Cao, L.: Differential study of sentinel-2a and landsat-8 images in oilseed rape identification. Remote Sens. Technol. Appl. **33**(5), 890–899 (2018)
34. Boosir, J., Ma, Q.: Wang: scale conversion of multi-sensor remote sensing digital images with different resolutions. Acta Geographica **59**(1), 101–110 (2004)
35. Guo, Y., Liu, Q., Liu, G.: Research on extraction of major crop planting information based on MODIS time-series NDVI. J. Nat. Resour. **30**(10), 1808–1818 (2017)
36. Lin, W.: Extraction based on modis spectrum analysis. Graduate School of Chinese Academy of Sciences (2006)
37. Hu, Z.: Research on the extraction of spatial and temporal distribution information of major food crops in China based on MODIS. University of Electronic Science and technology (2006)
38. Yang, X., Zhang, X., Jiang, D.: A method to extract multi-crop sown area based on MODIS time-series NDVI eigenvalues. Resour. Sci. **6**, 17–22 (2004)

39. Zhang, M.: Research on crop phenological monitoring and crop type identification model based on MODIS data. Huazhong Agricultural University (2013)
40. Liu, Y.: Oasis main food crops remote-sensing recognition and yield estimation based on multi-temporal GF-1 WFV images a case study in minqin oasis. Northwest Normal University (2016)
41. Liu, Z., Liu, L., Guo, H.: Extraction study of spring wheat based on GF1-NDVI time-series images. Beijing Surv. **32**(6), 643–646 (2018)
42. Ren, X.: Research on multi-source remote sensing classification methods for crops in Jiutai District. Jilin University, Changchun (2018)
43. Zhang, H.: Research on crop landscape model and its effects on crop identification and acreage estimation. Chinese Academy of Sciences (2017)
44. Shi, F., Lei, C., Xiao, J.: A comparative data-fusion analysis of multi-sensor satellite images. Geography Geo-inf. Sci. **34**(5), 49–55 (2018)
45. Ouyang, L., Mao, D., Wang, Z.: Analysis of crop planting structure and yield based on GF-1 and Landsat8 OLI image. Trans. Chin. Soc. Agric. Eng. **33**(11), 147–156 (2017)
46. Li, X., Wang, H., Wang, X.: Research on remote sensing classification of agricultural crops based on multi-temporWu Hongfeng. Research on crop pest and disease monitoring technology based on multi-source data fusion. Remote Sens. Technol. **34**(2), 389–397 (2019)
47. Wu, H.: Research on crop pest and disease monitoring technology based on multi-source data fusion. Mod. Agric. **5**, 59–60 (2015)
48. Li, Y.: Study on image recognition method of corn and soybean and rice. Heilongjiang Bayi Agricultural University (2017)
49. Sheng, Y., Chen, W., Xiao, Q.: Macroscopic classification of vegetation in China using meteorological satellite vegetation index. Chin. Sci. Bull. **40**(1), 68–71 (1995)
50. Arvor, D., Dubreuil, J.M.: V: A classification of MODIS EVI time series for crop mapping in the state of Mato Grosso. Brazi. Int. J. Remote Sens. **32**(22), 7847–7871 (2011)
51. Eastman, J.R., Sangermano, F., Machado, E.A.: Global trends in seasonality of normalized difference vegetation index (NDVI)1982–2011. Remote Sens. **5**(10), 4799–4818 (2013)
52. Yang, Y.: Extraction of winter wheat planting area based on NDVI time series data. Nanjing University (2019)
53. An, S.S., Jun, Y.: Zhao: extraction of winter wheat planting area based on NDVI time series data. J. Nat. Resour. **47**(15), 36 (2019)
54. Ma, C., Yang, F., Wang, X.: Extraction of tea gardens in southern hilly mountains based on mesoscale spectral and temporal phenological features. Remote Sens. Land Resour. **31**(1), 141–148 (2019)
55. Zhang, R., Wang, S., Ga, W.: Remote-sensing classification method of county-level agricultural crops using time-series NDVI. Trans. Chin. Soc. Agric. Mach. **46**(S1), 246–252 (2015)
56. Ping, Y., Zang, S.: Crop classification based on MODIS time series and phenological characteristics. J. Nat. Resour. **31**(3), 503–513 (2016)
57. Zhao, X., Wang, X., Cao, G., et al.: Extraction and application of crop growing season parameters based on time-series vegetation index in eastern Qinghai. Chin. Sci. Technol. Achievements **17**, 16–20 (2018)
58. Zhao, X., Wang, X., Cao, G.: Crop identification by using seasonal parameters extracted from time series Landsat images in a mountainous agricultural county of Qinghai Province. China. J. Agric. Sci. **9**(4), 116–127 (2017)
59. Yang, Y., Zhan, Y., Tia, Q.: Crop classification based on GF-1/WFV NDVI time series data. Trans. Chin. Soc. Agric. Eng. **31**(24), 155–161 (2019)
60. Wang, L., Wu, B., Zhang, M.: Winter wheat and rapeseed classification during key growth period by integrating multi-source remote sensing data. J. Geo-Inf. Sci. **21**(7), 1121–1131 (2019)

61. Zhao, Y.: Principles and Methods of Remote Sensing Application Analysis. Science Press, Beijing (2003)
62. Wang, D., Wu, J.: Research on hyperspectral remote sensing identification of crop species. Geography Geo-Inf. Sci. **31**(02), 29–33 (2015)
63. Yan, J., Chen, H., Liu, L.: Research progress of hyperspectral image classification. Opt. Precis. Eng. **27**(03), 680–693 (2019)
64. Zhu, L.: Research on crop classification and planting area extraction based on Sentinel multi-source remote sensing data. Northwest A&F University (2018)
65. Wang, L., Liu, J., Sha, J.: Automatic classification of winter wheat: based on geometry semantic knowledge. Chin. Agric. Sci. Bull. **35**, 120–130 (2019)
66. Xu, L., Wang, Q., Chen, Z.: A remote sensing interpretation method for fast differentiation of easily confused crops. Geospatial Inf. **15**(01), 59–62 (2017)
67. Jia, K., Li, Q.: Current status and prospect of research on the selection of crop remote sensing classification feature variables. Resour. Sci. **35**(12), 2507–2516 (2013)
68. Li, A., Bo, Y.: Comparative study of multi-source remote sensing thematic information: status, problems and prospects. Adv. Earth Sci. **26**(07), 741–750 (2011)
69. Zhou, Z., Li, S., Zhang, K., Shao, Y.: Crop distribution mapping based on CNN and crop spectral texture features. Remote Sens. Technol. Appl. **34**(04), 694–703 (2019)
70. Zhang, L.: Study on feature selection and ensemble learning based on feature selection for high-dimensional datasets. Tsinghua University (2004)
71. Wang, N., Li, Q., Du, X.: Univariate feature selection for remote sensing identification of major crops in northern Jiangsu Province. J. Remote Sens. **21**(04), 519–530 (2017)
72. Ban, S.: Remote sensing identification and extraction of county crop classification types. Northwest A&F University (2014)
73. Han, Y., Meng, J.: Research progress of remote sensing classification of crops for plots. Remote Sens. Land Resour. **31**(02), 1–9 (2019)
74. Jia, K., Wu, B., Li, Q.: Crop classification using HJ satellite multispectral data in the North China Plain. J. Appl. Remote Sens. **7**, 73–76 (2013)
75. Benediktsson, J.A., Chanussot, J., Fauvel, M.: Multiple classifier systems in remote sensing: from basics to recent developments. Multiple Classifier Syst.ss **44**(72), 501–512 (2007)
76. Du, P.J., Xia, J.S., Zhang, W.: Multiple classifier system for remote sensing image classification: a review. Sensors **12**(04), 4764–4792 (2012)

# Study on the Internet of Things Discipline in Civil Aviation

Jialei Chen[✉] and Huan Zhang

Civil Aviation Flight, University of China, Guanghan 618307, China
965353428@qq.com

**Abstract.** With the increasing development of computer science technology, the Internet of things technology is also maturing. Internet of things technology has great development prospects. At the same time, it has played its good influence and value in different fields. It will be of great significance to apply Internet of things discipline and technology to civil aviation work. This article briefly introduces the Internet of things discipline and technology. Then it introduces and discusses the research on the application of Internet of things discipline and technology in civil aviation. It is hoped that through the various applications of the current Internet of things technology in the civil aviation field, the Internet of things discipline and technology can give full play to its advantages in civil aviation, promote the economic development of the airport, and tap more possibilities for the actual development.

**Keywords:** Internet of things · Civil aviation · Direction

## 1 Introduction

Kevin Ashton, co-founder and executive director of MIT's Auto-ID Center, first mentioned the Internet of things in a speech to Procter and Gamble in 1999. The Internet of things refers to a system composed of interrelated computing devices, mechanical and digital machines, objects, animals or people [1–4]. These devices have unique identifiers and can transmit data through the network without human to human or human to computer interaction. The Internet of things makes the Internet connection between electronic devices and sensors easier. The Internet of things is a progress integrating a wide range of intelligent systems, architectures, many sensors and devices. It uses quantum and nanotechnology in terms of capacity, detection and computing speed, which is unimaginable in history. Comprehensive academic work and press releases are carried out on the network and in various article contents, showing the potential of the Internet of things revolution in efficiency and usefulness. Before designing a new business strategy, the Internet of things can be used as an initial step to take health, protection and interoperability into account.

## 2   Related Work

### 2.1   Intelligent Parking and Positioning

In 2013, Chen Xuan et al. designed a vehicle positioning system based on ZigBee wireless sensor network [5]. Through the research on wireless sensor network nodes, servers, and positioning technology and the design of relevant software, the system can be applied to vehicle positioning and tracking, which is ultimately conducive to solving the positioning problem after traffic accidents. In 2016, Atif et al. expanded the mode of Internet of things into the service scope based on intelligent parking in smart cities, and expounded the working problems of parking system from four dimensions: Interoperability of information and services in global interconnection, optimization of cloud agents, collection of real-time data flow of parking system and creation of language in specific dimension [6]. This law can facilitate namely car drivers and parking service providers, to improve the value-added services of parking and provide a new direction of cloud services for business models.

In 2017, Wei Ni designed a new algorithm to realize intersection control through vehicle self-organizing network, rather than using the combination of mutually exclusive methods to let the vehicles at the intersection compete for the right of way through information exchange [7]. Instead, based on the group method, the waiting vehicles in each lane are divided into groups. In the group, only the first vehicle needs to process requests from other lanes, and the member vehicles can follow the first vehicle, which significantly reduces the message cost, obtains better performance in terms of waiting time and system throughput, and realizes intersection control at less information cost, The superiority of r-mev algorithm is verified by NS3 simulation. In the same year, Zuo Yin proposed a GPS / WSN data fusion positioning system based on the Internet of things [8]. RSSI positioning is carried out based on ranging, the position information of airport vehicles is collected, and the joint Kalman filter algorithm is established to make the vehicle enter the GPS shield and still run the system. The system can improve the positioning accuracy and has good stability.

In 2020, Ghulam Ali et al. proposed a framework based on deep memory network, which integrates and develops a decision support system [9]. The system can not only predict the availability of parking spaces, but also predict the daytime and hourly occupancy rate of parking spaces, and finally provide guidance and help for drivers, select better routes and appropriate destinations, so as to realize the scalable development of more intelligent parking services. In 2021, Mohammad Peyman et al. developed a method based on agile optimization algorithm to solve the problem of dynamic ride sharing in edge or fog environment [10]. Through an example to verify the algorithm, it can be seen that in the traditional static scene and dynamic scene, the traffic system of the former has been optimized at the beginning, and the dynamic scene will use new data and randomly re optimize the system. In [11], Ou Yang proposed an indoor target recognition and tracking method based on RFID and CCD collaborative information to identify moving targets carrying electronic tags. The virtual reference tag is extended by RFID for rough positioning, and then the rough location information is used to guide the monitoring of different CCD open or sleep areas, so as to save the consumption of network and computing resources. Finally, CCD is used to realize more accurate positioning.

## 2.2   Runway Detection

In [12], Amedeo developed an innovative sensor to detect whether there is ice or water on the surface of the airport runway. In order to evaluate the repeatability, stability and reliability of the sensor, different simulations and experiments are carried out in the laboratory and in the field. By connecting GPRS modem, the collected data is sent to the public database. After three years of system testing, without any external help, the sensor can display correct operation and automatically reactivate after failure. At the same time, the state of runway surface is virtually represented in the Internet of things, and the function of the Internet of things is used to open a new situation. In 2017, Julien et al. realized the synchronous integrated operation of ground motion and take-off by integrating GPR and RSP management from push back to take-off [13]. Through the test of an airport data, it is proved that this method can significantly shorten the total completion time and taxiing time, and can be put into daily operation. Zhao Jian et al. Developed a runway intrusion prevention system that can provide the status of the ground protection area in real time and active alarm function, which can provide the real-time status and active alarm function of the ground protection area [14]. The design adopts to build the detection model of runway conflict area, and simulate to build a simple test platform based on laser detector at the airport, so as to achieve the actual effect of the test system, and finally verify the reliability and practicability of the system.

## 2.3   Airport Environmental Monitoring

In [15], Yang Dong proposed a design scheme of airport noise sensing node based on Internet of things. By using high-performance and low-power floating-point DSP, tms320c6747 is used as the core operation module, and ZigBee's short-range wireless transmission is used to send the noise data to the noise sensing node of the sink node. The system hardware adopts a programmable gain instrument amplifier which can improve the signal-to-noise ratio and automatically adjust the gain. In terms of software, it is filtered by eighth-order butter woods filter. Finally, a noise sensing node with low cost and low installation requirements that can accurately monitor the airport noise is obtained. In 2021, Lee et al. measured and analyzed the profile of overflight noise during typical takeoff and landing operations of aircraft at Changi Airport in Singapore by using the internally developed Smartphone Application noise explorer [16]. It was found that the one-third octave value of the scene was also much higher than the one-third octave value of aircraft combination data, it shows that there are significant differences in noise levels between aircraft taking off and landing and between different aircraft. At the same time, the study shows that a large amount of low-frequency noise will be generated during aircraft flying over. Therefore, the existence of such noise should be considered when planning a new airport and a new residential area or commercial development near the airport.

In [17], X. H. Wang et al. designed a noise sensing system suitable for airport environment based on Internet of things technology. Collect airport noise information by installing sensing nodes, transmit noise information through mobile communication or wired network through sink nodes, analyze the data collected by corresponding nodes on the data processing web platform, and query the node power, longitude and latitude position and other data. The system has the advantages of simple installation, strong mobility and low cost. It can collect and analyze more comprehensive and detailed data for assessing the impact of aircraft noise on the surrounding environment. In [18], Zhou Zhiyong proposed the framework of the alarm system for the airport perimeter by using the intelligent visual Internet of things, which is mainly to deploy the airport monitoring through the core technology of the intelligent visual Internet of things. Then, through the visual management platform technology of 3DGIS, integrating visual sensing technology, data transmission technology, video image processing technology, artificial intelligence technology, pattern recognition and machine learning technology, 3D virtual environment technology, a panoramic video browsing and monitoring system is designed and constructed to monitor the airport area and accurately track and locate the target object, Then it realizes the function of real-time display and timely alarm.

In [19], Sun Jian studied the application of Internet of things technology for Airport video perception. For airport business, research the application of Internet of things through video perception, mainly including the technology of detecting and intelligent analysis of airport passenger dense crowd by using high-point and wide-angle cameras; With the help of positioning technology, RFID technology and other technologies for accurate location and management of airport staff; Technology of monitoring and positioning special vehicles in flight area in combination with positioning system; Video surveillance, in-depth learning, technology for analyzing passengers' business behavior, etc.

### 2.4   Airport Perimeter Intrusion Prevention System

In [20], X. M. Cao et al. designed the airport perimeter security system based on the Internet of things. The core of "Internet of things (sensor network)" is gradually upgraded and applied to the construction of airport security system. In 2012, J. H. Lin analyzed the perimeter anti intrusion system of the flight area of Pudong Airport and designed the front section perceptron based on the principle of spider web bionics [21]. Through a specific algorithm, filter the error judgment, lock the target position and start the alarm, monitor and display the video screen, link the lighting and broadcasting system to warn the scene, and notify the security inspection team members to deal with the alarm on the scene according to the plan. The system effectively improves the airport safety factor and optimizes the airport safety management mode, which has great development and application space. In [22], S. J. Liu discussed and analyzed the surrounding anti-intrusion system, runway detection, monitoring and management of Internet of things in the airport, transportation of dangerous goods, personnel positioning and intelligent fighting.

### 2.5   Application and Management of Airport Facilities and Equipment

In 2010, Tang Ming proposed an application of Internet of things technology in Airlines. RFID is used to sense the life jacket tag on the aircraft, timely control the life of the life jacket, and improve the inspection efficiency and accuracy [23]. In this case, applying the extended development of Internet of things technology to the management of other time-lived parts, including lifeboat, slide, oxygen cylinder and PSU oxygen repeater, will save more costs, greatly improve work efficiency and avoid potential safety hazards. In [24], Z. H. Li designed a set of management process of aircraft protective articles based on RFID technology. Through this process, human errors can be eliminated. At the same time, in order to avoid interference between equipment signals, low-frequency tags (passive tags) are used to obtain working energy from the corresponding radiated near field through inductive coupling to start the memory. By scanning whether the protective articles on the aircraft are complete, we can finally ensure the safety of the aircraft.

In 2017, Ding Feng proposed to apply BIM Technology and Internet of things technology to airport operation and maintenance management [25]. Build a visual operation management platform based on BIM. Build a dynamic data platform through Internet of things technology to realize equipment and facilities account management, airport knowledge base management, equipment warranty management, business process control system, maintenance workflow management, equipment assets and maintenance management, query and statistics management. In [26], S. D. Guan in Guangzhou discussed the application of 5G Internet of things in airport facilities and equipment, and proposed to apply 5G to contactless services. In the epidemic era, it can not only save the corresponding paper cost, but also ensure the normal operation of production. In the high-definition video monitoring of the airport, 5G technology is used for high-precision face recognition of passengers to ensure work safety.

In 2020, J. Y. Lin analyzed and adopted the intelligent lighting control system based on Lora Internet of things technology, single lamp control system, operation and maintenance management system and mobile app in combination with Beijing new airport expressway [27].

## 2.6 Aviation Logistics

In [28] X. L. Zou et al. proposed and designed an aviation logistics query system based on the Internet of things. The cargo information is collected through RFID technology, the collected data is transmitted to ZigBee terminal node through RS232 serial port, and then transmitted to routing node through ZigBee wireless network for short distance. Finally, the information is transmitted through ZigBee gateway. The system can save the cost of cargo management, improve the staff work efficiency and the informatization degree of aviation logistics management, and realize the intelligent, visual and informatization management of aviation logistics.

In [29], W. J. Wang and others studied the whole process tracking of luggage. After the necessity analysis and feasibility analysis of the application, it constructively puts forward the ideas and schemes of smart civil aviation and new infrastructure construction, and pursues the goal of establishing a civil aviation baggage transportation standard system, so as to effectively improve the service quality of civil aviation baggage transportation and provide civil aviation baggage tracking information service with public benefits.

In 2020, Zhang Chao of Wuhan discussed the establishment of wireless identification system based on RFID technology [30]. Carry out warehousing management for airport goods, such as warehousing, storage, outbound and storage yard, so as to realize the large network function of interconnection of things, people and things, and people, improve work efficiency and ensure accuracy.

## 2.7 Smart Airport

In 2017, Men Chong proposed that aviation enterprises can speed up the construction of Internet of things system from ground infrastructure [31]. For example, the current airport realizes the personalized service of passengers with Internet of things technology, and the system will remind passengers of check-in matters, baggage check-in, boarding gate, boarding notice and other information. It is envisaged that in the future, aviation enterprises will enable passengers to get more boarding experience through innovative Internet of things technology, including conveniently confirming check-in information and providing corresponding navigation services for each passenger through sensors of wearable devices; Collect passenger body information through sensing elements and intelligently adjust comfortable temperature, seat height, angle and other cabin environment; Use Internet of things technology to quickly check baggage and transfer flights for passengers.

In [32], Wen Wei deeply explored the application of Internet of things technology in airport equipment and facilities. Among them, the warning system that maliciously blocks the lens of the monitoring system and the one click enable alarm button and connect the airport video monitoring to the alarm system of the public security department in real time can quickly and maximally avoid property losses and casualties. Based on radio frequency identification technology, independent bar codes and labels are set. Baggage identification can be realized by scanning the bar codes. The basic information of baggage can be automatically displayed on the platform. The baggage system connected with the monitoring system provides passengers with high-quality baggage transportation services, which greatly improves the applicability and automation of Airport facilities. In 2020, Zhang Hong introduced and analyzed the application of the joint Internet of things technology in the smart field of Pudong International Airport [33]. Based on the narrowband Internet of things technology, realize the synchronous display and query of PC segment management and mobile terminal app, including the construction projects of airport smart site such as airport electronic map system, airport operator and vehicle patrol system, flood control management and meteorological detection display terminal of Pudong Airport, site safety management, airport environmental management, etc.

In the same year, VAIO considered the meaning of Blockchain in the decision-making process of supply chain, and Italian airports used the collaborative decision-making platform based on Blockchain to promote the cooperation between air traffic controllers and the aviation industry [34]. In [35], Patil designed a street lamp system that can control the switch according to the external environment and set an emergency button to feed back the information cloud service in real time after triggering the alarm. Provide safety mechanism for roads on the basis of reducing power consumption. And Mobasshir studied the design system of intelligent autonomous lighting and air ventilation for IOT [36].

After testing the accuracy and practicability of the system, the subsystem composition and software architecture of perceptual autonomous lighting, air quality monitoring and ventilation system were described, the advantages of embedded autonomous lighting system replacing traditional lighting system are studied, and the future research challenges and directions are put forward. In [37], Mendes et al. proposed an IOT management system applied to airport toilet management. Using the organizational structure formed by intelligent monitoring organization, control center organization, application interface organization and PANGEA multi management system, they designed a multi-agent architecture based on Pangea platform. Under the epidemic situation, the cleanliness of airport services has been improved, and the possibility of infecting COVID-19 in bathroom facilities has been reduced to a minimum. In 2021, W. J. Li analyzed the application of Internet of things in smart airport, including monitoring the air through sensors, transmitting it to the information center via wireless network and displaying it in the information display of the terminal and the corresponding APP and official account of the smart airport [38].

## 3   Conclusion

In recent years, the Internet of things technology is becoming more and more mature. Driven by the current technical and economic environment, its related industries have become a trend all over the world, and its role value and influence are also expanding. The application of Internet of things technology in the airport greatly ensures the safety of the airport. And the work efficiency and quality of the airport have been greatly improved. In the field of airports, the application and development of Internet of things technology is not only the development trend required by the times, but also an effective way to improve airport service quality and ensure airport security. Therefore, for the rapid development of the airport, it is necessary to introduce Internet of things technology, and effectively apply it to the airport management to give full play to its role.

**Acknowledgement.** The authors gratefully acknowledge the helpful comments and suggestions of the reviewers.

**Funding Statement.** This work is partially supported by the Civil Aviation Professional Project under grant no. 0252109, and Project of Sichuan Provincial Department of Science and Technology under grant nos. 22ZDYF3574 and 22RKX0726.

**Conflicts of Interest.** The authors declare that they have no conflicts of interest to report regarding the present study.

## References

1. Mohan, A.: Application and usefulness of Internet of Things in information technology. Int. J. Eng. Manag. Res. (IJEMR) **8**(3), 57–61 (2018)
2. Berguiga, A., Harchay, A.: An IoT-based intrusion detection system approach for TCP syn attacks. Comput. Mater. Contin. **71**(2), 3839–3851 (2022)

3. Hemalatha, P., Dhanalakshmi, K.: Cellular automata based energy efficient approach for improving security in IoT. Intell. Autom. Soft Comput. **32**(2), 811–825 (2022)
4. Oliver, S.G., Purusothaman, T.: Lightweight and secure mutual authentication scheme for iot devices using coap protocol. Comput. Syst. Sci. Eng. **41**(2), 767–780 (2022)
5. Chen, X., Li, Y.: Vehicle positioning system based on ZigBee wireless sensor network. Autom. Appl. **2**(3), 79–80 (2014)
6. Atif, Y., Ding, J., Jeusfeld, M.A.: Internet of Things approach to cloud-based smart car parking. Procedia Comput. Sci. **5**(98), 193–198 (2016)
7. Ni, W., Wu, W., Li, K.: A message efficient intersection control algorithm for intelligent transportation in smart cities. Futur. Gener. Comput. Syst. **2**(76), 339–349 (2017)
8. Zuo, Y., Yuan, J.B., Xiao, X.: Research on Airport special vehicle positioning system based on Internet of Things. Mach. Manuf. Autom. **46**(1) 177–179 (2017)
9. Ali, G., et al.: IoT based smart parking system using deep long short memory network. Electronics **9**(10), 1–17 (2020)
10. Peyman, M., Copado, P.J., Tordecilla, R.D., Martins, L.D.C., Xhafa, F., Juan, A.A.: Edge computing and IoT analytics for agile optimization in intelligent transportation systems. Energies **14**(19), 1–26 (2021)
11. Yang, O.: Improved locating algorithm of railway tunnel personnel based on collaborative information fusion in Internet of Things. Trans. Inst. Meas. Control **39**(4), 446–454 (2017)
12. Pasero, A.T.E.: A runway surface monitor using Internet of Things. J. Electr. Eng. **65**(3), 169–173 (2014)
13. Guépet, J., Briant, O., Gayon, J.P., Acuna-Agost, R.: Integration of aircraft ground movements and runway operations. Transp. Res. Part E: Logist. Transp. Rev. **104**, 131–149 (2014)
14. Zhao, J., Feng, Z.H.: Research on runway intrusion prevention method and application under Internet of Things driving mode. Comput. Knowl. Technol. **13**(9), 44–46 (2017)
15. Yang, D., Yuan, J.B., Jin, J.L.: Design and implementation of airport noise sensing node based on Internet of Things. Mach. Manuf. Autom. **44**(2), 212–214 (2015)
16. Pue, L.H., Kumar, S., Garg, S., Meng, L.K.: Characteristics of aircraft flypast noise around Singapore Changi international airport. Appl. Acoust. **13**(185), 1–8 (2022)
17. Wang, X.H., Yuan, J.B., Yang, D., Xiao, X.: Airport noise perception system based on Internet of Things. Autom. Technol. Appl. **40**(4), 85–88 (2021)
18. Zhou, Z.Y.: Construction of airport perimeter alarm system using intelligent visual Internet of Things. China Public Secur. **11**(9), 162–165 (2012)
19. Sun, J.: Research on airport video perception application based on Internet of Things. Enterp. Technol. Dev. **34**(30), 40–42 (2015)
20. Cao, X.M., Wang, X.F., Liu, H.X.: Design of airport perimeter security system based on Internet of Things. Logist. Technol. **29**(19), 66–68 (2010)
21. Lin, J.H., Lu, K.: Application of perimeter intrusion prevention system for flight area of Pudong airport based on Internet of Things. East China Sci. Technol. **3**(7), 69–70 (2012)
22. Liu, S.J.: Thoughts on the application of Internet of Things technology in airports. Sci. Technol. Innov. Appl. **5**(8), 300 (2017)
23. Tang, M.: On how to use Internet of Things technology to improve the management quality of Airlines. Manag. Obs. **13**(22), 104–105 (2010)
24. Li, Z.H., Chen, Y.: Research on the application of RFID technology in civil aviation aircraft operation and maintenance. Traffic Inf. Secur. **29**(6), 124–126 (2011)
25. Ding, F.: Research on the application of Internet of Things technology in airport facilities. Mod. Transp. Technol. **14**(3), 111–114 (2017)
26. Guan, S.D.: Discussion on the application of 5G Internet of Things technology in airport facilities. Air Commer. **5**(12), 46–49 (2020)

27. Lin, J.Y.: Application of intelligent lighting control scheme based on Lora Internet of Things technology on expressway-taking Beijing new airport expressway (south fifth ring road - Beijing new airport) as an example. Wirel. Internet Technol. **17**(8), 165–168 (2020)
28. Zou, X.L., Pi, Y.B.: Aviation logistics query platform based on Internet of Things. Comput. Syst. Appl. **23**(11), 82–86 (2014)
29. Wang, W.J.: Juno explore the whole process of baggage tracking and promote the construction of civil aviation Internet of Things. Civ. Aviat. Manag. **10**(12), 38–41 (2020)
30. Zhang, C.: Application of RFID in cargo storage management of civil airport. Electron. World **5**(13), 176–177 (2020)
31. Men, C.: Information development of aviation enterprises in the era of Internet of Things. Electron. Technol. Softw. Eng. **5**(11), 214 (2017)
32. Wen, W.: Application analysis of Internet of Things technology in airport equipment and facilities. China Equip. Eng. **6**(18), 119–120 (2019)
33. Zhang, H., Zheng, W.L., Yin, C.R., Li, S.Z., Li, W.: Application of narrowband Internet of Things technology in the construction of airport smart field. Internet Things Technol. **10**(10), 95–98 (2020)
34. Di Vaio, A., Varriale, L.: Blockchain technology in supply chain management for sustainable performance: evidence from the airport industry. Int. J. Inf. Manag. **52**(4), 1–16 (2020)
35. Tanmay, P., Arjun, R.: Intelligent street lighting based on the Internet-improving energy efficiency and security. J. Res. Sci. Eng. **2**(5), 59–61 (2020)
36. Mahbub, M., Hossain, M.M., Gazi, M.S.A.: IoT-cognizant cloud-assisted energy efficient embedded system for indoor intelligent lighting, air quality monitoring, and ventilation. Internet Things **11**, 100266 (2020)
37. Sales-Mendes, A., Jiménez-Bravo, D.M., Navarro-Cáceres, M., Reis Quietinho Leithardt, V., Villarrubia González, G.: Multi-agent approach using LoRaWAN devices: an airport case study. Electronics **9**(9), 1430 (2020)
38. Li, W.J.: Application analysis of Internet of Things technology in smart airport. Digit. Commun. World **2**(3), 170–171 (2021)

# Reliability Evaluation of Smart DC Microgrid

Kai Zheng[1](✉), Xiang Yao[1], and Wei Wang[2]

[1] Jiangsu Key Construction Laboratory of IoT Application Technology, Wuxi Taihu University, Wuxi, China
534347752@qq.com
[2] Liverpool University, Liverpool, UK

**Abstract.** Nowadays, one of the main contributors of air pollution is thermal power plant. China want to develop renewable energy to solve the problem [1]. In many areas, roof photovoltaic (PV) energy systems, wind energy systems are built in last several years. In order to effective manage the renewable energy system, the concept of DC microgrid appeared, some of the roof PV energy systems also can be regarded as DC microgrids. It can manage the renewable energy system efficiently to reduce energy loss. For many DC microgrid, smart converter can upload temperature data, irradiation data and power data to the software. However, how to optimize the architecture design of smart DC microgrid is still wait to be solved. In this paper, continuous-time Markov chain (CTMC) models are built for evaluating the reliability of DC microgrid. The reliability of 3 typical architectures are evaluated and the most reliable one can be find out. What's more, the main influence factors for the reliability of DC microgrid are shown. Finally, strategies are given to optimize the architecture design of DC microgrid.

**Keywords:** Renewable energy system · CTMC · Smart DC microgrid

## 1 Introduction

In last 10 years, the air pollution all over the world became serious. One of the main contributors is thermal power plant. In order to solve this problem, many countries are interested in developing renewable energy sources, especially America and Germany [2]. Chinese government also want to use renewable energy sources to reduce air pollution, so the penetration of renewable energy sources in China increased fast [3].

However, how to efficiently manage the renewable energy systems is a problem. The concept of smart Direct Current (DC) microgrid [4] and Alternating Current (AC) microgrid [5] emerged about 10 years ago. Smart DC microgrid and AC microgrid help to improve the efficiency and safety of renewable energy system [6].

Compared with AC microgrid, DC microgrid has less complicated structure and less devices, the cost of DC microgrid is also less than AC microgrid [7, 8]. Thus, the proportion of DC microgrid is also increasing [9].

However, how to improve the architecture design of smart DC microgrid is still a challenge. For the reliability of smart DC microgrid, many researchers focused on

X. Sun et al. (Eds.): ICAIS 2022, CCIS 1588, pp. 595–605, 2022.
https://doi.org/10.1007/978-3-031-06764-8_46

islanding detection [10], low voltage LVRT ride through (LVRT) [11], hierarchical control [7]. Few of them did research on architecture optimization. In [12], the author used computing models to evaluate the reliability of PV energy system with Bluetooth remote reprogramming functions. However, he failed to compare his method with other reliability evaluation methods.

In this paper, Continuous time Markov chain (CTMC) model is used to evaluate the reliability of the smart DC microgrid. How to improve the reliability of DC microgrid is also illustrated. The contributions of this paper is shown below:

The reliability of 3 typical architectures of smart microgrid is evaluated, the most reliable one are found.

The influence factors of reliability are evaluated, which influence factor influence the reliability most is also given.

The CTMC models are compared with reliability block diagram (RBD) method (a typical computing method for reliability), the results shows that the efficiency of CTMC is better.

In Sect. 2, the structures and devices of DC microgrid are illustrated in detail. In Sect. 3, how to build CTMC models in software is given. In Sect. 4, the experiment results are shown and analyzed. Finally, the conclusion and future work are given.

## 2   Typical Architectures of Smart DC Sicrogrid

### 2.1   Smart DC Sicrogrid Architectures and Devices

DC microgrid can work at grid connected mode and islanding mode [13]. In main land, the DC microgrids are usually connected to the grid. However, for some remote island, the DC microgrids usually work at islanding mode [14]. Compared with grid-connected mode, islanding DC microgrid is difficult to repair, so in this paper, we focus on evaluating the reliability of roof islanding smart DC microgrid.

Usually DC microgrid has the following devices:

- PV panels: provide energy to the load and storage battery
- Storage batteries: store the energy provided by PV panels
- Converters: adjust the output voltage to a suitable one, the control algorithms in converters also can manage the operating of the DC microgrid. Most of the converters can communicate with control platform, so we can call this smart DC microgrid.
- Inverters: transfer DC current to AC current.
- Main grid: get the energy from PV panels

The typical DC microgrid is shown below in Fig. 1 [15].

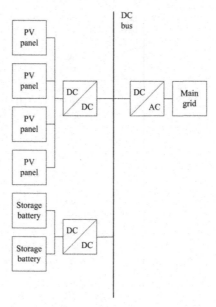

**Fig. 1.** Typical architecture of DC microgrid.

For islanding DC microgrid, the last 2 devices (inverter and main grid) do not exit, so the 3 typical architectures of islanding DC microgrid is shown in Fig. 2 [16, 17].

## 2.2 Continuous-Time Markov Chain

Continuous-time Markov chain (CTMC) model is used to study the reliability of DC microgrid in this paper. A CTMC is a four-tuple (S, s0, R, L):

- S is a finite set of states S = {s0, s1, s2, ..., sn}, where n is the number of states.
- s0 is the initial state.
- R is the transition rate matrix |S| × |S|.
- L is the labeling function.

Continuous stochastic logic (CSL) is the extension of non probabilistic continuous temporal logic used for specifying properties of CTMCs. It is defined by two types of syntaxes: state formula ($\Phi$) and path formula ($\Psi$).

CSL is used to verify the reliability of SDWSN. CSL statements that will be used are listed below.

P = ? [true U ≤ 12 * 3600 Down]: Probability of system failure occurring within 12 h.

P = ? [true U ≤ 15 * 24 * 3600 Down]: Probability of system failure occurring within 15 days.

In the CSL statements, "P" means the probability, "true" means the system is available. "U" means "until". "24 * 3600" means 1 day. "30 * 24 * 3600" means 30 days. "Down" means the system is down. For example, in ArchI,

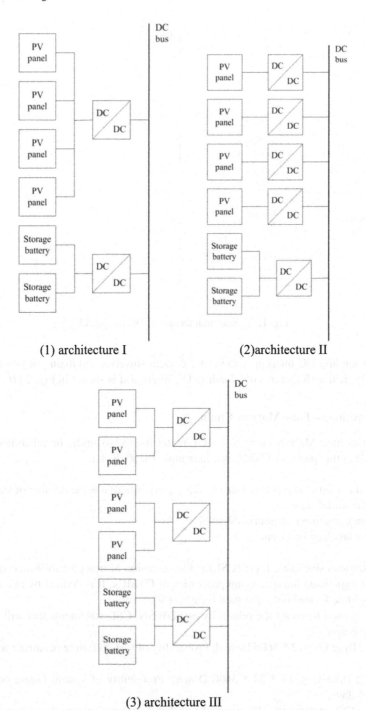

(1) architecture I                    (2)architecture II

(3) architecture III

**Fig. 2.** Typical architectures of DC microgrid.

Down = (np < 2) |( nc < 2) |( nb < 1)

It means that the system is down if (i) np is smaller than 2 or (ii) nc is smaller than 2 or (iii) nc is smaller than 1.

In this paper, CTMC models can be constructed in PRISM (a model checking software), and PRISM has its own language to build CTMC models.

## 2.3  Architecture Comparison of 3 Architectures

For architecture I is a centralized architecture, 4 PV panels are connected to the centralized DC/DC converter. Architecture II is much different from architecture I, each PV panels has a DC/DC converter, so it is a distributed architecture. Architecture III is an architecture between architecture I and II. The differences of the 3 Architectures are shown in Table 1.

**Table 1.** Differences between 3 architectures.

|                    | ArchI | ArchII | ArchII |
|--------------------|-------|--------|--------|
| PV panels          | 4     | 4      | 4      |
| Storage batteries  | 2     | 2      | 2      |
| Converters         | 2     | 5      | 3      |

# 3  CTMC Models for 3 Architectures

The 3 models for the 3 architectures are constructed in PRISM. Take Architecture I as an example, the modeling process of these CTMC models in PRISM is illustrated as follows.

**PV Panel Layer Module:** The initial value for PV panel layer is 4 (means all PV panels are available). If the PV panels fails with a failure rate "lambda_p", "p" will minus 1 (means available PV panels minus 1). The code for cloud layer is shown below:

```
p : [ 0 . . 4 ] i n i t 4 ;
[ ] p>0->p* lambda p : ( p'=p−1) ;
```

**Smart Converter Layer Module:** The initial number of applicable smart converters is 2. If each smart converter fails with a failure rate "lambda_c", "c" then minus 1. The code for converter layer is shown below:

```
c : [ 0 . . 2 ] i n i t 2 ;//number of available converter s
[ ] c>0 -> c * lambda_c  : ( c '= c −1) ; // f a i l u r e of
a s i ng l e converter
```

**Storage Battery Layer Module:** The initial available storage batteries is 2. Each storage battery fails with a failure rate "lambda_b" The code is shown below:

```
b : [0..2] init 2;
[ ] b >0 -> b* lambda_b : ( b'=b -1);
```

**Failure Conditions:** we need at least 2 PV panels, 1 battery are available, and their converters should be available and connected to the DC bus, so the failure conditions of Architecture I are show below:

formula down = ( c < 2) |( p < 2) |( b < 1);

The code for another 2 architectures are similar, but the reliability of another 2 architectures are different from the first one. According to the 2 architectures, the failure conditions also should be changed.

**Reliability Evaluation Index:** the CTMC models can be used to evaluate the reliability (failure rate) of the whole system within a period of time (for example, 1 year or 10 years). The influence of each component will be evaluated, which will be illustrated in detail.

## 4   Experiment Results

4 experiments are doing in PRISM. The failure rate parameters of different architectures are shown in Table 2. "fp" is the failure rate of PV panels, "fc" is the failure rate of converters, "fb" is the failure rate of batteries, "t" is the time period in experiments.

**Table 2.** Experiment perimeters.

|  | Architecture | fp (year$^{-1}$) | fc (year$^{-1}$) | fb(year$^{-1}$) | t (years) |
|---|---|---|---|---|---|
| Experiment 1 | I, II, III | 1/10 | 1/6 | 1/6 | 1,10 |
| Experiment 2 | III | 1/3, 1/5, 1/10, 1/15, 1/20 | 1/6 | 1/6 | 1,10 |
| Experiment 3 | III | 1/10 | 1/2, 1/4, 1/6, 1/8, 1/10 | 1/6 | 1,10 |
| Experiment 4 | III | 1/10 | 1/6 | 1/2, 1/4, 1/6, 1/8, 1/10 | 1,10 |

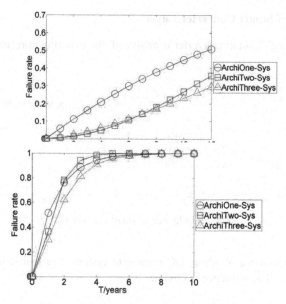

**Fig. 3.** Reliability comparison of 3 architectures.

## 4.1 Reliability Comparison of Architecture I, II and III

The CTMC models for the 3 architectures are constructed in PRISM. According to Fig. 3. The findings is shown below:

Remark. Before 8 months, the reliability of architecture II and III are similar, the reliability of architecture I is highest. However, after 8 months, architecture III is better than Architecture II. In a word, for long term, Architecture III is the best.

## 4.2 Influence of PV Panels Layer

After Architecture III is chosen, the influence of different devices can be analyzed. The influence of PV panels is analyzed first, the experiment results are shown in Fig. 4.

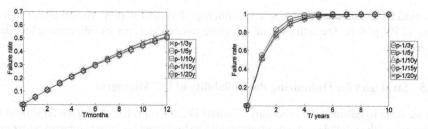

**Fig.4.** Influence of PV panels.

Remark. The failure rate of whole DC microgrid system is proportional to the failure rate of PV panels. However, the influence is not very obvious.

### 4.3  Influence of Smart Converter Layer

Then the influence of smart converter is analyzed, the experiment results are shown in Fig. 5.

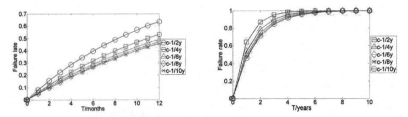

**Fig. 5.** Influence of smart converters.

Remark. The failure rate of whole DC microgrid system is proportional to the failure rate of converters. The influence is obvious.

### 4.4  Influence of Storage Battery Layer

Finally, the influence of storage battery is analyzed, the experiment results are shown in Fig. 6.

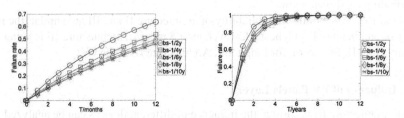

**Fig. 6.** Influence of storage battery

Remark. The failure rate of whole DC microgrid system is proportional to the failure rate of PV panels. The influence of it is close to converter, but its influence is less than converters.

### 4.5  Strategies for Optimizing the Reliability of DC Microgrid

If we want to enhance the reliability of smart DC microgrid, architecture III should be chosen and the reliability of converters should be improved because compared with other components, converter influence the reliability most.

**Table 3.** Failure rate of DC microgrid in 1 years using 3 methods.

|  | 3 months | 6 months | 9 months | 12 months | Average differences |
|---|---|---|---|---|---|
| CTMC | 0.1723 | 0.2932 | 0.3923 | 0.4825 | / |
| RBD | 0.1714 | 0.2928 | 0.3921 | 0.2823 | / |
| RBD-CTMC | −0.0009 | −0.0004 | −0.0002 | −0.0002 | −0.000425 |

### 4.6 Comparison Between CTMC Method and RBD Method

RBD method, which is a typical reliability evaluation method, is used as benchmark, we also did the 4 experiments by using RBD method in MATLAB. The differences between the 2 method are shown in Table 3.

The average difference is −0.000425, which is very close to CTMC method. In this way, we can think CTMC models are correct.

The efficiency of CTMC models are better than RBD method, the differences are shown in Table 4.

**Table 4.** Computing time comparison.

|  | CTMC | RBD |
|---|---|---|
| Experiment1 (1 year) | 0.0020 s | 0.0683 s |
| Experiment1 (10 years) | 0.0050 s | 0.0722 s |
| Experiment2 (1 year) | 0.0022 s | 0.0682 s |
| Experiment2 (10 years) | 0.0052 s | 0.0782 s |
| Experiment3 (1 year) | 0.0027 s | 0.0623 s |
| Experiment3 (10 years) | 0.0052 s | 0.0638 s |
| Experiment4 (1 year) | 0.0025 s | 0.0625 s |
| Experiment4 (10 years) | 0.0058 s | 0.0724 s |

## 5 Conclusion

In this paper, CTMC model is used to evaluate the reliability of smart DC microgrid. In 3 architectures, architecture III is the best one. Then the influences of different devices are analyzed, we find that the reliability of converter is the most important. In architecture design of DC microgrid, we should pay more attention to the converters.

For further study, more complex smart DC microgrid will be evaluated to meet different occasions. More real maintenance records will be found to support the verification of CTMC models.

**Acknowledgement.** The paper is supported by Taihu University of Wuxi, Jiangsu Key Construction Laboratory of IoT Application Technology. The paper is supported by Natural Science Foundation of Jiangsu Province No. 18KJB413009. I also should thank my previous supervisor an friends in Xi'an Jiaotong-Liverpool University, the research direction of this paper is supervised by him.

**Funding Statement.** The author(s) received no specific funding for this study.

**Conflicts of Interest.** The authors declare that they have no conflicts of interest to report regarding the present study.

# References

1. Anoune, K., Bouya, M., Astito, A., Abdellah, A.B.: Sizing methods and optimization techniques for PV-wind based hybrid renewable energy system: a review. Renew. Sustain. Energy Rev. **93**, 652–673 (2018)
2. Alawaji, S.: Evaluation of solar energy research and its applications in Saudi Arabia-20 years of experience. Renew. Sustain. Energy Rev. **5**(1), 59–77 (2001)
3. Li, X., Wang, W., Wang, H.: Dynamic environmental economic dispatch of hybrid renewable energy systems based on tradable green certificates. Energy **193**, 116699 (2020)
4. Kakigano, H., Miura, Y., Ise, T.: Low-voltage bipolar-type DC microgrid for super high quality distribution. IEEE Trans. Power Electron. **12**, 3066–3075 (2010)
5. Chakraborty, S., Simoes, M.G.: Experimental evaluation of active filtering in a single-phase high-frequency ac microgrid. IEEE Trans. Energy Convers. **24**(3), 673–682 (2009)
6. Heydari, R., Dragicevic, T., Blaabjerg, F.: High-bandwidth secondary voltage and frequency control of VSC-based AC microgrid. IEEE Trans. Power Electron. **34**(11), 11320–11331 (2019)
7. Shuai, Z., Fang, J., Ning, F., Shen, Z.J.: Hierarchical structure and bus voltage control of DC microgrid. Renew. Sustain. Energy Rev. **82**, 3670–3682 (2018)
8. Zhang, X., Wang, Z., Lu, Z.: Multi-objective load dispatch for microgrid with electric vehicles using modified gravitational search and particle swarm optimization algorithm. Appl. Energy **306**, 118018 (2022)
9. Mardani, M.M., Vafamand, N., Khooban, M.H.: Design of quadratic d-stable fuzzy controller for DC microgrids with multiple CPLs. IEEE Trans. Industr. Electron. **66**(6), 4805–4812 (2019)
10. Bekhradian, R., Davarpanah, M., Sanaye-Pasand, M.: Novel Approach for secure islanding detection in synchronous generator based microgrids. IEEE Trans. Power Deliv. **34**, 457–466 (2019)
11. Chen, L., Chen, H., Yang, J.: Comparison of superconducting fault current limiter and dynamic voltage restorer for LVRT improvement of high penetration microgrid. IEEE Trans. Appl. Supercond. **27**(4), 1–7 (2017)
12. Wu, S., Zheng, K., Huang, X.: Model checking PV energy system with remote reprogramming function. In: International Conference on Information Technology in Medicine & Education. IEEE Computer Society (2016)
13. Karimulla, S., Ravi, K.: Integration of renewable energy sources into the smart grid using enhanced SCA. Intell. Autom. Soft Comput. **32**(3), 1557–1572 (2022)
14. Dang, Q., Zhang, H., Zhao, B., He, Y., He, S., Kim, H.: Electrical data matrix decomposition in smart grid. J. Internet Things **1**(1), 1–7 (2019)

15. Asif, M., Ali, I., Ahmad, S., Irshad, A., Gardezi, A.A.: Industrial automation information analogy for smart grid security. Comput. Mater. Contin. **71**(2), 3985–3999 (2022)
16. Luo, J., Liao, J., Zhang, C., Wang, Z., Zhang, Y.: Fine-grained bandwidth estimation for smart grid communication network. Intell. Autom. Soft Comput. **32**(2), 1225–1239 (2022)
17. Varghese, L.J., Dhayalini, K., Jacob, S.S., Ali, I., Abdelmaboud, A.: Optimal load forecasting model for peer-to-peer energy trading in smart grids. Comput. Mater. Contin. **70**(1), 1053–1067 (2022)

# A Distributed Filtering Method Based on Adaptive Event Trigger

Peng Yan and Yao Xiang[✉]

Jiangsu Key Construction Laboratory of IoT Application Technology, Wuxi Taihu University, Wuxi, China
yx_cathy@qq.com

**Abstract.** This paper studies a kind of distributed robust state estimation problem based on adaptive event trigger mechanism. First, an adaptive trigger mechanism is introduced to reduce the communication burden between the sensor network and the filter network. Then, Markov chain is used to describe the random switching of the filter network communication topology. The purpose of this paper is to obtain a distributed full-order filter under the condition of linear matrix inequality (LMI), and to ensure the stability of the mean square exponential of the filtering dynamic system under the given l2-l∞ performance index. Finally, a simulation example verifies the effectiveness of the design method.

**Keywords:** Sensor networks · Switching topology · Adaptive event-triggered · Distributed filtering

## 1 Introduction

In the past few decades, wireless sensor networks (WSN) have been widely applied in many important fields, such as urban management, biomedicine, environmental monitoring, disaster relief and remote control of hazardous areas [1–4]. WSN is composed of a large number of sensors distributed in space, and each sensor node has certain intelligent computing functions. With the rapid development of science and technology, distributed filtering based on wireless sensor networks has attracted more and more scholars' attention [5, 6]. Distributed filter can fuse sampling information and estimation information of itself and its neighbors to achieve state estimation of the target object.

Event triggering is an effective method to save communication resources. It can determine whether to send new information to filter or controller by setting event triggering conditions. Compared with periodic sampling, event triggering can reduce communication frequency and maintain good system performance, such as system stability and convergence. Therefore, the study of event trigger has aroused extensive research by scholars [7–9]. In [7], the research focuses on the application of event triggering in networked control systems (NCS). In [8], a distributed event triggering strategy is studied in large networked systems and event triggering parameters are optimized. Unfortunately, in [7] and [9], the event-triggered threshold is a preset constant, which cannot

© The Author(s), under exclusive license to Springer Nature Switzerland AG 2022
X. Sun et al. (Eds.): ICAIS 2022, CCIS 1588, pp. 606–617, 2022.
https://doi.org/10.1007/978-3-031-06764-8_47

dynamically adjust the sampling interval and is difficult to adapt to changes in the system. This method of fixed event trigger threshold will undoubtedly lead to the waste of communication resources. Event trigger parameters should be adaptive. Therefore, filter/controller design with adaptive event triggering mechanism becomes a challenging problem. In [10] a class of nonlinear NCS control problem based on adaptive event triggering mechanism is studied. In [11] static output feedback control and improved adaptive event triggering mechanism of NCS are studied to save network bandwidth. In [10, 11] although the adaptive event triggering mechanism has been presented in the relevant research results of NCS, there are not many achievements in the application of distributed filter network.

In addition, in practical applications, many factors will lead to random changes in the topology of communication networks. For example, obstacles blocking, adding new nodes, unstable network communication and so on [4, 12–16]. For example, in [12], the problem of distributed state estimation for network topology switching without exceeding a given value is solved. In [4, 13] a new kind of distributed H is proposed $\infty$ State estimation framework, which combines partial information exchange and inhomogeneous Markov topology switching. The distributed state estimator designed in [14–16] not only considers random topology switching, but also embedded event triggering to reduce the communication frequency of the network. Literature [17] studies the distributed filtering problem with topological random switching when random loss is measured by sensors.

However, under the adaptive event triggering mechanism, the research results of distributed filtering in wireless sensor networks are not very rich. Based on the above discussion, the research objective of this paper is to embed adaptive event triggering mechanism for wireless sensor network, design a distributed state estimation method with random switching of communication topology, and realize the estimation or tracking of target system.

## 2 Problem Description

Consider a sensor network composed of N nodes. Its topological structure is expressed as a directed graph, where is the node set, is the boundary set and is the adjacency matrix $G = (V, E, A)V = \{1, 2, \cdots n\}E \subseteq V \times VA = [a_{ij}]_{n \times n}(a_{ij} \geq 0)$. If a directed graph has a boundary from node to node, then the ordered pair, and the node is called an adjacent node of the node $Gji\ (i, j) \in E\ a_{ij} > 0ji$. Also, assume that for all, $i \in Va_{ii} = 1$. So you can think of it as an additional boundary $(i, i)$. The set formed by all adjacent nodes of a node plus itself is called the adjacent node set of a node, denoted as $i\ iN_i = \{j \in V : (i, j) \in E\}$.

Consider the following discrete linear networked system:

$$\begin{cases} x(k + 1) = Ax(k) + Bw(k), x(0) = x_0 \\ z(k) = Mx(k), \end{cases} \tag{1}$$

Where is the system state, is the estimated system output signal, is the external interference of the system, and belongs to $x(k) \in \mathbb{R}^{n_x} z(k) \in \mathbb{R}^{n_z} w(k) \in \mathbb{R}^{n_w} l_2[0, \infty)$.

The measurement model of each sensor node is:

$$y_i(k) = C_i x(k) + D_i v_i(k), \tag{2}$$

Where is the measured value of sensor node I $y_i(k) \in \mathbb{R}^{n_y}$ $A, B, M, C_i$. And are known parameter matrices $D_i$.

In order to save network bandwidth resources, the following event triggering functions are designed:

$$g_i(\Upsilon_i(k), \delta_i) = \Upsilon_i^T(k)\Phi_i^{r(k)}\Upsilon_i(k) - \delta_i(k)r_i^T(k)\Phi_i^{r(k)}r_i(k). \tag{3}$$

And define

$$\begin{aligned} r_i(k) &= y_i(k) - C_i\hat{x}_i(k), \\ \Upsilon_i(k) &= r_i\left(k_u^j\right) - r_i(k). \end{aligned} \tag{4}$$

Where is the event-triggered positive definite matrix. $\Phi_i^{r(k)} > 0$ $K$ represents the current sampling time and the last event triggering time $k_u^i$.

Consider that the event triggering threshold is time-varying and satisfies the following equation: $\delta_i(k)$

$$\delta_i(k+1) = \delta_i(k) + d_i(k), \tag{5}$$

Where is given an initial event triggering threshold $\delta_i(0) \in [0, 1]$.
define

$$d_i(k) = \begin{cases} \varepsilon, & \Upsilon_i^T(k)\Upsilon(k) < \rho \\ 0, & \Upsilon_i^T(k)\Upsilon(k) = \rho \\ -\varepsilon, & \Upsilon_i^T(k)\Upsilon(k) > \rho \end{cases} \tag{6}$$

Where the sum is a non-negative constant $\rho\varepsilon$. For the convenience of calculation, it is assumed that the triggering threshold parameter of personal leave is bounded and the variation range is $\delta_i(k)$ $[\delta_m, \delta_M]\delta_m$. And indicate the lower and upper bounds of the threshold value respectively $\delta_M$.

Event triggering needs to satisfy the condition that each triggering moment is recorded in a sequence $g_i(\Upsilon_i(k), \delta_i) > 0$ $0 \le k_0^i \le k_1^i \le \cdots \le k_u^i \le \cdots$. Where is expressed as $k_{u+1}^i$

$$k_{u+1}^i = min\{k \in N | k > k_u^i, g_i(\Upsilon_i(k), \delta_i) > 0\}. \tag{7}$$

Therefore, the following distributed filter based on adaptive event triggering is designed:

$$\begin{cases} \hat{x}_i(k+1) = W_i^{r(k)}\hat{x}_i(k) + \sum_{j \in N_i^{r(k)}} a_{ij}^{r(k)}H_{ij}^{r(k)}r_j\left(k_k^j\right), \\ \hat{z}_i(k) = L_i^{r(k)}\hat{x}_i(k), \end{cases} \tag{8}$$

$\hat{x}_i \in \mathbb{R}^{n_x}$ and represent the state estimation and input estimation of the system respectively $\hat{z}_i(k) \in \mathbb{R}^{n_z}$.

Markov chains take values in finite sets $r(\cdot)S = \{1, 2, \cdots, n_0\}\Pi = [\pi_{st}]_{n_0 \times n_0}$. Represents the probability matrix that the communication topology of the filter network jumps from T to S, and satisfies

$$\pi_{st} = Prob(r(k+1) = t | r(k) = s), \forall s, t \in S \tag{9}$$

Among them, $\pi_{st} \geq 0 \sum_{t=1}^{n_0} \pi_{st} = 1$. Here the matrix, are the filter parameters that need to be designed $W_i^{r(k)} H_{ij}^{r(k)} L_i^{r(k)} \left( j \in \mathcal{N}_i^{r(k)} \right)$.

The state estimation error is defined as, and the system output estimation error is. The state estimation error of each node I can be obtained as: $e_i(k) = x(k) - \hat{x}_i(k)$ $\tilde{z}_i(k) = z(k) - \hat{z}_i(k)$.

$$
\begin{aligned}
e_i(k+1) &= \left[A - W_i^s\right] x(k) + W_i^s e_i(k) - \sum_{j \in \mathcal{N}_i^s} a_{ij}^s H_{ij}^s C_j e_j(k) \\
&- \sum_{j \in \mathcal{N}_i^{r(k)}} a_{ij}^s H_{ij}^s \Upsilon_j(k) - \sum_{j \in \mathcal{N}_i^s} a_{ij}^s H_{ij}^s D_j v_j(k) + Bw(k).
\end{aligned}
\tag{10}
$$

The output estimated error of each node is:

$$
\tilde{z}_i(k) = \left[M - L_i^s\right] e_i(k).
\tag{11}
$$

To simplify the analysis, define the following state matrix:

$$
\hat{x}(k) = vec_n^T \left\{ \hat{x}_i^T(k) \right\}, \ \bar{x}(k) = vec_n^T \left\{ x^T(k) \right\},
$$

$$
e(k) = vec_n^T \left\{ e_i^T(k) \right\}, \ \tilde{z}(k) = vec_n^T \left\{ \tilde{z}_i^T(k) \right\},
\tag{12}
$$

And parameter matrix

$$
\begin{aligned}
&\bar{A} = diag_n\{A\}, \bar{B} = vec^T\{B^T\}, \\
&\bar{C} = diag_n\{C_i\}, \bar{D} = diag_n\{D_i\}, \\
&\bar{M} = diag_n\{M\}, v(k) = vec_n^T\{v_i^T(k)\}, \\
&\Upsilon(k) = vec_n^T\{\Upsilon_i^T(k)\}, \delta(k) = diag_n\{\delta_i(k)\}, \\
&r(k) = vec_n^T\{r_i^T(k)\}, \tilde{C}_M = \left[0 \ \delta_M \bar{C}\right].
\end{aligned}
\tag{13}
$$

At the same time, define, $\eta(k) = \left[\bar{x}^T(k) \ e^T(k)\right]^T \bar{w}(k) = \left[w^T(k) \ v^T(k)\right]^T$. Then, it is easy to go to an augmented filter error system:

$$
\begin{cases}
\eta(k+1) = \mathscr{A}^s \eta(k) + \mathscr{F}^s \Upsilon(k) + \mathscr{B}^s \bar{w}(k), \\
\tilde{z}(k) = \mathscr{M}^s \eta(k),
\end{cases}
\tag{14}
$$

Among them

$$
\mathscr{A}^s = \begin{bmatrix} \bar{A} & 0 \\ \bar{A} - W^s & W^s - \bar{H}^s \bar{C} \end{bmatrix},
$$

$$
\mathscr{B}^s = \begin{bmatrix} \bar{B} & 0 \\ \bar{B} & -\bar{H}^s \bar{D} \end{bmatrix}, \ \mathscr{F}^s = \begin{bmatrix} 0 \\ -\bar{H}^s \end{bmatrix},
\tag{15}
$$

$$
\mathscr{M}^s = \left[0 \ \bar{M} - \bar{L}^s\right].
$$

and

$$
\bar{W}^s = diag\{W_i^s\}, \bar{L}^s = diag_n\{L_i^s\},
$$

$$
\bar{H}^s = [O_{ij}]_{n \times n}^s, O_{ij} = a_{ij}^s H_{ij}^s.
\tag{16}
$$

Apparently, at the time, $j \notin \mathcal{N}_i^s \ a_{ij} = 0$. Therefore, is a sparse matrix, expressed as $\bar{H}^s$:

$$
\bar{H}^s \in \mathcal{W}_{n_x \times n_y},
\tag{17}
$$

Among them

$$W_{p \times q} = \left\{ U = [U_{ij}] \in \mathbb{R}^{np \times nq} | U_{ij} \in \mathbb{R}^{p \times q}, U_{ij} = 0, \text{ if } j \notin N_i^s \right\}. \tag{18}$$

The purpose of the study is to find a set of distributed filter gain matrix and the filter error system (13) that makes the filter augmented both satisfy the following two conditions $\overline{W}^s \, \overline{H}^s \, \overline{L}^s (s = 1, 2, \cdots, n_0)$:

(a)  For any, at, the augmented filter error system is exponentially stable in mean square if there are constants and such that $\eta(0) \, \overline{w}(k) = 0 \, \lambda \geq 10 < \tau < 1$

$$\mathbb{E}\{\|\eta(k)\|\} \leq \lambda \tau^k \mathbb{E}\{\|\eta(0)\|\}. \tag{19}$$

(b)  Under zero initial conditions, for any non-zero, the filtering error satisfies $\overline{w}(k) \, \tilde{z}(k)$

$$\mathbb{E}\left\{ \|\tilde{z}(k)\|_\infty^2 \right\} < \gamma^2 \|\overline{w}(k)\|_2^2, \tag{20}$$

Among them

$$\|\tilde{z}(k)\|_\infty^2 = \sup_k \left\{ \tilde{z}^T(k) \tilde{z}(k) \right\},$$

$$\|\overline{w}(k)\|_2^2 = \sum_{k=0}^{\infty} \overline{w}^T(k) \overline{w}(k). \tag{21}$$

And is a given disturbance attenuation performance index $\gamma > 0$.

**Lemma 1.** Where is the invertible matrix $Q = diag\{Q_1, Q_2, \cdots, Q_n\}$ $Q_i \in \mathbb{R}^{p \times p} (1 \leq i \leq n)$. For any one of these, if theta, then theta $W \in \mathbb{R}^{np \times nq} X = QWW \in W_{p \times q} \Leftrightarrow X \in W_{p \times q}$.

## 3    Filter Performance Analysis

**Theorem 1.** Given $\gamma > 0$. Suppose there are matrices, and matrices that satisfy the following matrix inequality $\overline{L}^s \, \overline{W}^s \, \overline{\Phi}^s P(s) > 0 \, \overline{H}^s \, \overline{H}^s \in W_{n_x \times n_y}, s = 1, 2, \cdots, n_0$.

$$\begin{bmatrix} -P(s) & * & * & * & * \\ 0 & -\Phi(s) & * & * & * \\ 0 & 0 & -I & * & * \\ \Phi(s)\tilde{C}_M & 0 & 0 & -\Phi(s) & * \\ \overline{P}(s)\mathscr{A}^s & \overline{P}(s)\mathscr{F}^s & \overline{P}(s)\mathscr{B}^s & 0 & -\overline{P}(s) \end{bmatrix} < 0, \tag{22}$$

$$\begin{bmatrix} -P(s) & * \\ \mathscr{M}^s & -\gamma^2 I \end{bmatrix} < 0, \tag{23}$$

One of them $\overline{L}^s = diag_n\{L_i^s\}$, $\overline{W}^s = diag_n\{W_i^s\}$, $\overline{\Phi}^s = diag_n\{\Phi_i^s\}$. Then, it can be obtained that the augmented filtering error system (13) is exponentially stable in mean square and has $L_2 - l_\infty$ Performance.

**Firstly, consider and select the following Lyapunov functions $\overline{w}(k) = 0$:**

$$V(\eta(k), r(k)) = \eta^T(k)P(r(k))\eta(k). \tag{24}$$

Definition, can be obtained $\overline{P}(s) = \sum_{t=1}^{no} \pi_{st}P(t)$:

$$\begin{aligned}
\Delta V(\eta(k), s) &= \eta^T(k)\mathscr{A}^{s^T}\overline{P}(s)\mathscr{A}^s\eta(k) \\
&+ 2\eta^T(k)\mathscr{A}^{s^T}\overline{P}(s)\mathscr{F}^s\Upsilon(k) + \Upsilon^T(k)\mathscr{F}^{s^T}\overline{P}(s)\mathscr{F}^s\Upsilon(k) \\
&- \eta^T(k)P(s)\eta(k).
\end{aligned} \tag{25}$$

Considering the event trigger condition (3), it can be obtained:

$$\Upsilon^T(k)\Phi(s)\Upsilon(k) - \eta^T(k)\tilde{C}_M^T\Phi(s)\tilde{C}_M\eta(k) < 0. \tag{26}$$

Then, combining Eq. (25), we can get:

$$\Delta V(\eta(k), r(k)) \leq \xi^T(k)\Lambda^s\xi(k), \tag{27}$$

Among them.

$$\xi(k) = \left[ \eta^T(k) \ \Upsilon^T(k) \right]^T. \tag{28}$$

and

$$\Lambda^s = \begin{bmatrix} \Lambda_{11} & * \\ \Lambda_{21} & \Lambda_{22} \end{bmatrix}, \tag{29}$$

Among them

$$\begin{aligned}
\Lambda_{11} &= \mathscr{A}^{s^T}\overline{P}(s)\mathscr{A}^s + \tilde{C}_M^T\Phi(s)\tilde{C}_M - P(s), \\
\Lambda_{21} &= \mathscr{F}^{s^T}\overline{P}(s)\mathscr{A}^s, \\
\Lambda_{22} &= \mathscr{F}^{s^T}\overline{P}(s)\mathscr{F}^s - \Phi(s).
\end{aligned} \tag{30}$$

Then, by applying The Schur complementary lemma, Eq. (22) can obviously be obtained, so $\Lambda^s < 0$

$$\begin{aligned}
\mathbb{E}\{V(\eta(k+1), t|\eta(k)\} - V(\eta(k), s) &\leq \xi^T(k)\Lambda^s\xi(k) \\
&\leq -min\{\lambda s_{min}\{\}^T\} - \sigma\xi^T(k)\xi(k).
\end{aligned} \tag{31}$$

Among them

$$0 < \sigma \leq min\{\lambda s_{0\,min}\{\}\} \tag{32}$$

There is a constant such that $0 < \partial < v, v = max\{\lambda 0_{max}\{\}\}$

$$V(\eta(k), s) \leq v\xi^T(k)\xi(k). \tag{33}$$

Then, substitute Eq. (33) into Eq. (32) to obtain:

$$\mathbb{E}\{V(\eta(k+1), t)|\eta(k)\} - V(\eta(k), s) \\ \leq -\frac{\sigma}{v}V(\eta(k), s) = \lambda - \psi V(\eta(k), s). \tag{34}$$

One of them $0 < \psi = \frac{\sigma}{v} < 1$.

On the other hand, consider

$$\mu\|\eta(k)\|^2 \leq V(\eta(k), s) \leq v\|\eta(k)\|^2 \ \mu = min\{\lambda 0_{min}\{\}\} \tag{35}$$

You can get

$$\mathbb{E}\left\{\|\eta(k)\|^2\right\} \leq \frac{v}{\mu}(1 - \psi)\mathbb{E}\left\{\|\eta(0)\|^2\right\} + \frac{\lambda}{\mu\psi}. \tag{36}$$

Choice, so you can get $\lambda = 0$

$$\mathbb{E}\left\{\|\eta(k)\|^2\right\} \leq \frac{v}{\mu}(1 - \psi)^k\mathbb{E}\left\{\|\eta(0)\|^2\right\}. \tag{37}$$

Therefore, it can be concluded from Theorem 1 that the system (13) is exponentially stable with mean square.

Next, define the following performance functions:

$$J = \mathbb{E}\{V(k)\} - \mathbb{E}\left\{\sum_{i=0}^{k-1} \overline{w}^T(i)\overline{w}(i)\right\}. \tag{38}$$

Under zero initial conditions, it can be calculated

$$J = \mathbb{E}\{V(k)\} - \mathbb{E}\{V(0)\} - \mathbb{E}\left\{\sum_{i=0}^{k-1} \overline{w}^T(i)\overline{w}(i)\right\} \\ = \sum_{i=0}^{k-1}\left(\Delta V(i) - \overline{w}^T(i)\overline{w}(i)\right). \tag{39}$$

Further calculations will give you

$$\Delta V(k) \leq \xi^T(k)\Lambda^s\xi(k) + 2\overline{w}^T(k)\mathscr{B}^{sT}\overline{P}(s)\mathscr{A}^s\eta(k) \\ + 2\overline{w}^T(k)\mathscr{B}^{sT}\overline{P}(s)\mathscr{F}^s\Upsilon(k) + \overline{w}^T(k)\mathscr{B}^{sT}\overline{P}(s)\mathscr{B}^s\overline{w}(k). \tag{40}$$

Combining Eqs. (39) and (40), we have

$$J = \sum_{i=0}^{k-1}\left(\Delta V(i) - \overline{w}^T(i)\overline{w}(i)\right) \\ \leq \sum_{i=0}^{k-1}\left(\left[\xi^T(i) \ \overline{w}^T(i)\right]\begin{bmatrix} \Lambda^s & * \\ \Omega_{21}^s & \Omega_{22}^s \end{bmatrix}\begin{bmatrix} \xi(i) \\ \overline{w}(i) \end{bmatrix}\right), \tag{41}$$

Among them

$$\Omega_{21}^s = \left[\mathscr{B}^{sT}\overline{P}(s)\mathscr{A}^s \ \mathscr{B}^{sT}\overline{P}(s)\mathscr{F}^s\right], \ \Omega_{22}^s = \left[\mathscr{B}^{sT}\overline{P}(s)\mathscr{B}^s - I\right]. \tag{42}$$

After applying Schur's complementary lemma, Eq. (20) contains, i.e. $J < 0$

$$\mathbb{E}\{V(\eta(k), s\} - \sum_{i=0}^{k-1} \overline{w}^T(i)\overline{w}(i) < 0. \tag{43}$$

And then,

$$\mathbb{E}\left\{\eta^T(k)P(s)\eta(k)\right\} < \sum_{i=0}^{k-1} \overline{w}^T(i)\overline{w}(i). \tag{44}$$

Meanwhile, after applying Schur's complementary lemma, Eq. (23) can be obtained:

$$\mathcal{M}^{sT}\mathcal{M}^s < \gamma^2 P(s). \tag{45}$$

When, it is easy to get $k > 0$

$$\begin{aligned}\mathbb{E}\left\{\tilde{z}^T(k)\tilde{z}(k)\right\} &= \eta^T(k)\mathcal{M}^{sT}\mathcal{M}^s\eta(k) \\ &< \gamma^2\eta^T(k)P(s)\eta(k) = \gamma^2\mathbb{E}\left\{\eta^T(k)P(s)\eta(k)\right\} \\ &< \gamma^2 \sum_{i=0}^{k-1}\overline{w}^T(i)\overline{w}(i) \le \gamma^2\sum_{i=0}^{\infty}\overline{w}^T(i)\overline{w}(i).\end{aligned} \tag{46}$$

Through Eq. (46), get

$$\sup_k\left\{\mathbb{E}\left\{\tilde{z}^T(k)\tilde{z}(k)\right\}\right\} < \gamma^2 \sum_{i=0}^{\infty}\overline{w}^T(i)\overline{w}(i). \tag{47}$$

As a result,

$$\mathbb{E}\left\{\|\tilde{z}(k)\|_{\infty}^2\right\} < \gamma^2\mathbb{E}\|\overline{w}(k)\|_2^2. \tag{48}$$

At this point, the proof of Theorem 1 is completed.

## 4 Filter Design

**Theorem 2.** Given disturbance attenuation level $\gamma > 0$. The augmented filter error system is exponentially stable in mean square and has $L_2 - l_{\infty}$ Performance, if there are matrices, and, and matrices, and satisfy the following linear matrix inequalities $\overline{W}_f^s$ $\overline{L}_f^s R > 0 \, \Phi_i(s) > 0 \, Q_i(s) > 0 \overline{H}_f^s \overline{H}_f^s \in W_{n_x \times n_y}, s = 1, 2, \cdots, n_0.$

$$\begin{bmatrix} \Gamma_{11} & * & * & * & * & * & * & * \\ 0 & \Gamma_{22} & * & * & * & * & * & * \\ 0 & 0 & \Gamma_{33} & * & * & * & * & * \\ 0 & 0 & 0 & \Gamma_{44} & * & * & * & * \\ 0 & 0 & 0 & 0 & \Gamma_{55} & * & * & * \\ 0 & \Gamma_{62} & 0 & 0 & 0 & \Gamma_{66} & * & * \\ \Gamma_{71} & 0 & 0 & \Gamma_{74} & 0 & 0 & \Gamma_{77} & * \\ \Gamma_{81} & \Gamma_{82} & \Gamma_{83} & \Gamma_{84} & \Gamma_{85} & 0 & 0 & \Gamma_{88} \end{bmatrix} < 0, \tag{49}$$

$$\begin{bmatrix} -P_1(s) & * & * \\ 0 & -\overline{Q}(s) & * \\ 0 & M - \overline{L}_f^s & -\gamma^2 I \end{bmatrix} < 0, \tag{50}$$

Among them

$$
\begin{aligned}
&\overline{W}_f^s = diag_n\left\{W_{fi}^s\right\}, \overline{L}_f^s = diag_n\left\{L_{fi}^s\right\}, \\
&\overline{\Phi}(s) = diag_n\{\Phi_i(s)\}, \Gamma_{11} = -R, \\
&Q(s) = diag_n\{Q_i(s)\}, \Gamma_{22} = -\overline{Q}(s), \\
&\Gamma_{33} = -\overline{\Phi}(s), \Gamma_{44} = \Gamma_{55} = I, \\
&\Gamma_{62} = \delta_M \overline{\Phi}(s)\overline{C}, \Gamma_{66} = -\overline{\Phi}(s), \\
&\Gamma_{71} = R\overline{A}, \Gamma_{74} = R\overline{B}, \Gamma_{77} = -R, \\
&\Gamma_{81} = \overline{Q}(s)\overline{A} - \overline{W}_f^s, \Gamma_{82} = \overline{W}_f^s - \overline{H}_f^s\overline{C}, \\
&\Gamma_{83} = -\overline{H}_f^s, \Gamma_{84} = \overline{Q}(s)\overline{B}, \\
&\Gamma_{85} = -\overline{H}_f^s\overline{D}, \Gamma_{88} = -\overline{Q}(s).
\end{aligned}
\tag{51}
$$

The parameters of the distributed filter are expressed as follows:

$$
\overline{W}^s = \overline{Q}^{-1}(s)\overline{W}_f^s, \overline{H}^s = \overline{Q}^{-1}(s)\overline{H}_f^s, \overline{L}^s = \overline{L}_f^s.
\tag{52}
$$

By selecting formula (15), we can obtain: $P(s) = diag\{R, Q(s)\}$,

$$
\overline{Q}(s) = \sum_{t=1}^{n_0} \pi_{st} diag\{Q_1(t), Q_2(t), \cdots, Q_n(t)\},
\tag{53}
$$

$$
\begin{aligned}
&\overline{P}(s)\mathscr{A}^s = \begin{bmatrix} R\overline{A} & 0 \\ \overline{Q}(s)\overline{A} - \overline{Q}(s)\overline{W}^s & \overline{Q}(s)\overline{W}^s - \overline{Q}(s)\overline{H}^s\overline{C} \end{bmatrix}, \\
&\overline{P}(s)\mathscr{B}^s = \begin{bmatrix} R\overline{B} & 0 \\ \overline{Q}(s)\overline{B} & -\overline{Q}(s)\overline{H}^s\overline{D} \end{bmatrix}, \Phi(s)\check{C}_M = \begin{bmatrix} 0 & \delta_M \Phi(s)\overline{C} \end{bmatrix}, \\
&\overline{P}(s)\mathscr{F}^s = \begin{bmatrix} 0 \\ -\overline{Q}(s)\overline{H}^s \end{bmatrix}.
\end{aligned}
\tag{54}
$$

Substitute Eq. (54) into Eq. (22) and Eq. (23), and introduce a new variable, and $\overline{W}_f^s = \overline{Q}(s)\overline{W}^s \overline{H}_f^s = \overline{Q}(s)\overline{H}^s \overline{L}_f^s = \overline{L}^s$. Theorem 2 is easy to get. By Lemma 1, the constraint of Eq. (17) is satisfied $\overline{H}_f^s$. Theorem 2 is proved.

**Note 1.** Theorem 2 can be converted into the following convex optimization problem, which is convenient for Matlab to solve the optimal distributed filtering parameters $\delta = \gamma^2$.

$$
\min_{P_1(s),P_2(s),P_3(s),V_1^s,V_2^s,V_3^s,\overline{W}_f^s,\overline{H}_f^s,\overline{L}_f^s} \delta,
\tag{55}
$$
$$
s.t.(49)-(50)
$$

## 5  Digital Simulation

In order to prove the effectiveness of the distributed filtering method designed, a distributed filter network composed of four nodes is considered. Parameters of system (1) and sensor parameters are selected as follows:

$$
A = \begin{bmatrix} 0.4 & 0.7 \\ 0.8 & -0.5 \end{bmatrix}, B = \begin{bmatrix} 1 \\ 0.5 \end{bmatrix}, M = \begin{bmatrix} 1 & 1 \end{bmatrix},
$$

$$C_1 = \begin{bmatrix} -0.3 \ 0.9 \end{bmatrix}, C_2 = \begin{bmatrix} -0.4 \ 0.6 \end{bmatrix}, D_1 = 0.11,$$

$$C_3 = \begin{bmatrix} 0.5 \ 0.5 \end{bmatrix}, C_4 = \begin{bmatrix} 0.1 \ 0.4 \end{bmatrix}, D_2 = 0.15,$$

$$D_3 = 0.14, D_4 = 0.21, \varepsilon = 0.01, \rho = 0.4,$$

$v_i(k) = N\left(0, \frac{1}{k^2}\right)$, $w(k) = e^{-0.2k} \sin(k)$. Suppose the filter network has three different topologies:

$$A^1 = \begin{bmatrix} 1 & 0 & 0 & 1 \\ 0 & 1 & 1 & 0 \\ 1 & 0 & 1 & 0 \\ 0 & 1 & 0 & 1 \end{bmatrix}, A^2 = \begin{bmatrix} 1 & 0 & 1 & 0 \\ 0 & 1 & 0 & 1 \\ 0 & 0 & 1 & 0 \\ 0 & 0 & 1 & 1 \end{bmatrix}, A^3 = \begin{bmatrix} 1 & 1 & 0 & 1 \\ 1 & 1 & 1 & 0 \\ 0 & 1 & 1 & 0 \\ 1 & 0 & 0 & 1 \end{bmatrix}.$$

Let the initial filter topology, the initial state of the filter be zero $r_0 = 2$. The state transition matrix of the topology structure is:

$$\Pi = \begin{bmatrix} 0.4 \ 0.3 \ 0.3 \\ 0.3 \ 0.5 \ 0.2 \\ 0.2 \ 0.6 \ 0.2 \end{bmatrix}.$$

By using Matlab LMI toolbox, solve the convex optimization problem (55), get $\gamma = 0.46$.

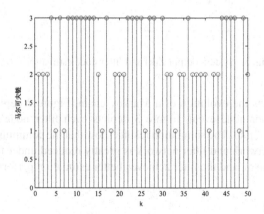

**Fig. 1.** Markov chain R (k).

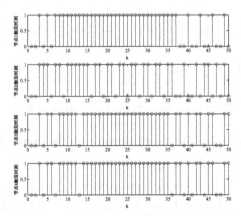

**Fig. 2.** Event trigger time.

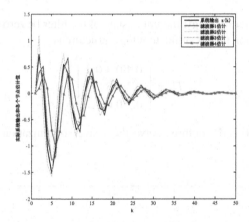

**Fig. 3.** System output Z(k) and filter node estimation $\hat{z}_i(k)$.

Figure 1 depicts the evolution of a Markov chain. Figure 2 depicts the triggering time of each sensor node event. Figure 3 depicts each filter node's estimate of the system output Z(k) $\hat{z}_i(k)$. The simulation results show that the communication frequency between sensor network and filter network is greatly reduced under the adaptive event triggering mechanism, and the filter achieves better estimation performance.

## 6   Conclusion

This paper discusses the distribution l of a class of filtering networks $_2$-$l_\infty$ State estimation problem. By embedding adaptive event triggering mechanism, the burden of network communication is greatly reduced. Considering the complex network environment, the designed distributed filter can still achieve the desired filtering performance even if the filter network communication topology switches randomly. Finally, the effectiveness of the design method is verified by numerical simulation.

**Acknowledgement.** This work was supported by National Key Research and Development Program of China, No. 2018YFD0400902, National Natural Science Foundation of China, No. 61873112, and Natural Science Research Project of Higher Education institutions of Jiangsu Province, No. 18KJB413009.

# References

1. Bruin, T.D., Verbert, K., Babuka, R.: Railway track circuit fault diagnosis using recurrent neural networks. IEEE Trans. Neural Netw. Learn. Syst. **28**(3), 523–533 (2016)
2. Bai, X., Wang, Z., Sheng, L., et al.: Reliable data fusion of hierarchical wireless sensor networks with asynchronous measurement for greenhouse monitoring. IEEE Trans. Control Syst. Technol. **2018**, 1–11 (2018)
3. Park, P., Di Marco, P., Johansson, K.H.: Cross-layer optimization for industrial control applications using wireless sensor and actuator mesh networks. IEEE Trans. Industr. Electron. **64**(4), 3250–3259 (2016)
4. Yang, F., Han, Q.L., Liu, Y.: Distributed $H_\infty$ state estimation over a filtering network with time-varying and switching topology and partial information exchange. IEEE Trans. Cybern. **49**(3), 870–882 (2018)
5. Dong, H., Bu, X., Wang, Z., et al.: Finite-horizon distributed state estimation under randomly switching topologies and redundant channels. IEEE Trans. Syst. Man Cybern.: Syst. **50**, 2938–2947 (2018)
6. Ge, X., Han, Q.L., Wang, Z.: A threshold-parameter-dependent approach to designing distributed event-triggered $H_\infty$ consensus filters over sensor networks. IEEE Trans. Cybern. **49**(4), 1148–1159 (2018)
7. Peng, C., Tian, E., Zhang, J., et al.: Decentralized event-triggering communication scheme for large-scale systems under network environments. Inf. Sci. **380**, 132–144 (2017)
8. Liu, H.: Mode-dependent event-triggered control of networked Takagi-Sugeno fuzzy systems. IET Control Theory (Chin. Appl.) **10**(6), 711–716 (2016)
9. Gu, Z., Tian, E., Liu, J.: Adaptive event-triggered control of a class of nonlinear networked systems. J. Franklin Inst. **354**(9), 3854–3871 (2017)
10. Gu, Z., Yue, D., Liu, J., et al.: $H_\infty$ tracking control of nonlinear networked systems with a novel adaptive event-triggered communication scheme. J. Franklin Inst. **354**(8), 3540–3553 (2017)
11. Ugrinovskii, V.: Distributed robust estimation over randomly switching networks using $H_\infty$ consensus. Automatica **49**(1), 160–168 (2013)
12. Yan, H., Yang, Q., Zhang, H., et al.: Distributed $H_\infty$ state estimation for a class of filtering networks with time-varying switching topologies and packet losses. IEEE Trans. Syst. Man Cybern.: Syst. **99**, 1–11 (2017)
13. Liu, B., Zhang, X.M., Han, Q.L.: Event-triggered H∞ filtering for networked systems with switching topologies. In: 2015 IEEE 13th International Conference on Industrial Informatics (INDIN), pp. 162–167, IEEE (2015)
14. Chi, X., Zhang, L., Jia, X.: Topologically switched multi-sensor networked system distributed $H_\infty$. J. Shaanxi Univ. Sci. Technol. **36**(1), 160–166 (2018)
15. Zhao, H., Zhang, D.: Distributed filtering based on event triggering in wireless sensor networks. J. Shaanxi Univ. Sci. Technol. (Nat. Sci. Ed.) **35**(02), 177–182 (2017)
16. Li, H., Gao, H., Shi, P., et al.: Fault-tolerant control of Markovian jump stochastic systems via the augmented sliding mode observer approach. Automatica **50**(7), 1825–1834 (2014)
17. Zhu, F., Wen, J., Peng, L., Yang, R.: Distributed sensor networks with random measurement data loss and switching topology $L_2$-$l_\infty$ design of filter. Control Decis. **35**(08), 1841–1848 (2020)

# Stratified Transfer Learning of Touchscreen Behavior on Cross-Device for User Identification

Huizhong Sun[1]([⊠]), Guosheng Xu[1], Xuanwen Zhang[2], Zhaonan Wu[1], and Bo Gao[3]

[1] School of Cyberspace Security, Beijing University of Posts and Telecommunication, Beijing 100786, China
sunhuizhong@bupt.edu.cn
[2] Comprehensive Research Center of Electronic Information Technology in the MIIT of China, Weihai 264200, China
[3] University of Technology Sydney, Sydney, Australia

**Abstract.** Recently, most continuous authentication study focuses on a single device, such as a smart phone or smart watch. However, as the cost of mobile smart devices decreases and it becomes more common for users to have more than one mobile device, authentication systems must adapt to an environment where users are constantly switching between multiple devices. And applying different authentication solutions to different devices can present usability challenges, where using the same authentication technology affects the security of other devices. Therefore, we propose Stratified Transfer Learning (STL) for cross-device user identification by using user-multi-device behavioral biometry and finding that the same user has the same number of dimensions and the same markers on smartphones and tablets, but follows different feature distributions. First, we collect the touch screen behaviors of users when interacting with multiple devices (tablets, phones) and extract features for keystroke and swipe, and then use STL to learn the correlation of features and transform the multi-device feature domain into a new shared feature space for user recognition in a cross-device environment. Finally, we perform validation on the SU-AIS BB-MAS dataset, which has same-user-multi-device behavioral data. The experimental results show that applying cross-device generation with similar interaction patterns enables cross-device user identification.

**Keywords:** Across-device · Keystroke · Swipe · User identification

## 1 Introduction

In recent years, with a large number of smart devices are used in mobile offices, more and more companies allow employees to bring their own computers to work, and tablets and smart phones are actively or passively used in various tasks. While mobile office brings fast and efficient office experience to the public, it also brings certain security risks.

In order to protect important data in mobile devices from being stolen by illegal users, smart devices use a combination of explicit (password, PIN, etc.) and implicit (touch screen gestures, keystroke dynamics, etc.) identity authentication methods. This

X. Sun et al. (Eds.): ICAIS 2022, CCIS 1588, pp. 618–631, 2022.
https://doi.org/10.1007/978-3-031-06764-8_48

approach has been confirmed by recent studies on the security and usability of a single mobile device. For example, sensor data generated by human-computer interaction is used to simulate the behavior of the user to identify unique users. One of the mechanisms is to apply the user's touch dynamics on the mobile device to create a unique behavior model and use it for authentication purposes. The user's touch gestures on the mobile device include horizontal and vertical swipes. Also using the touch sensors embedded in the screen features such as timestamps, touch coordinates (x-coordinates, y-coordinates), finger pressure and finger touch area can be extracted. These features are used to simulate the user's touch behavior on the touch screen. Another mechanism is keystroke dynamics, also known as typing dynamics, which is an analysis of a person's typing habits, such as the duration of a keystroke or the time between two keystrokes. In-depth observation of these habits can produce unique patterns or characteristics for each person, thereby identifying users. Unlike passwords, touchscreen gestures and keystroke dynamics do not require special hardware, which can enhance existing authentication systems, and user behaviors are not easy to be stolen or copied.

Research on continuous authentication on single smart devices has yielded a large number of efforts. Many authentication schemes meet the need for single-device scenarios, but little research has been done on combining behavioral data from smartphones and tablets, especially on how to leverage similarities in user touchscreen behavior on different devices to enable cross-device authentication. A. K. Belman [1] et al. focus on authentication in environments where users switch between multiple devices, exploring user interaction behaviors between different devices, and extracting the characteristics of the same behavior on different devices and the relationship between them. This paper proved that in a multi-device environment, these relationships can be used to authenticate users when users switch between devices. Finally, the authentication system is designed for three situations, exploiting the relationships between typing behaviors on desktop, mobile phone and tablet. Ngyuen [2] et al. presented a preliminary exploration to determine whether the biometric touch screen profiles can be applied to multiple mobile devices. The results of this small-scale study show that user behavior is consistent across different types of mobile hardware for playing and reading. This provides preliminary research demonstrating that behavioral biometrics can be applied across multiple mobile devices in a number of scenarios. For example, the use of sliding/keystroke behaviors, which in practice may be influenced by device hardware and software features (e.g., shape factors and virtual keyboard layout). For example, the size of the touchscreen may change the user's swipe behavior, while different virtual keyboard layouts may affect the input pattern. However, obtaining information from across devices can improve the applicability and flexibility of an authentication system, as it is necessary to access cross-device and simulate user behavior in each device.

Despite continuous authentication solutions based on mobile devices having many advantages, their design and implementation in new cross-device scenarios are still a challenging problem. For instance, how to use the user-multi-device similar interaction pattern to identify cross-device users. To this end, we have done the following work.

(1) We focus on the environment of switching between different devices, analyze the key factors of identifying users in cross-device scenarios, preprocess keystroke and

sliding behavior data, and explore the feasibility of migration learning to identify users across devices.

(2) There are significant differences in the interaction methods between different devices. We propose the STL method, which uses the source field data or features to enhance the training of the target field, and then achieve better training effects.

(3) Experiments show that under the same task, the STL method combined with the classification algorithm can effectively identify users with multiple devices, providing experience for future cross-device authentication research.

The rest of the paper is organized as follows. Section 2 discusses related work for continuous certification of cross-device scenarios and a single device. In Sect. 3, we study the cross-device scenario. Section 4 introduces the cross-device user identification scheme. Section 5 describes the experiment and analysis of the results. Section 6 presents the conclusions and future work.

## 2    Related Work

This section reviews recent continuous authentication solutions in the field. A variety of continuous authentication proposals for single and cross-device scenarios are analyzed, extracting common ideas and potential improvements.

### 2.1    Continuous Authentication in Single-Device Scenarios

In the field of continuous authentication for single device scenarios, Frank et al. [3] explored the feasibility of a continuous authentication mechanism based on a touch screen approach. In this paper, the authors first designed an experiment involving 41 volunteers whose experiments focused on collecting data on users' touch behaviors in activities such as browsing text and entering text, and then proposed a set of it has 30 kinds of behavior features based on the touch screen method. KNN and SVM are used to identify sliding behavior features. The experimental results show that this behavioral feature is feasible. Furthermore, Shen et al. [4] systematically investigated the reliability and applicability of the continuous authentication mechanism based on the touch screen, and analyzed the performance of the authentication mechanism in detail under various application scenarios and different authentication algorithms through more than 132,900 touch operations in 71 volunteers. In [5, 6] the same behavior is through the use of touch operations.

Shen et al. [7] investigated the reliability and applicability of using the built-in sensors of mobile phones, such as accelerometer, magnetometer, and gyroscope for continuous authentication. In this paper, the author not only proposed a set of features based on sensor data, but also built a sensor sequence distribution density model through a hidden Markov classifier, and finally constructs an authentication model for authentication. Experimental results show that the characteristics of behavioral biological data recorded by built-in sensors are stable and distinguishable, and in some scenarios, a false acceptance rate of 3.98% and a false rejection rate of 5.03% can be achieved.

Kayacik et al. [8] proposed a data-driven authentication scheme, which uses the built-in mobile phone sensor to perceive the user's behavior pattern to perform authentication. Through the authentication model running in the background, the current user's behavior pattern is compared with the initial user's behavior pattern. If the current user's behavior deviates from the established standard pattern and is higher than the set threshold, it will pass display authentication, such as password, etc. Way to further protect the security of the system. After the system model training is completed, in order to be able to support fast and lightweight deployment, the work shifts the training mode to the deployment model, that is, it allows the device to automatically select an appropriate detection threshold. Finally, this work further verifies that this sensor-based authentication method can effectively solve practical problems on the public data set, and proves the effectiveness of its model in a simulated attacker scenario.

## 2.2  Continuous Authentication in Cross-Device Scenarios

This section analyzes the continuous certification research work applied to cross-device scenarios. Most of the research focuses on multi-device certification. Currently, there are not many papers for cross-devices.

Sanchez et al. [9] designed a continuous certification scheme for smart offices. The authors deployed their architecture on smartphones and PCs as a proof of concept. Then, use Random Forest (RF) to test on different devices. The average accuracy rate on smart phones is 97.43%. The average accuracy rate on the computer is 96.32%. However, the author did not conduct any experiments combining different user behaviors.

Hintze D [10] et al. extended the concept of single sign-on from a single device to all users' devices, allowing trusted devices to share authentication information securely and transparently at close range in order to obtain sufficient information about the user's identity. Krašovec et al. [11] explored the possibilities provided by heterogeneous devices that collect non-sensitive data in a smart environment. A test platform for the Internet of Things is constructed, which collects data related to people's movement in space, interaction with specific equipment, computer terminal use, and typing, and builds a machine learning model that captures human behavior characteristics. Belman [12] et al. proposed a continuous authentication scheme for users of different handheld devices based on specific word features based on keystroke dynamics.

In a word, due to the frequency of device interaction and the increase in the number of mobile devices carried at the same time, one disadvantage of continuous authentication based on behavioral biometrics is that all users use a single device for research. Therefore, it is unclear whether the biometric model can be transferred between devices or applied to multiple devices at the same time.

Therefore, in cross-device scenarios, we use the behavioral biometric features of human-computer interaction to discover similar user habits, analyze the distribution of user touch screen behavioral features, and propose the feasibility of cross-device user identification based on Stratified Transfer Learning (STL) to reduce multi-device authentication time and improve user experience.

## 3   Proposed Method

This section describes the design details of a cross-device user identification based on transfer learning. The scheme consists of five parts: data collection, feature extraction, Common features for cross-device, classification, and verification of the feasibility of cross-device authentication (Fig. 1).

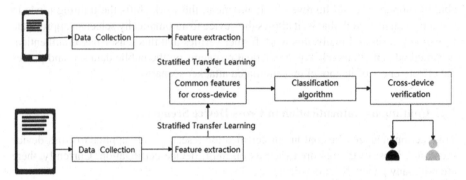

**Fig.1.** Cross-device user identification scenario based on stratified transfer learning.

**Data Collection:** Monitoring the data generated by user interaction with cross-device, collecting behavioral characteristics of tablets and smartphones, such as keystrokes and slide track information;

**Feature Extraction:** We biometrically measure slide and keystroke events in touch-screen behavior, and construct a sequence of features related to a single device and multiple devices by filtering and aggregating the characteristics of a single device.

**Common Features for Cross-Device:** Analyze patterns of similar behavior across devices, leverage the relevance of STL learning features, and transform multi-device feature domains into a new shared feature space for user identification across device environments.

**Classification Algorithm:** This paper uses SVM, random forest, KNN and other algorithms to build classification model in combination with STL.

**Cross-Device Validation:** Based on the experimental results, verify the feasibility of identifying similar behaviors across devices, and the impact of different activities on cross-device authentication results.

### 3.1   Data Collection

To study the feasibility of touch-screen behavior in cross-device authentication, we asked the same user to complete tasks on smartphones and tablets: swipe the screen, type free text, type fixed text, and so on, and the data collector records the user's behavior data when entering the touch screen. We extract keystrokes and slide features from each user's activity. Store the raw data for each sensor per user as a user ID. Keystroke data that collects time data for each key that the user presses and releases during a task. Time represents the timestamp of the keystroke event when typing is pressed or released. Touch data to extract a variety of features related to sliding speed and trajectory. EID: represents the touch-screen event ID, X value represents the X coordinates on the touch screen, Y value: represents the Y coordinates on the touch screen, pressure: represents touch-screen pressure, touch Major: represents the length of the long axis of the touch-screen area ellipse, touch Minor: represents the length of the short axis of the touch-screen area ellipse, pointer ID: represents the number of touch points in the touch-screen area, finger Orientation: Represents the direction of the finger's arc relative to the vertical plane of the device, action Type: indicates that the slide screen is beginning and ending, time: represents the timestamp of the touch screen event.

**Table 1.** Features extracted from keystroke and swipe.

| Features | Description |
|---|---|
| $f_1$-$f_5$ | Key hold latency is the down-up time between press and release of a key |
| $f_6$-$f_7$ | The minimum x and y coordinates in the entire swipe |
| $f_8$-$f_9$ | The maximum x and y coordinates in the entire swipe |
| $f_{10}$ | The Euclidean distance between the start and end points of the swipe |
| $f_{11}$ | Euclidean distance between points of a swipe |
| $f_{12}$ | The tangent angle of the swipe |
| $f_{13}$-$f_{14}$ | The mean and standard deviation of velocity during the swipe |
| $f_{15}$-$f_{s17}$ | The first, second and third quartiles of velocity during the swipe |
| $f_{18}$-$f_{s19}$ | The mean and standard deviation of acceleration during the swipe |
| $f_{20}$-$f_{s21}$ | Acceleration quartiles, standard deviation |
| $f_{22}$-$f_{24}$ | Pressure quartiles, Pressure mean and standard deviation |
| $f_{25}$-$f_{27}$ | The first, second and third quartiles of acceleration during the swipe |
| $f_{28}$-$f_{29}$ | The mean and standard deviation of pressure during the swipe |
| $f_{30}$-$f_{32}$ | The first, second and third quartiles of pressure during the swipe |
| $f_{33}$-$f_{34}$ | The mean and standard deviation of area during the swipe |
| $F_{35}$-$f_{37}$ | The first, second and third quartiles of area during the swipe |
| $f_{38}$-$f_{41}$ | The direction of the swipe comparing the displacement of the fingertip in x and y direction |
| $f_{42}$ | Length of the swipe |

### 3.2 Feature Extraction

Our experiments used SU-AIS BB-MAS dataset. In this paper, we consider touch-screen behavior data, such as slide screen and keystroke data, on smartphones and tablets for the same user. To get the identification information from the user's slide screen and keystrokes, we extract 84 features, as shown in Table 1. For keystroke events, because dynamic keystroke behavior recognition cannot rely on getting a fixed or free amount of text from each participant, nor is it guaranteed that all participants will type the same value, for each type, we extract the duration of the keystroke and the time between keystrokes. Swipe features extracted from swipe trajectories, pressure, acceleration and touch area data from smartphone and tablet.

To study more detailed information in the cross-device authentication process, we analyzed the following three scenarios based on the similarity of the same user's use of different devices. These three scenarios represent varying degrees of similarity across devices. We use S and T to represent domain activity, S to represent the domain of the smartphone, T to represent the domain of the tablet.

a) Similarity of the same device, which means that the user types different free or fixed text on the device while using a single device. Specifically, we extracted sensor data from typing fixed and free text and built two tasks: By answering questions, the user types fixed text/type free text on their smartphone.
b) Different operations of the same device, which refers to the sliding screen and keystroke operation performed by the user when using a single device. Specifically, we built two tasks based on the user's operation on the same device: the user's keystrokes and slide screens (vertical and horizontal) on the smartphone.
c) Similar operation of different devices, i.e. the same keystroke and slide screen operation on different devices. Specifically, we built four of these behaviors: keystrokes and slide screens (vertical and horizontal) on smartphones and tablets

We built a total of 8 tasks. Note that there are different touch-screen behaviors in this dataset. For scenarios a) and scenario b), we simply use a single device in the dataset to produce features, for scenario c) is a cross-device dataset, we extract three common subsets of the dataset (data set on tablet, dataset on smartphone, dataset across device).

### 3.3 Common Features for Cross-Device

Multi-device scenarios present new challenges, and when users interact with cross-devices, there are significant differences in the way different devices interact because of their heterogeneity. Therefore, how to move a single-device user authentication model from the source domain to the target domain for identification is a huge challenge. This is a typical cross-domain authentication problem, usually caused by a tag source domain $D_s$, an unlabeled target domain $D_t$, $D_s$ and $D_t$ having the same dimension and label space, i.e. $x_i$, $x_j \in R^d$, where d is the dimension, $Y_s = Y_t$, and in cross-domain learning they follow different characteristic distributions. Therefore, this paper proposes a Stratified Transfer Learning (STL) framework. STL can convert the same classes of both the source domain and the target domain into the same subspace to facilitate the use of their source domain data or characteristics to enhance training in the target area for better training results.

First, we label the target domain (tablet) by classifying the target domain (tablet) by a classifier trained on the source domain (smartphone). Acts as an initial classification. At the same time, in the classification process, there is a part that is difficult to classify and mark it as difficult to classify. There are many types of classifiers here, such as SVM, KNN, Random Forest (RF), etc., or it can make decisions together with multiple classifiers.

$$A_j = \begin{cases} majority(f_t(j), t) & \text{if majority holds} \\ -1 & otherwise \end{cases} \tag{1}$$

$A_j$ represents the result of majority voting on sample j, and $f_t(j)$ represents the prediction result of sample j by the t-th classifier. t represents the index of the classifier. "$-1$" means that the sample does not have a majority consensus, that is, a sample that is difficult to classify. The samples with this label are called residuals, and they will be annotated later.

The next step is to further excavate the intra-class relationship on the basis of pseudo-labels, so as to perform transfer learning. Feature migration is performed in each category of pseudo-tags, and finally the feature subspace of each category is synthesized into one subspace. We will use $x_{can}$ and $x_{res}$ to represent the candidate domain and residual respectively. $\tilde{y}_{can}$ represents the pseudo-label of the candidate. $D_s$ and $x_{can}$ are divided into G groups based on their (pseudo) labels, where G is the total number of classes. Then, feature conversion is performed in each class of the two domains. Finally, the results of different subspaces are merged.

The key to feature conversion is to use the similarity between the source domain and the target domain. Therefore, how to measure similarity (or divergence) is very important, so we use MMD (Maximum mean discrepancy) to measure the distance between the source domain and the target domain, and learn to find the subspace mapping with the smallest MMD distance.

$$D(D_s, D_t) = \left\| \frac{1}{n_s} \sum_{x_i \in D_s} \phi(x_i) - \frac{1}{n_t} \sum_{x_j \in D_t} \phi(x_j) \right\|_\delta^2 \tag{2}$$

$\delta$ represents the reconstructed kernel Hilbert space (RKHS), and $\varphi(x)$ represents some feature maps that map the original samples to RKHS. $D_s$ represents the source domain, and $D_t$ represents the target domain.

In order to achieve intra-class migration, we need to calculate the MMD distance between each class. Since the target domain has no tags, we use pseudo tags from majority voting. For the candidate domain $x_{can}$ and the source domain $D_s$, we express that their intra-class MMD distance as

$$D(D_s, x_{can}) = \sum_{g=1}^{G} \left\| \frac{1}{n_s^{(g)}} \sum_{x_i \in D_s^{(g)}} \phi(x_i) - \frac{1}{n_t^{(g)}} \sum_{x_i \in X_{can}^{(g)}} \phi(x_j) \right\|_\delta^2 \tag{3}$$

$$n_s^{(g)} = \left| D_s^{(g)} \right|, n_t^{(g)} = \left| X_{can}^{(g)} \right| \tag{4}$$

where g represents the label of the class, $D_s^{(c)}$ and $X_{can}^{(c)}$ represents the samples belonging to the g class in the source and candidate samples. At the same time, as with most pattern recognition problems, the kernel method can further increase the computational efficiency. We map the source data to the Hilbert space Calculate the distance in $\delta$.

$$K_{ij} = \langle \phi(x_i), \phi(x_j) \rangle = \phi(x_i)^T \phi(x_j) \tag{5}$$

where $\mathbf{x}_i$ and $\mathbf{x}_j$ are samples from either Ds or $\mathbf{X}_{can}$.

The above problem can be defined as:

$$\min_{w} \sum_{g=1}^{G} tr\left(W^T KL_g KW\right) + \lambda tr\left(W^T W\right) \tag{6}$$
$$s.t \qquad W^T KHKW = I$$

$tr(WTKL_g KW)$ represents the MMD distance between various source domains and target domains, and $tr(WTKL_g KW)$ denotes the regularization term to ensure the problem is well-defined with $\lambda$ the trade-off parameter. $W^T W$ is used to ensure that the converted data still retains the original data certain structural properties. $L_g$ is the MMD matrix within the class:

$$(L_g)_{ij} = \begin{cases} \dfrac{1}{(n_1^{(g)})^2} & x_i, x_j \in D_s^{(g)} \\[2ex] \dfrac{1}{(n_2^{(g)})^2} & x_i, x_j \in X_{can}^{(g)} \\[2ex] -\dfrac{1}{(n_1^{(g)})(n_2^{(g)})} & \begin{cases} x_i \in D_s^{(g)}, x_j \in X_{can}^{(g)} \\ x_i \in X_{can}^{(g)}, x_j \in D_s^{(g)} \end{cases} \\[3ex] 0 & otherwise \end{cases} \tag{7}$$

The Lagrangian method is used to transform the above problem into a universal eigen decomposition problem.

$$\left( K \sum_{g=1}^{G} L_c K^T + \lambda I \right) W = KHK^T W \phi \tag{8}$$

The finally obtained matrix W can map the data of the two domains into the same subspace. Then use different classifiers to annotate the remaining parts of the converted source domains and candidates. The majority voting system provides candidates with pseudo-labels $\widetilde{y}_{can}$, and transforms the pseudo-labels into the same subspace as the target domain through intra-class transfer.

### 3.4 Classification Algorithm

User identification aims to recognize who the current user is and further determine whether the current user has the legitimate right to access the mobile devices or applications. Formally, behavior-based user identification can be formulated as follows. Given a data set $\{(x_1, y_1), (x_n, y_n)\}$, where $x_i = [x^1{}_i,...,x^m{}_i]$ is the m-dimensional feature vector of samples; $y_i \in C$ is the corresponding class of one specific user; and C refers to the set of classes. The goal of the user identification task is to learn a mapping function that predicts the label information for one given behavior sequence with least biases. For user identification system, classification algorithms are SVM, KNN and RF [13–19].

## 4   Experimental Results and Analysis

Cross-device user identification is primarily the use of a single device authentication model to identify the behavior characteristics of the same user on other devices. In our experiment, we selected user behavior recognition for smartphones and tablets. Specifically, when users continue to switch between multiple devices, the same kind of activity, using a smartphone authentication model based on user behavior to mark other device user authentication information. Therefore, other similar user behaviors are used for cross-device user identification.

### 4.1   Effectiveness Verification of STL

In this section, to verify the validity of the STL from the following two aspects, first, the number of target domains on the algorithm. Second, will the choice of a majority voting classifier affect the framework. If we use different classifiers, performance may vary.

First, in each experiment, we limited the number of target domains to between 5% and 100%, with the rest attributed to the rest. Then the STL is tested for accuracy, and the basic classifier is a random forest (Fig. 2).

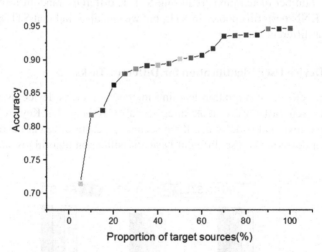

**Fig. 2.** Impact of number of target domains on STL performance.

As can be seen from the Fig. 3, the performance of the STL increases with the proportion of the target domain, but as the number of target domains increases, the improvement of accuracy decreases, i.e. as long as the target domain reaches a certain number, the accuracy of user identification can be improved.

In order to verify the effect of different classifiers on STL performance, we selected SVM, KNN, and RF classification algorithms. The results are shown in Fig. 4.

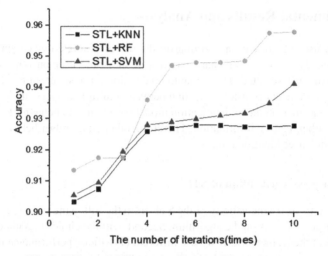

**Fig. 3.** Effects of different classifiers on STL performance.

From the figure we can see that different classifiers and STL combination, the same accuracy, the number of iterations requiring STL is different, random forests perform best in STL, KNN performs poorly in STL, but we can also find that STL has a certain robustness for different classifiers.

## 4.2 Cross-Device User Identification for Different Tasks

To explore the effects of migration learning methods on cross-device user identification under different tasks, we validate three scenarios in Sect. 4.1. Keystroke free text, keystroke fixed text, and slide screen three scenes represent different degrees of similarity between devices. We use different basic classification algorithms such as SVM,

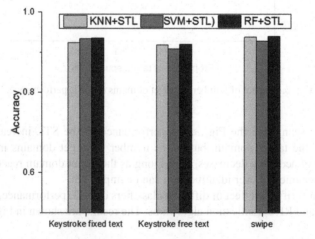

**Fig. 4.** Keystroke free text, keystroke fixed text and swipe for user identification.

KNN, RF, and STL combinations to identify user behavior across devices. The following figure is for each average classification accuracy.

From the figure above, we can see the features extracted when keystrokes are fixed on a smartphone, which better captures the similarity of keystrokes when the same user is using a virtual standard keyboard. Keystroke free text is susceptible to input characters, and there is a significant difference between keystroke fixed text. Sliding screens are susceptible to device size, but applying STL can capture the similarity of the same interaction mode between different devices.

### 4.3  Fusion Feature for Cross-Device User Identification

In this section, we'll show the results of a cross-device-multitasking scenario. Combine keystrokes and slide-screen behavior characteristics, train in a single-device scenario, and build a single-device user authentication model using RF classifiers. The learned model is then applied to the tablet and tested using touchscreen behavior data collected on the tablet. The test results are shown in Table 2 below.

**Table 2.**  STL + RF classification results for all tasks.

| Device | Task | Average EER |
|---|---|---|
| Cross-device | Swipe | 8.95% |
| | Keystroke | 7.57% |
| | Swipe + keystroke | 5.41% |

Equal error rate (EER) In order to balance the overall measure of error acceptance and error rejection rates when evaluating classification performance, the lower the value, the higher the accuracy of the verification system. As we can tell from the table, the EER value of the fusion feature is 2%–3% higher than the performance of a single device in cross-device user recognition.

## 5  Conclusion

In this paper, we focus on the environment in which multiple devices switch between, analyze the key factors for identifying users across device scenarios, preprocess keystrokes and slide-screen behavior data, and explore the feasibility of migration learning for cross-device user identification. There are significant differences in the way different devices interact, and we propose the STL method, which uses its source domain data or characteristics to enhance the training in the target area, so as to achieve better training results. Experiments show that under the same task, the STL method, combined with classification algorithm, can effectively identify users with multiple devices and provide experience for future cross-device certification research. We will continue to study device homologinity information for cross-device authentication.

**Funding Statement.** This work was financially supported by the National Natural Science Foundation of China under Grant No.6210070494, 61873069, China Postdoctoral Science Foundation under grant of No. 2021T140074. The National and the Key Scientific and Technological Innovation Projects in Shandong Province of China (No.: 2019JZZY010110).

**Conflicts of Interest.** The authors declare that they have no conflicts of interest to report regarding the present study.

# References

1. Belman, A.K., Phoha, V.V.: Doubletype: authentication using relationship between typing behavior on multiple devices. In: 2020 International Conference on Artificial Intelligence And Signal Processing, pp. 1–6 (2020)
2. Ngyuen, T., Voris, J.: Touchscreen biometrics across multiple devices. In: SOUPS (2017)
3. Frank, M., Biedert, R., Ma, E., Martinovic, I., Song, D.: Touchalytics: on the applicability of touchscreen input as a behavioral biometric for continuous authentication. IEEE Trans. Inf. Forensics Secur. **8**(1), 136–148 (2013)
4. Shen, C., Zhang, Y., Guan, X., Maxion, R.A.: Performance analysis of touch-interaction behavior for active smartphone authentication. IEEE Trans. Inf. Forensics Secur. **11**(3), 498–513 (2016)
5. Feng, T., Liu, Z., Kwon, K.A, et al.: Continuous mobile authentication using touchscreen gestures. In: IEEE International Conference on Technologies for Homeland Security, pp. 451–456 (2012)
6. Zhang, H., Patel, V.M, Fathy, M., et al.: Touch gesture-based active user authentication using dictionaries. In: IEEE Winter Conference on Applications of Computer Vision, pp. 207–214. IEEE (2015)
7. Shen, C., Li, Y., Chen, Y., et al.: Performance analysis of multi-motion sensor behavior for active smartphone authentication. IEEE Trans. Inf. Forensics Secur. **13**(1), 48–62 (2018)
8. Kayacik, H.G., et al.: Data driven authentication: on the effectiveness of user behaviour modelling with mobile device sensors. arXiv:1410.7743 (2014)
9. Sánchez, P.M.S., Celdrán, A.H., Maimó, L., Pérez, G.M., Wang, G.: Securing smart offices through an intelligent and multi-device continuous authentication system. In: International Conference on Smart City and Informatization, p. 7 (2019)
10. Hintze, D.: Towards transparent multi-device-authentication. In: Adjunct Proceedings of the 2015 ACM International Joint Conference on Pervasive and Ubiquitous Computing and Proceedings of the 2015 ACM International Symposium on Wearable Computers, pp. 435–440 (2015)
11. Krašovec, A., Pellarini, D., Geneiatakis, D., et al.: Not quite yourself today: behaviour-based continuous authentication in IoT environments. Proc. ACM Interact. Mob. Wearable Ubiquitous Technol. **4**(4), 1–29 (2020)
12. Belman, A.K., Phoha, V.V.: Discriminative power of typing features on desktops, tablets, and phones for user identification. ACM Trans. Privacy Secur. (TOPS) **23**(1), 1–36 (2020)
13. Sun, H.Z., Xu, G., Yu, H.W., Ma, M.Y., Guo, Y.H., Quan, R.J.: Malware detection based on multidimensional time distribution features. J. Quantum Comput. **3**(2), 55–63 (2021)
14. Xia, Z., Wang, L., Tang, J., Xiong, N.N., Weng, J.: A Privacy-preserving image retrieval scheme using secure local binary pattern in cloud computing. IEEE Trans. Netw. Sci. Eng. **8**(1), 318–330 (2020)
15. Sun, H., Xu, G., Wu, Z., Quan, R.: Android malware detection based on feature selection and weight measurement. Intell. Autom. Soft Comput. **33**(1), 585–600 (2022)

16. Bin, A., Ponnusamy, V., Sangodiah, A., Alroobaea, R., Jhanjhi, N.Z.: Smartphone security using swipe behavior-based authentication. Intell. Autom. Soft Comput. **29**(2), 571–585 (2021)
17. Aljuaid, S.M., Ansari, A.S.: Automated teller machine authentication using biometric. Comput. Syst. Sci. Eng. **41**(3), 1009–1025 (2022)
18. Alshammari, M., Nashwan, S.: Fully authentication services scheme for nfc mobile payment systems. Intell. Autom. Soft Comput. **32**(1), 401–428 (2022)
19. Malhotra, N., Bala, M.: Intelligent multilevel node authentication in mobile computing using clone node. Comput. Mater. Continua **70**(3), 5269–5284 (2022)

# EEMP: Architecture Design of Electrical Equipment Monitoring and Management Platform Oriented to Power Internet of Things

Xueming Qiao[1], Hao Chen[1], Weiyi Zhu[2], Ping Meng[1], Yansheng Fu[3], Xiaoyu He[3], Lechuan Hao[3], and Dongjie Zhu[3(✉)]

[1] State Grid Weihai Power Supply Company, No. 23, Kunming Road, Weihai 264209, China
[2] State Grid Shandong Electric Power Company, Jinan 250000, China
[3] School of Computer Science and Technology, Harbin Institute of Technology, Weihai 264209, China
zhudongjie@hit.edu.cn

**Abstract.** At present, electrical equipment is closely related to people's lives, and electrical equipment management has long become a key part of modern society. However, compared with other management systems, this type of system has the characteristics of long service life and complex management equipment. In order to accurately divide and manage the needs of the enterprise, a certain degree of understanding must be established in advance. This paper has realized a complete set of electrical equipment monitoring and management platform oriented to the power Internet of Things (EEMP) through the actual analysis of user needs and the main steps of outline design, detailed design and system implementation and testing. Through embedded intelligent Internet of Things equipment, EEMP realizes the main functions of intelligent inspection of electrical equipment, health detection of electrical equipment in use, and authenticity identification of electrical equipment. Experiments show that EEMP can help users get rid of traditional written records, eliminate safety hazards in a timely manner, quickly locate unexpected situations, accurately pursue responsibility, and ensure the safe use of equipment.

**Keywords:** Power Internet of Things · Electrical equipment · Intelligent inspection · Health detection · Authenticity identification

## 1  Introduction

As everyone knows, the development of computer science and technology has promoted the change of lifestyle. Nowadays, mobile phones, networks, and computers are even more inseparable from people, which greatly improves the quality of life and brings great convenience to people's lives [6]. Nowadays, the electrical equipment supervision system is an important part of modern life, escorting

X. Sun et al. (Eds.): ICAIS 2022, CCIS 1588, pp. 632–642, 2022.
https://doi.org/10.1007/978-3-031-06764-8_49

people's new life. However, there are still many companies that use manual methods to supervise electrical equipment. This method is time-consuming, laborious, inefficient, and has many regulatory problems in practical applications [15]. The design of EEMP is mainly to strengthen and manage the monitoring of electrical equipment, so that the on-site inspection personnel work more efficiently, the synchronization of equipment information is more rapid and accurate, and the management of electrical equipment is more comprehensive [2].

Because the current monitoring system lacks the function of employee behavior recognition or the behavior recognition function is weak, it is unable to perform dynamic recognition, so that the relevant personnel cannot accurately grasp the status of the employees, nor can they make abnormal judgments on the relevant equipment, thus failing to ensure the safety of the marketing site. In terms of external personnel control, precision marketing has not yet been achieved, nor has it been able to provide early warning of abnormal external behavior.

On the other hand, due to the large number of equipment in the marketing construction site, the wide range of points, and the huge workload of the acceptance inspection of the on-site construction situation, the application and promotion of an analysis technology for on-site construction images is very necessary. Using the analysis technology of on-site construction images, it is possible to analyze, screen and warn the conditions of personnel behavior, equipment authenticity, equipment integrity, construction process quality and wiring errors, and realize intelligent management [7].

The important purpose of using EEMP to manage electrical equipment is to keep up with the trend of advanced ideas and technologies, and to implement advanced technologies into actual production and life. At the same time, phase out the backward and inefficient way of using written records to manage [3], and establish a set of efficient and efficient supervision [13].

## 2  Related Work

Some developed countries in the world, such as the United States, the United Kingdom, etc., as well as some companies have taken the lead in the information management of capital [5], equipment, manpower, etc., and have developed their own distinctive development routes on this basis [9]. With the continuous expansion of the scale of the enterprise, the development speed of the enterprise or the country will become slower and slower until the bottleneck begins to restrict the development of the enterprise. In addition to the technological progress factors of key products [4], the restrictive factors often include management factors. The inefficiency and backwardness of the management mechanism will often cause the mobilization of resources, the feedback of information and the coordination of information to lag and deviation. Most of these are reflected in the process of the enterprise or the institutionalization of the company. Of course, information management also includes the management of electrical equipment. At present, the supervision system of electrical equipment has been improved day by day. It mainly includes two methods: First, electrical equipment does not undergo special processing [10], and every inspector can use a mobile terminal (special tablet or mobile phone) to perform inspection on electrical equipment. For inspection or status maintenance, the information will be uploaded to the database at the same time, and the company can learn about the latest information changes at any time. The other is to carry out technical upgrades to electrical equipment. Each electrical equipment can be linked to the management system via a local area network, and the status of each equipment can be dynamically viewed through the management system. But this method is still in the experimental stage, because there are many faulty systems that cannot be identified and the cost is too high. The first one is currently the mainstream solution.

Nowadays, some backward areas are still at the stage of passing written records and manual summarization to the superior department for equipment management. In this case, the supervision of electrical equipment should use the rapid development of technological achievements to create a system that meets its own needs. Electrical equipment is in all aspects of life and is directly related to us. In addition to facilitating inspections, users should also be able to conduct self-inspection or check on their own electrical equipment. Considering the popularity of mobile phones, you can consider using mobile apps as terminals to inspect electrical equipment and perform other operations.

## 3   EEMP: Electrical Equipment Monitoring and Management Platform Oriented to Power Internet of Things

This chapter will give a detailed description of the design of the electrical equipment monitoring and management platform oriented to the power Internet proposed by us. First, we will give a general introduction to the architecture of the entire system, and then introduce the design of each functional module in the system in detail.

### 3.1   System Overall Architecture Design

The electrical equipment supervision system is developed using the B/S architecture. The front-end uses the VUE framework, the front-end components use the element ui library components, and the back-end uses the spring boot architecture. The overall model of the project conforms to the Spring MVC framework model, where m is model, which is model, v is view, which is view, and c is controller, which is the controller, responsible for processing and forwarding requests. The writing of the back-end relies on the library functions of springboot, which makes the operation of the database very simple.

The architecture of the Android side is similar. The Android front-end uses the Hbuilder tool for programming, and the construction of the front-end interface relies on mui components. The main components are: scan the window, the interface of the underlying camera, various buttons and so on. Because the front and back ends are separated for development. The Android back-end and the web back-end share a project, and all the back-end interfaces are encapsulated

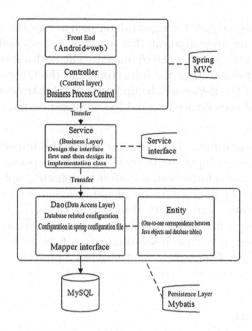

**Fig. 1.** EEMP system overall architecture diagram.

in one project. In this way, to run a back-end project, both the Android and the computer ports can work.

The basic functions of the entire system are meticulously divided, divided into modules, grouped according to function-related lines, and finally displayed with a chart, which is the functional structure diagram. There is no strict standard for the division of functional modules. According to the functions to be completed by the module, some are larger and some can be smaller. Generally speaking, larger modules can generally be run as a separate program, which is convenient code reuse and system structure are clearer, which facilitates subsequent development and upgrade. The system architecture is shown in Fig. 1.

### 3.2   Modular Design

**Employee Management.** The staff management module includes the account information of the management patrol personnel, and allows adding, deleting, checking and modifying staff information.

**Electrical Equipment Management.** Electrical equipment management mainly includes equipment storage. When the equipment is put into storage, each equipment must have its own anti-counterfeiting number, service life, production date and other attributes. The electrical equipment management module also has functions such as electrical equipment changes, electrical equipment scrapping, and electrical equipment maintenance records. In order to better meet actual needs, it is also required to export data, such as exporting a list of obsolete equipment, exporting all equipment that a person is responsible for, and performing statistical processing on the equipment. The health status of each device is stored in the database. After the inspectors scan the QR code of the device, the health status of the device will be updated. Administrators can directly see the health status of each device to avoid losses caused by poor device status.

**Inspection Management.** The inspector enters the inspection interface by scanning the QR code or inputting the device id. The inspector enters the corresponding device status information, and after the photo is uploaded, the device status information and the coordinates of the terminal device are uploaded to the database together. Authenticity detection is to compare the information obtained by scanning with the anti-counterfeiting serial number in the database. If they are consistent, it is true. If the comparison fails or the corresponding id or serial number is not found, then the device has a problem and a message will be reminded.

## 4   Experiments

In this chapter, we will explain in detail the deployment and testing of EEMP.

### 4.1   Experimental Environment

In order to test the capabilities of EEMP, we built a complete experimental system.

This system does not require high hardware performance, and only needs an Android phone and a computer that can be connected to the Internet. In order to make the system more comfortable, it is recommended that the computer configuration is as follows: win10 system, 8G memory, storage space above 256G, kernel intel i7, graphics card GTX1050 or above. The recommended mobile phone configuration is as follows: CPU Snapdragon 855 and above or other brand CPUs with the same computing power, system version Android 8, memory above 6G, storage space above 128G. On this basis, try to improve performance as much as possible to improve the efficiency of web page access.

### 4.2   Experimental Results

**Personnel Management Module.** The personnel management interface is not the focus of the system. The main function of personnel management of the system is to manage the accounts of inspectors, that is, to manage app users. Managers are senior administrators of the system. After successfully entering the system, they can view the detailed information of the inspectors, modify or delete part of the information. In order to be more practical, we also added the function of batch import and export. This can add a large number of users in

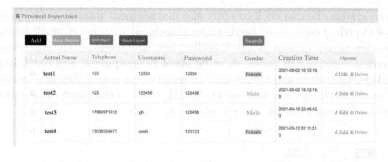

**Fig. 2.** Personnel management interface diagram.

a short time, and it can also export the list in batches, which is convenient for checking attendance and so on. The personnel management interface is shown in Fig. 2.

The staff adding interface is shown in Fig. 3.

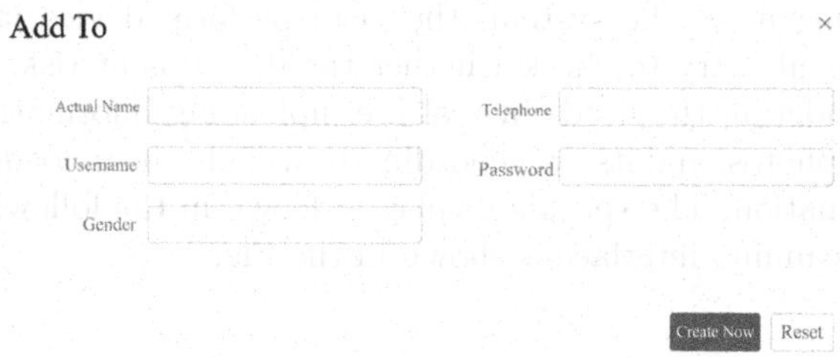

**Fig. 3.** Staff adding interface diagram.

The personnel deletion interface is shown in Fig. 4.

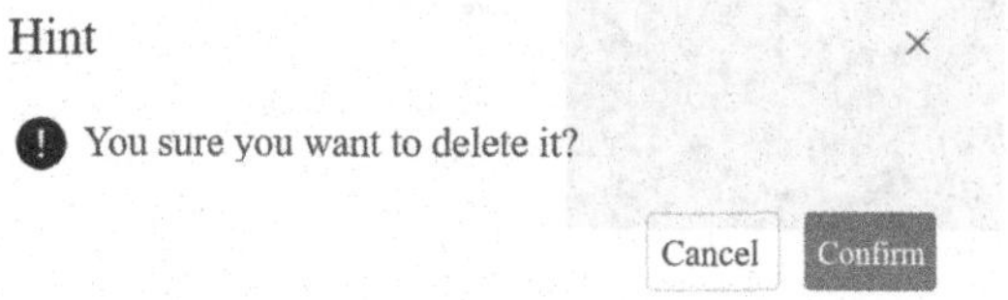

**Fig. 4.** Personnel deletion interface diagram.

**Device Management Module** Equipment management is the core part of the system, and electrical equipment information is managed in the electrical equipment supervision system. After the administrator has successfully logged in to the system, he can click to enter the management interface. The management of electrical equipment needs to be associated with many small functions, such as viewing equipment pictures, adding new equipment, changing equipment information, viewing QR codes, deleting obsolete equipment, and batch importing and deleting electrical equipment. In addition, a search function is needed, which can filter the devices and quickly find the devices that need to be managed. The device management interface is shown in Fig. 5.

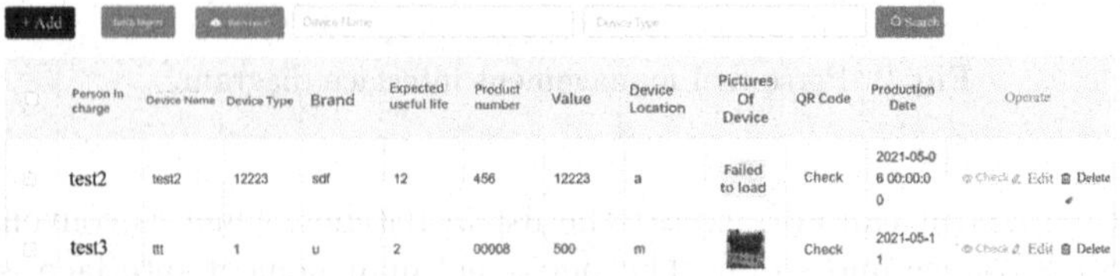

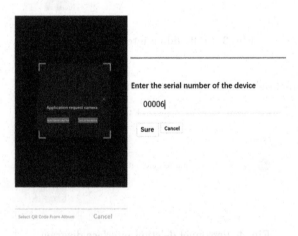

**Fig. 5.** Device management interface diagram.

After users log in to the system, they can perform device inspections by scanning or manual entry to check whether the device is at risk, and can also add notes. Considering the needs in real life, uploading information is allowed while uploading photos, and its own coordinates will also be uploaded along with the device information. The specific display is shown in the following figures.

The device scanning interface is shown in the Fig. 6.

**Fig. 6.** Device scan interface diagram.

The device status selection upload interface is shown in the Fig. 7.

**Fig. 7.** Device status selection interface diagram.

The device status upload result interface is shown in the Fig. 8.

**Fig. 8.** Device status upload result interface diagram.

The device does not exist prompt interface as shown in the Fig. 9.

**Fig. 9.** Device missing prompt interface diagram.

# 5   Conclusions

Compared with other management systems, the electrical equipment supervision system is characterized in that a large part of the management weight is concentrated on the two-dimensional code. Compared with simple management equipment, this system is more inclined to use two-dimensional codes for management. Whenever the electrical equipment is put into the warehouse, the equipment will generate a QR code based on the information of the electrical equipment. The image of the QR code can be printed, and the QR code can be pasted on the equipment that needs to be managed. Inspectors can scan the QR code through the Android app to perform operations such as patrolling and uploading the device, and the whole process does not require too high skills. The traditional book records were completely abandoned, and the written records were submitted to the company for statistics, and finally entered the system in this backward way. This new supervision method can effectively shorten the dissemination time of equipment information, which undoubtedly greatly improves the dissemination of information. Originally, equipment inspections required on-site personnel to submit all inspections to the company. Several days have passed since the company's statistics were completed. Moreover, on-site personnel may be lazy and absent from work, and these problems are difficult to solve. Even the equipment maintenance report process sometimes takes two to three days. After using the new management system, the inspection information is updated synchronously, and the coordinates of the mobile phone are also uploaded every time the inspection information is uploaded, which is also conducive to the supervision of employees. The synchronous transmission and update of information completely get rid of the dependence on writing. The combing and statistics of data also rely on computers, which reduces the participation of manpower, improves work efficiency, and the accuracy of information is also significantly improved.

**Funding Statement.** This work is supported by State Grid Shandong Electric Power Company Science and Technology Project Funding under Grant no. 520613200001,520613180002, 62061318C002, the Fundamental Research Funds for the Central Universities (Grant No. HIT. NSRIF.201714), Weihai Science and Technology Development Program (2016DX GJMS15), Future Network Scientific Research Fund Project (SN: FNSRFP-2021-YB-56) and Key Research and Development Program in Shandong Provincial (2017GGX90103).

**Conflicts of Interest.** The authors declare that they have no conflicts of interest to report regarding the present study.

**Acknowledgment.** The authors would like to thank the associate editor and the reviewers for the time and effort provided to review the manuscript.

# References

1. Chen, N., Li, H., Fan, X., Kong, W., Xie, Y.: Research on intelligent technology management and service platform. J. Artif. Intell. **2**(3), 149 (2020)
2. He, S., Zhang, H.: Design of intelligent supervision system for secondary equipment of power grid. Yunnan Electr. Power **39**(004), 46–49 (2011)
3. He, Z.: Design and Development of Real-Time Warehouse Supervision System Based on SSH Framework. Ph.D. thesis, Zhejiang University of Technology (2016)
4. Huang, A.: Research and Design of Plant Equipment Asset Management System. Ph.D. thesis, Nanchang University
5. Huang, H.: Design and Implementation of Electrical Equipment Management System for Coal-Fired Power Plants. Ph.D. thesis, South China University of Technology
6. Kuai, Y.: Investigation on the internal control of fixed assets management in colleges and universities. Fortune Today **24**, 119–120 (2020)
7. Lai, Y., Huang, K.: The application of electrical comprehensive supervision platform in campus. Intell. Build. **6**, 64–67 (2019)
8. Lee, J., Park, S.: Mobile memory management system based on user's application usage patterns. Comput. Mater. Continua **68**, 4031–4050 (2021)
9. Li, Y., Chen, C., Liu, X.: Design and implementation of power grid asset management system for operation efficiency optimization. Digital Technol. Appl. **38**(5), 2 (2020)
10. Lu, W.: Design and Application of SSH-based Human Resource Management System for Operators. Ph.D. thesis, Jilin University (2019)
11. Ortiz, J.H., García, J.F.C., Khalaf, O.I., Varela, F.V., Baron, P.J.B., Atehortúa, J.H.G.: Development of a module for measuring electrical variables in power transformers based in IoT, to manage and monitoring by telemetry mechanism. J. Internet Things **3**(2), 53 (2021)

12. Wang, Q., Dong, H.: Book retrieval method based on QR code and CBIR technology. J. Artif. Intell. **1**(2), 101 (2019)
13. Xu, H.: Analysis of the demand for a visual asset management system in a college. Shanxi Electron. Technol. **6**, 61–63+66 (2020)
14. Yu, X., Jiao, X., Wang, C., Chen, H., Aloqaily, M.: Analysis and design of university teaching equipment management information system. J. Cybersecur. **3**(3), 177 (2021)
15. Zhang, B., Li, J., Yong, H.: Research on the construction of the whole process supervision system of material supply based on mobile internet technology. Technol. Econ. Guide **28**(704)(06), 43+45 (2020)

# Virtual Network Resource Allocation Algorithm Based on Coefficient of Variation and Order Relationship

You Situ[1], Zhonglu Zou[1], and Yin Yuan[2(✉)]

[1] Dongguan Power Supply Bureau of Guangdong Power
Grid Co., Ltd., Dongguan 523120, China
[2] Guangdong Planning and Designing Institute of Telecommunications Co., Ltd.,
Guangzhou 510630, China
13826243083@139.com

**Abstract.** In the network slicing environment, how to improve the success rate of virtual network resource allocation has become an urgent problem to be solved. To solve this problem, this paper proposes a virtual network resource allocation algorithm based on the coefficient of variation and the order relationship under network slicing. The algorithm includes four steps: sorting the importance of the attributes of the underlying nodes, sorting the importance of the attributes of the virtual nodes, calculating the comprehensive attribute values of the underlying nodes and sorting them in descending order, fetching virtual network requests one by one and performing resource allocation. To improve the success rate of resource allocation, first allocate resources for important virtual nodes. When calculating the importance of a virtual node, first calculate the attribute value of the virtual node. After the attribute value is normalized by the min-max method, the comprehensive attribute value of each virtual node is calculated according to the weight and arranged in descending order. When allocating resources to virtual nodes one by one, nodes with large attribute values are preferentially allocated. In the performance analysis part, the algorithm of this paper is compared with the traditional algorithm, and it is verified that the algorithm of this paper has achieved good results in the two dimensions of the success rate of virtual network resource allocation and the utilization of underlying network resources.

**Keywords:** Network slicing · Resource allocation · Coefficient of variation · Order relationship

## 1 Introduction

With the rapid development and application of 5G network technology, smart grids have been rapidly constructed and applied. The number and types of power services carried on the smart grid have increased rapidly, meeting the diverse needs of users. In this context, power companies have invested more and more resources in the construction of communication networks in order to meet the needs of the power business for communication networks. In order to further improve the utilization rate of communication network resources, network slicing technology has become a key technology for communication network construction, and has been recognized by more and more power companies and network equipment manufacturers. In the network slicing environment, by dividing the traditional physical network into the underlying network and the virtual network, the utilization rate of physical network resources is effectively improved [1, 2]. In the network slicing environment, the underlying network provider is mainly responsible for the construction and operation of the underlying nodes and underlying link resources. The virtual network provider leases the underlying nodes and underlying links from the underlying network provider, and can quickly build a virtual network, thereby achieving the rapid construction and operation of power services [3–5].

In order to realize the efficient use of the underlying network resources and improve the construction and operation quality of the virtual network, how to efficiently allocate the underlying network resources to the virtual network has become a key issue that needs to be solved urgently [6]. In order to solve the problem of low efficiency of end-to-end network resource allocation algorithms, literature [7] proposed a service-oriented end-to-end resource allocation algorithm based on complex network theory, which improved the utilization of underlying network resources. Literature [8–10] proposed a heuristic virtual network resource allocation algorithm to improve the efficiency of the resource allocation algorithm. Literature [11] uses integer programming theory to model the resource allocation problem as an integer programming problem, which improves the utilization of underlying network resources. Literature [12] uses dynamic programming theory to further enhance the adaptability of the algorithm to the network environment. In order to solve the problem of low reliability of virtual network resources, literature [13] designed a virtual network resource allocation algorithm with adaptive capabilities based on artificial intelligence technology to improve the reliability of the virtual network. Literature [14] proposes a two-stage resource allocation algorithm, which improves the utilization of underlying network resources through the cooperation of node mapping and link mapping. Literature [15, 16] uses multi-link offloading technology to effectively solve the problem of low reliability of the virtual network when part of the link fails.

Through the analysis of the existing research, it can be known that the resource allocation algorithm of the virtual network in the existing research has achieved more results. However, existing research mainly solves the problem of algorithm optimization, which cannot reflect the disadvantages of objective information of actual data. To solve this problem, this paper proposes a network resource allocation algorithm based on the coefficient of variation and the order relationship under network slicing.

## 2 Problem Description

In the network slicing environment, network resources include underlying network resources and virtual network resources. The underlying network resources include underlying nodes and underlying links. The underlying network is represented by $G^S = (N^S, E^S)$. The bottom node is represented by $N^S$, and the bottom link is represented by $E^S$. In terms of underlying network resources, the underlying network includes the computing resources of the underlying nodes and the bandwidth resources of the underlying links. Use $CPU(n_i^S)$ to represent the computing resources of the underlying network node $n_i^S \in N^S$. Use $bw(e_j^S)$ to represent the bandwidth resource of the underlying link $e_j^S \in E^S$. In order to facilitate the description of the link between two specified bottom-level nodes, $e_{n_i^s n_j^s}^s$ can be used to represent the link between the bottom-level node $n_i^s$ and the bottom-level node $n_j^s$.

Virtual network providers need to rent the underlying nodes and underlying link resources to build virtual nodes and virtual links. This article describes the underlying network resources required by the virtual network as a virtual network resource request. The virtual network request is represented by $G^V = (N^V, E^V)$. The virtual node is represented by $N^V$. The virtual link is represented by $E^V$. In terms of virtual network resources, use $CPU(n_i^V)$ to represent the computing resource attributes of virtual network node $n_i^V \in N^V$. Use $bw(e_j^V)$ to represent the bandwidth resource attribute of virtual link $e_j^V \in E^V$.

In this paper, the process of requesting allocation of resources for the virtual network by the underlying node is called virtual network mapping. Virtual network mapping includes two processes: virtual node mapping and virtual link mapping. Virtual node mapping refers to selecting the underlying node that meets the resource requirements of the virtual node from the underlying nodes for resource allocation. Virtual link mapping refers to selecting the underlying link that meets the resource requirements of the virtual link from the underlying links for resource allocation. Use $M_N : (N^V \to N^S, E^V \to P^S)$ to represent the process of virtual network mapping. Use $N^V \to N^S$ to indicate that the resources of the virtual node $N^V$ are allocated by the underlying node $N^S$. Use $E^V \to P^S$ to indicate that the resources of the virtual link $E^V$ are allocated by the underlying path $P^S$. Wherein, the bottom path $P^S$ represents the end-to-end path between the two physical nodes mapped by the two virtual nodes of the virtual link $E^V$.

From the description of the virtual network mapping process, it can be seen that, on the premise of meeting the resource requirements of virtual nodes and virtual links, maximizing the resource utilization of the underlying nodes and improving the success rate of virtual network resource allocation are key issues that need to be solved in the virtual mapping process. Because the attributes of resources are the key factors that determine the success of resource allocation, this paper analyzes the attributes of resources and proposes a resource allocation algorithm that can improve the performance of resource allocation.

## 3  Resource Attribute Analysis

The following analyzes from the two dimensions of bottom-level node attributes and virtual node attributes. This is because the stronger the resource allocation capability of the underlying node is, the more resources can be allocated to the virtual network. In order to improve the success rate of virtual network resource allocation, first select important underlying nodes and allocate resources for virtual nodes. The key attributes of the underlying nodes include the degree, centrality, number of services, the number of historical failures, resource availability, and the number of resources of the underlying network nodes.

The degree of the bottom node is closely related to the number of links of the bottom node. When the degree of the bottom-layer node is larger, the number of links of the bottom-layer node is larger. Therefore, the degree of the bottom node is closely related to the resource allocation ability of the bottom node. The greater the degree of the bottom node, the stronger the resource allocation capability of the bottom node. Use $Deg_{n_i}$ to represent the degree of the bottom node $n_i \in N$, and the value is the number of edges directly connected to the bottom node. The centrality of the underlying network node refers to the distance between the network node and the center of the entire network. When the location of the bottom-level network node is more central, the distance between the node and other bottom-level nodes is closer, and the path distance for resource allocation will be shorter. Therefore, when allocating resources for virtual nodes, the node at the center of the network is preferred. Use $Cor_{n_i}$ to represent the centrality of the underlying network node, and use formula (1) for calculation. Among them, $dis_{n_i,n_j}$ represents the distance from the bottom node $n_i$ to the bottom node $n_j$, which is calculated using the end-to-end hop count of the two nodes.

$$Cor_{n_i} = \frac{1}{\sum_{n_j \in N} dis_{n_i,n_j}} \tag{1}$$

The number of services of the underlying nodes is closely related to the reliability of the underlying network. Because the opening, configuration, and adjustment of each power business will affect the reliable operation of the underlying network resources. When the number of services carried on the underlying nodes is large, the underlying network nodes will cause conflicts and errors due to more configurations and adjustments, which will greatly affect the reliability of the underlying network nodes. Therefore, the influence of the number of services of the bottom node on the reliability of the bottom node is called the configuration reliability of the bottom node, which is represented by $Q_{n_i}$ and calculated by formula (2). Among them, $\delta_j$ represents the number of services whose service type is j. z represents the number of power service types carried on the underlying node.

$$Q_{n_i} = \frac{1}{\sum_{j=1}^{z} \delta_j} \tag{2}$$

The number of historical failures of the underlying node indicates the number of failures of the underlying node. The larger the value, the higher the possibility that the current underlying node will fail again. When the underlying node fails, all virtual network services carried on it will be interrupted, causing major losses to business operations. According to network operation and maintenance experience, the possibility of failure of the underlying node is related to the time of the recent failure. When the underlying node fails, it is more likely to fail again, and the time for failure is shorter. Therefore, this article counts the number of failures of the bottom node in half a year, and uses $FN_{n_i}$ to represent the reciprocal of the number of failures of the bottom node $n_i$ in the past half a year. The larger the value of $FN_{n_i}$, the lower the number of historical failures and the failure frequency of the current underlying node, and the higher the reliability.

The resource availability rate of the bottom node refers to the proportion of the remaining resources of the bottom node in the total resources. Through analysis, it can be seen that the higher the availability of the resources of the underlying nodes, the better the performance of the current underlying nodes. When the utilization rate of the resources of the underlying node is too high, the performance of the entire underlying node will drop rapidly. For example, the utilization rate of network equipment is generally below 70% and can operate normally. When the utilization rate of resources is higher than 70%, the network equipment often crashes. The resource availability rate of the bottom node is represented by $RU_{n_i}$. The resource amount of the bottom node refers to the amount of computing resources that the bottom node can use. Because a key factor for the successful allocation of virtual network resources is that the computing resources of the underlying network need to satisfy the virtual network resource request. Therefore, the greater the number of resources of the underlying node, it indicates that the underlying node can satisfy more virtual network requests. Use $totResource_{n_i}$ to represent the resource amount of the underlying node. From the analysis of the attributes of the underlying nodes, it can be seen that the attributes of the underlying nodes determine the importance of the underlying nodes. First, important bottom nodes are selected to allocate resources for virtual nodes, thereby improving the success rate of virtual resource allocation.

In order to further improve the success rate of resource allocation, this paper proposes to allocate resources to important virtual nodes first. In order to evaluate the importance of virtual nodes, this paper analyzes the degree of virtual nodes, the centrality of virtual nodes, and the amount of virtual node resource requests. The degree of the virtual node is represented by $Deg_{n_i^v}$. The centrality of the virtual node is represented by $Cor_{n_i^v}$, and the resource request amount of the virtual node is represented by $totResource_{n_i^v}$. The meanings and calculation methods of these three attributes are similar to those of the underlying nodes.

In order to apply the attributes of the underlying network nodes to resource allocation and effectively improve the performance of the resource allocation algorithm, it is first necessary to determine the order relationship of the attributes. This article ranks the importance of resource attributes based on operational experience. In terms of ranking the importance of the attributes of the underlying nodes, the attributes of the underlying nodes are divided into three aspects: the success rate of resource allocation, reliability, and performance. In terms of the resource allocation success rate of the bottom node, the relevant attributes include resource amount, degree, and centrality. In terms of the reliability of the underlying nodes, the relevant attribute is the number of failures. The number of failures determines the reliability. This article takes the allocation success rate as the main evaluation factor. On the premise of ensuring the success of resource allocation, it is necessary to ensure the minimum number of failures. In terms of performance, the relevant attributes include the resource availability rate and the number of services of the underlying node. Availability and number of services are related to reliability. Relative to the number of services, the utilization rate determines the quality of resource allocation. The number of services determines the probability of resource allocation failure caused by unexpected events during resource allocation and use. Therefore, the attribute importance of the bottom node is ranked in descending order of resource amount, degree, centrality, number of failures, resource availability, and number of services.

In terms of ranking the importance of virtual node attributes, the amount of resources determines the success probability of resource allocation. The more resources are needed, the resources need to be allocated first. The degree determines that the underlying node that allocates resources to it needs to have a larger degree. First, allocate resources to it to prevent the resources of the underlying node with a large degree from being used up. Therefore, the attribute importance of virtual nodes is ranked in descending order of resource amount, degree, and centrality. In order to solve the importance of the underlying node and the virtual node, it is necessary to calculate the attribute value of the underlying node and the virtual node to obtain an evaluation value that can evaluate the importance of the node. First, the min-max method is used to normalize the attribute values of the underlying node and the virtual node. Second, the following strategy is used to solve the weight of each attribute.

Under normal circumstances, the common method of calculating attribute weights is the analytic hierarchy process. However, using the analytic hierarchy process to calculate attribute weights, the evaluation is mainly based on the importance of two attributes. This method cannot fully analyze the importance of multiple attributes. In order to solve this problem, this paper combines the coefficient of variation method with the attribute importance order relationship method to calculate the weight of the attribute. For each attribute, a more accurate attribute weight can be calculated by solving the coefficient of variation. The calculation method of the coefficient of variation $\lambda_k$ of the k-th attribute is shown in formula (3). Among them, $\beta_k$ represents the standard deviation of the k-th attribute, which is calculated using formula (4). $X_{ki}$ represents the value of the k-th attribute of the underlying node or virtual node i, and $\overline{X}_k$ represents the average value of the k-th attribute of the underlying node or virtual node. At this time, use formula (5) to calculate the rational assignment $\alpha_k$ of the k-th attribute.

$$\lambda_k = \beta_k \sqrt{X_k} \tag{3}$$

$$\beta_k = \sqrt{\sum_{k=1}^{m} (X_{ki} - \overline{X}_k)^2 / n}, k = 1, 2, ..., m \tag{4}$$

$$\alpha_k = \begin{cases} \dfrac{\lambda_{k-1}}{\lambda_k}, \lambda_{k-1} > \lambda_k \\ 1, \lambda_{k-1} \leq \lambda_k \end{cases} \tag{5}$$

Assuming that the most important attribute of the underlying node or virtual node is m, the weight $W_m$ of the m-th attribute of the underlying node or virtual node can be calculated using formula (6).

$$W_m = \frac{1}{1 + \sum_{k=1}^{m} \prod_{q=k}^{m} \alpha_q} \tag{6}$$

According to the weight $W_m$, the weight of the m−1, m−2,..., 1th index can be calculated using formula (7). Among them, m represents the number of attributes of the underlying node or virtual node. The m-th attribute is the most important.

$$W_{k-1} = d_k W_k, k = m, m - 1, \ldots, 3, 2, 1 \qquad (7)$$

# 4 Algorithm

The virtual network resource allocation algorithm based on coefficient of variation and order relationship (VNRAAoCVOR) under network slicing proposed in this paper is shown in Table 1. The algorithm includes four steps: sorting the importance of the attributes of the underlying nodes, sorting the importance of the attributes of the virtual nodes, calculating the comprehensive attribute values of the underlying nodes and sorting them in descending order, fetching virtual network requests one by one and performing resource allocation.

In step 1, according to the network operation and maintenance experience, it is combined with the goal of the resource allocation algorithm to rank the importance of the attributes of the underlying nodes. In step 2, according to network operation and maintenance experience, with the goal of improving the success rate of resource allocation, the importance of virtual node attributes is ranked. In step 3, the comprehensive attribute value of the bottom node is calculated and arranged in descending order. To improve the success rate of resource allocation, first allocate resources for important virtual nodes. When calculating the importance of a virtual node, first calculate the attribute value of the virtual node. After the attribute value is normalized by the min-max method, the comprehensive attribute value of each virtual node is calculated according to the weight and arranged in descending order. In step 4, for the virtual network request set, take out the virtual network requests one by one and perform resource allocation. When allocating resources to virtual nodes one by one, priority is given to virtual nodes with large comprehensive attribute values. Allocate resources for virtual links according to the shortest path strategy. During the node resource and link resource allocation process, if node resource allocation failure or link resource allocation failure occurs, the resource allocation of the virtual network fails.

# 5 Performance Analysis

In order to analyze the performance of the algorithm, the GT-ITM [17] tool was used to simulate the network topology environment in the experiment. The network topology environment includes the underlying network and the virtual network. The underlying network is composed of underlying nodes and underlying links. The number of bottom-layer nodes is 300, and the bottom-layer link is generated by connecting any two bottom-layer nodes with a probability of 0.2. To facilitate analysis, the computing resources of the underlying nodes and the bandwidth resources of the underlying links are uniformly distributed in [10, 30]. The virtual network includes virtual nodes and virtual links. The number of virtual nodes obeys the uniform distribution of [5, 15]. The virtual link is generated by connecting any two virtual nodes with a probability of 0.2. Both the computing resources of virtual nodes and the bandwidth resources of virtual links are uniformly distributed [1, 4]. The life cycle length of a virtual network is 10 time units, and the arrival of each virtual network service request obeys a Poisson distribution of 2 time units.

In order to verify the performance of the algorithm VNRAAoCVOR in this paper, it is compared with the virtual network resource allocation algorithm based on analytic hierarchy process (VNRAAoAHP). The comparison algorithm VNRAAoAHP calculates node attribute weights and ranks node resources according to the analytic hierarchy process. The dimensions of comparison include the success rate of virtual network resource allocation and the utilization of underlying network resources. The success rate of virtual network resource allocation refers to the proportion of the number of virtual networks that successfully obtain the underlying network resources in the total number of virtual networks that request resource allocation. The utilization rate of the underlying network resources is divided into the utilization rate of the underlying node resources and the utilization rate of the underlying link resources. The resource utilization rate of the underlying nodes refers to the proportion of the sum of the underlying network node resources allocated to the virtual network in the total underlying network node resources. The utilization rate of the underlying link resources refers to the proportion of the sum of the underlying network link resources allocated to the virtual network in the total underlying network link resources.

The comparison result of the virtual network resource allocation success rate is shown in Fig. 1. The X-axis in the figure indicates that the time the algorithm runs has increased from 500 time units to 3000 time units. The Y axis represents the success rate of virtual network resource allocation. It can be seen from the figure that the results of the virtual network resource allocation success rate under the two algorithms are relatively stable during different time periods when the algorithms are running. It shows that the resource allocation success rates of the two algorithms are relatively stable. In terms of comparison of the results of the two algorithms, the resource allocation success rate of VNRAAoCVOR under this algorithm is relatively high, because the algorithm in this

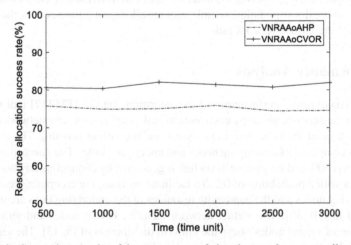

**Fig. 1.** Comparison results of the success rate of virtual network resource allocation

paper analyzes the attributes related to resource allocation in node attributes as the main attributes based on operating experience, thereby improving the success rate of resource allocation.

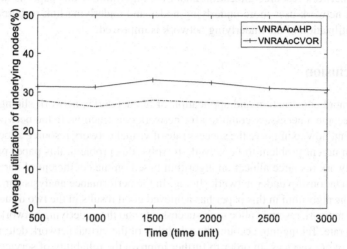

**Fig. 2.** Average utilization of node resources in the underlying network

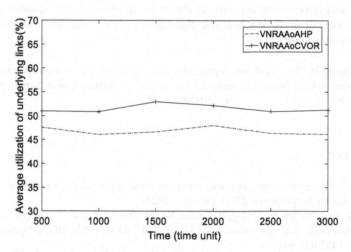

**Fig. 3.** Average utilization of link resources of the underlying network

The results of the average utilization of node resources and link resources of the underlying network are shown in Figs. 2 and 3. In Figs. 2 and 3, the X-axis represents the increase in the running time of the algorithm from 500 time units to 3000 time units. The Y axis in Fig. 2 represents the average utilization of the underlying node resources, and the Y axis in Fig. 3 represents the average utilization of the underlying link resources. It can be seen from Figs. 2 and 3 that the resource utilization rates of the two algorithms are relatively stable in different time periods, indicating that the two algorithms are relatively balanced in terms of resource allocation results. In terms of comparing the results of the two algorithms, the resource utilization rate under the algorithm in this paper is higher than that in the comparison algorithm. This is because the success rate of virtual network resource allocation under the algorithm of this paper is higher, and the virtual network uses more underlying nodes and underlying link resources, so the resource utilization of the underlying network is improved.

## 6  Conclusion

With the rapid construction and application of 5G networks, network slicing technology has become a necessary condition for network construction. In the network slicing environment, how to improve the success rate of virtual network resource allocation has become an urgent problem to be solved. To solve this problem, this paper proposes a virtual network resource allocation algorithm based on the coefficient of variation and the order relationship under network slicing. In the performance analysis part, it is verified that the algorithm in this paper has achieved good results in the two dimensions of the virtual network resource allocation success rate and the underlying network resource utilization rate. Taking into account the reliability of the virtual network determines the reliability of 5G services. In order to further improve the reliability of services, how to allocate high-reliability underlying network resources for the virtual network is a problem that needs to be solved urgently. In the next step, based on the research results of this paper, we will study new heuristic algorithms to further improve the reliability of virtual network resources.

**Acknowledgement.** This work was supported by Installation project of wireless service global access communication network management system of Dongguan Power Supply Bureau of Guangdong Power Grid Co., Ltd. (No. 031900GS62200248).

## References

1. Yuan, X.: Research on network resource optimal allocation algorithm based on game theory. Intell. Autom. Soft Comput. **27**(1), 249–257 (2021)
2. Tao, X., Han, Y., Xu, X., Zhang, P., Leung, V.C.M.: Recent advances and future challenges for mobile network virtualization. Sci. China Inf. Sci. **60**(4), 1–12 (2017). https://doi.org/10.1007/s11432-017-9045-1
3. Bannour, F., Souihi, S., Mellouk, A.: Distributed SDN control: survey, taxonomy, and challenges. IEEE Cummun. Surv. Tutor. **20**(1), 333–354 (2018)
4. Al-Wesabi, F.N., Khan, I., Alamgeer, M., Al-Sharafi, A.M., Choi, B.J.: A joint algorithm for resource allocation in D2D 5G wireless networks. Comput. Mater. Continua **69**(1), 301–317 (2021)
5. Mijumbi, R., Serrat, J., Gorricho, J., Bouten, N., Truck, F., Boutaba, R.: Network function virtualization: state-of-the-art and research challenges. IEEE Cummun. Surveys and Tutorials **18**(1), 236–262 (2016)
6. Amaldi, E., Coniglio, S., Koster, A.: On the computational complexity of the virtual network embedding problem. Electron. Notes Discrete Math. **52**, 213–220 (2016)

7. Guan, W., Wen, X., Wang, L.: A service-oriented deployment policy of end-to-end network slicing based on complex network theory. IEEE Access **6**, 19691–19701 (2018)
8. Cao, H., Zhu, Y., Yang, L., Zheng, G.: A efficient mapping algorithm with novel node-ranking approach for embedding virtual networks. IEEE Access **5**(1), 22054–22066 (2017)
9. Li, L., Wei, Y., Zhang, L., Wang, X.: Efficient virtual resource allocation in mobile edge networks based on machine learning. J. Cyber Secur. **2**(3), 141–150 (2020)
10. Al-Wesabi, F.N., Khan, I., Mohammed, S.L., Jameel, H.F., Alamgeer, M.: Optimal resource allocation method for device-to-device communication in 5G networks. Comput. Mater. Continua **71**(1), 1–15 (2022)
11. Chowdhury, S.R., Shahriar, N., Khan, A.: Revine: reallocation of virtual network embedding to eliminate substrate bottlenecks. In: IFIP/IEEE Symposium on Integrated Network and Service Management (IM), pp. 116–124 (2017)
12. Dehury, C.K., Sahoo, P.K.: DYVINE: fitness-based dynamic virtual network embedding in cloud computing. IEEE J. Sel. Areas Commun. **37**(5), 1029–1045 (2019)
13. Mijumbi, R., Serrat, J., Gorricho, J.L.: Design and evaluation of algorithms for mapping and scheduling of virtual network functions. In: Proceedings of the 2015 1st IEEE Conference on Network Softwarization (NetSoft), pp. 1–9 (2015)
14. Gong, L., Jiang, H., Wang, Y., Zhu, Z.: Novel location-constrained virtual network embedding (LC-VNE) algorithms towards integrated node and link mapping. IEEE/ACM Trans. Netw. **24**(6), 3648–3661 (2016)
15. Hamid, A.K., Al-Wesabi, F.N., Nemri, N., Zahary, A., Khan, I.: An optimized algorithm for resource allocation for d2d in heterogeneous networks. Comput. Mater. Continua **70**(2), 2923–2936 (2022)
16. Khan, M.M., Shahriar, N., Ahmed, R., Boutaba, R.: Multi-path link embedding for survivability in virtual networks. IEEE Trans. Netw. Serv. Manag. **13**(2), 253–266 (2016)
17. Zegura, E.W., Calvert, K.L., Bhattacharjee, S.: How to model an internetwork. In: Proceedings of IEEE INFOCOM 1996, Conference on Computer Communications, vol. 2, pp. 594–602 (1996)

# Security Threats and Countermeasures for Software-Defined Internet of Things

Xiaodan Guo[1]([⊠]) and Binhui Tang[2]

[1] Chendu Jincheng College, Chendu 610065, China
2250820357@qq.com
[2] School of Cyber Science and Engineering, Sichuan University, Chendu 610065, China

**Abstract.** Internet of Things (IoT) has been developed vigorously with the development of technology, and there is no way to solve many technical problems that come along with it. Software-defined network is the latest network architecture, which can solve many problems of traditional IoT, so some people propose IoT under software-defined architecture. In this paper, we analyze the common security problems under software-defined IoT architecture by combining the characteristics of software-defined network and IoT, and give the corresponding solution strategy suggestions for the reference of related scholars.

**Keywords:** Software-defined network · Internet of Things · Network security · Flow detection

## 1 Introduction

So far, along with the rapid development of sensing technology, embedded technology and wireless network technology, the Internet of Things (IoT) technology is spreading fast. Currently, people's acceptance of new technologies is getting faster and faster, and there is a great appreciation for intelligent living environment and social services. IoT is the basis for bringing substantial changes to the new needs [1]. Also, in the fields of intelligent transportation, industrial control and environmental monitoring, IoT can be found everywhere.

With the promotion of IoT applications, its scale is also expanding. The massive amount of IoT devices is not only large in number but also in variety, and security has become a problem that has to be faced in the evolution of IoT [2, 3].

Software Defined Network (SDN) is a new network architecture technology which is proposed latest [6]. Which differs from the traditional network in its architecture. SDN is generally considered as a three-layer architecture, which is based on the design concepts of control and forwarding separation, centralized control and programmability, enabling a flexible, adaptive and self-detecting network management approach [5]. Given the advantages of SDN in network management and network maintenance [6], academia and industry are gradually introducing the idea of software-defined networking into IoT applications. They want to take advantage of SDN to solve the security problems of

X. Sun et al. (Eds.): ICAIS 2022, CCIS 1588, pp. 654–662, 2022.
https://doi.org/10.1007/978-3-031-06764-8_51

traditional IoT. So a new field is currently emerging, which is called Software Defined Internet of Things (SDIoT).

The main architecture of SDN has three layers, and the architecture of traditional IoT also has three layers. They both have many things in common and some differences. Currently, researchers propose a series of specific architectures, such as software-defined data center network, software-defined distribution IoT, software-defined vehicle networking, software-defined intelligent buildings, etc.

These studies show that SDN can simplify the network maintenance and management of IoT, but also in the interconnection of heterogeneous networks, dynamic control of resources reflects its advantages.

The following sections will describe the organic combination of the two architectures.

## 2 Software Defined IoT System Architecture

The traditional IoT is mainly three layers: perception layer, network layer and application layer. The perception layer of IoT is the basis for realizing comprehensive perception of IoT through technologies such as sensors or radio frequency identification for intelligent perception and identification, information collection and processing and automatic control of the physical world [4]. Perception layer connects the physical world. It supports data for IoT applications. It is the entities to the network layer and applications through communication modules.

The network layer is responsible for the transmission of information, which may be a network or a combination of several networks.

The application layer is the interface between IoT system and users. This layer includes infrastructure, middleware, runtime environment and integration framework. For IoT applications, common base component libraries and industry-specific application suites are closely related to industry requirements.

The typical architecture of SDN is also a three-layer architecture: application layer, control layer and infrastructure layer.

The application for SDN is often a network requirement. The control layer contains controllers for SDN network. The infrastructure layer's main members are switches. The main advantage of SDN networks is the efficiency and reliability of network transmission.

The follow figure shows the combination architecture of SDN and IoT. This new architecture is proposed for resolving the new network problems for IoT system (Fig. 1).

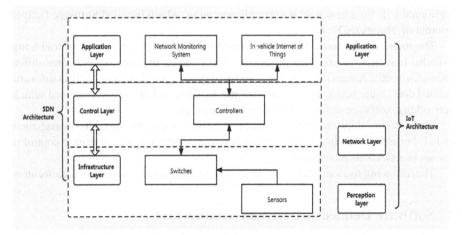

**Fig. 1.** SDN IoT architecture.

In this architecture, the perception layer called data-plane includes network devices, sensing nodes and other parts. the control plane is mainly controllers and network services; the application plane is various industry applications, user requirements of IoT and sensing applications [7].

Device nodes in the IoT system usually have limited power, computing, network and storage capabilities and are very sensitive to resource consumption, and this sensitivity is one of the main reasons for its security issues.

Current research on security analysis for SDN network architecture is still relatively small, but existing research shows that its main measures still rely on the deployment of security policies for controllers[8] and methods such as detection or traceability of data flows to ensure the security of its network, which all have one thing in common: high resource consumption. Although the introduction of SDN in IoT can help a lot in its network maintenance, in fact, it can also have a beneficial effect on IoT in terms of security.

The availability of IoT is the most prominent among all its features, so it requires higher security, and having stronger real-time performance can be one of the goals for software-defined network security policy development. IoT is a target for many attackers because of its network heterogeneity, scale variability and access diversity.

## 3   Security Threats and Countermeasures

With the introduction of software-defined networking into the IoT architecture, its security issues have attracted more attention. In this section, we will introduce the current typical threats and countermeasures one by one, taking into account the hierarchical relationship of the common architecture of Software Defined IoT that has been provided (Fig. 2).

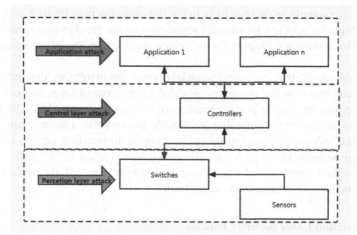

**Fig. 2.** Attack to the SDN IoT architecture.

## 3.1 Control Layer Security Policies

The network layer functions in Software Defined IoT are mainly controlled by SDN. Compared to the traditional IoT, it faces different security issues and its countermeasures are different. The security issues of the control layer mainly originate from its interface layer, which is mainly southbound infrastructure layer, northbound application layer, and east-west distributed controller [9–11].

(1) A common attack from the infrastructure layer is a DDoS attack. DDoS attacks on controllers often cause the entire software-defined network to go down, which has a bad impact and is often an important target for attackers. The attacker will use DDoS to consume the memory or computing resources of the controller, so that users cannot use the controller, and even further turn the whole IoT into a botnet to further attack other networks. sent to the controller [12]. There is no special and obvious difference between new traffic and normal traffic, and the constructed traffic packet headers only need to satisfy the corresponding part of information in the flow table matching field specified by the Openflow protocol.

  Malicious traffic detection is a common software-defined network attack defense means, not only to effectively identify DDoS attacks, worm attacks, etc., but also to predict unknown attacks in the network, thus ensuring the timely implementation of the early warning response mechanism of the Internet of Things.

(2) A common attack from the application layer is the theft of network information. The attacker takes advantage of the rule that the application layer needs to call the control layer interface to first infect the application layer program with a virus or worm, and then steal the network information when the application layer gets the network data from the control layer by calling the northbound interface. Because in software-defined IoT, the controller of the control layer has a full network view and global ownership of the information at the data level, its theft, once successful, may cause a large amount of IoT data leakage, resulting in unpredictable economic losses

[13]. For example, in the in-vehicle IoT, if the controller is stolen by the application APP with the vehicle's location information, then the attacker may further tamper with the information illegally for the vehicle that exposes the information.

The authors argue that since application layer programs in software-defined networks are developed based on the interfaces provided by the control layer, this consistency of interfaces can be used to provide mandatory security measures [14]. Although the applications running on the controller are flexible and versatile, a strong authentication mechanism or subscription mechanism can be set up on the interface, and any third-party applications authenticate or perform bulk authentication when invoking the interface provided by the controller, and when the authentication is passed, the application can access the network information on the controller.

### 3.2 Application Layer Security Policies

The success of Internet of Things (IoT) deployment has emerged important smart applications. These applications are running independently on different platforms, almost everywhere in the world [23]. For example, the healthcare IoT system is considered to be a significant and modern medical system. There is broad consensus that these systems will play a vital role in the achievement of economic growth in numerous growth countries [24]. Many researchers have found that with the focus on the healthcare IoT system, more and more security vulnerabilities are being exposed. From the patients to the doctors, there are so many chances for the cyber attackers. One of the characteristics of IoT is the wide range of application domains. Each application has its unique network features, so the application layer security issues are the most difficult to defend.

The common threats in the application layer of traditional IoT are identity impersonation, service abuse, privacy threats, signaling congestion, phishing, and DDoS attacks. Under the software-defined architecture, all applications are developed based on the interfaces provided by the controller [15], but each application is developed by a third party. Attackers exploit the vulnerabilities of the third party to insert malicious code into the application, and when the application accesses the controller, the malicious code will tamper with the network configuration on the controller, steal network information, or even directly steal and occupy network resources. These operations can affect the stability and availability of the entire software-defined IoT network.

Application layer problems can be borrowed from some traditional networks to deal with them by setting up firewalls in the corresponding places and adding checking mechanisms to ensure security. Independent third-party application security checking software can also be developed using the API provided by the controller [16]. By running these software separately on the controller to ensure the legality and reasonableness of the application's access to the network data, the application's access can be effectively monitored.

### 3.3 Security Policies for the Perception Layer

The sensing layer serves as the touch point for the IoT to connect to this world, it collects a lot of data, and this data is passed to the control layer through the switches in the infrastructure layer in the software-defined IoT. This layer belongs to the edge of the network, and the network threats at this layer mainly come from two points [17], one is the attack on the switch and the other is the attack on the sensing device.

(1) Recognizing that there is a threat of attack on the switch, we need to first understand the working principle of the switch in software-defined networks. Such switches generally have 3 components: data reception templates, flow tables and data forwarding templates. Take the commonly used Openflow switch as an example, after the receiving port receives a message, it tries to find the corresponding flow table entry in the flow table and get the corresponding operation action. If the operation action is forwarding [18], it will be given to the data forwarding template to forward the message out. If no corresponding flow table is found, the switch needs to encapsulate the message into a Packet In message as specified in the Openflow protocol and submit it to the controller, which will analyze and parse the message, and then send a new flow table to the switch after the controller's analysis, specifying the operation action of the message in the flow table [19]. At this time, the operation action may be forwarding or dropping. In this process, there is a possibility of DoS attack or DDoS attack, resulting in a large number of flow table generation, directly causing the switch's flow table overflow and stop working.

This threat then requires the controller and the switch to work together to make the appropriate rules to reduce the impact of such attacks. For example, using the intermediate platform FlowVisor, which acts as a network virtualization platform deployed between a standard OpenFlow controller and an OpenFlow switch, acting as a transparent proxy for both, FlowVisor is transparent to both the controller and the switch [20], neither of which are aware of FlowVisor's presence. It accepts rules from the controller and rewrites them, so that the generated rules affect only the parts of the network that allow control by a given controller. The switch then processes traffic according to the rules given by the FlowVisor, discarding packets that have no impact on the service and forwarding only those packets that are allowed by the rules.

(2) Attacks on sensing devices mainly target the data collected at the sensing layer. The attack behavior can cause the confidentiality, authenticity, integrity or freshness of the collected original data and other attributes to be damaged, such as data being illegally accessed, false data injection, data being tampered with, data transmission being delayed, etc.

The IoT requires high real-time and security of the collected data, and the conventional scheme for data protection relies on encryption algorithms and secret key management schemes. The device nodes in IoT are resource-constrained and do not have as much storage capacity and computing power as in communication networks [21]. In "Software Defined Work", the authors propose a lightweight encryption algorithm within the edge network, which ensures both real-time and security. Its real-time protection scheme is achieved by reducing the number of encryption rounds and simplifying the encryption function, while the security is also carried out by introducing non-linear functions in the encryption algorithm and increasing the secret key length.

This approach also provides a new way of thinking for solving security problems in software-defined IoT.

### 3.4 Botnet Threats and Countermeasures

Protecting individual devices or protecting individual levels of IoT devices no longer fully meets the modern IoT security needs. Because another important and prominent security threat of IoT is botnet. Due to the addition of mobile devices now, as well as the popularity of the Internet of Things after the perception layer devices are very large amounts of data [22], IoT applications and a wide variety of applications to protect measures there is no way to do unified, resulting in many IoT devices are attacked by attackers into a botnet. To the entire network protection to truly enhance the security of software-defined IoT.

Traditional botnet can only deploy botnet detection strategy on each node in the network, this fragmented detection will consume a large amount of network resources, including computing resources and communication resources. Moreover, the results of each node's individual detection are not reusable, and there is no way to use them as predictive data, and their usefulness is not maximized. The software-defined IoT can take advantage of the SDN controller's ability to globally manage the topology, and the general controller has powerful computing and communication capabilities, which just makes up for the limited resources of the traditional IoT.

In this way, there are two protection strategies: one is to place the detection work on the controller, freeing the resources of sensing devices and network devices; the other is to place the calculation of detection results on the controller, using the global view of the controller to analyze the source of the attack comprehensively.

Another important feature of SDN is that the controller has traffic forwarding control. The detection of traditional botnet generally needs to start after the end of the attack, and there is a delay in this detection, while the software-defined IoT can use the flow table mechanism to efficiently analyze the content in the data traffic in real time, using artificial intelligence and algorithms applied in big data, which can quickly track and predict the source of the attack. Because if there is a new traffic in the SDN network, the switch in the edge network will packetize this new traffic and send it to the controller through Packet In message, and the controller will judge the destination of this traffic, and the controller will send down the flow table to the switch after the analysis of the first packet of this traffic, and the switch will forward the data according to the newly sent flow table. In the process of turning IoT into a botnet, there will be a large number of new traffic, and the controller will also issue many such new flow table items, then the controller can identify the form of traffic through deep learning or using predictive algorithms to predict or detect the formation of botnet in advance, and take timely protective measures to interrupt network services in IoT to minimize the loss of IoT.

## 4   Summary

The introduction of software-defined networking technology into the Internet of Things has made the management of the Internet of Things greatly simplified, and also made the security problems of the Internet of Things effectively prevented. In this paper, starting from the architecture of software-defined networking, the security problems are categorized in layers and the corresponding prevention strategies are given in the hope that more attention can be drawn to them.

## References s

1. Ande, R., Adebisi, B., Hammoudeh, M.: Internet of Things: evolution and technologies from a security perspective. Sustain. Cities Soc. **2020**, 1–15 (2020)
2. Cisco. Cisco annual internet report (2018–2023) White Paper (2020)
3. Hazem, J., Badarmeh, Sri, D., Ravana, A.M., Mansoor: A survey on indexing techniques for mobility in Internet of Things': challenges, performances, and perspectives. Int J Network Mgmt (2020)
4. Mahbub, M.: Progressive researches on IoT security: an exhaustive analysis from the perspective of protocols, vuherabilties, and preemptive architectonics. J. Netw. Comput. Appl. **168**, 1–26 (2020)
5. Chen, M., Zhang, Y., Li, Y., et al.: EMC: Emotion-aware mobile cloud computing in 5G. IEEE Network **29**(2), 32–38 (2015)
6. Wan, J., Yan, H., Suo, H., et al.: Advances in cyber physical systems research. KSII Trans on Internet and Information System **5**(11), 1891–1908 (2019)
7. Ahmad, I., Namal, S.: Security in software defined networks: a survey. IEEE Com munications Surveys &. Tutorials **17**(4), 2317–2346 (2018)
8. Zhang, H.W.: A vision for cloud security. Netw. Secur. **15**(2), 12–15 (2014)
9. Benton. K.,Camp, L.J., Small, C.: Openflow vulnerability assessment. In: Proc of the 2nd ACM SIGCOMM Workshop on Hot Topics in Software Defined Networking, pp. 151–152 New York, ACM (2013)
10. Jing, Q., Vasilakos, A., Wan, J., et al.: Security of the Internet of things: perspectives and challenges. Wireless Netw. **20**(8), 2481–2501 (2014)
11. Namal, S., Ahmad, I.: SDN based inter-technology load balancing leveraged by flow admission control. In: Proc of IEEE SDN for Future Networks and Services. IEEE, Piscataway, NJ (2013)
12. Wei, D.D., Qiu, X.F.: Status-based Detection of malicious code in Internet of Things (IoT) devices. In: 2018 IEEE Conference on Communications and Network Security (CNS). pp. 1–7 (2018)
13. Ma, D.D., Shi, Y.J.: A lightweight encryption algorithm for edge networks in software defined industrial Internet of Things. In: 2019 IEEE 5th International Conference on Computer and Communications (ICCC 2019), pp. 1489–1493 (2019)
14. Huang, X., Chen, R.: A Survey of key management service in cloud. In: International Conference on Software Engineering (2018)
15. Zhand, C.K., Cui, Y., Tang, Y.Y.: Advances in software defined networking research. Journal of Software **2015**(1), 62–81 (2015)
16. Mohd, B.J., Hayajneh, T., Vasilakos, A.V.: A survey on lightweight block ciphers for low-resource devices: Comparative study and open issues. J. Netw. Comput. Appl. **58**, 73–93 (2015)
17. Chen, J., Cheng, X., Du, R.Y., Hu, L., Wang, C.H.: BotGuard: lightweight real-time botnet detection in software defined networks. Wuhan Univ. J. Nat. Sci. **02**, 103–113 (2017)
18. Liu, X.J., Liu, P.C.: Distributed denial-of-service attack detection method based on software-defined IoT. Journal of Computer Applications **40**(3), 753–759 (2020)

19. Cruz, T., Rosa, L., Proenca, J.: A Cybersecurity detection framework for supervisory control and data acquisition systems. IEEE Trans. Industr. Inf. **12**(6), 2236–2246 (2017)

20. Pranata, A.A., Jun, T.S., Kim, D.: Overhead reduction scheme for SDN-based data center networks. Computer Standards & Interfaces **2019**, 1–15 (2019)

21. Mckeown, N., Anderson, T., Balakrishnan, H.: OpenFlow: enabling innovation in campus networks. ACM SIGCOM M Computer Communication Review **38**(2), 69–74 (2008)

22. Poularak, I.K., Qin, Q., Nahum, E.M., et al.: Flexible SDN control in tactical ad hoc networks. In: Ad Hoc Networks, pp. 71–80 (2019)

23. Berguiga, A., Harchay, A.: An iot-based intrusion detection system approach for tcp syn attacks. Computers, Materials & Continua **71**(2), 3839–3851 (2022)

24. Nashwan, S.: Analysis of the desynchronization attack impact on the e2ea scheme. Comput. Syst. Sci. Eng. **41**(2), 625–644 (2022)

# Dynamic Backup Algorithm of Network Resources Based on Node Characteristics Under Network Slicing

Xuan Wang, Ziyuan Han[✉], and Jingyao Qin

China Power Construction Group Henan Electric Power Survey and Design Institute Co., Ltd.,
Zhengzhou 450007, China
hanziyuan-heny@powerchina.cn

**Abstract.** In order to solve the problem of the low success rate of virtual network resource allocation caused by the unreasonable resource backup strategy, this paper proposes a dynamic backup algorithm for network resources based on node characteristics under network slicing. The algorithm includes three processes: resource classification, resource backup trigger condition judgment, and resource backup execution. In the resource classification step, the importance of the under-lying network nodes is analyzed from three aspects: the type of the underlying node, the resource usage of the underlying node, and the distance between the underlying node and other underlying nodes, and the underlying network nodes are divided into key resources and common resources. In the resource backup trigger condition judgment step, judgment is made from two trigger conditions: a global trigger and a local trigger. In the resource backup step, different backup strategies are adopted for common resources and critical resources to make the backup effect more consistent with actual needs. In the experiment, it is verified that the algorithm in this paper has improved the bottom-level network revenue and the mapping success rate of the virtual network.

**Keywords:** Network slicing · Resource allocation · Resource backup · Underlying network · Virtual network

## 1 Introduction

With the rapid construction and operation of new application projects such as power Internet of Things and smart grid. The demand for network resources of power companies is increasing rapidly. In order to improve the utilization of network resources, network slicing technology has become a key technology of power companies [1–3]. Although network slicing technology has improved the utilization of network resources, how to improve the reliability of the network is an important issue. Literature [4] takes the optical network as the research object and proposes an intelligent resource allocation algorithm with automatic migration capability, which improves the resource utilization rate. Literature [5] uses deep learning algorithms to improve the self-learning ability of resource allocation algorithms. In order to improve the reliability of the resources

© The Author(s), under exclusive license to Springer Nature Switzerland AG 2022
X. Sun et al. (Eds.): ICAIS 2022, CCIS 1588, pp. 663–671, 2022.
https://doi.org/10.1007/978-3-031-06764-8_52

obtained by the virtual network, literature [6] uses a multi-route resource allocation mechanism to improve the utilization of the underlying network resources. Literature [7–9] takes the wireless network as the research object, and proposes the underlying network resource reconfiguration algorithm, which solves the problem of low resource utilization in the wireless network. Literature [10–12] adopts a targeted resource allocation strategy from the two dimensions of in-use resources and backup resources to improve the performance of the algorithm.

Through the analysis of existing research, it can be known that the main technology is to back up in advance to improve reliability. However, backing up in advance can easily lead to the problem of a large number of resources being occupied. To solve this problem, this paper proposes a dynamic backup algorithm for network resources based on node characteristics under network slicing. The algorithm includes three processes: resource classification, resource backup trigger condition judgment, and resource backup execution. In the experiment, it is verified that the algorithm in this paper can improve the bottom-level network revenue and the success rate of virtual network mapping.

## 2 Problem Description

In the network slicing environment, the original network resources are divided into the underlying network and the virtual network. The underlying network includes underlying nodes and underlying links. The virtual network includes virtual nodes and virtual links. The underlying network leases its resources to the virtual network. The virtual network can carry specific services according to business needs. In the formal description, use $G(N, E)$ to represent the underlying network and $G^v(N^v, E^v)$ to represent the virtual network. The bottom-layer node set and the bottom-layer link set of the bottom-layer network $G(N, E)$ are represented by N and E, respectively. The virtual node set and virtual link set of virtual network $G^v(N^v, E^v)$ are represented by $N^v$ and $E^v$, respectively. The bottom-level nodes included in the bottom-level node set N are represented by $n_i \in N$. The underlying links included in the underlying link set E are represented by $e_{ij} \in E$. The virtual nodes included in the virtual node set $N^v$ are represented by $n_i^v \in N^v$. The virtual links included in the virtual link set $E^v$ are represented by $e_{ij}^v \in E^v$.

For each bottom node $n_i \in N$, its resource attribute is CPU resources, which is represented by $C(n_i)$. The bottom node can allocate CPU resources to virtual nodes for use. Use $C_{re}(n_i^v)$ to represent the number of CPU resources that the virtual node $n_i^v \in N^v$ applies for from the underlying node. For each underlying link $e_{ij} \in E$, its resource attribute is bandwidth resource, which is represented by $B(e_{ij})$. The underlying link can allocate bandwidth resources to the virtual link. Use $B_{re}(e_{ij}^v)$ to indicate the amount of bandwidth resource requested by the virtual link $e_{ij}^v \in E^v$ from the underlying link.

The underlying link resource allocated by the virtual link is a path, and the starting endpoint of the path is the underlying node mapped by the two endpoints of the virtual link. Use $e_{ij}^v \rightarrow p(e_{ij}^v)$ to indicate that the virtual link $e_{ij}^v$ is mapped to the underlying path $p(e_{ij}^v)$. $e_{ij} \in p(e_{ij}^v)$ indicates that the bottom layer link $e_{ij}$ is the bottom layer link through which the bottom layer path $p(e_{ij}^v)$ passes.

The underlying network allocates resources for the virtual network, which is the key research content of the resource allocation problem in the network slicing environment.

For the performance of the average resource allocation algorithm, this paper defines the virtual network mapping revenue index for evaluation. For virtual network $G_i^y$, define its mapping income as $R_{G_i^y}$, and use formula (1) to calculate.

$$R_{G_i^y} = \sum_{n_i^y \in N^v} CPU(n_i^y) + \sum_{e_{ij}^y \in E^v} BW(e_{ij}^y) \qquad (1)$$

In formula (1), the first half represents the sum of resources allocated by all virtual nodes of virtual network $G_i^y$, and the second half represents the sum of resources allocated by all virtual links of virtual network $G_i^y$. Since the resources allocated by the virtual node and the virtual link are the same as the number of resources requested by the virtual node and the virtual link, the formula is the sum of the computing resources and bandwidth resources of the virtual node and the virtual link of the virtual network. In order to solve the problems of low network reliability and low utilization of network resources caused by regular backup of resources, this paper takes the backup of the underlying nodes as the research object and proposes a dynamic backup algorithm for network resources based on node characteristics.

# 3   Resource Allocation Model

In order to solve the best dynamic backup timing, the network management system needs to obtain the resource usage of the network node at a specific time node. Use to represent the resource utilization of x network nodes at time t. Among them, represents the node resource utilization rate of the underlying network node at time t.

## 3.1   Timing of Resource Backup

In order to obtain the timing for the resource backup of the underlying nodes, this article sets up two trigger conditions: a global trigger and a local trigger. Global triggering conditions refer to analysis from the dimensions of resource utilization of all underlying nodes. Use $TH_d$ to represent the threshold of resource utilization of all underlying nodes. The resource utilization rate of all the underlying nodes is too high, indicating that the resource utilization rate of more underlying nodes is too high, which easily leads to unreliable virtual network services. The local trigger condition refers to the evaluation from the instantaneous change of the resource utilization of a single bottom node. Use $\Delta_i$ to represent the threshold of change in resource utilization of a single underlying node in a specified time slice. When the instantaneous change in resource utilization of K underlying nodes exceeds this threshold, it indicates that there may be multiple underlying nodes in the network that are unreliable, which may easily cause abnormalities in virtual network services or increase the failure rate of virtual network mapping. Consider the instantaneous resource utilization of K underlying nodes as the triggering condition, because when the underlying node allocates resources to the virtual node, there are multiple underlying nodes that can meet the resource requirements of the virtual node.

When judging the global trigger condition, it is necessary to calculate the resource utilization of all underlying nodes, and use formula (2) to calculate. Formula (2) represents the sum of resource utilization of n underlying nodes at time t. $c_{i,t}$ represents the importance coefficient of each bottom node, and its value is related to the position of the bottom node in the network. This article divides the underlying nodes into two types: key nodes and ordinary nodes. For key nodes, the value of $c_{i,t}$ is 1.2. For ordinary nodes, the value of $c_{i,t}$ is 1. How to classify the underlying nodes is described in detail in the next section. $x_{i,t}$ represents the resource utilization of the underlying node i at time t, which is obtained by the network management system.

$$f_t = \sum_{i=1}^{n} c_{i,t} x_{i,t} \tag{2}$$

When judging the local trigger conditions, use formula (3) to calculate the instantaneous increase in resource utilization of each underlying node. Set the threshold of $\Delta_i$ to $\delta_i$. For each bottom node, when $x_{i,t} - x_{i,t-1} < \delta_i$, it indicates that the resource usage growth of the bottom node is relatively slow. When $x_{i,t} - x_{i,t-1} \geq \delta_i$, it indicates that the resource usage of the underlying node is increasing rapidly.

In order to distinguish the importance of key nodes and ordinary nodes, when the trigger mechanism of resource reconfiguration is set, the instantaneous change threshold $\Delta_i$ of key resources is denoted as $\delta_i^c$, and the instantaneous change threshold $\Delta_i$ of ordinary resources is denoted as $\delta_i^g$. And set the $\delta_i^c$ of the key resource to be smaller than the $\delta_i^g$ of the common resource. The next section will describe in detail how to divide resources into key resources and common resources.

$$\Delta_i = x_{i,t} - x_{i,t-1} \tag{3}$$

## 3.2 Resource Classification

In order to divide the bottom-level nodes into common bottom-level nodes and key bottom-level nodes, it is necessary to analyze the characteristics of the bottom-level nodes. For the key underlying node, it means that its position in the network is more important, resulting in a large number of virtual nodes that it carries. Moreover, when key nodes are unavailable, the resources allocated by the virtual network are not optimal resources. Through the above analysis, this article analyzes the three dimensions of the type of the bottom node, the resource usage rate of the bottom node, and the distance between the bottom node and other bottom nodes.

In different network environments, the location and function of each underlying node are different. Taking the power communication network as an example, the scale and load size of each bottom node are different. According to the importance of the underlying nodes, they can be divided into provincial dispatching center nodes, prefecture-level dispatching center nodes, county-level dispatching centers, and township-level dispatching centers. Use $s_i$ to represent the type coefficient of the bottom node i. According to the location of the bottom node, this article is divided into five levels: provincial, prefecture, county, township, and other. The type coefficients are 1.4, 1.3, 1.2, 1.1, 1.

The calculation method of the resource utilization rate of the bottom node is as formula (4). The first part of the formula represents the CPU resource usage of the underlying node, and the latter part represents the allocated resource amount of the link connected to the underlying node. $n_i^v \downarrow n_i^s$ represents the set of all virtual nodes

$n_i^v$ allocated by the underlying node $n_i^s$. $e_j^V \in E_i^S$ represents the amount of allocated resources of the link connected to the underlying node.

$$Used(n_i^s) = \sum_{n_i^v \downarrow n_i^s} C_{re}(n_i^v) + \sum_{e_j^V \in E_i^S} bw(e_j^V) \quad (4)$$

The larger the value of the resource usage of the underlying node is, it indicates that the current underlying node has carried more virtual node resources. Therefore, the larger the value of the resource usage of the underlying node, the more important the current underlying node.

The calculation method of the distance from the bottom node to other bottom nodes is as formula (5). $S_{MAP}$ represents the set of underlying nodes that have carried virtual nodes, and $hop(n_i^s, n_{si}^s)$ represents the number of links between the underlying node $n_i^s$ and the underlying node $n_{si}^s$. The greater the distance between the underlying node and other underlying nodes, the greater the underlying link bandwidth that needs to be consumed when virtual link resource allocation is performed, and the greater the underlying network resource overhead.

$$S(n_i^s) = \sum_{n_{si}^s \in S_{MAP}} hop(n_i^s, n_{si}^s) \quad (5)$$

In summary, the node importance evaluation method of the underlying network based on node characteristics proposed in this paper is shown in formula (6). In the formula, $Used_{max}(n^s)$ represents the maximum value of resource utilization in the underlying node, and $S_{max}(n^s)$ represents the maximum distance between the underlying node and other underlying nodes. Among them, $\frac{Used(n_i^s)}{Used_{max}(n^s)}$ represents the coefficient of resource usage. The larger the value, the more resources that the underlying node has allocated, and the more important. $\frac{S_{max}(n^s)}{S(n_i^s)}$ represents the distance coefficient from the underlying node to other underlying nodes. The larger the value, the greater the underlying node to other underlying nodes. The smaller the distance between the bottom nodes, the higher the centrality and the more important it is.

$$G_i = s_i \frac{Used(n_i^s)}{Used_{max}(n_i^s)} \frac{S_{max}(n_i^s)}{S(n_i^s)} \quad (6)$$

# 4   Algorithm

The dynamic backup algorithm of network resources based on node characteristics under network slicing (NRDBAoNC) proposed in this paper includes three processes: resource classification, resource backup trigger condition judgment, and resource backup execution.

1)   Divide the underlying network nodes into key resources and common resources

    a)   Using formula (4), calculate the resource usage of the underlying node;

b) Using formula (5), calculate the distance from the bottom node to other bottom nodes;
c) Use formula (6) to calculate the importance of the underlying network node;
d) Arrange the importance of the underlying network nodes in descending order, and take 20% of the nodes as key nodes, and the remaining nodes as ordinary nodes.

2) Determine whether resource backup needs to be executed

a) Determine whether the resource utilization rate of all nodes exceeds the threshold, if it exceeds, execute the resource backup mechanism, and go to step 3;
b) Determine whether the instantaneous change threshold of a single key resource exceeds the threshold. In case, no resource backup request is sent. When, the resource backup request coefficient increases by 1.
c) Determine whether the instantaneous change threshold of a single common resource exceeds the threshold. In case, no resource backup request is sent. When, the resource backup coefficient is increased by 1.
d) Determine whether the resource backup request coefficient exceeds K. If it exceeds K, execute the resource backup mechanism and go to step 3;

3) Implement resource backup mechanism

a) For nodes with a utilization rate of more than 70% among common resources, add 15% of their total resources as backup resources.
b) For nodes with a utilization rate of more than 60% among key resources, add 20% of their total resources as backup resources.

In the resource classification step, the importance of the underlying network nodes is analyzed from three aspects: the type of the underlying node, the resource usage of the underlying node, and the distance between the underlying node and other underlying nodes, and the underlying network nodes are divided into key resources and common resources. According to the descending order of the node importance $G_i$ of the underlying network, 20% of the nodes are selected as key nodes, and the remaining nodes are ordinary nodes. In the resource backup trigger condition judgment step, judgment is made from two trigger conditions: a global trigger and a local trigger. In terms of global triggering, it is determined whether the resource utilization rate $f_t$ of all nodes exceeds the threshold $TH_d$, and if it exceeds, the resource backup mechanism is executed. In terms of local triggering, firstly determine whether the instantaneous change threshold of a single key resource exceeds threshold $\delta_i^c$, secondly determine whether the instantaneous change threshold of a single common resource exceeds threshold $\delta_i^g$, and finally, determine whether the resource backup request coefficient exceeds K. If it exceeds, execute the resource backup mechanism. In the resource backup step, for nodes with a utilization rate of more than 70% among common resources, 15% of their total resources are added as backup resources. For nodes with a utilization rate of more than 60% among key resources, add 20% of their total resources as backup resources.

# 5   Performance Analysis

In order to verify the performance of the algorithm in this paper, the GT-ITM tool is used to generate the network environment [13]. The network environment includes the underlying network environment and the virtual network environment. The number of bottom-level nodes in the bottom-level network environment is 300, which is used to simulate a medium-level network environment. The number of links in the underlying network is the connection between any two underlying network nodes with a probability of 0.2. In order to facilitate the analysis of the experimental results, the number of computing resources of the underlying nodes and the number of bandwidth resources of the underlying links are set to the same scale, and both obey the uniform distribution of [30,50]. In terms of virtual network environment, each virtual network is randomly generated. The number of virtual nodes in each virtual network obeys the uniform distribution of [3, 6]. Any two virtual nodes generate virtual links with a probability of 0.2. The number of computing resources of virtual nodes and the number of bandwidth resources of virtual links obey the uniform distribution of [1, 6].

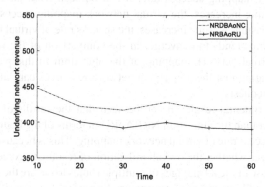

**Fig. 1.** Comparison of underlying network revenue.

In order to verify the performance of the algorithm NRDBAoNC in this paper, compare it with the network resource backup algorithm based on resource utilization (NRBAoRU). The algorithm NRBAoRU expands the underlying network resources when the utilization of k resources exceeds the threshold. The utilization rate of ordinary resources exceeds 70%, and the utilization rate of key resources exceeds 60%. In terms of evaluation indicators, the two algorithms are allocated the same scale of backup resources in the same time period, and the underlying network revenue and mapping success rate of the two algorithms are compared.

The bottom-level network revenue comparison results are shown in Fig. 1. The X-axis represents the time unit of network operation, and the Y-axis represents the bottom-level network revenue. It can be seen from the figure that as the network running time increases, the underlying network revenue of the two algorithms is decreasing and gradually converges. In terms of the results of the two algorithms, the bottom-layer network revenue of the algorithm in this paper is higher, indicating that the bottom-layer network resources can satisfy more virtual network resource requests.

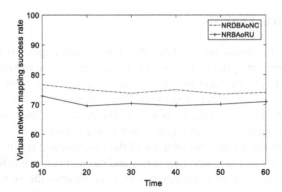

**Fig. 2.** Comparison of the success rate of virtual network mapping

The comparison result of the virtual network mapping success rate is shown in Fig. 2. The X axis represents the time unit of network operation, and the Y axis represents the virtual network mapping success rate. It can be seen from the figure that as the network running time increases, the virtual network mapping success rate of the two algorithms is decreasing. As time increases, the success rate of virtual network mapping of the two algorithms tends to converge. In the comparison of the results of the two algorithms, the virtual network mapping of the algorithm in this paper has a higher success rate, indicating that the underlying network resources can satisfy more virtual network resource requests.

From the experimental results, it can be seen that the results of the algorithm in this paper are better than the algorithm NRBAoRU in terms of the bottom-level network revenue and the success rate of virtual network mapping. This is because the algorithm in this paper first judges whether the overall utilization of resources exceeds the threshold, and can make full use of the advantages of multiple routes to ensure the success of virtual network mapping without capacity expansion. Secondly, the algorithm in this paper judges from the instantaneous rate of change of k resources exceeding the threshold, which can prevent the rapid increase in demand, which leads to the rapid exhaustion of resources and the problem of excessive resource utilization.

## 6    Conclusion

In the network slicing environment, the allocation of resources by the underlying network to the virtual network is an important research content. However, existing studies have selected unreasonable backup strategies during resource backup, resulting in a low success rate of virtual network resource allocation. To solve this problem, this paper proposes a dynamic backup algorithm of network resources based on node characteristics under network slicing. In the experimental link, it is verified that the algorithm in this paper has improved the bottom network revenue and the success rate of virtual network mapping. In the next step, based on the research results of this paper, deep learning algorithms are used to improve the self-learning ability of this algorithm, thereby enhancing the application value of the algorithm.

# References

1. Fischer, A., Botero, J.F., Beck, M.T.: Virtual network embedding: a survey. IEEE Commun. Surv. Tutorials **15**(4), 1888–1906 (2013)
2. Peng, M., Li, Y., Jiang, J., et al.: Heterogeneous cloud radio access networks: a new perspective for enhancing spectral and energy efficiencies. IEEE Wirel. Commun. **21**(6), 126–135 (2014)
3. Yuan, X.: Research on network resource optimal allocation algorithm based on game theory. Intell. Autom. Soft Comput. **27**(1), 249–257 (2021)
4. Soto, P., Botero, J.F.: Greedy randomized path-ranking virtual optical network embedding onto EON-based substrate networks. In: 2017 IEEE Colombian Conference on Communications and Computing (COLCOM), pp. 1–6. IEEE (2017)
5. Dolati, M., Hassanpour, S.B., Ghaderi, M.: Virtual network embedding with deep reinforcement learning. In: IEEE INFOCOM 2019-IEEE Conference on Computer Communications Workshops (INFOCOM WKSHPS), pp. 879–885 (2019)
6. Md, M., Nashid, S., Reaz, A., et al.: Multi-path link embedding for survivability in virtual networks. IEEE Trans. Netw. Serv. Manage. **13**(2), 253–266 (2016)
7. Raza, M.R., Fiorani, M., Rostami, A.: Dynamic slicing approach for multi-tenant 5G transport networks. IEEE/OSA J. Opt. Commun. Networking **10**(1), 77–90 (2018)
8. Al-Wesabi, F.N., Khan, I., Alamgeer, M., Al-Sharafi, A.M., Choi, B.J.: A joint algorithm for resource allocation in d2d 5g wireless networks. Comput. Mater. Continua **69**(1), 301–317 (2021)
9. Al-Wesabi, F.N., Khan, I., Mohammed, S.L., Jameel, H.F., Alamgeer, M.: Optimal resource allocation method for device-to-device communication in 5g networks. Comput. Mater. Continua **71**(1), 1–15 (2022)
10. Zheng, X., Tian, J., Xiao, X., Cui, X., Yu, X.: A heuristic survivable virtual network mapping algorithm. Soft. Comput. **23**(5), 1453–1463 (2018). https://doi.org/10.1007/s00500-018-3152-7
11. Almutairi, J., Aldossary, M.: Resource management and task offloading issues in the edge cloud environment. Intell. Autom. Soft Comput. **30**(1), 129–145 (2021)
12. Hamid, A.K., Al-Wesabi, F.N., Nemri, N., Zahary, A., Khan, I.: An optimized algorithm for resource allocation for d2d in heterogeneous networks. Comput. Mater. Continua **70**(2), 2923–2936 (2022)
13. Zegura, E.W., Calvert, K.L., Bhattacharjee, S.: How to model an internetwork. In: Proceedings of IEEE INFOCOM'96. Conference on Computer Communications 2, pp. 594–602 (1996)

# Smart Grid Information Security Assessment Model Based on Correlation Index

Yue Ma[1], Wenlong Sun[1], Yihong Guo[2(✉)], Shaocheng Wu[1], Tao Liu[1], Man Zhang[3], and Muhammad Shafiq[4]

[1] Shenzhen Power Supply Co., Ltd., Shenzhen 518001, China
[2] School of Cyberspace Security, Beijing University of Posts and Telecommunications, Beijing 100876, China
guoyihong@bupt.edu.cn
[3] Peng Cheng Laboratory, Shenzhen 518055, China
[4] School of Computer Science and Cyber Engineering, Guangzhou University, Guangzhou 510006, China

**Abstract.** Smart grid provides significant support for the safe and reliable operation of national transmission and distribution system. It has the characteristics of informatization, automation, and interaction, and its information security assessment model needs objectively exist. In view of this, a full-process smart grid information security assessment framework is proposed to provide guidance for the establishment of systematic and modularization of security. Based on the existing authoritative information security standards, combined with the actual situation of the target system, expand relevant security indices, and establish a smart grid information security index system. Considering the relevance of the indices, the ranking-based method is used to determine the weight of the indices, and the security level mapping is established through the fuzzy comprehensive assessment method, and the fuzzy set is used to replace the accurate value to weaken the subjective factor of the expert's score. Experimental verification has verified the effectiveness and adaptability of the model, which can provide a useful reference for safety assessment.

**Keywords:** Smart grid · Information security · Fuzzy theory · Security assessment

## 1 Introduction

Smart grid provides significant support for the safe and reliable operation of national transmission and distribution system, and can meet future growth, energy saving and diversified service requirements, and environmental constraints [1]. It has the characteristics of informatization, automation, and interaction [2]. Compared with traditional power grids, smart grids are characterized by a wide range of points and complex technology, which makes information security risks more prominent [3]. In addition, with the application of new technologies such as big data and artificial intelligence [4, 5],

X. Sun et al. (Eds.): ICAIS 2022, CCIS 1588, pp. 672–681, 2022.
https://doi.org/10.1007/978-3-031-06764-8_53

the security of Internet of things system represented by smart grid is facing greater challenges.

In the investigation of smart grid information security threats and protection technologies, IEEE SA [6] studied the network security of smart grids based on the value chain, and researched various technologies to mitigate threats. Amy Poh Ai Ling et al. [7] toke conceptual analysis methods as the core, fully analyzed the security requirements of smart grids, and provide a basis for solving smart grid cyber threats; Zhang Z et al. [8] analyzed the source of smart grid information security threats against user data security issues, and introduced identity authentication and security domain division mechanisms to improve the security of the user information exchange process; Meng F et al. [9] discussed user privacy protection issues in the areas of equipment safety, system authentication and access safety, and data communication safety.

In the research related to the assessment of power grid information security, to assess the distribution network security, Zhou Z et al. [10] applied the TOPSIS comprehensive assessment method and incorporate the second-level indices into the first-level indices; Wu R et al. [11] established a set of hierarchical assessment index system for the performance assessment of smart substation network, combining improved analytic hierarchy process and fuzzy comprehensive assessment method; Liu X et al. [12] used the gray correlation analysis method to evaluate the operation security of the power grid, established an index system, and passed the quality assessment. Sorting and sensitivity analysis obtain objective weights, calculate the correlation between safety indices, and complete the safety assessment of the operation of the interconnected power grid; Zeng M et al. [13] From the power grid's ability to safely supply power, static voltage security, and topology vulnerability, Transient security risks are evaluated based on five types of indices, AHP is used for index weighting, and dynamic fuzzy theory is applied to alleviate the impact of subjective factors of the assessment value; Gao J et al. [14] applied Markov chain analysis method to the operation of smart grid Safe and stable state prediction, a fast derivation method for system state prediction is proposed, and compared with the simulated system state distribution, which provides support for the smart grid security situation prediction technology.

Therefore, the detection and evaluation of security information for objects such as the Internet of things have attracted extensive attention [15–17], and the research on information security evaluation of smart grid has also made rapid progress. But most of the current assessment processes are simple and lack a complete and comprehensive assessment model framework. There are many existing security standards, but they are implemented in the index system of actual security assessment and the performance of grid operation safety, performance and other indices There are more, less attention to the security of data and information, lack of integration of the data flow process, consideration of corporate confidentiality, user privacy and other data security assessment; and the assessment method is more subjective in the determination of index weights, and it is mostly completed by expert assessment. And there is a lack of data relevance analysis. In view of this, this paper has established a further improvement of the smart grid information security assessment index system, comprehensively considers the potential threats affecting security in the process of smart grid data transfer. We refer to the Page

Rank algorithm, based on the ranking method, to determine the weight of the indices and uses fuzzy synthesis method completes the comprehensive assessment of system safety.

## 2    Smart Grid Information Security Assessment Frameworks

To ensure the assessment process's integrity and results' reliability, a series of important links such as the investigation and decomposition of target requirements in the assessment process, the establishment of an information security index system, the quantitative calculation of the assessment and the feedback of the results are proposed. The integrated framework of smart grid information security assessment shown in Fig. 1 serves as a framework guidance for the entire work.

### 2.1    Target Security Decomposition

Firstly, clarify the characteristics of the assessment target, and complete the investigation and analysis of the target system. Focusing on the informatization, automation, and interaction characteristics of smart grids compared to traditional grid systems, investigate the asset situation, operation records, existing security methods and information flow processes of the existing smart grid systems, and analyze and summarize the core information security associations of the smart grid system. feature. After clarifying the assessment of the target system, select the existing national authoritative standards for information security, power system security, etc. as guidance, and combine the characteristics of the target system to expand the selection of indices and eliminate redundancy, and clarify the assessment criteria of each index. Construct an assessment index system that matches the characteristics of the target system. This index system serves as the output of the security decomposition module to guide subsequent quantitative calculations.

### 2.2    Quantitative Calculation of Safety

The quantitative calculation module has two calculation processes: determination of index weights and comprehensive assessment calculations. The indices obtained by the target security decomposition have different degrees of influence on the system, and there are correlations between the indices. It is necessary to determine the appropriate index weights in accordance with the specific conditions to ensure the scientific and effective assessment results; obtain the clear index quantification of the index rights and the target system After the score, the comprehensive safety quantitative score and safety level of the system are obtained by the comprehensive assessment calculation process.

In the selection of the algorithm for determining the weight of the index, in view of the interrelationship between the indices, the correlation model is selected and the Page Rank algorithm [18] is used to determine the weight: the degree of influence is determined according to the collective assessment results of experts, and continuous iterative calculations, and finally reach a stable state to determine the weight. Using this algorithm to determine index weights not only considers the correlation between indices, but also integrates the assessment results of multiple experts, achieving the effect that

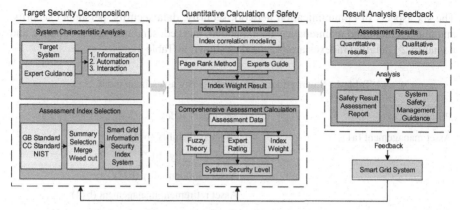

**Fig. 1.** Smart grid information security assessment model.

the larger the number of evaluators, the more objective the assessment results are, and the subjective problem of a single expert assessment is eliminated.

In the selection of algorithms for comprehensive assessment and calculation, many qualitative indexes lead to large errors in the quantitative assessment results using accurate values. Therefore, we choose to apply the fuzzy comprehensive assessment method of fuzzy theory for comprehensive assessment: construct an assessment level set, convert a single index into multiple levels, and conduct a questionnaire survey on professional reviewers or internal members of the department to select and score each index level. The normalized survey results participate in the calculation in the form of fuzzy sets. Finally, the comprehensive security level of the system is determined according to the selected membership function.

### 2.3 Assessment Result Analysis Feedback

In the process of quantitative calculation of system safety, quantitative results and grade results are produced. If the calculation process is retained, there will also be partial module results in the quantitative calculation process. The above results can clearly provide a scientific information security level and risk situation for the target system, which can be analyzed in combination with professional opinions, and can provide good information security improvement feedback for the target system, and further enhance the information security level of the target system, such as patches And software updates, optimized management measures, data classification protection, encryption level upgrade and other practical suggestions.

## 3   Smart Grid Information Security Objective Decomposition

By analyzing the characteristics of traditional information security assessment and smart grid application scenarios, combining with GB/T 32351-2015, CC standards, NIST and other power system and information security standards, the smart grid information security assessment indexes are divided into asset management, physical equipment security,

The six aspects of communication network security, data security, personnel security, and management and maintenance are expanded, merged, screened, and redundant, and a total of 24 detailed indexes are obtained as shown in Table 1.

**Table 1.** Smart grid information security assessment index.

| Primary index | Secondary index |
| --- | --- |
| Asset management (a1) | Asset availability (b11) |
| | Asset Integrity (b12) |
| | Asset confidentiality (b13) |
| | Asset retirement management (b14) |
| Physical device security (a2) | Operation safety of power facilities (b21) |
| | Embedded terminal security (b22) |
| | Equipment fault recovery capability (b23) |
| Communication network security (a3) | Internal system security (b31) |
| | External access security (b32) |
| | Cyber-attack threat (b33) |
| | Communication protocol security (b34) |
| | Network boundary isolation (b35) |
| Data security (a4) | Data encryption (b41) |
| | Data privacy protection (b42) |
| | Data access control (b43) |
| | Data backup (b44) |
| Personnel risk (a5) | Personnel safety awareness level (b51) |
| | Personnel management system (b52) |
| | Personnel operation standardization (b53) |
| | The signing of confidentiality agreement (b54) |
| Management and maintenance (a6) | Application system account and password management (b61) |
| | Information system security maintenance (b62) |
| | Emergency plan management (b63) |
| | System update management (b64) |

## 4    Calculation of Information Security Assessment of Smart Grid

### 4.1    Establish Evaluation Level Set

The assessment set refers to the set of possible assessment results that the evaluator finally produces on the target system. Combined security assessment process with the result of the assessment target, the final assessment set of the smart grid is determined to be V = {very low security, security Low, medium security, high security, very high security}, abbreviate very low, low, medium, high, very high.

## 4.2  Determine Weight

When calculating the weight of indexes, considering the impact of risk probability among different indexes, the weight of them is calculated by using the ranking based confirmation algorithm. This algorithm needs the following assumptions: A node which has greater weight pointing links is more important. At the same time, the quality of the linking nodes pointing to node $A$ is different, and the high-quality nodes pass more weight to other nodes through links.

The $PR$ value of each node can be calculated using formula (1).

$$PR_{(p_i)} = \alpha \sum_{p_j \in M_{p_i}} \frac{PR_{(p_i)}}{L_{(p_j)}} + \frac{(1-\alpha)}{N} \tag{1}$$

where, $M_{p_i}$ is all pairs of $p_i$ node has a node set out of the chain, $L_{(p_j)}$ is the number of outgoing nodes, and N is the total number of nodes, $\alpha$ is the probability the user randomly reaches a node, generally taken as 0.85. The $PR$ value can be calculated according to Eq. (1). When the iteration tends to be stable, the result can be obtained.

## 4.3  Fuzzy Comprehensive Judgment

Fuzzy comprehensive assessment is to make an overall evaluation of things with multiple attributes that can reasonably integrate these attributes or factors. Through the mapping relationship between a specific index and the assessment results of the assessment set, the membership degree of the evaluated index to the results of the assessment set is obtained.

Through the scoring of each index by professional reviewers or internal members of the department, and finally processing the data of the obtained effective scoring table, the fuzzy judgment membership matrix $R$ can be obtained, in which the value in row $i$ and column $j$ represents the membership of the $i$ index to the $j$ element in the assessment set, which is recorded as $r_{ij}$.

$$R = \begin{bmatrix} r_{11} & \cdots & r_{1m} \\ \vdots & \ddots & \vdots \\ r_{n1} & \cdots & r_{nm} \end{bmatrix}_{n \times m} \tag{2}$$

So, the result of fuzzy judgment is

$$B = WR = (b_1, b_2, \cdots, b_m) \tag{3}$$

The maximum membership methods $v = \{v_i | \max(b_i) \rightarrow v_i\}$ selected as the assessment result, that is, the assessment set with the largest membership in fuzzy assessment result B is taken as the final assessment result.

## 4.4 Experiment Results and Analysis

In the experimental part, we used a questionnaire survey to interview 10 experts of a smart grid system to assess the correlation of indicators and get the Table 2 after aggregating the results. Considering the number of indexes in Table 2, we take the quantitative assessment of asset management a1 and physical equipment security a2 in the primary indexes as the demonstration of the quantification of the overall security status of the smart grid.

## 4.5 Set Calculate Index Weight

Firstly, using the expert assessment results in Table 2 to construct the adjacency matrix $Q$. The value of row $i$ and column $j$ in the adjacency matrix represents the number of experts who believe that the $i$ index will affect the $j$ index. Such as $Q_{21}$. $Q_{21}$ is 1, indicating that the number of experts who consider that index $b12$ has an impact on $b11$ is 1. The adjacency matrix $Q$ is as follows.

**Table 2.** Scoring by experts on the relationship between indicators.

|      | b11 | b12 | b13 | b14 | b21 | b22 | b23 |
|------|-----|-----|-----|-----|-----|-----|-----|
| b11  | 0   | 3   | 3   | 1   | 2   | 1   | 8   |
| b12  | 1   | 0   | 1   | 1   | 3   | 1   | 1   |
| b13  | 10  | 8   | 0   | 8   | 9   | 5   | 6   |
| b14  | 3   | 3   | 8   | 0   | 1   | 1   | 1   |
| b21  | 8   | 8   | 6   | 1   | 0   | 1   | 5   |
| b22  | 1   | 1   | 1   | 1   | 5   | 0   | 4   |
| b23  | 3   | 4   | 1   | 1   | 3   | 1   | 0   |

$$Q = \begin{bmatrix} 0 & 3 & 3 & 1 & 2 & 1 & 8 \\ 1 & 0 & 1 & 1 & 3 & 1 & 1 \\ 10 & 8 & 0 & 8 & 9 & 5 & 6 \\ 3 & 3 & 8 & 0 & 1 & 1 & 1 \\ 8 & 8 & 6 & 1 & 0 & 1 & 5 \\ 1 & 1 & 1 & 1 & 5 & 0 & 4 \\ 3 & 4 & 1 & 1 & 3 & 1 & 0 \end{bmatrix}_{7 \times 7} \tag{4}$$

The probability transfer matrix $S$ obtained by normalizing the column of the matrix $Q$, and introducing the probability transfer matrix $S$ obtained above into formula (5), we can obtain the final transfer matrix $G$.

$$G = \alpha S + \frac{1 - \alpha}{N} U \tag{5}$$

where, $\alpha$ It is a random probability, generally 0.85. $N$ is the number of index nodes. $U$ is a matrix with all values of 1.

$$P_{n+1} = GP_n \tag{6}$$

Bring the final transfer matrix into formula (6). After continuous iteration, we can calculate the vector $W$ composed of $P_n$, as shown below.

$$W = \{w_{11}, w_{12}, \cdots, w_{23}\} = \{0.16, 0.17, \cdots, 0.16\} \tag{7}$$

## 4.6 Comprehensive Assessment

**Table 3.** Membership expert scoring.

| Assessment index | Very low | Low | Medium | High | Very high |
|---|---|---|---|---|---|
| b11 | 0.10 | 0.18 | 0.12 | 0.5 | 0.10 |
| b12 | 0.06 | 0.04 | 0.10 | 0.35 | 0.45 |
| b13 | 0.05 | 0.05 | 0.20 | 0.30 | 0.40 |
| b14 | 0.03 | 0.05 | 0.12 | 0.50 | 0.30 |
| b21 | 0.02 | 0.03 | 0.15 | 0.55 | 0.25 |
| b22 | 0.10 | 0.20 | 0.30 | 0.30 | 0.10 |
| b23 | 0.05 | 0.125 | 0.200 | 0.375 | 0.250 |

According to the scoring of each assessment index by experts and relevant review personnel, the effective scoring table obtained can be processed to obtain the expert scoring of the membership matrix, as shown in Table 3.

According to the above table, the fuzzy judgment matrix $R$ can be obtained as follows.

$$R = \begin{bmatrix} 0.10 & 0.18 & 0.12 & 0.5 & 0.10 \\ 0.06 & 0.04 & 0.10 & 0.35 & 0.45 \\ 0.05 & 0.05 & 0.20 & 0.30 & 0.40 \\ 0.03 & 0.05 & 0.12 & 0.50 & 0.30 \\ 0.02 & 0.03 & 0.15 & 0.55 & 0.25 \\ 0.10 & 0.20 & 0.30 & 0.30 & 0.10 \\ 0.05 & 0.125 & 0.200 & 0.375 & 0.250 \end{bmatrix}_{7x5} \tag{8}$$

Introducing the above fuzzy judgment matrix $R$ into formula (9), the security assessment results of smart grid can be obtained as follows.

$$B = WR = (0.057, 0.091, 0.162, 0.417, 0.274) \tag{9}$$

Membership distribution of safety assessment results is shown in Fig. 2 below.

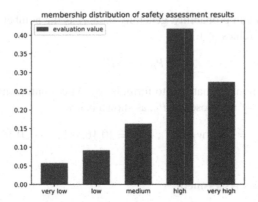

**Fig. 2.** Membership distribution map

According to the maximum membership method, the security assessment level of smart grid is high. The relationship between the degree of membership of the fuzzy comprehensive assessment results can be clearly obtained from the figure.

## 5    Conclusion

Aiming at the problem of simple information security assessment process and lack of complete and comprehensive assessment model of smart grid, this paper proposes a comprehensive security assessment model of smart grid. The model refers to GB standard, general criterion CC and NIST level protection standard, constructs the security assessment index system by analyzing and summarizing the core information security correlation characteristics of smart grid system, determines the index weight by using PageRank method based on ranking, and completes the comprehensive assessment of system security by using fuzzy comprehensive assessment method. Through experiments, it is finally determined that the security level assessment result of smart grid is high, which fully shows that the model has good availability and provides useful support for the security assessment of smart grid.

## References

1. Ding, D., Qi, W.: Realization of smart grid in China: challenges, problems and actions. Electr. Power **44**(11), 1–7 (2011)
2. Wang, Y.F., Zhang, B., Lin, W.M.: Smart grid information security - a research on standards. In: International Conference on Advanced Power System Automation & Protection, pp. 1188–1194 (2012)
3. Wang, H., Gu, Z.: Information security risk assessment of smart grid. Electr. Power IT **10**(11), 101–104 (2012)
4. Shafiq, M., Tian, Z., Bashir, A.K., Du, X., Guizani, M.: CorrAUC: a malicious bot-IoT traffic detection method in iot network using machine learning techniques. IEEE Internet Things J. **8**(5), 3242–3254 (2021)

5. Shafiq, M., Tian, Z., Sun, Y., Du, X., Guizani, M.: Selection of effective machine learning algorithm and Bot-IoT attacks traffic identification for Internet of Things in smart city. Future Gener. Comput. Syst. **107**, 433–442 (2020)
6. Bhat, K., Sundarraj, V., Sinha, S.: IEEE Cyber Security for the Smart Grid. IEEE 2013
7. Ling, A., Mukaidono, M.: Grid: Information security functional requirement. Academy & Industry Research Collaboration Center (AIRCC) **2**(2), 1–19 (2011)
8. Zhang, Z., Liu, H., Niu, S.: Information security requirements and challenges in smart grid. In: 6th IEEE Joint International Information Technology and Artificial Intelligence Conference, pp. 90–92 (2011)
9. Fanlin, M., Wei, Y.: Summary of research on security and privacy of smart grid. In: 2020 International Conference on Computer Communication and Network Security (ICCNS), pp. 39–42. IEEE (2020)
10. Zhou, Z., Wu, G., Dong, X.: A comprehensive assessment model for the distribution network with the new type of loads based on the topsis method. In: 2018 2nd IEEE Conference on Energy Internet and Energy System Integration (EI2), pp. 1–5 (2018)
11. Wu, R., Qi, A., Wu, M.: An assessment strategy based on AHP for intelligent substation network in power grid. In: IEEE International Conference on Network Infrastructure & Digital Content, pp. 512–516 (2013)
12. Liu, X., Wang, Q., Wang, T.: Assessment of interconnected power grid operation security based on grey correlation analysis. In: 2013 3rd International Conference on Consumer Electronics, Communications and Networks (CECNet), pp. 174–177 (2012)
13. Ming, Z., Shi, D., Song, X.: Indices system and methods for power grid security assessment based on dynamic fuzzy. In: International Conference on Electrical & Control Engineering, pp. 3830–3833. IEEE (2010)
14. Gao, J., Bai, H., Wang, D.: Rapid security situation prediction of smart grid based on markov chain. In: 2019 IEEE 3rd Information Technology, Networking, Electronic and Automation Control Conference (ITNEC), pp. 2386–2389 (2019)
15. Guo, Z., Lu, Y., Tian, H., Zuo, J., Lu, H.: A security evaluation model for multi-source heterogeneous systems based on IOT and edge computing. Clust. Comput. 1–15 (2021). https://doi.org/10.1007/s10586-021-03410-4
16. Lu, H., Jin, C., Helu, X., Zhu, C., Guizani, N., Tian, Z.: AutoD: intelligent blockchain application unpacking based on JNI layer deception call. IEEE Netw. **2021**, 215–221 (2021)
17. Hu, N., Tian, Z., Lu, H., Du, X., Guizani, M.: A multiple-kernel clustering based intrusion detection scheme for 5g and iot networks. Int. J. Mach. Learn. Cybern. **2021**, 1–16 (2021)
18. Pang, H., Liu, H.: Research on information engineering security surveillance risk assessment based on PageRank algorithm. Comput. Secur. **8**, 17–20 (2014)

# Hybrid Intrusion Detection System Supporting Dynamic Expansion

Honghao Liang[1], Tao Liu[1], Fanyao Meng[2(✉)], Sijian Li[1], Shaocheng Wu[1], Bo Lu[2], Man Zhang[3], and Muhammad Shafiq[4]

[1] Shenzhen Power Supply Co. Ltd., Shenzhen 518001, China
[2] School of Cyberspace Security, Beijing University of Posts and Telecommunications, Beijing 100876, China
mengfy@bupt.edu.cn
[3] Peng Cheng Laboratory, Shenzhen 518055, China
[4] Cyberspace Institute of Advanced Technology Guangzhou University, Guangzhou 510006, China

**Abstract.** Aiming at the problem of unknown security threats facing smart grids, Hybrid intrusion detection system supporting dynamic expansion is proposed. In the network context, network attack behaviors are detected based on network speed, protocol handshake, quintuple and other dimensions, and security response strategy deployment is automatically generated. Go to the firewall to execute. A formal method is used to analyze the Hybrid intrusion detection system supporting dynamic expansion, which verifies the feasibility of supporting the Hybrid intrusion detection system supporting dynamic expansion.

**Keywords:** Intrusion detection system · Detection and response · Cyberspace security · Security strategy

## 1 Introduction

Authors are required to adhere to this Microsoft Word template in preparing their manuscripts for submission. It will speed up the review and typesetting process.

The security requirements of smart grids change as the network context changes. Static deployment of security strategies can no longer adapt to this change. A detection and response strategy is needed to deal with known and unknown network attacks [1]. Intrusion detection technology can dynamically and proactively discover hidden network security hazards, prevent external network intrusions, and respond to security threats from inside the host. Intrusion detection technology includes anomaly detection and misuse detection [2].

The basic idea of anomaly detection is to establish an association between abnormal activities and computer security threats, so that intrusions can be detected. The advantage is that the establishment of the association does not require the analysis of the intruder's specific intrusion logic mechanism. The disadvantage is that there are many difficulties in establishing the selected characteristics of the association. After understanding the

X. Sun et al. (Eds.): ICAIS 2022, CCIS 1588, pp. 682–691, 2022.
https://doi.org/10.1007/978-3-031-06764-8_54

basis of feature detection, the person can adaptively adjust his own intrusion behavior characteristics [3–6]. Aiming at the shortcomings of anomaly detection, another technical route misuse detection [7, 8] is proposed, which describes all existing intrusions as a pattern and extracts detection features from it.

Aiming at the problem of using automated scripts to trigger network attacks on a regular basis, a combination of firewall and intrusion detection technology is used to construct an intrusion detection and response system (Intrusion Detection and Response System, IDRS), which can automatically respond to complex attacks in the network in real time and respond to network attacks reasonably and appropriately, And the response method will not cause system vulnerabilities to be exploited by attackers. From the perspective of the dynamic upgrade of the attacker and the defender, Hu H. et al. used a random evolutionary game model to simulate a network attacker [9], and added a parameter simulation to the Logit Quantal Response Dynamics (LQRD) equation. Together to quantify the cognitive differences of real users, through calculation of evolutionary stable equilibrium, an optimal decision-making method for balancing protection costs and benefits is proposed. The ransomware detection response experiment shows that it can help defenders predict possible attack behaviors and choose the best Optimal defense strategy, and get the maximum defense benefits. Vieira K. et al. proposed an intrusion detection and response method for large-scale distributed systems [10].

In order to achieve an attack goal, an intruder often achieves the intrusion goal gradually after a lot of attack events. In the traditional intrusion detection system output alarm log, the corresponding attack event sequence is often a pile of alarm records disorderly, and the attack event sequence constitutes an effective attack chain, which is buried in numerous attack alarms and cannot be discovered by maintenance personnel. Because this discrete alarm method cannot reveal the semantic association between attack events, it leads to unclear distinctions between many normal user behaviors and attack behaviors. Intrusion detection systems are required to recognize the entire sequence of attack events to constitute an effective attack and reduce the effective attack false alarm rate. In order to reduce the false alarm rate, Chkirbene Z. et al. proposed trust-based intrusion detection and classification [11], based on feature selection algorithms to reduce the number of input data features, randomly group features, and increase the probability of feature participation in different groups. Sorting according to feature accuracy scores and selecting top-ranked features to classify node data packets in the network provides higher accuracy, detection rate, and lower false alarm rate than current technologies. Sharma RK et al. proposed and implemented a plant-based network intrusion detection and response model, which is similar to the three-layer defense mechanism of plants against pathogens [12, 13]. They tested different network attacks and compared the results with the open-source intrusion detection system Snort. The experimental results showed, can reduce the detection false alarm rate and automatically respond [14].

The main contribution of this paper is that the intrusion detection system and the response system are combined with the formal semantic method, which can automatically respond to attacks from the network and the host, and uses the attack chain identification method to reduce the effective attack false alarm rate. Hybrid intrusion detection system has the following advantages:

1) The detection and response strategy is constructed in a formal way of attacker's ability, which can intuitively show the internal logic of attack behavior, and it is easy for engineers to maintain the strategy.

2) The use of logical system derivation to discover attack chains can detect existing attacks as well as unknown combined attacks, thereby improving the network's ability to respond to new combined attacks.

3) Use examples to substitute into the attack chain to automatically generate response strategies to block network attacks in real time.

4) Provide the analysis results in a readable form for the engineering personnel to read. While discovering intrusions and responding to attacks, it can also evaluate and analyze the vulnerable parts of the current system to provide enlightening guidance for subsequent system upgrades and improvements.

## 2   System Structure

The design content of the hybrid intrusion detection system includes four parts: network host intrusion event collection, attacker capability definition, intrusion event set evaluation, and intrusion behavior response. Figure 1 reveals the internal connection between these parts.

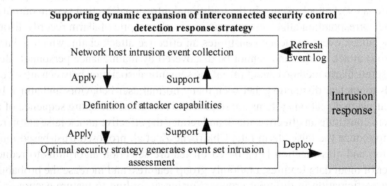

**Fig. 1.** Schematic diagram of the structure of the hybrid intrusion detection and response system.

The first part is the collection of network host intrusion events, which separately collects network transmission and host behavior events, and formalizes the intrusion event set into a first-order logic formula, determines the name of the generated item according to the event type, and formalizes it into a logical item according to the specific value of the attack event Parameters, the corresponding items of the event set are merged into a conjunctive formula and added to the logic system, completing the intrusion event detection and form conversion, and providing analysis targets for subsequent attack detection and analysis.

The second part is the definition of the attacker's ability, which provides a search space for the intrusion analysis engine, including the rules of the attacker's behavior in the existing host and network environment, and can determine whether an event constitutes an attack by searching the attack chain.

The third part is the intrusion evaluation of the event set. The expression of the intrusion event set is used as input, the possible intrusion trajectory is retrieved in the search engine, and the searched intrusion trajectory is analyzed to determine the attack type and attack effect.

The fourth part is the intrusion behavior response. The collected event instances are substituted into the logic system, and the intrusion trajectory is mapped to the response strategy according to the formula instantiation situation, and deployed to the response module composed of the fine-grained network firewall and the host security protection center to realize the intrusion behavior in real time response.

## 2.1 Calculation Process Steps

Figure 2 shows the method of detecting and responding to network attacks, which specifically includes the following steps:

First, map Snort rules to events to facilitate the construction of target propositions. The specific steps are as follows:

Step 1: After the attacker's intrusion generates a network intrusion event or a host intrusion event, the event record is stored in an event-driven manner, and the storage process publishes the event record to the message queue in a publish-subscribe manner.

Step 2: The main process circulates and subscribes to newly generated messages in the message queue, translates recent atomic events into expressions, and merges them into formal expressions in a conjunctive manner as the target formula to be verified. Next is the process of first-order logic automatic inference algorithm processing.

Step 3: Extract the atomic formulas of the logical system by analyzing the attacker's ability expressions, including constants, predicates, and functions. Use symbol reduction rules and formula reduction rules to gradually reduce the length of the formula until the length of the formula can no longer be reduced, and then determine whether the formula set for.

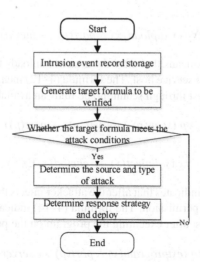

**Fig. 2.** Flow chart of hybrid intrusion detection system.

Step 3–1: Simplify the formula and subtract quantifiers and implication symbols from it.

Step 3–2: Set the maximum depth D of the semantic tree.

Step 3–3: Subtract the atomic formula of the formula set.

Step 3–4a: If the formula set is found to be, it means that the target proposition proof has been completed and the algorithm is terminated.

Step 3–4b: Select two common atomic formula expressions to apply the formula set reduction rule, add the generated new formula to the formula set, and jump to S3–3 to continue to subtract formulas from the formula set.

Finally, according to the attack chain search process, the logical system is deduced and mapped into fine-grained interconnection control rules and host authority commands. The specific steps are as follows:

Step 4: Analyze the space search proof process, and generate a new formula based on the proof process that satisfies the target formula, that is, the atomic formula is substituted into the existing formula, and the specific attack source and attack type are determined, thereby generating response rules and commands.

Step 5: Deploy the response strategy to the secure Internet gateway in real time through remote communication, so as to block the attacker's intrusion.

## 2.2  Scheme Example

The working process of the hybrid intrusion detection system is illustrated by scene examples, which specifically include the following steps:

The first step is to collect host network events and local attack events. Through rule scripts, file upload alarms and file authorization alarms are detected. After these actions are detected, event messages are generated and posted to the message queue.

The second step is to formalize the definition of the attacker's ability. This type of attack chain is formalized into the definition of the attacker's attack ability on the network:

$$\forall p \forall x \ (upload(x) \land port(p) \rightarrow file(x)) \tag{1}$$

The formula (4–11) means that after the attacker uploads the file through the port, the file will be left on the service host. The formula (4–12) means that when the attacker finds a service on the host through scanning, he finds an available port.

$$\forall p \ (scan(p) \land server(p) \rightarrow port(p)) \tag{2}$$

$$\forall x \ (sqlinject(x) \rightarrow chmod(x, \text{Exe})) \tag{3}$$

The formula (4–13) indicates that after the attacker injects the script file, he can grant the script file execution permission. The formula (4–14) indicates that the attacker will start a service on the host after executing the program on the port.

$$\forall x \forall p \ (extprogram(x) \land port(p) \rightarrow server(p)) \tag{4}$$

The formula (4–15) (4–16) represents the definition of the attacker's ability on the host:

$$\forall x \ (chmod\,(x, \text{Exe}) \wedge file(x) \rightarrow extprogram(x)) \qquad (5)$$

The formula (4–15) indicates that after the file has the execution permission, the attacker can execute the program remotely. The formula (4–16) indicates that the attacker launches an effective attack by executing the program remotely.

$$\forall x \ (extprogram(x) \rightarrow \text{Attack}) \qquad (6)$$

Formal attacker capabilities can be used to analyze whether an attack event constitutes an attack chain when the attacker's attack behavior is detected. The network attack behavior will generate file upload event messages, and the host file authorization execution event will generate host event messages. The two events are respectively formalized as.

The following is a specific attack implementation plan: First, the attacker scans the target machine to check the open ports; secondly, brute-forces the login page of the target machine's open website; thirdly, uses the website upload function to upload virus and Trojan horses; finally, the attacker uses The connection software remotely connects to the Trojan.

Through these attack event operations, the attacker successfully found the system vulnerabilities, and cleverly used the vulnerabilities to remotely connect to the target host to gain control of the target host.

Next, the above series of attack events can be expressed as formula (4–17). The attacker's ability is recorded as, the attack chain construction is equivalent to the previous attacker's network ability, host ability, and the formula for generating alarm events, which are connected by conjunctive operators. Together.

The third step is to formalize the target formula to be analyzed and proved as:

$$(C_a \wedge scan(9080) \wedge scan(8080) \wedge server(8080) \wedge upload(\text{Virus}) \wedge sqlinject(\text{Virus})) \rightarrow \text{Attack} \qquad (7)$$

The process of proving the target formula is the process of constructing an attack chain. When only the formula set is left, it indicates that the attacker has an attack chain in a series of events. Otherwise, the formula set cannot be further reduced, indicating that these events do not constitute an attack chain. The specific process as shown in Fig. 3.

The result of the derivation is $\{\perp\}$, Which shows that the target proposition has been proved. If there are non-formulas in the formula set and no rules can be applied to the formulas, so that the formula set is reduced, it means that this property proposition has not been proved.

In the fourth step, after the proof is completed, the detection response rules are generated and deployed in real time. By viewing the replacement of logical expressions, the predicate can be obtained $file(x)$ variable $x$ Substitute for Virus, predicate $port(p)$ variable $p$ Substitute for 8080 and 9080. From this analysis, the attack came from Virus file virus type, therefore, through the mapping algorithm, will check and kill Virus file response instruction is deployed to the host protection system to perform virus detection and isolation, and fine-grained blocking the remote host that uploads the file service,

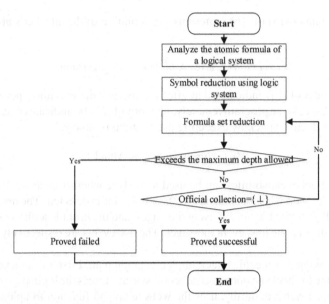

**Fig. 3.** Target formula proof flow chart.

and stops uploading Virus keyword file. In this way, by deploying network blocking rules and virus file killing rules, the attacker will be blocked from subsequent unknown attacks and cannot successfully perform subsequent intrusion operations.

## 3    Formal Semantic Analysis of Hybrid Intrusion Detection System

Use formal semantic methods to analyze hybrid intrusion detection systems in various situations to deepen the understanding of the working mechanism of hybrid intrusion detection systems. The specific manifestation is that in the configuration process, meeting configuration specifications makes the hybrid intrusion detection system have good endogenous security properties, That is, the initial state of the hybrid intrusion detection system remains flawless, safe and reliable, and provides protection for other functional safety.

### 3.1    Property 1 in the Initial State of the Hybrid Intrusion Detection System, if the Strategy Has Syntax Errors, the Hybrid Intrusion Detection System Can Self-check

In the parser of the hybrid intrusion detection system, on the one hand, since a formal method is used to define the grammatical rules of the policy, any policy that meets the grammatical specification must be able to be received by the parser; on the other hand, it is assumed that a policy is not Conforms to the grammatical specification, then the policy must not be received by the parser, so there is a one-to-one correspondence between the standard policy set policy elements and the parser receiving policy.

In this case, assuming that there is a grammatical error in the existing policy configuration within the program, the hybrid intrusion detection system will first check the grammatical norms through the parser before running, throw an exception at the position where the character stream cannot be parsed normally, and terminate the program. Next step.

## 3.2 Property 2 in the Initial State of the Hybrid Intrusion Detection System, if There Are Internal Loopholes, the Hybrid Intrusion Detection System Can Self-check

Assuming that within the hybrid intrusion detection system, the existing attacker capability definition, network environment definition, and host environment definition exist in the attack chain used by the attacker, then set the proof target as $\rightarrow$ Attack and use the reasoning engine to prove.

If the target is proven, it means that there are loopholes in the hybrid intrusion detection system; otherwise, it means that there is no attack chain in the hybrid intrusion detection system.

Secondly, the relationship between the internal modules of the strategy and the global nature of the strategy should also have corresponding knowledge and understanding, so that engineers can further correctly configure and use the program.

## 3.3 Property 3 if the Strategy of the Hybrid Intrusion Detection System Is Maintained Without Contradiction as a Whole, then the Sub-modules Are Also Maintained Without Contradiction

Suppose there are two clauses in the hybrid intrusion detection system module $c_1$, $c_2$ has a contradiction, that is, the corresponding structure is denoted as $c_1 := A \rightarrow B$, $c_2 := A \rightarrow \neg B$, the other module clauses remain unchanged and recorded as $c_3$, the overall strategy structure is $A \wedge c_3 \rightarrow B$ and $A \wedge c_3 \rightarrow \neg B$, that is, the two expressions with the same premise lead to opposite conclusions, which leads to contradictions in the overall strategy.

The first three properties are the nature of the hybrid intrusion detection system. When configuring the hybrid intrusion detection system, the hybrid intrusion detection system will automatically help engineers avoid and correct these errors. The following properties of the hybrid intrusion detection system need to be properly configured to meet, and these good properties can provide a safe and reliable quantitative evaluation for the program, and provide the fundamental guarantee of endogenous security for the hybrid intrusion detection system. Take the experimental configuration as an example to further analyze the nature of the special configuration instance.

## 3.4 Property 4 Any Effective Attack that Can Be Detected by a Hybrid Intrusion Detection System Has Corresponding Response Rules that Can Be Generated

Through the definition of attacker's ability, network environment, and host environment, the structural factors of attack chain construction can be obtained. They will be replaced by constants, which include: 8080, 8090, Virus, Exe, Attack, by looping through all formulas, Attack does not meet any predicate description, so exclude it from the replacement options, and use the same method, 8080, 8090 used to replace predicates $scan/1$, $server/1$, $port/1$, the port constant is the attacker starts the service through the network port to establish communication with the host, corresponding to it, Virus used to replace predicates $upload/1$, $chmod/2$, in other words, the virus file Virus attack chain structure will only be realized by uploading and authorization, and finally Exe, used to replace predicates $chmod/2$, Exe just grant executable permissions to virus files. Summarizing the previous constants, through the strategy-to-rule mapping algorithm, specific attack chain instances can be mapped to fine-grained firewall rules. The specific mapping method is:

Assign the IP address of the host to the rule destination IP segment, assign the source IP segment of the alarm event 5-tuple as the rule IP segment, in addition to the destination IP segment, and assign the corresponding protocol type. For example, the source IP segment of the alarm event is the target formula constant 8080, which is assigned to the rule source IP segment. In the Syslog host event, the constant Virus will generate the Shell command chmod -x Virus. In summary, any source port scan or file upload operation can be mapped to response rules.

### 3.5 Property 5 Generate Response Rules and Will Not Produce Mixed Intrusion Detection System Vulnerabilities

Like the existing policies, formalize the generation rules and add them to the policy configuration. They are: $\neg server(8080) \wedge \neg port(8080) \wedge \neg scan(8080) \wedge \neg chmod(Virus, Exe)$, after being merged into the target formula, many premises will be eliminated and become $scan(9080) \wedge upload(Virus) \rightarrow Attack$. Since the worst case is that the port and file are different, no elimination is done, but the length of the formula is increased without any preconditions that are conducive to the construction of the attack chain, so it does not make any contribution to the construction of the attack chain.

### 3.6 Property 6 the Hybrid Intrusion Detection System Can Detect Unknown Combined Attacks

To give a special example, by uploading a new file, executing a new file program, build an attack chain $attackchain_0$, on this basis, and then create a new service, port scanning for the new service, you can open a new port, upload a new file to execute the new program $attackchain_1$ constructs an attack chain, through repeated operations to achieve a new port attack chain sequence $attackchain_1$, $attackchain_2$, $attackchain_3$... You can see the attack chain set and the natural number set, indicating that the number of attacks is unlimited, and the rules cannot be established in an exhaustive manner. Set to detect. In contrast, the hybrid intrusion detection system strategy in the experiment can detect this type of combined attack through the inference engine.

## 4    Summary

A formal semantic method is adopted to design and implement hybrid intrusion detection. Its components can be flexibly replaced according to application scenarios. For example, Snort can be replaced with Suiricata, Kafka can be replaced with Pulsar, and the fine-grained firewall module can be replaced with IPFW, etc. The deployment of multiple operating systems provides flexibility in terms of high concurrency throughput and interface compatibility, and is compatible with existing network facilities as much as possible. In the process of strategy expansion, strategies should be added while verifying, and the interconnection that supports dynamic expansion should be continuously verified. The security target of the security control detection and response strategy can be checked from multiple angles during the static configuration stage.

# References

1. Shafiq, M., Tian, Z., Bashir, A.K., Du, X., Guizani, M.: CorrAUC: a malicious bot-IoT traffic detection method in IoT network using machine-learning techniques. IEEE Internet Things J. **8**(5), 3242–3254 (2020)
2. Shafiq, M., Tian, Z., Bashir, A.K., Jolfaei, A., Yu, X.: Data mining and machine learning methods for sustainable smart cities traffic classification: a survey. Sustain. Cities Soc. **60**, 102177 (2020)
3. Alhakami, W., Alharbi, A., Bourouis, S., Alroobaea, R., Bouguila, N.: Network anomaly intrusion detection using a nonparametric bayesian approach and feature selection. IEEE Access **7**, 52181–52190 (2019)
4. Ullah, I., Mahmoud, Q.: A two-level flow-based anomalous activity detection system for iot networks. Electronics **9**(3), 530 (2020)
5. Singh, P., Ranga, V.: Multilayer perceptron and genetic algorithm-based intrusion detection framework for cloud environment. IEEE Commun. Mag. **1**(3), 475–485 (2021)
6. Nobakht, M., Sivaraman, V., Boreli, R.: A Host-based intrusion detection and mitigation framework for smart home iot using openflow. In: 11th International Conference on Availability, Reliability and Security (ARES), pp. 147–156 (2016)
7. Papamartzivanos, D., Mármol, F., Kambourakis, G.: Introducing deep learning self-adaptive misuse network intrusion detection systems. IEEE Access **7**, 13546–13560 (2019)
8. Khan, A.A.Z., Serpen, G.: Misuse intrusion detection using machine learning for gas pipeline scada networks. In: IEEE, Las Vegas, NV, USA (2019)
9. Hu, H., Liu, Y., Chen, C., Zhang, H., Liu, Y.: Optimal decision making approach for cyber security defense using evolutionary game. IEEE Trans. Netw. Serv. Manage. **17**(3), 1683–1700 (2020)
10. Vieira, K., Koch, F.L., Sobral, J.B.M., Westphall, C.B., Leão, J.L.D.S.: Autonomic intrusion detection and response using big data. IEEE Syst. J. **14**(2), 1984–1991 (1984)
11. Chkirbene, Z., Erbad, A., Hamila, R., Mohamed, A., Guizani, M., Hamdi, M.: TIDCS: a dynamic intrusion detection and classification system based feature selection. IEEE Access **8**, 95864–95877 (2020)
12. Sharma, R.K., Issac, B., Kalita, H.K.: Intrusion detection and response system inspired by the defense mechanism of plants. IEEE Access **7**, 52427–52439 (2019)
13. Pan, M., et al.: DHPA: dynamic human preference analytics framework-a case study on taxi drivers' learning curve analysis. ACM Trans. Intell. Syst. Technol. **11**(1), 1–19 (2020)
14. Lu, H., Jin, C., Helu, X., Zhu, C., Guizani, N., Tian, Z.: AutoD: intelligent blockchain application unpacking based on jni layer deception call. IEEE Network **35**(2), 215–221 (2021)

# Research on Anti-tampering Mechanism of Massive Electric Energy Data Based on Blockchain

Hefang Jiang[1], Xiaowei Chen[1], Fenghui Duan[2]([⊠]), Shaocheng Wu[1], Tao Liu[1], Jin Li[2], Man Zhang[3], and Muhammad Shafiq[4]

[1] Shenzhen Power Supply Co. Ltd., Shenzhen 518001, China
[2] School of Cyberspace Security, Beijing University of Posts and Telecommunications, Beijing 100876, China
duanfh@bupt.edu.cn
[3] Peng Cheng Laboratory, Shenzhen 518055, China
[4] Guangzhou University, Guangzhou 510006, China

**Abstract.** Aiming at the problems of malicious tampering and difficult to identify, single point of failure attacks faced by massive electric energy data storage, a blockchain-based anti-tampering mechanism for massive electric energy data is proposed by combining the decentralized, tamper-proof and highly scalable features of blockchain. The mechanism mainly includes three parts: electric energy data metadata extraction, electric energy metadata deposition, and data tampering identification, and is developed and validated based on Hyperledger Fabric system. Based on the characteristics of large amount of electric energy data, strong timeliness, and complex data structure, the electric energy data deposition chain is constructed, and the hash value, data size, data storage location, and data The experiments prove that 10G data is stored on the chain, and the data is divided into 1 10G packet, 10 1G packets, 20 0.5G packets, 40 0.25G packets, and uploaded on the chain. The time required to calculate a 10G packet is about 19 s, the time required for concurrent calculation after data splitting is about 7.8 s, the time required for uploading operation is about 30 s, 74 s, 121 s, 236 s, and the time required to verify whether the 10G data is tampered is about 23 s, which provides strong support for trustworthy sharing of electric energy data.

**Keywords:** Blockchain · Tamper-proof · Fabric · Electric energy

## 1 Introduction

### 1.1 A Subsection Sample

Electricity metering is a key element in the evaluation of generation technologies and in influencing payments for electricity trading. With the smart grid, new energy devices and improved network information systems, distributed metering has become an important tool for accurate measurement of the power system. In order to store and share network data securely, reliably and efficiently, smart grids need to deploy wireless sensor networks to monitor the state of the power grid and respond to anomalies in a timely manner. Currently, smart grids need to upload data from wireless sensors to a trusted central storage and sharing node, but this centralized storage scheme is susceptible to malicious data tampering, single attacks that are difficult to identify, and other risks. In response to these information security issues, the use of blockchain distributed storage technology, such as protection against counterfeiting and tracking, provides an effective solution for the efficient storage and identification of counterfeit power measurements.

Blockchain technology supports key technologies such as distributed ledger for storage, decentralized computation, smart contracts, and consensus mechanisms. Blocks can be generated in a chronological order to form a chain of data that are then combined in a specific order. Data can also be generated and updated using consensus algorithms. Cryptographic encryption makes it impossible for data to be altered or tampered with, improving the integrity of power data and meeting the requirements for safe and secure sharing of complex power data. Blockchain technology has been used with much sucess in areas such as currency payments, e-commerce, and online finance. The energy industry has financing also used the technology to innovate and achieve breakthroughs [1].

Yang Dechang analyzed the compatibility of the blockchain and the energy Internet, and predicted the application prospects of the blockchain in the reform of the power system [2]. Wu Zhenquan et al. [3] Aimed at the problem that WSN sensing data in the current smart grid is vulnerable to node malicious attacks and single point failures when uploading data to trusted third-party nodes, they proposed to apply blockchain technology to smart grids. In the secure storage and sharing of grid data, it uses the alliance chain to select a number of nodes in the smart grid as collection base stations to form a data storage alliance chain that does not rely on third parties, thereby solving the security that occurs in the process of sensing node data storage in the smart grid. problem. Ouyang Xu discussed the introduction of blockchain into the demand-side reform of the electricity market, and initially constructed an access mechanism and transaction framework based on the direct purchase of electricity by large users of blockchain technology [4]. Li Bin analyzed the key factors of blockchain technology affecting automatic power demand response, and proposed the development idea of power response system from centralized to distributed management [5]. The conclusion shows that distributed management can more intelligently match the relationship between user power demand and power production, and improve the accuracy of demand response information [6]. Nevertheless, due to the complexity of grid systems and power data, there are still many problems in integrating block circuits with grid systems.

As the literature [7] single point of failure center for electricity storage center encountered, malicious manipulation and other issues, through the construction of an intelligent chain of data storage system alliance chain, in order to center the way to collectively maintain a secure and reliable database storage database, However, this document does not takes into account the data capacity problem encountered by electricity storage. Literature [8] Proposes a method of depositing evidence for transnational electricity transactions based on blockchain technology to ensure that private data of market entities and commercially confidential data such as transaction reporting, transaction settlement and transaction settlement cannot be manipulated and the process transactions can be tracked back. The center, regulators etc. provide reliable data. Taking the scenario of cross-border energy transactions in Northeast Asia as an example, a blockchain case was built to verify the viability of transnational energy transaction deposits and to ensure registration, declaration, clearing and settlement of data, certificates of deposit provide a solution. Literature [9] in relation to the risk of data manipulation, duplication and disclosure of data, electricity storage privacy, as well as user behavior risk and trade secret leakage in the data sharing process, blockchain decentralization use, tamper-proof, high level Expandable functions, build a chain electricity metadata alliance storage alliance and propose blockchain based trusted electricity data sharing privacy to provide protection for private data storage and provide great help for this article. The literature [10] proposes a five-part method of storing data that complements the design of interstellar chains for storing electricity data and includes identity verification to address the costly capacity issues of the blockchain itself. Electrical data. While the problem of extending the storage of electrical data blockchains can be effectively solved by a trusted storage mechanism, this article does not consider the identification of unauthorized handling of user data.

To address the above issues, this paper proposes a blockchain anti-counterfeiting mechanism for large-scale power data using blockchain technology with decentralized, open, autonomous, and anti-counterfeiting capabilities to store and manage critical data descriptions (metadata) in the power chain. We propose a blockchain anti-counterfeiting mechanism for large-scale power data using blockchain technology with anti-counterfeiting capabilities to store and manage critical data descriptions (metadata) in the power chain. It ensures accurate and complete consistency of power data within and across the power chain. The mechanism consists of three main components: metadata extraction, metadata storage, and data discovery, and is based on the HyperledgerFabric system. This system hash values of data, size of data, data storage location, and data. This scheme is based on fabric-sdk-go platform, using docker-compose to generate fabric image, instantiate chain code to interact with fabric platform, and at the same time use restful interface to The chain code is invoked, and the experiment proves that storing 10G data on the chain, dividing the data into storing 1 10G packet, 10 1G packets, 20 0.5G packets, 40 0.25G uploads on the chain, using SHA512 algorithm to calculate the hash, the time taken to calculate 1 10G packet is about 19s, the time taken to calculate concurrently after data division is about 7.8 s, and the time taken to upload the chain operation is about 30 s, 74 s, 121 s, 236 s. 74 s, 121 s, 236 s, and 23 s to verify whether the 10G data is tampered, which provides strong support for trustworthy sharing of electric energy data.

## 2 Background Technique

### 2.1 Hash Algorithm

Hash algorithm (Hash), also known as digest algorithm (Digest). SHA256 was developed by the National Security Agency and released by the National Institute of Standards and Technology (NIST) in 2001. The function of the hash algorithm is to pass a value through the hash algorithm to get a new value, and this value is the hash value. In the entire algorithm, the input binary value string can be of any length, but the final output value is a uniform length binary value string. This mapping rule is called a hash algorithm.

The three characteristics of the hash algorithm in the blockchain provide an important guarantee for the blockchain technology:

One is that the SHA256 algorithm has strong collision resistance (Collision-Resistance), and it is extremely difficult to crack. Even if the input data is only changed by one bit, the final hash value will not be the same. This also ensures that the same calculation method for the hash value of any two messages does not exist [11].

The second is to use hash value when transmitting information to ensure the privacy of the information (Hiding). The secrecy of the hash algorithm can ensure that even if an attacker obtains the hash value, the original text cannot be derived from the hash value.

The third is that in the known output and part of the input, the remaining input value can't be found, and it has better puzzle-friendliness. Puzzle-friendliness means that if an attacker wants to obtain a hash value that meets the conditions, he can only solve the original text by brute force, and there is no better solution. Encryption by using a hash algorithm can better ensure the stability of the blockchain system.

## 2.2  Asymmetric Encryption Algorithm

In blockchain, asymmetric encryption algorithms require each user to have two keys at the same time, a public key and a private key. The public and private key pairs are used together. Data encrypted with the public key needs to be decrypted with the corresponding private key. Therefore, data encrypted with a private key must be decrypted with the corresponding public key. The public key can be deduced from the private key, but the private key cannot be deduced from the public key. The public key is usually the public key [12]. Example: If you want to conduct a transaction between A and B, you need to apply for an electronic certificate from a licensing authority (CA). This digital license contains the public keys of both parties. A uses B's public key to encrypt the transmitted data, while B uses his private key to decrypt the data after receiving it. In a blockchain, both the public and private keys are written as hash values using a hashing algorithm. This hides the actual data on both sides and keeps it protected. Using this asymmetric encryption method ensures the security of the data in transit and protects the privacy of both parties in the transaction [13].

## 2.3  Digital Signature, Time Stamp Technology

The role of digital signature technology is to verify whether the transmitted data has been tampered with. In the blockchain, digital signature technology mainly uses asymmetric encryption algorithms. The sender of the information first uses the receiver's public key to encrypt the transmitted data or information, and at the same time uses its own private key to digitally sign the information or data to be transmitted; the receiver uses the sender's private key to decrypt and verify Whether the hash values are the same, use your own private key to decrypt the received information after checking it is correct [14].

A timestamp is a unique character used to identify the time in a digital signature. The function of the time stamp is to record the order of changes in each information record, which provides a basis for subsequent traceability and ensures traceability.

## 2.4  P2P Network

In the blockchain, the P2P network protocol is adopted. The P2P network protocol is peer-to-peer, and its operating mode adopts a point-to-point method to establish a connection between nodes. The network topology formed by this connection method is uncertain. The resources of the entire network are not completely concentrated on one node at the beginning, but are distributed on multiple devices [15]. Each node has the characteristics of freedom of entry and exit, and can obtain resources that it does not have but needed from the connected nodes. At the same time, each node can conduct transactions independently and broadcast on the entire network; after the node receives the required information, it can independently verify the information, and the information obtained by the correction is correct and reliable, and after the information is verified correctly, it is added to its own block. This weakly centralized P2P model can not only enhance the credibility of the information source, but also enable the information to exert greater derivative value [16].

## 2.5  Smart Contract

A smart contract is essentially an agreement, a computer transaction agreement that does not require an intermediary, self-verification, and automatically executes the terms of the contract. It is similar to a paper contract in reality [17]. In a smart contract, it contains all the information of a transaction. Only when the contract executor completes all the transaction goals, can the final result be produced and the transaction can be concluded. The weak third-party nature of smart contracts fits well with the decentralization of block-based technology. Smart contracts can make the exchange of information, value transfer and asset management more efficient [18].

In general, the blockchain uses an asymmetric encryption method for encryption. Each participant can use a public key to encrypt a piece of information and only the owner of the information can use the corresponding private key to decrypt it. Through the hash algorithm, the file can be processed to generate a string of hash values, and the hash values on the chain and off the chain can be compared to verify whether the file has been tampered with. In addition, the time stamp makes the difficulty of changing a record exponentially increased by time. These mechanisms make the blockchain tamper-proof. Through smart contract technology, human operations can be reduced, and the computer can automatically execute the content of the contract, which expands the application scope of blockchain.

## 3  Design

The anti-tampering mechanism for the safe storage of electrical energy data is shown in Fig. 1. The mechanism is composed of data sensor nodes [19], unlimited sensor networks, master station systems, blockchain systems, and distributed applications. Metering data, warning data, and other data are sent to the master station system through the wireless sensor network, and the master station system is used as a blockchain node to deploy distributed applications to realize data metadata description, data uploading and data tamper-proof detection. In it, an electrical energy data storage chain is built on the Hyperledger Fabric platform, and smart contracts perform drawing, querying, and identifying operations on the electrical energy data in the chain. DAPP, as a decentralized application, is a decentralized application on the blockchain. Implementing DAPP performs the following client-side operations Data forgery storage, query, and registration of metadata about the electrical energy in the chain.

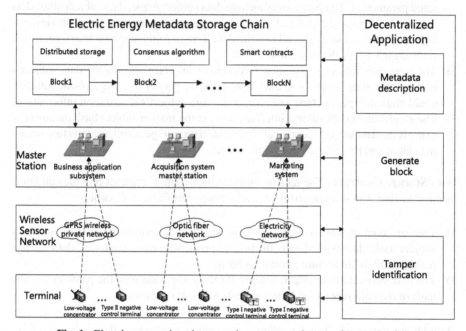

**Fig. 1.** Electric energy data data security storage anti-tampering mechanism.

## 3.1  Network Structure Design of Electric Energy Data Storage Chain

Electrical energy data storage chain certification network structure design [20], including organizational structure, network nodes, and smart contract deployment design. The division of the organizational structure is the basis for the design of the electric energy data storage chain network structure, which can be divided into trade organizations and regulatory authorities. Based on the organizational structure, the electric energy data storage chain network cluster node design. Cluster nodes include computation node clusters, ledger database clusters, authentication center clusters, and consensus clusters. Smart contracts are installed and instantiated on all nodes in the compute node cluster in a transaction setting. Smart contracts include data subject registration, data storage certificates, and three smart contracts for data acquisition. The data storage certificate contains only a hash of the affected data subject, a description of the data size, a description of the data, the data storage path, and other data about the chain.

## 3.2 Smart Contract Design

**Data Subject Registration Contract.** The data subject registration smart contract provides interfaces for writing data subject registration information, reading data subject registration information, and deregistering data subject.

1) The interface for writing data subject registration information accepts JSON structured parameters. The parameters include data subject name, data subject alias, data subject description, data subject's market role, address, person in charge phone number, email, etc., cross-chain call to write data storage Authentication interface, which returns the hash of the data subject;
2) The read data subject registration information interface accepts the data subject's hope, or the data subject's market role, address, person in charge phone number, email and other parameters, and returns the data subject's registration information;
3) The cancellation data subject interface accepts the market subject hash parameters, cancels the data subject record, calls the write data storage certificate interface across the chain, and returns the cancellation result.

**Data Storage Contract.** The data storage certificate smart contract provides an interface for writing data storage certificate and storage certificate verification.

1) The write data attestation interface accepts structured parameters, which include data subject hash, data type, data collection or processing time, data size, data storage path, data alias, and return attestation hash;
2) The data verification interface accepts JSON type parameters, the parameter is the hash of the data subject, and the verification result is returned.

**Data Query Contract.** The data query smart contract provides a data query interface, and the write data query interface accepts JSON structured parameters. The parameters include data subject hash, data type, data hash, and return block information where the data is located.

**Data Tampering Identification Contract.** The data tampering identification contract provides a data tampering identification interface. The written data tampering identification interface accepts JSON structured parameters. The parameters include the hash of the data subject, and the alias of the data subject, the data storage path and the tampering identification result are returned. The contract queries the original data according to the returned data storage path, and compares the hash operation result with the hash on the chain to determine whether it is consistent. If they are consistent, the tampered result is returned as not tampered, and if they are inconsistent, the tampered result is returned as tampered.

**Table 1.** Complete verification environment node configuration for electric energy data storage.

| Category | Node | Use |
|---|---|---|
| Contract calculation | Peer0.saveorg.genergy.net | Deploy smart contracts |
| | Peer1.saveorg.genergy.net | |
| | Peer2.saveorg.genergy.net | |
| | Peer3.saveorg.genergy.net | |
| | Peer0.regulatororg.genergy.net | |
| | Peer1.regulatororg.genergy.net | |
| Sorting | Order0. genergy.net | Consensus ordering |
| | Order1. genergy.net | |
| | Order2. genergy.net | |
| | Order3. genergy.net | |
| Distributed accounting | Couchdb0.saveorg.genergy.net | Deploy the ledger database |
| | Couchdb1.saveorg.genergy.net | |
| | Couchdb2.saveorg.genergy.net | |
| | Couchdb3.saveorg.genergy.net | |
| | Couchdb0.regulatororg.genergy.net | |
| | Couchdb1.regulatororg.genergy.net | |
| Certification | ca.saveorg.genergy.net | Certification services |
| | ca.regulatororg.genergy.net | |

## 4  System Implementation

This paper constructs a blockchain-based distributed electricity energy data security storage anti-tampering mechanism, the underlying blockchain adopts Hyperledger Fabric to build a depository chain, and uses 5 months of meter code table records within 1 year of the power grid as experimental data to complete the simulation experiment of blockchain-based distributed electricity energy data security storage anti-tampering scheme, and the development environment is Centos operating system, The development environment is Centos operating system, InterCorei6 processor, 32 GB of RAM, and 320 GB of hard disk space, which is sufficient to support the operation of related software. In order to verify the real effectiveness of the tamper-proof mechanism of electric energy data security storage, three key aspects of the storage scheme are selected for testing, namely, electric energy data metadata extraction, electric energy metadata data uploading to the blockchain and electric energy data tamper identification.

Based on the above cases, Hyperledger Fabric (release version 1.4.2) was used to build an electric energy data storage chain verification environment. Assuming that the organization involved in data storage is genergy.net, the organization that deposits the blockchain includes a storage organization (saveorg) and a regulator (regulatororg). The storage organization participates in the storage and query of data as the data subject, and the regulator participates as the regulator. and detecting the inquiry data consistency chain strand work, the cluster nodes contain 6 th peer computing nodes. 6 th couchdb books database node, 3 th ca authentication nodes. 4 th orderer sorted nodes; consensus mechanism employed raft algorithm. Fabric blockchain nodes include peer and orderer nodes. Table 1 shows the complete verification environment node configuration for electrical energy data storage.

Storing means. 4 nodes have been installed and registered body data instance, data storage and data query smart card contract, regulators 2 th peer nodes mounting data inquiry and contract smart identification data tampering, wherein peer0 node is set as an anchor node. Each peer node has a separate couchdb accounting database node.

*Four smart contracts are written using smart contracts, including data subject contract (register_cc), data storage certificate contract (audit_cc), data query contract (find_cc) and data tampering identification contract (Identify_cc) contract. China Southern Power Grid using the 2014 first half 1–5 TABLE stopwatch experimental data, experimental data generated each month about 2 Yi of data, the memory capacity of about 2G, dividing the data into memory 10 \*1G packet, 20 \*0.5G packet, 40 \*0.25G uploaded chain comparative tests, were recorded and calculated the hash time, winding time and tampering recognition time.*

### 4.1 Data Storage on the Chain Test

The client node issues a request to upload electrical energy data to the electrical energy data storage chain, and the blockchain node requests to call stub. PutState and pass in the electrical energy data hash value, original data size, data storage path, and data alias as parameters. After reaching a consensus between the nodes, the smart contract execution result is written into the blockchain ledger, and the information storage status of the client node is fed back. The key operations and functions are shown in Fig. 2 and Fig. 3.

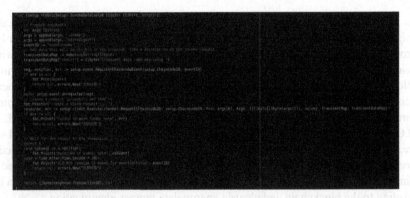

**Fig. 2.** The key code display of the electric energy data uploaded to the blockchain.

**Fig. 3.** Display of the function of uploading electrical energy data to the blockchain.

Measure its data to calculate the hash time and the data chain time as shown in Fig. 4.

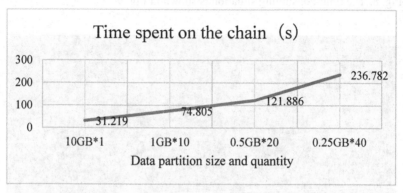

**Fig. 4.** Data calculation hash and time-consuming test on the chain.

## 4.2   Electric Energy Data Query Experiment Test

The node submits the electrical energy data query request, calls the smart contract to analyze the access request, extracts the original data hash as the query condition and passes it in as a parameter. The smart contract retrieves the corresponding data record from the blockchain ledger based on the query information and feeds it back to the client. The key codes and functions are shown in Fig. 5 and Fig. 6.

**Fig. 5.** Display of key codes for electric energy data query.

## 4.3   Electric Energy Data Tampering Identification Experiment Test

The node submits the electric energy data tampering identification request, calls the smart contract to analyze the access request, extracts the original data hash as the query

**Fig. 6.** Display of the query results of electric energy data.

condition and passes it in as a parameter, and returns the data subject's alias, data storage path, and tampering identification result. The key codes and functions are shown in Fig. 7 and Fig. 8. The time-consuming situation is shown in Fig. 9.

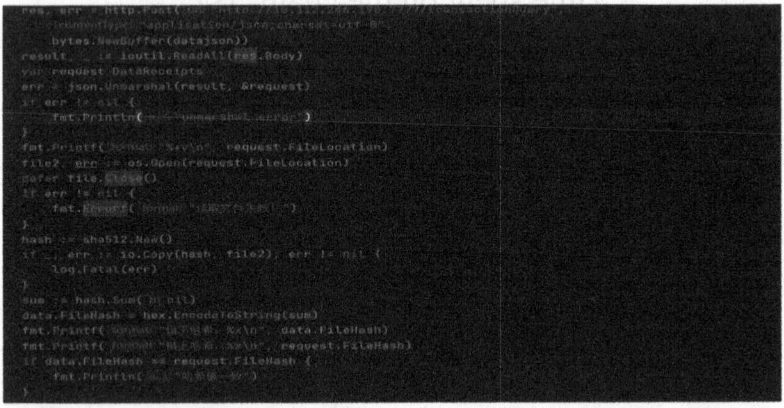

**Fig. 7.** Display of key codes for identification of electrical energy data tampering.

**Fig. 8.** Data tampering identification time consuming test.

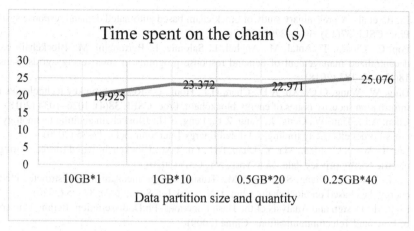

**Fig. 9.** Time-consuming test for data tampering identification.

## 5  Summary

Given the problems of malicious tampering and hard-to-identify single-point attacks associated with the storage of large-scale electrical energy data, an application scenario for storing large-scale electrical energy data is to combine a blockchain-based tamper-proof mechanism for large-scale electrical energy data with we propose. Considering the characteristics of large data volume, timeliness and complex data structure of electric energy data, the electric energy data storage chain is constructed by extracting electric energy metadata, storing the data hash, data size, data storage location and data name as metadata on the chain, and comparing the on-chain hash with the off-chain data hash to detect whether the data is consistent by using the tamper-evident characteristic of blockchain. In this paper, blockchain technology is applied to solve the problem of tamper-proof storage of electric energy data by combining the electric energy data storage scenario, and the implementation details are comprehensively described from three parts: electric energy data metadata extraction, metadata deposition, and data tamper identification. However, it is at the experimental stage, and further testing and verification are still needed to promote the application. In the future, we can try to combine the method with authentication sharing and other requirements to apply to the electric energy data trustworthy sharing application scenario.

## References

1. Li, Z., Kang, J., Yu, R., Ye, D., Deng, Q., Zhang, Y.: Consortium blockchain for secure energy trading in industrial internet of things. IEEE Trans. Industr. Inf. **14**(8), 3690–3700 (2018)
2. Yang, D.C., Zhao, X.Y., Xu, Z.X.: Developing status and prospect analysis of blockchain in energy internet. Proc. CSEE **37**(13), 3664–3671 (2017)
3. Wu, Z.Q., Liang, Y.H., Kang, J.W., Yu, R., He, Z.S.: Secure data storage and sharing system based on consortium blockchain in smart grid. J. Comput. Appl. **37**(10), 2742–2747 (2017)
4. Ouyang, X., Zhu, X.Q.: Preliminary applications of blockchain technique in large con- sumers direct power trading. Proc. CSEE **37**, 3737–3745 (2017)

5. Li, B., et al.: A preliminary study of block chain based automated demand response system. Proc. CSEE **37**(13), 3691–3702 (2017)
6. Pop, C., Cioara, T., Antal, M., Anghel, I., Salomie, I., Bertoncini, M.: Blockchain based decentralized management of demand response programs in smart energy grids. Sensors **18**(1), 162–183 (2018)
7. Ding, W., Wang, G.C., Xu, A.D., Chen, H.J., Hong, C.: Research on key technologies and information security issues of energy blockchain. Proc. CSEE **38**(4), 1026–1034 (2018)
8. Chen, A.L., Tian, W., Geng, J., Yang, Z.L., Feng, S.H.: Blockchain auditing technology for cross-border electricity trading. J. Global Energy Interconn. **3**(1), 79–85 (2020)
9. Liu, T., Wu, S.C., Li, J., Ma, Y., Duan, F.H., Lu, Y.M.: Blockchain-based trusted sharing of electric energy privacy data. New York, NY, USA (2020)
10. Li, J., Wu, S.Q., Zhang, S.L., Lu, Y.M.: Trusted storage mechanism of distributed electric energy data based on blockchain. Chin. J. Network Inf. Secur. **6**(2), 87–95 (2020)
11. Li, Z.M.: Design and Analysis of the Hash Functions. Ph.D. dissertation, Beijing University of Posts and Telecommunications, China (2009)
12. Zhang, P.X.: Application of data encryption technique in computer network information security. Heilongjiang Sci. **12**(12), 108–109 (2021)
13. Jiang, X., Wang, F.: Survey on blockchain technology and application. Comput. Telecommun. **1**(5), 25–29 (2021)
14. Yuan, Y., Wang, F.Y.: Blockchain: the state of the art and future trends. ACTA Automatica Sinica **42**(4), 481–494 (2016)
15. Cheng, G.S.: The evolution of block chain p2p network protocol. China Comput. Commun. **1**(22), 5–6 (2018)
16. Huang, J.Y.: Research on p2p network traversal strategy and optimization method. M.S. Thesis, Harbin Institute of Technology, China (2019)
17. Ouyang, L.W., Wang, S., Yuan, Y., Ni, X.C., Wang, F.Y.: Smart contracts: architecture and research progresses. Acta Automatica Sinica **45**(3), 445–457 (2019)
18. Han, X., Yuan, Y., Wang, F.Y.: Security problems on blockchain: the state of the art and future trends. Acta Automatica Sinica **45**(1), 206–225 (2019)
19. Li, J., Wu, S., Yang, Y., Duan, F., Lu, H., Lu, Y.: Controlled sharing mechanism of data based on the consortium blockchain. Secur. Commun. Networks **2021**, 5523489 (2021)
20. Shi, Q., Liu, K., Wen, M.: Interprovincial generation rights trading model based on blockchain technology. Electric Power Constr. **446**, 3 (2017)
21. Lu, H., Jin, C., Helu, X., Zhu, C., Guizani, N., Tian, Z.: AutoD: intelligent blockchain application unpacking based on jni layer deception call. IEEE Netw **35**(2), 215–221 (2021)
22. Hu, N., Tian, Z., Lu, H., Du, X., Guizani, M.: A multiple-kernel clustering based intrusion detection scheme for 5G and IoT networks. Int. J. Mach. Learn. Cybern. **12**(11), 3129–3144 (2021). https://doi.org/10.1007/s13042-020-01253-w
23. Shafiq, M., Tian, Z., Sun, Y., Du, X., Guizani, M.: Selection of effective machine learning algorithm and Bot-IoT attacks traffic identification for internet of things in smart city. Futur. Gener. Comput. Syst. **107**, 433–442 (2020)
24. Shafiq, M., Tian, Z., Bashir, A., Du, X., Guizani, M.: IoT malicious traffic identification using wrapper-based feature selection mechanisms. Comput. Secur. **94**, 101863 (2020)

# A True Random Number Generator Based on ADC Random Interval Sampling

Gang Li[ID], Haoyang Sun[ID], Peiqi Wu[ID], Zehua Li[ID], Zhenbing Li[ID], Xiaochuan Fang[ID], DeXu Chen, and Guangjun Wen[✉][ID]

University of Electronic Science and Technology of China, Xiyuan Ave. 2006, Chengdu, China
wgj@uestc.edu.cn

**Abstract.** This paper presents a true random number generator (TRNG) based on traditional Microcontroller Unit (MCU) with analog-to-digital converter (ADC). Within the proposed architecture, the MCU employs an ADC to continuously sample variational input signals (rise/fall process) for generating true random numbers (TRNs). In the process, the time interval between each ADC sampling is determined by the output signal sampled by the previous ADC (called a random interval). The method improves the randomness of ADC output data by using the altering input signal (including noise) and the non-linear feature of ADC. Additionally, the simulation results (base on NIST) show the proposed TRNG can be realized using conventional MCU.

**Keywords:** Microcontroller · ADC · Random interval · True random number

## 1 Introduction

In recent years, random numbers (RNs) has been widely used in encryption algorithm [1–8], radio frequency identification (RFID) and other fields [9–12]. RNs can be divided into pseudo-random numbers [13] and true random Numbers (TRNs) [14]. Pseudo-random numbers (PRNs) are realized by deterministic algorithms, and can be completely repeated. Their randomness is determined by the complexity of the algorithm and the calculation accuracy [15]. TRNs are often derived from physical phenomena (such as thermal noise and scintillation noise), and combined with certain algorithms and post-processing implementation, they have truly unpredictable characteristics [16].

TRNG uses the noise of analog circuit (easily affected by noise) as entropy source. According to the manifestation form of noise, the structure of TRNG can be divided into: 1) noise comparison structure based on thermal noise [17, 18], 2) Clock jitter based Beat Frequency Detection structure [19, 20], 3) ADC-based residual recycling structure [21–25, 26], also known as chaotic map.

Noise comparison structure collects random information of entropy source (resistance thermal noise) through comparator, and converts noise into random sequence, which need a high accuracy comparator. Beat frequency detection structure collects the random information of entropy source (oscillator clock jitter noise) in the register, which is a common method to realize TRNs [27, 28]. Compared with the noise comparison structure, beat detection is a more reliable noise sampling technique, but due to the lack of oscillator jitter, the randomness of the generated data is not strong enough. At the same time, two continuously oscillating clocks will also consume a lot of energy, increasing the power consumption of the system. In addition, it requires chip/FPGA, which cannot be used in general processors such as MCU, DSP and ARM.

TRNG based on ADC nonlinear chaotic map has been widely studied. In [9], SAR ADC and low-power dynamic residual amplifier were used to realize TRNG, and coarse SAR ADC was selectively activated to further reduce the system power consumption. [18] proposed a method that combines resistance thermal noise, oscillator sampling and discrete time chaotic system to realize TRNG, which has better performance. In [21–23], it proposed a method where multiple ADCs are used to realize TRNG with pipeline architecture. Each stage of ADC uses 1.5-bit resolution and output 1-bit RN, and the ADC input is the residual signal output by the previous stage ADC. In [24], after the completion of SAR ADC, the comparator is used to continue to compare the lowest point (residual) of ADC output, and the result of comparison is taken as a RN, which can complete ADC function and generate TRNs at the same time. In [10], a TRNG is also implemented by pipeline ADC, and compared with [21–23], dynamic residual amplifier with gain less than 2 (1.9 for simulation) is used to avoid system shock. In addition, a bit shuffling technique is used to replace the shift register and improve the statistical properties of generated sequences. However, the above methods are very complicated to implement, and they all need to provide special circuit structure, only suitable for chips, which increases the complexity and cost of system design.

This paper proposes a method based on ADC random interval sampling to realize a TRNG for solving the above problems, which can be realized by traditional MCU. The main innovation of this paper is that it proposes a mechanism combining variable analog input and ADC random interval sampling, which is very suitable for low-power application scenarios. In particular, in wireless sensor network nodes, the proposed method can greatly reduce the cost and power consumption (the sensor circuit can be directly used as entropy source, and they also need ADC to collect data, which).

The rest of the paper is arranged as follows: Section 2 describes the working principle of proposed TRNG. Section 3 introduces the simulation results. Section 4 concludes the paper.

## 2    The Operating Principle of Proposed TRNG

### 2.1    Structure Description of Proposed TRNG

Figure 1 shows the architecture of TRNG. It is composed of an external entropy source circuit and MCU. The external entropy source circuit may be an arbitrary circuit structure with a switch, which can realize energy-saving control and provide varying input signals for the MCU. And the MCU achieves functions, for instance analog-to-digital conversion, initial delay, random interval delay, random number generation, and post-processing. These functions can also be easily implemented on a custom chip. The initial delay provides the initial value to the system. The random interval delay will feedback the ADC output data recursively to the input, so as to realize a map system. The biggest advantage of this structure is that it can be used to realize both TRNG and information collection function (The input circuit in the external entropy source circuit is a sensor.). Therefore, in the WSNs equipment with sensors and ADC, this architecture is applied to achieve TRNG without adding any hardware circuit.

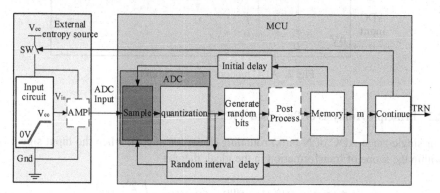

**Fig. 1.** TRNG proposed based on ADC.

When it is necessary to generate TRNs, the MCU connects the switch SW to power the input circuit and the amplifier, so that the $V_{in}$ voltage value starts to increase, thereby providing changing input signals for ADC. As illustrated, the simplest linear function is used to describe the changing process of the input signal, such as the red line segments in the input circuit in Fig. 1. Additionally, amplifiers (AMP) are used to amplify useful signals, like sensor signals. However, for TRNG, the AMP is an optional alternative. The initial delay module is applied to determine the time $t_0$ when the ADC starts sampling (the first sampling position $S_1$), as shown in Fig. 2. it is determined by the TRNs generated last time. The random interval delay module generates a waiting time according to the digital signal output from the ADC sampling this time, making the next sampling time $t_k$ of ADC, $k = 1, 2, \ldots$, m-1 present randomness. The random number generation module uses ADC output data to generate RNs (The method of generating RNs can be customized.). The Memory is employed to store the digital signals and TRNs generated by the ADC. The $m$ represents the total number of times that the ADC needs to sample during the rise of the input signal after each connection with SW. If the ADC generates 1-bit random number per sampling, then $m$ represents the TRN of $m$ bits, and the maximum value of m is limited by the rising time of the input signal and the average time that the ADC consumes once. The post-processing module is used to enhance the performance of RNs. The continue module represents the TRN of $m$ bits that needs to generate continuously.

The proposed TRNG will change the ADC output, even with the same input signals and identical initial sampling location, due to the noise of the input signals, the limited accuracy of the ADC and the quantization error. As a result, the next ADC sampling time changes accordingly, as the displayed $S_2$, $S_3$,..., $S_m$ in Fig. 2. Furthermore, even when the input circuit and the amplifier is enough good to make the effect of input circuit noise and amplifier noise negligible, the approach can also contribute to changes in the ADC output, and affect the subsequent delay time and the ADC sampling position, thus enhancing the randomness of the ADC output data, due to the clock jitter of the MCU, power supply voltage ripple and ADC quantization error factors.

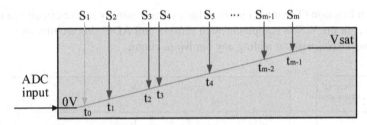

**Fig. 2.** ADC random interval sampling.

## 2.2 Principle Analysis of Proposed TRNG

For single-stage ADC of N bit(s) rounding-down for integer, when the input signal is within the scope of transformation in the ideal, there is

$$DADC = \{b^{(N-1)}...b^{(0)}\} = ADC(V) = \left\langle \frac{2^N}{V\text{ref}} Vin \right\rangle \tag{1}$$

where, $D_{ADC}$ represents the digital output signal of ADC, N represents ADC bit width, $ADC(\bullet)$ represents ADC conversion function, $\langle \bullet \rangle$ represents downward integration, $V_{ref}$ is ADC reference voltage, $V_{in}$ represents ADC analog input voltage. Based on the traditional ADC, which the map relationship between the input and output of the proposes system is

$$x_{n+1} = M(x_n) \tag{2}$$

where, $M(\bullet)$ represents the map function of the proposed system. The unit time of initial delay and random interval delay in Fig. 1 is the period of MCU working clock frequency, and the time of initial delay $t_0$ is determined by the TRNs ($RN_t$) in Memory.

$$t_0 = \frac{1}{fP} RNt \& const_1 \tag{3}$$

where $f_p$ is the operating frequency of the MCU, & is in bits and, $const_1$ is a constant ($const_1$ is 15 that takes the least significant four bits of $RN_t$). Similarly, we can get the random interval delay time is equal to

$$t_r^k = \frac{1}{fP} D_{ADC}^k \& const_2, (k \in R) \cap (0 < k \le m) \tag{4}$$

where, $t_r{}^k$ represents the interval of ADC sampling between the $k+1$ time and $k$ time, $D_{ADC}^k$ represents the output signal of ADC after the k time sampling, and $const_2$ is similar to $const_1$.

For simplicity, provided that a linear change in $V_{in}$ reveals, after SW is turned on, then

$$Vin = a_{slop} \times t + Nnoise \tag{5}$$

where $Nin$ is the thermal noise and power supply noise in the circuit, and $a_{slop}$ represents the slope of $V_{in}$. Then, the amplifier output can be calculated by the following equation:

$$Vamp = A \times a_{slop} \times t + Nnoise$$

where $A$ is the multiple of the amplifier. Since the $V_{amp}$ output is directly connected to the analog input of the ADC in the MCU, then, $x_n$ in Eq. (2) can be represented by $V_{amp}$. Hereby, the input voltage $V_{ADC}$ of the system of the TRNG proposed can be expressed as

$$VADC = \begin{cases} Nnoise, & t = 0 \\ A * a_{slop} * t + Nnoise, & 0 < t < \frac{V_{sat}}{A*a_{slop}} \\ V_{sat} + Nnoise, & t \geq \frac{V_{sat}}{A*a_{slop}} \end{cases} \tag{7}$$

where, $V_{sat}$ represents the maximum voltage that the amplifier output can achieve. When $t = 0$, the switch SW is off, $V_{ADC}$ only demonstrates noise. When $t \geq V_{sat}/(A \times a_{slop})$, assuming that the amplifier output is stable, $V_{ADC} = V_{amp} = V_{sat}$. When $t = 0$ and $t \geq VCC/(A \times a_{slop})$, if the circuit at the time is comprehended as a resistance voltage divider circuit (The resistance is infinite or infinitesimal.), the entropy source information input by the system is only provided by the noise [17]. In order to make the system possess higher randomness, it is therefore necessary to ensure that the total consumed time of the ADC sampling times is within $0 < t < VCC/(A * a_{slop})$ (setting the total time consumed by resistance and capacitance in the circuit or through $const_1$, $const_2$ and $m$). That is, the ADC needs to start sampling after $V_{ADC}$ is on the rise, and terminates before the $V_{ADC}$ is stable.

Therefore, during the rise of the input signal, the system relation between the voltage value of $V_{ADC}$ and the number of ADC sampling is

$$V_{ADC}(k) = \begin{cases} A * a_{slop} * (t0) + N^0 noise, & k = 0 \\ A * a_{slop} * (t0 + \sum_{i=1}^{k} (t_r^{i+1} + ts + tproc)) + N^k noise, & 0 < k \leq m - 1 \end{cases}$$

$$\tag{8}$$

The $t_s$ is the time required for ADC to perform analog-to-digital conversion, which can be calculated by the sampling frequency $fs$ of the built-in ADC in the MCU.

$$ts = \frac{1}{fS} \tag{9}$$

The $t_{proc}$ means the time that the MCU processes data after each sampling, which is determined by the working frequency of the MCU. Here, the assumption is that the MCU takes eight clocks to process data (The exact processing time depends on the specific application. In general, it consumes eight clocks.).

$$tproc = \frac{8}{fP} \tag{10}$$

When substituting Eqs. (1), (3), (4), (9) and (10) into (8), the expression of the proposed TRNG is as follows.

$$D_{ADC}^{k+1} = M(D_{ADC}^k) =$$

$$
\begin{cases}
\left\lfloor \frac{2^N}{Vcc} \left( A \times a_{slop} \times (\frac{1}{fP} RNt\&const_1) + Nnoise \right) \right\rfloor, & k = 0 \\[2ex]
\left\lfloor \frac{2^N}{Vcc} \left\{ A \times a_{slop} \times \left[ \frac{1}{fP} RNt\&const_1 + \sum_{i=1}^{k} \left( \frac{1}{fP} \left( D_{ADC}^i \&const_2 \right) + \frac{1}{fS} + \frac{8}{fP} \right) \right] + Nnoise \right\} \right\rfloor, & 0 < k \le m-1
\end{cases}
\tag{11}
$$

Equation (11) manifests the mapping relation of $D_{ADC}^{k+1}$ and $D_{ADC}^k$, and noise $Nnoise$ exerts immediate influence on the output of the map. Meanwhile, Eq. (1) suggest that the output signal $D_{ADC}$ of the ADC carries certain quantization error. With the application of the map in Eq. (1), the noise and quantization error are able to be sent to the ADC input signals, thus affecting the output data sampled by the next ADC sampling, which facilitates the divergence of the chaotic map (to obtain rapidly-changing $D_{ADC}$ data). Such process can improve TRNG performance.

At the same time, the total time which ADC performs sampling $m$ times takes to generate $m$-bit TRNs can be calculated.

$$
t = \frac{1}{fP} RNt\&const_1 + \frac{1}{fS} + \frac{8}{fP} + \sum_{i=1}^{m-1} \left( \frac{1}{fP} \left( D_{ADC}^i \&const_2 \right) + \frac{1}{fS} + \frac{8}{fP} \right)
\tag{12}
$$

After simplification,

$$
t = \frac{RNt\&const_1 + 8m}{fP} + \frac{m}{fS} + \sum_{i=1}^{m-1} \left( \frac{1}{fP} D_{ADC}^i \&const_2 \right)
\tag{13}
$$

To the best of our knowledge, the existing MCUs in the market, such as TMS320F2803x, its sampling frequency can reach 3 MHz, and the main frequency of the MCU can reach 60 MHz. When the choice is made $const_1 = const_1 = 15$, it indicates that the minimum four bits of $D_{ADC}^k$ and $RN_t$ are considered as the delay parameters. When the lowest four bits of $D_{ADC}^k$ and RNt both are one, the longest time consumed is 16 clocks, then

$$
t = \left( \frac{24m}{60} + \frac{m}{3} \right) us, \; m \ge 1
\tag{14}
$$

Therefore, it can be calculated that the slowest rate of generating TRNs is 1.36 Mbit/s. Similarly, the average rate is 1.67 Mbit/s.

## 3  Simulation and Verification

In consideration of the main differences lying between the TRNG proposed and the other TRNG using ADC are as follows. 1) Adoption of the changing signals using traditional ADC sampling; 2) Randomness of the time interval of each ADC sampling.

---

**Algorithm 1** TRNG simulation algorithm based on ADC
nonlinear effect and chaotic map

---

**Input:** $m$, continue_times, $const_1$, $const_2$, $A$, $a_{slop}$, $N_{noise}$

**Output:** TRNs

---

1. Turn on SW for obtaining input curve with $N_{noise}$,
   Had_sampling_times=0
2. Get $RN_t$ for intial delay, and $t_0 = (RN_t \ \& \ const_1)/f_P$.
3. Dealy_function ($t_0$).
4. ADC samples, $D_{ADC} = \lfloor 2^N V_{in}/V_{cc} \rfloor$ and
   Had_sampling_times **plus** one.
5. The lsb of TRNs **equals** the LSB of $D_{ADC}$
   The TRNs loop moves one bit to the left
6. **If** Had_sampling_times $== m$ **Then**
      Jump to step 7
   **Else**
      $t_r^k = (D_{ADC}^k \ \& \ const_2)/f_P$
      Dealy_function ($t_r^k$).
      **Jump** to step 4
   **End If**
7. **Save** TRNs
8. **If** Had_continue_times $==$ continue_times **Then**
      Jump to step 9
   **Else**
      Close SW
      Had_continue_times plus one
      **Jump** to step 1
   **End If**
9. **Return:** All TRNs

---

Therefore, targeted simulations are launched pertinent to the two aspects. Firstly, MATLAB was implemented to simulate the nonlinear and chaotic map of ADC as shown in Eq. (11), and a traditional ADC of 12 bits through Eq. (4) was simulated. The LSB of data output from of ADC each time was used to generate TRNs, and we set $A = a_{slop} = 1$, the means of $Nnoise = 1$ mV(mean value), $Vsat = 2$ V, and $m = 16$. The ADC system map algorithm is shown in algorithm 1.

The simulation was performed under the condition that the initial value $RN_t$ took a value of 20 and 21 respectively (The initial delay differs by one clock.). Consequently, the relationship between the number of iterations $n$ and $\overline{DADC}$ (representing the last four bits of $D_{ADC}$) and was obtained, as exhibited in Fig. 3. It is evident that when the initial delay is one clock different, the output data of the two simulations alters from the fifth iteration. And with the increase of the number of iterations, sharper distinctions emerge. Hence, the system is believed to have equipped with the characteristics of chaotic map.

In order to further verify the performance of the proposed TRNG, it is also imperative to verify whether the RN generated by simulation meets the randomness test requirements. So, the ADC input signals were divided into the following two situations: 1) a constant voltage of 1 V and $Nnoise = 1$ mV, and 2) $a_{slop} = 1$ and $Nnoise = 1$ mV.

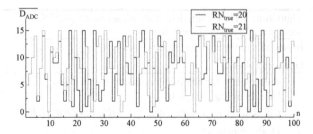

**Fig. 3.** Sensitivity of the system to initial delay.

Additionally, in the MCU, the processing process was separated into two situations: 1) ADC sampling fixed interval time, and 2) ADC sampling interval time. In other words, there were four cases to be simulated.

In this paper, the U.S. National Institute of Standards and Technology (NIST) test suite [25] was used to verify the randomness of random numbers. The test suite requires at least $10^6$ bits of data to meet the test data volume requirement, and $4 \times 10^6$ bits of data for each simulation case were generated. The NIST test was divided into 15 cases and multiple sub-cases, in which the *p-value* greater than 0.01 indicates that the randomness test requirements were met. In the case of multiple sub-cases, if the *p-value* of test results of all sub-cases is greater than 0.01, the test passes; otherwise, the test fails.

The Table 1 shows the test result of RN generated in four simulation situations. It can be seen from the Table that in whatever situation, the fixed 1 V voltage superimposing 1 mV noise for the input signal cannot pass the verification of NIST, no matter random interval delay was added or not. When the linear rising voltage with a slope rate of one superimposes 1 mV noise as input signals and without adding random delay interval, the generated RNs cannot pass the NIST test either. However, the test result turns better than that of 1 V constant voltage. After adding the random delay interval, the generated RNs can pass the NIST verification. Therefore, it is safe to say that the variable input signals and random interval delay mechanism can improve the randomness of the ADC output data.

**Table 1.** Verification result of TRNs generated.

| NIST-sts-2.1.2, randomness test | $x^* = 1 + \text{noise}$ | | $x^\# = 1 + \text{noise}$ | | $x^* = t + \text{noise}$ | | $x^\# = t + \text{noise}$ | |
|---|---|---|---|---|---|---|---|---|
| | *P-value* | Prop. | *P-value* | Prop. | *P-value* | Prop. | *P-value* | Prop. |
| Frequency | **0.000** | **0/10** | **0.0000** | **0/10** | **0.0000** | **6/10** | 0.2133 | 10/10 |
| Block Frequency | **0.0000** | **5/10** | **0.0000** | **3/10** | 0.35049 | 10/10 | 0.7399 | 10/10 |
| Cumulative Sums 0 | **0.0000** | **0/10** | **0.0000** | **0/10** | **0.0000** | **6/10** | 0.7399 | 10/10 |
| Cumulative Sums 1 | **0.0000** | **0/10** | **0.0000** | **0/10** | **0.00000** | **6/10** | 0.9114 | 10/10 |
| Runs | **0.0000** | **0/10** | **0.0000** | **0/10** | 0.2133 | 10/10 | 0.5342 | 10/10 |

*(continued)*

**Table 1.** (*continued*)

| NIST-sts-2.1.2, randomness test | $x^* = 1 +$ noise | | $x^\# = 1 +$ noise | | $x^* = t +$ noise | | $x^\# = t +$ noise | |
|---|---|---|---|---|---|---|---|---|
| | *P-value* | Prop. | *P-value* | Prop. | *P-value* | Prop. | *P-value* | Prop. |
| Longest Run | **0.0000** | **0/10** | **0.0000** | **0/10** | 0.7399 | 10/10 | 0.3505 | 10/10 |
| Rank | 0.3505 | 10/10 | 0.9114 | 10/10 | 0.5341 | 10/10 | 0.7399 | 10/10 |
| FFT | 0.3505 | 10/10 | 0.1223 | 10/10 | 0.7399 | 10/10 | 0.9114 | 10/10 |
| Non-Overlapping Template | **Fail** | **Fail** | **Fail** | **Fail** | **Fail** | Pass | – | Pass |
| Over lapping Template | **0.000** | **3/10** | **0.0000** | **4/10** | 0.7399 | 10/10 | 0.7399 | 10/10 |
| Universal | 0.3505 | 10/10 | 0.7399 | 10/10 | 0.1223 | 10/10 | 0.3505 | 10/10 |
| Approximate Entropy | **0.0000** | **0/10** | **0.0000** | **0/10** | 0.3505 | 10/10 | 0.7399 | 10/10 |
| Random Excursions | **Fail** | **Fail** | **Fail** | **Fail** | – | Pass | – | Pass |
| Random Excursions Variant | **Fail** | **Fail** | **Fail** | **Fail** | – | Pass | – | Pass |
| Serial 0 | 0.1223 | 8/10 | 0.2133 | 8/10 | 0.5342 | 10/10 | 0.9114 | 10/10 |
| Serial 1 | 0.1223 | 10/10 | 0.3505 | 10/10 | 0.3505 | 9/10 | 0.0669 | 10/10 |
| Linear Complexity | 0.3505 | 10/10 | 0.0179 | 10/10 | 0.2133 | 10/10 | 0.2133 | 10/10 |

## 4 Conclusion

This paper introduces the feasibility of implementing TRNG using ADC, and analyzes the shortcomings of implementing existing TRNG based on ADC. A TRNG based on ADC random interval sampling is proposed, which can be realized with traditional MCU. It does not need to add any circuit for sensor information acquisition equipment, greatly reducing the cost and power consumption of the system. It can be seen from the simulation results that the proposed circuit structure can realize TRNG, and the proposed method not only improves the compatibility of TRNG based on ADC, but also reduces the complexity of system, which has very high practical value.

## References

1. Shankar, K., Venkatraman, S.: A secure encrypted classified electronic healthcare data for public cloud environment. Intell. Autom. Soft Comput. **32**(2), 765–779 (2022)
2. Oliver, S.G., Purusothaman, T.: Lightweight and secure mutual authentication scheme for iot devices using coap protocol. Comput. Syst. Sci. Eng. **41**(2), 767–780 (2022)
3. Aljehane, N.O.: A secure intrusion detection system in cyberphysical systems using a parameter-tuned deep-stacked autoencoder. Comput. Mater. Continua **68**(3), 3915–3929 (2021)
4. Prabakaran, D., Ramachandran, S.: Multi-factor authentication for secured financial transactions in cloud environment. Comput. Mat. Continua **70**(1), 1781–1798 (2022)

5. Khan, S., Raza, A., Hwang, S.O.: An enhanced privacy preserving, secure and efficient authentication protocol for vanet. Comput. Mat. Continua **71**(2), 3703–3719 (2022)
6. Peng, X., Zhang, J., Zhang, S., Wan, W., Chen, H.: A secure signcryption scheme for electronic health records sharing in blockchain. Comput. Syst. Sci. Eng. **37**(2), 265–281 (2021)
7. Datta, D., Garg, L., Srinivasan, K., Inoue, A., Reddy, G.T.: An efficient sound and data steganography based secure authentication system. Comput. Mat. Continua **67**(1), 723–751 (2021)
8. Zhong, X.W., Xiong, L.Z., Xia, Z.H.: A secure visual secret sharing scheme with authentication based on QR Code. J. Big Data **3**(2), 85–95 (2021)
9. Kim, M., Ha, U., Lee, K.J., Lee, Y., Yoo, H.J.: A 82-nw chaotic map true random number generator based on a sub-ranging SAR ADC. IEEE J. Solid-State Circuits **52**(7), 1953–1965 (2017)
10. Gerosa, A., Bernardini, R., Pietri, S.: A fully integrated chaotic system for the generation of truly random numbers. IEEE Trans. Circuits Syst. I **49**(7), 993–1000 (2002)
11. Su, J., Chen, Y., Sheng, Z., Huang, Z., Liu, A.X.: From m-ary query to bit query: a new strategy for efficient large-scale rfid identification. IEEE Trans. Commun. **68**(4), 2381–2393 (2020)
12. Wang, C., Shao, X., Meng, Y., Gao, J.: A physical layer network coding based tag anti-collision algorithm for rfid system. Comput. Mat. Continua **66**(1), 931–945 (2021)
13. Pangratz, W.: Pseudo-random number generator based on binary and quinary maximal-length sequences. IEEE Trans. Comput **9**, 637–642 (1979)
14. Yang, K., Blaauw, D., Sylvester, D.: An all-digital edge racing true random number generator robust against pvt variations. IEEE J. Solid-State Circuits **51**(4), 1022–1031 (2016)
15. Li, D., Lu, Z., Zou, X., Liu, Z.: PUFKEY: A high-security and high-throughput hardware true random number generator for sensor networks. Sensors **15**(10), 26251–26266 (2015)
16. Ma, Y., Chen, T., Lin, J., Yang, J., Jing, J.: Entropy Estimation for ADC Sampling-Based True Random Number Generators. IEEE Trans. Inform. Forensic Secur **14**(11), 2887–2900 (2019)
17. Jinming, L., Jian, M. and Peiguo, L.: August. design and implement of a mcu based random number generater. In: 2016 11th International Conference on Computer Science & Education (ICCSE), pp. 945–948. IEEE (2016)
18. Petrie, C.S., Connelly, J.A.: A noise-based IC random number generator for applications in cryptography. IEEE Trans. Circuits Syst. I **47**(5), 615–621 (2000)
19. Liu, Y., Cheung, R.C.C., Wong, H.: A bias-bounded digital true random number generator architecture. IEEE Trans. Circuits Syst. I **64**(1), 133–144 (2017)
20. Bucci, M., Germani, L., Luzzi, R., Trifiletti, A., Varanonuovo, M.: A high-speed oscillator-based truly random number source for cryptographic applications on a smartcard IC. IEEE Trans. Comput **52**(4), 403–409 (2003)
21. Callegari, S., Rovatti, R., Setti, G.: Reconfigurable ADC/True-RNG for Secure Sensor Networks. In: IEEE Sensors. pp. 1072–1075 (2005)
22. Callegari, S., Rovatti, R., Setti, G.: Embeddable ADC-based true random number generator for cryptographic applications exploiting nonlinear signal processing and chaos. IEEE Trans. Signal Process **53**(2), 793–805 (2005)
23. Pareschi, F., Setti, G., Rovatti, R.: Implementation and testing of high-speed cmos true random number generators based on chaotic systems. IEEE Trans. Circuits Syst. I **57**(12), 3124–3137 (2010)
24. Jayaraj, A., Gujarathi, N.N., Venkatesh, I., Sanyal, A.: 0.6V-1.2V, 0.22pJ/bit true random number generator based on SAR ADC. IEEE Trans. Circuits Syst **67**(10), 1765–1769 (2019)
25. Rukhin, A., Soto, J., Nechvatal, J., Smid, M., Barker, E.: A statistical test suite for random and pseudorandom number generators for cryptographic applications. Booz-allen and hamilton inc mclean va. (2001)

# A Learning-Based Feature Extraction Method for Detecting Malicious Code

Zhiqiang Ruan[1($\boxtimes$)], Lixin Zhou[2], Haibo Luo[1], and Xiucai Ye[3]

[1] Minjiang University, Fuzhou 350108, China
rzq_911@163.com
[2] Fujian Jiangxia University, Fuzhou 350108, China
[3] Department of Computer Science, University of Tsukuba, Tsukuba 3058577, Japan

**Abstract.** The identification of new malicious code has become an important research direction in the field of network security, nevertheless, most malicious programs can only get a small amount of operation code after assembly, which is difficult to represent the malicious behavior of the program. This paper focuses on malicious code feature extraction and identification method, an improved malicious code recognition scheme is proposed by integrating the characteristics of assembly code and file structure. In particular, three sets of effective feature data sets are extracted from the collected sample data, and seven common machine learning classification models are used to evaluate them respectively. The experimental results show that the proposed scheme outperforms traditional methods in detecting the malicious program and its variants in terms of accuracy, accuracy, and recall ratio.

**Keywords:** Malicious code · Machine learning · Classifier · Algorithm

## 1 Introduction

Most network security incidents are caused by malicious code attacks, including the well-known malicious codes Trojans, viruses and worms. In 2020, the number of new mobile Internet malicious programs obtained by independent capture and manufacturer exchange was about 3028000, about 8.5% growth compared with the same period of the previous year. Through the statistics of malicious behavior of malicious programs, it is found that the top three are rogue behavior, tariff consumption and information theft, accounting for 48.4%, 21.1% and 12.7%, respectively [1]. Therefore, malicious code detection has become one of the key issues concerned by the network security community. However, the anti-detection technology is also accelerating the developing speed, which poses a great challenge to researchers.

Code analysis is a commonly used method to detect the intention and execution logic of malicious activities, it includes static and dynamic strategy depends on whether the program is executed to find effective features. For static analysis, it usually needs to check the disassembled code of the source to understand the behavior of the program from the semantic and code levels. The commonly used disassemblers include Ollydbg (OD),

Interactive Disassembler Professional (IDA), radare2, and DEBUG [2], sometimes, it only needs to analyze the binary stream, portable executable (PE) file header and other data of the program. Dynamic analysis needs to run the program in the virtual machine or via simulation to observe its behavior and record the characteristics during program execution, such as API call, network request, file operation, etc. The overhead of static analysis is small, but it is easy to be affected by confusion or shelling technology. The accuracy of dynamic analysis is relative higher, but the cost of testing the environment is large or the obtained information is incomplete. Currently, the most widely used method is still static analysis or the combination of these two technologies.

In this work, the features of the software to be check are extracted, and compared with the corresponding feature library. If the matching is successful, the software is cleared, otherwise, if the matching is unsuccessful, it is judged as normal software. In the actual scene, it usually needs to combine other technologies to distinguish whether malicious code is malignant or benign.

The machine learning is applied to train the recognition model and two types of malicious code features are used according to the characteristics of assembly code and file structure, namely, the opcode features extracted from assembly file and the static combination feature derived from the original file. The former needs to disassemble the original file to get its assembly file, and then uses n-gram and doc2vec methods [3] to extract opcode feature sequences independently. The latter extracts nine groups of effective features by parsing the original file, including six groups of format related features (PE basic information, PE header meta information, imported library and function information, section information, directory and its virtual address information) and three groups of PE format independent features (printable string information, byte / byte entropy histogram, joint distribution of byte and entropy). Finally, three sets of effective feature data sets are extracted from the collected sample data, and seven common machine learning classification models are used to evaluate them.

## 2  Feature Extraction

### 2.1  Assembly Opcode Extraction

Most of the static detection technologies of malicious code based on machine learning algorithm use assembly code to build classification model. The opcode sequence extracted in sequence can reflect the behavior characteristics of the program. The assembler code can be obtained after decomplication by using IDA pro to the original file, the following set of opcode sequences can be extracted: {push, push, sub, mov, xor, mov, cmp, jbe, mov, movzx, cmp, jz, setz, call, pop, retn}.

The opcode sequences obtained from the assembly text segmentation cannot be used for automatic analysis, they need to be digitized and vectorized. A suitable language model can be selected to preprocess opcode sequences, i.e., N-gram. In addition, we use doc2vec algorithm to vectorize the text and obtain the fixed length of opcode feature. The opcode sequence is transformed into text vector, where the semantic relationship between opcodes and their activities can be described.

In n-gram, n represents the length of sliding window, and different values of n will bring different effects. If the opcode sequence of an executable file is l, the n-ray syntax model will divide the opcode sequence into $l\text{-}n + 1$ feature sequence in the form of sliding windows. For example, when using the 3-g method to extract features on a set of opcode sequences {push, sub, mov, xor, cmp, call, pop}, in this case, $l = 7$, there are five feature sequences are obtained, and each sequence contains 3 words, such as {push, sub, mov}, {sub, mov, xor}, {mov xor cmp}, {xor, cmp, call}, and {cmp, call, pop}. Figure 1 is the frequency distribution histogram obtained from the statistics of the 3-g feature sequence of a malicious sample file. The experimental part will examine whether the assembly opcode features can better distinguish malicious programs from benign programs.

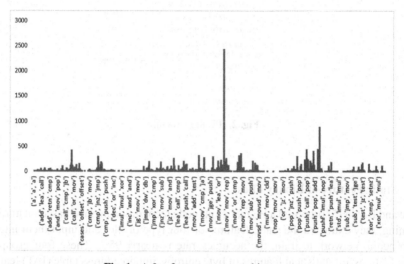

**Fig. 1.** A 3-g feature sequence histogram.

Doc2vec is a paragraph vector representation method based on word2vec language model. It can extract key features from sentences, paragraphs or documents, which indicates that each assembly file can get a vector representation. Doc2vec adds a paragraph vector on the input layer of word2vec, and this vector is shared by the same file. In the training process, the vector will gradually form the subject of the assembly opcode text according to the changes of different opcodes.

## 2.2  Executable File Structure

PE file is a general term for executable files of window systems, which includes the boot part and the data part [4]. The boot part is generally composed of DOS header, NT header and section table, as shown in Fig. 2. The MZ header in the DOS header contains the key information, as it is compatible with the MS-DOS system, furthermore, it provides the starting address of the file NT header, which contains the main information of PE files, such as identification, file header and optional header. The section table (block table) contains the name, attribute, location and other information of each section. Each section is an independent element for storing code and data, and all sections form the data part. The system will load all sections based on the section table after the program is executed.

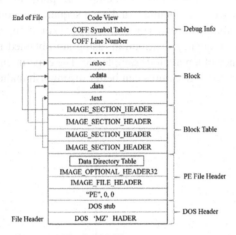

**Fig. 2.** PE file structure.

## 2.3 Static Feature of Binary Files

Saxe and Berlin [5] proposed a PE malicious code recognition method based on machine learning, they extracted the static features of four type of files and input them into the deep neural network to train, the accuracy rate is nearly 95%. These four groups of static features are statistical features of byte entropy, import address table (IAT) features of PE header, printable characters and PE meta information. Each group of features is extracted to form a 256-dimensional array, and then spliced to obtain a 1024-dimensional sample feature vector. However, this scheme only obtains a small amount of opcode after assembly.

We modify the window size, sliding step and other parameters of byte entropy feature, and add another 5 groups of features on the basis of the above four groups of features, and use executable file operation tool to parse binary files, four groups of file information are extracted, which includes file general information, export function table (EFT) feature, section information and data directory. The information entropy or hash method is used for digitization and quantization, and then the byte code of the binary file itself is counted to generate a byte histogram. Nine groups of features form a feature vector of no less than 2381 dimensions. Each sample can extract fixed features and input them into the classification model for training. The feature extraction process includes the following steps:

*1) Byte statistics.* The binary file is converted into byte stream, and the distribution histogram is obtained by calculating the frequency of all bytes. Compared with the traditional feature code, this feature is original and abstract.

*2) Statistical features of byte entropy.* First, the number of sliding windows (byte entropy pair) is computed, e.g., for a binary file, the sliding window size is 2048 bytes, the sliding step size is 1024 bytes, and the binary file size is 100kb, it takes 99 slides to calculate the entire binary file. Then, one needs to calculate the window size to obtain the entropy of a group of byte sequences. The information entropy $H(X)$ is calculated as follows:

$$H(X) = -\sum_{i=1}^{m} p_i log_2(p_i) \tag{1}$$

where $p_i$ is the byte frequency distribution [6].

The randomness of byte sequence is described by entropy. The greater the information entropy, the greater the randomness. Each sliding window has a fixed entropy value, which forms the byte frequency distribution of byte entropy pair. For instance, the above 99 groups of byte entropy pairs obtained by sliding are added by frequency accumulation, and a $16 \times 16$ dimensional distribution matrix is transformed into $1 \times 256$ dimensional feature vector to get the byte entropy pair distribution feature.

*3) Section information.* The attributes of each section are obtained by parsing the internal data of the file format, including section name, section size, section entropy, virtual size, string list of entry point function, etc. The name of the section is spliced with the size, entropy and virtual size of the section to form three new string lists. Those lists and the string lists of entry point function are vectorized by hash function and converted into 50-dimensional arrays. Then, we compute the total number of sections, the number of non-empty sections, the number of sections containing read and execute functions, the number of sections containing write functions, and obtains a 5-dimensional feature array. Next, for the overall information, the same hash method is used to extract a 50-dimensional array with the value ranges from 0 to 255. Finally, these six features are spliced to obtain a 256-dimensional vector.

*4) Import address table (IAT).* The IAT reflects the external functions that the binary file depends on, it reflects the malicious behavior of the program. The malicious code family usually has consistent behavior and depends on the same library function. Thus, we extract all library file names and called entry function names in IAT, and splice them in the format of "file: function" to obtain a new import function list, e.g., mscoree.dll:_ CorExeMain(). Then, we use the hash function to extract a 256-dimensional array from the library file name list, and extract a 1024-dimensional array from the import function list, and finally splice them to get a 1280-dimensional feature vector.

*5) Export function table (EFT).* The EFT records the related dependent functions called by the malicious code runtime. We directly extract the exported function list, and use the hash function to convert the list into a 128-dimensional vector.

*6) File description information.* we compute and return the basic information of the file and PE header, including file size, virtual size, debugging information, the number of imported functions, the number of exported functions, relocation table, resource table, digital signature, local thread storage table, and the number of symbols in the symbol table. The above information forms a 10-dimensional vector.

*7) PE meta information.* We collect the file compilation timestamp, compilation platform and flag list of file characteristics from the Object Common File Format (COFF) header of debugging information. Then, we obtain the following information from the optional header file: the subsystem required to run the PE file, the file attributes of the DLL, the type of optional header, the version number of the image, the version number of the linker, the version number of the operating system and its subsystem, the length of the code segment, and all file headers (including section tables), and the initial memory occupied by the runtime process heap. Later, the hash function is also used to convert the character type feature into a 10-dimensional vector, so that the PE information can be extracted to obtain a 62-dimensional feature vector.

*8) Printable string.* The binary code is converted into ASCII code, and only displayable strings are extracted, thus, the ASCII value range of characters is 32–127. Then, filter strings with less than five consecutive characters, and properly quantify the extracted strings, such as statistical length of extracted strings, average length of each string, histogram of printable characters and byte entropy pair. In addition, calculate the occurrence times of some sensitive information, including system file path, web address and executable file identification.

*9) Data directory table.* The data directory table consists of directory address and directory size. the data directory defines the index of each data directory area, there are 15 data directories such as import directory, export directory, resource directory, exception directory and redirection directory. Each extracted directory address and size are spliced to obtain a 30-dimensional feature vector.

## 3    The Classification and Identification Process

### 3.1    Design Principle

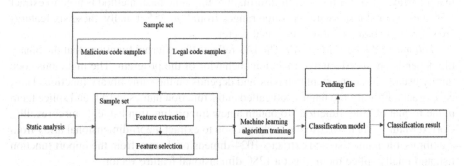

**Fig. 3.** Scheme flowchart.

The flowchart of the whole malicious code identification algorithm is shown in Fig. 3. First, the collected samples are preprocessed to obtain the static characteristics of the file. Then, specific methods are used to construct feature vectors according to different feature types and input them into the prediction model of machine learning algorithm. Finally, the prediction model is used to label the malicious code, and the prediction results are obtained.

### 3.2    Implement of Classification Model

Three features discussed in Sect. 2 are applied to seven different types of machine learning models for training, including decision tree (DT), random forest (RF), Light

Gradient Boosting Machine (LightGBM), support vector machine (SVM), K-nearest neighbor (KNN), Gaussian naive Bayes (GNB), and logistic regression (LR).

*1) DT.* It starts from the root node and generates branch nodes downward. The set of child nodes becomes smaller as the increase of the depth of the tree, and finally a simple measure set is obtained, where the leaf nodes represent the prediction results. After the model is trained, the imported samples can select different paths according to their own attributes, while the path selection is depending on the measurement value of its child node. The benefit value $D_i$ at node $i$ is calculated as follows:

$$Gain(D, a) = Entropy(D) - \sum\nolimits_{i=1}^{k} \frac{|D_i|}{|D|} Entropy(D_i) \qquad (2)$$

where $k$ is the depth of decision tree $D$ at child node $a$. In order to solve the inductive bias problem, we use the information gain rate to replace the original measurement, moreover, to prevent over fitting, it is necessary to prune when constructing the decision tree, the strategy of cutting branches and leaves has a great impact on the accuracy of decision tree.

*2) RF.* This strategy is to establish many decision trees like "forest" based on bagging algorithm, and determine the final prediction result by voting all decision trees. First, the bootstrap is used to put back sampling data set to obtain $n$ sample sets. The decision tree is constructed based on the training data set of each decision tree. In addition, $m$ features are randomly selected from the sampling set at each node. After obtaining the data set and decision characteristics, a single decision tree directly calculates the results without pruning. Finally, all the derived decision trees are voted, and the prediction results of the random forest model are obtained.

*3) LightGBM*, called LGBM for simplify hereafter, it is one of the implementations of Gradient Boosting Decision Tree (GBDT). LGBM is a gradient boosting framework that uses tree-based learning algorithm, it uses weak classifier (decision tree) for iterative training. The model has the advantages of high training efficiency and good fitting, because it uses histogram algorithm to transform the samples, which greatly reduces the time complexity. The leaf wise leaf growth strategy with depth constraints is used to construct the decision tree. In addition, the unilateral gradient algorithm filters out the samples with small gradient and reduces a lot of calculation.

*4) KNN.* The basic principle of KNN is that, there is a training sample set $A$, when a test sample $B$ is given, $K$ training samples closest to test sample $B$ in training set $A$ are found based on a certain distance measure, and then the type or value is predicted based on the information of $K$ training samples.

*5) SVM.* The basic idea of SVM learning is to solve the separation hyperplane which can correctly divide the training data set and has the largest geometric interval. The model trained by SVM completely depends on support vector, even if all non-support vector points in the training set are removed and the training process is repeated, the results will still get exactly the same model. SVM will find a partition hyperplane that can distinguish two categories and maximize the margin.

*6) GNB.* For the given item to be classified, GNB solves the problem of each item belongs to the category under the condition that the category with the largest probability. The information gain is obtained by calculating the corresponding conditional probability as follow:

$$P(Y|X) = \frac{P(X|Y) \times P(Y)}{P(X)} \tag{3}$$

The whole classification process is divided into three stages: *i) preparation stage*, which determines the feature attributes to form a training sample set. *ii) Classifier training stage*, which calculates the occurrence frequency of each category in the training sample and the conditional probability estimation of each feature attribute division, and record the results. *iii) application phase*, which uses the classifier to determine the items to be classified.

*7) LR.* It is a classification learning method that aims to distinguish different types of samples. For a two-classification problem, $y \in \{0, 1\}$, 1 indicates positive cases and 0 indicates negative cases. LR is based on the actual value predicted by the output of linear function $\theta^T x$, and find a hypothetical function $h_\theta(x) = g(\theta^T x)$ to map actual value to 0 or 1. If $h_\theta(x) \geq 0.5$, then $y = 1$, that is, $y$ belongs to the positive example. Otherwise, $y = 0$, and it is a negative example. The mathematical expression of the prediction function is

$$h_\theta(x) = g\left(\theta^T x\right) = \frac{1}{1 + e^{-\theta^T x}} \tag{4}$$

where $\theta$ is a parameter vector, the above equation can be further rewritten as

$$ln\frac{h_\theta(x)}{1 - h_\theta(x)} = \theta^T x \tag{5}$$

The numerator denotes the probability that $x$ belongs to positive example, while the denominator denotes the probability of $x$ belongs to the counterexample. The ratio of the two is called odds, for example, for a given $x$, $h_\theta(x) = 0.7$ is calculated from the determined parameters, then it means that there has 70% that $y$ is a positive example.

## 4  Evaluation

### 4.1  Experiment Setup

The experimental data are come from GitHub community and public platforms. The size of the sample set used is 13 Gb (including 10868 sample files), both benign samples and malicious samples are random sampling. The sample set is divided into training set, verification set and test set with the ratio of 7:2:1. Each simulation selects 10% of the samples randomly from the malicious samples and benign samples in the training set to form a training subset. The verification set is used for training evaluation, and the test set is used for the test of the final model.

The experiment environment is performed on AMD R5-4600H, six CPU cores of 3.00 GHz, 16 GB memory, Microsoft windows10 operating system. The algorithm is programmed in Python language, the development tool is Pycharm and machine learning toolkit is scikit-learn (sklearn). We define a confusion matrix as the evaluation basis, and use the receiver operating characteristic curve (ROC) as the measurement index of the final experimental results, we also introduce common indicators such as accuracy, accuracy, recall and F1 to evaluate the small set sample.

Let TP as the number of malicious codes that are correctly predicted, and FP be the number of non-malicious codes that are incorrectly predicted, TN refers to the number of non-malicious codes that are correctly predicted, and FN is the number of malicious codes that are incorrectly predicted, respectively. Let TPR be the proportion of malicious samples correctly identified (including the number of samples wrongly judged as benign), and FPR is the proportion of all benign samples judged as malicious. It has $TPR = TP/TP + FN$ and $FPR = FP/FP + TN$, respectively.

## 4.2 Experiment Results

In order to test whether the comprehensive static feature based on binary file can be applied to malicious code recognition and whether it is better than opcode feature. We use $n$-gram algorithm and doc2vec algorithm to extract the opcode features of malicious samples in the data set, and extract the comprehensive static features by parsing binary files. Then the three features are applied to seven different types of machine learning models in Sect. 3 for training. It is necessary to determine the size of the $n$-gram algorithm window size when comparing the three features. Figure 4 shows the detection accuracy of different window sizes on different models. Obviously, the performance of 3-g in each classify model is better than 2-g and 4-g.

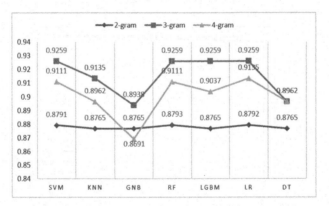

**Fig. 4.** N-gram accuracy.

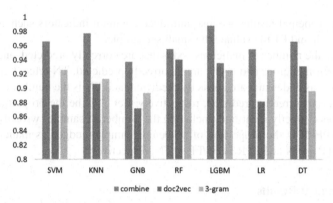

**Fig. 5.** Detection accuracy. (Color figure online)

Next, we combine with three features and seven models to form a total of 21 algorithms, and examine these algorithms on detection accuracy as shown in Fig. 5, where the green, blue and yellow columns represent the comprehensive static features, doc2vec opcode features and 3-g opcode features, respectively. It can be seen that the recognition accuracy of the comprehensive features is significantly higher than that of the other two features, as the fact that we combine with different classification algorithms rather than individual feature. It also shows that the proposed binary static feature extraction method has better performance in malicious code recognition.

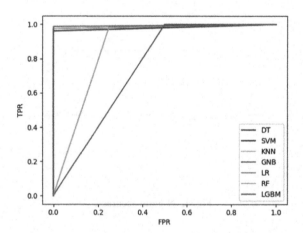

**Fig. 6.** Comprehensive feature comparison in ROC.

Figure 6 draws the ROC diagram of 21 algorithms according to the comprehensive static characteristics, including 7 different curves, and each curve corresponds to a classification model. The performance of each algorithm is judged by comparing the AUC value. It can be seen from Table 1 that the AUC value of LGBM is the highest. This is because the LGBM model combines the static characteristics of binary files and has better recognition ability of malicious code. In other words, it can accurately judge

**Table 1.** Evaluation value of different algorithms.

| Model | Index | | | |
|---|---|---|---|---|
| | AUC | Precision | Recall | F1 |
| RF | 0.8685 | 0.9536 | 0.9550 | 0.9533 |
| LGBM | 0.9935 | 0.9896 | 0.9887 | 0.9889 |
| SVM | 0.9805 | 0.9730 | 0.9662 | 0.9678 |
| LR | 0.8685 | 0.9536 | 0.9550 | 0.9533 |
| GNB | 0.75 | 0.9374 | 0.9325 | 0.9226 |
| DT | 0.9870 | 0.9730 | 0.9662 | 0.9678 |
| KNN | 0.9881 | 0.9807 | 0.9775 | 0.9782 |

malicious code and minimize the probability of misjudgment of benign files. Table 1 also shows that the accuracy, recall and F1 value of the seven algorithms are all higher than 0.9, indicating that the performance of the model obtained by using comprehensive static features are more stable.

## 5 Conclusions

This paper proposed a malicious code recognition algorithm based on machine learning, upon analyzing and integrating a large number of samples, various machine learning algorithms are used for classification and comparison. Experiments show that the proposed malicious code feature extraction method has a good effect on predicting whether the program is malicious, on this basis, we use LGBM learning model to train the comprehensive static features, and the detection accuracy and efficiency are better than the existing schemes. In the future, we will use the recognition model to design and implement a malicious code detection tool, expand the experimental samples, and compare with other schemes in the real applications.

**Acknowledgement.** This work was supported in part by the National Nature Science Foundation of China Under Grant 61871204 and 61902167, and the Natural Science Foundation of Fujian Province Under Grant 2021J011013 and 2021J011015.

## References

1. Venkateswaran, N., Umadevi, K.: Hybridized wrapper filter using deep neural network for intrusion detection. Comput. Syst. Sci. Eng. **42**(1), 1–14 (2022)
2. Gulivindala, A.K., Bahubalendruni, M.V.A.R., Chandrasekar, R., Ahmed, E., Abidi, M.H.: Automated disassembly sequence prediction for industry 4.0 using enhanced genetic algorithm. Comput. Mater. Continua **69**(2), 2531–2548 (2021)
3. Ghazal, T.M., Hussain, M.Z., Said, R.A., Nadeem, A., Hasan, M.K.: Performances of k-means clustering algorithm with different distance metrics. Intell. Autom. Soft Comput. **30**(2), 735–742 (2021)

4. Alghamdi, H.A.N.S., Alharbi, A.H.: Real time feature extraction deep-CNN for mask detection. Intell. Autom. Soft Comput. **31**(3), 1423–1434 (2022)
5. Chen, N., Xialihaer, N., Kong, W., Ren, J.: Research on prediction methods of energy consumption data. J. New Media **2**(3), 99–109 (2020)
6. Walaa, G., Anas, A., Waleed, N., Mustafa, A.S.: DLBT: deep learning-Based transformer to generate pseudo-code from source code. Comput. Mater. Continua **70**(2), 3117–3132 (2022)

# Author Index

Printed in the United States
by Baker & Taylor Publisher Services